THE
BOOK OF MORMON

An Account Written by

THE HAND OF MORMON
UPON PLATES

TAKEN FROM THE PLATES OF NEPHI

Wherefore, it is an abridgment of the record of the people of Nephi, and also of the Lamanites—Written to the Lamanites, who are a remnant of the house of Israel; and also to Jew and Gentile—Written by way of commandment, and also by the spirit of prophecy and of revelation—Written and sealed up, and hid up unto the Lord, that they might not be destroyed—To come forth by the gift and power of God unto the interpretation thereof—Sealed by the hand of Moroni, and hid up unto the Lord, to come forth in due time by way of the Gentile—The interpretation thereof by the gift of God.

An abridgment taken from the Book of Ether also, which is a record of the people of Jared, who were scattered at the time the Lord confounded the language of the people, when they were building a tower to get to heaven—Which is to show unto the remnant of the House of Israel what great things the Lord hath done for their fathers; and that they may know the covenants of the Lord, that they are not cast off forever—And also to the convincing of the Jew and Gentile that JESUS is the CHRIST, the ETERNAL GOD, manifesting himself unto all nations—And now, if there are faults they are the mistakes of men; wherefore, condemn not the things of God, that ye may be found spotless at the judgment-seat of Christ.

TRANSLATED BY JOSEPH SMITH, JUN.

PUBLISHED BY

The Church of Jesus Christ of Latter-day Saints
SALT LAKE CITY, UTAH, U. S. A.

A Marvelous Work and A Wonder Edition, May 2007
Printed in the United States of America
ISBN 1-60135-707-9

Copyright 1920
by
HEBER J. GRANT
Trustee-in-Trust for
The Church of Jesus Christ of Latter-day Saints
Salt Lake City, Utah, U. S. A.

First Edition published in
1830

First issued, as divided into chapters and verses
with references
By ORSON PRATT, in
1879

First issued in double-column pages, with
chapter headings, chronological data,
revised foot-note references,
pronouncing vocabulary
and index, in
1920

BRIEF ANALYSIS
OF THE
BOOK OF MORMON

Three classes of Record Plates are indicated on the title-page of The Book of Mormon, namely:

1. *The Plates of Nephi*, which, as the text of the Book makes clear, were of two kinds—(*a*) the Larger Plates; (*b*) the Smaller Plates. The former were more particularly devoted to the secular history of the peoples concerned, while the latter were occupied mostly by sacred records.

2. *The Plates of Mormon*, containing an abridgment from the Plates of Nephi, made by Mormon, with many commentaries and a continuation of the history by himself, and with further additions by Moroni, son of Mormon.

3. *The Plates of Ether*, containing a history of the Jaredites, which account was abridged by Moroni, who inserted comments of his own, and incorporated the record with the general history under the title, Book of Ether.

To these may be added another set of plates, which are of frequent mention in the Book of Mormon, namely:

4. *The Brass Plates of Laban*, brought by the people of Lehi from Jerusalem, and containing Hebrew Scriptures and genealogies, many extracts from which appear in the Nephite records.

The Book of Mormon comprises fifteen main parts or divisions, known, with one exception, as books, each designated by the name of its principal author. Of these, the first six books, namely, First Nephi, Second Nephi, Jacob, Enos, Jarom, and Omni, are translations from the corresponding sections of the Smaller Plates of Nephi. Between the books of Omni and Mosiah, we find *The Words of Mormon*, connecting the record of Nephi, as engraved on the Smaller Plates, with Mormon's abridgment of the Larger Plates for the periods following. *The Words of Mormon* constitute a brief explanation of the preceding portions of the record, and a preface to the parts following.

The body of the Book, from Mosiah to Mormon, chapter 7, inclusive, is the translation of Mormon's abridgment of the Plates of Nephi. The latter part of the Book of Mormon, from the beginning of Mormon, chapter 8, to the end of the volume, was engraved by Mormon's son, Moroni, who first proceeded to finish the record of his father's life, and then made an abridgment of the Jaredite record, as the Book of Ether. Later he added the parts known to us as the Book of Moroni.

The period covered by Book of Mormon annals extends from B. C. 600 to A. D. 421. In or about the latter year, Moroni, the last of the Nephite historians, sealed the sacred record, and hid it up unto the Lord, to be brought forth in the latter days, as predicted by the voice of God through his ancient prophets. In A. D. 1827, this same Moroni, then a resurrected personage, delivered the engraved plates to Joseph Smith.

ORIGIN OF
THE BOOK OF MORMON

Joseph Smith, through whom, by the gift and power of God, the ancient Scripture, known as THE BOOK OF MORMON, has been brought forth and translated into the English tongue, made personal and circumstantial record of the matter. He affirmed that during the night of September 21, 1823, he sought the Lord in fervent prayer, having previously received a Divine manifestation of transcendent import. His account follows:

"While I was thus in the act of calling upon God, I discovered a light appearing in my room, which continued to increase until the room was lighter than at noonday, when immediately a personage appeared at my bedside, standing in the air, for his feet did not touch the floor.

"He had on a loose robe of most exquisite whiteness. It was a whiteness beyond anything earthly I had ever seen; nor do I believe that any earthly thing could be made to appear so exceedingly white and brilliant. His hands were naked, and his arms also, a little above the wrists; so, also, were his feet naked, as were his legs, a little above the ankles. His head and neck were also bare. I could discover that he had no other clothing on but this robe, as it was open, so that I could see into his bosom.

"Not only was his robe exceedingly white, but his whole person was glorious beyond description, and his countenance truly like lightning. The room was exceedingly light, but not so very bright as immediately around his person. When I first looked upon him, I was afraid; but the fear soon left me.

"He called me by name, and said unto me that he was a messenger sent from the presence of God to me, and that his name was Moroni; that God had a work for me to do; and that my name should be had for good and evil among all nations, kindreds, and tongues, or that it should be both good and evil spoken of among all people.

"He said there was a book deposited, written upon gold plates, giving an account of the former inhabitants of this continent, and the source from whence they sprang. He also said that the fulness of the everlasting Gospel was contained in it, as delivered by the Savior to the ancient inhabitants;

"Also, that there were two stones in silver bows—and these stones, fastened to a breastplate, constituted what is called the Urim and Thummim —deposited with the plates; and the possession and use of these stones were what constituted *Seers* in ancient or former times; and that God had prepared them for the purpose of translating the book.

* * * * * * *

"Again, he told me, that when I got those plates of which he had spoken—for the time that they should be obtained was not yet fulfilled—I should not show them to any person; neither the breastplate with the Urim and Thummim; only to those to whom I should be commanded to show them; if I did I should be destroyed. While he was conversing with me about the plates, the vision was opened to my mind that I could see the place where the plates were deposited, and that so clearly and distinctly that I knew the place again when I visited it.

"After this communication, I saw the light in the room begin to gather immediately around the person of him who had been speaking to me, and it continued to do so, until the room was again left dark, except just around him, when instantly I saw, as it were, a conduit open right up into heaven, and he ascended until he entirely disappeared, and the room was left as it had been before this heavenly light had made its appearance.

"I lay musing on the singularity of the scene, and marveling greatly at what had been told to me by this extraordinary messenger; when, in the midst of my meditation, I suddenly discovered that my room was again beginning to get lighted, and in an instant, as it were, the same heavenly messenger was again by my bedside.

"He commenced, and again related the very same things which he had done at his first visit, without the least variation; which having done, he informed me of great judgments which were coming upon the earth, with great desolations by famine, sword, and pestilence; and that these grievous judgments would come on the earth in this generation. Having related these things, he again ascended as he had done before.

"By this time, so deep were the impressions made on my mind, that sleep had fled from my eyes, and I lay overwhelmed in astonishment at what I had both seen and heard. But what was my surprise when again I beheld the same messenger at my bedside, and heard him rehearse or repeat over again to me the same things as before; and added a caution to me, telling me that Satan would try to tempt me (in consequence of the indigent circumstances of my father's family), to get the plates for the purpose of getting rich. This he forbade me, saying that I must have no other object in view in getting the plates but to glorify God, and must not be influenced by any other motive than that of building His kingdom; otherwise I could not get them.

"After this third visit, he again ascended into heaven as before, and I was again left to ponder on the strangeness of what I had just experienced; when almost immediately after the heavenly messenger had ascended from me the third time, the cock crowed, and I found that day was approaching, so that our interviews must have occupied the whole of that night.

"I shortly after arose from my bed, and, as usual, went to the necessary labors of the day; but, in attempting to work as at other times, I found my strength so exhausted as to render me entirely unable. My father, who was laboring along with me, discovered something to be wrong with me, and told me to go home. I started with the intention of going to the house; but, in attempting to cross the fence out of the field where we were, my strength entirely failed me, and I fell helpless on the ground, and for a time was quite unconscious of anything.

"The first thing that I can recollect was a voice speaking unto me, calling me by name. I looked up, and beheld the same messenger standing over my head, surrounded by light as before. He then again related unto me all that he had related to me the previous night, and commanded me to go to my father and tell him of the vision and commandments which I had received.

"I obeyed; I returned to my father in the field, and rehearsed the whole matter to him. He replied to me that it was of God, and told me to go and do as commanded by the messenger. I left the field, and went to the place where the messenger had told me the plates were deposited; and owing to the distinctness of the vision which I had had concerning it, I knew the place the instant that I arrived there.

"Convenient to the village of Manchester, Ontario county, New York, stands a hill of considerable size, and the most elevated of any in the neighborhood. On the west side of this hill, not far from the top, under a stone of considerable size, lay the plates, deposited in a stone box. This stone was thick and rounding in the middle on the upper side, and thinner towards the edges, so that the middle part of it was visible above the ground, but the edge all around was covered with earth.

"Having removed the earth, I obtained a lever, which I got fixed under the edge of the stone, and with a little exertion raised it up. I looked in, and there indeed did I behold the plates, the Urim and Thummim, and the breastplate, as stated by the messenger. The box in which they lay was formed by laying stones together in some kind of cement. In the bottom of the box were laid two stones crossways of the box, and on these stones lay the plates and the other things with them.

"I made an attempt to take them out, but was forbidden by the messenger, and was again informed that the time for bringing them forth had not yet arrived, neither would it, until four years from that time; but he told me that I should come to that place precisely in one year from that time, and that he would there meet with me, and that I should continue to do so until the time should come for obtaining the plates.

"Accordingly, as I had been commanded, I went at the end of each year, and at each time I found the same messenger there, and received instruction and intelligence from him at each of our interviews, respecting what the Lord was going to do, and how and in what manner His kingdom was to be conducted in the last days.

* * * * * * *

"At length the time arrived for obtaining the plates, the Urim and Thummim, and the breastplate. On the twenty-second day of September, one thousand eight hundred and twenty-seven, having gone as usual at the end of another year to the place where they were deposited, the same heavenly messenger delivered them up to me with this charge: That I should be responsible for them; that if I should let them go carelessly, or through any neglect of mine, I should be cut off; but that if I would use all my endeavors to preserve them, until he, the messenger, should call for them, they should be protected.

"I soon found out the reason why I had received such strict charges to keep them safe, and why it was that the messenger had said that when I had done what was required at my hand, he would call for them. For no sooner was it known that I had them, than the most strenuous exertions were used to get them from me. Every stratagem that could be invented was resorted to for that purpose. The persecution became more bitter and severe than before, and multitudes were on the alert continually to get them from me if possible. But by the wisdom of God, they remained safe in my hands, until I had accomplished by them what was required at my hand. When, according to arrangements, the messenger called for them, I delivered them up to him; and he has them in his charge until this day, being the second day of May, one thousand eight hundred and thirty-eight."

For the complete record, see *Pearl of Great Price*, pages 50-54, and *History of the Church of Jesus Christ of Latter-day Saints*, volume 1, chapters 1 to 6 inclusive.

The ancient record, thus brought forth from the earth, as the voice of a people speaking from the dust, and translated into modern speech by the gift and power of God as attested by Divine affirmation, was first published to the world in the year 1830 as THE BOOK OF MORMON.

THE TESTIMONY OF THREE WITNESSES

BE IT KNOWN unto all nations, kindreds, tongues, and people, unto whom this work shall come: That we, through the grace of God the Father, and our Lord Jesus Christ, have seen the plates which contain this record, which is a record of the people of Nephi, and also of the Lamanites, their brethren, and also of the people of Jared, who came from the tower of which hath been spoken. And we also know that they have been translated by the gift and power of God, for his voice hath declared it unto us; wherefore we know of a surety that the work is true. And we also testify that we have seen the engravings which are upon the plates; and they have been shown unto us by the power of God, and not of man. And we declare with words of soberness, that an angel of God came down from heaven, and he brought and laid before our eyes, that we beheld and saw the plates, and the engravings thereon; and we know that it is by the grace of God the Father, and our Lord Jesus Christ, that we beheld and bear record that these things are true. And it is marvelous in our eyes. Nevertheless, the voice of the Lord commanded us that we should bear record of it; wherefore, to be obedient unto the commandments of God, we bear testimony of these things. And we know that if we are faithful in Christ, we shall rid our garments of the blood of all men, and be found spotless before the judgment-seat of Christ, and shall dwell with him eternally in the heavens. And the honor be to the Father, and to the Son, and to the Holy Ghost, which is one God. Amen.

OLIVER COWDERY
DAVID WHITMER
MARTIN HARRIS

AND ALSO
THE TESTIMONY OF EIGHT WITNESSES

BE IT KNOWN unto all nations, kindreds, tongues, and people, unto whom this work shall come: That Joseph Smith, Jun., the translator of this work, has shown unto us the plates of which hath been spoken, which have the appearance of gold; and as many of the leaves as the said Smith has translated we did handle with our hands; and we also saw the engravings thereon, all of which has the appearance of ancient work, and of curious workmanship. And this we bear record with words of soberness, that the said Smith has shown unto us, for we have seen and hefted, and know of a surety that the said Smith has got the plates of which we have spoken. And we give our names unto the world, to witness unto the world that which we have seen. And we lie not, God bearing witness of it.

CHRISTIAN WHITMER
JACOB WHITMER
PETER WHITMER, JUN.
JOHN WHITMER

HIRAM PAGE
JOSEPH SMITH, SEN.
HYRUM SMITH
SAMUEL H. SMITH

NAMES AND ORDER

OF BOOKS IN

THE BOOK OF MORMON

Name	Page	Designation in Foot-notes
First Book of Nephi	1	1 Ne.
Second Book of Nephi	49	2 Ne
Book of Jacob	107	Jac.
Book of Enos	125	Enos
Book of Jarom	127	Jar.
Book of Omni	129	Om.
The Words of Mormon	132	W. of Morm.
Book of Mosiah	134	Mos.
Book of Alma	195	Al.
Book of Helaman	359	He.
Third Nephi	399	3 Ne.
Fourth Nephi	456	4 Ne.
Book of Mormon	460	Morm.
Book of Ether	478	Eth.
Book of Moroni	510	Moro.

Other abbreviations in foot-notes:

Doctrine and Covenants	D. & C.
Pearl of Great Price	P. of G. P.

Books of the Holy Bible are designated by the usual abbreviations.

THE BOOK OF MORMON

THE FIRST BOOK OF NEPHI

HIS REIGN AND MINISTRY

An account of Lehi and his wife Sariah, and his four sons, being called, (beginning at the eldest) Laman, Lemuel, Sam, and Nephi. The Lord warns Lehi to depart out of the land of Jerusalem, because he prophesieth unto the people concerning their iniquity and they seek to destroy his life. He taketh three days' journey into the wilderness with his family. Nephi taketh his brethren and returneth to the land of Jerusalem after the record of the Jews. The account of their sufferings. They take the daughters of Ishmael to wife. They take their families and depart into the wilderness. Their sufferings and afflictions in the wilderness. The course of their travels. They come to the large waters. Nephi's brethren rebel against him. He confoundeth them, and buildeth a ship. They call the place Bountiful. They cross the large waters into the promised land, &c. This is according to the account of Nephi; or in other words, I, Nephi, wrote this record.

CHAPTER 1.

Lehi's vision of the pillar of fire and the book of prophecy—He predicts the impending fate of Jerusalem, and foretells the coming of the Messiah—The Jews seek his life.

1. I, Nephi, having been born of goodly parents, therefore I was taught somewhat in all the learning of my father; and having seen many afflictions in the course of my days, nevertheless, having been highly favored of the Lord in all my days; yea, having had a great knowledge of the goodness and the mysteries of God, therefore I make a record of my proceedings in my days.

2. Yea, I make a record in the language of my father, which consists of the learning of the Jews and the ªlanguage of the Egyptians.

3. And I know that the record which I make is true; and I make it with mine own hand; and I make it according to my knowledge.

4. For it came to pass in the commencement of the ᵇfirst year of the reign of Zedekiah, king of Judah, (my father, Lehi, having dwelt at Jerusalem in all his days); and in that same year there came ᶜmany prophets, prophesying unto the people that they must repent, or the great city Jerusalem must be destroyed.

5. Wherefore it came to pass that my father, Lehi, as he went forth prayed unto the Lord, yea,

---

a, Mos. 1:4. Morm. 9:32. b, 2 Kings 24:17, 18. c, 2 Chron. 36:15, 16.
ABOUT B. C. 600.

even with all his heart, in behalf of his people.

6. And it came to pass as he prayed unto the Lord, there came a pillar of fire and dwelt upon a rock before him; and he saw and heard much; and because of the things which he saw and heard he did quake and tremble exceedingly.

7. And it came to pass that he returned to his own house at Jerusalem; and he cast himself upon his bed, being overcome with the Spirit and the things which he had seen.

8. And being thus overcome with the Spirit, he was carried away in a vision, even that he saw the heavens open, and he thought he saw God sitting upon his throne, surrounded with numberless concourses of angels in the attitude of singing and praising their God.

9. And it came to pass that he saw one descending out of the midst of heaven, and he beheld that his luster was above that of the sun at noon-day.

10. And he also saw twelve others following him, and their brightness did exceed that of the stars in the firmament.

11. And they came down and went forth upon the face of the earth; and the first came and stood before my father, and gave unto him a book, and bade him that he should read.

12. And it came to pass that as he read, he was filled with the Spirit of the Lord.

13. And he read, saying: Wo, wo, unto Jerusalem, for I have seen thine abominations! Yea, and many things did my father read concerning Jerusalem—

^dthat it should be destroyed, and the inhabitants thereof; many should perish by the sword, and many should be carried away captive into Babylon.

14. And it came to pass that when my father had read and seen many great and marvelous things, he did exclaim many things unto the Lord; such as: Great and marvelous are thy works, O Lord God Almighty! Thy throne is high in the heavens, and thy power, and goodness, and mercy are over all the inhabitants of the earth; and, because thou art merciful, thou wilt not suffer those who come unto thee that they shall perish!

15. And after this manner was the language of my father in the praising of his God; for his soul did rejoice, and his whole heart was filled, because of the things which he had seen, yea, which the Lord had shown unto him.

16. And now I, Nephi, do not make a full account of the things which my *father hath written, for he hath written many things which he saw in visions and in dreams; and he also hath written many things which he prophesied and spake unto his children, of which I shall not make a full account.

17. But I shall make an account of my proceedings in my days. Behold, I make an *abridgment of the record of my father, upon plates which I have made with mine own hands; wherefore, after I have abridged the record of my father then will I make an account of mine own life.

18. Therefore, I would that ye should know, that after the

d, 2 Chron. 36:17—20. Jer. 39:1—9. *e*, 1 Ne. 6:1. *f*, 1 Ne. 6:1. 9:2—5. 10:1. 19:1—6. 2 Ne. 5:29—33. Jac. 1:1—4. 3:13, 14. 4:1, 2. 7:26, 27. Enos 13, 15—18. Jar. 14, 15. W. of Morm. 1—11. ABOUT B. C. 600.

Lord had shown so many marvelous things unto my father, Lehi, yea, concerning the destruction of Jerusalem, behold he went forth among the people, and began to prophesy and to declare unto them concerning the things which he had both seen and heard.

19. And it came to pass that the *g*Jews did mock him because of the things which he testified of them; for he truly testified of their wickedness and their abominations; and he testified that the things which he saw and heard, and also the things which he read in the book, manifested plainly of the coming of a Messiah, and also the redemption of the world.

20. And when the Jews heard these things they were angry with him; yea, even as with the prophets of old, whom they had cast out, and stoned, and slain; and they also sought his life, that they might take it away. But behold, I, Nephi, will show unto you that the tender mercies of the Lord are over all those whom he hath chosen, because of their faith, to make them mighty even unto the power of deliverance.

CHAPTER 2.

Lehi departs with his family into the wilderness bordering on the Red Sea—His elder sons, Laman and Lemuel, murmur against him—Nephi and Sam believe his words—The Lord's promises to Nephi.

1. For behold, it came to pass that the Lord spake unto my father, yea, even in a dream, and said unto him: Blessed art thou Lehi, because of the things which thou hast done; and because thou hast been faithful and declared unto this people the things which I commanded thee, behold, they seek to take away thy life.

2. And it came to pass that the Lord commanded my father, even in a dream, that he should take his family and depart into the wilderness.

3. And it came to pass that he was obedient unto the word of the Lord, wherefore he did as the Lord commanded him.

4. And it came to pass that he *departed into the wilderness. And he left his house, and the land of his inheritance, and his gold, and his silver, and his precious things, and took nothing with him, save it were his family, and provisions, and tents, and departed into the wilderness.

5. And he came down by the borders near the shore of the Red Sea; and he traveled in the wilderness in the borders which are nearer the Red Sea; and he did travel in the wilderness with his family, which consisted of my mother, Sariah, and my elder brothers, who were Laman, Lemuel, and Sam.

6. And it came to pass that when he had traveled three days in the wilderness, he pitched his tent in a valley by the side of a river of water.

7. And it came to pass that he built an altar of stones, and made an offering unto the Lord, and gave thanks unto the Lord our God.

8. And it came to pass that he called the name of the river, Laman, and it emptied into the Red Sea; and the valley was in the borders near the mouth thereof.

9. And when my father saw that the waters of the river emptied into the fountain of the Red Sea, he spake unto Laman, say-

---

g, 2 Chron. 36:16. Jer. 26:8—11.   * B. C. 600.

ing: O that thou mightest be like unto this river, continually running into the fountain of all righteousness!

10. And he also spake unto Lemuel: O that thou mightest be like unto this valley, firm and steadfast, and immovable in keeping the commandments of the Lord!

11. Now this he spake because of the stiffneckedness of Laman and Lemuel; for behold they did murmur in many things against their father, because he was a visionary man, and had led them out of the land of Jerusalem, to leave the land of their inheritance, and their gold, and their silver, and their precious things, to perish in the wilderness. And this they said he had done because of the foolish imaginations of his heart.

12. And thus Laman and Lemuel, being the eldest, did murmur against their father. And they did murmur because they knew not the dealings of that God who had created them.

13. Neither did they believe that Jerusalem, that great city, could be destroyed according to the words of the prophets. And they were like unto the Jews who were at Jerusalem, who sought to take away the life of my father.

14. And it came to pass that my father did speak unto them in the valley of Lemuel, with power, being filled with the Spirit, until their frames did shake before him. And he did confound them, that they durst not utter against him; wherefore, they did as he commanded them.

15. And my father dwelt in a tent.

16. And it came to pass that I, Nephi, being exceeding young, nevertheless being large in stature, and also having great desires to know of the mysteries of God, wherefore, I did cry unto the Lord; and behold he did visit me, and did soften my heart that I did believe all the words which had been spoken by my father; wherefore, I did not rebel against him like unto my brothers.

17. And I spake unto Sam, making known unto him the things which the Lord had manifested unto me by his Holy Spirit. And it came to pass that he believed in my words.

18. But, behold, Laman and Lemuel would not hearken unto my words; and being grieved because of the hardness of their hearts I cried unto the Lord for them.

19. And it came to pass that the Lord spake unto me, saying: Blessed art thou, Nephi, because of thy faith, for thou hast sought me diligently, with lowliness of heart.

20. And inasmuch as ye shall keep my commandments, ye shall prosper, *a*and shall be led to a land of promise; yea, even a land which I have prepared for you; yea, a land which is choice above all other lands.

21. And inasmuch as thy *b*brethren shall rebel against thee, they shall be cut off from the presence of the Lord.

22. And inasmuch as thou shalt keep my commandments, *c*thou shalt be made a ruler and a teacher over thy brethren.

23. For behold, in that day that they shall rebel against me, I will *d*curse them even with a

---

a, 1 Ne. 18:22, 23. Eth. 1:42. 2:7—12. *b*, 2 Ne. 5:20. Al. 9:13, 14. 38:1. *c*, 1 Ne. 3:20. 2 Ne. 5:19. *d*, 1 Ne. 12:22, 23. 2 Ne. 5:21—25. Al. 3:6—19. 17:15. 3 Ne. 2:15, 16. Morm. 5:15.

ABOUT B. C. 600.

I NEPHI, 3.

sore curse, and they shall have no power over thy seed except they shall rebel against me also.

24. And if it so be that they rebel against me, they shall be a scourge unto thy seed, to stir them up in the ways of remembrance.

CHAPTER 3.

Lehi's sons sent back to Jerusalem to obtain the plates of brass—Laban refuses to deliver the plates—Laman and Lemuel reproved by an angel.

1. And it came to pass that I, Nephi, returned from speaking with the Lord, to the tent of my father.

2. And it came to pass that he spake unto me, saying: Behold I have dreamed a dream, in the which the Lord hath commanded me that thou and thy brethren shall return to Jerusalem.

3. For behold, Laban hath the record of the Jews and also a genealogy of thy forefathers, and ᵃthey are engraven upon plates of brass.

4. Wherefore, the Lord hath commanded me that thou and thy brothers should go unto the house of Laban, and seek the records, and bring them down hither into the wilderness.

5. And now, behold thy brothers murmur, saying it is a hard thing which I have required of them; but behold I have not required it of them, but it is a commandment of the Lord.

6. Therefore go, my son, and thou shalt be favored of the Lord, because thou hast not murmured.

7. And it came to pass that I, Nephi, said unto my father: I will go and do the things which the Lord hath commanded, for I know that the Lord giveth no commandments unto the children of men, save he shall prepare a way for them that they may accomplish the thing which he commandeth them.

8. And it came to pass that when my father had heard these words he was exceeding glad, for he knew that I had been blessed of the Lord.

9. And I, Nephi, and my brethren took our journey in the wilderness, with our tents, to go up to the land of Jerusalem.

10. And it came to pass that when we had come up to the land of Jerusalem, I and my brethren did consult one with another.

11. And we ᵇcast lots—who of us should go in unto the house of Laban. And it came to pass that the lot fell upon Laman; and Laman went in unto the house of Laban, and he talked with him as he sat in his house.

12. And he desired of Laban the records which were engraven upon the plates of brass, which contained the ᶻgenealogy of my father.

13. And behold, it came to pass that Laban was angry, and thrust him out from his presence; and he would not that he should have the records. Wherefore, he said unto him: Behold thou art a robber, and I will slay thee.

14. But Laman fled out of his presence, and told the things which Laban had done, unto us. And we began to be exceeding sorrowful, and my brethren were about to return unto my father in the wilderness.

15. But behold I said unto them that: As the Lord liveth, and as we live, we will not go

a, 1 Ne. 3:12, 19, 20, 24. 4:24, 38. 5:10—22. 13:23. 19:22. 2 Ne. 4:2. 5:12. Mos. 1:3, 4. 28:20. Al. 37:3—12. 63:1, 11—14. 3 Ne. 1:2. *b*, Josh. 18:6, 10. Judg. 20:9. Acts 1:26. *z*, 1 Ne. 5:14. BETWEEN B. C. 600 AND 592.

down unto our father in the wilderness until we have accomplished the thing which the Lord hath commanded us.

16. Wherefore, let us be faithful in keeping the commandments of the Lord; therefore let us go down to the land of our father's inheritance, for behold he left ᶜgold and silver, and all manner of riches. And all this he hath done because of the commandments of the Lord.

17. For he knew that ᵈJerusalem must be destroyed, because of the wickedness of the people.

18. For behold, they have rejected the words of the prophets. Wherefore, if my father should dwell in the land after he hath been commanded to flee out of the land, behold, he would also perish. Wherefore, it must needs be that he flee out of the land.

19. And behold, it is wisdom in God that we should obtain these records, that we may preserve unto our children the ᵉlanguage of our fathers;

20. And also that we may preserve unto them the words which have been spoken by the mouth of all the holy prophets, which have been delivered unto them by the Spirit and power of God, since the world began, even down unto this present time.

21. And it came to pass that after this manner of language did I persuade my brethren, that they might be faithful in keeping the commandments of God.

22. And it came to pass that we went down to the land of our inheritance, and we did gather together our ᶠgold, and our silver, and our precious things.

23. And after we had gathered these things together, we went up again unto the house of Laban.

24. And it came to pass that we went in unto Laban, and desired him that he would give unto us the records which were engraven upon the ᵍplates of brass, for which we would give unto him our gold, and our silver, and all our precious things.

25. And it came to pass that when Laban saw our property, and that it was exceeding great, he did lust after it, insomuch that he thrust us out, and sent his servants to slay us, that he might obtain our property.

26. And it came to pass that we did flee before the servants of Laban, and we were obliged to leave behind our property, and it fell into the hands of Laban.

27. And it came to pass that we fled into the wilderness, and the servants of Laban did not overtake us, and we hid ourselves in the cavity of a rock.

28. And it came to pass that Laman was angry with me, and also with my father; and also was Lemuel, for he hearkened unto the words of Laman. Wherefore Laman and Lemuel did speak many hard words unto us, their younger brothers, and they did smite us even with a rod.

29. And it came to pass as they smote us with a rod, behold, an angel of the Lord came and stood before them, and he spake unto them, saying: Why do ye smite your younger brother with a rod? Know ye not that the Lord hath chosen him to be a ʰruler over you, and this because of your iniquities? Behold ye shall go up to Jerusalem again, and the Lord will deliver Laban into your hands.

---
c, 1 Ne. 2:4.   d, see d, 1 Ne. 1.   e, 1 Ne. 1:2, 3.   Mos. 1:4.   f, 1 Ne. 2:4.   3:16.
g, see a.   h, 1 Ne. 2:22.

BETWEEN B. C. 600 AND 592.

30. And after the angel had spoken unto us, he departed.

31. And after the angel had departed, Laman and Lemuel again began to murmur, saying: How is it possible that the Lord will deliver Laban into our hands? Behold, he is a mighty man, and he can command fifty, yea, even he can slay fifty; then why not us?

CHAPTER 4.

Nephi secures possession of the plates by stratagem—Laban slain with his own sword—Zoram accompanies Nephi and his brothers into the wilderness.

1. And it came to pass that I spake unto my brethren, saying: Let us go up again unto Jerusalem, and let us be faithful in keeping the commandments of the Lord; for behold he is mightier than all the earth, then why not mightier than Laban and his fifty, yea, or even than his tens of thousands?

2. Therefore let us go up; let us be strong like unto Moses; for he truly spake unto the waters of the Red Sea and they divided hither and thither, and our fathers came through, out of captivity, on dry ground, and the armies of Pharaoh did follow and were drowned in the waters of the Red Sea.

3. Now behold ye know that this is true; and ye also know that an angel hath spoken unto you; wherefore can ye doubt? Let us go up; the Lord is able to deliver us, even as our fathers, and to destroy Laban, even as the Egyptians.

4. Now when I had spoken these words, they were yet wroth, and did still continue to murmur; nevertheless they did follow me up until we came without the walls of Jerusalem.

5. And it was by night; and I caused that they should hide themselves without the walls. And after they had hid themselves, I, Nephi, crept into the city and went forth towards the house of Laban.

6. And I was led by the Spirit, not knowing beforehand the things which I should do.

7. Nevertheless I went forth, and as I came near unto the house of Laban I beheld a man, and he had fallen to the earth before me, for he was drunken with wine.

8. And when I came to him I found that it was Laban.

9. And I beheld his *a*sword, and I drew it forth from the sheath thereof; and the hilt thereof was of pure gold, and the workmanship thereof was exceeding fine, and I saw that the blade thereof was of the most precious steel.

10. And it came to pass that I was constrained by the Spirit that I should kill Laban; but I said in my heart: Never at any time have I shed the blood of man. And I shrunk and would that I might not slay him.

11. And the Spirit said unto me again: Behold the Lord hath delivered him into thy hands. Yea, and I also knew that he had sought to take away mine own life; yea, and he would not hearken unto the commandments of the Lord; and he also had taken away our property.

12. And it came to pass that the Spirit said unto me again: Slay him, for the Lord hath delivered him into thy hands;

13. Behold the Lord slayeth the wicked to bring forth his righteous purposes. It is better that one man should perish than

---

a, 2 Ne. 5:14. Jac. 1:10. Mos. 1:16. D. & C. 17:1. BET. B. C. 600 AND 592.

1 NEPHI, 4.

that a nation should dwindle and perish in unbelief.

14. And now, when I, Nephi, had heard these words, I remembered the words of the Lord which he spake unto me in the wilderness, saying that: Inasmuch as thy seed shall keep my commandments, [b]they shall prosper in the land of promise.

15. Yea, and I also thought that they could not keep the commandments of the Lord according to the law of Moses, save they should have the law.

16. And I also knew that the law was engraven upon the plates of brass.

17. And again, I knew that the Lord had delivered Laban into my hands for this cause—that I might obtain the records according to his commandments.

18. Therefore I did obey the voice of the Spirit, and took Laban by the hair of the head, and I smote off his head with his own sword.

19. And after I had smitten off his head with his own sword, I took the garments of Laban and put them upon mine own body; yea, even every whit; and I did gird on his armor about my loins.

20. And after I had done this, I went forth unto the treasury of Laban. And as I went forth towards the treasury of Laban, behold, I saw the servant of Laban who had the keys of the treasury. And I commanded him in the voice of Laban, that he should go with me into the treasury.

21. And he supposed me to be his master, Laban, for he beheld the garments and also the sword girded about my loins.

22. And he spake unto me concerning the elders of the Jews, he knowing that his master, Laban, had been out by night among them.

23. And I spake unto him as if it had been Laban.

24. And I also spake unto him that I should carry the engravings, which were upon the [c]plates of brass, to my elder brethren, who were without the walls.

25. And I also bade him that he should follow me.

26. And he, supposing that I spake of the brethren of the church, and that I was truly that Laban whom I had slain, wherefore he did follow me.

27. And he spake unto me many times concerning the elders of the Jews, as I went forth unto my brethren, who were without the walls.

28. And it came to pass that when Laman saw me he was exceedingly frightened, and also Lemuel and Sam. And they fled from before my presence; for they supposed it was Laban, and that he had slain me and had sought to take away their lives also.

29. And it came to pass that I called after them, and they did hear me; wherefore they did cease to flee from my presence.

30. And it came to pass that when the servant of Laban beheld my brethren he began to tremble, and was about to flee from before me and return to the city of Jerusalem.

31. And now I, Nephi, being a man large in stature, and also having received much strength of the Lord, therefore I did seize upon the servant of Laban, and held him, that he should not flee.

32. And it came to pass that I spake with him, that if he would

b, 1 Ne. 2:20. *c*, see *a*, 1 Ne. 3.

hearken unto my words, as the Lord liveth, and as I live, even so that if he would hearken unto our words, we would spare his life.

33. And I spake unto him, even with an oath, that he need not fear; that he should be a free man like unto us if he would go down in the wilderness with us.

34. And I also spake unto him, saying: Surely the Lord hath commanded us to do this thing; and shall we not be diligent in keeping the commandments of the Lord? Therefore, if thou wilt go down into the wilderness to my father thou shalt have place with us.

35. And it came to pass that Zoram did take courage at the words which I spake. Now ^{d}Zoram was the name of the servant; and he promised that he would go down into the wilderness unto my father. And he also made an oath unto us that he would tarry with us from that time forth.

36. Now we were desirous that he should tarry with us for this cause, that the Jews might not know concerning our flight into the wilderness, lest they should pursue us and destroy us.

37. And it came to pass that when Zoram had made an oath unto us, our fears did cease concerning him.

38. And it came to pass that we took the plates of brass and the servant of Laban, and departed into the wilderness, and journeyed unto the tent of our father.

CHAPTER 5.

Sariah's complaint against Lehi—Both rejoice over their sons' return—Contents of the brass plates—Lehi a descendant of Joseph—Laban also of that lineage—Lehi's prophecies.

1. And it came to pass that after we had come down into the wilderness unto our father, behold, he was filled with joy, and also my mother, Sariah, was exceeding glad, for she truly had mourned because of us.

2. For she had supposed that we had perished in the wilderness; and she also had complained against my father, telling him that he was a visionary man; saying: Behold thou hast led us forth from the land of our inheritance, and my sons are no more, and we perish in the wilderness.

3. And after this manner of language had my mother complained against my father.

4. And it had come to pass that my father spake unto her, saying: I know that I am a visionary man; for if I had not seen the things of God in a ^{a}vision I should not have known the goodness of God, but had tarried at Jerusalem, and had perished with my brethren.

5. But behold, I have obtained a land of promise, in the which things I do rejoice; yea, and I know that the Lord will deliver my sons out of the hands of Laban, and bring them down again unto us in the wilderness.

6. And after this manner of language did my father, Lehi, comfort my mother, Sariah, concerning us, while we journeyed in the wilderness up to the land of Jerusalem, to obtain the record of the Jews.

7. And when we had returned to the tent of my father, behold their joy was full, and my mother was comforted.

8. And she spake, saying: Now I know of a surety that the Lord hath ^{b}commanded my husband to

flee into the wilderness; yea, and I also know of a surety that the Lord hath protected my sons, and delivered them out of the hands of Laban, and given them power whereby they could accomplish the thing which the Lord hath commanded them. And after this manner of language did she speak.

9. And it came to pass that they did rejoice exceedingly, and did offer sacrifice and burnt offerings unto the Lord; and they gave thanks unto the God of Israel.

10. And after they had given thanks unto the God of Israel, my father, Lehi, took the records which were engraven upon ^cthe plates of brass, and he did search them from the beginning.

11. And he beheld that they did contain the five books of Moses, which gave an account of the creation of the world, and also of Adam and Eve, who were our first parents;

12. And also a record of the Jews from the beginning, even down to the commencement of the reign of Zedekiah, king of Judah;

13. And also the prophecies of the holy prophets, from the beginning, even down to the commencement of the reign of Zedekiah; and also many prophecies which have been spoken by the mouth of Jeremiah.

14. And it came to pass that my father, Lehi, also found upon the plates of brass a ^dgenealogy of his fathers; wherefore he knew that he was a descendant of Joseph; yea, even that Joseph who was the son of Jacob, who was sold into Egypt, and who was preserved by the hand of the Lord, that he might preserve his father,

Jacob, and all his household from perishing with famine.

15. And they were also led out of captivity and out of the land of Egypt, by that same God who had preserved them.

16. And thus my father, Lehi, did discover the genealogy of his fathers. And Laban also was a descendant of Joseph, wherefore he and his fathers had kept the records.

17. And now when my father saw all these things, he was filled with the Spirit, and began to prophesy concerning his seed—

18. That these plates of brass should go forth unto all nations, kindreds, tongues, and people who were of his seed.

19. Wherefore, he said that these plates of brass should never perish; neither should they be dimmed any more by time. And he prophesied many things concerning his seed.

20. And it came to pass that thus far I and my father had kept the commandments wherewith the Lord had commanded us.

21. And we had obtained the records which the Lord had commanded us, and searched them and found that they were desirable; yea, even of great worth unto us, insomuch that we could preserve the commandments of the Lord unto our children.

22. Wherefore, it was wisdom in the Lord that we should carry them with us, as we journeyed in the wilderness towards the land of promise.

CHAPTER 6.

Nephi's intent—He writes what is pleasing to God.

1. And now I, Nephi, do not give the genealogy of my fathers

c, see a, 1 Ne. 3. d, 1 Ne. 3:12. 5:16. 6:1. Al. 10:3. 37:3.
BETWEEN B. C. 600 AND 592.

in this part of my record; neither at any time shall I give it after upon these plates which I am writing; for it is given in the record which has been *a*kept by my father; wherefore, I do not write it in this work.

2. For it sufficeth me to say that we are a descendant of Joseph.

3. And it mattereth not to me that I am particular to give a full account of all the things of my father, for they cannot be written upon these plates, for I desire the room that I may write of the things of God.

4. For the fulness of mine intent is that I may persuade men to come unto the God of Abraham, and the God of Isaac, and the God of Jacob, and be saved.

5. Wherefore, the things which are pleasing unto the world I do not write, but the things which are pleasing unto God and unto those who are not of the world.

6. Wherefore, I shall give commandment unto my seed, that they shall not *b*occupy these plates with things which are not of worth unto the children of men.

CHAPTER 7.

Lehi's sons again sent back to Jerusalem—Ishmael and household agree to join Lehi's company—Dissension—Nephi, bound with cords, is freed through power of faith—His rebellious brethren repent.

1. And now I would that ye might know, that after my father, Lehi, had made an end of *a*prophesying concerning his seed, it came to pass that the Lord spake unto him again, saying that it was not meet for him, Lehi, that he should take his family into the wilderness alone; but that his sons should *b*take daughters to wife, that they might raise up seed unto the Lord in the land of promise.

2. And it came to pass that the Lord commanded him that I, Nephi, and my brethren, should again return unto the land of Jerusalem, and bring down *c*Ishmael and his family into the wilderness.

3. And it came to pass that I, Nephi, did again, with my brethren, go forth into the wilderness to go up to Jerusalem.

4. And it came to pass that we went up unto the house of Ishmael, and we did gain favor in the sight of Ishmael, insomuch that we did speak unto him the words of the Lord.

5. And it came to pass that the Lord did soften the heart of Ishmael, and also his household, insomuch that they took their journey with us down into the wilderness to the tent of our father.

6. And it came to pass that as we journeyed in the wilderness, behold Laman and Lemuel, and two of the daughters of Ishmael, and the two sons of Ishmael and their families, did rebel against us; yea, against me, Nephi, and Sam, and their father, Ishmael, and his wife, and his three other daughters.

7. And it came to pass in the which rebellion, they were desirous to return unto the land of Jerusalem.

8. And now I, Nephi, being grieved for the hardness of their hearts, therefore I spake unto them, saying, yea, even unto Laman and unto Lemuel: Behold

---

a, 1 Ne. 1:16. *b*, Jac. 1:1—4. 3:13, 14. 4:1—3. Enos 13—18. Jar. 1, 2, 14, 15. Om. 1, 3, 9, 11, 25. W. of Morm. 3—11. Chap. 7: *a*, 1 Ne. 1:16. 2:14. *b*, 1 Ne. 16:7. *c*, 1 Ne. 7:6, 19. Between B. C. 600 and 592.

ye are mine elder brethren, and how is it that ye are so hard in your hearts, and so blind in your minds, that ye have need that I, your younger brother, should speak unto you, yea, and set an example for you?

9. How is it that ye have not hearkened unto the word of the Lord?

10. How is it that ye have forgotten that ye have ^dseen an angel of the Lord?

11. Yea, and how is it that ye have forgotten what great things the Lord hath done for us, in ^edelivering us out of the hands of Laban, and also that we should obtain the record?

12. Yea, and how is it that ye have forgotten that the Lord is able to do all things according to his will, for the children of men, if it so be that they exercise faith in him? Wherefore, let us be faithful to him.

13. And if it so be that we are faithful to him, ^fwe shall obtain the land of promise; and ye shall know ^gat some future period that the word of the Lord shall be fulfilled concerning the destruction of Jerusalem; for all things which the Lord hath spoken concerning the destruction of Jerusalem must be fulfilled.

14. For behold, the Spirit of the Lord ceaseth soon to strive with them; for behold, they have ^hrejected the prophets, and ⁱJeremiah have they cast into prison. And they have sought to ^jtake away the life of my father, insomuch that they have driven him out of the land.

15. Now behold, I say unto you that if ye will return unto Jerusalem ye shall also perish with them. And now, if ye have choice, go up to the land, and remember the words which I speak unto you, that if ye go ye will also perish; for thus the Spirit of the Lord constraineth me that I should speak.

16. And it came to pass that when I, Nephi, had spoken these words unto my brethren, they were angry with me. And it came to pass that they did lay their hands upon me, for behold, they were exceeding wroth, and they did bind me with cords, for they sought to take away my life, that they might leave me in the wilderness to be devoured by wild beasts.

17. But it came to pass that I prayed unto the Lord, saying: O Lord, according to my faith which is in thee, wilt thou deliver me from the hands of my brethren; yea, even give me strength that I may burst these bands with which I am bound.

18. And it came to pass that when I had said these words, behold, the bands were loosed from off my hands and feet, and I stood before my brethren, and I spake unto them again.

19. And it came to pass that they were angry with me again, and sought to lay hands upon me; but behold, one of the daughters of Ishmael, yea, and also her mother, and one of the sons of Ishmael, did plead with my brethren, insomuch that they did soften their hearts; and they did cease striving to take away my life.

20. And it came to pass that they were sorrowful, because of their wickedness, insomuch that they did bow down before me,

---

d, 1 Ne. 3:20. *e*, 1 Ne. 4. *f*, 1 Ne. 2:20. 18:22, 23. *g*, 2 Ne. 6:8, 9. 25:10. Om. 15. He. 8:20, 21. *h*, Jer. 44:4—6. *i*, Jer. 37:15. *j*, 1 Ne. 2:1.
BETWEEN B. C. 600 AND 592.

and did plead with me that I would forgive them of the thing that they had done against me.

21. And it came to pass that I did frankly forgive them all that they had done, and I did exhort them that they would pray unto the Lord their God for forgiveness. And it came to pass that they did so. And after they had done praying unto the Lord we did again travel on our journey towards the tent of our father.

22. And it came to pass that we did come down unto the tent of our father. And after I and my brethren and all the house of Ishmael had come down unto the tent of my father, they did give thanks unto the Lord their God; and they did offer sacrifice and burnt offerings unto him.

CHAPTER 8.

Lehi's dream of the tree, the river, and the rod of iron—Laman and Lemuel partake not of the fruit of the tree.

1. And it came to pass that we had gathered together all manner of ªseeds of every kind, both of grain of every kind, and also of the seeds of fruit of every kind.

2. And it came to pass that while my father tarried in the wilderness he spake unto us, saying: Behold, I have dreamed a dream; or, in other words, I have seen a vision.

3. And behold, because of the thing which I have seen, I have reason to rejoice in the Lord because of Nephi and also of Sam; for I have reason to suppose that they, and also many of their seed, will be saved.

4. But behold, Laman and Lemuel, I fear exceedingly because of you; for behold, methought I saw in my dream, a dark and dreary wilderness.

5. And it came to pass that I saw a man, and he was dressed in a white robe; and he came and stood before me.

6. And it came to pass that he spake unto me, and bade me follow him.

7. And it came to pass that as I followed him I beheld myself that I was in a dark and dreary waste.

8. And after I had traveled for the space of many hours in darkness, I began to pray unto the Lord that he would have mercy on me, according to the multitude of his tender mercies.

9. And it came to pass after I had prayed unto the Lord I beheld a large and spacious field.

10. And it came to pass that I ᵇbeheld a tree, whose fruit was desirable to make one happy.

11. And it came to pass that I did go forth and partake of the fruit thereof; and I beheld that it was most sweet, above all that I ever before tasted. Yea, and I beheld that the fruit thereof was white, to exceed all the whiteness that I had ever seen.

12. And as I partook of the fruit thereof it filled my soul with exceeding great joy; wherefore, I began to be desirous that my family should partake of it also; for I knew that it was desirable above all other fruit.

13. And as I cast my eyes round about, that perhaps I might discover my family also, I beheld a ᶜriver of water; and it ran along, and it was near the tree of which I was partaking the fruit.

14. And I looked to behold from whence it came; and I saw the head thereof a little way off;

---

a, 1 Ne. 18:24. *b*, 1 Ne. 8:15, 20, 24, 25, 30. 11:8, 9, 21—23. 25. *c*, 1 Ne. 8:19. 12:16, 18. 15:26—29.
BETWEEN B. C. 600 AND 592.

and at the head thereof I beheld your mother, Sariah, and Sam, and Nephi; and they stood as if they knew not whither they should go.

15. And it came to pass that I beckoned unto them; and I also did say unto them with a loud voice that they should come unto me, and partake of the fruit, which was desirable above all other fruit.

16. And it came to pass that they did come unto me and partake of the fruit also.

17. And it came to pass that I was desirous that Laman and Lemuel should come and partake of the fruit also; wherefore, I cast mine eyes towards the head of the river, that perhaps I might see them.

18. And it came to pass that I saw them, but ^{d}they would not come unto me and partake of the fruit.

19. And I beheld a ^{e}rod of iron, and it extended along the bank of the river, and led to the tree by which I stood.

20. And I also beheld a straight and narrow path, which came along by the rod of iron, even to the tree by which I stood; and it also led by the head of the fountain, unto a large and spacious field, as if it had been a world.

21. And I saw numberless concourses of people, many of whom were pressing forward, that they might obtain the path which led unto the tree by which I stood.

22. And it came to pass that they did come forth, and commence in the path which led to the tree.

23. And it came to pass that there arose a mist of darkness; yea, even an exceeding great mist of darkness, insomuch that they who had commenced in the path did lose their way, that they wandered off and were lost.

24. And it came to pass that I beheld others pressing forward, and they came forth and caught hold of the end of the rod of iron; and they did press forward through the mist of darkness, clinging to the rod of iron, even until they did come forth and partake of the fruit of the tree.

25. And after they had partaken of the fruit of the tree they did cast their eyes about as if they were ashamed.

26. And I also cast my eyes round about, and beheld, on the other side of the river of water, ^{f}a great and spacious building; and it stood as it were in the air, high above the earth.

27. And it was filled with people, both old and young, both male and female; and their manner of dress was exceeding fine; and they were in the attitude of mocking and pointing their fingers towards those who had come at and were partaking of the fruit.

28. And after they had tasted of the fruit they were ashamed, because of those that were scoffing at them; and they fell away into forbidden paths and were lost.

29. And now I, Nephi, do not speak all the words of my father.

30. But, to be short in writing, behold, he saw other multitudes pressing forward; and they came and caught hold of the end of the ^{g}rod of iron; and they did press their way forward, continually holding fast to the rod of iron, until they came forth and fell

d, 2 Ne. 5:20.   *e,* 1 Ne. 8:24.   30. 15:23, 24.   *f,* vers. 31, 33.   1 Ne. 11:35, 36. 12:18.   *g,* 1 Ne. 8:19.   15:23, 24.   BETWEEN B. C. 600 AND 592.

1 NEPHI, 9.

down and partook of the fruit of the tree.

31. And he also saw other multitudes feeling their way towards that great and spacious building.

32. And it came to pass that many were ʰdrowned in the depths of the fountain; and many were lost from his view, wandering in strange roads.

33. And great was the multitude that did enter into that ⁱstrange building. And after they did enter into that building they did point the finger of scorn at me and those that were partaking of the fruit also; but we heeded them not.

34. These are the words of my father: For as many as heeded them, had fallen away.

35. And ʲLaman and Lemuel partook not of the fruit, said my father.

36. And it came to pass after my father had spoken all the words of his dream or vision, which were many, he said unto us, because of these things which he saw in a vision, he exceedingly feared for Laman and Lemuel; yea, he feared lest they should be ᵏcast off from the presence of the Lord.

37. And he did exhort them then with all the feeling of a tender parent, that they would hearken to his words, that perhaps the Lord would be merciful to them, and not cast them off; yea, my father did preach unto them.

38. And after he had preached unto them, and also prophesied unto them of many things, he bade them to keep the commandments of the Lord; and he did cease speaking unto them.

CHAPTER 9.

Concerning the plates of Nephi—Two sets of records, one of the ministry, the other of rulers, wars, etc.

1. And all these things did my father see, and hear, and speak, as he ᵃdwelt in a tent, in the valley of Lemuel, and also a great many more things, which cannot be written upon these plates.

2. And now, as I have spoken ᵇconcerning these plates, behold they are not the plates upon which I make a full account of the history of my people; for the plates upon which I make a full account of my people I have given the name of Nephi; wherefore, they are called the plates of Nephi, after mine own name; and these plates also are called the plates of Nephi.

3. Nevertheless, I have received a commandment of the Lord that I should make these plates, for the special purpose that there should be an account engraven of the ministry of my people.

4. Upon the other plates should be engraven an account of the reign of the kings, and the wars and contentions of my people; wherefore these plates are for the more part of the ministry; and the other plates are for the more part of the reign of kings and the wars and contentions of my people.

5. Wherefore, the Lord hath commanded me to make these plates for a ᶜwise purpose in him, which purpose I know not.

6. But the Lord knoweth all things from the beginning; wherefore, he prepareth a way to accomplish all his works among the children of men; for behold, he

---

h, 1 Ne. 8:13, 14. 15:26—29. *i,* 1 Ne. 8:26. *j,* vers. 4, 17, 18. *k,* 2 Ne. 5:20.
Chap. 9: *a,* 1 Ne. 2:6, 15. *b,* see *f,* 1 Ne. 1. *c,* W. of Morm. 7. Al. 37:2, 12, 14, 18.
D. & C. 3:19. 10:34—42. 1 Ne. 19:3.   Between B. C. 600 and 592.

1 NEPHI, 10.

hath all power unto the fulfilling of all his words. And thus it is. Amen.

CHAPTER 10.

Lehi predicts the Babylonian captivity, and the coming of the Lamb of God—The house of Israel likened to an olive-tree—Dispersion and subsequent gathering typified.

1. And now I, Nephi, proceed to give an account upon these plates of my proceedings, and my reign and ministry; wherefore, to proceed with mine account, I must speak somewhat of the things of my father, and also of my brethren.

2. For behold, it came to pass after my father had made an end of speaking the words of his dream, and also of exhorting them to all diligence, he spake unto them concerning the Jews—

3. That after they should be destroyed, even that great city Jerusalem, and many be carried away captive into Babylon, according to the own due time of the Lord, they should return again, yea, even be brought back out of captivity; and after they should be *a*brought back out of captivity they should possess again the land of their inheritance.

4. Yea, even *b*six hundred years from the time that my father left Jerusalem, a *c*prophet would the Lord God raise up among the Jews—even a Messiah, or, in other words, a Savior of the world.

5. And he also spake concerning the prophets, how *d*great a number had testified of these things, concerning this Messiah, of whom he had spoken, or this Redeemer of the world.

6. Wherefore, all mankind were in a *e*lost and in a fallen state, and ever would be save they should rely on this Redeemer.

7. And he spake also concerning a *f*prophet who should come before the Messiah, to prepare the way of the Lord—

8. Yea, even he should go forth and cry in the wilderness: Prepare ye the way of the Lord, and make his paths straight; for there standeth one among you whom ye know not; and he is mightier than I, whose shoe's latchet I am not worthy to unloose. And much spake my father concerning this thing.

9. And my father said he should baptize in Bethabara, beyond Jordan; and he also said he should baptize with water; even that he should baptize the Messiah with water.

10. And after he had baptized the Messiah with water, he should behold and bear record that he had baptized the Lamb of God, who should take away the sins of the world.

11. And it came to pass after my father had spoken these words he spake unto my brethren concerning the gospel which should be preached among the Jews, and also concerning the *g*dwindling of the Jews in unbelief. And after they had slain the Messiah, who should come, and after he had been slain he should rise from the dead, and should make himself manifest, by the Holy Ghost, unto the Gentiles.

12. Yea, even my father spake much concerning the Gentiles, and also concerning the house of

a, 2 Ne. 6:8—11. Dan. 9:2. *b*, 1 Ne. 19:8. 2 Ne. 25:19. 3 Ne. 1:1. *c*, 1 Ne. 22:20, 21. 3 Ne. 20:23. *d*, 3 Ne. 20:24. *e*, 2 Ne. 2:5—8. 9:6—38. 25:20. 31:21. Mos. 16:4, 5. Al. 9:30, 32. 12:22. *f*, 1 Ne. 11:27. 2 Ne. 31:4—18. *g*, Rom. 11. Jac. 4:15. 1 Ne. 4:13. 12:22. 13:35. Morm. 5:14. BETWEEN B. C. 600 AND 592.

Israel, that they should be compared like unto an ʰolive-tree, whose branches should be broken off and should be scattered upon all the face of the earth.

13. Wherefore, he said it must needs be that we should be led with one accord into the ⁱland of promise, unto the fulfilling of the word of the Lord, that we should be scattered upon all the face of the earth.

14. And after the house of Israel should be scattered they should be gathered together again; or, in fine, after ʲthe Gentiles had received the fulness of the Gospel, the natural branches of the olive-tree, or the remnants of the house of Israel, should be grafted in, or come to the knowledge of the true Messiah, their Lord and their Redeemer.

15. And after this manner of language did my father prophesy and speak unto my brethren, and also many more things which I do not write in this book; for I have ᵏwritten as many of them as were expedient for me in mine other book.

16. And all these things, of which I have spoken, were done as my father ˡdwelt in a tent, in the valley of Lemuel.

17. And it came to pass after I, Nephi, having heard all the words of my father, concerning the things which he saw in a vision, and also the things which he spake by the power of the Holy Ghost, which power he received by faith on the Son of God —and the Son of God was the Messiah who should come—I, Nephi, was desirous also that I might see, and hear, and know of these things, by the power of the Holy Ghost, which is the ᵐgift of God unto all those who diligently seek him, as well in times of old as in the time that he should manifest himself unto the children of men.

18. For he is the same yesterday, to-day, and forever; and the way is prepared for all men from the foundation of the world, if it so be that they repent and come unto him.

19. For he that diligently seeketh shall find; and the mysteries of God shall be unfolded unto them, by the power of the Holy Ghost, as well in these times as in times of old, and as well in times of old as in times to come; wherefore, the course of the Lord is one eternal round.

20. Therefore remember, O man, for all thy doings thou shalt be brought into judgment.

21. Wherefore, if ye have sought to do wickedly in the days of your probation, then ye are found unclean before the judgment-seat of God; and no unclean thing can dwell with God; wherefore, ye must be cast off forever.

22. And the Holy Ghost giveth authority that I should speak these things, and deny them not.

CHAPTER 11.

Nephi and the Spirit of the Lord— Lehi's prophetic dream interpreted— Nephi's vision of the Virgin and the Son of God—Christ's ministry foreshown.

1. For it came to pass after I had desired to know the things that my father had seen, and believing that the Lord was able to make them known unto me, as I sat pondering in mine heart I was caught away in the Spirit of the Lord, yea, into an exceeding high

---

h, Jac. chaps. 5, 6. *i*, 1 Ne. 2:20. 18:23. *j*, Jac. 5. 3 Ne. 16:4—7. 21:1—11. *k*, see *j*, 1 Ne. 1. *l*, see *a*, 1 Ne. 9. *m*, 2 Pet. 1:21. BETWEEN B. C. 600 AND 592.

mountain, which I never had before seen, and upon which I never had before set my foot.

2. And the Spirit said unto me: Behold, what desirest thou?

3. And I said: I desire to behold the things which my father saw.

4. And the Spirit said unto me: Believest thou that thy father saw the ªtree of which he hath spoken?

5. And I said: Yea, thou knowest that I believe all the words of my father.

6. And when I had spoken these words, the Spirit cried with a loud voice, saying: Hosanna to the Lord, the most high God; for he is God over all the earth, yea, even above all. And blessed art thou, Nephi, because thou believest in the Son of the most high God; wherefore, thou shalt behold the things which thou hast desired.

7. And behold this thing shall be given unto thee for a sign, that after thou hast beheld the tree which bore the fruit which thy father tasted, thou shalt also behold a man descending out of heaven, and him shall ye witness; and after ye have witnessed him ye shall bear record that it is the Son of God.

8. And it came to pass that the Spirit said unto me: Look! And I looked and beheld a tree; and it was like unto the tree which my father had seen; and the beauty thereof was far beyond, yea, exceeding of all beauty; and the whiteness thereof did exceed the whiteness of the driven snow.

9. And it came to pass after I had seen the tree, I said unto the Spirit: I behold thou hast shown unto me the tree which is precious above all.

10. And he said unto me: What desirest thou?

11. And I said unto him: To know the interpretation thereof —for I spake unto him as a man speaketh; for I beheld that he was in the ᵇform of a man; yet nevertheless, I knew that it was the Spirit of the Lord; and he spake unto me as a man speaketh with another.

12. And it came to pass that he said unto me: Look! And I looked as if to look upon him, and I saw him not; for he had gone from before my presence.

13. And it came to pass that I looked and beheld the great city of Jerusalem, and also other cities. And I beheld the city of Nazareth; and in the city of ᶜNazareth I beheld a virgin, and she was exceedingly fair and white.

14. And it came to pass that I saw the heavens open; and an angel came down and stood before me; and he said unto me: Nephi, what beholdest thou?

15. And I said unto him: A virgin, most beautiful and fair above all other virgins.

16. And he said unto me: Knowest thou the condescension of God?

17. And I said unto him: I know that he loveth his children; nevertheless, I do not know the meaning of all things.

18. And he said unto me: Behold, the virgin whom thou seest is the ᵈmother of the Son of God, after the manner of the flesh.

19. And it came to pass that I beheld that she was carried away in the Spirit; and after she had

a, 1 Ne. 8:10—12.   11:8, 9.   15:21, 22.   *b*, John 14:16, 17.   *c*, Luke 1:26, 27.
d, Luke 1:31, 32.   1 Ne. 11:20, 21.   Mos. 3:8.   15:2—5.   Eth. 3:9.
BETWEEN B. C. 600 AND 592.

been carried away in the Spirit for the space of a time the angel spake unto me, saying: Look!

20. And I looked and beheld the virgin again, bearing a child in her arms.

21. And the angel said unto me: Behold the Lamb of God, yea, even the Son of the Eternal Father! Knowest thou the meaning of the tree which thy father saw?

22. And I answered him, saying: Yea, it is the ^{e}love of God, which sheddeth itself abroad in the hearts of the children of men; wherefore, it is the most desirable above all things.

23. And he spake unto me, saying: Yea, and the most joyous to the soul.

24. And after he had said these words, he said unto me: Look! And I looked, and I beheld the Son of God going forth among the children of men; and I saw many fall down at his feet and worship him.

25. And it came to pass that I beheld that the ^{f}rod of iron, which my father had seen, was the word of God, which led to the fountain of living waters, or to the tree of life; which waters are a representation of the love of God; and I also beheld that the tree of life was a representation of the love of God.

26. And the angel said unto me again: Look and behold the condescension of God!

27. And I looked and beheld the Redeemer of the world, of whom my father had spoken; and I also beheld the ^{g}prophet who should prepare the way before him. And the Lamb of God went forth and was baptized of him; and after he was baptized, I beheld the heavens open, and the Holy Ghost come down out of heaven and abide upon him in the form of a dove.

28. And I beheld that he went forth ministering unto the people, in power and great glory; and the multitudes were gathered together to hear him; and I beheld that they cast him out from among them.

29. And I also beheld ^{h}twelve others following him. And it came to pass that they were carried away in the Spirit from before my face, and I saw them not.

30. And it came to pass that the angel spake unto me again, saying: Look! And I looked, and I beheld the heavens open again, and I saw angels descending upon the children of men; and they did minister unto them.

31. And he spake unto me again, saying: Look! And I looked, and I beheld the Lamb of God going forth among the children of men. And I beheld multitudes of people who were sick, and who were afflicted with all manner of diseases, and with devils and unclean spirits; and the angel spake and showed all these things unto me. And they were healed by the power of the Lamb of God; and the devils and the unclean spirits were cast out.

32. And it came to pass that the angel spake unto me again, saying: Look! And I looked and beheld the Lamb of God, that he was taken by the people; yea, the Son of the everlasting God was judged of the world; and I saw and bear record.

33. And I, Nephi, saw that he was lifted up upon the cross and slain for the sins of the world.

34. And after he was slain I

---

e, 1 Ne. 11:25. Moro. 8:26. f, 1 Ne. 8:19. g, 1 Ne. 10:7—10. 2 Ne. 31:4—14. h, 1 Ne. 11:34, 35, 36. 12:9. 13:24—26, 40, 41. 14:20. BET. B. C. 600 AND 592.

saw the multitudes of the earth, that they were gathered together to fight against the apostles of the Lamb; for thus were the twelve called by the angel of the Lord.

35. And the multitude of the earth was gathered together; and I beheld that they were in a large and spacious building, like unto the ¹building which my father saw. And the angel of the Lord spake unto me again, saying: Behold the world and the wisdom thereof; yea, behold the house of Israel hath gathered together to fight against the twelve apostles of the Lamb.

36. And it came to pass that I saw and bear record, that the great and spacious building was the pride of the world; and it fell, and the fall thereof was exceeding great. And the angel of the Lord spake unto me again, saying: Thus shall be the destruction of all nations, kindreds, tongues, and people, that shall fight against the twelve apostles of the Lamb.

CHAPTER 12.

Nephi's vision of the land of promise—The future appearing of the Savior to the people of Nephi—Their righteousness, iniquity, and downfall foreseen.

1. And it came to pass that the angel said unto me: Look, and behold thy seed, and also the seed of thy brethren. And I looked and beheld the land of promise; and I beheld multitudes of people, yea, even as it were in number as many as the sand of the sea.

2. And it came to pass that I beheld multitudes gathered together to battle, one against the other; and I beheld wars, and rumors of wars, and great slaughters with the sword among my people.

3. And it came to pass that I beheld many generations pass away, after the manner of wars and contentions in the land; and I beheld many cities, yea, even that I did not number them.

4. And it came to pass that I saw a mist of ªdarkness on the face of the land of promise; and I saw lightnings, and I heard thunderings, and earthquakes, and all manner of tumultuous noises; and I saw the earth and the rocks, that they rent; and I saw mountains tumbling into pieces; and I saw the plains of the earth, that they were broken up; and I saw many cities that they were sunk; and I saw many that they were burned with fire; and I saw many that did tumble to the earth, because of the quaking thereof.

5. And it came to pass after I saw these things, I saw the vapor of darkness, that it passed from off the face of the earth; and behold, I saw multitudes who had fallen because of the great and terrible judgments of the Lord.

6. And I saw the heavens open, and the Lamb of God ᵇdescending out of heaven; and he came down and showed himself unto them.

7. And I also saw and bear record that the Holy Ghost fell upon ᶜtwelve others; and they were ordained of God, and chosen.

8. And the angel spake unto me, saying: Behold the twelve disciples of the Lamb, who are chosen to minister unto thy seed.

i, 1 Ne. 8:26—28.   CHAP. 12: *a*, 1 Ne. 19:10—12. 2 Ne. 26:3—7. He. 14:20—27. 3 Ne. chaps. 8—10. *b*, 2 Ne. 26:1, 9. Al. 16:20. 3 Ne. 11:3—17. *c*, 3 Ne. 11:22. 12:1. 13:25. 15:11. 18:37. 19:4—36. Chaps. 27, 28. 4 Ne. 1—14.
BETWEEN B. C. 600 AND 592.

9. And he said unto me: Thou rememberest the twelve apostles of the Lamb? Behold they are they who shall judge the twelve tribes of Israel; wherefore, the twelve ministers of thy seed shall be judged of them; for ye are of the house of Israel.

10. And these twelve ministers whom thou beholdest shall judge thy seed. And, behold, they are righteous forever; for because of their faith in the Lamb of God their garments are made white in his blood.

11. And the angel said unto me: Look! And I looked, and beheld ᵈthree generations pass away in righteousness; and their garments were white even like unto the Lamb of God. And the angel said unto me: These are made white in the blood of the Lamb, because of their faith in him.

12. And I, Nephi, also saw many of the fourth generation who passed away in righteousness.

13. And it came to pass that I saw the multitudes of the earth gathered together.

14. And the angel said unto me: Behold thy seed, and also the seed of thy brethren.

15. And it came to pass that I looked and beheld the ᵉpeople of my seed gathered together in multitudes against the seed of my brethren; and they were gathered together to battle.

16. And the angel spake unto me, saying: Behold the fountain of filthy water which thy father saw; yea, even ᶠthe river of which he spake; and the depths thereof are the depths of hell.

17. And the mists of darkness are the temptations of the devil, which blindeth the eyes, and hardeneth the hearts of the children of men, and leadeth them away into broad roads, that they perish and are lost.

18. And the large and spacious building, which thy father saw, is vain imaginations and the pride of the children of men. And a great and a terrible gulf divideth them; yea, even the word of the justice of the Eternal God, and the Messiah who is the Lamb of God, of whom the Holy Ghost beareth record, from the beginning of the world until this time, and from this time henceforth and forever.

19. And while the angel spake these words, I beheld and saw that the seed of my brethren did contend against my seed, according to the word of the angel; and because of the pride of my seed, and the temptations of the devil, I beheld that the seed of my brethren did overpower the people of my seed.

20. And it came to pass that I beheld, and saw the people of the seed of my brethren that they had overcome my seed; and they went forth in multitudes upon the face of the land.

21. And I saw them gathered together in multitudes; and I saw wars and rumors of wars among them; and in wars and rumors of wars I saw ᵍmany generations pass away.

22. And the angel said unto me: Behold these shall dwindle in unbelief.

23. And it came to pass that I beheld, after they had dwindled in unbelief they became a ʰdark, and loathsome, and a filthy people, full of idleness and all manner of abominations.

d, 2 Ne. 26:9, 10. Al. 45:10—14. He. 13:5, 6, 9, 10. 3 Ne. 27:31, 32. Morm. 6.
e, Morm. 6. *f*, 1 Ne. 8:13, 14. 15:26—29. *g*, 1 Ne. 12:3. 2 Ne. 26:2. *h*, 2 Ne. 5:20—25. Al. 3:6—19. Morm. 5:15.
BETWEEN B. C. 600 AND 592.

CHAPTER 13.

The nations of the Gentiles—A great and abominable church—America's history foreshadowed—The Bible and the Book of Mormon.

1. And it came to pass that the angel spake unto me, saying: Look! And I looked and beheld many nations and kingdoms.

2. And the angel said unto me: What beholdest thou? And I said: I behold many nations and kingdoms.

3. And he said unto me: These are the nations and kingdoms of the Gentiles.

4. And it came to pass that I saw among the nations of the Gentiles the foundation of a *a*great church.

5. And the angel said unto me: Behold the foundation of a church which is most abominable above all other churches, which *b*slayeth the saints of God, yea, and tortureth them and bindeth them down, and yoketh them with a yoke of iron, and bringeth them down into captivity.

6. And it came to pass that I beheld this great and abominable church; and I *c*saw the devil that he was the foundation of it.

7. And I also *d*saw gold, and silver, and silks, and scarlets, and fine-twined linen, and all manner of precious clothing; and I saw many harlots.

8. And the angel spake unto me, saying: Behold the gold, and the silver, and the silks, and the scarlets, and the fine-twined linen, and the precious clothing, and the harlots, are the desires of this great and abominable church.

9. And also for the praise of the world do they destroy the saints of God, and bring them down into captivity.

10. And it came to pass that I looked and beheld many waters; and they divided the Gentiles from the seed of my brethren.

11. And it came to pass that the angel said unto me: Behold the wrath of God is upon the seed of thy brethren.

12. And I looked and beheld a man among the Gentiles, who was separated from the seed of my brethren by the many waters; and I beheld the Spirit of God, that it came down and wrought upon the man; and he went forth upon the many waters, even unto the seed of my brethren, who were in the promised land.

13. And it came to pass that I beheld the Spirit of God, that it wrought upon other Gentiles; and they went forth out of captivity, upon the many waters.

14. And it came to pass that I beheld many multitudes of the Gentiles upon the land of promise; and I beheld the wrath of God, that it was upon the seed of my brethren; and they were scattered before the Gentiles and were smitten.

15. And I beheld the Spirit of the Lord, that it was upon the Gentiles, and they did prosper and obtain the land for their inheritance; and I beheld that they were white, and exceeding fair and beautiful, like unto my *f*people before they were slain.

16. And it came to pass that I, Nephi, beheld that the Gentiles who had gone forth out of captivity did humble themselves before the Lord; and the power of the Lord was with them.

17. And I beheld that their

---

a, vers. 6, 26, 28, 32, 34. 1 Ne. 14:3, 9—17. *b*, ver. 9. 1·Ne. 14:13. Rev. 17:6. 18:24. *c*, 1 Ne. 14:9, 10. 22:22, 23. *d*, Morm. 8:36—38. Rev. 18:10—17. *f*, Morm. 6:17—22.

BETWEEN B. C. 600 AND 592.

mother Gentiles were gathered together upon the waters, and upon the land also, to battle against them.

18. And I beheld that the power of God was with them, and also that the wrath of God was upon all those that were gathered together against them to battle.

19. And I, Nephi, beheld that the *k*Gentiles that had gone out of captivity were delivered by the power of God out of the hands of all other nations.

20. And it came to pass that I, Nephi, beheld that they did prosper in the land; and I beheld a *l*book, and it was carried forth among them.

21. And the angel said unto me: Knowest thou the meaning of the book?

22. And I said unto him: I know not.

23. And he said: Behold it proceedeth out of the mouth of a Jew. And I, Nephi, beheld it; and he said unto me: The book that thou beholdest is a record of the Jews, which contains the covenants of the Lord, which he hath made unto the house of Israel; and it also containeth many of the prophecies of the holy prophets; and it is a record like unto the engravings which are upon the *m*plates of brass, save there are not so many; nevertheless, they contain the covenants of the Lord, which he hath made unto the house of Israel; wherefore, they are of great worth unto the Gentiles.

24. And the angel of the Lord said unto me: Thou hast beheld that the book proceeded forth from the mouth of a Jew; and when it proceeded forth from the mouth of a Jew it contained the plainness of the gospel of the Lord, of whom the twelve apostles bear record; and they bear record according to the truth which is in the Lamb of God.

25. Wherefore, these things go forth from the Jews in purity unto the Gentiles, according to the truth which is in God.

26. And after they go forth by the hand of the twelve apostles of the Lamb, from the Jews unto the Gentiles, thou seest the foundation of a great and abominable church, which is most abominable above all other churches; for behold, they have *n*taken away from the gospel of the Lamb many parts which are plain and most precious; and also many covenants of the Lord have they taken away.

27. And all this have they done that they might pervert the right ways of the Lord, that they might blind the eyes and harden the hearts of the children of men.

28. Wherefore, thou seest that after the book hath gone forth through the hands of the great and abominable church, that there are many plain and precious things taken away from the book, which is the book of the Lamb of God.

29. And after these plain and precious things were taken away it goeth forth unto all the nations of the Gentiles; and after it goeth forth unto all the nations of the Gentiles, yea, even across the many waters which thou hast seen with the Gentiles which have gone forth out of captivity, thou seest—because of the many plain and precious things which have been taken out of the book, which were plain unto the understanding of the children of men, ac-

---

k, 2 Ne. 10:10—12. *l*, vers. 23, 28, 38, 40. *m*, see *a*, 1 Ne. 3. *n*, vers. 28—32.

BETWEEN B. C. 600 AND 592.

cording to the plainness which is in the Lamb of God—because of these things which are taken away out of the gospel of the Lamb, an exceeding great many do stumble, yea, insomuch that Satan hath great power over them.

30. Nevertheless, thou beholdest that the °Gentiles who have gone forth out of captivity, and have been lifted up by the power of God above all other nations, upon the face of the land which is choice above all other lands, which is the land that the Lord God hath covenanted with thy father that his seed should have for the land of their inheritance; wherefore, thou seest that the Lord God will not suffer that the Gentiles will utterly destroy the ᵖmixture of thy seed, which are among thy brethren.

31. Neither will he suffer that the Gentiles shall destroy the ᵠseed of thy brethren.

32. Neither will the Lord God suffer that the Gentiles shall forever remain in that awful state of blindness, which thou beholdest they are in, because of the plain and most precious parts of the gospel of the Lamb which have been kept back by that abominable church, whose formation thou hast seen.

33. Wherefore saith the Lamb of God: I will be merciful unto the Gentiles, unto the visiting of the remnant of the house of Israel in great judgment.

34. And it came to pass that the angel of the Lord spake unto me, saying: Behold, saith the Lamb of God, after I have visited the remnant of the house of Israel —and this remnant of whom I speak is the seed of thy father— wherefore, after I have visited them in judgment, and smitten ʳthem by the hand of the Gentiles, and after the Gentiles do stumble exceedingly, because of the most plain and precious parts of the gospel of the Lamb which have been kept back by that abominable church, which is the mother of harlots, saith the Lamb—I will be merciful unto the Gentiles in that day, insomuch that I will bring forth unto them, in mine own power, much of my gospel, which shall be plain and precious, saith the Lamb.

35. For, behold, saith the Lamb: I will manifest myself unto thy seed, that they shall write many things which I shall minister unto them, which shall be plain and precious; and after thy seed shall be destroyed, and dwindle in unbelief, and also the seed of thy brethren, behold, these things shall be ˢhid up, to come forth unto the Gentiles, by the gift and power of the Lamb.

36. And in them shall be written my gospel, saith the Lamb, and my rock and my salvation.

37. And blessed are ᵗthey who shall seek to bring forth my Zion at that day, for they shall have the gift and the power of the Holy Ghost; and if they endure unto the end they shall be lifted up at the last day, and shall be saved in the everlasting kingdom of the Lamb; and whoso shall publish peace, yea, tidings of great joy, how beautiful upon the mountains shall they be.

38. And it came to pass that I beheld the remnant of the seed of my brethren, and also the ᵘbook of the Lamb of God, which

---

o, 2 Ne. 10:10—14. *p,* Al. 45:10—14. *q,* vers. 33, 34. Al. 45:14. 3 Ne. 16:7— 10. 21:4. Morm. 5:19—21. *r,* see *d. s,* 2 Ne. 27:6—26. 3 Ne. 16:4. Morm. 8:4. *t,* 2 Ne. 30:3. Jac. 5:70—75. 6:2, 8. *u,* ver. 40.   BETWEEN B. C. 600 AND 592.

had proceeded forth from the mouth of the Jew, that it came forth from the Gentiles unto the remnant of the seed of my brethren.

39. And after it had come forth unto them I beheld other *v*books, which came forth by the power of the Lamb, from the Gentiles unto them, unto the convincing of the Gentiles and the remnant of the seed of my brethren, and also the Jews who were scattered upon all the face of the earth, that the records of the prophets and of the twelve apostles of the Lamb are true.

40. And the angel spake unto me, saying: These last records, which thou hast seen among the Gentiles, shall establish the truth of the *w*first, which are of the twelve apostles of the Lamb, and shall make known the plain and precious things which have been taken away from them; and shall make known to all kindreds, tongues, and people, that the Lamb of God is the Son of the Eternal Father, and the Savior of the world; and that all men must come unto him, or they cannot be saved.

41. And they must come according to the words which shall be established by the mouth of the Lamb; and the words of the Lamb shall be made known in the records of thy seed, as well as in the records of the twelve apostles of the Lamb; wherefore they *x*both shall be established in one; for there is one God and one Shepherd over all the earth.

42. And the time cometh that he shall manifest himself unto all nations, both unto the Jews and also unto the Gentiles; and after he has manifested himself unto the Jews and also unto the Gentiles, then he shall manifest himself unto the Gentiles and also unto the Jews, and the last shall be first, and the first shall be last.

CHAPTER 14.

Alternative blessing or cursing for the Gentiles—Two churches only—Doom of the mother of harlots—Mission of John the Revelator—End of Nephi's vision.

1. And it shall come to pass, that if the Gentiles shall hearken unto the Lamb of God in that day that he shall manifest himself unto them in word, and also in *a*power, in very deed, unto the taking away of their stumbling blocks—

2. And harden not their hearts against the Lamb of God, they shall be *b*numbered among the seed of thy father; yea, they shall be numbered among the house of Israel; and they shall be a blessed people upon the promised land forever; they shall be no more brought *c*down into captivity; and the house of Israel shall no more be confounded.

3. And that great pit, which hath been digged for them by that great and abominable church, which was founded by the devil and his children, that he might lead away the souls of men down to hell—yea, that great pit which hath been digged for the destruction of men shall be filled by those who digged it, unto their utter destruction, saith the Lamb of God; not the destruction of the soul, save it be the casting of it into that hell which hath no end.

4. For behold, this is accord-

---

v, 3 Ne. 27:25, 26. *w*, ver. 38. *x*, 2 Ne. 3:12. 2 Ne. 29:13, 14. Ezek. 37:15—23. CHAP. 14: *a*, ver. 14. 1 Ne. 13:37. Jac. 6:2, 3. *b*, 3 Ne. 21:6, 22—25. Chap. 30. Eth. 13:10. *c*, 2 Ne. 10:10—14. BETWEEN B. C. 600 AND 592.

ing to the captivity of the devil, and also according to the justice of God, upon all those who will work wickedness and abomination before him.

5. And it came to pass that the angel spake unto me, Nephi, saying: Thou hast beheld that if the Gentiles repent it shall be well with them; and thou also knowest concerning the covenants of the Lord unto the house of Israel; and thou also hast heard that whoso repenteth not must perish.

6. Therefore, *d*wo be unto the Gentiles if it so be that they harden their hearts against the Lamb of God.

7. For the time cometh, saith the Lamb of God, that I will work a great and a *e*marvelous work among the children of men; a work which shall be everlasting, either on the one hand or on the other—either to the convincing of them unto peace and life eternal, or unto the deliverance of them to the hardness of their hearts and the blindness of their minds unto their being brought down into captivity, and also into destruction, both temporally and spiritually, according to the captivity of the devil, of which I have spoken.

8. And it came to pass that when the angel had spoken these words, he said unto me: Rememberest thou the covenants of the Father unto the house of Israel? I said unto him, Yea.

9. And it came to pass that he said unto me: Look, and behold that great and abominable church, which is the mother of abominations, whose foundation is the devil.

10. And he said unto me: Behold there are save *f*two churches only; the one is the church of the Lamb of God, and the other is the church of the devil; wherefore, whoso belongeth not to the church of the Lamb of God belongeth to that great church, which is the mother of abominations; and *g*she is the whore of all the earth.

11. And it came to pass that I looked and beheld the whore of all the earth, and she sat upon many waters; and she had dominion over all the earth, among all nations, kindreds, tongues, and people.

12. And it came to pass that I beheld the church of the Lamb of God, and its numbers were *h*few, because of the wickedness and abominations of the whore who sat upon many waters; nevertheless, I beheld that the church of the Lamb, who were the saints of God, were also upon all the face of the earth; and their dominions upon the face of the earth were small, because of the wickedness of the great whore whom I saw.

13. And it came to pass that I beheld that the great mother of abominations did gather together multitudes upon the face of all the earth, among all the nations of the Gentiles, to fight against the Lamb of God.

14. And it came to pass that I, Nephi, beheld the power of the Lamb of God, that it descended upon the saints of the church of the Lamb, and upon the covenant people of the Lord, who were scattered upon all the face of the earth; and they were armed with righteousness and

d, 2 Ne. 28:32. 3 Ne. 16:7—15. 21:11—21. *e*, Isa. 29:14. *f*, vers. 11—17. 22:14, 22—26. *g*, vers. 11—17. Rev. 17:5, 15. *h*, 3 Ne. 14:14. Isa. 24:6. Matt. 24:37.
BETWEEN B. C. 600 AND 592.

with the ^{i}power of God in great glory.

15. And it came to pass that I beheld that the wrath of God was poured out upon the great and abominable church, insomuch that there were wars and rumors of wars among all the nations and kindreds of the earth.

16. And as there began to be ^{j}wars and rumors of wars among all the nations which belonged to the mother of abominations, the angel spake unto me, saying: Behold, the wrath of God is upon the mother of harlots; and behold, thou seest all these things—

17. And when the day cometh that the ^{k}wrath of God is poured out upon the mother of harlots, which is the great and abominable church of all the earth, whose foundation is the devil, then, at that day, the work of the Father shall commence, in preparing the way for the fulfilling of his covenants, which he hath made to his people who are of the house of Israel.

18. And it came to pass that the angel spake unto me, saying: Look!

19. And I looked and beheld a man, and he was dressed in a white robe.

20. And the angel said unto me: Behold ^{l}one of the twelve apostles of the Lamb.

21. Behold, he shall see and write the remainder of these things; yea, and also many things which have been.

22. And he shall also write concerning the end of the world.

23. Wherefore, the things which he shall write are just and true; and behold they are written in the ^{m}book which thou beheld proceeding out of the mouth of the Jew; and at the time they proceeded out of the mouth of the Jew, or, at the time the book proceeded out of the mouth of the Jew, the things which were written were plain and pure, and most precious and easy to the understanding of all men.

24. And behold, the things which this apostle of the Lamb shall write are many things which thou hast seen; and behold, the remainder shalt thou see.

25. But the things which thou shalt see hereafter thou shalt not write; for the Lord God hath ordained the apostle of the Lamb of God that he should write them.

26. And also others who have been, to them hath he shown all things, and ^{n}they have written them; and they are sealed up to come forth in their purity, according to the truth which is in the Lamb, in the own due time of the Lord, unto the house of Israel.

27. And I, Nephi, heard and bear record, that the name of the apostle of the Lamb was ^{o}John, according to the word of the angel.

28. And behold, I, Nephi, am forbidden that I should write the remainder of the things which I saw and heard; wherefore the things which I have written sufficeth me; and I have written but a small part of the things which I saw.

29. And I bear record that I saw the things which my ^{p}father saw, and the angel of the Lord did make them known unto me.

30. And now I make an end of speaking concerning the things

i, 1 Ne. 13:37, 38. Jac. 6:2, 3. j, 1 Ne. 22:13, 14. Isa. 66:15, 16. k, 1 Ne. 22:15, 16. 3 Ne. 20:20, 21:20, 21. Morm. 8:41. l, ver. 27. m, 1 Ne. 13:20, 38, 40. n, 2 Ne. 27:6—23. Eth. 3:21—27. 12:21. o, ver. 20. p, 1 Ne. 8:2.

BETWEEN B. C. 600 AND 592.

which I saw while I was carried away in the spirit; and if all the things which I saw are not written, the things which I have written are true. And thus it is. Amen.

CHAPTER 15.

Lehi's teachings interpreted by Nephi—The olive-tree—The tree of life—The word of God.

1. And it came to pass that after I, Nephi, had been carried away in the spirit, and seen all these things, I returned to the tent of my father.

2. And it came to pass that I beheld my brethren, and they were disputing one with another concerning the things which my father had spoken unto them.

3. For he truly spake many great things unto them, which were hard to be understood, save a man should inquire of the Lord; and they being hard in their hearts, therefore they did not look unto the Lord as they ought.

4. And now I, Nephi, was grieved because of the hardness of their hearts, and also, because of the things which I had seen, and knew they must unavoidably come to pass because of the great wickedness of the children of men.

5. And it came to pass that I was overcome because of my afflictions, for I considered that mine afflictions were great above all, because of the destructions of ªmy people, for I had beheld their fall.

6. And it came to pass that after I had received strength I spake unto my brethren, desiring to know of them the cause of their disputations.

7. And they said: Behold, we cannot understand the words which ᵇour father hath spoken concerning the natural branches of the olive-tree, and also concerning the Gentiles.

8. And I said unto them: Have ye inquired of the Lord?

9. And they said unto me: We have not; for the Lord maketh no such thing known unto us.

10. Behold, I said unto them: How is it that ye do not keep the commandments of the Lord? How is it that ye will perish, because of the hardness of your hearts?

11. Do ye not remember the things which the Lord hath said?—If ye will not harden your hearts, and ask me in faith, believing that ye shall receive, with diligence in keeping my commandments, surely these things shall be made known unto you.

12. Behold, I say unto you, that the house of Israel was compared unto an ᶜolive-tree, by the Spirit of the Lord which was in our fathers; and behold are we not broken off from the house of Israel, and are we not a branch of the house of Israel?

13. And now, the thing which our father meaneth concerning the grafting in of the natural branches through the fulness of the Gentiles, is, that in the latter days, when our ᵈseed shall have dwindled in unbelief, yea, for the space of many years, and many generations after the Messiah shall be manifested in body unto the children of men, then shall the fulness of the gospel of the Messiah come unto the Gentiles, and from the Gentiles unto the remnant of our seed—

14. And at that day shall the

---

a, Enos 13. Morm. 6. b, 1 Ne. 9:1. 10:14. c, vers. 13, 16. 2 Ne. 3:5. Jac. 5. 6:1—4. d, 3 Ne. 21:4. Vers. 14—20. 1 Ne. 22:8—12. 3 Ne. 5:21—26. 16:10 —12. Chap. 21. Morm. 5:10—15, 20, 21. BETWEEN B. C. 600 AND 592.

remnant of our seed know that they are of the house of Israel, and that they are the covenant people of the Lord; and then shall they know and come to the knowledge of their forefathers, and also to the knowledge of the gospel of their Redeemer, which was ministered unto their fathers by him; wherefore, they shall come to the knowledge of their Redeemer and the very points of his doctrine, that they may know how to come unto him and be saved.

15. And then at that day will they not rejoice and give praise unto their everlasting God, their rock and their salvation? Yea, at that day, will they not receive the strength and nourishment from the true vine? Yea, will they not come unto the true fold of God?

16. Behold, I say unto you, Yea; they shall be remembered again among the house of Israel; they shall be grafted in, being a natural branch of the olive-tree, into the true olive-tree.

17. And this is what our father meaneth; and he meaneth that it will not come to pass until after they are scattered by the Gentiles; and he meaneth that it shall come by way of the Gentiles, that the Lord may show his power unto the Gentiles, for the very cause that he shall be rejected of the Jews, or of the house of Israel.

18. Wherefore, our father hath not spoken of our seed alone, but also of all the house of Israel, pointing to the covenant which should be fulfilled in the latter days; which covenant the Lord made to our father Abraham, saying: In thy seed shall all the kindreds of the earth be blessed.

19. And it came to pass that I, Nephi, spake much unto them concerning these things; yea, I spake unto them concerning the restoration of the *Jews in the latter days.

20. And I did rehearse unto them the words of Isaiah, who spake concerning the restoration of the Jews, or of the house of Israel; and after they were restored they should no more be confounded, neither should they be scattered again. And it came to pass that I did speak many words unto my brethren, that they were pacified and did humble themselves before the Lord.

21. And it came to pass that they did speak unto me again, saying: What meaneth this thing which our father saw in a dream? What meaneth the *tree which he saw?

22. And I said unto them: It was a representation of the tree of life.

23. And they said unto me: What meaneth the *rod of iron which our father saw, that led to the tree?

24. And I said unto them that it was the word of God; and whoso would hearken unto the word of God, and would hold fast unto it, they would never perish; neither could the temptations and the fiery darts of the adversary overpower them unto blindness, to lead them away to destruction.

25. Wherefore, I, Nephi, did exhort them to give heed unto the word of the Lord; yea, I did exhort them with all the energies of my soul, and with all the faculty which I possessed, that they would give heed to the word of

e, 1 Ne. 10:13—16. 22:11, 12. 2 Ne. 6:10—15. 9:1, 2. 10:5—9. 25:16, 17. 30:7, 8. 3 Ne. 5:21—26. 20:20—34. 21:26—29. 29:1, 8. Morm. 5:14. *f*, 1 Ne. 8:10—12. *g*, 1 Ne. 8:19.
BETWEEN B. C. 600 AND 592.

God and remember to keep his commandments always in all things.

26. And they said unto me: What meaneth the ʰriver of water which our father saw?

27. And I said unto them that the water which my father saw was filthiness; and so much was his mind swallowed up in other things that he beheld not the filthiness of the water.

28. And I said unto them that it was an awful ⁱgulf, which separated the wicked from the tree of life, and also from the saints of God.

29. And I said unto them that it was a representation of that awful hell, which the angel said unto me was prepared for the wicked.

30. And I said unto them that our father also saw that the justice of God did also divide the wicked from the righteous; and the brightness thereof was like unto the brightness of a flaming fire, which ascendeth up unto God forever and ever, and hath no end.

31. And they said unto me: Doth this thing mean the torment of the body in the days of probation, or doth it mean the final state of the soul after the death of the temporal body, or doth it speak of the things which are temporal?

32. And it came to pass that I said unto them that it was a representation of things both temporal and spiritual; for the day should come that they must be judged of their works, yea, even the works which were done by the temporal body in their days of probation.

33. Wherefore, if they should die in their wickedness they must be cast off also, as to the things which are spiritual, which are pertaining to righteousness; wherefore, they must be brought to stand before God, to be judged of their works; and if their works have been ʲfilthiness they must needs be filthy; and if they be filthy it must needs be that they cannot dwell in the kingdom of God; if so, the kingdom of God must be filthy also.

34. But behold, I say unto you, the kingdom of God is not filthy, and there cannot any unclean thing enter into the kingdom of God; wherefore there must needs be a place of filthiness prepared for that which is filthy.

35. And there is a place prepared, yea, even that ᵏawful hell of which I have spoken, and the devil is the foundation of it; wherefore the final state of the souls of men is to dwell in the kingdom of God, or to be cast out because of that ˡjustice of which I have spoken.

36. Wherefore, the wicked are rejected from the righteous, and also from that tree of life, whose fruit is most precious and most desirable above all other fruits; yea, and it is the greatest of all the gifts of God. And thus I spake unto my brethren. Amen.

CHAPTER 16.

Lehi's sons and the daughters of Ishmael intermarry—The journey continued—The ball or director given—Death of Ishmael.

1. And now it came to pass that after I, Nephi, had made an end of speaking to my breth-

---

h, 1 Ne. 8:13. i, 1 Ne. 12:18. 2 Ne. 1:13. Al. 26:20. He. 3:29. j, 2 Ne. 9:16.
Mos. 2:37. Al. 11:37. Morm. 9:4. 14. k, ver. 29. 2 Ne. 1:13. 2:29. 9:8—19.
26, 34, 36. 28:15, 21, 23. Jac. 6:10. Al. 12:16—18. 3 Ne. 27:11, 12. Moro. 8:13,
14, 21. l, ver. 30. D. & C. 29:37, 38. 86:36, 44, 84. Bet. B. C. 600 and 592.

ren, behold they said unto me: Thou hast declared unto us *hard things, more than we are able to bear.

2. And it came to pass that I said unto them that I knew that I had spoken hard things against the wicked, according to the truth; and the righteous have I justified, and testified that they should be lifted up at the last day; wherefore, the guilty taketh the truth to be hard, for it cutteth them to the very center.

3. And now my brethren, if ye were righteous and were willing to hearken to the truth, and give heed unto it, that ye might walk uprightly before God, then ye would not murmur because of the truth, and say: Thou speakest hard things against us.

4. And it came to pass that I, Nephi, did exhort my brethren, with all diligence, to keep the commandments of the Lord.

5. And it came to pass that they did humble themselves before the Lord; insomuch that I had joy and great hopes of them, that they would walk in the paths of righteousness.

6. Now, all these things were said and done as my father dwelt in a tent in the *b*valley which he called Lemuel.

7. And it came to pass that I, Nephi, took one of the daughters of *c*Ishmael to wife; and also, my brethren took of the daughters of Ishmael to wife; and also Zoram took the eldest daughter of Ishmael to wife.

8. And thus my father had fulfilled all the commandments of the Lord which had been given unto him. And also, I, Nephi, had been blessed of the Lord exceedingly.

9. And it came to pass that the voice of the Lord spake unto my father by night, and commanded him that on the morrow he should take his journey into the wilderness.

10. And it came to pass that as my father arose in the morning, and went forth to the tent door, to his great astonishment he beheld upon the ground a round *d*ball of curious workmanship; and it was of fine brass. And within the ball were two spindles; and the one pointed the way whither we should go into the wilderness.

11. And it came to pass that we did gather together whatsoever things we should carry into the wilderness, and all the remainder of our provisions which the Lord had given unto us; and we did take seed of every kind that we might carry into the wilderness.

12. And it came to pass that we did take our tents and depart into the wilderness, across the river Laman.

13. And it came to pass that we traveled for the space of four days, nearly a south-southeast direction, and we did pitch our tents again; and we did call the name of the place Shazer.

14. And it came to pass that we did take our bows and our arrows, and go forth into the wilderness to slay food for our families; and after we had slain food for our families we did return again to our families in the wilderness, to the place of Shazer. And we did go forth again in the wilderness, following the same direction, keeping in the most

a, vers. 2, 3. 2 Ne. 1:26, 27. Enos 23. Moro. 9:4. *b*, 1 Ne. 2:8, 14. 9:1. *c*, 1 Ne. 7:2—6, 19, 22. *d*, vers. 16, 26—30. 1 Ne. 18:12, 21. 2 Ne. 5:12. Al. 37:38—47. BETWEEN B. C. 600 AND 592.

fertile parts of the wilderness, which were in the borders near the Red Sea.

15. And it came to pass that we did travel for the space of many days, slaying food by the way, with our bows and our arrows and our stones and our slings.

16. And we did follow the directions of the ball, which led us in the more fertile parts of the wilderness.

17. And after we had traveled for the space of many days, we did pitch our tents for the space of a time, that we might again rest ourselves and obtain food for our families.

18. And it came to pass that as I, Nephi, went forth to slay food, behold, I did break my bow, which was made of *fine steel; and after I did break my bow, behold, my brethren were angry with me because of the loss of my bow, for we did obtain no food.

19. And it came to pass that we did return without food to our families, and being much fatigued, because of their journeying, they did suffer much for the want of food.

20. And it came to pass that Laman and Lemuel and the sons of Ishmael did begin to murmur exceedingly, because of their sufferings and afflictions in the wilderness; and also my father began to murmur against the Lord his God; yea, and they were all exceeding sorrowful, even that they did murmur against the Lord.

21. Now it came to pass that I, Nephi, having been afflicted with my brethren because of the loss of my bow, and their bows having lost their springs, it began to be exceedingly difficult, yea, insomuch that we could obtain no food.

22. And it came to pass that I, Nephi, did speak much unto my brethren, because they had hardened their hearts again, even unto complaining against the Lord their God.

23. And it came to pass that I, Nephi, did make out of wood a bow, and out of a straight stick, an arrow; wherefore, I did arm myself with a bow and an arrow, with a sling and with stones. And I said unto my father: Whither shall I go to obtain food?

24. And it came to pass that he did inquire of the Lord, for they had humbled themselves because of my word; for I did say many things unto them in the energy of my soul.

25. And it came to pass that the voice of the Lord came unto my father; and he was truly chastened because of his murmuring against the Lord, insomuch that he was brought down into the depths of sorrow.

26. And it came to pass that the voice of the Lord said unto him: Look upon the *f*ball, and behold the things which are written.

27. And it came to pass that when my father beheld the things which were written upon the ball, he did fear and tremble exceedingly, and also my brethren and the sons of Ishmael and our wives.

28. And it came to pass that I, Nephi, beheld the pointers which were in the ball, that they did *work according to the faith and diligence and heed which we did give unto them.

29. And there was also written

e, 1 Ne. 4:9. 2 Ne. 5:15. Jar. 8. Eth. 7:9. Ps. 18:34. *f*, 1 Ne. 16:10. *z*, Al. 37:40.

BETWEEN B. C. 600 AND 592.

upon them a new writing, which was plain to be read, which did give us understanding concerning the ways of the Lord; and it was written and changed from time to time, according to the faith and diligence which we gave unto it. And thus we see that by small means the Lord can bring about great things.

30. And it came to pass that I, Nephi, did go forth up into the top of the mountain, according to the directions which were given upon the ball.

31. And it came to pass that I did slay wild beasts, insomuch that I did obtain food for our families.

32. And it came to pass that I did return to our tents, bearing the beasts which I had slain; and now when they beheld that I had obtained food, how great was their joy! And it came to pass that they did humble themselves before the Lord, and did give thanks unto him.

33. And it came to pass that we did again take our journey, traveling nearly the same course as in the beginning; and after we had traveled for the space of many days we did pitch our tents again, that we might tarry for the space of a time.

34. And it came to pass that *Ishmael died, and was buried in the place which was called Nahom.

35. And it came to pass that the daughters of Ishmael did mourn exceedingly, because of the loss of their father, and because of their afflictions in the wilderness; and they did murmur against my father, because he had brought them out of the land of Jerusalem, saying: Our father is dead; yea, and we have wandered much in the wilderness, and we have suffered much affliction, hunger, thirst, and fatigue; and after all these sufferings we must perish in the wilderness with hunger.

36. And thus they did murmur against my father, and also against me; and they were desirous to return again to Jerusalem.

37. And Laman said unto Lemuel and also unto the sons of Ishmael: Behold, let us slay our father, and also our brother Nephi, who has taken it upon him to be our ruler and our teacher, who are his elder brethren.

38. Now, he says that the Lord has talked with him, and also that angels have ministered unto him. But behold, we know that he lies unto us; and he tells us these things, and he worketh many things by his cunning arts, that he may deceive our eyes, thinking, perhaps, that he may lead us away into some strange wilderness; and after he has led us away, he has thought to make himself a king and a ruler over us, that he may do with us according to his will and pleasure. And after this manner did my brother Laman stir up their hearts to anger.

39. And it came to pass that the Lord was with us, yea, even the voice of the Lord came and did speak many words unto them, and did chasten them exceedingly; and after they were chastened by the voice of the Lord they did turn away their anger, and did repent of their sins, insomuch that the Lord did bless us again with food, that we did not perish.

---

g, 1 Ne. 7:2—6, 19.

CHAPTER 17.

Irreantum or many waters—The Lord commands Nephi to build a ship—His brethren oppose him and are confounded.

1. And it came to pass that we did again take our journey in the wilderness; and we did travel nearly eastward from that time forth. And we did travel and wade through much affliction in the wilderness; and our women did bear children in the wilderness.

2. And so great were the blessings of the Lord upon us, that while we did live upon raw meat in the wilderness, our women did give plenty of suck for their children, and were strong, yea, even like unto the men; and they began to bear their journeyings without murmurings.

3. And thus we see that the commandments of God must be fulfilled. And if it so be that the children of men keep the commandments of God he doth nourish them, and strengthen them, and provide means whereby they can accomplish the thing which he has commanded them; wherefore, he did provide means for us while we did sojourn in the wilderness.

4. And we did sojourn for the space of many years, yea, *even eight years in the wilderness.

5. And we did come to the land which we called Bountiful, because of its much fruit and also wild honey; and all these things were prepared of the Lord that we might not perish. And we beheld the sea, which we called Irreantum, which, being interpreted, is many waters.

6. And it came to pass that we did pitch our tents by the seashore; and notwithstanding we had suffered many afflictions and much difficulty, yea, even so much that we cannot write them all, we were exceedingly rejoiced when we came to the seashore; and we called the place Bountiful, because of its much fruit.

7. And it came to pass that after I, Nephi, had been in the land of Bountiful for the space of many days, the voice of the Lord came unto me, saying: Arise, and get thee into the mountain. And it came to pass that I arose and went up into the mountain, and cried unto the Lord.

8. And it came to pass that the Lord spake unto me, saying: Thou shalt construct a ship, after the manner which I shall show thee, that I may carry thy people across these waters.

9. And I said: Lord, whither shall I go that I may find ore to molten, that I may make tools to construct the ship after the manner which thou hast shown unto me?

10. And it came to pass that the Lord told me whither I should go to find ore, that I might make tools.

11. And it came to pass that I, Nephi, did make a bellows wherewith to blow the fire, of the skins of beasts; and after I had made a bellows, that I might have wherewith to blow the fire, I did smite two stones together that I might make fire.

12. For the Lord had not hitherto suffered that we should make much fire, as we journeyed in the wilderness; for he said: I will make thy food become sweet, that ye cook it not;

13. And I will also be your light in the wilderness; and I will prepare the way before you,

---

* B. C. 592.

1 NEPHI, 17.

if it so be that ye shall keep my commandments; wherefore, inasmuch as ye shall keep my commandments ye shall be led towards the ªpromised land; and ye shall know that it is by me that ye are led.

14. Yea, and the Lord said also that: After ye have arrived in the promised land, ye shall know that I, the Lord, am God; and that I, the Lord, did deliver you from destruction; yea, that I did bring you out of the land of Jerusalem.

15. Wherefore, I, Nephi, did strive to keep the commandments of the Lord, and I did exhort my brethren to faithfulness and diligence.

16. And it came to pass that I did make ᵇtools of the ore which I did molten out of the rock.

17. And when my brethren saw that I was about to ᶜbuild a ship, they began to murmur against me, saying: Our brother is a fool, for he thinketh that he can build a ship; yea, and he also thinketh that he can cross these great waters.

18. And thus my brethren did complain against me, and were desirous that they might not labor, for they did not believe that I could build a ship; neither would they believe that I was instructed of the Lord.

19. And now it came to pass that I, Nephi, was exceeding sorrowful because of the hardness of their hearts; and now when they saw that I began to be sorrowful they were glad in their hearts, insomuch that they did rejoice over me, saying: We knew that ye could not construct a ship, for we knew that ye were lacking in judgment; wherefore, thou canst not accomplish so great a work.

20. And thou art like unto our father, led away by the foolish imaginations of his heart; yea, he hath led us out of the land of Jerusalem, and we have wandered in the wilderness for these many years; and our women have toiled, being big with child; and they have borne children in the wilderness and suffered all things, save it were death; and it would have been better that they had died before they came out of Jerusalem than to have suffered these afflictions.

21. Behold, these many years we have suffered in the wilderness, which time we might have enjoyed our possessions and the land of our inheritance; yea, and we might have been happy.

22. And we know that the people who were in the land of Jerusalem were a righteous people; for they kept the statutes and judgments of the Lord, and all his commandments, according to the law of Moses; wherefore, we know that they are a righteous people; and our father hath judged them, and hath led us away because we would hearken unto his words; yea, and our brother is like unto him. And after this manner of language did my brethren murmur and complain against us.

23. And it came to pass that I, Nephi, spake unto them, saying: Do ye believe that our fathers, who were the children of Israel, would have been led away out of the hands of the Egyptians if they had not hearkened unto the words of the Lord?

24. Yea, do ye suppose that they would have been led out of

a, 1 Ne. 2:20. 18:23. *b*, vers. 9, 10. *c*, vers. 8, 40, 51. 18:1—6.

ABOUT B. C. 591.

bondage, if the Lord had not commanded Moses that he should lead them out of bondage?

25. Now ye know that the children of Israel were in bondage; and ye know that they were laden with tasks, which were grievous to be borne; wherefore, ye know that it must needs be a good thing for them, that they should be brought out of bondage.

26. Now ye know that Moses was commanded of the Lord to do that great work; and ye know that by his word the waters of the Red Sea were divided hither and thither, and they passed through on dry ground.

27. But ye know that the Egyptians were drowned in the Red Sea, who were the armies of Pharaoh.

28. And ye also know that they were fed with manna in the wilderness.

29. Yea, and ye also know that Moses, by his word according to the power of God which was in him, smote the rock, and there came forth water, that the children of Israel might quench their thirst.

30. And notwithstanding they being led, the Lord their God, their Redeemer, going before them, leading them by day and giving light unto them by night, and doing all things for them which were expedient for man to receive, they hardened their hearts and blinded their minds, and reviled against Moses and against the true and living God.

31. And it came to pass that according to his word he did destroy them; and according to his word he did lead them; and according to his word he did do all things for them; and there was not any thing done save it were by his word.

32. And after they had crossed the river Jordan he did make them mighty unto the driving out of the children of the land, yea, unto the scattering them to destruction.

33. And now, do ye suppose that the children of this land, who were in the land of promise, who were driven out by our fathers, do ye suppose that they were righteous? Behold, I say unto you, Nay.

34. Do ye suppose that our fathers would have been more choice than they if they had been righteous? I say unto you, Nay.

35. Behold, the Lord esteemeth all flesh in one; he that is righteous is favored of God. But behold, this people had rejected every word of God, and they were ripe in iniquity; and the fulness of the wrath of God was upon them; and the Lord did curse the land against them, and bless it unto our fathers; yea, he did curse it against them unto their destruction, and he did bless it unto our fathers unto their obtaining power over it.

36. Behold, the Lord hath created the earth that it should be inhabited; and he hath created his children that they should possess it.

37. And he raiseth up a righteous nation, and destroyeth the nations of the wicked.

38. And he leadeth away the righteous into precious lands, and the wicked he destroyeth, and curseth the land unto them for their sakes.

39. He ruleth high in the heavens, for it is his throne, and this earth is his footstool.

40. And he loveth those who will have him to be their God.

ABOUT B. C. 591.

Behold, he loved our fathers, and he covenanted with them, yea, even Abraham, Isaac, and Jacob; and he remembered the covenants which he had made; wherefore, he did bring them out of the land of Egypt.

41. And he did straiten them in the wilderness with his rod; for they hardened their hearts, even as ye have; and the Lord straitened them because of their iniquity. He sent fiery flying serpents among them; and after they were bitten he prepared a way that they might be healed; and the labor which they had to perform was to look; and because of the simpleness of the way, or the easiness of it, there were many who perished.

42. And they did harden their hearts from time to time, and they did revile against Moses, and also against God; nevertheless, ye know that they were led forth by his matchless power into the land of promise.

43. And now, after all these things, the time has come that they have become wicked, yea, nearly unto ripeness; and I know not but they are at this day about to be destroyed; for I know that the day must surely come that they must be destroyed, save a few only, who shall be led away into captivity.

44. Wherefore, the Lord ^{d}commanded my father that he should depart into the wilderness; and the ^{e}Jews also sought to take away his life; yea, and ^{f}ye also have sought to take away his life; wherefore, ye are murderers in your hearts and ye are like unto them.

45. Ye are swift to do iniquity but slow to remember the Lord your God. ^{g}Ye have seen an angel, and he spake unto you; yea, ye have heard his voice from time to time; and he hath spoken unto you in a still small voice, but ye were past feeling, that ye could not feel his words; wherefore, he has spoken unto you like unto the voice of thunder, which did cause the earth to shake as if it were to divide asunder.

46. And ye also know that by the power of his almighty word he can ^{h}cause the earth that it shall pass away; yea, and ye know that by his word he can cause the ^{i}rough places to be made smooth, and smooth places shall be broken up. O, then, why is it, that ye can be so hard in your hearts?

47. Behold, my soul is rent with anguish because of you, and my heart is pained; I fear lest ye shall be cast off forever. Behold, I am full of the Spirit of God, insomuch that my frame has no strength.

48. And now it came to pass that when I had spoken these words they were angry with me, and were desirous to throw me into the depths of the sea; and as they came forth to lay their hands upon me I spake unto them, saying: In the name of the Almighty God, I command you that ye ^{j}touch me not, for I am filled with the power of God, even unto the consuming of my flesh; and whoso shall lay his hands upon me shall wither even as a dried reed; and he shall be as naught before the power of God, for God shall smite him.

49. And it came to pass that I, Nephi, said unto them that they should murmur no more against

d, 1 Ne. 2:2. e, 1 Ne. 2:1. f, 1 Ne. 16:37. g, 1 Ne. 3:29. h, 3 Ne. 26:3.
i, 1 Ne. 12:4. 19:11, 12. 2 Ne. 26:4—6. He. 14:21—24. 3 Ne. 8:5—19. j, vers.
52—55. 2 Ne. 1:26, 27.   About B. C. 591.

their father; neither should they withhold their labor from me, for God had commanded me that I should build a ship.

50. And I said unto them: [k]If God had commanded me to do all things I could do them. If he should command me that I should say unto this water, be thou earth, it should be earth; and if I should say it, it would be done.

51. And now, if the Lord has such great power, and has wrought so many miracles among the children of men, how is it that he cannot instruct me, that I should build a ship?

52. And it came to pass that I, Nephi, said many things unto my brethren, insomuch that they were confounded and could not contend against me; neither durst they lay their hands upon me nor touch me with their fingers, even for the space of many days. Now they durst not do this lest they should wither before me, so powerful was the Spirit of God; and thus it had wrought upon them.

53. And it came to pass that the Lord said unto me: Stretch forth thine hand again unto thy brethren, and they shall [l]not wither before thee, but I will shock them, saith the Lord, and this will I do, that they may know that I am the Lord their God.

54. And it came to pass that I stretched forth my hand unto my brethren, and they did not wither before me; but the Lord did shake them, even according to the word which he had spoken.

55. And now, they said: We know of a surety that the Lord is with thee, for we know that it is the power of the Lord that has shaken us. And they fell down before me, and were about to worship me, but I would not suffer them, saying: I am thy brother, yea, even thy younger brother; wherefore, worship the Lord thy God, and honor thy father and thy mother, that thy days may be long in the land which the Lord thy God shall give thee.

CHAPTER 18.

The ship completed—Jacob and Joseph—The voyage begun—Revelry and rebellion—A storm at sea—Arrival in the promised land.

1. And it came to pass that they did worship the Lord, and did go forth with me; and we did work timbers of curious workmanship. And the Lord did show me from time to time after what manner I should work the timbers of the ship.

2. Now I, Nephi, did not [a]work the timbers after the manner which was learned by men, neither did I build the ship after the manner of men; but I did build it after the manner which the Lord had shown unto me; wherefore, it was not after the manner of men.

3. And I, Nephi, did go into the mount oft, and I did pray oft unto the Lord; wherefore the Lord showed unto me great things.

4. And it came to pass that after I had finished the ship, according to the word of the Lord, my brethren beheld that it was good, and that the workmanship thereof was exceeding fine; wherefore, they did humble themselves again before the Lord.

5. And it came to pass that the voice of the Lord came unto my father, that we should arise and go down into the ship.

---

k, 1 Ne. 3:7. Jac. 4:6. Philip. 4:13. *l*, vers. 48, 54, 55.
CHAP. 18: *a*, 1 Ne. 17:8.
ABOUT B. C. 591.

6. And it came to pass that on the morrow, after we had prepared all things, much fruits and meat from the wilderness, and honey in abundance, and provisions according to that which the Lord had commanded us, we did go down into the ship, with all our loading and our *b*seeds, and whatsoever thing we had brought with us, every one according to his age; wherefore, we did all go down into the ship, with our wives and our children.

7. And now, my father had begat two sons in the wilderness; the elder was called Jacob and the younger Joseph.

8. And it came to pass after we had all gone down into the ship, and had taken with us our provisions and things which had been commanded us, we did put forth into the sea and were driven forth before the wind *c*towards the promised land.

9. And after we had been driven forth before the wind for the space of many days, behold, my brethren and the sons of Ishmael and also their wives began to make themselves merry, insomuch that they began to dance, and to sing, and to speak with much rudeness, yea, even that they did forget by what power they had been brought thither; yea, they were lifted up unto exceeding rudeness.

10. And I, Nephi, began to fear exceedingly lest the Lord should be angry with us, and smite us because of our iniquity, that we should be swallowed up in the depths of the sea; wherefore, I, Nephi, began to speak to them with much soberness; but behold they were angry with me, saying: We will not that our younger brother shall be a *d*ruler over us.

11. And it came to pass that Laman and Lemuel did take me and bind me with cords, and they did treat me with much harshness; nevertheless, the Lord did suffer it that he might show forth his power, unto the fulfilling of his word which he had spoken concerning the wicked.

12. And it came to pass that after they had bound me insomuch that I could not move, the *e*compass, which had been prepared of the Lord, did cease to work.

13. Wherefore, they knew not whither they should steer the ship, insomuch that there arose a great storm, yea, a great and terrible tempest, and we were driven back upon the waters for the space of three days; and they began to be frightened exceedingly lest they should be drowned in the sea; nevertheless they did not loose me.

14. And on the fourth day, which we had been driven back, the tempest began to be exceeding sore.

15. And it came to pass that we were about to be swallowed up in the depths of the sea. And after we had been driven back upon the waters for the space of four days, my brethren began to see that the judgments of God were upon them, and that they must perish save that they should repent of their iniquities; wherefore, they came unto me, and loosed the bands which were upon my wrists, and behold they had swollen exceedingly; and also mine ankles were much swollen, and great was the soreness thereof.

16. Nevertheless, I did look

---

b, 1 Ne. 8:1. 16:11. ver. 24. *c*, 1 Ne. 2:20. 5:5, 22. 7:13. 12:1, 4. 13:12, 14, 30. 14:2. 18:22, 23. *d*, 1 Ne. 2:22. 16:37, 38. 2 Ne. 1:25—27. 5:3, 19. *e*, see *d*, 1 Ne. 16. About B. C. 590.

unto my God, and I did praise him all the day long; and I did not murmur against the Lord because of mine afflictions.

17. Now my father, Lehi, had said many things unto them, and also unto the *f*sons of Ishmael; but, behold, they did breathe out much threatenings against anyone that should speak for me; and my parents being stricken in years, and having suffered much grief because of their children, they were brought down, yea, even upon their sick-beds.

18. Because of their grief and much sorrow, and the iniquity of my brethren, they were brought near even to be carried out of this time to meet their God; yea, their grey hairs were about to be brought down to lie low in the dust; yea, even they were near to be cast with sorrow into a watery grave.

19. And *g*Jacob and Joseph also, being young, having need of much nourishment, were grieved because of the afflictions of their mother; and also *h*my wife with her tears and prayers, and also my children, did not soften the hearts of my brethren that they would loose me.

20. And there was nothing save it were the power of God, which threatened them with destruction, could soften their hearts; wherefore, when they saw that they were about to be swallowed up in the depths of the sea they repented of the thing which they had done, insomuch that they loosed me.

21. And it came to pass after they had loosed me, behold, I took the *i*compass, and it did work whither I desired it. And it came to pass that I prayed unto the Lord; and after I had prayed the winds did cease, and the storm did cease, and there was a great calm.

22. And it came to pass that I, Nephi, did *j*guide the ship, that we sailed again towards the promised land.

23. And it came to pass that after we had sailed for the space of many days *we did arrive at the *k*promised land; and we went forth upon the land, and did pitch our tents; and we did call it the promised land.

24. And it came to pass that we did begin to till the earth, and we began to plant seeds; yea, we did put all our *l*seeds into the earth, which we had brought from the land of Jerusalem. And it came to pass that they did grow exceedingly; wherefore, we were blessed in abundance.

25. And it came to pass that we did find upon the land of promise, as we journeyed in the wilderness, that there were *m*beasts in the forests of every kind, both the cow and the ox, and the ass and the horse, and the goat and the wild goat, and all manner of wild animals, which were for the use of men. And we did find all manner of *n*ore, both of gold, and of silver, and of copper.

CHAPTER 19.

Nephi's record of his people—Sundry prophets mentioned—Zenos and his predictions.

1. And it came to pass that the Lord commanded me, wherefore I did make *a*plates of ore that I

---
f, 1 Ne. 7:6. *g*, ver. 7. *h*, 1 Ne. 16:7. *i*, ver. 12. *j*, ver. 13. *k*, 1 Ne. 2:20.
l, 1 Ne. 8:1. *m*, Enos 21. Al. 18:9. 20:6. 3 Ne. 3:22. 4:4. 6:1. Eth. 9:18,
19, 31—34. 10:19—21. *n*, 1 Ne. 19:1. 2 Ne. 5:14—16. Jac. 2:12, 13. He. 6:9—
11. Eth. 9:17. 10:7, 12, 23. CHAP. 19: *a*, see *f*, 1 Ne. 1.
* PROBABLY ABOUT B. C. 589.

might engraven upon them the record of my people. And upon the plates which I made I did engraven the [b]record of my father, and also our journeyings in the wilderness, and the prophecies of my father; and also many of mine own prophecies have I engraven upon them.

2. And I knew not at the time when I made them that I should be commanded of the Lord to make these plates; wherefore, the record of my father, and the genealogy of his fathers, and the more part of all our proceedings in the wilderness are engraven upon those plates of which I have spoken; wherefore, the things which transpired before I made these plates are, of a truth, more particularly made mention upon the first plates.

3. And after I had made [c]these plates by way of commandment, I, Nephi, received a commandment that the ministry and the prophecies, the more plain and precious parts of them, should be written upon these plates; and that the things which were written should be kept for the instruction of my people, who should possess the land, and also for other wise purposes, which purposes are known unto the Lord.

4. Wherefore, I, Nephi, did make a record upon the [d]other plates, which gives an account, or which gives a greater account of the wars and contentions and destructions of my people. And this have I done, and commanded my people what they should do after I was gone; and that these plates should be handed down from one generation to another, or from one prophet to another, until further commandments of the Lord.

5. And an account of my making [e]these plates shall be given hereafter; and then, behold, I proceed according to that which I have spoken; and this I do that the more sacred things may be kept for the knowledge of my people.

6. Nevertheless, I do not write anything upon plates save it be that I think it be sacred. And now, if I do err, even did they err of old; not that I would excuse myself because of other men, but because of the weakness which is in me, according to the flesh, I would excuse myself.

7. For the things which some men esteem to be of great worth, both to the body and soul, others set at naught and trample under their feet. Yea, even the very God of Israel do men trample under their feet; I say, trample under their feet but I would speak in other words—they set him at naught, and hearken not to the voice of his counsels.

8. And behold he cometh, according to the words of the angel, in [f]six hundred years from the time my father left Jerusalem.

9. And the world, because of their iniquity, shall judge him to be a thing of naught; wherefore they scourge him, and he suffereth it; and they smite him, and he suffereth it. Yea, they spit upon him, and he suffereth it, because of his loving kindness and his long-suffering towards the children of men.

10. And the God of our fathers, who were led out of Egypt, out of bondage, and also were preserved in the wilderness by him, yea, the God of Abraham,

b, 1 Ne. 1:16, 17. 19:2. *c*, 1 Ne. 9:2. *d*, 1 Ne. 9:4. *e*, 2 Ne. 5:30. D. & C. sec. 10. *f*, 1 Ne. 10:4. BETWEEN B. C. 588 AND 570.

and of Isaac, and the God of Jacob, yieldeth himself, according to the words of the angel, as a man, into the hands of wicked men, to be lifted up, according to the words of *g*Zenock, and to be crucified, according to the words of Neum, and to be buried in a sepulchre, according to the words of *h*Zenos, which he spake concerning the *i*three days of darkness, which should be a sign given of his death unto those who should inhabit the isles of the sea, more especially given unto those who are of the house of Israel.

11. For thus spake the prophet: The Lord God surely shall visit all the house of Israel at that day, some with his *j*voice, because of their righteousness, unto their great joy and salvation, and others *k*with the thunderings and the lightnings of his power, by tempest, by fire, and by smoke, and vapor of darkness, and by the opening of the earth, and by mountains which shall be carried up.

12. And all these things must surely come, saith the prophet Zenos. And the *l*rocks of the earth must rend; and because of the groanings of the earth, many of the kings of the isles of the sea shall be wrought upon by the Spirit of God, to exclaim: The God of nature suffers.

13. And as for those who are at Jerusalem, saith the prophet, they shall be scourged by all people, because they crucify the God of Israel, and turn their hearts aside, rejecting signs and wonders, and the power and glory of the God of Israel.

14. And because they turn their hearts aside, saith the prophet, and have despised the Holy One of Israel, they shall wander in the flesh, and perish, and become a hiss and a by-word, and be hated among all nations.

15. Nevertheless, when that day cometh, saith the prophet, that *m*they no more turn aside their hearts against the Holy One of Israel, then will he remember the covenants which he made to their fathers.

16. Yea, then will he remember the isles of the sea; yea, and all the people who are of the house of Israel, will I gather in, saith the Lord, according to the words of the prophet *n*Zenos, from the four quarters of the earth.

17. Yea, and all the earth shall see the salvation of the Lord, saith the prophet; every nation, kindred, tongue and people shall be blessed.

18. And I, Nephi, have written these things unto my people, that perhaps I might persuade them that they would remember the Lord their Redeemer.

19. Wherefore, I speak unto all the house of Israel, if it so be that they should obtain these things.

20. For behold, I have workings in the spirit, which doth weary me even that all my joints are weak, for those who are at Jerusalem; for had not the Lord been merciful, to show unto me concerning them, even as he had prophets of old, I should have perished also.

21. And he surely did show unto the prophets of old all things concerning them; and also

g, Al. 33:15. 34:7. He. 8:20. 3 Ne. 10:15—17. *h*, vers. 12, 16. Jac. 5:1. 6:1. Al. 33:3, 13, 15. 34:7. He. 8:19. 15:11. 3 Ne. 10:16. *i*, He. 14:20, 27. 3 Ne. 8:19—23. 10:9. *j*, 3 Ne. 9. *k*, He. 14:20—27. 3 Ne. 8:5—23. *l*, He. 14:21, 22. 3 Ne. 8:17, 18. *m*, see *e*, 1 Ne. 15. *n*, see *h*. BETWEEN B. C. 588 AND 570.

he did show unto many concerning us; wherefore, it must needs be that we know concerning them for they are °written upon the plates of brass.

22. Now it came to pass that I, Nephi, did teach my brethren these things; and it came to pass that I did read many things to them, which were engraven upon the ᵖplates of brass, that they might know concerning the doings of the Lord in other lands, among people of old.

23. And I did read many things unto them which were written in the book of Moses; but that I might more fully persuade them to believe in the Lord their Redeemer I did read unto them that which was written by the prophet Isaiah; for I did liken all scriptures unto us, that it might be for our profit and learning.

24. Wherefore I spake unto them, saying: Hear ye the words of the prophet, ye who are a remnant of the house of Israel, a branch who have been broken off; hear ye the words of the prophet, which were written unto all the house of Israel, and liken them unto yourselves, that ye may have hope as well as your brethren from whom ye have been broken off; for after this manner has the prophet written.

CHAPTER 20.

Prophecies recorded on the plates of brass—Compare Isaiah 48.

1. Hearken and hear this, O house of Jacob, who are called by the name of Israel, and are come forth ᵃout of the waters of Judah, or out of the waters of baptism, who ᵇswear by the name of the Lord, and make mention of the God of Israel, yet they swear ᶜnot in truth nor in righteousness.

2. Nevertheless, they call themselves ᵈof the holy city, but they do ᵉnot stay themselves upon the God of Israel, who is the Lord of Hosts; yea, the Lord of Hosts is his name.

3. Behold, ᶠI have declared the former things from the beginning; and they went forth out of my mouth, and I showed them. I did show them suddenly.

4. And I did it because I knew that thou art obstinate, and ᵍthy neck is an iron sinew, and thy brow brass;

5. And I have even ʰfrom the beginning declared to thee; before it came to pass I showed them thee; and I showed them for fear lest thou shouldst say—Mine idol hath done them, and my graven image, and my molten image hath commanded them.

6. Thou hast seen and heard all this; and will ye not declare them? And that I have showed thee new things from this time, even hidden things, and thou didst not know them.

7. They are created now, and not from the beginning, even before the day when thou heardest them not they were declared unto thee, lest thou shouldst say—Behold I knew them.

8. Yea, and thou heardest not; yea, thou knewest not; yea, from that time thine ear was not opened; for I knew that thou wouldst deal very treacherously, and wast called a ⁱtransgressor from the womb.

9. Nevertheless, for my name's sake will I defer mine anger, and

o, 3 Ne. 10:16, 17. *p*, see *a*, 1 Ne. 3. Chap. 20: *a*, Isa. 48:1. *b*, Deut. 6:13. Isa. 65:16. Zeph. 1:5. *c*, Jer. 4:2. 5:2. *d*, Isa. 52:1. *e*, Mic. 3:9—11. *f*, Isa. 41:22. 42:9. 43:9. 44:7, 8. 45:21. 46:9, 10. *g*, Ex. 32:9. Deut. 31:27. *h*, see *f*. *i*, Ps. 58:3.
Between B. C. 588 and 570.

for my praise will I refrain from thee, that I cut thee not off.

10. For, behold, I have refined thee, I have chosen thee in the furnace of affliction.

11. For mine own sake, yea, for mine own sake will I do this, for I will not suffer my name to be polluted, *j*and I will not give my glory unto another.

12. Hearken unto me, O Jacob, and Israel my called, for I am he; I am the *k*first, and I am also the last.

13. Mine *l*hand hath also laid the foundation of the earth, and my right hand hath spanned the heavens. *m*I call unto them and they stand up together.

14. *n*All ye, assemble yourselves, and hear; who among them hath declared these things unto them? The Lord hath loved him; yea, and he will fulfil his word which he hath declared by them; and *o*he will do his pleasure on Babylon, and his arm shall come upon the Chaldeans.

15. Also, saith the Lord; I the Lord, yea, I have spoken; yea, *p*I have called him to declare, I have brought him, and he shall make his way prosperous.

16. Come ye near unto me; *q*I have not spoken in secret; from the beginning, from the time that it was declared have I spoken; and the Lord God, and his Spirit, hath sent me.

17. And thus saith the Lord, thy Redeemer, the Holy One of Israel; I have sent him, the Lord thy God who teacheth thee to profit, who leadeth thee by the way thou shouldst go, hath done it.

18. O that thou hadst hearkened to my commandment—then had thy peace been as a river, and thy righteousness as the waves of the sea.

19. *r*Thy seed also had been as the sand; the offspring of thy bowels like the gravel thereof; his name should not have been cut off nor destroyed from before me.

20. *s*Go ye forth of Babylon, flee ye from the Chaldeans, with a voice of singing declare ye, tell this, utter to the end of the earth; say ye: *t*The Lord hath redeemed his servant Jacob.

21. And they *u*thirsted not; he led them through the deserts; he caused the waters to flow out of the rock for them; he clave the rock also and the waters gushed out.

22. And notwithstanding he hath done all this, and greater also, there is no peace, saith the Lord, unto the wicked.

CHAPTER 21.

Isaiah's writings, as recorded upon the plates of brass, continued—Compare Isaiah 49.

1. And again: Hearken, O ye house of Israel, all ye that are broken off and are driven out, because of the wickedness of the pastors of my people; yea, all ye that are broken off, that are scattered abroad, who are of my people, O house of Israel. Listen, *a*O isles, unto me, and hearken ye people from far; the Lord hath called me from the womb; from the bowels of my mother hath he made mention of my name.

2. And he hath made my mouth like a sharp sword; in the shadow of his hand hath he hid

---

j, Isa. 42:8. *k*, Isa. 41:4. Rev. 1:17. 22:13. *l*, Ps. 102:25. *m*, Isa. 40:26. *n*, see *f*. *o*, Isa. 44:28. *p*, Isa. 45:1—4. *q*, Isa. 45:19. *r*, Gen. 22:17. Hos. 1:10. *s*, Jer. 50:8. 51:6, 44, 45. Zech. 2:6, 7. *t*, Isa. 44:22, 23. *u*, Ps. 107:35—38. Isa. 35:6, 7. 41:17, 18. CHAP. 21: *a*, ver. 8. Isa. 51:5. 60:9. 66:19. 1 Ne. 22:4. 2 Ne. 10:20—22. BETWEEN B. C. 588 AND 570.

me, and made me a polished shaft; in his quiver hath he hid me;

3. And said unto me: Thou art my servant, O Israel, in whom I will be glorified.

4. Then I said, I have labored in vain, I have spent my strength for naught and in vain; surely my judgment is with the Lord, and my work with my God.

5. And now, saith the Lord— that formed me from the womb that I should be his servant, to bring Jacob again to him—though Israel be not gathered, yet shall I be glorious in the eyes of the Lord, and my God shall be my strength.

6. And he said: It is a light thing that thou shouldst be my servant to raise up the tribes of Jacob, and to restore the preserved of Israel. I will also give thee for a light ^cto the Gentiles, that thou mayest be my salvation unto the ends of the earth.

7. Thus saith the Lord, the Redeemer of Israel, his Holy One, to him whom man despiseth, to him whom the nations abhorreth, to servant of rulers: Kings shall see and arise, princes also shall worship, because of the Lord that is faithful.

8. Thus saith the Lord: In an acceptable time have I heard thee, ^dO isles of the sea, and in a day of salvation have I helped thee; and I will preserve thee, and give thee ^emy servant for a covenant of the people, to establish the earth, to cause to inherit the desolate heritages;

9. That thou mayest say to the prisoners: Go forth; ^fto them that sit in darkness: Show yourselves. They shall feed in the ways, and their ^gpastures shall be in all high places.

10. They shall not hunger nor thirst, neither shall the heat nor the sun smite them; for he that hath mercy on them shall lead them, even ^hby the springs of water shall he guide them.

11. And I will make ⁱall my mountains a way, and ^jmy highways shall be exalted.

12. And then, O house of Israel, behold, ^kthese shall come from far; and lo, these from the north and from the west; and these from the land of Sinim.

13. ^lSing, O heavens; and be joyful, O earth; for the feet of those who are in the east shall be established; and break forth into singing, O mountains; for they shall be smitten no more; for the Lord hath comforted his people, and will have mercy upon his afflicted.

14. But, behold, Zion hath said: The Lord hath forsaken me, and my Lord hath forgotten me— but he will show that he hath not.

15. ^mFor can a woman forget her sucking child, that she should not have compassion on the son of her womb? Yea, they may forget, yet will I not forget thee, O house of Israel.

16. Behold, I have graven thee upon the palms of my hands; thy walls are continually before me.

17. Thy children shall make haste against thy destroyers; and they that made thee waste shall go forth of thee.

18. Lift up thine eyes round about and behold; ⁿall these gather themselves together, and they shall come to thee. And as I live, saith the Lord, thou shalt surely clothe thee with them all,

c, 3 Ne. 21:11. *d,* see *a.* *e,* see *e,* 2 Ne. 3. *f,* 2 Ne. 3:5. *g,* Ezek. 34:14. 1 Ne. 22:25. *h,* see *u,* 1 Ne. 20. *i,* see *g.* *j,* Isa. 40:3. 62:10. *k,* Isa. 43:5—7. *l,* Isa. 44:23. *m,* Ps. 103:13. *n,* Mic. 4:11—13.

BETWEEN B. C. 588 AND 570.

as with an ornament, and bind them on even as a bride.

19. For thy waste and thy desolate places, and the land of thy destruction, shall even now be too narrow by reason of the inhabitants; and °they that swallowed thee up shall be far away.

20. The children whom thou shalt have, after thou hast ᵖlost the first, shall again in thine ears say: The place is too strait for me; give place to me that I may dwell.

21. Then shalt thou say in thine heart: Who hath begotten me these, seeing I have lost my children, and am desolate, a captive, and removing to and fro? And who hath brought up these? Behold, I was left alone; these, where have they been?

22. Thus saith the Lord God: Behold, I will lift up ʳmine hand to the Gentiles, and set up ˢmy standard to the people; and ᵗthey shall bring thy sons in their arms, and thy daughters shall be carried upon their shoulders.

23. And kings shall be thy nursing fathers, and their queens thy nursing mothers; they shall bow down to thee with their face towards the earth, and lick up the dust of thy feet; and thou shalt know that I am the Lord; for they shall not be ashamed that wait for me.

24. ᵘFor shall the prey be taken from the mighty, or the lawful captives delivered?

25. But thus saith the Lord, even the captives of the mighty shall be taken away, and the prey of the terrible shall be delivered; for I will contend with him that contendeth with thee, and I will save thy children.

26. ᵛAnd I will feed them that oppress thee with their own flesh; they shall be drunken with their own blood as with sweet wine; and all flesh shall know that I, the Lord, am thy Savior and thy Redeemer, the Mighty One of Jacob.

CHAPTER 22.

Nephi expounds the prophecies of Isaiah—Prediction of a mighty Gentile nation on the promised land—Lehi's descendants to be nourished by the Gentiles—The fate of those who fight against Zion.

1. And now it came to pass that after I, Nephi, had read these things which were engraven upon the ᵃplates of brass, my brethren came unto me and said unto me: What meaneth these things which ye have read? Behold, are they to be understood according to things which are spiritual, which shall come to pass according to the spirit and not the flesh?

2. And I, Nephi, said unto them: Behold they were manifest unto the prophet by the voice of the Spirit; for by the Spirit are all things made known unto the prophets, which shall come upon the children of men according to the flesh.

3. Wherefore, the things of which I have read are things pertaining to things both temporal and spiritual; for it appears that the house of Israel, sooner or later, will be scattered upon all the face of the earth, and also among all nations.

4. And behold, there are many who are already lost from the knowledge of those who are at Jerusalem. Yea, the more part of all the tribes have been led away; and they are scattered to

---

o, ver. 17. *p*, ver. 21. *r*, Isa. 66:18—20. *s*, Isa. 62:10. See *p*, 2 Ne. 15. *t*, 1 Ne. 22:8. 2 Ne. 6:6, 7. 10:8, 9. *u*, 1 Ne. 22:12—14. *v*, 1 Ne. 14:15—17. 22:13, 14. 2 Ne. 6:14—18. CHAP. 22: *a*, see *a*, 1 Ne. 3. BETWEEN B. C. 588 AND 570.

and fro upon the *b*isles of the sea; and whither they are none of us knoweth, save that we know that they have been led away.

5. And since they have been led away, these things have been prophesied concerning them, and also concerning all those who shall hereafter be scattered and be confounded, because of the Holy One of Israel; for against him will they harden their hearts; wherefore, they shall be scattered among all nations and shall be hated of all men.

6. Nevertheless, after they shall be nursed by the Gentiles, and the Lord has lifted up his hand upon the *c*Gentiles and set them up for a standard, and their children have been carried in their arms, and their daughters have been carried upon their shoulders, behold these things of which are spoken are temporal; for thus are the covenants of the Lord with our fathers; and it meaneth us in the days to come, and also all our brethren who are of the house of Israel.

7. And it meaneth that the time cometh that after all the house of Israel have been scattered and confounded, that the Lord God will raise up a *d*mighty nation among the Gentiles, yea, even upon the face of this land; and by them shall *e*our seed be scattered.

8. And after our seed is scattered the Lord God will proceed to do a *f*marvelous work among the Gentiles, which shall be of great worth unto our seed; wherefore, it is likened unto their being nourished by the Gentiles and being carried in their arms and upon their shoulders.

9. And it shall also be of *g*worth unto the Gentiles; and not only unto the Gentiles but unto *h*all the house of Israel, unto the making known of the covenants of the Father of heaven unto Abraham, saying: In thy seed shall all the kindreds of the earth be blessed.

10. And I would, my brethren, that ye should know that all the kindreds of the earth cannot be blessed unless he shall make bare his arm in the eyes of the nations.

11. Wherefore, the Lord God will proceed to make bare his arm in the eyes of all the nations, in bringing about his covenants and his gospel unto those who are of the house of Israel.

12. Wherefore, he will bring them again out of captivity, and they shall be gathered together to the lands of their inheritance; and they shall be brought out of obscurity and out of darkness; and they shall know that the Lord is their Savior and their Redeemer, the Mighty One of Israel.

13. And the blood of that great and abominable church, which is the whore of all the earth, shall turn upon their own heads; for *i*they shall war among themselves, and the sword of their own hands shall fall upon their own heads, and they shall be drunken with their own blood.

14. And every nation which shall war against thee, O house of Israel, shall be turned one against another, and they shall fall into the pit which they digged to ensnare the people of the Lord.

b, 2 Ne. 10:20—22. *c*, 1 Ne. 21:22. 23. *d*, 3 Ne. 20:27. *e*, 1 Ne. 13:12—20. 2 Ne. 1:11. 3 Ne. 16:4. *f*, 1 Ne. 13:35. 14:7. 2 Ne. 25:17. 27:26. 29:1, 2. 3 Ne. 21:1—9. Eth. 4:15. *g*, 1 Ne. 13:34—42. 14:1—5. 2 Ne. 28:2. 30:3. 3 Ne. 21:6. 23:4. *h*, 1 Ne. 13:39. 14:17. 2 Ne. 29:13, 14. 30:7, 8. 3 Ne. 5:23—26. 16:4, 5. 21:26—29. *i*, 1 Ne. 14:3, 15—17. 21:26. Between B. C. 588 and 570.

And all that ʲfight against Zion shall be destroyed, and that great whore, who hath perverted the right ways of the Lord, yea, that great and abominable church, shall tumble to the dust and great shall be the fall of it.

15. For behold, saith the prophet, the time cometh speedily that Satan shall have ᵏno more power over the hearts of the children of men; for the day soon cometh that all the proud and they who do wickedly shall be as stubble; and the day cometh that they must be ˡburned.

16. For the time soon cometh that the fulness of the wrath of God shall be poured out upon all the children of men; for he will not suffer that the wicked shall destroy the righteous.

17. Wherefore, he will preserve the righteous by his power, even if it so be that the fulness of his wrath must come, and the righteous be preserved, even unto the destruction of their enemies by fire. Wherefore, the righteous need not fear; for thus saith the prophet, they shall be saved, even if it so be as by fire.

18. Behold, my brethren, I say unto you, that these things must shortly come; yea, even blood, and fire, and vapor of smoke must come; and it must needs be upon the face of this earth; and it cometh unto men according to the flesh if it so be that they will harden their hearts against the Holy One of Israel.

19. For behold, the righteous shall not perish; for the time surely must come that all they who fight against Zion shall be cut off.

20. And the Lord will surely prepare a way for his people, unto the fulfilling of the words of Moses, which he spake, saying: A ᵐprophet shall the Lord your God raise up unto you, like unto me; him shall ye hear in all things whatsoever he shall say unto you. And it shall come to pass that all those who will not hear that prophet shall be cut off from among the people.

21. And now I, Nephi, declare unto you, that this prophet of whom Moses spake was the Holy One of Israel; wherefore, he shall execute judgment in righteousness.

22. And the ⁿrighteous need not fear, for they are those who shall not be confounded. But it is the kingdom of the devil, which shall be built up among the children of men, which kingdom is established among them which are in the flesh—

23. For the time speedily shall come that ᵒall churches which are built up to get gain, and all those who are built up to get power over the flesh, and those who are built up to become popular in the eyes of the world, and those who seek the lusts of the flesh and the things of the world, and to do all manner of iniquity; yea, in fine, all those who belong to the kingdom of the devil are they who need fear, and tremble, and quake; they are those who must be brought low in the dust; they are those who must be consumed as stubble; and this is according to the words of the prophet.

24. And the time cometh speedily that the righteous must be led up as ᵖcalves of the stall, and the

---

j, vers. 19, 20. 2 Ne. 27:2, 3. *k*, ver. 26. Jac. 5:76. *l*, vers. 17, 18. *m*, ver. 21. 3 Ne. 20:23. 21:11. *n*, vers. 16, 17, 19, 24, 28. *o*, 1 Ne. 14:10, 15—17. 2 Ne. 28:3—32. 3 Ne. 27:7—12. 4 Ne. 25—29. Morm. 8:28, 32, 33, 36—38. *p*, 3 Ne. 25:2.

BETWEEN B. C. 588 AND 570.

Holy One of Israel must reign in dominion, and might, and power, and great glory.

25. And he gathereth his ^qchildren from the four quarters of the earth; and he numbereth his sheep, and they know him; and there shall be one fold and one shepherd; and he shall feed his sheep, and in him they shall find pasture.

26. And because of the righteousness of his people, Satan has no power; wherefore, he cannot be loosed for the space of many years; for he hath no power over the hearts of the people, for they dwell in righteousness, and the Holy One of Israel reigneth.

27. And now behold, I, Nephi, say unto you that all these things must come according to the flesh.

28. But, behold, all nations, kindreds, tongues, and people shall dwell safely in the Holy One of Israel if it so be that they will repent.

29. And now I, Nephi, make an end; for I durst not speak further as yet concerning these things.

30. Wherefore, my brethren, I would that ye should consider that the things which have been written upon the ^rplates of brass are true; and they testify that a man must be obedient to the commandments of God.

31. Wherefore, ye need not suppose that I and my father are the only ones that have testified, and also taught them. Wherefore, if ye shall be obedient to the commandments, and endure to the end, ye shall be saved at the last day. And thus it is. Amen.

THE SECOND BOOK OF NEPHI

An account of the death of Lehi. Nephi's brethren rebel against him. The Lord warns Nephi to depart into the wilderness. His journeyings in the wilderness, &c.

CHAPTER 1.

A land of liberty, blessed for the righteous but cursed for the wicked—Lehi's exhortation.

1. And now it came to pass that after I, Nephi, had made an end of teaching my brethren, our father, Lehi, also spake many things unto them—how great things the Lord had done for them in bringing them out of the land of Jerusalem.

2. And he spake unto them concerning their ^arebellions upon the waters, and the mercies of God in sparing their lives, that they were not swallowed up in the sea.

3. And he also spake unto them concerning the ^bland of promise, which they had obtained—how merciful the Lord had been in warning us that we should flee out of the land of Jerusalem.

4. For, behold, said he, I have ^cseen a vision, in which I know that Jerusalem is destroyed; and had we remained in Jerusalem we should also have perished.

5. But, said he, notwithstand-

---

q, Ps. 50:5. Isa. 43:6, 7. Jer. 3:14. Eph. 1:10. Rev. 18:4, 5. *r*, see *a*, 1 Ne. 3. CHAP. 1: *a*, 1 Ne. 18:9—20. *b*, vers. 5—12. See *a*, 1 Ne. 2. *c*, 1 Ne. 17:14. He. 8:21, 22. BETWEEN B. C. 588 AND 570.

ing our afflictions, we have obtained a land of promise, a land which is choice above all other lands; a land which the Lord God hath covenanted with me should be a land for the inheritance of my seed. Yea, the Lord hath covenanted this land unto me, and to my children forever, and also all those who should be led out of other countries by the hand of the Lord.

6. Wherefore, I, Lehi, prophesy according to the workings of the Spirit which is in me, that there shall none come into this land save they shall be brought by the hand of the Lord.

7. Wherefore, this land is consecrated unto him whom he shall bring. And if it so be that they shall serve him according to the commandments which he hath given, it shall be a land of liberty unto them; wherefore, they shall never be brought down into captivity; if so, it shall be because of iniquity; for if iniquity shall abound *d*cursed shall be the land for their sakes, but unto the righteous it shall be blessed forever.

8. And behold, it is wisdom that this land should be kept as yet from the knowledge of other nations; for behold, many nations would overrun the land, that there would be no place for an inheritance.

9. Wherefore, I, Lehi, have obtained a promise, that inasmuch as those whom the Lord God shall bring out of the land of Jerusalem shall keep his commandments, they shall prosper upon the face of this land; and they shall be kept from all other nations, that they may possess this land unto themselves. And if it so be that they shall keep his commandments they shall be blessed upon the face of this land, and there shall be none to molest them, nor to take away the land of their inheritance; and they shall dwell safely forever.

10. But behold, when the time cometh that they shall dwindle in unbelief, after they have received so great blessings from the hand of the Lord—having a knowledge of the creation of the earth, and all men, knowing the great and marvelous works of the Lord from the creation of the world; having power given them to do all things by faith; having all the commandments from the beginning, and having been brought by his infinite goodness into this precious land of promise—behold, I say, if the day shall come that they will reject the Holy One of Israel, the true Messiah, their Redeemer and their God, behold, the judgments of him that is just shall rest upon them.

11. Yea, he will bring *e*other nations unto them, and he will give unto them power, and he will take away from them the lands of their possessions, and he will cause them to be scattered and smitten.

12. Yea, as one generation passeth to another there shall be bloodsheds, and great visitations among them; wherefore, my sons, I would that ye would remember; yea, I would that ye would hearken unto my words.

13. O that ye would awake; awake from a deep sleep, yea, even from the sleep of hell, and shake off the awful chains by which ye are bound, which are the chains which bind the chil-

d, Al. 45:10—14, 16. Morm. 1:17. 6:7—22. Eth. 2:8—12. *e*, 1 Ne. 13:12—20. Morm. 5:19, 20.   BETWEEN B. C. 588 AND 570.

dren of men, that they are carried away captive down to the eternal gulf of misery and woe.

14. Awake! and arise from the dust, and hear the words of a trembling parent, whose limbs ye must soon lay down in the cold and silent grave, from whence no traveler can return; a few more days and I go the way of all the earth.

15. But behold, the Lord hath redeemed my soul from hell; I have beheld his glory, and I am encircled about eternally in the arms of his love.

16. And I desire that ye should remember to observe the statutes and the judgments of the Lord; behold, this hath been the anxiety of my soul from the beginning.

17. My heart hath been weighed down with sorrow from time to time, for I have feared, lest for the hardness of your hearts the Lord your God should come out in the fulness of his wrath upon *f*you, that ye be cut off and destroyed forever;

18. Or, that a cursing should come upon you for the space of *g*many generations; and ye are visited by sword, and by famine, and are hated, and are led according to the will and captivity of the devil.

19. O my sons, that these things might not come upon you, but that ye might be a choice and a favored people of the Lord. But behold, his will be done; for his ways are righteousness forever.

20. And he hath said *h*that: Inasmuch as ye shall keep my commandments ye shall prosper in the land; but inasmuch as ye will not keep my commandments ye shall be cut off from my presence.

21. And now that my soul might have joy in you, and that my heart might leave this world with gladness because of you, that I might not be brought down with grief and sorrow to the grave, arise from the dust, my sons, and be men, and be determined in one mind and in one heart, united in all things, that ye may not come down into captivity;

22. That ye may not be cursed with a sore cursing; and also, that ye may not incur the displeasure of a just God upon you, unto the destruction, yea, the eternal destruction of both soul and body.

23. Awake, my sons; put on the armor of righteousness. Shake off the chains with which ye are bound, and come forth out of obscurity, and arise from the dust.

24. Rebel no more against your brother, whose views have been *i*glorious, and who hath kept the commandments from the time that we left Jerusalem; and who hath been an instrument in the hands of God, in bringing us forth into the land of promise; for were it not for him, we must have perished with *j*hunger in the wilderness; nevertheless, ye sought to *k*take away his life; yea, and he hath suffered much sorrow because of you.

25. And I exceedingly fear and tremble because of you, lest he shall suffer again; for behold, ye have accused him that he sought power and *l*authority over you; but I know that he hath not sought for power nor authority over you, but he hath sought the

---

f, 1 Ne. 2:23. 2 Ne. 5:21—24. Al. 3:6—19. Morm. 5:15. *g*, 1 Ne. 12:20—22.
h, Jar. 9. Om. 6. Mos. 1:7. 2:22, 31. Al. 9:13, 14. 36:1, 30. 37:13. 38:1.
3 Ne. 5:22. *i*, 1 Ne. 11, 18:3. *j*, 1 Ne. 16:32. *k*, 1 Ne. 16:37. *l*, 1 Ne. 16:38.
BETWEEN B. C. 588 AND 570.

glory of God, and your own eternal welfare.

26. And ye have murmured because he hath been plain unto you. Ye say that he hath used sharpness; ye say that he hath been angry with you; but behold, his sharpness was the ᵐsharpness of the power of the word of God, which was in him; and that which ye call anger was the truth, according to that which is in God, which he could not restrain, manifesting boldly concerning your iniquities.

27. And it must needs be that the power of God must be with him, even unto his commanding you that ye must obey. But behold, it was not he, but it was the Spirit of the Lord which was in him, which opened his mouth to utterance that he could not shut it.

28. And now my son, Laman, and also Lemuel and Sam, and also my sons who are the sons of Ishmael, behold, if ye will hearken unto the voice of Nephi ye shall not perish. And if ye will hearken unto him I leave unto you a blessing, yea, even my first blessing.

29. But if ye will not hearken unto him I take away my first blessing, yea, even my blessing, and it shall rest upon him.

30. And now, Zoram, I speak unto you: Behold, thou art the ⁿservant of Laban; nevertheless, thou hast been brought out of the land of Jerusalem, and I know that thou art a true friend unto my son, Nephi, forever.

31. Wherefore, because thou hast been faithful thy seed shall be blessed with his seed, that they dwell in prosperity long upon the face of this land; and nothing, save it shall be iniquity among them, shall harm or disturb their prosperity upon the face of this land forever.

32. Wherefore, if ye shall keep the commandments of the Lord, the Lord hath consecrated this land for the security of thy seed with the seed of my son.

CHAPTER 2.

Lehi to his son Jacob—Opposition necessary in all things—The forbidden fruit and the tree of life—Adam fell that men might be—Messiah, the great Mediator, to redeem mankind.

1. And now, Jacob, I speak unto you: Thou art my ᵃfirstborn in the days of my tribulation in the wilderness. And behold, in thy childhood thou hast suffered afflictions and much sorrow, because of the rudeness of thy brethren.

2. Nevertheless, Jacob, my firstborn in the wilderness, thou knowest the greatness of God; and he shall consecrate thine afflictions for thy gain.

3. Wherefore, thy soul shall be blessed, and thou shalt dwell safely with thy brother, Nephi; and thy days shall be spent in the service of thy God. Wherefore, I know that thou art redeemed, because of the righteousness of thy Redeemer; for thou hast beheld that in the fulness of time he cometh to bring salvation unto men.

4. And thou hast beheld in thy youth his glory; wherefore, thou art blessed even as they unto whom he shall minister in the flesh; for the Spirit is the same, yesterday, today, and forever. And the way is prepared from the fall of man, and salvation is free.

5. And men are instructed suf-

---

m, 1 Ne. 17:48. *n*, 1 Ne. 4:20, 35.   Chap. 2: *a*, 1 Ne. 18:7, 19.
BETWEEN B. C. 588 AND 570.

ficiently that they know good from evil. And the law is given unto men. And by the law no flesh is justified; or, by the law men are cut off. Yea, by the *b*temporal law they were cut off; and also, by the *c*spiritual law they perish from that which is good, and become miserable forever.

6. Wherefore, redemption cometh in and through the Holy Messiah; for he is full of grace and truth.

7. Behold he offereth himself a sacrifice for sin, to answer the ends of the law, unto all those who have a broken heart and a contrite spirit; and unto none else can the ends of the law be answered.

8. Wherefore, how great the importance to make these things known unto the inhabitants of the earth, that they may know that there is no flesh that can dwell in the presence of God, save it be through the merits, and mercy, and grace of the Holy Messiah, who layeth down his life according to the flesh, and taketh it again by the power of the Spirit, that he may bring to pass the *d*resurrection of the dead, being the first that should rise.

9. Wherefore, he is the firstfruits unto God, inasmuch as he shall make *e*intercession for all the children of men; and they that believe in him shall be saved.

10. And because of the intercession for all, all men come unto God; wherefore, they stand in the presence of him, to be judged of him according to the truth and holiness which is in him. Wherefore, the ends of the law which the Holy One hath given, unto the inflicting of the punishment which is affixed, which punishment that is affixed is in opposition to that of the happiness which is affixed, to answer the ends of the *f*atonement—

11. For it must needs be, that there is an *g*opposition in all things. If not so, my first-born in the wilderness, righteousness could not be brought to pass, neither wickedness, neither holiness nor misery, neither good nor bad. Wherefore, all things must needs be a compound in one; wherefore, if it should be one body it must needs remain as dead, having no life neither death, nor corruption nor incorruption, happiness nor misery, neither sense nor insensibility.

12. Wherefore, it must needs have been created for a thing of naught; wherefore there would have been no purpose in the end of its creation. Wherefore, this thing must needs destroy the wisdom of God and his eternal purposes, and also the power, and the mercy, and the justice of God.

13. And if ye shall say there is no law, ye shall also say there is no sin. If ye shall say there is no sin, ye shall also say there is no righteousness. And if there be no righteousness there be no happiness. And if there be no

b, 2 Ne. 9:4, 6, 7. Al. 11:42—45. 12:12, 16, 24, 27, 31, 36. 42:6—9. He. 14:16.
c, 2 Ne. 9:8—15, 26. Mos. 16:4—10. Al. 11:40—45. 12:16—18, 32, 36, 37. 40:13, 14, 26. 42:6—11, 14. He. 14:15—18. *d*, 2 Ne. 9:4, 6—19, 22. Mos. 13:35. 15:8, 9, 20—27. 16:7—11. Al. 5:15. 7:12. 11:41—45. 12:12—18, 24, 25. 22:14. 33:22. Chap. 40. 41:2—5. 42:23. He. 14:15—17, 25. 3 Ne. 23:9—13. 26:5. Morm. 6:21. 7:6. 9:13. Moro. 7:41. 10:34. Ezek. 37:3—10. Rom. 8:10. 1 Cor. 15:35—45.
e, ver. 10. Mos. 14:12. 15:8. Moro. 7:27, 28. *f*, 2 Ne. 9:7, 21, 22, 25, 26. 10:25. 25:16. Jac. 4:11, 12. Mos. 3:11, 15—19. 4:2, 6, 7. 13:28. 18:2. Al. 5:27. 13:5, 11. 21:9. 22:14. 24:13. 30:17. 33:22. 34:8—16, 36. 36:17. 42:15, 23. He. 14:15, 16. 3 Ne. 11:11. 27:19. Morm. 9:13. Moro. 7:41. 8:20. 10:33.
g, vers. 15, 16.   BETWEEN B. C. 588 AND 570.

righteousness nor happiness there be no punishment nor misery. And if these things are not there is no God. And if there is no God we are not, neither the earth; for there could have been no creation of things, neither to act nor to be acted upon; wherefore, all things must have vanished away.

14. And now, my sons, I speak unto you these things for your profit and learning; for there is a God, and he hath created all things, both the heavens and the earth, and all things that in them are, both things to act and things to be acted upon.

15. And to bring about his eternal purposes in the end of man, after he had created our first parents, and the beasts of the field and the fowls of the air, and in fine, all things which are created, it must needs be that there was an ^{h}opposition; even the forbidden fruit in opposition to the tree of life; the one being sweet and the other bitter.

16. Wherefore, the Lord God gave unto man that he should act for himself. Wherefore, man could not act for himself save it should be that he was enticed by the one or the other.

17. And I, Lehi, according to the things which I have read, must needs suppose that an angel of God, according to that ^{i}which is written, had fallen from heaven; wherefore, he became a devil, having sought that which was evil before God.

18. And because he had fallen from heaven, and had become miserable forever, he sought also the misery of all mankind. Wherefore, he said unto Eve, yea, even that old serpent, who is the devil, who is the father of all lies, wherefore he said: Partake of the forbidden fruit, and ye shall not die, but ye shall be as God, knowing good and evil.

19. And after Adam and Eve had partaken of the forbidden fruit they were driven out of the garden of Eden, to till the earth.

20. And they have brought forth children; yea, even the family of all the earth.

21. And the days of the children of men were prolonged, according to the will of God, that they might repent while in the flesh; wherefore, their state became a state of probation, and their time was lengthened, according to the commandments which the Lord God gave unto the children of men. For he gave commandment that all men must repent; for he showed unto all men that they were lost, because of the transgression of their parents.

22. And now, behold, if Adam had not transgressed he would not have fallen, but he would have remained in the garden of Eden. And all things which were created must have remained in the same state in which they were after they were created; and they must have remained forever, and had no end.

23. And they would have had ^{j}no children; wherefore they would have remained in a state of innocence, having no joy, for they knew no misery; doing no good, for they knew no sin.

24. But behold, all things have been done in the wisdom of him who knoweth all things.

25. Adam ^{k}fell that men might

---

h, ver. 11. i, ver. 18. 2 Ne. 9:8. Mos. 16:3. P. of G. P., Moses 4:3—4. Abraham 3:27, 28. Gen. 3:1. Rev. 12:9. 20:2. j, ver. 25. P. of G. P., Moses 5:11. k, ver. 23.

BETWEEN B. C. 588 AND 570.

be; and men are, that they might have joy.

26. And the Messiah cometh in the fulness of time, that he may redeem the children of men from the fall. And because that they are redeemed from the fall they have become ᶦfree forever, knowing good from evil; to act for themselves and not to be acted upon, save it be by the punishment of the law at the great and last day, according to the commandments which God hath given.

27. Wherefore, men are free according to the flesh; and all things are given them which are expedient unto man. And they are free to choose liberty and eternal life, through the great mediation of all men, or to choose captivity and death, according to the captivity and power of the devil; for he seeketh that all men might be miserable like unto himself.

28. And now, my sons, I would that ye should look to the great Mediator, and hearken unto his great commandments; and be faithful unto his words, and choose eternal life, according to the will of his Holy Spirit;

29. And not choose eternal death, according to the will of the flesh and the evil which is therein, which giveth the spirit of the devil power to captivate, to bring you down to hell, that he may reign over you in his own kingdom.

30. I have spoken these few words unto you all, my sons, in the last days of my probation; and I have chosen the good part, according to the words of the prophet. And I have none other object save it be the everlasting welfare of your souls. Amen.

CHAPTER 3.

Lehi to his son Joseph—A prophecy by Joseph in Egypt—A choice seer foretold—The mission of Moses—Hebrew and Nephite scriptures.

1. And now I speak unto you, Joseph, ᵃmy last-born. Thou wast born in the wilderness of mine afflictions; yea, in the days of my greatest sorrow did thy mother bear thee.

2. And may the Lord consecrate also unto thee ᵇthis land, which is a most precious land, for thine inheritance and the inheritance of thy seed with thy brethren, for thy security forever, if it so be that ye shall keep the commandments of the Holy One of Israel.

3. And now, Joseph, my last-born, whom I have brought out of the wilderness of mine afflictions, may the Lord bless thee forever, for thy seed shall not ᶜutterly be destroyed.

4. For behold, thou art the fruit of my loins; and I am a ᵈdescendant of Joseph who was carried captive into Egypt. And great were the covenants of the Lord which he made unto Joseph.

5. Wherefore, Joseph truly saw our day. And he obtained a promise of the Lord, that out of the fruit of his loins the Lord God would raise up a righteous branch unto the house of Israel; not the Messiah, but a branch which was to be broken off, nevertheless, to be remembered in the covenants of the Lord that the Messiah should be made manifest unto them in the latter days, in the spirit of power, unto the bringing of them out of darkness unto light—yea, out of hidden darkness and out of captivity unto freedom.

l, vers. 27—29. Al. chap. 29. 41:7. 42:27. He. 14:30. CHAP. 3: *a*, 1 Ne. 18:7, 19. *b*, 1 Ne. 2:20. 18:22, 23. *c*, 1 Ne. 13:30. *d*, 1 Ne. 5:14—16. Al. 10:3.
BETWEEN B. C. 588 AND 570.

6. For Joseph truly testified, saying: A *seer shall the Lord my God raise up, who shall be a choice seer unto the fruit of my loins.

7. Yea, Joseph truly said: Thus saith the Lord unto me: A choice seer will I raise up out of the fruit of thy loins; and he shall be esteemed highly among the fruit of thy loins. And unto him will I give commandment that he shall do a work for the fruit of thy loins, his brethren, which shall be of great worth unto them, even to the bringing of them to the knowledge of the covenants which I have made with thy fathers.

8. And I will give unto him a commandment that he shall do none other work, save the work which I shall command him. And I will make him great in mine eyes; for he shall do my work.

9. And he shall be great like unto Moses, whom I have said I would raise up unto you, to deliver my people, O house of Israel.

10. And Moses will I raise up, to deliver thy people out of the land of Egypt.

11. But a seer will I raise up out of the fruit of thy loins; and unto him will I give power to bring forth my word unto the seed of thy loins—and not to the bringing forth my word only, saith the Lord, but to the convincing them of my word, which shall have already gone forth among them.

12. Wherefore, the fruit of thy loins shall write; and the fruit of the loins of Judah shall write; and that which shall be written by the fruit of thy loins, and also that which shall be written by the fruit of the loins of Judah, shall *grow together, unto the confounding of false doctrines and laying down of contentions, and establishing peace among the fruit of thy loins, and bringing them to the *knowledge of their fathers in the latter days, and also to the knowledge of my covenants, saith the Lord.

13. And out of weakness he shall be made strong, in that day when my work shall commence among all my people, unto the restoring thee, O house of Israel, saith the Lord.

14. And thus prophesied Joseph, saying: Behold, that seer will the Lord bless; and they that seek to destroy him shall be confounded; for this promise, which I have obtained of the Lord, of the fruit of my loins, shall be fulfilled. Behold, I am sure of the fulfilling of this promise;

15. And his name shall be called *after me; and it shall be after the name of his father. And he shall be like unto me; for the thing, which the Lord shall bring forth by his hand, by the power of the Lord shall *bring my people unto salvation.

16. Yea, thus prophesied Joseph: I am sure of this thing, even as I am sure of the promise of Moses; for the Lord hath said unto me, I will preserve thy seed forever.

17. And the Lord hath said: I will raise up a Moses; and I will give power unto him in a rod; and I will give judgment unto him in writing. Yet I will not loose his tongue, that he shall speak much, for I will not make him mighty in speaking.

e, vers. 11, 14. Mos. 8:13—18. 3 Ne. 21:8—11. Morm. 8:16, 25. Eth. 3:21—28. *f*, Ezek. 37:16—20. *g*, 3 Ne. 5:23. Morm. 7:5, 10. *h*, ver. 14. *i*, 2 Ne. 27:6—26. Enos 12—18. Al. 37:1—20. 3 Ne. 16:10, 11. Morm. 7:8—10.

BETWEEN B. C. 588 AND 570.

But I will write unto him my law, by the finger of mine own hand; and I will make a spokesman for him.

18. And the Lord said unto me also: I will raise up unto the fruit of thy loins; and I will make for him a ʲspokesman. And I, behold, I will give unto him that he shall write the writing of the fruit of thy loins, unto the fruit of thy loins; and the spokesman of thy loins shall declare it.

19. And the words which he shall write shall be the words which are expedient in my wisdom should go forth unto the fruit of thy loins. And it shall be as if the fruit of thy loins had cried unto them from the dust; for I know their faith.

20. And they shall ᵏcry from the dust; yea, even repentance unto their brethren, even after many generations have gone by them. And it shall come to pass that their cry shall go, even according to the simpleness of their words.

21. Because of their faith their words shall proceed forth out of my mouth unto their brethren who are the fruit of thy loins; and the weakness of their words will I make strong in their faith, unto the remembering of my covenant which I made unto thy fathers.

22. And now, behold, my son Joseph, after this manner did my father of old prophesy.

23. Wherefore, because of this covenant thou art blessed; for thy seed shall not be destroyed, for they shall hearken unto the words of the book.

24. And there shall rise up one mighty among them, who shall do much good, both in word and in deed, being an instrument in the hands of God, with exceeding faith, to work mighty wonders, and do that thing which is great in the sight of God, unto the bringing to pass much restoration unto the house of Israel, and unto the seed of thy brethren.

25. And now, blessed art thou, Joseph. Behold, thou art little; wherefore hearken unto the words of thy brother, Nephi, and it shall be done unto thee even according to the words which I have spoken. Remember the words of thy dying father. Amen.

CHAPTER 4.

Lehi blesses the sons and daughters of Laman and Lemuel—Blessings upon Ishmael's household and upon Sam and his posterity—Death of Lehi—Further rebellion.

1. And now, I, Nephi, speak concerning the prophecies of which my father hath spoken, concerning Joseph, who was carried into Egypt.

2. For behold, he truly prophesied concerning all his seed. And the prophecies which he wrote, there are not many greater. And he prophesied concerning us, and our future generations; and they are written upon the ᵃplates of brass.

3. Wherefore, after my father had made an end of speaking concerning the prophecies of Joseph, he called the children of Laman, his sons, and his daughters, and said unto them: Behold, my sons, and my daughters, who are the sons and the daughters of my first-born, I would that ye should give ear unto my words.

4. For the Lord God hath said that: Inasmuch as ye shall keep my commandments ye shall prosper in the land; and inasmuch as

---

j, D. & C. 100:9, 11. *k*, 2 Ne. 26:16. Morm. 8:14—16, 23, 25, 26.
CHAP. 4: *a*, see *a*, 1 Ne. 3. BETWEEN B. C. 588 AND 570.

ye will not keep my commandments ye shall be cut off from my presence.

5. But behold, my sons and my daughters, I cannot go down to my grave save I should leave a blessing upon you; for behold, I know that if ye are brought up in the way ye should go ye will not depart from it.

6. Wherefore, if ye are cursed, behold, I leave my blessing upon you, that the cursing may be taken from you and be answered upon the heads of your parents.

7. Wherefore, because of my blessing the Lord God will not suffer that ye shall perish; wherefore, he *b*will be merciful unto you and unto your seed forever.

8. And it came to pass that after my father had made an end of speaking to the sons and daughters of Laman, he caused the sons and daughters of Lemuel to be brought before him.

9. And he spake unto them, saying: Behold, my sons and my daughters, who are the sons and the daughters of my second son; behold I leave unto you the *c*same blessing which I left unto the sons and daughters of Laman; wherefore, thou shalt not utterly be destroyed; but in the end thy seed shall be blessed.

10. And it came to pass that when my father had made an end of speaking unto them, behold, he spake unto the *d*sons of Ishmael, yea, and even all his household.

11. And after he had made an end of speaking unto them, he spake unto Sam, saying: Blessed art thou, and thy seed; for thou shalt inherit the land like unto thy brother Nephi. And thy seed shall be *e*numbered with his seed; and thou shalt be even like unto thy brother, and thy seed like unto his seed; and thou shalt be blessed in all thy days.

12. And it came to pass after my father, Lehi, had spoken unto all his household, according to the feelings of his heart and the Spirit of the Lord which was in him, he waxed old. And it came to pass that he died, and was buried.

13. And it came to pass that not many days after his death, Laman and Lemuel and the sons of Ishmael were angry with me because of the admonitions of the Lord.

14. For I, Nephi, was constrained to speak unto them, according to his word; for I had spoken many things unto them, and also my father, before his death; many of which sayings are written upon mine *f*other plates; for a more history part are written upon mine other plates.

15. And upon *g*these I write the things of my soul, and many of the scriptures which are engraven upon the plates of brass. For my soul delighteth in the scriptures, and my heart pondereth them, and writeth them for the learning and the profit of my children.

16. Behold, my soul delighteth in the things of the Lord; and my heart pondereth continually upon the things which I have seen and heard.

17. Nevertheless, notwithstanding the great goodness of the Lord, in showing me his great and marvelous works, my heart exclaimeth: O wretched man that I am! Yea, my heart sor-

b, 1 Ne. 13:31. 2 Ne. 10:18, 19. Jac. 3:3—9. He. 7:23, 24. 15:10—17. 3 Ne. 20:22. Morm. 5:20, 21. Eth. 13:6, 8—11. *c*, vers. 5—7. *d*, 1 Ne. 7:6. *e*, Jac. 1:12—14. *f*, 1 Ne. 9:4. *g*, 1 Ne. 6:1—6.   BETWEEN B. C. 588 AND 570.

roweth because of my flesh; my soul grieveth because of mine iniquities.

18. I am encompassed about, because of the temptations and the sins which do so easily beset me.

19. And when I desire to rejoice, my heart groaneth because of my sins; nevertheless, I know in whom I have trusted.

20. My God hath been my support; he hath led me through mine afflictions in the wilderness; and he hath preserved me upon the waters of the great deep.

21. He hath filled me with his love, even unto the consuming of my flesh.

22. He hath confounded mine enemies, unto the causing of them to quake before me.

23. Behold, he hath heard my cry by day, and he hath given me knowledge by visions in the nighttime.

24. And by day have I waxed bold in mighty prayer before him; yea, my voice have I sent up on high; and angels came down and ministered unto me.

25. And upon the wings of his Spirit hath my body been carried away upon exceeding high mountains. And mine eyes have beheld great things, yea, even too great for man; therefore I was bidden that I should not write them.

26. O then, if I have seen so great things, if the Lord in his condescension unto the children of men hath visited men in so much mercy, why should my heart weep and my soul linger in the valley of sorrow, and my flesh waste away, and my strength slacken, because of mine afflictions?

27. And why should I yield to sin, because of my flesh? Yea, why should I give way to temptations, that the evil one have place in my heart to destroy my peace and afflict my soul? Why am I angry because of mine enemy?

28. Awake, my soul! No longer droop in sin. Rejoice, O my heart, and give place no more for the enemy of my soul.

29. Do not anger again because of mine enemies. Do not slacken my strength because of mine afflictions.

30. Rejoice, O my heart, and cry unto the Lord, and say: O Lord, I will praise thee forever; yea, my soul will rejoice in thee, my God, and the rock of my salvation.

31. O Lord, wilt thou redeem my soul? Wilt thou deliver me out of the hands of mine enemies? Wilt thou make me that I may shake at the appearance of sin?

32. May the gates of hell be shut continually before me, because that my heart is broken and my spirit is contrite! O Lord, wilt thou not shut the gates of thy righteousness before me, that I may walk in the path of the low valley, that I may be strict in the plain road!

33. O Lord, wilt thou encircle me around in the robe of thy righteousness! O Lord, wilt thou make a way for mine escape before mine enemies! Wilt thou make my path straight before me! Wilt thou not place a stumbling block in my way—but that thou wouldst clear my way before me, and hedge not up my way, but the ways of mine enemy.

34. O Lord, I have trusted in thee, and I will trust in thee forever. I will not put my trust in the arm of flesh; for I know that cursed is he that putteth his trust in the arm of flesh. Yea, cursed

2 NEPHI, 5.

is he that putteth his trust in man or maketh flesh his arm.

35. Yea, I know that God will give liberally to him that asketh. Yea, my God will give me, if I ask not amiss; therefore I will lift up my voice unto thee; yea, I will cry unto thee, my God, the rock of my righteousness. Behold, my voice shall forever ascend up unto thee, my rock and mine everlasting God. Amen.

CHAPTER 5.

Nephi, warned of God, separates from those who seek his life—Zoram, Sam, Jacob and Joseph and others accompany him—The sword of Laban—A temple built—Nephi a king or protector—The rebellious cursed with a dark skin—Priests and teachers consecrated.

1. Behold, it came to pass that I, Nephi, did cry much unto the Lord my God, because of the ^{a}anger of my brethren.

2. But behold, their anger did increase against me, insomuch that they did seek to take away my life.

3. Yea, they did murmur against me, saying: Our younger brother thinks to rule over us; and we have had much trial because of him; wherefore, now let us slay him, that we may not be afflicted more because of his words. For behold, we will not have him to be our ruler; for it belongs unto us, who are the elder brethren, to rule over this people.

4. Now I do not write upon these plates all the words which they murmured against me. But it sufficeth me to say, that they did seek to take away my life.

5. And it came to pass that the Lord did warn me, that I, Nephi, should depart from them and flee into the wilderness, and all those who would go with me.

6. Wherefore, it came to pass that I, Nephi, did take my family, and also Zoram and his family, and Sam, mine elder brother and his family, and Jacob and Joseph, my younger brethren, and also my sisters, and all those who would go with me. And all those who would go with me were those who believed in the warnings and the revelations of God; wherefore, they did hearken unto my words.

7. And we did take our tents and whatsoever things were possible for us, and did journey in the wilderness for the space of many days. And after we had journeyed for the space of many days we did pitch our tents.

8. And my people would that we should call the name of the place ^{b}Nephi; wherefore, we did call it Nephi.

9. And all those who were with me did take upon them to call themselves the people of Nephi.

10. And we did observe to keep the judgments, and the statutes, and the commandments of the Lord in all things, according to the law of Moses.

11. And the Lord was with us; and we did prosper exceedingly; for we did sow seed, and we did reap again in abundance. And we began to raise flocks, and herds, and animals of every kind.

12. And I, Nephi, had also brought the records which were engraven upon the ^{c}plates of brass; and also the ^{d}ball, or compass, which was prepared for my father by the hand of the Lord, according to that which is written.

a, 2 Ne. 4:13. Enos 20. Mos. 10:15. *b*, Om. 12, 27. W. of Morm. 13. Mos. 7:6, 7, 9, 21. 9:1, 3, 4, 14. 11:13. 19:15, 19, 22. 21:26. 23:35—38. 28:1, 5. 29:3. Al. 2:24. 5:3. 17:8. 20:1, 2. 22:1, 26—34. 25:13. 27:14. 47:1, 20. 50:8, 11. 54:6. He. 4:12. 5:20, 21. *c*, see *a*, 1 Ne. 3. *d*, see *d*, 1 Ne. 16.

BETWEEN B. C. 588 AND 570.

13. And it came to pass that we began to prosper exceedingly, and to multiply in the land.

14. And I, Nephi, did take the *sword of Laban, and after the manner of it did make many swords, lest by any means the people who were now called Lamanites should come upon us and destroy us; for I knew their ᶠhatred towards me and my children and those who were called my people.

15. And I did teach my people to build buildings, and to work in all ᵍmanner of wood, and of iron, and of copper, and of brass, and of steel, and of gold, and of silver, and of precious ores, which were in great abundance.

16. And I, Nephi, did build a ʰtemple; and I did construct it after the manner of the temple of Solomon save it were not built of so many precious things; for they were not to be found upon the land, wherefore, it could not be built like unto Solomon's temple. But the manner of the construction was like unto the temple of Solomon; and the workmanship thereof was exceeding fine.

17. And it came to pass that I, Nephi, did cause my people to be industrious, and to labor with their hands.

18. And it came to pass that they would that I should be their ⁱking. But I, Nephi, was desirous that they should have no king; nevertheless, I did for them according to that which was in my power.

19. And behold, the words of the Lord had been fulfilled unto my brethren, which he spake concerning them, that I should be their ʲruler and their teacher. Wherefore, I had been their ruler and their teacher, according to the commandments of the Lord, until the time they sought to ᵏtake away my life.

20. Wherefore, the word of the Lord was fulfilled which he spake unto me, saying that: Inasmuch as they will not hearken unto thy words they shall be ˡcut off from the presence of the Lord. And behold, they were cut off from his presence.

21. And he had caused the ᵐcursing to come upon them, yea, even a sore cursing, because of their iniquity. For behold, they had hardened their hearts against him, that they had become like unto a flint; wherefore, as they were white, and exceeding fair and delightsome, that they might not be enticing unto my people the Lord God did cause a skin of blackness to come upon them.

22. And thus saith the Lord God: I will cause that they shall be loathsome unto thy people, save they shall repent of their iniquities.

23. And cursed shall be the seed of him that mixeth with their seed; for they shall be cursed even with the same cursing. And the Lord spake it, and it was done.

24. And because of their cursing which was upon them they did become an idle people, full of mischief and subtlety, and did seek in the wilderness for beasts of prey.

25. And the Lord God said unto me: They shall be a ⁿscourge unto thy seed, to stir them up in remembrance of me; and inasmuch

---

e, see a, 1 Ne. 4. f, see a, 2 Ne. 5. g, Jar. 8. Eth. 7:9. h, Jac. 1:17. Al. 16:13. 23:2. 26:29. He. 3:9, 14. 3 Ne. 11:1. i, 2 Ne. 6:2. Jac. 1:9, 11, 15. Jar. 7, 14. Om. 12, 19, 23, 24. Mos. 1:10. 6:4—7. j, see c, 1 Ne. 2. k, see ver. 2. l, see b, 1 Ne. 2. m, see d, 1 Ne. 2. n, 1 Ne. 2:24. 12:19. Al. 45:9—14. 46:24. Morm. 6.
BETWEEN B. C. 588 AND 570.

as they will not remember me, and hearken unto my words, they shall scourge them even unto destruction.

26. And it came to pass that I, Nephi, did consecrate Jacob and Joseph, that °they should be priests and teachers over the land of my people.

27. And it came to pass that we lived after the manner of happiness.

28. *And thirty years had passed away from the time we left Jerusalem.

29. And I, Nephi, had kept the ᵖrecords upon my plates, which I had made, of my people thus far.

30. And it came to pass that the Lord God said unto me: Make ᵠother plates; and thou shalt engraven many things upon them which are good in my sight, for the profit of thy people.

31. Wherefore, I, Nephi, to be obedient to the commandments of the Lord, went and made these plates upon which I have engraven these things.

32. And I engraved that which is pleasing unto God. And if my people are pleased with the things of God they will be pleased with mine engravings which are upon these plates.

33. And if my people desire to know the more particular part of the history of my people they must search mine other plates.

34. And it sufficeth me to say that †forty years had passed away, and we had already had wars and contentions with our brethren.

CHAPTER 6.

Jacob's exhortation to the people— He cites the prophecies of Isaiah.

1. The words of Jacob, the brother of Nephi, which he spake unto the people of Nephi:

2. Behold, my beloved brethren, I, Jacob, having been called of God, and ᵃordained after the manner of his holy order, and having been consecrated by my brother Nephi, unto whom ye look as a ᵇking or a protector, and on whom ye depend for safety, behold ye know that I have spoken unto you exceeding many things.

3. Nevertheless, I speak unto you again; for I am desirous for the welfare of your souls. Yea, mine anxiety is great for you; and ye yourselves know that it ever has been. For I have exhorted you with all diligence; and I have taught you the words of my father; and I have spoken unto you concerning all things which are written, from the creation of the world.

4. And now, behold, I would speak unto you concerning things which are, and which are to come; wherefore, I will read you the words of Isaiah. And they are the words which my brother has desired that I should speak unto you. And I speak unto you for your sakes, that ye may learn and glorify the name of your God.

5. And now, the words which I shall read are they which Isaiah spake concerning all the house of Israel; wherefore, they may be likened unto you, for ye are of the house of Israel. And there are many things which have been spoken by Isaiah which may be likened unto you, because ye are of the house of Israel.

6. And now, these are the words: ᶜThus saith the Lord God: Behold, I will lift up mine hand

---

o, 2 Ne. 6:2. Jac. 1:18, 19. *p*, see *f*, 1 Ne. 1. *q*, see *c*, 1 Ne. 9. CHAP. 6: *a*, 2 Ne. 5:26. Jac. 1:18, 19. *b*, see *i*, 2 Ne. 5. *c*, Isa. 49:22, 23. 2 Ne. 10:9. * B. C. 569. † B. C. 559.

to the Gentiles, and set up my standard to the people; and they shall bring thy sons in their arms, and thy daughters shall be carried upon their shoulders.

7. And kings shall be thy nursing fathers, and their queens thy nursing mothers; they shall bow down to thee with their faces towards the earth, and lick up the dust of thy feet; and thou shalt know that I am the Lord; for they shall not be ashamed that wait for me.

8. And now I, Jacob, would speak somewhat concerning these words. For behold, the Lord has ᵈshown me that those who were at Jerusalem, from whence we came, have been slain and carried away captive.

9. Nevertheless, the Lord has shown unto me that they should return again. And he also has shown unto me that the Lord God, the Holy One of Israel, should manifest himself unto them in the flesh; and after he should manifest himself they should scourge him and crucify him, according to the words of the angel who spake it unto me.

10. And after they have hardened their hearts and stiffened their necks against the Holy One of Israel, behold, the judgments of the Holy One of Israel shall come upon them. And the day cometh that they shall be smitten and afflicted.

11. Wherefore, after they are driven to and fro, for thus saith the angel, many shall be afflicted in the flesh, and shall not be suffered to perish, because of the prayers of the faithful; they shall be scattered, and smitten, and hated; nevertheless, the Lord will be merciful unto them, that ᵉwhen they shall come to the knowledge of their Redeemer, they shall be gathered together again to the lands of their inheritance.

12. And blessed are the ᶠGentiles, they of whom the prophet has written; for behold, if it so be that they shall repent and fight not against Zion, and do not unite themselves to that great and ᵍabominable church, they shall be saved; for the Lord God will fulfil his covenants which he has made unto his children; and for this cause the prophet has written these things.

13. Wherefore, ʰthey that fight against Zion and the covenant people of the Lord shall lick up the dust of their feet; and the people of the Lord shall not be ashamed. For the people of the Lord are they who wait for him; for they still wait for the coming of the Messiah.

14. And behold, according to the words of the prophet, the Messiah will set himself again the ⁱsecond time to recover them; wherefore, he will manifest himself unto them in power and great glory, unto the destruction of their enemies, when that day cometh when they shall believe in him; and none will he destroy that believe in him.

15. And they that believe ʲnot in him shall be destroyed, both by fire, and by tempest, and by earthquakes, and by bloodsheds, and by pestilence, and by famine. And they shall know that the Lord is God, the Holy One of Israel.

16. ᵏFor ˡshall the prey be

---

d, 1 Ne. 7:13, 14. *e*, see *c*, 1 Ne. 15. *f*, 1 Ne. 13:12—23, 30—35, 38—42. 14:1—5. 2 Ne. 10:8—14, 18, 19. 3 Ne. 16:6, 7. 20:27. 21:2—6, 22—25. Morm. 5:19. *g*, see *a*, 1 Ne. 13. *h*, see *j*, 1 Ne. 22. *i*, 2 Ne. 21:11, 25:17. 20:1. *j*, 1 Ne. 14:3, 15—17. 22:13—23. 2 Ne. 10:15, 16. 27:2—4. 28:15—32. 3 Ne. 16:8—15. 20:15—20. 21:11—21, 29. Morm. 5:22—24. Eth. 2:8—11. *k*, Isa. 49:24—26.

BETWEEN B. C. 559 AND 545.

2 NEPHI, 7.

taken from the mighty, or the lawful captive delivered?

17. But thus saith the Lord: Even the captives of the mighty shall be taken away, and the prey of the terrible shall be delivered; for the Mighty God shall deliver his covenant people. For thus saith the Lord: I will contend with them that contendeth with thee—

18. And I will feed them that oppress thee, with their own flesh; and they shall be drunken with their own blood as with sweet wine; and all flesh shall know that I the Lord am thy Savior and thy Redeemer, the Mighty One of Jacob.

CHAPTER 7.

Jacob's teachings continued—Compare Isaiah 50.

1. Yea, for thus saith the Lord: ^{a}Have I put thee away, or have I cast thee off forever? For thus saith the Lord: Where is the ^{b}bill of your mother's divorcement? To whom have I put thee away, or to which of my ^{c}creditors have I sold you? Yea, to whom have I sold you? Behold, for your iniquities ^{d}have ye sold yourselves, and for your transgressions is your mother put away.

2. Wherefore, when I came, there was no man; ^{e}when I called, yea, there was none to answer. O house of Israel, is my hand shortened at all that it cannot redeem, or have I no power to deliver? Behold, ^{f}at my rebuke I dry up the sea, I make ^{g}their rivers a wilderness and ^{h}their fish to stink because the waters are dried up, and they die because of thirst.

3. ^{i}I clothe the heavens with blackness, ^{j}and I make sackcloth their covering.

4. ^{k}The Lord God hath given me the tongue of the learned, that I should know how to speak a word in season unto thee, O house of Israel. When ye are weary he waketh morning by morning. He waketh mine ear to hear as the learned.

5. The Lord God hath opened mine ear, and I was not rebellious, neither turned away back.

6. I gave my back to the smiter, and my cheeks to them that plucked off the hair. I hid not my face from shame and spitting.

7. For the Lord God will help me, therefore shall I not be confounded. Therefore have I set my face like a flint, and I know that I shall not be ashamed.

8. And the Lord is near, and he justifieth me. Who will contend with me? Let us stand together. Who is mine adversary? Let him come near me, ^{l}and I will smite him with the strength of my mouth.

9. For the Lord God will help me. And all they who shall condemn me, behold, ^{m}all they shall wax old as a garment, and the moth shall eat them up.

10. Who is among you that feareth the Lord, that obeyeth the voice of his servant, that walketh in darkness and hath no light?

11. Behold all ye that kindle fire, that compass yourselves about with sparks, walk in the light of your fire and in the sparks which ye have kindled. ^{n}This shall ye have of mine hand —ye shall lie down in sorrow.

a, Mal. 2:16. Matt. 19:9. *b,* Deut. 24:1—4. Jer. 3:8. Hos. 2:2. *c,* 2 Kings 4:1. Matt. 18:25. *d,* Isa. 52:3. *e,* Prov. 1:24—27. Isa. 65:12. 66:4. Jer. 7:13. 35:15. D. & C. 133:67. *f,* Ex. 14:21. Ps. 106:9. Nah. 1:4. D. & C. 133:68. *g,* Josh. 3:15, 16. *h,* Ex. 7:18, 21. *i,* Ex. 10:21. *j,* Rev. 6:12. *k,* Ex. 4:11. *l,* Isa. 11:4. 2 Thess. 2:8. *m,* Job 13:28. Ps. 102:26. Isa. 51:6, 8. *n,* D. & C. 133:70.

BETWEEN B. C. 559 AND 545.

CHAPTER 8.

Jacob's teachings continued—Compare Isaiah 51.

1. Hearken unto me, ye that follow after righteousness. Look unto the rock from whence ye are hewn, and to the hole of the pit from whence ye are digged.

2. Look unto Abraham, your father, and unto Sarah, she that bare you; for I called him alone, and blessed him.

3. For the Lord ^ashall comfort Zion, he will comfort all ^bher waste places; and he will make her ^cwilderness like Eden, and ^dher desert like the garden of the Lord. Joy and gladness shall be found therein, thanksgiving and the voice of melody.

4. Hearken unto me, my people; and give ear unto me, O my nation; for a ^elaw shall proceed from me, and I will make my judgment to rest for a light for the people.

5. My righteousness is near; my salvation is gone forth, and mine arm shall judge the people. ^fThe isles shall wait upon me, and on mine arm shall they trust.

6. ^gLift up your eyes to the heavens, and look upon the earth beneath; for the heavens shall vanish away like smoke, and the earth shall wax old like a garment; and they that dwell therein shall die in like manner. But my salvation shall be forever, and my righteousness shall not be abolished.

7. Hearken unto me, ye that know righteousness, the people in whose heart I have written my ^hlaw, fear ye not the reproach of men, neither be ye afraid of their revilings.

8. ⁱFor the moth shall eat them up like a garment, and the worm shall eat them like wool. But my righteousness shall be forever, and my salvation from generation to generation.

9. ^jAwake, awake! ^kPut on strength, O arm of the Lord; awake ^las in the ancient days. Art thou not he that hath ^mcut Rahab, and wounded the dragon?

10. Art thou not he who hath dried the sea, the waters of the great deep; that hath made the depths of the sea a way for the ransomed to pass over?

11. ⁿTherefore, the redeemed of the Lord shall return, and come with singing unto Zion; and everlasting joy and holiness shall be upon their heads; and they shall obtain gladness and joy; sorrow and mourning shall flee away.

12. I am he; yea, I am he that comforteth you. Behold, who art thou, that thou shouldst be afraid of man, who shall die, and of the son of man, who shall be made like unto grass?

13. And forgetest the Lord thy maker, that hath stretched forth the heavens, and laid the foundations of the earth, ^oand hast feared continually every day, because of the fury of the oppressor, as if he were ready to destroy? ^pAnd where is the fury of the oppressor?

14. The ^qcaptive exile hasteneth, that he may be loosed, and that he should not die in the pit, nor that his bread should fail.

---

a, ver. 12. Ps. 102:13. Isa. 40:1. 52:9. *b*, Isa. 35:1. *c*, Ps. 107:3, 4, 35—37. Isa. 32:15—20. 35:1, 2, 6, 7. 43:19, 20. *d*, Isa. 35:1, 2, 6, 7. 43:19, 20. *e*, Isa. 2:3. Mic. 4:2. *f*, see *a*, 1 Ne. 21. *g*, Ps. 102:25, 26. Matt. 24:35. 2 Pet. 3:10—12. *h*, see *e*. *i*, see *m*, 2 Ne. 7. *j*, Ps. 44:23. Isa. 52:1. *k*, Ps. 93:1. Rev. 11:17. *l*, Ps. 44:1. *m*, Ps. 74:13, 14. 89:10. Isa. 27:1. Ezek. 29:3. *n*, Isa. 35:8—10. Jer. 31:12, 13. *o*, 1 Ne. 22:17. *p*, see *j*, 1 Ne. 22. *q*, ver. 25. 2 Ne. 9:12. Isa. 60:15. Zech. 9:11.

BETWEEN B. C. 559 AND 545.

15. But I am the Lord thy God, whose waves roared; the Lord of Hosts is my name.

16. And I have put my words in thy mouth, and have covered thee in the shadow of mine hand, 'that I may plant the heavens and lay the foundations of the earth, and say unto Zion: *Behold, thou art my people.

17. Awake, awake, stand up, O Jerusalem, 'which hast drunk at the hand of the Lord the cup of his fury—thou hast drunken the dregs of the cup of trembling wrung out—

18. And none to guide her among all the sons she hath brought forth; neither that taketh her by the hand, of all the sons she hath brought up.

19. These "two sons are come unto thee, who shall be sorry for thee—thy desolation and destruction, and the famine and the sword—and by whom shall I comfort thee?

20. Thy sons have fainted, save these two; they lie at the head of all the streets; as a wild bull in a net, they are full of the fury of the Lord, the rebuke of thy God.

21. Therefore hear now this, thou afflicted, and drunken, and not with wine:

22. Thus saith thy Lord, the Lord and thy God pleadeth the cause of his people; behold, I have taken out of thine hand the cup of trembling, the dregs of the cup of my fury; thou shalt no more drink it again.

23. But ᵛI will put it into the hand of them that afflict thee; who have said to thy soul: Bow down, that we may go over—and thou hast laid thy body as the ground and as the street to them that went over.

24. ʷAwake, awake, put on thy strength, O Zion; put on thy beautiful garments, O Jerusalem, the holy city; ˣfor henceforth there shall no more come into thee the uncircumcised and the unclean.

25. Shake thyself from the dust; arise, sit down, O Jerusalem; ʸloose thyself from the bands of thy neck, O captive daughter of Zion.

CHAPTER 9.

Jacob's teachings continued—The infinite atonement—The Savior's sufferings foreseen—Where there is no law there is no punishment.

1. And now, my beloved brethren, I have read these things that ye might know concerning the covenants of the Lord that he has covenanted with all the house of Israel—

2. That he has spoken unto the Jews, by the mouth of his holy prophets, even from the beginning down, from generation to generation, until the time comes that they shall be ᵃrestored to the true church and fold of God; when they shall be gathered home to the lands of their inheritance, and shall be established in all their lands of promise.

3. Behold, my beloved brethren, I speak unto you these things that ye may rejoice, and lift up your heads forever, because of the blessings which the Lord God shall bestow upon your children.

4. For I know that ye have searched much, many of you, to know of things to come; wherefore I know that ye know that our flesh must waste away and die;

---

r, Isa. 65:17. 66:22. s, ver. 3. Ps. 46:4—7. 48:1—3. 102:13—16. t, Jer. 25:15, 16. Luke 21:22—24. u, ver. 20. Rev. 11:3—13. v, Jer. 25:17. Joel 3:9—16. Zech. 12:2, 3, 8, 9. 14:3, 12—15. w, vers. 9, 17. Isa. 52:1, 2. x, Joel 3:17. Zech. 14:21. y, see q. CHAP. 9: a, see c, 1 Ne. 15. BETWEEN B. C. 559 AND 545.

nevertheless, in our *b*bodies we shall see God.

5. Yea, I know that ye know that in the body he shall show himself unto those at Jerusalem, from whence we came; for it is expedient that it should be among them; for it behooveth the great Creator that he suffereth himself to become subject unto man in the flesh, and *c*die for all men, that all men might become subject unto him.

6. For as death hath passed upon all men, to fulfil the merciful plan of the great Creator, there must needs be a power of resurrection, and the *d*resurrection must needs come unto man by reason of the fall; and the fall came by reason of transgression; and because man became fallen they were cut off *e*from the presence of the Lord.

7. Wherefore, it must needs be an infinite *f*atonement—save it should be an infinite atonement this corruption could not put on incorruption. Wherefore, the *g*first judgment which came upon man must needs have remained to an endless duration. And if so, this flesh must have laid down to rot and to crumble to its mother earth, to rise no more.

8. O the wisdom of God, his mercy and grace! For behold, if the flesh should rise no more our spirits must become subject to that *h*angel who fell from before the presence of the Eternal God, and became the devil, to rise no more.

9. And our spirits must have become *i*like unto him, and we become devils, angels to a devil, to be shut out from the presence of our God, and to remain with the father of lies, in misery, like unto himself; yea, to that being who beguiled our first parents, who transformeth himself nigh unto an angel of light, and stirreth up the children of men unto secret combinations of murder and all manner of secret works of darkness.

10. O how great the goodness of our God, who prepareth a way for our escape from the grasp of this awful monster; yea, that monster, *j*death and hell, which I call the death of the body, and also the death of the spirit.

11. And because of the way of deliverance of our God, the Holy One of Israel, this death, of which I have spoken, which is the temporal, shall deliver up its dead; which death is the grave.

12. And this death of which I have spoken, which is the spiritual death, shall deliver up its dead; which spiritual death is hell; wherefore, *k*death and hell must deliver up their dead, and hell must deliver up its captive spirits, and the grave must deliver up its captive bodies, and the bodies and the spirits of men will be restored one to the other; and it is by the power of the resurrection of the Holy One of Israel.

13. O how great the plan of our God! For on the other hand, the *l*paradise of God must deliver up the spirits of the righteous,

---

b, vers. 15, 22, 26, 38. Mos. 16:10. Al. 5:15, 22. 11:41—45. 12:12—18. 40:21. 42:23. He. 14:15—18. 3 Ne. 27:14, 15. Morm. 9:13. Moro. 10:34. *c*, vers. 21, 22. He. 14:15—18. 3 Ne. 27:14, 15. *d*, see *d*, 2 Ne. 2. *e*, ver. 9. Al. 42:7, 9, 11, 14, 23. He. 14:16, 17. *f*, see *f*, 2 Ne. 2. *g*, vers. 8—16. Mos. 3:26, 27. 16:4—11. Al. 11:45. 12:18, 26, 36. 42:6, 9, 14. He. 14:16, 17. Morm. 9:13. *h*, see *i*, 2 Ne. 2. *i*. vers. 16, 26, 37, 46. 1 Ne. 14:3, 4, 7. 2 Ne. 28:20—23. Mos. 16:2—5. 11. 3 Ne. 29:7. *j*, vers. 11—13, 26. Mos. 16:7, 8. Al. 12:24—27. 40:23—26. 42:6—15. He. 14:15 —19. Morm. 9:13. *k*, see *j*. *l*, Al. 40:12, 14. 4 Ne. 14. Moro. 10:34.

BETWEEN B. C. 559 AND 545.

and the grave deliver up the body of the righteous; and the spirit and the body is ᵐrestored to itself again, and all men become incorruptible, and immortal, and they are living souls, having a perfect knowledge like unto us in the flesh, save it be that our knowledge shall be perfect.

14. Wherefore, we shall have a "perfect knowledge of all our guilt, and our uncleanness, and our nakedness; and the righteous shall have a perfect knowledge of their enjoyment, and their righteousness, being clothed with purity, yea, even with the robe of righteousness.

15. And it shall come to pass that when all men shall have passed from this first death unto life, insomuch as they have become immortal, they must appear before the judgment-seat of the Holy One of Israel; and then cometh the judgment, and then must they be judged according to the holy judgment of God.

16. And assuredly, as the Lord liveth, for the Lord God hath spoken it, and it is his eternal word, which cannot pass away, that they who are righteous shall be righteous still, and they who are filthy shall be ᵒfilthy still; wherefore, they who are filthy are the devil and his angels; and they shall go away into everlasting fire, prepared for them; and their torment is as a lake of fire and brimstone, whose flame ascendeth up forever and ever and has no end.

17. O the greatness and the justice of our God! For he executeth all his words, and they have gone forth out of his mouth, and his law must be fulfilled.

18. But, behold, the righteous, the saints of the Holy One of Israel, they who have believed in the Holy One of Israel, they who have endured the crosses of the world, and despised the shame of it, they shall inherit the kingdom of God, which was prepared for them ᵖfrom the foundation of the world, and their joy shall be full forever.

19. O the greatness of the mercy of our God, the Holy One of Israel! For he delivereth his saints from that ᵠawful monster the devil, and death, and hell, and that lake of fire and brimstone, which is endless torment.

20. O how great the holiness of our God! For he knoweth all ʳthings, and there is not anything save he knows it.

21. And he cometh into the world that he may save all men if they will hearken unto his voice; for behold, he suffereth the pains of all men, yea, the ˢpains of every living creature, both men, women, and children, who belong to the family of Adam.

22. And he suffereth this that the ᵗresurrection might pass upon all men, that all might stand before him at the great and judgment day.

23. And he commandeth all men that ᵘthey must repent, and be baptized in his name, having

m, Al. 11:42—45. 40:21—24. Chap. 41. *n*, Mos. 3:25. Al. 11:43. 12:14. *o*, 1 Ne. 15:33—35. Al. 7:21. Morm. 9:14. *p*, Al. 13:3, 5. 7—9. 22:13. 42:26. He. 5:47. 3 Ne. 26:5. Eth. 3:14. 4:14, 15, 19. 12:32—34, 37. Moro. 8:12. *q*, see *k*, 1 Ne. 15. *r*, Al. 7:13. 13:7. 18:32. 26:35. He. 9:41. 3 Ne. 27:26. Morm. 8:17. Moro. 7:22. *s*, vers. 5, 7. Mos. 3:7. 15:10. Al. 7:11—13. 11:40. 22:14. 34:8—15. He. 14:15—17. 3 Ne. 9:22. 11:11, 14, 15. 27:14, 15. Morm. 9:13, 14. *t*, see *d*, 2 Ne. 2. *u*, Matt. 3:5, 6. Mark 1:4. Luke 3:3. John 3:5. Acts 2:38. 2 Ne. 31:5, 9—13, 17. Mos. 18:8—17. Al. 15:12—14. 19:35. 62:45. He. 3:24—26. 5:17, 19. 3 Ne. 7:23—26. 11:21—38. 12:1, 2. 18:5, 11, 30. 19:10—13. 23:5. 26:17, 21. 27:1, 16, 20. 28:18. Chap. 30. 4 Ne. 1. Morm. 7:8, 10. 9:23. Eth. 4:18. Moro. 6:1—4. 8:5—26.
BETWEEN B. C. 559 AND 545.

perfect faith in the Holy One of Israel, or they cannot be saved in the kingdom of God.

24. And if they will not repent and believe in his name, and be baptized in his name, and endure to the end, they must be damned; for the Lord God, the Holy One of Israel, has spoken it.

25. Wherefore, he has given a law; and where there is no law given there is no punishment; and where there is no punishment there is no condemnation; and where there is no condemnation the mercies of the Holy One of Israel have claim upon them, because of the *v*atonement; for they are delivered by the power of him.

26. For the atonement satisfieth the demands of his justice upon all those who have not the law given to them, that they are delivered from that awful monster, *w*death and hell, and the devil, and the lake of fire and brimstone, which is endless torment; and they are restored to that God who gave them breath, which is the Holy One of Israel.

27. But wo unto him that has the law given, yea, that has all the commandments of God, like unto us, and that transgresseth them, and that wasteth the days of his probation, for awful is his state!

28. O that cunning plan of the evil one! O the vainness, and the frailties, and the foolishness of men! When they *x*are learned they think they are wise, and they hearken not unto the counsel of God, for they set it aside, supposing they know of themselves, wherefore, their wisdom is foolishness and it profiteth them not. And they shall perish.

29. But to be learned is good if they hearken unto the counsels of God.

30. But wo unto the rich, who are rich as to the things of the world. For because they are rich they despise the poor, and they persecute the meek, and their hearts are upon their treasures; wherefore, their treasure is their God. And behold, their treasure shall perish with them also.

31. And wo unto the deaf that will not hear; for they shall perish.

32. Wo unto the blind that will not see; for they shall perish also.

33. Wo unto the uncircumcised of heart, for a knowledge of their iniquities shall smite them at the last day.

34. Wo unto the liar, for he shall be thrust down to hell.

35. Wo unto the murderer who deliberately killeth, for he shall die.

36. Wo unto them who commit *y*whoredoms, for they shall be thrust down to hell.

37. Yea, wo unto those that worship idols, for the devil of all devils delighteth in them.

38. And, in fine, wo unto all those who die in their sins; for they shall *z*return to God, and behold his face, and remain in their sins.

39. O, my beloved brethren, remember the awfulness in transgressing against that Holy God, and also the awfulness of yielding to the enticings of that cunning one. Remember, to be carnally-minded is death, and to be spiritually-minded is life eternal.

40. O, my beloved brethren,

v, see *f*, 2 Ne. 2. *w*, see *j*. *x*, vers. 29, 42. 2 Ne. 26:20. 27:15—26. 28:4, 15. *y*, 2 Ne. 28:15. Jac. 2:28. Al. 39:3, 9, 11. 3 Ne. 12:27—32. *z*, ver. 15. Al. 40:11.

give ear to my words. Remember the greatness of the Holy One of Israel. Do not say that I have spoken hard things against you; for if ye do, ye will revile against the truth; for I have spoken the words of your Maker. I know that the words of truth are hard against all uncleanness; but the righteous fear them not, for they love the truth and are not shaken.

41. O then, my beloved brethren, come unto the Lord, the Holy One. Remember that his paths are righteous. Behold, the way for man is ^{2a}narrow, but it lieth in a straight course before him, and the keeper of the gate is the Holy One of Israel; and he employeth no servant there; and there is none other way save it be by the gate; for he cannot be deceived, for the Lord God is his name.

42. And whoso knocketh, to him will he open; and the ^{2b}wise, and the learned, and they that are rich, who are puffed up because of their learning, and their wisdom, and their riches—yea, they are they whom he despiseth; and save they shall cast these things away, and consider themselves fools before God, and come down in the depths of humility, he will not open unto them.

43. But the things of the wise and the prudent shall be hid from them forever—yea, that happiness which is prepared for the saints.

44. O, my beloved brethren, remember my words. Behold, I take off my garments, and I shake them before you; I pray the God of my salvation that he view me with his all-searching eye; wherefore, ye shall know at the last day, when all men shall be judged of their works, that the God of Israel did witness that I shook your iniquities from my soul, and that I stand with brightness before him, and am rid of your blood.

45. O, my beloved brethren, turn away from your sins; shake off the chains of him that would bind you fast; come unto that God who is the rock of your salvation.

46. Prepare your souls for that glorious day when justice shall be administered unto the righteous, even the day of judgment, that ye may not shrink with awful fear; that ye may not remember your awful guilt in ^{2c}perfectness, and be constrained to exclaim: Holy, holy are thy judgments, O Lord God Almighty —but I know my guilt; I transgressed thy law, and my transgressions are mine; and the devil hath ^{2d}obtained me, that I am a prey to his awful misery.

47. But behold, my brethren, is it expedient that I should awake you to an awful reality of these things? Would I harrow up your souls if your minds were pure? Would I be plain unto you according to the plainness of the truth if ye were freed from sin?

48. Behold, if ye were holy I would speak unto you of holiness; but as ye are not holy, and ye look upon me as a teacher, it must needs be expedient that I teach you the consequences of sin.

49. Behold, my soul abhorreth sin, and my heart delighteth in righteousness; and I will praise the holy name of my God.

50. Come, my brethren, ^{2e}every one that thirsteth, come ye to the

2a, 2 Ne. 31:9, 17, 18. 33:9. Al. 37:44, 45. He. 3:29, 30. 3 Ne. 14:13, 14. 2b, ver. 29. 2 Ne. 28:4, 15. 2c, see n. 2d, see i. 2e, Isa. 55:1, 2.
BETWEEN B. C. 559 AND 545.

waters; and he that hath no money, come buy and eat; yea, come buy wine and milk without money and without price.

51. Wherefore, do not spend money for that which is of no worth, nor your labor for that which cannot satisfy. Hearken diligently unto me, and remember the words which I have spoken; and come unto the Holy One of Israel, and feast upon that which perisheth not, neither can be corrupted, and let your soul delight in fatness.

52. Behold, my beloved brethren, remember the words of your God; pray unto him continually by day, and give thanks unto his holy name by night. Let your hearts rejoice.

53. And behold how great the covenants of the Lord, and how great his condescensions unto the children of men; and because of his greatness, and his grace and mercy, he has promised unto us that our seed shall ²ᶠnot utterly be destroyed, according to the flesh, but that he would preserve them; and in future generations they shall become a righteous branch unto the house of Israel.

54. And now, my brethren, I would speak unto you more; but on the morrow I will declare unto you the remainder of my words. Amen.

CHAPTER 10.

Jacob's teachings continued—The coming of Christ—No kings upon the land of promise—They who fight against Zion shall perish.

1. And now I, Jacob, speak unto you again, my beloved brethren, concerning this ᵃrighteous branch of which I have spoken.

2. For behold, the promises which we have obtained are promises unto us according to the flesh; wherefore, as it has been shown unto me that ᵇmany of our children shall perish in the flesh because of unbelief, nevertheless, God will be merciful unto many; and our children shall be restored, that they may come to that which will give them the true knowledge of their Redeemer.

3. Wherefore, as I said unto you, it must needs be expedient that Christ—for in the last night the angel spake unto me that this should be his name—should come among the Jews, among those who are the more wicked part of the world; and they shall crucify him—for thus it behooveth our God, and there is none other nation on earth that would crucify their God.

4. For should the mighty miracles be wrought among other nations they would repent, and know that he be their God.

5. But because of priestcrafts and iniquities, they at Jerusalem will stiffen their necks against him, that he be crucified.

6. Wherefore, because of their iniquities, destructions, famines, pestilences, and bloodshed shall come upon them; and they who shall not be destroyed shall be scattered among all nations.

7. But behold, thus saith the Lord God: When the day cometh that they shall believe in me, that I am Christ, then have I covenanted with their fathers that ᶜthey shall be restored in the flesh, upon the earth, unto the lands of their inheritance.

8. And it shall come to pass that they shall be gathered in from their long dispersion, from

2f, see p, 1 Ne. 13. and ver. 31. 9:53. Jac. 5:25, 43—45. Al. 46:24, 25. CHAP. 10: a, 1 Ne. 15:12—17. 2 Ne. 3:5. b, see d, 1 Ne. 15. c, see e, 1 Ne. 15.
BETWEEN B. C. 559 AND 545.

the isles of the sea, and from the four parts of the earth; and the nations of the Gentiles shall be great in the eyes of me, saith God, in carrying them forth to the lands of their inheritance.

9. Yea, ^dthe kings of the Gentiles shall be nursing fathers unto them, and their queens shall become nursing mothers; wherefore, the promises of the Lord are great unto the Gentiles, for he hath spoken it, and who can dispute?

10. But behold, this land, said God, shall be a land of thine ^einheritance, and the Gentiles ^fshall be blessed upon the land.

11. And this land shall be a land of liberty unto the Gentiles, and there shall be no kings upon the land, who shall raise up unto the Gentiles.

12. And I will fortify this land ^gagainst all other nations.

13. And he that ^hfighteth against Zion shall perish, saith God.

14. For he that raiseth up a king against me shall perish, for I, the Lord, the king of heaven, will be their king, and I will be a light unto them forever, that hear my words.

15. Wherefore, for this cause, that my covenants may be fulfilled which I have made unto the children of men, that I will do unto them while they are in the flesh, I must needs destroy the ⁱsecret works of darkness, and of murders, and of abominations.

16. Wherefore, he that fighteth ^jagainst Zion, both Jew and Gentile, both bond and free, both male and female, shall perish; for they are they who are the ^kwhore of all the earth; for they who are not for me are against me, saith our God.

17. For I will fulfil my promises which I have made unto the children of men, that I will do unto them while they are in the flesh—

18. Wherefore, my beloved brethren, thus saith our God: I will afflict thy seed by the ^lhand of the Gentiles; nevertheless, I will soften the hearts of the Gentiles, that they shall be like unto a father to them; wherefore, the Gentiles shall be blessed and numbered among the house of Israel.

19. Wherefore, I will consecrate ^mthis land unto thy seed, and them who shall be numbered among thy seed, forever, for the land of their inheritance; for it is a choice land, saith God unto me, above all other lands, wherefore I will have all men that dwell thereon that they shall worship me, saith God.

20. And now, my beloved brethren, seeing that our merciful God has given us so great knowledge concerning these things, let us remember him, and lay aside our sins, and not hang down our heads, for we are not cast off; nevertheless, we have been driven out of the land of our inheritance; but we have been led to a better land, for the Lord has made the sea our path, and we are upon an isle of the sea.

d, 1 Ne. 13:35, 39. 15:17, 18. 22:5—9. 2 Ne. 6:6, 7. *e*, see *a*, 1 Ne. 2. *f*, 1 Ne. 13:15, 19, 34—42. 14:1—7. 15:13, 17. 22:6—10. 3 Ne. 16:4—7. 21:2—6, 22—25. Morm. 5:19. Eth. 2:12. *g*, 1 Ne. 13:19. *h*, ver. 16. 1 Ne. 22:14, 19. 2 Ne. 27:2, 3. *i*, 2 Ne. 9:9. 26:22. 27:27. Al. 37:21—32. He. 1:11, 12. 2:3—14. 3:23. 6:17—30, 37—41. 7:4, 5, 20, 21, 25. 8:1, 4, 27, 28. 9:6. 10:3. 11:2, 10, 25—33. 3 Ne. 1:27—30. 2:10—19. Chaps. 3, 4. 5:4—6. 6:28—30. 7:6, 9—12. 9:9. 4 Ne. 42, 46. Morm. 1:18. 2:8, 10, 27. 8:27, 40. Eth. 8:9—25. 9:1, 5, 6, 26. 10:33. 11:15, 22. 13:15, 18. 14:8—10. *j*, see *h*. *k*, see *g*, 1 Ne. 14. *l*, see *p* and *q*, 1 Ne. 13; also vers. 14, 15. *m*, 1 Ne. 13:15. See *a*, 1 Ne. 2. BETWEEN B. C. 559 AND 545.

21. But great are the promises of the Lord unto them who are upon the ⁿisles of the sea; wherefore as it says isles, there must needs be more than this, and they are inhabited also by our brethren.

22. For behold, the Lord God has ᵒled away from time to time from the house of Israel, according to his will and pleasure. And now behold, the Lord remembereth all them who have been broken off, wherefore he remembereth us also.

23. Therefore, cheer up your hearts, and remember that ye are free to act for yourselves—to choose the way of everlasting death or the way of eternal life.

24. Wherefore, my beloved brethren, reconcile yourselves to the will of God, and not to the will of the devil and the flesh; and remember, after ye are reconciled unto God, that it is only in and through the grace of God that ye are saved.

25. Wherefore, may God raise you from death by the power of the ᵖresurrection, and also from everlasting death by the power of the ᵍatonement, that ye may be received into the eternal kingdom of God, that ye may praise him through grace divine. Amen.

CHAPTER 11.

Jacob's teachings continued—Witnesses for the word of God—Types of the Redeemer.

1. And now, Jacob spake many more things to my people at that time; nevertheless only these things have I caused to be written, for the things which I have written sufficeth me.

2. And now I, Nephi, write more of the words of Isaiah, for my soul delighteth in his words. For I will liken his words unto my people, and I will send them forth unto all my children, for he verily ᵃsaw my Redeemer, even as I have seen him.

3. And my brother, Jacob, also has ᵇseen him as I have seen him; wherefore, I will send their words forth unto my children to prove unto them that my words are true. Wherefore, by the words of ᶜthree, God hath said, I will establish my word. Nevertheless, God sendeth ᵈmore witnesses, and he proveth all his words.

4. Behold, my soul delighteth in proving unto my people the truth of the coming of Christ; for, for this end hath the law of Moses been given; and all things which have been given of God from the beginning of the world, unto man, are the typifying of him.

5. And also my soul delighteth in the covenants of the Lord which he hath made to our fathers; yea, my soul delighteth in his grace, and in his justice, and power, and mercy in the great and eternal plan of ᵉdeliverance from death.

6. And my soul delighteth in proving unto my people that save Christ should come all men must perish.

7. For if there be no Christ there be ᶠno God; and if there be no God we are not, for there could have been no creation. But there is a God, and he is Christ, and

---

n, 1 Ne. 19:16. 22:3—5. Isa. 49:1. 51:5. 60:9. 66:19. o, 1 Ne. 22:4, 5. p, see d, 2 Ne. 2. q, see f, 2 Ne. 2. Chap. 11: a, 2 Ne. 16:1. Isa. 6:1, 5. b, 2 Ne. 2:3. 4. c, 2 Ne. 27:12. Eth. 5:3, 4. D. & C. 5:11, 15. See The Testimony of Three Witnesses in forepart of book. d, 2 Ne. 27:13, 14. Eth. 5:2. See The Testimony of Eight Witnesses in forepart of book. e, see f, 2 Ne. 2. f, 2 Ne. 2:13, 14. Al. 42:22, 23. Morm. 9:19. Between B. C. 559 and 545.

he cometh in the fulness of his own time.

8. And now I write some of the *g*words of Isaiah, that whoso of my people shall see these words may lift up their hearts and rejoice for all men. Now these are the words, and ye may liken them unto you and unto all men.

CHAPTER 12.

Prophecies as recorded on the brass plates—Compare Isaiah 2.

1. The word that Isaiah, the son of Amos, saw concerning Judah and Jerusalem:

2. And *a*it shall come to pass in the last days, when the mountain of the Lord's *b*house shall be established in the top of the mountains, and shall be exalted above the hills, and all nations shall flow unto it.

3. And many people shall go and say, Come ye, and let us go up to the *c*mountain of the Lord, to the house of the God of Jacob; and he will teach us of his ways, and we will walk in his paths; for out of Zion shall go forth the law, and the word of the Lord from Jerusalem.

4. And he shall *d*judge among the nations, and shall rebuke many people: and *e*they shall beat their swords into plow-shares, and their spears into pruning-hooks —nation shall not lift up sword against nation, neither shall they learn war any more.

5. O house of Jacob, come ye and let us walk in the light of the Lord; *f*yea, come, for ye have all gone astray, every one to his wicked ways.

6. Therefore, O Lord, thou hast forsaken thy people, the house of Jacob, because they be replenished *g*from the east, and *h*hearken unto soothsayers like the Philistines, and they please themselves in the children of strangers.

7. *i*Their land also is full of silver and gold, neither is there any end of their treasures; their land is also full of horses, neither is there any end of their chariots.

8. *j*Their land is also full of idols; they worship the work of their own hands, that which their own fingers have made.

9. And the mean man boweth *k*not down, and the great man humbleth himself not, therefore, forgive him not.

10. *m*O ye wicked ones, enter into the rock, and hide thee in the dust, for the fear of the Lord and the glory of his majesty shall smite thee.

11. And it shall come to pass that the *n*lofty looks of man shall be humbled, and the haughtiness of men shall be bowed down, and the Lord alone shall be exalted in that day.

12. For the *o*day of the Lord of Hosts soon cometh upon all nations, yea, upon every one; yea, upon the *p*proud and lofty, and upon every one who is lifted up, and he shall be brought low.

13. Yea, and the day of the Lord shall come upon all *q*the cedars of Lebanon, for they are high and lifted up; and upon all the oaks of Bashan;

14. And upon all the *r*high mountains, and upon all the hills, and upon all the nations which

---

g, see Isa. chaps. 2 to 14 inclusive, as quoted in the next 13 chapters, taken by Nephi from the brass plates. CHAP. 12: *a,* Mic. 4:1—3. *b,* ver. 3. 3 Ne. 24:1. *c,* D. & C. 133:13. *d,* 2 Ne. 21:2—5. *e,* 2 Ne. 21:9. *f,* Isa. 53:6. 1 Ne. 13. 2 Ne. 28:14. Mos. 14:6. Al. 5:37. *g,* Num. 23:7. *h,* Deut. 18:14. *i,* Deut. 17:16, 17. *j,* Jer. 2:28. *k,* Isa. 2:9. *m,* vers. 19, 21. Rev. 6:15, 16. *n,* ver. 17. 2 Ne. 15:15, 16. *o,* Zeph. 1:14—18. *p,* Mal. 4:1. *q,* Isa. 14:8. 37:24. Ezek. 31:3. Zech. 11:1, 2. *r,* Isa. 30:25. BETWEEN B. C. 559 AND 545.

are lifted up, and upon every people;

15. And upon ˢevery high tower, and upon every fenced wall;

16. And upon all the ships of the sea, and ᵗupon all the ships of Tarshish, and upon all pleasant pictures.

17. And ᵘthe loftiness of man shall be bowed down, and the haughtiness of men shall be made low; and the Lord alone shall be exalted in that day.

18. And the idols he shall ᵛutterly abolish.

19. And ʷthey shall go into the holes of the rocks, and into the caves of the earth, for the fear of the Lord shall come upon them and the glory of his majesty shall smite them, when he ariseth to shake terribly the earth.

20. In that day a ˣman shall cast his idols of silver, and his idols of gold, which he hath made for himself to worship, to the moles and to the bats;

21. To ʸgo into the clefts of the rocks, and into the tops of the ragged rocks, for the fear of the Lord shall come upon them and the majesty of his glory shall smite them, when he ariseth to shake terribly the earth.

22. Cease ye from man, whose breath is in his nostrils; for wherein is he to be accounted of?

CHAPTER 13.

Scriptures from the brass plates continued—Compare Isaiah 3.

1. For behold, the Lord, the Lord of Hosts, doth take away from Jerusalem, and from Judah, the stay and the staff, the whole staff of bread, and the whole stay of water—

2. The ᵃmighty man, and the man of war, the judge, and the prophet, and the prudent, and the ancient;

3. The captain of fifty, and the honorable man, and the counselor, and the cunning artificer, and the eloquent orator.

4. And I will ᵇgive children unto them to be their princes, and babes shall rule over them.

5. And the people shall be oppressed, every one by another, and every one by his neighbor; the child shall behave himself proudly against the ancient, and the base against the honorable.

6. When a man shall take hold of his brother of the house of his father, and shall say: Thou hast clothing, be thou our ruler, and let not this ruin come under thy hand—

7. In that day shall he swear, saying: I will not be a healer; for in my house there is neither bread nor clothing; make me not a ruler of the people.

8. For ᶜJerusalem is ruined, and Judah is fallen, because their tongues and their doings have been against the Lord, to provoke the eyes of his glory.

9. The show of their countenance doth witness against them, and doth declare their sin to be even as ᵈSodom, and they cannot hide it. Wo unto their souls, for they have rewarded evil unto themselves!

10. Say unto the righteous that it is well with them; for they shall eat the fruit of their doings.

11. Wo unto the wicked, for they shall perish; for the reward of their hands shall be upon them!

12. And my people, ᵉchildren

s, Isa. 33:18. 3 Ne. 21:15, 18. *t,* 1 Kings 10:22. *u,* ver. 11. *v,* ver. 20. *w,* see *m.* *x,* ver. 18. *y,* see *m.* CHAP. 13: *a,* 2 Kings 24:14. *b,* Eccl. 10:16. *c,* Mic. 3:12. *d,* Gen. 13:13. 18:20, 21. 19:5. *e,* ver. 4. BETWEEN B. C. 559 AND 545.

2 NEPHI, 14.

are their oppressors, and women rule over them. O my people, they *f*who lead thee cause thee to err and destroy the way of thy paths.

13. The Lord standeth up *g*to plead, and standeth to judge the people.

14. The Lord will enter into judgment with the ancients of his people and the princes thereof; for ye have eaten up *h*the vineyard and the spoil of the poor in your houses.

15. What mean ye? Ye *i*beat my people to pieces, and grind the faces of the poor, saith the Lord God of Hosts.

16. Moreover, the Lord saith: Because the daughters of Zion are haughty, and walk with stretched-forth necks and wanton eyes, walking and mincing as they go, and making a tinkling with their feet—

17. Therefore the Lord will smite with a *j*scab the crown of the head of the daughters of Zion, and the Lord will *k*discover their secret parts.

18. In that day the Lord will take away the bravery of their tinkling ornaments, and cauls, and round tires like the moon;

19. The chains and the bracelets, and the mufflers;

20. The bonnets, and the ornaments of the legs, and the headbands, and the tablets, and the ear-rings;

21. The rings, and nose jewels;

22. The changeable suits of apparel, and the mantles, and the wimples, and the crisping-pins;

23. The glasses, and the fine linen, and hoods, and the veils.

24. And it shall come to pass, instead of sweet smell there shall be stink; and instead of a girdle, a rent; and instead of well set hair, *l*baldness; and instead of a stomacher, a girding of sackcloth; burning instead of beauty.

25. Thy men shall fall by the sword and thy mighty in the war.

26. *m*And her gates shall lament and mourn; and she shall be desolate, and *n*shall sit upon the ground.

CHAPTER 14.

Scriptures from the brass plates continued—Compare Isaiah 4.

1. And in that day, seven women shall take hold of one man, saying: We will eat our own bread, and wear our own apparel; only let us be called by thy name to take away our reproach.

2. In that day shall *b*the branch of the Lord be beautiful and glorious; the fruit of the earth excellent and comely to them that are escaped of Israel.

3. And it shall come to pass, they that are *c*left in Zion and remain in Jerusalem shall be called holy, every one that is written among the living in Jerusalem—

4. When the Lord shall have *d*washed away the filth of the daughters of Zion, and shall have purged the blood of Jerusalem from the midst thereof by the spirit of judgment and by the *e*spirit of burning.

5. And *f*the Lord will create upon every dwelling-place of mount Zion, and upon her assemblies, a *g*cloud and smoke by day and the shining of a flaming fire

f, Isa. 9:16. *g*, Mic. 6:2. *h*, Isa. 5:7. *i*, Isa. 58:4. Mic. 3:2, 3. *j*, Deut. 28:27.
k, Jer. 13:22. Nah. 3:5. *l*, Isa. 22:12. Mic. 1:16. *m*, Jer. 14:2. Lam. 1:4.
n, Lam. 2:10. CHAP. 14: *b*, 2 Ne. 3:5. Isa. 60:21. 61:3. 2 Ne. 10:1. Jac. 2:25.
c, Matt. 13:41—43, 47—50. 25:1—12. *d*, 2 Ne. 13:10—26. *e*, Ezek. 20:37, 38.
Mal. 3:2. 4:1—3. *f*, Isa. 33:14, 15. 60:1—3, 19—21. Mal. 3:2, 3. *g*, Ex. 13:21.
Zech. 2:5. BETWEEN B. C. 559 AND 545.

by night; for upon all the glory of Zion shall be a defence.

6. And there shall be a tabernacle for a shadow in the daytime from the heat, and *h*for a place of refuge, and a covert from storm and from rain.

CHAPTER 15.

Scriptures from the brass plates continued—Compare Isaiah 5.

1. And then will I sing to my well-beloved a song of my beloved, touching *a*his vineyard. My well-beloved hath a vineyard in a very fruitful hill.

2. And he fenced it, and gathered out the stones thereof, and planted it with the choicest vine, and built a tower in the midst of it, and also made a wine-press therein; and he looked that it should bring forth grapes, and it brought forth *b*wild grapes.

3. And now, O inhabitants of Jerusalem, and men of Judah, judge, I pray you, betwixt me and my vineyard.

4. What could have been done more to my vineyard that I have not done in it? Wherefore, when I looked that it should bring forth grapes it brought forth wild grapes.

5. And now go to; I will tell you what I will do to my vineyard—I will *c*take away the hedge thereof, and it shall be eaten up; and I will break down the wall thereof, and it shall be trodden down;

6. And I will lay it waste; it shall not be pruned nor digged; but there shall come up *d*briers and thorns; I will also *e*command the clouds that they rain no rain upon it.

7. For the vineyard of the Lord of Hosts is the house of Israel, and the men of Judah his pleasant plant; and he looked for judgment, and behold, oppression; for righteousness, but behold, a cry.

8. Wo unto them that join *f*house to house, till there can be no place, that they may be placed alone in the midst of the earth!

9. In mine ears, said the Lord of Hosts, of a truth many houses shall be desolate, and great and fair cities without inhabitant.

10. Yea, ten acres of vineyard shall yield one *g*bath, and the seed of a homer shall yield an ephah.

11. *h*Wo unto them that rise up early in the morning, that they may follow strong drink, that continue until night, and wine inflame them!

12. *i*And the harp, and the viol, the tabret, and pipe, and wine are in their feasts; but they *j*regard not the work of the Lord, neither consider the operation of his hands.

13. Therefore, my people are gone into captivity, *k*because they have no knowledge; and their honorable men are famished, and their multitude dried up with thirst.

14. Therefore, hell hath enlarged herself, and opened her mouth without measure; and their glory, and their multitude, and their pomp, and he that rejoiceth, shall descend into it.

15. And *l*the mean man shall be brought down, and the mighty man shall be humbled, and the eyes of the lofty shall be humbled.

16. But the Lord of Hosts shall

h, Isa. 25:4. CHAP. 15: *a*, Ps. 80:8. Isa. 27:2. Jer. 2:21. Matt. 21:33. Mark 12:1. Luke 20:9. D. & C. 101:44—62. *b*, Jac. 5. *c*, Ps. 80:12. *d*, Isa. 7:23, 24. 32:13. *e*, Jer. 3:3. *f*, Mic. 2:2. *g*, Ezek. 45:11. *h*, ver. 22. Prov. 23:29—32. Eccl 10:17. *i*, Amos 6:5, 6. *j*, Job 34:27. Ps. 28:5. *k*, Isa. 1:3. Hos. 4:6. Luke 19:44. *l*, Isa. 2:9, 17.
BETWEEN B. C. 559 AND 545.

be ᵐexalted in judgment, and God that is holy shall be sanctified in righteousness.

17. Then shall the lambs feed after their manner, and the waste places of ⁿthe fat ones shall strangers eat.

18. Wo unto them that draw iniquity with cords of vanity, and sin as it were with a cart rope;

19. That say: Let him ᵒmake speed, hasten his work, that we may see it; and let the counsel of the Holy One of Israel draw nigh and come, that we may know it.

20. Wo unto them that call evil good, and good evil, that put darkness for light, and light for darkness, that put bitter for sweet, and sweet for bitter!

21. Wo unto the wise in their own eyes and prudent in their own sight!

22. Wo unto the mighty to drink wine, and men of strength to mingle strong drink;

23. Who justify the wicked for reward, and take away the righteousness of the righteous from him!

24. Therefore, as the fire devoureth the stubble, and the flame consumeth the chaff, their root shall be rottenness, and their blossoms shall go up as dust; because they have cast away the law of the Lord of Hosts, and despised the word of the Holy One of Israel.

25. Therefore, is the anger of the Lord kindled against his people, and he hath stretched forth his hand against them, and hath smitten them; and the hills did tremble, and their carcasses were torn in the midst of the streets. For all this his anger is not turned away, but his hand is stretched out still.

26. And he will lift up an ᵖensign to the nations from far, and will hiss unto them ʳfrom the end of the earth; and behold, they shall come with speed swiftly; none shall be weary nor stumble among them.

27. None shall slumber nor sleep; neither shall the girdle of their loins be loosed, nor the latchet of their shoes be broken;

28. Whose arrows shall be sharp, and all their bows bent, and their horses' hoofs shall be counted like flint, and their wheels like a whirlwind, their roaring like a lion.

29. They shall roar like young lions; yea, they shall roar, and lay hold of the prey, and shall carry away safe, and none shall deliver.

30. And in that day they shall roar against them like the roaring of the sea; and if they look unto the land, behold, darkness and sorrow, and the light is darkened in the heavens thereof.

CHAPTER 16.

Scriptures from the brass plates continued—Compare Isaiah 6.

1. In the year that king Uzziah died, I ᵃsaw also the Lord sitting upon a throne, high and lifted up, and his train filled the temple.

2. Above it stood the seraphim; each one had six wings; with twain he covered his face, and with twain he covered his feet, and with twain he did fly.

3. And one cried unto another, and said: Holy, holy, holy, is the Lord of Hosts; the ᵇwhole earth is full of his glory.

m, Isa. 2:11. *n,* Isa. 10:16. *o,* Jer. 17:15. *p,* Isa. 11:10, 12. 13:2. 18:3. 49:22. 66:19. Zech. 9:16. *r,* 2 Ne. 29:2. Moro. 10:28. CHAP. 16: *a,* ver. 5. 1 Kings 22:19. John 12:41. *b,* Ps. 72:19. BETWEEN B. C. 559 AND 545.

4. And the posts of the door moved at the voice of him that cried, and the house was filled with smoke.

5. Then said I: Wo is unto me! for I am undone; because I am a man of unclean lips; and I dwell in the midst of a people of unclean lips; for mine eyes have seen the King, the Lord of Hosts.

6. Then flew one of the seraphim unto me, having a live coal in his hand, which he had taken with the tongs from off the altar;

7. And he laid it upon my mouth, and said: Lo, this has touched thy lips; and thine iniquity is taken away, and thy sin purged.

8. Also I heard the voice of the Lord, saying: Whom shall I send, and who will go for us? Then I said: Here am I; send me.

9. And he said: Go and tell this people—*c*Hear ye indeed, but they understood not; and see ye indeed, but they perceived not.

10. Make the heart of this people fat, and make their ears heavy, and shut their eyes—lest they see with their eyes, and hear with their ears, and understand with their heart, and be converted and be healed.

11. Then said I: Lord, how long? And he said: *d*Until the cities be wasted without inhabitant, and the houses without man, and the land be utterly desolate;

12. And the Lord have removed men *e*far away, for there shall be a great forsaking in the midst of the land.

13. But yet there shall be a tenth, and they shall return, and shall be eaten, as a teil-tree, and as an oak whose substance is in them when they cast their leaves; so the *f*holy seed shall be the substance thereof.

CHAPTER 17.

Scriptures from the brass plates continued—Compare Isaiah 7.

1. And it came to pass in the days of *a*Ahaz the son of Jotham, the son of Uzziah, king of Judah, that Rezin, king of Syria, and Pekah the son of Remaliah, king of Israel, went up toward Jerusalem to war against it, but could not prevail against it.

2. And it was told the house of David, saying: Syria is confederate with Ephraim. And his heart was moved, and the heart of his people, as the trees of the wood are moved with the wind.

3. Then said the Lord unto Isaiah: Go forth now to meet Ahaz, thou and Shearjashub thy son, at the end of the *b*conduit of the upper pool in the highway of the fuller's field;

4. And say unto him: Take heed, and be quiet; fear not, neither be faint-hearted for the two tails of these smoking firebrands, for the fierce anger of Rezin with Syria, and of the son of Remaliah.

5. Because Syria, Ephraim, and the son of Remaliah, have taken evil counsel against thee, saying:

6. Let us go up against Judah and vex it, and let us make a breach therein for us, and set a king in the midst of it, yea, the son of Tabeal.

7. Thus saith the Lord God: *c*It shall not stand, neither shall it come to pass.

8. For *d*the head of Syria is Damascus, and the head of Damascus, Rezin; and within three

---

c, Matt. 13:14, 15. John 12:40. *d*, Mic. 3:12. *e*, 2 Kings 25:21. *f*, Ezra 9:2. CHAP. 17: *a*, 2 Kings 16:5. 2 Chron. 28:5, 6. *b*, 2 Kings 18:17. Isa. 36:2 *c*, Prov. 21:30. Isa. 8:10. *d*, 2 Sam. 8:6. BETWEEN B. C. 559 AND 545.

score and five years shall Ephraim be broken that it be not a people.

9. And the head of Ephraim is Samaria, and the head of Samaria is Remaliah's son. *If ye will not believe surely ye shall not be established.

10. Moreover, the Lord spake again unto Ahaz, saying:

11. *Ask thee a sign of the Lord thy God; ask it either in the depths, or in the heights above.

12. But Ahaz said: I will not ask, neither will I tempt the Lord.

13. And he said: Hear ye now, O house of David; is it a small thing for you to weary men, but will ye weary my God also?

14. Therefore, the Lord himself shall give you a sign—Behold, a *virgin shall conceive, and shall bear a son, and shall call his name *Immanuel.

15. Butter and honey shall he eat, that he may know to refuse the evil and to choose the good.

16. For *before the child shall know to refuse the evil and choose the good, the land that thou abhorrest shall be forsaken of *both her kings.

17. *The Lord shall bring upon thee, and upon thy people, and upon thy father's house, days that have not come from the day that *Ephraim departed from Judah, the king of Assyria.

18. And it shall come to pass in that day that the Lord shall hiss for the fly that is in the uttermost part of Egypt, and for the bee that is in the land of Assyria.

19. And they shall come, and shall rest all of them in the desolate valleys, and in the holes of the rocks, and upon all thorns, and upon all bushes.

20. In the same day shall the Lord shave with a *razor that is hired, by them beyond the river, by the king of Assyria, the head, and the hair of the feet; and it shall also consume the beard.

21. And it shall come to pass in that day, a man shall nourish a young cow and two sheep;

22. And it shall come to pass, for the abundance of milk they shall give he shall eat butter; for butter and honey shall every one eat that is left in the land.

23. And it shall come to pass in that day, every place shall be, where there were a thousand vines at a thousand silverlings, which shall be for *briers and thorns.

24. With arrows and with bows shall men come thither, because all the land shall become briers and thorns.

25. And all hills that shall be digged with the mattock, there shall not come thither the fear of briers and thorns; but it shall be for the sending forth of oxen, and the treading of lesser cattle.

CHAPTER 18.

Scriptures from the brass plates continued—Compare Isaiah 8.

1. Moreover, the word of the Lord said unto me: Take thee a great roll, and write in it with a man's pen, *concerning Maher-shalal-hash-baz.

2. And I took unto me faithful witnesses to record, Uriah the priest, and Zechariah the son of Jeberechiah.

3. And I went unto the prophetess; and she conceived and bare

---

e, 2 Chron. 20:20. *f*, Judg. 6:36—40. Matt. 12:38—40. *g*, Matt. 1:23. Luke 1:31, 34. See *f*, Al. 7. *h*, Isa. 8:8. *i*, Isa. 8:4. *j*, 2 Kings 15:30. 16:9. *k*, 2 Chron. 28:19—21. *l*, 1 Kings 12:16—19. *m*, 2 Kings 16:7, 8. 2 Chron. 28:20, 21. *n*, see *d*, 2 Ne. 15. CHAP. 18: *a*, ver. 3. BETWEEN B. C. 559 AND 545.

2 NEPHI, 18.

a son. Then said the Lord to me: Call his name, Maher-shalal-hash-baz.

4. *b*For behold, the child shall not have knowledge to cry, My father, and my mother, before *c*the riches of Damascus and the spoil of Samaria shall be taken away before the king of Assyria.

5. The Lord spake also unto me again, saying:

6. Forasmuch as this people refuseth the waters of *d*Shiloah that go softly, and rejoice in *e*Rezin and Remaliah's son;

7. Now therefore, behold, the Lord bringeth up upon them the waters of the river, strong and many, even the king *f*of Assyria and all his glory; and he shall come up over all his channels, and go over all his banks.

8. And he shall pass through Judah; he shall overflow and go over, *g*he shall reach even to the neck; and the stretching out of his wings shall fill the breadth of thy land, O *h*Immanuel.

9. *i*Associate yourselves, O ye people, and ye shall be broken in pieces; and give ear all ye of far countries; gird yourselves, and ye shall be broken in pieces; gird yourselves, and ye shall be broken in pieces.

10. Take counsel together, and it shall come to naught; speak the word, and it shall not stand; for God is with us.

11. For the Lord spake thus to me with a strong hand, and instructed me that I should not walk in the way of this people, saying:

12. Say ye not, A confederacy, to all to whom this people shall say, A confederacy; neither fear ye their fear, nor be afraid.

13. Sanctify the Lord of Hosts himself, and let him be your fear, and let him be your dread.

14. And he shall be for a sanctuary; but for a *j*stone of stumbling, and for a rock of offense to both the houses of Israel, for a gin and a snare to the inhabitants of Jerusalem.

15. And many among them shall *k*stumble and fall, and be broken, and be snared, and be taken.

16. Bind up the testimony, seal the law among my disciples.

17. And I will wait upon the Lord, that *l*hideth his face from the house of Jacob, and I will look for him.

18. Behold, I and the children whom the Lord hath given me are for signs and for wonders in Israel from the Lord of Hosts, which dwelleth in Mount Zion.

19. And when they shall say unto you: *m*Seek unto them that have familiar spirits, and unto wizards that peep and mutter—should not a people *n*seek unto their God for the living to hear from the dead?

20. To *o*the law and to the testimony; and if they speak not according to this word, it is because there is no light in them.

21. And they shall pass through it hardly bestead and hungry; and it shall come to pass that when they shall be hungry, they shall fret themselves, and curse their king and their God, and look upward.

22. And they shall look unto the earth and behold trouble, and darkness, *p*dimness of anguish, and shall be driven to darkness.

---

b, Isa. 7:16. *c*, 2 Kings 15:29, 30. *d*, Neh. 3:15. John 9:7. *e*, Isa. 7:1—6. *f*, Isa. 10:12. *g*, Isa. 30:28. *h*, Isa. 7:14. *i*, Joel 3:9—14. *j*, Isa. 28:16. Luke 2:34. Rom. 9:33. 1 Pet. 2:8. *k*, Matt. 21:44. Luke 20:18. Rom. 9:32. *l*, Isa. 54:8. *m*, 1 Sam. 28:8. Isa. 19:3. *n*, Isa. 29. See *c*, 2 Ne. 27. *o*, Luke 16:29—31. *p*, Isa. 5:30. 9:1.

BETWEEN B. C. 559 AND 545.

CHAPTER 19.

Scriptures from the brass plates continued—Compare Isaiah 9.

1. Nevertheless, the ᵃdimness shall not be such as was in her vexation, when at first he lightly afflicted the ᵇland of Zebulun, and the land of Naphtali, and afterwards did more grievously afflict by the way of the Red Sea beyond Jordan in Galilee of the nations.

2. The people that walked in darkness have seen a great light; they that dwell in the land of the shadow of death, upon them hath the light shined.

3. Thou hast multiplied the nation, and increased the joy—they joy before thee according to the joy in harvest, and as men rejoice when they divide the spoil.

4. For thou hast broken the yoke of his burden, and the staff of his shoulder, the rod of his oppressor.

5. For every battle of the warrior is with confused noise, and garments rolled in blood; but this shall be with burning and fuel of fire.

6. For ᶜunto us a child is born, unto us a son is given; and the ᵈgovernment shall be upon his shoulder; and his name shall be called, Wonderful, Counselor, The ᵉMighty God, The Everlasting Father, ᶠThe Prince of Peace.

7. Of the increase of government and peace ᵍthere is no end, upon the throne of David, and upon his kingdom to order it, and to establish it with judgment and with justice from henceforth, even forever. The zeal of the Lord of Hosts will perform this.

8. The Lord sent his word unto Jacob and it hath lighted upon Israel.

9. And all the people shall know, even Ephraim and the inhabitants of Samaria, that say in the pride and stoutness of heart:

10. The bricks are fallen down, but we will build with hewn stones; the sycamores are cut down, but we will change them into cedars.

11. Therefore the Lord shall set up the adversaries of Rezin against him, and join his enemies together;

12. The Syrians before and the Philistines behind; and they shall devour Israel with open mouth. ʰFor all this his anger is not turned away, but his hand is stretched out still.

13. For the people turneth not unto him that smiteth them, neither do they seek the Lord of Hosts.

14. Therefore will the Lord cut off from Israel ⁱhead and tail, branch and rush ʲin one day.

15. ᵏThe ancient, he is the head; and the prophet that teacheth lies, he is the tail.

16. ˡFor the leaders of this people cause them to err; and they that are led of them are destroyed.

17. Therefore the Lord shall have no ᵐjoy in their young men, neither shall have mercy on their fatherless and widows; for ⁿevery one of them is a hypocrite and an evildoer, and every mouth speaketh folly. ᵒFor all this his anger is not turned away, but his hand is stretched out still.

18. For wickedness ᵖburneth as the fire; it shall devour the briers and thorns, and shall kin-

a, Isa. 8:22. *b*, Matt. 4:15, 16. *c*, Isa. 7:14. Luke 2:11. *d*, Matt. 28:18. 1 Cor. 15:25—28. *e*, Tit. 2:13, see 2*b*, Mos. 7. *f*, Eph. 2:14—17. *g*, Dan. 2:44. *h*, vers. 17, 21. Isa. 5:25. 10:4. Jer. 4:8. *i*, ver. 15. *j*, Isa. 10:17. *k*, ver. 14. *l*, Isa. 3:12. *m*, Ps. 147:10, 11. *n*, Mic. 7:2, 3. *o*, see *h*. *p*, Isa. 10:17. Mal. 4:1.

BETWEEN B. C. 559 AND 545.

dle in the thickets of the forests, and they shall mount up like the lifting up of smoke.

19. Through the wrath of the Lord of Hosts is the ^qland darkened, and the people shall be as the fuel of the fire; ^rno man shall spare his brother.

20. ^sAnd he shall snatch on the right hand and be hungry; and he shall eat on the left hand and they shall not be satisfied; they shall eat every man the flesh of his own arm—

21. Manasseh, Ephraim; and Ephraim, Manasseh; they together shall be against Judah. ^tFor all this his anger is not turned away, but his hand is stretched out still.

CHAPTER 20.

Scriptures from the brass plates continued—Compare Isaiah 10.

1. Wo unto them that ^adecree unrighteous decrees, and that write grievousness which they have prescribed;

2. To turn away the needy from judgment, and to take away the right from the poor of my people, that widows may be their prey, and that they may rob the fatherless!

3. And ^bwhat will ye do in ^cthe day of visitation, and in the desolation which shall come from far? to whom will ye flee for help? and where will ye leave your glory?

4. Without me they shall bow down under the prisoners, and they shall fall under the slain. ^dFor all this his anger is not turned away, but his hand is stretched out still.

5. O Assyrian, the rod of mine anger, and the staff in their hand is their indignation.

6. I will send him against a ^ehypocritical nation, and against the people of my wrath will I give him a charge to take the spoil, and to take the prey, and to tread them down like the mire of the streets.

7. Howbeit he meaneth not so, neither doth his heart think so; but in his heart it is to destroy and cut off nations not a few.

8. For he saith: ^fAre not my princes altogether kings?

9. Is not ^gCalno as ^hCarchemish? Is not Hamath as Arpad? Is not Samaria ⁱas Damascus?

10. As my hand hath founded the kingdoms of the idols, and whose graven images did excel them of Jerusalem and of Samaria;

11. Shall I not, as I have done unto Samaria and her idols, so do to Jerusalem and to her idols?

12. Wherefore it shall come to pass that when the Lord hath performed his whole work ^jupon Mount Zion and upon Jerusalem, ^kI will punish the fruit of the stout heart of the king of Assyria, and the glory of his high looks.

13. For he saith: ^lBy the strength of my hand and by my wisdom I have done these things; for I am prudent; and I have moved the borders of the people, and have robbed their treasures, and I have put down the inhabitants like a valiant man;

14. And my hand hath found as a nest the riches of the people; and as one gathereth eggs that are left have I gathered all the earth; and there was none that moved the wing, or opened the mouth, or peeped.

15. Shall the ax boast itself against him that heweth there-

---

q, Isa. 8:22. *r*, Mic. 7:2—6. *s*, Lev. 26:26. *t*, see *h*. CHAP. 20: *a*, Ps. 58:2. 94:20. *b*, Job 31:14. *c*, Hos. 9:7. *d*, see *h*, 2 Ne. 19. *e*, Jer. 34:22. *f*, 2 Kings 18:24, 33—35. 19:10—13. *g*, Amos 6:2. *h*, 2 Chron. 35:20. *i*, 2 Kings 16:9. *j*, 2 Kings 19:31. *k*, Jer. 50:18. *l*, Isa. 37:24—38. BETWEEN B. C. 559 AND 545.

with? Shall the saw magnify itself against him that shaketh it? As if the rod should shake itself against them that lift it up, or as if the staff should lift up itself as if it were no wood!

16. Therefore shall the Lord, the Lord of Hosts, send among his fat ones, leanness; and under his glory he shall kindle a burning like the burning of a fire.

17. And the light of Israel shall be for a fire, and his Holy One for a flame, and ᵐshall burn and shall devour his thorns and his briers in one day;

18. And shall consume the glory of his forest, and of his fruitful field, both soul and body; and they shall be as when a standard-bearer fainteth.

19. And the rest of the trees of his forest shall be few, that a child may write them.

20. And it shall come to pass in that day, that the remnant of Israel, and such as are escaped of the house of Jacob, ⁿshall no more again stay upon him that smote them, but shall stay upon the Lord, the Holy One of Israel, in truth.

21. ᵒThe remnant shall return, yea, even the remnant of Jacob, unto the mighty God.

22. For ᵖthough thy people Israel be as the sand of the sea, ᵍyet a remnant of them shall return; the ʳconsumption decreed shall overflow with righteousness.

23. For the Lord God of Hosts shall make a consumption, even determined in all the land.

24. Therefore, thus saith the Lord God of Hosts: O my people that dwellest in Zion, ˢbe not afraid of the Assyrian; he shall smite thee with a rod, and shall lift up his staff against thee, ᵗafter the manner of Egypt.

25. For yet a very little while, and the ᵘindignation shall cease, and mine anger in their destruction.

26. And the Lord of Hosts shall ᵛstir up a scourge for him according to the slaughter of ʷMidian at the rock of Oreb; and ˣas his rod was upon the sea so shall he lift it up after the manner of Egypt.

27. And it shall come to pass in that day that ʸhis burden shall be taken away from off thy shoulder, and his yoke from off thy neck, and the yoke shall be destroyed because of the ᶻanointing.

28. He is come to Aiath, he is passed to Migron; at Michmash he hath laid up his carriages.

29. They are ²ᵃgone over the passage; they have taken up their lodging at Geba; Ramath is afraid; ²ᵇGibeah of Saul is fled.

30. Lift up the voice, O daughter of ²ᶜGallim; cause it to be heard unto ²ᵈLaish, O poor ²ᵉAnathoth.

31. ²ᶠMadmenah is removed; the inhabitants of Gebim gather themselves to flee.

32. As yet shall he remain at ²ᵍNob that day; he shall ²ʰshake his hand against the mount of the daughter of Zion, the hill of Jerusalem.

33. Behold, the Lord, the Lord of Hosts shall lop the bough with terror; and ²ⁱthe high ones of stature shall be hewn down; and the haughty shall be humbled.

34. And he shall cut down the

---

m, Isa. 9:18, 19. 37:36. *n*, 2 Kings 16:7—9. 2 Chron. 28:20, 21. *o*, Isa. 11:11. Joel 2:32. *p*, Rom. 9:27. *q*, Isa. 6:13. *r*, Isa. 28:22. *s*, Isa. 37:6, 7. *t*, Ex. 14. *u*, Dan. 11:36. *v*, 2 Kings 19:35. *w*, Judg. 7:25. Isa. 9:4. *x*, Ex. 14:26, 27. *y*, Isa. 14:25. *z*, Ps. 105:15. 2*a*, 1 Sam. 13:23. 2*b*, 1 Sam. 11:4. 2*c*, 1 Sam. 25:44. 2*d*, Judg. 18:7. 2*e*, Josh. 21:18. 2*f*, Josh. 15:31. 2*g*, 1 Sam. 21:1. 22:19. Neh. 11:32. 2*h*, Isa. 13:2. 2*i*, Amos 2:9. BETWEEN B. C. 559 AND 545.

2 NEPHI, 21.

thickets of the forests with iron, and Lebanon shall fall by a mighty one.

CHAPTER 21.

Scriptures from the brass plates continued—Compare Isaiah 11.

1. And ᵃthere shall come forth a rod out of the stem of Jesse, and a branch shall grow out of his roots.

2. ᵇAnd the Spirit of the Lord shall rest upon him, the spirit of wisdom and understanding, the spirit of counsel and might, the spirit of knowledge and of the fear of the Lord;

3. And shall make him of quick understanding in the fear of the Lord; and he shall not judge after the sight of his eyes, neither reprove after the hearing of his ears.

4. But ᶜwith righteousness shall he judge the poor, and reprove with equity for the meek of the earth; and he shall ᵈsmite the earth with the rod of his mouth, and with the breath of his lips shall he slay the wicked.

5. And ᵉrighteousness shall be the girdle of his loins, and faithfulness the girdle of his reins.

6. ᶠThe wolf also shall dwell with the lamb, and the leopard shall lie down with the kid, and the calf and the young lion and fatling together; and a little child shall lead them.

7. And the cow and the bear shall feed; their young ones shall lie down together; and the lion shall eat straw like the ox.

8. And the sucking child shall play on the hole of the asp, and the weaned child shall put his hand on the cockatrice's den.

9. ᵍThey shall not hurt nor destroy in all my holy mountain, for ʰthe earth shall be full of the knowledge of the Lord, as the waters cover the sea.

10. And in that day ⁱthere shall be a root of Jesse, which shall ʲstand for an ensign of the people; to it ᵏshall the Gentiles seek; and his rest shall be glorious.

11. And it shall come to pass in that day that the Lord shall set his hand again ˡthe second time to recover the remnant of his people which shall be left, ᵐfrom Assyria, and from Egypt, and from Pathros, and from Cush, and from Elam, and from Shinar, and from Hamath, and from the islands of the sea.

12. And he shall ⁿset up an ensign for the nations, and shall assemble the ᵒoutcasts of Israel, and ᵖgather together the dispersed of Judah from the four corners of the earth.

13. ᵠThe envy of Ephraim also shall depart, and the adversaries of Judah shall be cut off; Ephraim shall not envy Judah, and Judah shall not vex Ephraim.

14. But they shall fly upon the shoulders of the Philistines towards the west; they shall spoil them of the east together; they shall lay their hand upon Edom and Moab; and the children of Ammon shall obey them.

15. And the Lord ʳshall utterly destroy the tongue of the Egyptian sea; and with his mighty wind he shall shake his hand over the river, and shall smite it in the seven streams, and ˢmake men go over dry shod.

---

a, ver. 10. Isa. 53:2. Jer. 23:5, 6. Acts 13:23. Rev. 5:5. *b*, Isa. 61:1—3. *c*, Ps. 72:2, 4. Rev. 19:11. *d*, Job 4:9. Mal. 4:6. 2 Thess. 2:8. Rev. 1:16. 2:16. 19:15. *e*, Eph. 6:14. *f*, Isa. 65:25. Ezek. 34:25. Hos. 2:18. *g*, Job 5:23. Isa. 2:4. 35:9. *h*, Hab. 2:14. *i*, ver. 1. Rom. 15:12. *j*, ver. 12. See *p*, 2 Ne. 15. *k*, D. & C. 45:9, 10. *l*, see *i*, 2 Ne. 6. *m*, Zech. 10:10. *n*, see *p*, 2 Ne. 15. *o*, see *p*, 3 Ne. 15. *p*, see *e*, 1 Ne. 15. *q*, Jer. 3:18. *r*, Zech. 10:11. *s*, Rev. 16:12.

BETWEEN B. C. 559 AND 545.

16. ᵗAnd there shall be a highway for the remnant of his people which shall be left, from Assyria, ᵘlike as it was to Israel in the day that he came up out of the land of Egypt.

CHAPTER 22.

Scriptures from the brass plates continued—Compare Isaiah 12.

1. And ᵃin that day thou shalt say: O Lord, I will praise thee; though thou wast angry with me thine anger is turned away, and thou comfortedest me.

2. Behold, God is my salvation; I will trust, and not be afraid; for the Lord ᵇJEHOVAH is my ᶜstrength and my song; he also has become my salvation.

3. Therefore, with joy shall ye ᵈdraw water out of the wells of salvation.

4. And in that day shall ye say: ᵉPraise the Lord, call upon his name, declare his doings among the people, make mention that his name is exalted.

5. Sing unto the Lord; ᶠfor he hath done excellent things; this is known in all the earth.

6. ᵍCry out and shout, thou inhabitant of Zion; for great is the Holy One of Israel in the midst of thee.

CHAPTER 23.

Scriptures from the brass plates continued—Compare Isaiah 13.

1. The burden of Babylon, which Isaiah the son of Amos did see.

2. ᵃLift ye up a banner upon the high mountain, exalt the voice unto them, ᵇshake the hand, that they may go into the gates of the nobles.

3. I have commanded ᶜmy sanctified ones, I have also called my mighty ones, for mine anger is not upon them that rejoice in my highness.

4. The noise of the multitude in the mountains like as of a great people, a tumultuous noise of ᵈthe kingdoms of nations gathered together, the Lord of Hosts mustereth the hosts of the battle.

5. They come from a far country, from the end of heaven, yea, ᵉthe Lord, and the weapons of his indignation, to destroy the whole land.

6. Howl ye, for the ᶠday of the Lord is at hand; it shall come as a destruction from the Almighty.

7. Therefore shall all hands be faint, every man's heart shall melt;

8. And they shall be afraid; pangs and sorrows shall take hold of them; they shall be amazed one at another; their faces shall be as flames.

9. Behold, the day of the Lord cometh, cruel both with wrath and fierce anger, to lay the land desolate; and he shall destroy the sinners thereof out of it.

10. ᵍFor the stars of heaven and the constellations thereof shall not give their light; tho sun shall be darkened in her going forth, and the moon shall not cause her light to shine.

11. ʰAnd I will punish the world for evil, and the wicked for their iniquity; I will cause the

---

t, D. & C. 133:27. Zech. 10:11. Isa. 35:8—10. *u*, Ex. 14:29. Isa. 51:10. 63:12, 13. CHAP. 22: *a*, Isa. 2:11. *b*, Ps. 83:18. *c*, Ex. 15:2. Ps. 118:14. *d*, John 4:10, 14. 7:37, 38. *e*, 1 Chron. 16:8. Ps. 105:1—5. 145:4—6. *f*, Ps. 68:32—35. *g*, Isa. 54:1. Zeph. 3:14—20. Zech. 2:10—13. CHAP. 23: *a*, see *p*, 2 Ne. 15. *b*, Isa. 10:32. *c*, Joel 3:11. *d*, Joel 3:14. Zeph. 3:8. Zech. 12:2—9. 14:2, 3. *e*, Joel 3:11. Zeph. 3:8. Zech. 12:4, 8, 9. 14:3, 5, 9. *f*, ver. 9 Zeph. 1:14—18. Zech. 14:1, 5. *g*, Isa. 24:23. Ezek. 32:7, 8. Joel 2:31. 3:15. Matt. 24:29. Mark 13:24. Luke 21:25. Rev. 6:12. *h*, Isa. 2:17. 24:6. Mal. 4:1.

BETWEEN B. C. 559 AND 545.

arrogancy of the proud to cease, and will lay down the haughtiness of the terrible.

12. I will *make a man more precious than fine gold; even a man than the golden wedge of Ophir.

13. Therefore, I will ʲshake the heavens, and the earth shall remove out of her place, in the wrath of the Lord of Hosts, and in the day of his fierce anger.

14. And it shall be as the chased roe, and as a sheep that no man taketh up; and they shall ᵏevery man turn to his own people, and flee every one into his own land.

15. Every one that is proud shall be thrust through; yea, and every one that is joined to the wicked shall fall by the sword.

16. Their children also shall be ˡdashed to pieces before their eyes; their houses shall be spoiled and their wives ravished.

17. Behold, I will ᵐstir up the Medes against them, which shall not regard silver and gold, nor shall they delight in it.

18. Their bows shall also dash the young men to pieces; and they shall have no pity on the fruit of the womb; their eyes shall not spare children.

19. ⁿAnd Babylon, the glory of kingdoms, the beauty of the Chaldees' excellency, shall be as when God overthrew ᵒSodom and Gomorrah.

20. ᵖIt shall never be inhabited, neither shall it be dwelt in from generation to generation: neither shall the Arabian pitch tent there; neither shall the shepherds make their fold there.

21. ᑫBut wild beasts of the desert shall lie there; and their houses shall be full of doleful creatures; and owls shall dwell there, and satyrs shall dance there.

22. And the wild beasts of the islands shall cry in their desolate houses, and dragons in their pleasant palaces; and ʳher time is near to come, and her day shall not be prolonged. For I will destroy her speedily; yea, for I will be merciful unto my people, but the wicked shall perish.

CHAPTER 24.

Scriptures from the brass plates continued—Compare Isaiah 14.

1. For the Lord ᵃwill have mercy on Jacob, and will yet choose Israel, and set them in their own land; and the ᵇstrangers shall be joined with them, and they shall cleave to the house of Jacob.

2. And the people shall take them and bring them to their place; yea, from far unto the ends of the earth; and they shall return to their lands of promise. And the house of Israel shall possess them, and the land of the Lord shall be ᶜfor servants and handmaids; and they shall take them captives unto whom they were captives; and they shall rule over their oppressors.

3. And it shall come to pass in that day that the Lord shall give thee rest, from thy sorrow, and from thy fear, and from the hard bondage wherein thou wast made to serve.

4. And it shall come to pass in that day, that thou ᵈshalt take

i, Isa. 4:1—4. *j*, Isa. 24:17—20. Hag. 2:6, 7. Heb. 12:26. See *c*, 3 Ne. 26. *k*, Jer 50:16. 51:9. *l*, Ps. 137:8, 9. Nah. 3:10. *m*, Isa. 21:2. *n*, Isa. 14:4—27. *o*, Gen. 19:24, 25. Deut. 29:23. Jer. 49:18. 50:40. *p*, Jer. 50:3, 39. 51:29, 62. *q*, Isa. 34:11—15. Rev. 18:2. *r*, Jer. 51:33. CHAP. 24: *a*, Zech. 1:17. 2:12. *b*, Isa. 60:4, 5, 10. *c*, Isa. 60:10—12, 14. 61:5. *d*, Isa. 13:19. Hab. 2:6—8. Rev. 18:15—17.
BETWEEN B. C. 559 AND 545.

2 NEPHI, 24.

up this proverb against the king of Babylon, and say: How hath the oppressor ceased, the golden city ceased!

5. The Lord hath broken *the staff of the wicked, the scepters of the rulers.

6. He who smote the people in wrath with a continual stroke, he that ruled the nations in anger, is persecuted, and none hindereth.

7. The whole earth is at rest, and is quiet; they break forth nto singing.

8. Yea, ʳthe fir-trees rejoice at thee, and also the cedars of Lebanon, saying: Since thou art laid down no feller is come up against us.

9. ᵍHell from beneath is moved for thee to meet thee at thy coming; it stirreth up the dead for thee, even all the chief ones of the earth; it hath raised up from their thrones all the kings of the nations.

10. All they shall speak and say unto thee: Art thou also become weak as we? Art thou become like unto us?

11. Thy pomp is brought down to the grave; the noise of thy viols is not heard; the worm is spread under thee, and the worms cover thee.

12. ʰHow art thou fallen from heaven, O Lucifer, son of the morning! Art thou cut down to the ground, which did weaken the nations!

13. For thou hast said in thy heart: I will ascend into heaven, I will exalt my throne above the stars of God; I will sit also upon the mount of the congregation, ⁱin the sides of the north;

14. I will ascend above the heights of the clouds; ʲI will be like the Most High.

15. Yet thou shalt be brought down ᵏto hell, to the sides of the pit.

16. They that see thee shall narrowly look upon thee, and shall consider thee, and shall say: Is this the man that made the earth to tremble, that did shake kingdoms?

17. And made the world as a wilderness, and destroyed the cities thereof, and opened not the house of his prisoners?

18. All the kings of the nations, yea, all of them, lie in glory, every one of them in his own house.

19. But thou art cast out of thy grave like an abominable branch, and the remnant of those that are slain, thrust through with a sword, that go down to the stones of the pit; as a carcass trodden under feet.

20. Thou shalt not be joined with them in burial, because thou hast destroyed thy land and slain thy people; ˡthe seed of evil-doers shall never be renowned.

21. Prepare slaughter for his children ᵐfor the iniquities of their fathers, that they do not rise, nor possess the land, nor fill the face of the world with cities.

22. For I will rise up against them, saith the Lord of Hosts, and cut off from Babylon ⁿthe name, and remnant, ᵒand son, and nephew, saith the Lord.

23. ᵖI will also make it a possession for the bittern, and pools of water; and I will sweep it with the besom of destruction, saith the Lord of Hosts.

24. The Lord of Hosts hath sworn, saying: Surely as I have

e, Ps. 125:3. *f*, Isa. 55:12, 13. Ezek. 31:16. *g*, Ezek. 32:21. *h*, D. & C. 76:26. *i*, Ps. 48:2. *j*, Isa. 47:8. 2 Thess. 2:4. *k*, ver. 9. *l*, Job 18:16—21. Ps. 21:10. 37:28. 109:13. *m*, Ex. 20:5. Matt. 23:35. *n*, Prov. 10:7. Jer. 51:62. *o*, Job 18:19. *p*, Isa. 34:11—15.   BETWEEN B. C. 559 AND 545.

thought, so shall it come to pass; and as I have purposed, so shall it stand—

25. That I will bring the Assyrian in my land, and upon my mountains tread him under foot; then shall ⁹his yoke depart from off them, and his burden depart from off their shoulders.

26. This is the purpose that is ʳpurposed upon the whole earth; and this is the hand that is stretched out upon all nations.

27. For the Lord of Hosts hath purposed, and who shall disannul? And his hand is stretched out, and who shall turn it back?

28. In the year that ˢking Ahaz died was this burden.

29. Rejoice not thou, whole Palestina, ᵗbecause the rod of him that smote thee is broken; for out of the serpent's root shall come forth a cockatrice, and ᵘhis fruit shall be a fiery flying serpent.

30. And the first-born of the poor shall feed, and the needy shall lie down in safety; and I will kill thy root with famine, and he shall slay thy remnant.

31. Howl, O gate; cry, O city; thou, whole Palestina, art dissolved; for there shall come from the north a smoke, and none shall be alone in his appointed times.

32. What shall then answer the messengers of the nations? That ʷthe Lord hath founded Zion, and the poor of his people shall trust in it.

CHAPTER 25.

Nephi's comments—His prediction of the scattering and subsequent gathering of Israel—Time of the Messiah's advent specified.

1. Now I, Nephi, do speak somewhat concerning the words which I have written, which have been spoken by the mouth of Isaiah. For behold, Isaiah spake many things which were ᵃhard for many of my people to understand; for they know not concerning the manner of prophesying among the Jews.

2. For I, Nephi, have not taught them many things concerning the manner of the Jews; for their works were works of darkness, and their doings were doings of abominations.

3. Wherefore, I write unto my people, unto all those that shall receive hereafter these things which I write, that they may know the judgments of God, that they come upon all nations, according to the word which he hath spoken.

4. Wherefore, hearken, O my people, which are of the house of Israel, and give ear unto my words; for because the words of Isaiah are not plain unto you, nevertheless they are plain unto all those that are filled with the spirit of prophecy. But I give unto you a prophecy, according to the spirit which is in me; wherefore I shall prophesy according to the ᵇplainness which hath been with me from the time that I came out from Jerusalem with my father; for behold, my soul delighteth in plainness unto my people, that they may learn.

5. Yea, and my soul delighteth in the words of Isaiah, for I came out from Jerusalem, and mine eyes hath beheld the things of the Jews, and I know that the Jews do understand the things of the prophets, and there is none other people that understand the things which were spoken unto the Jews like unto them, save it

---

q, Isa. 10:27. *r*, Isa. 13:4—13. *s*, 2 Kings 16:20. *t*, 2 Chron. 26:6. *u*, 2 Kings 18:8. *w*, Ps. 87:1, 5. 102:16. Zeph. 3:12. Zech. 11:11. CHAP. 25: *a*, Jac. 4:14. *b*, vers. 7, 8. Jac. 4:13. BETWEEN B. C. 559 AND 545.

be that they are taught after the manner of the things of the Jews.

6. But behold I, Nephi, have not taught my children after the manner of the Jews; but behold, I, of myself, have dwelt at Jerusalem, wherefore I know concerning the regions round about; and I have made mention unto my children concerning the judgments of God, which hath come to pass among the Jews, unto my children, according to all that which Isaiah hath spoken, and I do not write them.

7. But behold, I proceed with mine own prophecy, according to my plainness; in the which I know that no man can err; nevertheless, in the days that the prophecies of Isaiah shall be fulfilled men shall know of a surety, at the times when they shall come to pass.

8. Wherefore, they are of worth unto the children of men, and he that supposeth that they are not, unto them will I speak particularly, and confine the words unto mine own people; for I know that they shall be of great worth unto them in the last days; for in that day shall they understand them; wherefore, for their good have I written them.

9. And as one generation hath been destroyed among the Jews because of iniquity, even so have they been destroyed from generation to generation according to their iniquities; and never hath any of them been destroyed save it were foretold them by the prophets of the Lord.

10. Wherefore, it hath been told them concerning the destruction which should come upon them, immediately after my father left Jerusalem; nevertheless, they hardened their hearts; and according to my prophecy they have been destroyed, save it be those which are ^ccarried away captive into Babylon.

11. And now this I speak because of the spirit which is in me. And notwithstanding they have been carried away they shall return again, and possess the land of Jerusalem; wherefore, they shall be restored again to the land of their inheritance.

12. But, behold, they shall have wars, and rumors of wars; and when the day cometh that the Only Begotten of the Father, yea, even the Father of heaven and of earth, shall manifest himself unto them in the flesh, behold, they will reject him, because of their iniquities, and the hardness of their hearts, and the stiffness of their necks.

13. Behold, they will crucify him; and after he is laid in a sepulchre for the space of three days he shall rise from the dead, with healing in his wings; and all those who shall believe on his name shall be saved in the kingdom of God. Wherefore, my soul delighteth to prophesy concerning him, for I have ^dseen his day, and my heart doth magnify his holy name.

14. And behold it shall come to pass that after the Messiah hath risen from the dead, and hath manifested himself unto his people, unto as many as will believe on his name, behold, Jerusalem shall be destroyed again; for wo unto them that fight against God and the people of his church.

15. Wherefore, the Jews shall be ^escattered among all nations; yea, and also Babylon shall be

---

c, 1 Ne. 1:13. 10:3. See *g,* 1 Ne. 7. *d,* 1 Ne. 11:13—34. *e,* 1 Ne. 10:12. 19:13, 14. 22:5. 2 Ne. 10:6. BETWEEN B. C. 559 AND 545.

destroyed; wherefore, the Jews shall be scattered by other nations.

16. And after they have been scattered, and the Lord God hath scourged them by other nations for the space of many generations, yea, even down from generation to generation until they shall be persuaded to *f*believe in Christ, the Son of God, and the *g*atonement, which is infinite for all mankind—and when that day shall come that they shall believe in Christ, and worship the Father in his name, with pure hearts and clean hands, and look not forward any more for another Messiah, then, at that time, the day will come that it must needs be expedient that they should believe these things.

17. And the Lord will set his hand again the *h*second time to restore his people from their lost and fallen state. Wherefore, he will proceed to do a *i*marvelous work and a wonder among the children of men.

18. Wherefore, he shall bring forth *j*his words unto them, which words shall judge them at the last day, for they shall be given them for the purpose of *k*convincing them of the true Messiah, who was rejected by them; and unto the convincing of them that they need not look forward any more for a Messiah to come, for there should not any come, save it should be a false Messiah which should deceive the people; for there is save one Messiah spoken of by the prophets, and that Messiah is he who should be rejected of the Jews.

19. For according to the words of the prophets, the Messiah cometh in *l*six hundred years from the time that my father left Jerusalem; and according to the words of the prophets, and also the word of the angel of God, his name shall be Jesus Christ, the Son of God.

20. And now, my brethren, I have spoken *m*plainly that ye cannot err. And as the Lord God liveth that brought Israel up out of the land of Egypt, and gave unto Moses power that he should heal the nations after they had been bitten by the poisonous serpents, if they would cast their eyes unto the serpent which he did raise up before them, and also gave him power that he should smite the rock and the water should come forth; yea, behold I say unto you, that as these things are true, and as the Lord God liveth, there is none other name given under heaven save it be this Jesus Christ, of which I have spoken, whereby man can be saved.

21. Wherefore, for this cause hath the Lord God promised unto me that these things which I write shall be kept and preserved, and handed down unto my seed, from generation to generation, that the promise may be fulfilled unto Joseph, that his seed should never perish as long as the earth should stand.

22. Wherefore, these things shall go from generation to generation as long as the earth shall stand; and they shall go according to the will and pleasure of God; and the nations who shall possess them shall be *n*judged of

---

f, 1 Ne. 10:14. 19:15—17. 2 Ne. 6:11, 14. 10:7—9. 25:18. 26:12. 30:7. 3 Ne. 5:26. 20:30—33 Morm. 3:21. 5:14. *g*, see *f*, 2 Ne. 2. *h*, 2 Ne. 6:14. 21:11. 29:1. Jac. 6:2. *i*, 1 Ne. 14:7. 1 Ne. 22:8. 2 Ne. 27:26. 29:1. 3 Ne. 21:9. 28:31 —33. Morm. 8:34. *j*, 1 Ne. 13:34, 35, 39, 40. 2 Ne. 27:6—26. 3 Ne. 16:4. Morm. 8:14—16, 25—34. *k*, 1 Ne. 13:39—42. 2 Ne. 25:16, 17. 26:12. Morm. 3:21. 5:12—15. *l*, see *b*, 1 Ne. 10. *m*, see *b*. *n*, ver. 18. 2 Ne. 33:10—15. 3 Ne. 27:23—27. 28:29—34. Eth. 4:8—10. BETWEEN B. C. 559 AND 545.

them according to the words which are written.

23. For we labor diligently to write, to persuade our children, and also our brethren, to believe in Christ, and to be reconciled to God; for we know that it is by grace that we are saved, after all we can do.

24. And, °notwithstanding we believe in Christ, we keep the law of Moses, and look forward with steadfastness unto Christ, until the law shall be fulfilled.

25. For, for this end was the law given; wherefore the law hath become dead unto us, and we are made alive in Christ because of our faith; yet we keep the law because of the commandments.

26. And we talk of Christ, we rejoice in Christ, we preach of Christ, we prophesy of Christ, and we write according to our prophecies, that our children may know to what source they may look for a remission of their sins.

27. Wherefore, we speak concerning the law that our children may know the deadness of the law; and they, by knowing the deadness of the law, may look forward unto that life which is in Christ, and know for what end the law was given. And after the law is fulfilled in Christ, that they need not harden their hearts against him when the law ought to be done away.

28. And now behold, my people, ye are a stiffnecked people; wherefore, I have spoken plainly unto you, that ye cannot misunderstand. And the words which I have spoken shall stand as a testimony against you; for they are sufficient to teach any man the right way; for the right way is to believe in Christ and deny him not; for by denying him ye also deny the prophets and the law.

29. And now behold, I say unto you that the right way is to believe in Christ, and deny him not; and Christ is the Holy One of Israel; wherefore ye must bow down before him, and worship him with all your might, mind, and strength, and your whole soul; and if ye do this ye shall in nowise be cast out.

30. And, inasmuch as it shall be expedient, ye must keep the performances and ordinances of God until the law shall be fulfilled which was given unto Moses.

CHAPTER 26.

Nephi's predictions continued — Christ to come to the Nephites — Their final destruction — The days of the Gentiles.

1. And after Christ shall have risen from the dead he shall ªshow himself unto you, my children, and my beloved brethren; and the words which he shall speak unto you shall be the law which ye shall do.

2. For behold, I say unto you that I have beheld that many generations shall pass away, and there shall be great wars and contentions among my people.

3. And after the Messiah shall come there shall be ᵇsigns given unto my people of his birth, and also of his death and resurrection; and great and terrible shall that day be unto the wicked, for they shall perish; and they perish because they cast out the prophets, and the saints, and stone them, and slay them; wherefore the ᶜcry

---

o, vers. 25—30. 1 Ne. 5:9. 2 Ne. 5:10. 26:1. Jac. 4:4, 5. Jar. 5. Mos. 2:3. 3:14—16. 12:28, 29, 31—37. 13:27—35. 16:14, 15. Al. 25:14—16. 30:3. 31:9. 34:13, 14. He. 15:5. 3 Ne. 1:24, 25. 9:17—19. 12:17, 18. 15:2—10.
CHAP. 26: *a*, ver. 9. 1 Ne. 11:7. 12:6. See *b*, 1 Ne. 12. *b*, see *a*, 1 Ne. 12. *c*, see *f*, 2 Ne. 28. 3 Ne. 6:23, 25. 7:10, 14, 19.   BETWEEN B. C. 559 AND 545.

of the blood of the saints shall ascend up to God from the ground against them.

4. Wherefore, all those who are proud, and that do wickedly, the day that cometh shall burn them up, saith the Lord of Hosts, for they shall be as stubble.

5. And they that kill the prophets, and the saints, the depths of the earth shall swallow them up, saith the Lord of Hosts; and mountains shall cover them, and whirlwinds shall carry them away, and buildings shall fall upon them and crush them to pieces and grind them to powder.

6. And they shall be visited with thunderings, and lightnings, and earthquakes, and all manner of destructions, for the fire of the anger of the Lord shall be kindled against them, and they shall be as stubble, and the day that cometh shall consume them, saith the Lord of Hosts.

7. O the pain, and the anguish of my soul for the loss of the slain of my people! For I, Nephi, have seen it, and it well nigh consumeth me before the presence of the Lord; but I must cry unto my God: Thy ways are just.

8. But behold, the righteous that hearken unto the words of the prophets, and destroy them not, but look forward unto Christ with steadfastness for the signs which are given, notwithstanding all persecution—behold, they are they which shall ^{d}not perish.

9. But the Son of righteousness shall ^{e}appear unto them; and he shall heal them, and they shall have peace with him, until three generations shall have passed away, and many of the ^{f}fourth generation shall have passed away in righteousness.

10. And when these things have passed away a speedy destruction cometh unto my people; for, notwithstanding the pains of my soul, I have seen it; wherefore, I know that it shall come to pass; and they sell themselves for naught; for, for the reward of their pride and their foolishness they shall reap destruction; for because they yield unto the devil and choose works of darkness rather than light, therefore they must go down to hell.

11. For the Spirit of the Lord will not always strive with man. And when the Spirit ceaseth to strive with man then cometh speedy destruction, and this grieveth my soul.

12. And as I spake concerning the ^{g}convincing of the Jews, that Jesus is the very Christ, it must needs be that the Gentiles ^{h}be convinced also that Jesus is the Christ, the Eternal God;

13. And that he manifesteth himself unto all those who believe in him, by the power of the Holy Ghost; yea, unto every nation, kindred, tongue, and people, working mighty miracles, signs, and wonders, among the children of men according to their faith.

14. But behold, I prophesy unto you concerning the last days; concerning the days when the Lord God ^{i}shall bring these things forth unto the children of men.

15. After my seed and the seed of my brethren ^{j}shall have dwindled in unbelief, and shall have been smitten by the Gentiles; yea, after ^{k}the Lord God shall have camped against them round about,

---

d, 3 Ne. 9:13. 10:12, 13. e, see b, 1 Ne. 12. f, 1 Ne. 12:12. Al. 45:10, 12. He. 13:5, 9, 10. 3 Ne. 27:32. Morm. 6:5—22. g, see f, 2 Ne. 25. h, see s, 1 Ne. 13. See 1 Ne. 13:34—38, 42. 14:1—3. Morm. 3:21. i, see j, 2 Ne. 25. j, 1 Ne. 12:22, 23. 15:13. Morm. 5:15, 20. 8:27. k, Isa. 29:3. BETWEEN B. C. 559 AND 545.

and shall have laid siege against them with a mount, and raised forts against them; and after they shall have been brought down low in the dust, even that they are not, yet the words of the righteous shall be written, and the prayers of the faithful shall be heard, and all those who have dwindled in unbelief shall not be forgotten.

16. For those who shall be destroyed shall *speak unto them out of the ground, and their speech shall be low out of the dust, and their voice shall be as one that hath a familiar spirit; for the Lord God will give unto him power, that he may whisper concerning them, even as it were out of the ground; and their speech shall whisper out of the dust.

17. For thus saith the Lord God: They shall write the things which shall be done among them, and they shall be written and sealed up in a book, and those who have dwindled in unbelief shall "not have them, for they seek to destroy the things of God.

18. Wherefore, as those who have been destroyed have been destroyed speedily; and the "multitude of their terrible ones shall be as chaff that passeth away— yea, thus saith the Lord God: It shall be at an instant, suddenly—

19. And it shall come to pass, that those who have °dwindled in unbelief shall be smitten by the hand of the Gentiles.

20. And the Gentiles are lifted up in the pride of their eyes, and have ᵖstumbled, because of the greatness of their stumbling block, that they have built up ᵍmany churches; nevertheless, they put down the ʳpower and miracles of God, and preach up unto themselves their own wisdom and their ˢown learning, that they may get 'gain and grind upon the face of the poor.

21. And there are many churches built up which cause envyings, and strifes, and malice.

22. And there are also ᵘsecret combinations, even as in times of old, according to the combinations of the devil, for he is the foundation of all these things; yea, the foundation of murder, and works of darkness; yea, and he leadeth them by the neck with a flaxen cord, until he bindeth them with his strong cords forever.

23. For behold, my beloved brethren, I say unto you that the Lord God worketh not in darkness.

24. He doeth not anything save it be for the benefit of the world; for he loveth the world, even that he layeth down his own life that he may ᵛdraw all men unto him. Wherefore, he commandeth none that they shall not partake of his salvation.

25. Behold, doth he cry unto any, saying: Depart from me? Behold, I say unto you, Nay; but he saith: Come unto me all ye ends of the earth, ʷbuy milk and honey, without money and without price.

26. Behold, hath he commanded any that they should depart out of the synagogues, or out of the houses of worship? Behold, I say unto you, Nay.

27. Hath he commanded any that they should not partake of

l, Isa. 29:4. *m*, Enos 14. Morm. 6:6. *n*, Isa. 29:5. Morm. 6:6—15. *o*, see *j*. *p*, 1 Ne. 13:29, 34. 14:1—3. *q*, 1 Ne. 14:9, 10. 22:23. 2 Ne. 28. Morm. 8:25—41. *r*, 2 Ne. 28:5, 6. Morm. 8:26. 9:7—26. Moro. 7:33—38. *s*, 2 Ne. 28:4. *t*, 1 Ne. 22:23. 2 Ne. 28:12, 13. Morm. 8:28, 32, 33, 36—39. *u*, see *i*, 2 Ne. 10. *v*, see *c*, 2 Ne. 9. *w*, Isa. 55:1.
BETWEEN B. C. 559 AND 545.

his salvation? Behold I say unto you, Nay; but he hath given it free for all men; and he hath commanded his people that they should persuade all men to repentance.

28. Behold, hath the Lord commanded any that they should not partake of his goodness? Behold I say unto you, Nay; but all men are privileged the one like unto the other, and none are forbidden.

29. He commandeth that there shall be no priestcrafts; for, behold, *priestcrafts are that men preach and set themselves up for a light unto the world, that they may get gain and praise of the world; but they seek not the welfare of Zion.

30. Behold, the Lord hath forbidden this thing; wherefore, the Lord God hath given a commandment that all men should have charity, which *y*charity is love. And except they should have charity they were nothing. Wherefore, if they should have charity they would not suffer the laborer in Zion to perish.

31. But the laborer in Zion shall labor for Zion; for if they labor for money they shall perish.

32. And again, the Lord God hath commanded that men should not murder; that they should not lie; that they should not steal; that they should not take the name of the Lord their God in vain; that they should not envy; that they should not have malice; that they should not contend one with another; that they should not commit whoredoms; and that they should do none of these things; for whoso doeth them shall perish.

33. For none of these iniquities come of the Lord; for he doeth that which is good among the children of men; and he doeth nothing save it be *plain unto the children of men; and he inviteth them all to come unto him and partake of his goodness; and he denieth none that come unto him, black and white, bond and free, male and female; and he remembereth the heathen; and all are alike unto God, both Jew and Gentile.

CHAPTER 27.

Nephi's predictions continued— God's judgments upon the wicked— The sealed book—The unlearned man —The three witnesses—A marvelous work and a wonder.

1. But, behold, in the last days, or in the days of the Gentiles— yea, behold all the nations of the Gentiles and also the Jews, both those who shall come upon this land and those who shall be upon other lands, yea, even upon all the lands of the earth, behold, they will be *a*drunken with iniquity and all manner of abominations—

2. And when that day shall come they shall be *b*visited of the Lord of Hosts, with thunder and with earthquake, and with a great noise, and with storm, and with tempest, and with the flame of devouring fire.

3. And all the nations that fight against Zion, and that distress her, shall be as a dream of a night vision; yea, it shall be unto them, even as unto a hungry man which dreameth, and behold he eateth but he awaketh and his soul is empty; or like unto a thirsty man which dreameth, and behold he drinketh but he awaketh and behold he is faint, and his soul hath appetite; yea, even so shall the multitude of all the na-

x, 3 Ne. 16:10. 21:19—21. Chap. 30.
Chap. 27: *a*, Isa. 29:9. *b*, Isa. 29:6—10.
y, Moro. 7:47, 48. 8:26. *z*, vers. 23, 24.
Between B. C. 559 and 545.

tions be that fight against Mount Zion.

4. For behold, all ye that doeth iniquity, stay yourselves and wonder, for ye shall cry out, and cry; yea, ye shall be drunken but not with wine, ye shall stagger but not with strong drink.

5. For behold, the Lord hath poured out upon you the spirit of deep sleep. For behold, ye have closed your eyes, and ye have rejected the prophets; and your rulers, and the seers hath he covered because of your iniquity.

6. And it shall come to pass that the Lord God shall bring forth unto you the words of a ᶜbook, and they shall be the words of them which have slumbered.

7. And behold the book shall be ᵈsealed; and in the book shall be a ᵉrevelation from God, from the beginning of the world to the ending thereof.

8. Wherefore, because of the things which are sealed up, the things which are sealed shall not be delivered in the ᶠday of the wickedness and abominations of the people. Wherefore the book shall be kept from them.

9. But the book shall be delivered unto a man, and he shall deliver the words of the book, which are the words of those who have slumbered in the dust, and he shall deliver these words unto another;

10. But the words which are sealed he shall not deliver, neither shall he deliver the book. For the book shall be sealed by the power of God, and the revelation which was sealed shall be kept in the book until the own ᵗdue time of the Lord, that they may come forth; for behold, they ʲreveal all things from the foundation of the world unto the end thereof.

11. And the day cometh that the words of the book which were sealed shall be read upon the house tops; and they shall be read by the power of Christ; and all things shall be ᵏrevealed unto the children of men which ever have been among the children of men, and which ever will be even unto the end of the earth.

12. Wherefore, at that day when the book shall be delivered unto the man of whom I have spoken, the book shall be hid from the eyes of the world, that the eyes of none shall behold it save it be that ᵐthree witnesses shall behold it, by the power of God, besides him to whom the book shall be delivered; and they shall testify to the truth of the book and the things therein.

13. And there is none other which shall view it, save it be a ⁿfew according to the will of God, to bear testimony of his word unto the children of men; for the Lord God hath said that the words of the faithful should speak as if it were from the ᵒdead.

14. Wherefore, the Lord God will proceed to bring forth the words of the book; and in the mouth of as ᵖmany witnesses as seemeth him good will he establish his word; and wo be unto him that ᵍrejecteth the word of God!

15. But behold, it shall come to pass that the Lord God shall say unto ʳhim to whom he shall deliver the book: Take these words which are not sealed and

---

c, 1 Ne. 13:34, 35, 39—42. 2 Ne. 3:6—23. 26:16, 17. 29:11. Enos 13—18. Morm. 5:12, 13. 8:14—16, 25—32. *d*, Isa. 29:11. *e*, Eth. 4:1—7. *f*, Eth. 4:6, 7. *i*, Eth. 4:7, 15. *j*, Eth. 4:15. *k*, Eth. 4:6, 7. 13—17. *m*, see *c*, 2 Ne. 11. *n*, see Testimony of Witnesses in forepart of Book. *o*, 2 Ne. 3:19, 20. 26:16, 17. 27:6. 33:13—15. Morm. 9:30. Moro. 10:27. Isa. 29:4. *p*, see *d*, 2 Ne. 11. *q*, 2 Ne. 28:29, 30. 33:13—15. Eth. 4:8. *r*, vers. 12, 19, 24. BETWEEN B. C. 559 AND 545.

deliver them to *another, that he may show them 'unto the learned, saying: "Read this, I pray thee. And the learned shall say: Bring hither the book, and I will read them.

16. And now, because of the glory of the world and to get gain will they say this, and not for the glory of God.

17. And the man shall say: I cannot bring the book, for it is sealed.

18. Then shall the learned say: I cannot read it.

19. Wherefore it shall come to pass, that the Lord God will deliver again the book and the words thereof to ᵛhim that is not learned; and the man that is not learned shall say: I am not learned.

20. Then shall the Lord God say unto him: The learned shall not read them, for they have rejected them, and I am able to do mine own work; wherefore thou shalt read the words which I shall give unto thee.

21. ʷTouch not the things which are sealed, for I will bring them forth in mine own due time; for I will show unto the children of men that I am able to do mine own work.

22. Wherefore, when thou hast read the words which I have commanded thee, and obtained the ˣwitnesses which I have promised unto thee, then shalt thou seal up the book again, and hide it up unto me, that I may preserve the words which thou hast not read, until I shall see fit in mine own wisdom ʸto reveal all things unto the children of men.

23. For behold, I am God; and I am a God of miracles; and I will show unto the world that I am the same yesterday, today, and forever; and I work not among the children of men save it be according to their faith.

24. And again it shall come to pass that the Lord shall say unto ᶻhim that shall read the words that shall be delivered him:

25. ²ᵃForasmuch as this people draw near unto me with their mouth, and with their lips do honor me, but have removed their hearts far from me, and their fear towards me is taught by the precepts of men—

26. Therefore, I will proceed to ²ᵇdo a marvelous work among this people, yea, a marvelous work and a wonder, for the wisdom of their wise and learned shall perish, and the understanding of their prudent shall be hid.

27. And wo unto them that seek deep to hide their counsel from the Lord! And their works are in the dark; and they say: Who seeth us, and who knoweth us? And they also say: Surely, your turning of things upside down shall be esteemed as the potter's clay. But behold, I will show unto them, saith the Lord of Hosts, that I know all their works. For shall the work say of him that made it, he made me not? Or shall the thing framed say of him that framed it, he had no understanding?

28. But behold, saith the Lord of Hosts: I will show unto the children of men that it is yet a very little while and Lebanon shall be turned into a fruitful field; and the fruitful field shall be esteemed as a forest.

29. ²ᶜAnd in that day shall the deaf hear the words of the book,

s, ver. 9. *t*, 1 Cor. 1:19—21. Hist. of the Church, Vol. 1, p. 20. *u*, Isa. 29:11. *v*, vers. 12, 15, 24. *w*, Eth. 5:1. *x*, see *c*, 2 Ne. 11. *y*, 2 Ne. 27:7, 8. Eth. 4:6, 7. *z*, vers. 12, 15, 19. 2*a*, Isa. 29:13—24. 2*b*, see *i*, 2 Ne. 25. 2*c*, see *c*.
BETWEEN B. C. 559 AND 545.

and the eyes of the blind shall see out of obscurity and out of darkness.

30. And the meek also shall increase, and their joy shall be in the Lord, and the poor among men shall rejoice in the Holy One of Israel.

31. ²ᵈFor assuredly as the Lord liveth they shall see that the terrible one is brought to naught, and the scorner is consumed, and all that watch for iniquity are cut off;

32. And they that make a man an offender for a word, and lay a snare for him that reproveth in the gate, and turn aside the just for a thing of naught.

33. Therefore, thus saith the Lord, who redeemed Abraham, concerning the house of Jacob: Jacob shall ²ᵉnot now be ashamed, neither shall his face now wax pale.

34. But when he seeth his children, the work of my hands, in the midst of him, they shall sanctify my name, and sanctify the Holy One of Jacob, and shall fear the God of Israel.

35. ²ᶠThey also that erred in spirit shall come to understanding, and they that murmured shall learn doctrine.

CHAPTER 28.

Nephi's predictions continued—Latter-day churches and conditions—The kingdom of the devil to be shaken—The misleading precepts of men.

1. And now, behold, my brethren, I have spoken unto you, according as the Spirit hath constrained me; wherefore, I know that they must surely come to pass.

2. The things which shall be written out of the ᵃbook shall be of great worth unto the children of men, and especially unto our seed, which is a remnant of the house of Israel.

3. For it shall come to pass in that day that the ᵇchurches which are built up, and not unto the Lord, when the one shall say unto the other: Behold, I, I am the Lord's; and the others shall say: I, I am the Lord's; and thus shall every one say that hath built up churches, and not unto the Lord—

4. And they shall contend one with another; and their priests shall contend one with another, and they shall teach with their ᶜlearning, and deny the Holy Ghost, which giveth utterance.

5. And they deny the ᵈpower of God, the Holy One of Israel; and they say unto the people: Hearken unto us, and hear ye our precept; for behold there is no God today, for the Lord and the Redeemer hath done his work, and he hath given his power unto men;

6. Behold, hearken ye unto my precept; if they shall say there is a miracle wrought by the hand of the Lord, believe it not; for this day he is not a God of miracles; he hath done his work.

7. Yea, and there shall be many which shall say: Eat, drink, and be merry, for tomorrow we die; and it shall be well with us.

8. And there shall also be many which shall say: Eat, drink, and be merry; nevertheless, fear God—he will ᵉjustify in committing a little sin; yea, lie a little, take the advantage of one because of his words, dig a pit for thy neighbor; there is no harm in this; and do all these

---

2d, see j, 1 Ne. 22. 2e, see e, 1 Ne. 15. 2f, 1 Ne. 13:35—38. 14:1—3.
CHAP. 28: a, see c, 2 Ne. 27. b, see q, 2 Ne. 26. c, 2 Ne. 26:20. d, see r, 2 Ne. 26.
e, vers. 21, 25, 26. Morm. 8:31.   BETWEEN B. C. 559 AND 545.

things, for tomorrow we die; and if it so be that we are guilty, God will beat us with a few stripes, and at last we shall be saved in the kingdom of God.

9. Yea, and there shall be many which shall teach after this manner, false and vain and foolish doctrines, and shall be puffed up in their hearts, and shall seek deep to hide their counsels from the Lord; and their works shall be in the dark.

10. And the *f*blood of the saints shall cry from the ground against them.

11. Yea, they have all gone out of the way; they have become corrupted.

12. Because of pride, and because of false teachers, and false doctrine, their *g*churches have become corrupted, and their churches are lifted up; because of pride they are puffed up.

13. They rob the poor because of their fine sanctuaries; they rob the poor because of their fine clothing; and they persecute the meek and the poor in heart, because in their pride they are puffed up.

14. They wear stiff necks and high heads; yea, and because of pride, and wickedness, and abominations, and whoredoms, they have all gone astray save it be a few, who are the humble followers of Christ; nevertheless, they are led, that in many instances they do err because they are *h*taught by the precepts of men.

15. O the wise, and the learned, and the rich, that are puffed up in the pride of their hearts, and all those who preach false doctrines, and all those who commit whoredoms, and pervert the right way of the Lord, *i*wo, wo, wo be unto them, saith the Lord God Almighty, for they shall be thrust down to hell!

16. Wo unto them that *j*turn aside the just for a thing of naught and revile against that which is good, and say that is of no worth! For the day shall come that the Lord God will speedily visit the inhabitants of the earth; and in that day that they are *k*fully ripe in iniquity they shall perish.

17. But behold, if the inhabitants of the earth shall repent of their wickedness and abominations they shall not be destroyed, saith the Lord of Hosts.

18. But behold, that great and abominable church, the whore of all the earth, must *l*tumble to the earth, and great must be the fall thereof.

19. For the kingdom of the devil *m*must shake, and they which belong to it must needs be stirred up unto repentance, or the devil will grasp them with his everlasting chains, and they be stirred up to anger, and perish;

20. For behold, at that day shall he *n*rage in the hearts of the children of men, and stir them up to anger against that which is good.

21. And others will he *o*pacify, and lull them away into carnal security, that they will say: All is well in Zion; yea, Zion prospereth, all is well—and thus the devil cheateth their souls, and leadeth them away carefully down to hell.

---

f, 1 Ne. 14:13. 22:14. 2 Ne. 5:16. Morm. 8:27, 40, 41. Eth. 8:22—24. D. & C. 58:53. 63:28—31. Rev. 6:9—11. 18:24. 19:2. *g*, see *q*, 2 Ne. 26. *h*, 2 Ne. 27:35. *i*, 1 Ne. 22:23. 2 Ne. 26:20—22, 32. Al. 39:5. 3 Ne. 29:4—9. Morm. 8:41. 9:26. *j*, 2 Ne. 27:32. *k*, 1 Ne. 22:16—23. Eth. 2:8—11. Morm. 8:41. *l*, 1 Ne. 14:3, 4, 6, 7, 15—17. See *k*, 1 Ne. 14. *m*, 1 Ne. 22:22, 23. 2 Ne. 28:20—32. *n*, ver. 28. *o*, 2 Ne. 26:29. 28:7—14, 25. Morm. 8:31.

BETWEEN B. C. 559 AND 545.

2 NEPHI, 29.

22. And behold, others he flattereth away, and telleth them there is no hell; and he saith unto them: I am no devil, for there is none—and thus he whispereth in their ears, until he grasps them with his awful *p*chains, from whence there is no deliverance.

23. Yea, they are *q*grasped with death, and hell; and death, and hell, and the devil, and all that have been seized therewith must stand before the throne of God, and be judged according to their works, from whence they must go into the place prepared for them, even a *r*lake of fire and brimstone, which is endless torment.

24. Therefore, wo be unto him that is at ease in Zion!

25. Wo be unto him that crieth: All is well!

26. Yea, wo be unto him that *s*hearkeneth unto the precepts of men, and denieth the power of God, and the gift of the Holy Ghost!

27. Yea, wo be unto him that saith: We have received, and we *t*need no more!

28. And in fine, wo unto all those who tremble, and are *u*angry because of the truth of God! For behold, he that is built upon the rock receiveth it with gladness; and he that is built upon a sandy foundation trembleth lest he shall fall.

29. Wo be unto him that shall say: We have received the word of God, and we *v*need no more of the word of God, for we have enough!

30. For behold, thus saith the Lord God: I will give unto the children of men *w*line upon line, precept upon precept, here a little and there a little; and blessed are those who hearken unto my precepts, and lend an ear unto my counsel, for they shall learn wisdom; *x*for unto him that receiveth I will give more; and from them that shall say, We have enough, from them shall be taken away even that which they have.

31. Cursed is he that putteth his trust in man, or maketh flesh his arm, or shall hearken unto the *y*precepts of men, save their precepts shall be given by the power of the Holy Ghost.

32. *z*Wo be unto the Gentiles, saith the Lord God of Hosts! For notwithstanding I shall lengthen out mine arm unto them from day to day, they will deny me; nevertheless, I will be merciful unto them, saith the Lord God, if they will repent and come unto me; for mine arm is lengthened out all the day long, saith the Lord God of Hosts.

CHAPTER 29.

Nephi's predictions continued—The Gentiles and the Bible—Other records—God's words to be gathered in one.

1. But behold, there shall be many—at that day when I shall proceed to do a *a*marvelous work among them, that I may remember my covenants which I have made unto the children of men, that I may set my hand again the *b*second time to recover my people, which are of the house of Israel;

2. And also, that I may remember the promises which I have made unto thee, Nephi, and also unto thy father, that I would remember your seed; and that the *c*words of your seed should pro-

p, 2 Ne. 1:13, 23. 9:45. Ver. 19. Al. 12:11, 17. 36:18. *q*, see *j*, 2 Ne. 9. *r*, see *k*, 1 Ne. 15. *s*, see *r*, 2 Ne. 26. 2 Ne. 28:31. *t*, vers. 29, 30. Al. 12:10, 11. 3 Ne. 26:9, 10. Eth. 4:8. *u*, ver. 20. *v*, ver. 27. Also see *t*. *w*, Isa. 28:10. *x*, Al. 12:10, 11. *y*, vers. 3—14. 2 Ne. 27:25. *z*, see *d*, 1 Ne. 14. CHAP. 29: *a*, see *i*, 2 Ne. 25. *b*, see *i*, 2 Ne. 6. *c*, 2 Ne. 3:21. See *l*, 2 Ne. 26. BET. B. C. 559 AND 545.

ceed forth out of my mouth unto your seed; and my words shall ᵈhiss forth unto the ends of the earth, for a ᵉstandard unto my people, which are of the house of Israel;

3. And because my words shall hiss forth—many of the Gentiles shall say: A ᶠBible! A Bible! We have got a Bible, and there cannot be any more Bible.

4. But thus saith the Lord God: O fools, they shall have a Bible; and it shall proceed forth from the Jews, mine ancient covenant people. And what thank they the Jews for the Bible which they receive from them? Yea, what do the Gentiles mean? Do they remember the travels, and the labors, and the pains of the Jews, and their diligence unto me, in bringing forth salvation unto the Gentiles?

5. O ye Gentiles, have ye remembered the Jews, mine ancient covenant people? Nay; but ye have cursed them, and have hated them, and have not sought to recover them. But behold, I will return all these things upon your own heads; for I the Lord have not forgotten my people.

6. Thou ᵍfool, that shall say: A Bible, we have got a Bible, and we need no more Bible. Have ye obtained a Bible save it were by the Jews?

7. Know ye not that there are more nations than one? Know ye not that I, the Lord your God, have created all men, and that I remember those who are upon the isles of the sea; and that I rule in the heavens above and in the earth beneath; and I bring forth my word unto the children of men, yea, even upon all the nations of the earth?

8. Wherefore murmur ye, because that ye shall receive more of my word? Know ye not that the testimony of two nations is a witness unto you that I am God, that I remember one nation like unto another? Wherefore, I speak the same words unto one nation like unto another. And when the two nations shall run together the testimony of the ʰtwo nations shall run together also.

9. And I do this that I may prove unto many that I am the same yesterday, today, and forever; and that I speak forth my words according to mine own pleasure. And because that I have spoken one word ye need not suppose that I cannot speak another; for my work is not yet finished; neither shall it be until the end of man, neither from that time henceforth and forever.

10. Wherefore, because that ye have a Bible ye need not suppose that it contains all my words; neither need ye suppose that I have not caused more to be written.

11. For I command all men, both in the east and in the west, and in the north, and in the south, and in the islands of the sea, that they shall write the words which I speak unto them; for out of the ⁱbooks which shall be written I will ʲjudge the world, every man according to their works, according to that which is written.

12. For behold, I shall speak unto the ᵏJews and they shall write it; and I shall also speak unto the ˡNephites and they shall write it; and I shall also ᵐspeak

---

d, Isa. 5:26. Moro. 10:28. *e*, Isa. 5:26. 18:3. 49:22. 62:10. D. & C. 45:9. 64:42. *f*, vers. 4. 6—14. *g*, ver. 3. *h*, 2 Ne. 3:12. Ezek. 37:15—20. *i*, see *c*, 2 Ne. 27. *j*, 2 Ne. 25:18, 22. 29:12—14. 3 Ne. 27:23—26. Rev. 20:12. *k*, 1 Ne. 13:23—29. 2 Ne. 3:12. *l*, 1 Ne. 13:39—42. 2 Ne. 3:12, 18—21. 26:16, 17. 27:6—26. *m*, 3 Ne. 16:1—3. 17:4.   BETWEEN B. C. 559 AND 545.

unto the other tribes of the house of Israel, which I have led away, and they shall write it; and I shall also speak unto ⁿall nations of the earth and they shall write it.

13. And it shall come to pass ^othat the Jews shall have the words of the Nephites, and the Nephites shall have the words of the Jews; and the Nephites and the Jews shall have the words of the lost tribes of Israel; and the lost tribes of Israel shall have the words of the Nephites and the Jews.

14. And it shall come to pass that my people, which are of the house of Israel, shall be gathered home unto the lands of their possessions; and my word also shall be ^pgathered in one. And I will show unto them that fight against my word and against my people, who are of the house of Israel, that I am God, and that I covenanted with Abraham that I would remember his seed forever.

CHAPTER 30.

Nephi's predictions continued—Converted Gentiles to be numbered with the covenant people—Jews and Lamanites to believe—The wicked to be destroyed.

1. And now behold, my beloved brethren, I would speak unto you; for I, Nephi, would not suffer that ye should suppose that ye are more righteous than the Gentiles shall be. For behold, except ye shall keep the commandments of God ye shall all likewise perish; and because of the words which have been spoken ye need not suppose that the Gentiles are utterly destroyed.

2. For behold, I say unto you that as many of the Gentiles as will repent are the covenant people of the Lord; and as many of the Jews as will not repent shall be cast off; for the Lord covenanteth with none save it be with them that repent and believe in his Son, who is the Holy One of Israel.

3. And now, I would prophesy somewhat more concerning the Jews and the Gentiles. For after the ^abook of which I have spoken shall come forth, and be written unto the Gentiles, and sealed up again unto the Lord, there shall be ^bmany which shall believe the words which are written; and they shall carry them forth unto the ^cremnant of our seed.

4. And then shall the remnant of our seed know concerning us, how that we came out from Jerusalem, and that they are descendants of the Jews.

5. And the gospel of Jesus Christ shall be declared ^damong them; wherefore, they shall be restored unto the ^eknowledge of their fathers, and also to the knowledge of Jesus Christ, which was had among their fathers.

6. And then shall they rejoice; for they shall know that it is a blessing unto them from the hand of God; and their scales of darkness shall begin to fall from their eyes; and many generations shall not pass away among them, save they shall be a ^fwhite and delightsome people.

7. And it shall come to pass that the Jews which are scattered also shall ^gbegin to believe in Christ; and they shall begin to

---

n, vers. 7—11. 2 Ne. 26:33. *o,* 2 Ne. 3:12. 29:8. Morm. 5:13, 14. *p,* see *o,* John 11:52. CHAP. 30: *a,* see *c,* 2 Ne. 27. *b,* 1 Ne. 13:34—42. 14:1, 2, 5, 12—14. 22:8, 9. 3 Ne. 16:6, 10, 11. 26:8. *c,* 1 Ne. 10:14. 15:13—18. 22:8—12. 3 Ne. 16:6—13. 20:13. *d,* 1 Ne. 13:38—42. 15:13—18. 3 Ne. 16:11, 12. 21:3—7, 24—26. Morm. 5:15. *e,* 1 Ne. 15:14. 2 Ne. 3:12. Morm. 7:1, 9, 10. *f,* 2 Ne. 5:21. Jac. 3:8. Al. 23:18. 3 Ne. 2:14—16. *g,* see *f,* 2 Ne. 25. BETWEEN B. C. 559 AND 545.

gather in upon the face of the land; and as many as shall believe in Christ shall also become a delightsome people.

8. And it shall come to pass that the Lord God shall commence his work among all nations, kindreds, tongues, and people, to bring about the *h*restoration of his people upon the earth.

9. *i*And with righteousness shall the Lord God judge the poor, and reprove with equity for the meek of the earth. And he shall smite the earth with the rod of his mouth; and with the breath of his lips shall he slay the wicked.

10. For the time speedily cometh that the Lord God shall cause a *j*great division among the people, and the wicked will he destroy; and he will spare his people, yea, even if it so be that he must destroy the wicked by fire.

11. *k*And righteousness shall be the girdle of his loins, and faithfulness the girdle of his reins.

12. And then shall the wolf dwell with the lamb; and the leopard shall lie down with the kid, and the calf, and the young lion, and the fatling, together; and a little child shall lead them.

13. And the cow and the bear shall feed; their young ones shall lie down together; and the lion shall eat straw like the ox.

14. And the sucking child shall play on the hole of the asp, and the weaned child shall put his hand on the cockatrice's den.

15. They shall not hurt nor destroy in all my holy mountain; for the earth shall be full of the knowledge of the Lord as the waters cover the sea.

16. *l*Wherefore, the things of all nations shall be made known; yea, all things shall be made known unto the children of men.

17. There is nothing which is secret save it shall be revealed; there is no work of darkness save it shall be made manifest in the light; and there is nothing which is *m*sealed upon the earth save it shall be loosed.

18. Wherefore, all things which have been revealed unto the children of men shall at that day be revealed; and Satan shall have power over the hearts of the children of men *n*no more, for a long time. And now, my beloved brethren, I must make an end of my sayings.

CHAPTER 31.

Nephi's predictions continued—Why the Savior would be baptized—The straight and narrow way.

1. .And now I, Nephi, make an end of my prophesying unto you, my beloved brethren. And I cannot write but a few things, which I know must surely come to pass; neither can I write but a few of the words of my brother Jacob.

2. Wherefore, the things which I have written sufficeth me, save it be a few words which I must speak concerning the doctrine of Christ; wherefore, I shall speak unto you plainly, according to the plainness of my prophesying.

3. For my soul delighteth in *a*plainness; for after this manner doth the Lord God work among the children of men. For the Lord God giveth light unto the understanding; for he speaketh unto men according to their language, unto their understanding.

4. Wherefore, I would that ye should remember that I have spoken unto you concerning *b*that

h, see *e*, 1 Ne. 15. *i*, Isa. 11:4. *j*, 1 Ne. 14:7. 22:16, 17. *k*, Isa. 11:5—9. *l*, 2 Ne. 29:6—14. Eth. 4:6, 7, 13—17. *m*, 1 Ne. 14:26. *n*, 1 Ne. 22:15, 26. Jac. 5:76. Eth. 8:26. CHAP. 31: *a*, see *b*, 2 Ne. 25. *b*, see *f*, 1 Ne. 10.

BETWEEN B. C. 559 AND 545.

prophet which the Lord showed unto me, that should baptize the Lamb of God, which should take away the sins of the world.

5. And now, if the Lamb of God, he being holy, should have need to be baptized by water, to ^cfulfil all righteousness, O then, how much more need have we, being unholy, to be baptized, yea, even by water!

6. And now, I would ask of you, my beloved brethren, wherein the Lamb of God did fulfil all righteousness in being baptized by water?

7. Know ye not that he was holy? But notwithstanding he being holy, he showeth unto the children of men that, according to the flesh he humbleth himself before the Father, and witnesseth unto the Father that he would be obedient unto him in keeping his commandments.

8. Wherefore, after he was baptized with water the Holy Ghost descended upon him in the ^dform of a dove.

9. And again, it showeth unto the children of men the ^estraightness of the path, and the narrowness of the gate, by which they should enter, he having set the example before them.

10. And he said unto the children of men: Follow thou me. Wherefore, my beloved brethren, can we follow Jesus save we shall be willing to keep the commandments of the Father?

11. And the Father said: Repent ye, repent ye, and be ^fbaptized in the name of my Beloved Son.

12. And also, the voice of the Son came unto me, saying: He that is baptized in my name, to him will the Father give the Holy Ghost, like unto me; wherefore, follow me, and do the things which ye have seen me do.

13. Wherefore, my beloved brethren, I know that if ye shall follow the Son, with full purpose of heart, acting no hypocrisy and no deception before God, but with real intent, repenting of your sins, witnessing unto the Father that ye are willing to take upon you the name of Christ, by baptism—yea, by following your Lord and your Savior down into the water, according to his word, behold, then shall ye receive the Holy Ghost; yea, then cometh the baptism of fire and of the Holy Ghost; and then can ye speak with the ^gtongue of angels, and shout praises unto the Holy One of Israel.

14. But, behold, my beloved brethren, thus came the voice of the Son unto me, saying: After ye have repented of your sins, and witnessed unto the Father that ye are willing to keep my commandments, by the baptism of water, and have received the baptism of fire and of the Holy Ghost, and can speak with a new tongue, yea, even with the tongue of angels, and after this should deny me, it would have been better for you that ye had not known me.

15. And I heard a voice from the Father, saying: Yea, the words of my Beloved are true and faithful. ^hHe that endureth to the end, the same shall be saved.

16. And now, my beloved brethren, I know by this that unless a man shall endure to the end, in following the example of the Son of the living God, he cannot be saved.

c, vers. 6, 7. *d*, 1 Ne. 11:27. Luke 3:22. John 1:32. D. & C. 93:15. *e*, see 2*a*, 2 Ne. 9. *f*, see *u*, 2 Ne. 9. *g*, ver. 14. 2 Ne. 32:2, 3. *h*, vers. 15, 16. Jac. 6:7—11. Mos. 5:11. 15:26, 27. Al. 24:30. 39:6. 3 Ne. 27:17. Morm. 1:16, 17. Heb. 6:4—6. 2 Pet. 2:21. D. & C. 132:27.

BETWEEN B. C. 559 AND 545.

17. Wherefore, do the things which I have told you I have seen that your Lord and your Redeemer should do; for, for this cause have they been shown unto me, that ye might know the ʲgate by which ye should enter. For the gate by which ye should enter is repentance and baptism by water; and then cometh a remission of your sins by fire and by the Holy Ghost.

18. And then are ye in this straight and narrow path which leads to eternal life; yea, ye have entered in by the gate; ye have done according to the commandments of the Father and the Son; and ye have received the Holy Ghost, which witnesses of the Father and the Son, unto the fulfilling of the promise which he hath made, that if ye entered in by the way ye should receive.

19. And now, my beloved brethren, after ye have gotten into this straight and narrow path, I would ask if all is done? Behold, I say unto you, Nay; for ye have not come thus far save it were by the word of Christ with unshaken faith in him, relying wholly upon the merits of him who is mighty to save.

20. Wherefore, ye must press forward with a steadfastness in Christ, having a perfect brightness of hope, and a love of God and of all men. Wherefore, if ye shall press forward, feasting upon the word of Christ, and endure to the end, behold, thus saith the Father: Ye shall have eternal life.

21. And now, behold, my beloved brethren, this is the ʲway; and there is none other way nor name given under heaven whereby man can be saved in the kingdom of God. And now, behold, this is the doctrine of Christ, and the only and true doctrine of the Father, and of the Son, and of the Holy Ghost, which is ᵏone God, without end. Amen.

CHAPTER 32.

Nephi's predictions continued—The tongue of angels—Office of the Holy Ghost.

1. And now, behold, my beloved brethren, I suppose that ye ponder somewhat in your hearts concerning that which ye should do after ye have entered in by the way. But, behold, why do ye ponder these things in your hearts?

2. Do ye not remember that I said unto you that after ye had received the Holy Ghost ye could speak with the tongue of angels? And now, how could ye speak with the ᵃtongue of angels save it were by the Holy Ghost?

3. Angels speak by the power of the Holy Ghost; wherefore, they speak the words of Christ. Wherefore, I said unto you, feast upon the words of Christ; for behold, the words of Christ will tell you all things what ye should do.

4. Wherefore, now after I have spoken these words, if ye cannot understand them it will be because ye ask not, neither do ye knock; wherefore, ye are not brought into the light, but must perish in the dark.

5. For behold, again I say unto you that if ye will enter in by the way, and receive the Holy Ghost, it will show unto you ᵇall things what ye should do.

6. Behold, this is the doctrine of Christ, and there will be no more doctrine given until after he shall manifest himself unto

---

i, see *e*. *j*, see *e*. *k*, Al. 11:44. 3 Ne. 11:27, 28, 36. 28:10. Morm. 7:7. Deut. 6:4. Gal. 3:20. Eph. 4:5, 6. CHAP. 32: *a*, see *g*, 2 Ne. 31. *b*, 1 Ne. 10:17—19. 13:37. 2 Ne. 31:13. Jar. 4. Al. 5:46—48. 3 Ne. 12:1, 2. 16:6. Chap. 30. Eth. 4:11, 12. Moro. 10:4—7. BETWEEN B. C. 559 AND 545.

8

you in the flesh. And when he shall manifest himself unto you in the flesh, the things which he shall say unto you shall ye observe to do.

7. And now I, Nephi, cannot say more; the Spirit stoppeth mine utterance, and I am left to mourn because of the unbelief, and the wickedness, and the ignorance, and the stiffneckedness of men; for they will not search knowledge, nor understand great knowledge, when it is given unto them in plainness, even as plain as word can be.

8. And now, my beloved brethren, I perceive that ye ponder still in your hearts; and it grieveth me that I must speak concerning this thing. For if ye would hearken unto the Spirit which teacheth a man to pray ye would know that ye must pray; for the evil spirit teacheth not a man to pray, but teacheth him that he must not pray.

9. But behold, I say unto you that ye must pray always, and not faint; that ye must not perform any thing unto the Lord save in the first place ye shall pray unto the Father in the name of Christ, that he will consecrate thy performance unto thee, that thy performance may be for the welfare of thy soul.

CHAPTER 33.

Nephi's parting testimony — Not mighty in writing as in speaking — His great concern for his people.

1. And now I, Nephi, cannot write all the things which were taught among my people; neither am I mighty in writing, like unto speaking; for when a man speaketh by the power of the Holy Ghost the power of the Holy Ghost carrieth it unto the hearts of the children of men.

2. But behold, there are many that harden their hearts against the Holy Spirit, that it hath no place in them; wherefore, they cast many things away which are written and esteem them as things of naught.

3. But I, Nephi, have written what I have written, and I esteem it as of great worth, and especially unto my people. For I pray continually for them by day, and mine eyes water my pillow by night, because of them; and I cry unto my God in faith, and I know that he will hear my cry.

4. And I know that the Lord God will consecrate my prayers for the gain of my people. And the words which I have written in weakness will be made strong unto them; for it persuadeth them to do good; it maketh known unto them of their fathers; and it speaketh of Jesus, and persuadeth them to believe in him, and to endure to the end, which is life eternal.

5. And it speaketh harshly against sin, according to the plainness of the truth; wherefore, no man will be angry at the words which I have written save he shall be of the spirit of the devil.

6. I glory in plainness; I glory

c, see b, 1 Ne. 12. d, see b, 2 Ne. 25. e, 1 Ne. 1:5. 6:21. 8:8. 15:8—11. 17:7. 18:3, 21. 2 Ne. 4:23, 24, 28—35. Jac. 7:22. Enos 4, 11. 15—18. Mos. 3:4. 4:1—3, 11, 19—22. 9:17—18. 21:14. 26:39. Al. 6:6. 17:3. 18:41—43. 19:14—16. 22:16. 27:11, 12. 31:10, 26—35. 33:4—11. 34:39. 38:8. 43:49, 50. 45:1. 46:13, 16. 58:10. 62:51. He. 11:3, 4, 10—16. 3 Ne. 1:11—14. 13:5—13. 14:7—11. 17:3, 15—17, 21. 18:15—24, 30. 19:6—10, 17—36. 20:1. 27:1, 2, 7, 9, 28, 29. 28:1—9, 30. Morm. 9:6, 21, 28, 36, 37. Eth. 1:34—43. 2:14, 15, 18—22. 3:1—5. Moro. 6:4, 5, 9. 7:6—10, 26, 48. 8:3, 26. 10:4, 5. Chap. 33: a, Eth. 12:23—27. b, see g, 2 Ne. 3. Also see e, 2 Ne. 30. c, 1 Ne. 16:1—3. 17:48. 2 Ne. 1:25—27. Enos 23. Jar. 12. W. of Morm. 17. Moro. 9:4. d, see b, 2 Ne. 25.

Between B. C. 559 and 545.

in truth; I glory in my Jesus, for he hath redeemed my soul from *hell.

7. I have charity for my people, and great faith in Christ that I shall meet many souls spotless at his judgment-seat.

8. I have charity for the Jew— I say Jew, because I mean them from whence I came.

9. I also have charity for the Gentiles. But behold, for none of these can I hope except they shall be reconciled unto Christ, and enter into the ʳnarrow gate, and walk in the straight path which leads to life, and continue in the path until the end of the day of probation.

10. And now, my beloved brethren, and also Jew, and all ye ends of the earth, hearken unto these words and believe in Christ; and if ye believe not in these words believe in Christ. And if ye shall believe in Christ ye will believe in these words, for they are the words of Christ, and he hath given them unto me; and they teach all men that they should do good.

11. And if they are not the words of Christ, judge ye—for Christ will show unto you, ᵍwith power and great glory, that they are his words, at the last day; and you and I shall stand face to face before his bar; and ye shall know that I have been commanded of him to write these things, notwithstanding my weakness.

12. And I pray the Father in the name of Christ that many of us, if not all, may be saved in his kingdom at that great and last day.

13. And now, my beloved brethren, all those who are of the house of Israel, and all ye ends of the earth, I speak unto you as the voice of one ʰcrying from the dust: Farewell until that great day shall come.

14. And you that will not partake of the goodness of God, and respect the words of the Jews, and also my words, and the words which shall proceed forth out of the mouth of the Lamb of God, behold, I bid you an everlasting farewell, for ⁱthese words shall condemn you at the last day.

15. For what I ʲseal on earth, shall be brought against you at the judgment bar; for thus hath the Lord commanded me, and I must obey. Amen.

THE BOOK OF JACOB
THE BROTHER OF NEPHI

The words of his preaching unto his brethren. He confoundeth a man who seeketh to overthrow the doctrine of Christ. A few words concerning the history of the people of Nephi.

CHAPTER 1.

Nephites and Lamanites—Death of Nephi, son of Lehi—Hardness of heart and wicked practices.

1. For behold, it came to pass that *fifty and five years had passed away from the time that Lehi left Jerusalem; wherefore, Nephi gave me, Jacob, a commandment concerning the ᵃsmall plates, upon which these things are engraven.

e, see k, 1 Ne. 15. f, see 2a, 2 Ne. 9. g, Eth. 4:8—10. 5:4—6. Moro. 7:35. 10:27. h, see l, 2 Ne. 26. i, see q, 2 Ne. 27. j, He. 10:5—11. See q, 2 Ne. 27. CHAP. 1: a, see b, 1 Ne. 6. *B. C. 544.

2. And he gave me, Jacob, a commandment that I should write upon these plates a few of the things which I considered to be most precious; that I should not touch, save it were lightly, concerning the history of this people which are called the people of Nephi.

3. For he said that the history of his people should be engraven upon his *b*other plates, and that I should preserve these plates and hand them down unto my seed, from generation to generation.

4. And if there were preaching which was sacred, or revelation which was great, or prophesying, that I should engraven the heads of them upon *c*these plates, and touch upon them as much as it were possible, for Christ's sake, and for the sake of our people.

5. For because of faith and great anxiety, it truly had been made manifest unto us concerning our people, *d*what things should happen unto them.

6. And we also had many revelations, and the spirit of much prophecy; wherefore, we knew of Christ and his kingdom, which should come.

7. Wherefore we labored diligently among our people, that we might persuade them to come unto Christ, and partake of the goodness of God, that they might enter into his rest, lest by any means he should swear in his wrath they should not enter in, as in the provocation in the days of temptation while the children of Israel were in the wilderness.

8. Wherefore, we would to God that we could persuade all men not to rebel against God, to provoke him to anger, but that all men would believe in Christ, and view his death, and suffer his cross and bear the shame of the world; wherefore, I, Jacob, take it upon me to fulfil *e*the commandment of my brother Nephi.

9. Now Nephi began to be old, and he saw that he must soon die; wherefore, he anointed a man to be a king and a ruler over his people now, according to the reigns of the kings.

10. The people having loved Nephi exceedingly, he having been a great protector for them, having wielded the sword of Laban in their defence, and having labored in all his days for their welfare—

11. Wherefore, the people were desirous to retain in remembrance his name. And whoso should reign in his stead were called by the people, *f*second Nephi, third Nephi, and so forth, according to the reigns of the kings; and thus they were called by the people, let them be of whatever name they would.

12. And it came to pass that Nephi died.

13. Now the people which were not Lamanites were Nephites; nevertheless, they were called Nephites, Jacobites, Josephites, Zoramites, Lamanites, Lemuelites, and Ishmaelites.

14. But I, Jacob, shall not hereafter distinguish them by these names, but I shall call them Lamanites that seek to destroy the people of Nephi, and those who are friendly to Nephi I shall call Nephites, or the people of Nephi, according to the reigns of the kings.

15. And now it came to pass that the people of Nephi, under

---

b, see *f*, 1 Ne. 1. *c*, ver. 1. See *b*, 1 Ne. 6. *d*, 1 Ne. chaps. 12—14. 15:1—18. 19:10—17. 22:7, 8. 2 Ne. 1:5—12. 2:3. Chap 3. 4:1—11. Chaps. 10,25—27. 29:11—14. 30:1—6. *e*, vers. 1—4. *f*, vers. 9, 14, 15. 2 Ne. 5:18.

BETWEEN B. C. 544 AND 421.

the reign of the *g*second king, began to grow hard in their hearts, and indulge themselves somewhat in wicked practices, such as like unto David of old desiring many wives and concubines, and also Solomon, his son.

16. Yea, and they also began to search much gold and silver, and began to be lifted up somewhat in pride.

17. Wherefore I, Jacob, gave unto them these words as I taught them in the *h*temple, having first obtained mine errand from the Lord.

18. For I, Jacob, and my brother Joseph *i*had been consecrated priests and teachers of this people, by the hand of Nephi.

19. And we did magnify our office unto the Lord, taking upon us the responsibility, answering the sins of the people upon our own heads if we did not teach them the word of God with all diligence; wherefore, by laboring with our might their *j*blood might not come upon our garments; otherwise their blood would come upon our garments, and we would not be found spotless at the last day.

CHAPTER 2.

Jacob's denunciation of unchastity and other sins—Plurality of wives forbidden because of iniquity.

1. The words which Jacob, the brother of Nephi, spake unto the people of Nephi, after the death of Nephi:

2. Now, my beloved brethren, I, Jacob, according to the responsibility which I am under to God, to magnify mine office with soberness, and that I might *a*rid my garments of your sins, I come up into the temple this day that I might declare unto you the word of God.

3. And ye yourselves know that I have hitherto been diligent in the office of my calling; but I this day am weighed down with much more desire and anxiety for the welfare of your souls than I have hitherto been.

4. For behold, as yet, ye have been obedient unto the word of the Lord, which I have given unto you.

5. But behold, hearken ye unto me, and know that by the help of the all-powerful Creator of heaven and earth I can tell you concerning your thoughts, how that ye are beginning to labor in sin, which sin appeareth very abominable unto me, yea, and abominable unto God.

6. Yea, it grieveth my soul and causeth me to shrink with shame before the presence of my Maker, that I might testify unto you concerning the wickedness of your hearts.

7. And also it grieveth me that I must use so much boldness of speech concerning you, before your wives and your children, many of whose *b*feelings are exceedingly tender and chaste and delicate before God, which thing is pleasing unto God;

8. And it supposeth me that they have come up hither to hear the pleasing word of God, yea, the word which healeth the wounded soul.

9. Wherefore, it burdeneth my soul that I should be constrained, because of the strict commandment which I have received from God, to admonish you according to your crimes, to enlarge the wounds of those who are already wounded, instead of consoling and

g, ver. 11. *h*, see *h*, 2 Ne. 5. *i*, 2 Ne. 5:26. *j*, 2 Ne. 9:44. Jac. 2:2.
CHAP. 2: *a*, see *j*, Jac. 1. *b*, vers. 9, 28, 33, 35. Jac. 3:7. Moro. 9:9, 10.
BETWEEN B. C. 544 AND 421.

healing their wounds; and those who have not been wounded, instead of feasting upon the pleasing word of God have daggers placed to pierce their souls and wound their delicate minds.

10. But, notwithstanding the greatness of the task, I must do according to the strict commands of God, and tell you concerning your wickedness and abominations, in the presence of the pure in heart, and the broken heart, and under the glance of the ^{c}piercing eye of the Almighty God.

11. Wherefore, I must tell you the truth according to the ^{d}plainness of the word of God. For behold, as I inquired of the Lord, thus came the word unto me, saying: Jacob, get thou up into the ^{e}temple on the morrow, and declare the word which I shall give thee unto this people.

12. And now behold, my brethren, this is the word which I declare unto you, that many of you have begun to search for gold, and for silver, and for all manner of precious ores, in the which this land, which is a ^{f}land of promise unto you and to your seed, doth ^{g}abound most plentifully.

13. And the hand of providence hath smiled upon you most pleasingly, that you have obtained many riches; and because some of you have obtained more abundantly than that of your brethren ye are lifted up in the pride of your hearts, and ^{h}wear stiff necks and high heads because of the costliness of your apparel, and persecute your brethren because ye suppose that ye are better than they.

14. And now, my brethren, do ye suppose that God justifieth you in this thing? Behold, I say unto you, Nay. But he condemneth you, and if ye persist in these things his judgments must speedily come unto you.

15. O that he would show you that he can pierce you, and with one ^{i}glance of his eye he can smite you to the dust!

16. O that he would rid you from this iniquity and abomination. And, O that ye would listen unto the word of his commands, and let not this pride of your hearts destroy your souls!

17. Think of your brethren like unto yourselves, and be familiar with all and free with your substance, that ^{j}they may be rich like unto you.

18. But before ye seek for riches, seek ye for the kingdom of God.

19. And after ye have obtained a hope in Christ ye shall obtain riches, if ye seek them; and ye will seek them for the intent to do good—to clothe the naked, and to feed the hungry, and to liberate the captive, and administer relief to the sick and the afflicted.

20. And now, my brethren, I have spoken unto you concerning pride; and those of you which have afflicted your neighbor, and persecuted him because ye were proud in your hearts, of the things which God hath given you, what say ye of it?

21. Do ye not suppose that such things are abominable unto him who created all flesh? And the one being is as precious in his sight as the other. And all flesh is of the dust; and for the selfsame end hath he created them, that they should keep his

BETWEEN B. C. 544 AND 421.

commandments and glorify him forever.

22. And now I make an end of speaking unto you concerning this pride. And were it not that I must speak unto you concerning a grosser crime, my heart would rejoice exceedingly because of you.

23. But the word of God burthens me because of your grosser crimes. For behold, thus saith the Lord: This people begin to wax in iniquity; they understand not the scriptures, for they seek to excuse themselves in committing whoredoms, because of the things which were written concerning David, and Solomon his son.

24. Behold, David and Solomon truly had ᵏmany wives and concubines, which thing was ˡabominable before me, saith the Lord.

25. Wherefore, thus saith the Lord, I have led this people forth out of the land of Jerusalem, by the power of mine arm, that I might raise up unto me a ᵐrighteous branch from the fruit of the loins of Joseph.

26. Wherefore, I the Lord God will not suffer that this people shall do like unto them of old.

27. Wherefore, my brethren, hear me, and hearken to the word of the Lord: For there shall not any man among you have save it be ⁿone wife; and concubines he shall have none;

28. For I, the Lord God, delight in the chastity of women. And ᵒwhoredoms are an abomination before me; thus saith the Lord of Hosts.

29. Wherefore, this people shall keep my commandments, saith the Lord of Hosts, or ᵖcursed be the land for their sakes.

30. For if I will, saith the Lord of Hosts, raise up seed unto me, I ᑫwill command my people; otherwise they shall hearken unto ʳthese things.

31. For behold, I, the Lord, have seen the sorrow, and heard the mourning of the daughters of my people in the land of Jerusalem, yea, and in all the lands of my people, because of the wickedness and abominations of ˢtheir husbands.

32. And I will not suffer, saith the Lord of Hosts, that the cries of the fair daughters of this people, which I have led out of the land of Jerusalem, shall come up unto me against the men of my people, saith the Lord of Hosts.

33. For they shall not lead away captive the daughters of my people because of their tenderness, save I shall visit them with a ᵗsore curse, even unto destruction; for they shall not commit ᵘwhoredoms, like unto them of old, saith the Lord of Hosts.

34. And now behold, my brethren, ye know that these commandments were ᵛgiven to our father, Lehi; wherefore, ye have known them before; and ye have come unto great condemnation; for ye have done these things which ye ought not to have done.

35. Behold, ye have done greater iniquities than the Lamanites, our brethren. Ye have broken the hearts of your tender wives, and lost the confidence of your children, because of your bad examples before them; and the sob-

---
k, 1 Kings 11:1—3. 2 Sam. 3:2—5, 14. 5:13. 11:26, 27. 12:7—12, 24. 15:16. 16:21, 22. 19:5. 20:3. 1 Kings 1:1—4. *l*, 1 Kings 11:9—11. Deut. 7:1—4. 17:14—17. Ezra 9:1, 2. Neh. 13:23—27. *m*, 2 Ne. 3:5. *n*, ver. 34. Jac. 3:5—7. *o*, see *l*, 2 Ne. 28. *p*, Jac. 3:3. Al. 45:16. Eth. 2:7—12. *q*, D. & C. 132. *r*, vers. 27, 34. Jac. 3:5. *s*, Ezek. 16:22—43. *t*, see *p*. *u*, see *t*, 2 Ne. 28. *v*, 1 Ne. 1:16, 17. 4:1.

BETWEEN B. C. 544 AND 421.

oings of their hearts ascend up to God against you. And because of the *strictness of the word of God, which cometh down against you, many hearts died, pierced with deep wounds.

CHAPTER 3.

Jacob's denunciation continued—Lamanites more righteous than Nephites—The former commended for fidelity in marriage—The latter again warned.

1. But behold, I, Jacob, would speak unto you that are pure in heart. Look unto God with firmness of mind, and ^apray unto him with exceeding faith, and he will console you in your afflictions, and he will plead your cause, and send down justice upon those who seek your destruction.

2. O all ye that are pure in heart, lift up your heads and receive the pleasing word of God, and feast upon his love; for ye may, if your minds are firm, forever.

3. But, wo, wo, unto you that are not pure in heart, that are filthy this day before God; for except ye repent the land is ^bcursed for your sakes; and the Lamanites, which are not filthy like unto you, nevertheless ^cthey are cursed with a sore cursing, shall scourge you even unto destruction.

4. And the time speedily cometh, that except ye repent they shall ^dpossess the land of your inheritance, and the Lord God will lead away the righteous out from among you.

5. Behold, the Lamanites your brethren, whom ye hate because of their filthiness and the ^ecursing which hath come upon their skins, are more righteous than you; for they have not forgotten the commandment of the Lord, which was given unto our fathers —that they should have save it were ^fone wife, and concubines they should have none, and there should not be whoredoms committed among them.

6. And now, this commandment they observe to keep; wherefore, because of this observance, in keeping this commandment, the Lord God will not destroy them, but will be merciful unto them; and one day they shall ^gbecome a blessed people.

7. Behold, their husbands love their wives, and their wives love their husbands; and their husbands and their wives love their children; and their unbelief and their hatred towards you is because of the iniquity of their fathers; wherefore, how much better are you than they, in the sight of your great Creator?

8. O my brethren, I fear that unless ye shall repent of your sins that their skins will be whiter than yours, when ye shall be brought with them before the throne of God.

9. Wherefore, a commandment I give unto you, which is the word of God, that ye revile no more against them because of the ^hdarkness of their skins; neither shall ye revile against them because of their filthiness; but ye shall remember your own filthiness, and remember that their filthiness came because of their fathers.

10. Wherefore, ye shall remember your children, how that ye have grieved their hearts because of the example that ye have set before them; and also, remember that ye may, because of your filth-

---

w, Jac. 2:27, 34.   3:5.   CHAP. 3: *a*, see *e*, 2 Ne. 32.   *b*, see *p*, Jac. 2.   *c*, see *d*, 1 Ne. 2.   *d*, Om. 5—7, 12, 13.   *e*, see *d*, 1 Ne. 2.   *f*, see *n*, Jac. 2.   *g*, 1 Ne. 15:13—18.   22:8.   See *i*, 2 Ne. 3.   *h*, see *d*, 1 Ne. 2.

BETWEEN B. C. 544 AND 421.

iness, bring your children unto destruction, and their sins be heaped upon your heads at the last day.

11. O my brethren, hearken unto my word; arouse the faculties of your soul; shake yourselves that ye may awake from the slumber of death; and loose yourselves from the pains of hell that ye may not become *i*angels to the devil, to be cast into that lake of *j*fire and brimstone which is the second death.

12. And now I, Jacob, spake many more things unto the people of Nephi, warning them against fornication and lasciviousness, and every kind of sin, telling them the awful consequences of them.

13. And a hundredth part of the proceedings of this people, which now began to be numerous, cannot be written upon *k*these plates; but many of their proceedings are written upon the *l*larger plates, and their wars, and their contentions, and the reigns of their kings.

14. These plates are called the plates of Jacob, and they were made by the *m*hand of Nephi. And I make an end of speaking these words.

CHAPTER 4.

Jacob's teachings continued—The law of Moses among the Nephites, pointing them to Christ—His rejection by the Jews foreseen.

1. Now behold, it came to pass that I, Jacob, having ministered much unto my people in word, (and I cannot write but a little of my words, because of the *a*difficulty of engraving our words upon plates) and we know that the things which we write upon plates must remain;

2. But whatsoever things we write upon anything save it be upon plates must perish and vanish away; but we can write a few words upon plates, which will give our children, and also our beloved brethren, a small degree of knowledge concerning us, or concerning their fathers—

3. Now in this thing we do rejoice; and we labor diligently to engraven these words upon plates, hoping that our beloved brethren and our children will receive them with thankful hearts, and look upon them that they may learn with joy and not with sorrow, neither with contempt, concerning their first parents.

4. For, for this intent have we written these things, that they may know that we knew of Christ, and we had a hope of his glory many hundred years before his coming; and not only we ourselves had a hope of his glory, but also all the holy prophets which were before us.

5. Behold, they believed in Christ and worshiped the Father in his name, and also we worship the Father in his name. And for this intent we *b*keep the law of Moses, it pointing our souls to him; and for this cause it is sanctified unto us for righteousness, even as it was accounted unto Abraham in the wilderness to be obedient unto the commands of God in offering up his son Isaac, which is a similitude of God and his Only Begotten Son.

6. Wherefore, we search the prophets, and we have many revelations and the spirit of prophecy; and having all these witnesses

i, see *i*, 2 Ne. 9. *j*, see *k*, 1 Ne. 15. *k*, see *b*, 1 Ne. 6. *l*, see *f*, 1 Ne. 1. *m*, 1 Ne. 19:2, 3. 2 Ne. 5:30—32. CHAP. 4: *a*, Eth. 12:23—26. *b*, see *o*, 2 Ne. 25.
BETWEEN B. C. 544 AND 421.

we obtain a hope, and our faith becometh unshaken, insomuch that we truly °can command in the name of Jesus and the very trees obey us, or the mountains, or the waves of the sea.

7. Nevertheless, the Lord God showeth us our weakness that we may know that it is by his grace, and his great condescensions unto the children of men, that we have power to do these things.

8. Behold, great and marvelous are the works of the Lord. How unsearchable are the depths of the mysteries of him; and it is impossible that man should find out all his ways. And no man knoweth of his ways save it be revealed unto him; wherefore, brethren, despise not the revelations of God.

9. For behold, by the ^dpower of his word man came upon the face of the earth, which earth was created by the power of his word. Wherefore, if God being able to speak and the world was, and to speak and man was created, O then, why not able to command the earth, or the workmanship of his hands upon the face of it, according to his will and pleasure?

10. Wherefore, brethren, seek not to counsel the Lord, but to take counsel from his hand. For behold, ye yourselves know that he counseleth in wisdom, and in justice, and in great mercy, over all his works.

11. Wherefore, beloved brethren, be reconciled unto him through the ^eatonement of Christ, his Only Begotten Son, and ye may obtain a ^fresurrection, according to the power of the resurrection which is in Christ, and be presented as the ^gfirst-fruits of Christ unto God, having faith, and obtained a good hope of glory in him before he manifesteth himself in the flesh.

12. And now, beloved, marvel not that I tell you these things; for why not speak of the ^hatonement of Christ, and attain to a perfect knowledge of him, as to attain to the knowledge of a ⁱresurrection and the world to come?

13. Behold, my brethren, he that prophesieth, let him prophesy to the understanding of men; for the Spirit speaketh the truth and lieth not. Wherefore, it speaketh of things as they really are, and of things as they really will be; wherefore, these things are manifested unto us ^jplainly, for the salvation of our souls. But behold, we are not witnesses alone in these things; for God also spake them unto prophets of old.

14. But behold, the Jews were a ^kstiffnecked people; and they despised the words of plainness, and killed the prophets, and sought for things that they could not understand. Wherefore, because of their blindness, which blindness came by looking beyond the mark, they must needs fall; for God hath taken away his ^lplainness from them, and delivered unto them many things which they cannot understand, because they desired it. And because they desired it God hath done it, that they may stumble.

15. And now I, Jacob, am led on by the Spirit unto prophesying; for I perceive by the workings of the Spirit which is in

c, 1 Ne. 7:17, 18. 17:48, 50, 53—55 29. He. 10:5—11. 3 Ne. 28:19—22. Mos. 2:25. Morm. 9:17. *c*, see *f*, 2 Ne. 2. Al. 40:16—21. He. 14:25. 3 Ne. 28:9—13. 20:4, 5. *h*, see *f*, 2 Ne. 2. *i*, see *d*, 2 Ne. 2. Jac. 6:4. *l*, see *b*, 2 Ne. 25.
Jac. 7:13—19. Mos. 13:3—6. Al. 14:26— Morm. 8:24. Eth. 12:30. *d*, 2 Ne. 2:14, 15. *f*, see *d*, 2 Ne. 2. *g*, Mos. 15:21—23. 1 Cor. 15:20. 1 Thess. 4:16. Rev. *j*, see *b*, 2 Ne. 25. *k*, 2 Ne. 25:2.
BETWEEN B. C. 544 AND 421.

me, that by the stumbling of the Jews they will ᵐreject the stone upon which they might build and have safe foundation.

16. But behold, according to the ⁿscriptures, this stone shall become the great, and the last, and the only sure foundation, upon which the Jews can build.

17. And now, my beloved, how is it possible that these, after having rejected the sure foundation, can ever build upon it, that it may become the ᵒhead of their corner?

18. Behold, my beloved brethren, I will unfold this mystery unto you; if I do not, by any means, get shaken from my firmness in the Spirit, and stumble because of my over anxiety for you.

CHAPTER 5.

Jacob quotes the prophet Zenos—Allegory of the tame and the wild olive-tree—Israel and the Gentiles.

1. Behold, my brethren, do ye not remember to have read the words of the prophet ᵃZenos, which he spake unto the house of Israel, saying:

2. Hearken, O ye house of Israel, and hear the words of me, a prophet of the Lord.

3. For behold, thus saith the Lord, I will liken thee, O house of Israel, like unto a ᵇtame olive-tree, which a man took and nourished in his vineyard; and it grew, and waxed old, and began to decay.

4. And it came to pass that the master of the vineyard went forth, and he saw that his olive-tree began to decay; and he said: I will prune it, and dig about it, and nourish it, that perhaps it may shoot forth young and tender branches, and it perish not.

5. And it came to pass that he pruned it, and digged about it, and nourished it according to his word.

6. And it came to pass that after many days it began to put forth somewhat a little, young and tender branches; but behold, the main top thereof began to perish.

7. And it came to pass that the master of the vineyard saw it, and he said unto his servant: It grieveth me that I should lose this tree; wherefore, go and pluck the branches from a ᶜwild olive-tree, and bring them hither unto me; and we will pluck off those main branches which are beginning to wither away, and we will cast them into the fire that they may be burned.

8. And behold, saith the Lord of the vineyard, I take away many of these ᵈyoung and tender branches, and I will graft them whithersoever I will; and it mattereth not that if it so be that the root of this tree will perish, I may preserve the fruit thereof unto myself; wherefore, I will take these young and tender branches, and I will graft them whithersoever I will.

9. Take thou the branches of the ᶜwild olive-tree, and graft them in, in the stead thereof; and these which I have plucked off I will cast into the fire and burn them, that they may not cumber the ground of my vineyard.

10. And it came to pass that the servant of the Lord of the vineyard did according to the word of the Lord of the vineyard,

---

m, 2 Ne. 18:14, 15. Isa. 8:14, 15. n, Ps. 118:22, 23. o, Ps. 118:22, 23.
CHAP. 5: a, see h; 1 Ne. 10. b, 1 Ne. 10:12, 14. 15:7, 12, 13, 16. 2 Ne. 3:5. Jac. 6:1—7. c, vers. 9, 10, 17, 18, 30—37, 46, 57, 65, 73. Rom. 11:17, 24. d, vers. 5, 13, 14, 19—27, 38—40, 43—46, 52, 54, 67, 68. c, see c. BET. B. C. 544 AND 421.

and grafted in the branches of the *f*wild olive-tree.

11. And the Lord of the vineyard caused that it should be digged about, and pruned, and nourished, saying unto his servant: It grieveth me that I should lose this tree; wherefore, that perhaps I might preserve the roots thereof that they perish not, that I might preserve them unto myself, I have done this thing.

12. Wherefore, go thy way; watch the tree, and nourish it, according to my words.

13. And *g*these will I place in the nethermost part of my vineyard, whithersoever I will, it mattereth not unto thee; and I do it that I may preserve unto myself the natural branches of the tree; and also, that I may lay up fruit thereof against the season, unto myself; for it grieveth me that I should lose this tree and the fruit thereof.

14. And it came to pass that the Lord of the vineyard went his way, and hid the natural branches of the tame olive-tree in the *h*nethermost parts of the vineyard, some in one and some in another, according to his will and pleasure.

15. And it came to pass that a *i*long time passed away, and the Lord of the vineyard said unto his servant: Come, let us go down into the vineyard, that we may labor in the vineyard.

16. And it came to pass that the Lord of the vineyard, and also the servant, went down into the vineyard to labor. And it came to pass that the servant said unto his master: Behold, look here; behold the tree.

17. And it came to pass that the Lord of the vineyard looked and beheld the tree in the which the wild olive branches had been grafted; and it had sprung forth and *j*begun to bear fruit. And he beheld that it was good; and the fruit thereof was like unto the natural fruit.

18. And he said unto the servant: Behold, the branches of the *k*wild tree have taken hold of the moisture of the root thereof, that the root thereof hath brought forth much strength; and because of the much strength of the root thereof the wild branches have brought forth tame fruit. Now, if we had not grafted in these branches, the tree thereof would have perished. And now, behold, I shall lay up much fruit, which the tree thereof hath brought forth; and the fruit thereof I shall lay up against the season, unto mine own self.

19. And it came to pass that the Lord of the vineyard said unto the servant: Come, let us go to the nethermost part of the vineyard, and behold if the natural branches of the tree have not brought forth much fruit also, that I may lay up of the fruit thereof against the season, unto mine own self.

20. And it came to pass that they went forth whither the master had hid the natural branches of the tree, and he said unto the servant: Behold these; and he beheld the first that it had brought forth much fruit; and he beheld also that it was good. And he said unto the servant: Take of the fruit thereof, and lay it up against the season, that I may preserve it unto mine own self; for behold, said he, this long time have I nourished it, and it hath brought forth much fruit.

---

f, see *c*. *g*, see *d*. *h*, vers. 13, 19, 38, 39, 52. *i*, vers. 25, 29, 76. *j*, Matt. 12:33. John 15:16. Rom. 11:16. *k*, see *c*. BETWEEN B. C. 544 AND 421.

21. And it came to pass that the servant said unto his master: How comest thou hither to plant this tree, or this branch of the tree? For behold, it was the poorest 'spot in all the land of the vineyard.

22. And the Lord of the vineyard said unto him: Counsel me not; I knew that it was a poor spot of ground; wherefore, I said unto thee, I have nourished it this long time, and thou beholdest that it hath brought forth much fruit.

23. And it came to pass that the Lord of the vineyard said unto his servant: Look hither; behold I have planted another branch of the tree also; and thou knowest that ᵐthis spot of ground was poorer than the first. But, behold the tree. I have nourished it this long time, and it hath brought forth much fruit; therefore, gather it, and lay it up against the season, that I may preserve it unto mine own self.

24. And it came to pass that the Lord of the vineyard said again unto his servant: Look hither, and behold ⁿanother branch also, which I have planted; behold that I have nourished it also, and it hath brought forth fruit.

25. And he said unto the servant: Look hither and behold the last. Behold, this have I planted in a °good spot of ground; and I have nourished it this long time, and only a ᵖpart of the tree hath brought forth tame fruit, and the ᑫother part of the tree hath brought forth wild fruit; behold, I have nourished this tree like unto the others.

26. And it came to pass that the Lord of the vineyard said unto the servant: Pluck off ʳthe branches that have not brought forth good fruit, and cast them into the fire.

27. But behold, the servant said unto him: Let us prune it, and dig about it, and nourish it a little longer, that perhaps it may bring forth good fruit unto thee, that thou canst lay it up against the season.

28. And it came to pass that the Lord of the vineyard and the servant of the Lord of the vineyard did nourish all the fruit of the vineyard.

29. And it came to pass that a ˢlong time had passed away, and the Lord of the vineyard said unto his ᵗservant: Come, let us go down into the vineyard, that we may labor again in the vineyard. For behold, the time draweth near, and the ᵘend soon cometh; wherefore, I must lay up fruit against the season, unto mine own self.

30. And it came to pass that the Lord of the vineyard and the servant went down into the vineyard; and they came to the tree whose natural branches had been broken off, and the wild branches had been grafted in; and behold all ᵛsorts of fruit did cumber the tree.

31. And it came to pass that the Lord of the vineyard did taste of the fruit, every sort according to its number. And the Lord of the vineyard said: Behold, this long time have we nourished this tree, and I have laid up unto myself against the season much fruit.

32. But behold, this time it hath brought forth much fruit, and there is ʷnone of it which is good. And behold, there are ˣall

---

l, ver. 22. *m*, vers. 21, 22, 25, 43, 44. *n*, Al. 16:17. *o*, ver. 43. 1 Ne. 2:20. *p*, He. 15:3. *q*, He. 15:4. *r*, ver. 25. *s*, vers. 15, 23, 76. *t*, 2 Ne. 27:9. D. & C. 101:55. 103:21. *u*, 1 Ne. 22:15—26. 2 Ne. 27:1—3. 30:10. Vers. 47, 62—64, 69, 71, 75, 76. 6:2. 3 Ne. 29:4. Morm. 8:41. Eth. 4:16. *v*, ver. 32. 4 Ne. 26. *w*, vers. 30, 35, 37, 42, 46. *x*, see *w*. BETWEEN B. C. 544 AND 421.

kinds of bad fruit; and it profiteth me nothing, notwithstanding all our labor; and now it grieveth me that I should lose this tree.

33. And the Lord of the vineyard said unto the servant: What shall we do unto the tree, that I may preserve again good fruit thereof unto mine own self?

34. And the servant said unto his master: Behold, because thou didst graft in the branches of the wild olive-tree they have nourished the roots, that they are alive and they have not perished; wherefore thou beholdest that they are yet good.

35. And it came to pass that the Lord of the vineyard said unto his servant: The tree profiteth me nothing, and the roots thereof profit me nothing so long as it shall bring forth evil fruit.

36. Nevertheless, I know that the roots are good, and for mine own purpose I have preserved them; and because of their much strength they have hitherto brought forth, from the ^{y}wild branches, good fruit.

37. But behold, the wild branches have grown and have overrun the roots thereof; and because that the wild branches have overcome the roots thereof it hath brought forth ^{z}much evil fruit; and because that it hath brought forth so much evil fruit thou beholdest that it beginneth to perish; and it will soon become ripened, that it may be cast into the fire, except we should do something for it to preserve it.

38. And it came to pass that the Lord of the vineyard said unto his servant: Let us go down into the ^{2a}nethermost parts of the vineyard, and behold if the natural branches have also brought forth evil fruit.

39. And it came to pass that they went down into the nethermost parts of the vineyard. And it came to pass that they beheld that the fruit of the natural branches had become corrupt also; yea, the ^{2b}first and the ^{2c}second and also the ^{2d}last; and they had all become corrupt.

40. And the ^{2e}wild fruit of the last had overcome that ^{2f}part of the tree which brought forth good fruit, even that the branch had withered away and died.

41. And it came to pass that the Lord of the vineyard ^{2g}wept, and said unto the servant: What could I have done more for my vineyard?

42. Behold, I knew that all the fruit of the vineyard, save it were these, had become corrupted. And now these which have once brought forth good fruit have also become corrupted; and now all the trees of my vineyard are good for ^{2h}nothing save it be to be hewn down and cast into the fire.

43. And behold this last, whose ^{2i}branch hath withered away, I did plant in a ^{2j}good spot of ground; yea, even that which was choice unto me above all other parts of the land of my vineyard.

44. And thou beheldest that I also cut down that which ^{2k}cumbered this spot of ground, that I might plant this tree in the stead thereof.

45. And thou beheldest that a ^{2l}part thereof brought forth good fruit, and a ^{2m}part thereof brought forth wild fruit; and because I plucked not the branches thereof and cast them into the fire, be-

---

y, see *c*. *z*, see *w*. 2*a*, see *h*. 2*b*, ver. 20. 2*c*, ver. 23. 2*d*, ver. 25. 2*e*, ver. 25. He. 15:4. 2*f*, ver. 25. He. 15:3. 2*g*, Isa. 5:4. 2*h*, see *w*. 2*i*, see *p*. 2*j*, ver. 25. 2*k*, Moro. 9:23. 2*l*, see *p*. 2*m*, see *q*.   BETWEEN B. C. 544 AND 421.

hold, they have overcome the good branch that it hath withered away.

46. And now, behold, notwithstanding all the care which we have taken of my vineyard, the trees thereof have become corrupted, that they bring forth ²ⁿno good fruit; and these I had hoped to preserve, to have laid up fruit thereof against the season, unto mine own self. But, behold, they have become like unto the wild olive-tree, and they are of ²ᵒno worth but to be hewn down and cast into the fire; and it grieveth me that I should lose them.

47. But what could I have done ²ᵖmore in my vineyard? Have I slackened mine hand, that I have not nourished it? Nay, I have nourished it, and I have digged about it, and I have pruned it, and I have dunged it; and I have stretched forth mine hand almost all the day long, and the ²qend draweth nigh. And it grieveth me that I should hew down all the trees of my vineyard, and cast them into the fire that they should be burned. Who is it that has corrupted my vineyard?

48. And it came to pass that the servant said unto his master: Is it not the loftiness of thy vineyard—have not the branches thereof overcome the roots which are good? And because the branches have overcome the roots thereof, behold they grew faster than the strength of the roots, taking strength unto themselves. Behold, I say, is not this the cause that the trees of thy vineyard have become corrupted?

49. And it came to pass that the Lord of the vineyard said unto the servant: Let us go to and hew down the trees of the vineyard and cast them into the fire, that they shall not cumber the ground of my vineyard, for I have done all. What could I have done ²ʳmore for my vineyard?

50. But, behold, the servant said unto the Lord of the vineyard: Spare it a little longer.

51. And the Lord said: Yea, I will spare it a little longer, for it grieveth me that I should lose the trees of my vineyard.

52. Wherefore, let us take of the ²ˢbranches of these which I have planted in the nethermost parts of my vineyard, and let us graft them into the ²ᵗtree from whence they came; and let us pluck from the tree those ²ᵘbranches whose fruit is most bitter, and graft in the natural branches of the tree in the stead thereof.

53. And this will I do that the tree may not perish, that, perhaps, I may preserve unto myself the roots thereof for mine own purpose.

54. And, behold, the ²ᵛroots of the natural branches of the tree which I planted whithersoever I would are yet alive; wherefore, that I may preserve them also for mine own purpose, I will take of the ²ʷbranches of this tree, and I will graft them in unto ²ˣthem. Yea, I will graft in unto them the branches of their mother tree, that I may preserve the ²ʸroots also unto mine own self, that when they shall be sufficiently strong perhaps they may bring forth good fruit unto me, and I may yet have glory in the fruit of my vineyard.

55. And it came to pass that they ²ᶻtook from the natural tree

2n, see w.   2o, 2 Ne. 20:33. Al. 5:52.   3 Ne. 27:11.   2p, vers. 41, 49.   2q, see u.
2r, vers. 41, 49.   2s, see d.   2t, see b.   2u, vers. 57, 65.   2v, vers. 11, 35, 37, 48, 54, 60.
2w, 3 Ne. 21:5, 6.   Morm. 5:15.   2x, see 2v.   2y, see 2v.   2z, see 2w.

BETWEEN B. C. 544 AND 421.

which had become wild, and grafted in unto the natural trees, which also had become wild.

56. And they also [3a]took of the natural trees which had become wild, and grafted into their mother tree.

57. And the Lord of the vineyard said unto the servant: Pluck not the wild branches from the trees, save it be those which are [3b]most bitter; and in them ye shall graft according to that which I have said.

58. And we will nourish again the trees of the vineyard, and we will trim up the branches thereof; and we will pluck from the trees those branches which [3c]are ripened, that must perish, and cast them into the fire.

59. And this I do that, perhaps, the roots thereof may take strength because of their goodness; and because of the change of the branches, that the good may overcome the evil.

60. And because that I have preserved the natural branches and the roots thereof, and that I have grafted in the natural branches again into their mother tree, and have preserved the roots of their mother tree, that, perhaps, the trees of my vineyard may bring forth again good fruit; and that I may have joy again in the fruit of my vineyard, and, perhaps, that I may rejoice exceedingly that I have preserved the [3d]roots and the branches of the first fruit—

61. Wherefore, go to, and call [3e]servants, that we may labor diligently with our might in the vineyard, that we may prepare the way, that I may bring forth again the natural fruit, which natural fruit is good and the most precious above all other fruit.

62. Wherefore, let us go to and labor with our might this [3f]last time, for behold the end draweth nigh, and this is for the last time that I shall prune my vineyard.

63. Graft in the branches; begin at the [3g]last that they may be first, and that the [3h]first may be last, and dig about the trees, both old and young, the first and the last; and the last and the first, that all may be nourished once again for the [3i]last time.

64. Wherefore, dig about them, and prune them, and dung them once more, for the last time, for the end draweth nigh. And if it be so that these last grafts shall grow, and bring forth the natural fruit, then shall ye prepare the way for them, that they may grow.

65. And as they begin to grow ye shall clear away the branches which bring forth [3j]bitter fruit, according to the strength of the good and the size thereof; and ye shall not clear away the bad thereof all at once, lest the roots thereof should be too strong for the graft, and the graft thereof shall perish, and I lose the trees of my vineyard.

66. For it grieveth me that I should lose the trees of my vineyard; wherefore ye shall clear away the bad according to the good shall grow, that the root and the top may be equal in strength, until the good shall overcome the bad, and the bad be hewn down and cast into the fire, that they cumber not the ground of my vineyard; and thus will I sweep away the bad out of my vineyard.

67. And the [3k]branches of the

3a, see 2v. 3b, vers. 58, 65, 66, 73, 74. 3c, see 3b. 3d, see 2v. 3e, vers. 70, 72, 74, 75. Jac. 6:2. 3f, see u. 3g, Matt. 20:10. 11:25, 26. 3h, D. & C. 88:51—62. 1 Ne. 13:42. 3i, see u. 3j, see 3b. 3k, ver. 56. BETWEEN B. C. 544 AND 421.

natural tree will I graft in again into the natural tree;

68. And the ³ᵗbranches of the natural tree will I graft into the natural branches of the tree; and thus will I bring them together again, that they shall bring forth the natural fruit, and they shall be ³ᵐone.

69. And the bad shall be cast away, yea, even out ³ⁿof all the land of my vineyard; for behold, only this once will I prune my vineyard.

70. And it came to pass that the Lord of the vineyard sent his ³ᵒservant; and the servant went and did as the Lord had commanded him, and brought ³ᵖother servants; and they were ³ᵠfew.

71. And the Lord of the vineyard said unto them: Go to, and ³ʳlabor in the vineyard, with your might. For behold, this is the last time that I shall nourish my vineyard; for the ³ˢend is nigh at hand, and the season speedily cometh; and if ye labor with your might with me ye shall have ³ᵗjoy in the fruit which I shall lay up unto myself against the time which will soon come.

72. And it came to pass that the ³ᵘservants did go and labor with their mights; and the Lord of the vineyard labored also with them; and they did obey the commandments of the Lord of the vineyard in all things.

73. And there began to be the natural fruit again in the vineyard; and the natural branches began to grow and thrive exceedingly; and the wild branches began to be plucked off and to be ³ᵛcast away; and they did keep the root and the top thereof ³ʷequal, according to the strength thereof.

74. And thus they labored, with all diligence, according to the commandments of the Lord of the vineyard, even until the ³ˣbad had been cast away out of the vineyard, and the Lord had preserved unto himself that the trees had become again the natural fruit; and they became like unto ³ʸone body; and the fruits were equal; and the Lord of the vineyard had preserved unto himself the natural fruit, which was most precious unto him from the beginning.

75. And it came to pass that when the Lord of the vineyard saw that his fruit was good, and that his vineyard was ³ᶻno more corrupt, he called up his servants, and said unto them: Behold, for this last time have we nourished my vineyard; and thou beholdest that I have done according to my will; and I have preserved the natural fruit, that it is good, even like as it was in the beginning. And blessed art thou; for because ye have been diligent in laboring with me in my vineyard, and have kept my commandments, and have brought unto me again the natural fruit, that my vineyard is no more corrupted, and the ⁴ᵃbad is cast away, behold ye shall have ⁴ᵇjoy with me because of the fruit of my vineyard.

76. For behold, for a ⁴ᶜlong time will I lay up of the fruit of my vineyard unto mine own self against the season, which speedily cometh; and for the ⁴ᵈlast time have I nourished my vineyard,

---

3*l*, ver. 55.   3*m*, vers. 66, 73, 74.   3*n*, vers. 66, 74, 75.   1 Ne. 22:15—17. 19—26. 2 Ne. 30:9, 10.   3*o*, D. & C. 101:55, 60.   103:21.   2 Ne. 27:9.   3*p*, see D. & C.   3*q*, 1 Ne. 14:12.   3*r*, D. & C. 6:3, 4.   11:3.   21:9.   24:19.   31:4, 5.   33:3, 4.   39:17.   43:28. 3*s*, see *u*.   3*t*, ver. 75.   1 Ne. 13:37, 38.   Jac. 6:3.   3*u*, see 3*p*.   3*v*, see 3*b*.   3*w*, see 3*m*.   3*x*, see 3*n*.   3*y*, see 3*m*.   3*z*, see 3*n*.   4*a*, see 3*n*.   4*b*, see 3*t*.   4*c*, D. & C. 101:62. 1 Ne. 22:26.   See *n*, 2 Ne. 30.   4*d*, see *u*.   BETWEEN B. C. 544 AND 421.

and pruned it, and dug about it, and dunged it; wherefore I will lay up unto mine own self of the fruit, for a long time, according to that which I have spoken.

77. And when the time cometh that evil fruit shall ^{4e}again come into my vineyard, then will I cause the good and the bad to be gathered; and the good will I preserve unto myself, and the bad will I cast away into its own place. And then cometh the season and the end; and my vineyard will I cause to be ^{4f}burned with fire.

CHAPTER 6.

Jacob expounds the allegory of the olive-tree—The pruning of the vineyard.

1. And now, behold, my brethren, as I said unto you that I would prophesy, behold, this is my prophecy—that the things which this prophet ^aZenos spake, concerning the house of Israel, in the which he likened them unto a ^btame olive-tree, must surely come to pass.

2. And the day that he shall set his hand again the ^csecond time to recover his people, is the day, yea, even the ^dlast time, that the servants of the Lord shall go forth in his ^epower, to nourish and prune his vineyard; and after that the ^fend soon cometh.

3. And how blessed are ^gthey who have labored diligently in his vineyard; and how ^hcursed are they who shall be cast out into their own place! And the world shall be ⁱburned with fire.

4. And how merciful is our God unto us, for he remembereth the house of Israel, both roots and branches; and he stretches forth his hands unto them all the day long; and they are a ^jstiffnecked and a gainsaying people; but as many as will not harden their hearts shall be saved in the kingdom of God.

5. Wherefore, my beloved brethren, I beseech of you in words of soberness that ye would repent, and come with full purpose of heart, and cleave unto God as he cleaveth unto you. And while his arm of mercy is extended towards you in the light of the day, harden not your hearts.

6. Yea, today, if ye will hear his voice, harden not your hearts; for why will ye die?

7. For behold, after ye have been nourished by the good word of God all the day long, will ye bring forth evil fruit, that ye must be hewn down and cast into the fire?

8. Behold, will ye reject these words? Will ye reject the words of the prophets; and will ye reject all the words which have been spoken concerning Christ, after so many have spoken concerning him; and deny the good word of Christ, and the power of God, and the gift of the Holy Ghost, and quench the Holy Spirit, and make a mock of the great plan of redemption, which hath been laid for you?

9. Know ye not that if ye will do these things, that the power of the redemption and the resurrection, which is in Christ, will bring you to stand with shame and ^kawful guilt before the bar of God?

10. And according to the power of justice, for justice cannot be denied, ye must go away into that

---

4*e*, Rev. 20:7, 8. 4*f*, Rev. 20:14, 15. Jac. 6:3. 3 Ne. 26:3, 4. D. & C. 29:23.
CHAP. 6: *a*, see *h*, 1 Ne. 19. *b*, see *b*, Jac. 5. *c*, see *i*, 2 Ne. 6. *d*, see *u*, Jac. 5.
e, see *t*, 1 Ne. 13. *f*, see *u*, Jac. 5. D. & C. 43:17—20, 28. *g*, see *t*, 1 Ne. 13. *h*, vers.
7—10. D. & C. 41:1. *i*, Jac. 5:77. 3 Ne. 26:3. *j*, see *k*, Jac. 4. *k*, Jac. 7:19. Mos.
15:26. Al. 39:5, 6. 3 Ne. 29:7.
BETWEEN B. C. 544 AND 421.

¹lake of fire and brimstone, whose flames are unquenchable, and whose smoke ascendeth up forever and ever, which lake of fire and brimstone is ᵐendless torment.

11. O then, my beloved brethren, repent ye, and enter in at the ⁿstrait gate, and continue in the way which is narrow, until ye shall obtain eternal life.

12. O be wise; what can I say more?

13. Finally, I bid you farewell, until I shall meet you before the ᵒpleasing bar of God, which bar striketh the wicked with awful dread and fear. Amen.

CHAPTER 7.

Sherem, denying the Christ, demands a sign and is stricken—He confesses his sin and dies—A reformation begins—Hatred of Lamanites for Nephites—Jacob gives the plates to his son Enos.

1. And now it came to pass after some years had passed away, there came a man among the people of Nephi, whose name was Sherem.

2. And it came to pass that he began to preach among the people, and to declare unto them that there should be no Christ. And he preached many things which were flattering unto the people; and this he did that he might overthrow the doctrine of Christ.

3. And he labored diligently that he might lead away the hearts of the people, insomuch that he did lead away many hearts; and he knowing that I, Jacob, had faith in Christ who should come, he sought much opportunity that he might come unto me.

4. And he was learned, that he had a perfect knowledge of the language of the people; wherefore, he could use much flattery, and much power of speech, according to the power of the devil.

5. And he had hope to shake me from the faith, notwithstanding the many revelations and the many things which I had seen concerning these things; for I truly had ᵃseen angels, and they had ministered unto me. And also, I had heard the voice of the Lord speaking unto me in very word, from time to time; wherefore, I could not be shaken.

6. And it came to pass that he came unto me, and on this wise did he speak unto me, saying: Brother Jacob, I have sought much opportunity that I might speak unto you; for I have heard and also know that thou goest about much, preaching that which ye call the gospel, or the doctrine of Christ.

7. And ye have led away much of this people that they pervert the right way of God, and keep not the law of Moses which is the right way; and convert the law of Moses into the worship of a being which ye say shall come many hundred years hence. And now behold, I, Sherem, declare unto you that this is blasphemy; for no man knoweth of such things; for he cannot tell of things to come. And after this manner did Sherem contend against me.

8. But behold, the Lord God poured in his Spirit into my soul, insomuch that I did confound him in all his words.

9. And I said unto him: Deniest

---

l, see *k*, 1 Ne. 15. *m*, D. & C. 19:10—12. Mos. 3:25, 27. 28:3. 1 Ne. 15:29, 30, 35. 2 Ne. 9:16, 19, 26. 28:23. Al. 12:17. 3 Ne. 27:11, 17. 29:7. Moro. 8:21. *n*, see 2*a*, 2 Ne. 9. *o*, Moro. 10:34. CHAP. 7: *a*, 2 Ne. 2:3, 4. 10:3. 11:3. Jac. 1:17. 2:11. 7:12. Al. 19:34. 24:14. He. 5:11. 13:37. 16:14. Moro. 7:22.

BETWEEN B. C. 544 AND 421.

thou the Christ who should come? And he said: If there should be a Christ, I would not deny him; but I know that there is no Christ, neither has been, nor ever will be.

10. And I said unto him: Believest thou the scriptures? And he said, Yea.

11. And I said unto him: Then ye do not understand them; for they truly testify of Christ. Behold, I say unto you that none of the prophets have written, nor prophesied, save they have spoken concerning this Christ.

12. And this is not all—it has been made manifest unto me, for I have heard and seen; and it also has been made manifest unto me by the power of the Holy Ghost; wherefore, I know if there should be no *b*atonement made all mankind must be lost.

13. And it came to pass that he said unto me: Show me a sign by this power of the Holy Ghost, in the which ye know so much.

14. And I said unto him: What am I that I should tempt God to show unto thee a sign in the thing which thou knowest to be true? Yet thou wilt deny it, because thou *c*art of the devil. Nevertheless, not my will be done; but if God shall smite thee, let that be a sign unto thee that he has power, both in heaven and in earth; and also, that Christ shall come. And thy will, O Lord, be done; and not mine.

15. And it came to pass that when I, Jacob, *d*had spoken these words, the power of the Lord came upon him, insomuch that he fell to the earth. And it came to pass that he was nourished for the space of many days.

16. And it came to pass that he said unto the people: Gather together on the morrow, *e*for I shall die; wherefore, I desire to speak unto the people before I shall die.

17. And it came to pass that on the morrow the multitude were gathered together; and he spake plainly unto them and denied the things which he had taught them, and confessed the Christ, and the power of the Holy Ghost, and the ministering of angels.

18. And he spake plainly unto them, that he had been deceived by the *f*power of the devil. And he spake of *g*hell, and of eternity, and of *h*eternal punishment.

19. And he said: I fear lest I have committed the *i*unpardonable sin, for I have lied unto God; for I denied the Christ, and said that I believed the scriptures; and they truly testify of him. And because I have thus lied unto God I greatly fear lest my case shall be awful; but I confess unto God.

20. And it came to pass that when he had said these words he could say no more, and he *j*gave up the ghost.

21. And when the *k*multitude had witnessed that he spake these things as he was about to give up the ghost, they were astonished exceedingly; insomuch that the power of God came down upon them, and they were overcome that they fell to the earth.

22. Now, this thing was pleasing unto me, Jacob, for I had requested it of my Father who was in heaven; for he had heard my cry and answered my prayer.

23. And it came to pass that peace and the love of God was restored again among the people; and they searched the *l*scriptures,

b, see f, 2 Ne. 2. c, vers. 4, 18. d, see c, Jac. 4. e, ver. 20. f, vers. 4, 14. g, see k, 1 Ne. 15. h, see m, Jac. 6. i, see k, Jac. 6. j, ver. 16. k, ver. 17. l, Al. 63:12. BETWEEN B. C. 544 AND 421.

and hearkened no more to the words of this wicked man.

24. And it came to pass that many means were devised to ᵐreclaim and restore the Lamanites to the knowledge of the truth; but it all was vain, for they delighted in wars and bloodshed, and they had an eternal ⁿhatred against us, their brethren. And they sought by the power of their arms to destroy us continually.

25. Wherefore, the people of Nephi did fortify against them with their armies, and with all their might, trusting in the God and rock of their salvation; wherefore, they became as yet, conquerors of their enemies.

26. And it came to pass that I, Jacob, began to be old; and the record of this people being kept on the ᵒother plates of Nephi, wherefore, I conclude this record, declaring that I have written according to the best of my knowledge, by saying that the time passed away with us, and also our lives passed away like as it were unto us a dream, we being a lonesome and a solemn people, wanderers, cast out from Jerusalem, born in tribulation, in a wilderness, and ᵖhated of our brethren, which caused wars and contentions; wherefore, we did mourn out our days.

27. And I, Jacob, saw that I must soon go down to my grave; wherefore, I said unto my son Enos: Take these ᵍplates. And I told him the ʳthings which my brother Nephi had commanded me, and he promised obedience unto the commands. And I make an end of my writing upon ˢthese plates, which writing has been small; and to the reader I bid farewell, hoping that many of my brethren may read my words. Brethren, adieu.

THE BOOK OF ENOS

The Lord's promise concerning a Nephite record to come forth to the Lamanites—Character, condition, and wars of the two peoples.

1. Behold, it came to pass that I, ᵃEnos, knowing my father that he was a just man—for he taught me in his language, and also in the nurture and admonition of the Lord—and blessed be the name of my God for it—

2. And I will tell you of the wrestle which I had before God, before I received a remission of my sins.

3. Behold, I went to hunt beasts in the forests; and the words which I had often heard my father speak concerning eternal life, and the joy of the saints, sunk deep into my heart.

4. And my soul hungered; and I kneeled down before my Maker, and I cried unto him in mighty prayer and supplication for mine own soul; and all the day long did I cry unto him; yea, and when the night came I did still raise my voice high that it reached the heavens.

5. And there came a voice unto me, saying: Enos, thy sins are forgiven thee, and thou shalt be blessed.

6. And I, Enos, knew that God

---

m, Enos 14, 20. n, ver. 26. Enos 14, 20. Jar. 6. Mos. 10:11—18, 28:2. Al. 26:23—25. o, see f, 1 Ne. 1. p, see n. q, see b, 1 Ne. 6. r, Jac. 1:1—4. s, see b, 1 Ne. 6. THE BOOK OF ENOS: a, Jac. 7:27. BETWEEN B. C. 544 AND 421.

could not lie; wherefore, my guilt was swept away.

7. And I said: Lord, how is it done?

8. And he said unto me: Because of thy faith in Christ, whom thou hast never before heard nor seen. And many years pass away before he shall manifest himself in the flesh; wherefore, go to, thy faith hath made thee whole.

9. Now, it came to pass that when I had heard these words I began to feel a desire for the welfare of my brethren, the Nephites; wherefore, I did pour out my whole soul unto God for them.

10. And while I was thus struggling in the spirit, behold, the voice of the Lord came into my mind again, saying: I will visit thy brethren according to their diligence in keeping my commandments. I have ^{b}given unto them this land, and it is a holy land; and I curse it not save it be for the cause of iniquity; wherefore, I will visit thy brethren according as I have said; and their transgressions will I bring down with sorrow upon their own heads.

11. And after I, Enos, had heard these words, my faith began to be unshaken in the Lord; and I prayed unto him with many long strugglings for my brethren, the Lamanites.

12. And it came to pass that after I had prayed and labored with all diligence, the Lord said unto me: I will grant unto thee according to thy desires, because of thy faith.

13. And now behold, this was the desire which I desired of him —that if it should so be, that my people, the Nephites, should fall into transgression, and by any means be destroyed, and the Lamanites should not be destroyed, that the Lord God would ^{c}preserve a record of my people, the Nephites; even if it so be by the power of his holy arm, that it might be brought forth at some future day unto the Lamanites, that, perhaps, they might be brought unto salvation—

14. For at the present our strugglings were ^{d}vain in restoring them to the true faith. And they swore in their wrath that, if it were possible, they would destroy our records and us, and also all the traditions of our fathers.

15. Wherefore, I knowing that the Lord God was able to preserve our records, I cried unto him continually, for he had said unto me: Whatsoever thing ye shall ask in faith, believing that ye shall receive in the name of Christ, ye shall receive it.

16. And I had faith, and I did cry unto God that he would ^{e}preserve the records; and he covenanted with me that he would ^{f}bring them forth unto the Lamanites in his own due time.

17. And I, Enos, knew it would be according to the covenant which he had made; wherefore my soul did rest.

18. And the Lord said unto me: Thy fathers have also required of me this thing; and it shall be done unto them according to their faith; for their faith was like unto thine.

19. And now it came to pass that I, Enos, went about among the people of Nephi, prophesying of things to come, and testifying of the things which I had heard and seen.

20. And I bear record that the people of Nephi did seek diligently

---

b, see a, 1 Ne. 2. c, vers. 15—18. See c, 2 Ne. 27. d, ver. 20. Jac. 7:24. e, ver. 13. f, see c, 2 Ne. 27. D. & C. 3:18—20. 10:48—51. BETWEEN B. C. 544 AND 421.

to ᵍrestore the Lamanites unto the true faith in God. But our labors were vain; their ʰhatred was fixed, and they were led by their evil nature that they became wild, and ferocious, and a bloodthirsty people, full of idolatry and filthiness; feeding upon beasts of prey; dwelling in tents, and wandering about in the wilderness with a short skin girdle about their loins and their heads shaven; and their skill was in the bow, and in the cimeter, and the ax. And many of them did eat nothing save it was raw meat; and they were continually seeking to destroy us.

21. And it came to pass that the people of Nephi did till the land, and ⁱraise all manner of grain, and of fruit, and flocks of herds, and flocks of all manner of cattle of every kind, and goats, and wild goats, and also many horses.

22. And there were exceeding many prophets among us. And the people were a stiffnecked people, hard to understand.

23. And there was nothing save it was ʲexceeding harshness, preaching and prophesying of wars, and contentions, and destructions, and continually reminding them of death, and the duration of eternity, and the judgments and the power of God, and all these things—stirring them up continually to keep them in the fear of the Lord. I say there was nothing short of these things, and exceeding great plainness of speech, would keep them from going down speedily to destruction. And after this manner do I write concerning them.

24. And I saw wars between the Nephites and Lamanites in the course of my days.

25. And it came to pass that I began to be old, *and an hundred and seventy and nine years had passed away from the time that our father Lehi ᵏleft Jerusalem.

26. And I saw that I must soon go down to my grave, having been wrought upon by the power of God that I must preach and prophesy unto this people, and declare the word according to the truth which is in Christ. And I have declared it in all my days, and have rejoiced in it above that of the world.

27. And I soon go to the place of my rest, which is with my Redeemer; for I know that in him I shall rest. And I rejoice in the day when my mortal shall put on ˡimmortality, and shall stand before him; then shall I see his face with pleasure, and he will say unto me: Come unto me, ye blessed, there is a place prepared for you in the ᵐmansions of my Father. Amen.

THE BOOK OF JAROM

Jarom, son of Enos, keeps the records—The Nephites serve the Lord and are prospered.

1. Now behold, I, Jarom, write a few words according to the commandment of my father, Enos, that our genealogy may be kept.

2. And as ᵃthese plates are small, and as these things are written for the intent of the benefit of our brethren the ᵇLamanites, wherefore, it must needs be that I write a little; but I shall not write the things of my prophesy-

---

g, ver. 14. Jac. 7:24. h, see n, Jac. 7. i, 1 Ne. 18:25. j, see a, 1 Ne. 16. k, 1 Ne. 1:4. 2:2. 3. l, see d, 2 Ne. 2. 1 Cor. 15:53. 2 Tim. 1:10. m, Eth. 12:32—34. D. & C. 72:4. 98:18. John 14:2, 3. THE BOOK OF JAROM: a, see b, 1 Ne. 6. b, see c, 2 Ne. 27. • B. C. 420.

ing, nor of my revelations. For what could I write more than my fathers have written? For have not they revealed the plan of salvation? I say unto you, Yea; and this sufficeth me.

3. Behold, it is expedient that much should be done among this people, ^cbecause of the hardness of their hearts, and the deafness of their ears, and the blindness of their minds, and the stiffness of their necks; nevertheless, God is exceeding merciful unto them, and has not as yet swept them off from the face of the land.

4. And there are many among us who have many revelations, for they are not all stiffnecked. And as many as are not stiffnecked and have faith, have communion with the Holy Spirit, which maketh manifest unto the children of men, according to their faith.

5. And now, behold, *two hundred years had passed away, and the people of Nephi had waxed strong in the land. They observed to ^dkeep the law of Moses and the sabbath day holy unto the Lord. And they profaned not; neither did they blaspheme. And the laws of the land were exceedingly strict.

6. And they were scattered upon much of the face of the land, and the Lamanites also. And they were exceeding more numerous than were they of the Nephites; and they ^eloved murder and would drink the blood of beasts.

7. And it came to pass that they came many times against us, the Nephites, to battle. But our kings and our leaders were mighty men in the faith of the Lord; and they taught the people the ways of the Lord; wherefore, we withstood the Lamanites and swept them away out of our lands, and began to fortify our cities, or whatsoever place of our inheritance.

8. And we multiplied exceedingly, and spread upon the face of the land, and became exceeding ^frich in gold, and in silver, and in precious things, and in fine workmanship of wood, in buildings, and in machinery, and also in iron and copper, and brass and steel, making all manner of tools of every kind to till the ground, and weapons of war—yea, the sharp pointed arrow, and the quiver, and the dart, and the javelin, and all preparations for war.

9. And thus being prepared to meet the Lamanites, they did not prosper against us. But the word of the Lord was verified, which he spake unto our fathers, saying that: ^gInasmuch as ye will keep my commandments ye shall prosper in the land.

10. And it came to pass that the prophets of the Lord did threaten the people of Nephi, according to the word of God, that if they did not keep the commandments, but should fall into transgression, they should be ^hdestroyed from off the face of the land.

11. Wherefore, the prophets, and the priests, and the teachers, did labor diligently, exhorting with all long-suffering the people to diligence; teaching the ⁱlaw of Moses, and the intent for which it was given; persuading them to look forward unto the Messiah, and believe in him to come as though he already was. And after this manner did they teach them.

c, Enos 23. d, see o, 2 Ne. 25. e, see n, Jac. 7. Enos 20. f, see n, 1 Ne. 18. g, see h, 2 Ne. 1. h, 1 Ne. 12:19, 20. Al. 45:10—14, He. 13:5—10. 3 Ne. 27:32. Morm. 6. i, see o, 2 Ne. 25.   * B. C. 399.

12. And it came to pass that by so doing they kept them from being destroyed upon the face of the land; for they did prick their hearts with the word, continually stirring them up unto repentance.

13. And it came to pass that *two hundred and thirty and eight years had passed away—after the manner of wars, and contentions, and dissensions, for the space of much of the time.

14. And I, Jarom, do not write more, for the plates are small. But behold, my brethren, ye can go to the ʲother plates of Nephi; for behold, upon them the records of our wars are engraven, according to the writings of the kings, or those which they caused to be written.

15. And I deliver these plates into the hands of my son Omni, that they may be kept according to the commandments of my fathers.

THE BOOK OF OMNI

Comprising records kept by Omni, Amaron, Chemish, Abinadom, and Amaleki—Mosiah, leaving the land of Nephi, discovers the land of Zarahemla, occupied by another colony from Jerusalem—He is made king—Coriantumr, the last of the Jaredites—King Benjamin—Other migrations.

1. Behold, it came to pass that I, Omni, being commanded by my father, Jarom, that I should write somewhat upon ᵃthese plates, to preserve our genealogy—

2. Wherefore, in my days, I would that ye should know that I fought much with the sword to preserve my people, the Nephites, from falling into the hands of their enemies, the Lamanites. But behold, I of myself am a wicked man, and I have not kept the statutes and the commandments of the Lord as I ought to have done.

3. And it came to pass that †two hundred and seventy and six years had passed away, and we had many seasons of peace; and we had many seasons of serious war and bloodshed. Yea, and in fine, ‡two hundred and eighty and two years had passed away, and I had kept these plates according to the ᵇcommandments of my fathers; and I conferred them upon my son Amaron. And I make an end.

4. And now I, Amaron, write the things whatsoever I write, which are few, in the book of my father.

5. Behold, it came to pass that §three hundred and twenty years had passed away, and the ᶜmore wicked part of the Nephites were destroyed.

6. For the Lord would not suffer, after he had led them out of the land of Jerusalem and kept and preserved them from falling into the hands of their enemies, yea, he would not suffer that the words should not be verified, which he spake unto our fathers, saying that: ᵈInasmuch as ye will not keep my commandments ye shall not prosper in the land.

7. Wherefore, the Lord did visit them in great judgment; nevertheless, he did spare the righteous that they should not perish, but did deliver them out of the hands of their enemies.

j, see *b,* 1 Ne. 6; also *f,* 1 Ne. 1.   THE BOOK OF OMNI: *a,* see *b,* 1 Ne. 6.   *b,* Jac. 1:1—4.   7:27.   Jar. 1, 2, 15.   *c,* Jar. 10.   *d,* see *h,* 2 Ne. 1.
* B. C. 361.   † B. C. 323.   ‡ B. C. 317.   § B. C. 279.

8. And it came to pass that I did deliver the plates unto my brother Chemish.

9. Now I, Chemish, write what few things I write, *e*in the same book with my brother; for behold, I saw the last which he wrote, that he wrote it with his own hand; and he wrote it in the day that he delivered them unto me. And after this manner we keep the *f*records, for it is according to the commandments of our fathers. And I make an end.

10. Behold, I, Abinadom, am the son of Chemish. Behold, it came to pass that I saw much war and contention between my people, the Nephites, and the Lamanites; and I, with my own sword, have taken the lives of many of the Lamanites in the defence of my brethren.

11. And behold, the record of this people is engraven upon plates which is had by the kings, according to the generations; and I know of no revelation save that which has been written, neither prophecy; wherefore, that which is sufficient is written. And I make an end.

12. Behold, I am Amaleki, the son of Abinadom. Behold, I will speak unto you somewhat concerning Mosiah, who was made king over the land of Zarahemla; for behold, he being warned of the Lord that he should flee out of the land of *g*Nephi, and as many as would hearken unto the voice of the Lord should also depart out of the land with him, into the wilderness—

13. And it came to pass that he did according as the Lord had commanded him. And they departed out of the land into the wilderness, as many as would hearken unto the voice of the Lord; and they were led by many preachings and prophesyings. And they were admonished continually by the word of God; and they were led by the power of his arm, through the wilderness, until they came down into the land which is called the land of *h*Zarahemla.

14. And they discovered a people, who were called the *i*people of Zarahemla. Now, there was great rejoicing among the people of Zarahemla; and also Zarahemla did rejoice exceedingly, because the Lord had sent the people of Mosiah with the *j*plates of brass which contained the record of the Jews.

15. Behold, it came to pass that Mosiah discovered that the people of Zarahemla came out from Jerusalem at the *k*time that Zedekiah, king of Judah, was carried away captive into Babylon.

16. And they journeyed in the wilderness, and were brought by the hand of the Lord across the great waters, into the land where Mosiah *l*discovered them; and they had dwelt there from that time forth.

17. And at the time that Mosiah discovered them, they had become exceeding numerous. Nevertheless, they had had many wars and serious contentions, and had fallen by the sword from time to time; and their language had become *m*corrupted; and they had brought no records with them; and they had denied the being of their Creator; and Mosiah, nor the people of Mosiah, could understand them.

18. But it came to pass that

---

e, see *b*. *f*, see *f*, 1 Ne. 1. *g*, see *b*, 2 Ne. 5. *h*, Al. 2:15. *i*, vers. 15—19. Mos. 25:2—4. Al. 22:30—32. He. 6:10. 8:21. *j*, see *a*, 1 Ne. 3. *k*, 2 Kings 25:1—7. See *i*. *l*, ver. 14. *m*, ver. 18.
BETWEEN B. C. 270 AND 130.

Mosiah caused that they should be taught in his language. And it came to pass that after they were taught in the language of Mosiah, Zarahemla gave a genealogy of his fathers, according to his memory; and they are written, but ⁿnot in these plates.

19. And it came to pass that the people of Zarahemla, and of Mosiah, did unite together; and Mosiah was appointed to be °their king.

20. And it came to pass in the days of Mosiah, there was a large stone brought unto him ᵖwith engravings on it; and he did ᑫinterpret the engravings by the gift and power of God.

21. And they gave an account of one ʳCoriantumr, and the slain of his people. And Coriantumr was ˢdiscovered by the ᵗpeople of Zarahemla; and he dwelt with them for the space of nine moons.

22. It also spake a few words concerning his fathers. And his first parents came out from the ᵘtower, at the time the Lord confounded the language of the people; and the severity of the Lord fell upon them according to his judgments, which are just; and their ᵛbones lay scattered in the land northward.

23. Behold, I, Amaleki, was born in the days of Mosiah; and I have lived to see his death; and Benjamin, his son, reigneth in his stead.

24. And behold, I have seen, in the days of king Benjamin, a serious war and much bloodshed between the Nephites and the Lamanites. But behold, the Nephites did obtain much advantage over them; yea, insomuch that king Benjamin did drive them out of the ʷland of Zarahemla.

25. And it came to pass that I began to be old; and, having no seed, and knowing king Benjamin to be a just man before the Lord, wherefore, I shall deliver up ˣthese plates unto him, exhorting all men to come unto God, the Holy One of Israel, and believe in prophesying, and in revelations, and in the ministering of angels, and in the gift of speaking with tongues, and in the gift of interpreting languages, and in all things which are good; for there is nothing which is good save it comes from the Lord; and that which is evil cometh from the devil.

26. And now, my beloved brethren, I would that ye should come unto Christ, who is the Holy One of Israel, and partake of his salvation, and the power of his redemption. Yea, come unto him, and offer your whole souls as an offering unto him, and continue in fasting and ʸpraying, and endure to the end; and as the Lord liveth ye will be saved.

27. And now I would speak somewhat concerning a certain number who went up into the wilderness to return to the land of ᶻNephi; for there was a large number who were desirous to possess the land of their inheritance.

28. Wherefore, they went up into the wilderness. And their leader being a strong and mighty man, and a stiffnecked man, wherefore he caused a contention among them; and ²ᵃthey were all slain, save fifty, in the wilderness, and

---

n, see j.　o, ver. 12.　p, ver. 21.　q, Mos. 8:13—18.　r, Eth. 12:1—3.　13:1, 2, 13—31.　Chaps. 14, 15.　s, Eth. 11:20, 21.　13:21.　t, see i.　u, Mos. 28:17.　Eth. 1:1—6.　Gen. 11:1—9.　v, Mos. 8:8—12.　See q.　w, see h.　x, see b, 1 Ne. 6. y, see e, 2 Ne. 32.　z, see b, 2 Ne. 5.　2a, Mos. 9:1, 2, 4.　Bet. B. C. 279 and 130.

they returned again to the ²ᵇland of Zarahemla.

29. And it came to pass that they also took ²ᶜothers to a considerable number, and took their journey again into the wilderness.

30. And I, Amaleki, had a brother, who also went with them; and I have not since known concerning them. And I am about to lie down in my grave; and these plates are ²ᵈfull. And I make an end of my speaking.

THE WORDS OF MORMON

Mormon's abridgment and the smaller plates of Nephi—Relation of the foregoing part of the Book of Mormon to that which follows.

1. And now I, Mormon, being about to deliver up the ᵃrecord which I have been making into the hands of my son Moroni, behold I have witnessed almost all the destruction of my people, the Nephites.

2. And it is ᵇmany hundred years after the coming of Christ *that I deliver these records into the ᶜhands of my son; and it supposeth me that he will witness the entire destruction of my people. But may God grant that he may survive them, that ᵈhe may write somewhat concerning them, and somewhat concerning Christ, that perhaps some day it may profit them.

3. And now, I speak somewhat concerning that which I have written; for after I had made an ᵉabridgment from the ᶠplates of Nephi, down to the ᵍreign of this king Benjamin, of whom Amaleki spake, I searched among the ʰrecords which had been delivered into my hands, and I found ⁱthese plates, which contained this small account of the prophets, from Jacob down to the reign of this king Benjamin, and also ᵏmany of the words of Nephi.

4. And the things which are upon these plates pleasing me, because of the prophecies of the coming of Christ; and my fathers knowing that many of them have been fulfilled; yea, and I also know that as many things as have been prophesied concerning us down to this day have been fulfilled, and as many as go beyond this day must surely come to pass—

5. Wherefore, I chose ˡthese things, to finish my record upon them, which remainder of my ᵐrecord I shall take from the ⁿplates of Nephi; and I cannot write the ᵒhundredth part of the things of my people.

6. But behold, I shall take ᵖthese plates, which contain these prophesyings and revelations, and put them with the remainder of my ᵠrecord, for they are choice unto me; and I know they will be choice unto my brethren.

7. And I do this for a ʳwise purpose; for thus it whispereth me, according to the workings of the Spirit of the Lord which is in me. And now, I do not know all

---

2b, see h. 2c, Mos. 9:3, 4. 2d, vers. 11, 19. THE WORDS OF MORMON: a, 3 Ne. 5:10. Morm. 1:1—4. 2:17, 18. 5:9. 6:1, 6. 8:1, 4, 5, 14—16. 9:32—36. Moro. 9:23, 24. 10:1—5. b, Morm. 6:5. c, Morm. 6:6. d, Morm. 8:1—8. e, Morm. 5:9. f, see f, 1 Ne. 1. g, Om. 23—25. h, Morm. 4:23. i, see b, 1 Ne. 6. k, see 1 and 2 Ne. l, ver. 6. m, 3 Ne. 5:14—18. Morm. 1:1. n, 1 Ne. 9:2. See f. See ver. 3; also see f, 1 Ne. 1. o, ver. 3. 3 Ne. 5:8—11. 26:6—12. Morm. 5:9. p, ver. 5. q, see c. r, D. & C. 3, 10. *ABOUT A. D. 385.

things; but the Lord knoweth all things which are to come; wherefore, he worketh in me to do according to his will.

8. And my prayer to God is concerning my brethren, that they may once again come to the knowledge of God, yea, the redemption of Christ; that they may once again be a *delightsome people.

9. And now I, Mormon, *proceed to finish out my ᵘrecord, which I take from the plates of Nephi; and I make it according to the knowledge and the understanding which God has given me.

10. Wherefore, it came to pass that after Amaleki had delivered up ᵛthese plates into the hands of king Benjamin, he took them and put them with the ʷother plates, which contained records which had been handed down by the kings, from generation to generation until the days of king Benjamin.

11. And they were handed down from king Benjamin, from generation to generation until they have fallen into ˣmy hands. And I, Mormon, pray to God that they may be preserved from this time henceforth. And I know that they will be preserved; for there are great things written upon them, out of which ʸmy people and ᶻtheir brethren shall be ²ᵃjudged at the great and last day, according to the word of God which is written.

12. And now, concerning this king Benjamin—he had somewhat of contentions among his own people.

13. And it came to pass also that the armies of the Lamanites came down out of the ²ᵇland of Nephi, to battle against his people. But behold, king Benjamin gathered together his armies, and he did stand against them; and he did fight with the strength of his own arm, with the ²ᶜsword of Laban.

14. And in the strength of the Lord they did contend against their enemies, until they had slain many thousands of the Lamanites. And it came to pass that they did contend against the Lamanites until they had driven them out of all the lands of their inheritance.

15. And it came to pass that after there had been false Christs, and their mouths had been shut, and they punished according to their crimes;

16. And after there had been false prophets, and false preachers and teachers among the people, and all these having been punished according to their crimes; and after there having been much contention and many dissensions away unto the Lamanites, behold, it came to pass that king Benjamin, with the assistance of the holy prophets who were among his people—

17. For behold, king Benjamin was a holy man, and he did reign over his people in righteousness; and there were many holy men in the land, and they did speak the word of God with power and with authority; and they did use much ²ᵈsharpness because of the stiffneckedness of the people—

18. Wherefore, with the help of these, king Benjamin, by laboring with all the might of his body and the faculty of his whole soul, and also the prophets, did once more establish peace in the land.

t, 2 Ne. 30:6. *u*, ver. 3. *v*, see *p*. *w*, see *f*. *x*, 3 Ne. 5:8—11. Morm. 4:23. *y*, He. 15:3. See *p*, Jac. 5. *z*, He. 15:4. See *q*, Jac. 5. 2*a*, 2 Ne. 25:18, 29:11. 33:11, 14, 15. 3 Ne. 27:23—27. Eth. 4:8—10. 5:4. 2*b*, see *b*, 2 Ne. 5. 2*c*, see *a*, 1 Ne. 4. 2*d*, see *a*, 1 Ne. 16. * About A. D. 385.

THE BOOK OF MOSIAH

CHAPTER 1.

King Benjamin's exhortation to his sons—Mosiah chosen to succeed his father—Mosiah receives the records, etc.

1. And now there was no more contention in all the ªland of Zarahemla, among all the people who belonged to king Benjamin, so that king Benjamin had continual peace all the remainder of his days.

2. And it came to pass that he had three sons; and he called their names Mosiah, and Helorum, and Helaman. And he caused that they should be taught in ᵇall the language of his fathers, that thereby they might become men of understanding; and that they might know concerning the prophecies which had been spoken by the mouths of their fathers, which were delivered them by the hand of the Lord.

3. And he also taught them concerning the records which were engraven on the ᶜplates of brass, saying: My sons, I would that ye should remember that were it not for these plates, which contain these records and these commandments, we must have suffered in ignorance, even at this present time, not knowing the mysteries of God.

4. For it were not possible that our father, Lehi, could have remembered all these things, to have taught them to his children, except it were for the help of these plates; for he having been ᵈtaught in the language of the Egyptians therefore he could read these engravings, and teach them to his children, that thereby they could teach them to their children, and so fulfilling the commandments of God, even down to this present time.

5. I say unto you, my sons, were it not for these things, which have been kept and preserved by the hand of God, that we might read and understand of his mysteries, and have his commandments always before our eyes, that even our fathers would have dwindled in unbelief, and we should have been like unto our brethren, the Lamanites, who know nothing concerning these things, or even do not believe them when they are taught them, because of the ᵉtraditions of their fathers, which are not correct.

6. O my sons, I would that ye should remember that these sayings are true, and also that these records are true. And behold, also the plates of Nephi, which contain the records and the sayings of our fathers from the time they left Jerusalem until now, and they are true; and we can know of their surety because we have them before our eyes.

7. And now, my sons, I would that ye should remember to search them diligently, that ye may profit thereby; and I would that ye should keep the commandments of God, that ye may prosper in the land according to the ᶠpromises which the Lord made unto our fathers.

8. And many more things did king Benjamin teach his sons, which are not written in this book.

---

a, Om. 13. *b*, ver. 4. 1 Ne. 1:2. Morm. 9:32. *c*, see *a*, 1 Ne. 3. *d*, see *b*. *e*, see *n*, Jac. 7. Al. 19:14. *f*, see *h*, 2 Ne. 1. ABOUT B. C. 130.

MOSIAH, 1.

9. And it came to pass that after king Benjamin had made an end of teaching his sons, that he waxed old, and he saw that he must very soon go the way of all the earth; therefore, he thought it expedient that he should confer the kingdom upon one of his sons.

10. Therefore, *he had Mosiah brought before him; and these are the words which he spake unto him, saying: My son, I would that ye should make a proclamation throughout all this land among all this people, or the ^gpeople of Zarahemla, and the ^hpeople of Mosiah who dwell in the land, that thereby they may be gathered together; for on the morrow I shall proclaim unto this my people out of mine own mouth that ⁱthou art a king and a ruler over this people, whom the Lord our God hath given us.

11. And moreover, I shall give this people a ^jname, that thereby they may be distinguished above all the people which the Lord God hath brought out of the land of Jerusalem; and this I do because they have been a diligent people in keeping the commandments of the Lord.

12. And I give unto them a name that never shall be blotted out, except it be through transgression.

13. Yea, and moreover I say unto you, that if this highly favored people of the Lord should fall into transgression, and become a wicked and an adulterous people, that the Lord will deliver them up, that thereby they become weak like unto their brethren; and he will no more preserve them by his matchless and marvelous power, as he has hitherto preserved our fathers.

14. For I say unto you, that if he had not extended his arm in the preservation of our fathers they must have fallen into the hands of the Lamanites, and become victims to their hatred.

15. And it came to pass that after king Benjamin had made an end of these sayings to his son, that he gave him charge concerning all the affairs of the kingdom.

16. And moreover, he also gave him charge concerning the records which were engraven on the ^kplates of brass; and also ^lthe plates of Nephi; and also, the ^msword of Laban, and the ⁿball or director, which led our fathers through the wilderness, which was prepared by the hand of the Lord that thereby they might be led, every one according to the heed and diligence which they gave unto him.

17. Therefore, as they were unfaithful they did not prosper nor progress in their journey, but were ^odriven back, and incurred the displeasure of God upon them; and therefore they were smitten with famine and sore afflictions, to stir them up in remembrance of their duty.

18. And now, it came to pass that Mosiah went and did as his father ^phad commanded him, and proclaimed unto all the people who were in the ^qland of Zarahemla that thereby they might gather themselves together, to go up to the ^rtemple to hear the words which his father should speak unto them.

---

g, Om. 14. *h*, see *p*. Mos. 27:35. 28:18. 29:40. He. 15:3. *i*, Mos. 2:30. 6:3, 4. *j*, ver. 12. Mos. 5:11. *k*, see *a*, 1 Ne. 3. *l*, see *f*, 1 Ne. 1. *m*, see *a*, 1. Ne. 4. *n*, see *d*, 1 Ne. 16. *o*, 1 Ne. 18:12, 13. *p*, ver. 10. Mos. 2:1. *q*, Om. 13. *r*, see *h*, 2 Ne. 5. * ABOUT B. C. 124.

CHAPTER 2.

King Benjamin builds a tower from which he addresses his people—The righteous reign of a God-fearing king.

1. And it came to pass that after Mosiah had done as his father ªhad commanded him, and had made a proclamation throughout all the land, that the people gathered themselves together throughout all the land, that they might go up to the ᵇtemple to hear the words which king Benjamin should speak unto them.

2. And there were a great number, even so many that they did not number them; for they had multiplied exceedingly and waxed great in the land.

3. And they also took of the firstlings of their flocks, that they might offer sacrifice and burnt offerings according to the ᶜlaw of Moses;

4. And also that they might give thanks to the Lord their God, who had brought them out of the land of Jerusalem, and who had delivered them out of the hands of their enemies, and had appointed just men to be their teachers, and also a just man to be their king, who had established peace in the ᵈland of Zarahemla, and who had taught them to keep the commandments of God, that they might rejoice and be filled with love towards God and all men.

5. And it came to pass that when they came up to the ᵉtemple, they pitched their tents round about, every man according to his family, consisting of his wife, and his sons, and his daughters, and their sons, and their daughters, from the eldest down to the youngest, every family being separate one from another.

6. And they pitched their tents round about the ᶠtemple, every man having his tent with the door thereof towards the temple, that thereby they might remain in their tents and hear the words which king Benjamin should speak unto them;

7. For the multitude being so great that king Benjamin could not teach them all within the walls of the temple, therefore he caused a ᵍtower to be erected, that thereby his people might hear the words which he should speak unto them.

8. And it came to pass that he began to speak to his people from the tower; and they could not all hear his words because of the greatness of the multitude; therefore he caused that the words which he spake should be written and sent forth among those that were not under the sound of his voice, that they might also receive his words.

9. And these are the words which he spake and caused to be written, saying: My brethren, all ye that have assembled yourselves together, you that can hear my words which I shall speak unto you this day; for I have not commanded you to come up hither to trifle with the words which I shall speak, but that you should hearken unto me, and open your ears that ye may hear, and your hearts that ye may understand, and your minds that the mysteries of God may be unfolded to your view.

10. I have not commanded you to come up hither that ye should fear me, or that ye should think that I of myself am more than a mortal man.

11. But I am like as yourselves,

---

a, Mos. 1:10, 18. *b*, see *h*, 2 Ne. 5. *c*, see *o*, 2 Ne. 25. *d*, Om. 13. *e*, see *h*, 2 Ne. 5. *f*, see *h*, 2 Ne. 5. *g*, ver. 8.

ABOUT B. C. 124.

MOSIAH, 2.

subject to all manner of infirmities in body and mind; yet I have been chosen by this people, and consecrated by ʰmy father, and was suffered by the hand of the Lord that I should be a ruler and a king over this people; and have been kept and preserved by his matchless power, to ⁱserve you with all the might, mind and strength which the Lord hath granted unto me.

12. I say unto you that as I have been suffered to spend my days in your service, even up to this time, and have not sought gold nor silver nor any manner of riches of you;

13. Neither have I suffered that ye should be confined in dungeons, nor that ye should make slaves one of another, nor that ye should murder, or plunder, or steal, or commit adultery; nor even have I suffered that ye should commit any manner of wickedness, and have taught you that ye should keep the commandments of the Lord, in all things which he hath commanded you—

14. And even I, myself, have labored with mine own hands that I might serve you, and that ye should not be laden with taxes, and that there should nothing come upon you which was grievous to be borne—and of all these things which I have spoken, ye yourselves are witnesses this day.

15. Yet, my brethren, I have not done these things that I might boast, neither do I tell these things that thereby I might accuse you; but I tell you these things that ye may know that I can answer a clear conscience before God this day.

16. Behold, I say unto you that because I said unto you that I had spent my days in your ʲservice, I do not desire to boast, for I have only been in the service of God.

17. And behold, I tell you these things that ye may learn wisdom; that ye may learn that when ye are in the service of your fellow beings ye are only in the service of your God.

18. Behold, ye have called me your king; and if I, whom ye call your king, do labor to serve you, then ought not ye to labor to serve one another?

19. And behold also, if I, whom ye call your king, who has spent his days in ᵏyour service, and yet has been in the service of God, do merit any thanks from you, O how you ought to thank your heavenly King!

20. I say unto you, my brethren, that if you should render all the thanks and praise which your whole soul has power to possess, to that God who has created you, and has kept and preserved you, and has caused that ye should rejoice, and has granted that ye should live in peace one with another—

21. I say unto you that if ye should serve him who has created you from the beginning, and is preserving you from day to day, by lending you breath, that ye may live and move and do according to your own will, and even supporting you from one moment to another—I say, if ye should serve him with all your whole souls yet ye would be unprofitable servants.

22. And behold, all that he requires of you is to keep his commandments; and he has ˡpromised you that if ye would keep his commandments ye should prosper in the land; and he never doth

---

h, Om. 23, 24. *i*, vers. 14, 16—19. *j*, vers. 11, 17—19. *k*, vers. 11, 16—18. *l*, see *h*, 2 Ne. 1. ABOUT B. C. 124.

vary from that which he hath said; therefore, if ye do keep his commandments he doth bless you and prosper you.

23. And now, in the first place, he hath created you, and granted unto you your lives, for which ye are indebted unto him.

24. And secondly, he doth require that ye should do as he hath commanded you; for which if ye do, he doth immediately bless you; and therefore he hath paid you. And ye are still indebted unto him, and are, and will be, forever and ever; therefore, of what have ye to boast?

25. And now I ask, can ye say aught of yourselves? I answer you, Nay. Ye cannot say that ye are even as much as the dust of the earth; yet ye were created of the ᵐdust of the earth; but behold, it belongeth to him who created you.

26. And I, even I, whom ye call your king, am no better than ye yourselves are; for I am also of the dust. And ye behold that I am old, and am about to yield up this mortal frame to its mother earth.

27. Therefore, as I said unto you that I had ⁿserved you, walking with a clear conscience before God, even so I at this time have caused that ye should assemble yourselves together, that I might be found blameless, and that your blood should not come upon me, when I shall stand to be judged of God of the things whereof he hath commanded me concerning you.

28. I say unto you that I have caused that ye should assemble yourselves together that I might rid my garments of your blood, at this period of time when I am about to go down to my grave, that I might go down in peace, and my immortal spirit may join the ᵒchoirs above in singing the praises of a just God.

29. And moreover, I say unto you that I have caused that ye should assemble yourselves together, that I might declare unto you that I can no longer be your teacher, nor your king;

30. For even at this time, my whole frame doth tremble exceedingly while attempting to speak unto you; but the Lord God doth support me, and hath suffered me that I should speak unto you, and hath commanded me that I should declare unto you this day, that my son Mosiah is a ᵖking and a ruler over you.

31. And now, my brethren, I would that ye should do as ye have hitherto done. As ye have kept my commandments, and also the commandments of my father, and have prospered, and have been kept from falling into the hands of your enemies, even so if ye shall keep the commandments of my son, or the commandments of God which shall be delivered unto you by him, ye shall prosper in the land, and your enemies shall have no power over you.

32. But, O my people, beware lest there shall arise contentions among you, and ye list to obey the ᑫevil spirit, which was spoken of by my father Mosiah.

33. For behold, there is a wo pronounced upon him who listeth to obey that spirit; for if he

m, 2 Ne. 2:15. 29:7. Jac. 2:21. 4:9. Mos. 4:21. 7:27. 28:17. Al. 18:28, 34, 36. 22:10—13. 42:2. Morm. 6:15. 9:11, 12, 17. Eth. 3:15, 16. Moro. 10:3. Gen. 2:7. 3:19. *n*, vers. 11, 12. 14—19. *o*, Morm. 7:7. *p*, Mos. 1:10. 6:3, 4. *q*, see *i*, 2 Ne. 2. 9:39. 18:19. 28:20—22. 32:8. Mos. 2:37. 3:6. 4:14. 16:3. Al. 3:26, 27. 5:20, 39—42. 30:42, 53. 34:34, 35, 39. 40:13, 14. He. 7:15, 16. 13:37. 3 Ne. 27:11, 32. Morm. 1:19. 5:18. Moro. 7:11—14, 17. 10:30. ABOUT B. C. 124.

listeth to obey him, and remaineth and dieth in his sins, the same drinketh damnation to his own soul; for he receiveth for his wages an ʳeverlasting punishment, having transgressed the law of God contrary to his own knowledge.

34. I say unto you, that there are not any among you, except it be your little children that have not been taught concerning these things, but what knoweth that ye are eternally indebted to your heavenly Father, to render to him all that you have and are; and also have been taught concerning the ˢrecords which contain the prophecies which have been spoken by the holy prophets, even down to the time our father, Lehi, left Jerusalem;

35. And also, all that has been spoken by our fathers until now. And behold, also, they spake that which was commanded them of the Lord; therefore, they are just and true.

36. And now, I say unto you, my brethren, that after ye have known and have been taught all these things, if ye should transgress and go contrary to that which has been spoken, that ye do withdraw yourselves from the Spirit of the Lord, that it may have no place in you to guide you in wisdom's paths that ye may be blessed, prospered, and preserved—

37. I say unto you, that the man that doeth this, the same cometh out in open rebellion against God; therefore he listeth to obey the ᵗevil spirit, and becometh an enemy to all righteousness; therefore, the Lord has no place in him, for he dwelleth not in unholy temples.

38. Therefore if that man repenteth not, and remaineth and dieth an enemy to God, the demands of divine justice do awaken his immortal soul to a lively sense of his own guilt, which doth cause him to shrink from the presence of the Lord, and doth fill his breast with guilt, and pain, and anguish, which is ᵘlike an unquenchable fire, whose flame ascendeth up forever and ever.

39. And now I say unto you, that mercy hath no claim on that man; therefore his final doom is to endure a ᵛnever-ending torment.

40. O, all ye old men, and also ye young men, and you little children who can understand my words, for I have spoken plainly unto you that ye might understand, I pray that ye should awake to a remembrance of the awful situation of those that have fallen into transgression.

41. And moreover, I would desire that ye should consider on the blessed and happy state of those that keep the commandments of God. For behold, they are blessed in all things, both temporal and spiritual; and if they hold out faithful to the end they are received into heaven, that thereby they may dwell with God in a state of never-ending happiness. O remember, remember that these things are true; for the Lord God hath spoken it.

CHAPTER 3.

King Benjamin's address continued —Another prophecy of the Christ— More concerning the atonement.

1. And again my brethren, I would call your attention, for I have somewhat more to speak unto you; for behold, I have

---

r, see m, Jac. 6. s, 1 Ne. 3:24. 5:14. t, see q. u, see m, Jac. 6. v, see m, Jac. 6.   ABOUT B. C. 124.

MOSIAH, 3.

things to tell you concerning that which is to come.

2. And the things which I shall tell you are made known unto me by an angel from God. And he said unto me: Awake; and I awoke, and behold he stood before me.

3. And he said unto me: Awake, and hear the words which I shall tell thee; for behold, I am come to declare unto you the glad tidings of great joy.

4. For the Lord hath heard thy prayers, and hath judged of thy righteousness, and hath sent me to declare unto thee that thou mayest rejoice; and that thou mayest declare unto thy people, that they may also be filled with joy.

5. For behold, the time cometh, and is not far distant, that with power, the Lord Omnipotent who reigneth, who was, and ^{a}is from all eternity to all eternity, shall come down from heaven among the children of men, and shall dwell in a ^{b}tabernacle of clay, and shall go forth amongst men, working ^{c}mighty miracles, such as healing the sick, raising the dead, causing the lame to walk, the blind to receive their sight, and the deaf to hear, and curing all manner of diseases.

6. And he shall cast out devils, or the ^{d}evil spirits which dwell in the hearts of the children of men.

7. And lo, he shall suffer temptations, and ^{e}pain of body, hunger, thirst, and fatigue, even more than man can suffer, except it be unto death; for behold, blood cometh from every pore, so great shall be his anguish for the wickedness and the abominations of his people.

8. And he shall be called Jesus Christ, the Son of God, the Father of heaven and earth, the Creator of all things from the beginning; and his mother shall be called ^{f}Mary.

9. And lo, he cometh unto his own, that salvation might come unto the children of men even through faith on his name; and even after all this they shall consider him a man, and say that he hath a devil, and shall scourge him, and shall ^{g}crucify him.

10. And he shall rise the ^{h}third day from the dead; and behold, he standeth to judge the world; and behold, all these things are done that a righteous judgment might come upon the children of men.

11. For behold, and also his blood ^{i}atoneth for the sins of those who have fallen by the transgression of Adam, who have died not knowing the will of God concerning them, or who have ^{j}ignorantly sinned.

12. But wo, wo unto him who knoweth that he rebelleth against God! For salvation cometh to none such except it be through repentance and faith on the Lord Jesus Christ.

13. And the Lord God hath sent his holy prophets among all the children of men, to declare these things to every kindred, nation, and tongue, that thereby whosoever should believe that

---

a, 2 Ne. 19:6. 26:12. Mos. 15:1—5. Al. 11:38, 39, 44. 13:7—9. He. 14:12. Moro. 7:22. 8:18. D. & C. 29:33. 39:1. 76:4. *b*, 2 Ne. 9:18—21. 2 Ne. 2:4. 6:9. 9:5, 21. 25:12. 32:6. Mos. 7:27. 15:1—7. Al. 7:9—13. 19:13. He. 14:4. 3 Ne. 1:14. 9:15, 16. 10:18, 19. Chaps. 11—28. Morm. 3:21. *c*, 1 Ne. 11:31. 2 Ne. 10:4. 26:13. Al. 7:11. *d*, see *q*, Mos. 2. *e*, see *s*, 2 Ne. 9. *f*, Al. 7:10. *g*, 1 Ne. 11:33. 19:10, 13. 2 Ne. 6:9. 10:3. 25:13. Mos. 15:7. 3 Ne. 11:14, 15. *h*, 1 Ne. 19:10. 2 Ne. 25:13. He. 14:20, 27. 3 Ne. 10:9. *i*, see *f*, 2 Ne. 2. *j*, 2 Ne. 9:25, 26. Mos. 3:20—22. 15:24, 25. Al. 9:15, 16. 29:5. 42:21. He. 15:14, 15. Moro. 8:22. About B. C. 124.

Christ should come, the same might receive remission of their sins, and rejoice with exceeding great joy, even as though he had already come among them.

14. Yet the Lord God saw that his people were a stiffnecked people, and he appointed unto them a law, even the ^{k}law of Moses.

15. And many signs, and wonders, and types, and shadows showed he unto them, concerning his coming; and also holy prophets spake unto them concerning his coming; and yet they hardened their hearts, and understood not that the law of Moses availeth nothing except it were through the ^{l}atonement of his blood.

16. And even if it were possible that little children could sin they could not be saved; but I say unto you they are blessed; for behold, as in Adam, or by nature, they fall, even so the blood of Christ atoneth for ^{m}their sins.

17. And moreover, I say unto you, that there shall be no other name given nor any other way nor means whereby salvation can come unto the children of men, only in and through the name of Christ, the Lord Omnipotent.

18. For behold he judgeth, and his judgment is just; and the ^{n}infant perisheth not that dieth in his infancy; but men drink damnation to their own souls except they humble themselves and become as little children, and believe that salvation was, and is, and is to come, in and through the ^{o}atoning blood of Christ, the Lord Omnipotent.

19. For the natural man is an enemy to God, and has been from the fall of Adam, and will be, forever and ever, unless he yields to the enticings of the Holy Spirit, and putteth off the natural man and becometh a saint through the atonement of Christ the Lord, and becometh as a child, submissive, meek, humble, patient, full of love, willing to submit to all things which the Lord seeth fit to inflict upon him, even as a child doth submit to his father.

20. And moreover, I say unto you, that the time shall come when the knowledge of a Savior shall spread throughout every nation, kindred, tongue, and people.

21. And behold, when that time cometh, none shall be found blameless before God, except it be ^{p}little children, only through repentance and faith on the name of the Lord God Omnipotent.

22. And even at this time, when thou shalt have taught thy people the things which the Lord thy God hath commanded thee, even then are they found no more blameless in the sight of God, only according to the words which I have spoken unto thee.

23. And now I have spoken the words which the Lord God hath commanded me.

24. And thus saith the Lord: They shall stand as a bright testimony against this people, at the judgment day; whereof they shall be judged, every man according to his works, whether they be good, or whether they be evil.

25. And if they be evil they are consigned to an awful view of their own guilt and abominations, which doth cause them to shrink from the presence of the Lord into a state of misery and ^{q}endless torment, from whence they can no more return; therefore they have drunk damnation to their own souls.

---

k, see o, 2 Ne. 25. l, see f, 2 Ne. 2. m, vers. 18, 19. Mos. 15:25. Moro. 8:8, 12, 22. n, see m. o, see f, 2 Ne. 2. p, see m. q, see m, Jac. 6. ABOUT B. C. 124.

26. Therefore, they have drunk out of the cup of the wrath of God, which justice could no more deny unto them than it could deny that Adam should fall because of his partaking of the forbidden fruit; therefore, mercy could have claim on them no more forever.

27. And their torment is ʳas a lake of fire and brimstone, whose flames are unquenchable, and whose smoke ascendeth up forever and ever. Thus hath the Lord commanded me. Amen.

CHAPTER 4.

King Benjamin's address concluded—The conditions of salvation—Man's dependence upon God—Liberality, wisdom and diligence enjoined.

1. And now, it came to pass that when king Benjamin had made an end of speaking the words which had been delivered unto him by the ᵃangel of the Lord, that he cast his eyes round about on the multitude, and behold they had fallen to the earth, for the fear of the Lord had come upon them.

2. And they had viewed themselves in their own carnal state, even less than the dust of the earth. And they all cried aloud with one voice, saying: O have mercy, and apply the ᵇatoning blood of Christ that we may receive forgiveness of our sins, and our hearts may be purified; for we believe in Jesus Christ, the Son of God, who created heaven and earth, and all things; who shall come down among the children of men.

3. And it came to pass that after they had spoken these words the Spirit of the Lord came upon them, and they were filled with joy, having received a remission of their sins, and having peace of conscience, because of the exceeding faith which they had in Jesus Christ who should come, according to the words which king Benjamin had spoken unto them.

4. And king Benjamin again opened his mouth and began to speak unto them, saying: My friends and my brethren, my kindred and my people, I would again call your attention, that ye may hear and understand the remainder of my words which I shall speak unto you.

5. For behold, if the knowledge of the goodness of God at this time has awakened you to a sense of your nothingness, and your worthless and fallen state—

6. I say unto you, if ye have come to a knowledge of the goodness of God, and his matchless power, and his wisdom, and his patience, and his long-suffering towards the children of men; and also, the ᶜatonement which has been prepared from the ᵈfoundation of the world, that thereby salvation might come to him that should put his trust in the Lord, and should be diligent in keeping his commandments, and continue in the faith even unto the end of his life, I mean the life of the mortal body—

7. I say, that this is the man who receiveth salvation, through the ᵉatonement which was prepared from the foundation of the world for all mankind, which ever were since the fall of Adam, or who are, or who ever shall be, even unto the end of the world.

8. And this is the means

---

r, see m, Jac. 6.   CHAP. 4: a, ver. 11.   Mos. 3:2.   b, see f, 2 Ne. 2.   c, see f, 2 Ne. 2.   d, ver. 7.   Mos. 18:13.   Al. 12:25, 30.   13:3, 5, 7, 8.   18:39.   22:13.   42:26. He. 5:47.   3 Ne. 1:14.   26:5.   Eth. 3:14.   e, see f, 2 Ne. 2.   ABOUT B. C. 124

MOSIAH, 4.

whereby salvation cometh. And there is none other salvation save this which hath been spoken of; neither are there any conditions whereby man can be saved except the conditions which I have told you.

9. Believe in God; believe that he is, and that he created all things, both in heaven and in earth; believe that he has all wisdom, and all power, both in heaven and in earth; believe that man doth not comprehend all the things which the Lord can comprehend.

10. And again, believe that ye must repent of your sins and forsake them, and humble yourselves before God; and ask in sincerity of heart that he would forgive you; and now, if you believe all these things see that ye do them.

11. And again I say unto you as I have said before, that as ye have come to the knowledge of the glory of God, or if ye have known of his goodness and have tasted of his love, and have received a remission of your sins, which causeth such exceeding great joy in your souls, even so I would that ye should remember, and always retain in remembrance, the greatness of God, and your own nothingness, and his goodness and long-suffering towards you, unworthy creatures, and humble yourselves even in the depths of humility, calling on the name of the Lord daily, and standing steadfastly in the faith of that which is to come, which was spoken by the mouth of the *f*angel.

12. And behold, I say unto you that if ye do this ye shall always rejoice, and be filled with the love of God, and always retain a remission of your sins; and ye shall grow in the knowledge of the glory of him that created you, or in the knowledge of that which is just and true.

13. And ye will not have a mind to injure one another, but to live peaceably, and to render to every man according to that which is his due.

14. And ye will not suffer your children that they go hungry, or naked; neither will ye suffer that they transgress the laws of God, and fight and quarrel one with another, and serve the *g*devil, who is the master of sin, or who is the evil spirit which hath been spoken of by our fathers, he being an enemy to all righteousness.

15. But ye will teach them to walk in the ways of truth and soberness; ye will teach them to love one another, and to serve one another.

16. And also, ye yourselves will succor those that stand in need of your succor; ye will administer of your substance unto him that standeth in need; and ye will not suffer that the *h*beggar putteth up his petition to you in vain, and turn him out to perish.

17. Perhaps thou shalt say: The man has brought upon himself his misery; therefore I will stay my hand, and will not give unto him of my food, nor impart unto him of my substance that he may not suffer, for his punishments are just—

18. But I say unto you, O man, whosoever doeth this the same hath great cause to repent; and except he repenteth of that which he hath done he perisheth forever, and hath no interest in the kingdom of God.

19. For behold, are we not all *i*beggars? Do we not all depend

f, see *a.* *g,* see *q,* Mos. 2. *h,* vers. 19, 20, 22—25. *i,* see *h.*   ABOUT B. C. 124.

upon the same Being, even God, for all the substance which we have, for both food and raiment, and for gold, and for silver, and for all the riches which we have of every kind?

20. And behold, even at this time, ye have been calling on his name, and begging for a remission of your sins. And has he suffered that ye have begged in vain? Nay; he has poured out his Spirit upon you, and has caused that your hearts should be filled with joy, and has caused that your mouths should be stopped that ye could not find utterance, so exceeding great was your joy.

21. And now, if God, who has created you, on whom you are dependent for your lives and for all that ye have and are, doth grant unto you ʲwhatsoever ye ask that is right, in faith, believing that ye shall receive, O then, how ye ought to impart of the substance that ye have one to another.

22. And if ye judge the man who putteth up his petition to you for your substance that he perish not, and condemn him, how much more just will be your condemnation for withholding your substance, which doth not belong to you but to God, to whom also your life belongeth; and yet ye put up no petition, nor repent of the thing which thou hast done.

23. I say unto you, wo be unto that man, for his substance shall perish with him; and now, I say these things unto those who are rich as pertaining to the things of this world.

24. And again, I say unto the poor, ye who have not and yet have sufficient, that ye remain from day to day; I mean all you who ᵏdeny the beggar, because ye have not; I would that ye say in your hearts that: I give not because I have not, but if I had I would give.

25. And now, if ye say this in your hearts ye remain guiltless, otherwise ye are condemned; and your condemnation is just for ye covet that which ye have not received.

26. And now, for the sake of these things which I have spoken unto you—that is, for the sake of retaining a remission of your sins from day to day, that ye may walk guiltless before God—I would that ye should impart of your substance to the poor, every man according to that which he hath, such ˡas feeding the hungry, clothing the naked, visiting the sick and administering to their relief, both spiritually and temporally, according to their wants.

27. And see that all these things are done in wisdom and order; for it is not requisite that a man should run faster than he has strength. And again, it is expedient that he should be diligent, that thereby he might win the prize; therefore, all things must be done in order.

28. And I would that ye should remember, that whosoever among you ᵐborroweth of his neighbor should return the thing that he borroweth, according as he doth agree, or else thou shalt commit sin; and perhaps thou shalt cause thy neighbor to commit sin also.

29. And finally, I cannot tell you all the things whereby ye may commit sin; for there are divers ways and means, even so

j, see *e*, 2 Ne. 32. *k*, see *h*. *l*, 2 Ne. 26:30. Jac. 2:19. Mos. 18:27—29. 21:17. Al. 1:27, 30. 4:12, 13. 34:28, 29. 3 Ne. 12:42. 13:1—4. 4 Ne. 3. Morm. 8:37, 39. Moro. 7:6—8. *m*, 3 Ne. 12:42. ABOUT B. C. 124.

MOSIAH, 5.

many that I cannot number them.

30. But this much I can tell you, that if ye do not watch yourselves, and your thoughts, and your words, and your deeds, and observe the commandments of God, and continue in the faith of what ye have heard concerning the coming of our Lord, even unto the end of your lives, ye must perish. And now, O man, remember, and perish not.

CHAPTER 5.

Effect of king Benjamin's address— The people repent and enter into covenant with Christ, and are called by his name.

1. And now, it came to pass that when king Benjamin had thus spoken to his people, he sent among them, desiring to know of his people if they believed the words which he had spoken unto them.

2. And they all cried with one voice, saying: Yea, we believe all the words which thou hast spoken unto us; and also, we know of their surety and truth, because of the Spirit of the Lord Omnipotent, which has wrought a mighty change in us, or in our hearts, that we have no more disposition to do evil, but to do good continually.

3. And we, ourselves, also, through the infinite goodness of God, and the manifestations of his Spirit, have great views of that which is to come; and were it expedient, we could prophesy of all things.

4. And it is the faith which we have had on the things which our king has spoken unto us that has brought us to this great knowledge, whereby we do rejoice with such exceeding great joy.

5. And we are willing to enter into a covenant with our God to do his will, and to be obedient to his commandments in all things that he shall command us, all the remainder of our days, that we may not bring upon ourselves a ^{a}never-ending torment, as has been spoken by the ^{b}angel, that we may not drink out of the cup of the wrath of God.

6. And now, these are the words which king Benjamin desired of them; and therefore he said unto them: Ye have spoken the words that I desired; and the covenant which ye have made is a righteous covenant.

7. And now, because of the covenant which ye have made ye shall be called the children of Christ, his sons, and his daughters; for behold, this day he hath spiritually begotten you; for ye say that your hearts are changed through faith on his name; therefore, ye are ^{c}born of him and have become his sons and his daughters.

8. And under this head ye are made free, and there is no other head whereby ye can be made free. There is no ^{d}other name given whereby salvation cometh; therefore, I would that ye should ^{e}take upon you the name of Christ, all you that have entered into the covenant with God that ye should be obedient unto the end of your lives.

9. And it shall come to pass that whosoever doeth this shall be found at the right hand of God, for he shall know the name by which he is called; for he

---

a, see *m*, Jac. 6. *b*, Mos. 3:2, 3. 4:1. *c*, Mos. 27:24—27. Al. 5:14, 49. 22:15. 36:23, 26. 38:6. John 1:13. 3:3. Tit. 3:5. *d*, 1 Ne. 10:6. 2 Ne. 2:8. 11:6. 25:20. 31:21. Mos. 4:8. 13:28. 15:19. 16:4. Al. 21:9. 34:9. 38:9. Acts 4:12. *e*, vers. 9—14. Mos. 26:18, 24. Al. 1:19. 5:38. 34:38. 3 Ne. 27:5—9. Morm. 8:38.
ABOUT B. C. 124.

shall be called by the *f*name of Christ.

10. And now it shall come to pass, that whosoever shall not take upon him the name of Christ must be called by some other name; therefore, he findeth himself on the left hand of God.

11. And I would that ye should remember also, that this is the name that I said I should give unto you that *g*never should be blotted out, except it be through transgression; therefore, take heed that ye do not transgress, that the name be not blotted out of your hearts.

12. I say unto you, I would that ye should remember to retain the *h*name written always in your hearts, that ye are not found on the *i*left hand of God, but that ye hear and know the voice by which ye shall be called, and also, the name by which he shall call you.

13. For how knoweth a man the master whom he has not served, and who is a stranger unto him, and is far from the thoughts and intents of his heart?

14. And again, doth a man take an ass which belongeth to his neighbor, and keep him? I say unto you, Nay; he will not even suffer that he shall feed among his flocks, but will drive him away, and cast him out. I say unto you, that even so shall it be among you if ye know not the *j*name by which ye are called.

15. Therefore, I would that ye should be steadfast and immovable, always abounding in good works, that Christ, the *k*Lord God Omnipotent, may seal you his, that you may be brought to heaven, that ye may have everlasting salvation and eternal life, through the wisdom, and power, and justice, and mercy of him who *l*created all things, in heaven and in earth, who is God above all. Amen.

CHAPTER 6.

Names of the people recorded—Priests appointed—Beginning of Mosiah's reign—Death of king Benjamin.

1. And now, king Benjamin thought it was expedient, after having finished speaking to the people, that he should take the names of all those who had entered into a covenant with God to keep his commandments.

2. And it came to pass that there was not one soul, except it were little children, but who had entered into the covenant and had taken upon them the *a*name of Christ.

3. And again, it came to pass that when king Benjamin had made an end of all these things, and had *b*consecrated his son Mosiah to be a ruler and a king over his people, and had given him all the charges concerning the kingdom, and also had appointed *c*priests to teach the people, that thereby they might hear and know the commandments of God, and to stir them up in remembrance of the *d*oath which they had made, he dismissed the multitude, and they returned, every one, according to their families, to their own houses.

---

f, see *e*. *g*, Mos. 1:11, 12. *h*, see *e*. *i*, ver. 10. *j*, see *e*. *k*, Mos. 3:5, 17, 18, 21. *l*, Mos. 3:8. 4:2. Al. 11:39. 3 Ne. 9:15. Morm. 9:17. Eth. 3:14—16. 4:7. Col. 1:16. CHAP. 6: *a*, see *e*, Mos. 5. *b*, see *i*, Mos. 1. *c*, see *o*, 2 Ne. 5. Mos. 18:18, 24, 28. 21:33. 23:16, 17. 25:19, 21. 26:7. 27:1, 5, 22. 29:42. Al. 1:3, 26. 4:7, 16, 18, 20. 5:3, 6:1, 8, 8:11, 23. 13:1—20. 15:13. 16:5, 18. 18:34. 23:4. 16. 24:7. 29:13. 30:20—23, 29, 31. 43:2. 46:38. 49:30. 3 Ne. 6:21, 22, 27. 11:21, 22. 12:1. 18:36, 87. 4 Ne. 14. Moro. 2:1—3. Chaps. 3, 4. 6:1, 7. 7:2. 8:1, 2, 28. *d*, vers. 1, 2, Mos. 5:5—7.

ABOUT B. C. 124.

4. And Mosiah began to ^ereign in his father's stead. *And he began to reign in the thirtieth year of his age, making in the whole, about four hundred and seventy-six years from the ^ftime that Lehi left Jerusalem.

5. And king Benjamin lived three years† and he died.

6. And it came to pass that king Mosiah did walk in the ways of the Lord, and did observe his judgments and his statutes, and did keep his commandments in all things whatsoever he commanded him.

7. And king Mosiah did cause his people that they should till the earth. And he also, himself, did till the earth, that thereby he might not become burdensome to his people, that he might do according to that which his father had done in all things. And there was no contention among all his people for the space of three years.

CHAPTER 7.

Expedition to the land of Lehi-Nephi—Ammon and king Limhi—People of Lehi-Nephi in bondage to Lamanites.

1. And now, it came to pass that after king Mosiah had had continual peace for the space of three years, he was desirous to know concerning the people who went up to dwell in the land of ^aLehi-Nephi, or in the city of Lehi-Nephi; for his people had heard nothing from them from the time they left the land of ^bZarahemla; therefore, they wearied him with their teasings.

2. And it came to pass that ‡king Mosiah granted that sixteen of their strong men might go up to the ^cland of Lehi-Nephi, to inquire concerning their brethren.

3. And it came to pass that on the morrow they started to go up, having with them one Ammon, he being a strong and mighty man, and a ^ddescendant of Zarahemla; and he was also their leader.

4. And now, they knew not the course they should travel in the wilderness to go up to the ^eland of Lehi-Nephi; therefore they wandered many days in the wilderness, even forty days did they wander.

5. And when they had wandered forty days they came to a hill, which is north of the land of ^fShilom, and there they pitched their tents.

6. And Ammon took three of his brethren, and their names were Amaleki, Helem, and Hem, and they went down into the ^gland of Nephi.

7. And behold, they met the king of the people who were in the land of Nephi, and in the land of Shilom; and they were surrounded by the king's guard, and were taken, and were bound, and were committed to prison.

8. And it came to pass when they had been in prison two days they were again brought before the king, and their bands were loosed; and they stood before the king, and were permitted, or rather commanded, that they should answer the questions which he should ask them.

9. And he said unto them: ^hBehold, I am Limhi, the son of Noah, who was the son of Zeniff, who came up out of the ⁱland of Zarahemla to inherit this land,

e, Mos. 1:10, 15. *f*, 1 Ne. 1:4. 2:4. CHAP. 7: *a*, see *b*, 2 Ne. 5. *b*, Om. 13. *c*, see *b*, 2 Ne. 5. *d*, Om. 14. *e*, see *b*, 2 Ne. 5. *f*, vers. 7, 16, 21. Mos. 9:6, 8, 14. 10:8. 11:12, 13. 22:8, 11. 24:1. Al. 23:12. *g*, see *b*, 2 Ne. 5. *h*, Mos. 11:1. 19:16. *i*, Om. 13. * ABOUT B. C. 124. † ABOUT B. C. 121. ‡ ABOUT B. C. 121.

which was the land of their fathers, who was made a king by the ʲvoice of the people.

10. And now, I desire to know the cause whereby ye were so ᵏbold as to come near the walls of the city, when I, myself, was with my guards without the gate?

11. And now, for this cause have I suffered that ye should be preserved, that I might inquire of you, or else I should have caused that my guards should have ˡput you to death. Ye are permitted to speak.

12. And now, when Ammon saw that he was permitted to speak, he went forth and ᵐbowed himself before the king; and rising again he said: O king, I am very thankful before God this day that I am yet alive, and am permitted to speak; and I will endeavor to speak with boldness;

13. For I am assured that if ye had known me ye would not have suffered that I should have worn these bands. For I am Ammon, and am a ⁿdescendant of Zarahemla, and have come up out of the ᵒland of Zarahemla to inquire concerning our brethren, whom ᵖZeniff brought up out of that land.

14. And now, it came to pass that after Limhi had heard the words of Ammon, he was exceeding glad, and said: Now, I know of a surety that my brethren who were in the land of Zarahemla ᑫare yet alive. And now, I will rejoice; and on the morrow I will cause that my people shall rejoice also.

15. For behold, we are in bondage to the Lamanites, and ʳare taxed with a tax which is grievous to be borne. And now, behold, our brethren will deliver us out of our bondage, or out of the hands of the Lamanites, and we will be their slaves; for it is better that we be slaves to the Nephites than to pay tribute to the king of the Lamanites.

16. And now, king Limhi commanded his guards that they should no more bind Ammon nor his brethren, but caused that they should go to the ˢhill which was north of Shilom, and bring their brethren into the city, that thereby they might eat, and drink, and rest themselves from the labors of their journey; for they ᵗhad suffered many things; they had suffered hunger, thirst, and fatigue.

17. And now, it came to pass on the morrow that king Limhi sent a proclamation among all his people, that thereby they might gather themselves together to the ᵘtemple, to hear the words which he should speak unto them.

18. And it came to pass that when they had gathered themselves together that he spake unto them in this wise, saying: O ye, my people, lift up your heads and be comforted; for behold, the time is at hand, or is not far distant, when we shall no longer be in subjection to our enemies, notwithstanding our many strugglings, which have been in vain; yet I trust there remaineth an effectual struggle to be made.

19. Therefore, lift up your heads, and rejoice, and put your trust in God, in that God who was the God of Abraham, and Isaac, and Jacob; and also, that God who brought the children of

---

j, Mos. 19:26. *k*, Mos. 21:23, 24. *l*, Mos. 21:23. *m*, Al. 47:22, 23. *n*, Om. 14. *o*, Om. 13. *p*, Mos. 9:1. *q*, Mos. 21:25, 26. *r*, ver. 22. Mos. 19:15. *s*, ver. 5. *t*, ver. 4. *u*, see *h*, 2 Ne. 5. ABOUT B. C. 121.

Israel out of the land of Egypt, and caused that they should walk through the Red Sea on dry ground, and fed them with manna that they might not perish in the wilderness; and many more things did he do for them.

20. And again, that same God has brought our fathers out of the land of Jerusalem, and has kept and preserved his people even until now; and behold, it is because of our iniquities and abominations that he has brought us into bondage.

21. And ye all are witnesses this day, that ^{v}Zeniff, who was made king over this people, he being ^{w}over-zealous to inherit the land of his fathers, therefore being deceived by the cunning and craftiness of king Laman, who having entered into a treaty with king Zeniff, and having yielded up into his hands the possessions of a part of the land, or even the city of ^{x}Lehi-Nephi, and the city of ^{y}Shilom; and the land round about—

22. And all this he did, for the sole purpose of bringing this people into subjection or into bondage. And behold, we at this time do pay tribute to the king of the Lamanites, to the ^{z}amount of one half of our corn, and our barley, and even all our grain of every kind, and one half of the increase of our flocks and our herds; and even one half of all we have or possess the king of the Lamanites doth exact of us, or our lives.

23. And now, is not this grievous to be borne? And is not this, our affliction, great? Now behold, how great reason we have to mourn.

24. Yea, I say unto you, great are the reasons which we have to mourn; for behold how many of our brethren have been slain, and their blood has been spilt in vain, and all because of iniquity.

25. For if this people had not fallen into transgression the Lord would not have suffered that this great evil should come upon them. But behold, they would not hearken unto his words; but there arose contentions among them, even so much that they did shed blood among themselves.

26. And a ^{2a}prophet of the Lord have they slain; yea, a chosen man of God, who told them of their wickedness and abominations, and prophesied of many things which are to come, yea, even the coming of Christ.

27. And because he said unto them that Christ ^{2b}was the God, the Father of all things, and said that he should take upon him the image of man, and it should be the image after which man was ^{2c}created in the beginning; or in other words, he said that man was created after the image of God, and that God should come down among the children of men, and ^{2d}take upon him flesh and blood, and go forth upon the face of the earth—

28. And now, because he said this, they did ^{2e}put him to death; and many more things did they do which brought down the wrath of God upon them. Therefore, who wondereth that they are in bondage, and that they are smitten with sore afflictions?

29. For behold, the Lord hath said: I will not succor my people in the day of their transgression; but I will hedge up their ways that they prosper not; and

v, Mos. 9:1. w, Mos. 9:3. x, see b, 2 Ne. 5. y, see f. z, see r. 2a, Mos. 17:12—20. 2b, 1 Ne. 19:7, 10. 2 Ne. 2:14, 15. 10:3. 25:12. 26:12. Mos. 3:5, 8. 15:1—5. 16:15. 27:30, 31. Al. 11:38, 39. 3 Ne. 9:15. 11:14. Morm. 3:21. 9:11, 12. Eth. 4:7. 2c, Al. 18:34. Eth. 3:15, 16. 2d, see b, Mos. 3. 2e, see 2a. ABOUT B. C. 121.

MOSIAH, 8.

their doings shall be as a stumbling block before them.

30. And again, he saith: If my people shall sow filthiness they shall reap the chaff thereof in the whirlwind; and the effect thereof is poison.

31. And again he saith: If my people shall sow filthiness they shall reap the ^{2f}east wind, which bringeth immediate destruction.

32. And now, behold, the promise of the Lord is fulfilled, and ye are smitten and afflicted.

33. But if ye will turn to the Lord with full purpose of heart, and put your trust in him, and serve him with all diligence of mind, if ye do this, he will, according to his own will and pleasure, deliver you out of bondage.

CHAPTER 8.

Ammon learns of the discovery of twenty-four gold plates with engravings—He suggests their submission to king Mosiah, prophet and seer.

1. And it came to pass that after king Limhi had made an end of speaking to his people, for he spake many things unto them and only a few of them have I written in this book, he told his people all the things concerning their brethren who were in the ^{a}land of Zarahemla.

2. And he caused that Ammon should stand up before the multitude, and rehearse unto them all that had happened unto their brethren from the time that ^{b}Zeniff went up out of the land even until the time that he ^{c}himself came up out of the land.

3. And he also rehearsed unto them the ^{d}last words which king Benjamin had taught them, and explained them to the people of king Limhi, so that they might understand all the words which he spake.

4. And it came to pass that after he had done all this, that king Limhi dismissed the multitude, and caused that they should return every one unto his own house.

5. And it came to pass that he caused that the ^{e}plates which contained the record of his people from the time that they left the ^{f}land of Zarahemla, should be brought before Ammon, that he might read them.

6. Now, as soon as Ammon had read the record, the king inquired of him to know if he could interpret languages, and Ammon told him that he could not.

7. And the king said unto him: Being grieved for the afflictions of my people, I caused that ^{g}forty and three of my people should take a journey into the wilderness, that thereby they might find the ^{h}land of Zarahemla, that we might appeal unto our brethren to deliver us out of bondage.

8. And they were lost in the wilderness for the space of many days, yet they were diligent, and found not the land of Zarahemla but returned to this land, having traveled in a land among ^{i}many waters, having discovered a land which was covered with ^{j}bones of men, and of beasts, and was also covered with ruins of buildings of every kind, having discovered a land which had been peopled with a people who were as numerous as the hosts of Israel.

9. And for a testimony that the things that they had said are

2*f*, Mos. 12:6. CHAP. 8: *a*, Om. 13. *b*, see *p*, Mos. 7. *c*, Mos. 7:3. *d*, Mos. chaps. 3—5. *e*, see Record of Zeniff, Mos. 9. *f*, Om. 13. *g*, Mos. 21:25. *h*, Om. 13. *i*, Al. 50:29. He. 3:3, 4. Morm. 6:4. *j*, Mos. 21:26, 27. He. 3:3—12. See Book of Ether.
ABOUT B. C. 121.

MOSIAH, 8.

true they have brought ᵏtwenty-four plates which are filled with engravings, and they are of pure gold.

10. And behold, also, they have brought ˡbreastplates, which are large, and they are of ᵐbrass and of copper, and are perfectly sound.

11. And again, they have brought swords, the hilts thereof have perished, and the blades thereof were cankered with rust; and there is no one in the land that is able to interpret the language or the engravings that are on the plates. Therefore I said unto thee: Canst thou translate?

12. And I say unto thee again: Knowest thou of any one that can translate? For I am desirous that these records should be translated into our language; for, perhaps, they will give us a knowledge of a remnant of the people who have been destroyed, from whence these records came; or, perhaps, they will give us a knowledge of this very people who have been destroyed; and I am desirous to know the cause of their destruction.

13. Now Ammon said unto him: I can assuredly tell thee, O king, of a man that can translate the records; for he has wherewith that he can look, and translate all records that are of ancient date; and it is a gift from God. And the things are called ⁿinterpreters, and no man can look in them except he be commanded, lest he should look for that he ought not and he should perish. And whosoever is commanded to look in them, the same is called seer.

14. And behold, the king of the people who are in the land of Zarahemla is the ᵒman that is commanded to do these things, and who has this high gift from God.

15. And the king said that a seer is ᵖgreater than a prophet.

16. And Ammon said that a seer is a revelator and a prophet also; and a gift which is greater can no man have, except he should possess the power of God, which no man can; yet a man may have great power given him from God.

17. But a seer can know of things which are past, and also of things which are to come, and by them shall all things be revealed, or, rather, shall secret things be made manifest, and hidden things shall come to light, and things which are not known shall be made known by them, and also things shall be made known by them which otherwise could not be known.

18. Thus God has provided a means that man, through faith, might work mighty miracles; therefore he becometh a great benefit to his fellow beings.

19. And now, when Ammon had made an end of speaking these words the king rejoiced exceedingly, and gave thanks to God, saying: Doubtless a ᵠgreat mystery is contained within these plates, and these interpreters were doubtless prepared for the purpose of unfolding all such mysteries to the children of men.

20. O how marvelous are the works of the Lord, and how long doth he suffer with his people; yea, and how blind and impenetrable are the understandings of

---

k, Mos. 21:27. 28:11. Al. 37:21—31. He. 6:26 Eth. 1:1—5. 15:33. *l*, Eth. 15:15. 24 *m*, Eth. 10:23. *n*, vers. 14—19. Om. 20—22. Mos. 21:27, 28. 28:11—19. Al. 10:2. 37:21—26. Eth. 3:23, 28. 4:5. D. & C. 17:1. *o*, Mos. 21:28. 28:17. *p*, vers. 16—19. D. & C. 21:1. *q*, 2 Ne. 27:7, 8, 10, 11. Eth. 3:21—28. 4:1—8. 5:1.

ABOUT B. C. 121.

the children of men; for they will not seek wisdom, neither do they desire that she should rule over them!

21. Yea, they are as a wild flock which fleeth from the shepherd, and scattereth, and are driven, and are devoured by the beasts of the forest.

THE RECORD OF ZENIFF.—*An account of his people, from the time they left the land of Zarahemla until the time that they were delivered out of the hands of the Lamanites.*
Comprising chapters 9 to 22 inclusive.

CHAPTER 9.

Zeniff goes to possess the land of Lehi-Nephi—A spy among the Lamanites—The craftiness of king Laman.

1. I, Zeniff, having been taught in all the language of the Nephites, and having had a knowledge of the ªland of Nephi, or of the land of our fathers' first inheritance, *and having been sent as a spy among the Lamanites that I might spy out their forces, that our army might come upon them and destroy them—but when I saw that which was good among them I was desirous that they should not be destroyed.

2. Therefore, I contended with my brethren in the wilderness, for I would that our ruler should make a treaty with them; but he being an austere and a bloodthirsty man commanded that I should be slain; but I was rescued by the shedding of much blood; for father fought against father, and brother against brother, until the ᵇgreater number of our army was destroyed in the wilderness; and we returned, those of us that were spared, to the land of Zarahemla, to relate that tale to their wives and their children.

3. And yet, I being ᶜover-zealous to inherit the land of our fathers, collected as many as were desirous to go up to possess the land, and started again on our journey into the wilderness to go up to the land; but we were smitten with famine and sore afflictions; for we were slow to remember the Lord our God.

4. Nevertheless, after many days' wandering in the wilderness we pitched our tents in the place where our brethren ᵈwere slain, which was near to the ᵉland of our fathers.

5. And it came to pass that I went again with four of my men into the city, in unto the king, that I might know of the disposition of the king, and that I might know if I might go in with my people and possess the land in peace.

6. And I went in unto the king, and he covenanted with me that I might possess the land of ᶠLehi-Nephi, and the land of ᵍShilom.

7. And he also commanded that his people should depart out of the land, and I and my people went into the land that we might possess it.

8. And we began to build buildings, and to repair the walls of the city, yea, even the walls of the city of Lehi-Nephi, and the city of Shilom.

9. And we began to till the ground, yea, even with ʰall manner of seeds, with seeds of corn, and of wheat, and of barley, and with neas, and with sheum, and with seeds of all manner of fruits;

a, see *b*, 2 Ne. 5. *b*, Om. 28. *c*, Mos. 7:21. Om. 29. *d*, ver. 2. Om. 28. *e*, see *b*, 2 Ne. 5. *f*, see *b*, 2 Ne. 5. *g*, see *f*, Mos. 7. *h*, 1 Ne. 8:1. 18:24. Enos 21.
*ABOUT B. C. 200.

and we did begin to multiply and prosper in the land.

10. Now it was the *k*cunning and the craftiness of king Laman, to bring my people into bondage, that he yielded up the land that we might possess it.

11. Therefore it came to pass, that after we had dwelt in the land for the space of *twelve years that king Laman began to grow uneasy, lest by any means my people should wax strong in the land, and that they could *l*not overpower them and bring them into bondage.

12. Now they were a *m*lazy and an idolatrous people; therefore they were desirous to bring us into *n*bondage, that they might glut themselves with the labors of our hands; yea, that they might feast themselves upon the flocks of our fields.

13. Therefore it came to pass that king Laman began to stir up his people that they should contend with my people; therefore there began to be wars and contentions in the land.

14. For, in the †thirteenth year of my reign in the land of Nephi, away on the south of the land of *o*Shilom, when my people were watering and feeding their flocks, and tilling their lands, a numerous host of Lamanites came upon them and began to slay them, and to take off their flocks, and the corn of their fields.

15. Yea, and it came to pass that they fled, all that were not overtaken, even into the *p*city of Nephi, and did call upon me for protection.

16. And it came to pass that I did arm them with bows, and with arrows, with swords, and with cimeters, and with clubs, and with slings, and with all manner of weapons which we could invent, and I and my people did go forth against the Lamanites to battle.

17. Yea, in the strength of the Lord did we go forth to battle against the Lamanites; for I and my people did cry mightily to the Lord that he would deliver us out of the hands of our enemies, for we were awakened to a remembrance of the deliverance of our fathers.

18. And God did hear our cries and did answer our prayers; and we did go forth in his might; yea, we did go forth against the Lamanites, and in one day and a night we did slay three thousand and forty-three; we did slay them even until we had driven them out of our land.

19. And I, myself, with mine own hands, did help to bury their dead. And behold, to our great sorrow and lamentation, two hundred and seventy-nine of our brethren were slain.

CHAPTER 10.

King Laman dies—Zeniff and his people prevail against their oppressors.

1. And it came to pass that we again began to establish the kingdom and we again began to possess the land in peace. And I caused that there should be weapons of war made of every kind, that thereby I might have weapons for my people against the time the Lamanites should come up again to war against my people.

2. And I set guards round about the land, that the Lamanites might not come upon us again unawares and destroy us; and thus I did guard my people and my flocks, and keep them from

k, vers. 11, 12. Mos. 7:22. 10:18. 19:26, 28. 21:3, 13. *l*, see *k*, *m*, Enos 20. *n*, see *k*. *o*, see *j*, Mos. 7. *p*, see *b*, 2 Ne. 5. *About B. C. 188. †About B. C. 187.

falling into the hands of our enemies.

3. And it came to pass that we did inherit the ᵃland of our fathers for many years, yea, *for the space of twenty and two years.

4. And I did cause that the men should till the ground, and raise ᵇall manner of grain and all manner of fruit of every kind.

5. And I did cause that the women should spin, and toil, and work, and work ᶜall manner of fine linen, yea, and cloth of every kind, that we might clothe our nakedness; and thus we did prosper in the land—thus we did have continual peace in the land for the space of twenty and two years.

6. And it came to pass that king Laman died, and his son began to reign in his stead. And he began to stir his people up in rebellion against my people; therefore they began to prepare for war, and to come up to battle against my people.

7. But I had sent my spies out round about the land of ᵈShemlon, that I might discover their preparations, that I might guard against them, that they might not come upon my people and destroy them.

8. And it came to pass that they came up upon the north of the land of ᵉShilom, with their numerous hosts, men ᶠarmed with bows, and with arrows, and with swords, and with cimeters, and with stones, and with slings; and they had their heads shaved that they were naked; and they were girded with a leathern girdle about their loins.

9. And it came to pass that I caused that the women and children of my people should be hid in the wilderness; and I also caused that all my old men that could bear arms, and also all my young men that were able to bear arms, should gather themselves together to go to battle against the Lamanites; and I did place them in their ranks, every man according to his age.

10. And it came to pass that we did go up to battle against the Lamanites; and I, even I, in my old age, did go up to battle against the Lamanites. And it came to pass that we did go up in the strength of the Lord to battle.

11. Now, the Lamanites knew nothing concerning the Lord, nor the strength of the Lord, therefore they depended upon their own strength. Yet they were a strong people, as to the strength of men.

12. They were a wild, and ferocious, and a blood-thirsty people, believing in the ᵍtradition of their fathers, which is this—Believing that they were driven out of the land of Jerusalem because of the iniquities of their fathers, and that they were wronged in the wilderness by their brethren, and they were also wronged while crossing the sea;

13. And again, that they were wronged while in the land of their ʰfirst inheritance, after they had crossed the sea, and all this because that Nephi was more faithful in keeping the commandments of the Lord—therefore he was favored of the Lord, for the Lord heard his prayers and answered them, and ⁱhe took the lead of their journey in the wilderness.

14. And his brethren were wroth with him because they understood not the dealings of

---

a, see *b*, 2 Ne. 5. *b*, see *h*, Mos. 9. *c*, Al. 1:29. He. 6:13. *d*, Mos. 11:12. 19:6. 20:1. 24:1. Al. 23:12. *e*, see *f*, Mos. 7. *f*, Enos 20. Al. 3:4, 5. 17:14, 15. 43:18 —21. *g*, see *n*, Jac. 7. *h*, 1 Ne. 18:23. *i*, 2 Ne. 5:5—9. * ABOUT B. C. 178

the Lord; they were also wroth with him upon the waters because they hardened their hearts against the Lord.

15 And again, they were wroth with him when they had arrived in the promised land, because they said that he had taken the ʲruling of the people out of their hands; and they sought to kill him.

16. And again, they were wroth with him because he departed into the wilderness as the Lord had commanded him, and ᵏtook the records which were engraven on the plates of brass, for they said that he robbed them.

17. And thus they have taught their children that they should hate them, and that they should murder them, and that they should rob and plunder them, and do all they could to destroy them; therefore they have an ˡeternal hatred towards the children of Nephi.

18. For this very cause has king Laman, by his ᵐcunning, and lying craftiness, and his fair promises, deceived me, that I have brought this my people up into this land, that they may destroy them; yea, and we have suffered these many years in the land.

19. And now I, Zeniff, after having told all these things unto my people concerning the Lamanites, I did stimulate them to go to battle with their might, putting their trust in the Lord; therefore, we did contend with them, face to face.

20. And it came to pass that we did drive them again out of our land; and we slew them with a great slaughter, even so many that we did not number them.

21. And it came to pass that we returned again to our own land, and my people again ⁿbegan to tend their flocks, and to till their ground.

22. And now I, being old, *did confer the kingdom upon one of my sons; therefore, I say no more. And may the Lord bless my people. Amen.

CHAPTER 11.

The wicked king Noah and his priests — The prophet Abinadi denounces the prevailing wickedness — King Noah seeks his life.

1. And now it came to pass that Zeniff conferred the kingdom upon Noah, one of his sons; therefore Noah began to reign in his stead; and he did not walk in the ways of his father.

2. For behold, he did not keep the commandments of God, but he did walk after the desires of his own heart. And he had ᵃmany wives and concubines. And he did cause his people to commit sin, and do that which was abominable in the sight of the Lord. Yea, and they did commit ᵇwhoredoms and all manner of wickedness.

3. And he laid a tax of one fifth part of all they possessed, a fifth part of their gold and of their silver, and a fifth part of their ziff, and of their copper, and of their brass and their iron; and a fifth part of their fatlings; and also a fifth part of all their grain.

4. And all this did he take to support himself, and his wives and his concubines; and also his priests, and ᵈtheir wives and their concubines; thus he had changed the affairs of the kingdom.

5. For he put down all the

---

j, 2 Ne. 5:1—4. *k*, 2 Ne. 5:12. *l*, see *n*, Jac. 7. *m*, see *k*, Mos. 9. *n*, Mos. 9:9, 14. CHAP. 11: *a*, see *n*, Jac. 2. *b*, see *i*, 2 Ne. 28. *d*, see *n*, Jac. 2.
* PROBABLY ABOUT B. C. 160.

*priests that had been consecrated by his father, and consecrated new *ones in their stead, such as were lifted up in the pride of their hearts.

6. Yea, and thus they were supported in their laziness, and in their idolatry, and in their whoredoms, by the *p*taxes which king Noah had put upon his people; thus did the people labor exceedingly to support iniquity.

7. Yea, and they also became idolatrous, because they were deceived by the vain and flattering words of the king and *h*priests; for they did speak flattering things unto them.

8. And it came to pass that king Noah built many elegant and spacious buildings; and he ornamented them with fine work of wood, and of all manner of precious things, of gold, and of silver, and of iron, and of brass, and of ziff, and of copper;

9. And he also built him a spacious palace, and a throne in the midst thereof, all of which was of fine wood and was ornamented with gold and silver and with precious things.

10. And he also caused that his workmen should work all manner of fine work within the walls of the *j*temple, of fine wood, and of copper, and of brass.

11. And the seats which were set apart for the *k*high priests, which were above all the other seats, he did ornament with pure gold; and he caused a breastwork to be built before them, that they might rest their bodies and their arms upon while they should speak lying and vain words to his people.

12. And it came to pass that he built a *l*tower near the *m*temple; yea, a very high tower, even so high that he could stand upon the top thereof and overlook the land of *n*Shilom, and also the land of *o*Shemlon, which was possessed by the Lamanites; and he could even look over all the land round about.

13. And it came to pass that he caused many buildings to be built in the land Shilom; and he caused a *p*great tower to be built on the hill north of the land Shilom, which had been a resort for the children of Nephi at the time they *q*fled out of the land; and thus he did do with the riches which he obtained by the taxation of his people.

14. And it came to pass that he placed his heart upon his riches, and he spent his time in riotous living with *r*his wives and his concubines; and so did also his *s*priests spend their time with harlots.

15. And it came to pass that he planted vineyards round about in the land; and he built winepresses, and made wine in abundance; and therefore he became a wine-bibber, and also his people.

16. And it came to pass that the Lamanites began to come in upon his people, upon small numbers, and to slay them in their fields, and while they were tending their flocks.

17. And king Noah sent guards round about the land to keep them off; but he did not send a sufficient number, and the Lamanites came upon them and killed them, and drove many of their flocks out of the land; thus the Lamanites began to destroy

---

e, see *c*, Mos. 6. *f*, vers. 7, 11, 14. Mos. 12:17, 25. 13:1. 17:1, 6, 12—18. 19:21, 23. 20:3, 18, 23. 21:20, 23. 23:9, 12, 31—35, 39. 24:1—6, 8—11. *g*, ver. 3. *h*, see *f*. *j*, see *h*, 2 Ne. 5. *k*, see *f*. *l*, Mos. 19:5, 6. *m*, see *h*, 2 Ne. 5. *n*, see *f*, Mos. 7. *o*, see *d*, Mos. 10. *p*, Mos. 7:5. *q*, Om. 12, 13. *r*, see *n*, Jac. 2. *s*, see *f*.

BETWEEN B. C. 160 AND 150.

them, and to exercise their hatred upon them.

18. And it came to pass that king Noah sent his armies against them, and they were driven back, or they drove them back for a time; therefore, they returned rejoicing in their spoil.

19. And now, because of this great victory they were lifted up in the pride of their hearts; they did boast in their own strength, saying that their fifty could stand against thousands of the Lamanites; and thus they did boast, and did delight in blood, and the shedding of the blood of their brethren, and this because of the wickedness of their king and 'priests.

20. And it came to pass that there was a man among them whose name was Abinadi; *and he went forth among them, and began to prophesy, saying: Behold, thus saith the Lord, and thus hath he commanded me, saying, Go forth, and say unto this people, thus saith the Lord—Wo be unto this people, for I have seen their abominations, and their wickedness, and their whoredoms; and except they repent I will visit them in mine anger.

21. And except they repent and turn to the Lord their God, behold, I will deliver them into the hands of their enemies; yea, and they shall be brought into ᵘbondage; and they shall be afflicted by the hand of their enemies.

22. And it shall come to pass that they shall know that I am the Lord their God, and am a jealous God, visiting the iniquities of my people.

23. And it shall come to pass that except this people repent and turn unto the Lord their God, they shall be brought into ᵛbondage; and none shall deliver them, except it be the Lord the Almighty God.

24. Yea, and it shall come to pass that when they shall cry unto me I will be ʷslow to hear their cries; yea, and I will suffer them that they be smitten by their enemies.

25. And except they repent in sackcloth and ashes, and cry mightily to the Lord their God, I will not hear their prayers, neither will I deliver them out of their afflictions; and thus saith the Lord, and thus hath he commanded me.

26. Now it came to pass that when Abinadi had spoken these words unto them they were wroth with him, and sought to take away his life; but the Lord delivered him out of their hands.

27. Now when king Noah had heard of the words which Abinadi had spoken unto the people, he was also wroth; and he said: Who is Abinadi, that I and my people should be judged of him, or who is the Lord, that shall bring upon my people such great affliction?

28. I command you to bring Abinadi hither, that I may slay him, for he has said these things that he might stir up my people to anger one with another, and to raise contentions among my people; therefore I will slay him.

29. Now the eyes of the people were blinded; therefore they hardened their hearts against the words of Abinadi, and they sought from that time forward to take him. And king Noah hardened his heart against the word of the Lord, and he did not repent of his evil doings.

t, see *f*. *u*, ver. 23. See *k*, Mos. 9. 12:2. *v*, see *u*. *w*, ver. 25. Mos. 21:14, 15.
* About B. C. 150.

MOSIAH, 12.

CHAPTER 12.

Abinadi, for denouncing evil-doers, is cast into prison—The false priests sit in judgment upon him—They are confounded.

1. And it came to pass that *after the space of two years that Abinadi came among them in disguise, that they knew him not, and began to prophesy among them, saying: Thus has the Lord commanded me, saying—Abinadi, go and prophesy unto this my people, for they have hardened their hearts against my words; they have repented not of their evil doings; therefore, I will visit them in my anger, yea, in my fierce anger will I visit them in their iniquities and abominations.

2. Yea, wo be unto this generation! And the Lord said unto me: Stretch forth thy hand and prophesy, saying: Thus saith the Lord, it shall come to pass that this generation, because of their iniquities, shall be brought into ^{a}bondage, and shall be smitten ^{b}on the cheek; yea, and shall be driven ^{c}by men, and shall be slain; and the vultures of the air, and the dogs, yea, and the wild beasts, shall devour their flesh.

3. And it shall come to pass that the life of king Noah shall be valued even as a ^{d}garment in a hot furnace; for he shall know that I am the Lord.

4. And it shall come to pass that I will smite this my people with sore afflictions, yea, with famine and with pestilence; and I will cause that they shall ^{e}howl all the day long.

5. Yea, and I will cause that they shall have burdens ^{f}lashed upon their backs; and they shall be driven before like a dumb ass.

6. And it shall come to pass that I will send forth hail among them, and it shall smite them; and they shall also be smitten with the ^{g}east wind; and insects shall pester their land also, and devour their grain.

7. And they shall be smitten with a great pestilence—and all this will I do because of their iniquities and abominations.

8. And it shall come to pass that except they repent I will ^{h}utterly destroy them from off the face of the earth; yet they shall ^{i}leave a record behind them, and I will preserve them for ^{j}other nations which shall possess the land; yea, even this will I do that I may discover the abominations of this people to other nations. And many things did Abinadi prophesy against this people.

9. And it came to pass that they were angry with him; and they took him and carried him bound before the king, and said unto the king: Behold, we have brought a man before thee who has prophesied evil concerning thy people, and saith that God will destroy them.

10. And he also prophesieth evil concerning thy life, and saith that thy life shall be as a ^{k}garment in a furnace of fire.

11. And again, he saith that thou shalt be as a stalk, even as a dry stalk of the field, which is run over by the beasts and trodden under foot.

12. And again, he saith thou shalt be as the blossoms of a thistle, which, when it is fully ripe, if the wind bloweth, it is driven forth upon the face of the land. And he pretendeth the Lord hath spoken it. And he saith all this

a, see *u*, Mos. 11. *b*, Mos. 21:3. *c*, ver. 5. Mos. 21:3, 4, 13. *d*, Mos. 19:20. *e*, Mos. 21:1—15. *f*, Mos. 21:3. *g*, Mos. 7:31. *h*, 1 Ne. 12:19. 2 Ne. 26:10, 11. Al. 45:9—14. He. 13:5, 6. 3 Ne. 27:32. Morm. 6. *i*, Morm. 8:14—16. See *c*, 2 Ne. 27. *j*, see *s*, 1 Ne. 13. *k*, ver. 3.

* ABOUT B. C. 148.

shall come upon thee except thou repent, and this because of thine iniquities.

13. And now, O king, what great evil hast thou done, or what great sins have thy people committed, that we should be condemned of God or judged of this man?

14. And now, O king, behold, we are guiltless, and thou, O king, hast not sinned; therefore, this man has lied concerning you, and he has prophesied in vain.

15. And behold, we are strong, we shall not come into bondage, or be taken captive by our enemies; yea, and thou hast prospered in the land, and thou shalt also prosper.

16. Behold, here is the man, we deliver him into thy hands; thou mayest do with him as seemeth thee good.

17. And it came to pass that king Noah caused that Abinadi should be cast into prison; and he commanded that the ^lpriests should gather themselves together that he might hold a council with them what he should do with him.

18. And it came to pass that he said unto the king: Bring him hither that we may question him; and the king commanded that he should be brought before them.

19. And they began to question him, that they might cross him, that thereby they might have wherewith to accuse him; but he answered them boldly, and withstood all their questions, yea, to their astonishment; for he did withstand them in all their questions, and did confound them in all their words.

20. And it came to pass that one of them said unto him: What meaneth the words which are written, and which have been taught by our fathers, saying:

21. ^mHow beautiful upon the mountains are the feet of him that bringeth good tidings; that publisheth peace; that bringeth good tidings of good; that publisheth salvation; that saith unto Zion, Thy God reigneth;

22. Thy watchman shall lift up the voice; with the voice together shall they sing; for they shall see eye to eye when the Lord shall bring again Zion;

23. Break forth into joy; sing together ye waste places of Jerusalem; for the Lord hath comforted his people, he hath redeemed Jerusalem;

24. The Lord hath made bare his holy arm in the eyes of all the nations, and all the ends of the earth shall see the salvation of our God?

25. And now Abinadi said unto them: Are you ⁿpriests, and pretend to teach this people, and to understand the spirit of prophesying, and yet desire to know of me what these things mean?

26. I say unto you, wo be unto you for perverting the ways of the Lord! For if ye understand these things ye have not taught them; therefore, ye have perverted the ways of the Lord.

27. Ye have not applied your hearts to understanding; therefore, ye have not been wise. Therefore, what teach ye this people?

28. And they said: We teach the law of Moses.

29. And again he said unto them: If ye teach the ^olaw of Moses why do ye not keep it? Why do ye set your hearts upon riches? Why do ye commit ^pwhoredoms and spend your strength with

---

l, see *f*, Mos. 11.   *m*, Isa. 52:7—10.   *n*, see *f*, Mos. 11.   *o*, see *o*, 2 Ne. 25.   *p*, see *i*, 2 Ne. 28.   ABOUT B. C. 148.

harlots, yea, and cause this people to commit sin, that the Lord has cause to send me to prophesy against this people, yea, even a great evil against this people?

30. Know ye not that I speak the truth? Yea, ye know that I speak the truth; and you ought to tremble before God.

31. And it shall come to pass that ye shall be smitten for your iniquities, for ye have said that ye teach the law of Moses. And what know ye concerning the law of Moses? Doth salvation come by the law of Moses? What say ye?

32. And they answered and said that salvation did come by the ᵠlaw of Moses.

33. But now Abinadi said unto them: I know if ye keep the commandments of God ye shall be saved; yea, if ye keep the commandments which the Lord delivered unto Moses in the mount of Sinai, saying:

34. ʳI am the Lord thy God, who hath brought thee out of the land of Egypt, out of the house of bondage.

35. Thou shalt have no other God before me.

36. Thou shalt not make unto thee any graven image, or any likeness of any thing in heaven above, or things which are in the earth beneath.

37. Now Abinadi said unto them, Have ye done all this? I say unto you, Nay, ye have not. And have ye taught this people that they should do all these things? I say unto you, Nay, ye have not.

CHAPTER 13.

Abinadi the prophet, protected by divine power, withstands the priests and cites the Law and the Gospel.

1. And now when the king had heard these words, he said unto ᵃhis priests: Away with this fellow, and slay him; for what have we to do with him, for he is mad.

2. And they stood forth and attempted to lay their hands on him; but he withstood them, and said unto them:

3. Touch me not, for God shall smite you if ye lay your hands upon me, for I have not delivered the message which the Lord sent me to deliver; neither have I told you that which ᵇye requested that I should tell; therefore, God will not suffer that I shall be destroyed at this time.

4. But I must fulfil the commandments wherewith God has commanded me; and because I have told you the truth ye are angry with me. And again, because I have spoken the word of God ye have judged me that I am ᶜmad.

5. Now it came to pass after Abinadi had spoken these words that the people of king Noah durst not lay their hands on him, for the Spirit of the Lord was upon him; and his face shone with exceeding luster, even as ᵈMoses' did while in the mount of Sinai, while speaking with the Lord.

6. And he spake with power and authority from God; and he continued his words, saying:

7. Ye see that ye have not power to slay me, therefore I finish my message. Yea, and I perceive that it cuts you to your hearts because I tell you the truth concerning your iniquities.

8. Yea, and my words fill you with wonder and amazement, and with anger.

9. But I finish my message; and then it matters not whither I go, if so be that I am saved.

---

q, see *o*, 2 Ne. 25. *r*, Ex. 20:2—4. 24. *c*, ver. 1. *d*, Ex. 34:29—35. CHAP. 13: *a*, see *f*, Mos. 11. *b*, Mos. 12:20— ABOUT B. C. 148.

10. But this much I tell you, what you do with me, after this, shall be as a *type and a shadow of things which are to come.

11. And now I read unto you the remainder of the commandments of God, for I perceive that they are not written in your hearts; I perceive that ye have studied and taught iniquity the most part of your lives.

12. And now, ye remember that I 'said unto you: Thou shalt not make unto thee any graven image, or any likeness of things which are in heaven above, or which are in the earth beneath, or which are in the water under the earth.

13. And again: ⁰Thou shalt not bow down thyself unto them, nor serve them; for I the Lord thy God am a jealous God, visiting the iniquities of the fathers upon the children, unto the third and fourth generations of them that hate me;

14. And showing mercy unto thousands of them that love me and keep my commandments.

15. Thou shalt not take the name of the Lord thy God in vain; for the Lord will not hold him guiltless that taketh his name in vain.

16. Remember the sabbath day, to keep it holy.

17. Six days shalt thou labor, and do all thy work;

18. But the seventh day, the sabbath of the Lord thy God, thou shalt not do any work, thou, nor thy son, nor thy daughter, thy man-servant, nor thy maid-servant, nor thy cattle, nor thy stranger that is within thy gates;

19. For in six days the Lord made heaven and earth, and the sea, and all that in them is; wherefore the Lord blessed the sabbath day, and hallowed it.

20. Honor thy father and thy mother, that thy days may be long upon the land which the Lord thy God giveth thee.

21. Thou shalt not kill.

22. Thou shalt not commit adultery. Thou shalt not steal.

23. Thou shalt not bear false witness against thy neighbor.

24. Thou shalt not covet thy neighbor's house, thou shalt not covet thy neighbor's wife, nor his man-servant, nor his maid-servant, nor his ox, nor his ass, nor anything that is thy neighbor's.

25. And it came to pass that after Abinadi had made an end of these sayings that he said unto them: Have ye taught this people that they should observe to do all these things for to keep these commandments?

26. I say unto you, Nay; for if ye had, the Lord would not have caused me to come forth and to prophesy evil concerning this people.

27. And now ye have said that salvation cometh by the law of Moses. I say unto you that it is expedient that ye should ʰkeep the law of Moses as yet; but I say unto you, that the time shall come when it shall ⁱno more be expedient to keep the law of Moses.

28. And moreover, I say unto you, that salvation doth not come by the law alone; and were it not for the ʲatonement, which God himself shall make for the sins and iniquities of his people, that they must unavoidably perish, notwithstanding the law of Moses.

29. And now I say unto you that it was expedient that there should be a law given to the chil-

e, Mos. 17:13—19. 19:20. Al. 25:7—12. *f*, Mos. 12:36. *g*, Ex. 20:5—17. *h*, see *o*, 2 Ne. 25. *i*, 3 Ne. 9:19, 20. 15:2—10. *j*, see *f*, 2 Ne. 2. ABOUT B. C. 148.

dren of Israel, yea, even a very strict law; for they were a stiffnecked people, quick to do iniquity, and slow to remember the Lord their God;

30. Therefore there was a law given them, yea, a ^{k}law of performances and of ordinances, a law which they were to observe strictly from day to day, to keep them in remembrance of God and their duty towards him.

31. But behold, I say unto you, that all these things were types of things to come.

32. And now, did they understand the law? I say unto you, Nay, they did not all understand the law; and this because of the hardness of their hearts; for they understood not that there could not any man be saved except it were through the redemption of God.

33. For behold, did not Moses prophesy unto them concerning the coming of the Messiah, and that God should redeem his people? Yea, and even all the prophets who have prophesied ever since the world began—have they not spoken more or less concerning these things?

34. Have they not said that ^{l}God himself should come down among the children of men, and take upon him the form of man, and go forth in mighty power upon the face of the earth?

35. Yea, and have they not said also that he should bring to pass the ^{m}resurrection of the dead, and that he, himself, should be oppressed and afflicted?

CHAPTER 14.

Abinadi quotes Isaiah to the priests of king Noah—Compare Isaiah 53.

1. Yea, even doth not Isaiah say: Who hath believed our report, and to whom is the arm of the Lord revealed?

2. For he shall grow up before him as a tender plant, and as a root out of dry ground; he hath no form nor comeliness; and when we shall see him there is no beauty that we should desire him.

3. He is despised and rejected of men; a man of sorrows, and acquainted with grief; and we hid as it were our face from him; he was despised, and we esteemed him not.

4. Surely he has borne our griefs, and carried our sorrows; yet we did esteem him stricken, smitten of God, and afflicted.

5. But he was wounded for our transgressions, he was bruised for our iniquities; the chastisement of our peace was upon him; and with his stripes we are healed.

6. All we, like sheep, have gone astray; we have turned every one to his own way; and the Lord hath laid on him the iniquities of us all.

7. He was oppressed, and he was afflicted, yet he opened not his mouth; he is brought as a lamb to the slaughter, and as a sheep before her shearers is dumb so he opened not his mouth.

8. He was taken from prison and from judgment; and who shall declare his generation? For he was cut off out of the land of the living; for the transgressions of my people was he stricken.

9. And he made his grave with the wicked, and with the rich in his death; because he had done no evil, neither was any deceit in his mouth.

10. Yet it pleased the Lord to bruise him; he hath put him to grief; when thou shalt make his soul an offering for sin he shall

---

k, see *o*, 2 Ne. 25. *l*, see *b*, Mos. 3. *m*, see *d*, 2 Ne. 2. ABOUT B. C. 148.

see his seed, he shall prolong his days, and the pleasure of the Lord shall prosper in his hand.

11. He shall see the travail of his soul, and shall be satisfied; by his knowledge shall my righteous servant justify many; for he shall bear their iniquities.

12. Therefore will I divide him a portion with the great, and he shall divide the spoil with the strong; because he hath poured out his soul unto death; and he was numbered with the transgressors; and he bore the sins of many, and made intercession for the transgressors.

CHAPTER 15.

Abinadi's prophecy—God himself to come down and redeem his people—Why Jesus Christ is called the Father and the Son.

1. And now Abinadi said unto them: I would that ye should understand that ªGod himself shall come down among the children of men, and shall redeem his people.

2. And because he ᵇdwelleth in flesh he shall be called the Son of God, and having subjected the flesh to the will of the Father, being the Father and the Son—

3. The Father, because he was ᶜconceived by the power of God; and the Son, ᵈbecause of the flesh; thus becoming the Father and Son—

4. And they are ᵉone God, yea, the very ᶠEternal Father of heaven and of earth.

5. And thus the flesh becoming ᵍsubject to the Spirit, or the Son to the Father, being ʰone God, ⁱsuffereth temptation, and yieldeth not to the temptation, but suffereth himself to be mocked, and scourged, and cast out, and disowned by his people.

6. And after all this, after working many ʲmighty miracles among the children of men, he shall be led, yea, even as Isaiah said, ᵏas a sheep before the shearer is dumb, so he opened not his mouth.

7. Yea, even so he shall be led, ˡcrucified, and slain, the flesh ᵐbecoming subject even unto death, the will of the Son being swallowed up in the will of the Father.

8. And thus God breaketh the ⁿbands of death, having gained the victory over death; giving the Son power to make ᵒintercession for the children of men—

9. Having ascended into heaven, having the bowels of mercy; being filled with compassion towards the children of men; standing betwixt them and justice; having ᵖbroken the bands of death, taken upon ᵠhimself their iniquity and their transgressions, having redeemed them, and satisfied the demands of justice.

10. And now I say unto you, who shall ʳdeclare his generation? Behold, I say unto you, that when his soul has been made an ˢoffering for sin he shall see his seed. And now what say ye? And who shall be ᵗhis seed?

11. Behold I say unto you, that whosoever has heard the words of the prophets, yea, all the holy prophets who have prophesied concerning the coming of the Lord—I say unto you, that all those who have hearkened unto their words, and believed that the

a, see 2*b,* Mos. 7. *b,* see *b,* Mos. 3. *c,* 1 Ne. 11:13—21. Mos. 3:8, 9. Al. 7:10. 19:13. 3 Ne. 1:14. Morm. 9:12. *d,* see *b,* Mos. 3. *e,* see *k,* 2 Ne. 31. *f,* see *a,* Mos. 3. *g,* ver. 2. *h,* see *k,* 2 Ne. 31. *i,* see *s,* 2 Ne. 9. *j,* see *c,* Mos. 3. *k,* Mos. 14:7. Isa. 53:7. *l,* see *g,* Mos. 3. *m,* vers. 2, 5. *n,* see *g* and *j,* 2 Ne. 9. *o,* see *e,* 2 Ne. 2. *p,* see *g* and *j,* 2 Ne. 9. *q,* Mos. 14:5—8, 11, 12. *r,* Mos. 14:8. *s,* Mos. 14:10. *t,* vers. 11—13. ABOUT B. C. 148.

Lord would redeem his people, and have looked forward to that day for a remission of their sins, I say unto you, that these are his seed, or they are the heirs of the kingdom of God.

12. For these are they whose sins he ᵘhas borne; these are they for whom he has died, to redeem them from their transgressions. And now, are they not his seed?

13. Yea, and are not the prophets, every one that has opened his mouth to prophesy, that has not fallen into transgression, I mean all the holy prophets ever since the world began? I say unto you that they are his seed.

14. And these are ᵛthey who have published peace, who have brought good tidings of good, who have published salvation; and said unto Zion: Thy God reigneth!

15. And O how beautiful upon the mountains were their feet!

16. And again, how beautiful upon the mountains are the feet of those that are still publishing peace!

17. And again, how beautiful upon the mountains are the feet of those who shall hereafter publish peace, yea, from this time henceforth and forever!

18. And behold, I say unto you, this is not all. For O how beautiful upon the mountains are the feet of him that bringeth good tidings, that is the founder of peace, yea, even the Lord, who has redeemed his people; yea, him who has granted salvation unto his people;

19. For were it not for the redemption which he hath made for his people, which was prepared from the ʷfoundation of the world, I say unto you, were it not for this, ˣall mankind must have perished.

20. But behold, the bands of death ʸshall be broken, and the Son reigneth, and hath power over the dead; therefore, he bringeth to pass the ᶻresurrection of the dead.

21. And there cometh a resurrection, even a ²ᵃfirst resurrection; yea, even a resurrection of those that have been, and who are, and who shall be, even until the resurrection of Christ—for so shall he be called.

22. And now, the resurrection of all the prophets, and all those that have believed in their words, or all those that have kept the commandments of God, shall come forth in the first resurrection; therefore, they are the first resurrection.

23. They are raised to dwell with God who has redeemed them; thus they have eternal life through Christ, who has broken the bands of death.

24. And these are those who have part in the first resurrection; and these are they that have died before Christ came, ²ᵇin their ignorance, not having salvation declared unto them. And thus the Lord bringeth about the restoration of these; and they have a part in the first resurrection, or have eternal life, being redeemed by the Lord.

25. And little children ²ᶜalso have eternal life.

26. But behold, and fear, and tremble before God, for ye ought to tremble; for the Lord redeemeth none such that rebel against him and die in their sins; yea, even all those that have perished

u, Mos. 14:12. *v*, Mos. 12:21—24. Isa. 52:7—10. *w*, see *d*, Mos. 4. *x*, see *e* and *g*, 2 Ne. 9. *y*, see *g* and *j*, 2 Ne. 9. *z*, see *d*, 2 Ne. 2. 2*a*, see *g*, Jac. 4. 2*b*, see *j*, Mos. 3. 2*c*, see *m*, Mos. 3. ABOUT B. C. 148.

in their sins ever since the world began, that have ²ᵈwilfully rebelled against God, that have known the commandments of God, and would not keep them; these are they that have ²ᵉno part in the first resurrection.

27. Therefore ought ye not to tremble? For salvation cometh to none such; for the Lord hath redeemed none such; yea, neither can the Lord redeem such; for he cannot deny himself; for he cannot ²ᶠdeny justice when it has its claim.

28. And now I say unto you that the time shall come that the salvation of the Lord shall be declared to every nation, kindred, tongue, and people.

29. Yea, Lord, ²ᵍthy watchmen shall lift up their voice; with the voice together shall they sing; for they shall see eye to eye, when the Lord shall bring again Zion.

30. Break forth into joy, sing together, ye waste places of Jerusalem; for the Lord hath comforted his people, he hath redeemed Jerusalem.

31. The Lord hath made bare his holy arm in the eyes of all the nations; and all the ends of the earth shall see the salvation of our God.

CHAPTER 16.

Abinadi continues his prophecy—Christ the only Redeemer—Resurrection and judgment.

1. And now, it came to pass that after Abinadi had spoken these words he stretched forth his hand and said: The time shall come when all shall see the salvation of the Lord; ᵃwhen every nation, kindred, tongue, and people shall see eye to eye and shall confess before God that his judgments are just.

2. And then shall the wicked be cast out, and they shall have ᵇcause to howl, and weep, and wail, and gnash their teeth; and this because they would not hearken unto the voice of the Lord; therefore the Lord redeemeth them not.

3. For they are carnal and devilish, and the devil ᶜhas power over them; yea, even that ᵈold serpent that did beguile our first parents, which was the cause of their fall; which was the cause of all mankind becoming carnal, sensual, devilish, knowing evil from good, subjecting themselves to the devil.

4. Thus ᵉall mankind were lost; and behold, they would have been endlessly lost were it not that God redeemed his people from their lost and fallen state.

5. But remember that he that persists in his own carnal nature, and goes on in the ways of sin and rebellion against God, remaineth in his fallen state and the devil hath ᶠall power over him. Therefore, he is as though there was no redemption made, being an enemy to God; and also is the devil an enemy to God.

6. And now if Christ had not come into the world, speaking of things to come as though they had already come, there could have been no redemption.

7. And if Christ had not risen from the dead, or have ᵍbroken the bands of death that the grave should have ʰno victory, and that death should have ⁱno sting, there could have been no resurrection.

8. But there is a ʲresurrection,

2d, see k, Jac. 6. 2e, ver. 24. 2f, Al. 42:1—26. 2g, Isn. 52:8—10. Mos. 12:22—24. CHAP. 16: a, Mos. 3:20, 21. 15:28, 31. b, see k, 1 Ne. 15. Matt. 13:42. c, see i, 2 Ne. 9. d, see i, 2 Ne. 2. e, see e and g, 2 Ne. 9. f, see i, 2 Ne. 9. g, see g and n, Mos. 15. h, Mos. 15:8, 20. Al. 22:14. 27:28. i, ver. 8. Al. 22:14. 24:23. Morm. 7:5. j, see d, 2 Ne. 2. ABOUT B. C. 148.

therefore the grave hath ^{k}no victory, and the ^{l}sting of death is swallowed up in Christ.

9. He is the ^{m}light and the life of the world; yea, a light that is endless, that can never be darkened; yea, and also a life which is endless, that there can be no more death.

10. Even ^{n}this mortal shall put on immortality, and this corruption shall put on incorruption, and shall be brought to stand before the bar of God, to be judged of him according to their works whether they be good or whether they be evil—

11. If they be good, to the resurrection of endless life and happiness; and if they be evil, to the resurrection of endless damnation, being delivered up ^{o}to the devil, who hath subjected them, which is damnation—

12. Having gone according to their own carnal wills and desires; having never called upon the Lord while the arms of mercy were extended towards them; for the arms of mercy were extended towards them, and they would not; they being warned of their iniquities and yet they would not depart from them; and they were commanded to repent and yet they would not repent.

13. And now, ought ye not to tremble and repent of your sins, and remember that only in and through Christ ye can be saved?

14. Therefore, if ye teach the ^{p}law of Moses, also teach that it is a shadow of those things which are to come—

15. Teach them that redemption cometh through Christ the Lord, who is the ^{q}very Eternal Father. Amen.

CHAPTER 17.

Martyrdom of Abinadi—While suffering death by fire he predicts retribution upon his murderers—Conversion of Alma.

1. And now it came to pass that when Abinadi had finished these sayings, that the king commanded that the ^{a}priests should take him and cause that he should be put to death.

2. But there was one among them whose name was Alma, he also being a descendant of Nephi. And he was a young man, and he believed the words which Abinadi had spoken, for he knew concerning the iniquity which Abinadi had testified against them; therefore he began to plead with the king that he would not be angry with Abinadi, but suffer that he might depart in peace.

3. But the king was more wroth, and caused that Alma should be cast out from among them, and sent his servants after him that they might slay him.

4. But he fled from before them and hid himself that they found him not. And he being concealed for many days did write all the words which Abinadi had spoken.

5. And it came to pass that the king caused that his guards should surround Abinadi and take him; and they bound him and cast him into prison.

6. And after three days, having counseled with his ^{b}priests, he caused that he should again be brought before him.

7. And he said unto him: Abinadi, we have found an accusation against thee, and thou art worthy of death.

---

k, ver. 7. l, ver. 7. m, Al. 38:9. 3 Ne. 9:18. 15:9. 18:16, 24. Eth. 3:14. 4:12. Moro. 7:18. John 8:12. 9:5. 14:6. D. & C. 84:45. 88:7—13. n, see d, 2 Ne. 2. Also j and m, 2 Ne. 9. o, see i, 2 Ne. 9. p, see o, 2 Ne. 25. q, see a, Mos. 3. Chap. 17: a, see f, Mos. 11. b, see f, Mos. 11. About B. C. 148.

MOSIAH, 18.

8. For thou hast said that ^cGod himself should come down among the children of men; and now, for this cause thou shalt be put to death unless thou wilt recall all the words which thou hast spoken evil concerning me and my people.

9. Now Abinadi said unto him: I say unto you, I will not recall the words which I have spoken unto you concerning this people, for they are true; and that ye may know of their surety I have suffered myself that I have fallen into your hands.

10. Yea, and I will suffer even until death, and I will not recall my words, and they shall stand as a testimony against you. And if ye slay me ye will shed innocent blood, and this shall also stand as a testimony against you at the last day.

11. And now king Noah was about to release him, for he feared his word; for he feared that the judgments of God would come upon him.

12. But the ^dpriests lifted up their voices against him, and began to accuse him, saying: He has reviled the king. Therefore the king was stirred up in anger against him, and he delivered him up that he might be slain.

13. And it came to pass that they took him and bound him, and scourged his skin with faggots, yea, even unto ^edeath.

14. And now when the flames began to scorch him, he cried unto them, saying:

15. Behold, even as ye have done unto me, so shall it come to pass that ^fthy seed shall cause that many shall suffer even the pains of death by fire; and this because they believe in the salvation of the Lord their God.

16. And it will come to pass that ye shall be afflicted with all manner of diseases because of your iniquities.

17. Yea, and ye shall be smitten on every hand, and shall be driven and scattered to and fro, even as a wild flock is driven by wild and ferocious beasts.

18. And in that day ye shall be ^ghunted, and ye shall be taken by the hand of your enemies, and then ye shall suffer, as I suffer, the pains of death by fire.

19. Thus God executeth vengeance upon those that destroy his people. O God, receive my soul.

20. And now, *when Abinadi had said these words, he fell, having suffered ^hdeath by fire; yea, having been put to death because he would not deny the commandments of God, having sealed the truth of his words by his death.

CHAPTER 18.

The waters of Mormon—Alma baptizes Helam and others—The church of Christ—King Noah sends an army to destroy Alma and his followers.

1. And now, it came to pass that Alma, who had fled from the servants of king Noah, repented of his sins and iniquities, and went about privately among the people, and began to teach the words of Abinadi—

2. Yea, concerning that which was to come, and also concerning the ^aresurrection of the dead, and the redemption of the people, which was to be brought to pass through the power, and sufferings, and death of Christ, and his resurrection and ascension into heaven.

---

c, Mos. 7:27. 13:34. *d*, see *f*, Mos. 11. *e*, vers. 18—20. Mos. 7:28. *f*, Mos. 13:10. Al. 25:7—12. *g*, Al. 25:8, 9. *h*, see *e*. CHAP. 18: *a*, see *d*, 2 Ne. 2. * ABOUT B. C. 148.

3. And as many as would hear his word he did teach. And he taught them privately, that it might not come to the knowledge of the king. And many did believe his words.

4. And it came to pass that as many as did believe him did go forth to a place which was called *b*Mormon, having received its name from the king, being in the borders of the land having been infested, by times or at seasons, by wild beasts.

5. Now, there was in *c*Mormon a fountain of pure water, and Alma resorted thither, there being near the water a thicket of small trees, where he did hide himself in the daytime from the searches of the king.

6. And it came to pass that as many as believed him went thither to hear his words.

7. And it came to pass *after many days there were a goodly number gathered together at the place of Mormon, to hear the words of Alma. Yea, all were gathered together that believed on his word, to hear him. And he did teach them, and did preach unto them repentance, and redemption, and faith on the Lord.

8. And it came to pass that he said unto them: Behold, here are the *d*waters of Mormon (for thus were they called) and now, as ye are desirous to come into the fold of God, and to be called his people, and are willing to bear one another's burdens, that they may be light;

9. Yea, and are willing to mourn with those that mourn; yea, and comfort those that stand in need of comfort, and to stand as witnesses of God at all times and in all things, and in all places that ye may be in, even until death, that ye may be redeemed of God, and be numbered with those of the *e*first resurrection, that ye may have eternal life—

10. Now I say unto you, if this be the desire of your hearts, what have you against being *f*baptized in the name of the Lord, as a witness before him that ye have entered into a covenant with him, that ye will serve him and keep his commandments, that he may pour out his Spirit more abundantly upon you?

11. And now when the people had heard these words, they clapped their hands for joy, and exclaimed: This is the desire of our hearts.

12. And now it came to pass that Alma took Helam, he being one of the first, and went and stood forth in the water, and cried, saying: O Lord, pour out thy Spirit upon thy servant, that he may do this work with holiness of heart.

13. And when he had said these words, the Spirit of the Lord was upon him, and he said: Helam, I baptize thee, *g*having authority from the Almighty God, as a testimony that ye have entered into a covenant to serve him until you are dead as to the mortal body; and may the Spirit of the Lord be poured out upon you; and may he grant unto you eternal life, through the redemption of Christ, whom he has prepared from the *h*foundation of the world.

14. And after Alma had said these words, both Alma and Helam were buried in the water; and they arose and came forth out of the water rejoicing, being filled with the Spirit.

---

b, vers. 5, 8, 16, 30. Al. 5:3. 3 Ne. 5:12. Morm. 1:5. *c*, ver. 4. *d*, ver. 5. *e*, see *g*, Jac. 4. *f*, see *u*, 2 Ne. 9. *g*, Al. 5:3. 3 Ne. 11:25. *h*, see *d*, Mos. 4.
* ABOUT B. C. 147.

MOSIAH, 18.

15. And again, Alma took another, and went forth a second time into the water, and baptized him according to the first, only he did not bury himself again in the water.

16. And after this manner he did baptize every one that went forth to the ⁱplace of Mormon; and they were in number about two hundred and four souls; yea, and they were baptized in the ʲwaters of Mormon, and were filled with the grace of God.

17. And they were called the church of God, or the church of Christ, from that time forward. And it came to pass that whosoever was ᵏbaptized by the power and authority of God was added to his church.

18. And it came to pass that Alma, having authority from God, ˡordained priests; even one priest to every fifty of their number did he ordain to preach unto them, and to teach them concerning the things pertaining to the kingdom of God.

19. And he commanded them that they should teach nothing save it were the things which he had taught, and which had been spoken by the mouth of the holy prophets.

20. Yea, even he commanded them that they should preach nothing save it were repentance and faith on the Lord, who had redeemed his people.

21. And he commanded them that there should be no contention one with another, but that they should look forward with one eye, having one faith and one baptism, having their hearts knit together in unity and in love one towards another.

22. And thus he commanded them to preach. And thus they became the children of God.

23. And he commanded them that they should observe the ᵐsabbath day, and keep it holy, and also every day they should give thanks to the Lord their God.

24. And he also commanded them that the ⁿpriests whom he had ordained should labor with their ᵒown hands for their support.

25. And there was ᵖone day in every week that was set apart that they should gather themselves together to teach the people, and to worship the Lord their God, and also, as often as it was in their power, to assemble themselves together.

26. And the priests were not to depend upon the people for ᵠtheir support; but for their labor they were to receive the grace of God, that they might wax strong in the Spirit, having the knowledge of God, that they might teach with power and authority from God.

27. And again Alma commanded that the people of the church should impart of their substance, ʳevery one according to that which he had; if he have more abundantly he should impart more abundantly; and of him that had but little, but little should be required; and to him that had not should be given.

28. And thus they should impart of their substance of their own free will and good desires towards God, and to those priests that stood in need, yea, and to every needy, naked soul.

29. And this he said unto them, having been commanded of God; and they did walk uprightly before God, imparting to one another both temporally and spir-

---
i, see *b*. *j*, vers. 5, 8. *k*, see *u*, 2 Ne. 9. *l*, see *c*, Mos. 6. *m*, Mos. 13:16—19. Mark 2:27, 28. D. & C. 59:9, 10. 68:29. *n*, see *c*, Mos. 6. *o*, ver. 26, 28. *p*, Ai. 32:11. *q*, ver. 24. *r*, see *j*, Jac. 2. ABOUT B. C. 147.

itually according to their needs and their wants.

30. And now it came to pass that all this was done in *Mormon, yea, by the 'waters of Mormon, in the ᵘforest that was near the waters of Mormon; yea, the place of Mormon, the waters of Mormon, the forest of Mormon, how beautiful are they to the eyes of them who there came to the knowledge of their Redeemer; yea, and how blessed are they, for they shall sing to his praise forever.

31. And these things were done in the ᵛborders of the land, that they might not come to the knowledge of the king.

32. But behold, it came to pass that the king, having discovered a movement among the people, sent his servants to watch them. Therefore on the day that they were assembling themselves together to hear the word of the Lord they were discovered unto the king.

33. And now the king said that Alma was stirring up the people to rebellion against him; therefore he sent his army to destroy them.

34. And it came to pass that Alma and the people of the Lord were ʷapprised of the coming of the king's army; therefore they took their tents and their families and departed into the wilderness.

35. And they were in number about four hundred and fifty souls.

CHAPTER 19.

A futile search—Gideon's insurrection—A Lamanite invasion — King Noah suffers death by fire—His son Limhi a tributary monarch.

1. And it came to pass that the ᵃarmy of the king returned, having searched in vain for the people of the Lord.

2. And now behold, the forces of the king were small, having been reduced, and there began to be a division among the remainder of the people.

3. And the lesser part began to breathe out threatenings against the king, and there began to be a great contention among them.

4. And now there was a man among them whose name was Gideon, and he being a strong man and an enemy to the king, therefore he drew his sword, and swore in his wrath that he would slay the king.

5. And it came to pass that he fought with the king; and when the king saw that he was about to overpower him, he fled and ran and got upon the ᵇtower which was near the ᶜtemple.

6. And Gideon pursued after him and was about to get upon the tower to slay the king, and the king cast his eyes round about towards the land of ᵈShemlon, and behold, the army of the Lamanites were within the borders of the land.

7. And now the king cried out in the anguish of his soul, saying: Gideon, spare me, for the Lamanites are upon us, and they will destroy us; yea, they will destroy my people.

8. And now the king was not so much concerned about his people as he was about his own life; nevertheless, Gideon did spare his life.

9. And the king commanded the people that they should flee before the Lamanites, and he himself did go before them, and they did flee into the wilderness,

---

s, see *b*, Mos. 18. *t*, vers. 5, 8. Mos. 23:1. Chap. 19: *a*, Mos. 18:33, 34. *b*, Mos. 11:12. *c*, see *h*, 2 Ne. 5. *d*, see *d*, Mos. 10.   Mos. 26:15. *u*, ver. 5. *v*, ver. 4. *w*, Mos.
About B. C. 145.

with their women and their children.

10. And it came to pass that the Lamanites did pursue them, and did overtake them, and began to slay them.

11. Now it came to pass that the king commanded them that all the men should *leave their wives and their children, and flee before the Lamanites.

12. Now there were many that would not leave them, but had rather stay and perish with them. And the rest left their wives and their children and fled.

13. And it came to pass that those who tarried with their wives and their children caused that their ⨍fair daughters should stand forth and plead with the Lamanites that they would not slay them.

14. And it came to pass that the Lamanites had compassion on them, for they were charmed with the ᵍbeauty of their women.

15. Therefore the Lamanites did spare their lives, and took them captives and carried them back to the ʰland of Nephi, and granted unto them that they might possess the land, under the conditions that they would deliver up king Noah into the hands of the Lamanites, and deliver up their property, even ⁱone half of all they possessed, one half of their gold, and their silver, and all their precious things, and thus they should pay tribute to the king of the Lamanites from year to year.

16. And now there was one of the sons of the king among those that were taken captive, whose name was ʲLimhi.

17. And now Limhi was desirous that his father should not be destroyed; nevertheless, Limhi was not ignorant of the iniquities of his father, he himself being a just man.

18. And it came to pass that Gideon sent men into the wilderness secretly, to search for the king and those that were with him. And it came to pass that they met the people in the wilderness, all save the king and his ᵏpriests.

19. Now they had sworn in their hearts that they would return to the land of Nephi, and if ˡtheir wives and their children were slain, and also ᵐthose that had tarried with them, that they would seek revenge, and also perish with them.

20. And the king commanded them that they should not return; and they were angry with the king, and caused that he should suffer, even unto death ⁿby fire.

21. And they were about to take the ᵒpriests also and put them to death, and they fled before them.

22. And it came to pass that they were about to return to the land of Nephi, and they met the men of Gideon. And the men of Gideon told them of all that had ᵖhappened to their wives and their children; and that the Lamanites had granted unto them that they might possess the land by paying a tribute to the Lamanites of ᵍone half of all they possessed.

23. And the people told the men of Gideon that they had ʳslain the king, and ˢhis priests had fled from them farther into the wilderness.

24. And it came to pass that

e, vers. 19, 21. *f*, ver. 14. *g*, ver. 13. *h*, see *b*, 2 Ne. 5. *i*, see *k*, Mos. 9. *j*, see *h*, Mos. 7. *k*, see *f*, Mos. 11. *l*, vers. 11, 12. *m*, ver. 12. *n*, Mos. 12:3, 10—12. *o*, see *f*, Mos. 11. *p*, vers. 14, 15. *q*, see *k*, Mos. 9. *r*, ver. 20. *s*, see *f*, Mos. 11.

BETWEEN B. C. 145 AND 123.

after they had ended the ceremony, that they returned to the land of Nephi, rejoicing, because 'their wives and their children were not slain; and they told Gideon what they had "done to the king.

25. And it came to pass that the king of the Lamanites made an oath unto them, that his people should not slay them.

26. And also Limhi, being the son of the king, having the kingdom conferred upon him by the people, made oath unto the king of the Lamanites that his people should pay tribute unto him, "even one half of all they possessed.

27. And it came to pass that Limhi began to establish the kingdom and to establish peace among his people.

28. And the king of the Lamanites set "guards round about the land, that he might keep the people of Limhi in the land, that they might not depart into the wilderness; and he did support his guards out of the *tribute which he did receive from the Nephites.

29. And now king Limhi did have continual peace in his kingdom for the space of two years, that the Lamanites did not molest them nor seek to destroy them.

CHAPTER 20.

Priests of king Noah carry off daughters of the Lamanites—Lamanites seek revenge upon king Limhi and his people—They are repulsed and pacified.

1. Now there was a place in "Shemlon where the daughters of the Lamanites did gather themselves together to sing, and to dance, and to make themselves merry.

2. And it came to pass that there was one day a small number of them gathered together to sing and to dance.

3. And now the *priests of king Noah, being ashamed to return to the *city of Nephi, yea, and also fearing that the people would *slay them, therefore they durst not return to their wives and their children.

4. And having tarried in the wilderness, and having discovered the daughters of the Lamanites, they laid and watched them;

5. And when there were but few of them gathered together to dance, they came forth out of their secret places and took them and carried them into the wilderness; yea, twenty and four of the *daughters of the Lamanites they carried into the wilderness.

6. And it came to pass that when the Lamanites found that their daughters had been missing, they were angry with the people of Limhi, for they thought it was the people of Limhi.

7. Therefore they sent their armies forth; yea, even the king himself went before his people; and they went up to the land of Nephi to destroy the people of Limhi.

8. And now Limhi had discovered them from the *tower, even all their preparations for war did he discover; therefore he gathered his people together, and laid wait for them in the fields and in the forests.

9. And it came to pass that when the Lamanites had come up, that the people of Limhi began to fall upon them from their

---

t, vers. 14, 15, 19, 22.   *u*, vers. 20, 23.   *v*, see *k*, Mos. 9.   *w*, Mos. 21:5.   22:6—10.
x, see *k*, Mos. 9.   CHAP. 20: *a*, see *d*, Mos. 10.   *b*, see *f*, Mos. 11.   *c*, see *b*, 2 Ne. 5.
d, Mos. 19:21.   *e*, vers. 6, 7, 15, 23.   Mos. 23:30—35.   *f*, Mos. 11:12.
BETWEEN B. C. 145 AND 123.

waiting places, and began to slay them.

10. And it came to pass that the battle became exceeding sore, for they fought like lions for their prey.

11. And it came to pass that the people of Limhi began to drive the Lamanites before them; yet they were not half so numerous as the Lamanites. But they fought for their lives, and for their wives, and for their children; therefore they exerted themselves and like dragons did they fight.

12. And it came to pass that they found the king of the Lamanites among the number of their dead; yet he was not dead, having been wounded and left upon the ground, so speedy was the flight of his people.

13. And they took him and bound up his wounds, and brought him before Limhi, and said: Behold, here is the king of the Lamanites; he having received a wound has fallen among their dead, and they have left him; and behold, we have brought him before you; and now let us slay him.

14. But Limhi said unto them: Ye shall not slay him, but bring him hither that I may see him. And they brought him. And Limhi said unto him: What cause have ye to come up to war against my people? Behold, my people have ^{g}not broken the oath that I made unto you; therefore, why should ye break the oath which ye made unto my people?

15. And now the king said: I have broken the oath because thy people did ^{h}carry away the daughters of my people; therefore, in my anger I did cause my people to come up to war against thy people.

16. And now Limhi had heard nothing concerning this matter; therefore he said: I will search among my people and whosoever has done this thing shall perish. Therefore he caused a search to be made among his people.

17. Now when Gideon had heard these things, he being the king's captain, he went forth and said unto the king: I pray thee forbear, and do not search this people, and lay not this thing to their charge.

18. For do ye not remember the ^{i}priests of thy father, whom this people sought to destroy? And are they not in the wilderness? And are not they the ones who have ^{j}stolen the daughters of the Lamanites?

19. And now, behold, and tell the king of these things, that he may tell his people that they may be pacified towards us; for behold they are already preparing to come against us; and behold also there are but few of us.

20. And behold, they come with their numerous hosts; and except the king doth pacify them towards us we must perish.

21. For are not the words of Abinadi ^{k}fulfilled, which he prophesied against us—and all this because we would not hearken unto the words of the Lord, and turn from our iniquities?

22. And now let us pacify the king, and we fulfil the ^{l}oath which we have made unto him; for it is better that we should be in bondage than that we should lose our lives; therefore, let us put a stop to the shedding of so much blood.

23. And now Limhi told the king all the things concerning his

---

g, Mos. 19:25, 26. h, vers. 1—6. i, see f, Mos. 11. j, ver. 5. k, Mos. 12:1—8. l, Mos. 19:26.

BETWEEN B. C. 145 AND 123.

father, and the ᵐpriests that had fled into the wilderness, and attributed the carrying away of their ⁿdaughters to them.

24. And it came to pass that the king was pacified towards his people; and he said unto them: Let us go forth to meet my people, without arms; and I swear unto you with an oath that my people shall not slay thy people.

25. And it came to pass that they followed the king, and went forth without arms to meet the Lamanites. And it came to pass that they did meet the Lamanites; and the king of the Lamanites did bow himself down before them, and did plead in behalf of the people of Limhi.

26. And when the Lamanites saw the people of Limhi, that they were without arms, they had compassion on them and were pacified towards them, and returned with their king in peace to their own land.

CHAPTER 21.

Abinadi's prophecy further fulfilled—Nephites in bondage suffer great affliction—The Lord softens the hearts of their enemies—More concerning the twenty-four plates.

1. And it came to pass that Limhi and his people returned to the city of Nephi, and began to dwell in the land again in peace.

2. And it came to pass that after many days the Lamanites began again to be stirred up in anger against the Nephites, and they began to come into the borders of the land round about.

3. Now they durst not slay them, because of the ᵃoath which their king had made unto Limhi; but they would smite them on ᵇtheir cheeks, and exercise authority over them; and began to put ᶜheavy burdens upon their backs, and ᵈdrive them as they would a dumb ass—

4. Yea, all this was done that the word of the Lord might be ᵉfulfilled.

5. And now the afflictions of the Nephites were great, and there was no way that they could deliver themselves out of their hands, for the Lamanites had ᶠsurrounded them on every side.

6. And it came to pass that the people began to murmur with the king because of their afflictions; and they began to be desirous to go against them to battle. And they did afflict the king sorely with their complaints; therefore he granted unto them that they should do according to their desires.

7. And they gathered themselves together again, and put on their armor, and went forth against the Lamanites to drive them out of their land.

8. And it came to pass that the Lamanites did beat them, and drove them back, and slew many of them.

9. And now there was a great mourning and lamentation among the people of Limhi, the widow mourning for her husband, the son and the daughter mourning for their father, and the brothers for their brethren.

10. Now there were a great many widows in the land, and they did cry mightily from day to day, for a great fear of the Lamanites had come upon them.

11. And it came to pass that their continual cries did stir up the remainder of the people of Limhi to anger against the La-

---

m, see *f*, Mos. 11. *n*, ver. 5. CHAP. 21: *a*, Mos. 19:25. *b*, Mos. 12:2. *c*, ver. 13. Mos. 12:5. *d*, ver. 13. Mos. 12:5. *e*, Mos. 12:2—7. 20:21. *f*, see *w*, Mos. 19.
BETWEEN B. C. 145 AND 123.

manites; and they went again to battle, but they were driven back again, suffering much loss.

12. Yea, they went again even the third time, and suffered in the like manner; and those that were not slain returned again to the city of Nephi.

13. And they did humble themselves even to the dust, subjecting themselves to the ^{g}yoke of bondage, submitting themselves to be smitten, and to be driven to and fro, and burdened, according to the desires of their enemies.

14. And they did humble themselves even in the depths of humility; and they did cry mightily to God; yea, even all the day long did they cry unto their God that he would deliver them out of their afflictions.

15. And now the Lord was ^{h}slow to hear their cry because of their iniquities; nevertheless the Lord did hear their cries, and began to soften the hearts of the Lamanites that they began to ease their burdens; yet the Lord did not see fit to deliver them out of bondage.

16. And it came to pass that they began to prosper by degrees in the land, and began to raise grain more abundantly, and flocks, and herds, that they did not suffer with hunger.

17. Now there was a great number of women, ^{i}more than there was of men; therefore king Limhi commanded that ^{j}every man should impart to the support of the widows and their children, that they might not perish with hunger; and this they did because of the greatness of their number that had been slain.

18. Now the people of Limhi kept together in a body as much as it was possible, and secured their grain and their flocks;

19. And the king himself did not trust his person without the walls of the city, unless he ^{k}took his guards with him, fearing that he might by some means fall into the hands of the Lamanites.

20. And he caused that his people should watch the land round about, that by some means they might take those ^{l}priests that fled into the wilderness, who had stolen the ^{m}daughters of the Lamanites, and that had caused such a great destruction to come upon them.

21. For they were desirous to take them that they might ^{n}punish them; for they had come into the land of Nephi by night, and carried off their grain and many of their precious things; therefore they laid wait for them.

22. And it came to pass that there was no more disturbance between the Lamanites and the people of Limhi, *even until the ^{o}time that Ammon and his brethren came into the land.

23. And the king having been without the gates of the city with his guard, discovered Ammon and his brethren; and supposing them to be priests of Noah therefore he caused that they should be taken, and bound, and cast into prison. And had they been the priests of Noah he would have caused that they should be put to death.

24. But when he found that they were not, but that they were his brethren, and had come ^{p}from the land of Zarahemla, he was filled with ^{q}exceeding great joy.

25. Now king Limhi had sent, previous to the coming of Ammon, a ^{r}small number of men to search

---
g, Mos. 12:2—8. h, Mos. 11:24, 25. i, vers. 10, 11. j, see j, Jac. 2. k, Mos. 7:7, 10. l, see l, Mos. 11. m, Mos. 20:5. n, ver. 23. Mos. 7:7—11. o, Mos. 7:6—13. p, Om. 13. q, Mos. 7:14. r, Mos. 8:7. * About B. C. 122.

for the land of Zarahemla; but they could not find it, and they were *lost in the wilderness.

26. Nevertheless, they did find a land which had been peopled; yea, a land which was ^tcovered with dry bones; yea, a land which had been peopled and which had been destroyed; and they, having ^usupposed it to be the land of Zarahemla, returned to the land of Nephi, having arrived in the borders of the land not many days before the ^vcoming of Ammon.

27. And they brought a ^wrecord with them, even a record of the people whose bones they had found; and it was engraven on plates of ore.

28. And now Limhi was again filled with joy on learning from the mouth of Ammon that king Mosiah had a ^xgift from God, whereby he could interpret such engravings; yea, and Ammon also did rejoice.

29. Yet Ammon and his brethren were filled with sorrow because so many of their brethren had been slain;

30. And also that king Noah and ^yhis priests had caused the people to commit so many sins and iniquities against God; and they also did mourn for the ^zdeath of Abinadi; and also for the ^{2a}departure of Alma and the people that went with him, who had formed a church of God through the strength and power of God, and faith on the words which had been spoken by Abinadi.

31. Yea, they did mourn for their departure, for they knew not whither they had fled. Now they would have gladly joined with them, for they themselves had entered into a covenant with God to serve him and keep his commandments.

32. And now since the coming of Ammon, king Limhi had also entered into a covenant with God, and also many of his people, to serve him and keep his commandments.

33. And it came to pass that king Limhi and many of his people were desirous to be baptized; but there was none in the land that had ^{2b}authority from God. And Ammon declined doing this thing, considering himself an unworthy servant.

34. Therefore they did not at that time form themselves into a church, ^{2c}waiting upon the Spirit of the Lord. Now they were desirous to become even as Alma and his brethren, who had fled into the wilderness.

35. They were desirous to be ^{2d}baptized as a witness and a testimony that they were willing to serve God with all their hearts; nevertheless they did prolong the time; and an account of their baptism shall be ^{2e}given hereafter.

36. And now all the study of Ammon and ^{2f}his people, and king Limhi and his people, was to deliver themselves out of the hands of the Lamanites and from ^{2g}bondage.

CHAPTER 22.

Plan to throw off Lamanite yoke—Gideon's proposal—Lamanites made drunk—The captive people escape and return to Zarahemla—End of Zeniff's record.

1. And now it came to pass that Ammon and king Limhi began to consult with the people how they should deliver themselves out of bondage; and even

---

s, Mos. 8:8. t, Mos. 8:7—11. u, Mos. 8:7, 8. v, Mos. 7:6—11. w, see k, Mos. 8.
x, see n, Mos. 8. y, see f, Mos. 11. z, Mos. 17:12—20. 2a, Mos. 18:34, 35. 2b, Mos. 18:13, 17. 3 Ne. 11:25. Ex. 28:1. Heb. 5:4. 2c, ver. 35. 2d, see u, 2 Ne. 9. 2e, Mos. 25:17, 18. 2f, Mos. 7:2, 3. 2g, Mos. 21:13.   ABOUT B. C. 122.

they did cause that all the people should gather themselves together; and this they did that they might have the voice of the people concerning the matter.

2. And it came to pass that they could find no way to deliver themselves out of bondage, except it were to take their women and children, and their flocks, and their herds, and their tents, and depart into the wilderness; for the Lamanites being so numerous, it was impossible for the people of Limhi to contend with them, thinking to deliver themselves out of bondage by the sword.

3. Now it came to pass that ᵃGideon went forth and stood before the king, and said unto him: Now O king, thou hast hitherto hearkened unto my words many times when we have been contending with our brethren, the Lamanites.

4. And now O king, if thou hast not found me to be an unprofitable servant, or if thou hast hitherto listened to my words in any degree, and they have been of ᵇservice to thee, even so I desire that thou wouldst listen to my words at this time, and I will be thy servant and deliver this people out of bondage.

5. And the king granted unto him that he might speak. And Gideon said unto him:

6. Behold the ᶜback pass, through the back wall, on the back side of the city. The Lamanites, or the guards of the Lamanites, by night are drunken; therefore let us send a proclamation among all this people that they gather together their flocks and herds, that they may drive them into the wilderness by night.

7. And I will go according to thy command and pay ᵈthe last tribute of wine to the Lamanites, and they will be ᵉdrunken; and we will pass through the ᶠsecret pass on the left of the camp when they are drunken and asleep.

8. Thus we will depart with our women and our children, our flocks, and our herds into the wilderness; a*d we will travel ᵍaround the land of Shilom.

9. And it came to pass that the king hearkened unto the words of Gideon.

10. And king Limhi caused that his people should gather their flocks together; and he sent the ʰtribute of wine to the Lamanites; and he also sent more wine, as a present unto them; and they did drink ⁱfreely of the wine which king Limhi did send unto them.

11. And it came to pass that the people of king Limhi did depart by night into the wilderness with their flocks and their herds, and they went ʲround about the land of Shilom in the wilderness, and bent their course towards the ᵏland of Zarahemla, being led by Ammon and ˡhis brethren.

12. And they had taken all their gold, and silver, and their precious things, which they could carry, and also their provisions with them, into the wilderness; and they pursued their journey.

13. And after being many days in the wilderness they arrived in the ᵐland of Zarahemla, and joined Mosiah's people, and became his subjects.

14. And it came to pass that Mosiah received them with joy; and he also received their ⁿrecords, and also the ᵒrecords which

---

a, Mos. 20:17. Al. 1:8, 9. *b*, Mos. 20:17—22. *c*, ver. 7. *d*, Mos. 19:26. *e*, vers. 6—10. *f*, ver. 6. *g*, ver. 11. See *f*, Mos. 7. *h*, ver. 7. *i*, vers. 6, 7. *j*, ver. 8. See *l*, Mos. 7. *k*, Om. 13. *l*, Mos. 7:2, 3. *m*, Om. 13. *n*, Record of Zeniff, Mos. 9. *o*, see *k*, Mos. 8.

ABOUT B. C. 122.

had been found by the people of Limhi.

15. And now it came to pass when the Lamanites had found that the people of Limhi had departed out of the land by night, that they sent an ^{p}army into the wilderness to pursue them;

16. And after they had pursued them two days, they could no longer follow their tracks; therefore they were ^{q}lost in the wilderness.

An account of Alma and the people of the Lord, who were driven into the wilderness by the people of king Noah.

Comprising chapters 23 and 24.

CHAPTER 23.

Alma refuses to be king—Land of Helam captured by Lamanites—Amulon, leader of king Noah's wicked priests, rules subject to the Lamanite monarch.

1. Now Alma, having been ^{a}warned of the Lord that the ^{b}armies of king Noah would come upon them, and having made it known to his people, therefore they gathered together their flocks, and took of their grain, and departed into the wilderness before the armies of king Noah.

2. And the Lord did strengthen them, that the people of king Noah could not overtake them to destroy them.

3. And they fled eight days' journey into the wilderness.

4. And they came to a land, yea, even a very beautiful and pleasant land, a land of pure water.

5. And they pitched their tents, and began to till the ground, and began to build buildings; yea, they were industrious, and did labor exceedingly.

6. And the people were desirous that Alma should be their king, for he was beloved by his people.

7. But he said unto them: Behold, it is not expedient that we should have a king; for thus saith the Lord: Ye shall ^{d}not esteem one flesh above another, or one man shall not think himself above another; therefore I say unto you it is not expedient that ye should have a king.

8. Nevertheless, if it were possible that ye could always have just men to be your kings it would be well for you to have a king.

9. But remember the ^{e}iniquity of king Noah and his priests; and I myself was ^{f}caught in a snare, and did many things which were abominable in the sight of the Lord, which caused me ^{g}sore repentance;

10. Nevertheless, after much tribulation, the Lord did hear my cries, and did answer my prayers, and has made me an instrument in his hands in bringing ^{h}so many of you to a knowledge of his truth.

11. Nevertheless, in this I do not glory, for I am unworthy to glory of myself.

12. And now I say unto you, ye have been oppressed by king Noah, and have been in ^{i}bondage to him and his priests, and have been brought into iniquity by them; therefore ye were bound with the bands of iniquity.

13. And now as ye have been delivered by the power of God out of these bonds; yea, even out of the ^{j}hands of king Noah and his

---

p, Mos. 23:30—39. *q,* Mos. 23:30, 36, 37. CHAP. 23: *a,* Mos. 18:34, 35. *b,* Mos. 18:33, 34. 19:1. *d,* vers. 8—15. Mos. 18:21—29. 27:3—5. See *j,* Jac. 2. *e,* Mos. 11:1—15. *f,* Mos. 17:1—4. 24:8—12. *g,* Mos. 18:1. *h,* Mos. 18:35. *i,* Mos. 11:2—15. *j,* vers. 1—3. Mos. 18:34, 35. BETWEEN B. C. 145 AND 123.

people, and also from the bonds of iniquity, even so I desire that ye should stand fast in this liberty wherewith ye have been made free, and that ye trust [k]no man to be a king over you.

14. And also trust [l]no one to be your teacher nor your minister, except he be a man of God, walking in his ways and keeping his commandments.

15. Thus did Alma teach his people, that every man should love his neighbor [m]as himself, that there should be no contention among them.

16. And now, Alma was their [n]high priest, he being the founder of their church.

17. And it came to pass that none received authority to preach or to teach except it were by him from God. Therefore he consecrated all their priests and all their teachers; and none were consecrated except they were just men.

18. Therefore they did watch over their people, and did nourish them with things pertaining to righteousness.

19. And it came to pass that they began to prosper exceedingly in the land; and they called the land [o]Helam.

20. And it came to pass that they did multiply and prosper exceedingly in the land of Helam; and they built a city, which they called the city of Helam.

21. Nevertheless the Lord seeth fit to chasten his people; yea, he trieth their patience and their faith.

22. Nevertheless — whosoever putteth his trust in him the same shall be [p]lifted up at the last day. Yea, and thus it was with this people.

23. For behold, I will show unto you that they were brought into bondage, and none could deliver them but the Lord their God, yea, even the God of Abraham and Isaac and of Jacob.

24. And it came to pass that he did deliver them, and he did show forth his mighty power unto them, and great were their rejoicings.

25. For behold, it came to pass that while they were in the land of Helam, yea, in the city of [q]Helam, while tilling the land round about, behold an army of the Lamanites was in the borders of the land.

26. Now it came to pass that the brethren of Alma fled from their fields, and gathered themselves together in the city of Helam; and they were much frightened because of the appearance of the Lamanites.

27. But Alma went forth and stood among them, and exhorted them that they should not be frightened, but that they should remember the Lord their God and he would deliver them.

28. Therefore they hushed their fears, and began to cry unto the Lord that he would soften the hearts of the Lamanites, that they would spare them, and their wives, and their children.

29. And it came to pass that the Lord did soften the hearts of the Lamanites. And Alma and his brethren went forth and delivered themselves up into their hands; and the Lamanites took possession of the [r]land of Helam.

30. Now the armies of the Lamanites, which had followed

---

k, vers. 6—9. Mos. 20:5—36. *l*, Mos. 18:18—29. *m*, Mos. 18:21. 3 Ne. 14:12. *n*, Mos. 18:18. See *c*, Mos. 6. *o*, vers. 20, 25, 26, 29, 35, 38, 39, 27:16. Al. 24:1. *p*, 1 Ne. 13:37. 16:2. Al. 26:7. 36:28. 38:5. 3 Ne. 15:1. 27:14, 15, 22. Morm. 2:19. Eth. 4:19. John 12:32. *q*, see *o*. *r*, see *o*.   BETWEEN B. C. 145 AND 123.

180 MOSIAH, 24.

after the people of king Limhi, had been *lost in the wilderness for many days.

31. And behold, they had found those ᵗpriests of king Noah, in a place which they called ᵘAmulon; and they had begun to possess the land of Amulon and had begun to till the ground.

32. Now the name of the leader of those priests was Amulon.

33. And it came to pass that Amulon did plead with the Lamanites; and he also sent forth their wives, who were the ᵛdaughters of the Lamanites, to plead with their brethren, that they should not destroy their husbands.

34. And the Lamanites had compassion on Amulon and his brethren, and did not destroy them, because of ʷtheir wives.

35. And Amulon and his brethren did join the Lamanites, and they were traveling in the wilderness in search of the land of Nephi when they discovered the land of ˣHelam, which was possessed by Alma and his brethren.

36. And it came to pass that the Lamanites promised unto Alma and his brethren, that if they would show them the way which led to the ʸland of Nephi that they would grant unto them their lives and their liberty.

37. But after Alma had shown them the way that led to the land of Nephi the Lamanites would not keep their promise; but they set ᶻguards round about the land of Helam, over Alma and his brethren.

38. And the remainder of them went to the land of Nephi; and a part of them returned to the land of Helam, and also brought with them the wives and the children of the guards who had been left in the land.

39. And the king of the Lamanites had granted unto ²ᵃAmulon that he should be a king and a ruler over his people, who were in the land of Helam; nevertheless he should have no power to do anything contrary to the will of the king of the Lamanites.

CHAPTER 24.

Amulon persecutes Alma and his followers—The Lord makes their burdens light and delivers them from bondage—They return to Zarahemla.

1. And it came to pass that Amulon did gain favor in the eyes of the king of the Lamanites; therefore, the king of the Lamanites granted unto him and his brethren that they should be appointed ᵃteachers over his people, yea, even over the people who were in the land of ᵇShemlon, and in the land of ᶜShilom, and in the land of ᵈAmulon.

2. For the Lamanites had taken possession of all these lands; therefore, the king of the Lamanites had appointed kings over all these lands.

3. And now the name of the king of the Lamanites was ᵉLaman, being called after the name of his father; and therefore he was called king Laman. And he was king over a numerous people.

4. And he appointed ᶠteachers of the brethren of Amulon in every land which was possessed by his people; and thus the language of Nephi began to be taught among all the people of the Lamanites.

5. And they were a people friendly one with another; never-

---

s, Mos. 22:16. *t*, see *f*, Mos. 11. *u*, vers. 32, 35, 39. Mos. 24:1, 4, 5, 8—11. 25:12. Al. 21:2—4. 23:14. 24:1, 28—30. 25:4—12. 43:13, 14. *v*, Mos. 20:5, 6, 18. *w*, ver. 33. *x*, see *o*. *y*, see *b*, 2 Ne. 5. *z*, ver. 38. 2*a*, see *u*.
Chap. 24: *a*, vers. 4—6. *b*, see *d*, Mos. 10. *c*, see *f*, Mos. 7. *d*, see *u*, Mos. 23. *e*, Mos. 9:10, 11. 10:6. *f*, ver. 1. Between B. C. 145 and 123.

MOSIAH, 24.

theless they knew not God; neither did the *h*brethren of Amulon teach them anything concerning the Lord their God, neither the law of Moses; nor did they teach them the words of Abinadi;

6. But they taught them that they should keep their record, and that they might write one to another.

7. And thus the Lamanites began to increase in riches, and began to trade one with another and wax great, and began to be a cunning and a wise people, as to the wisdom of the world, yea, a very cunning people, delighting in all manner of wickedness and plunder, except it were among their own brethren.

8. And now it came to pass that *k*Amulon began to exercise authority over Alma and his brethren, and began to persecute him, and cause that his children should persecute their children.

9. For Amulon knew Alma, that he had been *l*one of the king's priests, and that it was he that believed the words of Abinadi and was driven out before the king, and therefore he was wroth with him; for he was subject to king Laman, yet he exercised authority over them, and put tasks upon them, and put task-masters over them.

10. And it came to pass that so great were their afflictions that they began to cry mightily to God.

11. And Amulon commanded them that they should stop their cries; and he put guards over them to watch them, that whosoever should be found calling upon God should be put to death.

12. And Alma and his people did not raise their voices to the Lord their God, but did pour out their hearts to him; and he did know the thoughts of their hearts.

13. And it came to pass that the voice of the Lord came to them in their afflictions, saying: Lift up your heads and be of good comfort, for I know of the covenant which ye have made unto me; and I will covenant with my people and deliver them out of bondage.

14. And I will also *m*ease the burdens which are put upon your shoulders, that even you cannot feel them upon your backs, even while you are in bondage; and this will I do that ye may stand as witnesses for me hereafter, and that ye may know of a surety that I, the Lord God, do visit my people in their afflictions.

15. And now it came to pass that the burdens which were laid upon Alma and his brethren were made *n*light; yea, the Lord did strengthen them that they could bear up their burdens with ease, and they did submit cheerfully and with patience to all the will of the Lord.

16. And it came to pass that so great was their faith and their patience that the voice of the Lord came unto them again, saying: Be of good comfort, for on the morrow I will deliver you out of bondage.

17. And he said unto Alma: Thou shalt go before this people, and I will go with thee and deliver this people out of *o*bondage.

18. Now it came to pass that Alma and his people in the night-time gathered their flocks together, and also of their grain; yea, even all the night-time were they gathering their flocks together.

19. And in the morning the

h, see *f*, Mos. 11. *k*, Mos. 23:32. *l*, Mos. 17:2—4. *m*, vers. 9, 15. *n*, vers. 9, 14. *o*, vers. 13, 21. Mos. 25:10. 27:16. Al. 5:5, 6. 29:11, 12. 36:2, 29.

BETWEEN B. C. 145 AND 123.

Lord caused a ^{p}deep sleep to come upon the Lamanites, yea, and all their task-masters were in a profound sleep.

20. And Alma and his people departed into the wilderness; and when they had traveled all day they pitched their tents in a valley, and they called the valley Alma, because he led their way in the wilderness.

21. Yea, and in the valley of Alma they poured out their thanks to God because he had been merciful unto them, and eased their burdens, and had delivered them out of ^{q}bondage; for they were in bondage, and none could deliver them except it were the Lord their God.

22. And they gave thanks to God, yea, all their men and all their women and all their children that could speak lifted their voices in the praises of their God.

23. And now the Lord said unto Alma: Haste thee and get thou and this people out of this land, for the Lamanites have ^{r}awakened and do pursue thee; therefore get thee out of this land, and I will stop the Lamanites in this ^{s}valley that they come no further in pursuit of this people.

24. And it came to pass that they departed out of the valley, and took their journey into the wilderness.

25. And after they had been in the wilderness ^{t}twelve days *they arrived in the ^{u}land of Zarahemla; and king Mosiah did ^{v}also receive them with joy.

CHAPTER 25.

Zarahemla, a descendant of Mulek— The record of Zeniff and the account of Alma read to the people—Alma authorized to establish the church of Christ throughout the land.

1. And now king Mosiah caused that all the people should be gathered together.

2. Now there were not so many of the children of Nephi, or so many of those who were descendants of Nephi, as there were of the people of Zarahemla, who was a ^{a}descendant of Mulek, and those who came with him into the wilderness.

3. And there were not so many of the people of Nephi and of the people of Zarahemla as there were of the Lamanites; yea, they were not half so numerous.

4. And now all the people of Nephi were assembled together, and also all the people of Zarahemla, and ^{b}they were gathered together in two bodies.

5. And it came to pass that Mosiah did read, and caused to be read, the ^{c}records of Zeniff to his people; yea, he read the records of the people of Zeniff, from the time they ^{d}left the land of Zarahemla until they ^{e}returned again.

6. And he also read the account of Alma and his brethren, and all their afflictions, from the time they ^{f}left the land of Zarahemla until the time they ^{g}returned again.

7. And now, when Mosiah had made an end of reading the records, his people who tarried in the land were struck with wonder and amazement.

8. For they knew not what to think; for when they beheld those that had been delivered ^{h}out of bondage they were filled with exceeding great joy.

9. And again, when they

---

p, ver. 23. q, see o. r, ver. 19. s, vers. 20, 21. t, see c, Mos. 23. u, Om. 13. v, Mos. 22:14. CHAP. 25: a, Om. 14. b, ver. 13. c, see the heading of Mos. 9. d, Mos. 9:3, 4. e, Mos. 22:13. f, Mos. 9:3, 4. g, Mos. 24, 25. h, Mos. 22:11—13.
* ABOUT B. C. 122.

thought of their brethren who had been slain by the Lamanites they were filled with sorrow, and even shed many tears of sorrow.

10. And again, when they thought of the immediate goodness of God, and his power in *f*delivering Alma and his brethren out of the hands of the Lamanites and of bondage, they did raise their voices and give thanks to God.

11. And again, when they thought upon the Lamanites, who were their brethren, of their sinful and polluted state, they were filled with pain and anguish for the welfare of their souls.

12. And it came to pass that those who *j*were the children of Amulon and his brethren, who had taken to wife the *k*daughters of the Lamanites, were displeased with the conduct of their fathers, and they would no longer be called by the names of their fathers, therefore they took upon themselves the name of Nephi, that they might be called the children of Nephi and be numbered among those who were called Nephites.

13. And now *l*all the people of Zarahemla were numbered with the Nephites, and this because the kingdom had been conferred upon none but those who were descendants of Nephi.

14. And now it came to pass that when Mosiah had made an end of speaking and *m*reading to the people, he desired that Alma should also speak to the people.

15. And Alma did speak unto them, when they were assembled together in large bodies, and he went from one body to another, preaching unto the people repentance and faith on the Lord.

16. And he did exhort the people of Limhi and his brethren, all those that had been *n*delivered out of bondage, that they should remember that it was the Lord that did deliver them.

17. And it came to pass that after Alma had taught the people many things, and had made an end of speaking to them, that king Limhi was desirous that he might be baptized; and all his people were desirous that they might be baptized also.

18. Therefore, Alma did go forth into the water and did baptize them; yea, he did *o*baptize them after the manner he did his *p*brethren in the waters of Mormon; yea, and as many as he did baptize did belong to the church of God; and this because of their belief on the words of Alma.

19. And it came to pass that king Mosiah granted unto Alma that he might establish churches throughout all the land of Zarahemla; and gave him power to *q*ordain priests and teachers over every church.

20. Now this was done because there were so many people that they could not all be governed by one teacher; neither could they all hear the word of God in one assembly;

21. Therefore they did assemble themselves together in different bodies, being called churches; every church having their priests and their teachers, and every priest preaching the word according as it was delivered to him by the mouth of Alma.

22. And thus, notwithstanding there being many churches they were all one church, yea, even the church of God; for there was nothing preached in all the

f, Mos. 24:16—25. *j*, Mos. 20:3—5. *k*, Mos. 20:5. 23:33. *l*, Om. 19. *m*, vers. 5—7. *n*, Mos. 22:11—13. 24:16—25. *o*, see *u*, 2 Ne. 9. Mos. 21:32—35. *p*, Mos. 18:8—17. *q*, see *c*, Mos. 6. ABOUT B. C. 122.

churches except it were repentance and faith in God.

23. And now there were seven churches in the land of Zarahemla. And it came to pass that whosoever were desirous to take upon them the ʳname of Christ, or of God, they did join the churches of God;

24. And they were called the people of God. And the Lord did pour out his Spirit upon them, and they were blessed, and prospered in the land.

CHAPTER 26.

Concerning unbelievers and evildoers—The Lord instructs Alma how to deal with them.

1. Now it came to pass that there were many of the rising generation that could not understand the ᵃwords of king Benjamin, being little children at the time he spake unto his people; and they did not believe the tradition of their fathers.

2. They did not believe what had been said concerning the ᵇresurrection of the dead, neither did they believe concerning the coming of Christ.

3. And now because of their unbelief they could not understand the word of God; and their hearts were hardened.

4. And they would not be ᶜbaptized; neither would they ᵈjoin the church. And they were a separate people as to their faith, and remained so ever after, even in their carnal and sinful state; for they would not call upon the Lord their God.

5. And now in the reign of Mosiah they were not half so numerous as the people of God; but because of the dissensions among the brethren they became more numerous.

6. For it came to pass that they did deceive many with their flattering words, who were in the church, and did cause them to ᵉcommit many sins; therefore it became expedient that those who committed sin, that were in the church, should be admonished by the church.

7. And it came to pass that they were brought before the priests, and delivered up unto the ᶠpriests by the teachers; and the priests brought them before Alma, who was the ᵍhigh priest.

8. Now king Mosiah had given Alma the authority over the church.

9. And it came to pass that Alma did not know concerning them; but there were many witnesses against them; yea, the people stood and testified of their iniquity in abundance.

10. Now there had not any such thing happened before in the church; therefore Alma was troubled in his spirit, and he caused that they should be brought before the king.

11. And he said unto the king: Behold, here are many whom we have brought before thee, who are accused of their brethren; yea, and they have been taken in divers iniquities. And they do not repent of their iniquities; therefore we have brought them before thee, that thou mayest judge them according to their crimes.

12. But king Mosiah said unto Alma: Behold, I judge them not; therefore I deliver them into thy hands to be judged.

---

r, see *c*, Mos. 5.   CHAP. 26: *a*, Mos. chaps. 2—5.   *b*, see *d*, 2 Ne. 2.   *c*, see *u*, 2 Ne. 9.   *d*, Mos. 18:17.   25:18—23.   Al. 4:4, 5.   3 Ne. 26:21.   *e*, vers. 7—13, 19, 25—36.   Al. 5:57, 58.   6:3.   *f*, see *c*, Mos. 6.   *g*, Mos. 23:16.   29:42.   Al. 4:4, 18, 20.   5:3, 44, 49.   6:8.   8:11, 23.   13:1—20.   16:5.   30:21, 22, 23, 29.   43:2.   46:6, 38.   49:30.   He. 3:25.
PROBABLY BETWEEN B. C. 120 AND 100.

MOSIAH, 26.

13. And now the spirit of Alma was again troubled; and he went and inquired of the Lord what he should do concerning this matter, for he feared that he should do wrong in the sight of God.

14. And it came to pass that after he had poured out his whole soul to God, the voice of the Lord came to him, saying:

15. Blessed art thou, Alma, and blessed are they who were ʰbaptized in the ⁱwaters of Mormon. Thou art blessed because of thy exceeding faith in the words alone of my servant Abinadi.

16. And blessed are they because of their exceeding faith in the words alone which thou hast spoken unto them.

17. And blessed art thou because thou hast established a ʲchurch among this people; and they shall be established, and they shall be my people.

18. Yea, blessed is this people who are willing to bear my ᵏname; for in my name shall they be called; and they are mine.

19. And because thou hast inquired of me concerning the ˡtransgressor, thou art blessed.

20. Thou art my servant; and I covenant with thee that thou shalt have eternal life; and thou shalt serve me and go forth in my name, and shalt gather together my sheep.

21. And he that will hear my voice shall be my sheep; and him shall ye receive into the church, and him will I also receive.

22. For behold, this is my ᵐchurch; whosoever is ⁿbaptized shall be baptized unto repentance. And whomsoever ye receive shall believe in my name; and him will I freely forgive.

23. For it is I that taketh upon me the sins of the world; for it is I that hath °created them; and it is I that granteth unto him that believeth unto the end a place at my right hand.

24. For behold, in ᵖmy name are they called; and if they know me they shall come forth, and shall have a place eternally at my right hand.

25. And it shall come to pass that when the second trump shall sound then shall they that never knew me come forth and shall stand before me.

26. And then shall they know that I am the Lord their God, that I am their Redeemer; but they would not be redeemed.

27. And then I will confess unto them that I never knew them; and they shall depart into ᵠeverlasting fire prepared for the devil and his angels.

28. Therefore I say unto you, that he that will not hear my voice, the same shall ye ʳnot receive into my church, for him I will not receive at the last day.

29. Therefore I say unto you, Go; and whosoever ˢtransgresseth against me, him shall ye judge according to the sins which he has committed; and if he confess his sins before thee and me, and repenteth in the sincerity of his heart, him shall ye forgive, and I will forgive him also.

30. Yea, and as often as my people repent will I forgive them their trespasses against me.

31. And ye shall also forgive ᵗone another your trespasses; for verily I say unto you, he that forgiveth not his neighbor's trespasses when he says that he repents, the same hath brought himself under condemnation.

32. Now I say unto you, Go;

h, see *u*, 2 Ne. 9.   *i*, see *t*, Mos. 18.   *j*, Mos. 25:19—24.   *k*, see *e*, Mos. 5.   *l*, see *e*.
m, see *d*.   *n*, see *u*, 2 Ne. 9.   *o*, see *l*, Mos. 5.   *p*, see *e*, Mos. 5.   *q*, see *k*, 1 Ne. 15.
r, see *d*.   *s*, see *e*.   *t*, 3 Ne. 13:14, 15.   PROBABLY BETWEEN B. C. 120 AND 100.
13

and whosoever will not repent of his sins the same shall "not be numbered among my people; and this shall be observed from this time forward.

33. And it came to pass when Alma had heard these words he wrote them down that he might have them, and that he might judge the people of that church according to the *commandments of God.

34. And it came to pass that Alma went and judged those that had been taken in iniquity, according to the word of the Lord.

35. And whosoever repented of their sins and did "confess them, them he did number among the people of the church;

36. And those that would not confess their sins and repent of their iniquity, the same were *not numbered among the people of the church, and their names were blotted out.

37. And it came to pass that Alma did regulate all the affairs of the church; and they began again to have peace and to prosper exceedingly in the affairs of the church, walking circumspectly before God, receiving many, and *baptizing many.

38. And now all these things did Alma and his fellow laborers do who were over the church, walking in all diligence, teaching the word of God in all things, suffering all manner of afflictions, being persecuted by all those who did not belong to the church of God.

39. And they did admonish their brethren; and they were also admonished, every one by the word of God, according to his sins, or to the sins which he had committed, being commanded of God to *pray without ceasing, and to give thanks in all things.

CHAPTER 27.

Persecution forbidden and equality enjoined—Alma, the younger, and the four sons of Mosiah, among the unbelievers—Their miraculous conversion—They become preachers of righteousness.

1. And now it came to pass that the persecutions which were inflicted on the church by the unbelievers became so great that the church began to murmur, and complain to their leaders concerning the matter; and they did complain to Alma. And Alma laid the case before their king, Mosiah. And Mosiah consulted with his priests.

2. And it came to pass that king Mosiah sent a proclamation throughout the land round about that there should not any unbeliever persecute any of those who belonged to the church of God.

3. And there was a strict command throughout all the churches that there should be no persecutions among them, that there should be an *a*equality among all men;

4. That they should let no pride nor haughtiness disturb their peace; that every man should esteem his neighbor *b*as himself, laboring with their own hands for their support.

5. Yea, and all their *c*priests and teachers should labor with their *d*own hands for their support, in all cases save it were in sickness, or in much want; and doing these things, they did abound in the grace of God.

6. And there began to be much

---

u, vers. 34—36. Al. 1:24. *v*, vers. 28—32. *w*, vers. 29, 30. *x*, ver. 32. *y*, see *u*, 2 Ne. 9. *z*, see *e*, 2 Ne. 32. CHAP. 27: *a*, see *j*, Jac. 2. Mos. 29:32. Al. 30:11. *b*, see *l*, Mos. 4. See also *m*, Mos. 23. *c*, see *c*, Mos. 6. *d*, Mos. 18:24, 26.
PROBABLY BETWEEN B. C. 120 AND 100.

MOSIAH, 27.

peace again in the land; and the people began to be very numerous, and began to scatter abroad upon the face of the earth, yea, on the north and on the south, on the east and on the west, building large cities and villages in all quarters of the land.

7. And the Lord did visit them and prosper them, and they became a large and wealthy people.

8. Now the ^{e}sons of Mosiah were numbered among the unbelievers; and also one of the sons of Alma was numbered among them, he being called Alma, after his father; nevertheless, he became a very wicked and an idolatrous man. And he was a man of many words, and did speak much flattery to the people; therefore he led many of the people to do after the manner of his iniquities.

9. And he became a great hinderment to the prosperity of the church of God; stealing away the hearts of the people; causing much dissension among the people; giving a chance for the enemy of God to exercise his power over them.

10. And now it came to pass that while he was going about to destroy the church of God, for he did go about secretly with the sons of Mosiah ^{f}seeking to destroy the church, and to lead astray the people of the Lord, contrary to the commandments of God, or even the king—

11. And as I said unto you, as they were going about rebelling against God, behold, the angel of the Lord ^{g}appeared unto them; and he descended as it were in a cloud; and he spake as it were with a voice of thunder, which caused the ^{h}earth to shake upon which they stood;

12. And so great was their astonishment, that they fell to the earth, and understood not the words which he spake unto them.

13. Nevertheless he cried again, saying: Alma, arise and stand forth, for why persecutest thou the church of God? For the Lord hath said: ^{i}This is my church, and I will establish it; and nothing shall overthrow it, save it is the transgression of my people.

14. And again, the angel said: Behold, the Lord hath heard the prayers of his people, and also the prayers of his servant, Alma, who is thy father; for he has prayed with much faith concerning thee that thou mightest be brought to the knowledge of the truth; therefore, for this purpose have I come to convince thee of the power and authority of God, that the prayers of his servants might be answered according to their faith.

15. And now behold, can ye dispute the power of God? For behold, doth not my voice ^{j}shake the earth? And can ye not also ^{k}behold me before you? And I am sent from God.

16. Now I say unto thee: Go, and remember the captivity of thy fathers in the land of ^{l}Helam, and in the ^{m}land of Nephi; and remember how great things he has done for them; for they were in bondage, and he has ^{n}delivered them. And now I say unto thee, Alma, go thy way, and seek to destroy the church no more, that their prayers may be answered, and this even if thou wilt of thyself be cast off.

17. And now it came to pass that these were the last words

e, vers. 10, 34. *f*, Mos. 28:3, 4. Al. 26:17, 18. 36:6, 9, 11. 38:7. *g*, vers. 15, 18. Al. 36:5—11. 38:7. *h*, vers. 15, 18. Al. 36:7. 38:7. *i*, Mos. 26:22. *j*, see *h*. *k*, see *g*. *l*, see *o*. Mos. 23. *m*, see *b*, 2 Ne. 5. *n*, Mos. 18:34. 23:1—4, 24:17—21.
PROBABLY BETWEEN B. C. 100 AND 92.

which the angel spake unto Alma, and he departed.

18. And now Alma and those that were with him fell *again to the earth, for great was their astonishment; for with their own eyes they had *beheld an angel of the Lord; and his voice was as thunder, which *shook the earth; and they knew that there was nothing save the power of God that could shake the earth and cause it to tremble as though it would part asunder.

19. And now the astonishment of Alma was so great that he became *dumb, that he could not open his mouth; yea, and he became weak, even that he could not move his hands; therefore he was taken by those that were with him, and carried helpless, even until he was laid before his father.

20. And they rehearsed unto his father all that had happened unto them; and his father rejoiced, for he knew that it was the power of God.

21. And he caused that a multitude should be gathered together that they might witness what the Lord had done for his son, and also for those that were with him.

22. And he caused that the *priests should assemble themselves together; and they began to *fast, and to pray to the Lord their God that he would *open the mouth of Alma, that he might speak, and also that his *limbs might receive their strength—that the eyes of the people might be opened to see and know of the goodness and glory of God.

23. And it came to pass after they had *fasted and prayed for the space of two days and two nights, the limbs of Alma received their strength, and he stood up and began to speak unto them, bidding them to be of good comfort:

24. For, said he, I have repented of my sins, and have been redeemed of the Lord; behold I am *born of the Spirit.

25. And the Lord said unto me: Marvel not that all mankind, yea, men and women, all nations, kindreds, tongues and people, must be *born again; yea, born of God, changed from their carnal and fallen state, to a state of righteousness, being redeemed of God, becoming his sons and daughters;

26. And thus they become new creatures; and unless they do this, they can in nowise inherit the kingdom of God.

27. I say unto you, unless this be the case, they must be cast off; and this I know, because I was like to be cast off.

28. Nevertheless, after wandering through much tribulation, repenting nigh unto death, the Lord in mercy hath seen fit to snatch me out of an *everlasting burning, and I am born of God.

29. My soul hath been redeemed from the gall of bitterness and bonds of iniquity. I was in the darkest abyss; but now I behold the marvelous light of God. My soul was racked with ^{2a}eternal torment; but I am snatched, and my soul is pained no more.

30. I rejected my Redeemer, and denied that which had been spoken of by our fathers; but now that they may foresee that he will come, and that he remembereth

---

o, ver. 12.   *p*, see *g*.   *q*, see *h*.   *r*, ver. 22.   *s*, see *c*, Mos. 6.   *t*, ver. 23.   Al. 5:46. 6:6.   8:26.   10:7.   17:3, 9.   28:6.   30:2.   He. 3:35.   3 Ne. 13:16—18.   27:1.   4 Ne. 12.   Moro. 6:5.   *u*, vers. 19, 23.   *v*, vers. 19, 23.   *w*, ver. 22.   See *t*.   *x*, see *c*, Mos. 5.   *y*, see *c*, Mos. 5.   *z*, see *k*, 1 Ne. 15.   2*a*, see *m*, Jac. 6.
PROBABLY BETWEEN B. C. 100 AND 92.

every creature of his creating, he will make himself manifest unto all.

31. Yea, ²ᵇevery knee shall bow, and every tongue confess before him. Yea, even at the last day, when all men shall stand to be judged of him, then shall they confess that he is God; then shall they confess, who live without God in the world, that the judgment of an ²ᶜeverlasting punishment is just upon them; and they shall quake, and tremble, and shrink beneath the ²ᵈglance of his all-searching eye.

32. And now it came to pass that Alma began from this time forward to teach the people, and those who were with Alma at the time the angel appeared unto them, traveling round about through all the land, publishing to all the people the things which they had heard and seen, and preaching the word of God in much tribulation, being greatly persecuted by those who were unbelievers, being smitten by many of them.

33. But notwithstanding all this, they did impart much consolation to the church, confirming their faith, and exhorting them with long-suffering and much travail to keep the commandments of God.

34. And ²ᵉfour of them were the sons of Mosiah; and their names were Ammon, and Aaron, and Omner, and Himni; these were the names of the sons of Mosiah.

35. And they traveled throughout all the ²ᶠland of Zarahemla, and among all the people who were under the reign of king Mosiah, zealously striving to repair all the injuries which they had done to the church, confessing all their sins, and publishing all the ²ᵍthings which they had seen, and explaining the prophecies and the scriptures to all who desired to hear them.

36. And thus they were instruments in the hands of God in bringing many to the knowledge of the truth, yea, to the knowledge of their Redeemer.

37. And how blessed are they! For they did ²ʰpublish peace; they did publish good tidings of good; and they did declare unto the people that the Lord reigneth.

CHAPTER 28.

Mosiah permits his sons to preach to the Lamanites—The twenty-four plates translated—Alma, the younger, made the custodian of the records.

1. Now it came to pass that after the ᵃsons of Mosiah had done all these things, *they took a small number with them and returned to their father, the king, and desired of him that he would grant unto them that they might, with these whom they had selected, go up to the ᵇland of Nephi that they might preach the things which they had heard, and that they might impart the word of God to their brethren, the Lamanites—

2. That perhaps they might bring them to the knowledge of the Lord their God, and convince them of the iniquity of their fathers; and that perhaps they might cure them of their ᶜhatred towards the Nephites, that they might also be brought to rejoice in the Lord their God, that they might become friendly to one another, and that there should be

---

2b, Mos. 16:1, 2. D. & C. 88:104. 2c, see m, Jac. 6. 2d, see c, Jac. 2. 2e, ver. 10. 2f, Om. 13. 2g, vers. 10—17. 2h, Mos. 15:14—17. CHAP. 28: a, Mos. 27:34. b, see b, 2 Ne. 5. c, see n, Jac. 7. * ABOUT B. C. 92.

no more contentions in all the land which the Lord their God had given them.

3. Now they were desirous that salvation should be declared to every creature, for they could not bear that any human soul should perish; yea, even the very thoughts that any soul should endure *d*endless torment did cause them to quake and tremble.

4. And thus did the Spirit of the Lord work upon them, for they were the *e*very vilest of sinners. And the Lord saw fit in his infinite mercy to spare them; nevertheless they suffered much anguish of soul because of their iniquities, suffering much and fearing that they should be cast off forever.

5. And it came to pass that they did plead with their father many days that they might go up to the *f*land of Nephi.

6. And king Mosiah went and inquired of the Lord if he should let his sons go up among the Lamanites to preach the word.

7. And the Lord said unto Mosiah: Let them go up, for many shall believe on their words, and they shall have eternal life; and I will *g*deliver thy sons out of the hands of the Lamanites.

8. And it came to pass that Mosiah granted that they might go and do according to their request.

9. And they took their journey into the wilderness to go up to preach the word among the Lamanites; and I shall give an *h*account of their proceedings hereafter.

10. Now king Mosiah had no one to confer the kingdom upon, for there was not any of his sons who would accept of the kingdom.

11. Therefore he took the records which were engraven on the plates of *i*brass, and also the *j*plates of Nephi, and all the things which he had kept and preserved according to the commandments of God, after having translated and caused to be written the records which were on the *k*plates of gold which had been found by the people of Limhi, which were delivered to him by the hand of Limhi;

12. And this he did because of the great anxiety of his people; for they were desirous beyond measure to know concerning those people *l*who had been destroyed.

13. And now he translated them by the means of those *m*two stones which were fastened into the two rims of a bow.

14. Now these things were prepared from the beginning, and were handed down from generation to generation, for the purpose of interpreting languages;

15. And they have been kept and preserved by the hand of the Lord, that he should discover to every creature who should possess the land the iniquities and abominations of his people;

16. And whosoever has these things is called *n*seer, after the manner of old times.

17. Now after Mosiah had finished translating these records, behold, it gave an account of the people *o*who were destroyed, from the time that they were destroyed back to the building of the *p*great tower, at the time the Lord confounded the language of the people and they were scattered abroad upon the *q*face of all the

---

d, see *m*, Jac. 6. *e*, Mos. 27:8—11. *f*, see *b*, 2 Ne. 5. *g*, Al. 17:35. 19:22, 23. *h*, Al. chaps. 17—28. *i*, see *a*, 1 Ne. 3. *j*, see *f*, 1 Ne. 1. *k*, see *k*, Mos. 8. *l*, see *j*, Mos. 8. *m*, see *n*, Mos. 8. *n*, Mos. 8:13—18. *o*, see *j*, Mos. 8. *p*, Tower of Babel, Om. 20—22. Eth. 1:1—5. *q*, Eth. 1:33.

ABOUT B. C. 92.

earth, yea, and even from that time back until the 'creation of Adam.

18. Now this account did cause the people of Mosiah to mourn exceedingly, yea, they were filled with sorrow; nevertheless it gave them much knowledge, in the which they did rejoice.

19. And this account shall be *written hereafter; for behold, it is expedient that all people should know the things which are written in this account.

20. And now, as I said unto you, that after king Mosiah had done these things, he took the 'plates of brass, and all the things which he had kept, and conferred them upon Alma, who was the son of Alma; yea, "all the records, and also the 'interpreters, and conferred them upon him, and commanded him that he should keep and preserve them, and also keep a record of the people, handing them down from one generation to another, even as they had been handed down from the time that Lehi left Jerusalem.

CHAPTER 29.

King Mosiah discourses upon kingcraft — Recommends representative form of government—Judges elected—Death of Alma, the elder—Mosiah's death ends the reign of the Nephite kings.

1. Now when Mosiah had done this he sent out throughout all the land, among all the people, desiring to know their will concerning who should be their king.

2. And it came to pass that the voice of the people came, saying: We are desirous that Aaron thy son should be our king and our ruler.

3. Now Aaron had gone up to the "land of Nephi, therefore the king could not confer the kingdom upon him; neither would Aaron take upon him the kingdom; neither were any of the "sons of Mosiah willing to take upon them the kingdom.

4. Therefore king Mosiah sent again among the people; yea, even a written word sent he among the people. And these were the words that were written, saying:

5. Behold, O ye my people, or my brethren, for I esteem you as such, I desire that ye should consider the cause which ye are called to consider—for ye are desirous to have a king.

6. Now I declare unto you that he to whom the kingdom doth 'rightly belong has declined, and will not take upon him the kingdom.

7. And now if there should be another appointed in his stead, behold I fear there would rise contentions among you. And who knoweth but what my son, to whom the kingdom ᵈdoth belong, should turn to be angry and draw away a part of this people after him, which would cause wars and contentions among you, which would be the cause of shedding much blood and perverting the way of the Lord, yea, and destroy the souls of many people.

8. Now I say unto you let us be wise and consider these things, for we have no right to destroy my son, neither should we have any right to destroy another if he should be appointed in his stead.

9. And if my son should turn again to his pride and vain things he would recall the things which he had said, and claim his right

---

r, see *m*, Mos. 2. *s*, Book of Ether. *t*, see *a*, 1 Ne. 3. *u*, ver. 11. See also *k*, *l*, *m*, and *n*, Mos. 8. *v*, see *n*, Mos. 8. Chap. 29: *a*, see *b*, 2 Ne. 5. *b*, Mos. 27:34. *c*, vers. 2, 3, 7, 9. *d*, vers. 2, 3, 6, 9. About B. C. 92.

to the kingdom, which would cause him and also this people to commit much sin.

10. And now let us be wise and look forward to these things, and do that which will make for the peace of this people.

11. Therefore I will be your king the remainder of my days; nevertheless, let ᵉus appoint judges, to judge this people according to our law; and we will newly arrange the affairs of this people, for we will appoint wise men to be judges, that will judge this people according to the commandments of God.

12. Now it is better that a man should be judged of God than of man, for the judgments of God are always just, but the judgments of man are not always just.

13. Therefore, if it were possible that you could have just men to be your kings, who would establish the laws of God, and judge this people according to his commandments, yea, if ye could have men for your kings who would do even as my father ᶠBenjamin did for this people—I say unto you, if this could always be the case then it would be expedient that ye should always have kings to rule over you.

14. And even I myself have labored with all the power and faculties which I have possessed, to teach you the commandments of God, and to establish peace throughout the land, that there should be no wars nor contentions, no stealing, nor plundering, nor murdering, nor any manner of iniquity;

15. And whosoever has committed iniquity, him have I punished according to the law which has been given to us by our fathers.

16. Now I say unto you, that because all men are not just it is not expedient that ye should have a king or kings to rule over you.

17. For behold, how much iniquity doth one wicked king cause to be committed, yea, and what great destruction!

18. Yea, remember ᵍking Noah, his wickedness and his abominations, and also the wickedness and abominations of his people. Behold what great destruction did come upon them; and also because of their iniquities they were brought ʰinto bondage.

19. And were it not for the interposition of their all-wise Creator, and this because of their sincere repentance, they must unavoidably remain in bondage until now.

20. But behold, he did deliver them because ⁱthey did humble themselves before him; and because they cried mightily unto him he did deliver them out of bondage; and thus doth the Lord work with his power in all cases among the children of men, extending the arm of mercy towards them that put their trust in him.

21. And behold, now I say unto you, ye cannot dethrone an iniquitous king save it be through much contention, and the shedding of much blood.

22. For behold, he has his friends in iniquity, and he keepeth his guards about him; and he teareth up the laws of those who have reigned in righteousness before him; and he trampleth under

e, vers. 25—27, 34, 38, 39, 41. Al. 2:3—7. 4:16, 17. 50:39. He. 1:3—5, 13. 2:2. 3:37. 5:1, 2, 4. 6:15, 19, 39. 7:4. 8:27, 28. Chap. 9. 3 Ne. 1:1. 3:1. 6:10, 21—30. 7:1—3. *f*, Om. 23—25. W. of Morm. 3, 10—18. Mos. chaps. 1—6. *g*, Mos. 11:1—15. 12:17—19. 17:1—20. *h*, Mos. 12:2—8. *i*, Mos. 21:14. 22:5—14.
ABOUT B. C. 92.

his feet the commandments of God;

23. And he enacteth laws, and sendeth them forth among his people, yea, laws after the manner of his own wickedness; and whosoever doth not obey his laws he causeth to be destroyed; and whosoever doth rebel against him he will send his armies against them to war, and if he can he will destroy them; and thus an unrighteous king doth pervert the ways of all righteousness.

24. And now behold I say unto you, it is not expedient that such abominations should come upon you.

25. Therefore, choose you by the *j*voice of this people, judges, that ye may be judged according to the laws which have been given you by our fathers, which are correct, and which were given them by the hand of the Lord.

26. Now it is not common that the voice of the people desireth anything contrary to that which is right; but it is common for the lesser part of the people to desire that which is not right; therefore this shall ye observe and make it your law—to do your business by the voice of the people.

27. And if the time comes that the voice of the people doth *k*choose iniquity, then is the time that the judgments of God will come upon you; yea, then is the time he will visit you with great destruction even as he has hitherto visited this land.

28. And now if ye have judges, and they do not judge you according to the law which has been given, ye can cause that they may be judged of a higher judge.

29. If your higher judges do not judge righteous judgments, ye shall cause that a small number of your lower judges should be gathered together, and they shall judge your higher judges, according to the *l*voice of the people.

30. And I command you to do these things in the fear of the Lord; and I command you to do these things, and that ye have no king; that if these people commit sins and iniquities they shall be answered upon their own heads.

31. For behold I say unto you, the sins of many people have been caused by the iniquities of their kings; therefore their iniquities are answered upon the heads of their kings.

32. And now I desire that this inequality should be no more in this land, especially among this my people; but I desire that this land be a *m*land of liberty, and every man may enjoy his rights and privileges alike, so long as the Lord sees fit that we may live and inherit the land, yea, even as long as any of our posterity remains upon the face of the land.

33. And many more things did king Mosiah write unto them, unfolding unto them all the trials and troubles of a righteous king, yea, all the travails of soul for their people, and also all the murmurings of the people to their king; and he explained it all unto them.

34. And he told them that these things ought not to be; but that the burden should come upon *n*all the people, that every man might bear his part.

35. And he also unfolded unto them all the disadvantages they labored under, by having an unrighteous king to rule over them;

j, see *e*. *k*, Al. 2:3—7. 10:19. He. 5:2. 6:38—40. *l*, see *c*. *m*, 2 Ne. 1:7. Al. 46:10—28. 34—36. *n*, see *c*.   ABOUT B. C. 92.

36. Yea, all his iniquities and abominations, and all the wars, and contentions, and bloodshed, and the stealing, and the plundering, and the committing of whoredoms, and all manner of iniquities which cannot be enumerated—telling them that these things ought not to be, that they were expressly repugnant to the commandments of God.

37. And now it came to pass, after king Mosiah had sent these things forth among the people they were convinced of the truth of his words.

38. Therefore they relinquished their desires for a king, and became exceedingly anxious that every man should have an °equal chance throughout all the land; yea, and every man expressed a willingness to answer for his own sins.

39. Therefore, it came to pass that they assembled themselves together in bodies throughout the land, to cast in their voices concerning who should be their judges, to judge them according to the law which had been given them; and they were exceedingly rejoiced because of the ᵖliberty which had been granted unto them.

40. And they did wax strong in love towards Mosiah; yea, they did esteem him more than any other man; for they did not look upon him as a tyrant who was seeking for gain, yea, for that lucre which doth corrupt the soul; for he had not exacted riches of them, neither had he delighted in the shedding of blood; but he had established peace in the land, and he had granted unto his people that they should be delivered from all manner of bondage; therefore they did esteem him, yea, exceedingly, beyond measure.

41. And it came to pass that they did ᵍappoint judges to rule over them, or to judge them according to the law; and this they did throughout all the land.

42. And it came to pass that Alma was appointed to be the first chief judge, he being also the ʳhigh priest, his father having conferred the office upon him, and having given him the charge concerning all the affairs of the church.

43. And now it came to pass that Alma did walk in the ways of the Lord, and he did keep his commandments, and he did judge righteous judgments; and there was continual peace through the land.

44. And thus *commenced the ˢreign of the judges throughout all the ᵗland of Zarahemla, among all the people who were called the Nephites; and Alma was the first and chief judge.

45. And now it came to pass that his father died, being eighty and two years old, having lived to fulfil the commandments of God.

46. And it came to pass that Mosiah died also, in the thirty and third year of his reign, being ᵘsixty and three years old; making in the whole, five hundred and nine years from the time Lehi left Jerusalem.

47. And thus ended the ᵛreign of the kings over the people of Nephi; and thus ʷended the days of Alma, who was the founder of their church.

---

o, see *c*. *p*, see *m*. *q*, see *e*. *r*, see *g*, Mos. 26. *s*, see *e*. *t*, Om. 13. *u*, Mos. 6:4. *v*, vers. 41, 42. *w*, ver. 45. * B. C. 91.

THE BOOK OF ALMA

THE SON OF ALMA

The account of Alma, who was the son of Alma the first, and Chief Judge over the people of Nephi, and also the High Priest over the Church. An account of the reign of the Judges, and the wars and contentions among the people. And also an account of a war between the Nephites and the Lamanites, according to the record of Alma, the first and chief Judge.

CHAPTER 1.

Nehor, an enemy of the church, slays Gideon, and is brought to judgment and executed—Priestcraft and persecution—Improved conditions—Priests and people equal.

1. Now it came to pass that in the first year of the reign of the judges over the people of Nephi, from this time forward, king Mosiah having ^agone the way of all the earth, having warred a good warfare, walking uprightly before God, leaving none to reign in his stead; nevertheless he had established laws, and they were acknowledged by the people; therefore they were obliged to ^babide by the laws which he had made.

2. And it came to pass that in the first year of the reign of Alma in the judgment-seat, there was a ^cman brought before him to be judged, a man who was large, and was noted for his much strength.

3. And he had gone about among the people, preaching to them that which he termed to be the word of God, bearing down against the church; declaring unto the people that every priest and teacher ought to become popular; and they ought ^dnot to labor with their hands, but that they ought to be supported by the people.

4. And he also testified unto the people that ^eall mankind should be saved at the last day, and that they need not fear nor tremble, but that they might lift up their heads and rejoice; for the Lord had created all men, and had also redeemed all men; and, in the end, all men should have eternal life.

5. And it came to pass that he did teach these things so much that many did believe on his words, even so many that they began to support him and give him money.

6. And he began to be lifted up in the pride of his heart, and to wear very costly apparel, yea, and even began to establish a church after the manner of his preaching.

7. And it came to pass as he was going, to preach to those who believed on his word, he met a man who belonged to the church of God, yea, even one of their teachers; and he began to contend with him sharply, that he might lead away the people of the church; but the man withstood him, admonishing him with the words of God.

8. Now the name of the man was Gideon; and it was he who was an instrument in the hands of God ^fin delivering the people of Limhi out of bondage.

9. Now, because Gideon with-

---

a, Mos. 29:46. *b,* vers. 14, 18. *c,* ver. 15. *d,* Mos. 18:24, 26. 27:3—5. *e,* Al. 15:15. 21:6. *f,* Mos. 22:3—16.
ABOUT B. C. 91.

195

stood him with the words of God he was wroth with Gideon, and drew his sword and began to smite him. Now Gideon being stricken with many years, therefore he was not able to withstand his blows, therefore he was slain by the sword.

10. And the man who slew him was taken by the people of the church, and was brought before Alma, to be judged according to the crimes which he had committed.

11. And it came to pass that he stood before Alma and pleaded for himself with much boldness.

12. But Alma said unto him: Behold, this is the first time that priestcraft has been introduced among this people. And behold, thou art not only guilty of priestcraft, but hast endeavored to enforce it by the sword; and were priestcraft to be enforced among this people it would prove their entire destruction.

13. And thou hast shed the blood of a ^{g}righteous man, yea, a man who has done much good among this people; and were we to spare thee his blood would come upon us for vengeance.

14. Therefore thou art ^{h}condemned to die, according to the law which has been given us by Mosiah, our last king; and it has been acknowledged by this people; therefore this people must abide by the law.

15. And it came to pass that they took him; and his name was ^{i}Nehor; and they carried him upon the top of the hill Manti, and there he was caused, or rather did acknowledge, between the heavens and the earth, that what he had taught to the people was contrary to the word of God; and there he suffered an ignominious death.

16. Nevertheless, this did not put an end to the spreading of ^{j}priestcraft through the land; for there were many who loved the vain things of the world, and they went forth preaching false doctrines; and this they did for the ^{k}sake of riches and honor.

17. Nevertheless, they durst not lie, if it were known, for fear of the law, for liars were punished; therefore they pretended to preach according to their belief; and now the law could have no power on any man for ^{l}his belief.

18. And they ^{m}durst not steal, for fear of the law, for such were punished; neither durst they rob, nor murder, for he that murdered was punished unto death.

19. But it came to pass that whosoever did not belong to the church of God began to persecute those that did belong to the church of God, and had taken upon them the ^{n}name of Christ.

20. Yea, they did persecute them, and afflict them with all manner of words, and this because of their humility; because they were not proud in their own eyes, and because they did impart the word of God, one with another, without money and without price.

21. Now there was a strict law among the people of the church, that there should not any man, belonging to the church, arise and ^{o}persecute those that did not belong to the church, and that there should be no persecution among themselves.

22. Nevertheless, there were

g, ver. 9. h, vers. 1, 18. i, Al. 2:1, 20. 16:11. 24:28—30. j, vers. 5, 6, 12. k, vers. 5, 6. l, Al. 30:7—12. m, Al. 30:10. n, see c, Mos. 5. o, vers. 22—25.
ABOUT B. C. 91.

many among them who began to be proud, and began to contend warmly with their adversaries, even unto blows; yea, they would *r*smite one another with their fists.

23. Now this was in the *second year of the reign of Alma, and it was a cause of much affliction to the church; yea, it was the cause of much trial with the church.

24. For the hearts of many were hardened, and their names were *q*blotted out, that they were remembered no more among the people of God. And also many withdrew themselves from among them.

25. Now this was a great trial to those that did stand fast in the faith; nevertheless, they were steadfast and immovable in keeping the commandments of God, and they bore with patience the persecution which was heaped upon them.

26. And when the *r*priests left their *s*labor to impart the word of God unto the people, the people also left their labors to hear the word of God. And when the priest had imparted unto them the word of God they all returned again diligently unto their labors; and the priest, not esteeming himself above his hearers, for the preacher was no better than the hearer, neither was the teacher any better than the learner; and thus they were all equal, and they did all labor, every man according to his strength.

27. And they did impart of their substance, every man *t*according to that which he had, to the poor, and the needy, and the sick, and the afflicted; and they did not wear costly apparel, yet they were neat and comely.

28. And thus they did establish the affairs of the church; and thus they began to have continual peace again, notwithstanding all their persecutions.

29. And now, because of the steadiness of the church they began to be exceeding rich, having abundance of all things whatsoever they stood in need—and abundance of flocks and herds, and fatlings of every kind, and also abundance of grain, and of gold, and of silver, and of precious things, and abundance of *u*silk and fine-twined linen, and all manner of good homely cloth.

30. And thus, in their prosperous circumstances, they did not send away *v*any who were naked, or that were hungry, or that were athirst, or that were sick, or that had not been nourished; and they did not set their hearts upon riches; therefore they were liberal to all, both old and young, both bond and free, both male and female, whether out of the church or in the church, having no respect to persons as to those who stood in need.

31. And thus they did prosper and become far more wealthy than those who did not belong to their church.

32. For those who did not belong to their church did indulge themselves in sorceries, and in idolatry or idleness, and in babblings, and in envyings and strife; wearing costly apparel; being lifted up in the pride of their own eyes; lying, thieving, robbing, committing whoredoms, and murdering, and all manner of wickedness; nevertheless, the *w*law was

---

p, vers. 21, 23. *q*, Mos. 26:32, 36. *r*, see *c*, Mos. 6. *s*, Mos. 18:24, 26. 27:4, 5. *t*, see *j*, Jac. 2. *u*, Mos. 10:5. Al. 4:6. He. 6:13. *v*, see *j*, Jac. 2. *w*, vers. 14, 17, 18, 33. Mos. 29:15, 41. * ABOUT B. C. 90.

put in force upon all those who did transgress it, inasmuch as it was possible.

33. And it came to pass that by thus exercising the law upon them, every man suffering according to that which he had done, they became more still, and durst not commit any wickedness if it were known; therefore, there was much peace among the people of Nephi until the fifth year of the reign of the judges.

CHAPTER 2.

Amlici seeks to become king—Rejected by the majority, but is made king—He is defeated in battle—He joins the Lamanites—Alma slays Amlici and routs his forces.

1. And it came to pass in the commencement of the *fifth year of their reign there began to be a contention among the people; for a certain man, being called Amlici, he being a very cunning man, yea, a wise man as to the wisdom of the world, he being after the order of the ᵃman that slew ᵇGideon by the sword, who was ᶜexecuted according to the law—

2. Now this Amlici had, by his cunning, drawn away much people after him; even so much that they began to be very powerful; and they began to endeavor to establish Amlici to be a king over the people.

3. Now this was alarming to the people of the church, and also to all those who had not been drawn away after the persuasions of Amlici; for they knew that according to their law that such things must be established by the ᵈvoice of the people.

4. Therefore, if it were possible that Amlici should gain the voice of the people, he, being a wicked man, would deprive them of their rights and privileges of the church; for it was his intent to destroy the church of God.

5. And it came to pass that the people assembled themselves together throughout all the land, every man according to his mind, whether it were for or against Amlici, in separate bodies, having much dispute and wonderful contentions one with another.

6. And thus they did assemble themselves together to cast in their voices concerning the matter; and they were laid before the judges.

7. And it came to pass that the ᵉvoice of the people came against Amlici, that he was not made king over the people.

8. Now this did cause much joy in the hearts of those who were against him; but Amlici did stir up those who were in his favor to anger against those who were not in his favor.

9. And it came to pass that they gathered themselves together, and did consecrate Amlici to be their king.

10. Now when Amlici was made king over them he commanded them that they should take up arms against their brethren; and this he did that he might subject them to him.

11. Now the people of Amlici were distinguished by the name of Amlici, being called Amlicites; and the remainder were called Nephites, or the people of God.

12. Therefore the people of the Nephites were aware of the intent of the Amlicites, and therefore they did prepare to meet them; yea, they did ᶠarm them-

---

a, Al. 1:15. *b*, Al. 1:8. *c*, Al. 1:15. *d*, see *e*, Mos. 29. *e*, see *e*, Mos. 29:25—27. *f*, 2 Ne. 5:14. Enos 20. Jar. 8. Mos. 10:8. Al. 3:5. 43:18—20. He. 1:14. 3 Ne. 3:26. Morm. 6:9. * B. C. 87.

selves with swords, and with cimeters, and with bows, and with arrows, and with stones, and with slings, and with all manner of weapons of war, of every kind.

13. And thus they were prepared to meet the Amlicites at the time of their coming. And there were appointed captains, and higher captains, and chief captains, according to their numbers.

14. And it came to pass that Amlici did arm his men with all manner of weapons of war of every kind; and he also appointed rulers and leaders over his people, to lead them to war against their brethren.

15. And it came to pass that the Amlicites came upon the hill Amnihu, which was east of the ^{g}river Sidon, which ran by the ^{h}land of Zarahemla, and there they began to make war with the Nephites.

16. Now Alma, being the ^{i}chief judge and the governor of the people of Nephi, therefore he went up with his people, yea, with ^{j}his captains, and chief captains, yea, at the head of his armies, against the Amlicites to battle.

17. And they began to slay the Amlicites upon the ^{k}hill east of ^{l}Sidon. And the Amlicites did contend with the Nephites with great strength, insomuch that many of the Nephites did fall before the Amlicites.

18. Nevertheless the Lord did strengthen the hand of the Nephites, that they slew the Amlicites with great slaughter, that they began to flee before them.

19. And it came to pass that the Nephites did pursue the Amlicites all that day, and did slay them with much slaughter, insomuch that there were slain of the Amlicites twelve thousand five hundred thirty and two souls; and there were slain of the Nephites six thousand five hundred sixty and two souls.

20. And it came to pass that when Alma could pursue the Amlicites no longer he caused that his people should pitch their tents in the ^{m}valley of Gideon, the valley being called after that Gideon who was slain by the hand of ^{n}Nehor with the sword; and in this valley the Nephites did pitch their tents for the night.

21. And Alma sent spies to follow the remnant of the Amlicites, that he might know of their plans and their plots, whereby he might guard himself against them, that he might preserve his people from being destroyed.

22. Now those whom he had sent out to watch the camp of the Amlicites were called Zeram, and Amnor, and Manti, and Limher; these were they who went out with their men to watch the camp of the Amlicites.

23. And it came to pass that on the morrow they returned into the camp of the Nephites in great haste, being greatly astonished, and struck with much fear, saying:

24. Behold, we followed the camp of the ^{o}Amlicites, and to our great astonishment, in the land of Minon, above the ^{p}land of Zarahemla, in the course of the ^{q}land of Nephi, we saw a numerous host of the Lamanites; and

---

g, vers. 17, 27. 34. 35. Al. 3:3. 4:4. 6:7. 8:3. 16:6, 7. 22:27. 43:22, 27, 32, 35, 39—41, 50—53. 44:22. 49:16. 50:11. 56:25. Morm. 1:10. *h*, Om. 13. *i*, Mos. 29:42. *j*, vers. 13, 14. *k*, ver. 15. *l*, see *g*. *m*, ver. 26. Mos. 22:3—16. Al. 1:8, 9. 6:7. 8:1. *n*, see *i*, Al. 1. *o*, vers. 1, 11. 3:4, 13—18. *p*, Om. 13. *q*, see *b*, 2 Ne. 5.
B. C. 87.

behold, the Amlicites have joined them;

25. And they are upon our brethren in that land; and they are fleeing before them with their flocks, and their wives, and their children, towards ʳour city; and except we make haste they obtain possession of our city, and our fathers, and our wives, and our children be slain.

26. And it came to pass that the people of Nephi took their tents, and departed out of the ˢvalley of Gideon towards their city, which was the city of Zarahemla.

27. And behold, as they were crossing the ᵗriver Sidon, the Lamanites and the Amlicites, being as numerous almost, as it were, as the sands of the sea, came upon them to destroy them.

28. Nevertheless, the Nephites being strengthened by the hand of the Lord, having prayed mightily to him that he would deliver them out of the hands of their enemies, therefore the Lord did hear their cries, and did strengthen them, and the Lamanites and the Amlicites did fall before them.

29. And it came to pass that Alma fought with Amlici with the sword, face to face; and they did contend mightily, one with another.

30. And it came to pass that Alma, being a man of God, being exercised with much faith, cried, saying: O Lord, have mercy and spare my life, that I may be an instrument in thy hands to save and preserve this people.

31. Now when Alma had said these words he contended again with Amlici; and he was strengthened, insomuch that he slew Amlici with the sword.

32. And he also contended with the king of the Lamanites; but the king of the Lamanites fled back from before Alma and sent his guards to contend with Alma.

33. But Alma, with his guards, contended with the guards of the king of the Lamanites until he slew and drove them back.

34. And thus he cleared the ground, or rather the bank, which was on the west of the ᵘriver Sidon, throwing the bodies of the Lamanites who had been slain into the waters of Sidon, that thereby his people might have room to cross and contend with the Lamanites and the Amlicites on the west side of the river Sidon.

35. And it came to pass that when they had all crossed the river Sidon that the Lamanites and the Amlicites began to flee before them, notwithstanding they were so numerous that they could not be numbered.

36. And they fled before the Nephites towards the wilderness which was west and north, away beyond the borders of the land; and the Nephites did pursue them with their might, and did slay them.

37. Yea, they were met on every hand, and slain and driven, until they were scattered on the west, and on the north, until they had reached the wilderness, which was called Hermounts; and it was that part of the wilderness which was infested by wild and ravenous beasts.

38. And it came to pass that many died in the wilderness of their wounds, and were devoured by those beasts and also the vultures of the air; and their bones have been found, and have been heaped up on the earth.

---

r, Zarahemla.   *s*, see *m*.   *t*, see *g*.   *u*, see *g*.   B. C. 87.

CHAPTER 3.

The mark of the Amlicites, and the curse upon the Lamanites—Another Nephite victory.

1. And it came to pass that the Nephites who were not slain by the weapons of war, after having buried those who had been slain —now the number of the slain were not numbered, because of the greatness of their number— after they had finished burying their dead they all returned to their lands, and to their houses, and their wives, and their children.

2. Now many women and children had been slain with the sword, and also many of their flocks and their herds; and also many of their fields of grain were destroyed, for they were trodden down by the hosts of men.

3. And now as many of the Lamanites and the Amlicites who had been slain upon the ªbank of the river Sidon were cast into the ᵇwaters of Sidon; and behold their bones are in the depths of the ᶜsea, and they are many.

4. And the Amlicites were distinguished from the Nephites, for they had marked themselves with ᵈred in their foreheads after the manner of the Lamanites; nevertheless they had not ᵉshorn their heads like unto the Lamanites.

5. Now the heads of the Lamanites were shorn; and they were ᶠnaked, save it were skin which was girded about their loins, and also their ᵍarmor, which was girded about them, and their bows, and their arrows, and their stones, and their slings, and so forth.

6. And the skins of the Lamanites were ʰdark, according to the mark which was set upon their fathers, which was a curse upon them because of their transgression and their rebellion against their brethren, who consisted of Nephi, Jacob, and Joseph, and Sam, who were just and holy men.

7. And their brethren sought to destroy them, therefore they were cursed; and the Lord God set a ⁱmark upon them, yea, upon Laman and Lemuel, and also the sons of Ishmael, and Ishmaelitish women.

8. And this was done that their seed might be distinguished from the seed of their brethren, that thereby the Lord God might preserve his people, that they might not mix and believe in incorrect traditions which would prove their destruction.

9. And it came to pass that whosoever did mingle his seed with that of the Lamanites did bring the same curse upon his seed.

10. Therefore, whosoever suffered himself to be led away by the Lamanites was called under that head, and there was a mark set upon him.

11. And it came to pass that whosoever would not believe in the tradition of the Lamanites, but believed those records which were brought out of the land of Jerusalem, and also in the tradition of their fathers, which were correct, who believed in the commandments of God and kept them, were called the Nephites, or the people of Nephi, from that time forth—

12. And it is they who have kept the ʲrecords which are true of their people, and also of the people of the Lamanites.

13. Now we will return again

---

a, Al. 2:34. *b*, see *g*, Al. 2. *c*, Al. 44:22. *d*, vers. 13, 15, 16, 18, 19. *e*, ver. 5, Enos 20. *f*, Enos 20. Al. 43:20. *g*, see *f*, Al. 2. *h*, see *d*, 1 Ne. 2. *i*, see *d*, 1 Ne. 2. *j*, see *f*, 1 Ne. 1.   B. C. 87.

to the Amlicites, for they also had a mark set upon them; yea, they set the mark upon themselves, yea, even a ^{k}mark of red upon their foreheads.

14. Thus the word of God is fulfilled, for these are the words which he said to Nephi: Behold, the Lamanites have I cursed, and I will set a mark on them that they and their seed may be separated from thee and thy seed, from this time henceforth and forever, except they repent of their wickedness and turn to me that I may have mercy upon them.

15. And again: I will set a mark upon him that mingleth his seed with thy brethren, that they may be cursed also.

16. And again: I will set a ^{l}mark upon him that fighteth against thee and thy seed.

17. And again, I say he that departeth from thee shall no more be called thy seed; and I will bless thee, and whomsoever shall be called thy seed, henceforth and forever; and these were the promises of the Lord unto Nephi and to his seed.

18. Now the Amlicites knew not that they were fulfilling the words of God when they began to ^{m}mark themselves in their foreheads; nevertheless they had come out in open rebellion against God; therefore it was expedient that the curse should fall upon them.

19. Now I would that ye should see that they brought upon themselves the curse; and even so doth every man that is cursed bring upon himself his own condemnation.

20. Now it came to pass that not many days after the battle which was fought in the land of Zarahemla, by the Lamanites and the Amlicites, that there was another army of the Lamanites came in upon the people of Nephi, in the ^{n}same place where the first army met the Amlicites.

21. And it came to pass that there was an army sent to drive them out of their land.

22. Now Alma himself being afflicted with a wound did not go up to battle at this time against the Lamanites;

23. But he sent up a numerous army against them; and they went up and slew many of the Lamanites, and drove the remainder of them out of the borders of their land.

24. And then they returned again and began to establish peace in the land, being troubled no more for a time with their enemies.

25. Now *all these things were done, yea, all these wars and contentions were commenced and ended in the fifth year of the reign of the judges.

26. And in one year were thousands and tens of thousands of souls sent to the eternal world, that they might reap their rewards according to their works, whether they were good or whether they were bad, to reap eternal happiness or ^{o}eternal misery, according to the ^{p}spirit which they listed to obey, whether it be a good spirit or a bad one.

27. For every man receiveth wages of him whom he listeth to obey, and this according to the words of the spirit of prophecy; therefore let it be according to the truth. And thus endeth the fifth year of the reign of the judges.

---

k, see d. l, see d. m, ver. 4. n, Al. 2:24. o, see m, Jac. 6. p, see q, Mos. 2.
* B. C. 87.

CHAPTER 4.

Growth of the church—Prosperity, pride, and iniquity—Nephihah made chief judge.

1. Now it came to pass in the *sixth year of the reign of the judges over the people of Nephi, there were no contentions nor wars in the ᵃland of Zarahemla;

2. But the people were afflicted, yea, greatly afflicted for the ᵇloss of their brethren, and also for the loss of ᶜtheir flocks and herds, and also for the loss of their fields of grain, which were trodden under foot and destroyed by the Lamanites.

3. And so great were their afflictions that every soul had cause to mourn; and they believed that it was the judgments of God sent upon them because of their wickedness and their abominations; therefore they were awakened to a remembrance of their duty.

4. And they began to establish the church more fully; yea, and many were ᵈbaptized in the waters of ᵉSidon and were ᶠjoined to the church of God; yea, they were baptized by the hand of Alma, who had been consecrated the ᵍhigh priest over the people of the church, by the hand of his father Alma.

5. And it came to pass in the †seventh year of the reign of the judges there were about three thousand five hundred souls that united themselves to the church of God and were ʰbaptized. And thus endeth the seventh year of the reign of the judges over the people of Nephi; and there was continual peace in all that time.

6. And it came to pass in the ‡eighth year of the reign of the judges, that the people of the church began to wax proud, because of their exceeding riches, and ⁱtheir fine silks, and their fine-twined linen, and because of their many flocks and herds, and their gold and their silver, and all manner of precious things, which they had obtained by their industry; and in all these things were they lifted up in the pride of their eyes, for they began to wear very costly apparel.

7. Now this was the cause of much affliction to Alma, yea, and to many of the people whom Alma had ʲconsecrated to be teachers, and priests, and elders over the church; yea, many of them were sorely grieved for the wickedness which they saw had begun to be among their people.

8. For they saw and beheld with great sorrow that the people of the church began to be lifted up in the pride of their eyes, and to ᵏset their hearts upon riches and upon the vain things of the world, that they began to be scornful, one towards another, and they began to persecute those that did not believe according to their own will and pleasure.

9. And thus, in this eighth year of the reign of the judges, there began to be great contentions among the people of the church; yea, there were envyings, and strife, and malice, and persecutions, and ˡpride, even to exceed the pride of those who did not belong to the church of God.

10. And thus ended the eighth year of the reign of the judges; and the wickedness of the church was a great stumbling-block to those who did not belong to the church; and thus the church began to fail in its progress.

---

a, Om. 13. *b*, Al. 2:19. 3:1, 26. *c*, Al. 3:2. *d*, see *u*, 2 Ne. 9. *e*, see *g*, Al. 2. *f*, see *d*, Mos. 26. *g*, see *g*, Mos. 26. *h*, see *u*, 2 Ne. 9. *i*, see *u*, Al. 1. *j*, see *c*, Mos. 6. *k*, vers. 6, 9—12. *l*, see *k*.   * B. C. 86. † B. C. 85. ‡ B. C. 84.

11. And it came to pass in the *commencement of the ninth year, Alma saw the ᵐwickedness of the church, and he saw also that the example of the church began to lead those who were unbelievers on from one piece of iniquity to another, thus bringing on the destruction of the people.

12. Yea, he saw great inequality among the people, some lifting themselves up with their pride, despising others, turning their backs ⁿupon the needy and the naked and those who were hungry, and those who were athirst, and those who were sick and afflicted.

13. Now this was a great cause for lamentations among the people, while others were abasing themselves, succoring those who stood in need of their succor, ᵒsuch as imparting their substance to the poor and the needy, feeding the hungry, and suffering all manner of afflictions, for Christ's sake, who should come according to the spirit of prophecy;

14. Looking forward to that day, thus retaining a remission of their sins; being filled with great joy because of the ᵖresurrection of the dead, according to the will and power and deliverance of Jesus Christ from the ᑫbands of death.

15. And now it came to pass that Alma, having seen the afflictions of the humble followers of God, and the persecutions which were heaped upon them by the remainder of his people, and seeing ʳall their inequality, began to be very sorrowful; nevertheless the Spirit of the Lord did not fail him.

16. And he selected a wise man who was among the ˢelders of the church, and gave him power according to the ᵗvoice of the people, that he might have power to enact laws according to the ᵘlaws which had been given, and to put them in force according to the wickedness and the crimes of the people.

17. Now this man's name was Nephihah, and he was appointed chief judge; and he sat in the judgment-seat to judge and to govern the people.

18. Now Alma did not grant unto him the office of being ᵛhigh priest over the church, but he retained the office of high priest unto himself; but he delivered the judgment-seat unto Nephihah.

19. And this he did that he himself might go forth among his people, or among the people of Nephi, that he might preach the word of God unto them, to stir them up in remembrance of their duty, and that he might pull down, by the word of God, all the pride and craftiness and all the contentions which were among his people, seeing no way that he might reclaim them save it were in bearing down in pure testimony against them.

20. And thus in the commencement of the ninth year of the reign of the judges over the people of Nephi, Alma delivered up the judgment-seat to ʷNephihah, and confined himself wholly to the ˣhigh priesthood of the holy order of God, to the testimony of the word, according to the spirit of revelation and prophecy.

CHAPTER 5.

The words which Alma, the High Priest according to the holy order of

---

m, see *k*.   *n*, see *j*, Jac. 2.   *o*, see *j*, Jac. 2.   *p*, see *d*, 2 Ne. 2.   *q*, see *g* and *j*, 2 Ne. 9.   *r*, vers. 6—12.   *s*, ver. 7.   *t*, see *e*, Mos. 29.   *u*, Al. 1:1, 14, 18.   *v*, see *g*, Mos. 26.   *w*, vers. 17, 18.   Al. 8:12.   *x*, see *g*, Mos. 26.   * B. C. 83.

God, delivered to the people in their cities and villages throughout the land.

He recounts the experience of the church — Denounces iniquity — Calls upon the people to repent.

1. Now it came to pass that *Alma began to deliver the word of God unto the people, first in the ^aland of Zarahemla, and from thence throughout all the land.

2. And these are the words which he spake to the people in the church which was established in the city of Zarahemla, according to his own record, saying:

3. I, Alma, having been consecrated by my father, Alma, to be a ^bhigh priest over the church of God, he having ^cpower and authority from God to do these things, behold, I say unto you that he began to establish a church in the land which was in the borders of Nephi; yea, the land which was called the ^dland of Mormon; yea, and he did ^ebaptize his brethren in the waters of Mormon.

4. And behold, I say unto you, they were ^fdelivered out of the hands of the people of king Noah, by the mercy and power of God.

5. And behold, after that, they were brought into bondage by the hands of the Lamanites ^gin the wilderness; yea, I say unto you, they were in captivity, and again the Lord did ^hdeliver them out of bondage by the power of his word; and we were brought into this land, and here we began to establish the church of God throughout ⁱthis land also.

6. And now behold, I say unto you, my brethren, you that belong to this church, have you sufficiently retained in remembrance the ^jcaptivity of your fathers? Yea, and have you sufficiently retained in remembrance his mercy and long-suffering towards them? And moreover, have ye sufficiently retained in remembrance that he has delivered their souls from ^khell?

7. Behold, he changed their hearts; yea, he awakened them out of a deep sleep, and they awoke unto God. Behold, they were in the midst of darkness; nevertheless, their souls were illuminated by the light of the everlasting word; yea, they were encircled about by the ^lbands of death, and the ^mchains of hell, and an everlasting destruction did await them.

8. And now I ask of you, my brethren, were they destroyed? Behold, I say unto you, Nay, they were not.

9. And again I ask, were the ⁿbands of death broken, and the ^ochains of hell which encircled them about, were they loosed? I say unto you, Yea, they were loosed, and their souls did expand, and they did sing redeeming love. And I say unto you that they are saved.

10. And now I ask of you on what conditions are they saved? Yea, what grounds had they to hope for salvation? What is the cause of their being loosed from the ^pbands of death, yea, and also the ^qchains of hell?

11. Behold, I can tell you— did not my father Alma believe in the words which were delivered by the ^rmouth of Abinadi? And was he not a holy prophet? Did he not speak the words of

---

a, Om. 13. *b*, see *g*, Mos. 26. *c*, see *g*, Mos. 18. *d*, see *b*, Mos. 18. *e*, see *u*, 2 Ne. 9. *f*, Mos. 23:1—3. *g*, Mos. 23:37—39, 24:8—15. *h*, Mos. 24:17—25. *i*, ver. 1. *j*, see *f* and *g*. *k*, see *k*, 1 Ne. 15. *l*, see *g* and *j*, 2 Ne. 9. *m*, see *p*, 2 Ne. 28. *n*, see *g* and *j*, 2 Ne. 9. *o*, see *p*, 2 Ne. 28. *p* see *g* and *j*, 2 Ne. 9. *q*, see *p*, 2 Ne. 28. *r*, Mos. 17:2—4.   *ABOUT B. C. 83.

God, and my father Alma believe them?

12. And according to his faith there was a mighty change wrought in his heart. Behold I say unto you that this is all true.

13. And behold, he preached the word 'unto your fathers, and a mighty change was also wrought in their hearts, and they humbled themselves and put their trust in the true and living God. And behold, they were faithful 'until the end; therefore they were saved.

14. And now behold, I ask of you, my brethren of the church, have ye spiritually been "born of God? Have ye received his image in your countenances? Have ye experienced this mighty change in your hearts?

15. Do ye exercise faith in the redemption of him who 'created you? Do you look forward with an eye of faith, and view this mortal body "raised in immortality, and this corruption raised in incorruption, to stand before God to be judged according to the deeds which have been done in the mortal body?

16. I say unto you, can you imagine to yourselves that ye hear the voice of the Lord, saying unto you, in that day: Come unto me ye blessed, for behold, your works have been the works of righteousness upon the face of the earth?

17. Or do ye imagine to yourselves that ye can lie unto the Lord in that day, and say—Lord, our works have been righteous works upon the face of the earth —and that he will save you?

18. Or otherwise, can ye imagine yourselves brought before the tribunal of God with your souls filled with guilt and remorse, having a *remembrance of all your guilt, yea, a perfect remembrance of all your wickedness, yea, a remembrance that ye have set at defiance the commandments of God?

19. I say unto you, can ye look up to God at that day with a pure heart and clean hands? I say unto you, can you look up, having the image of God engraven upon your countenances?

20. I say unto you, can ye think of being saved when you have yielded yourselves to become ᵛsubjects to the devil?

21. I say unto you, ye will know at that day that ye cannot be saved; for there can no man be saved except his garments are washed white; yea, his garments must be purified until they are cleansed from all stain, through the ˢblood of him of whom it has been spoken by our fathers, who should come to redeem his people from their sins.

22. And now I ask of you, my brethren, how will any of you feel, if ye shall stand before the bar of God, having your garments stained with blood and all manner of filthiness? Behold, what will these things testify against you?

23. Behold will they not testify that ye are murderers, yea, and also that ye are guilty of all manner of wickedness?

24. Behold, my brethren, do ye suppose that such an one can have a place to sit down in the kingdom of God, with Abraham, with Isaac, and with Jacob, and also all the holy prophets, whose garments are cleansed and are spotless, pure and white?

25. I say unto you, Nay; except

---

s, Mos. 18:1—31. *t*, 2 Ne. 31:15. *u*, see *c*, Mos. 5. *v*, see *l*, Mos. 5. *w*, see *d*, 2 Ne. 2. Also *j* and *m*, 2 Ne. 9. *x*, see *n*, 2 Ne. 9. *y*, see *q*, Mos. 2. *z*, see *f*, 2 Ne. 2.

ABOUT B. C. 83.

ye make our Creator a liar from the beginning, or suppose that he is a liar from the beginning, ye cannot suppose that such can have place in the kingdom of heaven; but they shall be cast out for they are the [2a]children of the kingdom of the devil.

26. And now behold, I say unto you, my brethren, if ye have experienced a change of heart, and if ye have felt to sing the song of redeeming love, I would ask, can ye feel so now?

27. Have ye walked, keeping yourselves blameless before God? Could ye say, if ye were called to die at this time, within yourselves, that ye have been sufficiently humble? That your garments have been cleansed and made white through the [2b]blood of Christ, who will come to redeem his people from their sins?

28. Behold, are ye stripped of pride? I say unto you, if ye are not ye are not prepared to meet God. Behold ye must prepare quickly; for the kingdom of heaven is soon at hand, and such an one hath not eternal life.

29. Behold, I say, is there one among you who is not stripped of envy? I say unto you that such an one is not prepared; and I would that he should prepare quickly, for the hour is close at hand, and he knoweth not when the time shall come; for such an one is not found guiltless.

30. And again I say unto you, is there one among you that doth make a mock of his brother, or that heapeth upon him persecutions?

31. Wo unto such an one, for he is not prepared, and the time is at hand that he must repent or he cannot be saved!

32. Yea, even wo unto all ye workers of iniquity; repent, repent, for the Lord God hath spoken it!

33. Behold, he sendeth an invitation unto all men, for the arms of mercy are extended towards them, and he saith: Repent, and I will receive you.

34. Yea, he saith: Come unto me and ye shall partake of the [2c]fruit of the tree of life; yea, ye shall eat and drink of the bread and the waters of life freely;

35. Yea, come unto me and bring forth works of righteousness, and ye shall not be hewn down and [2d]cast into the fire—

36. For behold, the time is at hand that whosoever bringeth forth not good fruit, or whosoever doeth not the works of righteousness, the same have cause to wail and mourn.

37. O ye workers of iniquity; ye that are puffed up in the vain things of the world, ye that have professed to have known the ways of righteousness nevertheless have gone astray, as sheep having no shepherd, notwithstanding a shepherd hath called after you and is still calling after you, but ye will not hearken unto his voice!

38. Behold, I say unto you, that the [2e]good shepherd doth call you; yea, and in his own name he doth call you, which is the name of Christ; and if ye will not hearken unto the voice of the good shepherd, to the name by which ye are called, behold, ye are not the sheep of the good shepherd.

39. And now if ye are not the sheep of the [2f]good shepherd, of what fold are ye? Behold, I say unto you, that the devil is your

---

2a, see i, 2 Ne. 9. 2b, see f, 2 Ne. 2. 2c, see b, 1 Ne. 8. 2d, see k, 1 Ne. 15. 2e, vers. 39, 41, 57, 59, 60. He. 7:18. 3 Ne. 15:24. 16:1—5. 18:31. 2f, see 2e.

ABOUT B. C. 83.

ALMA, 5.

shepherd, and ye are of his fold; and now, who can deny this? Behold, I say unto you, whosoever denieth this is a liar and a ^{2g}child of the devil.

40. For I say unto you ^{2h}that whatsoever is good cometh from God, and whatsoever is evil cometh from the devil.

41. Therefore, if a man bringeth forth ^{2i}good works he hearkeneth unto the voice of the ^{2j}good shepherd, and he doth follow him; but whosoever bringeth forth ^{2k}evil works, the same becometh a ^{2l}child of the devil, for he hearkeneth unto his voice, and doth follow him.

42. And whosoever doeth this must receive his wages of him; therefore, for his wages he receiveth death, as to ^{2m}things pertaining unto righteousness, being dead unto all good works.

43. And now, my brethren, I would that ye should hear me, for I speak in the energy of my soul; for behold, I have spoken unto you plainly that ye cannot err, or have spoken according to the commandments of God.

44. For I am called to speak after this manner, according to the ^{2n}holy order of God, which is in Christ Jesus; yea, I am commanded to stand and testify unto this people the things which have been spoken by our fathers concerning the things which are to come.

45. And this is not all. Do ye not suppose that I know of these things myself? Behold, I testify unto you that I do know that these things whereof I have spoken are true. And how do ye suppose that I know of their surety?

46. Behold, I say unto you they are made known unto me by the Holy Spirit of God. Behold, I have ^{2o}fasted and prayed many days that I might know these things of myself. And now I do know of myself that they are true; for the Lord God hath made them manifest unto me by his Holy Spirit; and this is the spirit of revelation which is in me.

47. And moreover, I say unto you that it has thus been revealed unto me, that the words which have been spoken by our fathers are true, even so according to the spirit of prophecy which is in me, which is also by the manifestation of the Spirit of God.

48. I say unto you, that I know of myself that whatsoever I shall say unto you, concerning that which is to come, is true; and I say unto you, that I know that Jesus Christ shall come, yea, the Son, the Only Begotten of the Father, full of grace, and mercy, and truth. And behold, it is he that cometh to ^{2p}take away the sins of the world, yea, the sins of every man who steadfastly believeth on his name.

49. And now I say unto you that this is the ^{2q}order after which I am called, yea, to preach unto my beloved brethren, yea, and every one that dwelleth in the land; yea, to preach unto all, both old and young, both bond and free; yea, I say unto you the aged, and also the middle aged, and the rising generation; yea, to cry unto them that they must repent and be ^{2r}born again.

50. Yea, thus saith the Spirit: Repent, all ye ends of the earth, for the kingdom of heaven is soon

2g, see i, 2 Ne. 9. 2h, Om. 25. Eth. 4:12. Moro. 7:12—19. 10:6. 2i, 3 Ne. 14:16—20. 2j, see 2e. 2k, 3 Ne. 14:16—20. 2l, see i, 2 Ne. 9. 2m, see c, 2 Ne. 2. 2n, see g, Mos. 26. 2o, see t, Mos. 27. 2p, see f, 2 Ne. 2. 2q, see g, Mos. 26. 2r, see c, Mos. 5.

ABOUT B. C. 83.

at hand; yea, the Son of God cometh in his glory, in his might, majesty, power, and dominion. Yea, my beloved brethren, I say unto you, that the Spirit saith: Behold the glory of the King of all the earth; and also the King of heaven shall very soon shine forth among all the children of men.

51. And also the Spirit saith unto me, yea, crieth unto me with a mighty voice, saying: Go forth and say unto this people—Repent, for except ye repent ye can in nowise inherit the kingdom of heaven.

52. And again I say unto you, the Spirit saith: Behold, the ax is laid at the root of the tree; therefore every tree that bringeth not forth good fruit shall be ²ˢhewn down and cast into the fire, yea, a fire which cannot be consumed, even an unquenchable fire. Behold, and remember, the Holy One hath spoken it.

53. And now my beloved brethren, I say unto you, can ye withstand these sayings; yea, can ye lay aside these things, and trample the Holy One under your feet; yea, can ye be puffed up in the pride of your hearts; yea, will ye still persist in the wearing of ²ᵗcostly apparel and setting your hearts upon the vain things of the world, upon your riches?

54. Yea, will ye persist in supposing that ye are better one than another; yea, will ye persist in the persecution of your brethren, who humble themselves and do walk after the holy order of God, wherewith they have been brought into this church, having been sanctified by the Holy Spirit, and they do bring forth works which are meet for repentance—

55. Yea, and will you persist in turning your ²ᵘbacks upon the poor, and the needy, and in withholding your substance from them?

56. And finally, all ye that will persist in your wickedness, I say unto you that these are they who shall be ²ᵛhewn down and cast into the fire except they speedily repent.

57. And now I say unto you, all you that are desirous to follow the voice of the ²ʷgood shepherd, come ye out from the wicked, and be ye separate, and touch not their unclean things; and behold, their names shall be ²ˣblotted out, that the names of the wicked shall not be numbered among the names of the righteous, that the word of God may be fulfilled, which saith: The names of the wicked shall not be mingled with the names of my people;

58. For the names of the righteous shall be written in the book of life, and unto them will I grant an inheritance at my right hand. And now, my brethren, what have ye to say against this? I say unto you, if ye speak against it, it matters not, for the word of God must be fulfilled.

59. For what shepherd is there among you having many sheep doth not watch over them, that the wolves enter not and devour his flock? And behold, if a wolf enter his flock doth he not drive him out? Yea, and at the last, if he can, he will destroy him.

60. And now I say unto you that the ²ʸgood shepherd doth call after you; and if you will hearken

---

2s, vers. 35, 56. Jac. 6:7. 3 Ne. 27:11, 12. 2t, 2 Ne. 28:11—14. Morm. 8:36—30. 2u, see j, Jac. 2. 2v, see 2s. 2w, see 2e. 2x, Mos. 26:32—36. 2y, see 2e.

ABOUT B. C. 83.

unto his voice he will bring you into his fold, and ye are his sheep; and he commandeth you that ye suffer no ravenous wolf to enter among you, that ye may not be destroyed.

61. And now I, Alma, do command you in the language of him who hath commanded me, that ye observe to do the words which I have spoken unto you.

62. I speak by way of command unto you that belong to the church; and unto those who do not belong to the church I speak by way of invitation, saying: Come and be ^{2z}baptized unto repentance, that ye also may be partakers of the fruit of the ^{3a}tree of life.

CHAPTER 6.

The reform movement, begun in Zarahemla, is carried to the city of Gideon.

1. And now it came to pass that after Alma had made an end of speaking unto the people of the church, which was established in the city of Zarahemla, he ^{a}ordained priests and elders, by laying on his hands according to the order of God, to preside and watch over the church.

2. And it came to pass that whosoever did not belong to the church who repented of their sins were ^{b}baptized unto repentance, and were received into the church.

3. And it also came to pass that whosoever did belong to the church that did not repent of their wickedness and humble themselves before God—I mean those who were lifted up in the pride of their hearts—the same were rejected, and their names were ^{c}blotted out, that their names were not numbered among those of the righteous.

4. And thus they began to establish the order of the church in the city of ^{d}Zarahemla.

5. Now I would that ye should understand that the word of God was liberal unto all, that none were deprived of the privilege of assembling themselves together to hear the word of God.

6. Nevertheless the children of God were commanded that they should gather themselves together oft, and join in ^{e}fasting and mighty prayer in behalf of the welfare of the souls of those who knew not God.

7. And now it came to pass that when Alma had made these regulations he departed from them, yea, from the church which was in the city of Zarahemla, and went over upon the east of the ^{f}river Sidon, into the ^{g}valley of Gideon, there having been a city built, which was called the city of Gideon, which was in the valley that was called Gideon, being called after the man who was ^{h}slain by the hand of ^{i}Nehor with the sword.

8. And Alma went and began to declare the word of God unto the church which was established in the ^{j}valley of Gideon, according to the revelation of the truth of the word which had been spoken by his fathers, and according to the spirit of prophecy which was in him, according to the testimony of Jesus Christ, the Son of God, who should come to redeem his people from their sins, and the ^{k}holy order by which he was called. And thus it is written. Amen.

2z, see u, 2 Ne. 9. 3a, see b, 1 Ne. 8. 2 Ne. 9. c, Mos. 26:32—36. Al. 5:57, 58. f, see g, Al. 2. g, see m, Al. 2. h, Al. 1:9, g, Mos. 26.

CHAP. 6: a, see c, Mos. 6. b, see u, d, Om. 13. Al. 2:26. e, see t, Mos. 27. 15. i, Al. 1:15. j, see m, Al. 2. k, see

ABOUT B. C. 83.

CHAPTER 7.

The words of Alma which he delivered to the people in Gideon, according to his own record.

His testimony of the Redeemer—He commends the people for their righteousness.

1. Behold my beloved brethren, seeing that I have been permitted to come unto you, therefore I attempt to address you in my language; yea, by my own mouth, seeing that it is the first time that I have spoken unto you by the words of my mouth, I having been ªwholly confined to the judgment-seat, having had much business that I could not come unto you.

2. And even I could not have come now at this time were it not that the judgment-seat hath been ᵇgiven to another, to reign in my stead; and the Lord in much mercy hath granted that I should come unto you.

3. And behold, I have come having great hopes and much desire that I should find that ye had humbled yourselves before God, and that ye had continued in the supplicating of his grace, that I should find that ye were blameless before him, that I should find that ye were not in the awful dilemma that our brethren were in at Zarahemla.

4. But blessed be the name of God, that he hath given me to know, yea, hath given unto me the exceeding great joy of knowing that they are established again in the way of his righteousness.

5. And I trust, according to the Spirit of God which is in me, that I shall also have joy over you; nevertheless I do not desire that my joy over you should come by the cause of so much afflictions and sorrow which I have had for the brethren at ᶜZarahemla, for behold, my joy cometh over them after wading through much affliction and sorrow.

6. But behold, I trust that ye are not in a state of so much unbelief as were your brethren; I trust that ye are not lifted up in the pride of your hearts; yea, I trust that ye have not set your hearts ᵈupon riches and the vain things of the world; yea, I trust that you do not worship idols, but that ye do worship the true and the living God, and that ye look forward for the remission of your sins, with an everlasting faith, which is to come.

7. For behold, I say unto you there be many things to come; and behold, there is one thing which is of more importance than they all—for behold, the time is not far distant that the Redeemer liveth and cometh among his people.

8. Behold, I do not say that he will come among us at the time of his dwelling in his mortal tabernacle; for behold, the Spirit hath not said unto me that this should be the case. Now as to this thing I do not know; but this much I do know, that the Lord God hath power to do all things which are according to his word.

9. But behold, the Spirit hath said this much unto me, saying: Cry unto this people, saying— Repent ye, and prepare the way of the Lord, and walk in his paths, which are straight; for behold, the kingdom of heaven is at hand, and the Son of God cometh upon the face of the earth.

10. And behold, he shall be

---
a, Mos. 29:42. *b*, Al. 4:16—18. *c*, Om. 13. *d*, see 2*t*, Al. 5.   ABOUT B. C. 83.

born of *e*Mary, at Jerusalem which is the land of our forefathers, she being a *f*virgin, a precious and chosen vessel, who shall be overshadowed and conceive by the power of the Holy Ghost, and bring forth a son, yea, even the Son of God.

11. And he shall go forth, suffering pains and afflictions and temptations of every kind; and this that the word might be fulfilled which saith *g*he will take upon him the pains and the sicknesses of his people.

12. And he will take upon him death, that he may loose the *h*bands of death which bind his people; and he will take upon him their infirmities, that his bowels may be filled with mercy, according to the flesh, that he may know according to the flesh how to succor his people according to their infirmities.

13. Now the Spirit *i*knoweth all things; nevertheless the Son of God suffereth according to the flesh that he might *j*take upon him the sins of his people, that he might blot out their transgressions according to the power of his deliverance; and now behold, this is the testimony which is in me.

14. Now I say unto you that ye must repent, and be *k*born again; for the Spirit saith if ye are not born again ye cannot inherit the kingdom of heaven; therefore come and be *l*baptized unto repentance, that ye may be washed from your sins, that ye may have faith on the Lamb of God, who taketh *m*away the sins of the world, who is mighty to save and to cleanse from all unrighteousness.

15. Yea, I say unto you come and fear not, and lay aside every sin, which easily doth beset you, which doth bind you down to destruction, yea, come and go forth, and show unto your God that ye are willing to repent of your sins and enter into a covenant with him to keep his commandments, and witness it unto him this day by going into the *n*waters of baptism.

16. And whosoever doeth this, and keepeth the commandments of God from thenceforth, the same will remember that I say unto him, yea, he will remember that I have said unto him, he shall have eternal life, according to the testimony of the Holy Spirit, which testifieth in me.

17. And now my beloved brethren, do you believe these things? Behold, I say unto you, yea, I know that ye believe them; and the way that I know that ye believe them is by the manifestation of the Spirit which is in me. And now because your faith is strong concerning that, yea, concerning the things which I have spoken, great is my joy.

18. For as I said unto you from the beginning, that I had much desire that ye were not in the state of dilemma *o*like your brethren, even so I have found that my desires have been gratified.

19. For I perceive that ye are in the paths of righteousness; I perceive that ye are in the path which leads to the kingdom of God; yea, I perceive that ye are making his *p*paths straight.

20. I perceive that it has been made known unto you, by the testimony of his word, that he cannot walk in crooked paths;

e, Mos. 3:8. *f*, 1 Ne. 11:13—21. Mos. 3:8. *g*, Mos. 14:3—5. *h*, see *g*, and *j*, 2 Ne. 9. *i*, see *r*, 2 Ne. 9. *j*, Mos. 14:5, 8, 12. 15:12. *k*, see *c*, Mos. 5. *l*, see *u*, 2 Ne. 9. *m*, see *f*, 2 Ne. 2. *n*, see *u*, 2 Ne. 9. *o*, vers. 3—6. *p*, see 2*a*, 2 Ne. 9.

ABOUT B. C. 83.

neither doth he vary from that which he hath said; neither hath he a shadow of turning from the right to the left, or from that which is right to that which is wrong; therefore, his course is ⁿone eternal round.

21. And he doth not dwell in ʳunholy temples; neither can filthiness or anything which is unclean be received into the kingdom of God; therefore I say unto you the time shall come, yea, and it shall be at the last day, that he who is filthy ˢshall remain in his filthiness.

22. And now my beloved brethren, I have said these things unto you that I might awaken you to a sense of your duty to God, that ye may walk blameless before him, that ye may walk after the holy order of God, after which ye have been received.

23. And now I would that ye should be humble, and be submissive and gentle; easy to be entreated; full of patience and long-suffering; being temperate in all things; being diligent in keeping the commandments of God at all times; ᵗasking for whatsoever things ye stand in need, both spiritual and temporal; always returning thanks unto God for whatsoever things ye do receive.

24. And see that ye ᵘhave faith, hope, and charity, and then ye will always abound in good works.

25. And may the Lord bless you, and keep your garments spotless, that ye may at last be brought to sit down with Abraham, Isaac, and Jacob, and the holy prophets who have been ever since the world began, having your garments spotless even as their garments are spotless, in the kingdom of heaven to go no more out.

26. And now my beloved brethren, I have spoken these words unto you according to the Spirit which testifieth in me; and my soul doth exceedingly rejoice, because of the exceeding diligence and heed which ye have given unto my word.

27. And now, may the peace of God rest upon you, and upon your houses and lands, and upon your flocks and herds, and all that you possess, your women and your children, according to your faith and good works, from this time forth and forever. And thus I have spoken. Amen.

CHAPTER 8.

Alma's success in Melek—The people of Ammonihah cast him out—Comforted by an angel, he returns—Amulek joins him in the ministry—Great power given.

1. And now it came to pass that Alma returned from the ᵃland of Gideon, after having taught the people of Gideon many things which cannot be written, having established the order of the church, according as he had before done in the ᵇland of Zarahemla, yea, he returned to his own house at Zarahemla to rest himself from the labors which he had performed.

2. And thus ended the ninth year of the reign of the judges over the people of Nephi.

3. And it came to pass in the commencement of the *tenth year of the reign of the judges over the people of Nephi, that Alma departed from thence and took his journey over into the ᶜland of Melek, on the west of the ᵈriver

---

q, 1 Ne. 10:19. Al. 37:12. r, Mos. 2:37. Al. 34:36. He. 4:24. s, see o, 2 Ne 9.
t, see e, 2 Ne. 32. u, Al. 13:29. Eth. 12:31—34. Moro. 7. Chap. 8: a, see m, Al. 2.
b, Om. 13. c, vers. 4, 5, 6. Al. 31:6. 35:13. 45:18. d, see g, Al. 2. * B. C. 82.

Sidon, on the west by the borders of the wilderness.

4. And he began to teach the people in the land of Melek according to ᶜthe holy order of God, by which he had been called; and he began to teach the people throughout all the ᶠland of Melek.

5. And it came to pass that the people came to him throughout all the borders of the land which was by the wilderness side. And they were ᵍbaptized throughout all the land;

6. So that when he had finished his work at ʰMelek he departed thence, and traveled three days' journey on the north of the land of Melek; and he came to a city which was called ⁱAmmonihah.

7. Now it was the custom of the people of Nephi to call their lands, and their cities, and their villages, yea, even all their small villages, after the name of him who first possessed them; and thus it was with the land of ʲAmmonihah.

8. And it came to pass that when Alma had come to the city of Ammonihah he began to preach the word of God unto them.

9. Now Satan had gotten great hold upon the hearts of the people of the city of Ammonihah; therefore they would not hearken unto the words of Alma.

10. Nevertheless Alma labored much in the spirit, wrestling with God in ᵏmighty prayer, that he would pour out his Spirit upon the people who were in the city; that he would also grant that he might ˡbaptize them unto repentance.

11. Nevertheless, they hardened their hearts, saying unto him: Behold, we know that thou art Alma; and we know that thou art ᵐhigh priest over the church which thou hast established in many parts of the land, according to your tradition; and we are not of thy church, and we do not believe in such foolish traditions.

12. And now we know that because we are not of thy church we know that thou hast no power over us; and thou hast delivered up the ⁿjudgment-seat unto Nephihah; therefore thou art not the chief judge over us.

13. Now when the people had said this, and withstood all his words, and reviled him, and spit upon him, and caused that he should be cast out of their city, he departed thence and took his journey towards the city which was called Aaron.

14. And it came to pass that while he was journeying thither, being weighed down with sorrow, wading through much tribulation and anguish of soul, because of the wickedness of the people who were in the ᵒcity of Ammonihah, it came to pass while Alma was thus weighed down with sorrow, behold an angel of the Lord appeared unto him, saying:

15. Blessed art thou, Alma; therefore, lift up thy head and rejoice, for thou hast great cause to rejoice; for thou hast been faithful in keeping the commandments of God from the time which thou receivedst thy first message from him. Behold, I am he that ᵖdelivered it unto you.

16. And behold, I am sent to command thee that thou return to the city of Ammonihah, and preach again unto the people of the city; yea, preach unto them.

c, see *g*, Mos. 26. *f*, see *c*. *g*, see *u*, 2 Ne. 9. *h*, see *c*. *i*, vers. 7—9, 14, 16, 18, 19, Al. 9:1. 14:23. 15:1, 15, 16. 16:2, 3, 9, 11. 25:2. 49:1, 3, 10, 11, 14, 15, He. 5:10. *j*, see *i*. *k*, see *c*, 2 Ne. 32. *l*, see *u*, 2 Ne. 9. *m*, see *g*, Mos. 26. *n*, Al. 4:16, 17. *o*, see *i*. *p*, Mos. 27:11—16.

ABOUT B. C. 82.

Yea, say unto them, except they repent the Lord God will ^qdestroy them.

17. For behold, they do study at this time that they may destroy the liberty of thy people, (for thus saith the Lord) which is contrary to the statutes, and judgments, and commandments which he has given unto his people.

18. Now it came to pass that after Alma had received his message from the angel of the Lord he returned speedily to the land of Ammonihah. And he entered the city by another way, yea, by the way which is on the south of the ^rcity of Ammonihah.

19. And as he entered the city he was an hungered, and he said to a man: Will ye give to an humble servant of God something to eat?

20. And the man said unto him: I am a Nephite, and I know that thou art a holy prophet of God, for thou art the man whom an ^sangel said in a vision: Thou shalt receive. Therefore, go with me into my house and I will impart unto thee of my food; and I know that thou wilt be a ^tblessing unto me and my house.

21. And it came to pass that the man received him into his house; and the man was called Amulek; and he brought forth bread and meat and set before Alma.

22. And it came to pass that Alma ate bread and was filled; and he blessed Amulek and his house, and he gave thanks unto God.

23. And after he had eaten and was filled he said unto Amulek: I am Alma, and am the ^uhigh priest over the church of God throughout the land.

24. And behold, I have been called to preach the word of God among all this people, according to the spirit of revelation and prophecy; and I was in this land and they would not receive me, but they ^vcast me out and I was about to set my back towards this land forever.

25. But behold, I have been commanded that I should turn again and ^wprophesy unto this people, yea, and to testify against them concerning their iniquities.

26. And now, Amulek, because thou hast fed me and taken me in, thou art ^xblessed; for I was an hungered, for I had ^yfasted many days.

27. And Alma tarried many days with Amulek before he began to preach unto the people.

28. And it came to pass that the people did wax more gross in their iniquities.

29. And the word came to Alma, saying: Go; and also say unto my servant Amulek, go forth and prophesy unto this people, saying—Repent ye, for thus saith the Lord, except ye repent I will visit this people in mine anger; yea, and I will ^znot turn my fierce anger away.

30. And Alma went forth, and also Amulek, among the people, to declare the words of God unto them; and they were filled with the Holy Ghost.

31. And they had power given unto them, insomuch that they could not be confined in dungeons; neither was it possible that any man could slay them; nevertheless they did not exercise their power until they were ^{2a}bound in bands and cast into prison. Now, this was done that

---

q, ver. 29. Al. 9:4, 12, 18, 24. 10:19, 23, 27. 16:2, 3. 9—11. *r*, see *i*. *s*, Al. 10:7—9. *t*, vers. 22, 26. Al. 10:7, 11. *u*, see *g*, Mos. 26. *v*, ver. 13. *w*, ver. 16. *x*, see *t*. *y*, see *t*, Mos. 27. *z*, see *q*. 2a, Al. 14:17—29. ABOUT B. C. 82.

the Lord might show forth his power in them.

32. And it came to pass that they went forth and began to preach and to prophesy unto the people, according to the spirit and power which the Lord had given them.

The words of Alma, and also the words of Amulek, which were declared unto the people who were in the land of Ammonihah. And also they are cast into prison, and delivered by the miraculous power of God which was in them, according to the record of Alma.

Comprising chapters 9 to 14 inclusive.

CHAPTER 9.

Alma preaches to the people of Ammonihah and calls them to repentance—His testimony rejected.

1. And again, I, Alma, having been commanded of God that I should ªtake Amulek and go forth and preach again unto this people, or the people who were in the ᵇcity of Ammonihah, it came to pass as I began to preach unto them, they began to contend with me, saying:

2. Who art thou? Suppose ye that we shall believe the testimony of one man, although he should preach unto us that the earth should pass away?

3. Now they understood not the words which they spake; for they knew not that the earth should pass away.

4. And they said also: We will not believe thy words if thou shouldst prophesy that this great city should be destroyed in ᶜone day.

5. Now they knew not that God could do such marvelous works, for they were a hard-hearted and a stiffnecked people.

6. And they said: Who is God, that sendeth no more authority than one man among this people, to declare unto them the truth of such great and marvelous things?

7. And they stood forth to lay their hands on me; but behold, they did not. And I stood with boldness to declare unto them, yea, I did boldly testify unto them, saying:

8. Behold, O ye wicked and perverse generation, how have ye forgotten the tradition of your fathers; yea, how soon ye have forgotten the commandments of God.

9. Do ye not remember that our father, Lehi, was brought out of Jerusalem by the hand of God? Do ye not remember that they were all led by him through the wilderness?

10. And have ye forgotten so soon how many times he delivered our fathers out of the hands of their enemies, and preserved them from being destroyed, even by the hands of their own brethren?

11. Yea, and if it had not been for his matchless power, and his mercy, and his long-suffering towards us, we should unavoidably have been cut off from the face of the earth long before this period of time, and perhaps been consigned to a state of ᵈendless misery and woe.

12. Behold, now I say unto you that he commandeth you to repent; and except ye repent, ye can in nowise inherit the kingdom of God. But behold, this is not all—he has commanded you to repent, or he will ᵉutterly destroy you from off the face of the

---

a, Al. 8:29. *b*, see *i*, Al. 8. *c*, Al. 16:9, 10. *d*, see *m*, Jac. 6. *e*, see *q*, Al. 8.
ABOUT B. C. 82.

earth; yea, he will visit you in his anger, and in his *f*fierce anger he will not turn away.

13. Behold, do ye not remember the words which he spake unto Lehi, saying that: *g*Inasmuch as ye shall keep my commandments, ye shall prosper in the land? And again it is said that: Inasmuch as ye will not keep my commandments ye shall be cut off from the presence of the Lord.

14. Now I would that ye should remember, that inasmuch as the Lamanites have not kept the commandments of God, they have been cut off from the presence of the Lord. Now we see that the word of the Lord has been verified in this thing, and the *h*Lamanites have been cut off from his presence, from the beginning of their transgressions in the land.

15. Nevertheless I say unto you, that it shall be more tolerable for them in the day of judgment than for you, if ye remain in your sins, yea, and even more tolerable for them in this life than for you, except ye repent.

16. For there are many promises which are extended to the Lamanites; for it is because of the *i*traditions of their fathers that caused them to remain in their state of ignorance; therefore the Lord will be merciful unto them and *j*prolong their existence in the land.

17. And at some period of time they will be brought to believe in his word, and to know of the incorrectness of the traditions of their fathers; and many of them will be saved, for the Lord will be merciful unto all who call on his name.

18. But behold, I say unto you that if ye persist in your wickedness that your days shall not be prolonged in the land, for the Lamanites shall be sent upon you; and if ye repent not they shall come in a time when you know not, and ye shall be visited with *k*utter destruction; and it shall be according to the *l*fierce anger of the Lord.

19. For he will not suffer you that ye shall live in your iniquities, to destroy his people. I say unto you, Nay; he would rather suffer that the Lamanites might destroy *m*all his people who are called the people of Nephi, if it were possible that they could fall into sins and transgressions, after having had so much light and so much knowledge given unto them of the Lord their God;

20. Yea, after having been such a highly favored people of the Lord; yea, after having been favored above every other nation, kindred, tongue, or people; after having had all things made known unto them, according to their desires, and their faith, and prayers, of that which has been, and which is, and which is to come;

21. Having been visited by the Spirit of God; having conversed with angels, and having been spoken unto by the voice of the Lord; and having the spirit of prophecy, and the spirit of revelation, and also many gifts, the gift of speaking with tongues, and the gift of preaching, and the gift of the Holy Ghost, and the gift of *n*translation;

22. Yea, and after having been delivered of God out of the land of Jerusalem, by the hand of the Lord; having been saved from

f, Al. 8:29. *g*, 2 Ne. 1:9. 4:4. See *b*, 1 Ne. 2. *h*, see *b*, 1 Ne. 2. *i*, Mos. 10:11—17. *j*, Enos 13. See *c*, 2 Ne. 27. He. 15:10—16. *k*, Al. 16:2, 3, 9—11. *l*, Al. 8:29. 9:12. *m*, 1 Ne. 12:15, 19, 20. 15:5. Al. 45:10—14. He. 13:5—10. 15:17. Morm. 6. *n*, Om. 20—22. Mos. 8:13—19. 28:11—17. ABOUT B. C. 82.

15

famine, and from sickness, and all manner of diseases of every kind; and they having waxed strong in battle, that they might not be destroyed; having been brought °out of bondage time after time, and having been kept and preserved until now; and they have been prospered until they are rich in all manner of things—

23. And now behold I say unto you, that if this people, who have received so many blessings from the hand of the Lord, should transgress contrary to the light and knowledge which they do have, I say unto you that if this be the case, that if they should fall into transgression, it would be far more tolerable for the Lamanites than for them.

24. For behold, the promises of the Lord are ᵖextended to the Lamanites, but they are not unto you if ye transgress; for has not the Lord expressly promised and firmly decreed, that if ye will rebel against him that ye shall ᵠutterly be destroyed from off the face of the earth?

25. And now for this cause, that ye may not be destroyed, the Lord has sent his angel to visit many of his people, declaring unto them that they must go forth and cry mightily unto this people, saying: Repent ye, for the kingdom of heaven is nigh at hand;

26. And not many days hence the Son of God shall come in his glory; and his glory shall be the glory of the Only Begotten of the Father, full of grace, equity, and truth, full of patience, mercy, and long-suffering, quick to hear the cries of his people and to answer their prayers.

27. And behold, he cometh to redeem those who will be ʳbaptized unto repentance, through faith on his name.

28. Therefore, prepare ye the way of the Lord, for the time is at hand that all men shall reap a reward of their works, according to that which they have been—if they have been righteous they shall reap the salvation of their souls, according to the power and deliverance of Jesus Christ; and if they have been evil they shall reap the damnation of their souls, according to the ˢpower and captivation of the devil.

29. Now behold, this is the voice of the angel, crying unto the people.

30. And now, my beloved brethren, for ye are my brethren, and ye ought to be beloved, and ye ought to bring forth works which are meet for repentance, seeing that your hearts have been grossly hardened against the word of God, and seeing that ye are a ᵗlost and a fallen people.

31. Now it came to pass that when I, Alma, had spoken these words, behold, the people were wroth with me because I said unto them that they were a ᵘhardhearted and a stiffnecked people.

32. And also because I said unto them that they were a ᵛlost and a fallen people they were angry with me, and sought to lay their hands upon me, that they might cast me into prison.

33. But it came to pass that the Lord did not suffer them that they should take me at that time and cast me into prison.

34. And it came to pass that Amulek went and stood forth, and began to preach unto them also.

o, Mos. 22:11—13. 24:17—20. *p*, see *j*. *q*, see *m*. *r*, see *u*, 2 Ne. 9. *s*, see *t*, 2 Ne. 9. *t*, ver. 32. Al. 12:22. *u*, ver. 5. 2 Ne. 25:28. Mos. 3:14. *v*, ver. 30.

ABOUT B. C. 82.

And now the words of Amulek are not all written, nevertheless a part of his words are written in this book.

CHAPTER 10.

Amulek's lineage—Lehi a descendant of Joseph through Manasseh—Amulek tells of his conversion—His testimony—He denounces designing lawyers and judges—Zeezrom.

1. Now these are the words which Amulek preached unto the people who were in the ᵃland of Ammonihah, saying:

2. I am Amulek; I am the son of Giddonah, who was the son of Ishmael, who was a descendant of Aminadi; and it was that same Aminadi who interpreted the writing which was upon the wall of the temple, which was written by the finger of God.

3. And Aminadi was a descendant of Nephi, who was the son of Lehi, who came out of the land of Jerusalem, who was a descendant of Manasseh, who was the son of ᶻJoseph who was sold into Egypt by the hands of his brethren.

4. And behold, I am also a man of no small reputation among all those who know me; yea, and behold, I have ᵇmany kindreds and friends, and I have also acquired much riches by the hand of my industry.

5. Nevertheless, after all this, I never have known much of the ways of the Lord, and his mysteries and marvelous power. I said I never had known much of these things; but behold, I mistake, for I have seen much of his mysteries and his marvelous power; yea, even in the preservation of the lives of this people.

6. Nevertheless, I did harden my heart, for I was called many times and I would not hear; therefore I knew concerning these things, yet I would not know; therefore I went on rebelling against God, in the wickedness of my heart, even until the fourth day of this seventh month, which is in the tenth year of the reign of the judges.

7. As I was journeying to see a very near kindred, behold an angel of the Lord ᶜappeared unto me and said: Amulek, return to thine own house, for thou shalt feed a prophet of the Lord; yea, a holy man, who is a chosen man of God; for he has ᵈfasted many days because of the sins of this people, and he is an hungered, and thou shalt receive him into thy house and feed him, and he shall ᵉbless thee and thy house; and the blessing of the Lord shall rest upon thee and thy house.

8. And it came to pass that I obeyed the ᶠvoice of the angel, and returned towards my house. And as I was going thither I found the ᵍman whom the angel said unto me: Thou shalt receive into thy house—and behold it was this same man who has been speaking unto you concerning the things of God.

9. And the angel said unto me he is a ʰholy man; wherefore I know he is a holy man because it was said by an angel of God.

10. And again, I know that the things whereof he hath testified are true; for behold I say unto you, that as the Lord liveth, even so has he sent his angel to make these things manifest unto me; and this he has done while this Alma hath ⁱdwelt at my house.

11. For behold, he hath ʲblessed mine house, he hath blessed me, and my women, and my children, and my father and my kinsfolk;

---

a, see *i*, Al. 8. *z*, 1 Ne. 5:14. *b*, ver. 11. Al. 15:16. *c*, vers. 8, 9. Al. 8:20. *d*, see *t*, Mos. 27. *e*, see *t*, Al. 8. *f*, Al. 8:20. *g*, Al. 8:20. *h*, ver. 7. *i*, Al. 8:27. *j*, see *t*, Al. 8. ABOUT B. C. 82.

yea, even all my kindred hath he blessed, and the blessing of the Lord hath rested upon us according to the words which he spake.

12. And now, when Amulek had spoken these words the people began to be astonished, seeing there was *k*more than one witness who testified of the things whereof they were accused, and also of the things which were to come, according to the spirit of prophecy which was in them.

13. Nevertheless, there were some among them who thought to question them, that by their cunning devices they might catch them in their words, that they might find witness against them, that they might deliver them to their judges that they might be judged according to the law, and that they might be slain or cast into prison, according to the crime which they could make appear or witness against them.

14. Now it was those men who sought to destroy them, who were *l*lawyers, who were hired or appointed by the people to administer the law at their times of trials, or at the trials of the crimes of the people before the judges.

15. Now these lawyers were learned in all the arts and cunning of the people; and this was to enable them that they might be skilful in their profession.

16. And it came to pass that they began to question Amulek, that thereby they might make him cross his words, or contradict the words which he should speak.

17. Now they knew not that Amulek could know of their designs. But it came to pass as they began to question him, he perceived their thoughts, and he said unto them: O ye wicked and perverse generation, ye *m*lawyers and hypocrites, for ye are laying the foundations of the devil; for ye are laying traps and snares to catch the holy ones of God.

18. Ye are laying plans to pervert the ways of the righteous, and to bring down the wrath of God upon your heads, even to the utter destruction of this people.

19. Yea, well did Mosiah say, who was our last king, when he was about to deliver up the kingdom, having no one to confer it upon, causing that this people should be governed by their own voices—yea, well did he say that if the time should come that the *n*voice of this people should choose iniquity, that is, if the time should come that this people should fall into transgression, they would be ripe for destruction.

20. And now I say unto you that well doth the Lord judge of your iniquities; well doth he cry unto this people, by the voice of his angels: Repent ye, repent, for the kingdom of heaven is at hand.

21. Yea, well doth he cry, by the voice of his angels that: I will come down among my people, with equity and justice in my hands.

22. Yea, and I say unto you that if it were not for the prayers of the righteous, who are now in the land, that ye would even now be visited with utter destruction; yet it would not be by flood, as were the people in the days of Noah, but it would be by famine, and by pestilence, and the sword.

23. But it is by the *o*prayers of the righteous that ye are spared; now therefore, if ye will cast out the righteous from among you then will not the Lord stay his hand; but in his *p*fierce anger he

k, Al. 9:6. *l*, vers. 15—18, 24, 27, 29—32. Al. 11:20—37. 14:18, 23—28. *m*, see *l*. *n*, Mos. 29:27. *o*, see *e*, 2 Ne. 32. *p*, see *q*, Al. 8. ABOUT B. C. 82.

will come out against you; then ye shall be smitten by famine, and by pestilence, and by the sword; and the time is soon at hand except ye repent.

24. And now it came to pass that the people were more angry with Amulek, and they cried out, saying: This man doth revile against our laws which are just, and our wise ^qlawyers whom we have selected.

25. But Amulek stretched forth his hand, and cried the mightier unto them, saying: O ye wicked and perverse generation, why hath Satan got such great hold upon your hearts? Why will ye yield yourselves unto him that he may have power over you, to blind your eyes, that ye will not understand the words which are spoken, according to their truth?

26. For behold, have I testified against your law? Ye do not understand; ye say that I have spoken against your law; but I have not, but I have spoken in favor of your law, to your condemnation.

27. And now behold, I say unto you, that the foundation of the ^rdestruction of this people is beginning to be laid by the unrighteousness of your ^slawyers and your judges.

28. And now it came to pass that when Amulek had spoken these words the people cried out against him, saying: Now we know that this man is a child of the devil, for he hath lied unto us; for he hath spoken against our law. And now he says that he has not spoken against it.

29. And again, he has reviled against our lawyers, and our judges.

30. And it came to pass that the lawyers put it into their hearts that they should remember these things against him.

31. And there was one among them whose name was Zeezrom. Now he was the foremost to accuse Amulek and Alma, he being one of the most expert among them, having much business to do among the people.

32. Now the object of these lawyers was to *get gain; and they got gain *according to their employ.

CHAPTER 11.

Judges and their compensation—Nephite coins and measures—Zeezrom confounded by Amulek.

1. Now it was in the law of Mosiah that every man who was a judge of the law, or those who were appointed to be judges, should receive wages ^aaccording to the time which they labored to judge those who were brought before them to be judged.

2. Now if a man owed another, and he would not pay that which he did owe, he was complained of to the judge; and the judge executed authority, and sent forth officers that the man should be brought before him; and he judged the man according to the law and the evidences which were brought against him, and thus the man was compelled to pay that which he owed, or be stripped, or be cast out from among the people as a thief and a robber.

3. And the judge received for his wages according to ^bhis time —a ^csenine of gold for a day, or a ^dsenum of silver, which is equal to a senine of gold; and this is according to the law which was given.

4. Now these are the names of the different pieces of their gold, and of their silver, according to their value. And the names are given by the Nephites, for they did not reckon after the manner of the Jews who were at Jerusalem; neither did they measure after the manner of the Jews; but they altered their reckoning and their measure, according to the minds and the circumstances of the people, in every generation, until the reign of the judges, they having been established by ᵉking Mosiah.

5. Now the reckoning is thus—a ᶠsenine of gold, a seon of gold, a shum of gold, and a limnah of gold.

6. A ᵍsenum of silver, an amnor of silver, an ezrom of silver, and an onti of silver.

7. A senum of silver was ʰequal to a senine of gold, and either for a measure of barley, and also for a measure of every kind of grain.

8. Now the amount of a seon of gold was twice the value of a senine.

9. And a shum of gold was twice the value of a seon.

10. And a limnah of gold was the value of them all.

11. And an amnor of silver was as great as two senums.

12. And an ezrom of silver was as great as four senums.

13. And an ⁱonti was as great as them all.

14. Now this is the value of the lesser numbers of their reckoning—

15. A shiblon is half of a senum; therefore, a shiblon for half a measure of barley.

16. And a shiblum is a half of a shiblon.

17. And a leah is the half of a shiblum.

18. Now this is their number, according to their reckoning.

19. Now an antion of gold is equal to three shiblons.

20. Now, it was for the sole purpose to get gain, because they received their wages ʲaccording to their employ, therefore, they did stir up the people to riotings, and all manner of disturbances and wickedness, that they might have more employ, that they might get money according to the suits which were brought before them; therefore they did stir up the people against Alma and Amulek.

21. And this Zeezrom began to question Amulek, saying: Will ye answer me a few questions which I shall ask you? Now Zeezrom was a man who was expert in the devices of the devil, that he might destroy that which was good; therefore, he said unto Amulek: Will ye answer the questions which I shall put unto you?

22. And Amulek said unto him: Yea, if it be according to the Spirit of the Lord, which is in me; for I shall say nothing which is contrary to the Spirit of the Lord. And Zeezrom said unto him: Behold, here are six ᵏonties of silver, and all these will I give thee if thou wilt deny the existence of a Supreme Being.

23. Now Amulek said: O thou child of hell, why tempt ye me? Knowest thou that the righteous yieldeth to no such temptations?

24. Believest thou that there is no God? I say unto you, Nay, thou knowest that there is a God, but thou lovest that lucre more than him.

25. And now thou hast lied be-

---

e, Mos. 29. *f*, see *c*. *g*, see *d*. *h*, ver. 3. *i*, vers. 6, 22, 25. *j*, vers. 1, 3. Al. 10:32. *k*, see *i*.

ABOUT B. C. 82.

fore God unto me. Thou saidst unto me—Behold these ′sixonties, which are of great worth, I will give unto thee—when thou hadst it in thy heart to retain them from me; and it was only thy desire that I should deny the true and living God, that thou mightest have cause to destroy me. And now behold, for this great evil thou shalt have thy reward.

26. And Zeezrom said unto him: Thou sayest there is a true and living God?

27. And Amulek said: Yea, there is a true and living God.

28. Now Zeezrom said: Is there more than one God?

29. And he answered, No.

30. Now Zeezrom said unto him again: How knowest thou these things?

31. And he said: An ᵐangel hath made them known unto me.

32. And Zeezrom said again: Who is he that shall come? Is it the Son of God?

33. And he said unto him, Yea.

34. And Zeezrom said again: Shall he save his people ⁿin their sins? And Amulek answered and said unto him: I say unto you he shall not, for it is impossible for him to deny his word.

35. Now Zeezrom said unto the people: See that ye remember these things; for he said there is but one God; yet he saith that the Son of God shall come, but he shall not save his people—as though he had ᵒauthority to command God.

36. Now Amulek saith again unto him: Behold thou hast lied, for thou sayest that I spake as though I had authority to command God because I said he shall not save his people in their sins.

37. And I say unto you again that he cannot save them in their sins; for I cannot deny his word, and he hath said that no unclean thing can inherit the kingdom of heaven; therefore, how can ye be saved, except ye inherit the kingdom of heaven? Therefore, ye cannot be saved in your sins.

38. Now Zeezrom saith again unto him: Is the Son of God the ᵖvery Eternal Father?

39. And Amulek said unto him: Yea, he is the very ᶻEternal Father of heaven and of earth, and all things which in them are; he is the beginning and the end, the first and the last;

40. And he shall come into the world to redeem his people; and he shall take upon him the ᵠtransgressions of those who believe on his name; and these are they that shall have eternal life, and salvation cometh to none else.

41. Therefore the wicked remain as though there had been ʸno redemption made, ʳexcept it be the loosing of the bands of death; for behold, the day cometh that all shall rise from the dead and stand before God, and be judged according to their works.

42. Now, there is a death which is called a temporal death; and the death of Christ shall ˢloose the bands of this temporal death, that all shall be raised from this temporal death.

43. The spirit and the body shall be reunited again in its perfect form; ᵗboth limb and joint shall be restored to its proper frame, even as we now are at this time; and we shall be brought to stand before God, knowing even as we know now, and have a ᵘbright recollection of all our guilt.

l, see *i*. *m*, Al. 10:10. *n*, vers. 36, 37. He. 5:10, 11. *o*, ver. 36. *p*, ver. 39. See *a*, Mos. 3. *z*, Mos. 15:4. *q*, Mos. 14:5, 8. *y*, Al. 12:18. *r*, see *g* and *j*, 2 Ne. 9. *s*, see *g* and *j*, 2 Ne. 9. *t*, see *d*, 2 Ne. 2. *u*, see *n*, 2 Ne. 9. ABOUT B. C. 82.

44. Now, this ʷrestoration shall come to all, both old and young, both bond and free, both male and female, both the wicked and the righteous; and even there shall not so much as a hair of their heads be lost; but every thing shall be restored to its perfect frame, as it is now, or in the body, and shall be brought and be arraigned before the bar of Christ the Son, and God the Father, and the Holy Spirit, which is one ʷEternal God, to be judged according to their works, whether they be good or whether they be evil.

45. Now, behold, I have spoken unto you concerning the death of the mortal body, and also concerning the resurrection of the mortal body. I say unto you that this mortal body is ˣraised to an immortal body, that is from death, even from the first death unto life, that they can ʸdie no more; their spirits uniting with their bodies, never to be divided; thus the whole becoming spiritual and immortal, that they can no more see corruption.

46. Now, when Amulek had finished these words the people began again to be astonished, and also Zeezrom began to tremble. And thus ended the words of Amulek, or this is all that I have written.

CHAPTER 12.

Amulek's testimony confirmed by Alma—Doctrine of the tree of life—The plan of redemption expounded.

1. Now Alma, seeing that the words of Amulek had silenced Zeezrom, for he beheld that Amulek had caught him in his ᵃlying and deceiving to destroy him, and seeing that he began to ᵇtremble under a consciousness of his guilt, he opened his mouth and began to speak unto him, and to establish the words of Amulek, and to explain things beyond, or to unfold the scriptures beyond that which Amulek had done.

2. Now the words that Alma spake unto Zeezrom were heard by the people round about; for the multitude was great, and he spake on this wise:

3. Now Zeezrom, seeing that thou hast been taken in thy lying and craftiness, for thou hast not lied unto men only but thou hast lied unto God; for behold, he knows ᶜall thy thoughts, and thou seest that thy thoughts are made known unto us by his Spirit;

4. And thou seest that we know that thy plan was a ᵈvery subtle plan, as to the subtlety of the devil, for to lie and to deceive this people that thou mightest set them against us, to revile us and to cast us out—

5. Now this was a plan of thine adversary, and he hath exercised his power in thee. Now I would that ye should remember that what I say unto thee I say unto all.

6. And behold I say unto you all that this was a snare of the adversary, which he has laid to catch this people, that he might bring you into subjection unto him, that he might encircle you about with his ᵉchains, that he might chain you down to ᶠeverlasting destruction, according to the power of his captivity.

7. Now when Alma had spoken these words, Zeezrom began to tremble more exceedingly, for he was convinced more and more of the power of God; and he was also convinced that Alma and

v, see *d*, 2 Ne. 2. *w*, see *k*, 2 Ne. 31. *x*, see *d*, 2 Ne. 2. *y*, Al. 12:18, 20. CHAP. 12: *a*, Al. 11:20—38. *b*, Al. 11:46. *c*, see *r*, 2 Ne. 9. *d*, Al. 11:20—38. *e*, see *p*, 2 Ne. 28. *f*, see *m*, Jac. 6. ABOUT B. C. 82.

Amulek had a knowledge of him, for he was convinced that they °knew the thoughts and intents of his heart; for power was given unto them that they might know of these things according to the spirit of prophecy.

8. And Zeezrom began to inquire of them diligently, that he might know more concerning the kingdom of God. And he said unto Alma: What does this mean which Amulek hath spoken concerning the ʰresurrection of the dead, that all shall rise from the dead, both the just and the unjust, and are brought to stand before God to be judged according to their works?

9. And now Alma began to expound these things unto him, saying: It is given unto many to know the ᶻmysteries of God; nevertheless they are laid under a strict command that they shall not impart ⁱonly according to the portion of his word which he doth grant unto the children of men, according to the heed and diligence which they give unto him.

10. And therefore, he that will harden his heart, the same receiveth the ʲlesser portion of the word; and he that will not harden his heart, to him is given the greater ᵏportion of the word, until it is given unto him to know the mysteries of God until he know them in full.

11. And they that will harden their hearts, to them is given the lesser portion of the word until they know nothing concerning his mysteries; and then they are taken ˡcaptive by the devil, and led by his will down to destruction. Now this is what is meant by the ᵐchains of hell.

12. And Amulek hath spoken plainly ⁿconcerning death, and being °raised from this mortality to a state of immortality, and being brought before the bar of God, to be judged according to our works.

13. Then if our hearts have been hardened, yea, if we have hardened our hearts against the word, insomuch that it has not been found in us, then will our state be awful, for then we shall be condemned.

14. For our words will condemn us, yea, all our works will condemn us; we shall not be found spotless; and our thoughts will also condemn us; and in this awful state we shall not dare to look up to our God; and we would fain be glad if we could command the rocks and the mountains to fall upon us to hide us from his presence.

15. But this cannot be; we must come forth and stand before him in his glory, and in his power, and in his might, majesty, and dominion, and acknowledge to our everlasting shame that all his judgments are just; that he is just in all his works, and that he is merciful unto the children of men, and that he has all power to save every man that believeth on his name and bringeth forth fruit meet for repentance.

16. And now behold, I say unto you then cometh a death, even a second death, which is a ᵖspiritual death; then is a time that whosoever dieth in his sins, as to a temporal death, shall also die a spiritual death; yea, he shall ᵠdie as to things pertaining unto righteousness.

17. Then is the time when their

---

g, ver. 3. *h*, see *d*, 2 Ne. 2. *z*, vers. 10, 11. Al. 26:22. *i*, 3 Ne. 26:6—11. Eth. 4:1—7. *j*, see *i*. *k*, see *i*. *l*, see *i*, 2 Ne. 9. *m*, see *p*, 2 Ne. 28. *n*, Al. 11:41—45. *o*, see *d*, 2 Ne. 2. *p*, ver. 32. Al. 13:30. See *o*, 2 Ne. 9. Also see *k*, 1 Ne. 15. Jac. 3:11. *q*, ver. 32. 1 Ne. 15:33. Al. 40:26. He. 14:18. ABOUT B. C. 82.

torments shall be as a ʳlake of fire and brimstone, whose flame ascendeth up forever and ever; and then is the time that they shall be ˢchained down to an everlasting destruction, according to the power and captivity of Satan, he having subjected them according to his will.

18. Then, I say unto you, they shall be as though there had been no redemption made; for they cannot be redeemed according to God's justice; and they ᵗcannot die, seeing there is no more corruption.

19. Now it came to pass that when Alma had made an end of speaking these words, the people began to be more astonished;

20. But there was one Antionah, who was a chief ruler among them, came forth and said unto him: What is this that thou hast said, ᵘthat man should rise from the dead and be changed from this mortal to an immortal state, that the soul can never die?

21. What does the scripture mean, which saith that ᵛGod placed cherubim and a flaming sword on the east of the garden of Eden, lest our first parents should enter and partake of the fruit of the tree of life, and live forever? And thus we see that there was no possible chance that they should live forever.

22. Now Alma said unto him: This is the thing which I was about to explain. Now we see that Adam did fall by the partaking of the forbidden fruit, according to the word of God; and thus we see, that by his fall, all mankind became a ʷlost and fallen people.

23. And now behold, I say unto you that if it had been possible for Adam to have ˣpartaken of the fruit of the tree of life at that time, there would have been no death, and the word would have been void, making God a liar, for he said: ʸIf thou eat thou shalt surely die.

24. And we see that death comes upon mankind, yea, the death which has been ᶻspoken of by Amulek, which is the temporal death; nevertheless there was a space granted unto man in which he might repent; therefore this life became a ²ᵃprobationary state; a time to prepare to meet God; a time to prepare for that endless state which has been spoken of by us, which is after the ²ᵇresurrection of the dead.

25. Now, if it had not been for the plan of redemption, which was laid from the foundation of the world, there could have been no resurrection of the dead; but there was a plan of redemption laid, which shall bring to pass the ²ᶜresurrection of the dead, of which has been spoken.

26. And now behold, if it were possible that our first parents could have gone forth and ²ᵈpartaken of the tree of life they would have been forever miserable, having no preparatory state; and thus the plan of redemption would have been frustrated, and the word of God would have been void, taking none effect.

27. But behold, it was not so; but it was appointed unto men that they must die; and after death, they must come to judgment, even that same judgment of which we have spoken, which is the end.

28. And after God had ap-

---

r, see l, Jac. 6. s, see p, 2 Ne. 28. t, ver. 20. Al. 11:45. u, vers. 12—18.
v, Gen. 3:24. w, Al. 9:30, 32. See e and g, 2 Ne. 9. x, ver. 26. Al. 42:2—9.
y, Gen. 2:17. z, Al. 11:41—45. 2a, Al. 34:32—35. 42:4, 13. 2b, see d, 2 Ne. 2.
2c, see d, 2 Ne. 2. 2d, ver. 23. Al. 42:2—9.   ABOUT B. C. 82.

ALMA, 13.

pointed that these things should come unto man, behold, then he saw that it was expedient that man should know concerning the things whereof he had appointed unto them;

29. Therefore he sent angels [2e]to converse with them, who caused men to behold of his glory.

30. And they began from that time forth to call on his name; therefore God [2f]conversed with men, and made known unto them the plan of redemption, which had been prepared [2g]from the foundation of the world; and this he made known unto them according to their faith and repentance and their holy works.

31. Wherefore, he gave commandments unto men, they having first transgressed the [2h]first commandments as to things which were temporal, and becoming as Gods, knowing good from evil, placing themselves in a state to act, or being placed in a state to act [2i]according to their wills and pleasures, whether to do evil or to do good—

32. Therefore God gave unto them commandments, after having made [2j]known unto them the plan of redemption, that they should not do evil, the penalty thereof being a [2k]second death, which was an everlasting death as to [2l]things pertaining unto righteousness; for on such the plan of redemption could have no power, for the works of [2m]justice could not be destroyed, according to the supreme goodness of God.

33. But God did call on men, in the name of his Son, (this being the plan of redemption which was laid) saying: [2n]If ye will repent, and harden not your hearts, then will I have mercy upon you, through mine Only Begotten Son;

34. Therefore, whosoever repenteth, and hardeneth not his heart, he shall have claim on mercy through mine Only Begotten Son, unto a remission of his sins; and these shall enter into my rest.

35. And whosoever will [2o]harden his heart and will do iniquity, behold, I swear in my wrath that he shall not enter into my rest.

36. And now, my brethren, behold I say unto you, that if ye will harden your hearts ye shall not enter into the rest of the Lord; therefore your iniquity provoketh him that he sendeth down his wrath upon you as in the [2p]first provocation, yea, according to his word in the [2q]last provocation as well as the first, to the [2r]everlasting destruction of your souls; therefore, according to his word, unto the [2s]last death, as well as the [2t]first.

37. And now, my brethren, seeing we know these things, and they are true, let us repent, and harden not our hearts, that we provoke not the Lord our God to pull down his wrath upon us in these his [2u]second commandments which he has given unto us; but let us enter into the [2v]rest of God, which is prepared according to his word.

CHAPTER 13.

Alma's discourse continued—The holy order of the Son of God—High Priests—Why ordained—Melchizedek and Abraham.

1. And again, my brethren, I

2e, P. of G. P., Moses 5:6. 2f, P. of G. P., Moses 5:4, 5. 2g, see d, Mos. 4.
2h, 2 Ne. 2:18, 19. Gen. 2:16, 17. 2i, 2 Ne. 2:16. 2j, P. of G. P., Moses 5:4—9.
2k, vers. 16, 36. Jac. 3:11. Al. 13:30. See o, 2 Ne. 9. See k, 1 Ne. 15. 2l, see q.
2m, Mos. 15:27. Al. 34:15, 16. 42:13—25. 2n, P. of G. P., Moses 5:8. 2o, P. of
G. P., Moses 5:15. 2p, ver. 31. 2q, ver. 35. 2r, see 2k. 2s, see 2k. 2t, ver. 23.
2u, P. of G. P., Moses chaps. 4—7. 2v, vers. 34, 35. Al. 13:6, 12, 13, 16, 29. 16:17.
ABOUT B. C. 82.

would cite your minds forward to the time when the Lord God gave these commandments unto his children; and I would that ye should remember that the Lord God ordained *a*priests, after his holy order, which was after the order of his Son, to teach these things unto the people.

2. And those priests were ordained after the *b*order of his Son, in a manner that thereby the people might know in what manner to look forward to his Son for redemption.

3. And this is the manner after which they were ordained—being called and prepared *c*from the foundation of the world according to the *d*foreknowledge of God, on account of their exceeding faith and good works; in the first place being left to *e*choose good or evil; therefore they having chosen good, and exercising exceeding great faith, are called with a holy calling, yea, with that holy calling which was prepared with, and according to, a preparatory redemption for such.

4. And thus they have been called to this *f*holy calling on account of their faith, while others would reject the Spirit of God on account of the hardness of their hearts and blindness of their minds, while, if it had not been for this they might have had as great privilege as their brethren.

5. Or in fine, in the first place they were on the same standing with their brethren; thus this holy calling being prepared *g*from the foundation of the world for such as would not harden their hearts, being in and through the *h*atonement of the Only Begotten Son, who was prepared—

6. And thus being called by this holy calling, and ordained unto the *i*high priesthood of the holy order of God, to teach his commandments unto the children of men, that they also might enter into his *j*rest—

7. This *k*high priesthood being after the order of his Son, which order was *l*from the foundation of the world; or in other words, being *m*without beginning of days or end of years, being prepared *n*from eternity to all eternity, according to his *o*foreknowledge of all things—

8. Now they were ordained after this manner—being called with a holy calling, and ordained with a holy ordinance, and taking upon them the *p*high priesthood of the holy order, which calling, and ordinance, and high priesthood, is without *q*beginning or end—

9. Thus they become *r*high priests forever, after the order of the Son, the Only Begotten of the Father, who is *s*without beginning of days or end of years, who is full of grace, equity, and truth. And thus it is. Amen.

10. Now, as I said concerning the holy order of this *t*high priesthood, there were many who were ordained and became *u*high priests of God; and it was on account of their exceeding faith and repentance, and their righteousness before God, they choosing to repent and work righteousness rather than to perish;

11. Therefore they were called after this holy order, and were sanctified, and their garments

---

a, P. of G. P., Moses 6:7. 8:19. D. & C. 84:6—28, 107. *b*, see *a*. *c*, see *d*, Mos. 4. *d*, ver. 7. *e*, 2 Ne. 2:16. Al. 12:31. *f*, see *a*. *g*, see *d*, Mos. 4. *h*, see *f*, 2 Ne. 2. *i*, see *g*, Mos. 26. *j*, see 2*v*, Al. 12. *k*, see *g*, Mos. 26. *l*, see *d*, Mos. 4. *m*, P. of G. P., Abraham 3:2—4. *n*, see *a*, Mos. 3. *o*, ver. 3. See *r*, 2 Ne. 9. *p*, see *g*, Mos. 26. *q*, see *a*, Mos. 3. *r*, see *g*, Mos. 26. *s*, see *a*, Mos. 3. *t*, see *g*, Mos. 26. *u*, D. & C. 107:40—55. 84:6—22.

ABOUT B. C. 82.

were washed white through the ᵛblood of the Lamb.

12. Now they, after being sanctified by the Holy Ghost, having their garments made white, being pure and spotless before God, could not look upon sin save it were with abhorrence; and there were many, exceeding great many, who were made pure and entered into the ʷrest of the Lord their God.

13. And now, my brethren, I would that ye should humble yourselves before God, and bring forth fruit meet for repentance, that ye may also enter into that rest.

14. Yea, humble yourselves even as the people in the days of ˣMelchizedek, who was also a high priest after this same order which I have spoken, who also took upon him the high priesthood ʸforever.

15. And it was this same Melchizedek to whom Abraham paid tithes; yea, even our father Abraham paid tithes of ᶻone-tenth part of all he possessed.

16. Now these ordinances were given after this manner, that thereby the people might look forward on the Son of God, it being a type of his order, or it being his order, and this that they might look forward to him for a remission of their sins, that they might enter into the ²ᵃrest of the Lord.

17. Now this Melchizedek was a king over the land of Salem; and his people had waxed strong in iniquity and abomination; yea, they had all gone astray; they were full of all manner of wickedness;

18. But Melchizedek having exercised mighty faith, and received the office of the ²ᵇhigh priesthood according to the holy order of God, did preach repentance unto his people. And behold, they did repent; and Melchizedek did establish peace in the land in his days; therefore he was called the prince of peace, for he was the king of Salem; and he did reign under his father.

19. Now, there were ²ᶜmany before him, and also there were ²ᵈmany afterwards, but none were greater; therefore, of him they have more particularly made mention.

20. Now I need not rehearse the matter; what I have said may suffice. Behold, the ²ᵉscriptures are before you; if ye will wrest them it shall be to your own destruction.

21. And now it came to pass that when Alma had said these words unto them, he stretched forth his hand unto them and cried with a mighty voice, saying: Now is the time to repent, for the day of salvation draweth nigh;

22. Yea, and the voice of the Lord, by the ²ᶠmouth of angels, doth declare it unto all nations; yea, doth declare it, that they may have glad tidings of great joy; yea, and he doth sound these glad tidings among all his people, yea, even to them that are scattered abroad upon the face of the earth; wherefore they have come unto us.

23. And they are made known unto us in plain terms, that we may understand, that we ²ᵍcannot err; and this because of our being wanderers in a strange land; therefore, we are thus highly favored, for we have these glad tidings declared unto us in all parts of our vineyard.

---

v, see f, 2 No. 2. w, see 2v, Al. 12. x, vers. 15—18. y, vers. 7—9. See m. z, Gen. 14:20. 2a, see 2v, Al. 12. 2b, see g, Mos. 26. 2c, D. & C. 107:40—55. 2d, D. & C. 84:6—22. 2e, Al. 14:1, 8, 14. 2f, ver. 24. Mos. 3:2—27. Al. 8:14—17, 20. 10:7—10, 20. 11:31. 2g, see b, 2 Ne. 25. ABOUT B. C. 82.

24. For behold, angels are declaring it unto many at this time in our land; and this is for the purpose of preparing the hearts of the children of men to receive his word at the time of his coming in his glory.

25. And now we only wait to hear the joyful news declared unto us by the mouth of angels, of his coming; for the time cometh, we know not how soon. Would to God that it might be in my day; but let it be sooner or later, in it I will rejoice.

26. And it shall be made known unto just and holy men, by the ^{2h}mouth of angels, at the time of his coming, that the words of our fathers may be fulfilled, according to that which they have spoken concerning him, which was according to the spirit of prophecy which was in them.

27. And now, my brethren, I wish from the inmost part of my heart, yea, with great anxiety even unto pain, that ye would hearken unto my words, and cast off your sins, and not procrastinate the day of your repentance;

28. But that ye would humble yourselves before the Lord, and call on his holy name, and watch and ^{2i}pray continually, that ye may not be tempted above that which ye can bear, and thus be led by the Holy Spirit, becoming humble, meek, submissive, patient, full of love and all long-suffering;

29. ^{2j}Having faith on the Lord; having a hope that ye shall receive eternal life; having the love of God always in your hearts, that ye may be ^{2k}lifted up at the last day and enter into ^{2l}his rest.

30. And may the Lord grant unto you repentance, that ye may not bring down his wrath upon you, that ye may not be bound down by the ^{2m}chains of hell, that ye may not suffer the ^{2n}second death.

31. And Alma spake many more words unto the people, which are not written in this book.

CHAPTER 14.

Alma and Amulek imprisoned—Their adherents persecuted—Deaths by fire—Zeezrom, now repentant, pleads their cause and is cast out—The prophets delivered and their enemies slain.

1. And it came to pass after he had made an end of speaking unto the people many of them did believe on his words, and began to repent, and to search the ^{a}scriptures.

2. But the more part of them were desirous that they might destroy Alma and Amulek; for they were angry with Alma, because of the ^{b}plainness of his words unto Zeezrom; and they also said that ^{c}Amulek had lied unto them, and had reviled against their law and also against their lawyers and judges.

3. And they were also angry with Alma and Amulek; and because they had testified so plainly against their wickedness, they sought to put them away privily.

4. But it came to pass that they did not; but they took them and bound them with strong cords, and took them before the chief judge of the land.

5. And the people went forth and witnessed against them—^{d}testifying that they had reviled against the law, and their lawyers and judges of the land, and

2h, He. 13:7. 14:26, 28. 3 Ne. 7:18. 2i, see e, 2 Ne. 32. 2j, see u, Al. 7. 2k, see p, Mos. 23. 2l, see 2v, Al. 12. 2m, see p, 2 Ne. 28. 2n, see p, Al. 12.
CHAP. 14: a, vers. 8, 14. Al. 13:20. b, Al. 12:3—7. c, Al. 10:24—32. d, ver. 2.
ABOUT B. C. 82.

also of all the people that were in the land; and also testified that there was but one God, and that he should send his Son among the people, but he should ᵉnot save them; and many such things did the people testify against Alma and Amulek. Now this was done before the chief judge of the land.

6. And it came to pass that Zeezrom was astonished at the words which had been spoken; and he also knew concerning the blindness of the minds, which he had caused among the people by his ᶠlying words; and his soul began to be harrowed up under a consciousness of his own guilt; yea, he began to be encircled about by the pains of hell.

7. And it came to pass that he began to cry unto the people, saying: Behold, I am guilty, and these men are spotless before God. And he began to plead for them from that time forth; but they reviled him, saying: Art thou also possessed with the devil? And they spit upon him, and cast him out from among them, and also all those who believed in the words which had been spoken by Alma and Amulek; and they ᵍcast them out, and sent men to cast stones at them.

8. And they brought their wives and children together, and whosoever believed or had been taught to believe in the word of God they caused that they should be ʰcast into the fire; and they also brought forth their records which contained the ⁱholy scriptures, and cast them into the fire also, that they might be burned and destroyed by fire.

9. And it came to pass that they took Alma and Amulek, and carried them forth to the place of martyrdom, that they might witness the destruction of those who ʲwere consumed by fire.

10. And when Amulek saw the pains of the women and children who were consuming in the fire, he also was pained; and he said unto Alma: How can we witness this awful scene? Therefore let us stretch forth our hands, and exercise the ᵏpower of God which is in us, and save them from the flames.

11. But Alma said unto him: The Spirit constraineth me that I must not stretch forth mine hand; for behold the Lord receiveth them up unto himself, in glory; and he doth suffer that they may do this thing, or that the people may do this thing unto them, according to the hardness of their hearts, that the ˡjudgments which he shall exercise upon them in his wrath may be just; and the blood of the innocent shall stand as a witness against them, yea, and cry mightily against them at the last day.

12. Now Amulek said unto Alma: Behold, perhaps they will burn us also.

13. And Alma said: Be it according to the will of the Lord. But, behold, our work is not finished; therefore they burn us not.

14. Now it came to pass that when the bodies of those who had been cast into the fire ᵐwere consumed, and also the ⁿrecords which were cast in with them, the chief judge of the land came and stood before Alma and Amulek, as they were bound; and he smote them with his hand ᵒupon their cheeks, and said unto them:

---

e, Al. 11:33—37. *f*, Al. 10:31. 11:21—38. *g*, Al. 15:1. *h*, vers. 9—15. Al. 15:2. *i*, vers. 1, 14. Al. 13:20. *j*, see *h*. *k*, vers. 26—29. Al. 8:30, 31. *l*, vers. 26—29. Al. 16:2, 3, 9—11. *m*, see *h*. *n*, see *i*. *o*, vers. 15, 17, 20, 24, 25.

ABOUT B. C. 82.

ALMA, 14.

After what ye have seen, will ye preach again unto this people, that they shall be cast into a ᵖlake of fire and brimstone?

15. Behold, ye see that ye had not power to save those who had been cast into the fire; neither has God saved them because they were of thy faith. And the judge smote them again ᵍupon their cheeks, and asked: What say ye for yourselves?

16. Now this judge was after the order and faith of ʳNehor, who ˢslew Gideon.

17. And it came to pass that Alma and Amulek answered him nothing; and he ᵗsmote them again, and delivered them to the officers to be cast into prison.

18. And when they had been cast into prison three days, there came many lawyers, and judges, and priests, and teachers, who were of the profession of ᵘNehor; and they came in unto the prison to see them, and they questioned them about many words; but they answered them nothing.

19. And it came to pass that the judge stood before them, and said: Why do ye not answer the words of this people? Know ye not that I have power to deliver you up unto the flames? And he commanded them to speak; but they answered nothing.

20. And it came to pass that they departed and went their ways, but came again on the morrow; and the judge also smote them again on their cheeks. And many came forth also, and ᵛsmote them, saying: Will ye stand again and judge this people, and condemn ʷour law? If ye have such great power why do ye not ˣdeliver yourselves?

21. And many such things did they say unto them, gnashing their teeth upon them, and spitting upon them, and saying: How shall we look when we are damned?

22. And many such things, yea, all manner of such things did they say unto them; and thus they did mock them for many days. And they did withhold food from them that they might hunger, and water that they might thirst; and they also did take from them their clothes that they were naked; and thus they were bound with ʸstrong cords, and confined in prison.

23. And it came to pass after they had thus suffered for many days, (and it was on the twelfth day, in the tenth month, *in the tenth year of the reign of the judges over the people of Nephi) that the chief judge over the land of Ammonihah and many of their teachers and their lawyers went in unto the prison where Alma and Amulek were bound with cords.

24. And the chief judge stood before them, and smote them again, and said unto them: If ye have the power of God ᶻdeliver yourselves from these bands, and then we will believe that the Lord will destroy this people according to your words.

25. And it came to pass that they all went forth and smote them, saying the same words, even until the last; and when the last had spoken unto them the ²ᵃpower of God was upon Alma and Amulek, and they rose and stood upon their feet.

26. And Alma cried, saying: How long shall we suffer these great afflictions, O Lord? O Lord,

---

p, Al. 12:17. *q*, see *o*. *r*, Al. 1:15. *s*, Al. 1:7—14. 2:20. *t*, see *o*. *u*, Al. 1:15. *v*, see *o*. *w*, vers. 2, 5. *x*, ver. 24. *y*, vers. 4, 23, 26. Al. 8:31. *z*, ver. 20. 2*a*, Al. 8:30, 31.

B. C. 81.

ALMA, 15.

give us strength according to our faith which is in Christ, even unto deliverance. And they broke the ²ᵇcords with which they were bound; and when the people saw this, they began to flee, for the ²ᶜfear of destruction had come upon them.

27. And it came to pass that so great was their fear that they fell to the earth, and did not obtain the outer door of the prison; and the earth shook mightily, and the walls of the prison were rent in twain, so that they fell to the earth; and ²ᵈthe chief judge, and the lawyers, and priests, and teachers, who smote upon Alma and Amulek, were slain by the fall thereof.

28. And Alma and Amulek came forth out of the prison, and they were not hurt; for the Lord had granted unto them power, according to their faith which was in Christ. And they straightway came forth out of the prison; and they were ²ᵉloosed from their bands; and the prison had ²ᶠfallen to the earth, and ²ᵍevery soul within the walls thereof, save it were Alma and Amulek, was slain; and they straightway came forth into the city.

29. Now the people having heard a great noise came running together by multitudes to know the cause of it; and when they saw Alma and Amulek coming forth out of the prison, and the walls thereof ²ʰhad fallen to the earth, they were struck with great fear, and fled from the presence of Alma and Amulek even as a goat fleeth with her young from two lions; and thus they did flee from the presence of Alma and Amulek.

CHAPTER 15.

Zeezrom, miraculously healed, joins the church and preaches—Many baptized—Alma and Amulek return to Zarahemla.

1. And it came to pass that Alma and Amulek were commanded to depart out of that city; and they departed, and came out even into the land of ᵃSidom; and behold, there they found all the people who had departed out of the land of Ammonihah, who had been ᵇcast out and stoned, because they believed in the words of Alma.

2. And they related unto them all that had happened unto ᶜtheir wives and children, and also concerning themselves, and of their ᵈpower of deliverance.

3. And also Zeezrom lay sick at Sidom, with a burning fever, which was caused by the great tribulations of his mind on account of ᵉhis wickedness, for he supposed that Alma and Amulek were no more; and he supposed that they had been slain because of his iniquity. And this great sin, and his many other sins, did harrow up his mind until it did become exceeding sore, having no deliverance; therefore he began to be scorched with a burning heat.

4. Now, when he heard that Alma and Amulek were in the ᶠland of Sidom, his heart began to take courage; and he sent a message immediately unto them, desiring them to come unto him.

5. And it came to pass that they went immediately, obeying the message which he had sent unto them; and they went in unto the house unto Zeezrom; and they found him upon his bed, sick,

---
2b, see y. 2c, ver. 27. 2d, ver. 23. 2e, ver. 26. 2f, ver. 27. 2g, ver. 27. 2h, vers. 27, 28. Chap. 15: a, vers. 3, 4, 11, 13, 14, 17. b, Al. 14:7. c, Al. 14:8—14. d, Al. 14:26—29. e, Al. 10:31. 11:21—38. 14:6, 7. f, see a. About B. C. 81.

being ᵒvery low with a burning fever; and his mind also was ʰexceeding sore because of his iniquities; and when he saw them he stretched forth his hand, and besought them that they would heal him.

6. And it came to pass that Alma said unto him, taking him by the hand: Believest thou in the power of Christ unto salvation?

7. And he answered and said: Yea, I believe all the words that thou hast taught.

8. And Alma said: If thou believest in the redemption of Christ thou canst be healed.

9. And he said: Yea, I believe according to thy words.

10. And then Alma cried unto the Lord, saying: O Lord our God, have mercy on this man, and heal him according to his faith which is in Christ.

11. And when Alma had said these words, Zeezrom leaped upon his feet, and began to walk; and this was done to the great astonishment of all the people; and the knowledge of this went forth throughout all the ⁱland of Sidom.

12. And Alma ʲbaptized Zeezrom unto the Lord; and he began from that time forth to preach unto the people.

13. And Alma established a church in the ᵏland of Sidom, and consecrated ˡpriests and teachers in the land, to baptize unto the Lord whosoever were desirous to be baptized.

14. And it came to pass that they were many; for they did flock in from all the region round about Sidom, and were ᵐbaptized.

15. But as to the people that were in the ⁿland of Ammonihah, they yet remained a hard-hearted and a stiffnecked people; and they repented not of their sins, ascribing all the ᵒpower of Alma and Amulek to the devil; for they were of the profession of ᵖNehor, and did not believe in the repentance of their sins.

16. And it came to pass that Alma and Amulek, Amulek having ᵍforsaken all his gold, and silver, and his precious things, which were in the land of Ammonihah, for the word of God, he being rejected by those who were ʳonce his friends and also by his father and his kindred;

17. Therefore, after Alma having established the church at ˢSidom, seeing a great check, yea, seeing that the people were checked as to the pride of their hearts, and began to humble themselves before God, and began to assemble themselves together at their ᵗsanctuaries to worship God before the altar, watching and praying continually, that they might be delivered from Satan, and from death, and from destruction—

18. Now as I said, Alma having seen all these things, therefore he took Amulek and came over to the ᵘland of Zarahemla, and took him to his own house, and did administer unto him in his tribulations, and strengthened him in the Lord.

19. And thus ended the tenth year of the reign of the judges over the people of Nephi.

CHAPTER 16.

A cry of war—The wicked city Ammonihah destroyed by Lamanites—

---

g, ver. 3. *h*, ver. 3. Al. 14:6. *i*, see *a*. *j*, see *u*, 2 Ne. 9. *k*, see *a*. *l*, see *c*, Mos. 6. *m*, see *u*, 2 Ne. 9. *n*, see *i*, Al. 8. *o*, Al. 14:26—29. *p*, Al. 1:2—15. 2:20. *q*, Al. 10:4. *r*, Al. 10:4, 11. *s*, see *a*. *t*, Al. 16:13. 21:6. 22:7. 23:2. He. 3:9, 14. *u*, Om. 13. ABOUT B. C. 81.

ALMA, 16.

Zoram and his sons rout the enemy—Desolation of Nehors—The church widely established.

1. And it came to pass in the *eleventh year of the reign of the judges over the people of Nephi, on the fifth day of the second month, there having been much peace in the ^aland of Zarahemla, there having been no wars nor contentions for a certain number of years, even until the fifth day of the second month in the eleventh year, there was a cry of war heard throughout the land.

2. For behold, the armies of the Lamanites had come in upon the wilderness side, into the borders of the land, even into the ^bcity of Ammonihah, and began to slay the people and destroy the city.

3. And now it came to pass, before the Nephites could raise a sufficient army to drive them out of the land, they had ^cdestroyed the people who were in the city of Ammonihah, and also some around the borders of ^dNoah, and taken others captive into the wilderness.

4. Now it came to pass that the Nephites were desirous to obtain those who had been carried away captive into the wilderness.

5. Therefore, he that had been appointed chief captain over the armies of the Nephites, (and his name was Zoram, and he had two sons, Lehi and Aha)—now Zoram and his two sons, knowing that Alma was ^ehigh priest over the church, and having heard that he had the spirit of prophecy, therefore they went unto him and desired of him to know whether the Lord would that they should go into the wilderness in search of their brethren, who had been taken ^fcaptive by the Lamanites.

6. And it came to pass that Alma inquired of the Lord concerning the matter. And Alma returned and said unto them: Behold, the Lamanites will cross the ^griver Sidon in the south wilderness, away up beyond the borders of the ^hland of Manti. And behold there shall ye meet them, on the east of the ⁱriver Sidon, and there the Lord will deliver unto thee thy brethren who have been taken ^jcaptive by the Lamanites.

7. And it came to pass that ^kZoram and his sons crossed over the ^lriver Sidon, with their armies, and marched away beyond the borders of ^mManti into the south wilderness, which was on the east side of the river Sidon.

8. And they came upon the armies of the Lamanites, and the Lamanites were scattered and driven into the wilderness; and they took their brethren who had been taken captive by the Lamanites, and there was not one soul of them had been lost that were taken ⁿcaptive. And they were brought by their brethren to possess their ^oown lands.

9. And thus ended the eleventh year of the judges, the Lamanites having been driven out of the land, and the ^ppeople of Ammonihah were destroyed; yea, every living soul of the Ammonihahites was destroyed, and also their great city, which they said God could ^qnot destroy, because of its greatness.

10. But behold, in one day it

---

a, Om. 13. *b*, see *i*, Al. 8. *c*, vers. 9—11. Al. 9:18. 25:2. *d*, Al. 49:12—15. *e*, see *g*, Mos. 26. *f*, vers. 3, 4. *g*, see *g*, Al. 2. *h*, ver. 7. Al. 17:1. 22:27. 43:22, 24, 25, 42. 56:14. 57:22. 58:1, 13, 25—28, 39. 59:6. *i*, see *g*, Al. 2. *j*, vers. 3, 4. *k*, ver. 5. *l*, see *g*, Al. 2. *m*, see *h*. *n*, vers. 3—6. *o*, ver. 3. *p*, vers. 2, 3. Al. 9:18. *q*, Al. 9:4, 5.
* B. C. 81.

was left desolate; and the carcases were mangled by dogs and wild beasts of the wilderness.

11. Nevertheless, after many days their dead bodies were heaped up upon the face of the earth, and they were covered with a shallow covering. And now so great was the scent thereof that the people did not go in to possess the land of Ammonihah for many years. And it was called Desolation of 'Nehors; for they were of the profession of Nehor, who were slain; and their lands remained desolate.

12. And the Lamanites did not come again to war against the Nephites *until the fourteenth year of the reign of the judges over the people of Nephi. And thus for three years did the people of Nephi have continual peace in all the land.

13. And Alma and Amulek went forth preaching repentance to the people in their *temples, and in their 'sanctuaries, and also in their ^usynagogues, which were built ^vafter the manner of the Jews.

14. And as many as would hear their words, unto them they did impart the word of God, without any respect of persons, continually.

15. And thus did Alma and Amulek go forth, and also many more who had been chosen for the work, to preach the word throughout all the land. And the establishment of the church became general throughout the land, in all the region round about, among all the people of the Nephites.

16. And there was ^wno inequality among them; the Lord did pour out his Spirit on all the face of the land to prepare the minds of the children of men, or to prepare their hearts to receive the word which should be taught among them at the time of his coming—

17. That they might not be hardened against the word, that they might not be unbelieving, and go on to destruction, but that they might receive the word with joy, and as a branch be grafted into the true vine, that they might enter into the *rest of the Lord their God.

18. Now those ^ypriests who did go forth among the people did preach ^zagainst all lyings, and deceivings, and envyings, and strifes, and malice, and revilings, and stealing, robbing, plundering, murdering, committing adultery, and all manner of lasciviousness, crying that these things ought not so to be—

19. Holding forth things which must shortly come; yea, holding forth the coming of the Son of God, his sufferings and death, and also the ^{2a}resurrection of the dead.

20. And many of the people did inquire concerning the place where the Son of God should come; and they were taught that he would ^{2b}appear unto them after his resurrection; and this the people did hear with great joy and gladness.

21. And now after the church had been established throughout all the land—having got the victory over the devil, and the word of God being preached in its purity in all the land, and the

---

r, Al. 1:2—15. s, see h, 2 Ne. 5. t, see t, Al. 15. u, Al. 21:4, 5, 11, 16, 20. 23:2, 4. 26:29. 31:12, 13. 32:1, 2, 5, 9—12. 33:2. He. 3:9, 14. 3 Ne. 13:2. 5. v, 2 Ne. 5:16. w, Mos. 18:19—29. 23:15. 27:4. 4 Ne. 3. x, see 2v, Al. 12. y, see c, Mos. 6. See g, Mos. 26. z, 3 Ne. 30. 2a, see d, 2 Ne. 2. 2b, see b, 1 Ne. 12.
*ABOUT B. C. 78.

Lord pouring out his blessings upon the people—thus ended the fourteenth year of the reign of the judges over the people of Nephi.

An account of the sons of Mosiah, who rejected their rights to the kingdom for the word of God, and went up to the land of Nephi to preach to the Lamanites; their sufferings and deliverance—according to the record of Alma.

Comprising chapters 17 to 26 inclusive.

CHAPTER 17.

Ammon in the land of Ishmael—He becomes a servant to king Lamoni—His heroic defense of the king's flocks.

1. And now it came to pass that as Alma was journeying from the ^aland of Gideon southward, away to the ^bland of Manti, behold, to his astonishment, he met with the ^csons of Mosiah journeying towards the ^dland of Zarahemla.

2. Now these sons of Mosiah were with Alma at the time the angel ^efirst appeared unto him; therefore Alma did rejoice exceedingly to see his brethren; and what added more to his joy, they were still his brethren in the Lord; yea, and they had waxed strong in the knowledge of the truth; for they were men of a sound understanding and they had searched the ^fscriptures diligently, that they might know the word of God.

3. But this is not all; they had given themselves to ^gmuch prayer, and fasting; therefore they had the spirit of prophecy, and the spirit of revelation, and when they taught, they taught with power and authority of God.

4. And they had been teaching the word of God *for the space of fourteen years among the Lamanites, having had much success in bringing many to the knowledge of the truth; yea, by the power of their words many were brought before the altar of God, to call on his name and confess their sins before him.

5. Now these are the circumstances which attended them in their journeyings, for they had many afflictions; they did suffer much, both in body and in mind, such as hunger, thirst and fatigue, and also much labor in the spirit.

6. Now these were their journeyings: Having taken leave of their ^hfather, Mosiah, in the first year of the judges; having ⁱrefused the kingdom which their father was desirous to confer upon them, and also this was the minds of the people;

7. Nevertheless they departed out of the ^jland of Zarahemla, and took their swords, and their spears, and their bows, and their arrows, and their slings; and this they did that they might provide food for themselves while in the wilderness.

8. And thus they departed into the wilderness with their numbers which they had ^kselected, to go up to the ^lland of Nephi, to preach the word of God unto the Lamanites.

9. And it came to pass that they journeyed many days in the wilderness, and they ^mfasted much and prayed much that the Lord would grant unto them a portion of his Spirit to go with them, and abide with them, that they might be an instrument in the hands of

---

a, see *m*, Al. 2.   *b*, see *h*, Al. 16.   *c*, Mos. 27:34.   *d*, Om. 13.   *e*, Mos. 27:11—17.
f, Jac. 7:23. Al. 63:12.   *g*, see *e*, 2 Ne. 32. See *t*, Mos. 27.   *h*, Mos. 28:1, 5—9.
29:41—44.   *i*, Mos. 29:3.   *j*, Om. 13.   *k*, Mos. 28:1.   *l*, see *b*, 2 Ne. 5.   *m*, see *t*, Mos. 27.
* From about B. C. 91 to 77.

God to bring, if it were possible, their brethren, the Lamanites, to the knowledge of the truth, to the knowledge of the ⁿbaseness of the traditions of their fathers, which were not correct.

10. And it came to pass that the Lord did visit them with his Spirit, and said unto them: ᵒBe comforted. And they were comforted.

11. And the Lord said unto them also: ᵖGo forth among the Lamanites, thy brethren, and establish my word; yet ye shall be patient in long-suffering and afflictions, that ye may show forth good examples unto them in me, and I will make an instrument of thee in my hands unto the salvation of many souls.

12. And it came to pass that the hearts of the sons of Mosiah, and also those who were with them, took courage to go forth unto the Lamanites to declare unto them the word of God.

13. And it came to pass when they had arrived in the borders of the land of the Lamanites, that they separated themselves and departed one from another, trusting in the Lord that they should meet again at the close of their harvest; for they supposed that ᵠgreat was the work which they had undertaken.

14. And assuredly it was great, for they had undertaken to preach the word of God ʳto a wild and a hardened and a ferocious people; a people who delighted in murdering the Nephites, and robbing and plundering them; and their hearts were set upon riches, or upon gold and silver, and precious stones; yet they sought to obtain these things by murdering and plundering, that they might not labor for them with their own hands.

15. Thus they were a very indolent people, many of whom did worship idols, and the ˢcurse of God had fallen upon them because of the traditions of their fathers; notwithstanding the promises of the Lord were ᵗextended unto them on the conditions of repentance.

16. Therefore, this was the cause for which the sons of Mosiah had undertaken the ᵘwork, that perhaps they might bring them unto repentance; that perhaps they might bring them to know of the plan of redemption.

17. Therefore they ʳseparated themselves one from another, and went forth among them, every man alone, according to the word and power of God which was given unto him.

18. Now Ammon being the chief among them, or rather he did administer unto them, and he departed from them, after having blessed them according to their several stations, having imparted the word of God unto them, or administered unto them before his departure; and thus they took their several journeys throughout the land.

19. And Ammon went to the land of ʷIshmael, the land being called after the ˣsons of Ishmael, who also became Lamanites.

20. And as Ammon entered the land of Ishmael, the Lamanites took him and bound him, as was their custom to bind all the Nephites who fell into their hands, and carry them before the king; and thus it was left to the pleasure of the king to slay them,

n, see *n*, Jac. 7. *o*, ver. 12. Al. 26:27. *p*, Al. 26:27. *q*, vers. 14—16. *r*, see *n*, Jac. 7. *s*, see *d*, 1 Ne. 2. *t*, see *j*, Al. 9. *u*, see *q*. *v*, ver. 13. *w*, vers. 20, 21. Al. 20:14, 15. 21:18, 20. 22:1, 4. 23:9. 24:5. 25:13. *x*, see *c*, 1 Ne. 7.

ABOUT B. C. 90.

or to retain them in captivity, or to cast them into prison, or to cast them out of his land, according to his will and pleasure.

21. And thus Ammon was carried before the king who was over the ʸland of Ishmael; and his name was Lamoni; and he was a descendant of ᶜIshmael.

22. And the king inquired of Ammon if it were his desire to dwell in the land among the Lamanites, or among his people.

23. And Ammon said unto him: Yea, I desire to dwell among this people for a time; yea, and perhaps until the day I die.

24. And it came to pass that king Lamoni was much pleased with Ammon, and caused that his ²ᵃbands should be loosed; and he would that Ammon should take one of his daughters to wife.

25. But Ammon said unto him: Nay, but I will be thy servant. Therefore Ammon became a servant to king Lamoni. And it came to pass that he was set among other servants to watch the flocks of Lamoni, according to the custom of the Lamanites.

26. And after he had been in the service of the king three days, as he was with the Lamanitish servants going forth with their flocks to the place of water, which was called the ²ᵇwater of Sebus, and all the Lamanites drive their flocks hither, that they may have water—

27. Therefore, as Ammon and the servants of the king were driving forth their flocks to this place of water, behold, a certain number of the Lamanites, who had been with their flocks to water, stood and scattered the flocks of Ammon and the servants of the king, and they ²ᶜscattered them insomuch that they fled many ways.

28. Now the servants of the king began to murmur, saying: Now the king will slay us, as he ²ᵈhas our brethren because their flocks were scattered by the wickedness of these men. And they began to weep exceedingly, saying: Behold, our flocks are scattered already.

29. Now they wept because of the fear of being slain. Now when Ammon saw this his heart was swollen within him with joy; for, said he, I will show forth my power unto these my fellow-servants, or the power which is in me, in restoring these flocks unto the king, that I may win the hearts of these my fellow-servants, that I may lead them to believe in my words.

30. And now, these were the thoughts of Ammon, when he saw the afflictions of those whom he termed to be his brethren.

31. And it came to pass that he flattered them by his words, saying: My brethren, be of good cheer and let us go in search of the flocks, and we will ²ᵉgather them together and bring them back unto the place of water; and thus we will preserve the flocks unto the king and he will not slay us.

32. And it came to pass that they went in search of the flocks, and they did follow Ammon, and they rushed forth with much swiftness and did head the flocks of the king, and did gather them together again to the place of water.

33. And those ²ᶠmen again

y, see *w*. *z*, see *c*, 1 Ne. 7. 2*a*, ver. 20. 2*b*, ver. 34. Al. 18:7. 19:20, 21. 2*c*, vers. 29, 31—33, 35, 39. Al. 18:3. 19:20, 21. 2*d*, Al. 18:4—7. 19:20. 2*e*, ver. 32. 2*f*, vers. 27, 35.
ABOUT B. C. 90.

stood to scatter their flocks; but Ammon said unto his brethren: Encircle the flocks round about that they flee not; and I go and contend with these men who do scatter our flocks.

34. Therefore, they did as Ammon commanded them, and he went forth and stood to contend with those who stood by the ^{2g}waters of Sebus; and they were in number not a few.

35. Therefore they did not fear Ammon, for they supposed that one of their men could slay him according to their pleasure, for they knew not that the Lord had promised Mosiah that he would ^{2h}deliver his sons out of their hands; neither did they know anything concerning the Lord; therefore they delighted in the destruction of their brethren; and for this cause ^{2i}they stood to scatter the flocks of the king.

36. But Ammon stood forth and began to cast stones at them with his sling; yea, with mighty power he did sling stones amongst them; and thus he slew a ^{2j}certain number of them insomuch that they began to be astonished at his power; nevertheless they were angry because of the slain of their brethren, and they were determined that he should fall; therefore, seeing that they could not hit him with their stones, they came forth with clubs to slay him.

37. But behold, every man that lifted his club to smite Ammon, he smote off ^{2k}their arms with his sword; for he did withstand their blows by smiting their arms with the edge of his sword, insomuch that they began to be astonished, and began to flee before him; yea, and they were not few in number; and he caused them to flee by the strength of his arm.

38. Now six of them had fallen by the sling, but he slew none save it were their leader with his sword; and he smote off as many of their arms as were lifted against him, and they ^{2l}were not a few.

39. And when he had driven them afar off, he returned and they watered their flocks and returned them to the pasture of the king, and then went in unto the king, ^{2m}bearing the arms which had been smitten off by the sword of Ammon, of those who sought to slay him; and they were carried in unto the king for a testimony of the things which they had done.

CHAPTER 18.

King Lamoni mistakes Ammon for the Great Spirit—He is taught concerning the true God—Is overcome by the Spirit of the Lord.

1. And it came to pass that king Lamoni caused that his servants should stand forth and testify ^{a}to all the things which they had seen concerning the matter.

2. And when they had all testified to the things which they had seen, and he had learned of the faithfulness of Ammon in preserving his flocks, and also of his great power in contending against those who sought to slay him, he was astonished exceedingly, and said: Surely, this is more than a man. Behold, is not this the ^{b}Great Spirit who doth send such great punishments upon this people, because of their murders?

3. And they answered the king, and said: Whether he be the

2g, see 2b. 2h, Mos. 28:7. Al. 19:23. 2i, vers. 27, 33. 2j, ver. 38. Al. 18:16, 20. 2k, vers. 38, 39. Al. 18:16, 20. 2l, vers. 34, 38. 2m, vers. 37, 38. Al. 18:16, 20. CHAP. 18: a, Al. 17:31—38. b, vers. 3—5, 11, 18, 26—28. Al. 22:9—11.

ABOUT B. C. 90.

ALMA, 18.

Great Spirit or a man, we know not; but this much we do know, that he ᶜcannot be slain by the enemies of the king; neither can they scatter the king's flocks when he is with us, because of his expertness and great strength; therefore, we know that he is a friend to the king. And now, O king, we do not believe that a man has such great power, for we know he cannot be slain.

4. And now, when the king heard these words, he said unto them: Now I know that it is the ᵈGreat Spirit; and he has come down at this time to preserve your lives, that I might not slay you ᵉas I did your brethren. Now this is the Great Spirit of whom our fathers have spoken.

5. Now this was the tradition of Lamoni, which he had received from his father, that there was a Great Spirit. Notwithstanding they believed in a ᶠGreat Spirit, they supposed that whatsoever they did was right; nevertheless, Lamoni began to fear exceedingly, with fear lest he had done wrong in slaying his servants;

6. For he had slain ᵍmany of them because their brethren had scattered their flocks at the place of water; and thus, because they had had their flocks scattered they were slain.

7. Now it was the practice of the Lamanites to stand by the ʰwaters of Sebus to scatter the flocks of the people, that thereby they might drive away many that were scattered unto their own land, it being a practice of plunder among them.

8. And it came to pass that king Lamoni inquired of his servants, saying: Where is this man that has such great power?

9. And they said unto him: Behold, he is feeding thy ⁱhorses. Now the king had commanded his servants, previous to the time of the watering of their flocks, that they should prepare his horses and chariots, and conduct him forth to the ʲland of Nephi; for there had been a ᵏgreat feast appointed at the land of Nephi, by the father of Lamoni, who was king over all the land.

10. Now when king Lamoni heard that Ammon was preparing his horses and his ˡchariots he was more astonished, because of the faithfulness of Ammon, saying: Surely there has not been any servant among all my servants that has been so faithful as this man; for even he doth remember ᵐall my commandments to execute them.

11. Now I surely know that this is the ⁿGreat Spirit, and I would desire him that he come in unto me, but I durst not.

12. And it came to pass that when Ammon had made ready the ᵒhorses and the ᵖchariots for the king and his servants, he went in unto the king, and he saw that the countenance of the king was changed; therefore he was about to return out of his presence.

13. And one of the king's servants said unto him, Rabbanah, which is, being interpreted, powerful or great king, considering their kings to be powerful; and thus he said unto him: Rabbanah, the king desireth thee to stay.

14. Therefore Ammon turned himself unto the king, and said

---

c, Al. 17:34—38. *d*, see *b*. *e*, vers. 5, 6. Al. 17:28, 31. *f*, see *b*. *g*, see *e*. *h*, see 2*b*, Al. 17. *i*, ver. 10. See *m*, 1 Ne. 18. *j*, see *b*, 2 Ne. 5. *k*, Al. 20:9, 12. *l*, vers. 9, 12. Al. 20:6. 3 Ne. 3:22. *m*, ver. 9. *n*, see *b*. *o*, see *m*, 1 Ne. 18. *p*, see *l*. ABOUT B. C. 90.

unto him: What wilt thou that I should do for thee, O king? And the king answered him not for the space of an ^{q}hour, according to their time, for he knew not what he should say unto him.

15. And it came to pass that Ammon said unto him again: What desirest thou of me? But the king answered him not.

16. And it came to pass that Ammon, being filled with the Spirit of God, therefore he perceived the thoughts of the king. And he said unto him: Is it because thou hast heard that I ^{r}defended thy servants and thy flocks, and slew seven of their brethren with the sling and with the sword, and smote off the arms of others, in order to defend thy flocks and thy servants; behold, is it this that causeth thy marvelings?

17. I say unto you, what is it, that thy marvelings are so great? Behold, I am a man, and am thy servant; therefore, whatsoever thou desirest which is right, that will I do.

18. Now when the king had heard these words, he marveled again, for he beheld that Ammon could discern his thoughts; but notwithstanding this, king Lamoni did open his mouth, and said unto him: Who art thou? Art thou that ^{s}Great Spirit, who knows all things?

19. Ammon answered and said unto him: I am not.

20. And the king said: How knowest thou the thoughts of my heart? Thou mayest speak boldly, and tell me concerning these things; and also tell me by ^{t}what power ye slew and smote off the arms of my brethren that scattered my flocks—

21. And now, if thou wilt tell me concerning these things, whatsoever thou desirest I will give unto thee; and if it were needed, I would guard thee with my armies; but I know that thou art more powerful than all they; nevertheless, whatsoever thou desirest of me I will grant it unto thee.

22. Now Ammon being wise, yet harmless, he said unto Lamoni: Wilt thou hearken unto my words, if I tell thee by what power I do these things? And this is the thing that I desire of thee.

23. And the king answered him, and said: Yea, I will believe all thy words. And thus he was caught with guile.

24. And Ammon began to speak unto him with boldness, and said unto him: Believest thou that there is a God?

25. And he answered, and said unto him: I do not know what that meaneth.

26. And then Ammon said: Believest thou that there is a Great Spirit?

27. And he said, Yea.

28. And Ammon said: This is God. And Ammon said unto him again: Believest thou that this Great Spirit, who is God, created all things which are in heaven and in the earth?

29. And he said: Yea, I believe that he created all things which are in the earth; but I do not know the heavens.

30. And Ammon said unto him: The heavens is a place where God dwells and all his holy angels.

31. And king Lamoni said: Is it above the earth?

32. And Ammon said: Yea, and he looketh down upon all the children of men; and he knows all the thoughts and intents of

---

q, 3 Ne. 8:19. r, Al. 17:31—38. s, see b. t, Al. 17:31—38. ABOUT B. C. 90.

the heart; for by his hand were they all created from the beginning.

33. And king Lamoni said: I believe all these things which thou hast spoken. Art thou sent from God?

34. Ammon said unto him: I am a man; and man in the ᵘbeginning was created after the image of God, and I am called by his Holy Spirit to teach these things unto this people, that they may be brought to a knowledge of that which is just and true;

35. And a portion of that Spirit dwelleth in me, which giveth me knowledge, and also power according to my faith and desires which are in God.

36. Now when Ammon had said these words, he began at the creation of the world, and also the ᵛcreation of Adam, and told him all the things concerning the fall of man, and rehearsed and laid before him the ʷrecords and the holy scriptures of the people, which had been spoken by the prophets, even down to the time that their father, Lehi, left Jerusalem.

37. And he also rehearsed unto them (for it was unto the king and to his servants) all the ˣjourneyings of their fathers in the wilderness, and all their sufferings with hunger and thirst, and their travel, and so forth.

38. And he also rehearsed unto them concerning the rebellions of Laman and Lemuel, and the sons of Ishmael, yea, all their rebellions did he relate unto them; and he expounded unto them all the ʸrecords and scriptures from the time that Lehi left Jerusalem down to the present time.

39. But this is not all; for he expounded unto them the plan of redemption, which was prepared ᶻfrom the foundation of the world; and he also made known unto them concerning the coming of Christ, and all the works of the Lord did he make known unto them.

40. And it came to pass that after he had said all these things, and expounded them to the king, that the king ²ᵃbelieved all his words.

41. And he began to cry unto the Lord, saying: O Lord, have mercy; according to thy abundant mercy which thou hast had upon the people of Nephi, have upon me, and my people.

42. And now, when he had said this, he fell unto the earth, ²ᵇas if he were dead.

43. And it came to pass that his ²ᶜservants took him and carried him in unto his wife, and laid him upon a bed; and he lay as if he were dead for the ²ᵈspace of two days and two nights; and his wife, and his sons, and his daughters mourned over him, after the manner of the Lamanites, greatly lamenting his loss.

CHAPTER 19.

A wonderful conversion—Abish the Lamanite woman—Lamanite king and queen espouse the faith—Ammon establishes the church in Ishmael.

1. And it came to pass that ᵃafter two days and two nights they were about to take his body and lay it in a sepulchre, which they had made for the purpose of burying their dead.

2. Now the queen having heard of the fame of Ammon, therefore

---

u, ver. 32. Mos. 7:27. Eth. 3:13—16. *v*, ver. 34. See *m*, Mos. 2. *w*, see *a*, 1 Ne. 3. Al. 63:12. *x*, see First Book of Nephi. *y*, 1 Ne. 9:2. *z*, see *d*, Mos. 4. 2*a*, ver. 23. 2*b*, ver. 43. Al. 19:1, 5—12. 2*c*, Al. 19:4, 9. 2*d*, Al. 19:1, 5.
CHAP. 19: *a*, ver. 5. Al. 18:43. ABOUT B. C. 90.

she sent and desired that he should come in unto her.

3. And it came to pass that Ammon did as he was commanded, and went in unto the queen, and desired to know what she would that he should do.

4. And she said unto him: The *b*servants of my husband have made it known unto me that thou art a prophet of a holy God, and that thou hast power to do many mighty works in his name;

5. Therefore, if this is the case, I would that ye should go in and see my husband, for he has been laid upon his bed for the *c*space of two days and two nights; and some say that he is not dead, but others say that he is dead and that he stinketh, and that he ought to be placed in the *d*sepulchre; but as for myself, to me he doth not stink.

6. Now, this was what Ammon desired, for he knew that king Lamoni was under the power of God; he knew that the dark veil of unbelief was being cast away from his mind, and the light which did light up his mind, which was the light of the glory of God, which was a marvelous light of his goodness—yea, this light had infused such joy into his soul, the cloud of darkness having been dispelled, and that the light of everlasting life was lit up in his soul, yea, he knew that this had *e*overcome his natural frame, and he was carried away in God—

7. Therefore, what the queen desired of him was his only desire. Therefore, he went in to see the king according as the queen had desired him; and he saw the king, and he knew that he was not dead.

8. And he said unto the queen: He is not dead, but he sleepeth in God, and on the morrow he *f*shall rise again; therefore bury him not.

9. And Ammon said unto her: Believest thou this? And she said unto him: I have had no witness save thy word, and the word of our servants; nevertheless I believe that it shall be according as thou hast said.

10. And Ammon said unto her: Blessed art thou because of thy exceeding faith; I say unto thee, woman, there has not been such great faith among all the people of the Nephites.

11. And it came to pass that she watched over the bed of her husband, from that time even until that time on the morrow which Ammon had appointed that he should rise.

12. And it came to pass that he arose, *g*according to the words of Ammon; and as he arose, he stretched forth his hand unto the woman, and said: Blessed be the name of God, and blessed art thou.

13. For as sure as thou livest, behold, I have seen my Redeemer; and he shall come forth, and be born of a *h*woman, and he shall redeem all mankind who believe on his name. Now, when he had said these words, his heart was swollen within him, and he sunk again with joy; and the queen also sunk down, being overpowered by the Spirit.

14. Now Ammon seeing the Spirit of the Lord poured out according to his prayers upon the Lamanites, his brethren, who had been the cause of so much mourning among the Nephites, or among all the people of God because of

b, ver. 9.   Al. 18:43.   *c*, ver. 1.   Al. 18:43.   *d*, ver. 1.   *e*, Al. 18:42.   *f*, vers. 11, 12.   *g*, ver. 8.   *h*, see *d*, 1 Ne. 11.

ABOUT B. C. 90.

their iniquities and their traditions, he fell upon his knees, and began to pour out his soul in prayer and thanksgiving to God for what he had done for his brethren; and he was also overpowered with joy; and thus they all three had sunk to the earth.

15. Now, when the servants of the king had seen that they had fallen, they also began to cry unto God, for the fear of the Lord had come upon them also, for it was ⁱthey who had stood before the king and testified unto him concerning the great power of Ammon.

16. And it came to pass that they did call on the name of the Lord, in their might, even until they had all fallen to the earth, save it were ʲone of the Lamanitish women, whose name was Abish, she having been converted unto the Lord for many years, on account of a remarkable vision of her father—

17. Thus, having been converted to the Lord, and never having made it known, therefore, when she saw that all the servants of Lamoni had fallen to the earth, and also her mistress, the queen, and the king, and Ammon lay prostrate upon the earth, she knew that it was the power of God; and supposing that this opportunity, by making known unto the people what had happened among them, that by beholding this scene it would cause them to believe in the power of God, therefore she ran forth from house to house, making it known unto the people.

18. And they began to assemble themselves together unto the house of the king. And there came a multitude, and to their astonishment, they beheld the king, and the queen, and their servants prostrate upon the earth, and they all lay there as though they were dead; and they also saw Ammon, and behold, he was a Nephite.

19. And now the people began to murmur among themselves; some saying that it was a great evil that had come upon them, or upon the king and his house, because he had suffered that the Nephite should ᵏremain in the land.

20. But others rebuked them, saying: The king hath brought this evil upon his house, because he ˡslew his servants who had had their flocks scattered at the ᵐwaters of Sebus.

21. And they were also rebuked by those men who had stood at the waters of Sebus and scattered the flocks which belonged to the king, for ⁿthey were angry with Ammon because of the number which he had slain of their brethren at the waters of Sebus, while defending the flocks of the king.

22. Now, one of them, whose brother had been slain with the ᵒsword of Ammon, being exceedingly angry with Ammon, drew his sword and went forth that he might let it fall upon Ammon, to slay him; and as he lifted the sword to smite him, behold, he fell dead.

23. Now we see that Ammon could not be slain, for the Lord had said unto Mosiah, ᵖhis father: I will spare him, and it shall be unto him according to thy faith— therefore, Mosiah trusted him unto the Lord.

---

i, Al. 18:1, 2. *j*, vers. 17, 28, 29. *k*, Al. 17:22, 23. *l*, see 2*d*, Al. 17. *m*, see 2*b*, Al. 17. *n*, Al. 17:27. 18:7. *o*. Al. 17:38. *p*, Mos. 28:7. Al. 17:35.

ABOUT B. C. 90.

24. And it came to pass that when the multitude beheld that the man had qfallen dead, who lifted the sword to slay Ammon, fear came upon them all, and they durst not put forth their hands to touch him or any of those who had fallen; and they began to marvel again among themselves what could be the cause of this great power, or what all these things could mean.

25. And it came to pass that there were many among them who said that Ammon was the rGreat Spirit, and others said he was sent by the Great Spirit;

26. But others rebuked them all, saying that he was a monster, who had been sent from the Nephites to torment them.

27. And there were some who said that Ammon was sent by the Great Spirit to afflict them because of their iniquities; and that it was the Great Spirit that had always attended the Nephites, who had ever delivered them out of their hands; and they said that it was this Great Spirit who had destroyed so many of their brethren, the Lamanites.

28. And thus the contention began to be exceeding sharp among them. And while they were thus contending, the *woman servant who had caused the multitude to be gathered together came, and when she saw the contention which was among the multitude she was exceeding sorrowful, even unto tears.

29. And it came to pass that she went and took the queen by the hand, that perhaps she might raise her from the ground; and as soon as she touched her hand she arose and stood upon her feet, and cried with a loud voice, saying: O blessed Jesus, who has saved me from an tawful hell! O blessed God, have mercy on this people!

30. And when she had said this, she clasped her hands, being filled with joy, speaking many words which were not understood; and when she had done this, she took the king, Lamoni, by the hand, and behold he arose and stood upon his feet.

31. And he, immediately, seeing the contention among his people, went forth and began to rebuke them, and to teach them the uwords which he had heard from the mouth of Ammon; and as many as heard his words believed, and were converted unto the Lord.

32. But there were many among them who would not hear his words; therefore they went their way.

33. And it came to pass that when Ammon arose he also administered unto them, and also did all the servants of Lamoni; and they did all declare unto the people the selfsame thing—that their hearts had been changed; that they had no more desire to do evil.

34. And behold, many did declare unto the people that they had seen angels and had conversed with them; and thus they had told them things of God, and of his righteousness.

35. And it came to pass that there were many that did believe in their words; and as many as did believe were vbaptized; and they became a righteous people, and they did establish a church among them.

36. And thus the work of the Lord did commence among the Lamanites; thus the Lord did

---

q, ver. 22. *r*, see *b*, Al. 18. *s*, vers. 16, 17, 29. *t*, see *k*, 1 Ne. 15. *u*, Al. 18:36—39. *v*, see *u*, 2 Ne. 9.

ABOUT B. C. 90.

begin to pour out his Spirit upon them; and we see that his arm is extended to all people who will repent and believe on his name.

CHAPTER 20.

Ammon and king Lamoni journey to Middoni—They meet Lamoni's father who is king over all the land—Hostile at first, he relents, and grants great favors.

1. And it came to pass that when they had established a church in that land, that king Lamoni desired that Ammon should go with him to the *a*land of Nephi, that he might show him unto his father.

2. And the voice of the Lord came to Ammon, saying: Thou shalt not go up to the land of Nephi, for behold, the king will seek thy life; but thou shalt go to the *b*land of Middoni; for behold, thy brother Aaron, and also Muloki and Ammah *c*are in prison.

3. Now it came to pass that when Ammon had heard this, he said unto Lamoni: Behold, my brother and brethren *d*are in prison at Middoni, and I go that I may deliver them.

4. Now Lamoni said unto Ammon: I know, in the strength of the Lord thou canst do all things. But behold, I will go with thee to the *e*land of Middoni; for the king of the land of Middoni, whose name is Antiomno, is a friend unto me; therefore I go to the land of Middoni, that I may flatter the king of the land, and he will cast thy brethren out of *f*prison. Now Lamoni said unto him: Who told thee that thy brethren were in prison?

5. And Ammon said unto him: No one hath told me, save it be God; and he said unto me—*g*Go and deliver thy brethren, for they are in prison in the land of Middoni.

6. Now when Lamoni had heard this he caused that his servants should make ready *h*his horses and his *i*chariots.

7. And he said unto Ammon: Come, I will go with thee down to the *j*land of Middoni, and there I will plead with the king that he will cast thy brethren out of prison.

8. And it came to pass that as Ammon and Lamoni were journeying thither, they met the father of Lamoni, who was king *k*over all the land.

9. And behold, the father of Lamoni said unto him: Why did ye not come to the *l*feast on that great day when I made a feast unto my sons, and unto my people?

10. And he also said: Whither art thou going with this Nephite, who is one of the children of a liar?

11. And it came to pass that Lamoni rehearsed unto him whither he was going, for he feared to offend him.

12. And he also told him all the cause of his tarrying in his own kingdom, that he did not go unto his father to the *m*feast which he had prepared.

13. And now when Lamoni had rehearsed unto him all these things, behold, to his astonishment, his father was angry with him, and said: Lamoni, thou art going to *n*deliver these Nephites, who are sons of a liar. Behold, he

---

a, see *b*, 2 Ne. 5. *b*, vers. 3—7, 14, 15, 28, 30. Al. 21:12, 13, 18. 22:1, 3. 23:10. *c*, vers. 3—7, 13, 15, 22, 24, 26—30. Al. 21:13—15. 22:2. *d*, see *c*. *e*, see *b*. *f*, see *c*. *g*, ver. 2. *h*, see *m*, 1 Ne. 18. *i*, see *l*, Al. 18. *j*, see *b*. *k*, Al. 22:1. *l*, see *k*, Al. 18. *m*, see *k*, Al. 18. *n*, vers. 4, 7.   ABOUT B. C. 90,

robbed our fathers; and now his children are also come amongst us that °they may, by their cunning and their lyings, deceive us, that they again may rob us of our property.

14. Now the father of Lamoni commanded him that he should slay Ammon with the sword. And he also commanded him that he should not go to the ᵖland of Middoni, but that he should return with him to the ᑫland of Ishmael.

15. But Lamoni said unto him: I will not slay Ammon, neither will I return to the land of Ishmael, but I go to the land of Middoni that I may ʳrelease the brethren of Ammon, for I know that they are just men and holy prophets of the true God.

16. Now when his father had heard these words, he was angry with him, and he drew his sword that he might smite him to the earth.

17. But Ammon stood forth and said unto him: Behold, thou shalt not slay thy son; nevertheless, it were better that he should fall than thee, for behold, he has repented of his sins; but if thou shouldst fall at this time, in thine anger, thy soul could not be saved.

18. And again, it is expedient that thou shouldst forbear; for if thou shouldst slay thy son, he being an innocent man, his blood would cry from the ground to the Lord his God, for vengeance to come upon thee; and perhaps thou wouldst lose thy soul.

19. Now when Ammon had said these words unto him, he answered him, saying: I know that if I should slay my son, that I should shed innocent blood; for it is thou that hast sought to destroy him.

20. And he stretched forth his hand to slay Ammon. But Ammon withstood his blows, and also smote his arm that he could not use it.

21. Now when the king saw that Ammon could slay him, he began to plead with Ammon that he would spare his life.

22. But Ammon raised his sword, and said unto him: Behold, I will smite thee except thou wilt grant unto me that my brethren may be ˢcast out of prison.

23. Now the king, fearing he should lose his life, said: If thou wilt spare me I will grant unto thee whatsoever thou wilt ask, even to half of the kingdom.

24. Now when Ammon saw that he had wrought upon the old king according to his desire, he said unto him: If thou wilt grant that my brethren may be ᵗcast out of prison, and also that Lamoni may retain his kingdom, and that ye be not displeased with him, but grant that he may do according to his own desires in ᵘwhatsoever thing he thinketh, then will I spare thee; otherwise I will smite thee to the earth.

25. Now when Ammon had said these words, the king began to rejoice because of his life.

26. And when he saw that Ammon had no desire to destroy him, and when he also saw the great love he had for his son Lamoni, he was astonished exceedingly, and said: Because this is all that thou hast desired, that I would ᵛrelease thy brethren, and suffer that my son Lamoni should retain his kingdom, behold, I will grant unto you that my son may retain his kingdom from this time and

---

o, see n, Jac. 7. p, see b. q, see w, Al. 17. r, see n. s, vers. 24, 26, 27. t, see s. u, ver. 26. Al. 21:21, 22. 22:1. v, ver. 27. Al. 22:2. ABOUT B. C. 90.

forever; and I will govern him "no more—

27. And I will also grant unto thee that thy brethren *may be cast out of prison, and thou and thy brethren may come unto me, in my kingdom; for I shall greatly desire to see thee. For the king was greatly astonished at the words which he had spoken, and also at the words which had been spoken by his son Lamoni, therefore he was desirous to learn them.

28. And it came to pass that Ammon and Lamoni proceeded on their journey towards the ᵛland of Middoni. And Lamoni found favor in the eyes of the king of the land; therefore the brethren of Ammon were ᶻbrought forth out of prison.

29. And when Ammon did meet them he was exceeding sorrowful, for behold they were naked, and their skins were worn exceedingly because of being bound with ²ᵃstrong cords. And they also had ²ᵇsuffered hunger, thirst, and all kinds of afflictions; nevertheless they were patient in all their sufferings.

30. And, as it happened, it was their lot to have fallen into the hands of a more hardened and a more stiffnecked people; therefore they would not hearken unto their words, and they had cast them out, and had smitten them, and had driven them from house to house, and from place to place, even until they had arrived in the ²ᶜland of Middoni; and there they were taken and cast into prison, and bound with ²ᵈstrong cords, and kept in prison for many days, and were delivered by Lamoni and Ammon.

An account of the preaching of Aaron, and Muloki, and their brethren, to the Lamanites.

Comprising chapters 21 to 26 inclusive.

CHAPTER 21.

Rejected by the Amalekites, Aaron and Muloki go to Middoni—They are imprisoned—Their release and missionary labors—Ammon's further success—Synagogues built.

1. Now when Ammon and his brethren ᵃseparated themselves in the borders of the land of the Lamanites, behold Aaron took his journey towards the land which was called by the Lamanites, ᵇJerusalem, calling it after the land of their fathers' nativity; and it was away joining the ᶜborders of Mormon.

2. Now the Lamanites and the Amalekites and the ᵈpeople of Amulon had built a great city, which was called ᵉJerusalem.

3. Now the Lamanites of themselves were sufficiently hardened, but the Amalekites and the ᶠAmulonites were still harder; therefore they did cause the Lamanites that they should harden their hearts, that they should wax strong in wickedness and their abominations.

4. And it came to pass that Aaron came to the city of ᵍJerusalem, and first began to preach to the Amalekites. And he began to preach to them in their ʰsynagogues, for they had built synagogues after the ⁱorder of the Nehors; for many of the Amalekites and the Amulonites were after the order of the Nehors.

5. Therefore, as Aaron entered into one of their ʲsynagogues to preach unto the people, and as he

---

w, Al. 21:21, 22. 22:1. x, ver. 26. y, see b. z, vers. 4, 7. 2a, ver. 30. 2b, Al. 21:14. 2c, see b. 2d, ver. 29. Chap. 21; a, Al. 17:13. b, vers. 2, 4. Al. 24:1. 3 Ne. 9:7. c, see b, Mos. 18. d, see u, Mos. 23. e, vers. 1, 4. f, see u, Mos. 23. g, vers. 1, 2. h, see u, Al. 16. i, Al. 1:2—15. j, see u, Al. 16. About B. C. 90.

was speaking unto them, behold there arose an Amalekite and began to contend with him, saying: What is that thou hast testified? Hast thou *k*seen an angel? Why do not angels appear unto us? Behold are not this people as good as thy people?

6. Thou also sayest, except we repent we shall perish. How knowest thou the thought and intent of our hearts? How knowest thou that we have cause to repent? How knowest thou that we are not a righteous people? Behold, we have built *l*sanctuaries, and we do assemble ourselves together to worship God. We do believe that God will save *m*all men.

7. Now Aaron said unto him: Believest thou that the Son of God shall come to redeem mankind from their sins?

8. And the man said unto him: We do not believe that thou knowest any such thing. We do not believe in these foolish traditions. We do not believe that thou knowest of things to come, neither do we believe that thy fathers and also that our fathers did know concerning the things which they spake, of that which is to come.

9. Now Aaron began to open the scriptures unto them concerning the coming of Christ, and also concerning the *n*resurrection of the dead, and that there could be no redemption for mankind save it were through the death and sufferings of Christ, and the *o*atonement of his blood.

10. And it came to pass as he began to expound these things unto them they were angry with him, and began to mock him; and they would not hear the words which he spake.

11. Therefore, when he saw that they would not hear his words, he departed out of their *p*synagogue, and came over to a village which was called Ani-Anti, and there he *q*found Muloki preaching the word unto them; and also Ammah and his brethren. And they contended with many about the word.

12. And it came to pass that they saw that the people would harden their hearts, therefore they departed and came over into the *r*land of Middoni. And they did preach the word unto many, and few believed on the words which they taught.

13. Nevertheless, Aaron and a certain number of his brethren *s*were taken and cast into prison, and the remainder of them fled out of the land of Middoni unto the regions round about.

14. And those who were cast into prison suffered many things, and they were delivered by the hand of Lamoni and Ammon, and they were fed and clothed.

15. And they went forth again to declare the word, and thus they were delivered for the first time out of prison; and thus they had suffered.

16. And they went forth whithersoever they were led by the Spirit of the Lord, preaching the word of God in every *t*synagogue of the Amalekites, or in every assembly of the Lamanites where they could be admitted.

17. And it came to pass that the Lord began to bless them, insomuch that they brought many to the knowledge of the truth; yea, they did convince many of

---

k, Mos. 27:10—16, 34. *l*, see *t*, Al. 15. *m*, Al. 1:4. 15:15. *n*, see *d*, 2 Ne. 2. *o*, see *f*, 2 Ne. 2. *p*, see *u*, Al. 16. *q*, vers. 13, 14. Al. 20:2, 3, 28—30. *r*, see *b*, Al. 20. *s*, vers. 14, 15. Al. 20:26—30. *t*, see *u*, Al. 16. BETWEEN B. C. 90 AND 77.

ALMA, 22.

their sins, and of the traditions of their fathers, which were ᵘnot correct.

18. And it came to pass that Ammon and Lamoni returned from the ᵛland of Middoni to the ʷland of Ishmael, which was the land of their inheritance.

19. And king Lamoni would ˣnot suffer that Ammon should serve him, or be his servant.

20. But he caused that there should be ʸsynagogues built in the land of Ishmael; and he caused that his people, or the people who were under his reign, should assemble themselves together.

21. And he did rejoice over them, and he did teach them many things. And he did also declare unto them that they were a people who were under him, and that they were a free people, that they were ᶻfree from the oppressions of the king, his father; for that his father had granted unto him that he might reign over the people who were in the land of Ishmael, and in all the land round about.

22. And he also declared unto them that they might have the liberty of worshiping the Lord their God according to their desires, in whatsoever place they were in, if it were in the land which was under the reign of king Lamoni.

23. And Ammon did preach unto the people of king Lamoni; and it came to pass that he did teach them all things concerning things pertaining to righteousness. And he did exhort them daily, with all diligence; and they gave heed unto his word, and they were zealous for keeping the commandments of God.

CHAPTER 22.

Aaron in the land of Nephi—The king and all his household converted—Country divided between Nephites and Lamanites.

1. Now, as Ammon was thus teaching the people of Lamoni continually, we will return to the account of Aaron and his brethren; for after he departed from the ᵃland of Middoni he was led by the Spirit to the ᵇland of Nephi, even to the house of the king which was ᶜover all the land save it were the ᵈland of Ishmael; and he was the ᵉfather of Lamoni.

2. And it came to pass that he went in unto him into the king's palace, with his brethren, and bowed himself before the king, and said unto him: Behold, O king, we are the brethren of Ammon, whom thou hast ᶠdelivered out of prison.

3. And now, O king, if thou wilt spare our lives, we will be thy servants. And the king said unto them: Arise, for I will grant unto you your lives, and I will not suffer that ye shall be my servants; but I will insist that ye shall administer unto me; for I have been somewhat troubled in mind because of the ᵍgenerosity and the greatness of the words of thy brother Ammon; and I desire to know the cause why he has not come up out of ʰMiddoni with thee.

4. And Aaron said unto the king: Behold, the Spirit of the Lord has called him another way; he has gone to the ⁱland of Ishmael, to teach the people of Lamoni.

5. Now the king said unto them: What is this that ye have said concerning the ʲSpirit of the

---
u, see *n*, Jac. 7. *v*, see *b*, Al. 20. *w*, see *w*, Al. 17. *x*, Al. 17:25. *y*, see *u*, Al. 16. *z*, Al. 20:24, 26. 22:1. CHAP. 22: *a*, see *b*, Al. 20. *b*, see *b*, 2 Ne. 5. *c*, Al. 20:8. *d*, see *w*, Al. 17. *e*, Al. 20:8, 9. *f*, Al. 20:26, 27. *g*, Al. 20:26. *h*, see *b*, Al. 20. *i*, see *w*, Al. 17. *j*, ver. 4. BETWEEN B. C. 90 AND 77.

Lord? Behold, this is the thing which doth trouble me.

6. And also, what is this that Ammon said—*If ye will repent ye shall be saved, and if ye will not repent, ye shall be cast off at the last day?

7. And Aaron answered him and said unto him: Believest thou that there is a God? And the king said: I know that the Amalekites say that there is a God, and I have granted unto them that they should build *sanctuaries, that they may assemble themselves together to worship him. And if now thou sayest there is a God, behold I will believe.

8. And now when Aaron heard this, his heart began to rejoice, and he said: Behold, assuredly as thou livest, O king, there is a God.

9. And the king said: Is God that *Great Spirit that brought our fathers out of the land of Jerusalem?

10. And Aaron said unto him: Yea, he is that Great Spirit, and he created all things both in heaven and in earth. Believest thou this?

11. And he said: Yea, I believe that the Great Spirit created all things, and I desire that ye should tell me concerning all these things, and I will believe thy words.

12. And it came to pass that when Aaron saw that the king would believe his words, he began from the *creation of Adam, *reading the scriptures unto the king—how God created man after his own image, and that God gave him commandments, and that because of transgression, man had fallen.

13. And Aaron did expound unto him the scriptures from the creation of Adam, laying the fall of man before him, and their carnal state and also the plan of redemption, which was prepared from the *foundation of the world, through Christ, for all whosoever would believe on his name.

14. And since man had fallen he could not merit anything of himself; but the sufferings and death of Christ *atone for their sins, through faith and repentance, and so forth; and that he *breaketh the bands of death, that the grave shall have *no victory, and that the *sting of death should be swallowed up in the hopes of glory; and Aaron did expound all these things unto the king.

15. And it came to pass that after Aaron had expounded these things unto him, the king said: What shall I do that I may have this eternal life of which thou hast spoken? Yea, what shall I do that I may be *born of God, having this *wicked spirit rooted out of my breast, and receive his Spirit, that I may be filled with joy, that I may not be cast off at the last day? Behold, said he, I will give up all that I possess, yea, I will forsake my kingdom, that I may receive this great joy.

16. But Aaron said unto him: If thou desirest this thing, if thou wilt *bow down before God, yea, if thou wilt repent of all thy sins, and will bow down before God, and *call on his name in faith, believing that ye shall receive, then shalt thou receive the hope which thou desirest.

17. And it came to pass that when Aaron had said these words, the king did bow down before the Lord, upon his knees; yea, even

---

k, Al. 20:17, 18. *l*, see *t*, Al. 15. *m*, see *b*, Al. 18. *n*, ver. 13. See *m*, Mos. 2. *o*, see *a*, 1 Ne. 3. Al. 63:12. *p*, see *d*, Mos. 4. *q*, see *f*, 2 Ne. 2. *r*, see *g* and *j*, 2 Ne. 9. *s*, see *h*, Mos. 16. *t*, see *i*, Mos. 16. *u*, see *c*, Mos. 5. *v*, see *q*, Mos. 2. *w*, vers. 17, 18. *x*, see *e*, 2 Ne. 32.
BETWEEN B. C. 90 AND 77.

he did ʸprostrate himself upon the earth, and ᶻcried mightily, saying:

18. O God, Aaron hath told me that there is a God; and if there is a God, and if thou art God, wilt thou make thyself known unto me, and I will give away all my sins to know thee, and that I may be raised from the dead, and be saved at the last day. And now when the king had said these words, he was struck ²ᵃas if he were dead.

19. And it came to pass that his servants ran and told the queen all that had happened unto the king. And she came in unto the king; and when she saw him lay as if he were dead, and also Aaron and his brethren standing as ²ᵇthough they had been the cause of his fall, she was angry with them, and commanded that her servants, or the servants of the king, should take them and slay them.

20. Now the servants had seen the cause of the king's fall, therefore they durst not lay their hands on Aaron and his brethren; and they plead with the queen saying: Why commandest thou that we should slay these men, when behold one of them is mightier than us all? Therefore we shall fall before them.

21. Now when the queen saw the fear of the servants she also began to fear exceedingly, lest there should some evil come upon her. And she commanded her servants that they should go and ²ᶜcall the people, that they might slay Aaron and his brethren.

22. Now when Aaron saw the determination of the queen, he, also knowing the hardness of the hearts of the people, feared lest that a multitude should assemble themselves together, and there should be a great contention and a disturbance among them; therefore he put forth his hand and raised the king from the earth, and said unto him: Stand. And he stood upon his feet, receiving his strength.

23. Now this was done in the presence of the queen and many of the servants. And when they saw it they greatly marveled, and began to fear. And the king stood forth, and began to minister unto them. And he did minister unto them, insomuch that his ²ᵈwhole household were converted unto the Lord.

24. Now there was a ²ᵉmultitude gathered together because of the commandment of the queen, and there began to be great murmurings among them because of Aaron and his brethren.

25. But the king stood forth among them and administered unto them. And they were pacified towards Aaron and those who were with him.

26. And it came to pass that when the king saw that the people were pacified, he caused that Aaron and his brethren should stand forth in the midst of the multitude, and that they should preach the word unto them.

27. And it came to pass that the king sent a ²ᶠproclamation throughout all the land, amongst all his people who were in all his land, who were in all the regions round about, which was bordering even to the sea, on the east and on the west, and which was divided from the ²ᵍland of Zarahemla by a narrow strip of wilderness, which ran from the sea east even to the sea west, and

---

y, ver. 16. *z*, see *c*, 2 Ne. 32. 2*a*, ver. 19. 2*b*, ver. 18. 2*c*, ver. 24. 2*d*, Al. 23:3. 2*e*, ver. 21. 2*f*, Al. 23:1—4. 2*g*, Om. 13. BETWEEN B. C. 90 AND 77.

round about on the borders of the seashore, and the borders of the wilderness which was on the north by the land of Zarahemla, through the ^{2h}borders of Manti, by the head of the ^{2i}river Sidon, running from the east towards the west—and thus were the Lamanites and the Nephites divided.

28. Now, the more idle part of the Lamanites lived in the wilderness, and dwelt in tents; and they were spread through the wilderness on the west, in the ^{2j}land of Nephi; yea, and also on the west of the land of Zarahemla, in the borders by the seashore, and on the west in the land of Nephi, in the place of their fathers' first inheritance, and thus bordering along by the seashore.

29. And also there were many Lamanites on the east by the seashore, whither the Nephites had driven them. And thus the Nephites were nearly surrounded by the Lamanites; nevertheless the Nephites had taken possession of all the northern parts of the land bordering on the wilderness, at the head of the river Sidon, from the east to the west, round about on the wilderness side; on the north, even until they came to the land which they called ^{2k}Bountiful.

30. And it bordered upon the land which they called ^{2l}Desolation, it being so far northward that it came into the land which had ^{2m}been peopled and been destroyed, of whose ^{2n}bones we have spoken, which was discovered by the ^{2o}people of Zarahemla, it being the place of their ^{2p}first landing.

31. And they came from there ^{2q}up into the south wilderness. Thus the land on the northward was called ^{2r}Desolation, and the land on the southward was called ^{2s}Bountiful, it being the wilderness which is filled with all manner of wild animals of every kind, a part of which had ^{2t}come from the land northward for food.

32. And now, it was only the ^{2u}distance of a day and a half's journey for a Nephite, on the line Bountiful and the land Desolation, from the east to the west sea; and thus the land of Nephi and the land of Zarahemla were nearly surrounded by water, there being a small ^{2v}neck of land between the land northward and the land southward.

33. And it came to pass that the Nephites had inhabited the land Bountiful, even from the east unto the west sea, and thus the Nephites in their wisdom, with their guards and their armies, had hemmed in the Lamanites on the south, that thereby they should have no more possession on the north, that they might not overrun the land northward.

34. Therefore the Lamanites could have no more possessions only in the land of Nephi, and the wilderness round about. Now this was wisdom in the Nephites —as the Lamanites were an enemy to them, they would not suffer their afflictions on every hand, and also that they might have a country whither they might flee, according to their desires.

$2h$, see h, Al. 16. $2i$, see g, Al. 2. $2j$, see b, 2 Ne. 5. $2k$, vers. 31—33. Al. 50:32. 51:28, 30, 32. 52:9, 15, 17, 18, 27, 39. 53:3, 4. 55:26. 63:5. He. 1:23, 28, 29. 4:5, 6. 5:14. 3 Ne. 3:23. 11:1. $2l$, vers. 31, 32. Al. 46:17. 50:34. 63:5. 3 Ne. 3:23. Morm. 3:5, 7. 4:1—3, 8, 13, 19. $2m$, Book of Ether. $2n$, Mos. 8:7—12. 21:25—28. 28:11—19. Book of Ether. $2o$, Om. 20—22. $2p$, vers. 31, 32. Om. 14—22. He. 6:10. 8:21, 22. $2q$, He. 6:10. $2r$, see $2l$, also He. 3:5, 6. $2s$, see $2k$. $2t$, see m, 1 Ne. 18. $2u$, He. 4:7. $2v$, Al. 50:34. 52:9. 63:5. He. 4:7. Morm. 2:29. 3:5.

BETWEEN B. C. 90 AND 77.

35. And now I, after having said this, return again to the account of Ammon and Aaron, Omner and Himni, and their brethren.

CHAPTER 23.

Religious freedom is proclaimed— Many Lamanites converted—Amalekites and Amulonites reject the truth— The Anti-Nephi-Lehies.

1. Behold, now it came to pass that the king of the Lamanites sent a *a*proclamation among all his people, that they should not lay their hands on Ammon, or Aaron, or Omner, or Himni, nor either of their brethren who should go forth preaching the word of God, in whatsoever place they should be, in any part of their land.

2. Yea, he sent a decree among them, that they should not lay their hands on them to bind them, or to cast them into prison; neither should they spit upon them, nor smite them, nor cast them out of their *b*synagogues, nor scourge them; neither should they cast stones at them, but that they should have free access to their houses, and also their *c*temples, and their *d*sanctuaries.

3. And thus they might go forth and preach the word according to their desires, for the king had been converted unto the Lord, and *e*all his household; therefore he sent his *f*proclamation throughout the land unto his people, that the word of God might have no obstruction, but that it might go forth throughout all the land, that his people might be convinced concerning the *g*wicked traditions of their fathers, and that they might be convinced that they were all brethren, and that they ought not to murder, nor to plunder, nor to steal, nor to commit adultery, nor to commit any manner of wickedness.

4. And now it came to pass that when the king had sent forth this *h*proclamation, that Aaron and his brethren went forth from city to city, and from *i*one house of worship to another, establishing churches, and consecrating *j*priests and teachers throughout the land among the Lamanites, to preach and to teach the word of God among them; and thus they began to have great success.

5. And thousands were brought to the knowledge of the Lord, yea, thousands were brought to believe in the traditions of the Nephites; and they were taught the *k*records and prophecies which were handed down even to the present time.

6. And as sure as the Lord liveth, so sure as many as believed, or as many as were brought to the knowledge of the truth, through the preaching of Ammon and his brethren, according to the spirit of revelation and of prophecy, and the power of God working miracles in them— yea, I say unto you, as the Lord liveth, as many of the Lamanites as believed in their preaching, and were converted unto the Lord, *l*never did fall away.

7. For they became a righteous people; they did lay down the weapons of their rebellion, that they did not fight against God any more, neither against any of their brethren.

8. Now, these are they who were converted unto the Lord:

9. The people of the Laman-

---

a, vers. 2—4. Al. 22:27. *b*, see *u*, Al. 16. *c*, see *h*, 2 Ne. 5. *d*, see *t*, Al. 15. *e*, Al. 22:23. *f*, see *a*. *g*, see *n*, Jac. 7. *h*, see *a*. *i*, see *u*, Al. 16. See *h*, 2 Ne. 5. See *t*, Al. 15. *j*, see *c*, Mos. 6. *k*, see *a*, 1 Ne. 3. Al. 63:12. *l*, Al. 27:27. He. 15:6—10.

BETWEEN B. C. 90 AND 77.

ites who were in the ᵐland of Ishmael;

10. And also of the people of the Lamanites who were in the ⁿland of Middoni;

11. And also of the people of the Lamanites who were in the ᵒcity of Nephi;

12. And also of the people of the Lamanites who were in the ᵖland of Shilom, and who were in the land of ᵍShemlon, and in the city of Lemuel, and in the city of Shimnilom.

13. And these are the names of the cities of the Lamanites which were converted unto the Lord; and these are they that laid down the weapons of their rebellion, yea, all their weapons of war; and they were all Lamanites.

14. And the Amalekites were not converted, save only one; neither were any of the ʳAmulonites; but they did harden their hearts, and also the hearts of the Lamanites in that part of the land wheresoever they dwelt, yea, and all their villages and all their cities.

15. Therefore, we have named all the cities of the Lamanites in which they did repent and come to the knowledge of the truth, and were converted.

16. And now it came to pass that the king and those who were converted were desirous that they might have a name, that thereby they might be distinguished from their brethren; therefore the king consulted with Aaron and many of their ˢpriests, concerning the name that they should take upon them, that they might be distinguished.

17. And it came to pass that they called their names ᵗAnti-Nephi-Lehies; and they were called by this name and were no more called Lamanites.

18. And they began to be a very industrious people; yea, and they were friendly with the Nephites; therefore, they did open a correspondence with them, and the ᵘcurse of God did no more follow them.

CHAPTER 24.

Lamanites come against the people of God—Converted Lamanites refuse to take up arms—More conversions.

1. And it came to pass that the Amalekites and the ᵃAmulonites and the Lamanites who were in the land of Amulon, and also in the ᵇland of Helam, and who were in the ᶜland of Jerusalem, and in fine, in all the land round about, who had not been converted and had not taken upon them the name of ᵈAnti-Nephi-Lehi, were stirred up by the Amalekites and by the Amulonites to anger against their brethren.

2. And their hatred became exceeding sore against them, even insomuch that they began to rebel against their king, insomuch that they would not that he should be their king; therefore, they took up arms against the people of Anti-Nephi-Lehi.

3. Now the king conferred the kingdom upon his son, and he called his name Anti-Nephi-Lehi.

4. And the king died in that selfsame year that the Lamanites began to make preparations for war against the people of God.

5. Now when Ammon and his brethren and all those who had come up with him saw the preparations of the Lamanites to de-

---

m, see *w*, Al. 17. *n*, see *b*, Al. 20. *o*, see *b*, 2 Ne. 5. *p*, see *f*, Mos. 7. *q*, see *d*, Mos. 10. *r*, see *u*, Mos. 23. *s*, see *c*, Mos. 6. *t*, Al. 24:1—3, 5, 20. 25:1, 13. 27:2, 21, 25. 43:11. *u*, see *d*, 1 Ne. 2. 2 Ne. 30:6. 3 Ne. 2:14—16.
CHAP. 24: *a*, see *u*, Mos. 23. *b*, see *o*, Mos. 23. *c*, see *b*, Al. 21. *d*, see *t*, Al. 23.
BETWEEN B. C. 90 AND 77.

stroy their brethren, they came forth to the land of Midian, and there Ammon met all his brethren; and from thence they came to the *land of Ishmael that they might hold a council with Lamoni and also with his brother *Anti - Nephi - Lehi, what they should do to defend themselves against the Lamanites.

6. Now there was not one soul among all the people who had been converted unto the Lord that would take up arms against their brethren; nay, they would not even make any preparations for war; yea, and also their king commanded them that they should not.

7. Now, these are the words which he said unto the people concerning the matter: I thank my God, my beloved people, that our great God has in goodness sent these our brethren, the Nephites, unto us to preach unto us, and to convince us of the *traditions of our wicked fathers.

8. And behold, I thank my great God that he has given us a portion of his Spirit to soften our hearts, that we have *opened a correspondence with these brethren, the Nephites.

9. And behold, I also thank my God, that by opening this correspondence we have been convinced of our sins, and of the many murders which we have committed.

10. And I also thank my God, yea, my great God, that he hath granted unto us that we might repent of these things, and also that he hath forgiven us of those our many sins and murders which we have committed, and taken away the guilt from our hearts, through the merits of his Son.

11. And now behold, my brethren, since it has been all that we could do, (as we were the most lost of all mankind) to repent of all our sins and the many murders which we have committed, and to get God to take them away from our hearts, for it was all we could do to repent sufficiently before God that he would take away our stain—

12. Now, my best beloved brethren, since God hath taken away our stains, and our swords have become bright, then let us stain our swords *no more with the blood of our brethren.

13. Behold, I say unto you, Nay, let us retain our swords that they be not stained with the blood of our brethren; for perhaps, if we should stain our swords again they can no more be washed bright through the blood of the Son of our great God, which shall be shed for the *atonement of our sins.

14. And the great God has had mercy on us, and made these things known unto us that we might not perish; yea, and he has made these things known unto us beforehand, because he loveth our souls as well as he loveth our children; therefore, in his mercy he doth visit us by his angels, that the plan of salvation might be made known unto us as well as unto future generations.

15. Oh, how merciful is our God! And now behold, since it has been as much as we could do to get our *stains taken away from us, and our swords are made bright, let us *hide them away that they may be kept bright, as a testimony to our God at the last day, or at the day that we shall be brought to stand before him to be judged, that we

e, see *w*, Al. 17. *f*, see *t*, Al. 23. *g*, see *n*, Jac. 7. *h*, Al. 23:18. *i*, vers. 6, 13, 15—19. *j*, see *f*, 2 Ne. 2. *k*, see *i*. *l*, vers. 17—19. Al. 25:14. 26:32. 53:10, 11. 56:6—8.
BETWEEN B. C. 90 AND 77.

have not stained our swords in the blood of our brethren since he imparted his word unto us and has made us clean thereby.

16. And now, my brethren, if our brethren seek to destroy us, behold, we will hide away our swords, yea, even we will bury them ᵐdeep in the earth, that they may be kept bright, as a testimony that we have never used them, at the last day; and if our brethren destroy us, behold, we shall go to our God and shall be saved.

17. And now it came to pass that when the king had made an end of these sayings, and all the people were assembled together, they took their swords, and all the weapons which were used for the shedding of man's blood, and they did bury them up deep in the earth.

18. And this they did, it being in their view a testimony to God, and also to men, that they never would use weapons again for the shedding of man's blood; and this they did, vouching and covenanting with God, that rather than shed the blood of their brethren they would ⁿgive up their own lives; and rather than take away from a brother they would give unto him; and rather than spend their days in idleness they would labor abundantly with their hands.

19. And thus we see that, when these Lamanites were brought to believe and to know the truth, they were firm, and would °suffer even unto death rather than commit sin; and thus we see that they buried their weapons of peace, or they buried the weapons of war, for peace.

20. And it came to pass that their brethren, the Lamanites, made preparations for war, and came up to the land of Nephi for the purpose of destroying the king, and to place another in his stead, and also of destroying the people of ᵖAnti-Nephi-Lehi out of the land.

21. Now when the people saw that they were coming against them they went out to meet them, and prostrated themselves before them to the earth, and began to call on the name of the Lord; and thus they were in this attitude when the Lamanites began to fall upon them, and began to slay them with the sword.

22. And thus without meeting any resistance, they did slay a thousand and five of them; and we know that they are blessed, for they have gone to dwell with their God.

23. Now when the Lamanites saw that their brethren would not flee from the sword, neither would they turn aside to the right hand or to the left, but that they would lie down and perish, and praised God even in the very act of perishing under the sword—

24. Now when the Lamanites saw this they did forbear from slaying them; and there were many whose hearts had swollen in them for those of their brethren who had fallen under the sword, for they repented of the things which they had done.

25. And it came to pass that they threw down their weapons of war, and they would not take them again, for they were stung for the murders which they had committed; and they came down even as their brethren, relying upon the mercies of those whose arms were lifted to slay them.

---

m, see *l*.   *n*, vers. 16, 21—27.   *o*, see *n*.   *p*, see *t*, Al. 23.

BETWEEN B. C. 90 AND 77.

26. And it came to pass that the people of God were joined that day by more than the number who had been slain; and those who had been slain were righteous people, therefore we have no reason to doubt but what they were saved.

27. And there was not a wicked man slain among them; but there were more than a thousand brought to the knowledge of the truth; thus we see that the Lord worketh in many ways to the salvation of his people.

28. Now the greatest number of those of the Lamanites who slew so many of their brethren were Amalekites and Amulonites, the greatest number of whom were after the ^qorder of the Nehors.

29. Now, among those who joined the people of the Lord, there were none who were Amalekites or ^rAmulonites, or who were of the *order of Nehor, but they were actual descendants of Laman and Lemuel.

30. And thus we can plainly discern, that after a people have been once enlightened by the Spirit of God, and have had great knowledge of things pertaining to righteousness, and then have fallen away into sin and transgression, they become more hardened, and thus their state becomes ^sworse than though they had never known these things.

CHAPTER 25.

Lamanite aggressions—Vengeance by Amulonites — Martyrdoms — Further fulfilment of Abinadi's prophecy.

1. And behold, now it came to pass that those Lamanites were more angry because they had slain their brethren; therefore they swore vengeance upon the Nephites; and they did no more attempt to slay the people of ^aAnti-Nephi-Lehi at that time.

2. But they took their armies and went over into the borders of the land of Zarahemla, and fell upon the people who were in the ^bland of Ammonihah and ^cdestroyed them.

3. And after that, they had many battles with the Nephites, in the which they were driven and slain.

4. And among the Lamanites who were slain were almost all the ^dseed of Amulon and his brethren, who were the priests of Noah, and they were slain by the hands of the Nephites;

5. And the remainder, having fled into the east wilderness, and having usurped the power and authority over the Lamanites, caused that many of the Lamanites should ^eperish by fire because of their belief—

6. For many of them, after having suffered much loss and so many afflictions, began to be stirred up in remembrance of the ^fwords which Aaron and his brethren had preached to them in their land; therefore they began to disbelieve the ^gtraditions of their fathers, and to believe in the Lord, and that he gave great power unto the Nephites; and thus there were many of them converted in the wilderness.

7. And it came to pass that those rulers who were the remnant of the ^hchildren of Amulon caused that they should be ⁱput to death, yea, all those that believed in these things.

8. Now this martyrdom caused

---

q, Al. 1:2—15.   *r*, see *u*, Mos. 23.   *s*, Al. 1:2—15.   *t*, vers. 1, 28, 29.   See *h*, 2 Ne. 31. Al. 21:3—11. 23:14. 32:19. 47:36.   CHAP. 25: *a*, see *t*, Al. 23. *b*, see *i*, Al. 8. *c*, Al. 16:2, 3, 9—11. *d*, see *u*, Mos. 23. *e*, see *f*, Mos. 17. *f*, Al. 21:5—12. *g*, see *n*, Jac. 7. *h*, see *u*, Mos. 23. *i*, see *f*, Mos. 17.   BETWEEN B. C. 90 AND 77.

that many of their brethren should be stirred up to anger; and there began to be contention in the wilderness; and the Lamanites began to hunt the *j*seed of Amulon and his brethren and began to slay them; and they fled into the east wilderness.

9. And behold they are hunted at this day by the Lamanites. Thus the words of Abinadi *k*were brought to pass, which he said concerning the seed of the priests who caused that he should suffer death by fire.

10. For he said unto them: *l*What ye shall do unto me shall be a type of things to come.

11. And now Abinadi was the first that suffered *m*death by fire because of his belief in God; now this is what he meant, that many should suffer death by fire, *n*according as he had suffered.

12. And he said unto the priests of Noah that their seed should cause many to be put to death, in the like manner as he was, and that they should be scattered abroad and slain, even as a sheep having no shepherd is driven and slain by wild beasts; and now behold, these words were verified, for they were driven by the Lamanites, and they were *o*hunted, and they were smitten.

13. And it came to pass that when the Lamanites saw that they could not overpower the Nephites they returned again to their own land; and many of them came over to dwell in the *p*land of Ishmael and the *q*land of Nephi, and did join themselves to the people of God, who were the people of *r*Anti-Nephi-Lehi.

14. And they did also *s*bury their weapons of war, according as their brethren had, and they began to be a righteous people; and they did walk in the ways of the Lord, and did observe to keep his commandments and his statutes.

15. Yea, and they did keep the *t*law of Moses; for it was expedient that they should keep the law of Moses as yet, for it was not all fulfilled. But notwithstanding the law of Moses, they did look forward to the coming of Christ, considering that the law of Moses was a type of his coming, and believing that they must keep those outward performances until the time that he should be revealed unto them.

16. Now they did not suppose that salvation came by the law of Moses; but the law of Moses did serve to strengthen their faith in Christ; and thus they did retain a hope through faith, unto eternal salvation, relying upon the spirit of prophecy, which spake of those things to come.

17. And now behold, Ammon, and Aaron, and Omner, and Himni, and their brethren did rejoice exceedingly, for the success which they had had among the Lamanites, seeing that the Lord had granted unto them according to their *u*prayers, and that he had also verified his word unto them in every particular.

CHAPTER 26.

Ammon glories in the Lord—Boasting in righteousness—He recounts blessings to him and his brethren.

1. And now, these are the words of Ammon to his brethren, which say thus: My brothers and my brethren, behold I say unto

---

j, see *u*, Mos. 23. *k*, Mos. 17:15—20. *l*, Mos. 13:10. *m*, Mos. 17:13—20. *n*, vers. 5—7. *o*, vers. 8, 9. Mos. 17:18. *p*, see *w*, Al. 17. *q*, see *b*, 2 Ne. 5. *r*, see *t*, Al. 23. *s*, see *l*, Al. 24. *t*, see *o*, 2 Ne. 25. *u*, see *c*, 2 Ne. 32.

BETWEEN B. C. 90 AND 77

ALMA, 26.

you, how great reason have we to rejoice; for could we have supposed when we ᵃstarted from the ᵇland of Zarahemla that God would have granted unto us such great blessings?

2. And now, I ask, what great blessings has he bestowed upon us? Can ye tell?

3. Behold, I answer for you; for our brethren, the Lamanites, were in darkness, yea, even in the darkest abyss, but behold, how ᶜmany of them are brought to behold the marvelous light of God! And this is the blessing which hath been bestowed upon us, that we have been made instruments in the hands of God to bring about this great work.

4. Behold, ᵈthousands of them do rejoice, and have been brought into the fold of God.

5. Behold, the field was ripe, and blessed are ye, for ye did thrust in the sickle, and did reap with your might, yea, all the day long did ye labor; and behold the number of your sheaves! And they shall be gathered into the garners, that they are not wasted.

6. Yea, they shall not be beaten down by the ᵉstorm at the last day; yea, neither shall they be harrowed up by the whirlwinds; but when the storm cometh they shall be gathered together in their place, that the storm cannot penetrate to them; yea, neither shall they be driven with fierce winds whithersoever the enemy listeth ᶠto carry them.

7. But behold, they are in the hands of the Lord of the harvest, and they are his; and he will ᵍraise them up at the last day.

8. Blessed be the name of our God; let us sing to his praise, yea, let us give thanks to his holy name, for he doth work righteousness forever.

9. For if we had not come up out of the ʰland of Zarahemla, these our dearly beloved brethren, who have so dearly beloved us, would still have been ⁱracked with hatred against us, yea, and they would also have been strangers to God.

10. And it came to pass that when Ammon had said these words, his brother Aaron rebuked him, saying: Ammon, I fear that thy joy doth carry thee away unto boasting.

11. But Ammon said unto him: I do not boast in my own strength, nor in my own wisdom; but behold, my joy is full, yea, my heart is brim with joy, and I will rejoice in my God.

12. Yea, I know that I am nothing; as to my strength I am weak; therefore I will not boast of myself, but I will boast of my God, for in his strength I can do all things; yea, behold, many mighty miracles we have wrought in this land, for which we will praise his name forever.

13. Behold, how many thousands of our brethren has he loosed from the ʲpains of hell; and they are brought to sing redeeming love, and this because of the power of his word which is in us, therefore have we not great reason to rejoice?

14. Yea, we have reason to praise him forever, for he is the Most High God, and has loosed our brethren from the ᵏchains of hell.

15. Yea, they were encircled about with everlasting darkness

---

a, Mos. 28:9. Al. 17:6—9. *b*, Om. 13. *c*, Al. 23:8—13. *d*, Al. 23:5. *e*, He. 5:12. 3 Ne. 14:25, 27. *f*, see *i*, 2 Ne. 9. *g*, see *p*, Mos. 23. *h*, Om. 13. *i*, see *n*, Jac. 7. *j*, see *p*, 2 Ne. 28. *k*, see *p*, 2 Ne. 28. BETWEEN B. C. 90 AND 77.

and destruction; but behold, he has brought them into his everlasting light, yea, into everlasting salvation; and they are encircled about with the matchless bounty of his love; yea, and we have been instruments in his hands of doing this great and marvelous work.

16. Therefore, let us glory, yea, we will glory in the Lord; yea, we will rejoice, for our joy is full; yea, we will praise our God forever. Behold, who can glory too much in the Lord? Yea, who can say too much of his great power, and of his mercy, and of his long-suffering towards the children of men? Behold, I say unto you, I cannot say the smallest part which I feel.

17. Who could have supposed that our God would have been so merciful as to have snatched us from our awful, sinful, and polluted state?

18. Behold, we went forth even in wrath, with mighty threatenings to *l*destroy his church.

19. Oh then, why did he not consign us to an awful destruction, yea, why did he not let the sword of his justice fall upon us, and doom us to *m*eternal despair?

20. Oh, my soul, almost as it were, fleeth at the thought. Behold, he did not exercise his justice upon us, but in his great mercy hath brought us over that everlasting *n*gulf of death and misery, even to the salvation of our souls.

21. And now behold, my brethren, what natural man is there that knoweth these things? I say unto you, there is none that knoweth these things, save it be the penitent.

22. Yea, he that repenteth and exerciseth faith, and bringeth forth good works, and *o*prayeth continually without ceasing— unto such it is given to know the *z*mysteries of God; yea, unto such it shall be given to reveal things which never have been revealed; yea, and it shall be given unto such to bring thousands of souls to repentance, even as it has been given unto us to bring these our brethren to repentance.

23. Now do ye remember, my brethren, that we said unto our brethren in the land of Zarahemla, we go up to the land of Nephi, to preach unto our brethren, the Lamanites, and they laughed us to scorn?

24. For they said unto us: Do ye suppose that ye can bring the Lamanites to the knowledge of the truth? Do ye suppose that ye can convince the Lamanites of the *p*incorrectness of the traditions of their fathers, as stiffnecked a people as they are; whose hearts delight in the shedding of blood; whose days have been spent in the grossest iniquity; whose ways have been the ways of a transgressor from the beginning? Now my brethren, ye remember that this was their language.

25. And moreover they did say: Let us take up arms against them, that we destroy them and their iniquity out of the land, lest they overrun us and destroy us.

26. But behold, my beloved brethren, we came into the wilderness not with the intent to destroy our brethren, but with the intent that perhaps we might save some few of their souls.

27. Now when our hearts were *q*depressed, and we were about to turn back, behold, the Lord comforted us, and said: Go amongst

---

l, Mos. 27:10, 34. *m*, see *m*, Jac. 6. *n*, see *i*, 1 Ne. 15. *o*, see *e*, 2 Ne. 32. *z*, Al. 12:9. *p*, see *n*, Jac. 7. *q*, Al. 17:9—12. BETWEEN B. C. 90 AND 77.

thy brethren, the Lamanites, and bear with *patience thine afflictions, and I will give unto you success.

28. And now behold, we have come, and been forth amongst them; and we have been *patient in our sufferings, and we have suffered every privation; yea, we have traveled from house to house, relying upon the mercies of the world—not upon the mercies of the world alone but upon the mercies of God.

29. And we have entered into their houses and taught them, and we have taught them in their streets; yea, and we have taught them upon their hills; and we have also entered into their *temples and their *synagogues and taught them; and we have been *cast out, and mocked, and spit upon, and smote upon our cheeks; and we have been stoned, and taken and bound with *strong cords, and cast into prison; and through the power and wisdom of God we have been delivered again.

30. And we have suffered all manner of afflictions, and all this, that perhaps we might be the means of saving some soul; and we supposed that our joy would be full if perhaps we could be the means of *saving some.

31. Now behold, we can look forth and see the fruits of our labors; and are they few? I say unto you, Nay, they are *many; yea, and we can witness of their sincerity, because of their love towards their brethren and also towards us.

32. For behold, they had rather *sacrifice their lives than even to take the life of their enemy; and they have *buried their weapons of war deep in the earth, because of their love towards their brethren.

33. And now behold I say unto you, has there been so great love in all the land? Behold, I say unto you, Nay, there has not, even among the Nephites.

34. For behold, they would take up arms against their brethren; they would not suffer themselves to be slain. But behold how *many of these have laid down their lives; and we know that they have gone to their God, because of their love and of their hatred to sin.

35. Now have we not reason to rejoice? Yea, I say unto you, there never were men that had so great reason to rejoice as we, since the world began; yea, and my joy is carried away, even unto boasting in my God; for he has all power, all wisdom, and all understanding; he comprehendeth *all things, and he is a merciful Being, even unto salvation, to those who will repent and believe on his name.

36. Now if this is boasting, even so will I boast; for this is my life and my light, my joy and my salvation, and my redemption from everlasting wo. Yea, blessed is the name of my God, who has been mindful of this people, who are a *branch of the tree of Israel, and has been *lost from its body in a strange land; yea, I say, blessed be the name of my God, who has been mindful of us, *wanderers in a strange land.

37. Now my brethren, we see that God is mindful of every people, whatsoever land they may be in; yea, he numbereth his people,

and his bowels of mercy are over all the earth. Now this is my joy, and my great thanksgiving; yea, and I will give thanks unto my God forever. Amen.

CHAPTER 27.

People of Anti-Nephi-Lehi seek safety in Zarahemla—They are called the people of Ammon—Land of Jershon given to them.

1. Now it came to pass that when those Lamanites who had gone to war against the Nephites had found, after their ^amany struggles to destroy them, that it was in vain to seek their destruction, they returned again to the ^bland of Nephi.

2. And it came to pass that the Amalekites, because of their loss, were exceeding angry. And when they saw that they could not seek revenge from the Nephites, they began to stir up the people in anger against their brethren, the people of ^cAnti-Nephi-Lehi; therefore they began again to destroy them.

3. Now this people again refused to take their arms, and they suffered themselves to be slain according to the desires of their enemies.

4. Now when Ammon and his brethren saw this work of destruction among those whom they so dearly beloved, and among those who had so dearly beloved them—for they were treated as though they were angels sent from God to save them from everlasting destruction—therefore, when Ammon and his brethren saw this great work of destruction, they were moved with compassion, and they said unto the king:

5. Let us gather together this people of the Lord, and let us go down to the ^dland of Zarahemla to our brethren the Nephites, and flee out of the hands of our enemies, that we be not destroyed.

6. But the king said unto them: Behold, the Nephites will destroy us, because of the many murders and sins we have committed against them.

7. And Ammon said: I will go and inquire of the Lord, and if he say unto us, go down unto our brethren, will ye go?

8. And the king said unto him: Yea, if the Lord saith unto us go, we will go down unto our brethren, and we will be their slaves until we repair unto them the many murders and sins which we have committed against them.

9. But Ammon said unto him: It is against the law of our brethren, which was established by my father, that there should be ^eany slaves among them; therefore let us go down and rely upon the mercies of our brethren.

10. But the king said unto him: ^fInquire of the Lord, and if he saith unto us go, we will go; otherwise we will perish in the land.

11. And it came to pass that Ammon went and inquired of the Lord, and the Lord said unto him:

12. Get this people out of this land, that they perish not; for Satan has great hold on the hearts of the Amalekites, ^gwho do stir up the Lamanites to anger against their brethren to slay them; therefore get thee out of this land; and blessed are this people in this generation, for I will preserve them.

13. And now it came to pass that Ammon went and told the

---

a, Al. 25:2, 3. *b*, see *b*, 2 Ne. 5. *c*, see *t*, Al. 23. *d*, Om. 13. *e*, Mos. 29:32, 38, 40. *f*, ver. 11. *g*, vers. 2, 3. BETWEEN B. C. 90 AND 77.

king all the words which the Lord had ʰsaid unto him.

14. And they gathered together all their people, yea, all the people of the Lord, and did gather together all their flocks and herds, and departed out of the land, and came into the wilderness which divided the land of Nephi from the land of Zarahemla, and came over near the borders of the land.

15. And it came to pass that Ammon said unto them: Behold, I and my brethren will go forth into the land of Zarahemla, and ye shall remain here until we return; and we will try the hearts of our brethren, whether they will that ye shall come into their land.

16. And it came to pass that as Ammon was going forth into the land, that he and his brethren met Alma, over in the ⁱplace of which has been spoken; and behold, this was a joyful meeting.

17. Now the joy of Ammon was so great even that he was full; yea, he was swallowed up in the joy of his God, even to the exhausting of his strength; and he fell ʲagain to the earth.

18. Now was not this exceeding joy? Behold, this is joy which none receiveth save it be the truly penitent and humble seeker of happiness.

19. Now the joy of Alma in meeting his brethren was truly great, and also the joy of Aaron, of Omner, and Himni; but behold their joy was not that to exceed their strength.

20. And now it came to pass that Alma conducted his brethren back to the ᵏland of Zarahemla; even to his ˡown house. And they went and told the ᵐchief judge all the things that had happened unto them in the ⁿland of Nephi, among their brethren, the Lamanites.

21. And it came to pass that the chief judge sent a proclamation throughout all the land, desiring the ᵒvoice of the people concerning the admitting their brethren, who were the people of ᵖAnti-Nephi-Lehi.

22. And it came to pass that the voice of the people came, saying: Behold, we will give up the ᑫland of Jershon, which is on the east by the sea, which joins the ʳland Bountiful, which is on the south of the land Bountiful; and this land Jershon is the land which we will give unto our brethren for an inheritance.

23. And behold, we will set our armies between the land Jershon and the land Nephi, that we may protect our brethren in the land Jershon; and this we do for our brethren, on account of their fear to take up arms against their brethren lest they should commit sin; and this their great fear came because of their sore repentance which they had, on account of their many murders and their awful wickedness.

24. And now behold, this will we do unto our brethren, that they may inherit the land Jershon; and we will guard them from their enemies with our armies, on ˢcondition that they will give us a portion of their substance to assist us that we may maintain our armies.

25. Now, it came to pass that when Ammon had heard this, he

---

h, ver. 12. i, Al. 17:1—4. j, Al. 19:14, 17. k, Om. 13. l, Al. 15:18. m, Al. 4:16—18. n, see b, 2 Ne. 5. o, see e, Mos. 29. p, see t, Al. 23. q, vers. 23, 24, 26. Al. 28:1, 8. 30:1, 19. 31:3. 35:1, 2, 6, 8, 13, 14. 43:4, 15, 18, 22, 25. r, see 2k, Al. 22. s, Al. 43:13.

BETWEEN B. C. 90 AND 77.

266 ALMA, 28.

returned to the people of 'Anti-Nephi-Lehi, and also Alma with him, into the wilderness, where they had pitched their tents, and made known unto them all these things. And Alma also related unto them his "conversion, with Ammon and Aaron, and his brethren.

26. And it came to pass that it did cause great joy among them. And they went down into the 'land of Jershon, and took possession of the land of Jershon; and they were called by the Nephites the people of Ammon; therefore they were distinguished by that name ever after.

27. And they were among the people of Nephi, and also numbered among the people who were of the church of God. And they were also distinguished for their zeal towards God, and also towards men; for they were perfectly honest and upright in all things; and they were firm in the faith of Christ, "even unto the end.

28. And they did look upon shedding the blood of their brethren with the greatest abhorrence; and they never could be prevailed upon to take up arms against their brethren; and they never did look upon death with any degree of terror, for their hope and views of Christ and the 'resurrection; therefore, death was swallowed up to them by the ᵛvictory of Christ over it.

29. Therefore, they would suffer ᶻdeath in the most aggravating and distressing manner which could be inflicted by their brethren, before they would take the sword or cimeter to smite them.

30. And thus they were a zealous and beloved people, a highly favored people of the Lord.

CHAPTER 28.

Lamanites make war upon Nephites—A tremendous battle—Lamanites defeated—Deep mourning.

1. And now it came to pass that after the ᵃpeople of Ammon were established in the ᵇland of Jershon, and a church also established in the land of Jershon, and the armies of the Nephites were set round about the land of Jershon, yea, in all the borders round about the ᶜland of Zarahemla; behold the armies of the Lamanites had followed their brethren into the wilderness.

2. And thus there was a tremendous battle; yea, even such an one as never had been known among all the people in the land from the time Lehi left ᵈJerusalem; yea, and tens of thousands of the Lamanites were slain and scattered abroad.

3. Yea, and also there was a tremendous slaughter among the people of Nephi; nevertheless, the Lamanites were driven and scattered, and the people of Nephi returned again to their land.

4. And now this was a time that there was a great mourning and lamentation heard throughout all the land, among all the people of Nephi—

5. Yea, the cry of widows mourning for their husbands, and also of fathers mourning for their sons, and the daughter for the brother, yea, the brother for the father; and thus the cry of mourning was heard among all of them, mourning for their kindred who had been slain.

6. And now surely this was a

t, see *t*, Al. 23. *u*, Mos. 27:10—17. *v*, see *q*. *w*, see *l*, Al. 23. *x*, see *d*, 2 Ne. 11. *y*, see *h*, Mos. 16. *z*, Al. 24:20—23. 27:3. CHAP. 28: *a*, Al. 27:26. *b*, see *q*, Al. 27. *c*, Om. 13. *d*, 1 Ne. 2:2, 3. ABOUT B. C. 77.

sorrowful day; yea, a time of solemnity, and a time of much 'fasting and prayer.

7. And thus endeth the fifteenth year of the reign of the judges over the people of Nephi;

8. And this is the account of Ammon and his brethren, their journeyings in the land of Nephi, their sufferings in the land, their sorrows, and their afflictions, and their 'incomprehensible joy, and the reception and safety of the brethren in the ᵍland of Jershon. And now may the Lord, the Redeemer of all men, bless their souls forever.

9. And this is the account of the wars and contentions among the Nephites, and also the wars between the Nephites and the Lamanites; *and the fifteenth year of the reign of the judges is ended.

10. And ʰfrom the first year to the fifteenth has brought to pass the destruction of many thousand lives; yea, it has brought to pass an awful scene of bloodshed.

11. And the bodies of many thousands are laid low in the earth, while the bodies of many thousands are ⁱmoldering in heaps upon the face of the earth; yea, and many thousands are mourning for the loss of their kindred, because they have reason to fear, according to the promises of the Lord, that they are consigned to a state of endless wo.

12. While many thousands of others truly mourn for the loss of their kindred, yet they rejoice and exult in the hope, and even know, according to the promises of the Lord, that they are raised to dwell at the right hand of God, in a state of never-ending happiness.

13. And thus we see how great the inequality of man is because of sin and transgression, and the power of the devil, which comes by the cunning plans which he hath devised to ensnare the hearts of men.

14. And thus we see the great call of diligence of men to ʲlabor in the vineyards of the Lord; and thus we see the great reason of sorrow, and also of rejoicing— sorrow because of death and destruction among men, and joy because of the light of Christ unto life.

CHAPTER 29.

Alma's yearning desire to cry repentance to all—God's word apportioned in wisdom—Alma rejoices over success of his brethren.

1. O that I were an angel, and could have the wish of mine heart, that I might go forth and speak with the trump of God, with a voice to shake the earth, and cry repentance unto every people!

2. Yea, I would declare unto every soul, as with the voice of thunder, repentance and the plan of redemption, that they should repent and come unto our God, that there might not be more sorrow upon all the face of the earth.

3. But behold, I am a man, and do sin in my wish; for I ought to be content with the things which the Lord hath allotted unto me.

4. I ought not to harrow up in my desires, the firm decree of a just God, for I know that he granteth unto men according to their desire, whether it be unto death or unto life; yea, I know that he allotteth unto men according to their wills, whether

---

e, see f, Mos. 27. ƒ, Al. 26. 27:16—19. g, see q, Al. 27. h, Al. chaps. 1—28.
i, Al. 16:11. j, Jac. 5. * B. C. 76.

they be unto salvation or unto destruction.

5. Yea, and I know that good and evil have come before all men; he that ᵃknoweth not good from evil is blameless; but he that ᵇknoweth good and evil, to him it is given according to his desires, whether he desireth good or evil, life or death, joy or remorse of conscience.

6. Now, seeing that I know these things, why should I desire more than to perform the work to which I have been called?

7. Why should I ᶜdesire that I were an angel, that I could speak unto all the ends of the earth?

8. For behold, the Lord doth grant unto all nations, of their own nation and tongue, to teach his word, yea, in wisdom, ᵈall that he seeth fit that they should have; therefore we see that the Lord doth counsel in wisdom, according to that which is just and true.

9. I know that which the Lord hath commanded me, and I glory in it. I do ᵉnot glory of myself, but I glory in that which the Lord hath commanded me; yea, and this is my glory, that perhaps I may be an instrument in the hands of God to bring some soul to repentance; and this is my joy.

10. And behold, when I see many of my brethren truly penitent, and coming to the Lord their God, then is my soul filled with joy; then do I remember what the Lord has done ᶠfor me, yea, even that he hath heard my prayer; yea, then do I remember his merciful arm which he extended towards me.

11. Yea, and I also remember the captivity of my fathers; for I surely do know that the Lord did deliver them out of bondage, and by this did establish his church; yea, the Lord God, the God of Abraham, the God of Isaac, and the God of Jacob, did deliver them out of bondage.

12. Yea, I have always remembered the captivity of my fathers; and that same God who delivered them out of the hands of the Egyptians did deliver them ᵍout of bondage.

13. Yea, and that same God did establish his church among them; yea, and that same God hath called me by a ʰholy calling, to preach the word unto this people, and hath given me much success, in the which my joy is full.

14. But I do not joy in my own success alone, but my joy is more full because of the success of ⁱmy brethren, who have been up to the ʲland of Nephi.

15. Behold, they have labored exceedingly, and have brought forth much fruit; and how great shall be their reward!

16. Now, when I think of the success of these my brethren my soul is carried away, even to the separation of it from the body, as it were, so great is my joy.

17. And now may God grant unto these, my brethren, that they may sit down in the kingdom of God; yea, and also all those who are the fruit of their labors that they may go no more out, but that they may praise him forever. And may God grant that it may be done according to my words, even as I have spoken. Amen.

CHAPTER 30.

Korihor the Anti-Christ—Expelled from Jershon and arrested at Gideon

a, see j, Mos. 3.   b, see l, 2 Ne. 2.   c, ver. 1.   d, Al. 12:9—11.   e, Al. 26:12.
f, Mos. 27:11—31.   g, Mos. 24:16—22.   h, Al. 5:3.   i, Al. 17:1—8.   j, see b, 2 Ne. 5.
ABOUT B. C. 76.

ALMA, 30.

—*Arraigned in Zarahemla—He demands a sign and is stricken dumb—His miserable death.*

1. Behold, now it came to pass that after the ^apeople of Ammon were established in the ^bland of Jershon, yea, and also after the Lamanites were ^cdriven out of the land, and their dead were buried by the people of the land—

2. Now their dead were not numbered because of the ^dgreatness of their numbers; neither were the dead of the Nephites numbered—but it came to pass after they had buried their dead, and also after the days of ^efasting, and mourning, and prayer, (and it was in the sixteenth year of the reign of the judges over the people of Nephi) there began to be continual peace throughout all the land.

3. Yea, and the people did observe to keep the commandments of the Lord; and they were strict in observing the ordinances of God, according to the ^flaw of Moses; for they were taught to keep the law of Moses until it should be fulfilled.

4. And thus the people did have no disturbance in all the sixteenth year of the reign of the judges over the people of Nephi.

5. And it came to pass in the seventeenth year of the reign of the judges, there was continual peace.

6. But it came to pass in the *latter end of the seventeenth year, there came a man into the land of Zarahemla, and he was Anti-Christ, for he began to preach unto the people against the prophecies which had been spoken by the prophets, concerning the coming of Christ.

7. Now there was no ^glaw against a man's belief; for it was strictly contrary to the commands of God that there should be a law which should bring men on to unequal grounds.

8. For thus saith the scripture: ^hChoose ye this day, whom ye will serve.

9. Now if a man desired to serve God, it was his privilege; or rather, if he believed in God it was his privilege to serve him; but if he did not believe in him there was no law to punish him.

10. But if he murdered he was punished unto death; and if he robbed he was also punished; and if he stole he was also punished; and if he committed adultery he was also punished; yea, for all this wickedness they were punished.

11. For there was a law that men should be judged according to their crimes. Nevertheless, there was ⁱno law against a man's belief; therefore, a man was punished only for the crimes which he had done; therefore all men were on ^jequal grounds.

12. And this Anti-Christ, whose name was Korihor, (and the law could have no hold upon him) began to preach unto the people that there should be no Christ. And after this manner did he preach, saying:

13. O ye that are bound down under a foolish and a vain hope, why do ye yoke yourselves with such foolish things? Why do ye look for a Christ? For no man can know of anything which is to come.

14. Behold, these things which ye call prophecies, which ye say are handed down by holy prophets, behold, they are foolish traditions of your fathers.

---

a, Al. 27:26. *b*, see *q*, Al. 27. *c*, Al. 28:2, 3. *d*, see *c*. *e*, see *t*, Mos. 27. *f*, see *o*, 2 Ne. 25. *g*, vers. 9, 11. Al. 1:17. *h*, Josh. 24:15. *i*, vers. 7, 9. *j*, ver. 7. Mos. 27:3. 29:32. * B. C. 74.

15. How do ye know of their surety? Behold, ye cannot know of things which ye do not see; therefore ye cannot know that there shall be a Christ.

16. Ye look forward and say that ye see a remission of your sins. But behold, it is the effect of a frenzied mind; and this derangement of your minds comes because of the traditions of your fathers, which lead you away into a belief of things which are not so.

17. And many more such things did he say unto them, telling them that there could be no atonement made for the sins of men, but every man fared in this life according to the management of the creature; therefore every man prospered according to his genius, and that every man conquered according to his strength; and whatsoever a man did was no crime.

18. And thus he did preach unto them, leading away the hearts of many, causing them to lift up their heads in their wickedness, yea, leading away many women, and also men, to commit whoredoms—telling them that when a man was dead, that was the end thereof.

19. Now this man went over to the ^{k}land of Jershon also, to preach these things among the ^{l}people of Ammon, who were once the people of the Lamanites.

20. But behold they were more wise than many of the Nephites; for they took him, and bound him, and carried him before Ammon, who was a ^{m}high priest over that people.

21. And it came to pass that he caused that he should be carried out of the land. And he came over into the ^{n}land of Gideon, and began to preach unto them also; and here he did not have much success, for he was taken and bound and carried before the ^{o}high priest, and also the chief judge over the land.

22. And it came to pass that the high priest said unto him: Why do ye go about perverting the ways of the Lord? Why do ye teach this people that there shall be no Christ, to interrupt their rejoicings? Why do ye speak against all the prophecies of the holy prophets?

23. Now the high priest's name was Giddonah. And Korihor said unto him: Because I do not teach the foolish traditions of your fathers, and because I do not teach this people to bind themselves down under the foolish ordinances and performances which are laid down by ancient priests, to usurp power and authority over them, to keep them in ignorance, that they may not lift up their heads, but be brought down according to thy words.

24. Ye say that this people is a free people. Behold, I say they are in bondage. Ye say that those ancient prophecies are true. Behold, I say that ye do not know that they are true.

25. Ye say that this people is a guilty and a fallen people, because of the transgression of a parent. Behold, I say that a child is not guilty because of its parents.

26. And ye also say that Christ shall come. But behold, I say that ye do not know that there shall be a Christ. And ye say also that he shall be slain for the sins of the world—

27. And thus ye lead away this

---

k, see q, Al. 27. l, Al. 27:26. m, see g, Mos. 26. n, see m, Al. 2. o, see g, Mos. 26. ABOUT B. C. 74.

people after the foolish traditions of your fathers, and according to your own desires; and ye keep them down, even as it were in bondage, that ye may glut yourselves with the labors of their hands, that they durst not look up with boldness, and that they durst not enjoy their rights and privileges.

28. Yea, they durst not make use of that which is their own lest they should offend their priests, who do yoke them according to their desires, and have brought them to believe, by their traditions and their dreams and their whims and their visions and their pretended mysteries, that they should, if they did not do according to their words, offend some unknown being, who they say is God—a being who never has been seen or known, who never was nor ever will be.

29. Now when the high priest and the chief judge saw the hardness of his heart, yea, when they saw that he would revile even against God, they would not make any reply to his words; but they caused that he should be bound; and they delivered him up into the hands of the officers, and sent him to the *p*land of Zarahemla, that he might be brought before Alma, and the chief judge who was governor over all the land.

30. And it came to pass that when he was brought before Alma and the chief judge, he did go on in the *q*same manner as he did in the land of Gideon; yea, he went on to blaspheme.

31. And he did rise up in great swelling words before Alma, and did revile against the *r*priests and teachers, accusing them of leading away the people after the silly traditions of their fathers, for the sake of glutting on the labors of the people.

32. Now Alma said unto him: Thou knowest that we do not glut ourselves upon the labors of this people; for behold I have labored even from the commencement of the reign of the judges until now, with *s*mine own hands for my support, notwithstanding my many travels round about the land to declare the word of God unto my people.

33. And notwithstanding the many labors which I have performed in the church, I have never received so much as even one *t*senine for my labor; neither has any of my brethren, *u*save it were in the judgment-seat; and then we have received only according to law for our time.

34. And now, if we do not receive anything for our labors in the church, what doth it profit us to labor in the church save it were to declare the truth, that we may have rejoicings in the joy of our brethren?

35. Then why sayest thou that we preach unto this people to *v*get gain, when thou, of thyself, knowest that we receive no gain? And now, believest thou that we deceive this people, that causes such joy in their hearts?

36. And Korihor answered him, Yea.

37. And then Alma said unto him: Believest thou that there is a God?

38. And he answered, *w*Nay.

39. Now Alma said unto him: Will ye deny again that there is a God, and also deny the Christ? For behold, I say unto you, I know

p, Om. 13. *q,* vers. 23—28. *r,* see *c,* Mos. 6. *s,* Mos. 18:24. 27:5. *t,* see *c,* Al. 11. *u,* Al. 11:1, 3, 20. *v,* ver. 27. *w,* vers. 28, 29, 48. ABOUT B. C. 74.

there is a God, and also that Christ shall come.

40. And now what evidence have ye that there is no God, or that Christ cometh not? I say unto you that ye have none, save it be *your word only.

41. But, behold, I have all things as a testimony that these things are true; and ye also have all things as a testimony unto you that they are true; and will ye deny them? Believest thou that these things are true?

42. Behold, I know that thou believest, but thou art possessed with a lying spirit, and ye have put off the Spirit of God that it may have no place in you; but the devil has power over you, and he doth carry you about, working devices that he may destroy the children of God.

43. And now Korihor said unto Alma: If thou wilt show me a *sign, that I may be convinced that there is a God, yea, show unto me that he hath power, and then will I be convinced of the truth of thy words.

44. But Alma said unto him: Thou hast had signs enough; will ye tempt your God? Will ye say, Show unto me a sign, when ye have the testimony of all these thy brethren, and also all the holy prophets? The *scriptures are laid before thee, yea, and all things denote there is a God; yea, even the earth, and all things that are upon the face of it, yea, and ^{2a}its motion, yea, and also all the planets which move in their regular form do witness that there is a Supreme Creator.

45. And yet do ye go about, leading away the hearts of this people, testifying unto them there is no God? And yet will ye deny against all these witnesses? And he said: Yea, I will deny, except ye shall ^{2b}show me a sign.

46. And now it came to pass that Alma said unto him: Behold, I am grieved because of the hardness of your heart, yea, that ye will still resist the spirit of the truth, that thy soul may be destroyed.

47. But behold, it is better that thy soul should be lost than that thou shouldst be the means of bringing many souls down to destruction, by thy lying and by thy flattering words; therefore if thou shalt deny again, behold God shall smite thee, that thou shalt become ^{2c}dumb, that thou shalt never open thy mouth any more, that thou shalt not deceive this people any more.

48. Now Korihor said unto him: I do not deny the existence of a God, but I do not believe that there is a God; and I say also, that ye do not know that there is a God; and except ye ^{2d}show me a sign, I will not believe.

49. Now Alma said unto him: This will I give unto thee for a sign, that thou shalt be struck dumb, according to my words; and I say, that in the name of God, ye shall be struck dumb, that ye shall no ^{2e}more have utterance.

50. Now when Alma had said these words, Korihor was struck dumb, that he could not have utterance, according to the words of Alma.

51. And now when the chief judge saw this, he put forth his hand and wrote unto Korihor, saying: Art thou convinced of the power of God? In whom did ye desire that Alma should show forth his sign? Would ye that he

---

w, ver. 28. *y*, vers. 45, 48, 49, 50. *z*, see *a*, 1 Ne. 3. Al. 63:12. 2*a*, He. 12:11—15. 2*b*, see *y*. 2*c*, vers. 49, 50, 52. 2*d*, see *y*. 2*e*, vers. 47, 50. ABOUT B. C. 74.

should afflict others, to show unto thee a sign? Behold, he has showed unto you a sign; and now will ye dispute more?

52. And Korihor put forth his hand and wrote, saying: I know that I am dumb, for I cannot speak; and I know that nothing save it were the power of God could bring this upon me; yea, and I also ²ᶠknew that there was a God.

53. But behold, the devil hath deceived me; for he ²ᵍappeared unto me in the form of an angel, and said unto me: Go and reclaim this people, for they have all gone astray after an unknown God. And he said unto me: There is no God; yea, and he taught me that which I should say. And I have taught his words; and I taught them because they were pleasing unto the carnal mind; and I taught them, even until I had much success, insomuch that I verily believed that they were true; and for this cause I withstood the truth, even until I have brought this great curse upon me.

54. Now when he had said this, he besought that Alma should pray unto God, that the ²ʰcurse might be taken from him.

55. But Alma said unto him: If this curse should be taken from thee thou wouldst again lead away the hearts of this people; therefore, it shall be unto thee even as the Lord will.

56. And it came to pass that the curse was not taken off of Korihor; but he was cast out, and went about from house to house ²ⁱbegging for his food.

57. Now the knowledge of what had happened unto Korihor was immediately published throughout all the land; yea, the proclamation was sent forth by the chief judge to all the people in the land, declaring unto those who had believed in the words of Korihor that they must speedily repent, lest the same judgments would come unto them.

58. And it came to pass that they were all convinced of the wickedness of Korihor; therefore they were all converted again unto the Lord; and this put an end to the iniquity after the manner of Korihor. And Korihor did go about from house to house, begging food for his support.

59. And it came to pass that as he went forth among the people, yea, among a people who had separated themselves from the Nephites and called themselves ²ʲZoramites, being led by a man whose name was Zoram—and as he went forth amongst them, behold, he was run upon and trodden down, even until he was dead.

60. And thus we see the end of him who perverteth the ways of the Lord; and thus we see that the devil will not support his children at the last day, but doth speedily drag them down to ²ᵏhell.

CHAPTER 31.

Alma heads a mission to reclaim the apostate Zoramites—The Rameumptom or holy stand—The Zoramite form of worship.

1. Now it came to pass that after the end of Korihor, Alma having received tidings that the ᵃZoramites were perverting the ways of the Lord, and that Zoram, who was their leader, was leading the hearts of the people to bow down to dumb idols, his heart

---

2f, vers. 41, 42. 2g, 2 Ne. 9:9. 2h, ver. 56. 2i, ver. 58. 2j, Al. 31:1—4, 7—12. 35:2, 3, 7—11, 13, 14. 38:3. 39:2, 11. 43:4—6, 13, 20, 44. 52:20, 33. 2k, see k, 1 Ne. 15. CHAP. 31: a, see 2j, Al. 30. ABOUT B. C., 74.

again began to sicken because of the iniquity of the people.

2. For it was the cause of great sorrow to Alma to know of iniquity among his people; therefore his heart was exceeding sorrowful because of the separation of the Zoramites from the Nephites.

3. Now the Zoramites had gathered themselves together in a land which they called *b*Antionum, which was east of the *c*land of Zarahemla, which lay nearly bordering upon the seashore, which was south of the *d*land of Jershon, which also bordered upon the wilderness south, which wilderness was full of the Lamanites.

4. Now the Nephites greatly feared that the *e*Zoramites would enter into a correspondence with the Lamanites, and that it would be the means of great loss on the part of the Nephites.

5. And now, as the preaching of the word had a great tendency to lead the people to do that which was just—yea, it had had more powerful effect upon the minds of the people than the sword, or anything else, which had happened unto them—therefore Alma thought it was expedient that they should try the virtue of the word of God.

6. Therefore he took Ammon, and Aaron, and Omner; and Himni he did leave in the church in *f*Zarahemla; but the former three he took with him, and also Amulek and Zeezrom, who were at *g*Melek; and he also took two of his sons.

7. Now the eldest of his sons he took not with him, and his name was Helaman; but the names of those whom he took with him were *h*Shiblon and *i*Corianton; and these are the names of those who went with him among the *j*Zoramites, to preach unto them the word.

8. Now the Zoramites were dissenters from the Nephites; therefore they had had the word of God preached unto them.

9. But they had fallen into great errors, for they would not observe to keep the commandments of God, and his statutes, according to the *k*law of Moses.

10. Neither would they observe the performances of the church, to continue in *l*prayer and supplication to God daily, that they might not enter into temptation.

11. Yea, in fine, they did pervert the ways of the Lord in very many instances; therefore, for this cause, Alma and his brethren went into the land to preach the word unto them.

12. Now, when they had come into the land, behold, to their astonishment they found that the Zoramites had built *m*synagogues, and that they did gather themselves together on one day of the week, which day they did call the day of the Lord; and they did worship after a manner which Alma and his brethren had never beheld;

13. For they had a place built up in the center of their synagogue, a *n*place for standing, which was high above the head; and the top thereof would only admit one person.

14. Therefore, whosoever desired to worship must go forth and stand upon the top thereof, and stretch forth his hands towards heaven, and cry with a loud voice, saying:

---

b, Al. 43:5, 15, 22. *c*, Om. 13. *d*, see *q*, Al. 27. *e*, see 2*j*, Al. 30. *f*, Om. 13. *g*, see *c*, Al. 8. *h*, Al. 38. *i*, Al. 39—42. *j*, see 2*j*, Al. 30. *k*, see *o*, 2 Ne. 25. *l*, see *e*. 2 Ne. 32. *m*, see *u*, Al. 16. *n*, vers. 21, 23.   ABOUT B. C. 74.

15. Holy, holy God; we believe that thou art God, and we believe that thou art holy, and that thou wast a spirit, and that thou art a spirit, and that thou wilt be a spirit forever.

16. Holy God, we believe that thou hast separated us from our brethren; and we do not believe in the tradition of our brethren, which was handed down to them by the childishness of their fathers; but we believe that thou hast elected us to be thy holy children; and also thou hast made it known unto us that there shall be no Christ.

17. But thou art the same yesterday, today, and forever; and thou hast elected us that we shall be saved, whilst all around us are elected to be cast by thy wrath down to hell; for the which holiness, O God, we thank thee; and we also thank thee that thou hast elected us, that we may not be led away after the foolish traditions of our brethren, which doth bind them down to a belief of Christ, which doth lead their hearts to wander far from thee, our God.

18. And again we thank thee, O God, that we are a chosen and a holy people. Amen.

19. Now it came to pass that after Alma and his brethren and his sons had heard these prayers, they were astonished beyond all measure.

20. For behold, every man did go forth and offer up the same prayers.

21. Now the place was called by them Rameumptom, which, being interpreted, is the holy stand.

22. Now, from this stand they did offer up, every man, the self-same prayer unto God, thanking their God that they were °chosen of him, and that he did not lead them away after the *p*tradition of their brethren, and that their hearts were not stolen away to believe in things to come, which they knew nothing about.

23. Now, after the people had all offered up thanks after this manner, they returned to their homes, never speaking of their God again until they had assembled themselves together again to the *q*holy stand, to offer up thanks after their manner.

24. Now when Alma saw this his heart was grieved; for he saw that they were a wicked and a perverse people; yea, he saw that their hearts were set upon gold, and upon silver, and upon all manner of fine goods.

25. Yea, and he also saw that their hearts were lifted up unto great boasting, in their pride.

26. And he lifted up his voice to heaven, and cried, saying: O, how long, O Lord, wilt thou suffer that thy servants shall dwell here below in the flesh, to behold such gross wickedness among the children of men?

27. Behold, O God, they cry unto thee, and yet their hearts are swallowed up in their pride. Behold, O God, they cry unto thee with their mouths, while they are puffed up, even to greatness, with the vain things of the world.

28. Behold, O my God, their costly apparel, and their ringlets, and their bracelets, and their ornaments of gold, and all their precious things which they are ornamented with; and behold, their hearts are set upon them, and yet they cry unto thee and say—We *r*thank thee, O God, for

---

o, vers. 16, 17. *p*, ver. 16. *q*, vers. 13, 21. *r*, ver. 18. ABOUT B. C. 74.

we are a chosen people unto thee, while others shall perish.

29. Yea, and they say that thou hast made it *known unto them that there shall be no Christ.

30. O Lord God, how long wilt thou suffer that such wickedness and iniquity shall be among this people? O Lord, wilt thou give me strength, that I may bear with mine infirmities. For I am infirm, and such wickedness among this people doth pain my soul.

31. O Lord, my heart is exceeding sorrowful; wilt thou comfort my soul in Christ. O Lord, wilt thou grant unto me that I may have strength, that I may suffer with patience these afflictions which shall come upon me, because of the iniquity of this people.

32. O Lord, wilt thou comfort my soul, and give unto me success, and also my fellow laborers who are with me—yea, Ammon, and Aaron, and Omner, and also Amulek and Zeezrom, and also my *t*wo sons—yea, even all these wilt thou comfort, O Lord. Yea, wilt thou comfort their souls in Christ.

33. Wilt thou grant unto them that they may have strength, that they may bear their afflictions which shall come upon them because of the iniquities of this people.

34. O Lord, wilt thou grant unto us that we may have success in bringing them again unto thee in Christ.

35. Behold, O Lord, their souls are precious, and many of them are our brethren; therefore, give unto us, O Lord, power and wisdom that we may bring these, our brethren, again unto thee.

36. Now it came to pass that when Alma had said these words, that he *u*clapped his hands upon all them who were with him. And behold, as he clapped his hands upon them, they were filled with the Holy Spirit.

37. And after that they did separate themselves one from another, taking *v*no thought for themselves what they should eat, or what they should drink, or what they should put on.

38. And the Lord provided for them that they should hunger not, neither should they thirst; yea, and he also gave them strength, that they should suffer no manner of afflictions, *w*save it were swallowed up in the joy of Christ. Now this was according to the prayer of Alma; and this because he *x*prayed in faith.

CHAPTER 32.

The poor hearken to message of salvation—Alma's commendation and discourse—Faith developed by desire to believe.

1. And it came to pass that they did go forth, and began to preach the word of God unto the people, entering into their *a*synagogues, and into their houses; yea, and even they did preach the word in their streets.

2. And it came to pass that after much labor among them, they began to have success among the poor class of people; for behold, they were cast out of the synagogues because of the coarseness of their apparel—

3. Therefore they were not permitted to enter into their synagogues to worship God, being esteemed as filthiness; therefore they were poor; yea, they were esteemed by their brethren as dross; therefore they were *b*poor

s, ver. 16. *t*, ver. 7. *u*, 3 Ne. 18:37. *v*, 3 Ne. 13:25—34. *w*, ver. 32. *x*, vers. 26—35. CHAP. 32: *a*, see *u*, Al. 16. *b*, vers. 4, 5, 12. Al. 34:40. ABOUT B. C. 74.

as to things of the world; and also they were poor in heart.

4. Now, as Alma was teaching and speaking unto the people upon the hill Onidah, there came a great multitude unto him, who were those of whom we have been speaking, of whom were poor in heart, because of their poverty as to the things of the world.

5. And they came unto Alma; and the one who was the foremost among them said unto him: Behold, what shall these my brethren do, for they are despised of all men because of their poverty, yea, and more especially by our priests; for they have cast us out of our *c*synagogues which we have labored abundantly to build with our own hands; and they have cast us out because of our *d*exceeding poverty; and we have no place to worship our God; and behold, what shall we do?

6. And now when Alma heard this, he turned him about, his face immediately towards him, and he beheld with great joy; for he beheld that their afflictions had *e*truly humbled them, and that they were in a preparation to hear the word.

7. Therefore he did say no more to the other multitude; but he stretched forth his hand, and cried unto those whom he beheld, who were truly penitent, and said unto them:

8. I behold that ye are lowly in heart; and if so, blessed are ye.

9. Behold thy brother hath said, *f*What shall we do?—for we are cast out of our synagogues, that we cannot worship our God.

10. Behold I say unto you, do ye suppose that ye cannot worship God save it be in your *g*synagogues only?

11. And moreover, I would ask, do ye suppose that ye must not worship God only once in a *h*week?

12. I say unto you, it is well that ye are cast out of your *i*synagogues, that ye may be humble, and that ye may learn wisdom; for it is necessary that ye should learn wisdom; for it is because that ye are cast out, that ye are despised of your brethren because of your *j*exceeding poverty, that ye are brought to a lowliness of heart; for ye are necessarily brought to be humble.

13. And now, because ye are *k*compelled to be humble blessed are ye; for a man sometimes, if he is compelled to be humble, seeketh repentance; and now surely, whosoever repenteth shall find mercy; and he that findeth mercy and *l*endureth to the end the same shall be saved.

14. And now, as I said unto you, that because ye were *m*compelled to be humble ye were blessed, do ye not suppose that they are more blessed who truly humble themselves because of the word?

15. Yea, he that truly humbleth himself, and repenteth of his sins, and *n*endureth to the end, the same shall be blessed—yea, much more blessed than they who are compelled to be humble because of their exceeding poverty.

16. Therefore, blessed are they who humble themselves without being *o*compelled to be humble; or rather, in other words, blessed is he that believeth in the word of God, and is baptized without stubbornness of heart, yea, with-

---

c, see *u*, Al. 16. *d*, see *b*. *e*, vers. 12—16. *f*, ver. 5. *g*, see *u*, Al. 16. *h*, Mos. 18:25. *i*, see *u*, Al. 16. *j*, vers. 3—5. *k*, vers. 12, 14—16. *l*, see *h*, 2 Ne. 31. *m*, see *k*. *n*, see *h*, 2 Ne. 31. *o*, see *k*. ABOUT B. C. 74.

out being brought to know the word, or even compelled to know, before they will believe.

17. Yea, there are many who do say: If thou wilt show unto us a sign from heaven, then we shall know of a surety; then we shall believe.

18. Now I ask, is this faith? Behold, I say unto you, Nay; for if a man knoweth a thing he hath no cause to believe, for he knoweth it.

19. And now, how much [p]more cursed is he that knoweth the will of God and doeth it not, than he that only believeth, or only hath cause to believe, and falleth into transgression?

20. Now of this thing ye must judge. Behold, I say unto you, that it is on the one hand even as it is on the other; and it shall be unto every man according to his work.

21. And now as I said concerning faith—faith is not to have a [q]perfect knowledge of things; therefore if ye have faith ye hope for things which are not seen, which are true.

22. And now, behold, I say unto you, and I would that ye should remember, that God is merciful unto all who believe on his name; therefore he desireth, in the first place, that ye should believe, yea, even on his word.

23. And now, he imparteth his word by angels unto men, yea, not only men but women also. Now this is not all; little children do have words given unto them many times, which confound the wise and the learned.

24. And now, my beloved brethren, as ye have desired to know of me [r]what ye shall do because ye are afflicted and cast out—now I do not desire that ye should suppose that I mean to judge you only according to that which is true—

25. For I do not mean that ye all of you have been [s]compelled to humble yourselves; for I verily believe that there are some among you who would humble themselves, let them be in whatsoever circumstances they might.

26. Now, as I said concerning faith—that it was not a perfect knowledge—even so it is with my words. Ye cannot know of their surety at first, unto perfection, any more than faith is a perfect knowledge.

27. But behold, if ye will awake and arouse your faculties, even to an experiment upon my words, and exercise a particle of faith, yea, even if ye can no more than desire to believe, let this desire work in you, even until ye believe in a manner that ye can give place for a portion of my words.

28. Now, we will compare the word unto a seed. Now, if ye give place, that a seed may be planted in your heart, behold, if it be a true seed, or a good seed, if ye do not cast it out by your unbelief, that ye will resist the Spirit of the Lord, behold, it will begin to swell within your breasts; and when you feel these swelling motions, ye will begin to say within yourselves—It must needs be that this is a good seed, or that the word is good, for it beginneth to enlarge my soul; yea, it beginneth to enlighten my understanding, yea, it beginneth to be delicious to me.

29. Now behold, would not this increase your faith? I say unto you, Yea; nevertheless it hath not grown up to a perfect knowledge.

30. But behold, as the seed swelleth, and sprouteth, and be-

---

p, D. & C. 41:1.   *q*, vers. 17—19.   *r*, ver. 5.   *s*, see *k*.   ABOUT B. C. 74.

ginneth to grow, then you must needs say that the seed is good; for behold it swelleth, and sprouteth, and beginneth to grow.

31. And now, behold, are ye sure that this is a good seed? I say unto you, Yea; for every seed bringeth forth unto its own likeness.

32. Therefore, if a seed groweth it is good, but if it groweth not, behold it is not good, therefore it is cast away.

33. And now, behold, because ye have tried the experiment, and planted the seed, and it swelleth and sprouteth, and beginneth to grow, ye must needs know that the seed is good.

34. And now, behold, is your knowledge perfect? Yea, your knowledge is perfect in that thing, and your faith is dormant; and this because you know, for ye know that the word hath swelled your souls, and ye also know that it hath sprouted up, that your understanding doth begin to be enlightened, and your mind doth begin to expand.

35. O then, is not this real? I say unto you, Yea, because it is light; and whatsoever is light, is good, because it is discernible, therefore ye must know that it is good; and now behold, after ye have tasted this light is your knowledge perfect?

36. Behold I say unto you, Nay; neither must ye lay aside your faith, for ye have only exercised your faith to plant the seed that ye might try the experiment to know if the seed was good.

37. And behold, as the tree beginneth to grow, ye will say: Let us nourish it with great care, that it may get root, that it may grow up, and bring forth fruit unto us. And now behold, if ye nourish it with much care it will get root, and grow up, and bring forth fruit.

38. But if ye neglect the tree, and take no thought for its nourishment, behold it will not get any root; and when the heat of the sun cometh and scorcheth it, because it hath no root it withers away, and ye pluck it up and cast it out.

39. Now, this is not because the seed was not good, neither is it because the fruit thereof would not be desirable; but it is because your ground is barren, and ye will not nourish the tree, therefore ye cannot have the fruit thereof.

40. And thus, if ye will not nourish the word, looking forward with an eye of faith to the fruit thereof, ye can never pluck of the fruit of the tree of life.

41. But if ye will nourish the word, yea, nourish the tree as it beginneth to grow, by your faith with great diligence, and with patience, looking forward to the fruit thereof, it shall take root; and behold it shall be a tree springing up unto everlasting life.

42. And because of your diligence and your faith and your patience with the word in nourishing it, that it may take root in you, behold, by and by ye shall pluck the fruit thereof, which is 'most precious, which is sweet above all that is sweet, and which is white above all that is white, yea, and pure above all that is pure; and ye shall feast upon this fruit even until ye are filled, that ye hunger not, neither shall ye thirst.

43. Then, my brethren, ye shall reap the rewards of your faith, and your diligence, and patience, and long-suffering, waiting for the tree to bring forth fruit unto you.

t, see *b*, 1 Ne. 8.   ABOUT B. C. 74.

CHAPTER 33.

Alma's discourse continued—True worship not confined to sanctuaries— The prophets Zenos and Zenock again cited.

1. Now after Alma had spoken these words, they sent forth unto him desiring to know whether they should believe in one God, that they might obtain this fruit of which he had spoken, or how they should plant the seed, or the word of which he had spoken, which he said must be planted in their hearts; or in what manner they should begin to exercise their faith.

2. And Alma said unto them: Behold, ye have said *a*that ye could not worship your God because ye are cast out of your *b*synagogues. But behold, I say unto you, if ye suppose that ye cannot worship God, ye do greatly err, and ye ought to search the *c*scriptures; if ye suppose that they have taught you this, ye do not understand them.

3. Do ye remember to have read what *d*Zenos, the prophet of old, has said concerning *e*prayer or worship?

4. For he said: Thou art merciful, O God, for thou hast heard my prayer, even when I was in the wilderness; yea, thou wast merciful when I prayed concerning those who were mine enemies, and thou didst turn them to me.

5. Yea, O God, and thou wast merciful unto me when I did cry unto thee in my field; when I did cry unto thee in my prayer, and thou didst hear me.

6. And again, O God, when I did turn to my house thou didst hear me in my prayer.

7. And when I did turn unto my closet, O Lord, and prayed unto thee, thou didst hear me.

8. Yea, thou art merciful unto thy children when they cry unto thee, to be heard of thee and not of men, and thou wilt hear them.

9. Yea, O God, thou hast been merciful unto me, and heard my cries in the midst of thy congregations.

10. Yea, and thou hast also heard me when I have been cast out and have been despised by mine enemies; yea, thou didst hear my cries, and wast angry with mine enemies, and thou didst visit them in thine anger with speedy destruction.

11. And thou didst hear me because of mine afflictions and my sincerity; and it is because of thy Son that thou hast been thus merciful unto me, therefore I will cry unto thee in all mine afflictions, for in thee is my joy; for thou hast turned thy judgments away from me, because of thy Son.

12. And now Alma said unto them: Do ye believe those *f*scriptures which have been written by them of old?

13. Behold, if ye do, ye must believe what *g*Zenos said; for, behold he said: Thou hast turned away thy judgments because of thy Son.

14. Now behold, my brethren, I would ask if ye have *h*read the scriptures? If ye have, how can ye disbelieve on the Son of God?

15. For it is not written that *i*Zenos alone spake of these things, but *j*Zenock also spake of these things—

16. For behold, he said: Thou art angry, O Lord, with this people, because they will not under-

---

a, Al. 32:5. *b*, see *u*, Al. 16. *c*, see *a*, 1 Ne. 3. Al. 63:12. *d*, see *h*, 1 Ne. 19. *e*, see *e*, 2 Ne. 32. *f*, see *c*. *g*, see *h*, 1 Ne. 19. *h*, see *c*. *i*, see *h*, 1 Ne. 19. *j*, see *g*, 1 Ne. 19.   ABOUT B. C. 74.

stand thy mercies which thou hast bestowed upon them because of thy Son.

17. And now, my brethren, ye see that a second prophet of old has testified of the Son of God, and because the people would not understand his words they stoned him to death.

18. But behold, this is not all; these are not the only ones who have spoken concerning the Son of God.

19. Behold, he was spoken of by Moses; yea, and behold a type was *k*raised up in the wilderness, that whosoever would look upon it might live. And many did look and live.

20. But few understood the meaning of those things, and this because of the hardness of their hearts. But there were many who were so hardened that they would not look, therefore they perished. Now the reason they would not look is because they did not believe that it would heal them.

21. O my brethren, if ye could be healed by merely casting about your eyes that ye might be healed, would ye not behold quickly, or would ye rather harden your hearts in unbelief, and be slothful, that ye would not cast about your eyes, that ye might perish?

22. If so, wo shall come upon you; but if not so, then cast about your eyes and begin to believe in the Son of God, that he will come to redeem his people, and that he shall suffer and die to *l*atone for their sins; and that he shall rise again from the dead, which shall bring to pass the *m*resurrection, that all men shall stand before him, to be judged at the last and judgment day, according to their works.

23. And now, my brethren, I desire that ye shall plant this word in your hearts, and as it beginneth to swell even so nourish it by your faith. And behold, it will become a tree, springing up in you unto everlasting life. And then may God grant unto you that your burdens may be light, through the joy of his Son. And even all this can ye do if ye will. Amen.

CHAPTER 34.

Amulek's testimony—The great and last sacrifice—How mercy satisfies justice—Repentance not to be procrastinated.

1. And now it came to pass that after Alma had spoken these words unto them he sat down upon the ground, and Amulek arose and began to teach them, saying:

2. My brethren, I think that it is impossible that ye should be ignorant of the things which have been spoken concerning the coming of Christ, who is taught by us to be the Son of God; yea, I know that these things were taught unto you bountifully before your dissension from among us.

3. And as ye have desired of my beloved brother that he should make known unto you *a*what ye should do, because of your afflictions; and he hath spoken somewhat unto you to prepare your minds; yea, and he hath exhorted you unto faith and to patience—

4. Yea, even that ye would have so much faith as even to *b*plant the word in your hearts, that ye may try the experiment of its goodness.

5. And we have beheld that the great question which is in your

k, Num. 21:9. John 3:14. *l*, see *f*, 2 Ne. 2. *m*, see *d*, 2 Ne. 2.
CHAP. 34: *a*, Al. 32:5. *b*, Al. 33:23. ABOUT B. C. 74.
19

minds is whether the word be in the Son of God, or ^cwhether there shall be no Christ.

6. And ye also beheld that my brother has proved unto you, in many instances, that the word is in Christ unto salvation.

7. My brother has called upon the words of ^dZenos, that redemption cometh through the Son of God, and also upon the words of ^eZenock; and also he has appealed unto ^fMoses, to prove that these things are true.

8. And now, behold, I will testify unto you of myself that these things are true. Behold, I say unto you, that I do know that Christ shall come among the children of men, to take upon him the transgressions of his people, and that he shall ^gatone for the sins of the world; for the Lord God hath spoken it.

9. For it is expedient that an atonement should be made; for according to the great plan of the Eternal God there must be an atonement made, or else ^hall mankind must unavoidably perish; yea, all are hardened; yea, all are fallen and are lost, and must perish except it be through the ⁱatonement which it is expedient should be made.

10. For it is expedient that there should be a great and last sacrifice; yea, not a sacrifice of man, neither of beast, neither of any manner of fowl; for it shall not be a human sacrifice; but it must be an infinite and eternal sacrifice.

11. Now there is not any man that can sacrifice his own blood which will atone for the sins of another. Now, if a man murdereth, behold will our law, which is just, take the life of his brother? I say unto you, Nay.

12. But the law requireth the life of him who hath murdered; therefore there can be nothing which is short of an ^jinfinite atonement which will suffice for the sins of the world.

13. Therefore, it is expedient that there should be a great and ^klast sacrifice; and then shall there be, or it is expedient there should be, a ^lstop to the shedding of blood; then shall the ^mlaw of Moses be fulfilled; yea, it shall be all fulfilled, every jot and tittle, and none shall have passed away.

14. And behold, this is the whole meaning of the law, every whit pointing to that great and last sacrifice; and that great and ⁿlast sacrifice will be the Son of God, yea, ^oinfinite and eternal.

15. And thus he shall bring salvation to all those who shall believe on his name; this being the intent of this ^plast sacrifice, to bring about the bowels of mercy, which overpowereth justice, and bringeth about means unto men that they may have faith unto repentance.

16. And thus mercy can ^qsatisfy the demands of justice, and encircles them in the arms of safety, while he that exercises no faith unto repentance is exposed to the whole law of the demands of justice; therefore only unto him that has faith unto repentance is brought about the great and eternal plan of redemption.

17. Therefore may God grant unto you, my brethren, that ye may begin to exercise your faith unto repentance, that ye begin to call upon his holy name, that he would have mercy upon you;

---

c, Al. 31:16. *d*, Al. 33:3. See *h*, 1 Ne. 19. *e*, Al. 33:15. See *g*, 1 Ne. 19. *f*, Al. 33:19. *g*, see *f*, 2 Ne. 2. *h*, see *e* and *g*, 2 Ne. 9. *i*, see *f*, 2 Ne. 2. *j*, vers. 10, 14. *k*, vers. 14, 15. *l*, 3 Ne. 9:19. *m*, see *o*, 2 Ne. 25. *n*, vers. 13, 15. *o*, ver. 10. *p*, vers. 13, 14. *q*, see 2*m*, Al. 12.

ABOUT B. C. 74.

18. Yea, cry unto him for mercy; for he is mighty to save.

19. Yea, humble yourselves, and [r]continue in prayer unto him.

20. Cry unto him when ye are in your fields, yea, over all your flocks.

21. Cry unto him in your houses, yea, over all your household, both morning, mid-day, and evening.

22. Yea, cry unto him against the power of your enemies.

23. Yea, cry unto him against the devil, who is an enemy to all righteousness.

24. Cry unto him over the crops of your fields, that ye may prosper in them.

25. Cry over the flocks of your fields, that they may increase.

26. But this is not all; ye must pour out your souls in your closets, and your secret places, and in your wilderness.

27. Yea, and when you do not cry unto the Lord, let your hearts be full, drawn out in prayer unto him continually for your welfare, and also for the welfare of those who are around you.

28. And now behold, my beloved brethren, I say unto you, do not suppose that this is all; for after ye have done all these things, if ye [s]turn away the needy, and the naked, and visit not the sick and afflicted, and impart of your substance, if ye have, to those who stand in need—I say unto you, if ye do not any of these things, behold, your prayer is [t]vain, and availeth you nothing, and ye are as hypocrites who do deny the faith.

29. Therefore, if ye do not remember to be charitable, ye are as dross, which the refiners do cast out, (it being of no worth) and is trodden under foot of men.

30. And now, my brethren, I would that, after ye have received so many witnesses, seeing that the holy [u]scriptures testify of these things, ye come forth and bring fruit unto repentance.

31. Yea, I would that ye would come forth and harden not your hearts any longer; for behold, now is the time and the day of your salvation; and therefore, if ye will repent and harden not your hearts, immediately shall the great plan of redemption be brought about unto you.

32. For behold, this life is the time for men to prepare to meet God; yea, behold the day of this life is the [r]day for men to perform their labors.

33. And now, as I said unto you before, as ye have had so many witnesses, therefore, I beseech of you that ye do not procrastinate the day of your repentance until the end; for after this day of life, which is given us to prepare for eternity, behold, if we do not improve our time while in this life, then cometh the night of darkness wherein there can be no labor performed.

34. Ye cannot say, when ye are brought to that awful crisis, that I will repent, that I will return to my God. Nay, ye cannot say this; for that same spirit which doth possess your bodies at the time that ye go out of this life, that same spirit will have power to possess your body in that eternal world.

35. For behold, if ye have procrastinated the day of your repentance even until death, behold, ye have become subjected to the spirit of the devil, and he doth seal you his; therefore, the Spirit of the Lord hath withdrawn from

---

r, see *e*, 2 Ne. 32. *s*, see *l*, Mos. 4. *t*, Moro. 7:6—8. *u*, see *a*, 1 Ne. 3. Al. 63:12. *v*, see 2*a*, Al. 12.

ABOUT B. C. 74.

you, and hath no place in you, and the devil hath ^wall power over you; and this is the final state of the wicked.

36. And this I know, because the Lord hath said he dwelleth not in *unholy temples, but in the hearts of the righteous doth he dwell; yea, and he has also said that the righteous shall sit down in his kingdom, to go no more out; but their garments should be made white through the blood of the Lamb.

37. And now, my beloved brethren, I desire that ye should remember these things, and that ye should work out your salvation with fear before God, and that ye should no more deny the coming of Christ;

38. That ye contend no more against the Holy Ghost, but that ye receive it, and take upon you the *y*name of Christ; that ye humble yourselves even to the dust, and worship God, in whatsoever place ye may be in, in spirit and in truth; and that ye live in thanksgiving daily, for the many mercies and blessings which he doth bestow upon you.

39. Yea, and I also exhort you, my brethren, that ye be watchful unto *prayer continually, that ye may not be led away by the temptation of the devil, that he may not overpower you, that ye may not become his subjects at the last day; for behold, he rewardeth you no good thing.

40. And now my beloved brethren, I would exhort you to have patience, and that ye bear with all manner of afflictions; that ye do not revile against those who do cast you out because of your *z*aexceeding poverty, lest ye become sinners like unto them;

41. But that ye have patience, and bear with those afflictions, with a firm hope that ye shall one day rest from all your afflictions.

CHAPTER 35.

Nephite missionaries retire to land of Jershon—Their Zoramite converts, expelled from their own country, rejoin them—Preparations for war.

1. Now it came to pass that after Amulek had made an end of these words, they withdrew themselves from the multitude and came over into the *a*land of Jershon.

2. Yea, and the rest of the brethren, after they had preached the word unto the *b*Zoramites, also came over into the land of Jershon.

3. And it came to pass that after the more popular part of the Zoramites had consulted together concerning the words which had been preached unto them, they were angry because of the word, for it did destroy their craft; therefore they would not hearken unto the words.

4. And they sent and gathered together throughout all the land all the people, and consulted with them concerning the words which had been spoken.

5. Now their rulers and their priests and their teachers did not let the people know concerning their desires; therefore they found out privily the minds of all the people.

6. And it came to pass that after they had found out the minds of all the people, those who were in favor of the words which had been spoken by Alma and his brethren were cast out of the land; and they were many;

---

w, see *i*, 2 Ne. 9.   *x*, see *r*, Al. 7.   *y*, see *e*, Mos. 5.   *z*, see *e*, 2 Ne. 32.   2*a*, Al. 32:3—5.   CHAP. 35: *a*, see *q*, Al. 27.   *b*, see 2*j*, Al. 30   ABOUT B. C. 74.

and they came over also into the land of Jershon.

7. And it came to pass that Alma and his brethren did minister unto them.

8. Now the people of the Zoramites were angry with the ^dpeople of Ammon who were in Jershon, and the chief ruler of the ^eZoramites, being a very wicked man, sent over unto the people of Ammon desiring them that they should cast out of their land all those ^fwho came over from them into their land.

9. And he breathed out many threatenings against them. And now the ^opeople of Ammon did not fear their words; therefore they did not cast them out, but they did receive all the poor of the Zoramites that came over unto them; and ^hthey did nourish them, and did clothe them, and did give unto them lands for their inheritance; and they did administer unto them according to their wants.

10. Now this did stir up the Zoramites to anger against the people of Ammon, and they began to mix with the Lamanites and to stir them up also to anger against them.

11. And thus the ⁱZoramites and the Lamanites began to make preparations for war against the people of Ammon, and also against the Nephites.

12. And thus ended the *seventeenth year of the reign of the judges over the people of Nephi.

13. And the ^jpeople of Ammon departed out of the ^kland of Jershon, and came over into the ^lland of Melek, and gave place in the land of Jershon for the armies of the Nephites, that they might contend with the armies of the Lamanites and the armies of the Zoramites; and thus commenced a war betwixt the Lamanites and the Nephites, in the eighteenth year of the reign of the judges; and an account shall be given of their wars ^mhereafter.

14. And Alma, and Ammon, and their brethren, and also the ⁿtwo sons of Alma returned to the land of ^oZarahemla, after having been instruments in the hands of God of bringing many of the ^pZoramites to repentance; and as many as were brought to repentance were ^qdriven out of their land; but they have lands for their inheritance in the ^rland of Jershon, and they have taken up arms to defend themselves, and their wives, and children, and their lands.

15. Now Alma, being grieved for the iniquity of his people, yea for the wars, and the bloodsheds, and the contentions which were among them; and having been to declare the word, or sent to declare the word, among all the people in every city; and seeing that the hearts of the people began to wax hard, and that they began to be offended because of the strictness of the word, his heart was exceeding sorrowful.

16. Therefore, he caused that his sons should be gathered together, that he might give unto them every one his charge, separately, concerning the things pertaining unto righteousness. And we have an account of his commandments, which he gave unto them according to his own record.

---

c, see q, Al. 27. d, Al. 27:26. e, see 2j, Al. 30. f, ver. 6. g, Al. 27:26. h, see l, Mos. 4. i, see 2j, Al. 30. j, Al. 27:26. k, see q, Al. 27. l, see c, Al. 8. m, Al. chaps. 43, 44. n, Al. 31:7. o, Om. 13. p, see 2j, Al. 30. q, ver. 6. r, see q, Al. 27.
* B. C. 74.

The commandments of Alma to his son, Helaman.
Comprising chapters 36 and 37.

CHAPTER 36.

Alma recounts his sinful past, his miraculous conversion, and his subsequent zeal in the ministry.

1. My son, give ear to my words; for I swear unto you, that *a*inasmuch as ye shall keep the commandments of God ye shall prosper in the land.

2. I would that ye should do as I have done, in remembering the captivity of our fathers; for they were in *b*bondage, and none could deliver them except it was the God of Abraham, and the God of Isaac, and the God of Jacob; and he surely did deliver them in their afflictions.

3. And now, O my son Helaman, behold, thou art in thy youth, and therefore, I beseech of thee that thou wilt hear my words and learn of me; for I do know that whosoever shall put their trust in God shall be supported in their trials, and their troubles, and their afflictions, and shall be *c*lifted up at the last day.

4. And I would not that ye think that I know of myself—not of the temporal but of the spiritual, not of the carnal mind but of God.

5. Now, behold, I say unto you, if I had not been *d*born of God I should not have known these things; but God has, by the *e*mouth of his holy angel, made these things known unto me, not of any worthiness of myself;

6. For I went about with the *f*sons of Mosiah, seeking to destroy the church of God; but behold, God sent his *g*holy angel to stop us by the way.

7. And behold, he spake unto us, as it were the *h*voice of thunder, and the whole earth did tremble beneath our feet; and we all fell to the earth, for the fear of the Lord came upon us.

8. But behold, the voice said unto me: Arise. And I *i*arose and stood up, and beheld the angel.

9. And he said unto me: If thou wilt of thyself be *j*destroyed, seek no more to destroy the church of God.

10. And it came to pass that I *k*fell to the earth; and it was for the space of *l*three days and three nights that I could not open my mouth, neither had I the use of my limbs.

11. And the angel spake more things unto me, which were heard by my brethren, but I did not hear them; for when I heard the words—If thou wilt be *m*destroyed of thyself, seek no more to destroy the church of God—I was struck with such great fear and amazement lest perhaps I should be destroyed, that I fell to the earth and I did hear no more.

12. But I was racked with *n*eternal torment, for my soul was harrowed up to the greatest degree and racked with all my sins.

13. Yea, I did remember all my sins and iniquities, for which I was tormented with the pains of hell; yea, I saw that I had rebelled against my God, and that I had not kept his holy commandments.

14. Yea, and I had murdered many of his children, or rather led them away unto destruction; yea, and in fine so great had

---

a, see *h*, 2 Ne. 1. *b*, Mos. 23:23. 24:17—21. *c*, see *p*, Mos. 23. *d*, see *c*, Mos. 5. *e*, Mos. 27:11—17. *f*, Mos. 27:10. *g*, see *c*. *h*, Mos. 27:11. *i*, Mos. 27:13, 15. *j*, Mos. 27:16. *k*, Mos. 27:18. *l*, ver. 16. Mos. 27:19—23. *m*, Mos. 27:16. *n*, see *m*, Jac. 6. ABOUT B. C. 73.

ALMA, 36.

been my iniquities, that the very thought of coming into the presence of my God did rack my soul with inexpressible horror.

15. Oh, thought I, that I could be banished and become extinct both soul and body, that I might not be brought to stand in the presence of my God, to be judged of my deeds.

16. And now, for °three days and for three nights was I racked, even with the pains of a damned soul.

17. And it came to pass that as I was thus racked with torment, while I was harrowed up by the memory of my many sins, behold, I remembered also to have heard my father prophesy unto the people concerning the coming of one Jesus Christ, a Son of God, to ᵖatone for the sins of the world.

18. Now, as my mind caught hold upon this thought, I cried within my heart: O Jesus, thou Son of God, have mercy on me, who am in the gall of bitterness, and am encircled about by the everlasting ᑫchains of death.

19. And now, behold, when I thought this, I could remember my pains no more; yea, I was harrowed up by the memory of my sins no more.

20. And oh, what joy, and what marvelous light I did behold; yea, my soul was filled with joy as exceeding as was my pain!

21. Yea, I say unto you, my son, that there could be nothing so exquisite and so bitter as were my pains. Yea, and again I say unto you, my son, that on the other hand, there can be nothing so exquisite and sweet as was my joy.

22. Yea, methought I saw, even as our ʳfather Lehi saw, God sitting upon his throne, surrounded with numberless concourses of angels, in the attitude of singing and praising their God; yea, and my soul did long to be there.

23. But behold, my ˢlimbs did receive their strength again, and I stood upon my feet, and did manifest unto the people that I had been ᵗborn of God.

24. Yea, and from that time even until now, I have labored without ceasing, that I might bring souls unto repentance; that I might bring them to taste of the ᵘexceeding joy of which I did taste; that they might also be ᵛborn of God, and be ʷfilled with the Holy Ghost.

25. Yea, and now behold, O my son, the Lord doth give me exceeding great joy in the fruit of my labors;

26. For because of the word which he has imparted unto me, behold, many have been ˣborn of God, and have tasted as I have tasted, and have seen eye to eye as I have seen; therefore they do know of these things of which I have spoken, as I do know; and the knowledge which I have is of God.

27. And I have been supported under trials and troubles of every kind, yea, and in all manner of afflictions; yea, God has ʸdelivered me from prison, and from bonds, and from death; yea, and I do put my trust in him, and he will still deliver me.

28. And I know that he will ᶻraise me up at the last day, to dwell with him in glory; yea, and I will praise him forever, for he

---

o, ver. 10. Mos. 27:19—23. *p*, see *f*, 2 Ne. 2. *q*, see *p*, 2 Ne. 28. *r*, 1 Ne. 1:8. *s*, Mos. 27:23. *t*, see *c*, Mos. 5. *u*, vers. 20—22. *v*, see *c*, Mos. 5. *w*, 1 Ne. 10:17— 19. 2 Ne. 31:13, 14, 17, 18. 32:2, 5. Al. 31:36. 34:38. He. 5:45. 3 Ne. 9:20. 11:35, 36. 12:1, 2. 18:37. 19:13, 14. Chap. 30. 4 Ne. 1. *x*, see *c*, Mos. 5. *y*, Al. 14:26—29. *z*, see *p*, Mos. 23.

ABOUT B. C. 73.

has brought our fathers out of Egypt, and he has swallowed up the Egyptians in the Red Sea; and he led them by his power into the promised land; yea, and he has delivered them out of bondage and captivity from time to time.

29. Yea, and he has also brought our fathers out of the land of Jerusalem; and he has also, by his everlasting power, delivered them out of bondage and captivity, from time to time even down to the present day; and I have always retained in remembrance their captivity; yea, and ye also ought to retain in remembrance, as I have done, their captivity.

30. But behold, my son, this is not all; for ye ought to know as I do know, that ²ᵃinasmuch as ye shall keep the commandments of God ye shall prosper in the land; and ye ought to know also, that inasmuch as ye will not keep the commandments of God ye shall be cut off from his presence. Now this is according to his word.

CHAPTER 37.

Helaman entrusted with the records and other sacred relics—Gazelem—The Liahona a type of the word of Christ.

1. And now, my son Helaman, I command you that ye take the records which have been ᵃentrusted with me;

2. And I also command you that ye keep a record of this people, according as I have done, upon the ᵇplates of Nephi, and keep all these things sacred which I have kept, even as I have kept them; for it is for a ᶜwise purpose that they are kept.

3. And these plates of ᵈbrass, which contain these engravings, which have the records of the holy scriptures upon them, which have the ᵉgenealogy of our forefathers, even from the beginning—

4. Behold, it has been prophesied by our fathers, that they should be kept and ᶠhanded down from one generation to another, and be kept and preserved by the hand of the Lord until they should go forth unto every nation, kindred, tongue, and people, that they shall know of the mysteries contained thereon.

5. And now behold, if they are kept they must retain their ᵍbrightness; yea, and they will retain their brightness; yea, and also shall all the plates which do contain that which is holy writ.

6. Now ye may suppose that this is foolishness in me; but behold I say unto you, that by small and simple things are great things brought to pass; and small means in many instances doth confound the wise.

7. And the Lord God doth work by means to bring about his great and eternal purposes; and by ʰvery small means the Lord doth confound the wise and bringeth about the salvation of many souls.

8. And now, it has hitherto been wisdom in God that these things should be preserved; for behold, they have ⁱenlarged the memory of this people, yea, and convinced many of the error of their ways, and brought them to the knowledge of their God unto the salvation of their souls.

9. Yea, I say unto you, were it not for these things that these records do contain, which are on these plates, Ammon and his

---

2ᵃ, see ℎ, 2 Ne. 1. CHAP. 37: ᵃ, Mos. 28:20. ᵇ, see ƒ, 1 Ne. 1. ᶜ, vers. 12, 14, 18. Enos 13—18. W. of Morm. 6—11. ᵈ, see ᵃ, 1 Ne. 3. ᵉ, see ᵈ, 1 Ne. 5. ƒ, 1 Ne. 5:16—19. ᵍ, 1 Ne. 5:19. ʰ, D. & C. 64:33. ⁱ, Mos. 1:3—5.

ABOUT B. C. 73.

brethren ʲcould not have convinced so many thousands of the Lamanites of the incorrect tradition of their fathers; yea, these records and their words brought them unto repentance; that is, they brought them to the knowledge of the Lord their God, and to rejoice in Jesus Christ their Redeemer.

10. And who knoweth but what they will be the means of bringing many thousands of them, yea, and also many thousands of our stiffnecked brethren, the Nephites, who are now hardening their hearts in sin and iniquities, to the knowledge of their Redeemer?

11. Now these mysteries are not yet fully made known unto me; therefore I shall forbear.

12. And it may suffice if I only say they are preserved for a ᵏwise purpose, which purpose is known unto God; for he doth counsel in wisdom over all his works, and his paths ˡare straight, and his course is ᵐone eternal round.

13. O remember, remember, my son Helaman, how strict are the commandments of God. And he said: ⁿIf ye will keep my commandments ye shall prosper in the land—but if ye keep not his commandments ye shall be cut off from his presence.

14. And now remember, my son, that God has entrusted you with these things, which are sacred, which he has kept sacred, and also which he will keep and ᵒpreserve for a wise purpose in him, that he may show forth his power unto future generations.

15. And now behold, I tell you by the spirit of prophecy, that if ye transgress the commandments of God, behold, these things which are sacred shall be taken away from you by the power of God, and ye shall be delivered up unto Satan, that he may sift you as chaff before the wind.

16. But if ye keep the commandments of God, and do with these things which are sacred according to that which the Lord doth command you, (for you must appeal unto the Lord for all things whatsoever ye must do with them) behold, no power of earth or hell can take them from you, for God is powerful to the fulfilling of all his words.

17. For he will fulfil all his promises which he shall make unto you, for he has fulfilled his promises which he has made unto our fathers.

18. For he promised unto them that he would reserve these things for a wise purpose in him, that he might show forth his power unto ᵖfuture generations.

19. And now behold, one purpose hath he fulfilled, even to the restoration of ᑫmany thousands of the Lamanites to the knowledge of the truth; and he hath shown forth his power in them, and he will also still show forth his power in them unto ʳfuture generations; therefore they shall be preserved.

20. Therefore I command you, my son Helaman, that ye be diligent in fulfilling all my words, and that ye be diligent in keeping the commandments of God as they are written.

21. And now, I will speak unto you concerning those ˢtwenty-four plates, that ye keep them, that the mysteries and the works of darkness, and their secret works, or the ᵗsecret works of those peo-

j, Al. 18:36. 22:12. *k*, see *c*. *l*, see 2*a*, 2 Ne. 9. *m*, 1 Ne. 10:19. Al. 7:20. *n*, see *h*, 2 Ne. 1. *o*, vers. 2. 12. 18. See *c*. *p*, ver. 19. *q*, Al. 23:5—13. *r*, ver. 18. *s*, see *k*, Mos. 8. *t*, see *i*, 2 Ne. 10. ABOUT B. C. 73.

ple who have been destroyed, may be made manifest unto this people; yea, all their murders, and robbings, and their plunderings, and all their wickedness and abominations, may be made manifest unto this people; yea, and that ye preserve these *u*interpreters.

22. For behold, the Lord saw that his people began to work in darkness, yea, work *v*secret murders and abominations; therefore the Lord said, if they did not repent they should be *w*destroyed from off the face of the earth.

23. And the Lord said: I will prepare unto my servant Gazelem, a *x*stone, which shall shine forth in darkness unto light, that I may discover unto my people who serve me, that I may discover unto them the works of their brethren, yea, their *y*secret works, their works of darkness, and their wickedness and abominations.

24. And now, my son, these *z*interpreters were prepared that the word of God might be fulfilled, which he spake, saying:

25. I will bring forth out of darkness unto light all their ^{2a}secret works and their abominations; and except they repent I will ^{2b}destroy them from off the face of the earth; and I will bring to light all their secrets and abominations, unto every nation that shall hereafter possess the land.

26. And now, my son, we see that they did not repent; therefore ^{2c}they have been destroyed, and thus far the word of God has been fulfilled; yea, their secret abominations have been brought out of darkness and ^{2d}made known unto us.

27. And now, my son, I command you that ye retain all their oaths, and their covenants, and their agreements in their secret abominations; yea, and all their signs and their wonders ye shall keep from this people, that they know them not, lest peradventure they should fall into darkness also and be destroyed.

28. For behold, there is a curse upon all this land, that destruction shall come upon all those workers of darkness, according to the power of God, when they are fully ripe; therefore I desire that this people might not be destroyed.

29. Therefore ye shall keep these secret plans of their oaths and their covenants from this people, and only their wickedness and their murders and their abominations shall ye make known unto them; and ye shall teach them to abhor such wickedness and abominations and murders; and ye shall also teach them that these people were destroyed on account of their wickedness and abominations and their murders.

30. For behold, they murdered all the prophets of the Lord who came among them to declare unto them concerning their iniquities; and the blood of those whom they murdered did cry unto the Lord their God for vengeance upon those who were their murderers; and thus the judgments of God did come upon these workers of darkness and secret combinations.

31. Yea, and ^{2e}cursed be the land forever and ever unto those workers of darkness and secret combinations, even unto destruction, except they repent before they are fully ripe.

---

u, vers. 23—26. See *n*, Mos. 8. *v*, see *i*, 2 Ne. 10. *w*, see *j*, Mos. 8. *x*, see *n*, Mos. 8. *y*, see *i*, 2 Ne. 10. *z*, see *n*, Mos. 8. 2*a*, see *i*, 2 Ne. 10. 2*b*, see *j*, Mos. 8. 2*c*, see *j*, Mos. 8. 2*d*, see *i*, 2 Ne. 10. 2*e*, ver. 28. Al. 45:16. About B. C. 73.

32. And now, my son, remember the words which I have spoken unto you; trust not those secret plans unto this people, but teach them an everlasting hatred against sin and iniquity.

33. Preach unto them repentance, and faith on the Lord Jesus Christ; teach them to humble themselves and to be meek and lowly in heart; teach them to withstand every temptation of the devil, with their faith on the Lord Jesus Christ.

34. Teach them to never be weary of good works, but to be meek and lowly in heart; for such shall find rest to their souls.

35. O, remember, my son, and learn wisdom in thy youth; yea, learn in thy youth to keep the commandments of God.

36. Yea, and 2*f*cry unto God for all thy support; yea, let all thy doings be unto the Lord, and whithersoever thou goest let it be in the Lord; yea, let thy thoughts be directed unto the Lord; yea, let the affections of thy heart be placed upon the Lord forever.

37. Counsel with the Lord in all thy doings, and he will direct thee for good; yea, when thou liest down at night lie down unto the Lord, that he may watch over you in your sleep; and when thou risest in the morning let thy heart be full of thanks unto God; and if ye do these things, ye shall be 2*g*lifted up at the last day.

38. And now, my son, I have somewhat to say concerning the thing which our fathers call a 2*h*ball, or director—or our fathers called it Liahona, which is, being interpreted, a compass; and the Lord prepared it.

39. And behold, there cannot any man work after the manner of so curious a workmanship. And behold, it was prepared to show unto our fathers the course which they should travel in the wilderness.

40. And it did work for them according to their faith in God; therefore, if they had faith to believe that God could cause that those spindles should point the way they should go, behold, it was done; therefore they had this miracle, and also many other miracles wrought by the power of God, day by day.

41. Nevertheless, because those miracles were worked by small means it did show unto them marvelous works. They were slothful, and forgot to exercise their faith and diligence and then those marvelous works ceased, and they did not progress in their journey;

42. Therefore, they tarried in the wilderness, or did not travel a direct course, and were afflicted with hunger and thirst, because of their transgressions.

43. And now, my son, I would that ye should understand that these things are not without a shadow; for as our fathers were slothful to give heed to this compass (now these things were temporal) they did not prosper; even so it is with things which are spiritual.

44. For behold, it is as easy to give heed to the word of Christ, which will point to you a 2*i*straight course to eternal bliss, as it was for our fathers to give heed to this compass, which would point unto them a straight course to the promised land.

45. And now I say, is there not a type in this thing? For just as surely as this 2*j*director did bring

---

2*f*, see *e*, 2 Ne. 32. 2*g*, see *p*, Mos. 23. 2*h*, see *d*, 1 Ne. 16. 2*i*, see 2*a*, 2 Ne. 9.
2*j*, ver. 38. See *d*, 1 Ne. 16.   ABOUT B. C. 73.

our fathers, by following its course, to the ²ᵏpromised land, shall the words of Christ, if we follow their course, carry us beyond this vale of sorrow into a far better land of promise.

46. O my son, do not let us be slothful because of the easiness of the way; for so was it with our fathers; for so was it prepared for them, that if they would look they might live; even so it is with us. The way is prepared, and if we will look we may live forever.

47. And now, my son, see that ye take care of these sacred things, yea, see that ye look to God and live. Go unto this people and declare the word, and be sober. My son, farewell.

CHAPTER 38.

The commandments of Alma to his son, Shiblon.

Commended for faithfulness, and counseled to observe meekness and self-control.

1. My son, give ear to my words, for I say unto you, even as I said unto Helaman, that ᵃinasmuch as ye shall keep the commandments of God ye shall prosper in the land; and inasmuch as ye will not keep the commandments of God ye shall be cast off from his presence.

2. And now, my son, I trust that I shall have great joy in you, because of your steadiness and your faithfulness unto God; for as you have commenced in your youth to look to the Lord your God, even so I hope that you will continue in keeping his commandments; for blessed is he that ᵇendureth to the end.

3. I say unto you, my son, that I have had great joy in thee already, because of thy faithfulness and thy diligence, and thy patience and thy long-suffering among the people of the ᶜZoramites.

4. For I know that thou wast in bonds; yea, and I also know that thou wast stoned for the word's sake; and thou didst bear all these things with patience because the Lord was with thee; and now thou knowest that the Lord did deliver thee.

5. And now my son, Shiblon, I would that ye should remember, that as much as ye shall put your trust in God even so much ye shall be delivered out of your trials, and your troubles, and your afflictions, and ye shall be ᵈlifted up at the last day.

6. Now, my son, I would not that ye should think that I know these things of myself, but it is the Spirit of God which is in me which maketh these things known unto me; for if I had not been ᵉborn of God I should not have known these things.

7. But behold, the Lord in his great mercy sent his angel to declare unto me that I must stop the work of destruction among his people; yea, and I have ᶠseen an angel face to face, and he spake with me, and his voice was as thunder, and it shook the whole earth.

8. And it came to pass that I was ᵍthree days and three nights in the most bitter pain and anguish of soul; and never, until I did cry out unto the Lord Jesus Christ for mercy, did I receive a remission of my sins. But behold, I did cry unto him and I did find peace to my soul.

9. And now, my son, I have told you this that ye may learn wisdom, that ye may learn of me

---

2*k*, see *a*, 1 Ne. 2.   CHAP. 38: *a*, see *h*, 2 Ne. 1.   *b*, see *h*, 2 Ne. 31.   *c*, see 2*j*, Al. 30.   *d*, see *p*, Mos. 23.   *e*, see *c*, Mos. 5.   *f*, Mos. 27:11—17.   *g*, Mos. 27:19—23, Al. 36:10, 16.   ABOUT B. C. 73.

that there is ʰno other way or means whereby man can be saved, only in and through Christ. Behold, he ⁱis the life and the light of the world. Behold, he is the word of truth and righteousness.

10. And now, as ye have begun to teach the word even so I would that ye should continue to teach; and I would that ye would be diligent and temperate in all things.

11. See that ye are not lifted up unto pride; yea, see that ye do not boast in your own wisdom, nor of your much strength.

12. Use boldness, but not overbearance; and also see that ye bridle all your passions, that ye may be filled with love; see that ye refrain from idleness.

13. Do not pray as the ʲZoramites do, for ye have seen that they pray to be heard of men, and to be praised for their wisdom.

14. Do not say: O God, I thank thee that we are better than our brethren; but rather say: O Lord, forgive my unworthiness, and remember my brethren in mercy—yea, acknowledge your unworthiness before God at all times.

15. And may the Lord bless your soul, and receive you at the last day into his kingdom, to sit down in peace. Now go, my son, and teach the word unto this people. Be sober. My son, farewell.

The commandments of Alma to his son, Corianton.

Comprising chapters 39 to 42 inclusive.

CHAPTER 39.

Corianton reproved for harlotry—His sinful conduct had affected faith of the Zoramites—Christ's redemption retroactive.

1. And now, my son, I have somewhat more to say unto thee than what I said unto thy brother; for behold, have ye not observed the steadiness of thy brother, his faithfulness, and his diligence in keeping the commandments of God? Behold, has he not set a good example for thee?

2. For thou didst not give so much heed unto my words as did thy brother, among the people of the ᵃZoramites. Now this is what I have against thee; thou didst go on unto boasting in thy strength and thy wisdom.

3. And this is not all, my son. Thou didst do that which was grievous unto me; for thou didst forsake the ministry, and did go over into the land of Siron, among the borders of the Lamanites, after the harlot Isabel.

4. Yea, she did steal away the hearts of many; but this was no excuse for thee, my son. Thou shouldst have tended to the ministry wherewith thou wast entrusted.

5. Know ye not, my son, that these things are an abomination in the sight of the Lord; yea, ᵇmost abominable above all sins save it be the shedding of innocent blood or denying the Holy Ghost?

6. For behold, if ye deny the Holy Ghost when it once has had place in you, and ye know that ye deny it, behold, this is a sin which is ᶜunpardonable; yea, and whosoever murdereth ᵈagainst the light and knowledge of God, it is not easy for him to obtain forgiveness; yea, I say unto you, my son, that it is not easy for him to obtain a forgiveness.

7. And now, my son, I would to God that ye had not been guilty of so great a crime. I would not dwell upon your crimes, to har-

---

h, see *d,* Mos. 5. *i,* see *m,* Mos. 16. *j,* see 2*j,* Al. 30. CHAP. 39: *a,* see 2*j,* Al. 30. *b,* vers. 7, 11. See *i,* 2 Ne. 28. *c,* Moro. 8:28. *d,* ver. 5. ABOUT B. C. 73.

row up your soul, if it were not for your good.

8. But behold, ye cannot hide your crimes from God; and except ye repent they will stand as a testimony against you at the last day.

9. Now my son, I would that ye should repent and forsake your sins, and go no more after the lusts of your eyes, but *e*cross yourself in all these things; for except ye do this ye can in nowise inherit the kingdom of God. Oh, remember, and take it upon you, and cross yourself in these things.

10. And I command you to take it upon you to counsel with your elder brothers in your undertakings; for behold, thou art in thy youth, and ye stand in need to be nourished by your brothers. And give heed to their counsel.

11. Suffer not yourself to be led away by any vain or foolish thing; suffer not the devil to lead away your heart again after those *f*wicked harlots. Behold, O my son, how great iniquity ye brought upon the Zoramites; for when they saw your conduct they would not believe in my words.

12. And now the Spirit of the Lord doth say unto me: Command thy children to do good, lest they lead away the hearts of many people to destruction; therefore I command you, my son, in the fear of God, that ye refrain from your iniquities;

13. That ye turn to the Lord with all your mind, might, and strength; that ye lead away the hearts of no more to do wickedly; but rather return unto them, and acknowledge your faults and that wrong which ye have done.

14. Seek not after riches nor the vain things of this world; for behold, you cannot carry them with you.

15. And now, my son, I would say somewhat unto you concerning the coming of Christ. Behold, I say unto you, that it is he that surely shall come to take away the sins of the world; yea, he cometh to declare glad tidings of salvation unto his people.

16. And now, my son, this was the ministry unto which ye were called, to declare these glad tidings unto this people, to prepare their minds; or rather that salvation might come unto them, that they may prepare the minds of their children to hear the word at the time of his coming.

17. And now I will ease your mind somewhat on this subject. Behold, you marvel why these things should be known so long beforehand. Behold, I say unto you, is not a soul at this time as precious unto God as a soul will be at the time of his coming?

18. Is it not as necessary that the plan of redemption should be made known unto this people as well as unto their children?

19. Is it not as easy at this time for the Lord to *g*send his angel to declare these glad tidings unto us as unto our children, or as after the time of his coming?

CHAPTER 40.

Alma to Corianton continued—Resurrection universal—Separate states of righteous and wicked between death and resurrection—A literal restoration.

1. Now my son, here is somewhat more I would say unto thee; for I perceive that thy mind is worried concerning the *a*resurrection of the dead.

2. Behold, I say unto you, that

e, 3 Ne. 12:30. *f*, vers. 3, 7—9. *g*, Mos. 3:2—27. 27:11—17. Al. 11:31. 13:24.
CHAP. 40: *a*, see *d*, 2 Ne. 2. ABOUT B. C. 73.

there is no resurrection—or, I would say, in other words, that ^{b}this mortal does not put on immortality, this corruption does not put on incorruption—until after the coming of Christ.

3. Behold, he bringeth to pass the resurrection of the dead. But behold, my son, the resurrection is not yet. Now, I unfold unto you a mystery; nevertheless, there are many mysteries which are kept, that no one knoweth them save God himself. But I show unto you one thing which I have inquired diligently of God that I might know—that is concerning the resurrection.

4. Behold, there is a time appointed that all shall come forth from the dead. Now when this time cometh no one knows; but God knoweth the time which is appointed.

5. Now, whether there shall be one time, or a second time, or a third time, that men shall come forth from the dead, it mattereth not; for God knoweth all these things; and it sufficeth me to know that this is the case—that there is a time appointed that all shall rise from the dead.

6. Now there must needs be a space betwixt the time of death and the time of the resurrection.

7. And now I would inquire what becometh of the souls of men from this time of death to the time appointed for the resurrection?

8. Now whether there is more than one time appointed for men to rise it mattereth not; for all do not die at once, and this mattereth not; all is as one day with God, and time only is measured unto men.

9. Therefore, there is a time appointed unto men that they shall rise from the dead; and there is a space between the time of death and the resurrection. And now, concerning this space of time, what becometh of the souls of men is the thing which I have inquired diligently of the Lord to know; and this is the thing of which I do know.

10. And when the time cometh when all shall rise, then shall they know that God knoweth all the times which are appointed unto man.

11. Now, concerning the state of the soul between death and the resurrection—Behold, it has been made known unto me by an angel, that the spirits of all men, as soon as they are departed from this mortal body, yea, the spirits of ^{c}all men, whether they be good or evil, are taken home to that God who gave them life.

12. And then shall it come to pass, that the spirits of those who are righteous are received into a state of happiness, which is called ^{d}paradise, a state of rest, a state of peace, where they shall rest from all their troubles and from all care, and sorrow.

13. And then shall it come to pass, that the spirits of the wicked, yea, who are evil—for behold, they have no part nor portion of the Spirit of the Lord; for behold, they chose evil works rather than good; therefore the spirit of the devil did ^{e}enter into them, and take possession of their house—and these shall be cast out into outer darkness; ^{f}there shall be weeping, and wailing, and gnashing of teeth, and this because of their own iniquity,

b, Mos. 16:10. See *d*, 2 Ne. 2. Also *j* and *m*, 2 Ne. 9. *c*, vers. 15. 17. Eccl. 12:7. *d*, see *l*, 2 Ne. 9. *c*, see *i*, 2 Ne. 9. *f*, Mos. 16:2. See *k*, 1 Ne. 15.

ABOUT B. C. 73.

being led captive by the will of the devil.

14. Now this is the state of the souls of the wicked, yea, in ^gdarkness, and a state of awful, fearful looking for the fiery indignation of the wrath of God upon them; thus they remain in this state, as well as the righteous in ^hparadise, until the time of their resurrection.

15. Now, there are some that have understood that this state of happiness and this state of misery of the soul, before the resurrection, was a first resurrection. Yea, I admit it may be termed a resurrection, the ⁱraising of the spirit or the soul and their consignation to happiness or misery, according to the words which have been spoken.

16. And behold, again it hath been spoken, that there is a ^jfirst resurrection, a resurrection of all those who have been, or who are, or who shall be, down to the resurrection of Christ from the dead.

17. Now, we do not suppose that this first resurrection, which is spoken of in this manner, can be the resurrection ^kof the souls and their consignation to happiness or misery. Ye cannot suppose that this is what it meaneth.

18. Behold, I say unto you, Nay; but it meaneth the ^lreuniting of the soul with the body, of those ^mfrom the days of Adam down to the resurrection of Christ.

19. Now, whether the souls and the bodies of those of whom has been spoken shall all be reunited at once, the wicked as well as the righteous, I do not say; let it suffice, that I say that they all come forth; or in other words, their resurrection cometh to pass ⁿbefore the resurrection of those who die after the resurrection of Christ.

20. Now, my son, I do not say that their resurrection cometh at the resurrection of Christ; but behold, I give it as my opinion, that the souls and the bodies are ^oreunited, of the righteous, at the resurrection of Christ, and his ascension into heaven.

21. But whether it be at his resurrection or after, I do not say; but this much I say, that there is a ^pspace between death and the resurrection of the body, and a state of the soul in happiness or in misery until the time which is appointed of God that the dead shall come forth, and be reunited, both soul and body, and be brought to stand before God, and be judged according to their works.

22. Yea, this bringeth about the restoration of those things of which has been spoken by the mouths of the prophets.

23. The ^qsoul shall be restored to the body, and the body to the soul; yea, and every limb and joint shall be restored to its body; yea, even a hair of the head shall not be lost; but all things shall be restored to their proper and perfect frame.

24. And now, my son, this is the restoration of which has been spoken by the mouths of the prophets—

25. And then shall the righteous shine forth in the kingdom of God.

26. But behold, an awful ^rdeath cometh upon the wicked; for they die as to things pertaining to things of righteousness; for they are unclean, and ^sno unclean thing

g, ver. 13. *h*, see *l*, 2 Ne. 9. *i*, see *c*. *j*, see *g*, Jac. 4. *k*, see *c*. *l*, see *d*, 2 Ne. 2. *m*, vers. 19, 20. *n*, vers. 16, 18, 20. *o*, see *g*, Jac. 4. *p*, vers. 6, 9, 11—15. *q*, Al. 11:41—45, 41:2. See *d*, 2 Ne. 2. *r*, see *q*, Al. 12. *s*, Al. 11:37.

ABOUT B. C. 73.

can inherit the kingdom of God; but they are cast out, and consigned to partake of the fruits of their labors or their works, which have been evil; and they drink the dregs of a bitter cup.

CHAPTER 41.

Alma to Corianton continued—What restoration signifies—Men to be judged according to their deeds and desires—Self-judgment.

1. And now, my son, I have somewhat to say concerning the restoration of which has been spoken; for behold, some have wrested the scriptures, and have gone far astray because of this thing. And I perceive that thy mind has been worried also concerning this thing. But behold, I will explain it unto thee.

2. I say unto thee, my son, that the plan of restoration is requisite with the justice of God; for it is requisite that all things should be restored to their proper order. Behold, it is requisite and just, according to the power and resurrection of Christ, ^{a}that the soul of man should be restored to its body, and that every part of the body should be restored to itself.

3. And it is requisite with the justice of God that men should be judged according to their works; and ^{b}if their works were good in this life, and the desires of their hearts were good, that they should also, at the last day, be restored unto that which is good.

4. And ^{c}if their works are evil they shall be restored unto them for evil. Therefore, all things shall be restored to their proper order, every thing to its natural frame—mortality ^{d}raised to immortality, corruption to incorruption—raised to endless happiness to inherit the kingdom of God, or to ^{e}endless misery to inherit the kingdom of the devil, the one on one hand, the other on the other—

5. The one raised to ^{f}happiness according to his desires of happiness, or good according to his desires of good; and the other to ^{g}evil according to his desires of evil; for as he has desired to do evil all the day long even so shall he have his reward of evil when the night cometh.

6. And so it is on the other hand. If he hath repented of his sins, and ^{h}desired righteousness until the end of his days, even so he shall be rewarded unto righteousness.

7. These are they that are redeemed of the Lord; yea, these are they that are taken out, that are delivered from that ^{i}endless night of darkness; and thus they stand or fall; for behold, they are their own judges, whether to do good or do evil.

8. Now, the decrees of God are ^{j}unalterable; therefore, the way is prepared that whosoever will may walk therein and be saved.

9. And now behold, my son, do not risk one more offense against your God upon those points of doctrine, which ye have hitherto risked to commit sin.

10. Do not suppose, because it has been spoken concerning restoration, that ye shall be restored from sin to happiness. Behold, I say unto you, wickedness ^{k}never was happiness.

11. And now, my son, all men that are in a state of nature, or I would say, in a carnal state, are in the gall of bitterness and in the bonds of iniquity; they are

---

a, see *q*, Al. 40. *b*, vers. 6, 7, 14. *c*, vers. 10—13, 15. *d*, Mos. 16:10. See *d*, 2 Ne. 2. *e*, see *m*, Jac. 6. *f*, see *b*. *g*, see *c*. *h*, see *b*. *i*, see *m*, Jac. 6. *j*, Morm. 9:19. *k*, vers. 11, 12.

ABOUT B. C. 73.

without God in the world, and they have gone contrary to the nature of God; therefore, they are in a state *l*contrary to the nature of happiness.

12. And now behold, is the meaning of the word restoration to take a thing of a natural state and place it in an unnatural state, or to place it in a state opposite to its nature?

13. O, my son, this is not the case; but the meaning of the word *m*restoration is to bring back again evil for evil, or carnal for carnal, or devilish for devilish—*n*good for that which is good; righteous for that which is righteous; just for that which is just; merciful for that which is merciful.

14. Therefore, my son, see that you are merciful unto your brethren; deal justly, judge righteously, and do good continually; and if ye do all these things then shall ye receive your reward; yea, ye shall have mercy restored unto you again; ye shall have justice restored unto you again; ye shall have a righteous judgment restored unto you again; and ye shall have good rewarded unto you again.

15. For that which ye do send out shall return unto you again, and be restored; therefore, the word restoration *o*more fully condemneth the sinner, and justifieth him not at all.

CHAPTER 42.

Alma to Corianton continued—Justice and mercy expounded—The tree of life—Mortality a period of probation—Spiritual and temporal death—Repentance, atonement, law, punishment, all necessary.

1. And now, my son, I perceive there is somewhat more which doth worry your mind, which ye cannot understand—which is concerning the justice of God in the punishment of the sinner; for ye do try to suppose that it is injustice that the sinner should be consigned to a state of misery.

2. Now behold, my son, I will explain this thing unto thee. For behold, after the Lord God sent our first parents forth from the garden of Eden, to till the ground, from *a*whence they were taken— yea, he drew out the man, and he placed at the east end of the garden of Eden, cherubim, and a flaming sword which turned every way, to keep the tree of life—

3. Now, we see that the man had become as God, knowing good and evil; and lest he should put forth his hand, and take also of the tree of life, and eat and live forever, the Lord God placed cherubim and the flaming sword, that he should not partake of the fruit—

4. And thus we see, that there was a time granted unto man to repent, yea, a *b*probationary time, a time to repent and serve God.

5. For behold, if Adam had put forth his hand immediately, and partaken of the tree of life, he would have *c*lived forever, according to the word of God, having no space for repentance; yea, and also the word of God would have been *d*void, and the great plan of salvation would have been frustrated.

6. But behold, it was appointed unto man to die—therefore, as they were cut off from the tree of life they should be cut off from the face of the earth—and man became lost *e*forever, yea, they became fallen man.

l, vers. 10, 12. *m*, see *c*. *n*, see *b*. *o*, Al. 42:28. CHAP. 42: *a*, see *m*, Mos. 2. *b*, see 2*a*, Al. 12. *c*, ver. 3. *d*, vers. 6, 8. Al. 12:23, 26. *e*, see *w*, Al. 12.

ABOUT B. C. 73.

7. And now, ye see by this that our first parents were cut off both *f*temporally and *g*spiritually from the presence of the Lord; and thus we see they became subjects to follow after their *h*own will.

8. Now behold, it was not expedient that man should be *i*reclaimed from this temporal death, for that would destroy the great plan of happiness.

9. Therefore, as the soul could *j*never die, and the fall had brought upon all mankind a *k*spiritual death as well as a *l*temporal, that is, they were cut off from the presence of the Lord, it was expedient that mankind should be reclaimed from this spiritual death.

10. Therefore, as they had become carnal, sensual, and devilish, by nature, this *m*probationary state became a state for them to prepare; it became a preparatory state.

11. And now remember, my son, if it were not for the plan of redemption, (laying it aside) as soon as they were *n*dead their *o*souls were miserable, being cut off from the presence of the Lord.

12. And now, there was no means to reclaim men from this fallen state, which man had brought upon himself because of his own disobedience;

13. Therefore, according to justice, the plan of redemption could not be brought about, only on conditions of repentance of men in this *p*probationary state, yea, this preparatory state; for except it were for these conditions, mercy could not take effect *q*except it should destroy the work of justice. Now the work of justice could not be destroyed; if so, God would *r*cease to be God.

14. And thus we see that *s*all mankind were fallen, and they were in the grasp of justice; yea, the justice of God, which consigned them *t*forever to be cut off from his presence.

15. And now, the plan of mercy could not be brought about except an *u*atonement should be made; therefore God himself atoneth for the sins of the world, to bring about the plan of mercy, to *v*appease the demands of justice, that God might be a perfect, just God, and a merciful God also.

16. Now, repentance could not come unto men except there were a punishment, which also was *w*eternal as the *x*life of the soul should be, affixed opposite to the plan of happiness, which was as eternal also as the life of the soul.

17. Now, how could a man repent except he should sin? How could he sin if there was no law? How could there be a law save there was a punishment?

18. Now, there was a punishment affixed, and a just law given, which brought remorse of conscience unto man.

19. Now, if there was no law given—if a man murdered he should die—would he be afraid he would die if he should murder?

20. And also, if there was no law given against sin men would not be afraid to sin.

21. And if there was no law given, if *y*men sinned what could justice do, or mercy either, for they would have no claim upon the creature?

22. But there is a law given, and a punishment affixed, and a

f, see *b*, 2 Ne. 2. *g*, see *c*, 2 Ne. 2. *h*, see *l*, 2 Ne. 2. *i*, see *d*. *j*, ver. 11. *k*, see *c*, 2 Ne. 2. *l*, see *b*, 2 Ne. 2. *m*, see 2*a*, Al. 12. *n*, see *l*. *o*, see *k*. *p*, see 2*a*, Al. 12. *q*, see 2*m*, Al. 12. *r*, see *f*, 2 Ne. 11. *s*, see *e* and *g*, 2 Ne. 9. *t*, see *w*, Al. 12. *u*, see *f*, 2 Ne. 2. *v*, see 2*m*, Al. 12. *w*, see *m*, Jac. 6. *x*, vers. 8, 9. See *e* and *g*, 2 Ne. 9. *y*, see *j*, Mos. 3.

ABOUT B. C. 73.

repentance granted; which repentance, mercy claimeth; otherwise, *justice claimeth the creature and executeth the law, and the law inflicteth the punishment; if not so, the works of justice would be destroyed, and God would ²ᵃcease to be God.

23. But God ceaseth not to be God, and mercy claimeth the penitent, and mercy cometh because of the ²ᵇatonement; and the atonement bringeth to pass the ²ᶜresurrection of the dead; and the resurrection of the dead bringeth back men into the presence of God; and thus they are ²ᵈrestored into his presence, to be judged according to their works, according to the law and justice.

24. For behold, justice exerciseth all his demands, and also mercy claimeth all which is her own; and thus, none but the truly penitent are saved.

25. What, do ye suppose that mercy can rob justice? I say unto you, Nay; not one whit. If so, God would ²ᵉcease to be God.

26. And thus God bringeth about his great and eternal purposes, which were prepared ²ᶠfrom the foundation of the world. And thus cometh about the salvation and the redemption of men, and also their destruction and misery.

27. Therefore, O my son, whosoever will come may come and partake of the waters of life freely; and whosoever will not come the same is not compelled to come; but in the last day it shall be ²ᵍrestored unto him according to his deeds.

28. If he has desired to do evil, and has not repented in his days, behold, ²ʰevil shall be done unto him, according to the restoration of God.

29. And now, my son, I desire that ye should let these things trouble you no more, and only let your sins trouble you, with that trouble which shall bring you down unto repentance.

30. O my son, I desire ²ⁱthat ye should deny the justice of God no more. Do not endeavor to excuse yourself in the least point because of your sins, by denying the justice of God; but do you let the justice of God, and his mercy, and his long-suffering have full sway in your heart; and let it bring you down to the dust in humility.

31. And now, O my son, ye are called of God to preach the word unto this people. And now, my son, go thy way, declare the word with truth and soberness, that thou mayest bring souls unto repentance, that the great plan of mercy may have claim upon them. And may God grant unto you even according to my words. Amen.

CHAPTER 43.

Another Lamanite invasion—Armies of Moroni and Lehi surround and overpower the enemy.

1. And now it came to pass that the sons of Alma did go forth among the people, to declare the word unto them. And Alma, also, himself, could not rest, and he also went forth.

2. Now we shall say no more concerning their preaching, except that they preached the word, and the truth, according to the spirit of prophecy and revelation; and they preached after the ᵃholy order of God by which they were called.

3. And now I return to an account of the wars between the

g, see 2*m*, Al. 12. 2*a*, see *r*, also *f*, 2 Ne. 11. 2*b*, see *f*, 2 Ne. 2. 2*c*, see *d*, 2 Ne. 2. 2*d*, Al. 40:21—26. 2*e*, see *f*, 2 Ne. 11. 2*f*, see *d*, Mos. 4. 2*g*, Al. 41:15. 2*h*, see *c*, Al. 41. 2*i*, ver. 1. Chap. 43: *a*, see *g*, Mos. 26. About B. C. 73.

ALMA, 43.

Nephites and the Lamanites, in the *eighteenth year of the reign of the judges.

4. For behold, it came to pass that the ^bZoramites became Lamanites; therefore, in the commencement of the eighteenth year the people of the Nephites saw that the Lamanites were coming upon them; therefore they made preparations for war; yea, they gathered together their armies in the ^cland of Jershon.

5. And it came to pass that the Lamanites came with their thousands; and they came into the ^dland of Antionum, which is the ^eland of the Zoramites; and a man by the name of Zerahemnah was their leader.

6. And now, as the Amalekites were of a more wicked and murderous disposition than the Lamanites were, in and of themselves, therefore, Zerahemnah appointed chief captains over the Lamanites, and they were all Amalekites and ^fZoramites.

7. Now this he did that he might preserve their ^ghatred towards the Nephites, that he might bring them into subjection to the accomplishment of his designs.

8. For behold, his designs were to stir up the Lamanites to anger against the Nephites; this he did that he might usurp great power over them, and also that he might gain power over the Nephites by bringing them into bondage.

9. And now the design of the Nephites was to support their lands, and their houses, and their wives, and their children, that they might preserve them from the hands of their enemies; and also that they might preserve their rights and their privileges, yea, and also their ^hliberty, that they might worship God according to their desires.

10. For they knew that if they should fall into the hands of the Lamanites, that whosoever should worship God in spirit and in truth, the true and the living God, the Lamanites would destroy.

11. Yea, and they also knew the ⁱextreme hatred of the Lamanites towards their brethren, who were the people of ^jAnti-Nephi-Lehi, who were called the ^kpeople of Ammon—and they would not take up arms, yea, they had entered ^linto a covenant and they would not break it—therefore, if they should fall into the hands of the Lamanites they would be destroyed.

12. And the Nephites would not suffer ^mthat they should be destroyed; therefore they gave them ⁿlands for their inheritance.

13. And the people of Ammon did give unto the Nephites a ^olarge portion of their substance to support their armies; and thus the Nephites were compelled, alone, to withstand against the Lamanites, who were a compound of Laman and Lemuel, and the sons of Ishmael, and all those who had dissented from the Nephites, who were Amalekites and ^pZoramites, and the descendants of the ^qpriests of Noah.

14. Now those descendants were as numerous, nearly, as were the Nephites; and thus the Nephites were obliged to contend with their brethren, even unto bloodshed.

15. And it came to pass as the armies of the Lamanites had

---

b, see 2j, Al. 30.   c, see q, Al. 27.   d, see b, Al. 31.   e, Al. 31:3.   f, see 2j, Al. 30.
g, see n, Jac. 7.   h, see m, Mos. 29.   i, Al. 27:2.   j, see t, Al. 23.   k, Al. 27:26.
l, Al. 24:16—19.   m, Al. 27:23, 24.   n, Al. 27:22.   o, Al. 27:24.   p, see 2j, Al. 30.
q, see f, Mos. 11.   *About B. C. 74.

gathered together in the ^{r}land of Antionum, behold, the armies of the Nephites were prepared to meet them in the ^{s}land of Jershon.

16. Now, the leader of the Nephites, or the man who had been appointed to be the chief captain over the Nephites—now the chief captain took the command of all the armies of the Nephites—and his name was Moroni;

17. And Moroni took all the command, and the government of their wars. And he was only twenty and five years old when he was appointed chief captain over the armies of the Nephites.

18. And it came to pass that he met the Lamanites in the ^{t}borders of Jershon, and his people were armed ^{u}with swords, and with cimeters, and all manner of weapons of war.

19. And when the armies of the Lamanites saw that the people of Nephi, or that Moroni, had prepared his people with breastplates and with arm-shields, yea, and also shields to defend their heads, and also they were dressed with thick clothing—

20. Now the army of Zerahemnah was not prepared with any such thing; they had only their swords and their cimeters, their bows and their arrows, their stones and their slings; and they were naked, ^{v}save it were a skin which was girded about their loins; yea, all were naked, save it were the Zoramites and the Amalekites;

21. But they were not armed with breastplates, nor shields—therefore, they were exceedingly afraid of the armies of the Nephites because of their armor, notwithstanding their number being so much greater than the Nephites.

22. Behold, now it came to pass that they durst not come against the Nephites in the ^{w}borders of Jershon; therefore they departed out of the ^{x}land of Antionum into the wilderness, and took their journey round about in the wilderness, away by the head of the ^{y}river Sidon, that they might come into the ^{z}land of Manti and take possession of the land; for they did not suppose that the armies of Moroni would know whither they had gone.

23. But it came to pass, as soon as they had departed into the wilderness Moroni sent spies into the wilderness to watch their camp; and Moroni, also, knowing of the prophecies of Alma, sent certain men unto him, desiring him that he should inquire of the Lord whither the armies of the Nephites should go to defend themselves against the Lamanites.

24. And it came to pass that the word of the Lord came unto Alma, and Alma informed the messengers of Moroni, that the armies of the Lamanites were marching round about in the wilderness, that they might come over into the ^{2a}land of Manti, that they might commence an attack upon the weaker part of the people. And those messengers went and delivered the message unto Moroni.

25. Now Moroni, leaving a part of his army in the ^{2b}land of Jershon, lest by any means a part of the Lamanites should come into that land and take possession of the city, took the remaining part

---
r, see b, Al. 31. s, see q, Al. 27. t, see q, Al. 27. u, see f, Al. 2. v, ver. 37. Enos 20. Al. 3:4, 5. w, see q, Al. 27. x, see b, Al. 31. y, see g, Al. 2. z, see h, Al. 16. $2a$, see h, Al. 16. $2b$, see q, Al. 27. ABOUT B. C. 74.

of his army and marched over into the ²ᶜland of Manti.

26. And he caused that all the people in that quarter of the land should gather themselves together to battle against the Lamanites, to defend their lands and their country, their rights and their liberties; therefore they were prepared against the time of the coming of the Lamanites.

27. And it came to pass that Moroni caused that his army should be secreted in the valley which was near the bank of the ²ᵈriver Sidon, which was on the west of the river Sidon in the wilderness.

28. And Moroni placed spies round about, that he might know when the camp of the Lamanites should come.

29. And now, as Moroni knew the intention of the Lamanites, that it was their ²ᵉintention to destroy their brethren, or to subject them and bring them into bondage that they might establish a kingdom unto themselves over all the land;

30. And he also knowing that it was the ²ᶠonly desire of the Nephites to preserve their lands, and their liberty, and their church, therefore he thought it no sin that he should defend them by stratagem; therefore, he found by his ²ᵍspies which course the Lamanites were to take.

31. Therefore, he divided his army and brought a part over into the valley, and concealed them on the east, and on the south of the ²ʰhill Riplah;

32. And the remainder he concealed in the west valley, on the west of the ²ⁱriver Sidon, and so down into the ²ʲborders of the land Manti.

33. And thus having placed his army according to his desire, he was prepared to meet them.

34. And it came to pass that the Lamanites came up on the north of the ²ᵏhill, where a part of the army of Moroni was concealed.

35. And as the Lamanites had passed the ²ˡhill Riplah, and came into the valley, and began to cross the ²ᵐriver Sidon, the army which was concealed on the south of the hill, which was led by a man whose name was Lehi, and he led his army forth and encircled the Lamanites about on the east in their rear.

36. And it came to pass that the Lamanites, when they saw the Nephites coming upon them in their rear, turned them about and began to contend with the army of Lehi.

37. And the work of death commenced on both sides, but it was more dreadful on the part of the Lamanites, for their ²ⁿnakedness was exposed to the heavy blows of the Nephites ²ᵒwith their swords and their cimeters, which brought death almost at every stroke.

38. While on the other hand, there was now and then a man fell among the Nephites, by their swords and the loss of blood, they being shielded from the more vital parts of the body, or the more vital parts of the body being shielded from the strokes of the Lamanites, ²ᵖby their breastplates, and their arm-shields, and their head-plates; and thus the Nephites did carry

---

2c, see h, Al. 16. 2d, see g, Al. 2. 2e, vers. 8, 10. 2f, vers. 9, 45, 48, 49. See m, Mos. 29. Al. 44:5. 46:12—20. 48:10—16. 2g, vers. 23, 28. 2h, vers. 34, 35. 2i, see g, Al. 2. 2j, see h, Al. 16. 2k, vers. 31, 35. 2l, vers. 31, 34. 2m, see g, Al. 2. 2n, ver. 20. See v. 20, ver. 18. 2p, vers. 19, 21, 44. Al. 44:9. 46:13. 49:6, 24. He. 1:14. Morm. 6:9.

ABOUT B. C. 74,

on the work of death among the Lamanites.

39. And it came to pass that the Lamanites became frightened, because of the great destruction among them, even until they began to flee towards the ^{2q}river Sidon.

40. And they were pursued by Lehi and his men; and they were driven by Lehi into the waters of Sidon, and they crossed the waters of Sidon. And Lehi retained his armies upon the ^{2r}bank of the river Sidon that they should not cross.

41. And it came to pass that Moroni and his army met the Lamanites in the ^{2s}valley, on the ^{2t}other side of the river Sidon, and began to fall upon them and to slay them.

42. And the Lamanites did flee again before them, ^{2u}towards the land of Manti; and they were met again by the armies of Moroni.

43. Now in this case the Lamanites did fight exceedingly; yea, never had the Lamanites been known to fight with such exceeding great strength and courage, no, not even from the beginning.

44. And they were inspired by the ^{2v}Zoramites and the Amalekites, who were their chief captains and leaders, and by Zerahemnah, who was their chief captain, or their chief leader and commander; yea, they did fight like dragons, and many of the Nephites were slain by their hands, yea, for they did smite in two ^{2w}many of their head-plates, and they did pierce many of their breastplates, and they did smite off many of their arms; and thus the Lamanites did smite in their fierce anger.

45. Nevertheless, the Nephites were inspired by a better cause, for they were not fighting for monarchy nor power but they were ^{2x}fighting for their homes and their liberties, their wives and their children, and their all, yea, for their rites of worship and their church.

46. And they were doing that which they felt was the duty which they owed to their God; for the Lord had said unto them, and also unto their fathers, that: ^{2y}Inasmuch as ye are not guilty of the first offense, neither the second, ye shall not suffer yourselves to be slain by the hands of your enemies.

47. And again, the Lord has said that: Ye shall defend your families even unto bloodshed. Therefore for this cause were the Nephites contending with the Lamanites, to ^{2z}defend themselves, and their families, and their lands, their country, and their rights, and their religion.

48. And it came to pass that when the men of Moroni saw the ^{3a}fierceness and the anger of the Lamanites, they were about to shrink and flee from them. And Moroni, perceiving their intent, sent forth and inspired their hearts with these thoughts—yea, the ^{3b}thoughts of their lands, their liberty, yea, their freedom from bondage.

49. And it came to pass that they turned upon the Lamanites, and they cried with one voice unto the Lord their God, ^{3c}for their liberty and their freedom from bondage.

50. And they began to stand

2q, see g, Al 2. 2r, ver. 27. 2s, ver. 32. 2t, ver. 32. 2u, ver. 32. See h, Al. 16. 2v, ver. 6. 2w, see 2p. 2x, vers. 30, 47. Al. 44:5. 2y, D. & C. 98:23—48. Al. 48:14—16. 2z, see 2f. 3a, ver. 44. 3b, see 2f. 3c, see 2f. ABOUT B. C. 74.

against the Lamanites with power; and in that selfsame hour that they cried unto the Lord for their freedom, the Lamanites began to flee before them; and they fled even to the [3d]waters of Sidon.

51. Now, the Lamanites were more numerous, yea, by more than double the number of the Nephites; nevertheless, they were driven insomuch that they were gathered together in one body in the [3e]valley, upon the [3f]bank by the river Sidon.

52. Therefore the armies of Moroni encircled them about, yea, even on both sides of the river, for behold, on the east were the men of Lehi.

53. Therefore when Zerahemnah saw the men of Lehi on the east of the river Sidon, and the armies of Moroni on the west of the river Sidon, that they were encircled about by the Nephites, they were struck with terror.

54. Now Moroni, when he saw their terror, commanded his men that they should stop shedding their blood.

CHAPTER 44.

Moroni's magnanimity—Zerahemnah rejects his peace offer, but is compelled to accept terms—Lamanites make covenant of peace—End of Alma's record.

1. And it came to pass that they did stop and withdrew a pace from them. And Moroni said unto Zerahemnah: Behold, Zerahemnah, that we do not desire to be men of blood. Ye know that ye are in our hands, yet we do not desire to slay you.

2. Behold, we have not come out to battle against you that we might shed your blood for power; neither do we desire to bring any one to the yoke of bondage. But this is the [a]very cause for which ye have come against us; yea, and ye are angry with us because of our religion.

3. But now, ye behold that the Lord is with us; and ye behold that he has delivered you into our hands. And now I would that ye should understand that this is done unto us [b]because of our religion and our faith in Christ. And now ye see that ye cannot destroy this our faith.

4. Now ye see that this is the true faith of God; yea, ye see that God will support, and keep, and preserve us, so long as we are faithful unto him, and unto our faith, and our religion; and never will the Lord [c]suffer that we shall be destroyed except we should fall into transgression and deny our faith.

5. And now, Zerahemnah, I command you, in the name of that all-powerful God, who has strengthened our arms that we have gained power over you, [d]by our faith, by our religion, and by our rites of worship, and by our church, and by the sacred support which we owe to our wives and our children, by that liberty which binds us to our lands and our country; yea, and also by the maintenance of the sacred word of God, to which we owe all our happiness; and by all that is most dear unto us—

6. Yea, and this is not all; I command you by all the desires which ye have for life, that ye deliver up your weapons of war unto us, and we will seek not your blood, but we will spare your lives, if ye will go your way and come not again to war against us.

3d, see g, Al. 2. 3e, ver. 32. 3f, ver. 32. 43:49, 50. c, see h, 2 Ne. 1. d, see 2f, Al. 43. CHAP. 44: a, Al. 43:8. b, Al. ABOUT B. C. 74.

7. And now, if ye do not this, behold, ye are in our hands, and I will command my men that they shall fall upon you, and inflict the wounds of death in your bodies, that ye may become extinct; and then we will see who shall have power over this people; yea, we will see who shall be brought into bondage.

8. And now it came to pass that when Zerahemnah had heard these sayings he came forth and delivered *c*up his sword and his cimeter, and his bow into the hands of Moroni, and said unto him: Behold, here are our weapons of war; we will deliver them up unto you, but we will not suffer ourselves to *f*take an oath unto you, which we know that we shall break, and also our children; but take our weapons of war, and suffer that we may depart into the wilderness; otherwise we will retain our swords, and we will perish or conquer.

9. Behold, we are not of your faith; we do not believe that it is God that has delivered us into your hands; but we believe that it is your cunning that has preserved you from our swords. Behold, *g*it is your breastplates and your shields that have preserved you.

10. And now when Zerahemnah had made an end of speaking these words, Moroni returned the sword and the weapons of war, which he had received, unto Zerahemnah, saying: Behold, we will end the conflict.

11. Now I cannot recall the words which I have spoken, therefore as the Lord liveth, ye shall not depart *h*except ye depart with an oath that ye will not return again against us to war. Now as ye are in our hands we will spill your blood upon the ground, or ye shall submit to the conditions which I have proposed.

12. And now when Moroni had said these words, Zerahemnah retained his sword, and he was angry with Moroni, and he rushed forward that he might slay Moroni; but as he raised his sword, behold, one of Moroni's soldiers smote it even to the earth, and it broke by the hilt; and he also smote Zerahemnah that he *i*took off his scalp and it fell to the earth. And Zerahemnah withdrew from before them into the midst of his soldiers.

13. And it came to pass that the soldier who stood by, who smote off the scalp of Zerahemnah, took up the scalp from off the ground by the hair, and laid it upon the point of his sword, and stretched it forth unto them, saying unto them with a loud voice:

14. *j*Even as this scalp has fallen to the earth, which is the scalp of your chief, so shall ye fall to the earth except ye will deliver up your weapons of war and depart with a *k*covenant of peace.

15. Now there were many, when they heard these words and saw the *l*scalp which was upon the sword, that were struck with fear; and many came forth and threw down their weapons of war at the feet of Moroni, and entered into a covenant of peace. And as many as entered into a *m*covenant they suffered to depart into the wilderness.

16. Now it came to pass that Zerahemnah was exceeding wroth, and he did stir up the remainder

---

c, Al. 43:20. *f*, vers. 6, 11, 15, 19, 20. *g*, see 2*p*, Al. 43. *h*, see *f*. *i*, vers. 13—15. *j*, ver. 18. *k*, see *f*. *l*, see *i*. *m*, see *f*. ABOUT B. C. 74.

of his soldiers to anger, to contend more powerfully against the Nephites.

17. And now Moroni was angry, because of the stubbornness of the Lamanites; therefore he commanded his people that they should fall upon them and slay them. And it came to pass that they began to slay them; yea, and the Lamanites did contend with their swords and their might.

18. But behold, their ⁿnaked skins and their bare heads were exposed to the sharp swords of the Nephites; yea, behold they were pierced and smitten, yea, and did fall exceedingly fast before the swords of the Nephites; and they began to be swept down, even as the °soldier of Moroni had prophesied.

19. Now Zerahemnah, when he saw that they were all about to be destroyed, cried mightily unto Moroni, promising that he would covenant and also his people with them, if they would spare the remainder of their lives, that they ᵖnever would come to war again against them.

20. And it came to pass that Moroni caused that the work of death should cease again among the people. And he took the weapons of war from the Lamanites; and ᑋafter they had entered into a covenant with him of peace they were suffered to depart into the wilderness.

21. Now the number of their dead was not numbered because of the greatness of the number; yea, the number of their dead was exceeding great, both on the Nephites and on the Lamanites.

22. And it came to pass that they did cast their dead into the ʳwaters of Sidon, and they have gone forth and are buried in the depths of the sea.

23. And the armies of the Nephites, or of Moroni, returned and came to their houses and their lands.

24. And thus *ended the eighteenth year of the reign of the judges over the people of Nephi. And thus ended the record of Alma, which was written upon the ˢplates of Nephi.

The account of the people of Nephi, and their wars and dissensions, in the days of Helaman, according to the record of Helaman, which he kept in his days.

Comprising chapters 45 to 62 inclusive.

CHAPTER 45.

Nephite extinction again foretold—Alma's departure compared to that of Moses—Dissension in the church.

1. Behold, now it came to pass that the people of Nephi were exceedingly rejoiced, because the Lord had again delivered them out of the hands of their enemies; therefore they gave thanks unto the Lord their God; yea, and they did ᵃfast much and ᵇpray much, and they did worship God with exceeding great joy.

2. And it came to pass in the nineteenth year of the reign of the judges over the people of Nephi, that Alma came unto his son Helaman and said unto him: Believest thou the words which I spake unto thee ᶜconcerning those records which have been kept?

3. And Helaman said unto him: Yea, I believe.

4. And Alma said again: Believest thou in Jesus Christ, who shall come?

---

n, see v, Al. 43. o, ver. 14. p, see f. q, see f. r, see g, Al. 2. s, see f, 1 Ne. 1.
CHAP. 45: a, see t, Mos. 27. b, see e, 2 Ne. 32. c, Al. 37.   * B. C. 73.

5. And he said: Yea, I believe all the words which thou hast spoken.

6. And Alma said unto him again: Will ye keep my commandments?

7. And he said: Yea, I will keep thy commandments with all my heart.

8. Then Alma said unto him: Blessed art thou; and the Lord shall prosper thee in this land.

9. But behold, I have somewhat to prophesy unto thee; but what I prophesy unto thee ye shall not make known; yea, what I prophesy unto thee shall not be made known, even until the prophecy is fulfilled; therefore write the words which I shall say.

10. And these are the words: Behold, I perceive that this very people, the Nephites, according to the spirit of revelation which is in me, in ^{d}four hundred years from the time that Jesus Christ shall manifest himself unto them, shall ^{e}dwindle in unbelief.

11. Yea, and then shall they see wars and pestilences, yea, famines and bloodshed, even until the people of Nephi shall become ^{f}extinct—

12. Yea, and this because they shall dwindle in unbelief and fall into the works of darkness, and lasciviousness, and all manner of iniquities; yea, I say unto you, that because they shall sin against so great light and knowledge, yea, I say unto you, that from that day, even the ^{g}fourth generation shall not all pass away before this great iniquity shall come.

13. And when that great day cometh, behold, the time very soon cometh that those who are now, or the seed of those who are now numbered among the people of Nephi, shall no more be numbered among the people of Nephi.

14. But whosoever remaineth, and is not destroyed in that great and dreadful day, shall be ^{h}numbered among the Lamanites, and shall become like unto them, all, save it be a few who shall be called the disciples of the Lord; and them shall the Lamanites pursue even ^{i}until they shall become extinct. And now, because of iniquity, this prophecy shall be fulfilled.

15. And now it came to pass that after Alma had said these things to Helaman, he blessed him, and also his other sons; and he also blessed the earth for the righteous' sake.

16. And he said: Thus saith the Lord God—^{j}Cursed shall be the land, yea, this land, unto every nation, kindred, tongue, and people, unto destruction, which do wickedly, when they are fully ripe; and as I have said so shall it be; for this is the cursing and the blessing of God upon the land, for the Lord cannot look upon sin with the least degree of allowance.

17. And now, when Alma had said these words he blessed the church, yea, all those who should stand fast in the faith from that time henceforth.

18. And when Alma had done this he departed out of the ^{k}land of Zarahemla, as if to go into the ^{l}land of Melek. And it came to pass that he was never heard of more; as to his death or burial we know not of.

---

d, see d, 1 Ne. 12. e, Moro. 9. f, 2 Ne. 26:10. Morm. 6. g, see d, 1 Ne. 12. h, 1 Ne. 13:31. Moro. 9:24. i, Moro. 1:1—3. j, see d, 2 Ne. 1. k, Om. 13. l, see c, Al. 8.

B. C. 73.

19. Behold, this we know, that he was a righteous man; and the saying went abroad in the church that he was taken up by the Spirit, or buried by the hand of the Lord, even as Moses. But behold, the scriptures saith the Lord took Moses unto himself; and we suppose that he has also received Alma in the spirit, unto himself; therefore, for this cause we know nothing concerning his death and burial.

20. And now it came to pass in the *commencement of the nineteenth year of the reign of the judges over the people of Nephi, that Helaman went forth among the people to declare the word unto them.

21. For behold, because of their wars with the Lamanites and the many little dissensions and disturbances which had been among the people, it became expedient that the word of God should be declared among them, yea, and that a regulation should be made throughout the church.

22. Therefore, Helaman and his brethren went forth to establish the church again in all the land, yea, in every city throughout all the land which was possessed by the people of Nephi. And it came to pass that they did appoint ᵐpriests and teachers throughout all the land, over all the churches.

23. And now it came to pass that after Helaman and his brethren had appointed priests and teachers over the churches that there arose a dissension among them, and they would not give heed to the words of Helaman and his brethren;

24. But they grew proud, being lifted up in their hearts, because of their exceeding great riches; therefore they grew rich in their own eyes, and would not give heed to their words, to walk uprightly before God.

CHAPTER 46.

Amalickiah conspires to be king—Moroni and the title of liberty—The people covenant to maintain freedom—Flight of Amalickiah.

1. And it came to pass that as many as would not hearken to the words of Helaman and his brethren were gathered together against their brethren.

2. And now behold, they were exceeding wroth, insomuch that they were determined to slay them.

3. Now the leader of those who were wroth against their brethren was a large and a strong man; and his name was Amalickiah.

4. And Amalickiah was desirous to be a king; and those people who were wroth were also desirous that he should be their king; and they were the greater part of them the lower judges of the land, and they were seeking for power.

5. And they had been led by the flatteries of Amalickiah, that if they would support him and establish him to be their king that he would make them rulers over the people.

6. Thus they were led away by Amalickiah to dissensions, notwithstanding the preaching of Helaman and his brethren, yea, notwithstanding their exceeding great care over the church, for they were ᵃhigh priests over the church.

7. And there were many in the church who believed in the flat-

---

m, see *c*, Mos. 6.   Chap. 46: *a*, see *g*, Mos. 26.   • B. C. 73.

tering words of Amalickiah, therefore they dissented even from the church; and thus were the affairs of the people of Nephi exceedingly precarious and dangerous, notwithstanding their [b]great victory which they had had over the Lamanites, and their great rejoicings which they had had because of their deliverance by the hand of the Lord.

8. Thus we see how quick the children of men do forget the Lord their God, yea, how quick to do iniquity, and to be led away by the evil one.

9. Yea, and we also see the great wickedness one very wicked man can cause to take place among the children of men.

10. Yea, we see that Amalickiah, because he was a man of cunning device and a man of many flattering words, that he led away the hearts of many people to do wickedly; yea, and to seek to destroy the church of God, and to destroy the [c]foundation of liberty which God had granted unto them, or which blessing God had sent upon the face of the land for the righteous' sake.

11. And now it came to pass that when Moroni, who was the [d]chief commander of the armies of the Nephites, had heard of these dissensions, he was angry with Amalickiah.

12. And it came to pass that he [e]rent his coat; and he took a piece thereof, and wrote upon it —[f]In memory of our God, our religion, and freedom, and our peace, our wives, and our children—and he fastened it upon the end of a pole.

13. And he [g]fastened on his head-plate, and his breastplate, and his shields, and girded on his armor about his loins; and he took the pole, which had on the end thereof his rent coat, (and he called it the [h]title of liberty) and he bowed himself to the earth, and he [i]prayed mightily unto his God for the blessings of [j]liberty to rest upon his brethren, so long as there should a band of [k]Christians remain to possess the land—

14. For thus were all the true believers of Christ, who belonged to the church of God, called by those who did not belong to the church.

15. And those who did belong to the church were faithful; yea, all those who were true believers in Christ took upon them, gladly, the name of Christ, or Christians as they were called, because of their belief in Christ who should come.

16. And therefore, at this time, Moroni prayed that the cause of the Christians, and the [l]freedom of the land might be favored.

17. And it came to pass that when he had [m]poured out his soul to God, he named all the land which was [n]south of the [o]land Desolation, yea, and in fine, all the land, both [p]on the north and on the south—A chosen land, and the [q]land of liberty.

18. And he said: Surely God shall not suffer that we, who are despised because we take upon us the [r]name of Christ, shall be trodden down and destroyed, until we bring it upon us by our own transgressions.

19. And when Moroni had said

---

[b], Al. chaps. 43. 44. [c], see *m*, Mos. 29. [d], Al. 43:16. [e], vers. 13, 21—27. [f], see 2*f*, Al. 43. [g], see 2*p*, Al. 43. [h], see 2*f*, Al. 43. [i], see *e*, 2 Ne. 32. [j], see 2*f*, Al. 43. [k], vers. 14—16. Al. 48:10. [l], see 2*f*, Al. 43. [m], see *e*, 2 Ne. 32. [n], 3 Ne. 3:24. Morm. 3:5. [o], see 2*l*, Al. 22. [p], Al. 22:31. 63:4. [q], see 2*f*, Al. 43. [r], see *e*, Mos. 5.

B. C. 73.

these words, he went forth among the people, waving the *rent part of his garment in the air, that all might see the ᵗwriting which he had written upon the rent part, and crying with a loud voice, saying:

20. Behold, whosoever will maintain this title upon the land, let them come forth in the strength of the Lord, and enter into a covenant that they will ᵘmaintain their rights, and their religion, that the Lord God may bless them.

21. And it came to pass that when Moroni had proclaimed these words, behold, the people came running together with their armor girded about their loins, ʳrending their garments in token, or as a covenant, that they would not forsake the Lord their God; or, in other words, if they should transgress the commandments of God, or fall into transgression, and be ashamed to take upon them the ʷname of Christ, the Lord should rend them even as they had *rent their garments.

22. Now this was the covenant which they made, and they cast their garments at the feet of Moroni, saying: We covenant with our God, that we shall be destroyed, even as our brethren in the ʸland northward, if we shall fall into transgression; yea, he may cast us at the feet of our enemies, even as we have cast our garments at thy feet to be trodden under foot, if we shall fall into transgression.

23. Moroni said unto them: Behold, we are a remnant of the seed of Jacob; yea, we are a remnant of the seed of Joseph, whose ᶻcoat was rent by his brethren into many pieces; yea, and now behold, let us remember to keep the commandments of God, or our garments shall be rent by our brethren, and we be cast into prison, or be sold, or be slain.

24. Yea, let us preserve our ^{2a}liberty as a remnant of Joseph; yea, let us remember the words of Jacob, before his death, for behold, he saw that a part of the remnant of the coat of Joseph was preserved and had not decayed. And he said—^{2b}Even as this remnant of garment of my son hath been preserved, so shall a remnant of the seed of my son be preserved by the hand of God, and be taken unto himself, while the remainder of the seed of Joseph shall perish, even as the remnant of his garment.

25. Now behold, this giveth my soul sorrow; nevertheless, my soul hath joy in my son, because of that part of his seed which shall be taken unto God.

26. Now behold, this was the language of Jacob.

27. And now who knoweth but what the remnant of the seed of Joseph, which shall perish as his garment, are those who have dissented from us? Yea, and even it shall be ourselves if we do not stand fast in the faith of Christ.

28. And now it came to pass that when Moroni had said these words he went forth, and also sent forth in all the parts of the land where there were dissensions, and gathered together all the people who were desirous to maintain their ^{2c}liberty, to stand against Amalickiah and those who had dissented, who were called Amalickiahites.

29. And it came to pass that

s, see *e.* *t*, ver. 12. *u*, see 2*f*, Al. 43. *v*, see *e.* *w*, see *e*, Mos. 5. *x*, see *v.* *y*, see Book of Ether. *z*, Gen. 37:31—33. 2*a*, see 2*f*, Al. 43. 2*b*, ver. 27. 3 Ne. 5:23, 24. 10:17. 2*c*, see 2*f*, Al. 43.

B. C. 73.

when Amalickiah saw that the people of Moroni were more numerous than the Amalickiahites —and he also saw that his people were doubtful concerning the justice of the cause in which they had undertaken—therefore, fearing that he should not gain the point, he took those of his people who would and departed into the ^{2d}land of Nephi.

30. Now Moroni thought it was not expedient that the Lamanites should have any more strength; therefore he thought to cut off the people of Amalickiah, or to take them and bring them back, and put Amalickiah to death; yea, for he knew that he would stir up the Lamanites to anger against them, and cause them to come to battle against them; and this he knew that Amalickiah would do that he might obtain his purposes.

31. Therefore Moroni thought it was expedient that he should take his armies, who had gathered themselves together, and armed themselves, and entered into a covenant to keep the peace —and it came to pass that he took his army and marched out into the wilderness, to cut off the course of Amalickiah in the wilderness.

32. And it came to pass that he did according to his desires, and marched forth into the wilderness, and headed the armies of Amalickiah.

33. And it came to pass that Amalickiah fled with a small number of his men, and the remainder were delivered up into the hands of Moroni and were taken back into the land of Zarahemla.

34. Now, Moroni being a man who was appointed by the chief judges and the ^{2e}voice of the people, therefore he had power according to his will with the armies of the Nephites, to establish and to exercise authority over them.

35. And it came to pass that whomsoever of the Amalickiahites that would not enter into a covenant to support the ^{2f}cause of freedom, that they might maintain a free government, he caused to be put to death; and there were but few who denied the covenant of freedom.

36. And it came to pass also, that he caused the ^{2g}title of liberty to be hoisted upon every tower which was in all the land, which was possessed by the Nephites; and thus Moroni planted the standard of liberty among the Nephites.

37. And they began to have peace again in the land; and thus they did maintain peace in the land until nearly the *end of the nineteenth year of the reign of the judges.

38. And Helaman and the ^{2h}high priests did also maintain order in the church; yea, even for the space of four years did they have much peace and rejoicing in the church.

39. And it came to pass that there were many who died, firmly believing that their souls were redeemed by the Lord Jesus Christ; thus they went out of the world rejoicing.

40. And there were some who died with fevers, which at some seasons of the year were very frequent in the land—but not so much so with fevers, because of the excellent qualities of the many plants and roots which God

---

2d, see b, 2 Ne. 5. 2e, see e, Mos. 29. 2f, see 2f, Al. 43. 2g, vers. 12. 13. 2h, ver. 6. See g, Mos. 26.

* B. C. 72.

had prepared to remove the cause of diseases, to which men were subject by the nature of the climate—

41. But there were many who died with old age; and those who died in the faith of Christ are happy in him, as we must needs suppose.

CHAPTER 47.

Amalickiah, by treachery, becomes king of the Lamanites—His awful wickedness.

1. Now we will return in our record to Amalickiah and those who had ^afled with him into the wilderness; for, behold, he had taken those who went with him, and went up in the ^bland of Nephi among the Lamanites, and did stir up the Lamanites to anger against the people of Nephi, insomuch that the king of the Lamanites sent a proclamation throughout all his land, among all his people, that they should gather themselves together again to go to battle against the Nephites.

2. And it came to pass that when the proclamation had gone forth among them they were exceedingly afraid; yea, they feared to displease the king, and they also feared to go to battle against the Nephites lest they should lose their lives. And it came to pass that they would not, or the more part of them would not, obey the commandments of the king.

3. And now it came to pass that the king was wroth because of their disobedience; therefore he gave Amalickiah the command of that part of his army which was obedient unto his commands, and commanded him that he should go forth and compel them to arms.

4. Now behold, this was the desire of Amalickiah; for he being a very subtle man to do evil therefore he laid the plan in his heart to ^cdethrone the king of the Lamanites.

5. And now he had got the command of those parts of the Lamanites who were in favor of the king; and he sought to gain favor of those who were not obedient; therefore he went forward to the place which was called Onidah, for thither had all the Lamanites fled; for they discovered the army coming, and, supposing that they were coming to destroy them, therefore they fled to Onidah, to the place of arms.

6. And they had appointed a man to be a king and a leader over them, being fixed in their minds with a determined resolution that they would not be subjected to go against the Nephites.

7. And it came to pass that they had gathered themselves together upon the top of the mount which was called Antipas, in preparation to battle.

8. Now it was not Amalickiah's intention to give them battle according to the commandments of the king; but behold, it was his intention to gain favor with the armies of the Lamanites, that he might place himself at their head and ^ddethrone the king and take possession of the kingdom.

9. And behold, it came to pass that he caused his army to pitch their tents in the valley which was near the ^emount Antipas.

10. And it came to pass that when it was night he sent a secret embassy into the mount

---

^a, Al. 46:33.   ^b, see b, 2 Ne. 5.   ^c, vers. 8, 16, 35.   ^d, vers. 4, 16, 35.   ^e, vers. 7, 10.   B. C. 72.

ALMA, 47.

Antipas, desiring that the leader of those who were upon the mount, whose name was Lehonti, that he should come down to the foot of the mount, for he desired to speak with him.

11. And it came to pass that when Lehonti received the message he durst not go down to the foot of the mount. And it came to pass that Amalickiah sent again the second time, desiring him to come down. And it came to pass that Lehonti would not; and he sent again the third time.

12. And it came to pass that when Amalickiah found that he could not get Lehonti to come down off from the mount, he went up into the mount, nearly to Lehonti's camp; and he sent again the fourth time his message unto Lehonti, desiring that he would come down, and that he would bring his guards with him.

13. And it came to pass that when Lehonti had come down with his guards to Amalickiah, that Amalickiah desired him to come down with his army in the night-time, and surround those men in their camps over whom the king had given him command, and that he would deliver them up into Lehonti's hands, if he would make him (Amalickiah) a second leader over the whole army.

14. And it came to pass that Lehonti came down with his men and surrounded the men of Amalickiah, so that before they awoke at the dawn of day they were surrounded by the armies of Lehonti.

15. And it came to pass that when they saw that they were surrounded, they plead with Amalickiah that he would suffer them to fall in with their brethren, that they might not be destroyed. Now this was the very thing which Amalickiah desired.

16. And it came to pass that he delivered his men, *f*contrary to the commands of the king. Now this was the thing that Amalickiah desired, that he might accomplish his designs in *g*dethroning the king.

17. Now it was the custom among the Lamanites, if their chief leader was killed, to appoint the *h*second leader to be their chief leader.

18. And it came to pass that Amalickiah caused that one of his servants should administer poison by degrees to Lehonti, that he died.

19. Now, when Lehonti was dead, the Lamanites appointed Amalickiah to be their leader and their *i*chief commander.

20. And it came to pass that Amalickiah marched with his armies (for he had gained his desires) to the *j*land of Nephi, to the city of Nephi, which was the chief city.

21. And the king came out to meet him with his guards, for he supposed that Amalickiah had *k*fulfilled his commands, and that Amalickiah had gathered together so great an army to go against the Nephites to battle.

22. But behold, as the king came out to meet him Amalickiah caused that his servants should go forth to meet the king. And they went and bowed themselves before the king, as if to reverence him because of his greatness.

23. And it came to pass that the king put forth his hand to raise them, as was the custom with the Lamanites, as a token of

f, ver. 3. *g*, vers. 4, 8, 35. *h*, ver. 13. *i*, vers. 13, 17. *j*, see *b*, 2 Ne. 5. *k*, ver. 3.

B. C. 72.

ALMA, 47.

peace, which *l*custom they had taken from the Nephites.

24. And it came to pass that when he had raised the first from the ground, behold he stabbed the king to the heart; and he fell to the earth.

25. Now the servants of the king fled; and the servants of Amalickiah raised a cry, saying:

26. Behold, the servants of the king have stabbed him to the heart, and he has fallen and they have fled; behold, come and see.

27. And it came to pass that Amalickiah commanded that his armies should march forth and see what had happened to the king; and when they had come to the spot, and found the king lying in his gore, Amalickiah pretended to be wroth, and said: Whosoever loved the king, let him go forth, and pursue his servants that they may be slain.

28. And it came to pass that all they who loved the king, when they heard these words, came forth and pursued after the servants of the king.

29. Now when the servants of the king saw an army pursuing after them, they were frightened again, and fled into the wilderness, and came over into the *m*land of Zarahemla and joined the *n*people of Ammon.

30. And the army which pursued after them returned, having pursued after them in vain; and thus Amalickiah, by his fraud, gained the hearts of the people.

31. And it came to pass on the morrow he entered the *o*city Nephi with his armies, and took possession of the city.

32. And now it came to pass that the queen, when she had heard that the king was slain— for Amalickiah had sent an embassy to the queen informing her that the king had been slain by his servants, that he had pursued them with his army, but it was in vain, and they had made their escape—

33. Therefore, when the queen had received this message she sent unto Amalickiah, desiring him that he would spare the people of the city; and she also desired him that he should come in unto her; and she also desired him that he should bring witnesses with him to testify concerning the death of the king.

34. And it came to pass that Amalickiah took the *p*same servant that slew the king, and all *q*them who were with him, and went in unto the queen, unto the place where she sat; and they all testified unto her that the king was slain by his own servants; and they said also: They have fled; does not this testify against them? And thus they satisfied the queen concerning the death of the king.

35. And it came to pass that Amalickiah sought the favor of the queen, and took her unto him to wife; and thus by his fraud, and by the assistance of his cunning servants, he *r*obtained the kingdom; yea, he was acknowledged king throughout all the land, among all the people of the Lamanites, who were composed of the Lamanites and the Lemuelites and the Ishmaelites, and all the dissenters of the Nephites, from the reign of Nephi down to the present time.

36. Now these dissenters, having the same instruction and the same information of the Nephites, yea, having been instructed in the

l, Mos. 7:12. *m,* Om. 13. *n,* Al. 27:26. *o,* ver. 20. *p,* ver. 24. *q,* ver. 22. *r,* vers. 4, 8, 16. B. C. 72.

same knowledge of the Lord, nevertheless, it is strange to relate, not long after their dissensions *they became more hardened and impenitent, and more wild, wicked and ferocious than the Lamanites—drinking in with the traditions of the Lamanites; giving way to indolence, and all manner of lasciviousness; yea, entirely forgetting the Lord their God.

CHAPTER 48.

Amalickiah incites the Lamanites against Nephites—Moroni prepares for the conflict—A true patriot and a mighty man of God.

1. And now it came to pass that, as soon as Amalickiah had obtained the kingdom he began to inspire the hearts of the Lamanites against the people of Nephi; yea, he did appoint men to speak unto the Lamanites from their towers, against the Nephites.

2. And thus he did inspire their hearts against the Nephites, insomuch that in the *latter end of the nineteenth year of the reign of the judges, he having accomplished his designs thus far, yea, having been made king over the Lamanites, he sought also to reign over all the land, yea, and all the people who were in the land, the Nephites as well as the Lamanites.

3. Therefore he had accomplished his design, for he had hardened the hearts of the Lamanites and blinded their minds, and stirred them up to anger, insomuch that he had gathered together a numerous host to go to battle against the Nephites.

4. For he was determined, because of the greatness of the number of his people, to overpower the Nephites and to bring them into bondage.

5. And thus he did appoint chief captains of the ^aZoramites, they being the most acquainted with the strength of the Nephites, and their places of resort, and the weakest parts of their cities; therefore he appointed them to be chief captains over his armies.

6. And it came to pass that they took their camp, and moved forth toward the ^bland of Zarahemla in the wilderness.

7. Now it came to pass that while Amalickiah had thus been obtaining power by fraud and deceit, Moroni, on the other hand, had been preparing the minds of the people to be faithful unto the Lord their God.

8. Yea, he had been strengthening the armies of the Nephites, and erecting small ^cforts, or places of resort; throwing up banks of earth round about to enclose his armies, and also building walls of stone to encircle them about, round about their cities and the borders of their lands; yea, all round about the land.

9. And in their weakest fortifications he did place the greater number of men; and thus he did fortify and strengthen the land which was possessed by the Nephites.

10. And thus he was preparing to ^dsupport their liberty, their lands, their wives, and their children, and their peace, and that they might live unto the Lord their God, and that they might maintain that which was called by their enemies the cause of ^eChristians.

11. And Moroni was a strong and a mighty man; he was a man

---

s, see *t*, Al. 24:30. CHAP. 48: *a*, see 2*j*, Al. 30. *b*, Om. 13. *c*, Al. 49:13, 18—24. 50:1—6, 10. 51:23, 27. 52:2, 17. 53:3—7. 55:25, 26, 33. 56:15, 20, 21. 57:4. 58:23. 62:20—24. He. 1:20, 21, 22, 27. 4:7. 3 Ne. 3:14. Morm. 2:4, 21. 3:6. *d*, see 2*f*, Al. 43. *e*, see *k*, Al. 46.   * B. C. 72.

of a perfect understanding; yea, a man that did not delight in bloodshed; a man whose soul did joy in the *f*liberty and the freedom of his country, and his brethren from bondage and slavery;

12. Yea, a man whose heart did swell with thanksgiving to his God, for the many privileges and blessings which he bestowed upon his people; a man who did labor exceedingly for the welfare and safety of his people.

13. Yea, and he was a man who was firm in the faith of Christ, and he had sworn with an oath to *g*defend his people, his rights, and his country, and his religion, even to the loss of his blood.

14. Now the Nephites were *h*taught to defend themselves against their enemies, even to the shedding of blood if it were necessary; yea, and they were also taught never to give an offense, yea, and never to raise the sword except it were against an enemy, except it were to preserve their lives.

15. And this was their faith, that by so doing God would prosper them in the land, or in other words, *i*if they were faithful in keeping the commandments of God that he would prosper them in the land; yea, warn them to flee, or to prepare for war, according to their danger;

16. And also, that God would make it known unto them *j*whither they should go to defend themselves against their enemies, and by so doing, the Lord would deliver them; and this was the faith of Moroni, and his heart did glory in it; not in the shedding of blood but in doing good, in preserving his people, yea, in keeping the commandments of God, yea, and resisting iniquity.

17. Yea, verily, verily I say unto you, if all men had been, and were, and ever would be, like unto Moroni, behold, the very powers of hell would have been shaken forever; yea, the devil would *k*never have power over the hearts of the children of men.

18. Behold, he was a man like unto Ammon, the son of Mosiah, yea, and even the other sons of Mosiah, yea, and also Alma and his sons, for they were all men of God.

19. Now behold, Helaman and his brethren were no less serviceable unto the people than was Moroni; for they did preach the word of God, and they did *l*baptize unto repentance all men whosoever would hearken unto their words.

20. And thus they went forth, and the people did humble themselves because of their words, insomuch that they were highly favored of the Lord, and thus they were free from wars and contentions among themselves, yea, even for the space of four years.

21. But, as I have said, *m*in the latter end of the nineteenth year, yea, notwithstanding their peace amongst themselves, they were compelled reluctantly to contend with their brethren, the Lamanites.

22. Yea, and in fine, their wars never did cease for the space of many years with the Lamanites, notwithstanding their much reluctance.

23. Now, they were sorry to take up arms against the Lamanites, because they did not delight

---

f, see 2*f*, Al. 43. *g*, see 2*f*, Al. 43. *h*, see 2*y*, Al. 43. *i*, see *h*, 2 Ne. 1. *j*, Al. 16:5—8. 43:23, 24. 3 Ne. 3:18—21. *k*, 1 Ne. 22:26. *l*, see *u*, 2 Ne. 9. *m*. ver. 2.

B. C. 72.

in the shedding of blood; yea, and this was not all—they were sorry to be the means of sending so many of their brethren out of this world into an eternal world, unprepared to meet their God.

24. Nevertheless, they could not suffer to lay down their lives, that their wives and their children should be massacred by the barbarous cruelty of those who were once their brethren, yea, and had dissented from their church, and had left them and had gone to destroy them by joining the Lamanites.

25. Yea, they could not bear that their brethren should rejoice over the blood of the Nephites, so long as there were any who should keep the commandments of God, for the promise of the Lord was, ⁿif they should keep his commandments they should prosper in the land.

CHAPTER 49.

The invading Lamanites baffled and repulsed—Amalickiah's wrath over his failure—Prosperity of the church.

1. And now it came to pass in the *eleventh month of the nineteenth year, on the tenth day of the month, the armies of the Lamanites were seen approaching towards the ᵃland of Ammonihah.

2. And behold, the city had been rebuilt, and Moroni had stationed an army by the borders of the city, and they had ᵇcast up dirt round about to shield them from the arrows and the stones of the Lamanites; for behold, they fought with stones and with arrows.

3. Behold, I said that the city of Ammonihah had been rebuilt. I say unto you, yea, that it was in part rebuilt; and because the Lamanites had destroyed it ᶜonce, because of the iniquity of the people, they supposed that it would again become an easy prey for them.

4. But behold, how great was their disappointment; for behold, the Nephites had ᵈdug up a ridge of earth round about them, which was so high that the Lamanites could not cast their stones and their arrows at them that they might take effect, neither could they come upon them save it was by their place of entrance.

5. Now at this time the chief captains of the Lamanites were astonished exceedingly, because of the wisdom of the Nephites in preparing their places of security.

6. Now the leaders of the Lamanites had supposed, because of the greatness of their numbers, yea, they supposed that they should be privileged to come upon them as they had hitherto done; yea, and they had also prepared themselves ᵉwith shields, and with breastplates; and they had also prepared themselves with garments of skins, yea, very thick garments to cover their nakedness.

7. And being thus prepared they supposed that they should easily overpower and subject their brethren to the yoke of bondage, or slay and massacre them according to their pleasure.

8. But behold, to their uttermost astonishment, they were prepared for them, in a manner which never had been known among the children of Lehi. Now they were prepared for the Lamanites, to battle after the ᶠmanner of the instructions of Moroni.

n, see *h*, 2 Ne. 1.   CHAP. 49: *a*, see *i* and *j*, Al. 8.   *b*, see *c*, Al. 48.   *c*, Al. 16:2, 3, 9—11.   *d*, see *c*, Al. 48.   *e*, see 2*p*, Al. 43.   *f*, see *c*, Al. 48.   * B. C. 72.

9. And it came to pass that the Lamanites, or the Amalickiahites, were exceedingly astonished at their manner of preparation for war.

10. Now, if king Amalickiah had come down out of the *g*land of Nephi, at the head of his army, perhaps he would have caused the Lamanites to have attacked the Nephites at the city of *h*Ammonihah; for behold, he did care not for the blood of his people.

11. But behold, Amalickiah did not come down himself to battle. And behold, his chief captains durst not attack the Nephites at the city of Ammonihah, for Moroni had altered the management of affairs among the Nephites, insomuch that the Lamanites were disappointed in their places of retreat and they could not come upon them.

12. Therefore they retreated into the wilderness, and took their camp and marched towards the *i*land of Noah, supposing that to be the next best place for them to come against the Nephites.

13. For they knew not that Moroni had *j*fortified, or had built forts of security, for every city in all the land round about; therefore, they marched forward to the land of Noah with a firm determination; yea, their chief captains came forward and took an oath that they would destroy the people of that city.

14. But behold, to their astonishment, the city of *k*Noah, which had hitherto been a weak place, had now, by the means of Moroni, become strong, yea, even to exceed the strength of the *l*city Ammonihah.

15. And now, behold, this was wisdom in Moroni; for he had supposed that they would be frightened at the city Ammonihah; and as the *m*city of Noah had hitherto been the weakest part of the land, therefore they would march thither to battle; and thus it was according to his desires.

16. And behold, Moroni had appointed Lehi to be chief captain over the men of that city; and it was that *n*same Lehi who fought with the Lamanites in the valley on the east of the *o*river Sidon.

17. And now behold it came to pass, that when the Lamanites had found that Lehi commanded the city they were again disappointed, for they feared Lehi exceedingly; nevertheless their chief captains had sworn with an *p*oath to attack the city; therefore, they brought up their armies.

18. Now behold, the Lamanites could not get into their forts of security by any other way save by the entrance, because of the *q*highness of the bank which had been thrown up, and the depth of the ditch which had been dug round about, save it were by the entrance.

19. And thus were the Nephites prepared to destroy all such as should attempt to climb up to enter the fort by any other way, by casting over stones and arrows at them.

20. Thus they were prepared, yea, a body of their strongest men, with their swords and their slings, to smite down all who should attempt to come into their place of security by the place of *r*entrance; and thus were they prepared to defend themselves against the Lamanites.

---

g, see *b*, 2 Ne. 5. *h*, see *i*, Al. 8. *i*, vers. 13—15. Al. 16:3. *j*, see *c*, Al. 48. *k*, see *i*. *l*, see *i*, Al. 8. *m*, see *i*. *n*, Al. 43:35. *o*, see *g*, Al. 2. *p*, ver. 13. *q*, see *c*, Al. 48. *r*, vers. 4, 18, 21, 24.

B. C. 72.

21. And it came to pass that the captains of the Lamanites brought up their armies before the place of *entrance, and began to contend with the Nephites, to get into their place of security; but behold, they were driven back from time to time, insomuch that they were slain with an immense slaughter.

22. Now when they found that they could not obtain power over the Nephites by the pass, they began to 'dig down their banks of earth that they might obtain a pass to their armies, that they might have an equal chance to fight; but behold, in these attempts they were swept off by the stones and arrows which were thrown at them; and instead of filling up their ditches by pulling down the banks of earth, they were filled up in a measure with their dead and wounded bodies.

23. Thus the Nephites had all power over their enemies; and thus the Lamanites did attempt to destroy the Nephites until their 'chief captains were all slain; yea, and more than a thousand of the Lamanites were slain; while, on the other hand, there was not a single soul of the Nephites which was slain.

24. There were about fifty who were wounded, who had been exposed to the arrows of the Lamanites through the ʳpass, but they were ʷshielded by their shields, and their breastplates, and their head-plates, insomuch that their wounds were upon their legs, many of which were very severe.

25. And it came to pass, that when the Lamanites saw that their ˣchief captains were all slain they fled into the wilderness.

And it came to pass that they returned to the ʸland of Nephi, to inform their king, Amalickiah, who was a Nephite by birth, concerning their great loss.

26. And it came to pass that he was exceedingly angry with his people, because he had not obtained his desire over the Nephites; he had not subjected them to the yoke of bondage.

27. Yea, he was exceedingly wroth, and he did curse God, and also Moroni, swearing with an ᶻoath that he would drink his blood; and this because Moroni had kept the commandments of God in preparing for the safety of his people.

28. And it came to pass, that on the other hand, the people of Nephi did thank the Lord their God, because of his matchless power in delivering them from the hands of their enemies.

29. And thus ended the nineteenth year of the reign of the judges over the people of Nephi.

30. Yea, and there was continual peace among them, and exceeding great prosperity in the church because of their heed and diligence which they gave unto the word of God, which was declared unto them by Helaman, and Shiblon, and Corianton, and Ammon and his brethren, yea, and by all those who had been ordained by the ²ᵃholy order of God, being baptized unto repentance, and sent forth to preach among the people.

CHAPTER 50.

Moroni fortifies the line between land of Zarahemla and land of Nephi—Morianton plans to occupy the land northward—He is killed by Teancum—Pahoran succeeds Nephihah.

1. And now it came to pass

---

s, see *r*. *t*, see *c*, Al. 48. *u*, Al. 48:5. *v*, see *r*. *w*, see 2*p*, Al. 43. *x*, Al. 48:5. *y*, see *b*, 2 Ne. 5. *z*, Al. 51:9, 10. 2*a*, see *g*, Mos. 26. B. C. 72.

ALMA, 50.

that Moroni did not stop making preparations for war, or to defend his people against the Lamanites; for he caused that his armies should commence in the *commencement of the twentieth year of the reign of the judges, that they should commence in digging up ^aheaps of earth round about all the cities, throughout all the land which was possessed by the Nephites.

2. And upon the top of these ridges of earth he caused that there should be timbers, yea, works of timbers built up to the height of a man, round about the cities.

3. And he caused that upon those works of timbers there should be a frame of pickets built upon the timbers round about; and they were strong and high.

4. And he caused towers to be erected that overlooked those works of pickets, and he caused places of security to be built upon those towers, that the stones and the arrows of the Lamanites could not hurt them.

5. And they were prepared that they could cast stones from the top thereof, according to their pleasure and their strength, and slay him who should attempt to approach near the walls of the city.

6. Thus Moroni did prepare strongholds against the coming of their enemies, round about every city in all the land.

7. And it came to pass that Moroni caused that his armies should go forth into the east wilderness; yea, and they went forth and drove all the Lamanites who were in the east wilderness into their own lands, which were south of the ^bland of Zarahemla.

8. And the ^cland of Nephi did run in a straight course from the east sea to the west.

9. And it came to pass that when Moroni had driven all the Lamanites out of the east wilderness, which was north of the lands of their own possessions, he caused that the inhabitants who were in the land of Zarahemla and in the land round about should go forth into the east wilderness, even to the borders by the seashore, and possess the land.

10. And he also placed armies on the south, in the borders of their possessions, and caused them to erect ^dfortifications that they might secure their armies and their people from the hands of their enemies.

11. And thus he cut off all the strongholds of the Lamanites in the east wilderness, yea, and also on the west, fortifying the ^eline between the Nephites and the Lamanites, between the ^fland of Zarahemla and the ^gland of Nephi, from the west sea, running by the head of the ^hriver Sidon— the Nephites possessing all the land ⁱnorthward, yea, even all the land which was northward of the ^jland Bountiful, according to their pleasure.

12. Thus Moroni, with his armies, which did increase daily because of the assurance of protection which his works did bring forth unto them, did seek to cut off the strength and the power of the Lamanites from off the lands of their possessions, that they should have no power upon the lands of their possession.

13. And it came to pass that the Nephites began the foundation of a city, and they called the

---

a, see *c*, Al. 48. *b*, Om. 13. *c*, see *b*, 2 Ne. 5. *d*, see *c*, Al. 48. *e*, ver. 8. *f*, Om. 13. *g*, see *b*, 2 Ne. 5. *h*, see *g*, Al. 2. *i*, see *p*, Al. 46. *j*, see 2*k*, Al. 22.
* B. C. 72.

name of the ᵏcity Moroni; and it was by the east sea; and it was on the south by the line of the possessions of the Lamanites.

14. And they also began a foundation for a city between the city of Moroni and the city of Aaron, joining the borders of Aaron and Moroni; and they called the name of the city, or the land, ˡNephihah.

15. And they also began in that same year to build many cities on the north, one in a particular manner which they called ᵐLehi, which was in the north by the borders of the seashore.

16. And thus ended the twentieth year.

17. And in these prosperous circumstances were the people of Nephi in the *commencement of the twenty and first year of the reign of the judges over the people of Nephi.

18. And they did prosper exceedingly, and they became exceeding rich; yea, and they did multiply and were strong in the land.

19. And thus we see how merciful and just are all the dealings of the Lord, to the fulfilling of all his words unto the children of men; yea, we can behold that his words are verified, even at this time, which he spake unto Lehi, saying:

20. ⁿBlessed art thou and thy children; and they shall be blessed, inasmuch as they shall keep my commandments they shall prosper in the land. But remember, inasmuch as they will not keep my commandments they shall be cut off from the presence of the Lord.

21. And we see that these promises have been verified to the people of Nephi; for it has been their quarrelings and their contentions, yea, their murderings, and their plunderings, their idolatry, their whoredoms, and their abominations, which were among themselves, which brought upon them their wars and their destructions.

22. And those who were faithful in keeping the commandments of the Lord were delivered at all times, whilst thousands of their wicked brethren have been consigned to bondage, or to perish by the sword, or to dwindle in unbelief, and mingle with the Lamanites.

23. But behold there never was a happier time among the people of Nephi, since the days of Nephi, than in the days of Moroni, yea, even at this time, in the twenty and first year of the reign of the judges.

24. And it came to pass that the twenty and second year of the reign of the judges also ended in peace; yea, and also the twenty and third year.

25. And it came to pass that in the †commencement of the twenty and fourth year of the reign of the judges, there would also have been peace among the people of Nephi had it not been for a contention which took place among them concerning the ᵒland of Lehi, and the ᵖland of Morianton, which joined upon the borders of Lehi; both of which were on the borders by the seashore.

26. For behold, the people who possessed the ᵠland of Morianton did claim a part of the ʳland of Lehi; therefore there began to be a warm contention between them,

---

k, ver. 14. Al. 51:22—24. 59:5. 62:32, 34. 3 Ne. 8:9. 9:4. l, Al. 51:24—26. 59:5, 7—11. 62:14, 18, 26, 30. m, vers. 25.—28, 36. Al. 51:1, 24, 26. 59:5. 62:30. n, see h, 2 Ne. 1. o, see m. p, vers. 26, 28, 36. 51:26. 55:33. 59:5. q, see p. r, see m. * B. C. 71. † B. C. 68.

ALMA, 50.

insomuch that the people of Morianton took up arms against their brethren, and they were determined by the sword to slay them.

27. But behold, the people who possessed the ^{s}land of Lehi fled to the camp of Moroni, and appealed unto him for assistance; for behold they were not in the wrong.

28. And it came to pass that when the people of Morianton, who were led by a man whose name was Morianton, found that the people of Lehi had fled to the camp of Moroni, they were exceedingly fearful lest the army of Moroni should come upon them and destroy them.

29. Therefore, Morianton put it into their hearts that they should flee to the land which was ^{t}northward, which was ^{u}covered with large bodies of water, and take possession of the land which was northward.

30. And behold, they would have carried this plan into effect, (which would have been a cause to have been lamented) but behold, Morianton being a man of much passion, therefore he was angry with one of his maid servants, and he fell upon her and beat her much.

31. And it came to pass that she fled, and came over to the camp of Moroni, and told Moroni all things concerning the matter, and also concerning their intentions to flee into the land northward.

32. Now behold, the people who were in the land Bountiful, or rather Moroni, feared that they would hearken to the words of Morianton and unite with his people, and thus he would obtain possession of those parts of the land, which would lay a foundation for serious consequences among the people of Nephi, yea, which consequences would lead to the ^{r}overthrow of their liberty.

33. Therefore Moroni sent an army, with their camp, to head the people of Morianton, to stop their flight into the land northward.

34. And it came to pass that they did not head them until they had come to the borders of the ^{w}land Desolation; and there they did head them, by the ^{x}narrow pass which led by the sea into the land northward, yea, by the sea, on the west and on the east.

35. And it came to pass that the army which was sent by Moroni, which was led by a man whose name was Teancum, did meet the people of Morianton; and so stubborn were the people of Morianton, (being inspired by his wickedness and his flattering words) that a battle commenced between them, in the which Teancum did slay Morianton and defeat his army, and took them prisoners, and returned to the camp of Moroni. And thus ended the twenty and fourth year of the reign of the judges over the people of Nephi.

36. And thus were the people of Morianton brought back. And upon their covenanting to keep the peace they were restored to the ^{y}land of Morianton, and a union took place between them and the people of ^{z}Lehi; and they were also restored to their lands.

37. And it came to pass that in the same year that the people of Nephi had peace restored unto them, that Nephihah, the ^{2a}sec-

---

s, see m. t, see p, Al. 46. u, Mos. 8:8. He. 3:4. Morm. 6:4. v, see m, Mos. 29. w, see 2l, Al. 22. x, see 2v, Al. 22. y, see p. z, see m. 2a, Al. 4:16—18.
ABOUT B. C. 67.

ond chief judge, died, having filled the judgment-seat with perfect uprightness before God.

38. Nevertheless, he had refused Alma to take possession of ²ᵇthose records and those things which were esteemed by Alma and his fathers to be most sacred; therefore Alma had conferred them upon his son, Helaman.

39. Behold, it came to pass that the son of Nephihah was appointed to fill the judgment-seat, in the stead of his father; yea, he was appointed chief judge and governor over the people, with an oath and sacred ordinance to judge righteously, and to keep the peace and the ²ᶜfreedom of the people, and to grant unto them their sacred privileges to worship the Lord their God, yea, to support and maintain the cause of God all his days, and to bring the wicked to justice according to their crime.

40. Now behold, his name was Pahoran. And Pahoran did fill the seat of his father, and did commence his reign in the end of the twenty and fourth year, over the people of Nephi.

CHAPTER 51.

King-men and freemen—Pahoran, chief judge, is sustained by the freemen—King-men suppressed—Amalickiah's invasion, defeat, and death.

1. And now it came to pass in the *commencement of the twenty and fifth year of the reign of the judges over the people of Nephi, they having established peace between the people of ᵃLehi and the people of ᵇMorianton concerning their lands, and having commenced the twenty and fifth year in peace;

2. Nevertheless, they did not long maintain an entire peace in the land, for there began to be a contention among the people concerning the ᶜchief judge Pahoran; for behold, there were a part of the people who desired that a few ᵈparticular points of the law should be altered.

3. But behold, Pahoran would not alter nor suffer the law to be altered; therefore, he did not hearken to those who had sent in their voices with their petitions concerning the altering of the law.

4. Therefore, those who were desirous that the law should be altered were angry with him, and desired that he should no longer be chief judge over the land; therefore there arose a warm dispute concerning the matter, but not unto bloodshed.

5. And it came to pass that those who were desirous that Pahoran should be dethroned from the judgment-seat were called ᵉking-men, for they were desirous that the law should be altered in a manner to overthrow the free government and to establish a king over the land.

6. And those who were desirous that Pahoran should remain chief judge over the land took upon them the name of ᶠfreemen; and thus was the division among them, for the freemen had sworn or covenanted to maintain their rights and the privileges of their religion by a ᵍfree government.

7. And it came to pass that this matter of their contention was settled by the voice of the people And it came to pass that the voice of the people came in favor of the ʰfreemen, and Pahoran retained the judgment-seat, which caused much rejoicing among the breth-

---

2b, Al. 37. 2c, see m, Mos. 29. CHAP. 51: a, see m, Al. 50. b, see p, Al. 50. c, Al. 50:40. d, vers. 3, 5. e, vers. 7, 8, 13, 17—21. f, ver. 7. g, see m, Mos. 29. h, ver. 6. * B. C. 67.

ren of Pahoran and also many of the ʲpeople of liberty, who also put the ʲking-men to silence, that they durst not oppose but were obliged to maintain the ᵏcause of freedom.

8. Now those who were in favor of kings were those of high birth, and they sought to be kings; and they were supported by those who sought power and authority over the people.

9. But behold, this was a critical time for such contentions to be among the people of Nephi; for behold, Amalickiah had again stirred up the hearts of the people of the Lamanites against the people of the Nephites, and he was gathering together soldiers from all parts of his land, and arming them, and preparing for war with all diligence; for he had sworn to ˡdrink the blood of Moroni.

10. But behold, we shall see that his promise which he made was rash; nevertheless, he did prepare himself and his armies to come to battle against the Nephites.

11. Now his armies were not so great as they had hitherto been, because of the many thousands who had been slain by the hand of the Nephites; but notwithstanding their great loss, Amalickiah had gathered together a wonderfully great army, insomuch that he feared not to come down to the land of Zarahemla.

12. Yea, even Amalickiah did himself come down, at the head of the Lamanites. And it was in the twenty and fifth year of the reign of the judges; and it was at the same time that they had begun to settle the affairs of their contentions ᵐconcerning the chief judge, Pahoran.

13. And it came to pass that when the men who were called ⁿking-men had heard that the Lamanites were coming down to battle against them, they were glad in their hearts; and they refused to take up arms, for they were so wroth with the chief judge, and also with the ᵒpeople of liberty, that they would not take up arms to defend their country.

14. And it came to pass that when Moroni saw this, and also saw that the Lamanites were coming into the borders of the land, he was exceeding wroth because of the stubbornness of those people whom he had labored with so much diligence to preserve; yea, he was exceeding wroth; his soul was filled with anger against them.

15. And it came to pass that he sent a petition, with the ᵖvoice of the people, unto the governor of the land, desiring that he should read it, and give him (Moroni) power to compel those dissenters to defend their country or to put them to death.

16. For it was his first care to put an end to such contentions and dissensions among the people; for behold, this had been hitherto a cause of all their destruction. And it came to pass that it was granted according to the voice of the people.

17. And it came to pass that Moroni commanded that his army should go against those ᵠking-men, to pull down their pride and their nobility and level them with the earth, or they should take up arms and support the cause of liberty.

18. And it came to pass that the armies did march forth against them; and they did pull

---

i, see *m*, Mos. 29. *j*, see *c*. *k*, see *m*, Mos. 29. *l*, Al. 49:27. *m*, vers. 2—8. *n*, see *c*. *o*, see *m*, Mos. 29. *p*, see *e*, Mos. 29. *q*, see *e*.   ABOUT B. C. 67.

down their pride and their nobility, insomuch that as they did lift their weapons of war to fight against the men of Moroni they were hewn down and leveled to the earth.

19. And it came to pass that there were four thousand of those dissenters who were hewn down by the sword; and those of their leaders who were not slain in battle were taken and cast into prison, for there was no time for their trials at this period.

20. And the remainder of those dissenters, rather than be smitten down to the earth by the sword, yielded to the standard of liberty, and were compelled to hoist the *r*title of liberty upon their towers, and in their cities, and to take up arms in defence of their country.

21. And thus Moroni put an end to those king-men, that there were not any known by the appellation of *s*king-men; and thus he put an end to the stubbornness and the pride of those people who professed the blood of nobility; but they were brought down to humble themselves like unto their brethren, and to fight valiantly for their 'freedom from bondage.

22. Behold, it came to pass that while Moroni was thus breaking down the wars and contentions among his own people, and subjecting them to peace and civilization, and making regulations to prepare for war against the Lamanites, behold, the Lamanites had come into the *u*land of Moroni, which was in the borders by the seashore.

23. And it came to pass that the Nephites were not sufficiently strong in the city of Moroni; therefore Amalickiah did drive them, slaying many. And it came to pass that Amalickiah took possession of the city, yea, possession of all their fortifications.

24. And those who fled out of the *v*city of Moroni came to the *w*city of Nephihah; and also the people of the *x*city of Lehi gathered themselves together, and made preparations and were ready to receive the Lamanites to battle.

25. But it came to pass that Amalickiah would not suffer the Lamanites to go against the *y*city of Nephihah to battle, but kept them down by the seashore, leaving men in every city to maintain and defend it.

26. And thus he went on, taking possession of many cities, the *z*city of Nephihah, and the ^{2a}city of Lehi, and the ^{2b}city of Morianton, and the city of Omner, and the ^{2c}city of Gid, and the ^{2d}city of Mulek, all of which were on the east borders by the seashore.

27. And thus had the Lamanites obtained, by the cunning of Amalickiah, so many cities, by their numberless hosts, all of which were strongly ^{2e}fortified after the manner of the fortifications of Moroni; all of which afforded strongholds for the Lamanites.

28. ^{2f}And it came to pass that they marched to the borders of the land Bountiful, driving the Nephites before them and slaying many.

29. But it came to pass that they were met by Teancum, who had ^{2g}slain Morianton and had headed his people in his flight.

30. And it came to pass that

---

r, Al. 46:12, 13. *s*, see *c*. *t*, see *m*, Mos. 29. *u*, see *k*, Al. 50. *v*, see *k*, Al. 50. *w*, see *l*, Al. 50. *x*, see *m*, Al. 50. *y*, see *l*, Al. 50. *z*, see *l*, Al. 50. 2a, see *m*, Al. 50. 2b, see *p*, Al. 50. 2c, Al. 55:7, 16, 25, 26. He. 5:15. 2d, Al. 52:2, 16, 17, 19, 20, 22, 26, 28, 34. 53:2, 6. 2e, see *c*, Al. 48. 2f, see 2k, Al. 22. 2g, Al. 50:35.

ABOUT B. C. 67.

he headed Amalickiah also, as he was marching forth with his numerous army that he might take possession of the ^{2h}land Bountiful, and also the land ^{2i}northward.

31. But behold he met with a disappointment by being repulsed by Teancum and his men, for they were great warriors; for every man of Teancum did exceed the Lamanites in their strength and in their skill of war, insomuch that they did gain advantage over the Lamanites.

32. And it came to pass that they did harass them, insomuch that they did slay them even until it was dark. And it came to pass that Teancum and his men did pitch their tents in the borders of the ^{2j}land Bountiful; and Amalickiah did pitch his tents in the borders on the beach by the seashore, and after this manner were they driven.

33. And it came to pass that when the night had come, Teancum and his servant stole forth and went out by night, and went into the camp of Amalickiah; and behold, sleep had overpowered them because of their much fatigue, which was caused by the labors and heat of the day.

34. And it came to pass that Teancum stole privily into the tent of the king, and put a javelin to his heart; and he did cause the death of the king immediately that he did not awake his servants.

35. And he returned again privily to his own camp, and behold, his men were asleep, and he awoke them and told them all the things that he had done.

36. And he caused that his armies should stand in readiness, lest the Lamanites had awakened and should come upon them.

37. And thus endeth the twenty and fifth year of the reign of the judges over the people of Nephi; and thus endeth the days of Amalickiah.

CHAPTER 52.

Ammoron succeeds Amalickiah—Moroni, with Teancum and Lehi, retakes city of Mulek and wins great victory—Death of Jacob, the Lamanite general.

1. And now, it came to pass in the *twenty and sixth year of the reign of the judges over the people of Nephi, behold, when the Lamanites awoke on the first morning of the first month, behold, they found Amalickiah was dead in his own tent; and they also saw that Teancum was ready to give them battle on that day.

2. And now, when the Lamanites saw this they were affrighted; and they abandoned their design in marching into the ^{a}land northward, and retreated with all their army into the ^{b}city of Mulek, and sought protection in their ^{c}fortifications.

3. And it came to pass that the brother of Amalickiah was appointed king over the people; and his name was Ammoron; thus king Ammoron, the brother of king Amalickiah, was appointed to reign in his stead.

4. And it came to pass that he did command that his people should maintain those cities, which they had taken by the shedding of blood; for they had not taken any cities save they had lost much blood.

5. And now, Teancum saw that the Lamanites were determined

2h, see 2k, Al. 22. 2i, see p, Al. 46. 2j, see 2k, Al. 22. Chap. 52: a, see p, Al. 46. b, see 2d, Al. 51. c, see c, Al. 48. * B. C. 66.

to maintain those cities which they had taken, and those parts of the land which they had obtained possession of; and also seeing the enormity of their number, Teancum thought it was not expedient that he should attempt to attack them in their forts.

6. But he kept his men round about, as if making preparations for war; yea, and truly he was preparing to defend himself against them, by ᵈcasting up walls round about and preparing places of resort.

7. And it came to pass that he kept thus preparing for war until Moroni had sent a large number of men to strengthen his army.

8. And Moroni also sent orders unto him that he should retain all the prisoners who fell into his hands; for as the Lamanites had taken many prisoners, that he should retain all the prisoners of the Lamanites as a ransom for those whom the Lamanites had taken.

9. And he also sent orders unto him that he should fortify the ᵉland Bountiful, and secure the ᶠnarrow pass which led into the land ᵍnorthward, lest the Lamanites should obtain that point and should have power to harass them on every side.

10. And Moroni also sent unto him, desiring him that he would be faithful in maintaining that quarter of the land, and that he would seek every opportunity to scourge the Lamanites in that quarter, as much as was in his power, that perhaps he might take again by stratagem or some other way those cities which had been taken out of their hands; and that he also would ʰfortify and strengthen the cities round about, which had not fallen into the hands of the Lamanites.

11. And he also said unto him, I would come unto you, but behold, the Lamanites are upon us in the borders of the land by the west sea; and behold, I go against them, therefore I cannot come unto you.

12. Now, the king (Ammoron) had departed out of the ⁱland of Zarahemla, and had made known unto the queen concerning the death of his brother, and had gathered together a large number of men, and had marched forth against the Nephites on the borders by the west sea.

13. And thus he was endeavoring to harass the Nephites, and to draw away a part of their forces to that part of the land, while he had commanded those whom he had left to possess the cities which he had taken, that they should also harass the Nephites on the borders by the east sea, and should take possession of their lands as much as it was in their power, according to the power of their armies.

14. And thus were the Nephites in those dangerous circumstances in the ending of the twenty and sixth year of the reign of the judges over the people of Nephi.

15. But behold, it came to pass in the *twenty and seventh year of the reign of the judges, that Teancum, by the command of Moroni — who had established armies to protect the south and the west borders of the land, and had begun his march towards the ʲland Bountiful, that he might assist Teancum with his men in retaking the cities which they had lost—

16. And it came to pass that

---

d, see *c*, Al. 48.   *e*, see 2*k*, Al. 22.   *f*, see 2*v*, Al. 22.   *g*, see *p*, Al. 46.   *h*, see *c*, Al. 48.   *i*, Om. 13.   *j*, see 2*k*, Al. 22.
* B. C. 65.

Teancum had received orders to make an attack upon the ᵏcity of Mulek, and retake it if it were possible.

17. And it came to pass that Teancum made preparations to make an attack upon the city of Mulek, and march forth with his army against the Lamanites; but he saw that it was impossible that he could overpower them while they were in their ˡfortifications; therefore he abandoned his designs and returned again to the ᵐcity Bountiful, to wait for the coming of Moroni, that he might receive strength to his army.

18. And it came to pass that Moroni did arrive with his army at the land of Bountiful, in the latter end of the twenty and seventh year of the reign of the judges over the people of Nephi.

19. And in the *commencement of the twenty and eighth year, Moroni and Teancum and many of the chief captains held a council of war—what they should do to cause the Lamanites to come out against them to battle; or that they might by some means flatter them out of their strongholds, that they might gain advantage over them and take again the ⁿcity of Mulek.

20. And it came to pass they sent embassies to the army of the Lamanites, which protected the city of Mulek, to their leader, whose name was Jacob, desiring him that he would come out with his armies to meet them upon the plains between the two cities. But behold, Jacob, who was a ᵒZoramite, would not come out with his army to meet them upon the plains.

21. And it came to pass that Moroni, having no hopes of meeting them upon fair grounds, therefore, he resolved upon a plan that he might decoy the Lamanites out of their strongholds.

22. Therefore he caused that Teancum should take a small number of men and march down near the seashore; and Moroni and his army, by night, marched in the wilderness, on the west of the ᵖcity Mulek; and thus, on the morrow, when the guards of the Lamanites had discovered Teancum, they ran and told it unto Jacob, their leader.

23. And it came to pass that the armies of the Lamanites did march forth against Teancum, supposing by their numbers to overpower Teancum because of the smallness of his numbers. And as Teancum saw the armies of the Lamanites coming out against him he began to retreat down by the seashore, northward.

24. And it came to pass that when the Lamanites saw that he began to flee, they took courage and pursued them with vigor. And while Teancum was thus leading away the Lamanites who were pursuing them in vain, behold, Moroni commanded that a part of his army who were with him should march forth into the city, and take possession of it.

25. And thus they did, and slew all those who had been left to protect the city, yea, all those who would not yield up their weapons of war.

26. And thus Moroni had obtained possession of the ᑫcity Mulek with a part of his army, while he marched with the remainder to meet the Lamanites when they should return from the pursuit of Teancum.

---

k, see 2*d*, Al. 51. *l*, see *c*, Al. 48. *m*, see 2*k*, Al. 22. *n*, see 2*d*, Al. 51. *o*, see 2*j*, Al. 30. *p*, see 2*d*, Al. 51. *q*, see 2*d*, Al. 51. * B. C. 64.

27. And it came to pass that the Lamanites did pursue Teancum until they came near the rcity Bountiful, and then they were met by Lehi and a small army, which had been left to protect the city Bountiful.

28. And now behold, when the chief captains of the Lamanites had beheld Lehi with his army coming against them, they fled in much confusion, lest perhaps they should not obtain the scity Mulek before Lehi should overtake them; for they were wearied because of their march, and the men of Lehi were fresh.

29. Now the Lamanites did not know that Moroni had been in their rear with his army; and all they feared was Lehi and his men.

30. Now Lehi was not desirous to overtake them till they should meet Moroni and his army.

31. And it came to pass that before the Lamanites had retreated far they were surrounded by the Nephites, by the men of Moroni on one hand, and the men of Lehi on the other, all of whom were fresh and full of strength; but the Lamanites were wearied because of their long march.

32. And Moroni commanded his men that they should fall upon them until they had given up their weapons of war.

33. And it came to pass that Jacob, being their leader, being also a *t*Zoramite, and having an unconquerable spirit, he led the Lamanites forth to battle with exceeding fury against Moroni.

34. Moroni being in their course of march, therefore Jacob was determined to slay them and cut his way through to the *u*city of Mulek. But behold, Moroni and his men were more powerful; therefore they did not give way before the Lamanites.

35. And it came to pass that they fought on both hands with exceeding fury; and there were many slain on both sides; yea, and Moroni was wounded and Jacob was killed.

36. And Lehi pressed upon their rear with such fury with his strong men, that the Lamanites in the rear delivered up their weapons of war; and the remainder of them, being much confused, knew not whether to go or to strike.

37. Now Moroni seeing their confusion, he said unto them: If ye will bring forth your weapons of war and deliver them up, behold we will forbear shedding your blood.

38. And it came to pass that when the Lamanites had heard these words, their chief captains, all those who were not slain, came forth and threw down their weapons of war at the feet of Moroni, and also commanded their men that they should do the same.

39. But behold, there were many that would not; and those who would not deliver up their swords were taken and bound, and their weapons of war were taken from them, and they were compelled to march with their brethren forth into the *v*land Bountiful.

40. And now the number of prisoners who were taken exceeded more than the number of those who had been slain, yea, more than those who had been slain on both sides.

---

r, see 2*k*, Al. 22.   *s*, see 2*d*, Al. 51.   *t*, see 2*j*, Al. 30.   *u*, see 2*d*, Al. 51.   *v*, see 2*k*, Al. 22.

ABOUT B. C. 64.

CHAPTER 53.

City Bountiful fortified—Nephite dissension gives advantage to enemy —Helaman and his two thousand stripling warriors.

1. And it came to pass that they did set guards over the prisoners of the Lamanites, and did compel them to go forth and bury their dead, yea, and also the dead of the Nephites who were slain; and Moroni placed men over them to guard them while they should perform their labors.

2. And Moroni went to the ^acity of Mulek with Lehi, and took command of the city and gave it unto Lehi. Now behold, this Lehi was a man who had been with Moroni in the more part of all his battles; and he was a man like unto Moroni, and they rejoiced in each other's safety; yea, they were beloved by each other, and also beloved by all the people of Nephi.

3. And it came to pass that after the Lamanites had finished burying their dead and also the dead of the Nephites, they were marched back into the ^bland Bountiful; and Teancum, by the orders of Moroni, caused that they should commence laboring in ^cdigging a ditch round about the land, or the city, Bountiful.

4. And he caused that they should build a breastwork of timbers upon the inner bank of the ditch; and they cast up dirt out of the ditch against the breastwork of timbers; and thus they did cause the Lamanites to labor until they had encircled the ^dcity of Bountiful round about with a strong wall of timbers and earth, to an exceeding height.

5. And this city became an exceeding stronghold ever after; and in this city they did guard the prisoners of the Lamanites; yea, even within a wall which they had caused them to build with their own hands. Now Moroni was compelled to cause the Lamanites to labor, because it was easy to guard them while at their labor; and he desired all his forces when he should make an attack upon the Lamanites.

6. And it came to pass that Moroni had thus gained a victory over one of the greatest of the armies of the Lamanites, and had obtained possession of the ^ecity of Mulek, which was one of the strongest holds of the Lamanites in the land of Nephi; and thus he had also built a stronghold to retain his prisoners.

7. And it came to pass that he did no more attempt a battle with the Lamanites in that year, but he did employ his men in preparing for war, yea, and in making ^ffortifications to guard against the Lamanites, yea, and also delivering their women and their children from famine and affliction, and providing food for their armies.

8. And now it came to pass that the armies of the Lamanites, on the west sea, south, while in the absence of Moroni on account of some intrigue amongst the Nephites, which caused dissensions amongst them, had gained some ground over the Nephites, yea, insomuch that they had obtained possession of a number of their cities in that part of the land.

9. And thus because of iniquity amongst themselves, yea, because of dissensions and intrigue among themselves they were placed in the most dangerous circumstances.

---

a, see 2*d*, Al. 51. *b*, see 2*k*, Al. 22. *c*, see *c*, Al. 48. *d*, see 2*k*, Al. 22. *e*, see 2*d*, Al. 51. *f*, see *c*, Al. 48.   ABOUT B. C. 64.

10. And now behold, I have somewhat to say concerning the ^gpeople of Ammon, who, in the beginning, were Lamanites; but by Ammon and his brethren, or rather by the power and word of God, they had been ^hconverted unto the Lord; and they had been brought down into the ⁱland of Zarahemla, and had ever since been protected by the Nephites.

11. And because of their ^joath they had been kept from taking up arms against their brethren; for they had taken an oath that they never would shed blood more; and according to their oath they would have perished; yea, they would have suffered themselves to have fallen into the hands of their brethren, had it not been for the pity and the exceeding love which Ammon and his brethren had had for them.

12. And for this cause they were brought down into the land of Zarahemla; and they ever had been protected by the Nephites.

13. But it came to pass that when they saw the danger, and the many afflictions and tribulations which the Nephites bore for them, they were moved with compassion and were desirous to take up arms in the defence of their country.

14. But behold, as they were about to take their weapons of war, they were overpowered by the persuasions of Helaman and his brethren, for they were about to ^kbreak the oath which they had made.

15. And Helaman feared lest by so doing they should lose their souls; therefore all those who had entered into this covenant were compelled to behold their brethren wade through their afflictions, in their dangerous circumstances at this time.

16. But behold, it came to pass they had many sons, who had not entered into a covenant that they would not take their weapons of war to defend themselves against their enemies; therefore they did assemble themselves together at this time, as many as were able to take up arms, and they called themselves Nephites.

17. And they entered into a covenant to fight for the ^lliberty of the Nephites, yea, to protect the land unto the laying down of their lives; yea, even they covenanted that they never would give up their liberty, but they would fight in all cases to protect the Nephites and themselves from bondage.

18. Now behold, there were two thousand of those young men, who entered into this covenant and took their weapons of war to defend their country.

19. And now behold, as they never had hitherto been a disadvantage to the Nephites, they became now at this period of time also a great support; for they took their weapons of war, and they would that Helaman should be their leader.

20. And they were all young men, and they were exceedingly valiant for courage, and also for strength and activity; but behold, this was not all—they were men who were true at all times in whatsoever thing they were entrusted.

21. Yea, they were men of truth and soberness, for they had been taught to keep the commandments of God and to walk uprightly before him.

g, Al. 27:26. *h*, Al. 23:8—13. *i*, Om. 13. *j*, Al. 24:17—19. *k*, Al. 24:17—19. *l*, see *m*, Mos. 29.

ABOUT B. C. 64.

22. And now it came to pass that Helaman did march at the head of his two thousand stripling soldiers, to the support of the people in the borders of the land on the south by the west sea.

23. And thus ended the twenty and eighth year of the reign of the judges over the people of Nephi.

CHAPTER 54.

Ammoron asks for exchange of prisoners—Moroni grants request upon conditions—The Lamanite king's angry reply.

1. And now it came to pass in the *twenty and ninth year of the judges, that Ammoron sent unto Moroni desiring that he would exchange prisoners.

2. And it came to pass that Moroni felt to rejoice exceedingly at this request, for he desired the provisions which were imparted for the support of the Lamanite prisoners for the support of his own people; and he also desired his own people for the strengthening of his army.

3. Now the Lamanites had taken many women and children, and there was not a woman nor a child among all the prisoners of Moroni, or the prisoners whom Moroni had taken; therefore Moroni resolved upon a stratagem to obtain as many prisoners of the Nephites from the Lamanites as it were possible.

4. Therefore he wrote an epistle, and sent it by the servant of Ammoron, the same who had brought an epistle to Moroni. Now these are the words which he wrote unto Ammoron, saying:

5. Behold, Ammoron, I have written unto you somewhat concerning this war which ye have waged against my people, or rather which thy brother hath waged against them, and which ye are still determined to carry on after his death.

6. Behold, I would tell you somewhat concerning the justice of God, and the sword of his almighty wrath, which doth hang over you except ye repent and withdraw your armies into your own lands, or the land of your possessions, which is the ªland of Nephi.

7. Yea, I would tell you these things if ye were capable of hearkening unto them; yea, I would tell you concerning that ᵇawful hell that awaits to receive ᶜsuch murderers as thou and thy brother have been, except ye repent and withdraw your murderous purposes, and return with your armies to your own lands.

8. But as ye have rejected these things, and have fought against the people of the Lord, even so I may expect you will do it again.

9. And now behold, we are prepared to receive you; yea, and except you withdraw your purposes, behold, ye will pull down the wrath of that God whom you have rejected upon you, even to your utter destruction.

10. But, as the Lord liveth, our armies shall come upon you except ye withdraw, and ye shall soon be visited with death, for we will retain our cities and our lands; yea, and we will maintain our religion and the cause of our God.

11. But behold, it supposeth me that I talk to you concerning these things in vain; or it supposeth me that thou art a child of hell; therefore I will close my epistle by telling you that I will

---

a, see *b*, 2 Ne. 5. *b*, see *k*, 1 Ne. 15. *c*, Al. 47:18, 22—34.   • B. C. 63.

not exchange prisoners, save it be on conditions that ye will ^ddeliver up a man and his wife and his children, for one prisoner; if this be the case that ye will do it, I will exchange.

12. And behold, if ye do not this, I will come against you with my armies; yea, even I will arm my women and my children, and I will come against you, and I will follow you even into your own land, which is the land of our ^efirst inheritance; yea, and it shall be blood for blood, yea, life for life; and I will give you battle even until you are destroyed from off the face of the earth.

13. Behold, I am in my anger, and also my people; ye have sought to murder us, and we have only sought to defend ourselves. But behold, if ye seek to destroy us more we will seek to destroy you; yea, and we will seek ^four land, the land of our first inheritance.

14. Now I close my epistle. I am Moroni; I am a leader of the people of the Nephites.

15. Now it came to pass that Ammoron, when he had received this epistle, was angry; and he wrote another epistle unto Moroni, and these are the words which he wrote, saying:

16. I am Ammoron, the king of the Lamanites; I am the brother of Amalickiah whom ye have ^gmurdered. Behold, I will avenge his blood upon you, yea, and I will come upon you with my armies for I fear not your threatenings.

17. For behold, your fathers did wrong their brethren, insomuch that they did rob them of their ^hright to the government when it rightly belonged unto them.

18. And now behold, if ye will lay down your arms, and subject yourselves to be governed by those to whom the government doth rightly belong, then will I cause that my people shall lay down their weapons and shall be at war no more.

19. Behold, ye have breathed out many threatenings against me and my people; but behold, we fear not your threatenings.

20. Nevertheless, I will grant to exchange prisoners according to your request, gladly, that I may preserve my food for my men of war; and we will wage a war which shall be eternal, either to the subjecting the Nephites to our authority or to their eternal extinction.

21. And as concerning that God whom ye say we have ⁱrejected, behold, we know not such a being; neither do ye; but if it so be that there is such a being, we know not but that he hath made us as well as you.

22. And if it so be that there is a devil and a hell, behold will he not send you there to dwell with my ^jbrother whom ye have murdered, whom ye have hinted that he hath gone to such a place? But behold these things matter not.

23. I am Ammoron, and a descendant of ^kZoram, whom your fathers pressed and brought out of Jerusalem.

24. And behold now, I am a bold Lamanite; behold, this war hath been waged to avenge their wrongs, and to maintain and to obtain their ^lrights to the government; and I close my epistle to Moroni.

---

d, ver. 3. *e*, see *b*, 2 Ne. 5. *f*, see *b*, 2 Ne. 5. *g*, Al. 51:34. *h*, 2 Ne. 5:1—4. See *n*, Jac. 7. *i*, ver. 9. *j*, Al. 51:34. 52:3. *k*, 1 Ne. 4:35. *l*, see *h*

ABOUT B. C. 63.

CHAPTER 55.

Moroni, incensed at Ammoron's false assertions, refuses to exchange prisoners—Strategy secures release of captured Nephites—City of Gid taken without bloodshed.

1. Now it came to pass that when Moroni had received this epistle he was more angry, because he knew that Ammoron had a perfect knowledge of his fraud; yea, he knew that Ammoron knew that it was not a just cause that had caused him to wage a war against the people of Nephi.

2. And he said: Behold, I will not exchange prisoners with Ammoron save he will ^{a}withdraw his purpose, as I have stated in my epistle; for I will not grant unto him that he shall have any more power than what he hath got.

3. Behold, I know the place where the Lamanites do guard my people whom they have taken prisoners; and as Ammoron would not grant unto me mine epistle, behold, I will give unto him according to my words; yea, I will seek death among them until they shall sue for peace.

4. And now it came to pass that when Moroni had said these words, he caused that a search should be made among his men, that perhaps he might find a man who was a descendant of Laman among them.

5. And it came to pass that they found one, whose name was Laman; and he was ^{b}one of the servants of the king who was murdered by Amalickiah.

6. Now Moroni caused that Laman and a small number of his men should go forth unto the guards who were over the Nephites.

7. Now the Nephites were guarded in the ^{c}city of Gid; therefore Moroni appointed Laman and caused that a small number of men should go with him.

8. And when it was evening Laman went to the guards who were over the Nephites, and behold, they saw him coming and they hailed him; but he saith unto them: Fear not; behold, I am a Lamanite. Behold, we have escaped from the Nephites, and they sleep; and behold we have taken of their wine and brought with us.

9. Now when the Lamanites heard these words they received him with joy; and they said unto him: Give us of your wine, that we may drink; we are glad that ye have thus taken wine with you for we are weary.

10. But Laman said unto them: Let us keep of our wine till we go against the Nephites to battle. But this saying only made them more desirous to drink of the wine;

11. For, said they: We are weary, therefore let us take of the wine, and by and by we shall receive wine for our rations, which will strengthen us to go against the Nephites.

12. And Laman said unto them: You may do according to your desires.

13. And it came to pass that they did take of the wine freely; and it was pleasant to their taste, therefore they took of it more freely; and it was strong, having been prepared in its strength.

14. And it came to pass they did drink and were merry, and by and by they were all drunken.

15. And now when Laman and his men saw that they were all drunken, and were in a deep sleep, they returned to Moroni

---

a, Al. 54:6, 13.   *b*, Al. 47:29.   *c*, see 2c, Al. 51.   ABOUT B. C. 63.

and told him all the things that had happened.

16. And now this was according to the design of Moroni. And Moroni had prepared his men with weapons of war; and he sent to the ᵈcity Gid, while the Lamanites were in a deep sleep and drunken, and cast in weapons of war unto the prisoners, insomuch that they were all armed;

17. Yea, even to their women, and all those of their children, as many as were able to use a weapon of war, when Moroni had armed all those prisoners; and all those things were done in a profound silence.

18. But had they awakened the Lamanites, behold they were drunken and the Nephites could have slain them.

19. But behold, this was not the desire of Moroni; he did not delight in murder or bloodshed, but he delighted in the saving of his people from destruction; and for this cause he might not bring upon him injustice, he would not fall upon the Lamanites and destroy them in their drunkenness.

20. But he had obtained his desires; for he had armed those prisoners of the Nephites who were within the wall of the city, and had given them power to gain possession of those parts which were within the walls.

21. And then he caused the men who were with him to withdraw a pace from them, and surround the armies of the Lamanites.

22. Now behold this was done in the night-time, so that when the Lamanites awoke in the morning they beheld that they were surrounded by the Nephites without, and that their prisoners were armed within.

23. And thus they saw that the Nephites had power over them; and in these circumstances they found that it was not expedient that they should fight with the Nephites; therefore their chief captains demanded their weapons of war, and they brought them forth and cast them at the feet of the Nephites, pleading for mercy.

24. Now behold, this was the desire of Moroni. He took them prisoners of war, and took possession of the city, and caused that all the prisoners should be liberated, who were Nephites; and they did join the army of Moroni, and were a great strength to his army.

25. And it came to pass that he did cause the Lamanites, whom he had taken prisoners, that they should commence a labor in strengthening the ᵉfortifications round about the city Gid.

26. And it came to pass that when he had fortified the ᶠcity Gid, according to his desires, he caused that his prisoners should be taken to the ᵍcity Bountiful; and he also guarded that city with an exceeding strong force.

27. And it came to pass that they did, notwithstanding all the intrigues of the Lamanites, keep and protect all the prisoners whom they had taken, and also maintain all the ground and the advantage which they had retaken.

28. And it came to pass that the Nephites began again to be victorious, and to reclaim their rights and their privileges.

29. Many times did the Lamanites attempt to encircle them about by night, but in these at-

---

d, see 2*c*, Al. 51.   *e*, see *c*, Al. 48.   *f*, see 2*c*, Al. 51.   *g*, see 2*k*, Al. 22.

About B. C. 63.

ALMA, 56.

tempts they did lose many prisoners.

30. And many times did they attempt to administer of their wine to the Nephites, that they might destroy them with poison or with drunkenness.

31. But behold, the Nephites were not slow to remember the Lord their God in this their time of affliction. They could not be taken in their snares; yea, they would not partake of their wine, save they had first given to some of the Lamanite prisoners.

32. And they were thus cautious that no poison should be administered among them; for if their wine would poison a Lamanite it would also poison a Nephite; and thus they did try all their liquors.

33. And now it came to pass that it was expedient for Moroni to make preparations to attack the ^{h}city Morianton; for behold, the Lamanites had, by their labors, ^{i}fortified the city Morianton until it had become an exceeding stronghold.

34. And they were continually bringing new forces into that city, and also new supplies of provisions.

35. And thus ended the twenty and ninth year of the reign of the judges over the people of Nephi.

CHAPTER 56.

Helaman's epistle to Moroni—Wonderful faith and valor of the stripling Ammonites—Another great battle—Nephites victorious.

1. And now it came to pass in the *commencement of the thirtieth year of the reign of the judges, on the second day in the first month, Moroni received an epistle from Helaman, stating the affairs of the people in ^{a}that quarter of the land.

2. And these are the words which he wrote, saying: My dearly beloved brother, Moroni, as well in the Lord as in the tribulations of our warfare; behold, my beloved brother, I have somewhat to tell you concerning our warfare in this part of the land.

3. Behold, ^{b}two thousand of the sons of those men whom Ammon brought down out of the ^{c}land of Nephi—now ye have known that these were descendants of Laman, who was the eldest son of our father Lehi;

4. Now I need not rehearse unto you concerning their ^{d}traditions or their unbelief, for thou knowest concerning all these things—

5. Therefore it sufficeth me that I tell you that ^{e}two thousand of these young men have taken their weapons of war, and would that I should be their leader; and we have come forth to defend our country.

6. And now ye also know concerning the covenant which their fathers made, that they would not take up their weapons of war against their brethren to shed blood.

7. But in the twenty and sixth year, when they saw our afflictions and our tribulations for them, they were about to ^{f}break the covenant which they had made and take up their weapons of war in our defence.

8. But I would not suffer them that they should break this covenant which they had made, supposing that God would strengthen us, insomuch that we should not

---
h, see p, Al. 50. i, see c, Al. 48. CHAP. 56: a, Al. 53:8, 22. b, vers. 5, 10. Al. 53:22. c, see b, 2 Ne. 5, d, see n, Jac. 7. e, see b. f, Al. 24:17—19. 53:13—15.
*B. C. 62.

suffer more because of the fulfilling the oath which they had taken.

9. But behold, here is one thing in which we may have great joy. For behold, in the *twenty and sixth year, I, Helaman, did march at the head of these ^{g}two thousand young men to the ^{h}city of Judea, to assist Antipus, whom ye had appointed a leader over the people of that part of the land.

10. And I did join my ^{i}two thousand sons, (for they are worthy to be called sons) to the army of Antipus, in which strength Antipus did rejoice exceedingly; for behold, his army had been reduced by the Lamanites because their forces had slain a vast number of our men, for which cause we have to mourn.

11. Nevertheless, we may console ourselves in this point, that they have died in the cause of their country and of their God, yea, and they are happy.

12. And the Lamanites had also retained many prisoners, all of whom are chief captains, for none other have they spared alive. And we suppose that they are now at this time in the ^{j}land of Nephi; it is so if they are not slain.

13. And now these are the cities of which the Lamanites have obtained possession by the shedding of the blood of so many of our valiant men:

14. The ^{k}land of Manti, or the city of Manti, and the city of Zeezrom, and the ^{l}city of Cumeni, and the ^{m}city of Antiparah.

15. And these are the cities which they possessed when I arrived at the ^{n}city of Judea; and I found Antipus and his men toiling with their might to ^{o}fortify the city.

16. Yea, and they were depressed in body as well as in spirit, for they had fought valiantly by day and toiled by night to maintain their cities; and thus they had suffered great afflictions of every kind.

17. And now they were determined to conquer in this place or die; therefore you may well suppose that this little force which I brought with me, yea, those ^{p}sons of mine, gave them great hopes and much joy.

18. And now it came to pass that when the Lamanites saw that Antipus had received a greater strength to his army, they were compelled by the orders of Ammoron to not come against the ^{q}city of Judea, or against us, to battle.

19. And thus were we favored of the Lord; for had they come upon us in this our weakness they might have perhaps destroyed our little army; but thus were we preserved.

20. They were commanded by Ammoron to maintain those cities which they had taken. And thus ended the twenty and sixth year. And in the †commencement of the twenty and seventh year we had prepared our city and ourselves for defence.

21. Now we were desirous that the Lamanites should come upon us; for we were not desirous to make an attack upon them in their strongholds.

22. And it came to pass that we kept spies out round about, to watch the movements of the Lamanites, that they might not pass us by night nor by day to make

---
g, Al. 53:22. h, vers. 15, 18, 57. Al. 57:11. i, see b. j, see b, 2 Ne. 5. k, see h, Al. 16. l, Al. 57:7, 8, 12, 23, 31, 34. m, vers. 31, 33, 34. Al. 57:1–4. n, see k. o, see c, Al. 48. p, ver. 10. q, see h. *B. C. 66. †B. C. 65.

ALMA, 56.

an attack upon our other cities which were on the northward.

23. For we knew in those cities they were not sufficiently strong to meet them; therefore we were desirous, if they should pass by us, to fall upon them in their rear, and thus bring them up in the rear at the same time they were met in the front. We supposed that we could overpower them; but behold, we were disappointed in this our desire.

24. They durst not pass by us with their whole army, neither durst they with a part, lest they should not be sufficiently strong and they should fall.

25. Neither durst they march down against the *city of Zarahemla; neither durst they cross the head of ⁸Sidon, over to the city of Nephihah.

26. And thus, with their forces, they were determined to maintain those cities which they had taken.

27. And now it came to pass in the second month of this year, there was brought unto us many provisions from the ᵘfathers of those my ᵗtwo thousand sons.

28. And also there were sent two thousand men unto us from the ʷland of Zarahemla. And thus we were prepared with ten thousand men, and provisions for them, and also for their wives and their children.

29. And the Lamanites, thus seeing our forces increase daily, and provisions arrive for our support, they began to be fearful, and began to sally forth, if it were possible to put an end to our receiving provisions and strength.

30. Now when we saw that the Lamanites began to grow uneasy on this wise, we were desirous to bring a stratagem into effect upon them; therefore Antipus ordered that I should march forth with my little sons to a neighboring city, as if we were carrying provisions to a neighboring city.

31. And we were to march near the ˣcity of Antiparah, as if we were going to the city beyond, in the borders by the seashore.

32. And it came to pass that we did march forth, as if with our provisions, to go to that city.

33. And it came to pass that Antipus did march forth with a part of his army, leaving the remainder to maintain the city. But he did not march forth until I had gone forth with my little army, and came near the city Antiparah.

34. And now, in the ʸcity Antiparah were stationed the strongest army of the Lamanites; yea, the most numerous.

35. And it came to pass that when they had been informed by their spies, they came forth with their army and marched against us.

36. And it came to pass that we did flee before them, northward. And thus we did lead away the most powerful army of the Lamanites;

37. Yea, even to a considerable distance, insomuch that when they saw the army of Antipus pursuing them, with their might, they did not turn to the right nor to the left, but pursued their march in a straight course after us; and, as we suppose, it was their intent to slay us before Antipus should overtake them, and this that they might not be surrounded by our people.

38. And now Antipus, behold-

r, Om. 13. *s*, see *g*, Al. 2. *u*, Al. 27:26. *v*, vers. 3, 5, 10, 46. *w*, Om. 13.
x, see *m*. *y*, see *m*.

ABOUT B. C. 64.

ing our danger, did speed the march of his army. But behold, it was night; therefore they did not overtake us, neither did Antipus overtake them; therefore we did camp for the night.

39. And it came to pass that before the dawn of the morning, behold, the Lamanites were pursuing us. Now we were not sufficiently strong to contend with them; yea, I would not suffer that my little sons should fall into their hands; therefore we did continue our march, and we took our march into the wilderness.

40. Now they durst not turn to the right nor to the left lest they should be surrounded; neither would I turn to the right nor to the left lest they should overtake me, and we could not stand against them, but be slain, and they would make their escape; and thus we did flee all that day into the wilderness, even until it was dark.

41. And it came to pass that again, when the light of the morning came we saw the Lamanites upon us, and we did flee before them.

42. But it came to pass that they did not pursue us far before they halted; and it was in the morning of the third day of the seventh month.

43. And now, whether they were overtaken by Antipus we knew not, but I said unto my men: Behold, we know not but they have halted for the purpose that we should come against them, that they might catch us in their snare;

44. Therefore what say ye, my sons, will ye go against them to battle?

45. And now I say unto you, my beloved brother Moroni, that never had I seen so great courage, nay, not amongst all the Nephites.

46. For as I had ever called them *zmy* sons (for they were all of them very young) even so they said unto me: Father, behold our God is with us, and he will not suffer that we should fall; then let us go forth; we would not slay our brethren if they would let us alone; therefore let us go, lest they should overpower the army of Antipus.

47. Now they never had fought, yet they did not fear death; and they did think more upon the liberty of their ^{2a}fathers than they did upon their lives; yea, they had been taught by their mothers, ^{2b}that if they did not doubt, God would deliver them.

48. And they rehearsed unto me the words of their mothers, saying: We do not doubt our mothers knew it.

49. And it came to pass that I did return with my two thousand against these Lamanites who had pursued us. And now behold, the armies of Antipus had overtaken them, and a terrible battle had commenced.

50. The army of Antipus being weary, because of their long march in so short a space of time, were about to fall into the hands of the Lamanites; and had I not returned with my two thousand they would have obtained their purpose.

51. For Antipus had fallen by the sword, and many of his leaders, because of their weariness, which was occasioned by the speed of their march—therefore the men of Antipus, being confused because of the fall of their leaders, began to give way before the Lamanites.

---

z, vers. 10, 17, 27, 30, 39. 2*a*, Al. 27:26. 2*b*, Al. 57:21. ABOUT B. C. 64.

ALMA, 57.

52. And it came to pass that the Lamanites took courage, and began to pursue them; and thus were the Lamanites pursuing them with great vigor when Helaman came upon their rear with his [2c]two thousand, and began to slay them exceedingly, insomuch that the whole army of the Lamanites halted and turned upon Helaman.

53. Now when the people of Antipus saw that the Lamanites had turned them about, they gathered together their men and came again upon the rear of the Lamanites.

54. And now it came to pass that we, the people of Nephi, the people of Antipus, and I with my two thousand, did surround the Lamanites, and did slay them; yea, insomuch that they were compelled to deliver up their weapons of war and also themselves as prisoners of war.

55. And now it came to pass that when they had surrendered themselves up unto us, behold, I numbered those young men who had fought with me, fearing lest there were many of them slain.

56. But behold, to my great joy, there had [2d]not one soul of them fallen to the earth; yea, and they had fought as if with the strength of God; yea, never were men known to have fought with such miraculous strength; and with such mighty power did they fall upon the Lamanites, that they did frighten them; and for this cause did the Lamanites deliver themselves up as prisoners of war.

57. And as we had no place for our prisoners, that we could guard them to keep them from the armies of the Lamanites, therefore we sent them to the [2e]land of Zarahemla, and a part of those men who were not slain of Antipus, with them; and the remainder I took and joined them to my stripling [2f]Ammonites, and took our march back to the [2g]city of Judea.

CHAPTER 57.

Helaman's epistle continued—Antiparah retaken—City of Cumeni surrenders—Lamanites driven to Manti—A miraculous preservation—Escape of Lamanite prisoners.

1. And now it came to pass that I received an epistle from Ammoron, the king, stating that if I would deliver up those prisoners of war whom we had taken that he would deliver up the [a]city of Antiparah unto us.

2. But I sent an epistle unto the king, that we were sure our forces were sufficient to take the city of Antiparah by our force; and by delivering up the prisoners for that city we should suppose ourselves unwise, and that we would only deliver up our prisoners on exchange.

3. And Ammoron refused mine epistle, for he would not exchange prisoners; therefore we began to make preparations to go against the city of Antiparah.

4. But the people of [b]Antiparah did leave the city, and fled to their other cities, which they had possession of, to [c]fortify them; and thus the city of Antiparah fell into our hands.

5. And thus ended the twenty and eighth year of the reign of the judges.

6. And it came to pass that in the *commencement of the twenty and ninth year, we received a supply of provisions, and also an addition to our army, from the

---
2c, see b. 2d, Al. 57:25. 2e, Om. 13. 2f, Al. 27:26. 2g, see h.
CHAP 57: a, see m, Al. 56. b, see m, Al. 56. c, see c, Al. 48. * B. C. 63.

land of Zarahemla, and from the land round about, to the number of six thousand men, besides sixty of the sons of the Ammonites who had come to join their brethren, my little band of two thousand. And now behold, we were strong, yea, and we had also a plenty of provisions brought unto us.

7. And it came to pass that it was our desire to wage a battle with the army which was placed to protect the city Cumeni.

8. And now behold, I will show unto you that we soon accomplished our desire; yea, with our strong force, or with a part of our strong force, we did surround, by night, the city Cumeni, a little before they were to receive a supply of provisions.

9. And it came to pass that we did camp round about the city for many nights; but we did sleep upon our swords, and keep guards, that the Lamanites could not come upon us by night and slay us, which they attempted many times; but as many times as they attempted this their blood was spilt.

10. At length their provisions did arrive, and they were about to enter the city by night. And we, instead of being Lamanites, were Nephites; therefore, we did take them and their provisions.

11. And notwithstanding the Lamanites being cut off from their support after this manner, they were still determined to maintain the city; therefore it became expedient that we should take those provisions and send them to Judea, and our prisoners to the land of Zarahemla.

12. And it came to pass that not many days had passed away before the Lamanites began to lose all hopes of succor; therefore they yielded up the city unto our hands; and thus we had accomplished our designs in obtaining the city Cumeni.

13. But it came to pass that our prisoners were so numerous that, notwithstanding the enormity of our numbers, we were obliged to employ all our force to keep them, or to put them to death.

14. For behold, they would break out in great numbers, and would fight with stones, and with clubs, or whatsoever thing they could get into their hands, insomuch that we did slay upwards of two thousand of them after they had surrendered themselves prisoners of war.

15. Therefore it became expedient for us, that we should put an end to their lives, or guard them, sword in hand, down to the land of Zarahemla; and also our provisions were not any more than sufficient for our own people, notwithstanding that which we had taken from the Lamanites.

16. And now, in those critical circumstances, it became a very serious matter to determine concerning these prisoners of war; nevertheless, we did resolve to send them down to the land of Zarahemla; therefore we selected a part of our men, and gave them charge over our prisoners to go down to the land of Zarahemla.

17. But it came to pass that on the morrow they did return. And now behold, we did not inquire of them concerning the prisoners; for behold, the Lamanites were upon us, and they returned in season to save us

from falling into their hands. For behold, Ammoron had sent to their support a new supply of provisions and also a numerous army of men.

18. And it came to pass that ¹those men whom we sent with the prisoners did arrive in season to check them, as they were about to overpower us.

19. But behold, my little band of ᵐtwo thousand and sixty fought most desperately; yea, they were firm before the Lamanites, and did administer death unto all those who opposed them.

20. And as the remainder of our army were about to give way before the Lamanites, behold, those two thousand and sixty were firm and undaunted.

21. Yea, and they did obey and observe to perform every word of command with exactness; yea, and even according to their faith it was done unto them; and I did remember the words which they said unto me that their ⁿmothers had taught them.

22. And now behold, it was these my sons, and those men who had been ᵒselected to convey the prisoners, to whom we owe this great victory; for it was they who did beat the Lamanites; therefore they were driven back to the ᵖcity of Manti.

23. And we retained our ᵍcity Cumeni, and were not all destroyed by the sword; nevertheless, we had suffered great loss.

24. And it came to pass that after the Lamanites had fled, I immediately gave orders that my men who had been wounded should be taken from among the dead, and caused that their wounds should be dressed.

25. And it came to pass that there were two hundred, out of my two thousand and sixty, who had fainted because of the loss of blood; nevertheless, according to the goodness of God, and to our great astonishment, and also the foes of our whole army, there was ʳnot one soul of them who did perish; yea, and neither was there one soul among them who had not received many wounds.

26. And now, their preservation was astonishing to our whole army, yea, that they should be spared while there was a thousand of our brethren who were slain. And we do justly ascribe it to the miraculous power of God, because of their exceeding faith in that which they had been taught to believe—that there was a just God, and whosoever did not doubt, that they should be ˢpreserved by his marvelous power.

27. Now this was the faith of these of whom I have spoken; they are young, and their minds are firm, and they do put their trust in God continually.

28. And now it came to pass that after we had thus taken care of our wounded men, and had buried our dead and also the dead of the Lamanites, who were many, behold, we did inquire of Gid concerning the ᶠprisoners whom they had started to go down to the land of Zarahemla with.

29. Now Gid was the chief captain over the band who was appointed to guard them down to the land.

30. And now, these are the words which Gid said unto me: Behold, we did start to go down

---
l, ver. 16. *m,* ver. 6. See *b,* Al. 56. *n,* ver. 26. Al. 56:47, 48. *o,* vers. 16, 18. *p,* see *h,* Al. 16. *q,* see *l,* Al. 56. *r,* Al. 56:56. *s,* see *n.* *t,* ver. 16.

ABOUT B. C. 63.

to the ᵘland of Zarahemla with our prisoners. And it came to pass that we did meet the spies of our armies, who had been sent out to watch the camp of the Lamanites.

31. And they cried unto us, saying—Behold, the armies of the Lamanites are marching towards the ᵛcity of Cumeni; and behold, they will fall upon them, yea, and will destroy our people.

32. And it came to pass that our prisoners did hear their cries, which caused them to take courage; and they did rise up in rebellion against us.

33. And it came to pass because of their rebellion we did cause that our swords should come upon them. And it came to pass that they did in a body run upon our swords, in the which, the greater number of them were slain; and the remainder of them broke through and fled from us.

34. And behold, when they had fled and we could not overtake them, we took our march with speed towards the ʷcity Cumeni; and behold, we did arrive in time that we might assist our brethren in preserving the city.

35. And behold, we are again delivered out of the hands of our enemies. And blessed is the name of our God; for behold, it is he that has delivered us; yea, that has done this great thing for us.

36. Now it came to pass that when I, Helaman, had heard these words of Gid, I was filled with exceeding joy because of the goodness of God in preserving us, that we might not all perish; yea, and I trust that the souls of them who have been slain have entered into the rest of their God.

CHAPTER 58.

Helaman's epistle concluded—Nephite operations before Manti—A Lamanite sortie—Gid and Teomner capture the city—Enemy withdraws.

1. And behold, now it came to pass that our next object was to obtain the ᵃcity of Manti; but behold, there was no way that we could lead them out of the city by our small bands. For behold, they remembered that which we had hitherto done; therefore we could not decoy them away from their strongholds.

2. And they were so much more numerous than was our army that we durst not go forth and attack them in their strongholds.

3. Yea, and it became expedient that we should employ our men to the maintaining those parts of the land which we had regained of our possessions; therefore it became expedient that we should wait, that we might receive more strength from the ᵇland of Zarahemla and also a new supply of provisions.

4. And it came to pass that I thus did send an embassy to the governor of our land, to acquaint him concerning the affairs of our people. And it came to pass that we did wait to receive provisions and strength from the land of Zarahemla.

5. But behold, this did profit us but little; for the Lamanites were also receiving great strength from day to day, and also many provisions; and thus were our circumstances at this period of time.

6. And the Lamanites were sallying forth against us from time to time, resolving by stratagem to destroy us; nevertheless

---

u, Om. 13. v, see l, Al. 56. w, see l, Al. 56. CHAP. 58: a, see h, Al. 16.
b, Om. 13. ABOUT B. C. 63.

we could not come to battle with them, because of their retreats and their strongholds.

7. And it came to pass that we did wait in these difficult circumstances for the space of many months, even until we were about to perish for the want of food.

8. But it came to pass that we did receive food, which was guarded to us by an army of two thousand men to our assistance; and this is all the assistance which we did receive, to defend ourselves and our country from falling into the hands of our enemies, yea, to contend with an enemy which was innumerable.

9. And now the cause of these our embarrassments, or the cause why they did not send more strength unto us, we knew not; therefore we were grieved and also filled with fear, lest by any means the judgments of God should come upon our land, to our overthrow and utter destruction.

10. Therefore we did pour out our souls in ^cprayer to God, that he would strengthen us and deliver us out of the hands of our enemies, yea, and also give us strength that we might retain our cities, and our lands, and our possessions, for the support of our people.

11. Yea, and it came to pass that the Lord our God did visit us with assurances that he would deliver us; yea, insomuch that he did speak peace to our souls, and did grant unto us great faith, and did cause us that we should hope for our deliverance in him.

12. And we did take courage with our small force which we had received, and were fixed with a ^ddetermination to conquer our enemies, and to maintain our lands, and our possessions, and our wives, and our children, and the cause of our liberty.

13. And thus we did go forth with all our might against the Lamanites, who were in the ^ecity of Manti; and we did pitch our tents by the wilderness side, which was near to the city.

14. And it came to pass that on the morrow, that when the Lamanites saw that we were in the borders by the wilderness which was near the city, that they sent out their spies round about us that they might discover the number and the strength of our army.

15. And it came to pass that when they saw that we were not strong, according to our numbers, and fearing that we should cut them off from their support except they should come out to battle against us and kill us, and also supposing that they could easily destroy us with their numerous hosts, therefore they began to make preparations to come out against us to battle.

16. And when we saw that they were making preparations to come out against us, behold, I caused that Gid, with a small number of men, should secrete himself in the wilderness, and also that Teomner and a small number of men should secrete themselves also in the wilderness.

17. Now Gid and his men were on the right and the others on the left; and when they had thus secreted themselves, behold, I remained, with the remainder of my army, in that same place where we had first pitched our tents against the time that the Lamanites should come out to battle.

---

c, see *e*, 2 Ne. 32. *d*, see *m*, Mos. 29. *e*, see *h*, Al. 16. ABOUT B. C. 63.

18. And it came to pass that the Lamanites did come out with their numerous army against us. And when they had come and were about to fall upon us with the sword, I caused that my men, those who were with me, should retreat into the wilderness.

19. And it came to pass that the Lamanites did follow after us with great speed, for they were exceedingly desirous to overtake us that they might slay us; therefore they did follow us into the wilderness; and we did pass by in the *f*midst of Gid and Teomner, insomuch that they were not discovered by the Lamanites.

20. And it came to pass that when the Lamanites had passed by, or when the army had passed by, Gid and Teomner did rise up from their secret places, and did cut off the spies of the Lamanites that they should not return to the city.

21. And it came to pass that when they had cut them off, they ran to the city and fell upon the guards who were left to guard the city, insomuch that they did destroy them and did take possession of the city.

22. Now this was done because the Lamanites did suffer their whole army, save a few guards only, to be led away into the wilderness.

23. And it came to pass that Gid and Teomner by this means had obtained possession of their strongholds. And it came to pass that we took our course, after having traveled much in the wilderness towards the *g*land of Zarahemla.

24. And when the Lamanites saw that they were marching towards the land of Zarahemla, they were exceedingly afraid, lest there was a plan laid to lead them on to destruction; therefore they began to retreat into the wilderness again, yea, even back by the same way which they had come.

25. And behold, it was night and they did pitch their tents, for the chief captains of the Lamanites had supposed that the Nephites were weary because of their march; and supposing that they had driven their whole army therefore they took no thought concerning the *h*city of Manti.

26. Now it came to pass that when it was night, I caused that my men should not sleep, but that they should march forward by another way towards the land of Manti.

27. And because of this our march in the night-time, behold, on the morrow we were beyond the Lamanites, insomuch that we did arrive before them at the city of Manti.

28. And thus it came to pass, that by this stratagem we did take possession of the *i*city of Manti without the shedding of blood.

29. And it came to pass that when the armies of the Lamanites did arrive near the city, and saw that we were prepared to meet them, they were astonished exceedingly and struck with great fear, insomuch that they did flee into the wilderness.

30. Yea, and it came to pass that the armies of the Lamanites did flee out of all this quarter of the land. But behold, they have carried with them many women and children out of the land.

31. And those cities which had

f, vers. 16, 17, 20, 23.   *g*, Om. 13.   *h*, see *h*, Al. 16.   *i*, see *h*, Al. 16.

ABOUT B. C. 63.

been taken by the Lamanites, all of them are at this period of time in our possession; and our fathers and our women and our children are returning to their homes, all save it be those who have been taken prisoners and carried off by the Lamanites.

32. But behold, our armies are small to maintain so great a number of cities and so great possessions.

33. But behold, we trust in our God who has given us victory over those lands, insomuch that we have obtained those cities and those lands, which were our own.

34. Now we do not know the cause that the government does not grant us more strength; neither do ʲthose men who came up unto us know why we have not received greater strength.

35. Behold, we do not know but what ye are unsuccessful, and ye have drawn away the forces into that quarter of the land; if so, we do not desire to murmur.

36. And if it is not so, behold, we fear that there is some ᵏfaction in the government, that they do not send more men to our assistance; for we know that they are more numerous than that which they have sent.

37. But, behold, it mattereth not—we trust God will deliver us, notwithstanding the weakness of our armies, yea, and deliver us out of the hands of our enemies.

38. Behold, this is the twenty and ninth year, in the latter end, and we are in the possession of our lands; and the Lamanites have fled to the ˡland of Nephi.

39. And those sons of the ᵐpeople of Ammon, of whom I have so highly spoken, are with me in the ⁿcity of Manti; and the Lord has supported them, yea, and kept them from falling by the sword, insomuch that even ᵒone soul has not been slain.

40. But behold, they have received many wounds; nevertheless they stand fast in that liberty wherewith God has made them free; and they are strict to remember the Lord their God from day to day; yea, they do observe to keep his statutes, and his judgments, and his commandments continually; and their faith is strong in the prophecies concerning that which is to come.

41. And now, my beloved brother, Moroni, may the Lord our God, who has redeemed us and made us free, keep you continually in his presence; yea, and may he favor this people, even that ye may have success in obtaining the possession of all that which the Lamanites have taken from us, which was for our support. And now, behold, I close mine epistle. I am Helaman, the son of Alma.

CHAPTER 59.

Moroni writes to Pahoran, asking reenforcements for Helaman—City of Nephihah taken by Lamanites—Moroni's anger at seeming indifference of the government.

1. Now it came to pass in the *thirtieth year of the reign of the judges over the people of Nephi, after Moroni had received and had read Helaman's ᵃepistle, he was exceedingly rejoiced because of the welfare, yea, the exceeding success which Helaman had had, in obtaining those lands which were lost.

2. Yea, and he did make it known unto all his people, in all the land round about in that

---

j, ver. 8. *k*, Al. 61. *l*, see *b*, 2 Ne. 5. *m*, Al. 27:26. *n*, see *h*, Al. 16. *o*, Al. 56:56. 57:25. Chap. 59: *a*, Al. chaps. 56—58. * B. C. 62.

part where he was, that they might rejoice also.

3. And it came to pass that he immediately sent an epistle to ᵇPahoran, desiring that he should cause men to be gathered together to strengthen Helaman, or the armies of Helaman, insomuch that he might with ease maintain that part of the land which he had been so miraculously prospered in regaining.

4. And it came to pass when Moroni had sent this epistle to the ᶜland of Zarahemla, he began again to lay a plan that he might obtain the remainder of those possessions and cities which the Lamanites had taken from them.

5. And it came to pass that while Moroni was thus making preparations to go against the Lamanites to battle, behold, the people of ᵈNephihah, who were gathered together from the ᵉcity of Moroni and the ᶠcity of Lehi and the ᵍcity of Morianton, were attacked by the Lamanites.

6. Yea, even those who had been compelled to flee from the ʰland of Manti, and from the land round about, had come over and joined the Lamanites in this part of the land.

7. And thus being exceeding numerous, yea, and receiving strength from day to day, by the command of Ammoron they came forth against the people of ⁱNephihah, and they did begin to slay them with an exceeding great slaughter.

8. And their armies were so numerous that the remainder of the people of Nephihah were obliged to flee before them; and they came even and joined the army of Moroni.

9. And now as Moroni had supposed that there should be men sent to the ʲcity of Nephihah, to the assistance of the people to maintain that city, and knowing that it was easier to keep the city from falling into the hands of the Lamanites than to retake it from them, he supposed that they would easily maintain that city.

10. Therefore he retained all his force to maintain those places which he had recovered.

11. And now, when Moroni saw that the city of Nephihah was lost he was exceeding sorrowful, and began to doubt, because of the wickedness of the people, whether they should not fall into the hands of their brethren.

12. Now this was the case with all his chief captains. They doubted and marveled also because of the wickedness of the people, and this because of the success of the Lamanites over them.

13. And it came to pass that Moroni was angry with the government, because of their indifference concerning the ᵏfreedom of their country.

CHAPTER 60.

Moroni's second epistle to Pahoran—Complains of neglect—Demands immediate help on peril of reprisal.

1. And it came to pass that he wrote again to the governor of the land, ᵃwho was Pahoran, and these are the words which he wrote, saying: Behold, I direct mine epistle to Pahoran, in the ᵇcity of Zarahemla, who is the chief judge and the governor over the land, and also to all those who have been chosen by this

---

b, Al. 50:40. c, Om. 13. d, see l, Al. 50. e, see k, Al. 50. f, see m, Al. 50. g, see p, Al. 50. h, see h, Al. 16. 58:29, 30. i, see l, Al. 50. j, see l, Al. 50. k, see m, Mos. 29. Chap. 60: a, Al. 50:40. b, Om. 13. About B. C. 62.

ALMA, 60.

people to govern and manage the affairs of this war.

2. For behold, I have somewhat to say unto them by the way of condemnation; for behold, ye yourselves know that ye have been appointed to gather together men, and ^carm them with swords, and with cimeters, and all manner of weapons of war of every kind, and send forth against the Lamanites, in whatsoever parts they should come into our land.

3. And now behold, I say unto you that myself, and also my men, and also Helaman and his men, have suffered exceeding great sufferings; yea, even hunger, thirst, and fatigue, and all manner of afflictions of every kind.

4. But behold, were this all we had suffered we would not murmur nor complain.

5. But behold, great has been the slaughter among our people; yea, thousands have fallen by the sword, while it might have otherwise been if ye had rendered unto our armies sufficient strength and succor for them. Yea, great has been your neglect towards us.

6. And now behold, we desire to know the cause of this exceeding great neglect; yea, we desire to know the cause of your thoughtless state.

7. Can you think to sit upon your thrones in a state of thoughtless stupor, while your enemies are spreading the work of death around you? Yea, while they are murdering thousands of your brethren—

8. Yea, even they who have looked up to you for protection, yea, have ^dplaced you in a situation that ye might have succored them, yea, ye might have sent armies unto them, to have strengthened them, and have saved thousands of them from falling by the sword.

9. But behold, this is not all— ye have withheld your provisions from them, insomuch that many have fought and bled out their lives because of their great desires which they had for the welfare of this people; yea, and this they have done when they were about to perish with hunger, because of your exceeding great neglect towards them.

10. And now, my beloved brethren—for ye ought to be beloved; yea, and ye ought to have stirred yourselves more diligently for the welfare and the freedom of this people; but behold, ye have neglected them insomuch that the blood of thousands shall come upon your heads for vengeance; yea, for known unto God were all their cries, and all their sufferings—

11. Behold, could ye suppose that ye could sit upon your thrones, and because of the exceeding goodness of God ye could do nothing and he would deliver you? Behold, if ye have supposed this ye have supposed in vain.

12. Do ye suppose that, because so many of your brethren have been killed it is because of their wickedness? I say unto you, if ye have supposed this ye have supposed in vain; for I say unto you, there are many who have fallen by the sword; and behold it is to your condemnation;

13. For the Lord suffereth the ^erighteous to be slain that his justice and judgment may come upon the wicked; therefore ye need not suppose that the righteous are lost because they are slain; but behold, they do enter

c, see *f*, Al. 2.   *d*, see *e*, Mos. 29.   *e*, Mos. 17:10. Al. 14:11.   ABOUT B. C. 62.

into the ᶠrest of the Lord their God.

14. And now behold, I say unto you, I fear exceedingly that the judgments of God will come upon this people, because of their exceeding slothfulness, yea, even the slothfulness of our government, and their exceeding great neglect towards their brethren, yea, towards those who have been slain.

15. For were it not for the wickedness which first commenced at our head, we could have withstood our enemies that they could have gained no power over us.

16. Yea, had it not been for the war which broke out ᵍamong ourselves; yea, were it not for these ʰking-men, who caused so much bloodshed among ourselves; yea, at the time we were contending among ourselves, if we had united our strength as we hitherto have done; yea, had it not been for the desire of power and authority which those king-men had over us; had they been true to the cause of our freedom, and united with us, and gone forth against our enemies, instead of taking up their swords against us, which was the cause of so much bloodshed among ourselves; yea, if we had gone forth against them in the strength of the Lord, we should have dispersed our enemies, for it would have been done, according to the ⁱfulfilling of his word.

17. But behold, now the Lamanites are coming upon us, taking possession of our lands, and they are murdering our people with the sword, yea, our women and our children, and also carrying them away captive, causing them that they should suffer all manner of afflictions, and this because of the great wickedness of those who are seeking for power and authority, yea, even those ʲking-men.

18. But why should I say much concerning this matter? For we know not but what ye yourselves are seeking for authority. We know not but what ye are also traitors to your country.

19. Or is it that ye have neglected us because ye are in the heart of our country and ye are surrounded by security, that ye do not cause food to be sent unto us, and also men to strengthen our armies?

20. Have ye forgotten the commandments of the Lord your God? Yea, have ye forgotten the captivity of our fathers? Have ye forgotten the many times we have been delivered out of the hands of our enemies?

21. Or do ye suppose that the Lord will still deliver us, while we sit upon our thrones and do not make use of the ᵏmeans which the Lord has provided for us?

22. Yea, will ye sit in idleness while ye are surrounded with thousands of those, yea, and tens of thousands, who do also sit in idleness, while there are thousands round about in the borders of the land who are falling by the sword, yea, wounded and bleeding?

23. Do ye suppose that God will look upon you as guiltless while ye sit still and behold these things? Behold I say unto you, Nay. Now I would that ye should remember that God has said that the ˡinward vessel shall be cleansed first, and then shall the outer vessel be cleansed also.

---

f, see 2v, Al. 12. *g*, Al. 51:13—27. *h*, see *c*, Al. 51. *i*, see *h*, 2 Ne. 1. *j*, see *e*, Al. 51. *k*, ver. 11. *l*, ver. 24.

ABOUT B. C. 62.

24. And now, except ye do repent of that which ye have done, and begin to be up and doing, and send forth food and men unto us, and also unto Helaman, that he may support those parts of our country which he has regained, and that we may also recover the remainder of our possessions in these parts, behold it will be expedient that we contend no more with the Lamanites until we have first cleansed our inward vessel, yea, even the great head of our government.

25. And except ye grant mine epistle, and come out and show unto me a ᵐtrue spirit of freedom, and strive to strengthen and fortify our armies, and grant unto them food for their support, behold I will leave a part of my freemen to maintain this part of our land, and I will leave the strength and the blessings of God upon them, that none other power can operate against them—

26. And this because of their exceeding faith, and their patience in their tribulations—

27. And I will come unto you, and if there be any among you that has a desire for freedom, yea, if there be even a ⁿspark of freedom remaining, behold I will stir up insurrections among you, even until those who have desires to usurp power and authority shall become extinct.

28. Yea, behold I do not fear your power nor your authority, but it is my God whom I fear; and it is according to his commandments that I do take my sword to defend the cause of my country, and it is because of your iniquity that we have suffered so much loss.

29. Behold it is time, yea, the time is now at hand, that except ye do bestir yourselves in the defence of your country and your little ones, the sword of justice doth hang over you; yea, and it shall fall upon you and visit you even to your utter destruction.

30. Behold, I wait for assistance from you; and, except ye do administer unto our relief, behold, I come unto you, even in the ᵒland of Zarahemla, and smite you with the sword, insomuch that ye can have no more power to impede the progress of this people in the cause of our ᵖfreedom.

31. For behold, the Lord will not suffer that ye shall live and wax strong in your iniquities to destroy his righteous people.

32. Behold, can you suppose that the Lord will spare you and come out in judgment against the Lamanites, when it is the ᑫtradition of their fathers that has caused their hatred, yea, and it has been redoubled by those who have dissented from us, while your iniquity is for the cause of your love of glory and the vain things of the world?

33. Ye know that ye do transgress the laws of God, and ye do know that ye do trample them under your feet. Behold, the Lord saith unto me: If those whom ye have appointed your governors do not repent of their sins and iniquities, ye shall go up to battle against them.

34. And now behold, I, Moroni, am constrained, according to the covenant which I have made to keep the commandments of my God; therefore I would that ye should adhere to the word of God, and send speedily unto me of your provisions and of your men, and also to Helaman.

m, see 2*f*, Al. 43. *n*, see 2*f*, Al. 43. Jac. 7. *o*, Om. 13. *p*, see 2*f*, Al. 43. *q*, see *n*, ABOUT B. C. 62.

35. And behold, if ye will not do this I come unto you speedily; for behold, God will not suffer that we should perish with hunger; therefore he will give unto us of your food, even if it must be by the sword. Now see that ye ʳfulfil the word of God.

36. Behold, I am Moroni, your chief captain. I seek not for power, but to pull it down. I seek not for honor of the world, but for the glory of my God, and the ˢfreedom and welfare of my country. And thus I close mine epistle.

CHAPTER 61.

Pahoran's patriotic reply—He exonerates himself and the freemen—Nephite state tottering—Governor appeals for military aid against rebels.

1. Behold, now it came to pass that soon after Moroni had sent his epistle unto the chief governor, he received an epistle from ᵃPahoran, the chief governor. And these are the words which he received:

2. I, Pahoran, who am the chief governor of this land, do send these words unto Moroni, the chief captain over the army. Behold, I say unto you, Moroni, that I do not joy in your great afflictions, yea, it grieves my soul.

3. But behold, there are those who do joy in your afflictions, yea, insomuch that they have risen up in rebellion against me, and also those of my people who are ᵇfreemen, yea, and those who have risen up are exceeding numerous.

4. And it is those who have sought to take away the judgment-seat from me that have been the cause of this great iniquity; for they have used great flattery, and they have led away the hearts of many people, which will be the cause of sore affliction among us; they have withheld our provisions, and have daunted our freemen that they have not come unto you.

5. And behold, they have driven me out before them, and I have fled to the ᶜland of Gideon, with as many men as it were possible that I could get.

6. And behold, I have sent a proclamation throughout this part of the land; and behold, they are flocking to us daily, to their arms, in the defence of their country and their ᵈfreedom, and to avenge our wrongs.

7. And they have come unto us, insomuch that those who have risen up in rebellion against us are set at defiance, yea, insomuch that they do fear us and durst not come out against us to battle.

8. They have got possession of the land, or the ᵉcity, of Zarahemla; they have appointed a king over them, and he hath written unto the king of the Lamanites, in the which he hath joined an alliance with him; in the which alliance he hath agreed to maintain the city of Zarahemla, which maintenance he supposeth will enable the Lamanites to conquer the remainder of the land, and he shall be placed king over this people when they shall be conquered under the Lamanites.

9. And now, in your epistle you have censured me, but it mattereth not; I am not angry, but do rejoice in the greatness of your heart. I, Pahoran, do not seek for power, save only to retain my judgment-seat that I may

---

r, ver. 33. *s,* see 2*f,* Al. 43. CHAP. 61: *a,* Al. 50:40. *b,* see *m,* Mos. 29. *c,* see *m,* Al. 2. *d,* see *m,* Mos. 29. *e,* Om. 13. ABOUT B. C. 62.

preserve the rights and the [f]liberty of my people. My soul standeth fast in that liberty in the which God hath made us free.

10. And now, behold, we will resist wickedness even unto bloodshed. We would not shed the blood of the Lamanites if they would stay in their own land.

11. We would not shed the blood of our brethren if they would not rise up in rebellion and take the sword against us.

12. We would subject ourselves to the yoke of bondage if it were requisite with the justice of God, or if he should command us so to do.

13. But behold he doth not command us that we shall subject ourselves to our enemies, but that we should put our trust in him, and he will deliver us.

14. Therefore, my beloved brother, Moroni, let us resist evil, and whatsoever evil we cannot resist with our words, yea, such as rebellions and dissensions, let us resist them with our swords, that we may retain our freedom, that we may rejoice in the great privilege of our church, and in the cause of our Redeemer and our God.

15. Therefore, come unto me speedily with a few of your men, and leave the remainder in the charge of Lehi and Teancum; give unto them power to conduct the war in that part of the land, according to the Spirit of God, which is also the spirit of freedom which is in them.

16. Behold I have sent a few provisions unto them, that they may not perish until ye can come unto me.

17. Gather together whatsoever force ye can upon your march hither, and we will go speedily against those dissenters, in the strength of our God according to the faith which is in us.

18. And we will take possession of the [g]city of Zarahemla, that we may obtain more food to send forth unto Lehi and Teancum; yea, we will go forth against them in the strength of the Lord, and we will put an end to this great iniquity.

19. And now, Moroni, I do joy in receiving your epistle, for I was somewhat worried concerning what we should do, whether it should be just in us to go against our brethren.

20. But ye have said, except they repent the Lord [h]hath commanded you that ye should go against them.

21. See that ye strengthen Lehi and Teancum in the Lord; tell them to fear not, for God will deliver them, yea, and also all those who stand fast in that liberty wherewith God hath made them free. And now I close mine epistle to my beloved brother, Moroni.

CHAPTER 62.

Moroni marches to relief of Pahoran—Zarahemla recaptured from the rebels—Help sent to Helaman, Lehi, and Teancum—Lamanites concentrate in land of Moroni—Teancum slays Ammoron, at cost of his own life—Lamanites driven out of the land.

1. And now it came to pass that when Moroni had received this epistle his heart did take courage, and was filled with exceeding great joy because of the faithfulness of Pahoran, that he was not also a traitor to the freedom and cause of his country.

2. But he did also mourn exceedingly because of the iniquity of those who had driven Pahoran from the judgment-seat, yea, in

f, see *m*, Mos. 29. *g*, Om. 13. *h*, Al. 60:33. ABOUT B. C. 62.

fine because of those who had rebelled against their country and also their God.

3. And it came to pass that Moroni took a small number of men, according to the desire of Pahoran, and gave Lehi and Teancum command over the remainder of his army, and took his march towards the ᵃland of Gideon.

4. And he did raise the ᵇstandard of liberty in whatsoever place he did enter, and gained whatsoever force he could in all his march towards the ᶜland of Gideon.

5. And it came to pass that thousands did flock unto his standard, and did take up their swords in the defence of their ᵈfreedom, that they might not come into bondage.

6. And thus, when Moroni had gathered together whatsoever men he could in all his march, he came to the ᵉland of Gideon; and uniting his forces with those of Pahoran they became exceeding strong, even stronger than the men of Pachus, who was the king of those dissenters who had driven the ᶠfreemen out of the land of Zarahemla and had taken possession of the land.

7. And it came to pass that Moroni and Pahoran went down with their armies into the ᵍland of Zarahemla, and went forth against the city, and did meet the men of Pachus, insomuch that they did come to battle.

8. And behold, Pachus was slain and his men were taken prisoners, and Pahoran was restored to his judgment-seat.

9. And the men of Pachus received their trial, according to the law, and also those ʰking-men who had been taken and ⁱcast into prison; and they were executed according to the law; yea, those men of Pachus and those kingmen, whosoever would not take up arms in the defence of their country, but would fight against it, were put to death.

10. And thus it became expedient that this law should be strictly observed for the safety of their country; yea, and whosoever was found denying their freedom was speedily executed according to the law.

11. And thus ended the thirtieth year of the reign of the judges over the people of Nephi; Moroni and Pahoran having restored peace to the ʲland of Zarahemla, among their own people, having inflicted death upon all those who were not true to the ᵏcause of freedom.

12. And it came to pass in the *commencement of the thirty and first year of the reign of the judges over the people of Nephi, Moroni immediately caused that provisions should be sent, and also an army of six thousand men should be sent unto Helaman, to assist him in preserving that part of the land.

13. And he also caused that an army of six thousand men, with a sufficient quantity of food, should be sent to the armies of Lehi and Teancum. And it came to pass that this was done to fortify the land against the Lamanites.

14. And it came to pass that Moroni and Pahoran, leaving a large body of men in the ˡland of Zarahemla, took their march with a large body of men towards

---

a, see *m*, Al. 2. *b*, Al. 46:12, 13, 36. *c*, see *m*, Al. 2. *d*, see *m*, Mos. 29. *e*, see *m*, Al. 2. *f*, Al. 51:6, 7. 61:4. *g*, Om. 13. *h*, vers. 6, 10, 11. Al. 51:5, 7, 17. 21. 60:16. 61:8. *i*, Al. 51:19. *j*, Om. 13. *k*, Al. 46:12, 13, 36. *l*, Om. 13.
* B. C. 61.

the ᵐland of Nephihah, being determined to overthrow the Lamanites in that city.

15. And it came to pass that as they were marching towards the land, they took a large body of men of the Lamanites, and slew many of them, and took their provisions and their weapons of war.

16. And it came to pass after they had taken them, they caused them to enter into a covenant that they would no more take up their weapons of war against the Nephites.

17. And when they had entered into this covenant they sent them to dwell with the ⁿpeople of Ammon, and they were in number about four thousand who had not been slain.

18. And it came to pass that when they had sent them away they pursued their march towards the ᵒland of Nephihah. And it came to pass that when they had come to the city of Nephihah, they did pitch their tents in the plains of Nephihah, which is near the city of Nephihah.

19. Now Moroni was desirous that the Lamanites should come out to battle against them, upon the plains; but the Lamanites, knowing of their exceeding great courage, and beholding the greatness of their numbers, therefore they durst not come out against them; therefore they did not come to battle in that day.

20. And when the night came, Moroni went forth in the darkness of the night, and came upon the top of the wall to spy out in what part of the city the Lamanites did camp with their army.

21. And it came to pass that they were on the east, by the entrance; and they were all asleep. And now Moroni returned to his army, and caused that they should prepare in haste strong ᵖcords and ladders, to be let down from the top of the wall into the inner part of the wall.

22. And it came to pass that Moroni caused that his men should march forth and come upon the top of the wall, and let themselves down into that part of the city, yea, even on the west, where the Lamanites did not camp with their armies.

23. And it came to pass that they were all let down into the city by night, by the means of their strong cords and their ladders; thus when the morning came they were all within the walls of the city.

24. And now, when the Lamanites awoke and saw that the armies of Moroni were within the walls, they were affrighted exceedingly, insomuch that they did flee out by the pass.

25. And now when Moroni saw that they were fleeing before him, he did cause that his men should march forth against them, and slew many, and surrounded many others, and took them prisoners; and the remainder of them fled into the ᑫland of Moroni, which was in the borders by the seashore.

26. Thus had Moroni and Pahoran obtained the possession of the ʳcity of Nephihah without the loss of one soul; and there were many of the Lamanites who were slain.

27. Now it came to pass that many of the Lamanites that were prisoners were desirous to join the ˢpeople of Ammon and become a free people.

m, see *l*, Al. 50. *n*, Al. 27:26. *o*, see *l*, Al. 50. *p*, ver. 23. *q*, see *k*, Al. 50. *r*, see *l*, Al. 50. *s*, Al. 27:26.

28. And it came to pass that as many as were desirous, unto them it was granted according to their desires.

29. Therefore, all the prisoners of the Lamanites did join the people of Ammon, and did begin to labor exceedingly, tilling the ground, raising all manner of grain, and flocks and herds of every kind; and thus were the Nephites relieved from a great burthen; yea, insomuch that they were relieved from all the prisoners of the Lamanites.

30. Now it came to pass that Moroni, after he had obtained possession of the ᵗcity of Nephihah, having taken many prisoners, which did reduce the armies of the Lamanites exceedingly, and having regained many of the Nephites who had been taken prisoners, which did strengthen the army of Moroni exceedingly; therefore Moroni went forth from the land of Nephihah to the ᵘland of Lehi.

31. And it came to pass that when the Lamanites saw that Moroni was coming against them, they were again frightened and fled before the army of Moroni.

32. And it came to pass that Moroni and his army did pursue them from city to city, until they were met by Lehi and Teancum; and the Lamanites fled from Lehi and Teancum, even down upon the borders by the seashore, until they came to the ᵛland of Moroni.

33. And the armies of the Lamanites were all gathered together, insomuch that they were all in one body in the land of Moroni. Now Ammoron, the king of the Lamanites, was also with them.

34. And it came to pass that Moroni and Lehi and Teancum did encamp with their armies round about in the borders of the land of Moroni, insomuch that the Lamanites were encircled about in the borders by the wilderness on the south, and in the borders by the wilderness on the east.

35. And thus they did encamp for the night. For behold, the Nephites and the Lamanites also were weary because of the greatness of the march; therefore they did not resolve upon any stratagem in the night-time, save it were Teancum; for he was exceedingly angry with Ammoron, insomuch that he considered that Ammoron, and Amalickiah his brother, had been the cause of this great and lasting war between them and the Lamanites, which had been the cause of so much war and bloodshed, yea, and so much famine.

36. And it came to pass that Teancum in his anger did go forth into the camp of the Lamanites, and did let himself down over the walls of the city. And he went forth with a cord, from place to place, insomuch that he did find the king; and he did cast a ʷjavelin at him, which did pierce him near the heart. But behold, the king did awake his servant before he died, insomuch that they did pursue Teancum, and slew him.

37. Now it came to pass that when Lehi and Moroni knew that Teancum was dead they were exceeding sorrowful; for behold, he had been a man who had fought valiantly for his country, yea, a true friend to ˣliberty; and he had suffered very many exceedingly sore afflictions. But behold,

t, see *l*, Al. 50. *u*, see *m*, Al. 50. *v*, see *k*, Al. 50. *w*, Al. 51:34. *x*, Al. 46:12, 13, 36.
ABOUT B. C. 61.

he was dead, and had gone the way of all the earth.

38. Now it came to pass that Moroni marched forth on the morrow, and came upon the Lamanites, insomuch that they did slay them with a great slaughter; and they did drive them out of the land; and they did flee, even that they did not return at that time against the Nephites.

39. And thus *ended the thirty and first year of the reign of the judges over the people of Nephi; and thus they had had wars, and bloodsheds, and famine, and affliction, for the space of many years.

40. And there had been murders, and contentions, and dissensions, and all manner of iniquity among the people of Nephi; nevertheless for the righteous' sake, yea, because of the ʸprayers of the righteous, they were spared.

41. But behold, because of the exceeding great length of the war between the Nephites and the Lamanites many had become hardened, because of the exceeding great length of the war; and many were softened because of their afflictions, insomuch that they did humble themselves before God, even in the depth of humility.

42. And it came to pass that after Moroni had ᶻfortified those parts of the land which were most exposed to the Lamanites, until they were sufficiently strong, he returned to the ²ᵃcity of Zarahemla; and also Helaman returned to the place of his inheritance; and there was once more peace established among the people of Nephi.

43. And Moroni yielded up the command of his armies into the hands of his son, whose name was Moronihah; and he retired to his own house that he might spend the remainder of his days in peace.

44. And Pahoran did return to his judgment-seat; and Helaman did take upon him again to preach unto the people the word of God; for because of so many wars and contentions it had become expedient that a regulation should be made again in the church.

45. Therefore, Helaman and his brethren went forth, and did declare the word of God with much power unto the convincing of many people of their wickedness, which did cause them to repent of their sins and to be ²ᵇbaptized unto the Lord their God.

46. And it came to pass that they did establish again the church of God, throughout all the land.

47. Yea, and regulations were made concerning the law. ²ᶜAnd their judges, and their chief judges were chosen.

48. And the people of Nephi began to prosper again in the land, and began to multiply and to wax exceeding strong again in the land. And they began to grow exceeding rich.

49. But notwithstanding their riches, or their strength, or their prosperity, they were not lifted up in the pride of their eyes; neither were they slow to remember the Lord their God; but they did humble themselves exceedingly before him.

50. Yea, they did remember how great things the Lord had done for them, that he had delivered them from death, and from bonds, and from prisons, and from all manner of afflictions, and he had delivered them out of the hands of their enemies.

51. And they did ²ᵈpray unto the Lord their God continually,

---

y, see *e*, 2 Ne. 32.   *z*, see *c*, Al. 48.   2*a*, Om. 13.   2*b*, see *u*, 2 Ne. 9.   2*c*, Mos. 29:39.   2*d*, see *e*, 2 Ne. 32.   * B. C. 60.

insomuch that the Lord did bless them, according to his word, so that they did wax strong and prosper in the land.

52. And it came to pass that all these things were done. And Helaman died, in the *thirty and fifth year of the reign of the judges over the people of Nephi.

CHAPTER 63.

Shiblon succeeds Helaman—Death of Moroni—Hagoth, builder of ships—Nephite voyages to the land northward—Helaman, son of Helaman, keeps the records—Moronihah defeats Lamanites—End of Alma's account.

1. And it came to pass in the †commencement of the thirty and sixth year of the reign of the judges over the people of Nephi, that ªShiblon took possession of those ᵇsacred things which had been delivered unto Helaman by Alma.

2. And he was a just man, and he did walk uprightly before God; and he did observe to do good continually, to keep the commandments of the Lord his God; and also did his brother.

3. And it came to pass that Moroni died also. And thus ended the thirty and sixth year of the reign of the judges.

4. And it came to pass that in the ‡thirty and seventh year of the reign of the judges, there was a large company of men, even to the amount of five thousand and four hundred men, with their wives and their children, departed out of the ᵈland of Zarahemla into the land which was ᵉnorthward.

5. And it came to pass that Hagoth, he being an exceedingly curious man, therefore he went forth and built him an ᶠexceedingly large ship, on the borders of the ᵍland Bountiful, by the ʰland Desolation, and launched it forth into the west sea, by the ⁱnarrow neck which led into the ʲland northward.

6. And behold, there were many of the Nephites who did enter therein and did sail forth with much provisions, and also many women and children; and they took their course northward. And thus ended the thirty and seventh year.

7. And in the thirty and eighth year, this man built ᵏother ships. And the first ship did also return, and many more people did enter into it; and they also took much provisions, and set out again to the land northward.

8. And it came to pass that they were never heard of more. And we suppose that they were drowned in the depths of the sea. And it came to pass that one other ship also did sail forth; and whither she did go we know not.

9. And it came to pass that in this year there were many people who went forth into the land northward. And thus ended the thirty and eighth year.

10. And it came to pass in the §thirty and ninth year of the reign of the judges, ˡShiblon died also, and ᵐCorianton had gone forth to the land northward in a ⁿship, to carry forth provisions unto the people who had gone forth into that land.

11. Therefore it became expedient for Shiblon to confer those ᵒsacred things, before his death, upon the son of Helaman, who was called Helaman, being called after the name of his father.

---

a, Al. 38. *b*, Al. 37:3—12. *d*, Om. 13. *e*, Al. 46:17. *f*, vers. 6—10. He. 3:10, 14. *g*, see 2*k*, Al. 22. *h*, see 2*l*, Al. 22. *i*, see 2*v*, Al. 22. *j*, see *e*. *k*, see *f*. *l*, see *a*. *m*, see *c*. *n*, see *f*. *o*, Al. 37:3—12.
* B. C. 57. † B. C. 56. ‡ B. C. 55. § B. C. 53.

12. Now behold, all those engravings which were in the possession of Helaman ᵖwere written and sent forth among the children of men throughout all the land, save it were those parts which had been commanded by Alma should ᵍnot go forth.

13. Nevertheless, these things were to be kept sacred, and handed down from ʳone generation to another; therefore, in this year, they had been ˢconferred upon Helaman, before the ᵗdeath of Shiblon.

14. And it came to pass also in this year that there were some dissenters who had gone forth unto the Lamanites; and they were stirred up again to anger against the Nephites.

15. And also in this year they came down with a numerous army to war against the people of ᵘMoronihah, or against the army of Moronihah, in the which they were beaten and driven back again to their own lands, suffering great loss.

16. And thus ended the thirty and ninth year of the reign of the judges over the people of Nephi.

17. And thus ended the account of Alma, and Helaman his son, and also Shiblon, who was his son.

An account of the Nephites. Their wars and contentions, and their dissensions. And also the prophecies of many holy prophets, before the coming of Christ, according to the records of Helaman, who was the son of Helaman, and also according to the records of his sons, even down to the coming of Christ. And also many of the Lamanites are converted. An account of their conversion. An account of the righteousness of the Lamanites, and the wickedness and abominations of the Nephites, according to the record of Helaman and his sons, even down to the coming of Christ, which is called the book of Helaman, &c.

THE BOOK OF HELAMAN

CHAPTER 1.

Pahoran's sons contend for the judgment-seat—Pahoran the second is murdered by Kishkumen—Coriantumr, Nephite dissenter—Zarahemla captured and retaken.

1. And now behold, it came to pass in the *commencement of the fortieth year of the reign of the judges over the people of Nephi, there began to be a serious difficulty among the people of the Nephites.

2. For behold, ᵃPahoran had died, and gone the way of all the earth; therefore there began to be a serious contention concerning who should have the judgment-seat among the brethren, who were the sons of Pahoran.

3. Now these are their names who did contend for the judgment-seat, who did also cause the people to contend: Pahoran, Paanchi, and Pacumeni.

4. Now these are not all the sons of Pahoran, (for he had many) but these are they who did contend for the judgment-seat; therefore, they did cause three divisions among the people.

5. Nevertheless, it came to pass that Pahoran was appointed by the voice of the people to be chief

---

p, Al. 17:2.   q, Al. 37:27—32.   r, Al. 37:4.   s, ver. 11.   t, ver. 10.   u, Al. 62:43.
CHAP. 1: a, Al. 50:40.   * B. C. 52.

judge and a governor over the people of Nephi.

6. And it came to pass that Pacumeni, when he saw that he could not obtain the judgment-seat, he did unite with the voice of the people.

7. But behold, Paanchi, and that part of the people that were desirous that he should be their governor, was exceeding wroth; therefore, he was about to flatter away those people to rise up in rebellion against their brethren.

8. And it came to pass as he was about to do this, behold, he was taken, and was tried according to the ^{b}voice of the people, and condemned unto death; for he had raised up in rebellion and sought to destroy the liberty of the people.

9. Now when those people who were desirous that he should be their governor saw that he was condemned unto death, therefore they were angry, and behold, they sent forth one Kishkumen, even to the judgment-seat of Pahoran, and murdered Pahoran as he sat upon the judgment-seat.

10. And he was pursued by the servants of Pahoran; but behold, so speedy was the flight of Kishkumen that no man could overtake him.

11. And he went unto those that sent him, and they all entered into a covenant, yea, swearing by their everlasting Maker, that they would tell no man that Kishkumen had murdered Pahoran.

12. Therefore, Kishkumen was not known among the people of Nephi, for he was in disguise at the time that he murdered Pahoran. And Kishkumen and his band, who had covenanted with him, did mingle themselves among the people, in a manner that they all could not be found; but as many as were found were condemned unto death.

13. And now behold, Pacumeni was appointed, according to the ^{c}voice of the people, to be a chief judge and a governor over the people, to reign in the stead of his brother Pahoran; and it was according to his right. And all this was done in the fortieth year of the reign of the judges; and it had an end.

14. And it came to pass in the *forty and first year of the reign of the judges, that the Lamanites had gathered together an innumerable army of men, and ^{d}armed them with swords, and with cimeters and with bows, and with arrows, and with head-plates, and with breastplates, and with all manner of shields of every kind.

15. And they came down again that they might pitch battle against the Nephites. And they were led by a man whose name was Coriantumr; and he was a descendant of Zarahemla; and he was a dissenter from among the Nephites; and he was a large and a mighty man.

16. Therefore, the king of the Lamanites, whose name was Tubaloth, who was the son of Ammoron, supposing that Coriantumr, being a mighty man, could stand against the Nephites, with his strength and also with his great wisdom, insomuch that by sending him forth he should gain power over the Nephites—

17. Therefore he did stir them up to anger, and he did gather together his armies, and he did appoint Coriantumr to be their leader, and did cause that they

b, see c, Mos. 29. Al. 1:10—15. c, see c, Mos. 29. He. 2:2. d, see $2p$, Al. 43.
* B. C. 51.

should march down to the *land of Zarahemla to battle against the Nephites.

18. And it came to pass that because of so much contention and so much difficulty in the government, that they had not kept sufficient guards in the land of Zarahemla; for they had supposed that the Lamanites durst not come into the heart of their lands to attack that great city Zarahemla.

19. But it came to pass that Coriantumr did march forth at the head of his numerous host, and came upon the inhabitants of the city, and their march was with such exceedingly great speed that there was no time for the Nephites to gather together their armies.

20. Therefore Coriantumr did cut down the watch by the entrance of the city, and did march forth with his whole army into the city, and they did slay every one who did oppose them, insomuch that they did take possession of the whole city.

21. And it came to pass that Pacumeni, who was the chief judge, did flee before Coriantumr, even to the walls of the city. And it came to pass that Coriantumr did smite him against the wall, insomuch that he died. And thus ended the days of Pacumeni.

22. And now when Coriantumr saw that he was in possession of the city of Zarahemla, and saw that the Nephites had fled before them, and were slain, and were taken, and were cast into prison, and that he had obtained the possession of the strongest hold in all the land, his heart took courage insomuch that he was about to go forth against all the land.

23. And now he did not tarry in the land of Zarahemla, but he did march forth with a large army, even towards the ʲcity of Bountiful; for it was his determination to go forth and cut his way through with the sword, that he might obtain the north parts of the land.

24. And, supposing that their greatest strength was in the center of the land, therefore he did march forth, giving them no time to assemble themselves together save it were in small bodies; and in this manner they did fall upon them and cut them down to the earth.

25. But behold, this march of Coriantumr through the center of the land gave Moronihah great advantage over them, notwithstanding the greatness of the number of the Nephites who were slain.

26. For behold, Moronihah had supposed that the Lamanites durst not come into the center of the land, but that they would attack the cities round about in the borders as they had hitherto done; therefore Moronihah had caused that their strong armies should maintain those parts round about by the borders.

27. But behold, the Lamanites were not frightened according to his desire, but they had come into the center of the land, and had taken the capital city which was the city of Zarahemla, and were marching through the most capital parts of the land, slaying the people with a great slaughter, both men, women, and children, taking possession of many cities and of many strongholds.

28. But when Moronihah had discovered this, he immediately sent forth Lehi with an army round about to head them before

e, Om. 13. *f*, see 2*k*, Al. 22.   ABOUT B. C. 51.

they should come to the *g*land Bountiful.

29. And thus he did; and he did head them before they came to the land Bountiful, and gave unto them battle, insomuch that they began to retreat back towards the land of Zarahemla.

30. And it came to pass that Moronihah did head them in their retreat, and did give unto them battle, insomuch that it became an exceedingly bloody battle; yea, many were slain, and among the number who were slain Coriantumr was also found.

31. And now, behold, the Lamanites could not retreat either way, neither on the north, nor on the south, nor on the east, nor on the west, for they were surrounded on every hand by the Nephites.

32. And thus had Coriantumr plunged the Lamanites into the midst of the Nephites, insomuch that they were in the power of the Nephites, and he himself was slain, and the Lamanites did yield themselves into the hands of the Nephites.

33. And it came to pass that Moronihah took possession of the *h*city of Zarahemla again, and caused that the Lamanites who had been taken prisoners should depart out of the land in peace.

34. And thus ended the forty and first year of the reign of the judges.

CHAPTER 2.

Helaman the second is appointed chief judge—Kishkumen killed—Secret combinations — The Gadianton robbers.

1. And it came to pass in the *forty and second year of the reign of the judges, after Moronihah had established again peace between the Nephites and the Lamanites, behold there was no one to fill the judgment-seat; therefore there began to be a contention again among the people concerning who should fill the judgment-seat.

2. And it came to pass that Helaman, who was the son of Helaman, was appointed to fill the judgment-seat, by the *a*voice of the people.

3. But behold, Kishkumen, who had *b*murdered Pahoran, did lay wait to destroy Helaman also; and he was upheld by his band, who had entered into a covenant that no one should know his wickedness.

4. For there was one Gadianton, who was exceeding expert in many words, and also in his craft, to carry on the *c*secret work of murder and of robbery; therefore he became the leader of the band of Kishkumen.

5. Therefore he did flatter them, and also Kishkumen, that if they would place him in the judgment-seat he would grant unto those who belonged to his band that they should be placed in power and authority among the people; therefore Kishkumen sought to *d*destroy Helaman.

6. And it came to pass as he went forth towards the judgment-seat to destroy Helaman, behold one of the servants of Helaman, having been out by night, and having obtained, through disguise, a knowledge of those plans which had been laid by this band to *e*destroy Helaman—

7. And it came to pass that he met Kishkumen, and he gave unto him a sign; therefore Kishkumen made known unto him the object of his desire, desiring that he

---

g, see 2*k*, Al. 22. *h*, Om. 13. CHAP. 2: *a*, see *c*, Mos. 29. *b*, He. 1:9. *c*, see *l*, 2 Ne. 10. *d*, vers. 3, 6, 9. *e*, see *d*. *B. C. 50.

HELAMAN, 3.

would conduct him to the judgment-seat that he might murder Helaman.

8. And when the servant of Helaman had known all the heart of Kishkumen, and how that it was his object to murder, and also that it was the object of all those who belonged to his band to murder, and to rob, and to gain power, (and this was their *f*secret plan, and their combination) the servant of Helaman said unto Kishkumen: Let us go forth unto the judgment-seat.

9. Now this did please Kishkumen exceedingly, for he did suppose that he should accomplish his design; but behold, the servant of Helaman, as they were going forth unto the judgment-seat, did stab Kishkumen even to the heart, that he fell dead without a groan. And he ran and told Helaman all the things which he had seen, and heard, and done.

10. And it came to pass that Helaman did send forth to take this band of *g*robbers and secret murderers, that they might be executed according to the law.

11. But behold, when Gadianton had found that Kishkumen did not return he feared lest that he should be destroyed; therefore he caused that his band should follow him. And they took their flight out of the land, by a secret way, into the wilderness; and thus when Helaman sent forth to take them they could nowhere be found.

12. And more of this Gadianton shall be spoken hereafter. And thus ended the forty and second year of the reign of the judges over the people of Nephi.

13. And behold, in the end of this book ye shall see that this Gadianton did prove the overthrow, yea, almost the entire destruction of the people of Nephi.

14. Behold I do not mean the end of the book of Helaman, but I mean the end of the *h*book of Nephi, from which I have taken all the account which I have written.

CHAPTER 3.

More migrations to the north—A land of large waters—Buildings of cement—Many records kept—Helaman's son, Nephi, succeeds him.

1. And now it came to pass in the *forty and third year of the reign of the judges, there was no contention among the people of Nephi save it were a little pride which was in the church, which did cause some little dissensions among the people, which affairs were settled in the ending of the forty and third year.

2. And there was no contention among the people in the forty and fourth year; neither was there much contention in the forty and fifth year.

3. And it came to pass in the †forty and sixth, yea, there was much contention and many dissensions; in the which there were an exceeding great many who departed out of the *a*land of Zarahemla, and went forth unto the *b*land northward to inherit the land.

4. And they did travel to an exceeding great distance, insomuch that they came to *c*large bodies of water and many rivers.

5. Yea, and even they did spread forth into all parts of the land, into whatever parts it had not been rendered desolate and without timber, because of the *d*many inhabitants who had before inherited the land.

---

f, see *i,* 2 Ne. 10.   *g,* see *i,* 2 Ne. 10.   *h,* see *f,* 1 Ne. 1.   CHAP. 3: *a,* Om. 13.
b, Al. 46:17. 63:4.   *c,* see *i,* Mos. 8.   *d,* see *j,* Mos. 8.   * B. C. 49.   † B. C. 46.

HELAMAN, 3.

6. And now no part of the land was desolate, save it were for timber; but because of the greatness of the destruction of the people who had before inhabited the land it was called ᵉdesolate.

7. And there being but little timber upon the face of the land, nevertheless the people who went forth became exceeding expert in the working of cement; therefore they did build houses of ᶠcement, in the which they did dwell.

8. And it came to pass that they did multiply and spread, and did go forth from the land ᵍsouthward to the land ʰnortheward, and did spread insomuch that they began to cover the face of the whole earth, from the sea south to the sea ʲnorth, from the sea ᵏwest to the sea ˡeast.

9. And the people who were in the land ᵐnortheward did dwell in tents, and in houses of ⁿcement, and they did suffer whatsoever tree should spring up upon the face of the land that it should grow up, that in time they might have timber to build their houses, yea, their cities, and their ᵒtemples, and their ᵖsynagogues, and their ᑫsanctuaries, and all manner of their buildings.

10. And it came to pass as timber was exceeding ʳscarce in the land northward, they did send forth much by the way of ˢshipping.

11. And thus they did enable the people in the land ᵗnortheward that they might build many cities, both of wood and of ᵘcement.

12. And it came to pass that there were many of the ᵛpeople of Ammon, who were Lamanites by birth, did also go forth into this land.

13. And now there are many ʷrecords kept of the proceedings of this people, by many of this people, which are particular and very large, concerning them.

14. But behold, a ˣhundredth part of the proceedings of this people, yea, the account of the Lamanites and of the Nephites, and their wars, and contentions, and dissensions, and their preaching, and their prophecies, and their ʸshipping and their building of ships, and their building of ᶻtemples, and of ²ᵃsynagogues and their ²ᵇsanctuaries, and their righteousness, and their wickedness, and their murders, and their robbings, and their plundering, and all manner of abominations and whoredoms, cannot be contained in this work.

15. But behold, there ²ᶜare many books and many records of every kind, and they have been kept chiefly by the Nephites.

16. And they have been ²ᵈhanded down from one generation to another by the Nephites, even until they have fallen into transgression and have been murdered, plundered, and hunted, and driven forth, and slain, and scattered upon the face of the earth, and mixed with the Lamanites until they are ²ᵉno more called the Nephites, becoming wicked, and wild, and ferocious, yea, even becoming Lamanites.

17. And now I return again to mine account; therefore, what I have spoken had passed after there had been great contentions, and disturbances, and wars, and

e, see 2*l*, Al. 22. *f*, vers. 9, 11. *g*, see *n*, Al. 46. *h*, see *p*, Al. 46. *j*, 1 Ne. 21:12. *k*, Al. 22:27, 32, 33. He. 11:20. *l*, see *k*. *m*, see *h*. *n*, see *f*. *o*, see *h*, 2 Ne. 5. *p*, see *u*, Al. 16. *q*, see *t*, Al. 15. *r*, vers. 5, 9. *s*, see *f*, Al. 63. *t*, see *h*. *u*, see *f*. *v*, Al. 27:26. *w*, ver. 15. *x*, 3 Ne. 26:6—11. *y*, see *f*, Al. 63. *z*, see *h*, 2 Ne. 5. 2*a*, see *u*, Al. 16. 2*b*, see *t*, Al. 15. 2*c*, ver. 13. 2*d*, 1 Ne. 5:16—19. Al. 37:4. 2*e*, Al. 45:12—14.

ABOUT B. C. 46.

HELAMAN, 3.

dissensions, among the people of Nephi.

18. The *forty and sixth year of the reign of the judges ended;

19. And it came to pass that there was still great contention in the land, yea, even in the forty and seventh year, and also in the forty and eighth year.

20. Nevertheless [2f]Helaman did fill the judgment-seat with justice and equity; yea, he did observe to keep the statutes, and the judgments, and the commandments of God; and he did do that which was right in the sight of God continually; and he did walk after the ways of his father, insomuch that he did prosper in the land.

21. And it came to pass that he had two sons. He gave unto the eldest the name of Nephi, and unto the youngest, the name of Lehi. And they began to grow up unto the Lord.

22. And it came to pass that the wars and contentions began to cease, in a small degree, among the people of the Nephites, in the latter end of the forty and eighth year of the reign of the judges over the people of Nephi.

23. And it came to pass in the †forty and ninth year of the reign of the judges, there was continual peace established in the land, all save it were the [2g]secret combinations which Gadianton the robber had established in the more settled parts of the land, which at that time were not known unto those who were at the head of government; therefore they were not destroyed out of the land.

24. And it came to pass that in this same year there was exceeding great prosperity in the church,

insomuch that there were thousands who did join themselves unto the church and were [2h]baptized unto repentance.

25. And so great was the prosperity of the church, and so many the blessings which were poured out upon the people, that even the [2i]high priests and the teachers were themselves astonished beyond measure.

26. And it came to pass that the work of the Lord did prosper unto the [2j]baptizing and uniting to the church of God, many souls, yea, even tens of thousands.

27. Thus we may see that the Lord is merciful unto all who will, in the sincerity of their hearts, call upon his holy name.

28. Yea, thus we see that the gate of heaven is open unto all, even to those who will believe on the name of Jesus Christ, who is the Son of God.

29. Yea, we see that whosoever will may lay hold upon the word of God, which is quick and powerful, which shall divide asunder all the cunning and the snares and the wiles of the devil, and lead the man of Christ in a [2k]straight and narrow course across that everlasting [2l]gulf of misery which is prepared to engulf the wicked—

30. And land their souls, yea, their [2m]immortal souls, at the right hand of God in the kingdom of heaven, to sit down with Abraham, and Isaac, and with Jacob, and with all our holy fathers, to go no more out.

31. And in this year there was continual rejoicing in the [2n]land of Zarahemla, and in all the regions round about, even in all the land which was possessed by the Nephites.

2f, He. 2:2. 2g, see i, 2 Ne. 10. 2h, see u, 2 Ne. 9. 2i, see g, Mos. 26. 2j, see u, 2 Ne. 9. 2k, see e, 2 Ne. 31. 2l, see i, 1 Ne. 15. 2m, Al. 42:9, 11. See t, Al. 12. 2n, Om. 13.   * B. C. 45. † B. C. 43.

32. And it came to pass that there was peace and exceeding great joy in the remainder of the forty and ninth year; yea, and also there was continual peace and great joy in the fiftieth year of the reign of the judges.

33. And in the *fifty and first year of the reign of the judges there was peace also, save it were the pride which began to enter into the church—not into the church of God, but into the hearts of the people who professed to belong to the church of God—

34. And they were lifted up in pride, even to the persecution of many of their brethren. Now this was a great evil, which did cause the more humble part of the people to suffer great persecutions, and to wade through much affliction.

35. Nevertheless they did [2o]fast and pray oft, and did wax stronger and stronger in their humility, and firmer and firmer in the faith of Christ, unto the filling their souls with joy and consolation, yea, even to the purifying and the sanctification of their hearts, which sanctification cometh because of their yielding their hearts unto God.

36. And it came to pass that the fifty and second year ended in peace also, save it were the exceeding great pride which had gotten into the hearts of the people; and it was because of their exceeding great riches and their prosperity in the land; and it did grow upon them from day to day.

37. And it came to pass in the †fifty and third year of the reign of the judges, [2p]Helaman died, and his eldest son Nephi began to reign in his stead. And it came to pass that he did fill the judgment-seat with justice and equity; yea, he did keep the commandments of God, and did walk in the ways of his father.

CHAPTER 4.

Lamanites again invade land of Zarahemla—The city captured—Nephites driven into the land Bountiful—Moronihah fortifies the way—Weakened by wickedness, the Nephites prevail not.

1. And it came to pass in the ‡fifty and fourth year there were many dissensions in the church, and there was also a contention among the people, insomuch that there was much bloodshed.

2. And the rebellious part were slain and driven out of the land, and they did go unto the king of the Lamanites.

3. And it came to pass that they did endeavor to stir up the Lamanites to war against the Nephites; but behold, the Lamanites were exceedingly afraid, insomuch that they would not hearken to the words of those dissenters.

4. But it came to pass in the fifty and sixth year of the reign of the judges, there were dissenters who went up from the Nephites unto the Lamanites; and they succeeded with those others in stirring them up to anger against the Nephites; and they were all that year preparing for war.

5. And in the §fifty and seventh year they did come down against the Nephites to battle, and they did commence the work of death; yea, insomuch that in the fifty and eighth year of the reign of the judges they succeeded in obtaining possession of the [a]land of Zarahemla; yea, and also all the

---

2o, see t, Mos. 27. 2p, He. 2:2. Chap. 4: a, Om. 13.
* B. C. 41. † B. C. 39. ‡ B. C. 38. § B. C. 35.

lands, even unto the land which was near the ᵇland Bountiful.

6. And the Nephites and the armies of Moronihah were driven even into the land of Bountiful;

7. And there they did ᶜfortify against the Lamanites, from the west sea, even unto the east; it being a ᵈday's journey for a Nephite, on the line which they had ᵉfortified and stationed their armies to defend their north country.

8. And thus those dissenters of the Nephites, with the help of a numerous army of the Lamanites, had obtained all the possession of the Nephites which was in the land southward. And all this was done in the fifty and eighth and ninth years of the reign of the judges.

9. And it came to pass in the sixtieth year of the reign of the judges, Moronihah did succeed with his armies in obtaining many parts of the land; yea, they regained many cities which had fallen into the hands of the Lamanites.

10. And it came to pass in the *sixty and first year of the reign of the judges they succeeded in regaining even the half of all their possessions.

11. Now this great loss of the Nephites, and the great slaughter which was among them, would not have happened had it not been for their wickedness and their abomination which was among them; yea, and it was among those also who professed to belong to the church of God.

12. And it was because of the pride of their hearts, because of their exceeding riches, yea, it was because of their oppression to the poor, withholding their food ᶠfrom the hungry, withholding their clothing from the naked, and smiting their humble brethren upon the cheek, making a mock of that which was sacred, denying the spirit of prophecy and of revelation, murdering, plundering, lying, stealing, committing adultery, rising up in great contentions, and deserting away into the ᵍland of Nephi, among the Lamanites—

13. And because of this their great wickedness, and their boastings in their own strength, they were left in their own strength; therefore they did not prosper, but were afflicted and smitten, and driven before the Lamanites, until they had lost possession of almost all their lands.

14. But behold, Moronihah did preach many things unto the people because of their iniquity, and also Nephi and Lehi, who were the sons of Helaman, did preach many things unto the people, yea, and did prophesy many things unto them concerning their iniquities, and what should come unto them if they did not repent of their sins.

15. And it came to pass that they did repent, and inasmuch as they did repent they did begin to prosper.

16. For when Moronihah saw that they did repent he did venture to lead them forth from place to place, and from city to city, even until they had regained the ʰone-half of their property and the one-half of all their lands.

17. And thus ended the sixty and first year of the reign of the judges.

18. And it came to pass in the †sixty and second year of the reign of the judges, that Moroni-

b, see 2*k*, Al. 22. *c*, see *c*, Al. 48. *d*, Al. 22:32. *e*, see *c*, Al. 48. *f*, see *l*, Mos. 4. *g*, see *b*, 2 Ne. 5. *h*, ver. 10. * B. C. 31. † B. C. 30.

hah could obtain no more possessions over the Lamanites.

19. Therefore they did abandon their design to obtain the remainder of their lands, for so numerous were the Lamanites that it became impossible for the Nephites to obtain more power over them; therefore Moronihah did employ all his armies in maintaining those parts which he had taken.

20. And it came to pass, because of the greatness of the number of the Lamanites the Nephites were in great fear, lest they should be overpowered, and trodden down, and slain, and destroyed.

21. Yea, they began to remember the prophecies of Alma, and also the *i*words of Mosiah; and they saw that they had been a stiffnecked people, and that they had set at naught the commandments of God;

22. And that they had altered and trampled under their feet the *j*laws of Mosiah, or that which the Lord commanded him to give unto the people; and they saw that their laws had become corrupted, and that they had become a wicked people, insomuch that they were wicked even like unto the Lamanites.

23. And because of their iniquity the church had begun to dwindle; and they began to disbelieve in the *k*spirit of prophecy and in the spirit of revelation; and the judgments of God did stare them in the face.

24. And they saw that they had become weak, like unto their brethren, the Lamanites, and that the Spirit of the Lord did no more preserve them; yea, it had withdrawn from them because the Spirit of the Lord doth *l*not dwell in unholy temples—

25. Therefore the Lord did cease to preserve them by his miraculous and matchless power, for they had fallen into a state of unbelief and awful wickedness; and they saw that the Lamanites were exceedingly more numerous than they, and except they should cleave unto the Lord their God they must unavoidably perish.

26. For behold, they saw that the strength of the Lamanites was as great as their strength, even man for man. And thus had they fallen into this great transgression; yea, thus had they become weak, because of their transgression, in the space of not many years.

CHAPTER 5.

Nephi yields the judgment-seat to Cezoram—With his brother Lehi he devotes himself to the ministry—Marvelous manifestations—Converted Lamanites restore conquered Nephite lands.

1. And it came to pass that in this *same year, behold, Nephi *a*delivered up the judgment-seat to a man whose name was Cezoram.

2. For as their *b*laws and their governments were established by the voice of the people, and they who chose evil were more numerous than they who chose good, therefore they were ripening for destruction, for the laws had become corrupted.

3. Yea, and this was not all; they were a stiffnecked people, insomuch that they could not be governed by the law nor justice, save it were to their destruction.

4. And it came to pass that Nephi had become weary because

i, Mos. 29:27. *j*, Al. 1:1. *k*, ver. 12. *l*, see *r*, Al. 7. CHAP. 5: *a*, He. 3:37.
b, Mos. 29:27. * B. C. 30.

of their iniquity; and he yielded up the judgment-seat, and took it upon him to preach the word of God all the remainder of his days, and his brother Lehi also, all the remainder of his days;

5. For they remembered the words which their father Helaman spake unto them. And these are the words which he spake:

6. Behold, my sons, I desire that ye should remember to keep the commandments of God; and I would that ye should declare unto the people these words. Behold, I have given unto you the names of our first parents who came out of the land of Jerusalem; and this I have done that when you remember your names ye may remember them; and when ye remember them ye may remember their works; and when ye remember their works ye may know how that it is said, and also written, that they were good.

7. Therefore, my sons, I would that ye should do that which is good, that it may be said of you, and also written, even as it has been said and written of them.

8. And now my sons, behold I have somewhat more to desire of you, which desire is, that ye may not do these things that ye may boast, but that ye may do these things to lay up for yourselves a ^{c}treasure in heaven, yea, which is eternal, and which fadeth not away; yea, that ye may have that ^{d}precious gift of eternal life, which we have reason to suppose hath been given to our fathers.

9. O remember, remember, my sons, the ^{e}words which king Benjamin spake unto his people; yea, remember that there is no other way nor means whereby man can be saved, only through the ^{f}atoning blood of Jesus Christ, who shall come; yea, remember that he cometh to redeem the world.

10. And remember also the words which Amulek spake unto Zeezrom, in the ^{g}city of Ammonihah; for he said unto him that the Lord surely should come to redeem his people, but that he should ^{h}not come to redeem them in their sins, but to redeem them from their sins.

11. And he hath power given unto him from the Father to redeem them from their sins because of repentance; therefore he hath ^{i}sent his angels to declare the tidings of the conditions of repentance, which bringeth unto the power of the Redeemer, unto the salvation of their souls.

12. And now, my sons, remember, remember that it is upon the rock of our Redeemer, who is Christ, the Son of God, that ye must build your foundation; that when the devil shall ^{j}send forth his mighty winds, yea, his shafts in the whirlwind, yea, when all his hail and his mighty storm shall beat upon you, it shall have no power over you to drag you down to the gulf of misery and endless wo, because of the rock upon which ye are built, which is a sure foundation, a foundation whereon if men build they cannot fall.

13. And it came to pass that these were the words which Helaman taught to his sons; yea, he did teach them many things which are not written, and also many things which are written.

14. And they did remember his words; and therefore they went forth, keeping the commandments

---

c, He. 8:25. 3 Ne. 13:19—21. d, 1 Ne. 15:36. e, Mos. 2—5. f, Mos. 3:17. See f, 2 Ne. 2. g, see i, Al. 8. h, Al. 11:33—37. i, Al. 13:24, 25. 39:19. j, see e, Al. 26. ABOUT B. C. 30.

of God, to teach the word of God among all the people of Nephi, beginning at the ^kcity Bountiful;

15. And from thenceforth to the ^lcity of Gid; and from the city of Gid to the ^mcity of Mulek;

16. And even from one city to another, until they had gone forth among all the people of Nephi who were in the ⁿland southward; and from thence into the ^oland of Zarahemla, ^pamong the Lamanites.

17. And it came to pass that they did preach with great power, insomuch that they did confound many of ^qthose dissenters who had gone over from the Nephites, insomuch that they came forth and did confess their sins and were ^rbaptized unto repentance, and immediately returned to the Nephites to endeavor to repair unto them the wrongs which they had done.

18. And it came to pass that Nephi and Lehi did preach unto the Lamanites with such great power and authority, for they had power and authority given unto them that they might speak, and they also had what they should speak given unto them—

19. Therefore they did speak unto the great astonishment of the Lamanites, to the convincing them, insomuch that there were eight thousand of the Lamanites who were in the ^sland of Zarahemla and round about ^tbaptized unto repentance, and were convinced of the wickedness of the ^utraditions of their fathers.

20. And it came to pass that Nephi and Lehi did proceed from thence to go to the ^vland of Nephi.

21. And it came to pass that they were taken by an army of the Lamanites and cast into prison; yea, even in that same prison ^win which Ammon and his brethren were cast by the servants of Limhi.

22. And after they had been cast into prison many days without food, behold, they went forth into the prison to take them that they might slay them.

23. And it came to pass that Nephi and Lehi were encircled about as if by fire, even insomuch that ^xthey durst not lay their hands upon them for fear lest they should be burned. Nevertheless, Nephi and Lehi were not burned; and they were as standing in the midst of fire and were not burned.

24. And when they saw that they were encircled about with a pillar of fire, and that it burned them not, their hearts did take courage.

25. For they saw that the Lamanites durst not lay their hands upon them; neither durst they come near unto them, but stood as if they were struck dumb with amazement.

26. And it came to pass that Nephi and Lehi did stand forth and began to speak unto them, saying: Fear not, for behold, it is God that has shown unto you this marvelous thing, in the which is shown unto you that ye cannot lay your hands on us to slay us.

27. And behold, when they had said these words, the earth shook exceedingly, and the walls of the prison did shake as if they were about to tumble to the earth; but behold, they did not fall. And behold, they that were in the prison were Lamanites and Nephites who were dissenters.

---

k, see 2*k*, Al. 22. *l*, see 2*c*, Al. 51. *m*, see 2*d*, Al. 51. *n*, see *n*, Al. 46. *o*, Om. 13. *p*, He. 4:5. *q*, He. 4:2, 4. *r*, see *u*, 2 Ne. 9. *s*, Om. 13. *t*, see *u*, 2 Ne. 9. *u*, see *n*, Jac. 7. *v*, see *b*, 2 Ne. 5. *w*, Mos. 7:6—8. 21:22—24. *x*, ver. 25.

ABOUT B. C. 30.

28. And it came to pass that they were overshadowed with a cloud of darkness, and an awful solemn fear came upon them.

29. And it came to pass that there came a voice as if it were above the cloud of darkness, saying: Repent ye, repent ye, and seek no more to destroy my servants whom I have sent unto you to declare good tidings.

30. And it came to pass when they heard this voice, and beheld that it was not a voice of thunder, neither was it a voice of a great tumultuous noise, but behold, *y*it was a still voice of perfect mildness, as if it had been a whisper, and it did pierce even to the very soul—

31. And notwithstanding the mildness of the voice, behold the earth shook exceedingly, and the walls of the prison trembled again, as if it were about to tumble to the earth; and behold the cloud of darkness, which had overshadowed them, did not disperse—

32. And behold the voice came again, saying: Repent ye, repent ye, for the kingdom of heaven is at hand; and seek no more to destroy my servants. And it came to pass that the earth shook again, and the walls trembled.

33. And also again the third time the voice came, and did speak unto them marvelous words which cannot be uttered by man; and the walls did tremble again, and the earth shook as if it were about to divide asunder.

34. And it came to pass that the Lamanites could not flee because of the cloud of darkness which did overshadow them; yea, and also they were immovable because of the fear which did come upon them.

35. Now there was one among them who was a Nephite by birth, who had once belonged to the church of God but had dissented from them.

36. And it came to pass that he turned him about, and behold, he saw through the cloud of darkness the faces of Nephi and Lehi; and behold, they did shine exceedingly, even as the faces of angels. And he beheld that they did lift their eyes to heaven; and they were in the attitude as if talking or lifting their voices to some being whom they beheld.

37. And it came to pass that this man did cry unto the multitude, that they might turn and look. And behold, there was power given unto them that they did turn and look; and they did behold the faces of Nephi and Lehi.

38. And they said unto the man: Behold, what do all these things mean, and who is it with whom these men do converse?

39. Now the man's name was Aminadab. And Aminadab said unto them: They do converse with the angels of God.

40. And it came to pass that the Lamanites said unto him: What shall we do, that this cloud of darkness may be removed from overshadowing us?

41. And Aminadab said unto them: You must repent, and cry unto the voice, even until ye shall have faith in Christ, who was taught unto you by Alma, and Amulek, and Zeezrom; and when ye shall do this, the cloud of darkness shall be removed from overshadowing you.

42. And it came to pass that they all did begin to cry unto the voice of him who had shaken the earth; yea, they did cry even until

y, 3 Ne. 11:3.

the cloud of darkness was dispersed.

43. And it came to pass that when they cast their eyes about, and saw that the cloud of darkness was dispersed from overshadowing them, behold, they saw that they were encircled about, yea every soul, by a pillar of fire.

44. And Nephi and Lehi were in the midst of them; yea, they were encircled about; yea, they were as if in the midst of a flaming fire, yet it did harm them not, neither did it take hold upon the walls of the prison; and they were filled with that joy which is unspeakable and full of glory.

45. And behold, the *Holy Spirit of God did come down from heaven, and did enter into their hearts, and they were filled as if with fire, and they could speak forth marvelous words.

46. And it came to pass that there came a voice unto them, yea, a pleasant voice, as if it were a whisper, saying:

47. Peace, peace be unto you, because of your faith in my Well Beloved, who was from the ^{2a}foundation of the world.

48. And now, when they heard this they cast up their eyes as if to behold from whence the voice came; and behold, they saw the heavens open; and angels came down out of heaven and ministered unto them.

49. And there were about three hundred souls who saw and heard these things; and they were bidden to go forth and marvel not, neither should they doubt.

50. And it came to pass that they did go forth, and did minister unto the people, declaring throughout all the regions round about all the things which they had heard and seen, insomuch that the more part of the Lamanites were convinced of them, because of the greatness of the evidences which they had received.

51. And as many as were convinced did lay down their weapons of war, and also their ^{2b}hatred and the tradition of their fathers.

52. And it came to pass that they did ^{2c}yield up unto the Nephites the lands of their possession.

CHAPTER 6.

Lamanites send missionaries to Nephites—Peace and freedom abound—The land Lehi and the land Mulek—Cezoram and his son murdered—Gadianton robbers seize government.

1. And it came to pass that when the sixty and second year of the reign of the judges *had ended, all these things had happened and the Lamanites had become, the more part of them, a righteous people, insomuch that their righteousness did exceed that of the Nephites, because of their firmness and their steadiness in the faith.

2. For behold, there were many of the Nephites who had become hardened and impenitent and grossly wicked, insomuch that they did reject the word of God and all the preaching and prophesying which did come among them.

3. Nevertheless, the people of the church did have great joy because of the conversion of the Lamanites, yea, because of the church of God, which had been established among them. And they did fellowship one with another, and did rejoice one with another, and did have great joy.

---

z, 3 Ne. 9:20. Eth. 12:14. 2a, see d, Mos. 4. 2b, see n, Jac. 7. 2c, He. 4:5, 9, 10, 18, 19. *B. C. 29.

HELAMAN, 6.

4. And it came to pass that many of the Lamanites did come down into the ᵃland of Zarahemla, and did declare unto the people of the Nephites the manner of their conversion, and did exhort them to faith and repentance.

5. Yea, and many did preach with exceedingly great power and authority, unto the bringing down many of them into the depths of humility, to be the humble followers of God and the Lamb.

6. And it came to pass that many of the Lamanites did go into the ᵇland northward; and also Nephi and Lehi went into the land northward, to preach unto the people. And thus ended the sixty and third year.

7. And behold, there was peace in all the land, insomuch that the Nephites did go into whatsoever part of the land they would, whether among the Nephites or the Lamanites.

8. And it came to pass that the Lamanites did also go whithersoever they would, whether it were among the Lamanites or among the Nephites; and thus they did have free intercourse one with another, to buy and to sell, and to get gain, according to their desire.

9. And it came to pass that they became exceeding rich, both the Lamanites and the Nephites; and they did have an ᶜexceeding plenty of gold, and of silver, and of all manner of precious metals, both in the ᵈland south and in the ᵉland north.

10. Now the land south was ᶠcalled Lehi, and the land north was ᵍcalled Mulek, which was after the ʰson of Zedekiah; for the Lord did bring ⁱMulek into the land north, and ʲLehi into the land south.

11. And behold, there was ᵏall manner of gold in both these lands, and of silver, and of precious ore of every kind; and there were also curious workmen, who did work all kinds of ore and did refine it; and thus they did become rich.

12. They did raise grain in abundance, both in the north and in the south; and they did flourish exceedingly, both in the north and in the south. And they did multiply and wax exceedingly strong in the land. And they did raise many flocks and herds, yea, many fatlings.

13. Behold their women ˡdid toil and spin, and did make all manner of cloth, of fine-twined linen and cloth of every kind, to clothe their nakedness. And thus the sixty and fourth year did pass away in peace.

14. And in the *sixty and fifth year they did also have great joy and peace, yea, much preaching and many prophecies concerning that which was to come. And thus passed away the sixty and fifth year.

15. And it came to pass that in the †sixty and sixth year of the reign of the judges, behold, ᵐCezoram was murdered by an unknown hand as he sat upon the judgment-seat. And it came to pass that in the same year, that his son, who had been appointed by the people in his stead, was also murdered. And thus ended the sixty and sixth year.

16. And in the ‡commencement of the sixty and seventh

---

a, Om. 13. *b,* see *p,* Al. 46. *c,* see *n,* 1 Ne. 18. *d,* see *n,* Al. 46. *e,* see *p,* Al. 46. *f,* Al. 50:25. *g,* Al. 51:26. *h,* Om. 14, 15. *i,* see *e.* *j,* see *d.* *k,* see *n,* 1 Ne. 18. *l,* see *c,* Mos. 10. *m,* He. 5:1.   * B. C. 27.   † B. C. 26.   ‡ B. C. 25.

year the people began to grow exceedingly wicked again.

17. For behold, the Lord had blessed them so long with the riches of the world that they had not been stirred up to anger, to wars, nor to bloodshed; therefore they began to set their hearts upon their riches; yea, they began to seek to get gain that they might be lifted up one above another; therefore they began to ⁿcommit secret murders, and to rob and to plunder, that they might get gain.

18. And now behold, those murderers and plunderers were a band who had been formed by Kishkumen and Gadianton. And now it had come to pass that there were many, even among the Nephites, of ᵒGadianton's band. But behold, they were more numerous among the more wicked part of the Lamanites. And they were called Gadianton's robbers and murderers.

19. And it was they who did murder the ᵖchief judge Cezoram, and ᑫhis son, while in the judgment-seat; and behold, they were not found.

20. And now it came to pass that when the Lamanites found that there were robbers among them they were exceeding sorrowful; and they did use every means in their power to destroy them off the face of the earth.

21. But behold, Satan did stir up the hearts of the more part of the Nephites, insomuch that they did unite with those ʳbands of robbers, and did enter into their covenants and their oaths, that they would protect and preserve one another in whatsoever difficult circumstances they should be placed, that they should not suffer for their murders, and their plunderings, and their stealings.

22. And it came to pass that they did have their signs, yea, their ˢsecret signs, and their secret words; and this that they might distinguish a brother who had entered into the covenant, that whatsoever wickedness his brother should do he should not be injured by his brother, nor by those who did belong to his band, who had taken this covenant.

23. And thus they might murder, and plunder, and steal, and commit whoredoms and all manner of wickedness, contrary to the laws of their country and also the laws of their God.

24. And whosoever of those who belonged to their band should reveal unto the world of their wickedness and their abominations, should be tried, not according to the laws of their country, but according to the laws of their wickedness, which had been given by Gadianton and Kishkumen.

25. Now behold, it is these ᵗsecret oaths and covenants which Alma commanded his son should not go forth unto the world, lest they should be a means of bringing down the people unto destruction.

26. Now behold, those secret oaths and covenants did not come forth unto Gadianton from the records which were delivered unto Helaman; but behold, they were put into the heart of Gadianton by that ᵘsame being who did entice our first parents to partake of the forbidden fruit—

27. Yea, that same being who did plot with Cain, that if he would murder his brother Abel it

---

n, see t, 2 Ne. 10. o, He. 2:12, 13. p, ver. 15. q, ver. 15. r, see t, 2 Ne. 10. s, Al. 37:27. t, Al. 37:27—32. u, P. of G. P., Moses 4:6—12. ABOUT B. C. 25.

should not be known unto the world. And he did ^vplot with Cain and his followers from that time forth.

28. And also it is that same being who put it into the hearts of the people to ^wbuild a tower sufficiently high that they might get to heaven. And it was that same being who led on the people who came from that tower ^xinto this land; who spread the works of darkness and abominations over all the face of the land, until he dragged the people down to an ^yentire destruction, and to an ^zeverlasting hell.

29. Yea, it is that same being who put it into the heart of ^{2a}Gadianton to still carry on the work of darkness, and of secret murder; and he has brought it forth from the beginning of man even down to this time.

30. And behold, it is he who is the author of all sin. And behold, he doth carry on his works of darkness and secret murder, and doth hand down their plots, and their oaths, and their covenants, and their plans of awful wickedness, from generation to generation according as he can get hold upon the hearts of the children of men.

31. And now behold, he had got great hold upon the hearts of the Nephites; yea, insomuch that they had become exceedingly wicked; yea, the more part of them had turned out of the way of righteousness, and did trample under their feet the commandments of God, and did turn unto their own ways, and did build up unto themselves idols of their gold and their silver.

32. And it came to pass that all these iniquities did come unto them in the space of not many years, insomuch that a more part of it had come unto them in the sixty and seventh year of the reign of the judges over the people of Nephi.

33. And they did grow in their iniquities in the *sixty and eighth year also, to the great sorrow and lamentation of the righteous.

34. And thus we see that the Nephites did begin to dwindle in unbelief, and grow in wickedness and abominations, while the Lamanites began to grow exceedingly in the knowledge of their God; yea, they did begin to keep his statutes and commandments, and to walk in truth and uprightness before him.

35. And thus we see that the Spirit of the Lord began to withdraw from the Nephites, because of the wickedness and the hardness of their hearts.

36. And thus we see that the Lord began to pour out his Spirit upon the Lamanites, because of their easiness and willingness to believe in his words.

37. And it came to pass that the Lamanites did hunt the ^{2b}band of robbers of Gadianton; and they did preach the word of God among the more wicked part of them, insomuch that this band of robbers was utterly destroyed from among the Lamanites.

38. And it came to pass on the other hand, that the Nephites did build them up and support them, beginning at the more wicked part of them, until they had overspread all the land of the Nephites, and had seduced the more part of the righteous until they had come down to believe in their works and partake of their spoils, and to join with them in

---

v, P. of G. P., Moses 5:29—31. *w*, see Eth. 1. *x*, Book of Ether. *y*, Eth. 8:9, 15—25. *z*, see *k*, 1 Ne. 15. *2a*, He. 2:10—13. *2b*, see *t*, 2 Ne. 10. * B. C. 24.

their secret murders and combinations.

39. And thus they did obtain the sole management of the government, insomuch that they did trample under their feet and smite and rend and turn their backs upon the poor and the meek, and the humble followers of God.

40. And thus we see that they were in an awful state, and ripening for an everlasting destruction.

41. And it came to pass that thus ended the sixty and eighth year of the reign of the judges over the people of Nephi.

THE PROPHECY OF NEPHI, THE SON OF HELAMAN.—*God threatens the people of Nephi that he will visit them in his anger, to their utter destruction except they repent of their wickedness. God smiteth the people of Nephi with pestilence; they repent and turn unto him. Samuel, a Lamanite, prophesies unto the Nephites.* Comprising chapters 7 to 16 inclusive.

CHAPTER 7.

Nephi, rejected by the people in the north, returns to Zarahemla—From his garden tower he prays to God and addresses the multitude.

1. Behold, now it came to pass in the *sixty and ninth year of the reign of the judges over the people of the Nephites, that Nephi, the son of Helaman, returned to the ªland of Zarahemla from the ᵇland northward.

2. For he had been forth among the people who were in the land northward, and did preach the word of God unto them, and did prophesy many things unto them;

3. And they did reject all his words, insomuch that he could not stay among them, but returned again unto the land of his nativity.

4. And seeing the people in a state of such awful wickedness, and those ᶜGadianton robbers filling the judgment-seats—having usurped the power and authority of the land; laying aside the commandments of God, and not in the least aright before him; doing no justice unto the children of men;

5. Condemning the righteous because of their righteousness; letting the guilty and the wicked go unpunished because of their money; and moreover to be held in office at the head of government, to rule and do according to their wills, that they might get gain and glory of the world, and, moreover, that they might the more easily commit adultery, and steal, and kill, and do according to their own wills—

6. Now this great iniquity had come upon the Nephites, in the space of not many years; and when Nephi saw it, his heart was swollen with sorrow within his breast; and he did exclaim in the agony of his soul:

7. Oh, that I could have had my days in the days when my father Nephi first came out of the land of Jerusalem, that I could have joyed with him in the ᵈpromised land; then were his people easy to be entreated, firm to keep the commandments of God, and slow to be led to do iniquity; and they were quick to hearken unto the words of the Lord—

8. Yea, if my days could have been in those days, then would

---

a, Om. 13. *b*, see *p*, Al. 46. *c*, see *i*, 2 Ne. 10. He. 2:10—13. *d*, see *a*, 1 Ne. 2.
* B. C. 23.

my soul have had joy in the righteousness of my brethren.

9. But behold, I am consigned that these are my days, and that my soul shall be filled with sorrow because of this the wickedness of my brethren.

10. And behold, now it came to pass that it was upon a tower, which was in the garden of Nephi, which was by the highway which led to the chief market, which was in the *city of Zarahemla; therefore, Nephi had bowed himself upon the tower which was in his garden, which tower was also near unto the garden gate by which led the highway.

11. And it came to pass that there were certain men passing by and saw Nephi as he was pouring out his soul unto God upon the tower; and they ran and told the people what they had seen, and the people came together in multitudes that they might know the cause of so great mourning for the wickedness of the people.

12. And now, when Nephi arose he beheld the multitudes of people who had gathered together.

13. And it came to pass that he opened his mouth and said unto them: Behold, why have ye gathered yourselves together? That I may tell you of your iniquities?

14. Yea, because I have got upon my tower that I might pour out my soul unto my God, because of the exceeding sorrow of my heart, which is because of your iniquities!

15. And because of my mourning and lamentation ye have gathered yourselves together, and do marvel; yea, and ye have great need to marvel; yea, ye ought to marvel because ye are given away that the devil has got so great hold upon your hearts.

16. Yea, how could you have given way to the enticing of him who is seeking to hurl away your souls down to *everlasting misery and endless wo?

17. O repent ye, repent ye! Why will ye die? Turn ye, turn ye unto the Lord your God. Why has he forsaken you?

18. It is because you have hardened your hearts; yea, ye will not hearken unto the voice of the *good shepherd; yea, ye have provoked him to anger against you.

19. And behold, instead of gathering you, except ye will repent, behold, he shall scatter you forth that ye shall become meat for dogs and wild beasts.

20. O, how could you have forgotten your God in the very day that he has delivered you?

21. But behold, it is to get gain, to be praised of men, yea, and that ye might get gold and silver. And ye have set your hearts upon the riches and the vain things of this world, for the which ye do murder, and plunder, and steal, and bear false witness against your neighbor, and do all manner of iniquity.

22. And for this cause wo shall come unto you except ye shall repent. For if ye will not repent, behold, this great city, and also all those great cities which are round about, which are in the land of our possession, shall be taken away that ye shall have no place in them; for behold, the Lord will not grant unto you strength, as he has hitherto done, to withstand against your enemies.

23. For behold, thus saith the

c, Om. 13.   *f*, see *m*, Jac. 6.   *g*, see 2*e*, Al. 5.   BETWEEN B. C. 23 AND 20.

Lord: I will not show unto the wicked of my strength, to one more than the other, save it be unto those who repent of their sins, and hearken unto my words. Now therefore, I would that ye should behold, my brethren, that it shall be better for the Lamanites than for you except ye shall repent.

24. For behold, they are more righteous than you, for they have not sinned against that great knowledge which ye have received; therefore the Lord will be merciful unto them; yea, he will *h*lengthen out their days and increase their seed, even when thou shalt be *i*utterly destroyed except thou shalt repent.

25. Yea, wo be unto you because of that great abomination which has come among you; and ye have united yourselves unto it, yea, to that *j*secret band which was established by Gadianton!

26. Yea, wo shall come unto you because of that pride which ye have suffered to enter your hearts, which has lifted you up beyond that which is good because of your exceeding great riches!

27. Yea, wo be unto you because of your wickedness and abominations!

28. And except ye repent ye shall perish; yea, even your lands shall be taken from you, and ye shall be *k*destroyed from off the face of the earth.

29. Behold now, I do not say that these things shall be, of myself, because it is not of myself that I know these things; but behold, I know that these things are true because the Lord God has made them known unto me, therefore I testify that they shall be.

CHAPTER 8.

Nephi's address continued—Corrupt judges vainly endeavor to incite people against him—By inspiration he announces the murder of the chief judge.

1. And now it came to pass that when Nephi had said these words, behold, there were men who were judges, who also belonged to the *a*secret band of Gadianton, and they were angry, and they cried out against him, saying unto the people: Why do ye not seize upon this man and bring him forth, that he may be condemned according to the crime which he has done?

2. Why seest thou this man, and hearest him revile against this people and against our law?

3. For behold, Nephi had spoken unto them concerning the corruptness of their law; yea, many things did Nephi speak which cannot be written; and nothing did he speak which was contrary to the commandments of God.

4. And those judges were angry with him because he spake plainly unto them concerning their *b*secret works of darkness; nevertheless, they durst not lay their own hands upon him, for they feared the people lest they should cry out against them.

5. Therefore they did cry unto the people, saying: Why do you suffer this man to revile against us? For behold he doth condemn all this people, even unto destruction; yea, and also that these our *c*great cities shall be taken from us, that we shall have no place in them.

6. And now we know that this is impossible, for behold, we are powerful, and our cities great, therefore our enemies can have no power over us.

h, see *j*, Al. 9. *i*, see *m*, Al. 9. *j*, see *c*. See also *i*, 2 Ne. 10. *k*, see *m*, Al. 9.
CHAP. 8: *a*, see *b*. See also *i*, 2 Ne. 10. *b*, see *i*, 2 Ne. 10. *c*, He. 7:22.
BETWEEN B. C. 23 AND 20.

7. And it came to pass that thus they did stir up the people to anger against Nephi, and raised contentions among them; for there were some who did cry out: Let this man alone, for he is a good man, and those things which he saith will surely come to pass except we repent;

8. Yea, behold, all the judgments will come upon us which he has testified unto us; for we know that he has testified aright unto us concerning our iniquities. And behold they are many, and he knoweth as well all things which shall befall us as he knoweth of our iniquities;

9. Yea, and behold, if he had not been a prophet he could not have testified concerning those things.

10. And it came to pass that those people who sought to destroy Nephi were compelled because of their fear, that they did not lay their hands on him; therefore he began again to speak unto them, seeing that he had gained favor in the eyes of some, insomuch that the remainder of them did fear.

11. Therefore he was constrained to speak more unto them saying: Behold, my brethren, have ye not read that God gave power unto one man, even Moses, to smite upon the waters of the Red Sea, and they parted hither and thither, insomuch that the Israelites, who were our fathers, came through upon dry ground, and the waters closed upon the armies of the Egyptians and swallowed them up?

12. And now behold, if God gave unto this man such power, then why should ye dispute among yourselves, and say that he hath given unto me no power whereby I may ^dknow concerning the judgments that shall come upon you except ye repent?

13. But, behold, ye not only deny my words, but ye also deny all the words which have been spoken by our fathers, and also the words which were spoken by this man, Moses, who had such great power given unto him, yea, the words which he hath spoken concerning the coming of the Messiah.

14. Yea, did he not bear record that the Son of God should come? And as he ^elifted up the brazen serpent in the wilderness, even so shall he be lifted up who should come.

15. And as many as should look upon that serpent should live, even so as many as should look upon the Son of God with faith, having a contrite spirit, might live, even unto that life which is eternal.

16. And now behold, Moses did not only testify of these things, but also all the holy prophets, from his days even to the days of Abraham.

17. Yea, and behold, Abraham saw of his coming, and was filled with gladness and did rejoice.

18. Yea, and behold I say unto you, that Abraham not only knew of these things, but there were many before the days of Abraham who were called by the ^forder of God; yea, even after the order of his Son; and this that it should be shown unto the people, a great many thousand years before his coming, that even redemption should come unto them.

19. And now I would that ye should know, that even since the

---

d, He. 7:28, 20. *e*, Al. 33:19—22. *f*, see *g*, Mos. 26. Al. 13:19. D. & C. 84:6—16. BETWEEN B. C. 23 AND 20.

days of Abraham there have been many prophets that have testified these things; yea, behold, the prophet *g*Zenos did testify boldly; for the which he was slain.

20. And behold, also *h*Zenock, and also *i*Ezias, and also Isaiah, and Jeremiah, (Jeremiah being that same prophet who testified of the destruction of Jerusalem) and now we know that Jerusalem was destroyed according to the words of Jeremiah. O then why not the Son of God come, according to his prophecy?

21. And now will you dispute that Jerusalem was destroyed? Will ye say that the sons of Zedekiah were not slain, all except it were *j*Mulek? Yea, and do ye not behold that the seed of Zedekiah are with us, and they were driven out of the land of Jerusalem? But behold, this is not all—

22. Our father Lehi was driven out of Jerusalem because he testified of these things. Nephi also testified of these things, and also almost all of our fathers, even down to this time; yea, they have testified of the coming of Christ, and have looked forward, and have rejoiced in his day which is to come.

23. And behold, he is God, and he is with them, and he did manifest himself unto them, that they were redeemed by him; and they gave unto him glory, because of that which is to come.

24. And now, seeing ye know these things and cannot deny them except ye shall lie, therefore in this ye have sinned, for ye have rejected all these things, notwithstanding so many evidences which ye have received; yea, even ye have received all things, both things in heaven, and all things which are in the earth, as a witness that they are true.

25. But behold, ye have rejected the truth, and rebelled against your holy God; and even at this time, instead of laying up for yourselves *k*treasures in heaven, where nothing doth corrupt, and where nothing can come which is unclean, ye are heaping up for yourselves wrath against the day of judgment.

26. Yea, even at this time ye are ripening, because of your murders and your fornication and wickedness, for everlasting destruction; yea, and except ye repent it will come unto you soon.

27. Yea, behold it is now even at your doors; yea, go ye in unto the judgment-seat, and search; and behold, your judge is murdered, and he lieth in his blood; and he hath been murdered *l*by his brother, who seeketh to sit in the judgment-seat.

28. And behold, they both belong to your *m*secret band, whose author is Gadianton and the evil one who seeketh to destroy the souls of men.

CHAPTER 9.

Nephi's word verified—Chief judge found dead at the judgment-seat—Nephi and five others accused—Their innocence established—The murderer made known.

1. Behold, now it came to pass that when Nephi had spoken these words, certain men who were among them ran to the judgment-seat; yea, even there were *a*five who went, and they said among themselves, as they went:

g, see *h*, 1 Ne. 19. *h*, see *g*, 1 Ne. 19. *i*, D. & C. 84:11—13. *j*, He. 6:10. Om. 13. Ezek. 17:22, 23. Om. 14. *k*, see *c*, He. 5. *l*, He 9:6, 26—38. *m*, see *i*, 2 Ne. 10. Chap. 9: *a*, vers. 7—9, 12—18. BETWEEN B. C. 23 AND 20.

HELAMAN, 9.   381

2. Behold, now we will know of a surety whether this man be a prophet and God hath commanded him to prophesy such marvelous things unto us. Behold, we do not believe that he hath; yea, we do not believe that he is a prophet; nevertheless, if this thing which he has said concerning the chief judge be true, that he be dead, then will we believe that the other words which he has spoken are true.

3. And it came to pass that they ran in their might, and came in unto the judgment-seat; and behold, the chief judge had fallen to the earth, and did *b*lie in his blood.

4. And now behold, when they saw this they were astonished exceedingly, insomuch that they fell to the earth; for they had not believed the words which Nephi had spoken concerning the chief judge.

5. But now, when they saw they believed, and fear came upon them lest all the judgments which Nephi had spoken should come upon the people; therefore they did quake, and had fallen to the earth.

6. Now, immediately when the judge had been murdered—he being stabbed by *c*his brother by a garb of secrecy, and he fled, and the servants ran and told the people, raising the cry of murder among them;

7. And behold the people did gather themselves together unto the place of the judgment-seat— and behold, to their astonishment they saw those *d*five men who had fallen to the earth.

8. And now behold, the people knew nothing concerning the multitude who had gathered together at the *e*garden of Nephi; therefore they said among themselves: *f*These men are they who have murdered the judge, and God has smitten them that they could not flee from us.

9. And it came to pass that they laid hold on them, and bound them and cast them into prison. And there was a proclamation sent abroad that the judge was slain, and that the murderers had been taken and were cast into prison.

10. And it came to pass that on the morrow the people did assemble themselves together to mourn and to *g*fast, at the burial of the great chief judge who had been slain.

11. And thus also those judges who were at the garden of Nephi, and heard his words, were also gathered together at the burial.

12. And it came to pass that they inquired among the people, saying: Where are the *h*five who were sent to inquire concerning the chief judge whether he was dead? And they answered and said: Concerning the five whom ye say ye have sent, we know not; but there are five who are the murderers, whom we have cast into prison.

13. And it came to pass that the judges desired that they should be brought; and they were brought, and behold they were the *i*five who were sent; and behold the judges inquired of them to know concerning the matter, and they told them all that they had done, saying:

14. We ran and came to the place of the judgment, and when we saw all things even as Nephi had testified, we were astonished insomuch that we fell to the

---
b, He. 8:27. *c*, see *l*, He. 8. *d*, see *a*. *e*, He. 7:10, 11, 14. *f*, see *a*. *g*, see *t*, Mos. 27. *h*, see *a*. *i*, see *a*.   BETWEEN B. C. 23 AND 20.

earth; and when we were recovered from our astonishment, behold they ʲcast us into prison.

15. Now, as for the murder of this man, we know not who has done it; and only this much we know, we ran and came according as ye desired, and behold he was ᵏdead, according to the words of Nephi.

16. And now it came to pass that the judges did expound the matter unto the people, and did cry out against Nephi, saying: Behold, we know that this Nephi must have agreed with some one to slay the judge, and then he might declare it unto us, that he might convert us unto his faith, that he might raise himself to be a great man, chosen of God, and a prophet.

17. And now behold, we will detect this man, and he shall confess his fault and make known unto us the true murderer of this judge.

18. And it came to pass that the ˡfive were liberated on the day of the burial. Nevertheless, they did rebuke the judges in the words which they had spoken against Nephi, and did contend with them one by one, insomuch that they did confound them.

19. Nevertheless, they caused that Nephi should be taken and bound and brought before the multitude, and they began to question him in divers ways that they might cross him, that they might accuse him to death—

20. Saying unto him: Thou art confederate; who is this man that hath done this murder? Now tell us, and acknowledge thy fault; saying, Behold here is money; and also we will grant unto thee thy life if thou wilt tell us, and acknowledge the agreement which thou hast made with him.

21. But Nephi said unto them: O ye fools, ye uncircumcised of heart, ye blind, and ye stiffnecked people, do ye know how long the Lord your God will suffer you that ye shall go on in this your way of sin?

22. O ye ought to begin to howl and mourn, because of the great destruction which at this time doth await you, except ye shall repent.

23. Behold ye say that I have agreed with a man that he should murder Seezoram, our chief judge. But behold, I say unto you, that this is because I have testified unto you that ye might know concerning this thing; yea, even for a witness unto you, that I did know of the wickedness and abominations which are among you.

24. And because I have done this, ye say that I have agreed with a man that he should do this thing; yea, because I showed unto you this sign ye are angry with me, and seek to destroy my life.

25. And now behold, I will show unto you another sign, and see if ye will in this thing seek to destroy me.

26. Behold I say unto you: Go to the house of Seantum, who is the ᵐbrother of Seezoram, and say unto him—

27. Has Nephi, the pretended prophet, who doth prophesy so much evil concerning this people, agreed with thee, in the which ye have murdered Seezoram, who is your brother?

28. And behold, he shall say unto you, Nay.

29. And ye shall say unto him: Have ye murdered your brother?

j, ver. 9.   *k*, He. 8:27.   *l*, see *a*.   *m*, see *l*, He. 8.   BETWEEN B. C. 23 AND 20.

30. And he shall stand with fear, and wist not what to say. And behold, he shall deny unto you; and he shall make as if he were astonished; nevertheless, he shall declare unto you that he is innocent.

31. But behold, ye shall examine him, and ye shall find blood upon the skirts of his cloak.

32. And when ye have seen this, ye shall say: From whence cometh this blood? Do we not know that it is the blood of your brother?

33. And then shall he tremble, and shall look pale, even as if death had come upon him.

34. And then shall ye say: Because of this fear and this paleness which has come upon your face, behold, we know that thou art guilty.

35. And then shall greater fear come upon him; and then shall he confess unto you, and deny no more that he has done this murder.

36. And then shall he say unto you, that I, Nephi, know nothing concerning the matter save it were given unto me by the power of God. And then shall ye know that I am an honest man, and that I am sent unto you from God.

37. And it came to pass that they went and did, even according as Nephi had said unto them. And behold, the words which he had said were true; for according to the words he did deny; and also according to the words he did confess.

38. And he was brought to prove that he himself was the very murderer, insomuch that the five were set at liberty, and also was Nephi.

39. And there were some of the Nephites who believed on the words of Nephi; and there were some also, who believed because of the testimony of the ⁿfive, for they had been converted while they were in prison.

40. And now there were some among the people, who said that Nephi was a prophet.

41. And there were others who said: Behold, he is a god, for except he was a god he could not know of all things. For behold, he has told us the thoughts of our hearts, and also has told us things; and even he has brought unto our knowledge the true murderer of our chief judge.

CHAPTER 10.

Nephi is comforted by the Lord with promise of great power—He preaches repentance and warns the wicked of impending judgments.

1. And it came to pass that there arose a division among the people, insomuch that they divided hither and thither and went their ways, leaving Nephi alone, as he was standing in the midst of them.

2. And it came to pass that Nephi went his way towards his own house, pondering upon the things which the Lord had shown unto him.

3. And it came to pass as he was thus pondering—being much cast down because of the wickedness of the people of the Nephites, their ᵃsecret works of darkness, and their murderings, and their plunderings, and all manner of iniquities—and it came to pass as he was thus pondering in his heart, behold, a voice came unto him saying:

4. Blessed art thou, Nephi, for those things which thou hast done; for I have beheld how thou hast with unwearyingness

---

n, see a.   CHAP. 10: a, see i, 2 Ne. 10.   BETWEEN B. C. 23 AND 20.

declared the word, which I have given unto thee, unto this people. And thou hast not feared them, and hast not sought thine own life, but hast sought my will, and to keep my commandments.

5. And now, because thou hast done this with such unwearyingness, behold, I will bless thee forever; and I will make thee mighty in word and in deed, in faith and in works; yea, even that all things shall be done unto thee according to thy word, for thou shalt not ask that which is contrary to my will.

6. Behold, thou art Nephi, and I am God. Behold, I declare it unto thee in the presence of mine angels, that ye shall have power over this people, and shall smite the earth with *b*famine, and with pestilence, and destruction, according to the wickedness of this people.

7. Behold, I give unto you power, that whatsoever ye shall seal on earth shall be sealed in heaven; and whatsoever ye shall loose on earth shall be loosed in heaven; and thus shall ye have power among this people.

8. And thus, if ye shall say unto this temple it shall be rent in twain, it shall be done.

9. And if ye shall say *c*unto this mountain, Be thou cast down and become smooth, it shall be done.

10. And behold, if ye shall say that God shall smite this people, it shall come to pass.

11. And now behold, I command you, that ye shall go and declare unto this people, that thus saith the Lord God, who is the Almighty: Except ye repent ye shall be smitten, *d*even unto destruction.

12. And behold, now it came to pass that when the Lord had spoken these words unto Nephi, he did stop and did not go unto his own house, but did return unto the multitudes who were scattered about upon the face of the land, and began to declare unto them the word of the Lord which had been spoken unto him, concerning their destruction if they did not repent.

13. Now behold, notwithstanding that great miracle which Nephi had done in telling them *e*concerning the death of the chief judge, they did harden their hearts and did not hearken unto the words of the Lord.

14. Therefore Nephi did declare unto them the word of the Lord, saying: Except ye repent, thus saith the Lord, ye shall be *f*smitten even unto destruction.

15. And it came to pass that when Nephi had declared unto them the word, behold, they did still harden their hearts and would not hearken unto his words; therefore they did revile against him, and did seek to lay their hands upon him that they might cast him into prison.

16. But behold, the power of God was with him, and they could not take him to cast him into prison, for he was taken by the Spirit and *g*conveyed away out of the midst of them.

17. And it came to pass that thus he did go forth *h*in the Spirit, from multitude to multitude, declaring the word of God, even until he had declared it unto them all, or sent it forth among all the people.

18. And it came to pass that they would not hearken unto his words; and there began to be

b, He. 11:4—18. *c*, Eth. 12:30. See *c*, Jac. 4. Matt. 17:20. *d*, vers. 12—14. *e*, He. 8:27. 9:26—38. *f*, ver. 11. *g*, Acts 8:39, 40. *h*, ver 16.
BETWEEN B. C. 23 AND 20.

contentions, insomuch that they were divided against themselves and began to slay one another with the sword.

19. And thus ended the seventy and first year of the reign of the judges over the people of Nephi.

CHAPTER 11.

A great famine—The people turn to the Lord and are again prospered—Dissension and strife follow—The Gadianton band revived.

1. And now it came to pass in the *seventy and second year of the reign of the judges that the contentions did increase, insomuch that there were wars throughout all the land among all the people of Nephi.

2. And it was this ^asecret band of robbers who did carry on this work of destruction and wickedness. And this war did last all that year; and in the †seventy and third year it did also last.

3. And it came to pass that in this year Nephi did cry unto the Lord, saying:

4. O Lord, do not suffer that this people shall be destroyed by the sword; but O Lord, rather let there be a ^bfamine in the land, to stir them up in remembrance of the Lord their God, and perhaps they will repent and turn unto thee.

5. And so it was done, according to the words of Nephi. And there was a great famine upon the land, among all the people of Nephi. And thus in the ‡seventy and fourth year the famine did continue, and the work of destruction did cease by the sword but became sore by famine.

6. And this work of destruction did also continue in the §seventy and fifth year. For the earth was smitten that it was dry, and did not yield forth grain in the season of grain; and the whole earth was smitten, even among the Lamanites as well as among the Nephites, so that they were smitten that they did perish by thousands in the more wicked parts of the land.

7. And it came to pass that the people saw that they were about to perish by famine, and they began to remember the Lord their God; and they began to remember the words of Nephi.

8. And the people began to plead with their chief judges and their leaders, that they would say unto Nephi: Behold, we know that thou art a man of God, and therefore cry unto the Lord our God that he turn away from us this famine, lest all the words which thou hast spoken ^cconcerning our destruction be fulfilled.

9. And it came to pass that the judges did say unto Nephi, according to the words which had been desired. And it came to pass that when Nephi saw that the people had repented and did humble themselves in sackcloth, he cried again unto the Lord, saying:

10. O Lord, behold this people repenteth; and they have swept away the ^dband of Gadianton from amongst them insomuch that they have become extinct, and they have concealed their secret plans in the earth.

11. Now, O Lord, because of this their humility wilt thou turn away thine anger, and let thine anger be appeased in the destruction of those wicked men whom thou hast already destroyed.

12. O Lord, wilt thou turn

a, see *i*, 2 Ne. 10.   *b*, see *b*, He. 10.   *c*, He. 10:11—14.   *d*, see *i*, 2 Ne. 10.
* B. C. 20.   † B. C. 19.   ‡ B. C. 18.   § B. C. 17.

away thine anger, yea, thy fierce anger, and cause that this famine may cease in this land.

13. O Lord, wilt thou hearken unto me, and cause that it may be done according to my words, and send forth rain upon the face of the earth, that she may bring forth her fruit, and her grain in the season of grain.

14. O Lord, thou didst hearken unto my words when I said, Let there be a *f*famine, that the pestilence of the sword might cease; and I know that thou wilt, even at this time, hearken unto my words, for thou saidst that: If this people repent I will spare them.

15. Yea, O Lord, and thou seest that they have repented, because of the famine and the pestilence and destruction which has come unto them.

16. And now, O Lord, wilt thou turn away thine anger, and try again if they will serve thee? And if so, O Lord, thou canst bless them according to thy words which thou hast said.

17. And it came to pass that in the *seventy and sixth year the Lord did turn away his anger from the people, and caused that rain should fall upon the earth, insomuch that it did bring forth her fruit in the season of her fruit. And it came to pass that it did bring forth her grain in the season of her grain.

18. And behold, the people did rejoice and glorify God, and the whole face of the land was filled with rejoicing; and they did no more seek to destroy Nephi, but they did esteem him as a great prophet, and a man of God, having *f*great power and authority given unto him from God.

19. And behold, Lehi, his brother, was not a whit behind him as to things pertaining to righteousness.

20. And thus it did come to pass that the people of Nephi began to prosper again in the land, and began to build up their waste places, and began to multiply and spread, even until they did cover the whole face of the land, both on the *g*northward and on the *h*southward, from the sea west to the sea east.

21. And it came to pass that the seventy and sixth year did end in peace. And the seventy and seventh year began in peace; and the church did spread throughout the face of all the land; and the more part of the people, both the Nephites and the Lamanites, did belong to the church; and they did have exceeding great peace in the land; and thus ended the seventy and seventh year.

22. And also they had peace in the seventy and eighth year, save it were a few contentions concerning the points of doctrine which had been laid down by the prophets.

23. And in the †seventy and ninth year there began to be much strife. But it came to pass that Nephi and Lehi, and many of their brethren who knew concerning the true points of doctrine, having many revelations daily, therefore they did preach unto the people, insomuch that they did put an end to their strife in that same year.

24. And it came to pass that in the ‡eightieth year of the reign of the judges over the people of Nephi, there were a certain number of the dissenters from the people of Nephi, who had some

---

c, see *b*, He. 10. *f*, He. 10:5—11. *g*, see *p*, Al. 46. *h*, see *n*, Al. 46.
* B. C. 16. † B. C. 13. ‡ B. C. 12.

HELAMAN, 11.

years before gone over unto the Lamanites, and taken upon themselves the name of Lamanites, and also a certain number who were real descendants of the Lamanites, being stirred up to anger by them, or by those dissenters, therefore they commenced a war with their brethren.

25. And they did commit murder and plunder; and then they would retreat back into the mountains, and into the wilderness and secret places, hiding themselves that they could not be discovered, receiving daily an addition to their numbers, inasmuch as there were dissenters that went forth unto them.

26. And thus in time, yea, even in the space of not many years, they became an exceeding great band of robbers; and they did search out all the ⁱsecret plans of Gadianton; and thus they became robbers of Gadianton.

27. Now behold, these robbers did make great havoc, yea, even great destruction among the people of Nephi, and also among the people of the Lamanites.

28. And it came to pass that it was expedient that there should be a stop put to this work of destruction; therefore they sent an army of strong men into the wilderness and upon the ʲmountains to search out this band of robbers, and to destroy them.

29. But behold, it came to pass that in that same year they were driven back even into their own lands. And thus ended the eightieth year of the reign of the judges over the people of Nephi.

30. And it came to pass in the *commencement of the eighty and first year they did go forth again against this band of robbers, and did destroy many; and they were also visited with much destruction.

31. And they were again obliged to return out of the wilderness and out of the mountains unto their own lands, because of the exceeding greatness of the numbers of those robbers who infested the mountains and the wilderness.

32. And it came to pass that thus ended this year. And the robbers did still increase and wax strong, insomuch that they did defy the whole armies of the Nephites, and also of the Lamanites; and they did cause great fear to come unto the people upon all the face of the land.

33. Yea, for they did visit many parts of the land, and did do great destruction unto them; yea, did kill many, and did carry away others captive into the wilderness, yea, and more especially their women and their children.

34. Now this great evil, which came unto the people because of their iniquity, did stir them up again in remembrance of the Lord their God.

35. And thus ended the eighty and first year of the reign of the judges.

36. And in the eighty and second year they began again to forget the Lord their God. And in the eighty and third year they began to wax strong in iniquity. And in the eighty and fourth year they did not mend their ways.

37. And it came to pass in the †eighty and fifth year they did wax stronger and stronger in their pride, and in their wickedness; and thus they were ripening again for destruction.

38. And thus ended the eighty and fifth year.

---
i, see *i*, 2 Ne. 10.   *j*, ver. 25.   * B. C. 11.   † B. C. 7.

CHAPTER 12.

Human frailty and the goodness and power of God—Blessed are the penitent—Men to be judged according to their works.

1. And thus we can behold how false, and also the unsteadiness of the hearts of the children of men; yea, we can see that the Lord in his great infinite goodness doth bless and prosper those who put their trust in him.

2. Yea, and we may see at the very time when he doth prosper his people, yea, in the increase of their fields, their flocks and their herds, and in ^agold, and in silver, and in all manner of precious things of every kind and art; sparing their lives, and delivering them out of the hands of their enemies; softening the hearts of their enemies that they should not declare wars against them; yea, and in fine, doing all things for the welfare and happiness of his people; yea, then is the time that they do harden their hearts, and do forget the Lord their God, and do trample under their feet the Holy One—yea, and this because of their ease, and their exceedingly great prosperity.

3. And thus we see that except the Lord doth chasten his people with many afflictions, yea, except he doth visit them with death and with terror, and with famine and with all manner of pestilence, they will not remember him.

4. O how foolish, and how vain, and how evil, and devilish, and how quick to do iniquity, and how slow to do good, are the children of men; yea, how quick to hearken unto the words of the evil one, and to set their hearts upon the vain things of the world!

5. Yea, how quick to be lifted up in pride; yea, how quick to boast, and do all manner of that which is iniquity; and how slow are they to remember the Lord their God, and to give ear unto his counsels, yea, how slow to walk in wisdom's paths!

6. Behold, they do not desire that the Lord their God, who hath created them, should rule and reign over them; notwithstanding his great goodness and his mercy towards them, they do set at naught his counsels, and they will not that he should be their guide.

7. O how great is the nothingness of the children of men; yea, even they are less than the dust of the earth.

8. For behold, the dust of the earth moveth hither and thither, to the dividing asunder, at the command of our great and everlasting God.

9. Yea, behold at his voice do the hills and the mountains tremble and quake.

10. And by the power of his voice they are broken up, and become smooth, yea, even like unto a valley.

11. Yea, by the power of his voice doth the whole earth shake;

12. Yea, by the power of his voice, do the foundations rock, even to the very center.

13. Yea, and if he say unto the earth—Move—it is moved.

14. Yea, if he say unto the earth—Thou shalt go back, that it ^blengthen out the day for many hours—it is done;

15. And thus, according to his word the earth goeth back, and it appeareth unto man that the sun standeth still; yea, and behold,

---

a, see *n*, 1 Ne. 18. *b*, Josh. 10:12—14. 2 Kings 20:8—11. Isa. 38:7, 8. See 2*a*, Al. 30. ABOUT B. C. 7

this is so; for surely it is the earth that moveth and not the sun.

16. And behold, also, if he say unto the waters of the great deep—*c*Be thou dried up—it is done.

17. Behold, if he say unto this mountain—Be thou raised up, and *d*come over and fall upon that city, that it be buried up—behold it is done.

18. And behold, if a man hide up a treasure in the earth, and the Lord shall say—*e*Let it be accursed, because of the iniquity of him who hath hid it up—behold, it shall be accursed.

19. And if the Lord shall say—Be thou accursed, that no man shall find thee from this time henceforth and forever—behold, no man getteth it henceforth and forever.

20. And behold, if the Lord shall say unto a man—Because of thine iniquities, thou shalt be *f*accursed forever—it shall be done.

21. And if the Lord shall say—Because of thine iniquities thou shalt be cut off *g*from my presence—he will cause that it shall be so.

22. And wo unto him to whom he shall say this, for it shall be unto him that will do iniquity, and he cannot be saved; therefore, for this cause, that men might be saved, hath repentance been declared.

23. Therefore, blessed are they who will repent and hearken unto the voice of the Lord their God; for these are they that shall be saved.

24. And may God grant, in his great fulness, that men might be brought unto repentance and good works, that they might be restored unto grace for grace, according to their works.

25. And I would that all men might be saved. But we read that in the great and last day there are some who shall be cast out, yea, who shall be cast off *h*from the presence of the Lord;

26. Yea, who shall be consigned to a state of *i*endless misery, fulfilling the words which say: They that have done good shall have everlasting life; and they that have done evil shall have *j*everlasting damnation. And thus it is. Amen.

The prophecy of Samuel, the Lamanite, to the Nephites.

Comprising chapters 13 to 15 inclusive.

CHAPTER 13.

Samuel proclaims his prophecies from the city wall—Sword of justice to fall on fourth generation—Nephite cities spared for sake of the righteous—Land to be cursed—Slippery treasures.

1. And now it came to pass in the *eighty and sixth year, the Nephites did still remain in wickedness, yea, in great wickedness, while the Lamanites did observe strictly to keep the commandments of God, according to the *a*law of Moses.

2. And it came to pass that in this year there was one Samuel, a Lamanite, came into the *b*land of Zarahemla, and began to preach unto the people. And it came to pass that he did preach, many days, repentance unto the people, and they did cast him out, and he was about to return to his own land.

---

c, Isa. 44:27. 51:10. *d*, 3 Ne. 8:10, 25. 9:5, 6, 8. *e*, ver. 19. He. 13:17—23, 30—37. Morm. 1:17—19. 2:10—14. Eth. 14:1, 2. *f*, see *k*, Jac. 6. *g*, vers. 25, 26. See *b*, 1 Ne. 2. *h*, see *g*. *i*, see *m*, Jac. 6. *j*, see *m*, Jac. 6.   Chap. 13: *a*, see *o*, 2 Ne. 25. *b*, Om. 13.   * B. C. 6.

3. But behold, the voice of the Lord came unto him, that he should return again, and prophesy unto the people whatsoever things should come into his heart.

4. And it came to pass that they would not suffer that he should enter into the city; therefore he went and got upon the wall thereof, and stretched forth his hand and cried with a loud voice, and prophesied unto the people whatsoever things the Lord put into his heart.

5. And he said unto them: Behold, I, Samuel, a Lamanite, do speak the words of the Lord which he doth put into my heart; and behold he hath put it into my heart to say unto this people that the sword of justice hangeth over this people; and ^{c}four hundred years pass not away save the sword of justice falleth upon this people.

6. Yea, heavy destruction awaiteth this people, and it surely cometh unto this people, and nothing can save this people save it be repentance and faith on the Lord Jesus Christ, who surely shall come into the world, and shall suffer many things and shall be slain for his people.

7. And behold, an angel of the Lord hath declared it unto me, and he did bring glad tidings to my soul. And behold, I was sent unto you to declare it unto you also, that ye might have glad tidings; but behold ye ^{d}would not receive me.

8. Therefore, thus saith the Lord: Because of the hardness of the hearts of the people of the Nephites, except they repent I will take away my word from them, and I will withdraw my Spirit from them, and I will suffer them no longer, and I will turn the hearts of their brethren against them.

9. And ^{e}four hundred years shall not pass away before I will cause that they shall be smitten; yea, I will visit them with the sword and with famine and with pestilence.

10. Yea, I will visit them in my fierce anger, and there shall be those of the fourth generation who shall live, of your enemies, to behold your utter destruction; and this shall surely come except ye repent, saith the Lord; and those of the fourth generation shall visit your destruction.

11. But if ye will repent and return unto the Lord your God I will turn away mine anger, saith the Lord; yea, thus saith the Lord, blessed are they who will repent and turn unto me, but wo unto him that repenteth not.

12. Yea, ^{f}wo unto this great city of Zarahemla; for behold, it is because of those who are righteous that it is saved; yea, wo unto this great city, for I perceive, saith the Lord, that there are many, yea, even the more part of this great city, that will harden their hearts against me, saith the Lord.

13. But blessed are they who will repent, for them will I spare. But behold, if it were not for the righteous who are in this great city, behold, I would cause that fire should come down out of heaven and destroy it.

14. But behold, it is for the righteous' sake that it is spared. But behold, the time cometh, saith the Lord, that when ye shall cast out the righteous from among you, then shall ye be ripe for destruction; yea, wo be unto this great city, because of the wicked-

---

c, see *d,* 1 Ne. 12.   *d,* ver. 2.   *e,* see *d,* 1 Ne. 12.   *f,* 3 Ne. 8:8, 24.   9:3.
ABOUT B. C. 6.

ness and abominations which are in her.

15. Yea, and wo be unto the *g*city of Gideon, for the wickedness and abominations which are in her.

16. Yea, and wo be unto all the cities which are in the land round about, which are possessed by the Nephites, because of the wickedness and abominations which are in them.

17. And behold, a *h*curse shall come upon the land, saith the Lord of Hosts, because of the peoples' sake who are upon the land, yea, because of their wickedness and their abominations.

18. And it shall come to pass, saith the Lord of Hosts, yea, our great and true God, that whoso shall hide up treasures in the earth shall find them again no more, because of the great curse of the land, save he be a righteous man and shall hide it up unto the Lord.

19. For I will, saith the Lord, that they shall hide up their treasures unto me; and cursed be they who hide not up their treasures unto me; for none hideth up their treasures unto me save it be the righteous; and he that hideth not up his treasures unto me, *i*cursed is he, and also the treasure, and none shall redeem it because of the curse of the land.

20. And the day shall come that they shall hide up their treasures, because they have set their hearts upon riches; and because they have set their hearts upon their riches, I will hide up their treasures when they shall flee before their enemies; because they will not hide them up unto me, cursed be they and also their treasures; and in that day shall they be smitten, saith the Lord.

21. Behold ye, the people of this great city, and hearken unto my words; yea, hearken unto the words which the Lord saith; for behold, he saith that ye are cursed because of your riches, and also are your riches cursed because ye have set your hearts upon them, and have not hearkened unto the words of him who gave them unto you.

22. Ye do not remember the Lord your God in the things with which he hath blessed you, but ye do always remember your riches, not to thank the Lord your God for them; yea, your hearts are not drawn out unto the Lord, but they do swell with great pride, unto boasting, and unto great swelling, envyings, strifes, malice, persecutions, and murders, and all manner of iniquities.

23. For this cause hath the Lord God caused that a curse should come upon the land, and also upon your riches, and this because of your iniquities.

24. Yea, wo unto this people, because of this time which has arrived, that ye do *j*cast out the prophets, and do mock them, and cast stones at them, and do slay them, and do all manner of iniquity unto them, even as they did of old time.

25. And now when ye talk, ye say: If our days had been in the days of our fathers of old, we would not have slain the prophets; we would not have stoned them, and cast them out.

26. Behold ye are worse than they; for as the Lord liveth, if a prophet come among you and declareth unto you the word of the Lord, which testifieth of your sins and iniquities, ye are angry with

g, see *m*, Al. 2. *h*, see *e*, He. 12. *i*, see *e*, He. 12. *j*, ver. 26. He. 16:6.

ABOUT B. C. 6.

him, and cast him out and seek all manner of ways to destroy him; yea, you will say that he is a false prophet, and that he is a sinner, and of the devil, because he testifieth that your deeds are evil.

27. But behold, if a man shall come among you and shall say: Do this, and there is no iniquity; do that and ye shall not suffer; yea, he will say: Walk after the pride of your own hearts; yea, walk after the pride of your eyes, and do whatsoever your heart desireth—and if a man shall come among you and say this, ye will receive him, and say that he is a prophet.

28. Yea, ye will lift him up, and ye will give unto him of your substance; ye will give unto him of your gold, and of your silver, and ye will clothe him with costly apparel; and because he speaketh flattering words unto you, and he saith that all is well, then ye will not find fault with him.

29. O ye wicked and ye perverse generation; ye hardened and ye stiffnecked people, how long will ye suppose that the Lord will suffer you? Yea, how long will ye suffer yourselves to be led by foolish and blind guides? Yea, how long will ye choose darkness rather than light?

30. Yea, behold, the anger of the Lord is already kindled against you; behold, he hath ^{k}cursed the land because of your iniquity.

31. And behold, the time cometh that he curseth your riches, that they become ^{l}slippery, that ye cannot hold them; and in the days of your poverty ye cannot retain them.

32. And in the days of your poverty ye shall cry unto the Lord; and in vain shall ye cry, for your desolation is already come upon you, and your destruction is made sure; and then shall ye weep and howl in that day, saith the Lord of Hosts. And then shall ye lament, and say:

33. ^{m}O that I had repented, and had not killed the prophets, and stoned them, and cast them out. Yea, in that day ye shall say: O that we had remembered the Lord our God in the day that he gave us our riches, and then they would not have become slippery that we should lose them; for behold, our riches are gone from us.

34. Behold, we lay a tool here and on the morrow it is gone; and behold, our swords are taken from us in the day we have sought them for battle.

35. Yea, we have hid up our treasures and they have slipped away from us, because of the curse of the land.

36. O that we had repented in the day that the word of the Lord came unto us; for behold the land is cursed, and ^{n}all things are become slippery, and we cannot hold them.

37. Behold, we are surrounded by ^{o}demons, yea, we are encircled about by the angels of him who hath sought to destroy our souls. Behold, our iniquities are great. O Lord, canst thou not turn away thine anger from us? And this shall be your language in those days.

38. But behold, your ^{p}days of probation are past; ye have procrastinated the day of your salvation until it is everlastingly too late, and your ^{q}destruction

---

k, see e, He. 12. l, vers. 33—37. Morm. 1:17—19. See c, He. 12. m, Morm. 2:10—15. n, see l. o, Morm. 2:10. p, Morm. 2:13—15. q, Morm. 2:15.

ABOUT B. C. 6.

is made sure; yea, for ye have sought all the days of your lives for that which ye could not obtain; and ye have sought for happiness in doing iniquity, which thing is ʳcontrary to the nature of that righteousness which is in our great and Eternal Head.

39. O ye people of the land, that ye would hear my words! And I pray that the anger of the Lord be turned away from you, and that ye would repent and be saved.

CHAPTER 14.

Samuel the Lamanite predicts the Christ—The sign of Christ's birth to be given in five years—Sign of his death also foretold.

1. And now it came to pass that Samuel, the Lamanite, did prophesy a great many more things which cannot be written.

2. And behold, he said unto them: Behold, I give unto you a sign; for ᵃfive years more cometh, and behold, then cometh the Son of God to redeem all those who shall believe on his name.

3. And behold, this will I give unto you for a sign at the time of his coming; for behold, there shall be great lights in heaven, insomuch that in the night before he cometh there shall be ᵇno darkness, insomuch that it shall appear unto man as if it was day.

4. Therefore, there shall be one day and a night and a day, as if it were one day and there were no night; and this shall be unto you for a sign; for ye shall know of the rising of the sun and also of its setting; therefore they shall know of a surety that there shall be two days and a night; nevertheless the night shall not be darkened; and it shall be the night before he is born.

5. And behold, there shall a ᶜnew star arise, such an one as ye never have beheld; and this also shall be a sign unto you.

6. And behold this is not all, there shall be ᵈmany signs and wonders in heaven.

7. And it shall come to pass that ye shall all be amazed, and wonder, insomuch that ye shall ᵉfall to the earth.

8. And it shall come to pass that whosoever shall believe on the Son of God, the same shall have everlasting life.

9. And behold, thus hath the Lord ᶠcommanded me, by his angel, that I should come and tell this thing unto you; yea, he hath commanded that I should prophesy these things unto you; yea, he hath said unto me: Cry unto this people, repent and prepare the way of the Lord.

10. And now, because I am a Lamanite, and have spoken unto you the words which the Lord hath commanded me, and because it was hard against you, ye are angry with me and do seek to destroy me, and have ᵍcast me out from among you.

11. And ye shall hear my words, for, for this intent have I come up ʰupon the walls of this city, that ye might hear and know of the judgments of God which do await you because of your iniquities, and also that ye might know the conditions of repentance;

12. And also that ye might know of the coming of Jesus Christ, the Son of God, the ⁱFather of heaven and of earth, the Creator of all things from the beginning; and that ye might know

---

r, Al. 41:10—12. Chap. 14: *a*, 3 Ne. 1:5—21. *b*, ver. 4. 3 Ne. 1:8, 13—20. *c*, 3 Ne. 1:21. *d*, 3 Ne. 1:20. 2:1—3. *e*, 3 Ne. 1:16, 17. *f*, He. 13:3, 7. *g*, He. 13:2. *h*, He. 13:4. *i*, Mos. 3:8. 15:4. Al. 11:39. 3 Ne. 9:15. Eth. 4:7.

About B. C. 6.

of the signs of his coming, to the intent that ye might believe on his name.

13. And if ye believe on his name ye will repent of all your sins, that thereby ye may have a remission of them through his merits.

14. And behold, again, another sign I give unto you, yea, a sign of his death.

15. For behold, he surely must die that salvation may come; yea, it behooveth him and becometh expedient that he dieth, to bring to pass the ʲresurrection of the dead, that thereby men may be brought into the presence of the Lord.

16. Yea, behold, this death bringeth to pass the resurrection, and redeemeth ᵏall mankind from the first death—that spiritual death; for all mankind, by the fall of Adam being cut off from the presence of the Lord, are considered as dead, ˡboth as to things temporal and to things spiritual.

17. But behold, the resurrection of Christ redeemeth mankind, yea, even ᵐall mankind, and bringeth them back into the presence of the Lord.

18. Yea, and it bringeth to pass the condition of repentance, that whosoever repenteth the same is not hewn down and cast into the fire; but whosoever repenteth not is hewn down and cast into the fire; and there cometh upon them ⁿagain a spiritual death, yea, a second death, for they are cut off ᵒagain as to things pertaining to righteousness.

19. Therefore repent ye, repent ye, lest by knowing these things and not doing them ye shall suffer yourselves to come under condemnation, and ye are brought down unto this ᵖsecond death.

20. But behold, as I said unto you ᑫconcerning another sign, a sign of his death, behold, in that day that he shall suffer death ʳthe sun shall be darkened and refuse to give his light unto you; and also the moon and the stars; and there shall be no light upon the face of this land, even from the time that he shall suffer death, for the space of three days, to the time that he shall rise again from the dead.

21. Yea, at the time that he shall yield up the ghost there ˢshall be thunderings and lightnings for the space of many hours, and the earth shall shake and tremble; and the ᵗrocks which are upon the face of this earth, which are both above the earth and beneath, which ye know at this time are solid, or the more part of it is one solid mass, shall be broken up;

22. Yea, they shall be rent in twain, and shall ever after be ᵘfound in seams and in cracks, and in broken fragments upon the face of the whole earth, yea, both above the earth and beneath.

23. And behold, there shall be great ᵛtempests, and there shall be many mountains ʷlaid low, like unto a valley, and there shall be many places which are now called valleys which shall become mountains, whose height is great.

24. And many ˣhighways shall be broken up, and ʸmany cities shall become desolate.

---

j, see *d*, 2 Ne. 2.   *k*, see *j*, 2 Ne. 9.   *l*, see *b* and *c*, 2 Ne. 2.   *m*, see *j*, 2 Ne. 9.
n, see *p*, Al. 12.   *o*, see *q*, Al. 12.   *p*, see *p*, Al. 12.   *q*, ver. 14.   *r*, see *i*, 1 Ne. 19.
s, vers. 26, 27.   1 Ne. 12:4.   19:11, 12.   3 Ne. 8:5—7, 19.   *t*, 1 Ne. 12:4.   19:12.
3 Ne. 8:18.   10:9.   *u*, 3 Ne. 8:18.   *v*, 1 Ne. 19:11.   3 Ne. 8:6, 12, 19.   10:14.   *w*,
1 Ne. 12:4.   19:11.   3 Ne. 8:10—19.   *x*, 3 Ne. 8:13.   *y*, 1 Ne. 12:4.   3 Ne. 8:8—10,
14, 24, 25.   9:3—12.   10:7.   ABOUT B. C. 6.

25. And ᶠmany graves shall be opened, and shall yield up many of their dead; and ²ᵃmany saints shall appear unto many.

26. And behold, thus hath the angel spoken unto me; for he said unto me that there ²ᵇshould be thunderings and lightnings for the space of many hours.

27. And he said unto me that while the thunder and the lightning lasted, and the tempest, that these things should be, and that darkness should cover the face of the whole earth for the space of ²ᶜthree days.

28. And the angel said unto me that many shall see greater things than these, to the intent that they might believe that these signs and these wonders should come to pass upon all the face of this land, to the intent that there should be no cause for unbelief among the children of men—

29. And this to the intent that whosoever will believe might be saved, and that whosoever will not believe, a righteous judgment might come upon them; and also if they are condemned they bring upon themselves their own condemnation.

30. And now remember, remember, my brethren, that whosoever perisheth, perisheth unto himself; and whosoever doeth iniquity, doeth it unto himself; for behold, ye are ²ᵈfree; ye are permitted to act for yourselves; for behold, God hath given unto you a knowledge and he hath made you free.

31. He hath given unto you that ye might know good from evil, and he hath given unto you that ye might choose life or death; and ye can do good and be ²ᵉrestored unto that which is good, or have that which is good restored unto you; or ye can do evil, and have that which is evil restored unto you.

CHAPTER 15.

Samuel the Lamanite continues his warning words—A remnant of his people to be preserved—Nephites to be utterly destroyed unless they repent.

1. And now, my beloved brethren, behold, I declare unto you that except ye shall repent your ᵃhouses shall be left unto you desolate.

2. Yea, except ye repent, your women shall have great cause to mourn in the day that they shall give suck; for ye shall attempt to flee and there shall be no place for refuge; yea, and wo unto them which are with child, for they shall be heavy and cannot flee; therefore, they shall be trodden down and shall be left to perish.

3. Yea, wo unto this people who are called the people of Nephi except they shall repent, when they shall see all these signs and wonders which shall be showed unto them; for behold, they have been a chosen people of the Lord; yea, the people of Nephi hath he loved, and also hath he chastened them; yea, in the days of their iniquities hath he chastened them because he loveth them.

4. But behold my brethren, the Lamanites hath he hated because their deeds have been evil continually, and this because of the iniquity of the ᵇtradition of their fathers. But behold, salvation hath come unto them through the preaching of the Nephites; and for this intent hath the Lord prolonged their days.

5. And I would that ye should

---

z, see *g*, Jac. 4. 2*a*, 3 Ne. 23:7—13. 2*b*, see *s*. 2*c*, see *i*, 1 Ne. 19. 2*d*, see *l*, 2 Ne. 2. 2*e*, Al. 41. CHAP. 15: *a*, see *y*, He. 14. *b*, see *n*, Jac. 7. ABOUT B. C. 6.

behold that the more part of them are in the path of their duty, and they do walk circumspectly before God, and they do observe to keep his commandments and his statutes and his judgments according to the ᶜlaw of Moses.

6. Yea, I say unto you, that the more part of them are doing this, and they are striving with unwearied diligence that they may bring the remainder of their brethren to the knowledge of the truth; therefore there are many who do add to their numbers daily.

7. And behold, ye do know of yourselves, for ye have witnessed it, that as many of them as are brought to the knowledge of the truth, and to know of the ᵈwicked and abominable traditions of their fathers, and are led to believe the holy scriptures, yea, the prophecies of the holy prophets, which are written, which leadeth them to faith on the Lord, and unto repentance, which faith and repentance bringeth a change of heart unto them—

8. Therefore, as many as have come to this, ye know of yourselves are firm and steadfast in the faith, and in the thing wherewith they have been made free.

9. And ye know also that they have ᵉburied their weapons of war, and they fear to take them up lest by any means they should sin; yea, ye can see that they fear to sin—for behold they will suffer themselves that they be trodden down and ᶠslain by their enemies, and will not lift their swords against them, and this because of their faith in Christ.

10. And now, because of their steadfastness when they do believe in that thing which they do believe, for because of their firmness when they are once enlightened, behold, the Lord shall bless them and prolong their days, notwithstanding their iniquity—

11. Yea, even if they should dwindle in unbelief the Lord shall ᵍprolong their days, until the time shall come which hath been spoken of by our fathers, and also by the prophet ʰZenos, and many other prophets, concerning the restoration of our brethren, the Lamanites, again to the knowledge of the truth—

12. Yea, I say unto you, that in the latter times the ⁱpromises of the Lord have been extended to our brethren, the Lamanites; and notwithstanding the many afflictions which they shall have, and ʲnotwithstanding they shall be driven to and fro upon the face of the earth, and be hunted, and shall be smitten and scattered abroad, having no place for refuge, the Lord shall be merciful unto them.

13. And this is according to the prophecy, that they shall be brought to the true knowledge, which is the knowledge of their Redeemer, and their great and ᵏtrue shepherd, and be numbered among his sheep.

14. Therefore I say unto you, it shall be better for them than for you except ye repent.

15. For behold, had the mighty works been shown unto them which have been shown unto you, yea, unto them who have dwindled in unbelief because of the traditions of their fathers, ye can see of yourselves that they never would again have dwindled in unbelief.

---

c, see *a*, 2 Ne. 25. *d*, see *n*, Jac. 7. *e*, Al. 24:17—19. *f*, Al. 24:21—23. *g*, Enos 13. See *c*, 2 Ne. 27. *h*, see *h*, 1 Ne. 19. *i*, Enos 13. See *c*, 2 Ne. 27. *j*, Morm. 5:15. *k*, see 2*c*, Al. 5. ABOUT B. C. 6.

16. Therefore, saith the Lord: I will not utterly destroy them, but I will cause that in the day of my wisdom they shall ⁱreturn again unto me, saith the Lord.

17. And now behold, saith the Lord, concerning the people of the Nephites: If they will not repent, and observe to do my will, I will ᵐutterly destroy them, saith the Lord, because of their unbelief notwithstanding the many mighty works which I have done among them; and as surely as the Lord liveth shall these things be, saith the Lord.

CHAPTER 16.

Some of the Nephites join the church of Christ—The majority reject Samuel's testimony—They attempt to assault and bind him—He escapes and returns to his own country—Nephi's further ministry—Skepticism abounds.

1. And now, it came to pass that there were many who heard the words of Samuel, the Lamanite, which he spake upon the "walls of the city. And as many as believed on his word went forth and sought for Nephi; and when they had come forth and found him they confessed unto him their sins and denied not, desiring that they might be ᵇbaptized unto the Lord.

2. But as many as there were who did not believe in the words of Samuel were angry with him; and they cast stones at him upon the wall, and also many shot arrows at him as he stood upon the wall; but the Spirit of the Lord was with him, insomuch that they could not hit him with their stones neither with their arrows.

3. Now when they saw this, that they could not hit him, there were many more who did believe on his words, insomuch that they went away unto Nephi to be baptized.

4. For behold, Nephi was baptizing, and prophesying, and preaching, crying repentance unto the people, showing signs and wonders, working miracles among the people, that they might know that the Christ must shortly come—

5. Telling them of things which must shortly come, that they might know and remember at the time of their coming that they had been made known unto them beforehand, to the intent that they might believe; therefore as many as believed on the words of Samuel went forth unto him to be baptized, for they came repenting and confessing their sins.

6. But the more part of them did not believe in the words of Samuel; therefore when they saw that they could ᶜnot hit him with their stones and their arrows, they cried unto their captains, saying: Take this fellow and bind him, for behold he hath a devil; and because of the power of the devil which is in him we cannot hit him with our stones and our arrows; therefore take him and bind him, and away with him.

7. And as they went forth to lay their hands on him, behold, he did cast himself down from the ᵈwall, and did flee out of their lands, yea, even unto his own country, and began to preach and to prophesy among his own people.

8. And behold, he was never heard of more among the Nephites; and thus were the affairs of the people.

9. And thus ended the eighty and sixth year of the reign of the

---

l, Enos 13. Also *c*, 2 Ne. 27. *m*, see *m*, Al. 9.   CHAP. 16: *a*, He. 13:4.   *b*, see *u*, 2 Ne. 9.   *c*, ver. 2.   *d*, He. 13:4.   ABOUT B. C. 6.

judges over the people of Nephi.

10. And thus ended also the *eighty and seventh year of the reign of the judges, the more part of the people remaining in their pride and wickedness, and the lesser part walking more circumspectly before God.

11. And these were the conditions also, in the eighty and eighth year of the reign of the judges.

12. And there was but little alteration in the affairs of the people, save it were the people began to be more hardened in iniquity, and do more and more of that which was contrary to the commandments of God, in the eighty and ninth year of the reign of the judges.

13. But it came to pass in the †ninetieth year of the reign of the judges, there were great signs given unto the people, and wonders; and the words of the prophets began to be fulfilled.

14. And *c*angels did appear unto men, wise men, and did declare unto them glad tidings of great joy; thus in this year the scriptures began to be fulfilled.

15. Nevertheless, the people began to harden their hearts, all save it were the most believing part of them, both of the Nephites and also of the Lamanites, and began to depend upon their own strength and upon their own wisdom, saying:

16. Some things they may have guessed right, among so many; but behold, we know that all these great and marvelous works cannot come to pass, of which has been spoken.

17. And they began to reason and to contend among themselves, saying:

18. That it is not reasonable that such a being as a Christ shall come; if so, and he be the Son of God, *f*the Father of heaven and of earth, as it has been spoken, why will he not show himself unto us as well as unto them who shall be at Jerusalem?

19. Yea, why will he not show himself in this land as well as in the land of Jerusalem?

20. But behold, we know that this is a wicked tradition, which has been handed down unto us by our fathers, to cause us that we should believe in some great and marvelous thing which should come to pass, but not among us, but in a land which is far distant, a land which we know not; therefore they can keep us in ignorance, for we cannot witness with our own eyes that they are true.

21. And they will, by the cunning and the mysterious arts of the evil one, work some great mystery which we cannot understand, which will keep us down to be servants to their words, and also servants unto them, for we depend upon them to teach us the word; and thus will they keep us in ignorance if we will yield ourselves unto them, all the days of our lives.

22. And many more things did the people imagine up in their hearts, which were foolish and vain; and they were much disturbed, for Satan did stir them up to do iniquity continually; yea, he did go about spreading rumors and contentions upon all the face of the land, that he might harden the hearts of the people against that which was good and against that which should come.

23. And *g*notwithstanding the signs and the wonders which were wrought among the people of the Lord, and the many miracles

---

c, Al. 13:20.   *f*, see *a*, Mos. 3.   *g*, ver. 13.   * B. C. 5.   † B. C. 2.

3 NEPHI, 1.

which they did, Satan did get great hold upon the hearts of the people upon all the face of the land.

24. And thus *ended the nine-tieth year of the reign of the judges over the people of Nephi.

25. And thus ended the book of Helaman, according to the record of Helaman and his sons.

THIRD NEPHI
THE BOOK OF NEPHI
THE SON OF NEPHI, WHO WAS THE SON OF HELAMAN

And Helaman was the son of Helaman, who was the son of Alma, who was the son of Alma, being a descendant of Nephi who was the son of Lehi, who came out of Jerusalem in the first year of the reign of Zedekiah, the king of Judah.

CHAPTER 1
Nephi, son of Helaman, departs—Signs given of the Savior's birth—Opposite effects manifest—Again, the Gadianton band.

1. Now it came to pass that the †ninety and first year had passed away and it was ᵃsix hundred years from the time that Lehi left Jerusalem; and it was in the year that Lachoneus was the chief judge and the governor over the land.

2. And Nephi, the son of Helaman, had departed out of the land of ᵇZarahemla, giving charge unto his son Nephi, who was his eldest son, concerning the ᶜplates of brass, and all the records which had been kept, and ᵈall those things which had been kept sacred from the departure of Lehi out of Jerusalem.

3. Then he departed out of the land, and ᵉwhither he went, no man knoweth; and his son Nephi did keep the records in his stead, yea, the record of this people.

4. And it came to pass that in the commencement of the ninety and second year, behold, the prophecies of the prophets began to be fulfilled more fully; for there began to be ᶠgreater signs and greater miracles wrought among the people.

5. But there were some who began to say that the time was past for the words to be fulfilled, which were ᵍspoken by Samuel, the Lamanite.

6. And they began to rejoice over their brethren, saying: Behold the time is past, and the words of Samuel are not fulfilled; therefore, your joy and your faith concerning this thing hath been vain.

7. And it came to pass that they did make a great uproar throughout the land; and the people who believed began to be very sorrowful, lest by any means those things which had been spoken might not come to pass.

8. But behold, they did watch steadfastly ʰfor that day and that night and that day which should be as one day as if there were no night, that they might know that their faith had not been vain.

9. Now it came to pass that there was a day set apart by the unbelievers, that all those who be-

---
a, 1 Ne. 10:4. *b*, Om. 13. *c*, see *a*, 1 Ne. 3. *d*, Al. 37. *e*, 3 Ne. 2:9. *f*, He. 16:13, 23. *g*, He. 14:2—7. *h*, He. 14:3, 4. * B. C. 1. † A. D. 1.

lieved in those traditions ^{t}should be put to death except the ^{j}sign should come to pass, which had been given by Samuel the prophet.

10. Now it came to pass that when Nephi, the son of Nephi, saw this wickedness of his people, his heart was exceedingly sorrowful.

11. And it came to pass that he went out and bowed himself down upon the earth, and cried mightily to his God in behalf of his people, yea, those who were about ^{k}to be destroyed because of their faith in the tradition of their fathers.

12. And it came to pass that he cried mightily unto the Lord, all the day; and behold, the voice of the Lord came unto him, saying:

13. Lift up your head and be of good cheer; for behold, the time is at hand, and on ^{l}this night shall the sign be given, and on the morrow come I into the world, to show unto the world that I will fulfil all that which I have caused to be spoken by the mouth of my holy prophets.

14. Behold, I come unto my own, to fulfil all things which I have made known unto the children of men ^{m}from the foundation of the world, and to do the will, both of the Father and of the Son—^{n}of the Father because of me, and ^{o}of the Son because of my flesh. And behold, the time is at hand, and ^{p}this night shall the sign be given.

15. And it came to pass that the words which came unto Nephi were fulfilled, according as they had been spoken; for behold, ^{q}at the going down of the sun there was no darkness; and the people began to be astonished because there was no darkness when the night came.

16. And there were many, who had not believed the words of the prophets, who ^{r}fell to the earth and became as if they were dead, for they knew that the great ^{s}plan of destruction which they had laid for those who believed in the words of the prophets had been frustrated; for the signal which had been given was already at hand.

17. And they began to know that the Son of God must shortly appear; yea, in fine, all the people upon the face of the whole earth from the west to the east, both in the land ^{t}north and in the land ^{u}south, were so exceedingly astonished that they ^{v}fell to the earth.

18. For they knew that the prophets had testified of these things for many years, and that the sign which had been given was already at hand; and they began to fear because of their iniquity and their unbelief.

19. And it came to pass that there was ^{w}no darkness in all that night, but it was as light as though it was mid-day. And it came to pass that the sun did rise in the morning again, according to its proper order; and they knew that it was the day that the Lord should be born, because of the sign which had been given.

20. And it had come to pass, yea, all things, every whit, according to the words of the prophets.

21. And it came to pass also that a ^{x}new star did appear, according to the word.

22. And it came to pass that from this time forth there began

---

i, vers. 11, 16. j, He. 14:2—7. k, vers. 9, 16. l, ver. 8. He. 14:3, 4. m, see d, Mos. 4. n, see c, Mos. 15. o, see b, Mos. 3. p, He. 14:3, 4. q, He. 14:3, 4. r, ver. 17. He. 14:7. s, vers. 9, 11. t, see p, Al. 46. u, see n, Al. 46. v, ver. 16. He. 14:7. w, He. 14:3, 4. x, He. 14:5.

A. D. 1.

to be lyings sent forth among the people, by Satan, to harden their hearts, to the intent that they might not believe in those signs and wonders which they had seen; but notwithstanding these lyings and deceivings the more part of the people did believe, and were converted unto the Lord.

23. And it came to pass that Nephi went forth among the people, and also many others, ᵛbaptizing unto repentance, in the which there was a great remission of sins. And thus the people began again to have peace in the land.

24. And there were no contentions, save it were a few that began to preach, endeavoring to prove by the scriptures that it was no more expedient to observe the law of Moses. Now in this thing they did err, having not understood the scriptures.

25. But it came to pass that they soon became converted, and were convinced of the error which they were in, for it was made known unto them that the ᶻlaw was not yet fulfilled, and that it must be fulfilled in every whit; yea, the word came unto them that it must be fulfilled; yea, that one jot or tittle should not pass away till it should all be fulfilled; therefore in this same year were they brought to a knowledge of their error and did confess their faults.

26. And thus the ninety and second year did pass away, bringing glad tidings unto the people because of the signs which did come to pass, according to the words of the prophecy of all the holy prophets.

27. And it came to pass that the ninety and third year did also pass away in peace, save it were for the ²ᵃGadianton robbers, who dwelt upon the mountains, who did infest the land; for so strong were their holds and their secret places that the people could not overpower them; therefore they did commit many murders, and did do much slaughter among the people.

28. And it came to pass that in the ninety and fourth year they began to increase in a great degree, because there were many dissenters of the Nephites who did flee unto them, which did cause much sorrow unto those Nephites who did remain in the land.

29. And there was also a cause of much sorrow among the Lamanites; for behold, they had many children who did grow up and began to wax strong in years, that they became for themselves, and were led away by some who were Zoramites, by their lyings and their flattering words, to join those Gadianton robbers.

30. And thus were the Lamanites afflicted also, and began to decrease as to their faith and righteousness, because of the wickedness of the rising generation.

CHAPTER 2.

Nephite degeneracy—White Lamanites—Both peoples unite for defence against robbers and murderers.

1. And it came to pass that thus passed away the ninety and fifth year also, and the people began to forget ᵃthose signs and wonders which they had heard, and began to be less and less astonished at a sign or a wonder from heaven, insomuch that they

---

y, see *u*, 2 Ne. 9. *z*, see *o*, 2 Ne. 25. 2*a*, He. 2:11—13, CHAP. 2: *a*, He. 14:3—7.
3 Ne. 1:8, 13—21.   A. D. 3—5.

began to be hard in their hearts, and blind in their minds, and began to disbelieve all which they had heard and seen—

2. Imagining up some vain thing in their hearts, that it was wrought by men and by the power of the devil, to lead away and deceive the hearts of the people; and thus did Satan get possession of the hearts of the people again, insomuch that he did blind their eyes and lead them away to believe that the doctrine of Christ was a foolish and a vain thing.

3. And it came to pass that the people began to wax strong in wickedness and abominations; and they did not believe that there should be any more signs or wonders given; and Satan did go about, leading away the hearts of the people, tempting them and causing them that they should do great wickedness in the land.

4. And thus did pass away the ninety and sixth year; and also the ninety and seventh year; and also the ninety and eighth year; and also the ninety and ninth year;

5. And also an hundred years had passed away since the days of *b*Mosiah, who was king over the people of the Nephites.

6. And six hundred and nine years had passed away since Lehi left Jerusalem.

7. And nine years had passed away from the time when the *c*sign was given, which was spoken of by the prophets, that Christ should come into the world.

8. Now the Nephites began to *d*reckon their time from this period when the sign was given, or from the coming of Christ; therefore, nine years had passed away.

9. And Nephi, who was the father of Nephi, who had the charge of the records, *e*did not return to the land of *f*Zarahemla, and could nowhere be found in all the land.

10. And it came to pass that the people did still remain in wickedness, notwithstanding the much preaching and prophesying which was sent among them; and thus passed away the tenth year also; and the eleventh year also passed away in iniquity.

11. And it came to pass in the thirteenth year there began to be wars and contentions throughout all the land; for the *g*Gadianton robbers had become so numerous, and did slay so many of the people, and did lay waste so many cities, and did spread so much death and carnage throughout the land, that it became expedient that all the people, both the Nephites and the Lamanites, should take up arms against them.

12. Therefore, all the Lamanites who had become converted unto the Lord did unite with their brethren, the Nephites, and were compelled, for the safety of their lives and their women and their children, to take up arms against those Gadianton robbers, yea, and *h*also to maintain their rights, and the privileges of their church and of their worship, and their freedom and their liberty.

13. And it came to pass that before this thirteenth year had passed away the Nephites were threatened with utter destruction because of this war, which had become exceedingly sore.

14. And it came to pass that those Lamanites who had united

---

b, Mos. 29:46, 47. *c*, see *a*. *d*, ver. 7. *e*, 3 Ne. 1:2, 3. *f*, Om. 13. *g*, He. 2:11—13. *h*, see *m*, Mos. 29.

A. D. 10—14.

with the Nephites were numbered among the Nephites;

15. And ʲtheir curse was taken from them, and their skin became ʲwhite like unto the Nephites;

16. And their young men and their daughters became exceedingly fair, and they were numbered among the Nephites, and were called Nephites. And thus ended the thirteenth year.

17. And it came to pass in the commencement of the fourteenth year, the war between the ᵏrobbers and the people of Nephi did continue and did become exceedingly sore; nevertheless, the people of Nephi did gain some advantage of the robbers, insomuch that they did drive them back out of their lands into the mountains and into their secret places.

18. And thus ended the fourteenth year. And in the *fifteenth year they did come forth against the people of Nephi; and because of the wickedness of the people of Nephi, and their many contentions and dissensions, the Gadianton robbers did gain many advantages over them.

19. And thus ended the fifteenth year, and thus were the people in a state of many afflictions; and the sword of destruction did hang over them, insomuch that they were about to be smitten down by it, and this because of their iniquity.

CHAPTER 3.

Lachoneus, governor of the land, receives epistle from Giddianhi, the robber chieftain—Surrender demanded—Lachoneus ignores demand and prepares for defence.

1. And now it came to pass that in the sixteenth year from the coming of Christ, ᵃLachoneus, the governor of the land, received an epistle from the leader and the governor of this band of robbers; and these were the words which were written, saying:

2. Lachoneus, most noble and chief governor of the land, behold, I write this epistle unto you, and do give unto you exceeding great praise because of your firmness, and also the firmness of your people, in maintaining that which ye suppose to be your ᵇright and liberty; yea, ye do stand well, as if ye were supported by the hand of a god, in the defence of your liberty, and your property, and your country, or that which ye do call so.

3. And it seemeth a pity unto me, most noble Lachoneus, that ye should be so foolish and vain as to suppose that ye can stand against so many brave men who are at my command, who do now at this time stand in their arms, and do await with great anxiety for the word—Go down upon the Nephites and destroy them.

4. And I, knowing of their unconquerable spirit, having proved them in the field of battle, and knowing of their everlasting hatred towards you because of the many wrongs which ye have done unto them, therefore if they should come down against you they would visit you with utter destruction.

5. Therefore I have written this epistle, sealing it with mine own hand, feeling for your welfare, because of your firmness in that which ye believe to be right, and your noble spirit in the field of battle.

6. Therefore I write unto you, desiring that ye would yield up unto this my people, your cities,

---

i, see *d,* 1 Ne. 2. *j,* see *f,* 2 Ne. 30. *k,* He. 2:11—13. Chap. 3: *a,* 3 Ne. 1:1. *b,* see *m,* Mos. 29. *A. D 15.

your lands, and your possessions, rather than that they should visit you with the sword and that destruction should come upon you.

7. Or in other words, yield yourselves up unto us, and unite with us and become acquainted with our ^csecret works, and become our brethren that ye may be like unto us—not our slaves, but our brethren and partners of all our substance.

8. And behold, I swear unto you, if ye will do this, with an oath, ye shall not be destroyed; but if ye will not do this, I swear unto you with an oath, that on the morrow month I will command that my armies shall come down against you, and they shall not stay their hand and shall spare not, but shall slay you, and shall let fall the sword upon you even until ye shall become extinct.

9. And behold, I am Giddianhi; and I am the governor of this the ^dsecret society of Gadianton; which society and the works thereof I know to be good; and they are of ancient date and they have been handed down unto us.

10. And I write this epistle unto you, Lachoneus, and I hope that ye will deliver up your lands and your possessions, without the shedding of blood, that this my people may recover their rights and government, who have dissented away from you because of your wickedness in retaining from them their rights of government, and except ye do this, I will avenge their wrongs. I am Giddianhi.

11. And now it came to pass when Lachoneus received this epistle he was exceedingly astonished, because of the boldness of Giddianhi demanding the possession of the land of the Nephites, and also of threatening the people and avenging the wrongs of those that had received no wrong, save it were they had wronged themselves by dissenting away unto those wicked and abominable robbers.

12. Now behold, this Lachoneus, the governor, was a just man, and could not be frightened by the demands and the threatenings of a robber; therefore he did not hearken to the epistle of Giddianhi, the governor of the robbers, but he did cause that his people should cry unto the Lord for strength against the time that the robbers should come down against them.

13. Yea, he sent a proclamation among all the people, that they should ^egather together their women, and their children, their flocks and their herds, and all their substance, save it were their land, unto one place.

14. And he caused that ^ffortifications should be built round about them, and the strength thereof should be exceeding great. And he caused that armies, both of the Nephites and of the Lamanites, or of all them who were numbered among the Nephites, should be placed as guards round about to watch them, and to guard them from the robbers day and night.

15. Yea, he said unto them: As the Lord liveth, except ye repent of all your iniquities, and cry unto the Lord, ye will in nowise be delivered out of the hands of those ^gGadianton robbers.

16. And so great and marvel-

c, see *i*, 2 Ne. 10.   *d*, see *i*, 2 Ne. 10.   *e*, vers. 22—24.   *f*, see *c*, Al. 48.   *g*, He. 2:11—13.   A. D. 16.

ous were the words and prophecies of Lachoneus that they did cause fear to come upon all the people; and they did exert themselves in their might to do according to the words of Lachoneus.

17. And it came to pass that Lachoneus did appoint chief captains over all the armies of the Nephites, to command them at the time that the robbers should come down out of the wilderness against them.

18. Now the chiefest among all the captains and the great commander of all the armies of the Nephites was appointed, and his name was ^{h}Gidgiddoni.

19. Now it was the custom among all the Nephites to appoint for their chief captains, (save it were in their times of wickedness) some one that had the spirit of revelation and also prophecy; therefore, this Gidgiddoni was a great prophet among them, as also was the chief judge.

20. Now the people said unto Gidgiddoni: Pray unto the Lord, and let us go up upon the mountains and into the wilderness, that we may fall upon the robbers and destroy them in their own lands.

21. But Gidgiddoni saith unto them: The Lord forbid; for if we should go up against them the Lord would deliver us into their hands; therefore we will prepare ourselves in the center of our lands, and we will gather all our armies together, and we will not go against them, but we will wait till they shall come against us; therefore as the Lord liveth, if we do this he will deliver them into our hands.

22. And it came to pass in the *seventeenth year, in the latter end of the year, the proclamation of ^{i}Lachoneus had gone forth throughout all the face of the land, and they had taken their ^{j}horses, and their ^{k}chariots, and their cattle, and all their flocks, and their herds, and their grain, and all their substance, and did march forth by thousands and by tens of thousands, until they had all gone forth to the place which ^{l}had been appointed that they should gather themselves together, to defend themselves against their enemies.

23. And the land which was appointed was the ^{m}land of Zarahemla and the ^{n}land Bountiful, yea, to the line which was between the land Bountiful and the land ^{o}Desolation.

24. And there were a great many thousand people who were called Nephites, who did gather themselves together in this land. Now Lachoneus did cause that they should gather themselves together in the land ^{p}southward, because of the great curse which was upon the ^{q}land northward.

25. And they did ^{r}fortify themselves against their enemies; and they did dwell in one land, and in one body, and they did fear the words which had been spoken by Lachoneus, insomuch that they did repent of all their sins; and they did put up their prayers unto the Lord their God, that he would deliver them in the time that their enemies should come down against them to battle.

26. And they were exceedingly sorrowful because of their enemy. And ^{s}Gidgiddoni did cause that they should make weapons of

---

h, vers. 20, 21, 26. 3 Ne. 4:13, 24, 26. *i*, 3 Ne. 1:1. *j*, see *m*, 1 Ne. 18. *k*, see *l*, Al. 18. *l*, vers. 13, 23, 24. *m*, Om. 13. *n*, see 2*k*, Al. 22. *o*, see 2*l*, Al. 22. *p*, see *n*, Al. 46. *q*, see *p*, Al. 46. *r*, see *c*, Al. 48. *s*, see *h*. * A. D. 17.

war of 'every kind, and they should be strong with armor, and with shields, and with bucklers, after the manner of his instruction.

CHAPTER 4.

The robbers beaten and their leader slain—His successor, Zemnarihah, hanged—Gidgiddoni's military prowess.

1. And it came to pass that in the latter end of the eighteenth year those ^aarmies of robbers had prepared for battle, and began to come down and to sally forth from the hills, and out of the mountains, and the wilderness, and their strongholds, and their secret places, and began to take possession of the lands, both which were in the land ^bsouth and which were in the land ^cnorth, and began to take possession of all the lands which had been ^ddeserted by the Nephites, and the cities which had been left desolate.

2. But behold, there were no wild beasts nor game in those lands which had been deserted by the Nephites, and there was no game for the robbers ^esave it were in the wilderness.

3. And the robbers could not exist save it were in the wilderness, for the want of food; for the Nephites had left their lands desolate, and had gathered their flocks and their herds and all their substance, and they were in ^fone body.

4. Therefore, there was no chance for the robbers to plunder and to obtain food, save it were to come up in open battle against the Nephites; and the Nephites being in one body, and having so great a number, and having ^greserved for themselves provisions, and ^hhorses and cattle, and flocks of every kind, that they might subsist for the space of seven years, in the which time they did hope to destroy the robbers from off the face of the land; and thus the eighteenth year did pass away.

5. And it came to pass that in the nineteenth year Giddianhi found that it was expedient that he should go up to battle against the Nephites, for there was no way that they could subsist save it were to plunder and rob and murder.

6. And they durst not spread themselves upon the face of the land insomuch that they could raise grain, lest the Nephites should come upon them and slay them; therefore Giddianhi gave commandment unto his armies that in this year they should go up to battle against the Nephites.

7. And it came to pass that they did come up to battle; and it was in the sixth month; and behold, great and terrible was the day that they did come up to battle; and they were girded about after the manner of robbers; and they had a lamb-skin about their loins, and they were dyed in blood, and their heads were shorn, and they had headplates upon them; and great and terrible was the appearance of the armies of Giddianhi, because of their armor, and because of their being dyed in blood.

8. And it came to pass that the armies of the Nephites, when they saw the appearance of the army of Giddianhi, had all fallen to the earth, and did lift their cries to the Lord their God, that he would spare them and deliver them out of the hands of their enemies.

---

t, see 2*p*, Al. 43.   CHAP. 4: *a*, He. 2:11—13.   *b*, see *n*, Al. 46.   *c*, see *p*, Al. 46.   *d*, 3 Ne. 3:13, 14, 22—24.   *e*, see *m*, 1 Ne. 18.   *f*, see *d*.   *g*, vers. 16—18.   *h*, see *m*, 1 Ne. 18.

A. D. 18—19.

9. And it came to pass that when the armies of Giddianhi saw this they began to shout with a loud voice, because of their joy, for they had supposed that the Nephites had fallen with fear because of the terror of their armies.

10. But in this thing they were disappointed, for the Nephites did not fear them; but they did fear their God and did supplicate him for protection; therefore, when the armies of Giddianhi did rush upon them they were prepared to meet them; yea, in the strength of the Lord they did receive them.

11. And the battle commenced in this the sixth month; and great and terrible was the battle thereof, yea, great and terrible was the slaughter thereof, insomuch that there never was known so great a slaughter among all the people of Lehi since he left Jerusalem.

12. And notwithstanding the *threatenings and the oaths which Giddianhi had made, behold, the Nephites did beat them, insomuch that they did fall back from before them.

13. And it came to pass that *Gidgiddoni commanded that his armies should pursue them as far as the borders of the wilderness, and that they should not spare any that should fall into their hands by the way; and thus they did pursue them and did slay them, to the borders of the wilderness, even until they had fulfilled the commandment of Gidgiddoni.

14. And it came to pass that Giddianhi, who had stood and fought with boldness, was pursued as he fled; and being weary because of his much fighting he was overtaken and slain. And thus was the end of Giddianhi the robber.

15. And it came to pass that the armies of the Nephites did return again to their place of security. And it came to pass that this nineteenth year did pass away, and the robbers did not come again to battle; neither did they come again in the twentieth year.

16. And in the *twenty and first year they did not come up to battle, but they came up on all sides to lay siege round about the people of Nephi; for they did suppose that if they should cut off the people of Nephi from their lands, and should hem them in on every side, and if they should cut them off from all their outward privileges, that they could cause them to yield themselves up according to their wishes.

17. Now they had appointed unto themselves another leader, whose name was Zemnarihah; therefore it was Zemnarihah that did cause that this siege should take place.

18. But behold, this was an advantage to the Nephites; for it was impossible for the robbers to lay siege sufficiently long to have any effect upon the Nephites, because of *their much provision which they had laid up in store.

19. Because of the scantiness of provisions among the robbers —for behold, they had nothing save it were meat for their subsistence, which meat they did obtain in the wilderness;

20. And it came to pass that the wild game became scarce in the wilderness—insomuch that the robbers were about to perish with hunger.

21. And the Nephites were con-

---

i, 3 Ne. 3:4—10. *j*, see *h*, 3 Ne. 3. *k*, ver. 4. * A. D. 21.

tinually marching out by day and by night, and falling upon their armies, and cutting them off by thousands and by tens of thousands.

22. And thus it became the desire of the people of Zemnarihah to withdraw from their design, because of the great destruction which came upon them by night and by day.

23. And it came to pass that Zemnarihah did give command unto his people that they should withdraw themselves from the siege, and march into the furthermost parts of the land ^{l}northward.

24. And now, Gidgiddoni being aware of their design, and knowing of their weakness because of the want of food, and the great slaughter which had been made among them, therefore he did send out his armies in the night-time, and did cut off the way of their retreat, and did place his armies in the way of their retreat.

25. And this did they do in the night-time, and got on their march beyond the robbers, so that on the morrow, when the robbers began their march, they were met by the armies of the Nephites both in their front and in their rear.

26. And the robbers who were on the south were also cut off in their places of retreat. And all these things were done by command of Gidgiddoni.

27. And there were many thousands who did yield themselves up prisoners unto the Nephites, and the remainder of them were slain.

28. And their leader, Zemnarihah, was taken and hanged upon a tree, yea, even upon the top thereof until he was dead. And when they had hanged him until he was dead they did fell the tree to the earth, and did cry with a loud voice, saying:

29. May the Lord preserve his people in righteousness and in holiness of heart, that they may cause to be felled to the earth all who shall seek to slay them because of power and ^{m}secret combinations, even as this man hath been felled to the earth.

30. And they did rejoice and cry again with one voice, saying: May the God of Abraham, and the God of Isaac, and the God of Jacob, protect this people in righteousness, so long as they shall call on the name of their God for protection.

31. And it came to pass that they did break forth, all as one, in singing, and praising their God for the great thing which he had done for them, in preserving them from falling into the hands of their enemies.

32. Yea, they did cry: Hosanna to the Most High God. And they did cry: Blessed be the name of the Lord God Almighty, the Most High God.

33. And their hearts were swollen with joy, unto the gushing out of many tears, because of the great goodness of God in delivering them out of the hands of their enemies; and they knew it was because of their repentance and their humility that they had been delivered from an everlasting destruction.

CHAPTER 5.

Nephites repent and seek to end works of wickedness—Mormon's account of himself and of the plates kept by him—Another allusion to the gathering of Israel.

1. And now behold, there was

---

l, see p, Al. 46. m, see i, 2 Ne. 10.   A. D. 21—22.

3 NEPHI, 5.

not a living soul among all the people of the Nephites who did doubt in the least the words of all the holy prophets who had spoken; for they knew that it must needs be that they must be fulfilled.

2. And they knew that it must be expedient that Christ had come, because of the many signs which had been given, according to the words of the prophets; and because of the things which had come to pass already they knew that it must needs be that all things should come to pass according to that which had been spoken.

3. Therefore they did forsake all their sins, and their abominations, and their whoredoms, and did serve God with all diligence day and night.

4. And now it came to pass that when they had taken all the robbers prisoners, insomuch that none did escape who were not slain, they did cast their prisoners into prison, and did cause the word of God to be preached unto them; and as many as would repent of their sins and enter into a covenant that they would murder no more were set at liberty.

5. But as many as there were who did not enter into a covenant, and who did still continue to have those *a*secret murders in their hearts, yea, as many as were found breathing out threatenings against their brethren were condemned and punished according to the law.

6. And thus they did put an end to all those wicked, and secret, and abominable combinations, in the which there was so much wickedness, and so many murders committed.

7. And thus had the twenty and second year passed away, and the twenty and third year also, and the twenty and fourth, and the twenty and fifth; and thus had *^btwenty and five years passed away.

8. And there had many things transpired which, in the eyes of some, would be great and marvelous; nevertheless, they cannot all be written in this book; yea, *^cthis book cannot contain even a hundredth part of what was done among so many people in the space of twenty and five years;

9. But behold there are *^drecords which do contain all the proceedings of this people; and a shorter but true account was given by Nephi.

10. Therefore I have made my record of these things according to the *^erecord of Nephi, which was engraven on the plates which were called the *^fplates of Nephi.

11. And behold, I do make the record on *^gplates which I have made with mine own hands.

12. And behold, I am called Mormon, being called after the *^hland of Mormon, the land in which *ⁱAlma did establish the church among the people, yea, the first church which was established among them after their transgression.

13. Behold, I am a disciple of Jesus Christ, the Son of God. I have been called of him to declare his word among his people, that they might have everlasting life.

14. And it hath become expedient that I, according to the will of God, that the prayers of those

---

a, see *i*, 2 Ne. 10. *b*, 3 Ne. 2:8. *c*, vers. 10, 11. W. of Morm. 5—7, 9. He. 3:14. *d*, He. 3:13, 15, 16. *e*, He. 2:14. *f*, see *f*, 1 Ne. 1. *g*, vers. 14—18. W. of Morm. 1—11. He. 3:13—17. Morm. 1:1. 3:16—22. 5:9, 12, 13. 7:8—10. 8:5, 12—16. *h*, see *b*, Mos. 18. *i*, Mos. 18. • A. D. 21—26.

who have gone hence, who were the holy ones, should be fulfilled according to their faith, should make a record of these things which have been done—

15. Yea, a ^{k}small record of that which hath taken place from the time that Lehi left Jerusalem, even down until the present time.

16. Therefore I do make my record from the accounts which have been given by those who were before me, until the commencement of my day;

17. And then I do make a ^{l}record of the things which I have seen with mine own eyes.

18. And I know the record which I make to be a just and a true record; nevertheless there are many things which, according to our language, we are not able to write.

19. And now I make an end of my saying, which is of myself, and proceed to give my account of the things which have been before me.

20. I am Mormon, and a pure descendant of Lehi. I have reason to bless my God and my Savior Jesus Christ, that he brought our fathers out of the land of Jerusalem, (and no one knew it save it were himself and those whom he brought out of that land) and that he hath given me and my people so much knowledge unto the salvation of our souls.

21. Surely he hath blessed the house of Jacob, and hath been merciful unto the seed of Joseph.

22. And ^{m}insomuch as the children of Lehi have kept his commandments he hath blessed them and prospered them according to his word.

23. Yea, and surely shall he again bring a ^{n}remnant of the seed of Joseph to the knowledge of the Lord their God.

24. And as surely as the Lord liveth, will he gather in from the four quarters of the earth ^{o}all the remnant of the seed of Jacob, who are scattered abroad upon all the face of the earth.

25. And as he hath covenanted with all the house of Jacob, even so shall the covenant wherewith he hath covenanted with the house of Jacob be fulfilled in his own due time, unto the restoring all the house of Jacob unto the knowledge of the covenant that he hath covenanted with them.

26. And then shall they know their Redeemer, who is Jesus Christ, the Son of God; and then shall they be gathered in from the four quarters of the earth unto their own lands, from whence they have been dispersed; yea, as the Lord liveth so shall it be. Amen.

CHAPTER 6.

The people are prospered—Pride, wealth, and class distinctions follow—The church rent by dissension—Deeds of darkness.

1. And now it came to pass that the people of the Nephites did all return to their own lands in the *twenty and sixth year, every man, with his family, his flocks and his herds, his ^{a}horses and his cattle, and all things whatsoever did belong unto them.

2. And it came to pass that they had not eaten up all their provisions; therefore they did take with them all that they had not devoured, of all their grain of every kind, and their gold, and their silver, and all their

---

k, see g. l, Morm. 1—7. m, see h, 2 Ne. 1. n, see g, 2 Ne. 3. o, see e, 1 Ne. 15.
CHAP. 6: a, see m, 1 Ne. 18. *A. D. 26.

precious things, and they did return to their own lands and their possessions, both on the north and on the south, both on the *b*land northward and on the *c*land southward.

3. And they granted unto those robbers who had *d*entered into a covenant to keep the peace, of the band who were desirous to remain Lamanites, lands, according to their numbers, that they might have, with their labors, wherewith to subsist upon; and thus they did establish peace in all the land.

4. And they began again to prosper and to wax great; and the twenty and sixth and seventh years passed away, and there was great order in the land; and they had formed their laws according to equity and justice.

5. And now there was nothing in all the land to hinder the people from prospering continually, except they should fall into transgression.

6. And now it was *e*Gidgiddoni, and the *f*judge, Lachoneus, and those who had been appointed leaders, who had established this great peace in the land.

7. And it came to pass that there were many cities built anew, and there were many old cities repaired.

8. And there were *g*many highways cast up, and many roads made, which led from city to city, and from land to land, and from place to place.

9. And thus passed away the twenty and eighth year, and the people had continual peace.

10. But it came to pass in the twenty and ninth year there began to be some disputings among the people; and some were lifted up unto pride and boastings because of their exceeding great riches, yea, even unto great persecutions;

11. For there were many *h*merchants in the land, and also many *i*lawyers, and many officers.

12. And the people began to be distinguished by ranks, according to their riches and their chances for learning; yea, some were ignorant because of their poverty, and others did receive great learning because of their riches.

13. Some were lifted up in pride, and others were exceedingly humble; some did return railing for railing, while others would receive railing and persecution and all manner of afflictions, and would not turn and revile again, but were humble and penitent before God.

14. And thus there became a great inequality in all the land, insomuch that the church began to be broken up; yea, insomuch that in the thirtieth year the church was broken up in all the land save it were among a few of the Lamanites who were converted unto the true faith; and they would not depart from it, for they were firm, and steadfast, and immovable, willing with all diligence to keep the commandments of the Lord.

15. Now the cause of this iniquity of the people was this—Satan had great power, unto the stirring up of the people to do all manner of iniquity, and to the puffing them up with pride, tempting them to seek for power, and authority, and riches, and the vain things of the world.

---

b, see *p*, Al. 46. *c*, see *n*, Al. 46. *d*, 3 Ne. 5:4. *e*, see *h*, 3 Ne. 3. *f*, 3 Ne. 1:1. 3:1. *g*, He. 14:24. 3 Ne. 8:13. *h*, He. 6:8. *i*, vers. 21, 22, 27. Al. 10:14, 15, 17, 27, 32. 14:5, 18, 23 27.

A. D. 29—30.

16. And thus Satan did lead away the hearts of the people to do all manner of iniquity; therefore they had enjoyed peace but a few years.

17. And thus, in the commencement of the ʲthirtieth year —the people having been delivered up for the space of a long time to be carried about by the temptations of the devil whithersoever he desired to carry them, and to do whatsoever iniquity he desired they should—and thus in the commencement of this, the thirtieth year, they were in a state of awful wickedness.

18. Now they did not sin ignorantly, for they knew the will of God concerning them, for it had been taught unto them; therefore they did wilfully rebel against God.

19. And now it was in the days of Lachoneus, the son of ᵏLachoneus, for Lachoneus did fill the seat of his father and did govern the people that year.

20. And there began to be men inspired from heaven and sent forth, standing among the people in all the land, preaching and testifying boldly of the sins and iniquities of the people, and testifying unto them concerning the redemption which the Lord would make for his people, or in other words, the resurrection of Christ; and they did testify boldly of his death and sufferings.

21. Now there were many of the people who were exceeding angry because of those who testified of these things; and those who were angry were chiefly the chief judges, and they who had been ˡhigh priests and ᵐlawyers; yea, all those who were lawyers were angry with those who testified of these things.

22. Now there was no ⁿlawyer nor ᵒjudge nor ᵒhigh priest that could have power to condemn any one to death save their condemnation was signed by the ᵖgovernor of the land.

23. Now there were many of those who testified of the things pertaining to Christ who testified boldly, who were taken and put to death secretly by the judges, that the knowledge of their death came not unto the ᑫgovernor of the land until after their death.

24. Now behold, this was contrary to the laws of the land, that any man should be put to death except they had power from the governor of the land—

25. Therefore a complaint came up unto the land of ʳZarahemla, to the governor of the land, against these judges who had condemned the prophets of the Lord unto death, not according to the law.

26. Now it came to pass that they were taken and brought up before the judge, to be judged of the crime which they had done, according to the law which had been given by the ˢpeople.

27. Now it came to pass that those judges had many friends and kindreds; and the remainder, yea, even almost all the ᵗlawyers and the ᵘhigh priests, did gather themselves together, and unite with the kindreds of those judges who were to be tried according to the law.

28. And they did enter into a covenant one with another, yea, even into that covenant which was given by them of old, which covenant was given and admin-

j, 3 Ne. 2:8. *k*, 3 Ne. 1:1. *l*, see *g*, Mos. 26. *m*, see *i*. *n*, see *i*. *o*, see *g*, Mos. 26. *p*, ver. 19. *q*, ver. 19. *r*, Om. 13. *s*, see *e*, Mos. 29. *t*, see *i*. *u*, see *g*, Mos. 26.

A. D. 29—30.

istered by the devil, to combine against all righteousness.

29. Therefore they did combine against the people of the Lord, and enter into a covenant to destroy them, and to deliver those who were guilty of murder from the grasp of justice, which was about to be administered according to the law.

30. And they did set at defiance the law and the rights of their country; and they did covenant one with another to destroy the governor, and to establish a king over the land, that the land should no more be at *v*liberty but should be subject unto kings.

CHAPTER 7.

Chief judge murdered and government overthrown—Division into tribes—King Jacob—Nephi's powerful ministry.

1. Now behold, I will show unto you that they did not establish a king over the land; but in this same year, yea, the thirtieth year, they did destroy upon the judgment-seat, yea, did murder the chief judge of the land.

2. And the people were divided one against another; and they did separate one from another into tribes, every man according to his family and his kindred and friends; and thus they did destroy the government of the land.

3. And every tribe did appoint a chief or a leader over them; and thus they became tribes and leaders of tribes.

4. Now behold, there was no man among them save he had much family and many kindreds and friends; therefore their tribes became exceeding great.

5. Now all this was done, and there were no wars as yet among them; and all this iniquity had come upon the people because they did yield themselves unto the power of Satan.

6. And the regulations of the government were destroyed, because of the *a*secret combination of the friends and kindreds of those who murdered the prophets.

7. And they did cause a great contention in the land, insomuch that the more righteous part of the people had nearly all become wicked; yea, there were but few righteous men among them.

8. And thus *b*six years had not passed away since the more part of the people had turned from their righteousness, like the dog to his vomit, or like the sow to her wallowing in the mire.

9. Now this *c*secret combination, which had brought so great iniquity upon the people, did gather themselves together, and did place at their head a man whom they did call Jacob;

10. And they did call him their king; therefore he became a king over this wicked band; and he was one of the chiefest who had given his voice against the prophets who testified of Jesus.

11. And it came to pass that they were not so strong in number as the tribes of the people, who were united together save it were their leaders did establish their laws, every one according to his tribe; nevertheless they were enemies; notwithstanding they were not a righteous people, yet they were united in the hatred of those who had entered into a covenant to destroy the government.

12. Therefore, Jacob seeing that their enemies were more nu-

v, see *m*, Mos. 29.   Chap. 7: *a*, see *i*, 2 Ne. 10.   *b*, 3 Ne. 5:7.   *c*, see *i*, 2 Ne. 10.

A. D. 29—30.

merous than they, he being the king of the band, therefore he commanded his people that they should take their flight into the northernmost part of the land, and there build up unto themselves a kingdom, until they were joined by dissenters, (for he flattered them that there would be many dissenters) and they become sufficiently strong to contend with the tribes of the people; and they did so.

13. And so speedy was their march that it could not be impeded until they had gone forth out of the reach of the people. And thus ended the thirtieth year; and thus were the affairs of the people of Nephi.

14. And it came to pass in the thirty and first year that they were divided into tribes, every man according to his family, kindred and friends; nevertheless they had come to an agreement that they would not go to war one with another; but they were not united as to their laws, and their manner of government, for they were established according to the minds of those who were their chiefs and their leaders. But they did establish very strict laws that one tribe should not trespass against another, insomuch that in some degree they had peace in the land; nevertheless, their hearts were turned from the Lord their God, and they did *d*stone the prophets and did cast them out from among them.

15. And it came to pass that Nephi—having been visited by angels and also the voice of the Lord, therefore having seen angels, and being eye-witness, and having had power given unto him that he might know concerning the ministry of Christ, and also being eye-witness to their *e*quick return from righteousness unto their wickedness and abominations;

16. Therefore, being grieved for the hardness of their hearts and the blindness of their minds —went forth among them in that same year, and began to testify, boldly, repentance and remission of sins through faith on the Lord Jesus Christ.

17. And he did minister many things unto them; and all of them cannot be written, and a part of them would not suffice, therefore they are not written in this book. And Nephi did minister with power and with great authority.

18. And it came to pass that they were angry with him, even because he had greater power than they, for it were not possible that they could disbelieve his words, for so great was his faith on the Lord Jesus Christ that *f*angels did minister unto him daily.

19. And in the name of Jesus did he cast out devils and unclean spirits; and even his *g*brother did he raise from the dead, after he had been stoned and suffered death by the people.

20. And the people saw it, and did witness of it, and were angry with him because of his power; and he did also do many more miracles, in the sight of the people, in the name of Jesus.

21. And it came to pass that the thirty and first year did pass away, and there were but few who were converted unto the Lord; but as many as were converted did truly signify unto the people that they had been visited by the power and Spirit of God, which

---

d, ver. 10. 3 Ne. 6:23—25. *e*, ver. 8. *f*, ver. 15. *g*, 3 Ne. 19:4. A. D. 31—32.

was in Jesus Christ, in whom they believed.

22. And as many as had ʰdevils cast out from them, and were healed of their sicknesses and their infirmities, did truly manifest unto the people that they had been wrought upon by the Spirit of God, and had been healed; and they did show forth signs also and did do some miracles among the people.

23. Thus passed away the thirty and second year also. And Nephi did cry unto the people in the commencement of the thirty and third year; and he did preach unto them repentance and remission of sins.

24. Now I would have you to remember also, that there were none who were brought unto repentance who were not ⁱbaptized with water.

25. Therefore, there were ordained of Nephi, men unto this ministry, that all such as should come unto them should be baptized with water, and this as a witness and a testimony before God, and unto the people, that they had repented and received a remission of their sins.

26. And there were many in the commencement of this year that were ʲbaptized unto repentance; and thus the more part of the year did pass away.

CHAPTER 8.

Christ's crucifixion attested by predicted signs—Tempest and earthquake, whirlwind and fire—A great and terrible destruction—Three days of darkness.

1. And now it came to pass that according to our record, and we know our record to be true, for behold, it was a ᵃjust man who did keep the record—for he truly did ᵇmany miracles in the name of Jesus; and there was not any man who could do a miracle in the name of Jesus save he were cleansed every whit from his iniquity—

2. And now it came to pass, if there was no mistake made by this man in the reckoning of our time, the ᶜthirty and third year had passed away;

3. And the people began to look with great earnestness for the sign which had been given by the prophet Samuel, the Lamanite, yea, for the time that there should be ᵈdarkness for the space of three days over the face of the land.

4. And there began to be great doubtings and disputations among the people, notwithstanding so many signs had been given.

5. And it came to pass in the ᵉthirty and fourth year, in the first month, on the fourth day of the month, there arose a great storm, such an one as never had been known in all the land.

6. And there was also a ᶠgreat and terrible tempest; and there was ᵍterrible thunder, insomuch that it did shake the whole earth as if it was about to divide asunder.

7. And there were exceeding ʰsharp lightnings, such as never had been known in all the land.

8. And the ⁱcity of Zarahemla did take fire.

9. And the ʲcity of Moroni did sink into the depths of the sea, and the inhabitants thereof were drowned.

h, ver. 19. *i*, see *u*, 2 Ne. 9. *j*, see *u*, 2 Ne. 9. CHAP. 8: *a*, 3 Ne. 23:7, 12. *b*, 3 Ne. 7:19, 20. *c*, 3 Ne. 2:8. *d*, ver. 23. 1 Ne. 19:10. He. 14:20, 27. 3 Ne. 10:9. *e*, 3 Ne. 2:8. *f*, see *v*, He. 14. *g*, see *s*, He. 14. *h*, see *k*, 1 Ne. 19. *i*, Om. 13. Al. 2:26. *j*, see *k*, Al. 50.
A. D. 32—34.

3 NEPHI, 8.

10. And the earth was carried up upon the *k*city of Moronihah, that in the place of the city there became a great mountain.

11. And there was a great and terrible destruction in the land *l*southward.

12. But behold, there was a more great and terrible destruction in the land *m*northward; for behold, the whole face of the land was changed, because of the *n*tempest and the *o*whirlwinds, and the *p*thunderings and the *q*lightnings, and the exceeding great quaking of the whole earth;

13. And the *r*highways were broken up, and the level roads were spoiled, and many smooth places *s*became rough.

14. And many great and notable cities were *t*sunk, and many were *u*burned, and many were shaken till the buildings thereof had *v*fallen to the earth, and the inhabitants thereof were slain, and the places were left desolate.

15. And there were some cities which remained; but the damage thereof was exceeding great, and there were many in them who were slain.

16. And there were some who were carried away in the *w*whirlwind; and whither they went no man knoweth, save they know that they were carried away.

17. And thus the face of the whole earth became deformed, because of the *x*tempests, and the *y*thunderings, and the *z*lightnings, and the quaking of the earth.

18. And behold, the ^{2a}rocks were rent in twain; they were broken up upon the face of the whole earth, insomuch that they were found in ^{2b}broken fragments, and in seams and in cracks, upon all the face of the land.

19. And it came to pass that when the ^{2c}thunderings, and the ^{2d}lightnings, and the ^{2e}storm, and the ^{2f}tempest, and the quakings of the earth did cease—for behold, they did last for about the space of ^{2g}three hours; and it was said by some that the time was greater; nevertheless, all these great and terrible things were done in about the space of three hours—and ^{2h}then behold, there was darkness upon the face of the land.

20. And it came to pass that there was thick darkness upon all the face of the land, insomuch that the inhabitants thereof who had not fallen could ^{2i}feel the vapor of darkness;

21. And there could be no light, because of the darkness, neither candles, neither torches; neither could there be fire kindled with their fine and exceedingly dry wood, so that there could not be any light at all;

22. And there was not any light seen, neither fire, nor glimmer, neither the sun, nor the moon, nor the stars, for so great were the mists of darkness which were upon the face of the land.

23. And it came to pass that it did last for the space of ^{2j}three days that there was no light seen; and there was great mourning and howling and weeping among all the people continually;

k, ver. 25. He. 12:17. 3 Ne. 9:5. *l*, see *n*, Al. 46. *m*, see *p*, Al. 46. *n*, see *v*, He. 14. *o*, ver. 16. 3 Ne. 10:13, 14. *p*, see *s*, He. 14. *q*, see *k*, 1 Ne. 19. *r*, see *g*, 3 Ne. 6. *s*, 1 Ne. 12:4. *t*, 1 Ne. 12:4. *u*, 1 Ne. 12:4. *v*, 1 Ne. 12:4. *w*, ver. 12. *x*, see *v*, He. 14. *y*, see *s*, He. 14. *z*, see *k*, 1 Ne. 19. 2*a*, see *t*, He. 14. 2*b*, He. 14:22. 2*c*, see *s*, He. 14. 2*d*, see *k*, 1 Ne. 19. 2*e*, ver. 5. 2*f*, see *v*, He. 14. 2*g*, Luke 23:44, 45. 2*h*, see *t*, 1 Ne. 19. 2*i*, vers. 3, 22, 23. 1 Ne. 12:5. 19:11. He. 14:20, 27. 3 Ne. 10:9. 2*j*, see *t*, 1 Ne. 19. A. D. 34.

yea, great were the groanings of the people, because of the darkness and the great destruction which had come upon them.

24. And in one place they were heard to cry, saying: O that we had repented before this great and terrible day, and then would our brethren have been spared, and they would not have been [2k]burned in that great city Zarahemla.

25. And in another place they were heard to cry and mourn, saying: O that we had repented before this great and terrible day, and had not killed and stoned the prophets, and cast them out; then would our mothers and our fair daughters, and our children have been spared, and not have been buried up in that great [2l]city Moronihah. And thus were the howlings of the people great and terrible.

CHAPTER 9.

The voice of God proclaims the extent of the disaster and declares the causes thereof—The Law of Moses fulfilled—The acceptable sacrifice of a broken heart and a contrite spirit.

1. And it came to pass that there was a [a]voice heard among all the inhabitants of the earth, upon all the face of this land, crying:

2. Wo, wo, wo unto this people; wo unto the inhabitants of the whole earth except they shall repent; for the devil laugheth, and his angels rejoice, because of the slain of the fair sons and daughters of my people; and it is because of their iniquity and abominations that they are fallen!

3. Behold, that [b]great city Zarahemla have I [c]burned with fire, and the inhabitants thereof.

4. And behold, that great [d]city Moroni have I caused to be [e]sunk in the depths of the sea, and the inhabitants thereof to be drowned.

5. And behold, that great [f]city Moronihah have I covered with earth, and the inhabitants thereof, to hide their iniquities and their abominations from before my face, that the blood of the prophets and the saints shall not come any more unto me against them.

6. And behold, the city of Gilgal have I caused to be sunk, and the inhabitants thereof to be buried up in the depths of the earth;

7. Yea, and the city of Onihah and the inhabitants thereof, and the city of Mocum and the inhabitants thereof, and the [g]city of Jerusalem and the inhabitants thereof; and waters have I caused to come up in the stead thereof, to hide their wickedness and abominations from before my face, that the blood of the prophets and the saints shall not come up any more unto me against them.

8. And behold, the city of Gadiandi, and the city of Gadiomnah, and the city of Jacob, and the city of Gimgimno, all these have I caused to be sunk, and made [h]hills and valleys in the places thereof; and the inhabitants thereof have I buried up in the depths of the earth, to hide their wickedness and abominations from before my face, that the blood of the prophets and the saints should not come up any more unto me against them.

9. And behold, that great city

2k, ver. 8. He. 13:12—14. 2l, see k. CHAP. 9: a, 1 Ne. 10:11. b, Om. 13. c, 3 Ne. 8:8. d, see k, Al. 50. e, 3 Ne. 8:9. f, see k, 3 Ne. 8. g, see b, Al. 21. h, 1 Ne. 19:11. He. 12:17. 14:23. 3 Ne. 8:10. 10:13, 14. A. D. 34.

Jacobugath, which was inhabited by the people of king Jacob, have I caused to be ⁱburned with fire because of their sins and their wickedness, which was above all the wickedness of the whole earth, because of their ʲsecret murders and combinations; for it was they that did destroy the ᵏpeace of my people and the government of the land; therefore I did cause them to be burned, to destroy them from before my face, that the ˡblood of the prophets and the saints should not come up unto me any more against them.

10. And behold, the city of Laman, and the city of Josh, and the city of Gad, and the city of Kishkumen, have I caused to be ᵐburned with fire, and the inhabitants thereof, because of their wickedness in casting out the prophets, and stoning those whom I did send to declare unto them concerning their wickedness and their abominations.

11. And because they did cast them all out, that there were none righteous among them, I did send down ⁿfire and destroy them, that their wickedness and abominations might be hid from before my face, that the blood of the prophets and the saints whom I sent among them might not cry unto me from the ground against them.

12. And many great destructions have I caused to come upon this land, and upon this people, because of their wickedness and their abominations.

13. O all ye that are spared because ye were more righteous than they, will ye not now return unto me, and repent of your sins, and be converted, that I may heal you?

14. Yea, verily I say unto you, if ye will come unto me ye shall have eternal life. Behold, mine arm of mercy is extended towards you, and whosoever will come, him will I receive; and blessed are those who come unto me.

15. Behold, I am Jesus Christ the Son of God. I ᵒcreated the heavens and the earth, and all things that in them are. I was with the Father from the beginning. ᵖI am in the Father, and the Father in me; and ᵍin me hath the Father glorified his name.

16. I came unto ʳmy own, and my own received me not. And the scriptures ˢconcerning my coming are fulfilled.

17. And as many as have received me, to them have I ᵗgiven to become the sons of God; and even so will I to as many as shall believe on my name, for behold, by me ᵘredemption cometh, and ᵛin me is the law of Moses fulfilled.

18. I ʷam the light and the life of the world. I am Alpha and Omega, the beginning and the end.

19. And ye shall offer up unto me ˣno more the shedding of blood; yea, your sacrifices and your burnt offerings shall be done away, for I will accept none of your sacrifices and your burnt offerings.

20. And ye shall offer for a sacrifice unto me a broken heart and a contrite spirit. And whoso cometh unto me with a broken heart and a contrite spirit, him

i, ver. 10. **1** Ne. 12:4. **3** Ne. 8:14. *j*, see *i*, 2 Ne. 10. *k*, 3 Ne. 7:9—13. *l*, 3 Ne. 6:23—25. 7:10. *m*, see *i*. *n*, see *i*. *o*, Mos. 3:8. 4:2. See *i*, He. 14. *p*, 3 Ne. 11:27. 19:23, 29. Eth. 3:14. *q*, 3 Ne. 11:7, 11. *r*, John 1:11. *s*, 3 Ne. 15:4, 5. *t*, John 1:12. *u*, ver. 21. 2 Ne. 31:21. Mos. 3:17. 4:7, 8. See *d*, Mos. 5. *v*, 3 Ne. 15:2—8. *w*, see *m*, Mos. 16. *x*, 3 Ne. 15:2—8. A. D. 34.

will I baptize ʸwith fire and with the Holy Ghost, even as the Lamanites, because of their faith in me at the time of ᶻtheir conversion, were baptized with fire and with the Holy Ghost, and they knew it not.

21. Behold, I have come unto the world to bring ²ᵃredemption unto the world, to save the world from sin.

22. Therefore, whoso repenteth and cometh unto me as a ²ᵇlittle child, him will I receive, for of such is the kingdom of God. Behold, for such I have laid down my life, and have taken it up again; therefore repent, and come unto me ye ends of the earth, and be saved.

CHAPTER 10.

Silence in the land—Again the voice from heaven—The darkness disperses—Only the more righteous of the people are spared.

1. And now behold, it came to pass that all the people of the land did ᵃhear these sayings, and did witness of it. And after these sayings there was silence in the land for the space of many hours;

2. For so great was the astonishment of the people that they did cease lamenting and howling for the loss of their kindred which had been slain; therefore there was silence in all the land for the space of many hours.

3. And it came to pass that there came a voice again unto the people, and all the people did hear, and did witness of it, saying:

4. O ye people of these ᵇgreat cities which have fallen, who are descendants of Jacob, yea, who are of the house of Israel, how oft have I gathered you as a hen gathereth her chickens under her wings, and have nourished you.

5. And again, how oft would I have gathered you as a hen gathereth her chickens under her wings, yea, O ye people of the house of Israel, who have fallen; yea, O ye people of the house of Israel, ye that dwell at Jerusalem, as ye that have fallen; yea, how oft would I have gathered you as a hen gathereth her chickens, and ye would not.

6. O ye house of Israel whom I have ᶜspared, how oft will I gather you as a hen gathereth her chickens under her wings, if ye will repent and return unto me with full purpose of heart.

7. But if not, O house of Israel, the places of your dwellings shall become desolate until the ᵈtime of the fulfilling of the covenant to your fathers.

8. And now it came to pass that after the people had heard these words, behold, they began to weep and howl again because of the loss of their kindred and friends.

9. And it came to pass that thus did the ᵉthree days pass away. And it was in the ᶠmorning, and the darkness dispersed from off the face of the land, and the earth did cease to tremble, and the ᵍrocks did cease to rend, and the dreadful groanings did cease, and all the tumultuous noises did pass away.

10. And the earth did cleave

y, 1 Ne. 10:17, 19, 22. 13:37. 2 Ne. 31:11—14. 17, 18. 32:2—5. 33:1, 2. Jac. 6:8. 7:12. Al. 13:28. 34:38. 36:24. He. 5:45. 3 Ne. 7:21. 11:35, 36. 12:1, 2. 15:23. 16:4, 6. 18:37. 19:9, 13, 14, 20—22. 26:17. 28:11, 18. 30:2. 4 Ne. 1, 3, 48. Morm. 1:14. 7:10. Eth. 5:4. 12:14, 23, 41. Moro. 2. 3:4. 4:3. 5:2. 6:4, 9. 7:32, 36. 8:7, 9, 23, 26. 10:4—7, 9—19. *z*, He. 5:45. Eth. 12.14. 2*a*, see *u*. 2*b*, 3 Ne. 11:37, 38. CHAP. 10: *a*, 1 Ne. 19:11. *b*, 3 Ne. 8:8—10, 24, 25. 9:3—12. *c*, vers. 12, 13. 3 Ne. 9:13. *d*, see *e*, 1 Ne. 15. *e*, see *t*, 1 Ne. 19. *f*, 3 Ne. 8:19—23. *g*, see *t*, He. 14. A. D. 34.

together again, that it stood; and the mourning, and the weeping, and the wailing of the people who were spared alive did cease; and their mourning was turned into joy, and their lamentations into the praise and thanksgiving unto the Lord Jesus Christ, their Redeemer.

11. And thus far were the ^{h}scriptures fulfilled which had been spoken by the prophets.

12. And it was the ^{i}more righteous part of the people who were saved, and it was they who received the prophets and stoned them not; and it was they who had not shed the blood of the saints, who were spared—

13. And they were spared and were ^{j}not sunk and buried up in the earth; and they were ^{k}not drowned in the depths of the sea; and they were ^{l}not burned by fire, neither were they fallen upon and crushed to death; and they were not carried away in the ^{m}whirlwind; neither were they overpowered by the ^{n}vapor of smoke and of darkness.

14. And now, whoso readeth, let him understand; he that hath the scriptures, let him ^{o}search them, and see and behold if all these deaths and destructions by ^{p}fire, and by ^{q}smoke, and by ^{r}tempests, and by ^{s}whirlwinds, and by the ^{t}opening of the earth to receive them, and all these things are not unto the fulfilling of the prophecies of many of the holy prophets.

15. Behold, I say unto you, Yea, many have testified of these things at the coming of Christ, and were slain because they testified of these things.

16. Yea, the prophet ^{u}Zenos did testify of these things, and also ^{v}Zenock spake concerning these things, because they testified particularly concerning us, who are the remnant of their seed.

17. Behold, our father Jacob also testified ^{w}concerning a remnant of the seed of Joseph. And behold, are not we a remnant of the seed of Joseph? And these things which testify of us, are they not written upon the ^{x}plates of brass which our father Lehi brought out of Jerusalem?

18. And it came to pass that in the ending of the thirty and fourth year, behold, I will show unto you that the people of Nephi who were spared, and also those who had been called Lamanites, who had been spared, did have great favors shown unto them, and great blessings poured out upon their heads, insomuch that soon after the ascension of Christ into heaven he did truly manifest himself unto them—

19. ^{y}Showing his body unto them, and ministering unto them; and an account of his ministry shall be ^{z}given hereafter. Therefore for this time I make an end of my sayings.

Jesus Christ did show himself unto the people of Nephi, as the multitude were gathered together in the land Bountiful, and did minister unto them; and on this wise did he show himself unto them.

Comprising chapters 11 to 26 inclusive.

CHAPTER 11.

The Eternal Father proclaims the Christ—The Resurrected Christ ap-

---

h, 1 Ne. 12:4, 5. 19:10—12. He. 14:20—28. i, ver. 13. 3 Ne. 9:13. j, 3 Ne. 8:9. 9:4—8. k, 3 Ne. 8:9. 9:4, 7. l, 3 Ne. 8:8, 24. 9:3, 9. 10. m, ver. 14. 3 Ne. 8:16. n, see 2i, 3 Ne. 8. o, see h. p, see l. q, see 2i, 3 Ne. 8. r, see v, He. 14. s, see m. t, see h, 3 Ne. 9. u, see h, 1 Ne. 19. v, see g, 1 Ne. 19. w, Al. 46:24—26. 3 Ne. 20:22. x, see a, 1 Ne. 3. y, see b, 1 Ne. 12. z, 3 Ne. chaps. 11—30. A. D. 34.

3 NEPHI, 11.

pears—The multitude permitted to feel his wounds—Mode of baptism prescribed—Contention and disputation forbidden—Christ the rock.

1. And now it came to pass that there were a great multitude gathered together, of the people of Nephi, round about the ^atemple which was in the ^bland Bountiful; and they were marveling and wondering one with another, and were showing one to another the ^cgreat and marvelous change which had taken place.

2. And they were also conversing about this Jesus Christ, of whom the ^dsign had been given concerning his death.

3. And it came to pass that while they were thus conversing one with another, they heard a voice as if it came out of heaven; and they cast their eyes round about, for they understood not the voice which they heard; and it was not a harsh voice, neither was it a loud voice; nevertheless, and notwithstanding it being a ^esmall voice it did pierce them that did hear to the center, insomuch that there was no part of their frame that it did not cause to quake; yea, it did pierce them to the very soul, and did cause their hearts to burn.

4. And it came to pass that again they heard the voice, and they understood it not.

5. And again the third time they did hear the voice, and did open their ears to hear it; and their eyes were towards the sound thereof; and they did look steadfastly towards heaven, from whence the sound came.

6. And behold, the third time they did understand the voice which they heard; and it said unto them:

7. Behold my Beloved Son, in whom I am well pleased, in whom I ^fhave glorified my name—hear ye him.

8. And it came to pass, as they understood they cast their eyes up again towards heaven; and behold, they saw a ^gMan descending out of heaven; and he was clothed in a white robe; and he came down and stood in the midst of them; and the eyes of the whole multitude were turned upon him, and they durst not open their mouths, even one to another, and wist not what it meant, for they thought it was an angel that had appeared unto them.

9. And it came to pass that he stretched forth his hand and spake unto the people, saying:

10. Behold, I am Jesus Christ, whom the prophets testified shall come into the world.

11. And behold, ^hI am the light and the life of the world; and I have drunk out of that ⁱbitter cup which the Father hath given me, and have ^jglorified the Father in taking upon me the ^ksins of the world, in the which I have suffered the will of the Father in all things from the beginning.

12. And it came to pass that when Jesus had spoken these words the whole multitude fell to the earth; for they remembered that it had been ^lprophesied among them that Christ should show himself unto them after his ascension into heaven.

13. And it came to pass that the Lord spake unto them saying:

14. Arise and come forth unto

---

a, see *h*, 2 Ne. 5. *b*, see 2k, Al. 22. *c*, 3 Ne. 8:11—14. *d*, He. 14:20—27. 3 Ne. 8:5—25. 9:10. *e*, He. 5:30, 31, 46, 47. *f*, ver. 11. 3 Ne. 9:15. *g*, see *b*, 1 Ne. 12. *h*, see *m*, Mos. 16. *i*, John 18:11. *j*, ver. 7. 3 Ne. 9:15. *k*, ver. 14. * *r. * 21. John 1:29. *l*, see *b*, 1 Ne. 12. A. D. 34.

me, that ye may ᵐthrust your hands into my side, and also that ye may feel the prints of the nails in my hands and in my feet, that ye may know that I am the God of Israel, and the ⁿGod of the whole earth, and have been slain for the ᵒsins of the world.

15. And it came to pass that the multitude went forth, and ᵖthrust their hands into his side, and did feel the prints of the nails in his hands and in his feet; and this they did do, going forth one by one until they had all gone forth, and did see with their eyes and did feel with their hands, and did know of a surety and did bear record, that it was he, of whom it was written by the ᑫprophets, that should come.

16. And when they had all gone forth and had witnessed for themselves, they did cry out with one accord, saying:

17. Hosanna! Blessed be the name of the ʳMost High God! And they did fall down at the feet of Jesus, and did worship him.

18. And it came to pass that he spake unto Nephi (for ˢNephi was among the multitude) and he commanded him that he should come forth.

19. And Nephi arose and went forth, and bowed himself before the Lord and did ᵗkiss his feet.

20. And the Lord commanded him that he should arise. And he arose and stood before him.

21. And the Lord said unto him: I give unto you ᵘpower that ye shall ᵛbaptize this people when I am ʷagain ascended into heaven.

22. And again the Lord called others, and said unto them likewise; and he gave unto them ˣpower to baptize. And he said unto them: On this wise shall ye baptize; and there shall be ʸno disputations among you.

23. Verily I say unto you, that whoso repenteth of his sins through your words, and desireth to be baptized in my name, on this wise shall ye baptize them— Behold, ye shall go down and ᶻstand in the water, and in my name shall ye baptize them.

24. And now behold, these are the words which ye shall say, calling them by name, saying:

25. Having ²ᵃauthority given me of Jesus Christ, ²ᵇI baptize you in the name of the Father, and of the Son, and of the Holy Ghost. Amen.

26. And then shall ye immerse them in the water, and come forth again out of the water.

27. And after this manner shall ye baptize in my name; for behold, verily I say unto you, ²ᶜthat the Father, and the Son, and the Holy Ghost are one; ²ᵈand I am in the Father, and the Father in me, and the Father and I are ²ᵉone.

28. And according as I have commanded you ²ᶠthus shall ye baptize. And there shall be ²ᵍno disputations among you, as there have hitherto been; neither shall there be disputations among you concerning the points of my doctrine, as there have hitherto been.

29. For verily, verily I say unto you, he that hath the spirit of ²ʰcontention is not of me, but is of the devil, who is the father of contention, and he stirreth up the hearts of men to contend with anger, one with another.

30. Behold, this is not my doc-

m, ver. 15. John 20:27. *n*, see 2*b*, Mos. 7. *o*, see *k*. *p*, ver. 14. *q*, ver. 10. *r*, see 2*b*, Mos. 7. *s*, 3 Ne. 1:2, 3, 10. 7:15, 20, 23—26. *t*, 3 Ne. 17:10. *u*, see *g*, Mos. 18. *v*, see *u*, 2 Ne. 9. *w*, 3 Ne. 18:39. *x*, see *g*, Mos. 18. *y*, vers. 28—30. 3 Ne. 18:34. *z*, Mos. 18:12. 3 Ne. 19:10—13. 2*a*, see *g*, Mos. 18. 2*b*, see *u*, 2 Ne. 9. 2*c*, see *k*, 2 Ne. 31. 2*d*, see *p*, 3 Ne. 9. 2*e*, see *k*, 2 Ne. 31. 2*f*, vers. 25, 26. 2*g*, vers. 22, 29, 30. 2*h*, vers. 22, 28, 30.

A. D. 34.

trine, to stir up the hearts of men with anger, one against another; but this is my doctrine, that ²ᶦsuch things should be done away.

31. Behold, verily, verily, I say unto you, I will declare unto you my doctrine.

32. And this is my doctrine, and it is the doctrine which the Father hath given unto me; ²ʲand I bear record of the Father, and the Father beareth record of me, and the Holy Ghost beareth record of the Father and me; and I bear record that the Father commandeth all men, everywhere, to repent and believe in me.

33. And whoso believeth in me, and is ²ᵏbaptized, the same shall be saved; and they are they who shall inherit the kingdom of God.

34. And whoso believeth not in me, and is not baptized, shall be damned.

35. Verily, verily, I say unto you, that this is my doctrine, ²ᶦand I bear record of it from the Father; and ²ᵐwhoso believeth in me believeth in the Father also; and unto him will the Father ²ⁿbear record of me, for he will visit him ²ᵒwith fire and with the Holy Ghost.

36. And thus will the Father ²ᵖbear record of me, and the Holy Ghost will bear record unto him of the Father and me; ²ᑫfor the Father, and I, and the Holy Ghost are one.

37. And again I say unto you, ye must repent, and become as a little child, and be ²ʳbaptized in my name, or ye can in nowise receive these things.

38. And again I say unto you, ye must repent, and be baptized in my name, and become as a ²ˢlittle child, or ye can in nowise inherit the kingdom of God.

39. Verily, verily, I say unto you, that this is my doctrine, and whoso buildeth upon this buildeth upon my rock, and ²ᵗthe gates of hell shall not prevail against them.

40. And whoso shall declare more or less than this, and establish it for my doctrine, the same cometh of evil, and is not built upon my rock; but he buildeth upon a ²ᵘsandy foundation, and the gates of hell stand open to receive such when the floods come and the winds beat upon them.

41. Therefore, go forth unto this people, and declare the words which I have spoken, unto the ends of the earth.

CHAPTER 12.

The Savior's teachings to the Nephites—He calls and commissions the twelve disciples—His words to the multitude—The Sermon on the Mount retold—Compare Matthew 5.

1. And it came to pass that when Jesus had spoken these words unto ᵃNephi, and to those who had been called, (now the number of them who had been called, and received ᵇpower and authority to baptize, was ᶜtwelve) and behold, he stretched forth his hand unto the multitude, and cried unto them, saying: Blessed are ye if ye shall give heed unto the words of these twelve whom I have chosen from among you to minister unto you, and to be your servants; and unto them I have ᵈgiven power that they may baptize you with water; and after

2i, vers. 22, 28, 29. 2j, vers. 35, 36. 3 Ne. 28:11. Eth. 5:4. 2k, see u, 2 Ne. 9.
2l, vers. 32, 36. 2m, Eth. 4:12. 2n, vers. 32, 36. 2o, see y, 3 Ne. 9. 2p, see 2j.
2q, see k, 2 Ne. 31. 2r, see u, 2 Ne. 9. 2s, see 2b, 3 Ne. 9. 2t, Matt. 16:18. 3 Ne.
18:12, 13. 2u, Matt. 7:24—27. 3 Ne. 14:24—27. 18:12, 13. CHAP. 12: a, see s,
3 Ne. 11. b, see g, Mos. 18. c, 3 Ne. 13:25. 15:11. 18:1—17. 26—39. 19:4—36.
20:1—6. 26:17. Chaps. 27, 28. 4 Ne. 1, 5, 13, 14, 30—33, 37, 44, 46. Morm. 1:13.
3:19. 8:10, 11. 9:22, 25. Eth. 12:17. Moro. 2:3. d, see g, Mos. 18. A. D. 34.

that ye are baptized with water, behold, I will baptize you ᶜwith fire and with the Holy Ghost; therefore blessed are ye if ye shall believe in me and be baptized, after that ye have seen me and know that I am.

2. And again, more blessed are they who shall believe in your words because that ye shall testify that ye have seen me, and that ye know that I am. Yea, blessed are they who shall believe in your words, and come down into the depths of humility and be ᶠbaptized, for they shall be visited ᵍwith fire and with the Holy Ghost, and shall receive a remission of their sins.

3. Yea, blessed are the ʰpoor in spirit who come unto me, for theirs is the kingdom of heaven.

4. And again, blessed are all they that mourn, for they shall be comforted.

5. And blessed are the meek, for they shall inherit the earth.

6. And blessed are all they who do hunger and thirst after righteousness, for they shall be ⁱfilled with the Holy Ghost.

7. And blessed are the merciful, for they shall obtain mercy.

8. And blessed are all the pure in heart, for they shall see God.

9. And blessed are all the peacemakers, for they shall be called the children of God.

10. And blessed are all they who are ʲpersecuted for my name's sake, for theirs is the kingdom of heaven.

11. And blessed are ye when men shall revile you and persecute, and shall say all manner of evil against you falsely, for my sake;

12. For ye shall have ᵏgreat joy and be exceeding glad, for great shall be your reward in heaven; for so persecuted they the prophets who were before you.

13. Verily, verily, I say unto you, I give unto you to be the salt of the earth; but if the salt shall lose its savor wherewith ˡshall the earth be salted? The salt shall be thenceforth good for nothing, but to be cast out and to be trodden under foot of men.

14. Verily, verily, I say unto you, I give unto you to be the light of this people. A city that is set on a hill cannot be hid.

15. Behold, do men light a candle and put it under a bushel? Nay, but on a candlestick, and it giveth light to all that are in the house;

16. Therefore let your light so shine before this people, that they may see your good works and glorify your Father who is in heaven.

17. Think not that I am come to destroy the law or the prophets. I am not come to destroy but to fulfil;

18. For verily I say unto you, one jot nor one tittle ᵐhath not passed away from the law, but in me it hath all been fulfilled.

19. And behold, I have given you the law and the commandments of my Father, that ye shall believe in me, and that ye shall repent of your sins, and come unto me with a ⁿbroken heart and a contrite spirit. Behold, ye have the commandments before you, and the ᵒlaw is fulfilled.

20. Therefore come unto me and be ye saved; for verily I say unto you, that except ye shall keep my ᵖcommandments, which

---

c, see *y*, 3 Ne. 9. *f*, see *u*, 2 Ne. 9. *g*, see *y*, 3 Ne. 9. *h*, Matt. 5:3. *i*, Matt. 5:6. *j*, Matt. 5:10. *k*, Matt. 5:12. *l*, Matt. 5:13. *m*, Matt. 5:18. *n*, 3 Ne. 9:20. *o*, vers. 18, 46. 3 Ne. 9:17. 15:4—10. *p*, ver. 19. 3 Ne. 15:10.   A. D. 34.

I have commanded you at this time, ye shall in no case enter into the kingdom of heaven.

21. Ye have heard that it hath been said by them of old time, and it is also written before you, that thou shalt not kill, and whosoever shall kill shall be in danger of the qjudgment of God;

22. But I say unto you, that whosoever is angry with his brother shall be in danger of rhis judgment. And whosoever shall say to his brother, Raca, shall be in danger of the council; and whosoever shall say, Thou fool, shall be in danger of hell fire.

23. Therefore, if ye shall come unto me, or shall sdesire to come unto me, and rememberest that thy brother hath aught against thee—

24. Go thy way unto thy brother, and first be reconciled to thy brother, and then come unto me with full purpose of heart, and I will receive you.

25. Agree with thine adversary quickly while thou art in the way with him, lest at any time he shall get thee, and thou shalt be cast into prison.

26. Verily, verily, I say unto thee, thou shalt by no means come out thence until thou hast paid the uttermost tsenine. And while ye are in prison can ye pay even one senine? Verily, verily, I say unto you, Nay.

27. Behold, it is written by them of old time, that thou shalt not commit adultery;

28. But I say unto you, that whosoever looketh on a woman, to lust after her, hath committed adultery already in his heart.

29. Behold, I give unto you a commandment, that ye suffer unone of these things to enter into your heart;

30. For it is better that ye should deny yourselves of these things, wherein ye will take up your cross, than that ye should be cast into hell.

31. It hath been written, that whosoever shall put away his wife, let him give her a writing of divorcement.

32. Verily, verily, I say unto you, that whosoever vshall put away his wife, saving for the cause of fornication, causeth her to commit adultery; and whoso shall marry her who is divorced committeth adultery.

33. And again it is written, thou shalt not forswear thyself, but shalt perform unto the Lord thine oaths;

34. But verily, verily, I say unto you, swear not at all; neither by heaven, for it is God's throne;

35. Nor by the earth, for it is his footstool;

36. Neither shalt thou swear by the head, because thou canst not make one hair black or white;

37. But let your communication be Yea, yea; Nay, nay; for whatsoever cometh of more than these is evil.

38. And behold, it is written, an eye for an eye, and a tooth for a tooth;

39. But I say unto you, that ye shall not resist evil, but whosoever shall smite thee on thy right cheek, turn to him the other also;

40. And if any man will sue thee at the law and take away thy coat, let him have thy cloak also;

41. And whosoever shall com-

---

q, Matt. 5:21. *r*, Matt. 5:22. *s*, Matt. 5:23, 24. *t*, see *c*, Al. 11. *u*, D. & C. 42:23. 43:10, 17. See *i*, 2 Ne. 28. *v*, Matt. 5:32. Mark 10:11, 12. Luke 16:18.
A. D. 34.

pel thee to go a mile, go with him twain.

42. Give to him that asketh thee, and from him that would borrow of thee turn thou not away.

43. And behold it is written also, that thou shalt love thy neighbor and hate thine enemy;

44. But behold I say unto you, love your enemies, bless them that curse you, do good to them that hate you, and pray for them who despitefully use you and persecute you;

45. That ye may be the children of your Father who is in heaven; for he maketh his sun to rise on the evil and on the good.

46. Therefore those things which were of old time, which were under the law, in me are ʷall fulfilled.

47. Old things ˣare done away, and all things have become new.

48. Therefore I would that ye should be perfect even ʸas I, or your Father who is in heaven is perfect.

CHAPTER 13.

The Savior's sermon to the Nephites continued—His commandments to the twelve—Compare Matthew 6.

1. Verily, verily, I say that I would that ye should do alms unto the poor; but take heed that ye do not your alms before men to be seen of them; otherwise ye have no reward of your Father who is in heaven.

2. Therefore, when ye shall do your alms do not sound a trumpet before you, as will hypocrites do in the ᵃsynagogues and in the streets, that they may have glory of men. Verily I say unto you, they have their reward.

3. But when thou doest alms let not thy left hand know what thy right hand doeth;

4. That thine alms may be in secret; and thy Father who seeth in secret, himself shall reward thee openly.

5. And when thou prayest thou shalt not do as the hypocrites, for they love to pray, standing in the synagogues and in the corners of the streets, that they may be seen of men. Verily I say unto you, they have their reward.

6. But thou, when thou prayest, enter into thy closet, and when thou hast shut thy door, pray to thy Father who is in secret; and thy Father, who seeth in secret, shall reward thee openly.

7. But when ye pray, use not vain repetitions, as the heathen, for they think that they shall be heard for their much speaking.

8. Be not ye therefore like unto them, for your Father knoweth what things ye have need of before ye ask him.

9. After this manner therefore pray ye: Our Father who art in heaven, hallowed be thy name.

10. Thy will be done on earth as it is in heaven.

11. And forgive us our debts, as we forgive our debtors.

12. And lead us not into temptation, but deliver us from evil.

13. For thine is the kingdom, and the power, and the glory, forever. Amen.

14. For, if ye forgive men their trespasses your heavenly Father will also forgive you;

15. But if ye forgive not men their trespasses neither will your Father forgive your trespasses.

16. Moreover, when ye ᵇfast be not as the hypocrites, of a sad countenance, for they disfigure their faces that they may appear

---

w, see *o. x*, 3 Ne. 15:2, 3. *y*, Matt. 5:48. 3 Ne. 19:25—29. 27:27.
CHAP. 13: *a*, see *u*, Al. 16. *b*, see *t*, Mos. 27. A. D. 34.

unto men to fast. Verily I say unto you, they have their reward.

17. But thou, when thou fastest, anoint thy head, and wash thy face;

18. That thou appear not unto men to fast, but unto thy Father, who is in secret; and thy Father, who seeth in secret, shall reward thee openly.

19. Lay not up for yourselves treasures upon earth, where moth and rust doth corrupt, and thieves break through and steal;

20. But lay up for yourselves treasures in heaven, where neither moth nor rust doth corrupt, and where thieves do not break through nor steal.

21. For where your treasure is, there will your heart be also.

22. The light of the body is the eye; if, therefore, thine eye be single, thy whole body shall be full of light.

23. But if thine eye be evil, thy whole body shall be full of darkness. If, therefore, the light that is in thee be darkness, how great is that darkness!

24. No man can serve two masters; for either he will hate the one and love the other, or else he will hold to the one and despise the other. Ye cannot serve God and Mammon.

25. And now it came to pass that when Jesus had spoken these words he looked upon the twelve whom he had chosen, and said unto them: Remember the words which I have spoken. For behold, ^cye are they whom I have chosen to minister unto this people. Therefore I say unto you, take no thought for your life, what ye shall eat, or what ye shall drink; nor yet for your body, what ye shall put on. Is not the life more than meat, and the body than raiment?

26. Behold the fowls of the air, for they sow not, neither do they reap nor gather into barns; yet your heavenly Father feedeth them. Are ye not much better than they?

27. Which of you by taking thought can add one cubit unto his stature?

28. And why take ye thought for raiment? Consider the lilies of the field how they grow; they toil not, neither do they spin;

29. And yet I say unto you, that even Solomon, in all his glory, was not arrayed like one of these.

30. Wherefore, if God so clothe the grass of the field, which today is, and tomorrow is cast into the oven, even so will he clothe you, if ye are not of little faith.

31. Therefore take no thought, saying, What shall we eat? or, What shall we drink? or, Wherewithal shall we be clothed?

32. For your heavenly Father knoweth that ye have need of all these things.

33. But seek ye first the kingdom of God and his righteousness, and all these things shall be added unto you.

34. Take therefore no thought for the morrow, for the morrow shall take thought for the things of itself. Sufficient is the day unto the evil thereof.

CHAPTER 14.

The Savior's sermon continued— Further instructions to the multitude —Compare Matthew 7.

1. And now it came to pass that when Jesus had spoken these words he turned again to the multitude, and did open his mouth unto them again, saying:

c, Matt. 6:25. See c, 3 Ne. 12.

A. D. 34.

Verily, verily, I say unto you, Judge not, that ye be not judged.

2. For with what judgment ye judge, ye shall be judged; and with what measure ye mete, it shall be measured to you again.

3. And why beholdest thou the mote that is in thy brother's eye, but considerest not the beam that is in thine own eye?

4. Or how wilt thou say to thy brother: Let me pull the mote out of thine eye—and behold, a beam is in thine own eye?

5. Thou hypocrite, first cast the beam out of thine own eye; and then shalt thou see clearly to cast the mote out of thy brother's eye.

6. Give not that which is holy unto the dogs, neither cast ye your pearls before swine, lest they trample them under their feet, and turn again and rend you.

7. *a*Ask, and it shall be given unto you; seek, and ye shall find; knock, and it shall be opened unto you.

8. For every one that asketh, receiveth; and he that seeketh, findeth; and to him that knocketh, it shall be opened.

9. Or what man is there of you, who, if his son ask bread, will give him a stone?

10. Or if he ask a fish, will he give him a serpent?

11. If ye then, being evil, know how to give good gifts unto your children, how much more shall your Father who is in heaven give good things to them that ask him?

12. Therefore, all things whatsoever ye would that men should do to you, do ye even so to them, for this is the law and the prophets.

13. Enter ye in at the *b*strait gate; for wide is the gate, and broad is the way, which leadeth to destruction, and many there be who go in thereat;

14. Because strait is the gate, and narrow is the way, which leadeth unto life, and few there be that find it.

15. Beware of false prophets, who come to you in sheep's clothing, but inwardly they are ravening wolves.

16. Ye shall know them by their fruits. Do men gather grapes of thorns, or figs of thistles?

17. Even so every good tree bringeth forth good fruit; but a corrupt tree bringeth forth evil fruit.

18. A good tree cannot bring forth evil fruit, neither a corrupt tree bring forth good fruit.

19. Every tree that bringeth not forth good fruit is hewn down, and cast into the fire.

20. Wherefore, by their fruits ye shall know them.

21. Not every one that saith unto me, Lord, Lord, shall enter into the kingdom of heaven; but he that doeth the will of my Father who is in heaven.

22. Many will say to me in that day: Lord, Lord, have we not prophesied in thy name, and in thy name have cast out devils, and in thy name done many wonderful works?

23. And then will I profess unto them: I never knew you; depart from me, ye that work iniquity.

24. Therefore, whoso heareth these sayings of mine and doeth them, I will liken him unto a wise man, who built his house upon a rock—

25. And the *c*rain descended, and the floods came, and the

---

a, 3 Ne. 27:20. *b*, see 2*a*, 2 Ne. 9. 3 Ne. 27:33. *c*, see *c*, Al. 26. A. D. 34.

winds blew, and beat upon that house; and it fell not, for it was founded upon a rock.

26. And every one that heareth these sayings of mine and doeth them not shall be likened unto a foolish man, who built his house upon the sand—

27. And the rain descended, and the floods came, and the winds blew, and beat upon that house; and it fell, and great was the fall of it.

CHAPTER 15.

The Law of Moses superseded—The Giver of the Law fulfils the Law—The sheep of another fold.

1. And now it came to pass that when Jesus had ended these sayings he cast his eyes round about on the multitude, and said unto them: Behold, ye have heard the things which I *a*taught before I ascended to my Father; therefore, whoso remembereth these sayings of mine and doeth them, him will I *b*raise up at the last day.

2. And it came to pass that when Jesus had said these words he perceived that there were some among them who marveled, and wondered what he would concerning the *c*law of Moses; for they understood not the *d*saying that old things had passed away, and that all things had become new.

3. And he said unto them: Marvel not that I said unto you that old things had passed away, and that all things had become new.

4. Behold, I say unto you that the *e*law is fulfilled that was given unto Moses.

5. Behold, *f*I am he that gave the law, and I am he who covenanted with my people Israel; therefore, the *g*law in me is fulfilled, for I have come to fulfil the law; therefore it hath an end.

6. Behold, I do *h*not destroy the prophets, for as many as have not been fulfilled in me, verily I say unto you, shall all be fulfilled.

7. And because I said unto you that *i*old things have passed away, I do not destroy that which hath been spoken concerning things which are to come.

8. For behold, the *j*covenant which I have made with my people is not all fulfilled; but the *k*law which was given unto Moses hath an end in me.

9. Behold, I am the law, and the *l*light. Look unto me, and endure to the end, and ye shall live; for unto him that *m*endureth to the end wi'l I give eternal life.

10. Behold, I have given unto you the commandments; therefore keep my commandments. And this is the law and the prophets, for they truly testified of me.

11. And now it came to pass that when Jesus had spoken these words, he said unto *n*those twelve whom he had chosen:

12. Ye are my disciples; and ye are a light unto this people, who are a remnant of the house of Joseph.

13. And behold, *o*this is the land of your inheritance; and the Father hath given it unto you.

14. And not at any time hath the Father given me commandment that I should tell it unto your brethren at Jerusalem.

15. Neither at any time hath the Father given me command-

a, Matt. chaps. 5—7. *b*, see *p*, Mos. 23. *c*, see *o*, 2 Ne. 25. *d*, 3 Ne. 12:46, 47. *e*, 3 Ne. 9:17. *f*, 1 Cor. 10:4. *g*, 3 Ne. 12:46, 47. *h*, vers. 7, 8. *i*, 3 Ne. 20:11, 12. 23:1—3. *i*, 3 Ne. 12:46, 47. *j*, 3 Ne. 5:24—26. 16:5. See *c*, 1 Ne. 15. *k*, see *o*, 2 Ne. 25. *l*, see *m*, Mos. 16. *m*, see 2 Ne. 31:20. *n*, 3 Ne. 12:1. *o*, see *k*, 1 Ne. 18.

A. D. 34.

ment that I should tell unto them concerning the *p*other tribes of the house of Israel, whom the Father hath led away out of the land.

16. This much did the Father command me, that I should tell unto them:

17. That *q*other sheep I have which are not of this fold; them also I must bring, and they shall hear my voice; and there shall be one fold, and one shepherd.

18. And now, because of stiffneckedness and unbelief they understood not my word; therefore I was commanded to say no more of the Father concerning this thing unto them.

19. But, verily, I say unto you that the Father hath commanded me, and I tell it unto you, that ye were separated from among them because of their iniquity; therefore it is because of their iniquity that they know not of you.

20. And verily, I say unto you again that the *r*other tribes hath the Father separated from them; and it is because of their iniquity that they know not of them.

21. And verily I say unto you, that *s*ye are they of whom I said: Other sheep I have which are not of this fold; them also I must bring, and they shall hear my voice; and there shall be one fold, and one shepherd.

22. And they understood me not, for they supposed it had been the Gentiles; for they understood not that the Gentiles should be *t*converted through their preaching.

23. And they understood me not that I said they shall hear my voice; and they understood me not that the Gentiles should not at any time hear my voice—that I should not manifest myself unto them *u*save it were by the Holy Ghost.

24. But behold, ye have both heard my voice, and seen me; and ye are my *v*sheep, and ye are numbered among those whom the Father hath given me.

CHAPTER 16.

Yet another fold to hear the Savior —Blessings upon the believing Gentiles—The state of those who reject the Gospel—The prophet Isaiah cited.

1. And verily, verily, I say unto you that I have *a*other sheep, which are not of this land, neither of the land of Jerusalem, neither in any parts of that land round about whither I have been to minister.

2. For they of whom I speak are they who have *b*not as yet heard my voice; neither have I at any time manifested myself unto them.

3. But I have received a commandment of the Father that I shall go unto them, and that they shall *c*hear my voice, and shall be numbered among my sheep, that there may be one fold and one shepherd; therefore I go to show myself unto them.

4. And I command you that ye shall write these sayings after I am gone, that if it so be that my people at Jerusalem, they who have seen me and been with me in my ministry, do not ask the Father in my name, that they may receive a knowledge of you by the Holy Ghost, and also of the *d*other tribes whom they know not of, that these sayings which ye shall write shall be kept and shall be manifested *e*unto the

p, ver. 20. 2 Ne. 21:12. 3 Ne. 16:1—4. 17:4. *q*, vers. 21—24. John 10:16. *r*, see *p*. *s*, ver. 17. *t*, Acts 10:34—43. *u*, Acts 10:44, 48. *v*, vers. 17, 21. Chap. 16: *a*, see *p*, 3 Ne. 15. *b*, 3 Ne. 15:17, 21, 23, 24. *c*, see *b*. *d*, see *p*, 3 Ne. 15. *c*, see *c*, 2 Ne. 27.   A. D. 34.

Gentiles, that through the ᶠfulness of the Gentiles, the remnant of their seed, who shall be scattered forth upon the face of the earth because of their unbelief, may be brought in, or may be brought to a knowledge of me, their Redeemer.

5. And ᵍthen will I gather them in from the four quarters of the earth; and then will I fulfil the ʰcovenant which the Father hath made unto all the people of the house of Israel.

6. And blessed are the Gentiles, because of their belief in me, in and ⁱof the Holy Ghost, which witnesses unto them ʲof me and of the Father.

7. Behold, because of their belief in me, saith the Father, and because of the unbelief of you, O house of Israel, in the ᵏlatter day shall the truth come unto the Gentiles, that the fulness of these things shall be made known unto them.

8. But ˡwo, saith the Father, unto the unbelieving of the Gentiles—for notwithstanding they have come forth upon the face of this land, and have scattered my people who are of the house of Israel; and my people who are of the house of Israel have been cast out from among them, and have been trodden under feet by them;

9. And because of the mercies of the Father unto the Gentiles, and also the judgments of the Father upon my people who are of the house of Israel, verily, verily, I say unto you, that ᵐafter all this, and I have caused my people who are of the house of Israel to be smitten, and to be afflicted, and to be slain, and to be cast out from among them, and to become hated by them, and to become a hiss and a byword among them—

10. And thus commandeth the Father that I should say unto you: At that day when the Gentiles shall sin against my ⁿgospel, and shall be lifted up in the pride of their hearts above ᵒall nations, and above all the people of the whole earth, and shall be filled with all manner of lyings, and of deceits, and of mischiefs, and all manner of hypocrisy, and murders, and ᵖpriestcrafts, and ᵠwhoredoms, and of ʳsecret abominations; and if they shall do all those things, and shall reject the ˢfulness of my gospel, behold, saith the Father, I will ᵗbring the fulness of my gospel from among them.

11. And then will I remember my covenant which I have made unto my people, O house of Israel, and I will bring my gospel unto ᵘthem.

12. And I will show unto thee, O house of Israel, that the Gentiles shall not have power over you; but I will remember my ᵛcovenant unto you, O house of Israel, and ye shall come unto the ʷknowledge of the fulness of my gospel.

13. But if the Gentiles will repent and return unto me, saith the Father, behold they shall be ˣnumbered among my people, O house of Israel.

14. And I will not suffer my people, who are of the house of Israel, to go through among

---

f, 1 Ne. 10:14. See *c*, 2 Ne. 27. *g*, see *e*, 1 Ne. 15. *h*, see *j*, 3 Ne. 15. *i*, see *u*, 3 Ne. 15. *j*, 3 Ne. 11:32, 35, 36. *k*, see *c*, 2 Ne. 27. *l*, 2 Ne. 28:32. See *d*, 1 Ne. 14. *m*, see *j*, 2 Ne. 26. *n*, 1 Ne. 13:34, 36. 3 Ne. 27:9—12. *o*, Morm. 8:35—41. *p*, 2 Ne. 26:29. *q*, see *i*, 2 Ne. 28. *r*, see *t*, 2 Ne. 10. *s*, see *n*. *t*, 3 Ne. 20:27, 28. *u*, see *v*, 3 Ne. 20:29. *v*, see *j*, 3 Ne. 15. *w*, He. 15:13. *x*, 2 Ne. 10:18, 19. 3 Ne. 21:22—25. Chap. 30.

A. D. 34.

them, and tread them down, saith the Father.

15. But if they will not turn unto me, and hearken unto my voice, I will suffer them, yea, I will suffer my people, O house of Israel, that they shall go through among them, and shall tread them down, and they shall be as *y*salt that hath lost its savor, which is thenceforth good for nothing but to be cast out, and to be trodden under foot of my people, O house of Israel.

16. Verily, verily, I say unto you, thus hath the Father commanded me—that *z*I should give unto this people this land for their inheritance.

17. And then the words of the prophet Isaiah shall be fulfilled, which say:

18. ²*ª*Thy watchmen shall lift up the voice; with the voice together shall they sing, for they shall see eye to eye when the Lord shall bring again Zion.

19. Break forth into joy, sing together, ye waste places of Jerusalem; for the Lord hath comforted his people, he hath redeemed Jerusalem.

20. The Lord hath made bare his holy arm in the eyes of all the nations; and all the ends of the earth shall see the salvation of God.

CHAPTER 17.

The Savior's instructions continued—The lost tribes—The Savior heals the sick and blesses little children—A marvelous and touching scene.

1. Behold, now it came to pass that when Jesus had spoken these words he looked round about again on the multitude, and he said unto them: Behold, my time is at hand.

2. I perceive that ye are weak, that ye cannot understand all my words which I am commanded of the Father to speak unto you at this time.

3. Therefore, go ye unto your homes, and ponder upon the things which I have said, and ask of the Father, in my name, that ye may understand, and prepare your minds for the morrow, and I come unto you again.

4. But now I *ª*go unto the Father, and also to show myself unto the *b*lost tribes of Israel, for they are not lost unto the Father, for he knoweth whither he hath taken them.

5. And it came to pass that when Jesus had thus spoken, he cast his eyes round about again on the multitude, and beheld they were in tears, and did look steadfastly upon him as if they would ask him to tarry a little longer with them.

6. And he said unto them: Behold, my bowels are filled with compassion towards you.

7. *c*Have ye any that are sick among you? Bring them hither. Have ye any that are lame, or blind, or halt, or maimed, or leprous, or that are withered, or that are deaf, or that are afflicted in any manner? Bring them hither and I will heal them, for I have compassion upon you; my bowels are filled with mercy.

8. For I perceive that ye desire that I should show unto you what I have done unto your brethren at Jerusalem, for I see that your faith is *d*sufficient that I should heal you.

9. And it came to pass that when he had thus spoken, all the multitude, with one accord, did go forth with their sick and their afflicted, and their lame, and with

y, 3 Ne. 12:13. *z,* see *o,* 3 Ne. 15. 2*a,* Isa. 52:8—10. CHAP. 17: *a,* 3 Ne. 18:39. *b,* see *p,* 3 Ne. 15. *c,* vers. 9, 10. *d,* 2 Ne. 27:23. Eth. 12:12. A. D. 34.

their blind, and with their dumb, and with all them that were afflicted in any manner; and he did *heal them every one as they were brought forth unto him.

10. And they did all, both they who had been healed and they who were whole, bow down at his feet, and did worship him; and as many as could come for the multitude did ′kiss his feet, insomuch that they did bathe his feet with their tears.

11. And it came to pass that he commanded that their *little children should be brought.

12. So they brought their little children and set them down upon the ground round about him, and Jesus stood in the midst; and the multitude gave way till they had all been brought unto him.

13. And it came to pass that when they had all been brought, and Jesus stood in the midst, he commanded the multitude that they should ʰkneel down upon the ground.

14. And it came to pass that when they had knelt upon the ground, Jesus groaned within himself, and said: Father, I am ⁱtroubled because of the wickedness of the people of the house of Israel.

15. And when he had said these words, he himself also ʲknelt upon the earth; and behold he prayed unto the Father, and the things which he prayed cannot be written, and the multitude did bear record who heard him.

16. And after this manner do they bear record: ᵏThe eye hath never seen, neither hath the ear heard, before, so great and marvelous things as we saw and heard Jesus speak unto the Father;

17. And no tongue can speak, neither can there be written by any man, neither can the hearts of men conceive so great and marvelous things as we both saw and heard Jesus speak; and no one can conceive of the joy which filled our souls at the time we heard him pray for us unto the Father.

18. And it came to pass that when Jesus had made an end of praying unto the Father, he arose; but so great was the joy of the multitude that they were overcome.

19. And it came to pass that Jesus spake unto them, and bade them arise.

20. And they arose from the earth, and he said unto them: Blessed are ye because of your faith. And now behold, my joy is full.

21. And when he had said these words, he wept, and the multitude bare record of it, and ˡhe took their little children, one by one, and blessed them, and prayed unto the Father for them.

22. And when he had done this he wept again;

23. And he spake unto the multitude, and said unto them: Behold your little ones.

24. And as they looked to behold they cast their eyes towards heaven, and they saw the heavens open, and they saw angels descending out of heaven as it were in the midst of fire; and they came down and encircled those little ones about, and they ᵐwere encircled about with fire; and the angels did minister unto them.

25. And the multitude did see

e, 3 Ne. 26:15. *f*, 3 Ne. 11:19. *g*, vers. 12, 21, 23, 24. 3 Ne. 26:14, 16. *h*, 3 Ne. 19:6, 16, 17. *i*, 3 Ne. 27:32. *j*, 3 Ne. 19:19, 27. *k*, 3 Ne. 19:32—34. *l*, see *g*. *m*, see *g*. A. D. 34.

and hear and bear record; and they know that their record is true for they all of them did see and hear, every man for himself; and they were in number about two thousand and five hundred souls; and they did consist of men, women, and children.

CHAPTER 18.

Sacrament of bread and wine instituted among the Nephites—Necessity of prayer emphasized—Authority given to confer the Holy Ghost.

1. And it came to pass that Jesus commanded his ^adisciples that they should bring forth ^bsome bread and wine unto him.

2. And while they were gone for bread and wine, he commanded the multitude that they should sit themselves down upon the earth.

3. And when the disciples had come with bread and wine, he took of the bread and brake and blessed it; and he gave unto the disciples and commanded that they should eat.

4. And when they had eaten and were filled, he commanded that they should give unto the multitude.

5. And when the multitude had eaten and were filled, he said unto the disciples: Behold there shall one be ^cordained among you, and to him will I give power that he shall break bread and bless it and give it unto the people of my church, unto all those who shall believe and ^dbe baptized in my name.

6. And this shall ye always observe to do, even as I have done, even as I have broken bread and blessed it and given it unto you.

7. And this shall ye do in ^eremembrance of my body, which I have shown unto you. And it shall be a testimony unto the Father that ye do always remember me. And if ye do ^falways remember me ye shall have my Spirit to be with you.

8. And it came to pass that when he said these words, he commanded his disciples that they should take of the wine of the cup and drink of it, and that they should also give unto the multitude that they might drink of it.

9. And it came to pass that they did so, and did drink of it and were filled; and they gave unto the multitude, and they did drink, and they were filled.

10. And when the disciples had done this, Jesus said unto them: Blessed are ye for this thing which ye have done, for this is fulfilling my commandments, and this doth witness unto the Father that ye are willing to do that which I have commanded you.

11. And this shall ye always do to those who repent and are ^gbaptized in my name; and ye shall do it in ^hremembrance of my blood, which I have shed for you, that ye may witness unto the Father that ye do always remember me. And if ye do ⁱalways remember me ye shall have my Spirit to be with you.

12. And I give unto you a commandment that ye shall do these things. And if ye shall always do these things blessed are ye, for ye are built upon my rock.

13. But whoso among you shall do more or less than these ^jare not built upon my rock, but are built upon a sandy foundation; and when the rain descends,

---

a, see *c*, 3 Ne. 12. *b*, vers. 2—14. 28—34. 3 Ne. 20:3—9. 26:13. 4 Ne. 27. Morm. 9:29. Moro. chaps. 4, 5. *c*, 4 Ne. 14. See *g*, Mos. 18. Morm. 3:4. *d*, see *u*, 2 Ne. 9. *e*, ver. 11. 3 Ne. 20:8. Moro. 4:3. 5:2. *f*, ver. 11. Moro. 4:3. 5:2. *g*, see *u*, 2 Ne. 9. *h*, see *e*. *i*, see *f*. *j*, see *e*, Al. 26. A. D. 34.

and the floods come, and the winds blow, and beat upon them, they shall fall, and the gates of hell are ready open to receive them.

14. Therefore blessed are ye if ye shall keep my commandments, which the Father hath commanded me that I should give unto you.

15. Verily, verily, I say unto you, ye must watch and [k]pray always, lest ye be tempted by the devil, and ye be led away captive by him.

16. And as I have prayed among you even so shall ye pray in my church, among my people who do repent and are baptized in my name. Behold [l]I am the light; I have set an example for you.

17. And it came to pass that when Jesus had spoken these words unto his disciples, he turned again unto the multitude and said unto them:

18. Behold, verily, verily, I say unto you, ye must watch and [m]pray always lest ye enter into temptation; for Satan desireth to have you, that he may sift you as wheat.

19. Therefore ye must always pray unto the Father in my name;

20. And whatsoever ye shall ask the Father in my name, which is right, believing that ye shall receive, behold it shall be given unto you.

21. [n]Pray in your families unto the Father, always in my name, that your wives and your children may be blessed.

22. And behold, ye shall meet together oft; and ye shall not forbid any man from coming unto you when ye shall meet together, but suffer them that they may come unto you and forbid them not;

23. But ye shall pray for them, and shall not cast them out; and if it so be that they come unto you oft ye shall pray for them unto the Father, in my name.

24. Therefore, hold up your light that it may shine unto the world. Behold I am the [o]light which ye shall hold up—that which ye have seen me do. Behold ye see that I have prayed unto the Father, and ye all have witnessed.

25. And ye see that I have commanded that [p]none of you should go away, but rather have commanded that ye should come unto me, that ye might [q]feel and see; even so shall ye do unto the world; and whosoever breaketh this commandment suffereth himself to be led into temptation.

26. And now it came to pass that when Jesus had spoken these words, he turned his eyes again upon the [r]disciples whom he had chosen, and said unto them:

27. Behold verily, verily, I say unto you, I give unto you another commandment, and then I must go unto my Father that I may fulfil [s]other commandments which he hath given me.

28. And now behold, this is the commandment which I give unto you, that ye shall not suffer any one knowingly to [t]partake of my flesh and blood unworthily, when ye shall minister it;

29. For whoso eateth and drinketh my flesh and blood unworthily eateth and drinketh

---

k, see e, 2 Ne. 32. l, see m, Mos. 16. m, see e, 2 Ne. 32. n, Al. 34:21. See o, 2 Ne. 32. o, see m, Mos. 16. p, vers. 22, 23. q, 3 Ne. 11:14, 16. r, see c, 3 Ne. 12. s, 3 Ne. 16:3. t, vers. 29, 30. 3 Ne. 20:8. Morm. 9:29.   A. D. 34.

damnation to his soul; therefore if ye know that a man is unworthy to eat and drink of my flesh and blood ye shall forbid him.

30. Nevertheless, ye shall not cast him out from among you, but ye shall minister unto him and shall pray for him unto the Father, in my name; and if it so be that he repenteth and is ^ubaptized in my name, then shall ye receive him, and shall minister unto him of my flesh and blood.

31. But if he repent not he shall not be numbered among my people, that he may not destroy my people, for behold I ^vknow my sheep, and they are numbered.

32. Nevertheless, ye shall not cast him out of your ^wsynagogues, or your places of worship, for unto such shall ye continue to minister; for ye know not but what they will return and repent, and come unto me with full purpose of heart, and I shall heal them; and ye shall be the means of bringing salvation unto them.

33. Therefore, keep these sayings which I have commanded you that ye come not under condemnation; for wo unto him whom the Father condemneth.

34. And I give you these commandments because of the disputations which have been among you. And blessed are ye if ye have ^xno disputations among you.

35. And ^ynow I go unto the Father, because it is expedient that I should go unto the Father for your sakes.

36. And it came to pass that when Jesus had made an end of these sayings, he touched with his hand the disciples whom he had chosen, one by one, even until he had touched them all, and spake unto them as he touched them.

37. And the multitude heard not the words which he spake, therefore they did not bear record; but the disciples bare record that he gave them ^zpower to give the ^{2a}Holy Ghost. And I will show unto you ^{2b}hereafter that this record is true.

38. And it came to pass that when Jesus had touched them all, there came a cloud and overshadowed the multitude that they could not see Jesus.

39. And while they were overshadowed he departed from them, and ascended into heaven. And the ^{2c}disciples saw and did bear record that he ascended again into heaven.

CHAPTER 19.

Names of the Nephite twelve—Their baptism—The Holy Ghost given—The Savior's second visitation—An ineffable outpouring of prayer.

1. And now it came to pass that when Jesus had ^aascended into heaven, the multitude did disperse, and every man did take his wife and his children and did return to his own home.

2. And it was noised abroad among the people immediately, before it was yet dark, that the multitude had seen Jesus, and that he had ministered unto them, and that he would also show himself on the ^bmorrow unto the multitude.

3. Yea, and even all the night it was noised abroad concerning Jesus; and insomuch did they send forth unto the people that there were many, yea, an exceeding great number, did labor ex-

---

u, see *u*, 2 Ne. 9.   *v*, 1 Ne. 22:25.   *w*, see *u*, Al. 16.   *x*, 3 Ne. 11:28—30.   *y*, 3 Ne. 17:4.   *z*, Moro. 2.   *2a*, see *y*, 3 Ne. 9.   *2b*, Moro. 2.   *2c*, see *c*, 3 Ne. 12.
CHAP. 19: *a*, 3 Ne. 18:39.   *b*, 3 Ne. 17:3.   A. D. 34.

ceedingly all that night, that they might be on the morrow in the place where Jesus should show himself unto the multitude.

4. And it came to pass that on the morrow, when the multitude was gathered together, behold, Nephi and ᶜhis brother whom he had raised from the dead, whose name was Timothy, and also his son, whose name was Jonas, and also Mathoni, and Mathonihah, his brother, and Kumen, and Kumenonhi, and Jeremiah, and Shemnon, and Jonas, and Zedekiah, and Isaiah—now these were the names of the ᵈdisciples whom Jesus had chosen—and it came to pass that they went forth and stood in the midst of the multitude.

5. And behold, the multitude was so great that they did cause that they should be separated into twelve bodies.

6. And the twelve did teach the multitude; and behold, they did cause that the multitude should ᵉkneel down upon the face of the earth, and should pray unto the Father in the name of Jesus.

7. And the disciples did pray unto the Father also in the name of Jesus. And it came to pass that they arose and ministered unto the people.

8. And when they had ministered those same words which Jesus had spoken—nothing ᶠvarying from the words which Jesus had spoken—behold, they knelt again and prayed to the Father in the name of Jesus.

9. And they did pray for that which they most desired; and they desired that the ᵍHoly Ghost should be given unto them.

10. And when they had thus prayed they went down unto the water's edge, and the multitude followed them.

11. And it came to pass that Nephi went down into the water and was baptized.

12. And he came up out of the water and began to baptize. And he baptized all those whom Jesus had chosen.

13. And it came to pass when they were ʰall baptized and had come up out of the water, the ⁱHoly Ghost did fall upon them, and they were filled with the Holy Ghost and with fire.

14. And behold, they were ʲencircled about as if it were by fire; and it came down ᵏfrom heaven, and the multitude did witness it, and did bear record; and angels did come down out of heaven and did minister unto them.

15. And it came to pass that while the angels were ministering unto the disciples, behold, Jesus came and stood in the midst and ministered unto them.

16. And it came to pass that he spake unto the multitude, and commanded them that they should ˡkneel down again upon the earth, and also that his disciples should kneel down upon the earth.

17. And it came to pass that when they had all knelt down upon the earth, he commanded his disciples that ᵐthey should pray.

18. And behold, they began to pray; and they did pray unto Jesus, calling him their Lord and their God.

19. And it came to pass that Jesus departed out of the midst of them, and went a little way off

---

c, 3 Ne. 7:19.   *d*, see *c*, 3 Ne. 12.   *e*, see *h*, 3 Ne. 17.   *f*, 3 Ne. chaps. 11—18.
g, see *y*, 3 Ne. 9.   *h*, see *u*, 2 Ne. 9.   *i*, see *y*, 3 Ne. 9.   *j*, He. 5:23, 24, 36, 43—45.
3 Ne. 17:24.   *k*, He. 5:45.   *l*, see *h*, 3 Ne. 17.   *m*, see *e*, 2 Ne. 32.   A. D. 34.

from them and bowed himself to the earth, and he said:

20. Father, I thank thee that thou hast ⁿgiven the Holy Ghost unto these whom I have chosen; and it is because of their belief in me that I have °chosen them out of the world.

21. Father, I pray thee that thou wilt ᵖgive the Holy Ghost unto all them that shall believe in their words.

22. Father, thou hast given them the Holy Ghost because they believe in me; and thou seest that they believe in me because thou hearest them, and they pray unto me; and they pray unto me because I am with them.

23. And now Father, I pray unto thee for them, and also for all those who shall believe on their words, that they may believe in me, that ᑫI may be in them as thou, Father, art in me, that we may be ʳone.

24. And it came to pass that when Jesus had thus prayed unto the Father, he came unto his disciples, and behold, they did still continue, without ceasing, to pray unto him; and they did not multiply many words, for it was given unto them ˢwhat they should pray, and they were filled with desire.

25. And it came to pass that Jesus blessed them as they did pray unto him; and his countenance did smile upon them, and the light of his countenance did shine upon them, and behold they were as white as the countenance and also the garments of Jesus; and behold the whiteness thereof ᵗdid exceed all the whiteness, yea, even there could be nothing upon earth so white as the whiteness thereof.

26. And Jesus said unto them: Pray on; nevertheless they did not cease to pray.

27. And he turned from them again, and went a little way off and bowed himself to the earth; and he prayed again unto the Father, saying:

28. Father, I thank thee that thou hast purified those whom I have chosen, because of their faith, and I pray for them, and also for them who shall believe on their words, that they may be purified in me, through faith on their words, even as they are purified in me.

29. Father, I pray not for the world, but for those whom thou hast given me out of the world, because of their faith, that they may be purified in me, that I may be ᵘin them as thou, Father, art in me, that we may be one, that I may be glorified in them.

30. And when Jesus had spoken these words he came again unto his disciples; and behold they did pray steadfastly, without ceasing, unto him; and he did smile upon them again; and behold they were ᵛwhite, even as Jesus.

31. And it came to pass that he went again a little way off and prayed unto the Father;

32. And ʷtongue cannot speak the words which he prayed, neither can be written by man the words which he prayed.

33. And the multitude did hear and do bear record; and their hearts were open and they did understand in their hearts the words which he prayed.

34. Nevertheless, so great and marvelous were the words which

---

n, see *y*, 3 Ne. 9. *o*, see *c*, 3 Ne. 12. *p*, see *y*, 3 Ne. 9. *q*, see *p*, 3 Ne. 9. *r*, see *k*, 2 Ne. 31. *s*, ver. 9. *t*, ver. 30. *u*, see *p*, 3 Ne. 9. *v*, ver. 25. *w*, 3 Ne. 17:16, 17, 26:14. 28:14, 16.

A. D. 84.

he prayed that they cannot be written, neither can they be uttered by man.

35. And it came to pass that when Jesus had made an end of praying he came again to the disciples, and said unto them: So great faith have I never seen among all the Jews; wherefore I could not show unto them so *great miracles, because of their unbelief.

36. Verily I say unto you, there are none of them that have seen so great things as ye have seen; neither have they heard so great things as ye have heard.

CHAPTER 20.

Bread and wine, miraculously provided, again administered—The remnant of Jacob—The Savior proclaims himself to be the prophet spoken of as like unto Moses—Many prophets cited.

1. And it came to pass that he commanded the multitude that they should cease to pray, and also his disciples. And he commanded them that they should not cease to pray in their hearts.

2. And he commanded them that they should arise and stand up upon their feet. And they arose up and stood upon their feet.

3. And it came to pass that he *brake bread again and blessed it, and gave to the disciples to eat.

4. And when they had eaten he commanded them that they should break bread, and give unto the multitude.

5. And when they had given unto the multitude he also gave them wine to drink, and commanded them that they should give unto the multitude.

6. Now, there had been no bread, neither wine, brought by the disciples, neither by the multitude;

7. But he truly gave unto them bread to eat, and also wine to drink.

8. And he said unto them: He that eateth this bread eateth of *b*my body to his soul; and he that drinketh of this wine drinketh of my blood to his soul; and his soul shall never hunger nor thirst, but shall be filled.

9. Now, when the multitude had all eaten and drunk, behold, they were *c*filled with the Spirit; and they did cry out with one voice, and gave glory to Jesus, whom they both saw and heard.

10. And it came to pass that when they had all given glory unto Jesus, he said unto them: Behold now I finish the commandment which the Father hath commanded me concerning this people, who are a remnant of the house of Israel.

11. Ye remember that I spake unto you, and said that *d*when the words of Isaiah should be fulfilled—behold they are written, ye have them before you, therefore search them—

12. And verily, verily, I say unto you, that when they shall be fulfilled then is the fulfilling of the *e*covenant which the Father hath made unto his people, O house of Israel.

13. And then shall the remnants, which shall be scattered abroad upon the face of the earth, be *f*gathered in from the east and from the west, and from the south and from the north; and they shall be brought to the knowledge of the Lord their God, who hath redeemed them.

14. And the Father hath com-

---

x, see *d*, 3 Ne. 17.   CHAP. 20: *a*, see *b*, 3 Ne. 18.   *b*, see *t*, 3 Ne. 18.   *c*, see *y*, 3 Ne. 9.   *d*, 3 Ne. 16:17.   Isa. 52:9, 10.   *e*, see *j*, 3 Ne. 15.   *f*, see *e*, 1 Ne. 15.

A. D. 34.

manded me that I should give unto *ⁿ*you this land, for your inheritance.

15. And I say unto you, that if the Gentiles do *ʰ*not repent after the *ᵐ*blessing which they shall receive, after they have scattered *ⁿ*my people—

16. Then shall *ᵒ*ye, who are a remnant of the house of Jacob, go forth among them; and ye shall be in the midst of them who shall be many; and ye shall be among them as a lion among the beasts of the forest, and as a young lion among the flocks of sheep, who, if he goeth through both treadeth down and teareth in pieces, and none can deliver.

17. Thy hand shall be lifted up upon thine adversaries, and all thine enemies shall be cut off.

18. And I will *ᵖ*gather my people together as a man gathereth his sheaves into the floor.

19. For I will make my people with whom the Father hath covenanted, yea, I will make thy horn iron, and I will make thy hoofs brass. And thou shalt beat in pieces many people; and I will consecrate their gain unto the Lord, and their substance unto the Lord of the whole earth. And behold, I am he who doeth it.

20. And it shall come to pass, saith the Father, that the sword of my justice shall hang over them at that day; and except they repent it shall fall upon them, saith the Father, yea, even upon *ᵍ*all the nations of the Gentiles.

21. And it shall come to pass that I will establish my people, O house of Israel.

22. And behold, this people will I establish *ʳ*in this land, unto the fulfilling of the *ˢ*covenant which I made with your father Jacob; and it shall be a *ᵗ*New Jerusalem. And the *ᵘ*powers of heaven shall be in the midst of this people; yea, even *ᵛ*I will be in the midst of you.

23. Behold, I am he of whom Moses spake, saying: *ʷ*A prophet shall the Lord your God raise up unto you of your brethren, like unto me; him shall ye hear in all things whatsoever he shall say unto you. And it shall come to pass that every soul who will not hear that prophet shall be cut off from among the people.

24. Verily I say unto you, yea, and *ˣ*all the prophets from Samuel and those that follow after, as many as have spoken, have testified of me.

25. And behold, ye are the children of the prophets; and ye are of the house of Israel; and ye are of the covenant which the Father made with your fathers, saying unto Abraham: And *ʸ*in thy seed shall all the kindreds of the earth be blessed.

26. The Father having raised me up unto you first, and sent me to bless you in turning away every one of you from his iniquities; and this because ye are the children of the covenant—

27. And after that ye were blessed then fulfilleth the Father the covenant which he made with Abraham, saying: *ᶻ*In thy seed shall all the kindreds of the earth be blessed—unto the pouring out of the *²ᵃ*Holy Ghost through me upon the Gentiles, which blessing

g, see *o*, 3 Ne. 15. *h*, see *l*, 3 Ne. 16. *m*, see *c*, 2 Ne. 27. *n*, 3 Ne. 16:10—14. *o*, 3 Ne. 16:14, 15. 21:11—21. Morm. 5:22—24. Mic. 4:12, 13. 5:8—15. *p*, Mic. 4:12, 13. *q*, see *j*, 1 Ne. 14. *r*, see *o*, 3 Ne. 15. *s*, Gen. 49:22—26. *t*, 3 Ne. 21:23, 24. Eth. 13:1—12. *u*, 3 Ne. 21:25. *v*, 3 Ne. 21:25. *w*, see *m*, 1 Ne. 22. Deut. 18:15, 18, 19. Acts 3:19—26. *x*, Acts 3:19—26. *y*, ver. 27. Gen. 22:18. Acts 3:25. *z*, see *y*. *2a*, 3 Ne. 15:23. Acts 10:44—48. A. D. 34.

upon the Gentiles [2b]shall make them mighty above all, unto the scattering of my people, O house of Israel.

28. And they shall be a [2c]scourge unto the people of this land. Nevertheless, when they shall have received the [2d]fulness of my gospel, then if they shall harden their hearts against me I will [2e]return their iniquities upon their own heads, saith the Father.

29. And I will remember the [2f]covenant which I have made with my people; and I have covenanted with them that I would [2g]gather them together in mine own due time, that I would give unto them again the land of their fathers for their inheritance, which is the land of Jerusalem, which is the promised land unto them forever, saith the Father.

30. And it shall come to pass that the time cometh, when the fulness of my gospel shall be [2h]preached unto them;

31. And they shall believe in me, that I am Jesus Christ, the Son of God, and shall pray unto the Father in my name.

32. Then shall [2i]their watchmen lift up their voice, and with the voice together shall they sing; for they shall see eye to eye.

33. Then will the Father [2j]gather them together again, and give unto them Jerusalem for the land of their inheritance.

34. Then shall they break forth into joy—Sing together, ye waste places of Jerusalem; for the Father hath comforted his people, he hath redeemed Jerusalem.

35. The Father hath made bare his holy arm in the eyes of all the nations; and all the ends of the earth shall see the salvation of the Father; and the Father and I [2k]are one.

36. And then shall be brought to pass that which is written: [2l]Awake, awake again, and put on thy strength, O Zion; put on thy beautiful garments, O Jerusalem, the holy city, for henceforth there shall no more come into thee the uncircumcised and the unclean.

37. Shake thyself from the dust; arise, sit down, O Jerusalem; loose thyself from the bands of thy neck, O captive daughter of Zion.

38. For thus saith the Lord: Ye have sold yourselves for naught, and ye shall be redeemed without money.

39. Verily, verily, I say unto you, that my people shall know my name; yea, in that day they shall know that I am he that doth speak.

40. And then shall they say: [2m]How beautiful upon the mountains are the feet of him that bringeth good tidings unto them, that publisheth peace; that bringeth good tidings unto them of good, that publisheth salvation; that saith unto Zion: Thy God reigneth!

41. And then shall a cry go forth: [2n]Depart ye, depart ye, go ye out from thence, touch not that which is unclean; go ye out of the midst of her; be ye clean that bear the vessels of the Lord.

42. For ye shall not go out with haste nor go by flight; for the Lord will go before you, and the God of Israel shall be your rearward.

43. Behold, my servant shall deal prudently; he shall be exalted and extolled and be very high.

2b, 1 Ne. 13:11—15. 2c, 1 Ne. 13:11, 14. 3 Ne. 16:8, 9. 2d, 3 Ne. 16:10. 2e, 3 Ne. 16:15. 20:15—20. 2f, see j. 3 Ne. 15. 2g, see e, 1 Ne. 15. 2h, see f, 2 Ne. 25. 2i, Isa. 52:9, 10. 3 Ne. 16:18—20. 2j, see e, 1 Ne. 15. 2k, see k, 2 Ne. 31. 2l, Isa. 52:1—3, 6. 2m, Isa. 52.7. 2n, Isa. 52:11—15.   A. D. 34.

44. As many were astonished at thee—his visage was so marred, more than any man, and his form more than the sons of men—

45. So shall he sprinkle many nations; the kings shall [2o]shut their mouths at him, for that which had not been told them shall they see; and that which they had not heard shall they consider.

46. Verily, verily, I say unto you, all these things shall surely come, even as the Father hath commanded me. Then shall [2p]this covenant which the Father hath covenanted with his people be fulfilled; and [2q]then shall Jerusalem be inhabited again with my people, and it shall be the land of their inheritance.

CHAPTER 21.

Sign of the Father's work—Glorious destiny of repentant Gentiles—Condemnation predicted for the impenitent—The New Jerusalem.

1. And verily I say unto you, I give unto you a [a]sign, that ye may know the time when these things shall be about to take place—that I shall [b]gather in, from their long dispersion, my people, O house of Israel, and shall establish again among them my Zion;

2. And behold, this is the thing which I will give unto you for a [c]sign—for verily I say unto you that when these things which I declare unto you, and which I shall declare unto you hereafter of myself, and by the [d]power of the Holy Ghost which shall be given unto you of the Father, shall be made [e]known unto the Gentiles that they may know concerning [f]this people who are a remnant of the house of Jacob, and concerning this my people who [g]shall be scattered by them;

3. Verily, verily, I say unto you, when these things shall be made known unto them of the Father, and shall come forth of the Father, [h]from them unto you;

4. For it is wisdom in the Father that they should be established in this land, and be set up as a [i]free people by the power of the Father, that these things might come forth from them [j]unto a remnant of your seed, that the [k]covenant of the Father may be fulfilled which he hath covenanted with his people, O house of Israel;

5. Therefore, when these works and the works which shall be wrought among you hereafter shall come forth from the Gentiles, [l]unto your seed which shall [m]dwindle in unbelief because of iniquity;

6. For thus it behooveth the Father that it should come forth from the Gentiles, that he may show forth his [n]power unto the Gentiles, for this cause that the Gentiles, if they will not harden their hearts, that they may repent and come unto me and be [o]baptized in my name and know of the true points of my doctrine, that they may be [p]numbered among my people, O house of Israel;

7. And when these things come to pass that thy seed shall [q]begin to know these things—it shall be a [r]sign unto them, that they may know that the work of the Father

---

2o, 3 Ne. 21:8. 2p, see f, 3 Ne. 15. 2q, see e, 1 Ne. 15. Chap. 21: a, vers. 2, 7. Isa. 66:19. b, see c, 1 Ne. 15. c, see a. d, see y, 3 Ne. 9. e, see c, 2 Ne. 27. f, see o, 3 Ne. 20. g, see 2c, 3 Ne. 20. h, see b, 2 Ne. 30. i, 1 Ne. 13:17—19. See f, 2 Ne. 10. j, see b, 2 Ne. 30. k, see f, 3 Ne. 15. l, see b, 2 Ne. 30. m, see g and h, 1 Ne. 12. n, see i, 1 Ne. 14. o, see u, 2 Ne. 9. p, see x, 3 Ne. 16. q, 3 Ne. 16:10—13. r, see a. A. D. 34.

hath *already commenced unto the fulfilling of the covenant which he hath made unto the people who are of the house of Israel.

8. And when that day shall come, it shall come to pass that *kings shall shut their mouths; for that which had not been told them shall they see; and that which they had not heard shall they consider.

9. For in that day, for my sake shall the Father work a work, which shall be a ᵘgreat and a marvelous work among them; and there shall be among them those who will not believe it, although a man shall declare it unto them.

10. But behold, the life of my ᵛservant shall be in my hand; therefore they shall not hurt him, although he shall be ʷmarred because of them. Yet I will heal him, for I will show unto them that my wisdom is greater than the ˣcunning of the devil.

11. Therefore it shall come to pass that whosoever will not believe in my words, who am Jesus Christ, which the Father shall cause ʸhim to bring forth unto the Gentiles, and shall give unto him power that he shall bring them forth unto the Gentiles, (it shall be done even as ᶻMoses said) they shall be cut off from among my people who are of the covenant.

12. And ²ᵃmy people who are a remnant of Jacob shall be among the Gentiles, yea, in the midst of them as a lion among the beasts of the forest, as a young lion among the flocks of sheep, who, if he go through both treadeth down and teareth in pieces, and none can deliver.

13. Their hand shall be lifted up upon their adversaries, and all their enemies shall be cut off.

14. Yea, wo be unto the Gentiles except they repent; for it shall come to pass in that day, saith the Father, that I will cut off thy horses out of the midst of thee, and I will destroy thy chariots;

15. And I will cut off the cities of thy land, and throw down all thy strongholds;

16. And I will cut off witchcrafts out of thy land, and thou shalt have no more soothsayers;

17. Thy graven images I will also cut off, and thy standing images out of the midst of thee, and thou shalt no more worship the works of thy hands;

18. And I will pluck up thy groves out of the midst of thee; so will I destroy thy cities.

19. And it shall come to pass that all ²ᵇlyings, and deceivings, and envyings, and strifes, and priestcrafts, and whoredoms, shall be done away.

20. For it shall come to pass, saith the Father, that at that day whosoever will not repent and come unto my Beloved Son, them will I ²ᶜcut off from among my people, O house of Israel;

21. And I will execute ²ᵈvengeance and fury upon them, even as upon the heathen, such as they have not heard.

22. But if they will repent and hearken unto my words, and harden not their hearts, I will establish ²ᵉmy church among them, and they shall come in unto the ²ᶠcovenant and be ²ᵍnumbered

---

s, vers. 26—29. *t*, 3 Ne. 20:45. *u*, see *i*, 2 Ne. 25. *v*, ver. 11. 3 Ne. 20:43, 45.
w, 3 Ne. 20:44. *x*, D. & C. 10:43. *y*, see *c*, 2 Ne. 3. *z*, see *w*, 3 Ne. 20. 2*a*, see *o*,
3 Ne. 20. 2*b*, vers. 11, 20, 21. 3 Ne. 29:4, 9. Chap. 30. Morm. 8:21, 41. 2*c*, see *w*,
3 Ne. 20. 2*d*, see 2*b*. 2*e*, 1 Ne. 14:12, 14. 2*f*, see *j*, 3 Ne. 15. 2*g*, see *x*, 3 Ne. 16.
A. D. 34.

among this the remnant of Jacob, unto whom I have given ²ʰthis land for their inheritance;

23. And they shall ²ⁱassist my people, the remnant of Jacob, and also as many of the house of Israel as shall come, that they may build a city, which shall be ²ʲcalled the New Jerusalem.

24. And then shall ²ᵏthey assist my people that they may be gathered in, who are scattered upon all the face of the land, in unto the ²ᵐNew Jerusalem.

25. And then shall the ²ⁿpower of heaven come down among them; and I ²ᵒalso will be in the midst.

26. And then shall the work of the Father commence at that day, even ²ᵖwhen this gospel shall be preached among the remnant of this people. Verily I say unto you, at that day shall the work of the Father commence among all the dispersed of my people, yea, ²qeven the tribes which have been lost, which the Father hath led away out of Jerusalem.

27. Yea, the work shall commence among all the dispersed of my people, with the Father, to prepare the way whereby they may come unto me, that they may call on the Father in my name.

28. Yea, and then shall the work commence, with the Father, among all nations, in preparing the way whereby ²ʳhis people may be gathered home to the land of their inheritance.

29. And they shall go out from all nations; and they ²ˢshall not go out in haste, nor go by flight, for I will go before them, saith the Father, and I will be their rearward.

CHAPTER 22.

The Savior further quotes the prophecies of Isaiah—Compare Isaiah 54.

1. And then shall that which is written come to pass: Sing, O ᵃbarren, thou that didst not bear; break forth into singing, and cry aloud, thou that didst not travail with child; for more are the children of the ᵇdesolate than the children of the married wife, saith the Lord.

2. ᵈEnlarge the place of thy tent, and let them stretch forth the curtains of thy habitations; spare not, lengthen thy cords and strengthen thy stakes;

3. For thou shalt break forth on the right hand and on the left, and thy seed shall inherit the Gentiles and make the desolate cities to be inhabited.

4. Fear not, for thou shalt not be ashamed; neither be thou confounded, for thou shalt not be put to shame; for thou shalt forget the shame of thy youth, and shalt not remember the reproach of thy youth, and shalt not remember the reproach of thy widowhood any more.

5. For thy maker, thy husband, the Lord of Hosts is his name; and thy Redeemer, the Holy One of Israel—the God of the who'e earth shall he be called.

6. For the Lord hath called ᵉthee as a woman forsaken and grieved in spirit, and a wife of youth, when thou wast refused, saith thy God.

7. For a small moment have I forsaken thee, but with great mercies will I ᶠgather thee.

8. In a little wrath I hid my face from thee for a moment, but

---

2ʰ, see o, 3 Ne. 15. 2ⁱ, Eth. 13:10. 2ʲ, vers. 24, 25. 3 Ne. 20:22. Eth. 13:1—12. 2ᵏ, ver. 6. 2ᵐ, see 2ʲ. 2ⁿ, 3 Ne. 20:22. 2ᵒ, 3 Ne. 20:22. 2ᵖ, see b, 2 Ne. 30. 2q, see p, 3 Ne. 15. 2ʳ, see e, 1 Ne. 15. 2ˢ, 3 Ne. 20:42. Isa. 52:11—15.
Chap. 22: a. Zeph. 3:14. b, Isa. 49:21. d, Isa. 49:19, 20. e, Isa. 62:4. f, see e, 1 Ne. 15.   A. D. 34.

with everlasting kindness will I have mercy on thee, saith the Lord thy Redeemer.

9. For this, the waters of Noah unto me, for as I have sworn that the waters of Noah should no more go over the earth, so have I sworn that I would not be wroth with thee.

10. For the *g*mountains shall depart and the hills be removed, but my kindness shall not depart from thee, neither shall the *h*covenant of my people be removed, saith the Lord that hath mercy on thee.

11. O thou afflicted, *i*tossed with tempest, and not comforted! Behold, I *j*will lay thy stones with fair colors, and lay thy foundations with sapphires.

12. And I will make thy windows of agates, and thy gates of carbuncles, and all thy borders of pleasant stones.

13. And *k*all thy children shall be taught of the Lord; and great shall be the peace of thy children.

14. In righteousness shalt thou be established; thou shalt be far from oppression for thou shalt not fear, and from terror for it shall not come near thee.

15. Behold, they shall surely gather together against thee, not by me; whosoever shall gather together *l*against thee shall fall for thy sake.

16. Behold, I have created the smith that bloweth the coals in the fire, and that bringeth forth an instrument for his work; and I have created the waster to destroy.

17. No weapon that is formed against thee shall prosper; and every tongue that shall rise against thee in judgment thou shalt condemn. This is the heritage of the servants of the Lord, and their righteousness is of me, saith the Lord.

CHAPTER 23.

The Savior commands that omissions from Nephite records be supplied—Prophecy of Samuel the Lamanite added.

1. And now, behold, I say unto you, that ye ought to search these things. Yea, a commandment I give unto you that ye search these things diligently; for great are the words of Isaiah.

2. For surely he spake as touching all things concerning my people which are of the house of Israel; therefore it must needs be that he must speak also to the Gentiles.

3. And all things that he spake have been and shall be, even *a*according to the words which he spake.

4. Therefore give heed to my words; write the things which I have told you; and according to the time and the will of the Father *b*they shall go forth unto the Gentiles.

5. And whosoever will hearken unto my words and repenteth and is *c*baptized, the same shall be saved. Search the prophets, for many there be that testify of these things.

6. And now it came to pass that when Jesus had said these words he said unto them again, after he had expounded all the scriptures unto them which they had received, he said unto them: Behold, other scriptures I would that ye should write, that ye have not.

7. And it came to pass that he

---

g, He. 12:8—12. Isa. 40:4, 5. *h*, see *j*, 3 Ne. 15. *i*, Isa. 49:21. *j*, Rev. 21:18—21. *k*, Isa. 60:21. Jer. 31:33, 34. *l*, see *j*, 1 Ne. 22. Chap. 23; *a*, 2 Pet. 1:19—21. *b*, see *c*, 2 Ne. 27. *c*, see *u*, 2 Ne. 9.　　　　A. D. 34.

said unto ᵈNephi: Bring forth the record which ye have kept.

8. And when Nephi had brought forth the records, and laid them before him, he cast his eyes upon them and said:

9. Verily I say unto you, I commanded my servant Samuel, the Lamanite, that he should testify unto this people, that at the day that the Father should glorify his name in me that there were ᵉmany saints who should arise from the dead, and should appear unto many, and should minister unto them. And he said unto them: Was it not so?

10. And his disciples answered him and said: Yea, Lord, Samuel did prophesy according to thy words, and they were all fulfilled.

11. And Jesus said unto them: How be it that ye have not written this thing, that many saints did arise and appear unto many and did minister unto them?

12. And it came to pass that Nephi remembered that this thing had not been written.

13. And it came to pass that Jesus commanded that it should be written; therefore it was written according as he commanded.

14. And now it came to pass that when Jesus had expounded all the scriptures in one, which they had written, he commanded them that they should teach the things which he had expounded unto them.

CHAPTER 24.

Malachi's words given to the Nephites—The law of tithes and offerings—Compare Malachi 3.

1. And it came to pass that he commanded them that they should write the words which the Father had given unto Malachi, which he should tell unto them. And it came to pass that after they were written he expounded them. And these are the words which he did tell unto them, saying: Thus said the Father unto Malachi—ᵃBehold, I will send my messenger, and he shall prepare the way before me, and the Lord whom ye seek shall ᵇsuddenly come to his temple, even the messenger of the covenant, whom ye delight in; behold, he shall come, saith the Lord of Hosts.

2. But who may ᶜabide the day of his coming, and who shall stand when he appeareth? For he is like a refiner's fire, and like fuller's soap.

3. And he shall sit as a refiner and purifier of silver; and he shall purify the ᵈsons of Levi, and purge them as gold and silver, that they may offer unto the Lord an offering in righteousness.

4. Then shall the offering of Judah and Jerusalem be pleasant unto the Lord, as in the days of old, and as in former years.

5. And I will come ᵉnear to you to judgment; and I ᶠwill be a swift witness against the sorcerers, and against the adulterers, and against false swearers, and against those that oppress the hireling in his wages, the widow and the fatherless, and that turn aside the stranger, and fear not me, saith the Lord of Hosts.

6. For I am the Lord, I change not; therefore ye sons of Jacob are not consumed.

7. Even from the days of your fathers ye are gone away from

---

d, 3 Ne. 8:1, 2.   *e*, see *g*, Jac. 4.   He. 14:25, 26.   Chap. 24: *a*, D. & C. 45:9. Isa. 66:6,   40:3—5, 9—11.   59:20, 21.   *b*, Isa. 2:2—4.   Mic. 4:1—4.   3 Ne. 20:22. 21:25,   *c*, 3 Ne. 25.   *d*, D. & C. sec. 13.   84:31—34.   *e*, Ezek. 43:1, 2, 4—7.   *f*, 3 Ne. 25:1, 3, 6.   See *w*, 3 Ne. 20.   A. D. 34.

mine ordinances, and have not kept them. Return unto me and I will return unto you, saith the Lord of Hosts. But ye say: Wherein shall we return?

8. Will a man rob God? Yet ye have robbed me. But ye say: Wherein have we robbed thee? In tithes and offerings.

9. Ye are cursed with a curse, for ye have robbed me, even this whole nation.

10. Bring ye *g*all the tithes into the storehouse, that there may be meat in my house; and prove me now herewith, saith the Lord of Hosts, if I will not open you the windows of heaven, and pour you out a blessing that there shall not be room enough to receive it.

11. And I will rebuke the devourer for your sakes, and he shall not destroy the fruits of your ground; neither shall your vine cast her fruit before the time in the fields, saith the Lord of Hosts.

12. And all nations shall call you blessed, for ye shall be a delightsome land, saith the Lord of Hosts.

13. Your words have been stout against me, saith the Lord. Yet ye say: What have we spoken against thee?

14. Ye have said: It is vain to serve God, and what doth it profit that we have kept his ordinances and that we have walked mournfully before the Lord of Hosts?

15. And now we call the proud happy; yea, they that work wickedness are set up; yea, they that tempt God are even delivered.

16. Then they that feared the Lord spake *h*often one to another, and the Lord hearkened and heard; and a *i*book of remembrance was written before him for them that feared the Lord, and that thought upon his name.

17. And they shall be mine, saith the Lord of Hosts, in that day when I *j*make up my jewels; and I will spare them as a man spareth his own son that serveth him.

18. Then shall ye return and discern between the righteous and the wicked, between him that serveth God and him that serveth him not.

CHAPTER 25.

Malachi's words continued—Elijah and his mission—The great and dreadful day of the Lord—Compare Malachi 4.

1. For behold, the day cometh that shall *a*burn as an oven; and all the proud, yea, and all that do wickedly, shall be stubble; and the day that cometh shall burn them up, saith the Lord of Hosts, that it shall leave them neither root nor branch.

2. But unto you that *b*fear my name, shall the Son of Righteousness arise with healing in his wings; and ye shall go forth and grow up as *c*calves in the stall.

3. And ye shall tread down the wicked; for they shall be *d*ashes under the soles of your feet in the day that I shall do this, saith the Lord of Hosts.

4. Remember ye the law of Moses, my servant, which I commanded unto him in Horeb for all Israel, with the statutes and judgments.

5. Behold, I will send you *e*Elijah the prophet before the *f*coming of the great and dreadful day of the Lord;

g, D. & C. 64:23. 119, 120. *h*, Moro. 6:5, 6. *i*, 3 Ne. 27:25, 26. *j*, D. & C. 101:3. Chap. 25: *a*, ver. 3. 1 Ne. 22:15, 17, 18, 23. 2 Ne. 27:2. 30:10. Jac. 6:3. Isa. 24:6. 66:16. *b*, 3 Ne. 24:16. *c*, 1 Ne. 22:24. *d*, ver. 1. *e*, D. & C. 110:13. *f*, 3 Ne. 25:3.

A. D. 34.

6. And he shall °turn the heart of the fathers to the children, and the heart of the children to their fathers, lest I come and smite the earth with a curse.

CHAPTER 26.

The Savior expounds all things from the beginning—Marvels spoken by the mouths of babes—The work of the disciples.

1. And now it came to pass that when Jesus had told these things he expounded them unto the multitude; and he did expound all things unto them, both great and small.
2. And he saith: "These scriptures, which ye had not with you, the Father commanded that I should give unto you; for it was wisdom in him that they should be given unto future generations.
3. And he did expound all things, even from the beginning until the time that he should ᵇcome in his glory—yea, even all things which should come upon the face of the earth, even until the ᶜelements should melt with fervent heat, and the earth should be wrapt together as a scroll, and the heavens and the earth should pass away;
4. And even unto the great and last day, ᵈwhen all people, and all kindreds, and all nations and tongues shall stand before God, to be judged of their works, whether they be good or whether they be evil—
5. If they be good, to the ᵉresurrection of everlasting life; and if they be evil, to the resurrection of damnation; being on a parallel, the one on the one hand and the other on the other hand, according to the mercy, and the justice, and the holiness which is in Christ, who was ᶠbefore the world began.
6. And now there cannot be written in this ᵍbook even a hundredth part of the things which Jesus did truly teach unto the people;
7. But behold the ʰplates of Nephi do contain the more part of the things which he taught the people.
8. And these things have I written, which are a ⁱlesser part of the things which he taught the people; and I have written them to the intent that they may be brought again unto this people, ʲfrom the Gentiles, according to the words which Jesus hath spoken.
9. And when they shall have received this, which is expedient that they should have first, to try their faith, and if it shall so be that they shall believe ᵏthese things then shall the ˡgreater things be made manifest unto them.
10. And if it so be that they will not believe these things, then shall the greater things ᵐbe withheld from them, unto their condemnation.
11. Behold, I was about to write them, ⁿall which were engraven upon the plates of Nephi, but the Lord forbade it, saying: I will ᵒtry the faith of my people.
12. Therefore I, Mormon, do write the things which have been commanded me of the Lord. And now I, Mormon, make an end of my sayings, and proceed to write

g, D. & C. 98:16, 17   CHAP. 26: *a,* 3 Ne. 24, 25.   *b,* see *f,* 3 Ne. 25.   *c,* Morm. 5:23.   2 Pet. 1:10, 12.   Isa. 24:1—4, 17—20.   Rev. 20:11.   *d,* Mos. 16:1, 2, 10. Al. 12:12.   40:21.   3 Ne. 27:14, 15.   Morm. 9:13, 14.   *e,* Mos. 16:11.   See *d,* 2 Ne. 2. *f,* see *d,* Mos. 4.   *g,* W. of Morm. 5.   He. 3:14.   3 Ne. 5:8.   Eth. 15:33.   *h,* see *f,* 1 Ne. 1.   *i,* see *g.*   *j,* see *b,* 2 Ne. 30.   *k,* see *i.*   *l,* D. & C. 128:18.   Eth. 4:6—8, 13. *m,* Eth. 4:8—10.   *n,* ver. 7.   *o,* Eth. 11:6.   A. D. 34.

the things which have been commanded me.

13. Therefore, I would that ye should behold that the Lord truly did teach the people, for the space of three days; and after that he did show himself unto them oft, and did ᵖbreak bread oft, and bless it, and give it unto them.

14. And it came to pass that he did teach and minister unto the ᵠchildren of the multitude of whom hath been spoken, and he did loose their tongues, and they did speak unto their fathers ʳgreat and marvelous things, even greater than he had revealed unto the people; and he loosed their tongues that they could utter.

15. And it came to pass that after he had ascended into heaven —the second time that he showed himself unto them, and had gone unto the Father, after having ˢhealed all their sick, and their lame, and opened the eyes of their blind and unstopped the ears of the deaf, and even had done all manner of cures among them, and raised a man from the dead, and had shown forth his power unto them, and had ascended unto the Father—

16. Behold, it came to pass on the morrow that the multitude gathered themselves together, and they both saw and heard these children; yea, ᵗeven babes did open their mouths and utter marvelous things; and the things which they did utter were forbidden that there should not any man write them.

17. And it came to pass that the ᵘdisciples whom Jesus had chosen began from that time forth to ᵛbaptize and to teach as many as did come unto them; and as many as were baptized in the name of Jesus were ʷfilled with the Holy Ghost.

18. And many of them saw and heard unspeakable things, which are ˣnot lawful to be written.

19. And they taught, and did minister one to another; and they had ʸall things common among them, every man dealing justly, one with another.

20. And it came to pass that they did do all things even as Jesus had commanded them.

21. And they who were ᶻbaptized in the name of Jesus ²ᵃwere called the church of Christ.

CHAPTER 27.

Jesus Christ names his church—All things are written by the Father—Men to be judged by what is written in the books.

1. And it came to pass that as the ᵃdisciples of Jesus were journeying and were preaching the things which they had both heard and seen, and were baptizing in the name of Jesus, it came to pass that the disciples were gathered together and were united in mighty ᵇprayer and ᶜfasting.

2. And Jesus again showed himself unto them, for they were praying unto the Father in his name; and Jesus came and stood in the midst of them, and said unto them: What will ye that I shall give unto you?

3. And they said unto him: Lord, we will that thou wouldst tell us the name whereby we shall call this church; for there are disputations among the people concerning this matter.

4. And the Lord said unto

---

p, see *b*, 3 Ne. 18. *q*, see *g*, 3 Ne. 17. *r*, see *w*, 3 Ne. 19. *s*, 3 Ne. 17:7—10. *t*, see *w*, 3 Ne. 19. *u*, see *c*, 3 Ne. 12. *v*, 4 Ne. 1. See *u*, 2 Ne. 9. *w*, see *y*, 3 Ne. 9. *x*, see *w*, 3 Ne. 19. *y*, 4 Ne. 2, 3, 25, 26. *z*, see *u*, 2 Ne. 9. 2*a*, see *d*, Mos. 26. CHAP. 27: *a*, see *c*, 3 Ne. 12. *b*, see *e*, 2 Ne. 32. *c*, see *t*, Mos. 27. A. D. 34—35.

them: Verily, verily, I say unto you, why is it that the people should murmur and dispute because of this thing?

5. Have they not read the scriptures, which say ye must take upon you the ᵈname of Christ, which is my name? For by this name shall ye be called at the last day;

6. And whoso taketh upon him my name, and endureth to the end, the same shall be saved at the last day.

7. Therefore, whatsoever ye shall do, ye shall do it in my name; therefore ye shall call the church in my name; and ye shall call upon the Father in my name that he will bless the church for my sake.

8. And how be it my church save it be called in my name? For if a church be called in Moses' name then it be Moses' church; or if it be called in the name of a man then it be the church of a man; but if it be called in my name then it is my church, if it so be that they are built upon my gospel.

9. Verily I say unto you, that ye are built upon my gospel; therefore ye shall call whatsoever things ye do call, in my name; therefore if ye call upon the Father, for the church, if it be in my name the Father will hear you;

10. And if it so be that the church is built upon my gospel then will the Father show forth his own works in it.

11. But if it be not built upon my gospel, and is built upon the works of men, or upon the works of the devil, verily I say unto you they have joy in their works for a season, and by and by the end cometh, and they are ᵉhewn down and cast into the fire, from whence there is no return.

12. For their works do follow them, for it is because of their works that they are hewn down; therefore remember the things that I have told you.

13. Behold I have given unto you my gospel, and this is the gospel which I have given unto you—that I came into the world to do the will of my Father, because my Father sent me.

14. And my Father sent me that I might be lifted up upon the cross; and after that I had ᶠbeen lifted up upon the cross, that I might draw all men unto me, that as I have been lifted up by men even so should men ᵍbe lifted up by the Father, to stand before me, to be judged of their works, whether they be good or whether they be evil—

15. And for this cause have I been lifted up; therefore, according to the power of the Father I will draw all men unto me, that they may be judged according to their works.

16. And it shall come to pass, that whoso repenteth and is ʰbaptized in my name shall be filled; and if he ⁱendureth to the end, behold, him will I hold guiltless before my Father at that day when I shall stand to judge the world.

17. And he that endureth not unto the end, the same is he that is also ʲhewn down and cast into the fire, from whence they can no more return, because of the justice of the Father.

18. And this is the word which he hath given unto the children

---

d, vers. 6—10. See *c*, Mos. 5. *e*, see *k*, 1 Ne. 15. *f*, ver. 15. 1 Ne. 19:10. 3 Ne. 28:6. *g*, see *f*. *h*, see *u*, 2 Ne. 9. *i*, 1 Ne. 13:37. See *h*, 2 Ne. 31. *j*, see *k*, 1 Ne. 15.

A. D. 34—35.

of men. And for this cause he fulfilleth the words which he hath given, and he lieth not, but 'fulfilleth all his words.

19. And ^{k}no unclean thing can enter into his kingdom; therefore nothing entereth into his rest save it be those who have washed their garments in my blood, because of their faith, and the repentance of all their sins, and their faithfulness unto the ^{l}end.

20. Now this is the commandment: Repent, all ye ends of the earth, and come unto me and be ^{m}baptized in my name, that ye may be sanctified by the ^{n}reception of the Holy Ghost, that ye may stand spotless before me at the last day.

21. Verily, verily, I say unto you, this is my gospel; and ye know the things that ye must do in my church; for the works which ye have seen me do that shall ye also do; for that which ye have seen me do even that shall ye do;

22. Therefore, if ye do these things blessed are ye, for ye shall be ^{o}lifted up at the last day.

23. Write the things which ye have seen and heard, save it be those ^{p}which are forbidden.

24. Write the works of this people, which shall be, even as hath been written, of that which hath been.

25. For behold, ^{q}out of the books which have been written, and which shall be written, shall this people ^{r}be judged, for by them shall their works be known unto men.

26. And behold, all things are ^{s}written by the Father; therefore ^{t}out of the books which shall be written shall the world be judged.

27. And know ye that ^{u}ye shall be judges of this people, according to the judgment which I shall give unto you, which shall be just. Therefore, what manner of men ought ye to be? Verily I say unto you, even as I am.

28. And now I go unto the Father. And verily I say unto you, whatsoever things ye shall ask the Father in my name shall be given unto you.

29. Therefore, ^{v}ask, and ye shall receive; knock, and it shall be opened unto you; for he that asketh, receiveth; and unto him that knocketh, it shall be opened.

30. And now, behold, my joy is great, even unto fulness, because of you, and also this generation; yea, and even the Father rejoiceth, and also all the holy angels, because of you and this generation; for none of them are lost.

31. Behold, I would that ye should understand; for I mean them who are now alive of this generation; and none of them are lost; and in them I have fulness of joy.

32. But behold, it sorroweth me because of the ^{w}fourth generation from this generation, for they are led away captive by him even as was the ^{x}son of perdition; for they will sell me for silver and for gold, and for that which ^{y}moth doth corrupt and which thieves can break through and steal. And in that day will I visit them, even in ^{z}turning their works upon their own heads.

33. And it came to pass that

k, Al. 11:37. See *r*, Al. 7. *l*, see *t*. *m*, see *u*, 2 Ne. 9. *n*, see *y*, 3 Ne. 9. *o*, see *p*, Mos. 23. *p*, 3 Ne. 26:16, 18. *q*, ver. 26. See *c*, 2 Ne. 27. *r*, see *j*, 2 Ne. 29. *s*, 3 Ne. 24:16. *t*, ver. 25. See *c*, 2 Ne. 27. *u*, 1 Ne. 12:9, 10. Morm. 3:19. *v*, 3 Ne. 14:7, 8. *w*, see *d*, 1 Ne. 12. *x*, 3 Ne. 29:7. *y*, 3 Ne. 13:19—21. *z*, Morm. 5.
A. D. 34—35.

when Jesus had ended these sayings he said unto his disciples: ²ᵃEnter ye in at the strait gate; for strait is the gate, and narrow is the way that leads to life, and few there be that find it; but wide is the gate, and broad the way which leads to death, and many there be that travel therein, until the night cometh, wherein no man can work.

CHAPTER 28.

Each of the twelve is granted his heart's desire—Three elect to remain on earth until the Lord comes in his glory—Marvelous manifestations to the three—They are made immune to death and disaster.

1. And it came to pass when Jesus had said these words, he spake unto his disciples, one by one, saying unto them: What is it that ye desire of me, after that I am gone to the Father?

2. And they all spake, save it were three, saying: We desire that after we have lived unto the age of man, that our ministry, wherein thou hast called us, may have an end, that we may speedily come unto thee in thy kingdom.

3. And he said unto them: Blessed are ye because ye desired this thing of me; therefore, after that ye are ᵃseventy and two years old ye shall come unto me in my kingdom; and with me ye shall find rest.

4. And when he had spoken unto them, he turned himself unto the three, and said unto them: What will ye that I should do unto you, when I am gone unto the Father?

5. And they sorrowed in their hearts, for they durst not speak unto him the thing which they desired.

6. And he said unto them: Behold, I know your thoughts, and ye have desired the thing which ᵇJohn, my beloved, who was with me in my ministry, before that I was ᶜlifted up by the Jews, desired of me.

7. Therefore, more blessed are ye, for ye shall ᵈnever taste of death; but ye shall live to behold all the doings of the Father unto the children of men, even until all things shall be fulfilled according to the will of the Father, when I shall ᵉcome in my glory with the powers of heaven.

8. And ye shall never ᶠendure the pains of death; but when I shall come in my glory ye shall be ᵍchanged in the twinkling of an eye from mortality to immortality; and then shall ye be blessed in the kingdom of my Father.

9. And again, ye shall not have ʰpain while ye shall dwell in the flesh, neither sorrow ⁱsave it be for the sins of the world; and all this will I do because of the thing which ye have desired of me, for ye have desired that ye might bring the souls of men unto me, while the world shall stand.

10. And for this cause ye shall have fulness of joy; and ye shall sit down in the kingdom of my Father; yea, your joy shall be full, even as the Father hath given me fulness of joy; and ye shall be even as I am, and I am even as the Father; and the Father and I are ʲone;

11. And the Holy Ghost beareth record of the Father and me; and the Father ᵏgiveth the Holy Ghost unto the children of men, because of me.

2a, 3 Ne. 14:13, 14. See 2a, 2 Ne. 9. CHAP. 28: a, 4 Ne. 14. b, D. & C. 7. c, see f, 3 Ne. 27. d, vers. 8, 9, 19—22, 25, 37—40. 4 Ne. 14, 37. Morm. 8:10--12. e, th 12:17. e, 3 Ne. 20:22. 21:25. f, see d. g, vers. 15, 17, 36—40. h, see d. i, 4 Ne. 44. Morm. 8:10. j, see k, 2 Ne. 31. k, see y, 3 Ne. 9. A. D. 34—35.

3 NEPHI, 28.

12. And it came to pass that when Jesus had spoken these words, he touched every one of them with his finger save it were the three who were to tarry, and then he departed.

13. And behold, the heavens were opened, and *they were caught up into heaven, and saw and heard unspeakable things.

14. And it was ᵐforbidden them that they should utter; neither was it given unto them power that they could utter the things which they saw and heard;

15. And whether they were in the body or out of the body, they could not tell; for it did seem unto them like a transfiguration of them, that they were changed from this body of flesh into an immortal state, that they could behold the things of God.

16. But it came to pass that they did again minister upon the face of the earth; nevertheless they did not minister of the things which they had heard and seen, because of the ⁿcommandment which was given them in heaven.

17. And now, ᵒwhether they were mortal or immortal, from the day of their transfiguration, I know not;

18. But this much I know, according to the record which hath been given—they did go forth upon the face of the land, and did minister unto all the people, uniting as many to the church as would believe in their preaching; ᵖbaptizing them, and as many as were baptized did ᵍreceive the Holy Ghost.

19. And they were cast into prison by them who did not belong to the church. And the ʳprisons could not hold them, for they were rent in twain.

20. And they were cast down into the earth; but they did smite the earth with the word of God, insomuch that by his power they were delivered out of the depths of the earth; and therefore they could not dig pits sufficient to hold them.

21. And thrice they were cast into a furnace and received no harm.

22. And twice were they cast into a den of wild beasts; and behold they did play with the beasts as a child with a suckling lamb, and received no harm.

23. And it came to pass that thus they did go forth among all the people of Nephi, and did preach the gospel of Christ unto all people upon the face of the land; and they were converted unto the Lord, and were united unto the church of Christ, and thus the people of ˢthat generation were blessed, according to the word of Jesus.

24. And now I, Mormon, make an end of speaking concerning these things for a time.

25. Behold, I was about to write the ᵗnames of those who were never to taste of death, but the Lord forbade; therefore I write them not, for they are hid from the world.

26. But behold, ᵘI have seen them, and they have ministered unto me.

27. And behold they will be among the Gentiles, and the Gentiles shall know them not.

28. They will also be among the Jews, and the Jews shall know them not.

29. And it shall come to pass, when the Lord seeth fit in his

---

l, vers. 2, 4—8, 12, 36.   4 Ne. 14, 37.   *m*, see *w*, 3 Ne. 19.   *n*, ver. 14.   *o*, vers. 36—40.   *p*, see *u*, 2 Ne. 9.   *q*, see *y*, 3 Ne. 9.   *r*, 4 Ne. 5, 30—33.   Morm. 8:24.   *s*, 3 Ne. 27:30, 31.   *t*, 3 Ne. 19:4.   *u*, Morm. 8:11.   A. D. 34—35.

wisdom that they shall minister unto all the scattered tribes of Israel, and unto all nations, kindreds, tongues and people, and shall bring out of them unto Jesus many souls, that their ʳdesire may be fulfilled, and also because of the ʷconvincing power of God which is in them.

30. And they are as the angels of God, and if they shall pray unto the Father in the name of Jesus they can show themselves unto whatsoever man it seemeth them good.

31. Therefore, ˣgreat and marvelous works shall be wrought by them, before the great and coming day when all people must surely stand before the judgment-seat of Christ;

32. Yea even among the Gentiles shall there be a great and marvelous work wrought by them, before that judgment day.

33. And if ye had ʸall the scriptures which give an account of all the marvelous works of Christ, ye would, according to the words of Christ, know that these things must surely come.

34. And wo be unto him that will ᶻnot hearken unto the words of Jesus, and also to them whom he hath chosen and sent among them; for whoso receiveth not the words of Jesus and the words of those whom he hath sent receiveth not him; and therefore he will not receive them at the last day;

35. And it would be better for them if they had not been born. For do ye suppose that ye can get rid of the justice of an offended God, who hath been trampled under feet of men, that thereby salvation might come?

36. And now behold, as I spake concerning those whom the Lord hath chosen, yea, even three who were ²ᵃcaught up into the heavens, that I knew not ²ᵇwhether they were cleansed from mortality to immortality—

37. But behold, since I wrote, I have inquired of the Lord, and he hath made it manifest unto me that there must needs be a change wrought upon their bodies, or ²ᶜelse it needs be that they must taste of death;

38. Therefore, that they might not taste of death there was a change wrought upon their bodies, that they might ²ᵈnot suffer pain nor sorrow save it were for the sins of the world.

39. Now this change was not equal to that which shall take place at the last day; but there was a change wrought upon them, insomuch that Satan could have no power over them, that he could not tempt them; and they were sanctified in the flesh, that they were holy, and that the ²ᵉpowers of the earth could not hold them.

40. And in this state they were to remain until the judgment day of Christ; and at that day they were to receive a ²ᶠgreater change, and to be received into the kingdom of the Father to go no more out, but to dwell with God eternally in the heavens.

CHAPTER 29.

Mormon's warning to those who spurn the words and works of the Lord.

1. And now behold, I say unto you that when the Lord shall see fit, in his wisdom, that these sayings shall ᵃcome unto the Gen-

---

v, ver. 9.   w, vers. 30—33.   x, see w.   y, 3 Ne. 26:6—12.   z, Eth. 4:8—12.   2a, vers. 13—16.   2b, ver. 17.   2c, see d.   2d, ver. 9.   2e, ver. 20.   2f, ver. 8.
CHAP. 29: a, see c, 2 Ne. 27.

A. D. 34—35.

tiles according to his word, then ye may know that the [b]covenant which the Father hath made with the children of Israel, concerning their restoration to the lands of their inheritance, is already beginning to be fulfilled.

2. And ye may know that the words of the Lord, which have been spoken by the holy prophets, shall all be fulfilled; and ye need not say that the Lord delays his coming unto the children of Israel.

3. And ye need not imagine in your hearts that the words which have been spoken are vain, for behold, the Lord will remember his covenant which he hath made unto his people of the house of Israel.

4. And [c]when ye shall see these sayings coming forth among you, then ye need not any longer spurn at the doings of the Lord, for the sword of his justice is in his right hand; and behold, at that day, if ye shall spurn at his doings he will cause that [d]it shall soon overtake you.

5. Wo unto him that spurneth at the doings of the Lord; yea, wo unto him that shall deny the Christ and his works!

6. Yea, [e]wo unto him that shall deny the revelations of the Lord, and that shall say the Lord no longer worketh by revelation, or by prophecy, or by gifts, or by tongues, or by healings, or by the power of the Holy Ghost!

7. Yea, and wo unto him that shall say at that day, to get gain, that there can be no miracle wrought by Jesus Christ; for he that doeth this shall become like unto the [f]son of perdition, for whom there was no mercy, according to the word of Christ!

8. Yea, and ye need not any longer hiss, nor spurn, nor make game of the Jews, nor any of the remnant of the house of Israel; for behold, the Lord remembereth his [g]covenant unto them, and he will do unto them according to that which he hath sworn.

9. Therefore ye need not suppose that ye can turn the right hand of the Lord unto the left, that he may not [h]execute judgment unto the fulfilling of the [i]covenant which he hath made unto the house of Israel.

CHAPTER 30.

Mormon calls the Gentiles to repentance.

1. Hearken, O ye Gentiles, and hear the words of Jesus Christ, the Son of the living God, which he hath commanded [a]me that I should speak concerning you, for, behold he commandeth me that I should write, saying:

2. Turn, all ye Gentiles, from your wicked ways; and repent of your evil doings, of your [b]lyings and deceivings, and of your [c]whoredoms, and of your [d]secret abominations, and your idolatries, and of your murders, and your [e]priestcrafts, and your envyings, and your strifes, and from all your wickedness and abominations, and come unto me, and be [f]baptized in my name, that ye may receive a remission of your sins, and be [g]filled with the Holy Ghost, that ye may be [h]numbered with my people who are of the house of Israel.

---

b, see j, 3 Ne. 15. c, see j, 3 Ne. 15. d, see 2b, 3 Ne. 21. e, Morm. 9:7—11, 15—26. Moro. 7:35—38. 10:19—29. f, 3 Ne. 27:32. g, see j, 3 Ne. 15. h, see 2b, 3 Ne. 21. i, see j, 3 Ne. 15. Chap. 30: a, 3 Ne. 5:12, 13. b, 3 Ne. 21:19—21. c, see y, 2 Ne. 9. d, see i, 2 Ne. 10. e, see x, 2 Ne. 26. f, see u, 2 Ne. 9. g, see y, 3 Ne. 9. h, see x, 3 Ne. 16.   A. D. 34—35.

FOURTH NEPHI
THE BOOK OF NEPHI

WHO IS THE SON OF NEPHI—ONE OF THE DISCIPLES OF JESUS CHRIST

An account of the people of Nephi, according to his record.

The church of Christ flourishes—Nephites and Lamanites converted—They have all things in common—Two centuries of righteousness followed by division and degeneracy—Amos and Ammaron in turn keep the records.

1. And it came to pass that the ^athirty and fourth year passed away, and also the thirty and fifth, and behold the ^bdisciples of Jesus had formed a church of Christ in all the lands round about. And as many as did come unto them, and did truly repent of their sins, were ^cbaptized in the name of Jesus; and they did also ^dreceive the Holy Ghost.

2. And it came to pass in the thirty and sixth year, the people were all converted unto the Lord, upon all the face of the land, both Nephites and Lamanites, and there were no contentions and disputations among them, and every man did deal justly one with another.

3. And they had ^eall things common among them; therefore there were not rich and poor, bond and free, but they were all made free, and partakers of the ^fheavenly gift.

4. And it came to pass that the thirty and seventh year passed away also, and there still continued to be peace in the land.

5. And there were great and marvelous works ^gwrought by the disciples of Jesus, insomuch that they did heal the sick, and raise the dead, and cause the lame to walk, and the blind to receive their sight, and the deaf to hear; and all manner of miracles did they work among the children of men; and in nothing did they work miracles save it were in the name of Jesus.

6. And thus did the thirty and eighth year pass away, and also the thirty and ninth, and forty and first, and the forty and second, yea, even until forty and nine years had passed away, and also the fifty and first, and the fifty and second; yea, and even until fifty and nine years had passed away.

7. And the Lord did prosper them exceedingly in the land; yea, insomuch that they did build cities again where there had been cities burned.

8. Yea, even that great ^hcity Zarahemla did they cause to be built again.

9. But there were many cities which had ⁱbeen sunk, and waters came up in the stead thereof; therefore these cities could not be renewed.

10. And now, behold, it came to pass that the people of Nephi did wax strong, and did multiply exceedingly fast, and became an exceedingly fair and delightsome people.

11. And they were married, and given in marriage, and were

---

a, 3 Ne. 2:6—8. *b*, see *c*, 3 Ne. 12. *c*, see *u*, 2 Ne. 9. *d*, see *y*, 3 Ne. 9. *e*, see *y*, 3 Ne. 26. *f*, see *y*, 3 Ne. 9. *g*, see *r*, 3 Ne. 28. *h*, Om. 13. 3 Ne. 8:8, 24. 9:3. *i*, 3 Ne. 8:9. 9:4, 7.

A. D. 36—60.

blessed according to the multitude of the promises which the Lord had made unto them.

12. And they did not walk any more after the performances and ordinances of the *ʲ*law of Moses; but they did walk after the commandments which they had received from their Lord and their God, continuing in *ᵏ*fasting and prayer, and in *ˡ*meeting together oft both to *ᵐ*pray and to hear the word of the Lord.

13. And it came to pass that there was no contention among all the people, in all the land; but there were *ⁿ*mighty miracles wrought among the disciples of Jesus.

14. And it came to pass that the *seventy and first year passed away, and also the seventy and second year, yea, and in fine, till the seventy and ninth year had passed away; yea, even an hundred years had passed away, and the disciples of Jesus, whom he had chosen, had all gone to the *ᵒ*paradise of God, save it were the *ᵖ*three who should tarry; and there were other disciples ordained in their stead; and also many of that generation had passed away.

15. And it came to pass that there was no contention in the land, because of the love of God which did dwell in the hearts of the people.

16. And there were no envyings, nor strifes, nor tumults, nor whoredoms, nor lyings, nor murders, nor any manner of lasciviousness; and surely there could not be a happier people among all the people who had been created by the hand of God.

17. There were no robbers, nor murderers, neither were there Lamanites, nor any manner of -ites; but they were in one, the children of Christ, and heirs to the kingdom of God.

18. And how blessed were they! For the Lord did bless them in all their doings; yea, even they were blessed and prospered until †an hundred and ten years had passed away; and the first generation from Christ had passed away, and there was no contention in all the land.

19. And it came to pass that *ʳ*Nephi, he that kept this last record, (and he kept it upon the *ˢ*plates of Nephi) died, and his son Amos kept it in his stead; and he kept it upon the plates of Nephi also.

20. And he kept it eighty and four years, and there was still peace in the land, save it were a small part of the people who had revolted from the church and taken upon them the name of Lamanites; therefore there began to be Lamanites again in the land.

21. And it came to pass that Amos died also, (and it was an hundred and ninety and four years from the coming of Christ) and his son Amos kept the record in his stead; and he also kept it upon the plates of Nephi; and it was also written in the book of Nephi, which is this book.

22. And it came to pass that ‡two hundred years had passed away; and the second generation had all passed away save it were a few.

23. And now I, Mormon, would that ye should know that the people had multiplied, insomuch that they were spread upon all the face of the land, and that they

---

j, see *o*, 2 Ne. 25. 3 Ne. 9:19. 15:2—8. *k*, see *t*, Mos. 27. *l*, 3 Ne. 24:16. *m*, see *e*, 2 Ne. 32. *n*, see *r*, 3 Ne. 28. *o*, see *l*, 2 Ne. 9. *p*, see *d*, 3 Ne. 28. *r*, see heading of 4 Nephi. *s*, see *f*, 1 Ne. 1:17. *A. D. 72. †A. D. 111. ‡A. D. 201.

30

had become exceeding rich, because of their prosperity in Christ.

24. And now, in this *two hundred and first year there began to be among them those who were lifted up in pride, such as the wearing of costly apparel, and all manner of fine pearls, and of the fine things of the world.

25. And from that time forth they did have their goods and their substance 'no more common among them.

26. And they began to be divided into classes; and they began to build up churches unto themselves to get gain, and began to deny the true church of Christ.

27. And it came to pass that when †two hundred and ten years had passed away there were many churches in the land; yea, there were many churches which professed to know the Christ, and yet they did deny the more parts of his gospel, insomuch that they did receive all manner of wickedness, and did administer that which was sacred unto him to whom it had "been forbidden because of unworthiness.

28. And this church did multiply exceedingly because of iniquity, and because of the power of Satan who did get hold upon their hearts.

29. And again, there was another church which denied the Christ; and they did persecute the true church of Christ, because of their humility and their belief in Christ; and they did despise them because of the many miracles which were wrought among them.

30. Therefore they did exercise power and authority over the ʳdisciples of Jesus who did tarry with them, and they did cast them into prison; but by the power of the word of God, which was in them, the ʷprisons were rent in twain, and they went forth doing mighty miracles among them.

31. Nevertheless, and notwithstanding all these miracles, the people did harden their hearts, and did seek to kill them, even as the Jews at Jerusalem sought to kill Jesus, according to his word.

32. And they did cast them into ˣfurnaces of fire, and they came forth receiving no harm.

33. And they also cast them into ʸdens of wild beasts, and they did play with the wild beasts even as a child with a lamb; and they did come forth from among them, receiving no harm.

34. Nevertheless, the people did harden their hearts, for they were led by many priests and false prophets to build up many churches, and to do all manner of iniquity. And they did smite upon the people of Jesus; but the people of Jesus did not smite again. And thus they did dwindle in unbelief and wickedness, from year to year, even until two hundred and thirty years had passed away.

35. And now it came to pass in this year, yea, in the ‡two hundred and thirty and first year, there was a great division among the people.

36. And it came to pass that in this year there arose a people who were called the Nephites, and they were true believers in Christ; and among them there were those who were called by the Lamanites—Jacobites, and Josephites, and Zoramites;

37. Therefore the true believers in Christ, and the true

---

t, see *y*, 3 Ne. 26. *u*, 3 Ne. 18:28. 29. *v*, see *d*, 3 Ne. 28. *w*, ver. 5. 3 Ne. 28:19. *x*, 3 Ne. 28:21. *y*, 3 Ne. 28:22. * A. D. 201. † A. D. 211. ‡ A. D. 231.

worshipers of Christ, (among whom were the *three disciples of Jesus who should tarry) were called Nephites, and Jacobites, and Josephites, and Zoramites.

38. And it came to pass that they who rejected the gospel were called Lamanites, and Lemuelites, and Ishmaelites; and they did not dwindle in unbelief, but they did ²ᵃwilfully rebel against the gospel of Christ; and they did teach their children that they should not believe, even as their fathers, from the beginning, did dwindle.

39. And it was because of the wickedness and abomination of their fathers, even as it was in the beginning. And they were taught to hate the children of God, even as the Lamanites were taught to ²ᵇhate the children of Nephi from the beginning.

40. And it came to pass that *two hundred and forty and four years had passed away, and thus were the affairs of the people. And the more wicked part of the people did wax strong, and became exceedingly more numerous than were the people of God.

41. And they did still continue to build up churches unto themselves, and adorn them with all manner of precious things. And thus did two hundred and fifty years pass away, and also two hundred and sixty years.

42. And it came to pass that the wicked part of the people began again to build up the ²ᶜsecret oaths and combinations of Gadianton.

43. And also the people who were called the people of Nephi began to be proud in their hearts, because of their exceeding riches, and become vain like unto their brethren, the Lamanites.

44. And from this time the ²ᵈdisciples began to sorrow for the sins of the world.

45. And it came to pass that when three hundred years had passed away, both the people of Nephi and the Lamanites had become exceeding wicked one like unto another.

46. And it came to pass that the ²ᵉrobbers of Gadianton did spread over all the face of the land; and there were none that were righteous save it were the disciples of Jesus. And gold and silver did they lay up in store in abundance, and did traffic in all manner of traffic.

47. And it came to pass that after †three hundred and five years had passed away, (and the people did still remain in wickedness) Amos died; and his brother, Ammaron, did keep the record in his stead.

48. And it came to pass that when ‡three hundred and twenty years had passed away, Ammaron, being constrained by the Holy Ghost, did hide up the records which were sacred—yea, even ²ᶠall the sacred records which had been handed down from generation to generation, which were sacred—even until the three hundred and twentieth year from the coming of Christ.

49. And he did hide them up unto the Lord, that they might come again ²ᵍunto the remnant of the house of Jacob, according to the prophecies and the promises of the Lord. And thus is the end of the record of Ammaron.

---

z, see d, 3 Ne. 28. 2a, 3 Ne. 27:32. Morm. 1:16. 2b, see n, Jac. 7. 2c, see i, 2 Ne. 10. He. 2:3—14. 2d, 3 Ne. 28:9. 2e, see 2c. 2f, Al. 37:2—4. He. 3:13, 15, 16. 2g, 3 Ne. 21:26. * A. D. 245. † A. D. 306. ‡ A. D. 321.

THE BOOK OF MORMON

CHAPTER 1.

Ammaron's charge to Mormon respecting the sacred engravings—War and wickedness—The three Nephite disciples depart—Mormon restrained from preaching—Predictions of Abinadi and Samuel the Lamanite fulfilled.

1. And now I, Mormon, make a record of the things which I have both seen and heard, and call it the ᵃBook of Mormon.

2. And about the time that ᵇAmmaron hid up the records unto the Lord, he came unto me, (I being about ten years of age, and I began to be learned somewhat after the manner of the learning of my people) and Ammaron said unto me: I perceive that thou art a sober child, and art quick to observe;

3. Therefore, when ye are about twenty and four years old I would that ye should remember the things that ye have observed concerning this people; and when ye are of that age go to the land ᶜAntum, unto a hill which shall be called ᵈShim; and there have I ᵉdeposited unto the Lord all the sacred engravings concerning this people.

4. And behold, ye shall take the ᶠplates of Nephi unto yourself, and the remainder shall ye leave in the place where they are; and ye shall engrave on the plates of Nephi ᵍall the things that ye have observed concerning this people.

5. And I, Mormon, being a descendant of ʰNephi, (and my father's name was Mormon) I remembered the things which Ammaron commanded me.

6. And it came to pass that I, being *eleven years old, was carried by my father into the ⁱland southward, even to the ʲland of Zarahemla.

7. The whole face of the land had become covered with buildings, and the people were as numerous almost, as it were the sand of the sea.

8. And it came to pass in this year there began to be a war between the Nephites, who consisted of the Nephites and the Jacobites and the Josephites and the Zoramites; and this war was between the Nephites, and the Lamanites and the Lemuelites and the Ishmaelites.

9. Now the Lamanites and the Lemuelites and the Ishmaelites were called Lamanites, and the two parties were Nephites and Lamanites.

10. And it came to pass that the war began to be among them in the borders of Zarahemla, by the ᵏwaters of Sidon.

11. And it came to pass that the Nephites had gathered together a great number of men, even to exceed the number of thirty thousand. And it came to pass that they did have in this same year a number of battles, in which the Nephites did beat the Lamanites and did slay many of them.

12. And it came to pass that the Lamanites withdrew their design, and there was peace settled in the land; and peace did remain for the space of about four years, that there was no bloodshed.

13. But wickedness did prevail

---

a, Morm. 2:17, 18. 5:9. *b*, 4 Ne. 47—49. *c*, Morm. 2:17. *d*, Morm. 4:23. Eth. 9:3. *e*, 4 Ne. 48. *f*, see *f*, 1 Ne. 1. *g*, Morm. 2:18. *h*, 3 Ne. 5:12, 20. See *b*, Mos. 18. *i*, see *n*, Al. 46. *j*, Om. 13. *k*, see *g*, Al. 2. *ABOUT A. D. 322.

MORMON, 2.

upon the face of the whole land, insomuch that the Lord did take away his ˡbeloved disciples, and the work of miracles and of healing did cease because of the iniquity of the people.

14. And there were no gifts from the Lord, and the Holy Ghost did not come upon any, because of their wickedness and unbelief.

15. And I, *being fifteen years of age and being somewhat of a sober mind, therefore I was visited of the Lord, and tasted and knew of the goodness of Jesus.

16. And I did endeavor to preach unto this people, but my mouth was shut, and I was forbidden that I should preach unto them; for behold they had ᵐwilfully rebelled against their God; and the ⁿbeloved disciples were taken away out of the land, because of their iniquity.

17. But I did remain among them, but I was forbidden to preach unto them, because of the hardness of their hearts; and because of the hardness of their hearts the land was ᵒcursed for their sake.

18. And these ᵖGadianton robbers, who were among the Lamanites, did infest the land, insomuch that the inhabitants thereof began to hide up their treasures in the earth; and they became slippery, because the Lord had ᑫcursed the land, that they could not hold them, nor retain them again.

19. And it came to pass that there were sorceries, and witchcrafts, and magics; and the power of the evil one was wrought upon all the face of the land, even unto the fulfilling of all the ʳwords of Abinadi, and also Samuel the Lamanite.

CHAPTER 2.

Mormon leads the Nephite armies— More of the Gadianton robbers—By treaty the land northward is given to the Nephites, and the land southward to the Lamanites.

1. And it came to pass in that ᵃsame year there began to be a war again between the Nephites and the Lamanites. And notwithstanding I being young, was large in stature; therefore the people of Nephi appointed me that I should be their leader, or the leader of their armies.

2. Therefore it came to pass that †in my sixteenth year I did go forth at the head of an army of the Nephites, against the Lamanites; therefore three hundred and twenty and six years ᵇhad passed away.

3. And it came to pass that in the three hundred and twenty and seventh year the Lamanites did come upon us with exceeding great power, insomuch that they did frighten my armies; therefore they would not fight, and they began to retreat towards the ᶜnorth countries.

4. And it came to pass that we did come to the city of Angola, and we did take possession of the city, and make preparations to defend ourselves against the Lamanites. And it came to pass that we did ᵈfortify the city with our might; but notwithstanding all our fortifications the Lamanites did come upon us and did drive us out of the city.

5. And they did also drive us forth out of the land of David.

---

l, 3 Ne. 28:2—12. See *d*, 3 Ne. 28. *m*, see 2*a*, 4 Ne. *n*, see *l*. *o*, see *d*, 2 Ne. 1. *p*, see 2*c*, 4 Ne. *q*, see *d*, 2 Ne. 1. *r*, He. 13:18—23, 30—37. Morm. 2:10—15.
CHAP. 2: *a*, Morm. 1:12, 15. *b*, 3 Ne. 2:7, 8. *c*, see 2*r*, Al. 22. See also *p*, Al. 46. *d*, see *c*, Al. 48. * ABOUT A. D. 326. † A. D. 327—328.

6. And we marched forth and came to the land of Joshua, which was in the borders west by the seashore.

7. And it came to pass that we did gather in our people as fast as it were possible, that we might get them together in one body.

8. But behold, the land was filled with ᶜrobbers and with Lamanites; and notwithstanding the great destruction which hung over my people, they did not repent of their evil doings; therefore there was blood and carnage spread throughout all the face of the land, both on the part of the Nephites and also on the part of the Lamanites; and it was one complete revolution throughout all the face of the land.

9. And now, the Lamanites had a king, and his name was ᶠAaron; and he came against us with an army of forty and four thousand. And behold, I withstood him with forty and two thousand. And it came to pass that I beat him with my army that he fled before me. And behold, all this was done, and *three hundred and thirty years had passed away.

10. And it came to pass that the Nephites began to repent of their iniquity, and began to cry even as had been prophesied by ᵍSamuel the prophet; for behold no man could keep that which was his own, for the thieves, and the robbers, and the murderers, and the magic art, and the witchcraft which was in the land.

11. Thus there began to be a mourning and a lamentation in all the land because of these things, and more especially among the people of Nephi.

12. And it came to pass that when I, Mormon, saw their lamentation and their mourning and their sorrow before the Lord, my heart did begin to rejoice within me, knowing the mercies and the long-suffering of the Lord, therefore supposing that he would be merciful unto them that they would again become a righteous people.

13. But behold this my joy was vain, for their sorrowing was not unto repentance, because of the goodness of God; but it was rather the sorrowing of the damned, because the Lord would not always suffer them to take happiness in sin.

14. And they did not come unto Jesus with broken hearts and contrite spirits, but they did curse God, and wish to die. Nevertheless they would struggle with the sword for their lives.

15. And it came to pass that my sorrow did return unto me again, and I saw that the day of grace was passed with them, both temporally and spiritually; for I saw thousands of them hewn down in open rebellion against their God, and heaped up as dung upon the face of the land. And thus †three hundred and forty and four years had passed away.

16. And it came to pass that in the three hundred and forty and fifth year the Nephites did begin to flee before the Lamanites; and they were pursued until they came even to the land of Jashon, before it was possible to stop them in their retreat.

17. And now, the ʰcity of Jashon was near the land where Ammaron had ⁱdeposited the records unto the Lord, that they might not be destroyed. And behold I had gone according to the word of Ammaron, and taken the

---

c, see 2c, 4 Ne. 48, 49. *f*, Moro. 9:17. *g*, see *r*, Morm. 1. *h*, Morm. 1:3. 4:23. *i*, 4 Ne.
*A. D. 331. †A. D. 345.

MORMON, 3.   463

ʲplates of Nephi, and did make a record according to the words of Ammaron.

18. And upon the plates of Nephi I did make a ᵏfull account of all the wickedness and abominations; but upon ˡthese plates I did forbear to make a full account of their wickedness and abominations, for behold, a continual scene of wickedness and abominations has been before mine eyes ever since I have been sufficient to behold the ways of man.

19. And wo is me because of their wickedness; for my heart has been filled with sorrow because of their wickedness, all my days; nevertheless, I know that I shall be ᵐlifted up at the last day.

20. And it came to pass that in this year the people of Nephi again were hunted and driven. And it came to pass that we were driven forth until we had come northward to the land which was called Shem.

21. And it came to pass that we did ⁿfortify the city of Shem, and we did gather in our people as much as it were possible, that perhaps we might save them from destruction.

22. And it came to pass in the *three hundred and forty and sixth year they began to come upon us again.

23. And it came to pass that I did speak unto my people, and did urge them with great energy, that they would stand boldly before the Lamanites and fight for their wives, and their children, and their houses, and their homes.

24. And my words did arouse them somewhat to vigor, insomuch that they did not flee from before the Lamanites, but did stand with boldness against them.

25. And it came to pass that we did contend with an army of thirty thousand against an army of fifty thousand. And it came to pass that we did stand before them with such firmness that they did flee from before us.

26. And it came to pass that when they had fled we did pursue them with our armies, and did meet them again, and did beat them; nevertheless the strength of the Lord was not with us; yea, we were left to ourselves, that the Spirit of the Lord did not abide in us; therefore we had become weak like unto our brethren.

27. And my heart did sorrow because of this the great calamity of my people, because of their wickedness and their abominations. But behold, we did go forth against the Lamanites and the ᵒrobbers of Gadianton, until we had again taken possession of the lands of our inheritance.

28. And the †three hundred and forty and ninth year had passed away. And in the three hundred and fiftieth year we made a treaty with the Lamanites and the robbers of Gadianton, in which we did get the lands of our inheritance divided.

29. And the Lamanites did give unto us the ᵖland northward, yea, even to the ᑫnarrow passage which led into the ʳland southward. And we did give unto the Lamanites all the land southward.

CHAPTER 3.

Nephites continue in wickedness—Mormon refuses to be their military leader—His address to future generations—The twelve to judge the house of Israel.

1. And it came to pass that the Lamanites did not come to

ʲ, Morm. 1:4. See ʲ, 1 Ne. 1. ᵏ, Morm. 1:4. ˡ, see g, 3 Ne. 5. ᵐ, see p, Mos. 23.
ⁿ, see c, Al. 48. ᵒ, see 2c, 4 Ne. ᵖ, see c. ᑫ, see 2v, Al. 22. ʳ, see n, Al. 46.
* A. D. 346. † A. D. 350.

battle again *until ten years more had passed away. And behold, I had employed my people, the Nephites, in preparing their lands and their arms against the time of battle.

2. And it came to pass that the Lord did say unto me: Cry unto this people—Repent ye, and come unto me, and be ye ᵃbaptized, and build up again my church, and ye shall be spared.

3. And I did cry unto this people, but it was in vain; and they did not realize that it was the Lord that had spared them, and granted unto them a chance for repentance. And behold they did harden their hearts against the Lord their God.

4. And it came to pass that after this tenth year had passed away, making, in the whole, three hundred and sixty years from the coming of Christ, the king of the Lamanites sent an epistle unto me, which gave unto me to know that they were preparing to come again to battle against us.

5. And it came to pass that I did cause my people that they should gather themselves together at the ᵇland Desolation, to a city which was in the borders, by the ᶜnarrow pass which led into the ᵈland southward.

6. And there we did place our armies, that we might stop the armies of the Lamanites, that they might not get possession of any of our lands; therefore we did ᵉfortify against them with all our force.

7. And it came to pass that in the three hundred and sixty and first year the Lamanites did come down to the ᶠcity of Desolation to battle against us; and it came to pass that in that year we did beat them, insomuch that they did return to their own lands again.

8. And in the †three hundred and sixty and second year they did come down again to battle. And we did beat them again, and did slay a great number of them, and their dead were cast into the sea.

9. And now, because of this great thing which my people, the Nephites, had done, they began to boast in their own strength, and began to swear before the heavens that they would avenge themselves of the blood of their brethren who had been slain by their enemies.

10. And they did swear by the heavens, and also by the throne of God, that they would go up to battle against their enemies, and would cut them off from the face of the land.

11. And it came to pass that I, Mormon, did utterly refuse from this time forth to be a commander and a leader of this people, because of their wickedness and abomination.

12. Behold, I had led them, notwithstanding their wickedness I had led them many times to battle, and had loved them, according to the love of God which was in me, with all my heart; and my soul had been poured out in prayer unto my God all the day long for them; nevertheless, it was without faith, because of the hardness of their hearts.

13. And ᵍthrice have I delivered them out of the hands of their enemies, and they have repented not of their sins.

14. And when they had ʰsworn

a, see *u*, 2 Ne. 9. *b*, see 2*l*, Al. 22. *c*, see 2*v*, Al. 22. *d*, see *n*, Al. 46. *e*, see *c*, Al. 48. *f*, see 2*l*, Al. 22. *g*, vers. 7, 8. Morm. 2:27—29. *h*, vers. 9, 10.
* A. D. 360. † A. D. 362.

by all that had been forbidden them by our Lord and Savior Jesus Christ, that they would go up unto their enemies to battle, and avenge themselves of the blood of their brethren, behold the voice of the Lord came unto me, saying:

15. Vengeance is mine, and I will repay; and because this people repented not after I had delivered them, behold, they shall be ʲcut off from the face of the earth.

16. And it came to pass that I utterly refused to go up against mine enemies; and I did even as the Lord had commanded me; and I did stand as an idle witness to manifest unto the world the things which I saw and heard, according to the manifestations of the Spirit which had testified of things to come.

17. Therefore I ʲwrite unto you, Gentiles, and also unto you, house of Israel, when the work shall ᵏcommence, that ye shall be about to prepare to return to the land of your inheritance;

18. Yea, behold, I write unto all the ends of the earth; yea, unto you, twelve tribes of Israel, who shall be judged according to your works ˡby the twelve whom Jesus chose to be his disciples in the land of Jerusalem.

19. And I write also unto the remnant of this people, who shall also be judged ᵐby the twelve whom Jesus chose in this land; and ⁿthey shall be judged by the other twelve whom Jesus chose in the land of Jerusalem.

20. And these things doth the Spirit manifest unto me; therefore I write unto you all. And for this cause I write unto you, that ye may know that ye must ᵒall stand before the judgment-seat of Christ, yea, every soul who belongs to the whole human family of Adam; and ye must stand to be judged of your works, whether they be good or evil;

21. And also that ye may believe the gospel of Jesus Christ, which ye shall ᵖhave among you; and also that the Jews, the covenant people of the Lord, shall have ᑫother witness besides him whom they saw and heard, that Jesus, whom they slew, was the very Christ and the ʳvery God.

22. And I would that I could persuade all ye ends of the earth to repent and prepare to stand before the judgment-seat of Christ.

CHAPTER 4.

Nephites begin a war of revenge upon Lamanites—Nephites no longer prevail—Sacred records taken from the hill Shim.

1. And now it came to pass that in the *three hundred and sixty and third year the Nephites did go up with their armies to battle against the Lamanites, out of the ᵃland Desolation.

2. And it came to pass that the armies of the Nephites were driven back again to the land of Desolation. And while they were yet weary, a fresh army of the Lamanites did come upon them; and they had a sore battle, insomuch that the Lamanites did take possession of the ᵇcity Desolation, and did slay many of the Nephites, and did take many prisoners.

i, Morm. 6. *j*, see *c*, 2 Ne. 27. *k*, see *e*, 1 Ne. 15. *l*, 1 Ne. 12:9. *m*, 1 Ne. 12:10. 3 Ne. 27:27. *n*, 1 Ne. 12:9. *o*, see *d*, 3 Ne. 26. *p*, 1 Ne. 13:20—29, 41, 42. *q*, see *k*, 2 Ne. 25. *r*, 2 Ne. 26:12. See *b*, Mos. 3. Chap. 4: *a*, see 2*l*, Al. 22. *b*, see 2*l*, Al. 22. * A. D. 363.

3. And the remainder did flee and join the inhabitants of the ᶜcity Teancum. Now the city Teancum lay in the borders by the seashore; and it was also near the ᵈcity Desolation.

4. And it was because the armies of the Nephites went up unto the Lamanites that they began to be smitten; for were it not for that, the Lamanites could have had no power over them.

5. But, behold, the judgments of God will overtake the wicked; and it is by the wicked that the wicked are punished; for it is the wicked that stir up the hearts of the children of men unto bloodshed.

6. And it came to pass that the Lamanites did make preparations to come against the city Teancum.

7. And it came to pass in the three hundred and sixty and fourth year the Lamanites did come against the ᵉcity Teancum, that they might take possession of the city Teancum also.

8. And it came to pass that they were repulsed and driven back by the Nephites. And when the Nephites saw that they had driven the Lamanites they did ᶠagain boast of their strength; and they went forth in their own might, and took possession again of the ᵍcity Desolation.

9. And now all these things had been done, and there had been thousands slain on both sides, both the Nephites and the Lamanites.

10. And it came to pass that the three hundred and sixty and sixth year had passed away, and the Lamanites came again upon the Nephites to battle; and yet the Nephites repented not of the evil they had done, but persisted in their wickedness continually.

11. And it is impossible for the tongue to describe, or for man to write a perfect description of the horrible scene of the blood and carnage which was among the people, both of the Nephites and of the Lamanites; and every heart was hardened, so that they delighted in the shedding of blood continually.

12. And there never had been so great wickedness among all the children of Lehi, nor even among all the house of Israel, according to the words of the Lord, as was among this people.

13. And it came to pass that the Lamanites did take possession of the ʰcity Desolation, and this because their number did exceed the number of the Nephites.

14. And they did also march forward against the ⁱcity Teancum, and did drive the inhabitants forth out of her, and did take many prisoners both women and children, and did offer ʲthem up as sacrifices unto their idol gods.

15. And it came to pass that in the three hundred and sixty and seventh year, the Nephites being angry because the Lamanites had ᵏsacrificed their women and their children, that they did go against the Lamanites with exceeding great anger, insomuch that they did beat again the Lamanites, and drive them out of their lands.

16. And the Lamanites did not come again against the Nephites until the three hundred and seventy and fifth year.

17. And in this year they did come down against the Nephites

---

c, vers. 6, 7, 14. *d*, see 2*l*, Al. 22. *e*, see *c*. *f*, Morm. 3:9. *g*, see 2*l*, Al. 22.
h, see 2*l*, Al. 22. *i*, see *c*. *j*, vers. 15, 21. *k*, see *j*.   A. D. 364—375.

with all their powers; and they were not numbered because of the greatness of their number.

18. And from this time forth did the Nephites gain no power over the Lamanites, but began to be swept off by them even as a dew before the sun.

19. And it came to pass that the Lamanites did come down against the [l]city Desolation; and there was an exceedingly sore battle fought in the land Desolation, in the which they did beat the Nephites.

20. And they fled again from before them, and they came to the city Boaz; and there they did stand against the Lamanites with exceeding boldness, insomuch that the Lamanites did not beat them until they had come again the second time.

21. And when they had come the second time, the Nephites were driven and slaughtered with an exceedingly great slaughter; their women and their children were [m]again sacrificed unto idols.

22. And it came to pass that the Nephites did again flee from before them, taking all the inhabitants with them, both in towns and villages.

23. And now I, Mormon, seeing that the Lamanites were about to overthrow the land, therefore I did go to the hill [n]Shim, and did take up all the records which Ammaron had [o]hid up unto the Lord.

CHAPTER 5.

Mormon relents and again leads Nephites—Lamanites outnumber Nephites — Crime and carnage — Mormon's abridgment of the records.

1. And it came to pass that I did go forth among the Nephites, and did repent of the [a]oath which I had made that I would no more assist them; and they gave me command again of their armies, for they looked upon me as though I could deliver them from their afflictions.

2. But behold, I was without hope, for I knew the judgments of the Lord which should come upon them; for they repented not of their iniquities, but did struggle for their lives without calling upon that Being who created them.

3. And it came to pass that the Lamanites did come against us as we had fled to the city of Jordan; but behold, they were driven back that they did not take the city at that time.

4. And it came to pass that they came against us again, and we did maintain the city. And there were also other cities which were maintained by the Nephites, which strongholds did cut them off that they could not get into the country which lay before us, to destroy the inhabitants of our land.

5. But it came to pass that whatsoever lands we had passed by, and the inhabitants thereof were not gathered in, were destroyed by the Lamanites, and their towns, and villages, and cities were burned with fire; and thus three hundred and seventy and nine years passed away.

6. And it came to pass that in the three hundred and eightieth year the Lamanites did come again against us to battle, and we did stand against them boldly; but it was all in vain, for so great were their numbers that they did tread the people of the Nephites under their feet.

7. And it came to pass that we

---
l, see 2*l*, Al. 22. *m*, see *j*. *n*, Morm. 1:3. Eth. 9:3. *o*, see 2*f*, 4 Ne.
CHAP. 5: *a*, Morm. 3:11, 16. A. D. 375—380

did again take to flight, and those whose flight was swifter than the Lamanites' did escape, and those whose flight did not exceed the Lamanites' were swept down and destroyed.

8. And now behold, I, Mormon, do not desire to harrow up the souls of men in casting before them such an awful scene of blood and carnage as was laid before mine eyes; but I, knowing that [b]these things must surely be made known, and that all things which are hid [c]must be revealed upon the house-tops—

9. And also that a knowledge of these things must come unto the remnant of these people, and also unto the Gentiles, who the Lord hath said should [d]scatter this people, and this people should be counted as naught among them—therefore I write a [e]small abridgment, daring not to give a full account of the things which I have seen, because of the commandment which I have received, and also that ye might not have too great sorrow because of the wickedness of this people.

10. And now behold, this I speak unto [f]their seed, and also to the Gentiles who have care for the house of Israel, that realize and know from whence their blessings come.

11. For I know that such will sorrow for the calamity of the house of Israel; yea, they will sorrow for the destruction of this people; they will sorrow that this people had not repented that they might have been clasped in the arms of Jesus.

12. Now these things are written unto the remnant of the house of Jacob; and they are written after this manner, because it is known of God that wickedness will not bring them forth unto them; and they are to be [g]hid up unto the Lord that they may come forth in his own due time.

13. And this is the commandment which I have received; and behold, they shall [h]come forth according to the commandment of the Lord, when he shall see fit, in his wisdom.

14. And behold, they shall go unto the unbelieving of the Jews; and for this intent shall they go —that they may be [i]persuaded that Jesus is the Christ, the Son of the living God; that the Father may bring about, through his most Beloved, his great and eternal purpose, in [j]restoring the Jews, or all the house of Israel, to the land of their inheritance, which the Lord their God hath given them, unto the fulfilling of his covenant;

15. And also that the [k]seed of this people may more fully believe his [l]gospel, which shall go forth unto them from the Gentiles; for this people shall be [m]scattered, and shall [n]become a dark, a filthy, and a loathsome people, beyond the description of that which ever hath been amongst us, yea, even that which hath been among the Lamanites, and this because of their unbelief and [o]idolatry.

16. For behold, the Spirit of the Lord hath already ceased to strive with their fathers; and they are without Christ and God in the world; and they are driven about as chaff before the wind.

b, vers. 9—15. *c*, see *c*, 2 Ne. 27. *d*, vers. 19, 20. 1 Ne. 13:14. 22:7. 2 Ne. 1:11, 12. 10:18. 26:19. 3 Ne. 16:8, 9. 20:27, 28. *e*, see *a*, Morm. 1. *f*, 2 Ne. 1:31. *g*, Morm. 8:4, 13, 14. Moro. 10:2. *h*, see *c*, 2 Ne. 27. *i*, see *f*, 2 Ne. 25. *j*, see *e*, 1 Ne. 15. *k*, see *f*. *l*, 1 Ne. 13:20—29, 38—41. Morm. 7:8, 9. *m*, see *d*. *n*, see *d*, 1 Ne. 2. *o*, see *j*, Morm. 4.

A. D. 380 TO 384.

17. They were once a delightsome people, and they had Christ for their shepherd; yea, they were led even by God the Father.

18. But now, behold, they are led about by Satan, even as chaff is driven before the wind, or as a vessel is tossed about upon the waves, without sail or anchor, or without anything wherewith to steer her; and even as she is, so are they.

19. And behold, the Lord hath reserved their blessings, which they might have received in the land, for the Gentiles ᵖwho shall possess the land.

20. But behold, it shall come to pass that they shall be ᵍdriven and scattered by the Gentiles; and after they have been driven and scattered by the Gentiles, behold, ʳthen will the Lord remember the covenant which he made unto Abraham and unto all the house of Israel.

21. And also the Lord will remember the ˢprayers of the righteous, which have been put up unto him for them.

22. And then, O ye Gentiles, how can ye stand before the power of God, except ye shall repent and turn from your evil ways?

23. Know ye not that ye are in the hands of God? Know ye not that he hath all power, and at his great command the ᵗearth shall be rolled together as a scroll?

24. Therefore, repent ye, and humble yourselves before him, lest he shall come out in justice against you—lest a ᵘremnant of the seed of Jacob shall go forth among you as a lion, and tear you in pieces, and there is none to deliver.

CHAPTER 6.

The hill Cumorah and its records—The final struggle between the two nations—Lamanites victorious—Twenty-four Nephites survive.

1. And now I finish my record concerning the destruction of my people, the Nephites. And it came to pass that we did march forth before the Lamanites.

2. And I, Mormon, wrote an epistle unto the king of the Lamanites, and desired of him that he would grant unto us that we might gather together our people unto the ᵃland of Cumorah, by a hill which was called Cumorah, and there we could give them battle.

3. And it came to pass that the king of the Lamanites did grant unto me the thing which I desired.

4. And it came to pass that we did march forth to the land of Cumorah, and we did pitch our tents round about the hill Cumorah; and it was in a land of many waters, rivers, and fountains; and here we had hope to gain advantage over the Lamanites.

5. And *when ᵇthree hundred and eighty and four years had passed away, we had gathered in all the remainder of our people unto the land Cumorah.

6. And it came to pass that when we had gathered in all our people in one to the land of Cumorah, behold I, Mormon, ᶜbegan to be old; and knowing it to be the last struggle of my people, and having been commanded of the Lord that I should not suf-

---
p, 1 Ne. 13:12—19. 2 Ne. 1:11. 10:10—14, 18, 19. 26:19, 20. 30:3. *q,* see *d.*
r, 3 Ne. 16:8—12. 21:1—11. *s,* Enos 12—18. Morm. 8:24—26. Morm. 9:36, 37.
t, see *c,* 3 Ne. 26. *u,* see *o,* 3 Ne. 20. Chap. 6: *a,* vers. 4—6, 11. Morm. 8:2.
b, 3 Ne. 2:7, 8. *c,* 4 Ne. 48. Morm. 1:2. 8:1. * A. D. 385.

fer the ^drecords which had been handed down by our fathers, which were sacred, to fall into the hands of the Lamanites, (for the Lamanites would destroy them) therefore I made ^ethis record out of the ^fplates of Nephi, and ^ghid up in the ^hhill Cumorah ⁱall the records which had been entrusted to me by the hand of the Lord, save it were ^jthese few plates which I gave unto my son Moroni.

7. And it came to pass that my people, with their wives and their children, did now behold the armies of the Lamanites marching towards them; and with that awful fear of death which fills the breasts of all the wicked, did they await to receive them.

8. And it came to pass that they came to battle against us, and every soul was filled with terror because of the greatness of their numbers.

9. And it came to pass that they did fall upon my people ^kwith the sword, and with the bow, and with the arrow, and with the ax, and with all manner of weapons of war.

10. And it came to pass that my men were hewn down, yea, even my ten thousand who were with me, and I fell wounded in the midst; and they passed by me that they did not put an end to my life.

11. And when they had gone through and hewn down all my people save it were twenty and four of us, (among whom was my son Moroni) and we having survived the dead of our people, did behold on the morrow, when the Lamanites had returned unto their camps, from the top of the ^lhill Cumorah, the ten thousand of my people who were hewn down, being led in the front by me.

12. And we also beheld the ten thousand of my people who were led by my son Moroni.

13. And behold, the ten thousand of Gidgiddonah had fallen, and he also in the midst.

14. And Lamah had fallen with his ten thousand; and Gilgal had fallen with his ten thousand; and Limhah had fallen with his ten thousand; and Joneam had fallen with his ten thousand; and Camenihah, and Moronihah, and Antionum, and Shiblom, and Shem, and Josh, had fallen with their ten thousand each.

15. And it came to pass that there were ten more who did fall by the sword, with their ten thousand each; yea, even all my people, save it were ^mthose twenty and four who were with me, and also a ⁿfew who had escaped into the south countries, and a few who ^odissented over unto the Lamanites, had fallen; and their flesh, and bones, and blood lay upon the face of the earth, being left by the hands of those who slew them to molder upon the land, and to crumble and to return to their mother earth.

16. And my soul was rent with anguish, because of the slain of my people, and I cried:

17. O ye fair ones, how could ye have departed from the ways of the Lord! O ye fair ones, how could ye have rejected that Jesus, who stood with open arms to receive you!

18. Behold, if ye had not done this, ye would not have fallen. But behold, ye are fallen, and I mourn your loss.

d, see 2*f*, 4 Ne. *e*, see *a*, Morm. 1. *f*, see *f*, 1 Ne. 1. *g*, see *g*, Morm. 5. *h*, see *a*.
i, see 2*f*, 4 Ne. *j*, see *a*, Morm. 1. *k*, see 2*p*, Al. 43. *l*, see *a*. *m*, ver. 11. *n*, Morm.
8:2. *o*, see *h*, Al. 45.

A. D. 385.

19. O ye fair sons and daughters, ye fathers and mothers, ye husbands and wives, ye fair ones, how is it that ye could have fallen!

20. But behold, ye are gone, and my sorrows cannot bring your return.

21. And the day soon cometh that your mortal must put on immortality, and these bodies which are now ᵖmoldering in corruption must soon become incorruptible bodies; and then ye must stand before the judgment-seat of Christ, to be judged according to your works; and if it so be that ye are righteous, then are ye blessed with your fathers who have gone before you.

22. O that ye had repented before this great destruction had come upon you. But behold, ye are gone, and the Father, yea, the Eternal Father of heaven, knoweth your state; and he doeth with you according to his justice and mercy.

CHAPTER 7.

Mormon affirms to Lamanites that they are of the house of Israel—Admonishes them for their salvation.

1. And now, behold, I would speak somewhat unto the remnant of this people who are spared, if it so be that God may give unto them my words, that they may know of the things of their fathers; yea, I speak unto you, ye remnant of the house of Israel; and these are the words which I speak:

2. Know ye that ye are of the house of Israel.

3. Know ye that ye must come unto repentance, or ye cannot be saved.

4. Know ye that ye must lay down your weapons of war, and delight no more in the shedding of blood, and take them not again, save it be that God shall command you.

5. Know ye that ye must come to the ᵇknowledge of your fathers, and repent of all your sins and iniquities, and believe in Jesus Christ, that he is the Son of God, and that he was slain by the Jews, and by the power of the Father he hath risen again, whereby he hath gained the ᶜvictory over the grave; and also in him is the ᵈsting of death swallowed up.

6. And he bringeth to pass the ᵉresurrection of the dead, whereby man must be raised to stand before his judgment-seat.

7. And he hath brought to pass the redemption of the world, whereby he that is found guiltless before him at the judgment day hath it given unto him to dwell in the presence of God in his kingdom, to sing ceaseless praises with the ᶠchoirs above, unto the Father, and unto the Son, and unto the Holy Ghost, which are ᵍone God, in a state of happiness which hath no end.

8. Therefore repent, and be ʰbaptized in the name of Jesus, and lay hold upon the gospel of Christ, which shall be set before you, not only in ⁱthis record but also in the record which shall come unto the Gentiles ʲfrom the Jews, which record shall come from the Gentiles unto you.

9. For behold, ᵏthis is written for the intent that ye may believe ˡthat; and if ye believe that ye will believe this also; and if ye believe this ye will ᵐknow concerning your fathers, and also

---

p, see *d*, 2 Ne. 2. CHAP. 7: *b*, see *g*, 2 Ne. 3. *c*, see *h*, Mos. 16. *d*, see *i*, Mos. 16. *e*, see *d*, 2 Ne. 2. *f*, Mos. 2:28. *g*, see *k*, 2 Ne. 31. *h*, see *u*, 2 Ne. 9. *i*, see *a*, Morm. 1. *j*, see *l*, Morm. 5. *k*, 3 Ne. 5:12—17. See *a*, Morm. 1. *l*, see *l*, Morm. 5. *m*, see *g*, 2 Ne. 3. ABOUT A. D. 385.

MORMON, 8.

the marvelous works which were wrought by the power of God among them.

10. And ye will also know that ye are a remnant of the seed of Jacob; therefore ye are numbered among the people of the first covenant; and if it so be that ye believe in Christ, and are ⁿbaptized, first with water, then ᵒwith fire and with the Holy Ghost, following the example of our Savior, according to that which he hath commanded us, it shall be well with you in the day of judgment. Amen.

CHAPTER 8.

Moroni finishes his father's record—After the carnage of Cumorah—Mormon among the slain—Lamanites and robbers possess the land—Mormon's record to come out of the earth—Conditions and calamities of latter days depicted.

1. Behold I, ᵃMoroni, do finish the record of my father, Mormon. Behold, I have but few things to write, which things I have been commanded by my father.

2. And now it came to pass that after the ᵇgreat and tremendous battle at ᶜCumorah, behold, the Nephites who had ᵈescaped into the country southward were hunted by the Lamanites, until they were all destroyed.

3. And my father also was killed by them, and I even remain alone to write the sad tale of the destruction of my people. But behold, they are gone, and I fulfil the commandment of my father. And whether they will slay me, I know not.

4. Therefore I will write and ᵉhide up the records in the earth; and whither I go it matureth not.

5. Behold, my father hath ᶠmade this record, and he hath written the intent thereof. And behold, I would write it also if I had room upon the ᵍplates, but I have not; and ore I have none, for I am alone. My father hath been ʰslain in battle, and all my kinsfolk, and I have not friends nor whither to go; and ⁱhow long the Lord will suffer that I may live I know not.

6. Behold, *four hundred years have passed away since the coming of our Lord and Savior.

7. And behold, the Lamanites have hunted my people, the Nephites, down from city to city and from place to place, even until they are ʲno more; and great has been their fall; yea, great and marvelous is the destruction of my people, the Nephites.

8. And behold, it is the hand of the Lord which hath done it. And behold also, the Lamanites are at war one with another; and the whole face of this land is one continual round of murder and bloodshed; and no one knoweth the ᵏend of the war.

9. And now, behold, I say no more concerning them, for there are none save it be the Lamanites and ˡrobbers that do exist upon the face of the land.

10. And there are none that do know the true God save it be the ᵐdisciples of Jesus, who did tarry in the land until the wickedness of the people was so great that the Lord would not suffer them to ⁿremain with the people; and whether they be upon the face of the land no man knoweth.

11. But behold, my ᵒfather and I have seen them, and they have ministered unto us.

---

n, see u, 2 Ne. 9. o, see y, 3 Ne. 9. CHAP. 8: a, Morm. 6:6. Moro. 9:24. b, Morm. 6:8—15. c, see a, Morm. 6. d, Morm. 6:15. e, see g, Morm. 5. f, see a, Morm. 1. g, Morm. 6:6. h, ver. 3. i, Moro. 1. 10:1, 2. j, see d, 1 Ne. 12. k, 1 Ne. 12:20—23. l, see 2c, 4 Ne. m, see d, 3 Ne. 28. n, Morm. 1:16. o, 3 Ne. 28:26.
* A. D. 401.

12. And whoso receiveth ᵖthis record, and shall not condemn it because of the imperfections which are in it, the same shall know of ᵍgreater things than these. Behold, I am Moroni; and were it possible, I would make all things known unto you.

13. Behold, I make an end of speaking concerning this people. I am the son of Mormon, and my father was a ʳdescendant of Nephi.

14. And I am the same who ˢhideth up this record unto the Lord; the plates thereof are of no worth, because of the commandment of the Lord. For he truly saith that no one shall have them to get gain; but the record thereof is of great worth; and whoso shall bring it to light, ᵗhim will the Lord bless.

15. For none can have power to bring it to light save it be given him of God; for God wills that it shall be done with an eye single to his glory, or the welfare of the ancient and long dispersed covenant people of the Lord.

16. And blessed be ᵘhe that shall bring this thing to light; for it shall be brought out of darkness unto light, according to the word of God; yea, it shall be brought ᵛout of the earth, and it shall shine forth out of darkness, and come unto the knowledge of the people; and it shall be done by the power of God.

17. And if there be faults they be the ʷfaults of a man. But behold, we know no fault; nevertheless God knoweth all things; therefore, he that ˣcondemneth, let him be aware lest he shall be in danger of hell fire.

18. And he that saith: Show unto me, or ye shall be ʸsmitten—let him beware lest he commandeth that which is forbidden of the Lord.

19. For behold, the same that judgeth rashly shall be judged rashly again; for according to his works shall his wages be; therefore, he that smiteth shall be smitten again, of the Lord.

20. Behold what the scripture says—man shall not smite, neither shall he judge; for judgment is mine, saith the Lord, and vengeance is mine also, and I will repay.

21. And he that shall breathe out wrath and strifes against the work of the Lord, and against the covenant people of the Lord who are the house of Israel, and shall say: We will destroy the work of the Lord, and the Lord will not remember his covenant which he hath made unto the house of Israel—the same is in danger to be ᶻhewn down and cast into the fire;

22. For the eternal purposes of the Lord shall roll on, until all his promises shall be fulfilled.

23. Search the prophecies of Isaiah. Behold, I cannot write them. Yea, behold I say unto you, that those saints who have gone before me, who have possessed this land, shall cry, yea, even from the ²ᵃdust will they cry unto the Lord; and as the Lord liveth he will remember the covenant which he hath made with them.

24. And he knoweth their prayers, that they were in behalf of their brethren. And he knoweth their faith, for in ²ᵇhis name

---

p, 3 Ne. 5:8—11, 13—18. See *a*, Morm. 1. *q*, 3 Ne. 26:6—11. Eth. 4:8, 13. *r*, 3 Ne. 5:20. *s*, see *s*, 1 Ne. 13. Moro. 10:1, 2. *t*, see *e*, 2 Ne. 3. *u*, see *e*, 2 Ne. 3. *v*, see *c*, 2 Ne. 27. *w*, see Title-page. Morm. 9:31, 33. Eth. 12:22—28, 35. *x*, see Title-page. Vers. 19, 21. 2 Ne. 28:29, 30. 3 Ne. 29. Eth. 4:8—10. *y*, vers. 19, 20. *z*, see *x*. 2*a*, see *s*, Morm. 5. 2*b*, see *c*, Jac. 4. BETWEEN A. D. 400 AND 421.

31

could they remove mountains; and in his name could they cause the earth to shake; and by the power of his word did they cause prisons to tumble to the earth; yea, even the fiery furnace could not harm them, neither wild beasts nor poisonous serpents, because of the power of his word.

25. And behold, [2c]their prayers were also in behalf of [2d]him that the Lord should suffer to bring these things forth.

26. And no one need say they shall not come, for they surely shall, for the Lord hath spoken it; for [2e]out of the earth shall they come, by the hand of the Lord, and none can stay it; and it shall come in a day when it shall be said that [2f]miracles are done away; and it shall come even as if [2g]one should speak from the dead.

27. And it shall come in a day when the [2h]blood of saints shall cry unto the Lord, because of [2i]secret combinations and the works of darkness.

28. Yea, it shall come in a day when the power of God shall be [2j]denied, and churches [2k]become defiled and be lifted up in the pride of their hearts; yea, even in a day when leaders of churches and teachers shall rise in the pride of their hearts, even to the envying of them who belong to their churches.

29. Yea, it shall come in a day when [2l]there shall be heard of fires, and tempests, and vapors of smoke in foreign lands;

30. And there shall also be [2m]heard of wars, rumors of wars, and [2n]earthquakes in divers places.

31. Yea, it shall come in a day when there shall be great pollutions upon the face of the earth; there [2o]shall be murders, and robbing, and lying, and deceivings, and whoredoms, and all manner of abominations; when there shall be many who will say, Do this, or do that, and it mattereth not, for the Lord will uphold such at the last day. But wo unto such, for they are in the gall of bitterness and in the bonds of iniquity.

32. Yea, it shall come in a day when there shall be churches built up that shall say: Come unto me, and for your money you shall be forgiven of your sins.

33. O ye wicked and perverse and stiffnecked people, [2p]why have ye built up churches unto yourselves to get gain? Why have ye [2q]transfigured the holy word of God, that ye might bring damnation upon your souls? Behold, look ye unto the [2r]revelations of God; for behold, the time cometh at that day when all these things must be fulfilled.

34. Behold, the Lord hath shown unto me [2s]great and marvelous things concerning that which must shortly come, at that day when these things shall come forth among you.

35. Behold, I speak unto you as if ye were present, and yet ye are not. But behold, Jesus Christ hath shown you unto me, and I know your doing.

36. And I know that ye do walk in the [2t]pride of your hearts; and there are none save a [2u]few only who do not lift themselves up in

---

2c, see s, Morm. 5. 2d, see e, 2 Ne. 3. 2e, see c, 2 Ne. 27. 2f, 2 Ne. 28:4—6. 3 Ne. 29:7. Morm. 8:28. 9:15—26. See r, 2 Ne. 26. 2g, 2 Ne. 26:15, 16. 33:13. Morm. 9:30. Moro. 10:27. 2h, see f, 2 Ne. 28. 2i, see i, 2 Ne. 10. 2j, see 2f. 2k, vers. 32—38. See q, 2 Ne. 26. 2l, 1 Ne. 22:18. 2 Ne. 27:1—3. 2m, 1 Ne. 14:15—17. 22:13—15. Isa. 66:15, 16. 2n, 2 Ne. 27:2. 2o, 3 Ne. 16:10. 21:19. Chap. 30. 2p, see 2k. 2q, 1 Ne. 13:20—29, 32, 34, 35, 40, 41. 2r, 1 Ne. 14:18—27. Eth. 4:16. 2s, see i, 2 Ne. 25. 2t, 2 Ne. 28. 3 Ne. 16:10. 2u, 2 Ne. 28:14.

BETWEEN A. D. 400 AND 421.

the pride of their hearts, unto the wearing of very fine apparel, unto envying, and strifes, and malice, and persecutions, and all manner of iniquities; and your churches, yea, even every one, have become polluted because of the pride of your hearts.

37. For behold, ye do love money, and your substance, and your fine apparel, and the adorning of your churches, more than ye ^{2v}love the poor and the needy, the sick and the afflicted.

38. O ye pollutions, ye hypocrites, ye teachers, who sell yourselves for that which will canker, why have ye polluted the holy church of God? Why are ye ashamed to take upon you the ^{2w}name of Christ? Why do ye not think that greater is the value of an endless happiness than that misery which never dies—because of the praise of the world?

39. Why do ye adorn yourselves with that which hath no life, and yet ^{2x}suffer the hungry, and the needy, and the naked, and the sick and the afflicted to pass by you, and notice them not?

40. Yea, why do ye build up your ^{2y}secret abominations to get gain, and cause that widows should mourn before the Lord, and also orphans to mourn before the Lord, and also the ^{2z}blood of their fathers and their husbands to cry unto the Lord from the ground, for vengeance upon your heads?

41. Behold, the ^{3a}sword of vengeance hangeth over you; and the time soon cometh that he avengeth the ^{3b}blood of the saints upon you, for he will not suffer their cries any longer.

CHAPTER 9.

Moroni's address to unbelievers—His testimony concerning the Christ—The Nephite language known as reformed Egyptian.

1. And now, I speak also concerning those who do not believe in Christ.

2. Behold, will ye believe in the day of your visitation—behold, when the Lord shall come, yea, even that great day when the ^{a}earth shall be rolled together as a scroll, and the elements shall melt with fervent heat, yea, in that great day when ye shall be brought to stand before the Lamb of God—then will ye say that there is no God?

3. Then will ye longer deny the Christ, or can ye behold the Lamb of God? Do ye suppose that ye shall dwell with him under a consciousness of your guilt? Do ye suppose that ye could be happy to dwell with that holy Being, when your souls are racked with a consciousness of guilt that ye have ever abused his laws?

4. Behold, I say unto you that ye would be more miserable to dwell with a holy and just God, under a consciousness of your filthiness before him, than ye would to dwell with the damned souls in hell.

5. For behold, when ye shall be brought to see your nakedness before God, and also the glory of God, and the holiness of Jesus Christ, it will kindle a flame of unquenchable fire upon you.

6. O then ye unbelieving, turn ye unto the Lord; cry mightily unto the Father in the name of Jesus, that perhaps ye may be found spotless, pure, fair, and white, having been cleansed by

2v, see l, Mos. 4.   2w, see c, Mos. 5.   2x, see l, Mos. 4.   2y, see i, 2 Ne. 10.
2z, see f, 2 Ne. 28.   3a, see k, 1 Ne. 14.   3b, see f, 2 Ne. 28.   CHAP. 9: a, see c,
3 Ne. 26.   BETWEEN A. D. 400 AND 421.

MORMON, 9.

the *b*blood of the Lamb, at that great and last day.

7. And again I speak unto you who deny the revelations of God, and say that they are done away, that there *c*are no revelations, nor prophecies, nor gifts, nor healing, nor speaking with tongues, and the interpretation of tongues;

8. Behold I say unto you, he that denieth these things knoweth not the gospel of Christ; yea, he has not read the scriptures; if so, he does not understand them.

9. For do we not read that God is the *d*same yesterday, today, and forever, and in him there is no variableness neither shadow of changing?

10. And now, if ye have imagined up unto yourselves a god who doth vary, and in whom there is shadow of changing, then have ye imagined up unto yourselves a god who is not a God of miracles.

11. But behold, I will show unto you a God of miracles, even the God of Abraham, and the God of Isaac, and the God of Jacob; and it is that same God who created the heavens and the earth, and all things that in them are.

12. Behold, he *e*created Adam, and by *f*Adam came the fall of man. And because of the fall of man came Jesus Christ, even the *g*Father and the *h*Son; and because of Jesus Christ came the redemption of man.

13. And because of the redemption of man, which came by Jesus Christ, they are brought back into the presence of the Lord; yea, this is wherein *i*all men are redeemed, because the death of Christ bringeth to pass the *j*resurrection, which bringeth to pass a redemption from an *k*endless sleep, from which sleep all men shall be awakened by the power of God when the trump shall sound; and they shall come forth, both small and great, and all shall stand before his bar, being redeemed and loosed from this eternal band of death, which death is a temporal death.

14. And then cometh the judgment of the Holy One upon them; and then cometh the time that he that is *l*filthy shall be filthy still; and he that is righteous shall be righteous still; he that is happy shall be happy still; and he that is unhappy shall be unhappy still.

15. And now, O all ye that have imagined up unto yourselves a god who can do *m*no miracles, I would ask of you, have all these things passed, of which I have spoken? Has the end come yet? Behold I say unto you, Nay; and God has not ceased to be a God of miracles.

16. Behold, are not the things that God hath wrought marvelous in our eyes? Yea, and who can comprehend the marvelous works of God?

17. Who shall say that it was not a miracle that by his word the heaven and the earth should be; and by the power of his word man was created of the *n*dust of the earth; and by the power of his word have miracles been wrought?

18. And who shall say that Jesus Christ did not do many mighty miracles? And there were many mighty miracles wrought by the hands of the apostles.

19. And if there were miracles wrought then, why has God ceased

b, see *f*, 2 Ne. 2. *c*, see *e*, 3 Ne. 29. See 2*f*, Morm. 8. *d*, vers. 10. 19. 1 Ne. 10:18. 19. Al. 7:20. Moro. 8:18. *e*, see *m*, Mos. 2. *f*, 2 Ne. 2:18, 19, 21. 9:6—9. Mos. 3:26. 16:3—5. Al. 12:22, 26. He. 14:16. Eth. 3:13. Moro. 8:8. *g*, see *c*, Mos. 15. *h*, see *b*, Mos. 3. *i*, see *j*, 2 Ne. 9. *j*, see *d*, 2 Ne. 2. *k*, see *g*, 2 Ne. 9. *l*, see *o*, 2 Ne. 9. *m*, see *c*. *n*, see *m*, Mos. 2. BETWEEN A. D. 400 AND 421.

to be a God of miracles and yet be an unchangeable Being? And behold, I say unto you he °changeth not; if so he would ᵖcease to be God; and he ceaseth not to be God, and is a God of miracles.

20. And the reason why he ceaseth to do miracles among the children of men is ᵩbecause that they dwindle in unbelief, and depart from the right way, and know not the God in whom they should trust.

21. Behold, I say unto you that whoso believeth in Christ, doubting nothing, ʳwhatsoever he shall ask the Father in the name of Christ it shall be granted him; and this promise is unto all, even unto the ends of the earth.

22. For behold, thus said Jesus Christ, the Son of God, unto his disciples ˢwho should tarry, yea, and also to ᵗall his disciples, in the hearing of the multitude: Go ye into all the world, and preach the gospel to every creature;

23. And he that believeth and is ᵘbaptized shall be saved, but he that believeth not shall be damned;

24. And ᵛthese signs shall follow them that believe—in my name shall they cast out devils; they shall speak with new tongues; they shall take up serpents; and if they drink any deadly thing it shall not hurt them; they shall lay hands on the sick and they shall recover;

25. And whosoever shall believe in my name, doubting nothing, unto him will I confirm all my words, even unto the ends of the earth.

26. And now, behold, who can stand against the works of the Lord? Who can deny his sayings? Who will rise up against the almighty power of the Lord? Who will despise the works of the Lord? Who will despise the children of Christ? Behold, all ye who are despisers of the works of the Lord, for ye shall ʷwonder and perish.

27. O then despise not, and wonder not, but hearken unto the words of the Lord, and ask the Father in the name of Jesus for what things soever ye shall stand in need. Doubt not, but be believing, and begin as in times of old, and come unto the Lord with all your heart, and work out your own salvation with fear and trembling before him.

28. Be wise in the days of your probation; strip yourselves of all uncleanness; ask not, that ye may consume it on your lusts, but ask with a firmness unshaken, that ye will yield to no temptation, but that ye will serve the true and living God.

29. See that ye are not ˣbaptized unworthily; see that ye partake not of the sacrament of Christ ʸunworthily; but see that ye do all things in worthiness, and do it in the name of Jesus Christ, the Son of the living God; and if ye do this, and ᶻendure to the end, ye will in nowise be cast out.

30. Behold, I speak unto you as though I spake ²ᵃfrom the dead; for I know that ye shall hear my words.

31. Condemn me not because of mine imperfection, neither my father, because of his imperfection, neither them who have written before him; but rather give thanks unto God that he hath made manifest unto you ²ᵇour

---

o, see *d*. *p*, see *f*, 2 Ne. 11. *q*, see *d*, 3 Ne. 17. See *c*. *r*, 3 Ne. 18:20. *s*, see *d*, 3 Ne. 28. *t*, see *c*, 3 Ne. 12. *u*, see *u*, 2 Ne. 9. *r*, see *c*; also Mark 16:17, 18. *w*, ver. 27. *x*, see *u*, 2 Ne. 9. *y*, see *t*, 3 Ne. 18. *z*, see *h*, 2 Ne. 31. *2a*, see *2g*, Morm. 8. *2b*, see *w*, Morm. 8. BETWEEN A. D. 400 AND 421.

imperfections, that ye may learn to be more wise than we have been.

32. And now, behold, we have written this record according to our knowledge, in the characters which are called among us the ^{2c}reformed Egyptian, being handed down and altered by us, according to our manner of speech.

33. And if ^{2d}our plates had been sufficiently large we should have written in Hebrew; but the Hebrew hath been ^{2e}altered by us also; and if we could have written in Hebrew, behold, ye would have had ^{2f}no imperfection in our record.

34. But the Lord knoweth the things which we have written, and also that none other people knoweth our language; therefore he hath prepared ^{2g}means for the interpretation thereof.

35. And these things are written that we may rid our garments of the blood of our brethren, who have ^{2h}dwindled in unbelief.

36. And behold, these things which we have desired concerning our brethren, yea, even their restoration to the knowledge of Christ, are ^{2i}according to the prayers of all the saints who have dwelt in the land.

37. And may the Lord Jesus Christ grant that their prayers may be answered according to their faith; and may God the Father remember the ^{2j}covenant which he hath made with the house of Israel; and may he bless them forever, through faith on the name of Jesus Christ. Amen.

THE BOOK OF ETHER

The record of the Jaredites, taken from the twenty-four plates found by the people of Limhi in the days of king Mosiah.

CHAPTER 1.

The prophet Ether's genealogy—The great tower—Jared and his brother—Their language not confounded—Preparing for migration as directed by the Lord.

1. And now I, Moroni, proceed to give an account of those ancient inhabitants who were destroyed by the hand of the Lord upon the face of this ^{a}north country.

2. And I take mine account from the ^{b}twenty and four plates which were found by the people of Limhi, which is called the Book of Ether.

3. And as I suppose that the first part of this record, which speaks ^{c}concerning the creation of the world, and also of Adam, and an account from that time even to the ^{d}great tower, and whatsoever things transpired among the children of men until that time, is had among the Jews—

4. Therefore I do not write those things which transpired from the days of Adam until that time; but they are had upon the plates; and whoso findeth them, the same will have power that he may get the full account.

5. But behold, I give not the full account, but a ^{e}part of the account I give, from the ^{f}tower down until they were destroyed.

2c, see a, 1 Ne. 1. 2d, see a, Morm. 1. See g, Morm. 8. 2e, 1 Ne. 1:2. 2f, see w, Morm. 8. 2g, Mos. 8:13—18. Eth. 3:23, 28. D. & C. 17:1. 2h, see d, 1 Ne. 2. 2i, see s, Morm. 5. 2j, see j, 3 Ne. 15. Chap. 1: a, see p, Al. 46. b, see k, Mos. 8. c, Mos. 28:17. d, vers. 5, 33. Om. 20—22. Mos. 28:17. e, Eth. 3:17. 15:33. f, see d.

6. And on this wise do I give the account. He that wrote this record was Ether, and he was a descendant of Coriantor.

7. Coriantor was the son of Moron.

8. And Moron was the son of Ethem.

9. And Ethem was the son of Ahah.

10. And Ahah was the son of Seth.

11. And Seth was the son of Shiblon.

12. And Shiblon was the son of Com.

13. And Com was the son of Coriantum.

14. And Coriantum was the son of Amnigaddah.

15. And Amnigaddah was the son of Aaron.

16. And Aaron was a descendant of Heth, who was the son of Hearthom.

17. And Hearthom was the son of Lib.

18. And Lib was the son of Kish.

19. And Kish was the son of Corom.

20. And Corom was the son of Levi.

21. And Levi was the son of Kim.

22. And Kim was the son of Morianton.

23. And Morianton was a descendant of Riplakish.

24. And Riplakish was the son of Shez.

25. And Shez was the son of Heth.

26. And Heth was the son of Com.

27. And Com was the son of Coriantum.

28. And Coriantum was the son of Emer.

29. And Emer was the son of Omer.

30. And Omer was the son of Shule.

31. And Shule was the son of Kib.

32. And Kib was the son of Orihah, who was the son of Jared;

33. Which Jared came forth with his brother and their families, with some others and their families, from the *g*great tower, at the time the Lord *h*confounded the language of the people, and swore in his wrath that *i*they should be scattered upon all the face of the earth; and according to the word of the Lord the people were scattered.

34. And the brother of Jared being a large and mighty man, and a man highly favored of the Lord, Jared, his brother, said unto him: Cry unto the Lord, that he will *j*not confound us that we may not understand our words.

35. And it came to pass that the brother of Jared did cry unto the Lord, and the Lord had compassion upon Jared; therefore he did not confound the language of Jared; and Jared and his brother were not confounded.

36. Then Jared said unto his brother: Cry again unto the Lord, and it may be that he will turn away his anger from them who are our friends, that he confound not their language.

37. And it came to pass that the brother of Jared did cry unto the Lord, and the Lord had compassion upon their friends and their families also, that they *k*were not confounded.

38. And it came to pass that Jared spake again unto his brother, saying: Go and inquire of the Lord whether he will *l*drive us

---

g, see *d*. *h*, vers. 34—37. Gen. 11:7, 9. Om. 22. Mos. 28:17. *i*, vers. 38—43. Om. 22. Mos. 28:17. Gen. 11:8, 9. *j*, see *h*. *k*, see *h*. *l*, see *i*.

out of the land, and if he will drive us out of the land, cry unto him whither we shall go. And who knoweth but the Lord will carry us forth into a land which is choice above all the earth? And if it so be, let us be faithful unto the Lord, that we may receive it for our inheritance.

39. And it came to pass that the brother of Jared did cry unto the Lord according to that which had been spoken by the mouth of Jared.

40. And it came to pass that the Lord did hear the brother of Jared, and had compassion upon him, and said unto him:

41. Go to and gather together thy flocks, both male and female, of every kind; and also of the seed of the earth of every kind; and ᵐthy families; and also Jared thy brother and his family; and ⁿalso thy friends and their families, and the friends of Jared and their families.

42. And when thou hast done this thou shalt go at the head of them down into the valley which is northward. And there will I meet thee, and I will go before thee ᵒinto a land which is choice above all the lands of the earth.

43. And there will I bless thee and thy seed, and raise up unto me of thy seed,•and of the seed of thy brother, and they who shall go with thee, a great nation. And there shall be none ᵖgreater than the nation which I will raise up unto me of thy seed, upon all the face of the earth. And thus I will do unto thee because this long time ye have cried unto me.

CHAPTER 2.

In the valley of Nimrod—Deseret, the honey bee—The Lord again talks with the brother of Jared—Divine decree concerning the land of promise—The place Moriancumer—Barges built.

1. And it came to pass that Jared and his brother, and their families, and also the friends of Jared and his brother and their families, went down into the valley which ᵃwas northward, (and the name of the valley was Nimrod, being called after the mighty hunter) with their flocks which they had gathered together, male and female, of ᵇevery kind.

2. And they did also lay snares and catch fowls of the air; and they did also prepare a vessel, in which they did carry with them the fish of the waters.

3. And they did also carry with them deseret, which, by interpretation, is a honey bee; and thus they did carry with them swarms of bees, and all manner of that which was upon the face of the land, ᶜseeds of every kind.

4. And it came to pass that when they had come down into the ᵈvalley of Nimrod the Lord came ᵉdown and talked with the brother of Jared; and he was in a ᶠcloud, and the brother of Jared saw him not.

5. And it came to pass that the Lord commanded them that they should go forth into the wilderness, yea, into that quarter where there never had man been. And it came to pass that the Lord did go ᵍbefore them, and did talk with them as he stood in a cloud, and gave directions whither they should travel.

6. And it came to pass that they did travel in the wilderness, and did build barges, in which they did cross many waters, being directed continually by the hand of the Lord.

m, Eth. 6:20. n, Eth. 6:16. o, see a, 1 Ne. 2. p, Eth. 15:2. CHAP. 2: a, Eth. 1:42. b, Eth. 1:41. 6:4. 9:18, 19. c, Eth. 1:41. d, ver. 1. e, Eth. 1:42. f, vers. 5, 14. g, Eth. 1:42.

7. And the Lord would not suffer that they should stop beyond the sea in the wilderness, but he would that they should come forth even unto the ᶦland of promise, which was choice above all other lands, which the Lord God had preserved for a righteous people.

8. And he had sworn in his wrath unto the brother of Jared, that whoso should possess this land of promise, from that time henceforth and forever, should serve him, the true and only God, or they should be swept off when the fulness of his wrath should come upon them.

9. And now, we can behold the ʲdecrees of God concerning this land, that it is a land of promise; and whatsoever nation shall possess it shall serve God, or they shall be swept off when the fulness of his wrath shall come upon them. And the fulness of his wrath cometh upon them when they are ripened in iniquity.

10. For behold, this is a land which is choice above all other lands; wherefore he that doth possess it shall serve God or shall be swept off; for it is the everlasting decree of God. And it is not until the fulness of iniquity among the children of the land, that they are swept off.

11. And this cometh unto you, O ye Gentiles, that ye may know the decrees of God—that ye may repent, and not continue in your iniquities until the fulness come, that ye may not bring down the fulness of the wrath of God upon you as the inhabitants of the land have hitherto done.

12. Behold, this is a choice land, and whatsoever nation shall possess it shall be ᵏfree from bondage, and from captivity, and from all other nations under heaven, if they will but serve the God of the land, who is Jesus Christ, who hath been manifested by the things which we have written.

13. And now I proceed with my record; for behold, it came to pass that the Lord did bring Jared and his brethren forth even to that great sea which divideth the lands. And as they came to the sea they pitched their tents; and they called the name of the place Moriancumer; and they dwelt in tents, and dwelt in tents upon the seashore for the space of four years.

14. And it came to pass at the end of four years that the Lord came again unto the brother of Jared, and stood ᶦin a cloud and talked with him. And for the space of three hours did the Lord talk with the brother of Jared, and chastened him because he remembered not to call upon the name of the Lord.

15. And the brother of Jared repented of the evil which he had done, and did call upon the name of the Lord for his brethren who were with him. And the Lord said unto him: I will forgive thee and thy brethren of their sins; but thou shalt not sin any more, for ye shall remember that my Spirit will not always strive with man; wherefore, if ye will sin until ye are fully ripe ye shall be cut off from the presence of the Lord. And these ᵐare my thoughts upon the land which I shall give you for your inheritance; for it shall be a land choice above all other lands.

16. And the Lord said: Go to work and build, after the manner

---

i, vers. 8, 12—15. See *o*, Eth. 1. Also see *d*, 2 Ne. 1. *j*, vers. 10, 11. See *i*. *k*, 1 Ne. 13:19. 2 Ne. 1:7. 10:10—14. *l*, see *f*. *m*, see *i*.

of barges which ye have ⁿhitherto built. And it came to pass that the brother of Jared did go to work, and also his brethren, and built barges after the manner which they had built, according to the instructions of the Lord. And they were small, and they were light upon the water, even like unto the lightness of a fowl upon the water.

17. And they were built after a manner that they were exceeding °tight, even that they would hold water like unto a dish; and the bottom thereof was tight like unto a dish; and the sides thereof were tight like unto a dish; and the ends thereof were peaked; and the top thereof was tight like unto a dish; and the length thereof was the length of a tree; and the door thereof, when it was shut, was tight like unto a dish.

18. And it came to pass that the brother of Jared cried unto the Lord, saying: O Lord, I have performed the work which thou hast commanded me, and I have made the barges according as thou hast directed me.

19. And behold, O Lord, in them there is no light; whither shall we steer? And also we shall perish, for in them we cannot breathe, save it is the air which is in them; therefore we shall perish.

20. And the Lord said unto the brother of Jared: Behold, thou shalt make a hole in the top, and also in the qbottom; and when thou shalt suffer for air thou shalt unstop the hole and receive air. And if it be so that the water come in upon thee, behold, ye shall stop the hole, that ye may not perish in the flood.

21. And it came to pass that the brother of Jared did so, according as the Lord had commanded.

22. And he cried again unto the Lord saying: O Lord, behold I have done even as thou hast commanded me; and I have prepared the vessels for my people, and behold there is no light in them. Behold, O Lord, wilt thou suffer that we shall cross this great water in darkness?

23. And the Lord said unto the brother of Jared: What will ye that I should do that ye may have light in your vessels? For behold, ye cannot have windows, for they will be dashed in pieces; neither shall ye take fire with you, for ye shall not go by the light of fire.

24. For behold, ye shall be as a whale ʳin the midst of the sea; for the mountain waves shall dash upon you. Nevertheless, I will bring you up again out of the depths of the sea; for the winds have gone forth out of my mouth, and also the rains and the floods have I sent forth.

25. And behold, I prepare you against these things; for ye cannot cross this great deep save I prepare you against the waves of the sea, and the winds which have gone forth, and the floods which shall come. Therefore what will ye that I should prepare for you that ye may have light when ye are swallowed up in the depths of the sea?

CHAPTER 3.

The finger of the Lord—Jesus Christ shows himself in the spirit to the brother of Jared—The luminous stones—The interpreters—A record yet to come.

1. And it came to pass that the brother of Jared, (now the number of the vessels which had been

n, ver. 6.   *o,* Eth. C:7.   *q,* vers. 24, 25.   *r,* ver. 25.   Eth. 6:6, 7, 10.

prepared was eight) went forth unto the mount, which they called the mount Shelem, because of its exceeding height, and did molten out of a rock sixteen small stones; and they were white and clear, even as transparent glass; and he did carry them in his hands upon the top of the mount, and cried again unto the Lord, saying:

2. O Lord, thou hast said ^{b}that we must be encompassed about by the floods. Now behold, O Lord, and do not be angry with thy servant because of his weakness before thee; for we know that thou art holy and dwellest in the heavens, and that we are unworthy before thee; because of ^{c}the fall our natures have become evil continually; nevertheless, O Lord, thou hast given us a commandment that we must call upon thee, that from thee we may receive according to our desires.

3. Behold, O Lord, thou hast smitten us because of our iniquity, and hast driven us forth, and for these many years we have been in the wilderness; nevertheless, thou hast been merciful unto us. O Lord, look upon me in pity, and turn away thine anger from this thy people, and suffer not that they shall go forth across this raging deep in darkness; but behold these ^{d}things which I have molten out of the rock.

4. And I know, O Lord, that thou hast all power, and can do whatsoever thou wilt for the benefit of man; therefore touch these stones, O Lord, with ^{e}thy finger, and prepare them that they may shine forth in darkness; and they shall shine forth unto us in the vessels which we have prepared, that we may have light while we shall cross the sea.

5. Behold, O Lord, thou canst do this. We know that thou art able to show forth great power, which looks small unto the understanding of men.

6. And it came to pass that when the brother of Jared had said these words, behold, the Lord stretched forth his hand and touched the stones one by one with his finger. And the ^{f}veil was taken from off the eyes of the brother of Jared, and he ^{g}saw the finger of the Lord; and it was as the finger of a man, like unto flesh and blood; and the brother of Jared fell down before the Lord, for he was struck with fear.

7. And the Lord saw that the brother of Jared had fallen to the earth; and the Lord said unto him: Arise, why hast thou fallen?

8. And he saith unto the Lord: I saw the finger of the Lord, and I feared lest he should smite me; for I knew not that the Lord had flesh and blood.

9. And the Lord said unto him: Because of thy faith thou hast seen that I shall take upon me flesh and blood; and never has man come before me with such exceeding faith as thou hast; for were it not so ye could not have seen my finger. Sawest thou more than this?

10. And he answered: Nay; Lord, show thyself unto me.

11. And the Lord said unto him: Believest thou the words which I shall speak?

12. And he answered: Yea, Lord, I know that thou speakest the truth, for thou art a God of truth, and canst not lie.

13. And when he had said these words, behold, the Lord showed himself unto him, and said: Because thou knowest these

---

b, Eth. 2:24, 25.   *c*, see *f*, Morm. 9.   *d*, vers. 1, 4, 6.   Eth. 6:2, 3, 10.   *e*, vers. 6—9, 19.   Eth. 12:10—21.   *f*, vers. 19, 20.   Eth. 12:10, 21.   *g*, see *e*.

things ye are redeemed ^{h}from the fall; therefore ye are brought back into my presence; therefore I show myself unto you.

14. Behold, I am he who was prepared ^{i}from the foundation of the world to redeem my people. Behold, I am Jesus Christ. I am ^{j}the Father and the ^{k}Son. In me shall all mankind have light, and that eternally, even they who shall believe on my name; and they shall become my sons and my daughters.

15. And ^{l}never have I showed myself unto man whom I have created, for never has man believed in me as thou hast. Seest thou that ye are created after mine own image? Yea, even ^{m}all men were created in the beginning after mine own image.

16. Behold, this body, which ye now behold, is the ^{n}body of my spirit; and ^{o}man have I created after the body of my spirit; and even as I appear unto thee to be in the spirit will I appear unto my people in the flesh.

17. And now, as I, Moroni, said I could ^{p}not make a full account of these things which are written, therefore it sufficeth me to say that Jesus showed himself unto this man in the spirit, even after the manner and in the likeness of the same body even as he showed himself unto the Nephites.

18. And he ministered unto him even as he ministered unto the Nephites; and all this, that this man might know that he was God, because of the many great works which the Lord had showed unto him.

19. And because of the knowledge of this man he could not be kept from beholding ^{r}within the veil; and he ^{s}saw the finger of Jesus, which, when he saw, he ^{t}fell with fear; for he knew that it was the finger of the Lord; and he had faith no longer, for he knew, nothing doubting.

20. Wherefore, having this perfect knowledge of God, he could not be kept ^{u}from within the veil; therefore he saw Jesus; and he did ^{v}minister unto him.

21. And it came to pass that the Lord said unto the brother of Jared: Behold, thou shalt not suffer these things which ye have seen and heard to go forth unto the world, until the ^{w}time cometh that I shall glorify my name in the flesh; wherefore, ye shall treasure up the things which ye have seen and heard, and show it to no man.

22. And behold, when ye shall come unto me, ye shall ^{x}write them and shall seal them up, that no one can interpret them; for ye shall write them in a language that they cannot be read.

23. And behold, these ^{y}two stones will I give unto thee, and ye shall seal them up also with the things which ye shall write.

24. For behold, the ^{z}language which ye shall write I have ^{2a}confounded; wherefore I will cause in my own due time that these stones shall ^{2b}magnify to the eyes of men these things which ye shall write.

25. And when the Lord had said these words, he ^{2c}showed unto the brother of Jared all the inhabitants of the earth which had been, and also all that would be; and he withheld them not

---

h, Eth. 12:19, 21. i, see d, Mos. 4. j, see c, Mos. 15. k, see b, Mos. 3. l, see D. & C. 107:54. m, ver. 16. Mos. 7:27. Al. 18:34. n, 1 Ne. 11:11. o, see m. p, see e, Eth. 1. r, see f. s, see e. t, ver. 6. u, see f. v, ver. 18. w, Eth. 4:1, 2. x, ver. 27. y, see n, Mos. 8. z, ver. 22. 2a, see h, Eth. 1. 2b, see n, Mos. 8. 2c, ver. 26. Eth. 4:4.

ETHER, 4.

from his sight, even unto the ends of the earth.

26. For he had said unto him in times before, that if he would believe in him that he could show unto him all things—it should be shown unto him; therefore the Lord could not withhold anything from him, for he knew that the Lord could show him all things.

27. And the Lord said unto him: Write these things and ²ᵈseal them up; and I will show them in mine own due time unto the children of men.

28. And it came to pass that the Lord commanded him that he should ²ᵉseal up the two stones which he had received, and show them not, until the Lord should show them unto the children of men.

CHAPTER 4.

The brother of Jared commanded to write—Moroni's solemn admonition—Cursed is he who contends against the word of the Lord—Whatsoever persuades men to do good is of God.

1. And the Lord commanded the brother of Jared to go down out of the ᵃmount from the presence of the Lord, and write the things which he had seen; and they were ᵇforbidden to come unto the children of men until after that he should be lifted up upon the cross; and for this cause did king ᶜMosiah keep them, that they should not come unto the world until after Christ should show himself unto his people.

2. And after Christ truly had showed himself unto his people he commanded that they should be made manifest.

3. And now, after that, they have all dwindled in unbelief; and there is none save it be the Lamanites, and they have rejected the gospel of Christ; therefore I am commanded that I should ᵈhide them up again in the earth.

4. Behold, I have written upon these plates the ᵉvery things which the brother of Jared saw; and there never were greater things made manifest than those which were made manifest unto the brother of Jared.

5. Wherefore the Lord hath commanded me to write them; and I have written them. And he commanded me that I should seal them up; and he also hath commanded that I should seal up the interpretation thereof; wherefore I have sealed up the ᶠinterpreters, according to the commandment of the Lord.

6. For the Lord said unto me: They shall not go forth unto the Gentiles ᵍuntil the day that they shall repent of their iniquity, and become clean before the Lord.

7. And in that day that they shall exercise faith in me, saith the Lord, ʰeven as the brother of Jared did, that they may become sanctified in me, then will I manifest unto them the things which the brother of Jared saw, even to the unfolding unto them all my revelations, saith Jesus Christ, the Son of God, ⁱthe Father of the heavens and of the earth, and all things that in them are.

8. And he that will contend against the word of the Lord, ʲlet him be accursed; and he that shall deny these things, let him be accursed; for unto them will I show ᵏno greater things, saith

2d, 2 Ne. 27:6—23. Mos. 28:11—20. Al. 37:21—31. 2e, see n, Mos. 8.
Chap. 4: a, Eth. 3:1. b, Eth. 3:21. c, Mos. 28:11—20. d, see s, 1 Ne. 13. Morm. 8:14. Moro. 10:1, 2. e, vers. 5—7, 13—16. 2 Ne. 27:6—11, 15, 17, 21, 22. Eth. 5:1. f, see n, Mos. 8. g, vers. 7—16. 2 Ne. 27:7, 8, 11. 21. h, Eth. 3. i, see a, Mos. 3. Mos. 3:8. 4:2. 7:27. He. 16:18. j, 2 Ne. 27:14. 28:20, 30. 33:11—15.
k, vers. 13—16. 3 Ne. 26:6—12.

Jesus Christ; for I am he who speaketh.

9. And at my command the heavens are opened and are shut; and at my word ^{l}the earth shall shake; and at my command the inhabitants thereof shall pass away, even so as ^{m}by fire.

10. And he that believeth not my words believeth not my disciples; and if it so be that I do not speak, judge ye; for ye shall know that it is I that speaketh, at the last day.

11. But he that believeth these things which I have spoken, him will I visit with the ^{n}manifestations of my Spirit, and he shall know and bear record. For because of my Spirit he shall know that these things are true; for it persuadeth men to do good.

12. And whatsoever thing ^{o}persuadeth men to do good is of me; for good cometh of none save it be of me. I am the same that leadeth men to all good; he that will not believe my words will ^{p}not believe me—that I am; and he that will not believe me will not believe the Father who sent me. For behold, I am ^{q}the Father, I ^{r}am the light, and the life, and the truth of the world.

13. Come unto me, O ye Gentiles, and I will show unto you the ^{s}greater things, the knowledge which is hid up because of unbelief.

14. Come unto me, O ye house of Israel, and it shall be made manifest unto you how great things the Father hath laid up for you, from the foundation of the world; and it hath not come unto you, because of unbelief.

15. Behold, when ye shall rend that veil of unbelief which doth cause you to remain in your awful state of wickedness, and hardness of heart, and blindness of mind, then shall the ^{t}great and marvelous things which have been hid up from the ^{u}foundation of the world from you—yea, when ye shall call upon the Father in my name, with a broken heart and a contrite spirit, then shall ye know that the Father hath remembered the ^{v}covenant which he made unto your fathers, O house of Israel.

16. And then shall my revelations which I have caused to be written by my servant ^{w}John be unfolded in the eyes of all the people. Remember, when ye see these things, ye shall know that the time is at hand that they shall be made manifest in very deed.

17. Therefore, ^{x}when ye shall receive this record ye may know that the work of the Father has commenced upon all the face of the land.

18. Therefore, repent all ye ends of the earth, and come unto me, and believe in my gospel, and be ^{y}baptized in my name; for he that believeth and is baptized shall be saved; but he that believeth not shall be damned; and ^{z}signs shall follow them that believe in my name.

19. And blessed is he that is found faithful unto my name at the last day, for he shall be ^{2a}lifted up to dwell in the kingdom prepared for him ^{2b}from the foundation of the world. And behold it is I that hath spoken it. Amen.

---

l, He. 12:8—18. 3 Ne. 26:3. Morm. 5:23. 9:2. m, see a, 3 Ne. 25. n, Eth. 5:4. Moro. 10:4, 5. o, Moro. 7:5—22. 10:6, 7. p, ver. 10. 3 Ne. 28:34, 35. q, see c, Mos. 15. r, see m, Mos. 16. s, see k. t, see t, 2 Ne. 25. u, see d, Mos. 4. v, see j, 3 Ne. 15. w, 1 Ne. 14:18—28. x, 3 Ne. 21:1—11, 26—29. y, see u, 2 Ne. 9. z, see e, 3 Ne. 29. See 2f, Morm. 8. 2a, see p, Mos. 23. 2b, see d, Mos. 4.

CHAPTER 5.

Moroni to the future translator of his writings.

1. And now I, Moroni, have written the words which were commanded me, according to my memory; and I have told ^ayou the things which I have ^bsealed up; therefore touch them not in order that ^cye may translate; for that thing is forbidden you, except by and by it shall be wisdom in God.

2. And behold, ye may be privileged that ye may show the plates unto ^dthose who shall assist to bring forth this work;

3. And unto ^ethree shall they be shown by the power of God; wherefore they shall know of a surety that these things are true.

4. And in the mouth of ^fthree witnesses shall these things be established; and the testimony of three, and this work, in the which shall be shown forth the ^gpower of God and also his word, ^hof which the Father, and the Son, and the Holy Ghost bear record—and all this shall stand as a testimony against the world at the last day.

5. And if it so be that they repent and come unto the Father in the name of Jesus, they shall be received into the kingdom of God.

6. And now, if I have no authority for these things, judge ye; for ye shall know that I have authority ⁱwhen ye shall see me, and we shall stand before God at the last day. Amen.

CHAPTER 6.

The story of the Jaredites continued—Their vessels lighted by miracle—Through the depths of the sea to the promised land—The people desire a king—Their leaders foresee evil but yield to the popular will—Death of Jared and his brother.

1. And now I, Moroni, proceed to give the record of Jared and his brother.

2. For it came to pass after the Lord had prepared ^athe stones which the brother of Jared had carried up into the mount, the brother of Jared came down out of the mount, and he did put forth the stones into the ^bvessels which were prepared, one in each end thereof; and behold, they did give light unto the vessels.

3. And thus the Lord caused ^cstones to shine in darkness, to give light unto men, women, and children, that they might not cross the great waters in darkness.

4. And it came to pass that when they had prepared all manner of food, that thereby they might subsist upon the water, and also food for their ^dflocks and herds, and whatsoever beast or animal or fowl that they should carry with them—and it came to pass that when they had done all these things they got aboard of their vessels or barges, and set forth into the sea, commending themselves unto the Lord their God.

5. And it came to pass that the Lord God caused that there should be a ^efurious wind blow upon the face of the waters, towards the promised land; and thus they were tossed upon the waves of the sea before the wind.

6. And it came to pass that they were many times buried in the depths of the sea, because of the mountain waves which broke upon them, and also the great

---

a, 2 Ne. 27:7—12. b, see c, Eth. 4. c, see a. d, see d, 2 Ne. 11. e, ver. 4. See c, 2 Ne. 11. f, see c. g, see t, 1 Ne. 13. See c, 3 Ne. 29. See 2f, Morm. 8. h, 3 Ne. 11:32—36. i, see g, 2 Ne. 33. Chap. 6: a, see d, Eth. 3. b, Eth. 3. c, see d, Eth. 3. d, see b, Eth. 2. e, ver. 6. Eth. 2:24, 25.

and terrible tempests which were caused by the fierceness of the wind.

7. And it came to pass that when they were buried in the deep there was no water that could hurt them, their vessels being *tight like unto a dish, and also they were tight like unto the ark of Noah; therefore when they were encompassed about by many waters they did cry unto the Lord, and he did bring them forth again upon the top of the waters.

8. And it came to pass that the wind did never cease to blow towards the promised land while they were upon the waters; and thus they were driven forth before the wind.

9. And they did sing praises unto the Lord; yea, the brother of Jared did sing praises unto the Lord, and he did thank and praise the Lord all the day long; and when the night came, they did not cease to praise the Lord.

10. And thus they were driven forth; and no monster of the sea could break them, neither whale that could mar them; and they did have *light continually, whether it was above the water or under the water.

11. And thus they were driven forth, three hundred and forty and four days upon the water.

12. And they did land upon the ʰshore of the promised land. And when they had set their feet upon the shores of the promised land they bowed themselves down upon the face of the land, and did humble themselves before the Lord, and did shed tears of joy before the Lord, because of the multitude of his tender mercies over them.

13. And it came to pass that they went forth upon the face of the land, and began to till the earth.

14. And Jared had four sons; and they were called Jacom, and Gilgah, and Mahah, and Orihah.

15. And the brother of Jared also begat sons and daughters.

16. And the friends of Jared and his brother were in number about twenty and two souls; and they also begat sons and daughters before they came to the promised land; and therefore they began to be many.

17. And they were taught to walk humbly before the Lord; and they were also taught from on high.

18. And it came to pass that they began to spread upon the face of the land, and to multiply and to till the earth; and they did wax strong in the land.

19. And the brother of Jared began to be old, and saw that he must soon go down to the grave; wherefore he said unto Jared: Let us gather together our people that we may number them, that we may know of them what they will ⁱdesire of us before we go down to our graves.

20. And accordingly the people were gathered together. Now the number of the sons and the daughters of the brother of Jared ʲwere twenty and two souls; and the number of sons and daughters of Jared were twelve, he having four sons.

21. And it came to pass that they did number their people; and after that they had numbered them, they did desire of them the things which they would that they should do before they went down to their graves.

22. And it came to pass that

---

f, Eth. 2:17, 20.   *g*, see *d*, Eth. 3.   *h*, Eth. 7:6.   Al. 22:29—34.   *i*, vers. 21, 22.   *j*, Eth. 1:41.

the people ᵏdesired of them that they should anoint one of their sons to be a king over them.

23. And now behold, this was grievous unto them. And the brother of Jared said unto them: Surely this thing ˡleadeth into captivity.

24. But Jared said unto his brother: Suffer them that they may have a king. And therefore he said unto them: Choose ye out from among our sons a king, even whom ye will.

25. And it came to pass that they chose even the firstborn of the brother of Jared; and his name was Pagag. And it came to pass that he refused and would not be their king. And the people would that his father should constrain him, but his father would not; and he commanded them that they should constrain no man to be their king.

26. And it came to pass that they chose all the brothers of Pagag, and they would not.

27. And it came to pass that neither would the sons of Jared, even all save it were one; and ᵐOrihah was anointed to be king over the people.

28. And he began to reign, and the people began to prosper; and they became exceedingly rich.

29. And it came to pass ⁿthat Jared died, and his brother also.

30. And it came to pass that Orihah did walk humbly before the Lord, and did remember how great things the Lord had done for his father, and also taught his people how great things the Lord had done for their fathers.

CHAPTER 7.

Orihah's righteous reign, followed by rebellion, usurpation and strife—The rival kingdoms of Shule and Cohor—Wickedness and idolatry—Prophets appear and the people repent.

1. And it came to pass that Orihah did execute judgment upon the land in righteousness all his days, whose days were exceeding many.

2. And he begat sons and daughters; yea, he begat thirty and one, among whom were twenty and three sons.

3. And it came to pass that he also begat ᵇKib in his old age. And it came to pass that Kib reigned in ˙his stead; and Kib begat ᶜCorihor.

4. And when Corihor was thirty and two years old he rebelled against his father, and went over and dwelt in the ᵈland of Nehor; and he begat sons and daughters, and they became exceeding fair; wherefore Corihor drew away many people after him.

5. And when he had gathered together an army he came up unto the land of ᵉMoron where the king dwelt, and took him captive, which brought to pass the saying of the brother of Jared that they would be ᶠbrought into captivity.

6. Now the land of ᵍMoron, where the king dwelt, was near the land which is called ʰDesolation by the Nephites.

7. And it came to pass that Kib dwelt in captivity, and his people under Corihor his son, until he became exceeding old; nevertheless Kib begat Shule in his old age, while he was yet in captivity.

8. And it came to pass that Shule was angry with his brother; and Shule waxed strong, and became mighty as to the strength of

---

k, vers. 19, 21. *l,* Eth. 7:5. *m,* vers. 14, 30. Eth. 1:32. 7:1. *n,* ver. 19. CHAP. 7: *b,* vers. 3—10. Eth. 1:31, 32. *c,* vers. 3—15. *d,* ver. 9. *e,* vers. 6, 16, 17. Eth. 14:6, 11. *f,* Eth. 6:23. *g,* see *e.* *h,* see 2*l,* Al. 22.

a man; and he was also mighty in judgment.

9. Wherefore, he came to the hill Ephraim, and he did molten out of the hill, and made swords out of ⁱsteel for those whom he had drawn away with him; and after he had armed them with swords he returned to the ʲcity Nehor, and gave battle unto his brother Corihor, by which means he obtained the kingdom and restored it unto his father Kib.

10. And now because of the thing which Shule had done, his father bestowed upon him the kingdom; therefore he began to reign in the stead of his father.

11. And it came to pass that he did execute judgment in righteousness; and he did spread his kingdom upon all the face of the land, for the people had become exceeding numerous.

12. And it came to pass that Shule also begat many sons and daughters.

13. And Corihor repented of the many evils which he had done; wherefore Shule gave him power in his kingdom.

14. And it came to pass that Corihor had many sons and daughters. And among the sons of Corihor there was one whose name was Noah.

15. And it came to pass that Noah rebelled against Shule, the king, and also his father Corihor, and drew away Cohor his brother, and also all his brethren and many of the people.

16. And he gave battle unto Shule, the king, in which he did obtain the land of their ᵏfirst inheritance; and he became a king over that part of the land.

17. And it came to pass that he gave battle again unto Shule, the king; and he took Shule, the king, and carried him away captive into ˡMoron.

18. And it came to pass as he was about to put him to death, the sons of Shule crept into the house of Noah by night and slew him, and broke down the door of the prison and brought out their father, and placed him upon his throne in his own kingdom.

19. Wherefore, the son of Noah did build up his kingdom in his stead; nevertheless they did not gain power any more over Shule the king, and the people who were under the reign of Shule the king did prosper exceedingly and wax great.

20. And the country was divided; and there were two kingdoms, the kingdom of Shule, and the kingdom of Cohor, the son of Noah.

21. And Cohor, the son of Noah, caused that his people should give battle unto Shule, in which Shule did beat them and did slay Cohor.

22. And now Cohor had a son who was called Nimrod; and Nimrod gave up the kingdom of Cohor unto Shule, and he did gain favor in the eyes of Shule; wherefore Shule did bestow great favors upon him, and he did do in the kingdom of Shule according to his desires.

23. And also in the reign of Shule there ᵐcame prophets among the people, who were sent from the Lord, prophesying that the wickedness and idolatry of the people was bringing a curse upon the land, and they should be destroyed if they did not repent.

24. And it came to pass that the people did revile against the prophets, and did mock them. And it came to pass that king

i, see *c*, 1 Ne. 16.   *j*, ver. 4.   *k*, ver. 17. See *e*.   *l*, see *k*.   *m*, vers. 24—26.

Shule did execute judgment against all those who did revile against the prophets.

25. And he did execute a law throughout all the land, which gave power unto the prophets that they should go whithersoever they would; and by this cause the people were brought unto repentance.

26. And because the people did repent of their iniquities and idolatries the Lord did spare them, and they began to prosper again in the land. And it came to pass that Shule begat sons and daughters in his old age.

27. And there were no more wars in the days of Shule; and he remembered the great things that the Lord had done for his fathers in bringing them ⁿacross the great deep into the promised land; wherefore he did execute judgment in righteousness all his days.

CHAPTER 8.

The good king Omer—His son Jared conspires with Akish to obtain the crown—Strife and bloodshed—Secret and murderous combinations—Modern Gentiles warned against such.

1. And it came to pass that he begat Omer, and Omer reigned in his stead. And Omer begat Jared; and Jared begat sons and daughters.

2. And Jared rebelled against his father, and came and dwelt in the land of Heth. And it came to pass that he did flatter many people, because of his cunning words, until he had gained the half of the kingdom.

3. And when he had gained the half of the kingdom he gave battle unto his father, and he did carry away his father into captivity, and did make him serve in captivity;

4. And now, in the days of the reign of Omer he was in captivity the half of his days. And it came to pass that he begat sons and daughters, among whom were Esrom and Coriantumr;

5. And they were exceedingly angry because of the doings of Jared their brother, insomuch that they did raise an army and gave battle unto Jared. And it came to pass that they did give battle unto him by night.

6. And it came to pass that when they had slain the army of Jared they were about to slay him also; and he plead with them that they would not slay him, and he would give up the kingdom unto his father. And it came to pass that they did grant unto him his life.

7. And now Jared became exceeding sorrowful because of the loss of the kingdom, for he had set his heart upon the kingdom and upon the glory of the world.

8. Now the daughter of Jared being exceeding expert, and seeing the sorrows of her father, thought to devise a plan whereby she could redeem the kingdom unto her father.

9. Now the daughter of Jared was exceeding fair. And it came to pass that she did talk with her father, and said unto him: Whereby hath my father so much sorrow? Hath he not read the ᵃrecord which our fathers brought across the great deep? Behold, is there not an account concerning them of old, that they by their ᵇsecret plans did obtain kingdoms and great glory?

10. And now, therefore, let my father send for Akish, the son of Kimnor; and behold, I am fair, and I will dance before him, and

---

n, Eth. 6:1—12. Chap. 8: *a*, Eth. 1:3. *b*, ver. 15. P. of G. P., Moses 5:18—33. He. 6:27. See *i*, 2 Ne. 10.

I will please him, that he will desire me to wife; wherefore if he shall desire of thee that ye shall give unto him me to wife, then shall ye say: I will give her if ye will bring unto me the head of my father, the king.

11. And now Omer was a friend to Akish; wherefore, when Jared had sent for Akish, the daughter of Jared danced before him that she pleased him, insomuch that he desired her to wife. And it came to pass that he said unto Jared: Give her unto me to wife.

12. And Jared said unto him: I will give her unto you, if ye will bring unto me the head of my father, the king.

13. And it came to pass that Akish gathered in unto the house of Jared all his kinsfolk, and said unto them: Will ye swear unto me that ye will be faithful unto me in the thing which I shall desire of you?

14. And it came to pass that they all ᶜsware unto him, by the God of heaven, and also by the heavens, and also by the earth, and by their heads, that whoso should vary from the assistance which Akish desired should lose his head; and whoso should divulge whatsoever thing Akish made known unto them, the same should lose his life.

15. And it came to pass that thus they did agree with Akish. And Akish did administer unto them the oaths which were given by ᵈthem of old who also sought power, which had been handed down even from Cain, who was a murderer from the beginning.

16. And they were kept up by the power of the devil to administer these oaths unto the people, to keep them in darkness, to help such as sought power to gain power, and to murder, and to plunder, and to lie, and to commit all manner of wickedness and whoredoms.

17. And it was the daughter of Jared who put it into his heart to search up these things of old; and Jared put it into the heart of Akish; wherefore, Akish administered it unto his kindred and friends, leading them away by fair promises to do whatsoever thing he desired.

18. And it came to pass that they formed a ᵉsecret combination, even as they of old; which combination is most abominable and wicked above all, in the sight of God;

19. For the Lord worketh not in secret combinations, neither doth he will that man should shed blood, but in all things hath forbidden it, from the beginning of man.

20. And now I, Moroni, do not write the manner of their oaths and combinations, for it hath been made known unto me that they are had among all people, and they are had among the Lamanites.

21. And they have caused the destruction of this people of whom I am now speaking, and also the destruction of the people of Nephi.

22. And whatsoever nation shall uphold such secret combinations, to get power and gain, until they shall spread over the nation, behold, they shall be destroyed; for the Lord will not suffer that the ᶠblood of his saints, which shall be shed by them, shall always cry unto him from the ground for vengeance upon them and yet he avenge them not.

23. Wherefore, O ye Gentiles,

c, see *i*, 2 Ne. 10.   *d*, see *b*.   *e*, see *i*, 2 Ne. 10.   *f*, see *f*, 2 Ne. 28.

it is wisdom in God that these things should be shown unto you, that thereby ye may repent of your sins, and suffer not that these *g*murderous combinations shall get above you, which are built up to get power and gain— and the work, yea, even the work of destruction come upon you, yea, even the *h*sword of the justice of the Eternal God shall fall upon you, to your overthrow and destruction if ye shall suffer these things to be.

24. Wherefore, the Lord commandeth you, when ye shall see these things come among you that ye shall awake to a sense of your awful situation, because of this *i*secret combination which shall be among you; or wo be unto it, because of the *j*blood of them who have been slain; for they cry from the dust for vengeance upon it, and also upon those who built it up.

25. For it cometh to pass that whoso buildeth it up seeketh to *k*overthrow the freedom of all lands, nations, and countries; and it bringeth to pass the destruction of all people, for it is built up by the devil, who is the father of all lies; even that same liar who beguiled our first parents, yea, even that same liar who hath caused man to commit murder from the beginning; who hath hardened the hearts of men that they have murdered the prophets, and stoned them, and cast them out from the beginning.

26. Wherefore, I, Moroni, am commanded to write these things that evil may be done away, and that the time may come that *l*Satan may have no power upon the hearts of the children of men, but that they may be persuaded to do good continually, that they may come unto the fountain of all righteousness and be saved.

CHAPTER 9.

Omer loses and regains his crown—Emer's prosperous reign—Cureloms and cumoms, animals of that period—Sundry kings—Famine and poisonous serpents.

1. And now I, Moroni, proceed with my record. Therefore, behold, it came to pass that because of the *a*secret combinations of Akish and his friends, behold, they did overthrow the kingdom of Omer.

2. Nevertheless, the Lord was merciful unto Omer, and also to his sons and to his daughters who did not seek his destruction.

3. And the Lord warned Omer in a dream that he should depart out of the land; wherefore Omer departed out of the land with his family, and traveled many days, and came over and passed by the *b*hill of Shim, and came over by the place where the Nephites *c*were destroyed, and from thence eastward, and came to a place which was called Ablom, by the seashore, and there he pitched his tent, and also his sons and his daughters, and all his household, save it were Jared and his family.

4. And it came to pass that Jared was anointed king over the people, by the hand of wickedness; and he gave unto Akish his daughter to wife.

5. And it came to pass that Akish sought the life of his father-in-law; and he applied unto those whom he had sworn by the *e*oath of the ancients, and they obtained the head of his father-in-law, as he sat upon his throne, giving audience to his people.

g, see *i*, 2 Ne. 10. *h*, see *k*, 1 Ne. 14. *i*, see *i*, 2 Ne. 10. *j*, see *f*, 2 Ne. 28. *k*, vers. 21, 22. *l*, see *n*, 2 Ne. 30. CHAP. 9: *a*, see *i*, 2 Ne. 10. *b*, see *a*, Morm. 1. *c*, Morm. 6:1—15. *e*, see *i*, 2 Ne. 10.

6. For so great had been the spreading of this wicked and secret society that it had corrupted the hearts of all the people; therefore Jared was murdered upon his throne, and Akish reigned in his stead.

7. And it came to pass that Akish began to be jealous of his son, therefore he shut him up in prison, and kept him upon little or no food until he had suffered death.

8. And now the brother of him that suffered death, (and his name was Nimrah) was angry with his father because of that which his father had done unto his brother.

9. And it came to pass that Nimrah gathered together a small number of men, and fled out of the land, and came over and dwelt *f*with Omer.

10. And it came to pass that Akish begat other sons, and they won the hearts of the people, notwithstanding they had sworn unto him to do all manner of iniquity according to that which he desired.

11. Now the people of Akish were desirous for gain, even as Akish was desirous for power; wherefore, the sons of Akish did offer them money, by which means they drew away the more part of the people after them.

12. And there began to be a war between the sons of Akish and Akish, which lasted for the space of many years, yea, unto the destruction of nearly all the people of the kingdom, yea, even all, save it were thirty souls, and they who fled with the house of Omer.

13. Wherefore, Omer was restored again to the *g*land of his inheritance.

14. And it came to pass that Omer began to be old; nevertheless, in his old age he begat Emer; and he anointed Emer to be king to reign in his stead.

15. And after that he had anointed Emer to be king he saw peace in the land for the space of two years, and he died, having seen exceeding many days, which were full of sorrow. And it came to pass that Emer did reign in his stead, and did fill the steps of his father.

16. And the Lord began again to take the curse from off the land, and the house of Emer did prosper exceedingly under the reign of Emer; and in the space of sixty and two years they had become exceeding strong, insomuch that they became exceeding rich—

17. Having *h*all manner of fruit, and of grain, *i*and of silks, and of fine linen, *j*and of gold, and of silver, and of precious things;

18. And also *k*all manner of cattle, of oxen, and cows, and of sheep, and of swine, and of goats, and also many other kinds of animals which were useful for the food of man.

19. And they also had *l*horses, and asses, and there were elephants and cureloms and cumoms; all of which were useful unto man, and more especially the elephants and cureloms and cumoms.

20. And thus the Lord did pour out his blessings upon this land, which was *m*choice above all other lands; and he commanded that whoso should possess the land should possess it unto the Lord, or they should be *n*destroyed when

---

f, ver. 3. *g*, see *e*, Eth. 7. *h*, Eth. 1:41. *i*, Eth. 10:24. *j*, Eth. 10:12, 23. *k*, vers. 31, 34. Eth. 10:12, 19, 20, 26. *l*, see *m*, 1 Ne. 18. *m*, see *i*, Eth. 2. *n*, Eth. 2:8—11.

they were ripened in iniquity; for upon such, saith the Lord: I will pour out the fulness of my wrath.

21. And Emer did execute judgment in righteousness all his days, and he begat many sons and daughters; and he begat Coriantum, and he anointed Coriantum to reign in his stead.

22. And after he had anointed Coriantum to reign in his stead he lived four years, and he saw peace in the land; yea, and he even saw the Son of Righteousness, and did rejoice and glory in his day; and he died in peace.

23. And it came to pass that Coriantum did walk in the steps of his father, and did build many mighty cities, and did administer that which was good unto his people in all his days. And it came to pass that he had no children even until he was exceeding old.

24. And it came to pass that his wife died, being an hundred and two years old. And it came to pass that Coriantum took to wife, in his old age, a young maid, and begat sons and daughters; wherefore he lived until he was an hundred and forty and two years old.

25. And it came to pass that he begat Com, and Com reigned in his stead; and he reigned forty and nine years, and he begat Heth; and he also begat other sons and daughters.

26. And the people had spread again over all the face of the land, and there began again to be an exceeding great wickedness upon the face of the land, and Heth began to embrace the °secret plans again of old, to destroy his father.

27. And it came to pass that he did dethrone his father, for he slew him with his own sword; and he did reign in his stead.

28. And there came prophets in the land ᵖagain, crying repentance unto them—that they must prepare the way of the Lord or there should come a curse upon the face of the land; yea, even there should be a ᵍgreat famine, in which they should be destroyed if they did not repent.

29. But the people believed not the words of the prophets, but they cast them out; and some of them they cast into pits and left them to perish. And it came to pass that they did all these things according to the commandment of the king, Heth.

30. And it came to pass that there began to be a great dearth upon the land, and the inhabitants began to be destroyed exceeding fast because of the dearth, for there was no rain upon the face of the earth.

31. And there came forth ʳpoisonous serpents also upon the face of the land, and did poison many people. And it came to pass that their flocks began to flee before the poisonous serpents, towards the land ˢsouthward, which was called by the Nephites ᵗZarahemla.

32. And it came to pass that there were many of them which did perish by the way; nevertheless, there were some which fled into the land southward.

33. And it came to pass that the Lord did cause the serpents that they should pursue them no more, but that they should hedge up the way that the people could not pass, that whoso should attempt to pass might fall by the poisonous serpents.

---

o, see *i*, 2 Ne. 10. *p*, ver. 29. Eth. 7:23. 11:1, 12, 20. *q*, vers. 30—35. *r*, vers. 32—34. Eth. 10:19. *s*, see *n*, Al. 46. *t*, Om. 13.

34. And it came to pass that the people did follow the course of the beasts, and did devour the carcasses of them which fell by the way, until they had devoured them all. Now when the people saw that they must perish they began to repent of their iniquities and cry unto the Lord.

35. And it came to pass that when they had humbled themselves sufficiently before the Lord he did send rain upon the face of the earth; and the people began to revive again, and there began to be fruit in the north countries, and in all the countries round about. And the Lord did show forth his power unto them in preserving them from famine.

CHAPTER 10.

Riplakish the wrong-doer—Morianton the reformer—Other monarchs and their wars—The land southward a wilderness—The land northward inhabited.

1. And it came to pass that Shez, who was a descendant of Heth—for Heth had perished by the famine, and all his household save it were Shez—wherefore, Shez began to build up again a broken people.

2. And it came to pass that Shez did remember the destruction of his fathers, and he did build up a righteous kingdom; for he remembered what the Lord had done in bringing Jared and his brother ªacross the deep; and he did walk in the ways of the Lord; and he begat sons and daughters.

3. And his eldest son, whose name was Shez, did rebel against him; nevertheless, Shez was smitten by the hand of a robber, because of his exceeding riches, which brought peace again unto his father.

4. And it came to pass that his father did build up many cities upon the face of the land, and the people began again to spread over all the face of the land. And Shez did live to an exceeding old age; and he begat Riplakish. And he died, and Riplakish reigned in his stead.

5. And it came to pass that Riplakish did not do that which was right in the sight of the Lord, for he did have ᵇmany wives and concubines, and did lay that upon men's shoulders which was grievous to be borne; yea, he did tax them with heavy taxes; and with the taxes he did build many spacious buildings.

6. And he did erect him an exceedingly beautiful throne; and he did build many prisons, and whoso would not be subject unto taxes he did cast into prison; and whoso was not able to pay taxes he did cast into prison; and he did cause that they should labor continually for their support; and whoso refused to labor he did cause to be put to death.

7. Wherefore he did obtain all his fine work, yea, even his fine gold he did cause to be refined in prison; and all manner of fine workmanship he did cause to be wrought in prison. And it came to pass that he did afflict the people with his ᶜwhoredoms and abominations.

8. And when he had reigned for the space of forty and two years the people did rise up in rebellion against him; and there began to be war again in the land, insomuch that Riplakish was killed, and his descendants were driven out of the land.

9. And it came to pass after the space of many years, Morianton, (he being a descendant of

a, Eth. 6:1—12. 7:27. *b*, see *k, l,* and *q,* Jac. 2. *c,* see *i,* 2 Ne. 28.

Riplakish) gathered together an army of outcasts, and went forth and gave battle unto the people; and he gained power over many cities; and the war became exceeding sore, and did last for the space of many years; and he did gain power over all the land, and did establish himself king over all the land.

10. And after that he had established himself king he did ease the burden of the people, by which he did gain favor in the eyes of the people, and they did anoint him to be their king.

11. And he did do justice unto the people, but not unto himself because of his ^{d}many whoredoms; wherefore he was cut off from the presence of the Lord.

12. And it came to pass that Morianton built up many cities, and the people became exceeding rich under his reign, both in buildings, and in ^{e}gold and silver, and in raising grain, and in ^{f}flocks, and herds, and such things which had been restored unto them.

13. And Morianton did live to an exceeding great age, and then he begat Kim; and Kim did reign in the stead of his father; and he did reign eight years, and his father died. And it came to pass that Kim did not reign in righteousness, wherefore he was not favored of the Lord.

14. And his brother did rise up in rebellion against him, by which he did bring him into captivity; and he did remain in captivity all his days; and he begat sons and daughters in captivity, and in his old age he begat Levi; and he died.

15. And it came to pass that Levi did serve in captivity after the death of his father, for the space of forty and two years. And he did make war against the king of the land, by which he did obtain unto himself the kingdom.

16. And after he had obtained unto himself the kingdom he did that which was right in the sight of the Lord; and the people did prosper in the land; and he did live to a good old age, and begat sons and daughters; and he also begat Corom, whom he anointed king in his stead.

17. And it came to pass that Corom did that which was good in the sight of the Lord all his days; and he begat many sons and daughters; and after he had seen many days he did pass away, even like unto the rest of the earth; and Kish reigned in his stead.

18. And it came to pass that Kish passed away also, and Lib reigned in his stead.

19. And it came to pass that Lib also did that which was good in the sight of the Lord. And in the days of Lib the ^{g}poisonous serpents were destroyed. Wherefore they did go into the land ^{h}southward, to hunt food for the people of the land, for the land was covered with ^{i}animals of the forest. And Lib also himself became a great hunter.

20. And they built a great city by the narrow neck of land, by the place where the sea divides the land.

21. And they did preserve the land ^{j}southward for a wilderness, to get game. And the whole face of the ^{k}land northward was covered with inhabitants.

22. And they were exceedingly industrious, and they did buy and

d, see c. e, see j, Eth. 9. f, see k, Eth. 9. g, see r, Eth. 9. h, see n, Al. 46. i, Eth. 9:32. j, see n, Al. 46. k, see p, Al. 46.

sell and traffic one with another, that they might get gain.

23. And they did work in all *l* manner of ore, and they did make gold, and silver, and iron, and brass, and all manner of metals; and they did dig it out of the earth; wherefore, they did cast up *m* mighty heaps of earth to get ore, of gold, and of silver, and of iron, and of copper. And they did work all manner of fine work.

24. And they did *n* have silks, and fine-twined linen; and they did work all manner of cloth, that they might clothe themselves from their nakedness.

25. And they did make all manner of *o* tools to till the earth, both to plow and to sow, to reap and to hoe, and also to thrash.

26. And they did make all manner of tools with which they did work their beasts.

27. And they did make all manner of weapons of war. And they did work all manner of work of exceedingly curious workmanship.

28. And never could be a people more blessed than were they, and more prospered by the hand of the Lord. And they were in a land that was *p* choice above all lands, for the Lord had spoken it.

29. And it came to pass that Lib did live many years, and begat sons and daughters; and he also begat Hearthom.

30. And it came to pass that Hearthom reigned in the stead of his father. And when Hearthom had reigned twenty and four years, behold, the kingdom was taken away from him. And he served many years in captivity, yea, even all the remainder of his days.

31. And he begat Heth, and Heth lived in captivity all his days. And Heth begat Aaron, and Aaron dwelt in captivity all his days; and he begat Amnigaddah, and Amnigaddah also dwelt in captivity all his days; and he begat Coriantum, and Coriantum dwelt in captivity all his days; and he begat Com.

32. And it came to pass that Com drew away the half of the kingdom. And he reigned over the half of the kingdom forty and two years; and he went to battle against the king, Amgid, and they fought for the space of many years, during which time Com gained power over Amgid, and obtained power over the remainder of the kingdom.

33. And in the days of Com there began to be robbers in the land; and they adopted the old plans, and administered *q* oaths after the manner of the ancients, and sought again to destroy the kingdom.

34. Now Com did fight against them much; nevertheless, he did not prevail against them.

CHAPTER 11.

Jaredite prophets predict utter destruction of their people except they repent—The warning unheeded.

1. And there came also in the days of Com *a* many prophets, and prophesied of the destruction of that great people except they should repent, and turn unto the Lord, and forsake their murders and wickedness.

2. And it came to pass that the prophets were rejected by the people, and they fled unto Com for protection, for the people sought to destroy them.

3. And they prophesied unto

l, see *j*, Eth. 9. *m*, see *l*. *n*, Eth. 9:17. *o*, ver. 25. *p*, see *i*, Eth. 2. *q*, see *i*, 2 Ne. 10, Chap. 11: *a*, see *p*, Eth. 9.

Com many things; and he was blessed in all the remainder of his days.

4. And he lived to a good old age, and begat Shiblom; and Shiblom reigned in his stead. And the brother of Shiblom rebelled against him, and there began to be an exceeding great war in all the land.

5. And it came to pass that the brother of Shiblom caused that ᵇall the prophets who prophesied of the destruction of the people should be put to death;

6. And there was great calamity in all the land, for they had testified that a great curse should come upon the land, and also upon the people, and that there should be a great destruction among them, such an one as never had been upon the face of the earth, and their bones should become as heaps of earth upon the face of the land except they should repent of their wickedness.

7. And they hearkened not unto the voice of the Lord, because of their ᵈwicked combinations; wherefore, there began to be wars and contentions in all the land, and also many famines and pestilences, insomuch that there was a great destruction, such an one as never had been known upon the face of the earth; and all this came to pass in the days of Shiblom.

8. And the people began to repent of their iniquity; and inasmuch as they did the Lord did have mercy on them.

9. And it came to pass that Shiblom was slain, and Seth was brought into captivity, and did dwell in captivity all his days.

10. And it came to pass that Ahah, his son, did obtain the kingdom; and he did reign over the people all his days. And he did do all manner of iniquity in his days, by which he did cause the shedding of much blood; and few were his days.

11. And Ethem, being a descendant of Ahah, did obtain the kingdom; and he also did do that which was wicked in his days.

12. And it came to pass that in the days of Ethem there came ᵉmany prophets, and prophesied again unto the people; yea, they did prophesy that the Lord would utterly destroy them from off the face of the earth except they repented of their iniquities.

13. And it came to pass that the people hardened their hearts, and would not hearken unto their words; and the prophets mourned and withdrew from among the people.

14. And it came to pass that Ethem did execute judgment in wickedness all his days; and he begat Moron. And it came to pass that Moron did reign in his stead; and Moron did that which was wicked before the Lord.

15. And it came to pass that there arose a rebellion among the people, because of that ᶠsecret combination which was built up to get power and gain; and there arose a mighty man among them in iniquity, and gave battle unto Moron, in which he did overthrow the half of the kingdom; and he did maintain the half of the kingdom for many years.

16. And it came to pass that Moron did overthrow him, and did obtain the kingdom again.

17. And it came to pass that there arose another mighty man; and he was a descendant of the brother of Jared.

18. And it came to pass that he

---

b, ver. 1. *d*, see *i*, 2 Ne. 10. *e*, see *p*, Eth. 9. *f*, see *i*, 2 Ne. 10.

did overthrow Moron and obtain the kingdom; wherefore, Moron dwelt in captivity all the remainder of his days; and he begat Coriantor.

19. And it came to pass that Coriantor dwelt in captivity all his days.

20. And in the days of Coriantor there *g*also came many prophets, and prophesied of great and marvelous things, and cried repentance unto the people, and except they should repent the Lord God would execute judgment against them to their utter destruction;

21. And that the Lord God would send or bring forth *h*another people to possess the land, by his power, after the manner by which he brought their fathers.

22. And they did reject all the words of the prophets, because of their *i*secret society and wicked abominations.

23. And it came to pass that Coriantor begat Ether, and he died, having dwelt in captivity all his days.

CHAPTER 12.

The prophet Ether and king Coriantumr—The Jaredite and Nephite languages—God gives weaknesses that men may be humble—Moroni's farewell to the Gentiles.

1. And it came to pass that the days of Ether were in the days of Coriantumr; and Coriantumr was king over all the land.

2. And Ether was a prophet of the Lord; wherefore Ether came forth in the days of Coriantumr, and began to prophesy unto the people, for he could not be restrained because of the Spirit of the Lord which was in him.

3. For he did cry from the morning, even until the going down of the sun, exhorting the people to believe in God unto repentance lest they *a*should be destroyed, saying unto them that by faith all things are fulfilled—

4. Wherefore, whoso believeth in God might with *b*surety hope for a better world, yea, even a place at the right hand of God, which hope cometh of faith, maketh an anchor to the souls of men, which would make them sure and steadfast, always abounding in good works, being led to glorify God.

5. And it came to pass that Ether did prophesy great and marvelous things unto the people, which they did not believe, because they saw them not.

6. And now, I, Moroni, would speak somewhat concerning these things; I would show unto the world that faith is things which are hoped for and not seen; wherefore, dispute not because ye see not, for ye receive no witness until after the trial of your faith.

7. For it was by faith that Christ showed himself unto our fathers, after he had risen from the dead; and he showed not himself unto them until after they had faith in him; wherefore, it must needs be that some had faith in him, for he showed himself not unto the world.

8. But because of the faith of men he has shown himself unto the world, and glorified the name of the Father, and prepared a way that thereby others might be partakers of the heavenly gift, that they might hope for those things which they have not seen.

9. Wherefore, ye may also have hope, and be partakers of the gift, if ye will but have faith.

10. Behold it was by faith that

g, see *p*, Eth. 9. *h*, Eth. 13:20, 21. *i*, see *i*, 2 Ne. 10. CHAP. 12; *a*, Eth. 11:12, 20—22. *b*, vers. 6, 8, 9, 32. Moro. 7:40—44. 8:26. 10:20—22.

they of old were called ᶜafter the holy order of God.

11. Wherefore, by faith was the law of Moses given. But in the gift of his Son hath God prepared a more excellent way; and it is by faith that it hath been fulfilled.

12. For if there be no faith among the children of men God can do ᵈno miracle among them; wherefore, he showed not himself until after their faith.

13. Behold, it was the faith of Alma and Amulek that caused the ᵉprison to tumble to the earth.

14. Behold, it was the faith of Nephi and Lehi that ᶠwrought the change upon the Lamanites, that they were baptized with fire and with the Holy Ghost.

15. Behold, it was the ᵍfaith of Ammon and his brethren which wrought so great a miracle among the Lamanites.

16. Yea, and even all they who wrought miracles wrought them by faith, even those who were before Christ and also those who were after.

17. And it was by faith that the three disciples obtained a promise that they should ʰnot taste of death; and they obtained not the promise until after their faith.

18. And neither at any time hath any wrought miracles until after their faith; wherefore they first believed in the Son of God.

19. And there were many whose faith was so exceeding strong, even before Christ came, who could not be kept from ⁱwithin the veil, but truly saw with their eyes the things which they had beheld with an eye of faith, and they were glad.

20. And behold, we have seen in this record that one of these was the brother of Jared; for so great was his faith in God, that when God put ʲforth his finger he could not hide it from the sight of the brother of Jared, because of his word which he had spoken unto him, which word he had obtained by faith.

21. And after the brother of Jared had beheld the finger of the Lord, because of the ᵏpromise which the brother of Jared had obtained by faith, the Lord could ˡnot withhold anything from his sight; wherefore he showed him all things, for he could ᵐno longer be kept without the veil.

22. And it is by faith that my fathers have obtained the ⁿpromise that these things should come unto their brethren through the Gentiles; therefore the Lord hath commanded me, yea, even Jesus Christ.

23. And I said unto him: Lord, the Gentiles will ᵒmock at these things, because of our weakness in writing; for Lord thou hast made us mighty in word by faith, but thou hast not made us mighty in writing; for thou hast made all this people that they could speak much, because of the Holy Ghost which thou hast given them;

24. And thou hast made us that we could write but little, because of the ᵖawkwardness of our hands. Behold, thou hast not made us mighty in writing like unto the brother of Jared, for thou madest him that the things ᵍwhich he wrote were mighty even as thou art, unto the overpowering of man to read them.

25. Thou hast also made our

---

c, see *g*, Mos. 26. *d*, see *d*, 3 Ne. 17. *e*, Al. 14:26—29. *f*, He. 5:20—52. 3 Ne. 9:20. *g*, Al. 17:29—39. *h*, see *d*, 3 Ne. 28. *i*, see *f*, Eth. 3. *j*, see *e*, Eth. 3. *k*, Eth. 3:26. *l*, Eth. 3:25, 26. *m*, see *f*, Eth. 3. *n*, Enos 13. *o*, vers. 26—28. See *w*, Morm. 8. *p*, see *w*, Morm. 8. *q*, Eth. 3:27. 4:1.

words powerful and great, even that we ʳcannot write them; wherefore, when we write we behold our weakness, and stumble because of the placing of our words; and I fear lest the Gentiles shall ˢmock at our words.

26. And when I had said this, the Lord spake unto me, saying: Fools mock, but they shall mourn; and my grace is sufficient for the meek, that they shall take no advantage of your weakness;

27. And if men come unto me I will show unto them their weakness. I give unto men weakness that they may be humble; and my grace is sufficient for all men that humble themselves before me; for if they humble themselves before me, and have faith in me, then will I make weak things become strong unto them.

28. Behold, I will show unto the Gentiles their weakness, and I will show unto them that faith, hope and charity bringeth unto me—the fountain of all righteousness.

29. And I, Moroni, having heard these words, was comforted, and said: O Lord, thy righteous will be done, for I know that thou workest unto the children of men according to their faith;

30. For the brother of Jared said unto the mountain Zerin, Remove—and ᵗit was removed. And if he had not had faith it would not have moved; wherefore thou workest after men have faith.

31. For thus didst thou manifest thyself unto thy disciples; for after they had faith, and did speak in thy name, thou didst show thyself unto them in great power.

32. And I also remember that thou hast said that thou hast prepared a house for man, yea, even among the ᵘmansions of thy Father, in which man might have a more excellent ᵛhope; wherefore man must hope, or he cannot receive an inheritance in the place which thou hast prepared.

33. And again, I remember that thou hast said that thou hast loved the world, even unto the laying down of thy life for the world, that thou mightest take it again to prepare a place for the children of men.

34. And now I know that this love which thou hast had for the children of men is charity; wherefore, except men shall have ʷcharity they cannot inherit that place which thou hast prepared in the mansions of thy Father.

35. Wherefore, I know by this thing which thou hast said, that if the Gentiles have not charity, because of our weakness, that thou wilt prove them, and take away their talent, yea, even that which they have received, and give unto them who shall have more abundantly.

36. And it came to pass that I prayed unto the Lord that he would give unto the Gentiles grace, that they might have charity.

37. And it came to pass that the Lord said unto me: If they have not charity it mattereth not unto thee, thou hast been faithful; wherefore, thy garments shall be made clean. And because thou hast ˣseen thy weakness thou shalt be made strong, even unto the sitting down in the place which I have prepared in the ʸmansions of my Father.

38. And now I, Moroni, bid farewell unto the Gentiles, yea,

r, vers. 23, 24, 40. 2 Ne. 33:1. *s*, vers. 23, 27. *t*, see *c*, Jac. 4. *u*, vers. 33, 34, 37. Enos 27. *v*, see *b*. *w*, vers. 35—37. *x*, vers. 26—28, 35, 40. *y*, see *u*.

and also unto my brethren whom I love, until we shall meet before the judgment-seat of Christ, where all men shall know that my garments are not spotted with your blood.

39. And then shall ye know that I have seen Jesus, and that he hath talked with me face to face, and that he told me in plain humility, even as a man telleth another in mine own language, concerning these things;

40. And only a *few have I written, because of my weakness in writing.

41. And now, I would commend you to seek this Jesus of whom the prophets and apostles have written, that the grace of God the Father, and also the Lord Jesus Christ, and the Holy Ghost, which beareth ²ᵃrecord of them, may be and abide in you forever. Amen.

CHAPTER 13.

Moroni continues the Jaredite history—Ether and his predictions—His life sought—He dwells in the cavity of a rock—Views by night the destruction falling upon his people.

1. And now I, Moroni, proceed to finish my record concerning the destruction of the people of whom I have been writing.

2. For behold, they rejected all the words of Ether; for he truly told them of all things, from the beginning of man; and that after the waters had receded from off the face of this land it became a choice land above all other lands, a chosen land of the Lord; wherefore the Lord would have that all men should serve him who dwell upon the face thereof;

3. And that it was the ᵃplace of the New Jerusalem, which should ᵇcome down out of heaven, and the holy sanctuary of the Lord.

4. Behold, Ether saw the days of Christ, and he spake concerning a ᶜNew Jerusalem upon this land.

5. And he spake also concerning the house of Israel, and the Jerusalem from whence ᵈLehi should come—after it should be destroyed it should be built up again, a ᵉholy city unto the Lord; wherefore, it could not be a new Jerusalem for it had been in a time of old; but it should be built up again, and become a holy city of the Lord; and it should be built unto the house of Israel.

6. And that a ᶠNew Jerusalem should be built up upon this land, unto the remnant of the seed of Joseph, for which things there has been a type.

7. For as Joseph brought his father down into the land of Egypt, even so he died there; wherefore, the Lord brought a remnant of the seed of Joseph out of the land of Jerusalem, that he might be merciful unto the seed of Joseph that ᵍthey should perish not, even as he was merciful unto the father of Joseph that he should perish not.

8. Wherefore, the remnant of the house of Joseph shall be built upon this land; and it shall be a land of ʰtheir inheritance; and they shall build up a ⁱholy city unto the Lord, like unto the Jerusalem of old; and they shall no more be confounded, until the end come when the earth shall pass away.

9. ʲAnd there shall be a new heaven and a new earth; and

g, see *e*, Eth. 1. 2*a*, 3 Ne. 11:32, 36. CHAP. 13: *a*, see *t*, 3 Ne. 20. *b*, ver. 10, Rev. 3:12. 21:2. *c*, see *t*, 3 Ne. 20. *d*, 1 Ne. chaps. 1—18. *e*, ver. 11. Rev. 21:10—27. *f*, see *t*, 3 Ne. 20. *g*, 2 Ne. 3:5—24. Al. 46:24—26. *h*, see *o*, 3 Ne. 15. *i*, see *t*, 3 Ne. 20. *j*, Rev. 21:1.

they shall be like unto the old save the old have passed away, and all things have become new.

10. And ᵏthen cometh the New Jerusalem; and blessed are they who dwell therein, for it is they whose garments are white through the blood of the Lamb; and they are they who are ˡnumbered among the remnant of the seed of Joseph, who were of the house of Israel.

11. And ᵐthen also cometh the Jerusalem of old; and the inhabitants thereof, blessed are they, for they have been washed in the blood of the Lamb; and they are they who were scattered and gathered in from the four quarters of the earth, and from the ⁿnorth countries, and are partakers of the fulfilling of the covenant which God made with their father, Abraham.

12. And when these things come, bringeth to pass the scripture which saith, ᵒthere are they who were first, who shall be last; and there are they who were last, who shall be first.

13. And I was about to write more, but I am forbidden; but great and marvelous were the prophecies of Ether; but they esteemed him as naught, and cast him out; and he hid himself in the ᵖcavity of a rock by day, and by ᑫnight he went forth viewing the things which should come upon the people.

14. And as he dwelt in the cavity of a rock he made the ʳremainder of this record, viewing the destructions which came upon the people, by night.

15. And it came to pass that in that same year in which he was cast out from among the people there began to be a great war among the people, for there were many who rose up, who were mighty men, and sought to destroy Coriantumr by their ˢsecret plans of wickedness, of which hath been spoken.

16. And now Coriantumr, having studied, himself, in all the arts of war and all the cunning of the world, wherefore he gave battle unto them who sought to destroy him.

17. But he repented not, neither his fair sons nor daughters; neither the fair sons and daughters of Cohor; neither the fair sons and daughters of Corihor; and in fine, there were none of the fair sons and daughters upon the face of the whole earth who repented of their sins.

18. Wherefore, it came to pass that in the first year that Ether dwelt in the ᵗcavity of a rock, there were many people who were slain by the sword of those ᵘsecret combinations, fighting against Coriantumr that they might obtain the kingdom.

19. And it came to pass that the sons of Coriantumr fought much and bled much.

20. And in the second year the word of the Lord came to Ether, that he should go and prophesy unto Coriantumr that, if he would repent, and all his household, the Lord would give unto him his kingdom and spare the people—

21. Otherwise they should be destroyed, and all his household save it were himself. And he should only live to see the fulfilling of the prophecies which had been spoken concerning ᵛanother people receiving the land for their inheritance; and Coriantumr should receive a burial by them; and every soul should be

destroyed save it were Coriantumr.

22. And it came to pass that Coriantumr repented not, neither his household, neither the people; and the wars ceased not; and they sought to kill Ether, but he fled from before them and hid again in the *cavity of the rock.

23. And it came to pass that there arose up Shared, and he also gave battle unto Coriantumr; and he did beat him, insomuch that in the third year he did bring him into captivity.

24. And the sons of Coriantumr, in the fourth year, did beat Shared, and did obtain the kingdom again unto their father.

25. Now there began to be a war upon all the face of the land, every man with his band fighting for that which he desired.

26. And there were robbers, and in fine, all manner of wickedness upon all the face of the land.

27. And it came to pass that Coriantumr was exceedingly angry with Shared, and he went against him with his armies to battle; and they did meet in great anger, and they did meet in the valley of Gilgal; and the battle became exceeding sore.

28. And it came to pass that Shared fought against him for the space of three days. And it came to pass that Coriantumr beat him, and did pursue him until he came to the plains of Heshlon.

29. And it came to pass that Shared gave him battle again upon the plains; and behold, he did beat Coriantumr, and drove him back again to the valley of Gilgal.

30. And Coriantumr gave Shared battle again in the valley of Gilgal, in which he beat Shared and slew him.

31. And Shared wounded Coriantumr in his thigh, that he did not go to battle again for the space of two years, in which time all the people upon the face of the land were shedding blood, and there was none to restrain them.

CHAPTER 14.

A curse upon the land—Continued strife and bloodshed—Coriantumr not to fall by the sword.

1. And now there began to be a great *curse upon all the land because of the iniquity of the people, in which, if a man should lay his tool or his sword upon his shelf, or upon the place whither he would keep it, behold, upon the morrow, he could not find it, so great was the curse upon the land.

2. Wherefore every man did cleave unto that which was his own, with his hands, and would not borrow neither would he lend; and every man kept the hilt of his sword in his right hand, in the defence of his property and his own life and of his wives and children.

3. And now, after the space of two years, and after the death of Shared, behold, there arose the brother of Shared and he gave battle unto Coriantumr, in which Coriantumr did beat him and did pursue him to the wilderness of Akish.

4. And it came to pass that the brother of Shared did give battle unto him in the wilderness of Akish; and the battle became exceeding sore, and many thousands fell by the sword.

5. And it came to pass that Coriantumr did lay siege to the wilderness; and the brother of Shared did march forth out of the wilderness by night, and slew a

w, Eth. 15:29—32. *x*, see *p*. CHAP. 14: *a*, see *k*, He. 13.

part of the army of Coriantumr, as they were drunken.

6. And he came forth to the *b*land of Moron, and placed himself upon the throne of Coriantumr.

7. And it came to pass that Coriantumr dwelt with his army in the wilderness for the space of two years, in which he did receive great strength to his army.

8. Now the brother of Shared, whose name was Gilead, also received great strength to his army, because of *c*secret combinations.

9. And it came to pass that his high priest murdered him as he sat upon his throne.

10. And it came to pass that one of the secret combinations murdered him in a secret pass, and obtained unto himself the kingdom; and his name was Lib; and Lib was a man of great stature, more than any other man among all the people.

11. And it came to pass that in the first year of Lib, Coriantumr came up unto the *d*land of Moron, and gave battle unto Lib.

12. And it came to pass that he fought with Lib, in which Lib did smite upon his arm that he was wounded; nevertheless, the army of Coriantumr did press forward upon Lib, that he fled to the borders upon the seashore.

13. And it came to pass that Coriantumr pursued him; and Lib gave battle unto him upon the seashore.

14. And it came to pass that Lib did smite the army of Coriantumr, that they fled again to the wilderness of Akish.

15. And it came to pass that Lib did pursue him until he came to the plains of Agosh. And Coriantumr had taken all the people with him as he fled before Lib in that quarter of the land whither he fled.

16. And when he had come to the plains of Agosh he gave battle unto Lib, and he smote upon him until he died; nevertheless, the brother of Lib did come against Coriantumr in the stead thereof, and the battle became exceeding sore, in the which Coriantumr fled again before the army of the brother of Lib.

17. Now the name of the brother of Lib was called Shiz. And it came to pass that Shiz pursued after Coriantumr, and he did overthrow many cities, and he did slay both women and children, and he did burn the cities.

18. And there went a fear of Shiz throughout all the land; yea, a cry went forth throughout the land—Who can stand before the army of Shiz? Behold, he sweepeth the earth before him!

19. And it came to pass that the people began to flock together in armies, throughout all the face of the land.

20. And they were divided; and a part of them fled to the army of Shiz, and a part of them fled to the army of Coriantumr.

21. And so great and lasting had been the war, and so long had been the scene of bloodshed and carnage, that the whole face of the land was covered with the bodies of the dead.

22. And so swift and speedy was the war that there was none left to bury the dead, but they did march forth from the shedding of blood to the shedding of blood, leaving the bodies of both men, women, and children strewed upon the face of the land, to become a prey to the worms of the flesh.

23. And the scent thereof went

---

b, see *e*, Eth. 7.   *c*, see *i*, 2 Ne. 10.   *d*, see *e*, Eth. 7.

forth upon the face of the land, even upon all the face of the land; wherefore the people became troubled by day and by night, because of the scent thereof.

24. Nevertheless, Shiz did not cease to pursue Coriantumr; for he had sworn to avenge himself upon Coriantumr of the ᵉblood of his brother, who had been slain, and the word of the Lord which came to Ether that Coriantumr should ᶠnot fall by the sword.

25. And thus we see that the Lord did visit them in the fulness of his wrath, and their wickedness and abominations had prepared a way for their everlasting destruction.

26. And it came to pass that Shiz did pursue Coriantumr eastward, even to the borders of the seashore, and there he gave battle unto Shiz for the space of three days.

27. And so terrible was the destruction among the armies of Shiz that the people began to be frightened, and began to flee before the armies of Coriantumr; and they fled to the land of Corihor, and swept off the inhabitants before them, all them that would not join them.

28. And they pitched their tents in the valley of Corihor; and Coriantumr pitched his tents in the valley of Shurr. Now the valley of Shurr was near the hill Comnor; wherefore, Coriantumr did gather his armies together upon the hill Comnor, and did sound a trumpet unto the armies of Shiz to invite them forth to battle.

29. And it came to pass that they came forth, but were driven again; and they came the second time, and they were driven again the second time. And it came to pass that they came again the third time, and the battle became exceeding sore.

30. And it came to pass that Shiz smote upon Coriantumr that he gave him many deep wounds; and Coriantumr, having lost his blood, fainted, and was carried away as though he were dead.

31. Now the loss of men women and children on both sides was so great that Shiz commanded his people that they should not pursue the armies of Coriantumr; wherefore, they returned to their camp.

CHAPTER 15.

The hill Ramah or Cumorah—Preparations for a mighty struggle—Millions go down to death—Shiz slain by Coriantumr—Ether's concluding words—End of the Jaredite record.

1. And it came to pass when Coriantumr had recovered of his wounds, he began to remember the ᵃwords which Ether had spoken unto him.

2. He saw that there had been slain by the sword already nearly two millions of his people, and he began to sorrow in his heart; yea, there had been slain two millions of mighty men, and also their wives and their children.

3. He began to repent of the evil which he had done; he began to remember the words which had been spoken by the mouth of all the prophets, and he saw them that they were fulfilled thus far, every whit; and his soul mourned and refused to be comforted.

4. And it came to pass that he wrote an epistle unto Shiz, desiring him that he would spare the people, and he would give up the kingdom for the sake of the lives of the people.

5. And it came to pass that

e, ver. 16. *f,* Eth. 13:21.   CHAP. 15; *a,* Eth. 13:20, 21.

when Shiz had received his epistle he wrote an epistle unto Coriantumr, that if he would give himself up, that he might slay him with his own sword, that he would spare the lives of the people.

6. And it came to pass that the people repented not of their iniquity; and the people of Coriantumr were stirred up to anger against the people of Shiz; and the people of Shiz were stirred up to anger against the people of Coriantumr; wherefore, the people of Shiz did give battle unto the people of Coriantumr.

7. And when Coriantumr saw that he was about to fall he fled again before the people of Shiz.

8. And it came to pass that he came to the waters of Ripliancum, which, by interpretation, is large, or to exceed all; wherefore, when they came to these waters they pitched their tents; and Shiz also pitched his tents near unto them: and therefore on the morrow they did come to battle.

9. And it came to pass that they fought an exceedingly sore battle, in which Coriantumr was wounded again, and he fainted with the loss of blood.

10. And it came to pass that the armies of Coriantumr did press upon the armies of Shiz that they beat them, that they caused them to flee before them; and they did flee *d*southward, and did pitch their tents in a place which was called Ogath.

11. And it came to pass that the army of Coriantumr did pitch their tents by the hill Ramah; and it was that same hill where my father Mormon did *f*hide up the records unto the Lord, which were sacred.

12. And it came to pass that they did gather together all the people upon all the face of the land, who had not been slain, save it was Ether.

13. And it came to pass that Ether *g*did behold all the doings of the people; and he beheld that the people who were for Coriantumr were gathered together to the army of Coriantumr; and the people who were for Shiz were gathered together to the army of Shiz.

14. Wherefore, they were for the space of four years gathering together the people, that they might get all who were upon the face of the land, and that they might receive all the strength which it was possible that they could receive.

15. And it came to pass that when they were all gathered together, every one to the army which he would, with their wives and their children—both men women and children being *h*armed with weapons of war, having shields, and breastplates, and head-plates, and being clothed after the manner of war—they did march forth one against another to battle; and they fought all that day, and conquered not.

16. And it came to pass that when it was night they were weary, and retired to their camps; and after they had retired to their camps they *i*took up a howling and a lamentation for the loss of the slain of their people; and so great were their cries, their howlings and lamentations, that they did rend the air exceedingly.

17. And it came to pass that on the morrow they did go again to battle, and great and terrible was that day; nevertheless, they conquered not, and when the night came again they did *j*rend the air with their cries, and their howl-

d, see *a*, Morm. 6.   *f*, Morm. 6:6.   *g*, Eth. 13:14.   *h*, Eth. 10:27.   *i*, ver. 17.   *j*, ver. 16.

ings, and their mournings, for the loss of the slain of their people.

18. And it came to pass that Coriantumr wrote [k]again an epistle unto Shiz, desiring that he would not come again to battle, but that he would take the kingdom, and spare the lives of the people.

19. But behold, the Spirit of the Lord had ceased striving with them, and Satan had full power over the hearts of the people; for they were given up unto the hardness of their hearts, and the blindness of their minds that they might be destroyed; wherefore they went again to battle.

20. And it came to pass that they fought all that day, and when the night came they slept upon their swords.

21. And on the morrow they fought even until the night came.

22. And when the night came they were drunken with anger, even as a man who is drunken with wine; and they slept again upon their swords.

23. And on the morrow they fought again; and when the night came they had all fallen by the sword save it were fifty and two of the people of Coriantumr, and sixty and nine of the people of Shiz.

24. And it came to pass that they slept upon their swords that night, and on the morrow they fought again, and they contended in their might with their swords and with their shields, all that day.

25. And when the night came there were thirty and two of the people of Shiz, and twenty and seven of the people of Coriantumr.

26. And it came to pass that they ate and slept, and prepared for death on the morrow. And they were large and mighty men as to the strength of men.

27. And it came to pass that they fought for the space of three hours, and they fainted with the loss of blood.

28. And it came to pass that when the men of Coriantumr had received sufficient strength that they could walk, they were about to flee for their lives; but behold, Shiz arose, and also his men, and he swore in his wrath that he would slay Coriantumr or he would perish by the sword.

29. Wherefore, he did pursue them, and on the morrow he did overtake them; and they fought again with the sword. And it came to pass that when they had all fallen by the sword, save it were Coriantumr and Shiz, behold Shiz had fainted with the loss of blood.

30. And it came to pass that when Coriantumr had leaned upon his sword, that he rested a little, he smote off the head of Shiz.

31. And it came to pass that after he had smitten off the head of Shiz, that Shiz raised upon his hands and fell; and after that he had struggled for breath, he died.

32. And it came to pass that [l]Coriantumr fell to the earth, and became as if he had no life.

33. And the Lord spake unto Ether, and said unto him: Go forth. And he went forth, and beheld that the words of the Lord had all been fulfilled; and he [m]finished his record; (and the [n]hundredth part I have not written) and he hid them in a manner that the [o]people of Limhi did find them.

34. Now the last words which are written by Ether are these:

---

k, ver. 4. *l*, Om. 20—22. *m*, Eth. 13:14. *n*, see *c*, Eth. 1. *o*, see *k*, Mos. 8.

Whether the Lord will that I be translated, or that I suffer the will of the Lord in the flesh, it mattereth not, if it so be that I am saved in the kingdom of God. Amen.

THE BOOK OF MORONI

CHAPTER 1.

Moroni's desolate state—He writes, hoping for the welfare of the Lamanites.

1. Now I, Moroni, after having made an end of ᵃabridging the account of the people of Jared, I had supposed not to have written more, but I have not as yet perished; and I make not myself known to the Lamanites lest they should destroy me.

2. For behold, their wars are ᵇexceedingly fierce among themselves; and because of their hatred they put to death every Nephite that will not deny the Christ.

3. And I, Moroni, will not deny the Christ; wherefore, I wander whithersoever I can for the safety of mine own life.

4. Wherefore, I write a few more things, contrary to that which I had supposed; for I had supposed not to have written any more; but I write a few more things, that perhaps they may be of ᶜworth unto my brethren, the Lamanites, in some future day, according to the will of the Lord.

CHAPTER 2.

Concerning the bestowal of the Holy Ghost by the Nephite twelve.

1. The words of Christ, which he spake unto his ᵃdisciples, the twelve whom he had chosen, as he laid his hands upon them—

2. And he called them by name, saying: Ye shall call on the Father in my name, in mighty prayer; and after ye have done this ye shall have power that to him upon whom ye shall lay your hands, ᵇye shall give the Holy Ghost; and in my name shall ye give it, for thus do mine apostles.

3. Now Christ spake these words unto them at the time of his first appearing; and the multitude ᶜheard it not, but the disciples heard it; and on as many as they ᵈlaid their hands, fell the Holy Ghost.

CHAPTER 3.

Concerning the ordination of priests and teachers.

1. The manner which the ᵃdisciples, who were called the elders of the church, ᵇordained priests and teachers—

2. After they had prayed unto the Father in the name of Christ, they laid their hands upon them, and said:

3. In the name of Jesus Christ I ordain you to be a priest, (or, if he be a teacher) I ordain you to be a teacher, to preach repentance and remission of sins through Jesus Christ, by the endurance of faith on his name to the end. Amen.

4. And after this manner did they ordain priests and teachers, according to the gifts and callings of God unto men; and they

---

a, see Book of Ether. *b,* 1 Ne. 12:20—23. Morm. 5:15. *c,* 2 Ne. 3:7, 11, 12, 19—21. See *c,* 2 Ne. 27. CHAP. 2: *a,* see *c,* 3 Ne. 12. *b,* ver. 3. 3 Ne. 18:37. *c,* 3 Ne. 18:37. *d,* see *b.* CHAP. 3: *a,* see *c,* 3 Ne. 12. *b,* vers. 2—4. See *c,* Mos. 6.

BETWEEN A. D. 400 AND 421.

MORONI, 4, 5, 6. 511

ordained them by the ^cpower of the Holy Ghost, which was in them.

CHAPTER 4.
Mode of administering the sacramental bread.

1. The manner of their ^aelders and priests administering the ^bflesh and blood of Christ unto the church; and they administered it according to the commandments of Christ; wherefore we know the manner to be true; and the elder or priest did minister it—

2. And they did ^ckneel down with the church, and pray to the Father in the name of Christ, saying:

3. O God, the Eternal Father, we ask thee in the name of thy Son, Jesus Christ, to bless and sanctify this bread to the souls of all those who partake of it; that they may eat in remembrance of the ^dbody of thy Son, and witness unto thee, O God, the Eternal Father, that they are willing to take upon them the ^ename of thy Son, and always remember him, and keep his commandments which he hath given them, that they may always have his Spirit to be with them. Amen.

CHAPTER 5.
Mode of administering the sacramental wine.

1. The manner of administering the wine—Behold, they took the cup, and said:

2. O God, the Eternal Father, we ask thee, in the name of thy Son, Jesus Christ, to bless and sanctify this wine to the souls of all those who drink of it, that they may do it in remembrance of the ^ablood of thy Son, which was shed for them; that they may witness unto thee, O God, the Eternal Father, that they do always remember him, that they may have his Spirit to be with them. Amen.

CHAPTER 6.
Conditions and mode of baptism—Church discipline.

1. And now I speak concerning baptism. Behold, ^aelders, ^bpriests, and teachers were baptized; and they were not ^cbaptized save they brought forth fruit meet that they were worthy of it.

2. Neither did they receive any unto baptism save they came forth with a broken heart and a contrite spirit, and witnessed unto the church that they truly repented of all their sins.

3. And none were received unto baptism save they took upon them the ^dname of Christ, having a determination to serve him to the end.

4. And after they had been received unto baptism, and were wrought upon and cleansed by the ^epower of the Holy Ghost, they were numbered among the people of the church of Christ; and their names were taken, that they might be remembered and nourished by the good word of God, to keep them in the right way, to keep them continually watchful unto ^fprayer, relying alone upon the merits of Christ, who was the author and the finisher of their faith.

5. And the church did meet together oft, to ^gfast and to pray, and to speak one with another concerning the welfare of their souls.

---

c, 1 Ne. 13:37. Moro. 6:9.   CHAP. 4: *a*, Moro. 3:1. *b*, see *t*, 3 Ne. 18. *c*, D. & C. 20:76. *d*, see *t*, 3 Ne. 18. *e*, see *e*, Mos. 5.   CHAP. 5: *a*, see *t*, 3 Ne. 18. D. & C. 20:79. 27:2—4.   CHAP. 6: *a*, Moro. 3:1. *b*, see *c*, Mos. 6. *c*, see *u*, 2 Ne. 9. *d*, see *e*, Mos. 5. *e*, see *y*, 3 Ne. 9. *f*, see *e*, 2 Ne. 32. *g*, see *t*, Mos. 27.
BETWEEN A. D. 400 AND 421.

6. And they did meet together oft to ^hpartake of bread and wine, in remembrance of the Lord Jesus.

7. And they were strict to observe that there should be no iniquity among them; and whoso was found to commit iniquity, and ⁱthree witnesses of the church did condemn them before the elders, and if they repented not, and confessed not, their names were blotted out, and they were not numbered among the people of Christ.

8. But as ^joft as they repented and sought forgiveness, with real intent, they were forgiven.

9. And their meetings were conducted by the church after the manner of the workings of the Spirit, and by the power of the Holy Ghost; for as the ^kpower of the Holy Ghost led them whether to preach, or to exhort, or to pray, or to supplicate, or to sing, even so it was done.

CHAPTER 7.

Moroni presents Mormon's teachings on faith, hope, charity.

1. And now I, Moroni, write a few of the words of my father Mormon, which he spake ^aconcerning faith, hope, and charity; for after this manner did he speak unto the people, as he taught them in the ^bsynagogue which they had built for the place of worship.

2. And now I, Mormon, speak unto you, my beloved brethren; and it is by the grace of God the Father, and our Lord Jesus Christ, and his holy will, because of the ^cgift of his calling unto me, that I am permitted to speak unto you at this time.

3. Wherefore, I would speak unto you that are of the church, that are the peaceable followers of Christ, and that have obtained a sufficient hope by which ye can enter into the rest of the Lord, from this time henceforth until ye shall rest with him in heaven.

4. And now my brethren, I judge these things of you because of your peaceable walk with the children of men.

5. For I remember the word of God, which saith ^dby their works ye shall know them; for if their works be good, then they are good also.

6. For behold, God hath said a man being evil cannot do that which is good; for if he offereth a gift, or prayeth unto God, except he shall do it with real intent it profiteth him nothing.

7. For behold, it is not counted unto him for righteousness.

8. For behold, if a man being evil giveth a gift, he doeth it grudgingly; wherefore it is counted unto him the same as if he had retained the gift; wherefore he is counted evil before God.

9. And likewise also is it counted evil unto a man, if he shall pray and not with real intent of heart; yea, and it profiteth him nothing, for God receiveth none such.

10. Wherefore, a man being evil cannot do that which is good; neither will he give a good gift.

11. For behold, a bitter fountain cannot bring forth good water; neither can a good fountain bring forth bitter water; wherefore, a man being a servant of the devil cannot follow Christ; and if he follow Christ he cannot be a servant of the devil.

h, see *b*, 3 Ne. 18. *i*, D. & C. 42:80, 81. *j*, Mos. 26:31. *k*, see *c*, Moro. 3. Chap. 7: *a*, vers. 21—39, 40—44, 45—48. Eth. 12:3—37. Moro. 8:14, 26. 10:20—23. *b*, see *u*, Al. 16. *c*, 3 Ne. 5:13. *d*, 3 Ne. 14:15—20. Between A. D. 400 and 421.

12. Wherefore, all things which are good cometh of God; and that which is evil cometh of the devil; for the devil is an enemy unto God, and fighteth against him continually, and inviteth and enticeth to sin, and to do that which is evil continually.

13. But behold, that which is of God inviteth and enticeth to do good continually; wherefore, every thing which inviteth and enticeth to do good, and to love God, and to serve him, is inspired of God.

14. Wherefore, take heed, my beloved brethren, that ye do not judge that which is evil to be of God, or that which is good and of God to be of the devil.

15. For behold, my brethren, it is given unto you to judge, that ye may know good from evil; and the way to judge is as plain, that ye may know with a perfect knowledge, as the daylight is from the dark night.

16. For behold, the Spirit of Christ is given to every man, that he may know good from evil; wherefore, I show unto you the way to judge; for every thing which inviteth to do good, and to persuade to believe in Christ, is sent forth by the power and gift of Christ; wherefore ye may know with a perfect knowledge it is of God.

17. But whatsoever thing persuadeth men to do evil, and believe not in Christ, and deny him, and serve not God, then ye may know with a perfect knowledge it is of the devil; for after this manner doth the devil work, for he persuadeth no man to do good, no, not one; neither do his angels; neither do they who subject themselves unto him.

18. And now, my brethren, seeing that ye know the light by which ye may judge, which light is the light of Christ, see that ye do not judge wrongfully; for with that same judgment which ye judge ye shall also be judged.

19. Wherefore, I beseech of you, brethren, that ye should search diligently in the light of Christ that ye may know good from evil; and if ye will lay hold upon every good thing, and condemn it not, ye certainly will be a child of Christ.

20. And now, my brethren, how is it possible that ye can lay hold upon every good thing?

21. And now I come to that faith, of which I said I would speak; and I will tell you the way whereby ye may lay hold on every good thing.

22. For behold, God knowing all things, being from everlasting to everlasting, behold, he sent angels to minister unto the children of men, to make manifest concerning the coming of Christ; and in Christ there should come every good thing.

23. And God also declared unto prophets, by his own mouth, that Christ should come.

24. And behold, there were divers ways that he did manifest things unto the children of men, which were good; and all things which are good cometh of Christ; otherwise men were fallen, and there could no good thing come unto them.

25. Wherefore, by the ministering of angels, and by every word which proceeded forth out of the mouth of God, men began to exercise faith in Christ; and thus by faith, they did lay hold upon every good thing; and thus

it was until the coming of Christ.

26. And after that he came men also were saved by faith in his name; and by faith, they become the sons of God. And as sure as Christ liveth he spake these words unto our fathers, saying: ⁿWhatsoever thing ye shall ask the Father in my name, which is good, in faith believing that ye shall receive, behold, it shall be done unto you.

27. Wherefore, my beloved brethren, have miracles ceased because Christ hath ascended into heaven, and hath sat down on the right hand of God, to °claim of the Father his rights of mercy which he hath upon the children of men?

28. For he hath answered the ends of the law, and he claimeth all those who have ^pfaith in him; and they who have faith in him will cleave unto every good thing; wherefore he ^qadvocateth the cause of the children of men; and he dwelleth eternally in the heavens.

29. And because he hath done this, my beloved brethren, ^rhave miracles ceased? Behold I say unto you, Nay; neither have angels ^sceased to minister unto the children of men.

30. For behold, they are subject unto him, to minister according to the word of his command, showing themselves unto them of strong faith and a firm mind in every form of godliness.

31. And the office of their ministry is to call men unto repentance, and to fulfil and to do the work of the covenants of the Father, which he hath made unto the children of men, to prepare the way among the children of men, by declaring the word of Christ unto the chosen vessels of the Lord, that they may bear testimony of him.

32. And by so doing, the Lord God prepareth the way that the residue of men may have faith in Christ, that the ^tHoly Ghost may have place in their hearts, according to the power thereof; and after this manner bringeth to pass the Father, the ^ucovenants which he hath made unto the children of men.

33. And Christ hath said: If ye will have faith in me ye shall have power to do whatsoever thing is expedient in me.

34. And he hath said: ^vRepent all ye ends of the earth, and come unto me, and be ^wbaptized in my name, and have faith in me, that ye may be saved.

35. And now, my beloved brethren, if this be the case that these things are true which I have spoken unto you, and God will show unto you, ^xwith power and great glory at the last day, that they are true, and if they are true has the ^yday of miracles ceased?

36. Or have angels ^zceased to appear unto the chi'dren of men? Or has he ^{2a}withheld the power of the Holy Ghost from them? Or will he, so long as time shall last, or the earth shall stand, or there shall be one man upon the face thereof to be saved?

37. Behold I say unto you, Nay; for it is by ^{2b}faith that miracles are wrought; and it is by faith that ^{2c}angels appear and minister unto men; wherefore, if these things have ceased wo be unto the children of men, for it is

---

n, 3 Ne. 18:20. *o*, see *e*, 2 Ne. 2. *p*, see *a*. *q*, see *e*, 2 Ne. 2. *r*, see *r*, 2 Ne. 26.
s, vers. 30—32, 36, 37. *t*, see *y*, 3 Ne. 9. *u*, see *j*, 3 Ne. 15. *v*, 3 Ne. 27:20. Eth. 4:18.
w, see *u*, 2 Ne. 9. *x*, see *g*, 2 Ne. 33. *y*, see *r*, 2 Ne. 26. *z*, see *s*. *2a*, 1 Ne. 10:17—19.
2 Ne. 28:4. Moro. 10:4, 5, 7, 19, 24—27. *2b*, see *a*. *2c*, see *s*.

BETWEEN A. D. 400 AND 421.

MORONI, 8.

[2d]because of unbelief, and all is vain.

38. For no man can be saved, according to the words of Christ, save they shall have faith in his name; wherefore, if these things have ceased, then has [2e]faith ceased also; and awful is the state of man, for they are as though there had been no redemption made.

39. But behold, my beloved brethren, I judge better things of you, for I judge that ye have faith in Christ because of your meekness; for if ye have not faith in him then ye are not fit to be numbered among the people of his church.

40. And again, my beloved brethren, I would speak unto you concerning [2f]hope. How is it that ye can attain unto faith, save ye shall have hope?

41. And what is it that ye shall hope for? Behold I say unto you that ye shall have hope through the [2g]atonement of Christ and the power of his resurrection, to be [2h]raised unto life eternal, and this because of your faith in him according to the promise.

42. Wherefore, if a man have faith he must needs have hope; for without faith there cannot be any hope.

43. And again, behold I say unto you that he cannot have faith and hope, save he shall be meek, and lowly of heart.

44. If so, his faith and hope is vain, for none is acceptable before God, save the meek and lowly in heart; and if a man be meek and lowly in heart, and confesses by the power of the Holy Ghost that Jesus is the Christ, he must needs have [2i]charity; for if he have not charity he is nothing; wherefore he must needs have charity.

45. And charity suffereth long, and is kind, and envieth not, and is not puffed up, seeketh not her own, is not easily provoked, thinketh no evil, and rejoiceth not in iniquity but rejoiceth in the truth, beareth all things, believeth all things, hopeth all things, endureth all things.

46. Wherefore, my beloved brethren, if ye have not charity, ye are nothing, for charity never faileth. Wherefore, cleave unto charity, which is the greatest of all, for all things must fail—

47. But charity is the pure love of Christ, and it endureth forever; and whoso is found possessed of it at the last day, it shall be well with him.

48. Wherefore, my beloved brethren, pray unto the Father with all the energy of heart, that ye may be filled with this love, which he hath bestowed upon all who are true followers of his Son, Jesus Christ; that ye may become the sons of God; that when he shall appear we shall [2j]be like him, for we shall see him as he is; that we may have this hope; that we may be purified [2k]even as he is pure. Amen.

CHAPTER 8.

Mormon's epistle to Moroni—Little children have no need of repentance or baptism.

1. An epistle of my father Mormon, written to me, Moroni; and it was written unto me soon after my calling to the ministry. And on this wise did he write unto me, saying:

2. My beloved son, Moroni, I rejoice exceedingly that your

2d, ver. 38. Moro. 10:19, 23—27. 2e, see 2d. 2f, see a. 2g, see f, 2 Ne. 2. 2h, see d, 2 Ne. 2. 2i, see a. 2j, 3 Ne. 27:27. 1 John 3:2. 2k, 3 Ne. 19:28, 29.

BETWEEN A. D. 400 AND 421.

Lord Jesus Christ hath been mindful of you, and hath called you to his ministry, and to his holy work.

3. I am mindful of you always in my prayers, continually praying unto God the Father in the name of his Holy Child, Jesus, that he, through his infinite goodness and grace, will keep you through the *a*endurance of faith on his name to the end.

4. And now, my son, I speak unto you concerning that which grieveth me exceedingly; for it grieveth me that there should disputations rise among you.

5. For, if I have learned the truth, there have been disputations among you concerning the *b*baptism of your little children.

6. And now, my son, I desire that ye should labor diligently, that this gross error should be removed from among you; for, for this intent I have written this epistle.

7. For immediately after I had learned these things of you I inquired of the Lord concerning the matter. And the word of the Lord came to me by the *c*power of the Holy Ghost, saying:

8. Listen to the words of Christ, your Redeemer, your Lord and your God. Behold, I came into the world not to call the righteous but sinners to repentance; the whole need no physician, but they that are sick; wherefore, little children are whole, for they are not capable of committing sin; wherefore the curse of Adam is *d*taken from them in me, that it hath no power over them; and the *e*law of circumcision is done away in me.

9. And after this manner did the Holy Ghost manifest the word of God unto me; wherefore, my beloved son, I know that it is *f*solemn mockery before God, that ye should baptize little children.

10. Behold I say unto you that this thing shall ye teach—repentance and baptism unto those who are accountable and capable of committing sin; yea, teach parents that they must repent and be baptized, and humble themselves as their little children, and they shall all be saved with their little children.

11. And their little children need no repentance, neither baptism. Behold, baptism is unto repentance to the fulfilling the commandments unto *g*the remission of sins.

12. But little children are alive in Christ, even *h*from the foundation of the world; if not so, God is a partial God, and also a changeable God, and a respecter to persons; for how many little children have died without baptism!

13. Wherefore, if little children could not be saved without baptism, these must have gone to an endless hell.

14. Behold I say unto you, that he that supposeth that little children need baptism is in the gall of bitterness and in the bonds of iniquity; for he hath *i*neither faith, hope, nor charity; wherefore, should he be cut off while in the thought, he must go down to *j*hell.

15. For awful is the wickedness to suppose that God saveth one child because of baptism, and the other must perish because he hath no baptism.

16. Wo be unto them that shall pervert the ways of the Lord

---

a, see *h*, 2 Ne. 31. *b*, vers. 9—26. *c*, see *c*, Moro. 3. *d*, see *m*, Mos. 3. *e*, Gen. 17:9—14. *f*, vers. 14, 23. See *b*, *g*, 3 Ne. 12:2. 30:2. *h*, see *d*, Mos. 4. *i*, see *a*, Moro. 7. *j*, see *k*, 1 Ne. 15.

BETWEEN A. D. 400 AND 421.

after this manner, for they shall perish except they repent. Behold, I speak with boldness, having authority from God; and I fear not what man can do; for perfect love casteth out all fear.

17. And I am filled with charity, which is everlasting love; wherefore, all children are alike unto me; wherefore, I love little children with a perfect love; and they are all alike and ᵏpartakers of salvation.

18. For I know that God is not a partial God, neither a changeable being; but he is ˡunchangeable from ᵐall eternity to all eternity.

19. Little children cannot repent; wherefore, it is awful wickedness to deny the pure mercies of God unto them, for they are ⁿall alive in him because of his ᵒmercy.

20. And he that saith that little children need baptism denieth the mercies of Christ, and setteth at naught the ᵖatonement of him and the power of his redemption.

21. Wo unto such, for they are in danger of death, ᵠhell, and an endless torment. I speak it boldly; God hath commanded me. Listen unto them and give heed, or they stand against you at the judgment-seat of Christ.

22. For behold that all little children are ʳalive in Christ, and also all ˢthey that are without the law. For the power of redemption cometh on all them that have no law; wherefore, he that is not condemned, or he that is under no condemnation, cannot repent; and unto such baptism availeth nothing—

23. But it is ᵗmockery before God, denying the ᵘmercies of Christ, and the power of his Holy Spirit, and putting trust in dead works.

24. Behold, my son, this thing ought not to be; for repentance is unto them that are under condemnation and under the curse of a broken law.

25. And the first fruits of repentance is baptism; and baptism cometh by faith unto the fulfilling the commandments; and the ʳfulfilling the commandments bringeth remission of sins;

26. And the remission of sins bringeth meekness, and lowliness of heart; and because of meekness and lowliness of heart cometh the ʷvisitation of the Holy Ghost, which Comforter filleth ˣwith hope and perfect love, which love endureth by diligence unto ʸprayer, until the end shall come, when all the saints shall dwell with God.

27. Behold, my son, I will write unto you again if I go not out soon against the Lamanites. Behold, the pride of this nation, or the people of the Nephites, hath proven their destruction except they should repent.

28. Pray for them, my son, that repentance may come unto them. But behold, I fear lest the Spirit hath ceased striving with them; and in this part of the land they are also seeking to put down all power and authority which cometh from God; and they are ᶻdenying the Holy Ghost.

29. And after rejecting so great a knowledge, my son, they must perish soon, unto the fulfilling of the prophecies which were ²ᵃspoken by the prophets, as well as the words of our Savior himself.

---

k, see *m*, Mos. 3. *l*, see *d*, Morm. 9. *m*, see *a*, Mos. 3. *n*, ver. 22. *o*, vers. 20, 23. *p*, see *f*, 2 Ne. 2. *q*, see *k*, 1 Ne. 15. *r*, ver. 19. *s*, see *j*, Mos. 3. *t*, see *f*. *u*, vers. 19, 20, 23. *v*, see *g*. *w*, see *y*, 3 Ne. 9. *x*, see *a*, Moro. 7. *y*, see *c*, 2 Ne. 32. *z*, Al. 39:5, 6. 2*a*, see *d*, 1 Ne. 12. BETWEEN A. D. 400 AND 421.

30. Farewell, my son, until I shall write unto you, or shall meet you again. Amen.

CHAPTER 9.

The second epistle of Mormon to his son, Moroni.

Atrocities committed by Lamanites and Nephites—A Father's last and affectionate admonition.

1. My beloved son, I write unto you again that ye may know that I am yet alive; but I write somewhat of that which is grievous.

2. For behold, I have had a sore battle with the Lamanites, in which we did not conquer; and Archeantus has fallen by the sword, and also Luram and Emron; yea, and we have lost a great number of our choice men.

3. And now behold, my son, I fear lest the Lamanites shall ªdestroy this people; for they do not repent, and Satan stirreth them up continually to anger one with another.

4. Behold, I am laboring with them continually; and when I speak the word of God with ᵇsharpness they tremble and anger against me; and when I use no sharpness they harden their hearts against it; wherefore, I fear ᶜlest the Spirit of the Lord hath ceased striving with them.

5. For so exceedingly do they anger that it seemeth me that they have no fear of death; and they have lost their love, one towards another; and they ᵈthirst after blood and revenge continually.

6. And now, my beloved son, notwithstanding their hardness, let us labor diligently; for if we should cease to labor, we should be brought under condemnation; for we have a labor to perform whilst in this tabernacle of clay, that we may conquer the enemy of all righteousness, and rest our souls in the kingdom of God.

7. And now I write somewhat concerning the sufferings of this people. For according to the knowledge which I have received from Amoron, behold, the Lamanites have many prisoners, which they took from the tower of Sherrizah; and there were men, women, and children.

8. And the husbands and fathers of those women and children they have slain; and they feed the women upon the flesh of their husbands, and the children upon the flesh of their fathers; and no water, save a little, do they give unto them.

9. And notwithstanding this great abomination of the Lamanites, it doth not exceed that of our people in Moriantum. For behold, many of the daughters of the Lamanites have they taken prisoners; and after depriving them of that which was most dear and precious above all things, which is chastity and virtue—

10. And after they had done this thing, they did murder them in a most cruel manner, torturing their bodies even unto death; and after they have done this, they devour their flesh like unto wild beasts, because of the hardness of their hearts; and they do it for a token of bravery.

11. O my beloved son, how can a people like this, that are without civilization—

12. (And only a few years have passed away, and they were a civil and a delightsome people)

13. But O my son, how can a people like this, whose delight is in so much abomination—

---

a, see *d*, 1 Ne. 12. *b*, see *a*, 1 Ne. 16. *c*, Moro. 8:28. *d*, Morm. 4:11, 12.
BETWEEN A. D. 400 AND 421.

14. How can we expect that God will stay his hand in judgment against us?

15. Behold, my heart cries: Wo unto this people. Come out in judgment, O God, and hide their sins, and wickedness, and abominations from before thy face!

16. And again, my son, there are many widows and their daughters who remain in Sherrizah; and that part of the provisions which the Lamanites did not carry away, behold, the army of Zenephi has carried away, and left them to wander whithersoever they can for food; and many old women do faint by the way and die.

17. And the army which is with me is weak; and the armies of the Lamanites are betwixt Sherrizah and me; and as many as have fled to the army of *e*Aaron have fallen victims to their awful brutality.

18. O the depravity of my people! They are without order and without mercy. Behold, I am but a man, and I have but the strength of a man, and I cannot any longer enforce my commands.

19. And they have become strong in their perversion; and they are alike brutal, sparing none, neither old nor young; and they delight in everything save that which is good; and the suffering of our women and our children upon all the face of this land doth exceed everything; yea, tongue cannot tell, neither can it be written.

20. And now, my son, I dwell no longer upon this horrible scene. Behold, thou knowest the wickedness of this people; thou knowest that they are without principle, and past feeling; and their wickedness doth exceed that of the Lamanites.

21. Behold, my son, I cannot recommend them unto God lest he should smite me.

22. But behold, my son, I recommend thee unto God, and I trust in Christ that thou wilt be saved; and I pray unto God that he will *f*spare thy life, to witness the return of his people unto him, or their utter destruction; for I know that they must perish except they repent and return unto him.

23. And if they perish it will be *g*like unto the Jaredites, because of the wilfulness of their hearts, seeking *h*for blood and revenge.

24. And if it so be that they perish, we know that many of our brethren have *i*dissented over unto the Lamanites, and many more will also dissent over unto them; wherefore, write somewhat a few things, if thou art spared and I shall perish and not see thee; but I trust that I may see thee soon; for I have sacred records that I would *j*deliver up unto thee.

25. My son, be faithful in Christ; and may not the things which I have written grieve thee, to weigh thee down unto death; but may Christ lift thee up, and may his sufferings and death, and the showing his body unto our fathers, and his mercy and longsuffering, and the hope of his glory and of eternal life, rest in your mind forever.

26. And may the grace of God the Father, whose throne is high in the heavens, and our Lord Jesus Christ, who sitteth on the right hand of his power, until all

---

e, Morm. 2:9. *f*, Morm. 8:3. *g*, Eth. chaps. 13—15. *h*, ver. 5. Morm. 4:11, 12. *i*, 1 Ne. 13:31. Al. 45:14. *j*, Morm. 6:6.   BETWEEN A. D. 400 AND 421.

things shall become subject unto him, be, and abide with you forever. Amen.

CHAPTER 10.

Moroni's farewell to the Lamanites—Conditions on which individual testimony of the truth of the Book of Mormon may be obtained—Moroni seals up the record of his people.

1. Now I, Moroni, write somewhat as seemeth me good; and I write unto my brethren, the Lamanites; and I would that they should know that *more than four hundred and twenty years have passed away since the ªsign was given of the coming of Christ.

2. And I seal up ᵇthese records, after I have spoken a few words by way of exhortation unto you.

3. Behold, I would exhort you that when ye shall read these things, if it be wisdom in God that ye should read them, that ye would remember how merciful the Lord hath been unto the children of men, from the ᶜcreation of Adam even down until the time that ye shall receive these things, and ponder it in your hearts.

4. And when ye shall receive these things, I would exhort you that ye would ask God, the Eternal Father, in the name of Christ, if these things are not true; and if ye shall ask with a sincere heart, with real intent, having faith in Christ, he will manifest the truth of it unto you, ᵈby the power of the Holy Ghost.

5. And by the power of the Holy Ghost ye may know the truth of all things.

6. And whatsoever thing is good is just and true; wherefore, nothing that is good denieth the Christ, but acknowledgeth that he is.

7. And ye may know that he is, by the power of the Holy Ghost; wherefore I would exhort you that ye deny ᵉnot the power of God; for he worketh by power, ᶠaccording to the faith of the children of men, the ᵍsame today and tomorrow, and forever.

8. And again, I exhort you, my brethren, that ye ʰdeny not the gifts of God, for they are many; and they come from the same God. And there are different ways that these gifts are administered; but it is the same God who worketh all in all; and they are given by the manifestations of the Spirit of God unto men, to profit them.

9. ⁱFor behold, to one is given by the Spirit of God, that he may teach the word of wisdom;

10. And to another, that he may teach the word of knowledge by the same Spirit;

11. And to another, exceeding great faith; and to another, the gifts of healing by the same Spirit;

12. And again, to another, that he may work mighty miracles;

13. And again, to another, that he may prophesy concerning all things;

14. And again, to another, the beholding of angels and ministering spirits;

15. And again, to another, all kinds of tongues;

16. And again, to another, the interpretation of languages and of divers kinds of tongues.

17. And all these gifts come by the Spirit of Christ; and they come unto every man severally, according as he will.

18. And I would exhort you, my beloved brethren, that ye re-

---

a, 3 Ne. 2:8. *b*, Morm. 6:6. *c*, see *m*, Mos. 2. *d*, vers. 5, 7. See *c*, Moro. 3. *e*, see *r*, 2 Ne. 26. *f*, see *d*, 3 Ne. 17. *g*, see *d*, Morm. 9. *h*, see *c*, 3 Ne. 29. *i*, see *e*, 3 Ne. 29. 1 Cor. 12:8—11. D. & C. 46:8—30. *About A. D. 421.

member that ^jevery good gift cometh of Christ.

19. And I would exhort you, my beloved brethren, that ye remember that he is the ^ksame yesterday, today, and forever, and that all these gifts of which I have spoken, which are spiritual, ^lnever will be done away, even as long as the world shall stand, only according to the unbelief of the children of men.

20. ^mWherefore, there must be faith; and if there must be faith there must also be hope; and if there must be hope there must also be charity.

21. And except ye have charity ye can in nowise be saved in the kingdom of God; neither can ye be saved in the kingdom of God if ye have not faith; neither can ye if ye have no hope.

22. And if ye have no hope ye must needs be in despair; and despair cometh because of iniquity.

23. And Christ truly said unto our fathers: ⁿIf ye have faith ye can do all things which are expedient unto me.

24. And now I speak unto all the ends of the earth—^othat if the day cometh that the power and gifts of God shall be done away among you, it shall be because of unbelief.

25. And wo be unto the children of men if this be the case; for there shall be none that doeth good among you, no not one. For if there be one among you that doeth good, he shall work by the power and gifts of God.

26. And wo unto them who shall do these things away and die, for they die in their sins, and they cannot be saved in the kingdom of God; and I speak it according to the words of Christ; and I lie not.

27. And I exhort you to remember these things; for the time speedily cometh that ye shall ^pknow that I lie not, for ye shall see me at the bar of God; and the Lord God will say unto you: Did I not declare my words unto you, which were written by this man, like as one ^qcrying from the dead, yea, even as one speaking out of the dust?

28. I declare these things unto the fulfilling of the prophecies. And behold, they shall proceed forth out of the mouth of the everlasting God; and his word shall ^rhiss forth from generation to generation.

29. And God shall ^sshow unto you, that that which I have written is true.

30. And again I would exhort you that ye would come unto Christ, and lay hold upon every ^tgood gift, and ^utouch not the evil gift, nor the unclean thing.

31. And awake, and ^varise from the dust, O Jerusalem; yea, and put on thy beautiful garments, O daughter of Zion; and strengthen thy stakes and enlarge thy borders forever, that thou mayest ^wno more be confounded, that the ^xcovenants of the Eternal Father which he hath made unto thee, O house of Israel, may be fulfilled.

32. Yea, come unto Christ, and be perfected in him, and deny yourselves of all ungodliness; and if ye shall deny yourselves of all ungodliness, and love God with all your might, mind and strength, then is his grace sufficient for you, that by his grace ye may be perfect in Christ; and if by the

---

j, see *o*, Eth. 4. *k*, see *d*, Morm. 9. *l*, see 2*d*, Moro. 7. *m*, see *a*, Moro. 7.
n, Moro. 7:33. *o*, see 2*d*, Moro. 7. *p*, see *g*, 2 Ne. 33. *q*, see *s*, Morm. 5. See also
2*g*, Morm. 8. *r*, see *d*, 2 Ne. 29. *s*, see *g*, 2 Ne. 33. *t*, see *o*, Eth. 4. *u*, 2 Ne.
18:19. *v*, Isa. 52:1, 2. *w*, Eth. 13:8. *x*, see *j*, 3 Ne. 15. ABOUT A. D. 421.

grace of God ye are perfect in Christ, ye can in ʸnowise deny the power of God.

33. And again, if ye by the grace of God are perfect in Christ, and deny not his power, then are ye sanctified in Christ by the grace of God, through the ᶻshedding of the blood of Christ, which is in the covenant of the Father unto the remission of your sins, that ye become holy, without spot.

34. And now I bid unto all, farewell. I soon go to rest in the ²ᵃparadise of God, until my spirit and body shall again ²ᵇreunite, and I am brought forth triumphant through the air, to meet you before the ²ᶜpleasing bar of the great Jehovah, the Eternal Judge of both quick and dead. Amen.

y, see *e*, 3 Ne. 29. *z*, see *f*, 2 Ne. 2. 2*a*, see *l*, 2 Ne. 9. Rev. 2:7. 2*b*, see *d*, 2 Ne. 2. 2*c*, Jac. 6:13.

ABOUT A. D. 421.

THE END

SYNOPSIS OF CHAPTERS

Figures at end of paragraphs denote pages.

THE FIRST BOOK OF NEPHI

Chap. 1—Beginning of the record of Nephi, which dates from B. C. 600—Lehi has a vision of the pillar of fire and the book of prophecy—He predicts the impending fate of Jerusalem, and foretells the coming of the Messiah—The Jews seek his life.............. **1**

Chap. 2—Lehi departs with his family into the wilderness bordering on the Red Sea—Lehi's elder sons, Laman and Lemuel, murmur—His younger sons, Nephi and Sam, believe his words—The Lord's promises to Nephi............ **3**

Chap. 3—By command of the Lord, Lehi's sons are sent back to Jerusalem to obtain certain plates of brass—Laban refuses to deliver the plates and seeks to kill Nephi and his brothers—Laman and Lemuel reproved by an angel... **5**

Chap. 4—Nephi secures the plates by stratagem—by command of the Spirit he slays Laban with the latter's own sword—Zoram accompanies Nephi and his brothers into the wilderness.... **7**

Chap. 5—Sariah complains against Lehi—Both rejoice over their sons' return—Contents of the plates of brass—Lehi a descendant of Joseph—Laban also of that lineage—Lehi's prophecies...... **9**

Chap. 6—Nephi's intent—He writes what is pleasing to God.................. **10**

Chap. 7—Lehi's sons sent back to Jerusalem—Ishmael and household agree to join Lehi's company—Dissension—Nephi, bound with cords, is freed through power of faith—His rebellious brethren repent **11**

Chap. 8—Lehi's dream of the tree, the river, and the rod of iron—Laman and Lemuel partake not of the fruit...... **13**

Chap. 9—Concerning the plates of Nephi—Two sets of records, one of the ministry, the other of rulers, wars, etc.. **15**

Chap. 10—Lehi predicts the Babylonian captivity, and the coming of the Lamb of God—The house of Israel likened to an olive-tree—Dispersion and subsequent gathering typified............. **16**

Chap. 11—Nephi and the Spirit of the Lord—Lehi's prophetic dream interpreted—Nephi's vision of the Virgin and the Son of God—Christ's ministry foreshown **17**

Chap. 12—Nephi's vision of the land of promise—The future appearing of the Savior to the people of Nephi—Their righteousness, iniquity, and downfall foreseen **20**

Chap. 13—The nations of the Gentiles—A great and abominable church—America's history foreshadowed—The Holy Bible to proceed from the Jews—The Book of Mormon to come forth unto the Gentiles **22**

Chap. 14—Alternative blessing or cursing for the Gentiles—Two churches only—Doom of the mother of harlots—Mission of John the Revelator—End of Nephi's vision **25**

Chap. 15—Lehi's teachings interpreted by Nephi—The olive-tree—The tree of life —The word of God................... **28**

Chap. 16—Lehi's sons and Zoram intermarry with the daughters of Ishmael—The journey continued—The ball or director given—Death of Ishmael.... **30**

Chap. 17—Irreantum or many waters—The Lord commands Nephi to build a ship—His brethren oppose him and are confounded **34**

Chap. 18—The ship completed—Jacob and Joseph—The voyage begun—Revelry and rebellion aboard—A storm at sea—Arrival in the promised land........ **38**

Chap. 19—Nephi's record of his people—Sundry prophets mentioned—Zenos and his predictions **40**

Chap. 20—Prophecies recorded on the plates of brass—Compare Isaiah 48.. **43**

Chap. 21—Isaiah's writings, as recorded upon the plates of brass, continued—Compare Isaiah 49.................... **44**

Chap. 22—Nephi expounds the prophecies of Isaiah—Prediction of a mighty Gentile nation on the promised land—Lehi's descendants to be nourished by the Gentiles—The fate of those who fight against Zion.................... **46**

THE SECOND BOOK OF NEPHI

Chap. 1—The promised land a land of liberty, blessed for the righteous but cursed for the wicked—Lehi's exhortation **49**

Chap. 2—Lehi to his son Jacob—Opposition necessary in all things—The forbidden fruit and the tree of life—Adam fell that men might be—Messiah, the great Mediator, to redeem mankind **52**

Chap. 3—Lehi to his son Joseph—A prophecy by Joseph in Egypt—A choice seer foretold—The mission of Moses—Hebrew and Nephite scriptures..... **55**

523

SYNOPSIS OF CHAPTERS

Chap. 4—Lehi blesses the sons and daughters of Laman and Lemuel—Blessings upon Ishmael's household and upon Sam and his posterity—Death of Lehi—Further rebellion... **57**
Chap. 5—Nephi, warned of God, separates from those who seek his life—Zoram, Sam, Jacob and Joseph and others accompany him—The sword of Laban—A temple built—Nephi a king or protector—The rebellious cursed with a dark skin—Priests and teachers are consecrated **60**
Chap. 6—Jacob's exhortation to the people—He cites the prophecies of Isaiah **62**
Chap. 7—Jacob's teachings continued—Compare Isaiah 50..................... **64**
Chap. 8—Jacob's teachings continued—Compare Isaiah 51..................... **65**
Chap. 9—Jacob's teachings continued—The atonement infinite—Where there is no law there is no punishment.. **66**
Chap. 10—Jacob's teachings continued—The coming of Christ—No kings upon the land of promise—They who fight against Zion shall perish............ **71**
Chap. 11—Jacob's teachings continued—Witnesses for the word of God—Types of the Redeemer..................... **73**
Chap. 12—Prophecies as recorded on the brass plates—Compare Isaiah 2...... **74**
Chap. 13—Scriptures from the brass plates continued—Compare Isaiah 3........ **75**
Chap. 14—Scriptures from the brass plates continued—Compare Isaiah 4........ **76**
Chap. 15—Scriptures from the brass plates continued—Compare Isaiah 5........ **77**
Chap. 16—Scriptures from the brass plates continued—Compare Isaiah 6........ **78**
Chap. 17—Scriptures from the brass plates continued—Compare Isaiah 7........ **79**
Chap. 18—Scriptures from the brass plates continued—Compare Isaiah 8........ **80**
Chap. 19—Scriptures from the brass plates continued—Compare Isaiah 9........ **82**
Chap. 20—Scriptures from the brass plates continued—Compare Isaiah 10....... **83**
Chap. 21—Scriptures from the brass plates continued—Compare Isaiah 11....... **85**
Chap. 22—Scriptures from the brass plates continued—Compare Isaiah 12....... **86**
Chap. 23—Scriptures from the brass plates continued—Compare Isaiah 13....... **86**
Chap. 24—Scriptures from the brass plates continued—Compare Isaiah 14....... **87**
Chap. 25—Nephi's comments—His prediction of the scattering and subsequent gathering of Israel—Time of the Messiah's advent again specified........ **89**
Chap. 26—Nephi's predictions continued—Christ to come to the Nephites—Their final destruction—The days of the Gentiles **92**
Chap. 27—Nephi's predictions continued—God's judgments upon the wicked—The sealed book—The unlearned man—The three witnesses—A marvelous work and a wonder................... **95**
Chap. 28—Nephi's predictions continued—Latter-day churches and conditions—The kingdom of the devil to be shaken—The misleading precepts of men.. **98**
Chap. 29—Nephi's predictions continued—The Gentiles and the Bible—Other records—God's words to be gathered in one **100**
Chap. 30—Nephi's predictions continued—Converted Gentiles to be numbered with the covenant people—Jews and Lamanites to believe—The wicked to be destroyed **102**
Chap. 31—Nephi's predictions continued—Why the Savior would be baptized—The straight and narrow way...... **103**
Chap. 32—Nephi's predictions continued—The tongue of angels—Office of the Holy Ghost **105**
Chap. 33—Nephi's parting testimony—Not mighty in writing as in speaking—His great concern for his people.. **106**

THE BOOK OF JACOB

Chap. 1—Nephites and Lamanites—Death of Nephi, son of Lehi—Hardness of heart and wicked practices........ **107**
Chap. 2—Jacob's denunciation of unchastity and other sins—Plurality of wives forbidden because of iniquity **109**
Chap. 3—Jacob's denunciation continued—Lamanites more righteous than Nephites—The former commended for fidelity in marriage—The latter again warned **112**
Chap. 4—Jacob's teachings continued—The law of Moses among the Nephites, pointing them to Christ—His rejection by the Jews foreseen................ **113**
Chap. 5—Jacob quotes the prophet Zenos—Allegory of the tame and wild olive-tree—Israel and the Gentiles....... **115**
Chap. 6—Jacob expounds the allegory of the olive-tree—The pruning of the vineyard **122**
Chap. 7—Sherem, denying the Christ, demands a sign and is stricken—He confesses his sin and dies—A reformation begins—Hatred of Lamanites for Nephites—Jacob gives the plates to his son Enos **123**

THE BOOK OF ENOS

The Lord's promise concerning a Nephite record to come forth to the Lamanites—Character, condition, and wars of the two peoples............ **125**

THE BOOK OF JAROM

Jarom, son of Enos, keeps the records—The Nephites serve the Lord and are prospered **127**

SYNOPSIS OF CHAPTERS

THE BOOK OF OMNI

Comprising records kept by Omni, Amaron, Chemish, Abinadom, and Amaleki—Mosiah, the first, leaving the land of Nephi, discovers the land of Zarahemla, occupied by another colony from Jerusalem—He is made king—Coriantumr, the last of the Jaredites—King Benjamin—Other migrations **129**

THE WORDS OF MORMON

Mormon's abridgment and the smaller plates of Nephi—Relation of the foregoing part of the Book of Mormon to that which follows **132**

THE BOOK OF MOSIAH

Chap. 1—King Benjamin's exhortation to his sons—Mosiah chosen to succeed his father—He receives the records, etc. **134**
Chap. 2—King Benjamin builds a tower from which he addresses his people—The righteous reign of a God-fearing king **136**
Chap. 3—King Benjamin's address continued—Another prophecy of the Christ, —More concerning the atonement.. **139**
Chap. 4—King Benjamin's address concluded—The conditions of salvation—Man's dependence upon God—Liberality, wisdom and diligence enjoined **142**
Chap. 5—Effect of king Benjamin's address—The people repent and enter into covenant with Christ, and are called by his name...................... **145**
Chap. 6—Names of the people recorded—Priests appointed—Beginning of Mosiah's reign—Death of king Benjamin **146**
Chap. 7—Expedition to the land of Lehi-Nephi—Ammon and king Limhi—People of Lehi-Nephi in bondage to Lamanites **147**
Chap. 8—Ammon learns of the discovery of twenty-four gold plates with engravings—He suggests they be submitted to king Mosiah, prophet and seer **150**
Chap. 9—Beginning of the Record of Zeniff—Zeniff goes to possess the land of Lehi-Nephi—A spy among the Lamanites—The craftiness of king Laman **152**
Chap. 10—King Laman dies—Zeniff and his people prevail against their oppressors **153**
Chap. 11—The wicked king Noah and his priests—The prophet Abinadi denounces the prevailing wickedness—King Noah seeks his life...................... **155**
Chap. 12—Abinadi, for denouncing evil-doers, is cast into prison—The false priests sit in judgment upon him—They are confounded............... **158**
Chap. 13—Abinadi the prophet, protected by divine power, withstands the priests and cites the law and the gospel.. **160**
Chap. 14—Abinadi quotes Isaiah to the priests of king Noah—Compare Isaiah 53 .... **162**
Chap. 15—Abinadi's prophecy—God himself to come down and redeem his people—Why Jesus Christ is called the Father and the Son................. **163**
Chap. 16—Abinadi's prophecy continued —Christ the only Redeemer—Resurrection and judgment............... **165**
Chap. 17—Martyrdom of Abinadi—While suffering death by fire he predicts retribution upon his murderers—Conversion of Alma..................... **166**
Chap. 18—The waters of Mormon—Alma baptizes Helam and others—The church of Christ—King Noah sends an army to destroy Alma and his followers.... **167**
Chap. 19—A futile search—Gideon's insurrection—A Lamanite invasion—King Noah suffers death by fire—His son Limhi a tributary monarch......... **170**
Chap. 20—Priests of king Noah carry off daughters of the Lamanites—Lamanites seek revenge upon king Limhi and his people—They are repulsed and pacified **172**
Chap. 21—Abinadi's prophecy further fulfilled—Nephites in bondage suffer great affliction—The Lord softens the hearts of their enemies—More concerning the twenty-four plates **174**
Chap. 22—Plan to throw off Lamanite yoke — Gideon's proposal — Lamanites made drunk—The captive people escape and go to Zarahemla—End of Zeniff's record **176**
Chap. 23—Alma refuses to be king—Land of Helam captured by Lamanites —Amulon, leader of king Noah's wicked priests, rules subject to the Lamanite monarch **178**
Chap. 24—Amulon persecutes Alma and his followers—The Lord makes their burdens light and delivers them from bondage—They go to Zarahemla.. **180**
Chap. 25—Zarahemla, a descendant of Mulek—The record of Zeniff and the account of Alma read to the people—Alma authorized to establish the church of Christ throughout the land...... **182**
Chap. 26—Concerning unbelievers and evil-doers—The Lord instructs Alma how to deal with them............. **184**
Chap. 27—Persecution forbidden and equality enjoined—Alma, the younger, and the four sons of Mosiah, among the unbelievers—Their miraculous conversion—They become preachers of righteousness **186**
Chap. 28—Mosiah permits his sons to preach to the Lamanites—The twenty-four plates translated — Alma, the younger, made the custodian of the records **189**

SYNOPSIS OF CHAPTERS

Chap. 29—King Mosiah discourses upon kingcraft—Recommends representative form of government—Judges elected—Death of Alma, the elder—Mosiah's death ends the reign of the Nephite kings **191**

THE BOOK OF ALMA

Chap. 1—Nehor, an enemy of the church, slays Gideon, and is brought to judgment and executed—Priestcraft and persecution — Improved conditions — Priests and people equal............ **195**

Chap. 2—Amlici seeks to become king—Rejected by the majority, but is made king—He is defeated in battle—He joins the Lamanites—Alma slays Amlici and routs his forces............ **198**

Chap. 3—The mark of the Amlicites, and the curse upon the Lamanites—Another Nephite victory.............. **201**

Chap. 4—Growth of the church—Prosperity, pride, and iniquity—Nephihah made chief judge.................... **203**

Chap. 5—Alma recounts the experience of the church—Denounces iniquity—Calls upon the people to repent.... **204**

Chap. 6—The reform movement, begun in Zarahemla, is carried to the city of Gideon **210**

Chap. 7—Alma's testimony of the Redeemer—He commends the people for their righteousness **211**

Chap. 8—Alma's success in Melek—The people of Ammonihah cast him out—Comforted by an angel, he returns—Amulek joins him in the ministry—Great power given................... **213**

Chap. 9—Alma preaches to the people of Ammonihah and calls them to repentance—His testimony rejected...... **216**

Chap. 10—Amulek's lineage—Lehi a descendant of Joseph through Manasseh—Amulek tells of his conversion—His testimony—He denounces designing lawyers and judges—Zeezrom...... **219**

Chap. 11—Judges and their compensation—Nephite coins and measures—Zeezrom confounded by Amulek.. **221**

Chap. 12—Amulek's testimony confirmed by Alma—Doctrine of the tree of life—The plan of redemption expounded **224**

Chap. 13—Alma's discourse continued—The holy order of the Son of God—High priests—Why ordained—Melchizedek and Abraham.................... **227**

Chap. 14—Alma and Amulek imprisoned—Their adherents persecuted—Deaths by fire—Zeezrom, now repentant, pleads their cause and is cast out—The prophets are delivered from prison—Their enemies slain **230**

Chap. 15—Zeezrom, miraculously healed, joins the church and preaches—Many baptized—Alma and Amulek return to Zarahemla **233**

Chap. 16—A cry of war—The wicked city Ammonihah destroyed by Lamanites—Zoram and his sons rout the enemy—Desolation of Nehors—The church widely established **234**

Chap. 17—Ammon in the land of Ishmael—He becomes a servant to the king—His heroic rescue and defence of the king's flocks **237**

Chap. 18—King Lamoni mistakes Ammon for the Great Spirit—He is taught concerning the true God—Overcome by the Spirit of the Lord, he falls as if dead **240**

Chap. 19—A wonderful conversion—Abish the Lamanite woman—Lamanite king and queen espouse the faith—Ammon establishes the church in Ishmael **243**

Chap. 20—Ammon and king Lamoni journey to Middoni—They meet Lamoni's father who is king over all the land—Hostile at first, he relents and grants great favors **247**

Chap. 21—Rejected by the Amalekites, Aaron and Muloki go to Middoni—They are imprisoned—Their release and missionary labors—Ammon's further success—Synagogues built **249**

Chap. 22—Aaron in the land of Nephi—The king and all his household converted—Country divided between Nephites and Lamanites............... **251**

Chap. 23—Religious freedom proclaimed—Many Lamanites converted—Amalekites and Amulonites reject the truth—The Anti-Nephi-Lehies **255**

Chap. 24—Lamanites come against the people of God—Converted Lamanites refuse to take up arms—More conversions **256**

Chap. 25—Lamanite aggressions — Vengeance by Amulonites—Martyrdoms—Further fulfilment of Abinadi's prophecy **259**

Chap. 26—Ammon glories in the Lord—Boasting in righteousness—He recounts blessings to himself and his brethren **260**

Chap. 27—People of Anti-Nephi-Lehi seek safety in Zarahemla—They are called the people of Ammon—Land of Jershon given to them...................... **264**

Chap. 28—Lamanites make war upon Nephites—A tremendous battle—Lamanites defeated—Deep mourning...... **266**

Chap. 29—Alma's yearning desire to cry repentance to all—God's word is apportioned in wisdom—Alma rejoices over success of his brethren...... **267**

Chap. 30—Korihor the Anti-Christ—Expelled from Jershon and arrested at Gideon—Arraigned in Zarahemla—He demands a sign and is stricken dumb—His miserable death.............. **268**

Chap. 31—Alma heads a mission to reclaim the Zoramite dissenters—The

SYNOPSIS OF CHAPTERS 527

Rameumptom or holy stand—The Zoramite form of worship.......... 273
Chap. 32—The poor hearken to message of salvation—Alma's commendation and discourse—Faith developed by desire to believe 276
Chap. 33—Alma's discourse continued—True worship not confined to sanctuaries—The prophets Zenos and Zenock again cited................... 280
Chap. 34—Amulek's testimony—The great and last sacrifice—How mercy satisfies justice—Repentance not to be procrastinated 281
Chap. 35—Nephite missionaries retire to land of Jershon—Their Zoramite converts, expelled from their own country, rejoin them—Preparations made for war 284
Chap. 36—Alma recounts his sinful past, his miraculous conversion, and his subsequent zeal in the ministry.. 286
Chap. 37—Helaman entrusted with the records and other sacred relics—Gazelem—Liahona a type of the word of Christ 288
Chap. 38—Shiblon commended for faithfulness, and counseled to observe meekness and self-control................ 292
Chap. 39—Corianton reproved for harlotry—His sinful conduct had affected faith of the Zoramites—Christ's redemption retroactive 293
Chap. 40—Alma to Corianton continued—Resurrection universal—Separate states of righteous and wicked between death and resurrection—Paradise—A literal restoration assured 294
Chap. 41—Alma to Corianton continued—What restoration signifies—Men to be judged according to their deeds and desires—Self-judgment 297
Chap. 42—Alma to Corianton concluded—Justice and mercy expounded—The tree of life—Mortality a period of probation—Spiritual and temporal death—Repentance, atonement, law, punishment, all necessary.................. 298
Chap. 43—Alma and his sons severally go forth to preach and teach—Another Lamanite invasion—Armies of Moroni and Lehi overpower and surround the enemy 300
Chap. 44—Moroni's magnanimity—Zerahemnah rejects his peace offer, but is compelled to accept terms—Lamanites make covenant of peace—End of Alma's record 305
Chap. 45—Nephite extinction again foretold—Alma's departure compared to that of Moses—Dissension in the church 307
Chap. 46—Amalickiah conspires to be king—Moroni and the title of liberty—His stirring protest and appeal—The people covenant to maintain freedom—Flight of Amalickiah................ 309

Chap. 47—Amalickiah, by treachery, becomes king of the Lamanites—His awful wickedness 313
Chap. 48—Amalickiah incites Lamanites against Nephites—Moroni prepares for the conflict—A true patriot and a mighty man of God................ 316
Chap. 49—Lamanites attack city of Noah—The invaders baffled and repulsed—Amalickiah's wrath over his failure—Prosperity of the church.......... 318
Chap. 50—Moroni fortifies the line between land of Zarahemla and land of Nephi—Morianton plans to occupy the land northward—He is killed by Teancum—Pahoran succeeds Nephihah.. 320
Chap. 51—King-men and freemen—Pahoran, chief judge, is sustained by the freemen—King-men suppressed—Amalickiah's invasion, defeat, and death 324
Chap. 52—Ammoron succeeds Amlickiah—Moroni, with Teancum and Lehi, retakes city of Mulek and wins great victory—Death of Jacob, the Lamanite general 327
Chap. 53—City Bountiful fortified—Nephite dissension gives advantage to enemy—Helaman and his two thousand stripling warriors 331
Chap. 54—Ammoron asks for exchange of prisoners—Moroni grants request upon conditions—The Lamanite king's angry reply 333
Chap. 55—Moroni, incensed at Ammoron's false assertions, refuses to exchange prisoners—Strategy secures release of captured Nephites—City of Gid taken without bloodshed 335
Chap. 56—Helaman's epistle to Moroni—Wonderful faith and valor of the stripling Ammonites—Another great battle—Nephites victorious 337
Chap. 57—Helaman's epistle continued—Antiparah retaken—City of Cumeni surrenders—Lamanites driven to Manti—A miraculous preservation—Escape of many Lamanite prisoners....... 341
Chap. 58—Helaman's epistle concluded—Nephite operations before Manti—A Lamanite sortie—Gid and Teomner capture the city—Enemy withdraws 344
Chap. 59—Moroni writes to Pahoran, asking reenforcements for Helaman—City of Nephihah taken by Lamanites—Moroni's anger at seeming indifference of the government............ 347
Chap. 60—Moroni's second epistle to Pahoran—Complains of neglect—Demands immediate help on peril of reprisal 348
Chap. 61—Pahoran's patriotic reply—He exonerates himself and the freemen—He shows the Nephite state to be tottering—Governor appeals for military aid against rebels............ 352
Chap. 62—Moroni marches to relief of Pahoran—Zarahemla recaptured from

the rebels—Help sent to Helaman, Lehi, and Teancum—Lamanites concentrate in land of Moroni—Teancum slays Ammoron, at cost of his own life—Lamanites driven out of the land 353

Chap. 63—Shiblon succeeds Helaman—Death of Moroni—Hagoth, builder of ships—Nephite voyages to the land northward—Helaman, son of Helaman, keeps the records—Moronihah defeats Lamanites—End of Alma's account 358

THE BOOK OF HELAMAN

Chap. 1—Pahoran's sons contend for the judgment-seat—Pahoran the second is murdered by Kishkumen—Coriantumr, Nephite dissenter, is leader of the Lamanites—Zarahemla captured and retaken 359

Chap. 2—Helaman the second is appointed chief judge—Kishkumen slain by Helaman's servant—Secret combinations—The Gadianton robbers escape 362

Chap. 3—More migrations to the north—A land of large waters—Buildings of cement—Many records kept—Helaman dies—His son, Nephi, succeeds him 363

Chap. 4—Many dissensions in the church—Lamanites again invade land of Zarahemla—The city captured—Nephites driven into the land Bountiful—Moronihah fortifies the way—Weakened by wickedness, the Nephites prevail not 366

Chap. 5—Nephi yields judgment-seat to Cezoram—With his brother Lehi he devotes himself to the ministry—Marvelous manifestations—Converted Lamanites restore conquered Nephite lands 368

Chap. 6—Lamanites send missionaries to Nephites—Peace and freedom abound—The land Lehi and the land Mulek—Cezoram murdered—His son also murdered—Gadianton robbers seize government 372

Chap. 7—Beginning of the prophecy of Nephi, son of Helaman—Nephi, rejected by the people in the north, returns to Zarahemla—From his garden tower he prays to God and addresses the multitude 376

Chap. 8—Nephi's address continued—Corrupt judges vainly endeavor to incite people against him—By inspiration he announces the murder of the chief judge 378

Chap. 9—Nephi's words verified—Chief judge found dead at the judgment-seat—Nephi and five others accused—Their innocence established—The murderer made known................ 380

Chap. 10—Nephi is comforted by the Lord with promise of great power—He preaches repentance and warns the wicked of impending judgments... 383

Chap. 11—Further depredations by the secret band of robbers—A great famine—The famishing people turn to the Lord and are again prospered—Dissension and strife follow—The Gadianton band more active................ 385

Chap. 12—Mormon's commentary on the condition of the people—Human frailty and the goodness and power of God—Blessed are the penitent—Men to be judged according to their works.. 388

Chap. 13—Beginning of the prophecy of Samuel the Lamanite—Samuel proclaims his prophecies from the city wall—Sword of justice to fall on fourth generation—Nephite cities spared for sake of the righteous—Land to be cursed—Slippery treasures.......... 389

Chap. 14—Samuel the Lamanite predicts the Christ—The signs of Christ's birth to be given in five years—Signs of his death also foretold.............. 393

Chap. 15—Samuel the Lamanite continues his warning words—A remnant of his people to be preserved—Nephites to be utterly destroyed unless they repent 395

Chap. 16—Some of the Nephites join the church of Christ—The majority reject Samuel's testimony—They attempt to assault and bind him—He escapes and returns to his own country—Nephi's further ministry—Skepticism abounds 397

THIRD NEPHI

Chap. 1—Nephi, son of Helaman, departs —Signs of the Savior's birth actually appear—Opposite effects manifest—Again, the Gadianton band........ 399

Chap. 2—Nephite degeneracy—Nephite reckoning of time changed—White Lamanites—Both peoples unite for defence against the bands of robbers and murderers 401

Chap. 3—Lachoneus, governor of the land, receives epistle from Gaddianhi, the robber chieftain—Surrender demanded—Lachoneus ignores demand and prepares for defence............ 403

Chap. 4—The robbers beaten and their leader slain—His successor, Zemnarihah, hanged—Gidgiddoni's military prowess 406

Chap. 5—Nephites repent and seek to end works of wickedness—Mormon's account of himself and of the plates kept by him—Another allusion to the gathering of Israel................ 408

Chap. 6—The people are prospered—Pride, wealth, and class distinctions follow—The church rent by dissension —Deeds of darkness............ 410

Chap. 7—Chief judge murdered and government overthrown—Division into

SYNOPSIS OF CHAPTERS 529

tribes—King Jacob—Nephi's powerful ministry 413
Chap. 8—Christ's crucifixion attested by predicted signs—Tempest and earthquake, whirlwind and fire—A great and terrible destruction—Three days of darkness 415
Chap. 9—The voice of God proclaims the extent of the disaster and declares the causes thereof—The law of Moses fulfilled—The acceptable sacrifice of a broken heart and a contrite spirit.. 417
Chap. 10—Silence in the land for many hours—Again the voice from heaven—The darkness disperses—Only the more righteous of the people had been spared 419
Chap. 11—Beginning of the record of the personal ministry of the resurrected Christ among the Nephites—The Eternal Father proclaims the Christ—The Resurrected Christ appears—The multitude permitted to feel his wounds—Mode of baptism prescribed—Contention and disputation forbidden—Christ the rock 420
Chap. 12—The Savior's teachings to the Nephites continued—He calls and commissions the twelve disciples—His words to the multitude—The Sermon on the Mount retold—Compare Matthew 5 423
Chap. 13—The Savior's sermon to the Nephites continued—His commandments to the twelve—Compare Matthew 6 426
Chap. 14—The Savior's sermon continued —Further instructions to the multitude —Compare Matthew 7............ 427
Chap. 15—The Law of Moses superseded —The Giver of the Law fulfils the Law —The people there present were declared to be the sheep of another fold, spoken of to the Jews.............. 429
Chap. 16—Yet another fold to hear the Savior—Blessings upon the believing Gentiles—The state of those who reject the Gospel—The prophet Isaiah cited 430
Chap. 17—The Savior's instructions continued—The lost tribes of Israel—The Savior heals the sick and blesses little children—A marvelous and touching scene 432
Chap. 18—Sacrament of bread and wine instituted among the Nephites—Necessity of prayer emphasized—Authority given to the twelve disciples to confer the Holy Ghost................ 434
Chap. 19—Names of the Nephite twelve —Their baptism—The Holy Ghost given —The Savior's second visitation—An ineffable outpouring of prayer.... 436
Chap. 20—Bread and wine, miraculously provided, again administered—The remnant of Jacob—The Savior proclaims himself to be the prophet spoken of as like unto Moses—Many prophets cited 439
Chap. 21—Sign of the Father's work—Glorious destiny of repentant Gentiles —Condemnation predicted for the impenitent—The New Jerusalem...... 442
Chap. 22—The Savior further quotes the prophecies of Isaiah—Compare Isaiah 54 444
Chap. 23—The Savior commands that omissions from Nephite records be supplied—Prophecy of Samuel the Lamanite added 445
Chap. 24—Malachi's words given to the Nephites—The law of tithes and offerings—Compare Malachi 3........... 446
Chap. 25—Malachi's words continued—Elijah and his mission—The great and dreadful day of the Lord—Compare Malachi 4 447
Chap. 26—The Savior expounds all things from the beginning—Marvels spoken by the mouths of babes—The work of the disciples 448
Chap. 27—Jesus Christ names his church —All things are written by the Father—Men to be judged by what is written in the books............... 449
Chap. 28—Each of the twelve is granted his heart's desire—Three elect to remain on earth until the Lord comes in his glory—Marvelous manifestations to the three—They are made immune to death and disaster............... 452
Chap. 29—Mormon's warning to those who spurn the words and works of the Lord 454
Chap. 30—Mormon calls the Gentiles to repentance 455

FOURTH NEPHI

The church of Christ flourishes—Nephites and Lamanites converted—They have all things in common—Two centuries of righteousness followed by division and degeneracy—Amos and Ammaron in turn keep the records 456

THE BOOK OF MORMON

Chap. 1—Ammaron's charge to Mormon respecting the sacred engravings—War and wickedness—The three Nephite disciples depart—Mormon restrained from preaching—Predictions of Abinadi and Samuel the Lamanite fulfilled.. 460
Chap. 2—Mormon leads the Nephite armies—More of the Gadianton robbers—By treaty the land northward is given to the Nephites, and the land southward to the Lamanites....... 461
Chap. 3—Nephites continue in wickedness—Mormon refuses to be their military leader—His address to future generations—The twelve to judge the house of Israel..................,,, 463

SYNOPSIS OF CHAPTERS

Chap. 4—Nephites begin a war of revenge upon Lamanites—Nephites no longer prevail—The sacred record taken from the hill Shim **465**
Chap. 5—Mormon relents and again leads Nephites—Lamanites outnumber Nephites—Crime and carnage—Mormon's abridgment of the records **467**
Chap. 6—The hill Cumorah and its records—The final struggle between the two nations—Lamanites victorious—Twenty-four Nephites survive..... **469**
Chap. 7—Mormon affirms to Lamanites that they are of Israel—Admonishes them for their salvation **471**
Chap. 8—Moroni finishes his father's record—After the carnage of Cumorah—Mormon among the slain—Lamanites and robbers possess the land—Mormon's record to come out of the earth—Conditions and calamities of latter days depicted **472**
Chap. 9—Moroni's address to unbelievers—His testimony concerning the Christ—The Nephite language known as reformed Egyptian **475**

THE BOOK OF ETHER

Chap. 1—The prophet Ether's genealogy—The great tower—Jared and his brother—Their language not confounded—Preparing for migration as directed by the Lord **478**
Chap. 2—In the valley of Nimrod—Deseret, the honey bee—The Lord again talks with the brother of Jared—Divine decree concerning the land of promise—The place Moriancumer—Barges built **480**
Chap. 3—The finger of the Lord—Jesus Christ shows himself in the spirit to the brother of Jared—The luminous stones—The interpreters—A record yet to come **482**
Chap. 4—The brother of Jared commanded to write—Moroni's solemn admonition—Cursed is he who contends against the word of the Lord—Whatsoever persuades men to do good is of God **485**
Chap. 5—Moroni to the future translator of his writings **487**
Chap. 6—The story of the Jaredites continued—Their vessels lighted by miracle—Through the depths of the sea to the promised land—The people desire a king—Their leaders foresee evil but yield to the popular will—Death of Jared and his brother **487**
Chap. 7—Orihah's righteous reign, followed by rebellion, usurpation and strife—The rival kingdoms of Shule and Cohor—Wickedness and idolatry—Prophets appear and the people repent **489**
Chap. 8—The good king Omer—His son Jared conspires with Akish to obtain the crown—Strife and bloodshed—Secret and murderous combinations—Modern Gentiles warned against such dangers **491**
Chap. 9—Omer loses and regains his crown—Emer's prosperous reign—Cureloms and cumoms, animals of that period—Sundry kings—Famine and poisonous serpents **493**
Chap. 10—Riplakish the wrong-doer—Morianton the reformer—Other monarchs and their wars—The land southward a wilderness—The land northward inhabited **496**
Chap. 11—Jaredite prophets predict utter destruction of their people except they repent—The warning unheeded.... **498**
Chap. 12—The prophet Ether and king Coriantumr—The Jaredite and Nephite languages—God gives weaknesses that men may be humble—Moroni's farewell to the Gentiles **500**
Chap. 13—Moroni continues the Jaredite history—Ether and his predictions—His life sought—He dwells in the cavity of a rock—Views by night the destruction falling upon his people **503**
Chap. 14—A curse upon the land—Continued strife and bloodshed—Coriantumr not to fall by the sword.... **505**
Chap. 15—The hill Ramah or Cumorah—Preparations for a mighty struggle—Millions go down to death—Shiz slain by Coriantumr—Ether's concluding words—End of the Jaredite record.. **507**

THE BOOK OF MORONI

Chap. 1—Moroni's desolate state—He writes, hoping for the welfare of the Lamanites **510**
Chap. 2—Concerning the bestowal of the Holy Ghost by the Nephite twelve.. **510**
Chap. 3—Concerning the ordination of priests and teachers **510**
Chap. 4—Mode of administering the sacramental bread **511**
Chap. 5—Mode of administering the sacramental wine **511**
Chap. 6—Conditions and mode of baptism—Church discipline **511**
Chap. 7—Moroni presents Mormon's teachings on faith, hope, charity.. **512**
Chap. 8—Mormon's epistle to Moroni—Little children have no need of repentance or baptism **515**
Chap. 9—The second epistle of Mormon to his son, Moroni—Atrocities committed by Lamanites and Nephites—A father's last and affectionate admonition **518**
Chap. 10—Moroni's farewell to the Lamanites—Conditions on which individual testimony of the truth of the Book of Mormon may be obtained—Moroni seals up the record of his people **520**

PRONOUNCING VOCABULARY

MOSTLY PROPER NAMES OF BOOK OF MORMON ORIGIN

With some Biblical names included

Aaron—ăr'ŏn
Abel—ā'bel
Abinadi—à-bĭn'à-dĭ
Abinadom—à-bĭn'à-dŏm
Abish—ā'bĭsh
Ablom—ăb'lŏm
Abraham—ā'brà-hăm
Agosh—ā'gŏsh
Aha—ā'hă
Ahah—ā'hä
Ahaz—ā'hăz
Aiath—a-ī'ath
Akish—ā'kĭsh
Alma—ăl'mà
Amaleki—à-măl'ĕ-kī
Amalekites—à-măl'ĕ-kītes
Amalickiah—à-mă-lĭ-kī'ä
Amalickiahites—à-mă-lĭ-kī'ä-hītes
Amaron—ă-mā'rŏn
Amgid—ăm'gĭd
Aminadab—à-mĭn'à-dăb
Aminadi—à-mĭn'à-dĭ
Amlici—ăm'lĭ-cī
Amlicites—ăm'lĭ-cītes
Ammah—ăm'mä
Ammaron—ăm'ăr-on

Ammon—ăm'ŏn
Ammonites—ăm'ŏn-ītes
Ammonihah—ăm-ŏn-ī'hä
Ammonihahites—ăm-ŏn-ī'hä-hītes
Ammoron—ăm'ōr-ŏn
Amnigaddah—ăm-nĭ-găd'dä
Amnihu—ăm-nī'hū
Amnor—ăm'nôr
Amoron—à-mō'rŏn
Amos—ā'mŏs
Amulek—ăm'ū-lĕk
Amulon—ăm'ū-lŏn
Amulonites—ăm'ū-lŏn-ītes
Anathoth—àn'a-thoth
Angola—ăn-gō'là
Ani-Anti—ăn'i-ăn'tĭ
Anti-Nephi-Lehi—ăn'tĭ-nē'phĭ-lē'hĭ
Anti-Nephi-Lehies
—ăn'tĭ-nē'phĭ-lē'hīes
Antiomno—ăn-tĭ-ŏm'nō
Antion—ăn'ti-ŏn
Antionah—ăn-tĭ-ōn'ä
Antionum—ăn-tĭ-ōn'ŭm
Antiparah—ăn-tĭ-pâr'ä
Antipas—ăn'tĭ-pàs
Antipus—ăn'tĭ-pŭs

PRONOUNCING VOCABULARY

Antum—ăn'tŭm
Archeantus—àr-kĕ-ăn'tŭs
Arpad—àr'păd

Babylon—băb'ĭ-lŏn
Bashan—bā'shan
Benjamin—ben'ja-min
Bethabara—beth-äb'ä-rä
Boaz—bō'ăz
Bountiful—boun'tĭ-fŭl

Camenihah—kă-mĕ-nī'hä
Carchemish—kàr-kĕm'ĭsh
Cezoram—cē-zō'răm
Chaldeans—kăl-dē'ăns
Chemish—kĕm'ish
Cohor—kō'hôr
Com—kôm
Comnor—kôm'nôr
Corianton—kō-rĭ-ăn'tŏn
Coriantor—kō-rĭ-ăn'tôr
Coriantum—kō-rĭ-ăn'tŭm
Coriantumr—kō-rĭ-ăn'tŭ-mŭr
Corihor—kō'rĭ-hôr
Corom—kō'rŏm
Cumeni—kū-mē'nĭ
Cumom—kū'mŏm
Cumorah—kụ-mōr'ä
Curelom—kụ-rē'lōm

Deseret—dĕṣ-êr-ĕt'
Desolation—dĕs-ō-lā'tion

Edom—ē'dȯm
Elam—ē'lăm
Elijah—ē-lī'jä
Emer—ē'mēr
Emron—ĕm'rŏn
Enos—ē'nŏs
Ephah—ē'-fä
Ephraim—ēf'rā-ĭm
Esrom—ĕs-rŏm
Ethem—ēth'ĕm

Ether—ēth'ēr
Ezias—ē-zī'ȧs
Ezrom—ĕz'rŏm

Gad—găd
Gadiandi—găd-ĭ-ăn'dĭ
Gadianton—găd-ĭ-ăn'tŏn
Gadiomnah—găd-ĭ-ŏm'nä
Gallim—găl'lĭm
Gazelem—gā'zĕl-ĕm
Geba—gē'bȧ
Gebim—gē'bĭm
Gibeah—gib'e-ä
Gid—gĭd
Giddonah—gĭd-dō'nä
Giddianhi—gĭd-dĭ-ăn'hĭ
Gidgiddonah—gĭd-gĭd-dō'nä
Gidgiddoni—gĭd-gĭd-dō'nĭ
Gilead—gĭl'ē-ăd
Gilgah—gĭl'gä
Gilgal—gĭl'găl
Gimgimno—gĭm-gĭm'nō
Gomorrah—gō-mōr'rä

Hagoth—hā'gȯth
Hamath—hā'măth
Hearthom—hē-är'thŏm
Helam—hē'lăm
Helaman—hē'lȧ-măn
Helem—hē'lĕm
Helorum—hē-lō'rum
Hem—hĕm
Hermounts—hēr'mounts
Heshlon—hĕsh'lŏn
Himni—hĭm'nĭ
Horeb—hōr'ĕb

Immanuel—ĭm-măn'ū-ĕl
Irreantum—ir-rē-ăn'tŭm
Ishmaelites—ĭsh'mā-ĕl-ītes

Jacobites—jā'cŏb-ītes
Jacobugath—jā-cō-bū'găth

PRONOUNCING VOCABULARY

Jacom—jā'kŏm
Jared—jā'red
Jaredites—jā'rĕd-ītes
Jarom—jā'rŏm
Jashon—jā'shŏn
Jeberechiah—jĕb-ĕr-ĕ-kī'ä
Jershon—jer'shŏn
Jonas—jō'näs
Joneam—jō'nē'ăm
Jordan—jôr'dan
Josephites—jō'sĕf-ītes
Jothan—jō'thăn

Kib—kĭb
Kim—kĭm
Kimnor—kĭm'nôr
Kishkumen—kĭsh-kū'mĕn
Korihor—kō'rĭ-hôr
Kumen—kū'mĕn
Kumenonhi—kū-mĕn-ŏn'hĭ

Laban—lā'băn
Lachoneus—lā-kōn'ē-ŭs
Laish—lā'ĭsh
Lamah—lā'mä
Laman—lā'măn
Lamanites—lā'măn-ītes
Lamoni—lä-mō'nī
Lauram—läu'răm
Lehi—lē'hī
Lehi-Nephi—lē'hī-nē'fī
Lehonti—lē-hŏn'tī
Lemuel—lĕm'ū-ĕl
Lemuelites—lĕm'ū-ĕl-ītes
Liahona—lē-á-hō'nä
Limhah—lĭm'hä
Limher—lĭm'hēr
Limhi—lĭm'hī
Limnah—lim-nä

Madmenah—măd-mĕn'ä
Mahah—mā'hä

Maher-shalal-hash-baz
 —mā'her-shăl-ăl-hăsh'băz
Manasseh—măn-ăs'sĕ
Manti—măn'tī
Mathoni—mă-thō'nī
Mathonihah—mă-thō-nī'hä
Medes—mēdes
Melchizedek—mĕl-kiz'ĕ-dĕk
Melek—mē-lĕk
Michmash—mĭk'măsh
Middoni—mĭd-dō'nī
Midian—mĭ'di-ăn
Migron—mī'grŏn
Minon—mī'nŏn
Moab—mō'ăb
Mocum—mō'kŭm
Moriancumer—mō-rĭ-ăn'kū-mer
Morianton—mō-rĭ-ăn'tŏn
Moriantum—mō-rĭ-ăn'tŭm
Mormon—môr'mŏn
Moron—mō'rŏn
Moroni—mō-rō'nī
Moronihah—mō-rō-nī'hä
Mosiah—mō-sī'ä
Mulek—mū'lĕk
Muloki—mū-lō'kī

Nahom—nā'hŏm
Naphtali—naf'ta-lī
Nazareth—náz'a-rĕth
Neas—nē-ăs
Nehor—nē'hōr
Nephi—nē'fī
Nephihah—nē-fī'hä
Nephites—nē'fītes
Neum—nē'ŭm
Nimrah—nĭm'rä
Nimrod—nĭm'rŏd

Ogath—ō'găth
Omer—ō'mēr
Omner—ŏm'nēr

PRONOUNCING VOCABULARY

Omni—ŏm'nĭ
Onidah—ō-nī'dä
Onihah—ō-nī'hä
Ophir—ō'fer
Oreb—ō'rĕb
Orihah—ō-rī'há

Paanchi—pā-ăn'kĭ
Pachus—pā'kŭs
Pacumeni—pā-kū'mĕ-nĭ
Pagag—pā'găg
Pahoran—pā-hō'răn
Palestina—păl-ĕs-tī'nä
Pathros—pā'thrŏs
Pekah—pē'kä
Pharaoh—fā'rō
Philistines—fĭl-ĭs'tĭns

Rabbanah—răb-băn'ä
Rahab—rā'hăb
Ramah—rā'mä
Ramath—rā'math
Rameumptom—răm-ē-ŭmp'tŏm
Riplah—rĭp'lä
Riplakish—rĭp-lā'kĭsh
Ripliancum—rĭp-lĭ-ăn'kŭm

Salem—sā'lĕm
Samaria—să-mā'rĭ-ä
Sarah—sā'rä
Sariah—să-rī'ä
Seantum—sē-ăn'tŭm
Sebus—sē'bŭs
Seezoram—sē-ĕ-zō'-răm
Shared—shā'rĕd
Shazer—shā'zĕr
Shearjashub—shē-är-jā'shŭb
Shelem—shĕl'ĕm
Shemlon—shĕm'lŏn
Shemnon—shĕm'nŏn
Sherem—shē'rĕm

Sherrizah—shĕr-rī'zā
Sheum—she'ŭm
Shez—shĕz
Shiblom—shĭb'lŏm
Shiblon—shĭb'lŏn
Shiloah—shī'lo-ä
Shilom—shī'lŏm
Shim—shĭm
Shimnilon—shĭm-nĭ'lŏn
Shinar—shī'när
Shiz—shĭz
Shule—shūl
Shum—shŭm
Shurr—shŭr
Sidom—sīd'ŏm
Sidon—sīd'ŏn
Sinai—sī'nā-ī
Sinim—sī'nĭm
Siron—sī'rŏn

Tarshish—tär'shĭsh
Teancum—tē-ăn'kŭm
Teomner—tē-ŏm'nĕr
Tubaloth—tū'bá-lŏth

Uriah—ū-rī'ä
Uzziah—ŭz-zī'ä

Zarahemla—zā-rá-hĕm'lá
Zebulun—zĕb'ū-lŭn
Zeezrom—zē-ĕz'rŏm
Zemnarihah—zĕm-nä-rī'hä
Zenephi—zē'nĕ-fī
Zeniff—zē'nĭf
Zenoch—zē'nok
Zenos—zē'nŏs
Zerahemnah—zĕr-ä-hĕm'nä
Zeram—zē'răm
Zerim—zē'rĭm
Ziff—zĭf
Zoram—zō'răm
Zoramites—zō'răm-ītes

INDEX

Numbers refer to pages and verses. Thus, 189-34 indicates page 189, and verse 34 on that page. In general, the verse in which the beginning of the subject-matter occurs is the only one specified.

Aaron, son of Mosiah, 189-34; chosen king by people; refuses kingdom, 191-2; goes to Jerusalem, 249-1; ministry of, among Lamanites, 249-4; preaches atonement, 250-7; goes to Ani-Anti, 250-11; goes to Middoni, 250-12; imprisoned in Middoni, 247-2, 250-13; released, 250-14; preaches in synagogues, 250-16; goes to land of Nephi, 251-1; teaches the king, 251-2; rebukes Ammon, 261-10; meets Alma, 265-16. See also **Mosiah, sons of.**
Aaron, Jaredite king, son of Heth, 479-16, 498-31.
Aaron, king of Lamanites, defeated by army of Mormon, 462-9; brutality of army of, 519-17.
Aaron, city of, 214-13, 322-14.
Abel, 374-27.
Abhorrence, sin looked upon with, by the righteous, 229-12, 266-28, 70-49.
Abinadi, prophesies to people of king Noah, 157-20, 158-1; brought before king Noah, 159-16, 166-6; imprisoned, 159-17; confounds questioners, 159-19; quotes Isaiah, 159-21, 162-1; quotes from ten commandments, 160-35, 161-13; face of, shines, 160-5; preaches atonement, 161-18; foretells crucifixion, 163-7; proclaims divine justice, 165-1; preaches redemption and resurrection, 165-6; condemned by Noah, 160-1, 166-1; prophesies death of many by fire, 167-15; first martyr by fire, 167-13, 260-11; means of blessing to Alma, 185-15; words of, fulfilled, 173-21, 260-9, 461-19.
Abinadom, Nephite historian, son of Chemish, 130-10.
Abish, a Lamanitish woman, conversion of, 245-16; calls people to house of king, 245-17; grieved because of tumult, 246-28; raises the queen, 246-29.
Ablom, Omer pitches tent at, 493-3.
Abominable church, the, 26-9.
Abominable combinations, secret and, 67-6, 94-22, 289-21, 409-6, 500-22.
Abominations, the mother of, 26-9; of church of the devil, 26-12; of Jews, 89-2; in last days, 95-1; to be discovered through a divinely prepared stone, 290-23; of Lamanites and Nephites not fully recorded, 364-14; of Lamanites and Nephites in days of Mormon, 518-9.

Abraham, covenant with, 29-18, 36-40, 102-14; kindreds of earth blessed through, 29-18, 47-9, 440-25; God of, to be crucified, 41-10; and Isaac, similitude of God and Christ, 113-5; paid tithes, 229-15; saw of Christ's coming, 379-17.
Abridgment, of Lehi's record, by Nephi, 2-17; of plates of Nephi, by Mormon, 132-3, 410-15; of Jaredite record, by Moroni, 478-5, 484-17, 509-33.
Abyss, the, of spiritual darkness, 188-29, 261-3.
Account, made by Nephi, 2-17; by Zeniff, 152; of Alma and his people, 178; of sons of Mosiah, 237; of Aaron and brethren, 249; by Helaman, 307.
Accountable, baptism for those only who are, 516-10.
Accursed, treasure may be, 389-18; all who contend against the Lord may be, 485-8.
Act, to, or to be acted upon, 53-13, 55-26; mankind free to, 227-31, 395-30.
Adam, fell that man might be, 54-25; his children redeemed, 68-21, 142-7; fell by partaking of forbidden fruit, 226-22; restrained from partaking of tree of life, 298-3; account of, on Jaredite plates, 478-4.
Adam and Eve, plates of brass contain account of, 10-11; their fall, 54-19.
Admonition, of the Lord, 58-13, 125-1.
Adultery, a most abominable sin, 293-5; forbidden, 161-22, 236-18, 255-3, 425-27.
Adversary, the, 29-24, 224-5.
Advocate, Christ, the, 514-28.
Affixed, punishment and blessing are, 53-10, 299-16.
Afflictions, diverse effects of, 357-41; consecrated for blessing, 52-2.
Agony, of soul, 376-6.
Agosh, battleground of Lib and Coriantumr, 506-15.
Aha, son of Zoram, 235-5.
Ahah, Jaredite king, son of Seth, 479-10, 499-10.
Akish, son of Kimnor, 491-10; daughter of Jared dances before, 492-11; oaths administered by, 492-13; overthrows kingdom of Omer, 493-1; marries daughter of Jared, 493-4; causes death of Jared and obtains kingdom, 493-5; wars with sons, 494-12.

535

INDEX

Akish, wilderness of, battleground of Gilead and Coriantumr, 505-3.
Alive, in Christ, 92-25, 516-12, 517-19, 22.
Allowance, Lord cannot look upon sin with, 308-16.
All things, known to the Lord, 15-6, 54-24, 68-20; God's foreknowledge of, 228-7; known to the Spirit, 212-13; God, Christ created, 54-14, 140-8, 393-12, 418-15; need of opposition in, 53-11; a compound in one, 53-11; to be revealed, 96-10, 11; to be restored, 297-2, 4; denote there is a God, 272-44; are written by the Father, 451-26; to become new, 503-9.
All things in common, among disciples of Christ, 449-19, 456-3.
Alma, and his people, account of, 178.
Alma, Book of, 195; words of, 205.
Alma, the first, 166-2; life sought by king Noah, 166-3; teaches words of Abinadi, 167-1; resorts to the place of Mormon, 168-5; teaches believers, 168-7; baptizes Helam, 168-13; baptizes many, 169-16; ordains priests, 169-18, 179-17; admonishes priests not to depend on people for support, 169-26; discovered by servants of king Noah, 170-32; departs into wilderness, 170-34; declines to be king, 178-7; high priest, founder of church, 179-16; and people surrender to Lamanites, 179-29; and people oppressed by Amulon, 181-8; leads people out of bondage into wilderness, 181-17; and people arrive at Zarahemla, 182-25; record of, read by king Mosiah, 182-6; preaches to Nephites, 183-14; baptizes Limhi and people, 183-18; permitted to establish churches, 183-19; dissenters brought before, 184-7; given authority over church by Mosiah, 184-8; receives direction from the Lord, 185-29; regulates affairs of church, 186-37; church complains to, 186-1; prays for son, 187-14; ordained son high priest, 194-42; dies, 194-45.
Alma, son of Alma, seeks to destroy church, 187-8; with sons of Mosiah sees angel, 187-11; becomes helpless and dumb, 188-19; his father rejoices over him, 188-20; relates terrifying experience, 188-29; teaches people, 189-32; receives from king Mosiah the plates, records, and interpreters, 191-20; is appointed the first chief judge, 194-42; ordained high priest by his father, 194-42; sentences Nehor, 196-14; leads army of Nephites, 199-16; slays Amlici, 200-31; contends with king of Lamanites, 200-32; sends army to repulse Lamanites, 202-23; baptizes in Sidon, 203-4; ordains elders, priests, and teachers, 203-7, 210-1; resigns judgment-seat to Nephihah, 204-17; retains office of high priest, 204-18; preaches in land of Zarahemla, 205-1; preaches in valley of Gideon, 210-7; addresses people of Gideon, 211-1; preaches the Redeemer's coming, 211-7; having established church in Gideon, he returns to Zarahemla, 213-1; teaches and baptizes at Melek, 214-4; preaches at Ammonihah, 214-8; visited by an angel, 214-14; returns to Ammonihah as commanded, 214-16; meets Amulek, 215-19; see **Alma and Amulek;** heals and baptizes Zeezrom, 234-10; establishes church at Sidom, 234-13; on journey from Gideon to Manti, meets sons of Mosiah, 237-1, 265-16; conducts sons of Mosiah to Zarahemla, 265-20; relates his conversion to people of Ammon, 265-25; wishes he were angel, 267-1; says Lord raises up men in all nations to teach truth, 268-8; tries Korihor, 271-30; his work in the ministry was not for pay, 271-33; gives Korihor a sign—that of dumbness, 272-49; takes missionary party to Zoramites, 274-6; astonished at Zoramite prayers, 275-19; lays hands on companions, 276-36; and brethren separate, 276-37; preaches on hill Onidah, 277-4; preaches to poor, 277-12; and brethren go to Jershon, 284-1; gives commandments to Helaman, 286-1; recounts conversion, 286-6, 292-7; describes his awful state prior to repentance, 286-12; had experienced exquisite pain and joy, 287-21; recounts his labors, 287-24; commits the sacred plates to Helaman, 288-1; gives commandments to Shiblon, 292-1; counsels Shiblon to bridle passions, 293-12; advises humility and penitence, 293-14; gives commandments to Corianton, 293-1; chides Corianton, 293-2; denounces unchastity, 293-5; expounds the resurrection, 294-1; explains state between death and resurrection, 295-11; explains doctrine of restoration, 296-22, 297-1; shows necessity of punishment, 298-1; explains the fall of Adam, 298-3; discourses on the atonement, 299-15; explains relation of justice and mercy, 300-24; sends Corianton forth to preach, 300-31; receives word of Lord directing Moroni, 302-24; instructs Helaman, 307-2; prophesies concerning wickedness and consequent extinction of people of Nephi, 308-10; blesses sons, and the earth for the sake of the righteous, 308-16; blesses the church, 308-17; departs toward Melek, not known of afterward, 308-18; thought to have been taken up by the Spirit, 309-19; his teachings cited by Aminadab, 371-41.
Alma, teachings of, on prayer, the prophet Zenos cited, 280-3; on resurrection, 294-1; on state of man between death and resurrection, 295-11; on paradise, 295-12; on state of wicked,

INDEX 537

296-14; on restoration, 296-22, 297-1; on mortality as a probationary state, 298-4; on redemption, 299-13; on claims of justice, 299-14; on atonement, 299-15; on claims of mercy, 300-23; on free agency, 300-27.

Alma and Amulek, in Ammonihah, 216-1; speak to Zeezrom and people, 224-1; questioned by Antionah, 226-20; teach repentance, 227-33; bound with cords by people of Ammonihah, 230-4; see converts burned, 231-10; smitten by chief judge, 231-14, 232-24; imprisoned and bound, 232-17; smitten by many, 232-25; break cords, 232-26; delivered when prison fell, 233-28; go from Ammonihah to Sidom, 233-1; return to Zarahemla, 234-18; preach repentance, 236-13.

Alma, valley of, 182-20.

Almighty, God the, 86-ch. 23:6, 157-23, 384-11.

Alpha and Omega, Christ called, 418-18.

Altar, built by Lehi, 3-7; in sanctuaries at Sidom, 234-17; penitent Lamanites brought before, 237-4.

Amaleki, son of Abinadom, 130-12; gives plates to king Benjamin, 131-25; ends his record, 132-30.

Amaleki, one of the brethren of Ammon, 147-6.

Amalekites, helped to build city of Jerusalem, 249-2; more hardened and hateful than Lamanites, 249-3; preached to by Aaron, 249-4; after the order of Nehors, 249-4; not converted, 256-14; rebel, 256-2; evil character of, 264-12; chosen for chief captains because of their murderous disposition, 301-6; dissenters from the Nephites, 301-13.

Amalickiah, leader of revolt against Helaman, 309-3; man of cunning, 310-10; flees from Moroni, 311-29; army of, captured, 312-33; unyielding people of, put to death, 312-35; stirs up Lamanites, 313-1; head of Lamanite army, 313-3; seeks king's overthrow, 313-4; sends message to Lehonti, 313-10; his army surrounded by that of Lehonti, 314-14; causes Lehonti's death, 314-18; appointed commander of army, 314-19; marches to city of Nephi, 314-20; causes king's death, 315-24; takes city of Nephi, 315-31; called before queen, 315-33; made king, 315-35; foments hatred of Lamanites toward Nephites, 316-1; makes Zoramites captains, 316-5; orders advance on land of Zarahemla, 316-6; loses many soldiers, 320-25; enraged over defeat of army he curses Moroni, 320-27; heads army in person, 325-12; takes city of Moroni, 326-23; takes many cities, 326-26; meets Teancum, 326-29; slain by Teancum, 327-34; brother of, made king, 327-3.

Amalickiahites, see **Amalickiah.**

Amaron, son of Omni, receives plates from his father, 129-3; delivers plates to Chemish, 130-8.

Amgid, Jaredite king, overcome by Com, 498-32.

Aminadab, Nephite dissenter, teaches Lamanites, 371-39.

Aminadi, ancestor of Amulek, interpreted handwriting in temple, 219-2.

Amlici, seeks to be king, 198-1; rejected by votes, 198-7; made king of rebellious faction, 198-9; slain by Alma in battle, 200-31.

Amlicites, revolting Nephite faction, 198-11; defeated, 200-35; marked in foreheads, 201-13.

Ammah, a Nephite missionary to the Lamanites, imprisoned at Middoni, 247-2; released from prison, 249-28; preaches at Ani-Anti, 250-11; goes to Middoni, 250-12.

Ammaron, keeps the records, 459-47; hides records, 459-48; tells Mormon of records, 460-2; his instructions followed by Mormon, 467-23.

Ammon, descendant of Zarahemla, 147-3; with his brethren meets king Limhi, who binds and imprisons them, 147-7; is arraigned before the king and is honored, 147-8; addresses people of Limhi, 150-2; reads record of Limhi, 150-6; learns of discovery of records and relics of a more ancient people, 150-7; informs king Limhi of a seer who could translate, 151-13; suspected of being a priest of Noah, 175-23; leads Limhi and his people to freedom, 177-11.

Ammon, son of Mosiah, 189-34; chief of missionaries, 238-18; enters land of Ishmael, bound by Lamanites, 238-20; becomes servant of king Lamoni, 239-25; contends with enemies in protection of the king's flocks, 240-34; could not be slain, 240-3; thought to be the Great Spirit, 241-4; prepares chariots, 241-9; discerns the king's thoughts, 242-18; teaches king Lamoni, 242-24; gives history of Laman and Lemuel, 243-38; overcome by Spirit, 244-14; threatened by a Lamanite, 245-22; revives and ministers to the people, 246-33; organizes church, 246-35; invited to visit father of king Lamoni, 247-1; forbidden by the Lord to go to the land of Nephi, 247-2; starts for Middoni to deliver his brethren from prison, 247-3; meets father of king Lamoni, 247-8; overcomes king of Lamanites, 248-24; secures release of his brethren, 249-28; returns to land of Ishmael, 251-18; teaches people of king Lamoni, 251-23; and brethren hold council with king Lamoni and brother, 256-5; reviews their success, 260-1; rebuked by Aaron, 261-10; praises God, 261-12, 263-35; proposes migration of

35

538 INDEX

converts to land of Zarahemla, 264-5; inquires of Lord, 264-11; enters land of Zarahemla with his brethren, 265-15; meets Alma, 265-16; overcome with joy, 265-17; returns with Alma, 265-25; high priest over the people, 270-20; banishes Korihor, 270-21. See also **Mosiah, sons of.**
Ammon, people of, called Anti-Nephi-Lehies, 256-17; called Ammonites, 341-57, 341-6; friendly with Nephites, 256-18; king of, dies, 256-4; refuse to fight, bury weapons, 257-12, 258-16; Lamanites attack, 258-20; passively submit, even to death, 258-21, 264-3; enemies of, repent, 258-24; joined by Lamanites, 259-26, 355-27; slain by Amalekites, 259-28, 264-2; observe law of Moses, 260-15, 269-3; look forward to Christ, 260-16; offer to become slaves to Nephites, 264-8; proclamation concerning, 265-21; given land of Jershon, 265-22; protected by Nephites, 265-23; numbered with church, 266-27; receive converts from Zoramites, 284-6; remove to Melek, 285-13; hated by Lamanites, 301-11; succored by Nephites, 301-12; support army, 301-13, 339-27; about to break their covenant, 332-13; sons of, prepare for battle, 332-16; sons of, choose Helaman their leader, 332-19; sons of, defeat Lamanites, 341-54; sons of, miraculously preserved from death, 341-56; go to land northward, 364-12.
Ammonites, see **Ammon, people of.**
Ammonihah, city of, 214-6; Alma preaches at, 214-8, 216-1; Alma cast out of, 214-13; Alma returns to, 215-18; Amulek predicts destruction of people of, 220-23; people of, burn holy scriptures, 231-8; converts in, martyred, 231-8; leaders of, bind Alma and Amulek, 232-22; prison at, falls, 233-27; people of, flee from prophets, 233-29; Alma and Amulek banished from, 233-1; people of, impenitent, 234-15; people of, destroyed, 235-9, 259-2; called Desolation of Nehors, 236-11; Lamanites approach, 318-1; rebuilt by Nephites, 318-2; fortified, 318-4.
Ammonihahites, 235-9.
Ammonihah, land of, see **Ammonihah, city of.**
Ammoron, king of Lamanites, 327-3; reports to Lamanitish queen, 328-12; attacks Nephites by west sea, 328-12; proposes exchange of prisoners, 333-1; epistle of Moroni to, 333-4; his reply, 334-15; abandons attack on city of Judea, 338-18; in land of Moroni, 356-33; slain by Teancum, 356-36.
Amnigaddah, Jaredite king, son of Aaron, 479-15; dwells in captivity, 498-31.
Amnihu, hill of, 199-15.
Amnor, Nephite spy, 199-22.
Amnor, a silver coin, 222-6, 11.

Amoron, reports to Mormon, 518-7.
Amos, son of Nephi, keeps records, 457-19; dies, 457-21.
Amos, son of Amos, keeps the records, 457-21; dies, 459-47.
Amulek, visited by angel, 215-20, 219-7; receives Alma, 215-21; blessed by Alma, 215-26; preaches to people of Ammonihah, 219-1; son of Giddonah, 219-2; reputation of, 219-4; prophesies destruction of people of Ammonihah, 220-23; questioned by Zeezrom, 222-21; preaches Christ, 223-39; rejected by relatives and friends, 234-16; goes on mission to Zoramites, 274-6; preaches to the poor, 281-1; explains supreme sacrifice of Christ, 282-10; teaches prayer, 282-17; goes to Jershon, 284-1; quoted on redemption, 369-10. See also **Alma and Amulek.**
Amulon, land of, 180-31; teachers appointed in, 180-1.
Amulon, leader of priests of Noah, 180-32; sends wives of himself and brethren to plead with Lamanites, 180-33; and brethren join Lamanites, 180-35; made king over people in Helam, 180-39; made teacher of Lamanites, 180-1; oppresses Alma's people, 181-8; orders people to cease praying, 181-11; children of people of, change name to Nephites, 183-12; people of, help to build city of Jerusalem, 249-2; descendants of, hunted down and slain, 259-8, 260-12.
Amulonites, more wicked than Lamanites, 249-3; not converted, 256-14, 259-29; stir up Lamanites, 256-1; rebel against Ammonites, 256-2; slain by Nephites, 259-4; usurp leadership and persecute Lamanites, 259-5; slain by Lamanites, 260-8; fulfil Abinadi's prophecy, 260-9.
Anchor (figurative), 469-18, 500-4.
Ancient covenant people, 101-4, 5.
Ancients, evil oaths of the, 493-5, 498-33.
Angel, speaks to Laman and Lemuel, 6-29, 7-3, 12-10, 37-45; appears to Nephi, son of Lehi, 18-14; of God, fallen, 54-17, 67-8; appears to Jacob, 71-3, 123-5; speaks to king Benjamin, 140-2, 142-1; appears to Alma and sons of Mosiah, 187-11, 286-8; appears to Alma, 214-14; appears to Amulek, 219-7; appears to Samuel the Lamanite, 390-7.
Angels, in vision of Lehi, 2-8; minister to Nephi, 59-24; to the devil, 67-9, 113-11; speak by the power of Holy Ghost, 105-3; declare word to many, 230-24; appear to Lamanites, 246-34; doctrine of, challenged, 249-5; visit people of Ammon, 257-14; declare repentance, 369-11; faces of Nephi and Lehi like, 371-36; minister to people, 372-48; appear to wise men, 398-14; visit Nephi, son of Helaman, 414-15, 18; of devil rejoice, 417-2; minister to little

INDEX 539

children in presence of Christ, 433-24; minister to the twelve disciples, 437-14; the three disciples like, 454-30; office of, 514-29.
Anger, of Laman and Lemuel, 58-13, 60-1; of the Lord, 93-6; stirred up by devil, 99-20; Jaredite armies drunken with, 509-22; of Nephites, 518-5.
Angola, city of, fortified, 461-4; Nephites driven from, 461-4.
Anguish, of soul, 37-47, 93-7, 190-4, 214-14, 292-8, 470-16.
Ani-Anti, Aaron goes to, 250-11; Muloki and his brethren preach at, 250-11.
Animals, in land of promise, 40-25; raised by Nephites, 60-11; ferocious, to become gentle, 103-12; carried by Jaredites, 487-ch. 6:4; domesticated by Jaredites, 494-18.
Anti-Christ, Sherem, 123-1; Nehor, 195-2; Korihor in Zarahemla, 269-6; in Jershon, 270-19; in Gideon, 270-21.
Anti-Nephi-Lehi, made king, 256-3; holds council with Ammon and Lamoni, 256-5; forbids war, 257-6.
Anti-Nephi-Lehies, see **Ammon, people of.**
Antiomno, king of Middoni, 247-4.
Antion, a gold coin, 222-19.
Antionah, a ruler in Ammonihah, 226-20.
Antionum, land of, settled by Zoramites, 274-3; Lamanites enter, 301-5; Lamanites retire from, 302-22.
Antionum, a Nephite chieftain, slain, 470-14.
Antiparah, city of, taken by Lamanites, 338-14; army of, decoyed by Helaman, 339-31; recovered by Nephites, 341-4.
Antipas, a mount, Lamanites assemble on, 313-7.
Antipus, Helaman goes to assist, 338-9; pursues Lamanites, 339-33; overtakes Lamanites, 340-49; slain, 340-51; Helaman rescues army of, 341-52.
Antum, land of, plates hidden in, by Ammaron, 460-3.
Apostle, seen by Nephi, 27-20; John, to write of end of world, 27-22, 27.
Apostles, seen in vision of Lehi, 2-10; seen in vision of Nephi, 19-29; Israel and nations fight, 20-35; to judge tribes of Israel, 21-9; book goes forth from, 23-24; miracles wrought by, 476-18.
Apparel, costly, worn by Nehor, 195-6; costly, worn by Nephites, 203-6; coarseness of, cause of persecution, 276-2.
Archeantus, a Nephite officer, slain by sword, 518-2.
Arm of the Lord, power of, 126-13, 111-25; made bare, 159-24, 165-31, 441-35; extended in mercy, 122-5, 418-14. See **Arms,** of God's love.
Arm, of flesh not to be trusted, 59-34.
Arms, of God's love, 51-15; of mercy extended, 207-33.
Arms, see **Weapons.**

Armor, of righteousness, 51-23; of war, 201-5, 302-19.
Ascension, of Christ, predicted, 167-2, 296-20; affirmed by Christ, 429-1; after visitation to the Nephites, witnessed, 436-39, 449-15.
Asp, to become harmless, 103-14.
Ass, in land of promise, 40-25.
Atonement, the, infinite, 67-7, 91-16; satisfies justice, 69-26; law of Moses worthless without, 141-15; people of king Benjamin convinced of, 142-2; prepared from beginning, 142-6; without it there is no salvation, 142-8; taught by Aaron, 250-9; by Alma, 281-22; by Amulek, 282-9; by Moroni, 515-41; no salvation without, 282-9; brings mercy, and the resurrection, 300-23; for children without baptism, 517-20.
Authority from God, baptism denied through lack of, 176-33; sons of Mosiah taught with, 237-3.
Ax, at root of tree, 209-52.

Babes, utter marvelous things, 449-16.
Babblings, of non-church members, 197-32.
Babylon, Jewish captives taken to, 16-3, 130-15; to be destroyed, 90-15.
Ball of Brass, see **Liahona.**
Baptism, a prophet to administer, at Bethabara as predicted by Lehi, 16-9; of Lamb of God, foreseen, 16-10, 19-27; commanded, 68-23; all men need to accept, 104-5; of Christ, why necessary, 104-7; Holy Ghost follows, 104-12; of fire and Holy Ghost, 104-13, 423-35, 423-1, 437-13, 449-17; gate by which to enter, 105-17, 511-4; the witness of a covenant with the Lord, 168-10; administered by Alma, 168-13, 214-5; of Zeezrom, 234-12; at Sidom, 234-14; of 8,000 Lamanites, 370-19; preached by sons of Helaman, 370-17; twelve disciples authorized to perform, 422-22; 423-1; form of ordinance specified, 422-25; of Nephi, son of Helaman, 437-11; by Nephi, 437-12; necessary to salvation, 423-33, 486-18; by twelve disciples, 449-17; humility prerequisite to, 511-6. 6:2; of little children, wrong, 516-9; to be administered to those who are accountable, 516-10.
Bar, of God, 107-11, 15, 122-9, 123-13, 166-10, 206-22, 224-44, 225-12, 476-13, 522-34.
Barges, built by Jared, 480-6; description of, 481-16; number of, 482-1; people sail in, 487-ch. 6:4; driven before wind, 487-ch. 6:5.
Battle, among Nephites foreseen by Nephi, 20-2, 21-15; with the Lamanites, fought by Mormon, 518-2; final, of Nephites, 470-8; final, of Jaredites, 508-15.
Beasts, wild, slain for food by Nephi, 33-31; in land of promise, 40-25;

540 INDEX

created by God, 54-15; hunted by Enos, 125-3; Lamanites drink blood of, 128-6; at Mormon, 168-4; in Hermounts, 200-37; mangle human carcasses, 235-10.
Beatitudes, given to Nephites by Christ, 424-3.
Bees, deseret, carried by Jaredites, 480-3.
Beggar, not to be allowed to ask in vain, 143-16.
Belief, individual, not punishable by law, 196-17, 269-7.
Believers in Christ, called Christians, 310-14; true, again called Nephites, 458-36.
Bellows, of skins, made by Nephi, 34-11.
Benjamin, Nephite prophet-king, succeeds Mosiah the first, 131-23; given plates by Amaleki, 131-25; has other plates, 133-10; uses sword of Laban against Lamanites, 133-13; defeats Lamanites, 133-14; enjoys continued peace, 134-1; sons of, 134-2; teaches sons from records, 134-3; confers kingdom on Mosiah, 135-10, 138-30; confers sacred things on Mosiah, 135-16; addresses people from tower, 136-8; had labored with his own hands, 137-14; urges service to fellow man, 137-17; people of, covenant with the Lord, 145-5; takes names of covenant people, 146-1; consecrates Mosiah, appoints priests, 146-3; dies, 147-ch. 6:5; good example of, cited, 192-13; teachings of cited, 369-9.
Bethabara, prophet to baptize at, 16-9.
Bible, Gentiles shall say: A Bible! 101-3; to proceed from Jews, 101-4; does not contain all the words of God, 101-10.
Birth of Christ, foreshadowed in vision of Nephi, 18-15; signs of, predicted by Nephi, 92-3; by Samuel, the Lamanite, 393-3; sign given, 400-15.
Blasphemy, Sherem wickedly says that the gospel is, 123-7; by Korihor before Alma, 271-30.
Blind, that will not see, 69-32; shall see out of obscurity, 97-29; to receive their sight, 140-5, 449-15, 456-5.
Block, stumbling (figurative), 59-33, 94-20.
Blood, atoning, of Christ, 21-10, 140-11, 250-9; sacramental cup in remembrance of, 434-11, 511-ch. 5:2; people of the abominable church to be drunken with their own, 47-13, oppressors to be drunken with their own, 64-18; of the saints shall cry from the ground, 99-10.
Bloodshed, predicted, 50-12, 63-15, 71-6; defend families even unto, 304-47.
Boasting, in strength of man, 157-19, 388-5, 411-10, 464-9, 466-8; in righteousness, 261-12, 263-36.
Boaz, city of, Nephites flee to, 467-20; driven from, 467-21.
Body, Christ shall show his, 67-5; mortal, raised in immortality, 206-15; spirit shall be reunited with, 223-43; every part of, to be restored, 223-43, 297-2; of Christ's spirit, 484-16.
Bondage, Israel led out of, 35-24, 41-10; of Limhi to the Lamanites, 148-15; predicted by Abinadi, 158-2; Limhi seeks freedom from, 176-36; Alma and people delivered from, 181-17.
Bones, of Jaredites scattered in land northward, 131-22; found by Limhi's explorers, 150-8.
Book, in vision of Lehi, 2-11; contains record of Jews, 23-23; of great worth to Gentiles, 23-23; shorn of many plain and precious parts by the abominable church, 23-26; a blessing to Joseph's seed, 57-23; to be sealed up unto Lord, 94-17, 96-10, 97-22; words of, to be brought forth, 96-6; words of, to be read on housetops, 96-11; three witnesses of, 96-12; other witnesses of, 96-13; words of, delivered to learned, 96-15; unlearned to read words of, 97-20; to be carried among Gentiles, 102-5; of life contains names of righteous, 209-58; of Mormon to try faith, 448-9.
Books, the five of Moses, on plates of brass, 10-11; to come forth to Israel, 25-39; sealed, to come forth, 27-26; world to be judged out of, 101-11; many, kept by Nephites, 364-15.
Born of God, 188-25, 28, 206-14, 252-15, 286-5, 287-23, 292-6.
Borrowing, 144-28, 426-42.
Boundary, disputes lead to war, 322-25.
Bountiful, city of, see **Bountiful, land of.**
Bountiful, land of (in Arabia), 34-5, 6, 7.
Bountiful, land of (in the promised land), 254-29; inhabited by Nephites, 254-33; Nephites driven to borders of, 326-28; Teancum goes to, 326-29, 328-15; fortified, 328-9, 331-4; occupied by Teancum and army, 329-17; Moroni arrives at, 329-18; Lehi meets Lamanites near, 330-27; prisoners marched to, 330-39; prisoners labor in, 331-3; Hagoth builds ships in, 358-5; Coriantumr marches toward, 361-23; Lamanites get lands near, 366-5; Christ appears in, 421-1.
Bow, Nephi breaks his, 32-18. See also **Weapons.**
Branch, seed of Lehi to become a righteous, 71-53.
Brass, ball of, see **Liahona.**
Brass, plates of, in possession of Laban, 5-3, 6-24; secured by Nephi, 9-38; Lehi's prophecy concerning, 10-18, 19; contents of, 10-11; people of Zarahemla rejoice over, 130-14; description of, by Alma, 288-3.
Bread, sacramental, called for by Jesus, 434-1; broken and blessed, 434-3, 439-3; miraculously provided for adminis-

INDEX

tration to Nephites, 439-6; blessing on, 511-ch. 4:3.
Breastplates, brought by Limhi's explorers, 151-10; used by Nephites, 302-19, 303-38, 306-9; by Lamanites, 360-14; by Jaredites, 508-15.
Brimstone, fire and, the torment of the wicked, 68-16, 69-26, 100-23, 113-11, 123-10, 226-17.
Brother of Jared, record of, as made by Ether, found by Limhi's explorers, 150-9, 176-27; Ether's record of, translated by Mosiah, 190-11; record of people of, by Ether, 478-2; Jaredite record abridged by Moroni, 478-5; highly favored of the Lord, 479-34; language of, and of the people, not confounded, 479-35; promised a choice land, 480-42, 481-7; posterity to be great nation, 480-43; takes deseret, or honey bee, 480-3; talks with Lord, 480-4; commanded to go into wilderness, 480-5; dwelt at Moriancumer, 481-13; chastened and repents, 481-14; commanded to build barges, 481-16; melts stones on mount Shelem, 482-1; sees finger of the Lord, 483-6; sees Christ, 483-13; told that Christ will appear in the flesh, 484-16; told to write and seal records, 484-22; given two stones, as interpreters, 484-23; shown inhabitants of earth, 484-25; commanded to seal up writing and stones, 485-27; writings of, and translation, sealed up by Moroni, 485-5; puts stones, which the Lord had touched, into vessels for lights, 487-ch. 6:2; sails for promised land, with his people, 487-4; driven by wind, 487-5; reaches promised land, 488-12; tills the earth, 488-13; family of, 488-20; warns against monarchical rule, 489-23; sons of, refuse kingdom, 489-26; death of, 489-29; causes the mountain, Zerin, to be removed, 502-30.
Brutality, of Lamanites and degenerate Nephites, 518-10, 519-17, 19.
Building, spacious, in vision of Lehi, 14-26; in vision of Nephi, 20-35; interpreted, 21-18.
Burdens, of Nephites in bondage made light, 181-14.
Burnt offerings, by Lehi and family, 10-9, 13-22; by people of king Benjamin, 136-3; done away after Christ, 418-19.

Cain, son of Adam, 374-27; a murderer from the beginning, 492-15.
Calling, of priests and high priests, 228-3, 228-8; a holy, 228-4, 268-13.
Calno, 83-9.
Camenihah, a Nephite chieftain, killed, 470-14.
Camp, of Amlicites watched, 199-22.
Capital city, Zarahemla, of the land, 361-27.

Captain, Gideon, king Limhi's, 173-17; Zoram, of Nephites, 235-5; Moroni, of Nephites, 302-16, 352-36; Zerahemnah, of Lamanites, 304-44; Lehi, of Nephites, 319-16; Gid, over Lamanite prisoners, 343-29.
Captains, appointed by Nephites, 199-13; Amalekites and Zoramites appointed as, by Zerahemnah, 301-6; from Zoramites and Amalekites, to lead the Lamanites, 304-44; from Zoramites, because of knowledge of Nephite cities, 316-5; of Lamanites astonished at Nephite fortifications, 318-5; appointed by Lachoneus, 405-17.
Captivation, of devil, 55-29, 218-28.
Captivity, of Jews, predicted, 2-13, 16-3; of Jews, realized, 63-8, 130-15; of Nephites, 235-3, 350-17, 387-33; of the fathers, 187-16, 205-6, 268-11, 286-2, 350-20; brother of Jared warns against kings as cause of, 489-23; of Kib, 489-7; of Shule, 490-17; of Omer, 491-4; of Kim, 497-14; of Levi, 497-15; of Hearthom, 498-30; of Heth, Aaron, Amnigaddah, and Coriantum, 498-31; of Seth, 499-9; of Moron, 500-18; of Coriantor, 500-19.
Carbuncles, gates of, 445-12.
Carcass, trodden under feet, 88-19.
Carcasses, mangled by dogs, 235-10; devoured by people, 496-34.
Carchemish, 83-9.
Carnage, spread by Gadianton robbers, 402-11; spread in Mormon's day, 462-8, 466-11, 468-8; in Ether's day, 506-21.
Carnal, a sinful state, 142-2, 165-3, 5, 166-12, 184-4, 188-25, 252-13, 297-11, 298-13.
Cattle, raised by Nephites, 127-21; gathered for safety, 405-22, 406-4; returned with, to their own lands, 410-1; among the Jaredites, 494-18.
Cavity, of a rock, Nephi and brothers hide in, 6-27; Ether hides in, 504-13, 18, 505-22.
Cement, Nephites expert in use of, 364-7, 9, 11.
Cezoram, becomes chief judge, 368-1; murdered, 373-15; son of, murdered, 373-15.
Chains, of sin, 50-13, 70-45; of hell, 205-7, 225-11, 230-30, 261-14.
Chance, equal, for every man, 194-38.
Chances, for learning unequal, 411-12.
Change, brought about by repentance, 145-2, 206-12, 13, 14, 396-7; wrought on bodies of the three Nephite disciples, 454-37.
Changes, in laws desired by king-men, 324-2.
Characters, written, reformed Egyptian, 478-32.
Chariots, of king Lamoni, 241-9, 247-6; of the Nephites, 405-22; of the Gentiles, to be destroyed, 443-14.

Charity, all men should have, 95-30; Nephi has, for his people, and for Jew and Gentile, 107-7, 8, 9; faith, hope, and, 213-24, 230-29, 502-28; men cannot inherit kingdom without, 502-34; Mormon on faith, hope, and, 512-1.
Chastened, by the Lord, Lehi, 32-25; Laman, Lemuel, and others, 33-39; people of Nephi, 395-3; brother of Jared, 481-14; for wise purposes, 179-21, 388-3.
Chastisement, of our peace, 162-5.
Chastity, God delights in, 111-28; precious above all things, 518-9.
Chemish, receives plates from Amaron, 130-8; writes in book of Omni, 130-9.
Cherubim, and a flaming sword, 226-21, 298-2.
Chickens, as a hen gathers her, 419-4, 5, 6.
Chiefs, and leaders, Lamanite custom concerning, 314-17; over tribes, 413-3, 414-14.
Chief judges, see **Judges.**
Child, of virgin in vision of Nephi, 19-20; little, shall lead them, 85-6; of the devil, 208-39; of hell, 222-23, 333-11; little, type of humility, 423-37; Mormon a sober, 460-2; the Holy, 516-3.
Children, born in wilderness, to Lehi's people, 35-20; to Lehi, 39-7; Lehi's posterity, many to be restored, 71-2; of men to have word of God, 98-2, 100-30; care of, 143-14; of Christ, 145-7; little, have eternal life, 164-25; confound the wise, 278-23; brought to Jesus, 433-11; blessed by Jesus, 433-21; ministered to by angels, 433-24; speak marvelous things, 449-14; and women, sacrificed to idols, 466-14, 467-21; baptism of, a mockery before God, 516-9; saved, 516-12; little, alive in Christ, 517-22.
Choice, the promised land, 4-20, 24-30, 50-5, 72-19, 481-7, 10, 12, 15, 503-2; seer, a, 56-6; plates, 132-6; people, 51-19.
Christ, names of, 71-3, 91-19, 140-8, 421-10; **coming of,** predicted, 124-11, 379-19, 440-24; by Lehi, 3-19, 17-17, 380-22; by Nephi, son of Lehi, 18-6; by Alma, 167-2; by Ammon, 243-39; by Aaron, 250-7, 9; by Samuel the Lamanite, 393-2; by Nephi, son of Helaman, 414-16; by Moses, 440-23; time of coming predicted, 16-4, 393-2, 400-13; time reckoned from coming of, 402-8; not manifest personally unto Gentiles, 430-23; church to be called in name of, 450-8. **Accepted:** by king Benjamin's people, 142-2; by Lamoni, 244-13; by Lamoni's queen, 246-29; by Anti-Nephi-Lehi, 257-10; by 8,000 Lamanites, 370-19. **Types of:** Law of Moses, 73-4; the brazen serpent, 281-19, 379-14. **Titles of:** Messiah, 17-17; Savior, 25-40, 47-12, 104-13, 141-20; Redeemer, 28-14, 42-18, 47-12, 52-3, 63-11, 73-2, 127-27, 211-7, 516-8; Son of God, 91-16, 163-2, 209-50, 281-2, 282-14; Son of Righteousness, 93-9, 447-2, 495-22; Only Begotten, 113-5, 227-33, 228-9; Holy One of Israel, 42-14, 44-17, 47-5, 50-10, 92-29; Mighty One, 46-26, 47-12, 64-18; Father and Son, 163-2, 476-12, 484-14; good shepherd, 207-38, 377-18; king of heaven, 209-50; Eternal Father of heaven and earth, 223-39; author and finisher of faith, 511-4. **Signs,** of his first advent predicted, 92-3; of his birth, 393-4; of his death, 394-14, 20; given, fulfilled, 400-19; destruction at his death, 415-5. **Life and death of:** Born of woman, 18-18, 244-13; baptized by John, 19-27; is rejected, 90-12; mocked, scourged and cast out, 163-5; lifted up on the cross, 19-33, 90-13, 140-9, 450-14; rises from the dead, 90-13; breaks the bands of death, 163-8; shows himself to the Nephites, 92-1, 420-18; announcement by a voice from heaven, 417-1, 419-3, 421-3; the people understand the voice, 421-6; descends out of heaven, 421-8; calls Nephi, 422-18; commissions Nephi and others to baptize, 422-21; commissions the twelve disciples, 422-22, 423-1; works miracles, 140-5, 432-7, 449-15; to show himself to the lost tribes of Israel, 432-4; is worshiped, 433-10; prays and blesses little children, 433-21; institutes sacrament of bread and wine, 434-1; lays hands on his disciples, 436-36; ascends into heaven, 436-39; appears again, 437-15; miraculous providing of sacramental emblems, 439-6; appears to disciples, 449-2; predicts degeneracy in the fourth generation, 451-32. **Mission and work of:** The giver of the law of Moses, 429-5; fulfiller of law, 429-4, 8; is the law and the light, 429-9; atones for the sins of those who have fallen through Adam, 140-11, 207-27, 252-14; redeems his people, 163-1; but not in their sins, 223-34; satisfies the demands of justice, 163-9; brings resurrection from the dead, 204-14, 295-3, 394-15; will manifest himself to all, 188-30; gives little children eternal life, 164-25; shall see his seed, 163-10; means of salvation to the Gentiles, 107-9; by the house of Israel, 441-31; by all men, 450-14; will manifest himself a second time, 63-14; to Jerusalem, 67-5; is the judge, 107-7, 11, 140-10; will reject those who reject him, 454-34; word of, to the Gentiles, 455-1. **Teachings of,** on baptism: mode of ordinance, 422-23; authority to baptize, 422-21; all must repent and be baptized, 423-37; fire and the Holy Ghost after, 424-2; those baptized called the church, 169-17, 449-21. On the sacrament: in remembrance of his

INDEX   543

body, 434-7; of his blood, 434-11; forbids unworthy to partake, 435-28. On the unity of the Godhead, 422-27, 423-32. On sundry subjects: forbids disputation, 422-28; all men must repent and believe, 423-32; become as a little child, 423-37; the rock, 423-39; repeats sermon on the mount, 424-3; the beatitudes, 424-3; his sheep, 430-24; still other sheep, 430-1; the gathering of Israel, 431-5; Gentiles to be numbered with the people of God, 431-13; watch and pray always, 435-15; prayer in families, 435-21; meet together oft, 435-22; search scriptures, 445-1; his teachings to be written, 445-4; expounds prophecies of Malachi, 446-1.

Disciples of, a light unto the people, 429-12; names of the Nephite twelve, 437-4; their desire asked for, 452-1; desires expressed save by three, 452-2; desires granted, 452-3; the promise given to the three, 452-7; the three go forth upon the face of the land, 453-18; their miraculous deliverances, 453-21; names of the three not given, 453-25; they minister to Mormon, 453-26; and Moroni, 472-11; among the Gentiles, but unknown, 453-27.

Christians, name taken by believers, 310-15; cause of, defended, 316-10; executed secretly, 412-23.

Christs, false, 133-15.

Church of God, 26-10; and fold, 66-2; entered through baptism, 203-4, 449-21; pride enters, 203-6; people of, become wicked, 204-11; among Gentiles, 443-22; to be called by name of Christ, 450-8; organized by disciples, 456-1; meets often, 511-5.

Church of the Devil, 26-10; called great and abominable, 22-5, 25-3, 27-17, 47-13, 63-12; called whore of all the earth, 26-10, 47-13, 72-16, 99-18; denies Christ, 458-29.

Churches, many, among Gentiles, 94-20; contend, saying: I am the Lord's, 98-3; many branches among Nephites, all one church, 183-22; built up to get gain, 458-26; to forgive sins for money, 474-32.

Cimeter, Lamanites' skill in, 127-20; surrendered by Zerahemnah, 306-8. See also **Weapons.**

Circumcision, law of done away in Christ, 516-8.

Cities, destruction of, in Nephi's vision, 20-4; called after those who first possessed them, 214-7; fortified, 321-1; many, built by Nephites, 322-15; of Nephites captured by Lamanites, 326-26; built anew and repaired, 411-7; destroyed at time of crucifixion, 415-8, 417-3, 456-9; many, built by Coriantum, 495-23.

City of Nephi, of Desolation, of Zarahemla, etc., see **Nephi, city of; Desolation, city of,** etc.

Civilization, rebellious Nephites subjected to, 326-22; degenerate Nephites without, 518-11.

Classes, among people, 276-2, 458-26.

Clefts, of rocks, 75-21.

Climate, diseases due to, 313-40.

Closet, prayer in, 280-7, 283-26, 426-6.

Cloth, made by people of Zeniff, 154-5; by Nephites, 373-13; by Jaredites, 498-24.

Clothing, of Moroni's army, 302-19; withheld from naked, 367-12; wolves in sheep's, 428-15.

Cloud, angel descended in a, 187-11; of darkness over Lamoni, 244-6; of darkness over multitude, 371-28; overshadowed multitude while Christ ascended, 436-38; the Lord talks to brother of Jared from a, 480-4.

Coat, Moroni's, rent for title of liberty, 310-12; of Joseph, 311-24.

Cockatrice, 85-8, 89-29, 103-14.

Cohor, brother of Noah, a Jaredite, 490-15.

Cohor, son of Noah, becomes king of Jaredites, 490-20.

Com, Jaredite king, father of Heth, 479-26, 495-25; dethroned and slain, 495-27.

Com, Jaredite king, born in captivity, 498-31; subdues Amgid and gains part of kingdom, 498-32; fought robbers, 498-34; protected prophets, 498-2.

Combination, secret, of Kishkumen, 363-8; of murderers, 413-6; among Jaredites, 492-18, 499-15.

Combinations, secret, 94-22. See also **Gadianton Robbers.** Judgments of God upon, 290-30; origin of, among Nephites, 374-18; signs and words among, 374-22; their secret oaths to be kept from people, 374-25; oaths of, given by devil to Cain, 374-27, 492-15; Nephites make end of, 409-6; given by devil, 412-28; destroy government, 413-6; gather and appoint king, 413-9; among Jaredites, 492-18; cause destruction of Nephites, 363-13; of Jaredites, 492-21; Gentiles warned against, 492-23; built up by devil, 493-25; instigated by daughter of the dethroned king, Jared, 492-17; Jared murdered by, 494-6; Heth embraces, 495-26; Com fights against, 498-34; prophets rejected because of, 495-29; many people slain because of, 504-18; Gilead receives recruits by, 506-8; cause murder of Gilead, 506-9.

Comforter, 517-26; see **Holy Ghost.**

Coming of Christ, see **Christ.**

Commander, 304-44; Moroni chief, 310-11; Amalickiah chief, 314-19; Gidgiddoni chief, 405-18; Mormon refused to be, 464-11.

Commandments, Lord opens way to fulfil his, 5-7; keeping of, brings blessings, 50-9; Nephites kept law because of, 92-25; summarized, 95-32; to be kept by Nephites, 102-1; keeping of, prospers people, 128-9; taught by king Benjamin, 137-13; the ten, 161-12; disobeyers of, to be cut off, 217-13.
Commencement, of reign of judges, 194-44.
Comnor, hill, scene of great Jaredite battle, 507-28.
Compass, see **Liahona.**
Compassion, divine, towards children of men, 163-9; Lamanites had, 171-14, 174-26, 180-34; Ammon moved with, 264-4; Jesus filled with, 432-6; of the Lord for Jared, 479-35.
Complaint, against unrighteous judges, 412-25.
Concubines, of David and Solomon, 108-15, 111-24; prohibited, 111-27; of king Noah and his wicked priests, 156-14; among Jaredites, 496-5.
Condemnation, none where there is no law, 69-25.
Conditions, of salvation, 143-8, 205-10; Moroni's, for exchange of prisoners, 333-11.
Consignation, to happiness or misery, 296-15, 17.
Contentions, and wars, recorded on larger plates, 15-4, 41-4; foreseen by Nephi, 20-3; prophesied of by Nephi, 92-2; witnessed by Jacob, 125-26; by Enos, 127-23; by Jarom, 129-13; by Benjamin, 133-12; by Zeniff, 153-13; warning against, by Mosiah, 191-7; among people of Zarahemla, 130-17; people warned against, 138-32; forbidden, 169-21; regarding Amlici, 198-5; in church, 203-9; among Lamanites regarding Ammon, 246-28; concerning lands of Lehi and Morianton, 322-25; cause of wars and destruction of Nephites, 325-9; caused by Gadianton robbers, 402-11; the devil the father of, 422-29; among Jaredites, 499-7.
Contrite, spirit and broken heart, 59-32, 486-15, 511-ch. 6:2; an acceptable offering in place of Mosaic sacrifices, 418-20, 424-19.
Conversion, of Alma through Abinadi, 167-1, 205-11; of Alma and sons of Mosiah, 187-11; of Zeezrom, 233-5; of Abish, 245-16; of Lamoni's household, 253-23; of Lamoni's father, 252-15; of one Amalekite, 256-14.
Converts, burned, 231-8; many, made by sign of Christ's birth, 400-16.
Copper, found in promised land, 40-25; used by Nephi, 61-15; fine workmanship in, 128-8.
Cords, Nephi bound with, 12-16, 39-11; of the devil, 94-22; and ladders used by Moroni, 355-21.

Corianton, goes to Zoramites, 274-7; instructed by Alma, 293-1; had forsaken the ministry, 293-3; had injured the mission, 294-11; encouraged by Alma, 298-14; instructed by Alma on probation, 298-4; on redemption, 299-11; on justice, 299-14; on atonement, 299-15; on repentance, 299-16; on free agency, 300-27; called to preach again, 300-31; sails northward, 358-10.
Coriantor, son of Moron, 479-7; born in captivity, 499-18; begets Ether, dies in captivity, 500-23.
Coriantum, son of Amnigaddah, 479-14; dwells in captivity, 498-31.
Coriantum, son of Emer, 479-28; anointed king, 495-21; reigns righteously, 495-23.
Coriantumr, son of Omer, 491-4; defeats Jared, 491-6.
Coriantumr, last Jaredite survivor, dwells with people of Zarahemla, 131-21; account of his people, 131-21; king of Jaredites, 500-1; his destruction sought, 504-15; skilled in warfare, 504-16; warned by Ether, 504-20; to be buried by another people, 504-21; captured by Shared, 505-23; liberated by sons, 505-24; meets Shared in battle, 505-28; wounded, 505-31; defeats brother of Shared, 505-3; throne of, taken by Gilead, 506-6; battles with Lib, 506-12; flees to Agosh, 506-15; slays Lib, 506-16; battles with Shiz, 506-16; flees before Shiz, 506-17; not to fall by sword, 507-24; meets Shiz at Comnor, 507-28; wounded by Shiz, 507-30, 508-9; repentance of, 507-3; writes to Shiz, 507-4, 509-18; flees before Shiz, 508-7; goes to Ripliancum, 508-8; defeats Shiz, 508-10; camps at hill Ramah, 508-11; watched by Ether, 508-13; final battle with Shiz, 508-15; slays Shiz, 509-30; falls wounded, 509-32.
Coriantumr, Nephite dissenter, Lamanite commander, 360-15; takes Zarahemla, 361-20; kills the judge, Pacumeni, 361-21; marches toward Bountiful, 361-23; killed, 362-30; army of, captured, 362-32.
Corihor, land of, 507-27.
Corihor, son of Kib, 489-3; rebels against Kib, 489-4; makes captive of father, 489-7; loses kingdom to Shule, 490-9; repents and gains favor of Shule, 490-13.
Corihor, an associate of Coriantumr, 504-17.
Corom, son of Levi, 479-20, 497-16.
Correspondence, between Lamanites and Nephites, 256-18, 257-8; fear of Zoramites entering into a, 274-4.
Corruption, of mortality to put on incorruption, 67-7, 166-10, 295-2, 297-4.
Corruptness, of law under Gadianton sway, 378-3.

Council of war, called by Moroni and Teancum, 329-19.
Counsel, of God, 69-28; dark, hidden from the Lord, 97-27, 99-9.
Countenance, of Nephi and Lehi, 371-36; of Jesus, 438-25.
Covenant, to Abraham, 29-18; to Lehi, 50-5; of baptism, to Helam, 168-13; of evil, 412-28; not all fulfilled by Christ then, 429-8; to be fulfilled in last days, 442-7.
Covenants, in record of Jews, 23-23, 42-15, 63-12; taken away from record of Jews, 23-26; to house of Israel, 26-5, 66-1, 71-7, 73-5; to Abraham, 47-9; to children of men, 72-15, 100-1; evil and secret, to be kept from people, 290-27.
Cow, on the land of promise, 40-25; among Jaredites, 494-18.
Cracks, in earth, 394-22, 416-18.
Craftiness, of king Laman, 149-21, 153-10, 155-18; of Zeezrom, 224-3.
Creation, of the earth, 36-36, 50-10, 54-14, 73-7; of Adam, 190-17; of man, 114-9; of man in image of God, 484-15.
Creator, see **Christ.**
Creature, salvation for every, 190-3; justice claims the, 300-22; gospel for every, 477-22.
Cries, of unrepentant, God slow in hearing, 157-24; of righteous, God quick to hear, 218-26; of Nephite spies heard by prisoners, 344-32; at destruction of Jaredites, 508-16.
Crimes, preached against by Jacob, 109-9; grosser, 111-22; judgment by Alma according to, 184-11; Korihor defends, 270-17.
Crisis, the awful, at judgment, 283-34.
Cross, of crucifixion, seen in vision of Nephi, 19-33; Christ speaks of, 450-14.
Crosses, of the world, 68-18.
Crucifixion, foreseen by Nephi, 19-33, 63-9, 71-3, 90-13; by king Benjamin, 140-9; affirmed by Christ, 421-14; see **Christ.**
Cumeni, city of, 338-14, 342-7.
Cumoms, animals known to Jaredites, 494-19.
Cumorah, hill, named by Nephites, 469-2; Mormon hides records in, 469-6; scene of final battle between Nephites and Lamanites, 472-2; called Ramah by Jaredites, 508-11.
Cunning, of Amlici, 198-2; of Amalickiah, 326-27; of devil, 443-10.
Cup, bitter (figurative), 66-17, 142-26, 296-26, 421-11; sacramental, 434-8, 511-ch. 5:1.
Cures, miraculous, 140-5, 449-15.
Cureloms, animals known to Jaredites, 494-19.
Curse, on Lamanites if they rebel, 4-23; of Lamanites seen by Nephi, 21-23; comes upon Lamanites, 61-21, 112-5, 201-6; on the land, 392-30, 405-24, 505-1; of Adam taken from children, 516-8.

Cush, 85-11.
Custom, as to naming of cities, 214-7; of arresting strangers, 238-20; of succession in leadership, 314-17; of appointing gifted leaders, 405-19.

Daggers (figurative), to pierce souls, 109-9.
Damascus, 79-ch. 17:8.
Damnation, drunk to their souls, 141-25, 435-29; subjection to the devil, 166-11; for evil-doers, 389-26; resurrection of, 448-5; for corrupters of the word, 474-33.
Dance, Lehi's company, on the ship, 39-9; of Lamanitish daughters, 172-1; of daughter of Jared, the dethroned king, 492-11.
Dark, and dreary waste, in Lehi's vision, 13-4, 7; and loathsome people, the Lamanites, 21-23, 468-15; works of wicked, in the, 97-27; veil of unbelief, 244-6.
Darkness, on land of promise seen in vision by Nephi, 20-4; to be visited upon Israel, 42-11; Israel to be brought out of, 47-12; secret works of, to be destroyed, 72-15; scales of, shall fall, 102-6; stone to shine in, 290-23; night without, sign of Christ's birth, 393-3, 400-15; for three days, sign of Christ's death, 415-3; vapor of, could be felt, 416-20; disappeared, 419-9.
Dart, a weapon, 128-8.
Darts, of adversary, 29-24.
Daughters, of Ishmael, 11-6; married by Zoram and sons of Lehi, 31-7; of Lamanites captured by priests of king Noah, 172-5; of Lamanites maltreated, 518-9.
David, king of Israel, evil practices, 108-15; concubinage of, abominable, 111-24; house of, 79-2, 80-13.
David, land of, 461-5.
Day, cloud by, 76-5; of judgment, 141-24; journey of a, for a Nephite, 367-7; of execution set, of believers, 399-9; Ether hid in cavity of rock by, 504-13.
Dead, the living to hear from the, 81-19; raised from the, by Nephi, son of Nephi, 437-4; raised from the, by Christ, 449-15; Christ's resurrection from the, see **Christ, life and death of; Resurrection.**
Deadness, of Mosaic law, 92-27.
Deaf, that will not hear, 69-31; to hear word of book, 97-29; to hear, 140-5; healed by Christ, 432-7; healed by the disciples, 456-5.
Dealings, of God not understood by Laman and Lemuel, 4-12, 154-14; merciful and just, 322-19.
Dearth, famine in days of Heth, 495-30.
Death, passed upon all men, 67-6; of spirit, hell as the, 67-10; bands of, broken by God, 163-8; swallowed up

546 INDEX

in Christ, 166-8; murder punished by, 196-18; spiritual, 225-16.
Debtors, 426-11.
Decoy, Lamanites out of strongholds, 329-21; inability to, 344-1.
Decree, protecting sons of Mosiah, 255-2.
Decrees, unrighteous, 83-1; of God unalterable, 297-8; of God concerning land of promise, 481-9, 11.
Deeds, to be watched, 145-30; done in the body, 206-15; judged according to, 287-15, 300-27; evil, 391-26.
Defiance, to commands of God, 206-18; to law, 413-30.
Degree, of allowance, none with God, for sin, 308-16.
Delight, of the Lord in chastity, 111-28.
Delightsome, people, 133-8, 469-17; fair and, 61-21, 456-10; white and, 102-6; civil and, 518-12.
Deliverance, from death, 73-5; from Lamanites, 153-17; from bands of death, 204-14; from foes, by the Lord, 309-7.
Demands, of justice, 139-38; atonement satisfies, 69-26; mercy satisfies, 282-16; to appease, 299-15; of a robber, refused by Lachoneus, 404-12.
Demons, 392-37.
Den, of the cockatrice, 85-8; of wild beasts, three disciples cast into, 453-22, 458-33.
Depravity, of Nephites, 519-18.
Depths, of hell, 21-16; of sorrow, 32-25; of humility, 70-42, 143-11, 357-41, 373-5; of the earth, 93-5, 417-6; of God's mysteries, 114-8.
Descendants, of the Jews, 102-4; of Nephi, 182-2, 183-13; of Mulek, 182-2; of Laman and Lemuel, 259-29; of priests of Noah, 301-13; of Laman, 337-3; of Lamanites, 386-24; of Jacob, 419-4; of Riplakish, 496-8.
Deseret, honey bee, 480-3.
Desolation, city of, Lamanites march to, 464-7; Lamanites take possession of, 465-2, 466-13; retaken by Nephites, 466-8.
Desolation, land of, 254-30; near Bountiful, 254-32; people gathered at, 464-5; near Moron, 489-6.
Desolation of Nehors, 236-11.
Despair, because of iniquity, 262-19, 521-22.
Despisers, of works of God shall perish, 477-26.
Destruction, of Nephites predicted, 93-6, 127-23; at death of Christ, 415-5; because of wickedness, 418-12; occurred, 418-12, 420-14; of Moroni's people, 472-3; of Jaredites, 490-23, 498-1, 503-1, 504-14; caused by secret combinations, 492-21.
Devil, founder of the abominable church, 22-6, 25-3; captivity by, 26-7, 51-18; a fallen angel, 54-17, 67-8; beguiled first parents, 67-9; transforms himself, 67-9; and angels filthy, 68-16; father

of secret combinations, 94-22, 374-26; to be shorn of power, 103-18; deceived Sherem, 124-18; evil comes from, 131-25, 400-22, 513-12; master of sin, 143-14; captivation of, 218-28; appeared to Korihor, 273-53; takes possession of wicked, 295-13; destroyer of souls, 380-28; an enemy of God, 513-12.
Devils, to be cast out, 140-6; cast out, 414-19.
Dilemma, the awful, of guilt, 211-3, 212-18.
Diligence, wins prize, 144-27; in keeping commandments, 213-23.
Dimmed, plates not to be, by time, 10-19, 288-5.
Directions, given on Liahona, 33-30; given brother of Jared, 480-5.
Director, see **Liahona**.
Dirt, cast up for fortification, 318-2, 331-4.
Disciple, Mormon a, 409-13.
Disciples, the twelve, foreseen by Nephi, 20-8, 21-10; chosen, 422-22, 423-1, 429-12; names of, 437-4; teach in twelve assemblies, 437-5; promise of Jesus to, 452-1; the three, not to taste death, 452-7; found a church, 456-1; miracles wrought by, 456-5, 458-30; imprisoned and delivered, 458-30; in furnace, 458-32; in dens of beasts, 458-33; taken away, 461-13, 472-10; seen by Mormon and Moroni, 453-26, 472-11.
Diseases, cures of, by Christ predicted, 140-5; effected, 432-7; certain plants a remedy for, 312-40.
Disguise, Abinadi in, 158-1; of Kishkumen, 360-12; of servant of Helaman, 362-6.
Dispersion, see **Scattering**.
Displeasure, of God, 51-22, 135-17.
Disposition, of King Benjamin's converts, 145-2; of Lamanite king, 152-5; of Amalekites, 301-6.
Disputations, forbidden by Christ, 422-22, 28, 436-34; concerning name of the church, 449-3; concerning infant baptism, 516-4, 5; see **Contentions**.
Dissension, caused by Alma, 187-9; by Amalickiah, 309-6.
Dissensions, in Mosiah's time, 184-5; followed by wickedness, 315-36.
Dissenter, Coriantumr a, 360-15.
Dissenters, names blotted out, 197-24; not converted, 259-29; persecute Lamanites, 259-5; hunted down by Lamanites, 259-8; the Zoramites, 274-8; join Lamanites, 301-13, 315-35, 386-24; a menace to Nephites, 318-24; kingmen, refuse to fight, 325-15, 354-6; one converted, 371-35; Jacob and conspirators, 413-12.
Division, among people prophesied, 103-10; among king Noah's people, 170-2; between freemen and king-men, 324-4; following death of Pahoran, 359-4; between church and unbelievers, 458-35.

INDEX   547

Divorcement, figurative of apostasy, 64-1; condemned by Christ, save because of fornication, 425-31.
Doctrines, false, 99-9, 12, 196-16; false, to be confounded by combined Nephite and Jewish scriptures, 56-12; of Christ, 105-21, 6, 423-32. See also **Christ, teachings of.**
Dominions, of church of Christ to be small, 26-12.
Doors, of tents toward temple, 136-6; prayer behind closed, 426-6.
Dormant, faith may be, 279-34.
Doubtings, over prophecy of Samuel the Lamanite, 415-4.
Dove, descent of Holy Ghost upon Christ in form of a, 19-27, 104-8.
Dragons (figurative), 65-9, 87-22; people of Limhi fight like, 173-11; Lamanites fight like, 304-44.
Dream, see **Vision.**
Dross (figurative), 276-3, 283-29.
Drunkenness, as a military ruse, 335-8, 337-30.
Dumb, Alma made temporarily, 188-19; Korihor stricken, 272-50; healed by Christ, 432-9.
Dust, figurative of humiliation, 48-14, 51-14, 93-15; records shall speak from, 57-19, 96-9, 107-13, 521-27; man created from, 138-25.
Dwindling in Unbelief, Laban slain to prevent nation, 7-13; of Lehi's seed predicted, 21-22, 24-35, 50-10, 308-10, 442-5; among Nephites, 322-22, 375-34, 458-34; followed by curse, 21-23; distinguished from wilful rebellion, 459-38; causes cessation of miracles, 477-20.

Earthquakes, predicted, 20-4, 63-15, 93-6, 95-2, 474-30; occurred at Christ's death, 416-12.
Ease, in Zion, slothful, 100-24.
Eat, drink and be merry, the wicked say, 98-7; the twelve disciples to take no thought what to, 427-25, 31.
Eden, Adam and Eve driven from, 54-19, 226-21, 298-2; type of perfection, 65-3.
Edom, 85-14.
Egypt, Joseph sold into, 10-14, 55-4, 57-1, 219-3; Israel delivered from, 10-15, 37-40.
Egyptian, reformed, writing, 478-32.
Egyptians, language of the, 1-2, 134-4.
Elam, 85-11.
Elders, of the Jews, 8-22; over the church, 203-7; ordained, 210-1; disciples called, 510-ch. 3:1; baptized, 511-ch. 6:1; judge iniquity, 512-7.
Elements, to melt with fervent heat, 448-3, 475-2.
Elephants, 494-19.
Elijah, return of, promised, 447-5.
Embassy, Amalickiah to Lehonti, 313-10; Amalickiah to Lamanite queen, 315-32; Moroni to Jacob, 329-20; Helaman to governor, 344-4.
Emer, son of Omer, 479-29; anointed king of Jaredites, 494-14.
Emron, a Nephite soldier, slain, 518-2.
Enemy, of soul, 59-28; to all righteousness, 139-37; to God, 141-19, 165-5.
Enemies, confounded, 59-22; deliverance from, 59-31, 280-4.
Engraving, upon plates, difficulty of, 113-1.
Engravings, on plates, 8-24, 10-11, 62-32, 150-9; on stone, 131-20; characters used in the, 478-32.
Enos, given plates, 125-27; sins forgiven, 125-5; gives plates to Jarom, 127-1.
Enos, Book of, 125.
Ensign, to the nations, 78-26; of the people, 85-10.
Enticings, of the devil, 69-39; of the Holy Spirit, 141-19.
Envy, of Ephraim, 85-13; condemned, 207-29.
Envyings, produced by dissension, 94-21, 197-32, 391-22; forbidden, 236-18, 443-19, 455-ch. 30:2; abolished by righteous living, 457-16.
Ephraim, Syria confederate with, 79-2; to know word of God, 82-9; to be purged of envy, 85-13.
Ephraim, hill, 490-9.
Epistle, Moroni to Ammoron, 333-4; Ammoron to Moroni, 334-15; Helaman to Moroni, 337-1; Ammoron to Helaman, 341-1; Helaman to Ammoron, 341-2; Moroni to Pahoran, 348-3; Pahoran to Moroni, 352-1; Giddianhi to Lachoneus, 403-1; Lamanite king to Mormon, 464-4; Mormon to Lamanite king, 469-2; Coriantumr to Shiz, 507-4, 509-18; Shiz to Coriantumr, 508-5; Mormon to Moroni, 515-1, 518-1.
Equality, among people, 186-3, 236-16, 269-11.
Error, conviction of, 288-8, 401-25; Zoramites in, 274-9; infant baptism a gross, 516-6.
Esrom, a Jaredite, son of Omer, 491-4; battles with Jared, 491-5.
Establishment, of the church by Alma and Amulek, 236-15.
Eternal life, men free to choose, 55-27, 73-23; teachings regarding, 69-39, 105-18, 125-3; hope for, 123-11, 515-41.
Eternal Father, the, 163-4, 166-15, 223-39; sacramental prayers addressed to, 511-ch. 4:3, 511-ch. 5:2; covenants with Israel, 521-31; Christ the Son of the, 19-21, 25-40.
Eternity, of priesthood, 228-7; life preparation for, 283-33; God unchangeable throughout, 517-18.
Ethem, Jaredite king, son of Ahah, 479-9, 499-11.
Ether, Book of, taken from record on the 24 plates, 478-2.

Ether, son of Coriantor, 479-6, 500-23; prophecies of, 500-5; words of, rejected, 503-2; sees days of Christ, 503-4; dwells in cavity of a rock, 504-18, 505-22; word of the Lord to, 507-24; words of, remembered, 507-1; hides records, 509-33; last words of, 509-34.
Eve, see **Adam and Eve.**
Evidence, demanded of Korihor, 272-40.
Evidences, basis of law, 221-2; of truth, 372-50, 380-24.
Evil one, see **Devil.**
Evil, comes from devil, 131-25, 208-4C, 513-12; men quick to do, 388-4.
Evil-doers, 82-17, 88-20.
Example, set by Nephi, 11-8; set by Christ, 104-16.
Examples, bad, 111-35, 112-10, 204-11; good, 238-11, 293-1.
Exhortation, Moroni's final, 520-2.
Experiment, with faith, 278-27, 281-4.
Expert, in wickedness, Zeezrom, 221-31, 222-21; Gadianton, 362-4; people, in working of cement, 364-7.
Expertness, of Ammon, 240-3.
Exquisite, bitterness and sweetness, 287-21.
Eye, of God, searching, 70-44, 189-31; piercing, 110-10; see eye to, 159-22, 165-29, 1, 287-26, 432-18, 441-32; of faith, 169-21, 206-15, 279-40, 501-19; for an eye, 425-38; is light of body, 427-22; mote in brother's, 428-3; change in twinkling of, 452-8; single to glory of God, 473-15.
Eyes, of world, book hid from, 96-12; of the blind, 97-29; of blind opened, 449-15.
Ezias, 380-20.
Ezrom, a silver coin, 222-6, 12.

Faction, in government feared, 347-36.
Faith, necessary to salvation, 68-23, 140-12; in Christ, 105-19, 168-7, 183-15, 211-6, 234-10, 281-4, 291-33, 379-15; brings knowledge, 108-5, 145-4, 243-35, 262-22, 396-7, 484-19, 485-7; in words of prophets, 176-30, 206-12; protects, 305-4, 317-16, 343-27, 390-6, 427-30, 516-3; a power in prayer, 187-14, 200-30, 234-10; in righteous doing, 343-27, 353-17, 414-18, 520-7; not perfect knowledge, 278-18; hope and charity, 500-4, 512-1.
Fall of man, way prepared from, 52-4; evil tendencies followed, 165-3, 483-2; explained by Aaron, 252-13; by Alma, 298-2; by Samuel the Lamanite, 394-16; by Mormon, 476-12.
Families, to be defended, 304-47; prayer in, enjoined, 435-21.
Famine, predicted, 51-18, 63-15, 71-6, 89-30, 384-6, 390-9, 495-28; suffered by people of Zeniff, 152-3; by Nephites, 356-35, 385-4; by Jaredites, 495-30, 499-7; people saved from, 218-22, 220-22, 331-7.

Fasting, and prayer enjoined, 131-26, 210-6; and prayer brought revelation, 237-3.
Father, Eternal, Lamb of God, Son of, 19-21, 25-40. See also **Eternal Father;** pray unto, 520-4; Everlasting, 82-6; Only Begotten of the, 90-12, 208-48, 218-26, 228-5, 9; of lies, devil the, 54-18, 67-9, 493-25; of contention, devil the, 422-29; of heaven and earth, 140-8, 393-12, 485-7; and Son, 163-2, 422-27, 441-35, 452-10, 484-14.
Fathers, nursing, 72-9; iniquities of, 161-13; mourn for sons, 266-5; hearts of, turned, 448-ch. 25:6; children fed on flesh of, 518-8.
Faults, confession of, urged, 294-13; confessed, 401-25; in record, are of men, 473-17.
Fear, of the Lord, 74-10, 142-1, 245-15, 286-7; of death, 470-7; of destruction, 233-26.
Feet, of Christ, men worship at, 19-24, 433-10; prints of nails in, 422-14; beautiful upon mountains, 164-15.
Fevers, among Nephites, 312-40.
Field, spacious, in Lehi's vision, 13-9; Lebanon a fruitful, 97-28; prayer in, 280-5, 283-20; lilies of, 427-28.
Fifty, of Laban, 7-31, 7-1; captain of, 75-3; all of company from Zarahemla slain save, 131-28; persons to one priest, 169-18; Nephites wounded at siege of city of Noah, 320-24.
Fight, against apostles, in vision of Nephi, 20-34; against Lamb of God, in vision of Nephi, 26-13; against Zion brings disaster, 47-14, 63-12, 95-3; against God, 90-14.
Figs, not gathered from thistles, 428-16.
Filthiness, in vision of Nephi, 30-27; of Lamanites, 112-5; poor esteemed as, 276-3; moral, 150-30, 206-22, 213-21, 475-4.
Finger, of God wrote upon wall, 219-2; of the Lord seen by Jared, 483-6; Christ touches disciples with, 453-12.
Fire, pillar of, seen by Lehi, 2-6; and brimstone, figurative of punishment, 68-16, 100-23, 113-11, 122-10, 142-27, 226-17, 232-14; unquenchable, 139-38, 209-52, 475-5; Abinadi suffers death by, 167-13; king Noah put to death by, 171-20; Lamanites perish by, 259-5; in danger of hell, 425-22; 473-17; Nephi and Lehi encircled by, 370-23, 372-43; little children encircled with, 433-24; like a refiner's, 446-2; the three Nephite disciples cast into, 458-32; baptism of, see **Holy Ghost.**
Firstlings, offered as sacrifice, 136-3.
Fish, mentioned by Christ, 428-10; carried by Jaredites, 480-2.
Flattery, of Sherem, 123-4; of Alma, 187-8; of Amalickiah, 309-5; of king-men, 352-4.

Flesh, lust of the, 48-23; Christ the Son because of the, 163-3; and blood of Christ, how administered, 511-ch. 4:1, ch. 5:1; human, fed to women and children, 518-8.

Flight, of Lehi from Jerusalem, 9-36; of Lamanites before Limhi's army, 173-12; of Morianton, 323-33; of Kishkumen, 360-10; of Gadianton robbers, 363-11; of king Jacob, 413-12; of Mormon, 468-7.

Flocks, in time of Enos, 127-21; as, fleeing from shepherd, 152-21; of Nephites desired by Lamanites, 153-12; guarded from Lamanites, 153-2; as, driven by beasts, 167-17; shepherd would protect from wolves, 209-59; of Lamoni preserved by Ammon, 239-25, 240-2; protected from robbers, 406-4; of brother of Jared, 480-41; Jaredites rich in, 497-12.

Flood, destruction of Nephites not by, 220-22; Jared and his people not to perish in, 482-20.

Fold, one, and one shepherd, 49-25, 430-3; of God, 66-2, 261-4; of the devil, 207-39; other sheep not of this, 430-17, 430-1.

Followers, of Christ, 99-14, 512-3, 515-48; of God, 204-15, 373-5.

Food, supplied Alma by Amulek, 215-20; withheld from Alma and Amulek in prison, 232-22; begged by Korihor, 273-56; Helaman's army suffers for want of, 345-7; not sent by the rulers, 350-19; received by Lehi and Teancum, 354-13; Nephi and Lehi imprisoned without, 370-22; of Nephites kept from robbers, 406-3; animals used as, by Jaredites, 494-18; hunted for people, 497-19.

Fool, Nephi called a, 35-17; misunderstanding Bible, 101-6; calling brother, forbidden, 425-22.

Foolishness, of men, 69-28, 93-10.

Fools, to consider selves as, before God, 70-42; wicked Nephites called, 382-21; mocking, shall mourn, 502-26.

Forefathers, Lehi's, genealogy of, on brass plates, 5-3, 288-3; knowledge of, 28-14.

Foreheads, marked red by Amlicites, 201-4.

Foreknowledge, of God, men chosen and ordained according to, 228-3; God's, of all things, 228-7.

Forgiveness, to be prayed for, 13-21; of sins, 142-2; not easy to obtain, 293-6; granted as often as sought, 512-ch. 6:8.

Form, of man, Spirit of the Lord in the, 18-11; of man, God in the, 162-34; of a dove, Holy Ghost manifest as, 19-27, 104-8; in resurrection, 223-43; of nature, a testimony of God, 272-44; of godliness, 514-30.

Fornication, condemned, 113-12, 380-26; sole justification for divorce, 425-32.

Fortifications, prepared by Nephites, 316-8, 319-13, 321-10, 331-7, 404-14; taken by Lamanites, 326-23; prisoners work on, 336-25; of Angola insufficient, 461-4.

Foundation, of great and abominable church, 22-4, 26-9; sandy (figurative), 100-28, 423-40, 429-26, 434-13; Christ the one and safe, 114-15, 369-12; of destruction, 221-27.

Founder, of peace, 164-18; of the church, Alma, 179-16, 194-47.

Fountain, in vision of Nephi, 21-16; rod of iron leading by, 14-20, 19-25; at Mormon, 168-5; of all righteousness, 493-26, 502-28; a bitter, cannot bring good water, 512-11.

Fragments, rocks broken into at time of crucifixion, 394-22, 416-18.

Fraud, of Amalickiah, 313-4, 315-30.

Freedom, from captivity, for house of Joseph, 55-5; from bondage, worth fighting for, 304-48; cause of, supported, 312-35; striven for by Moroni, 316-11; oath of, by Pahoran, 324-39; enforced, 324-7; indifference concerning, 348-13; defended by Pahoran, 352-6, 353-1; defended against Gadianton robbers, 402-12; secret combinations threaten to overthrow, 493-25.

Freemen, name of, taken, 324-6; support Pahoran, 352-3; driven from Zarahemla, 354-6.

Fruit, desirable, seen in Lehi's vision, 13-10; evil, 118-35, 122-7, 428-17; forbidden, 54-15, 142-26, 226-22; good, 117-26, 207-36, 428-17; wild and tame, 116-18, 117-25; of tree of life, 30-36, 210-62; bitter, 119-52.

Fruits, first, of the resurrection, 53-9; of Christ, 114-11; of repentance, 517-25; of labors, 263-31, 296-26; men known by their, 428-16.

Fulness, of gospel, 17-14, 441-28; of the Gentiles, 28-13, 430-4; of the wrath of God, 36-35, 48-16, 481-11, 494-20; of time, 52-3, 73-7; of joy, 451-30, 452-10; of iniquity, 481-10.

Furnace, of affliction, 44-10; life of king Noah as garment in, 158-3; the three disciples cast into a, 453-21, 458-32, 473-24.

Fury, of the oppressor, 65-13; of Jacob the Zoramite in battle, 330-33; to be executed, 443-21.

Gad, city of, 418-10.

Gadiandi, city of, 417-8.

Gadianton, expert in wickedness, 362-4; flees from Helaman, 363-11; proves overthrow of people, 363-13; secret combinations of, 365-23; secrets of, 374-24; oaths of, 374-26; inspired by Satan, 375-29; author of secret band, 380-28; band of, swept away, 385-10; secret plans of, 387-26.

Gadianton robbers, band of, 374-18, 459-42; hunted down by Lamanites, 375-37; control judgment-seat, 376-4, 378-1; destroyed, 385-10; re-established in mountains, 401-27; among Lamanites, 401-29, 461-18; become numerous, 402-11; gain advantage, 403-18.
Gadiomnah, city of, 417-8.
Gain, churches built for, 48-23, 94-20, 95-29, 458-26, 474-33; object of Nephite lawyers, 221-32, 222-20; through plunder, 374-17; plates not to be used for, 473-14; through traffic, 497-22.
Gall of bitterness, soul redeemed from, 188-29; Alma in, 287-18; wicked in, 297-11; for wicked, 474-31, 516-14.
Game, none found in lands deserted by Nephites, 406-2; scarcity of, hinders robbers, 407-20; wilderness preserved for, by Jaredites, 497-21.
Garden, of Eden, first parents driven from, 54-19, 298-2; of Nephi, multitude instructed at, 377-10, 381-8, 11.
Garment, life of king Noah compared to, 158-3.
Garments, of Laban worn by Nephi, 8-19; of the twelve disciples, white in blood of Christ, 21-10; to be kept spotless (figurative), 109-19, 2, 138-28, 206-21; of skins worn by Lamanites, 318-6.
Gate, to kingdom of God, 70-41, 104-9, 107-9, 123-11, 428-13, 451-33.
Gates, of hell, 59-32, 423-39, 434-13.
Gathering, of Israel, 431-5, 442-1.
Gazelem, 290-23.
Geba, 84-29.
Gebim, 84-31.
Genealogy, of Lehi, 5-3, 12, 10-14, 16, 288-3; of Zarahemla, 130-18; of Jaredite kings, 478-6.
Generation, the fourth from birth of Christ, 21-12; 93-9, 308-12, 390-10, 451-32; visiting sins until third and fourth, 161-13; wicked and perverse, 216-8, 220-17, 221-25, 392-29.
Generations, three, from time of Christ pass in righteousness, 21-11, 93-9; prophecies concerning future, 57-2, 71-53, 289-14, 448-2.
Gentiles, a man among, to cross the great waters, 22-12; record among, 25-40; mighty nation among, 47-7; a marvelous work among, 47-8, 454-32; remnant of Jacob among, 443-12; the three disciples among, 453-27; to scatter remnant of house of Israel, 29-17, 93-15; to nurse house of Israel, 47-6; to bring forth book, 24-38, 471-8; gospel to come through, 28-13, 442-5, 448-8, 468-15, 471-8; great church seen among, 22-4; receive scriptures in purity from Jews; corrupted scriptures, 23-29; to afflict seed of Nephi, 72-18; to smite unbelievers, 94-19; shall say: A Bible! and reject other scriptures, 101-3; to be shown mercy, 24-32; to get Nephite record, 24-35, 102-3; to receive manifestation of Christ, 25-42; to have gospel, 28-13; promises unto, 72-9; the promised land a land of liberty unto, 72-11; prayed for by Moroni, 502-36; prosperity of, seen in vision of Nephi, 22-15; to mock, 501-23; written to by Moroni, 465-17.
Gid, city of, captured by Lamanites, 326-26; retaken by Nephites, 335-7, 336-16, 23; strongly fortified, 336-25.
Gid, captain over Lamanite prisoners, 343-29; loses prisoners, 344-32; in ambush before Manti, 345-16; takes possession of Manti, 346-21.
Giddianhi, writes to Lachoneus, 404-9; plunders, 406-5; hideous appearance of soldiers of, 406-7; people of, slaughtered, 407-11; beaten, 407-12.
Giddonah, father of Amulek, 219-2.
Giddonah, high priest in land of Gideon, 270-23; sends Korihor to Alma for judgment, 271-29.
Gideon, a Nephite patriot, 170-4; his plan of freedom, 177-6; a teacher of the people, 195-7; withstands Nehor, 195-7, 9; slain by Nehor, 195-9, 196-13; valley and city named after, 199-20, 210-7.
Gideon, city of, 210-7.
Gideon, valley of, 199-20; church established in, 210-8.
Gidgiddonah, Nephite commander, 470-13.
Gidgiddoni, chief captain of Nephite armies, 405-18; a prophet, 405-19; defeats Gadianton robbers, 407-14; establishes peace, 411-6.
Gift, lay hold on the good, touch not the evil, 521-30; every good, cometh of Christ, 520-18; of interpreting languages, 131-25; of translation, 217-21; of eternal life, 369-8; the heavenly, 456-3, 500-8; see also **Gifts;** of the Holy Ghost, see **Holy Ghost.**
Gifts, spiritual, Amaleki exhorts men to believe in, 131-25; spiritual, Alma speaks of different, 217-21; varied manifestations of, 520-8; taken from people through unbelief, 521-24.
Gilgah, son of Jared, 488-14.
Gilgal, a Nephite chieftain, killed, 470-14.
Gilgal, city of, sunk, 417-6.
Gilgal, valley of, 505-27; Coriantumr defeats Shared in, 505-28; Shared slain in, 505-30.
Gilead, brother of Shared, 506-8; fights Coriantumr, 505-3; ascends throne, 506-6; murdered by his high priest, 506-9.
Gimgimno, city of, sunk, 417-8.
Glass, as clear as, molten stones prepared by the brother of Jared, 482-1.
Glory, the Son of God to come in great, 48-24, 208-50, 218-26, 230-24, 448-3; rendered unto Jesus at his visitation to the Nephites, 439-9, 10.

INDEX 551

Goats, found upon promised land, 40-25; raised by Nephites, 127-21.
God, love of, 19-22; justice of, 21-18; yields himself up to be crucified, 41-10; to do marvelous work among Gentiles, 47-8; greatness of, 52-2; commandments given by, 54-21; sin abominable unto, 109-5; commands there shall be no priestcrafts, 95-29; of miracles, 476-15; unchangeable, 517-18.
Gold, desired by the abominable church, 22-7; found in promised land, 40-25; people taught to work in, 61-15; people lifted up in pride because of, 110-12; people of Limhi pay tribute of, 171-15; people have abundance of, 197-29; coins, 222-5.
Good, inspired of God, 208-40, 513-13; children of men slow to do, 388-4.
Gospel, to go to Gentiles, 24-34; precious parts of, taken away, 24-32; to be written for Gentiles, 24-35; declared among remnant of seed of Lehi, 102-5; church built upon, 450-10; denied by those who do not know it, 476-8.
Government, overthrown by secret combinations, 413-6.
Governor, Alma the, 199-16; Lachoneus the, 399-1.
Grace, of God, 67-8, 71-53, 114-7; for Gentiles, prayed for, 502-36.
Grains, raised by Nephites, 127-21, 152-9.
Grapes, not gathered of thorns, 428-16; wild, figurative of recreant Israel, 77-2, 4.
Grave, no traveler can return from, 51-14; must deliver up dead, 67-12; shall have no victory, 252-14.
Graves, opened, 395-25.
Great and abominable church, see Church of the Devil.
Great Spirit, Ammon supposed to be the, 240-2, 241-11, 246-25; Lamanites believe in, 241-5; is God, 242-28, 252-9.
Guilt, men to have a consciousness of their, 68-14, 122-9, 139-38, 141-25, 206-18, 223-43; racked with consciousness of, 475-3.
Guilty, the, take the truth to be hard, 31-2.
Gulf, awful, separates wicked from tree of life, 30-28; of misery and woe, 50-13.

Hagoth, builds and launches ships, 358-5.
Hail, to smite people of king Noah, 158-6.
Happiness, state of righteous, 140-4, 202-26, 295-12, 471-7.
Harlots, priests of king Noah with, 156-14; Isabel, 293-3.
Head-plates, worn by Nephites, 303-38, 304-44; by Lamanites, 360-14; by Jaredites, 508-15.
Healing, of Zeezrom by Alma, 234-6; of sick and afflicted by Christ, 432-9, 449-15; by the disciples, 456-5.
Hearthom, son of Lib, king of Jaredites, 479-17, 498-29.

Heat, fervent, to melt the elements, 448-3, 475-2.
Heathen, remembered, 95-33; vengeance to be visited upon, 443-21.
Heavens, opened, to Lehi, 2-8; to Nephi, 18-14, 19-27; to penitent Lamanites, 372-48; where God dwells, 242-30.
Helam, a follower of king Noah, baptized by Alma, 168-12.
Helam, city of, 179-20.
Helaman, Book of, 359.
Helaman, son of king Benjamin, 134-2.
Helaman, son of Alma, 274-7; instructed by Alma, 286-1; receives the plates, 288-2, 289-21, 324-38; forbidden to reveal secret oaths, 290-27; instructed about Liahona, 291-38; appoints priests, 309-22; preaches, 309-1, 357-45; maintains order in church, 312-38; persuades people of Ammon not to break oath, 332-14; leads 2,000 sons of Ammonites, 332-19; writes to Moroni, 337-1; assists Antipus, 338-9; marches by Antiparah as a ruse, 339-31; returns to help men of Antipus, 340-50; victorious, 341-54; receives letter from king Ammoron, 341-1; makes conditions as to exchange of prisoners, 341-2; army of, strengthened, 341-6; surrounds Cumeni, 342-7; complains about indifference of the rulers, 345-7; decoys Lamanites at Manti, 345-17, 346-18; returns to Zarahemla, 357-42; dies, 358-52.
Helaman, son of Helaman, receives the records, 358-11; appointed judge, 362-2; saved by servant, 362-6; character of, 365-20; had instructed his sons, 369-5; dies, 366-37.
Helem, one of the brethren of Ammon, 147-6.
Hell, devil leads souls of men to, 25-3, 55-29; spiritual death is, 67-12; to deliver up its dead, 67-12; pains of, 113-11, 261-13; chains of, 205-7, 9; gates of, shall not prevail, 423-39.
Helorum, son of king Benjamin, 134-2.
Hem, one of the brethren of Ammon, 147-6.
Hermounts, Lamanites fled to, 200-37.
Herds, of Nephites, 60-11, 127-21, 197-29; people of Zeniff pay tribute of half of, 149-22; of Jaredites, 487-ch. 6:4, 497-12.
Heshlon, plains of, 505-28.
Heth, land of, 491-2.
Heth, son of Com, 479-26, 495-25; rebels and takes throne, 495-27; death of, 496-1.
Heth, son of Hearthom, 479-16, 498-31.
Highways, built by Nephites, 411-8.
Hill, of Amnihu, etc., see **Amnihu,** hill of, etc.
Himni, son of Mosiah, 189-34; mission of, among Lamanites, 260-17; presides over church in Zarahemla, 274-6. See **Mosiah, sons of.**

Hiss, a, and a by-word, the Jews to be, 42-14, 431-9; the word of the Lord to hiss forth, 78-26, 80-18, 100-2, 521-28.
History, of people engraven on the larger plates, 15-2, 58-14, 108-3.
Holiness, the, of God, of Christ, 53-10, 68-20, 448-5, 475-5.
Holy Ghost, Christ to manifest himself by, to the Gentiles, 16-11, 93-13; Nephi saw, abiding upon Christ, 19-27; Nephi saw, upon the twelve, 20-7; beareth record of Christ, 21-18, 452-11; denial of, 100-26, 293-6; given after baptism, 104-12, 423-37; gifts of, 105-2, 520-5; Mary conceived by power of, 211-10; sanctification by, 229-12; Nephi and Lehi filled with, 372-45; the twelve disciples receive power to give, 436-37; the disciples receive, 437-13, 438-20; to Gentiles, 440-27; gives truth of all things, 520-5.
Holy order of God, Jacob ordained after, 62-2; Alma called by, 210-8; priests ordained after, 227-1; people to walk after, 213-22; high priests ordained after, 228-8. See also **Priesthood.**
Holy stand, of the Zoramites, 275-21.
Honey, in the land Bountiful, in Arabia, 34-5; taken on the ship, 39-6; butter and, 80-15; milk and, 94-25.
Honey bee, deseret, carried by Jaredites, 480-3.
Hope, enjoined, 213-24, 515-41.
Horses, found upon land of promise, 40-25; had by Nephites and Lamanites, 127-21, 241-9, 247-6; by Jaredites, 494-19.
Houses, of worship, see **Synagogues.**
House tops, sealed book to be read upon, 96-11.
House of Israel, Nephites of the, 101-12; promises to, 100-1, 431-11; Lord to remember, 455-8.
Howling, howlings, in mourning, among the Nephites, 416-23, 417-25; among the Jaredites, 508-16, 17.
Humility, enjoined, 70-42, 143-11; people became strong through, 366-35.
Hunger, of the soul, 125-4, 424-6; to be appeased, 439-8.

Idleness, a Lamanite trait, 21-23, 61-24, 254-28; admonition against, 293-12.
Idolatry, of the Lamanites, 126-20, 153-12; among the Nephites, 156-6, 7, 197-32, 322-21; Alma guilty of, 187-8; among the Jaredites, 490-23; see **Idols.**
Idols, worship of, condemned, 69-37; by Nephites, 375-31; by Lamanites, 238-15; by Zoramites, 273-1; sacrifices to, by Lamanites, 466-14, 467-21.
Images, graven, 443-17.
Immanuel, a title of the Christ, 80-14, 81-8.
Immortality, mortality changed to, 67-13, 127-27, 166-10, 224-45, 226-20, 452-8.

Incorrectness, of Lamanite traditions, 201-8, 217-17, 262-24, 288-9.
Incorruptible, mortal bodies to become, 67-13, 166-10, 206-15, 294-2, 297-4.
Industry, Nephites show much, 61-17; Amulek gained riches by his, 219-4.
Inequality, should be no, 193-32, 411-14; among the Nephites, 204-12, 15; abolished, 236-16; because of sin, 267-13.
Inheritance, lands of, to Nephites, 47-12, 49-5, 50-9; confirmed by Christ, 439-14; Jews to be gathered to their, 71-8; Lamanites to possess, 112-4; righteous to have, with God, 209-58.
Iniquity, iniquities, Christ to suffer because of, 161-28, 162-5, 6, 163-ch. 14:11; quick to do, 161-29, 310-8, 388-4; in gall of bitterness and bonds of, 188-29, 297-11, 474-31, 516-14.
Insects, land to be pestered by, 158-6.
Interpreters, used by a seer, 151-13; prepared to unfold mysteries, 151-19; Alma receives, 191-20; Helaman entrusted with, 289-21, 290-24; Moroni seals up, 485-5.
Iron, Nephites work in, 128-8.
Iron rod, vision of, by Lehi, 14-19; seen by Nephi, 19-25; explanation of, 29-23.
Irreantum, many waters, 34-5.
Isaac, God covenanted with, 36-40; God of, 41-10; intended sacrifice of, 113-5.
Isabel, harlot of Siron, 293-3.
Isaiah, one of the twelve disciples, 437-4.
Isaiah, prophet of Israel, Nephi teaches words of, 29-20, 43-23; Nephi reads words of, 43-1, 44-1; Nephi expounds writings of, 46-1; Nephi writes words of, 74 to 89; Abinadi quotes, 162-1; people instructed to search prophecies of, 473-23.
Ishmael, and family join Lehi's company, 11-5, 13-22; daughters of, marry sons of Lehi, 31-7; Zoram married eldest daughter of, 31-7; death of, at Nahom, 33-34; Lamoni descendant of, 239-21.
Ishmael, descendant of Aminadi, 219-2.
Ishmael, land of, 238-19; Ammon in, 238-20, 239-21; synagogues built in, 251-20.
Isles, of sea, to suffer, 42-12; Israel scattered upon, 46-4; people of Israel to be gathered from, 71-8; to be remembered, 101-7; promises of God to people upon, 73-21.
Israel, house of, likened unto olive-tree, 16-12; to be scattered, then gathered, 17-14; to be judged by the apostles, 21-9; fight against apostles, 20-35; Gentiles to be numbered among, 25-2; covenants of Lord unto, 26-5; work of God to commence among, 27-17; to be a hiss and by-word, 42-14; righteous branch to be raised up unto, 55-5; to be restored, 56-13; tribes of, to write words of the Lord, 101-12; Christ speaks to, 419-5; Christ goes to lost tribes of, 432-4.
Ites, none left, 457-17.

INDEX 553

Jacob, Book of, 107-1.
Jacob, city of, sunk in sea, 417-8.
Jacob, son of Lehi, 39-7; flees with Nephi, 60-6; made a priest, 62-26; preaches to people, 62-1, 73-1, 109-1; to write history of people upon the plates, 108-2; confounds Sherem, 123-8; concludes his record, 125-26.
Jacob, Zoramite leader, 329-20; and army surrounded, 330-31; killed, 330-35.
Jacob, king of robbers, 413-9; flees northward, 413-12.
Jacob, House of, 43-1, 74-5, 98-33, 410-21, 25, 440-16, 442-2.
Jacobites, one of the divisions of the Nephites, 108-13.
Jacobugath, city of, burned, 417-9.
Jacom, son of Jared, 488-14.
Jared, came forth from the great tower, 479-33; language of, not confounded, 479-35; promised a choice land, 480-42; goes into valley of Nimrod, 480-1; embarks, 487-ch. 6:4; reaches promised land, 488-12; numbers people, 488-19; death of, 489-29. See also **Brother of Jared.**
Jared, son of Omer, 491-1; rebels against father, 491-2; defeated in battle, 491-6; murderous proposal to Akish, 492-12; anointed king, 493-4; killed, 493-5.
Jaredites, account of, 478-1; perished because of wilfulness of their hearts, 519-23.
Jarom, Book of, 127.
Jarom, son of Enos, 127-1.
Jashon, land of, 462-16.
Javelin, made by Nephites for war, 128-8; Amalickiah killed with, 327-34; Ammoron killed with, 356-36.
Jealous, God is, 157-22, 161-13.
Jehovah, 86-ch. 22:2, 522-34.
Jeremiah, one of the twelve disciples, 437-4.
Jeremiah, a prophet of Israel, brass plates contain some prophecies of, 10-13; cast into prison, 12-14.
Jershon, land of, 265-22; given to people of Anti-Nephi-Lehi, 265-22, see **Ammon, people of;** church established in, 266-1; Korihor in, 270-19; Alma and Amulek enter, 284-1; people of Ammon depart out of, 285-13; Nephites gather armies in, 301-4.
Jerusalem, Lamanite city, 249-1; Aaron came to city of, 249-4; submerged, 417-7.
Jerusalem, in Palestine, destruction of, predicted by prophets, 1-4; Lehi prophesies against, 2-18; Lehi and family leave, 3-4; prophecies concerning, to be fulfilled, 12-13; Lehi's sons return to, for the brass plates, 5-2; Lehi's sons return to, to fetch family of Ishmael, 11-2; destroyed, 49-4, 63-8, 90-10; people of Zarahemla came from, 130-14; covenant people to return to, 441-29; to be redeemed, 441-34.
Jerusalem, the New, see **New Jerusalem.**
Jesse, 85-1, 10.
Jesus, see **Christ.**
Jew, book proceeds from mouth of, 23-23, 27-23; Nephi has charity for, 107-8.
Jews, mock Lehi, 3-19; Laban had record of, 5-3; the plates of brass contain record of, 10-12; prophet to be raised up among, 16-4; gospel to be preached to, 16-11; record of, beheld by Nephi, 23-23; to be scourged, 42-13; God spoke to, by prophets, 66-2; understand prophecies, 89-5; to be scattered, 90-15; to become drunken with iniquity, 95-1; cursed by Gentiles, 101-5; to have words of Nephites and of the lost tribes, 102-13; cast off unless they repent, 102-2; eventually to accept Christ, 441-31.
John, the apostle, 27-27, 452-6; ordained to write, 27-25; written revelations of, 486-16.
Jonas, one of the twelve disciples, 437-4.
Joneam, Nephite leader, killed, 470-14.
Jordan, city of, Lamanites repulsed at, 467-3.
Joseph, who was sold into Egypt, Lehi descendant of, 55-4; seer to be raised up from, 56-11, 14; prophecies of, 57-1; seed should never perish, 91-21; righteous branch from, 111-25; Amulek descendant of, 219-2; part of coat of, preserved, 311-24; Lehi's posterity a remnant of the seed of, 311-23, 27, 420-17, 503-6, 504-10.
Joseph, son of Lehi, born in wilderness, 39-7; made to grieve, 40-19; Lehi blesses, 55-1; to hearken unto words of Nephi, 57-25; flees with Nephi, 60-6; made a priest, 62-26, 109-18.
Josephites, a division of the Nephites, 108-13.
Josh, city of, burned, 418-10.
Josh, a Nephite leader, killed, 470-14.
Joshua, land of, Nephites come to, 462-6.
Jot, nor tittle, of the law, not to pass away void, 282-13, 401-25; Christ affirms none had passed, 424-18.
Journey, a day's, for a Nephite, 254-32, 367-7.
Joy, men are that they might have, 54-25; of righteous shall be full, 68-18, 98-30.
Judea, city of, Helaman arrives at, 338-9; fortified, 338-15.
Judge, Alma first chief, 194-42; Nephihah second chief, 204-16; of Ammonihah after order of Nehor, 232-16; smites Alma and Amulek, 232-24; killed by falling of prison walls, 233-27; proclamation of, concerning people of Anti-Nephi-Lehi, 265-21; Nephihah the, dies, 323-37; Pahoran appointed chief, 324-39; Pahoran the, dies, 359-2; Pahoran, son of Pahoran, chief, 359-5; Pahoran

36

the, murdered by Kishkumen, 360-9; Pacumeni appointed chief, 360-13; Pacumeni the, killed by Coriantumr, 361-21; Helaman chief, 362-2; Nephi appointed, 366-37; Cezoram chief, 368-1; son of Cezoram chief, 373-15; Seezoram chief, 382-23; Lachoneus chief, 399-1; Lachoneus, son of Lachoneus, chief, 412-19.

Judges, suggested by Mosiah, 192-11; chosen by voice of people, 193-25, 194-39, 359-5, 360-13, 362-2; reign of begun, 195-1.

Judgment, doings of men brought to, 17-20, 107-15; God executes, in righteousness, 48-21; first, 67-7; after death come to, 226-27; murderer in danger of, 425-21; out of books, 451-25; of God against wicked, 500-20; Moroni prays for, of God, 519-15.

Judgments, of God, 20-5, 50-10, 68-15, 89-3, 225-15, 231-11.

Justice, of God, 30-35, 68-17, 69-26, 70-46, 139-38, 298-1; cannot be denied, 122-10; work of, cannot be destroyed, 227-32, 299-13; mercy cannot rob, 300-25.

Keeper, the, of the gate is the Holy One of Israel, 70-41.

Kib, Jaredite king, son of Orihah, 479-32, 489-3; captive under Corihor, 489-7; receives kingdom again, 490-9; bestows kingdom on Shule, 490-10.

Kid, leopard to lie down with, 103-12.

Kim, Jaredite king, son of Morianton, 479-22, 497-13; brought into captivity, 497-14.

Kimnor, father of Akish, 491-10.

King, of Nephites, called Nephi, 108-11; of heaven and earth, 208-50; of Salem, Melchizedek, 229-18.

Kingdom, of devil built up among men, 48-22; must shake, 99-19; wicked belong to, 206-25; of God, 24-37, 68-23, 105-21, 122-4; no filthiness in, 30-34; seek the, 110-18; of Nephites ends, 194-47; of heaven, 208-50; who may inherit, 423-38.

King-men, 324-5; executed, 354-9.

Kings, Mosiah's warning against rule by, 192-16; the iniquities of some, 193-31; wanted by wicked Nephites, 413-30.

Kish, Jaredite king, son of Corom, 479-19, 497-17.

Kishkumen, murders Pahoran, 360-9; seeks to murder Helaman, 362-3; killed by servant of Helaman, 363-9.

Kishkumen, city of, burned, 418-10.

Knee, every, shall bow before Christ, 189-31.

Knowledge, of the Lord, penitent brought to the, 255-5, 288-9, 315-36; 410-23, 439-13; earth shall be full of, 85-9, 103-15.

Korihor, an Anti-Christ, 269-12; in Jershon, 270-19; in Gideon, 270-21; before Giddonah, 270-23; makes accusations, 270-24; sent to Alma, 271-29; asks for sign, 272-43; sign given, stricken dumb, 272-50; deceived by devil, 273-53; cast out, 273-56; killed among Zoramites, 273-59.

Kumen, one of the twelve disciples, 437-4.

Kumenonhi, one of the twelve disciples, 437-4.

Laban, possessor of brass plates, 5-3; treasure offered him for the plates, 6-24; a robber, 6-25; slain, 8-18; sword of, 8-18, 61-14, 108-10, 133-13, 135-16; descendant of Joseph, 10-16.

Lachoneus, chief judge, 399-1; receives letter from robber band, 403-1; assembles his people, 404-13; fortifies camp, 404-14; character of, 403-2, 404-12, 404-16, 405-19.

Lachoneus, son of Lachoneus, chief judge, 412-19; receives complaints of illegal executions, 412-25; slain by rebels, 413-1.

Ladders, used by Moroni's army, 355-21.

Lamah, a Nephite chieftain, killed, 470-14.

Laman, eldest son of Lehi, 3-5; admonished by his father, 3-9; posterity of, cursed, as seen in vision, 21-23; meets Laban, 5-11; flees from Laban, 5-14; rebels against Nephi and Sam, 11-ch. 7:6; marries, 31-7; plots against lives of Lehi and Nephi, 33-37; assisted by Lemuel, binds Nephi, 39-11; Lehi's blessing on children of, 57-4; seed of, not to perish, 58-9; angry towards Nephi, 58-13.

Laman, king over Lamanites, 149-21, 180-3.

Laman, one of Moroni's soldiers, 335-5.

Laman, city of, burned, 418-10.

Laman, river of, 3-8, 31-12.

Lamanite, Samuel the, see **Samuel.**

Lamanites, cursed, 21-23, 61-21, 112-5; seek to destroy Nephites, 108-14; Enos prays for, 126-11; dress of, 154-8; illfounded belief of, 154-12; daughters of, captured by priests of Noah, 172-1; prosper when they heed good instruction, 181-7; shave heads, 154-8, 201-4; dissenters to, were marked, 201-10; merciful promises to, 217-16; converts among, 237-4, 255-3, 8; traditions of, base, 237-9; divided from Nephites by wilderness, 253-27; after conversion, steadfast in truth, 255-6; lay weapons down, 255-7, 257-6; converts take new name, 256-16, 256-3; unconverted, slaughter converts, 256-1, 258-21; swear vengeance anew upon Nephites, 259-1; destroy people of Ammonihah, 259-2; many perish by fire, 259-5; follow converts, great slaughter results,

INDEX   555

266-1; approach Ammonihah, 318-1; fight with stones, 318-2; astonished at Nephite fortifications, 318-4; prepared for war, 318-6; attack city of Noah, 319-15, 320-21; defeated, 320-25; driven by Moroni's army, 321-7; retreat to captured cities and fortifications, 327-2; by west sea, 328-11; decoyed by Teancum, 329-23; defeated, 330-39; made prisoners, guarded in labor, 331-1; took women and children as prisoners, 333-3; attempt strategy, 336-29; fortify Morianton, 337-33; slay all prisoners but captains, 338-12; fearful of Nephites, 339-24; lose city of Manti, 346-28; attack city of Nephihah, 348-5; many captured by Moroni and Pahoran, 355-15; driven back to own lands, 359-15; capture Zarahemla, 361-22; many converted by sons of Helaman, 370-19, 372-50; yield up lands, 372-52; many became more righteous than Nephites, 372-1, 375-36; preach to Nephites, 373-4; go northward, 373-6; when converted, relieved of curse, 402-14; name of, abolished, 457-17; name revived, 457-20; unbelievers called, 459-38; taught to hate, 459-39; utterly destroy Nephite nation, 470-7, 11; dissension among, 472-8; reject gospel of Christ, 485-3; secret combinations among, 492-20.

Lamb of God, see **Christ**.

Lamb, to dwell with wolf, 103-12.

Lamb-skin, worn by Gadianton robbers, 406-7.

Lamentation, among people of Limhi, 174-9; among all people of Nephi, 266-4; of righteous Nephites, 375-33; of Nephi, son of Helaman, 377-15; in sin, 462-11; Jaredite, 508-16.

Lamoni, king over land of Ishmael, 239-21; slays servants, 239-28, 241-4; meets Ammon, 239-21; supposes Ammon to be the Great Spirit, 240-2; prayer of, 243-41; appears to be dead, 243-1; revives, and testifies of Christ, 244-12; overcome by joy, queen also, 244-13; multitude astonished over, 245-18; church organized among people of, 246-35; meets his father, king of the whole people, 247-8; returns to Ishmael, 251-18; causes synagogues to be built, 251-20; counsels with Anti-Nephi-Lehi, 256-5.

Land of promise, Nephi to be led to, 4-20, 17-13; Lehi rejoices over, 9-5; Nephi and brethren to obtain, 12-13; Nephi beholds in vision, 20-1; Gentiles to be led to seed of Lehi in, 22-13; choice above all lands, 24-30, 49-5; see **Choice;** Lehi's colony driven toward, 39-8; arrival at, 40-23; seed of Lehi prosper in, 50-9; gold, silver and precious ores abound in, 110-12; Jared's colony carried toward, 487-ch. 6:5; Jaredites reach the, 488-12.

Language, of Nephites, 1-2, 134-2; Nephites unable to write in full on account of, 410-18; of records, called reformed Egyptian, 478-32; no other people know, 478-34; of people confounded at the great tower, 479-33; of Jared's people not confounded, 479-35.

Lasciviousness, Jacob warns people against, 113-12; Nephites fall into, 308-12; people free from during a period of blessing, 457-16.

Last days, words of Nephi written for good of people in, 90-8; God's words to judge in, 91-18; Nephi prophesies concerning, 93-14; to be terrible, 95-1.

Law of Moses, on the brass plates, 8-16, 10-11; Laman and Lemuel speak of, 35-22; priests of Noah falsely claim to teach, 159-28; a type of Christ, 260-15; not then fulfilled, 401-24; fulfilled in and by Jesus Christ, who was the giver of the law, 418-17, 429-4, 5; not followed as to performances after Christ's visitation, 457-12.

Laws, of Nephites very strict, 128-5; established by Mosiah, 195-1; enforced upon transgressors, 197-32, 221-2, 269-10; trampled under feet of Nephites, 368-22; corrupted, 368-2; overthrown when Gadianton band usurped power, 376-4.

Lawyers, hired at trials, 220-14; many among Nephites, 411-11.

Laying on of hands, to ordain, 210-1.

Leah, a lesser coin, 222-17.

Learning, Gentiles puffed up in, 94-20; priests teach their, and deny Holy Ghost, 98-4.

Lebanon, to become a fruitful field, 97-1.

Lehi, of Jerusalem, sees pillar of fire, 2-6; has vision of heaven, 2-8; sees Christ and the apostles, 2-9; foresees destruction of Jerusalem, 2-13, 16-3; record of, 2-17, 40-1; preaches in Jerusalem, 2-18; dream of, 3-1; leaves Jerusalem, 3-4; family of, 3-5; speaks with power in valley of Lemuel, 4-14; sends for the brass plates, 5-4; receives the brass plates, 10-10; descendant of Joseph, 10-14; prophecy of, concerning the plates, 10-18; sees vision of the tree and the rod of iron, 13-2; predicts Christ, 16-4; finds Liahona, 31-10; sons of, born in wilderness, 39-7; and company arrive in promised land, 40-23; prophesies, 49-1; blesses Jacob, 52-1; blesses Joseph, 55-3; blesses children of Laman, 57-3; blesses sons and daughters of Lemuel, 58-8; blesses Sam, 58-11; dies, 58-12; daughters of, 60-6.

Lehi, son of Zoram, 235-5.

Lehi, Nephite commander, 303-35; pursues Lamanites, 304-40; made chief captain, 319-16; at city of Noah, 319-17; meets Lamanites, 330-28; attacks army of Jacob, 330-36; in command at Mulek, 331-2; Lamanites flee from, 356-32; intercepts enemy, protects land Bountiful, 361-28.

Lehi, son of Helaman, 365-21; preaches to Nephites, 367-14; preaches to Lamanites, 370-18; goes to land of Nephi, 370-20; cast into prison, 370-21; encircled about as if with fire, 370-23; face of, shines, 371-36; goes into land northward, 373-6.

Lehi, city of, 322-15; people of, prepare for battle, 326-24; captured by Amalickiah, 326-26.

Lehi, land of, 322-25; people in appeal to Moroni, 323-27.

Lehi-Nephi, land of, 147-1.

Lehi, land southward called, 373-10.

Lehonti, leader of Lamanites, 313-10; poisoned at command of Amalickiah, 314-18.

Lemuel, second son of Lehi, rebuked, 4-14; threatened with curse, 4-21; rebels, 11-6; marries, 31-7; plots against lives of Lehi and Nephi, 33-37; with Laman binds Nephi, 39-11; Lehi blesses sons and daughters of, 58-9; angry, 58-13; mark placed upon seed of, 201-7.

Lemuel, valley of, 4-14; Lehi dwells in, 15-1.

Lemuelites, a division of the Lamanites, 108-13; reject gospel, 459-38.

Leopard, to lie down with the kid, 103-12.

Levi, a Jaredite, son of Kim, 479-21; serves in captivity, then becomes king, 497-15.

Liahona, Lehi finds, 31-10; instructions upon, 32-27; worked according to faith, 32-28; ceases to work because of wickedness, 39-12; works by faith of Nephi, 40-21; Nephi takes, with him, 60-12; known as ball, and compass, 31-10, 32-26, 60-12; called also director, 135-16, 291-38, 45; name thus called, 291-38.

Liar, thrust down to hell, 69-34.

Lib, son of Kish, 479-18; becomes king, 497-18; a great hunter, 497-19.

Liberty, promised land a land of, 50-7; of belief and worship, 196-17, 251-22, 269-9; Nephites desire to preserve, 303-30; Moroni's title of, 310-13; title of, hoisted on every tower, 312-36; Moroni planted standard of, 312-36; king-men forced to acknowledge standard of, 326-20; youthful Ammonites covenant to fight for, 332-17.

Life eternal, to be spiritually minded is, 69-39; hope to be raised up unto, 515-41.

Light, throughout night, sign of Christ's birth, 393-3, 399-8, 400-15; in the wilderness, Lord to be, 34-13; choose darkness rather than, 93-10; priestcraft set up as, 95-29; miraculously provided for Jaredite barges, 483-4, 487-ch. 6:2.

Lightnings, and thunderings, shown in vision to Nephi, 20-4; God to visit Israel with, 42-11; wicked to be visited with, 93-6; at death of Christ, 415-7.

Limnah, a Nephite chieftain, slain, 470-14.

Limnah, a gold coin, 222-5.

Limher, a Nephite soldier, 199-22.

Limhi, son of Noah, meets Ammon, 147-9; sends proclamation for people to assemble, 148-17; and people in bondage to Lamanites, 149-22; captured, 171-16; made king, 172-26; fights with Lamanites, 172-9; sends men to find land of Zarahemla, 175-25; explorers of, bring back record of Jaredites, 176-27; and people escape with aid of Ammon, 177-11; arrive at land of Zarahemla, 177-13.

Linen, fine-twined, 22-8, 197-29, 203-6, 373-13, 498-24.

Lion, 103-12, 440-16.

Loathsome, people, Lamanites a, 21-23, 61-22, 468-15.

Looking, awful, fearful, state of wicked awaiting resurrection, 296-14.

Lord, the Gentiles to humble before, 22-16; to understand, a man should inquire of the, 28-3; covenant of, with fathers, 47-6; to raise up mighty Gentile nation, 47-7; prepares way for his people, 48-20; statutes of the, 51-16; anger of, kindled against wicked, 93-6; Spirit of, not always to strive with man, 93-11; the, and the Redeemer, 98-5; dwelleth not in unholy temples, 284-36; talks with brother of Jared, 481-14, 482-20. See also **Christ.**

Lord's prayer, 426-9.

Lost tribes, of Israel, 429-15, 432-4.

Love, arms of God's, 51-15; charity is, 95-30.

Lucre, corrupts the soul, 194-40; love, more than God, 222-24.

Luram, a Nephite soldier, slain, 518-2.

Lusts, of flesh, sought by wicked, 48-23; of eyes, 294-9; ask not for things to consume on, 477-28.

Machinery, employed by Nephites, 128-8.

Mad, Abinadi misjudged to be because of his testimony, 160-1, 4.

Madmenah, a village in Palestine, 84-31.

Mahah, son of Jared, 488-14.

Majesty, of God, 74-10, 75-19, 21, 208-50, 225-15.

Maker, the Lord, so named, 65-13, 69-40, 109-6, 125-4, 360-11, 444-5.

Malachi, Jewish prophet cited, 446-1.

Malice, caused by opposing churches, 94-21; forbidden, 95-32.

Man, angel as, 13-5; Son of God as, 18-7; Jesus Christ showed himself to the brother of Jared in form of a, 484-15;

INDEX 557

Jesus Christ visited the Nephites as a, 421-8; Spirit of the Lord manifest to Nephi in form of a, 18-11.
Manasseh, Aminadi a descendant of, 219-3; Lehi a descendant of, 219-3.
Mankind, became lost and fallen, 226-22; Christ shall redeem all, 244-13, 394-16.
Manna, Israel fed with, 148-19.
Mansions, of the Father, 127-27, 502-32, 34, 37.
Manti, hill, Nehor executed on, 196-15.
Manti, Nephite soldier, 199-22.
Manti, land of, 235-6.
Manti, city of, 343-22; taken by stratagem, 345-13, 346-28.
Mark, set by God upon Lamanites, 201-6, 202-15; red, on Amlicites, 201-4, 13.
Marriage, of sons of Lehi, 31-7.
Mary, mother of Jesus, 18-18, 140-8, 211-10. See also **Virgin.**
Mathoni, one of the twelve disciples, 437-4.
Mathonihah, one of the twelve disciples, 437-4.
Measure, of money among Nephites, 222-4.
Mediator, the great, Christ so called, 55-28.
Meek, the, persecuted by the rich, 69-30, 99-13; the, shall increase, 98-30; God shall judge for the, 103-9; teach to be, 291-33; the, blessed, 424-5.
Melchizedek, 229-14.
Melek, land of, 213-3; Amulek and Zeezrom at, 274-6; people of Ammon go to, 285-13.
Men, Christ suffers pains of all, 68-21; becoming as Gods, 227-31.
Merchants, 411-11.
Mercy, Lord visited men in, 59-26, 71-53; hath no claim on unrepentant, 139-39; he who repents has claim on, 227-34, 282-15.
Mercy and justice, 299-22.
Messenger, of the Lord, 446-1.
Messiah, see **Christ.**
Metals, specified, 373-9, 498-23.
Middoni, land of, 247-2.
Midian, land of, 256-5.
Milk, and honey, 94-25; wine and, 70-50.
Ministers, twelve to judge, 21-10.
Minon, land of, 199-24.
Miracles, if among other nations would cause repentance, 71-4; Jesus to work mighty, 93-13, 140-5; God of, 98-6; Nephi, son of Helaman, works, 397-4; great among the people, 399-4; wrought by Christ among Nephites, 432-7, 449-15; all manner of, wrought by the disciples, 456-5; God has not ceased to be God of, 476-15; day of, 514-27, 35.
Misery, eternal, 202-26, 216-11.
Mist of darkness, see **Darkness.**
Mockery, baptism of little children a, 516-9, 517-23.
Mocum, city of, destroyed, 417-7.

Money, of the Nephites, 222-4; wicked unpunished because of, under Gadianton rule, 376-5; priestly laborers for, shall perish, 95-31; forgiveness of sins for, promised by wicked church, 474-32.
Monster, Ammon called a, 246-26. See also **Devil.**
Moriancumer, temporary abiding place of Jaredites, 481-13.
Morianton, proposes to flee northward, 323-29; maid informs Moroni of plans of, 323-31; slain, 323-35.
Morianton, Jaredite, descendant of Riplakish, 479-23; becomes king, 496-9.
Morianton, city of, captured by Amalickiah, 326-26; fortified by Lamanites, 337-33.
Morianton, land of, 322-25.
Mormon, Book of, 460.
Mormon, father of Mormon, 460-5.
Mormon, last great leader of Nephites, 409-12, 460-1; incorporates smaller plates of Nephi with his own abridgment of the larger plates, 132-6; instructed by Ammaron concerning the records, 460-2; goes to Zarahemla, 460-6; visited of the Lord, 461-15; is restrained from preaching, 461-16; appointed military leader, 461-1; retreats into the land of Joshua, 462-6; takes charge of the plates of Nephi, 462-17; makes treaty dividing land with Lamanites, 463-28; resigns leadership because of wickedness of the people, 464-11; writes for future generations, 465-17; takes charge of records hidden by Ammaron, 467-23; writes abridgment of record preserved on the plates of Nephi, 132-3; records history of his times, 460-1; gathers Nephites at Cumorah, 469-4; hides records in hill Cumorah, 469-6; teachings of, on faith, hope, and charity, recorded by Moroni, 512-1; first epistle of, to Moroni, 515-1; second epistle of, to Moroni, 518-1; battles with Lamanites, 518-2; killed, 472-3.
Mormon, forest of, 170-30.
Mormon, land of, 205-3.
Mormon, waters of, 168-8, 183-18, 205-3.
Mormon, Words of, 132.
Moron, Jaredite king, 479-7, 499-14.
Moroni, Nephite commander, 302-16; equipment of army of, 302-19; sends spies into wilderness, 302-23; marches into Manti, 302-25; stratagem of, 303-27; defeats Lamanites, 305-51; demands surrender of Zerahemnah, 305-5; ends the conflict, 307-20; raises title of liberty, 310-13; gathers army, 311-21, 28; cuts off armies of Amalickiah, 312-32; establishes liberty and peace, 312-36; strengthens his armies, 316-8; character of, 316-11; prepares army, 318-8; cursed by Amalickiah, 320-27; builds more fortifications, 320-1; con-

flict of, with king-men, 325-13; gains victory, 326-19; sends re-enforcements to Teancum, 328-7; enters Bountiful, 329-18; joins Teancum, 329-19; wounded, 330-35; fortifies Bountiful, 331-4; has correspondence with Ammoron, 333-4, 334-15; sends Laman with wine to Lamanites, 335-6; arms prisoners in Gid, 336-16; receives epistle from Helaman, 337-1; writes to Pahoran, 348-3, 1; receives answer, 352-1; marches towards Gideon, 354-3; joins Pahoran, 354-6, 14; takes city of Nephihah, 355-21; returns to Zarahemla, 357-42; dies, 358-3.

Moroni, son of Mormon, 132-1, 469-6; finishes record of his father, 472-1; testifies of the three Nephite disciples, 472-10; on the bringing forth of the records, 473-12; makes abridgment of Jaredite record, 478-1; seals record and interpreters, 485-5; speaks on faith, 500-6; will not deny Christ even to escape death, 510-ch. 1:3; records mode of administering ordinances, conferring the Holy Ghost, 510-ch. 2; ordaining priests and teachers, 510-ch. 3; administering sacrament of bread and wine, 511-ch. 4, 5; on baptism and church discipline, 511-ch. 6; quotes his father on faith, hope and charity, 512-1; letters of Mormon to, 515-1, 518-1; writes to Lamanites, 520-1; his prophetic promise to the faithful reader of the record, 520-3; on spiritual gifts, 520-8; commends faith, hope, and charity, 521-20; his concluding testimony, 522-34; seals and hides up the records, 473-14, 520-2.

Moroni, city of, 321-13; destroyed, 415-9.
Moroni, land of, 326-22, 355-25.
Moronihah, commander, son of and successor to Moroni, 357-43; surprised by Lamanite invasion, 361-26; defeats and captures enemy, 362-30; driven into land Bountiful, 367-6; regains half of lost possessions, 367-10.
Moronihah, Nephite chieftain, slain at Cumorah, 470-14.
Moronihah, city of, buried, 416-10.
Mortality, to be followed by immortality, 225-12, 297-4, 452-8, 454-36, 127-27, 166-10.
Moses, commanded to do a great work, 36-26; a prophet like unto, 48-20, 440-23; God gave power unto, 56-17, 379-11; Christ the prophet of whom Moses spoke, 48-21, 440-23.
Moses, Books of, the five, on plates of brass, 10-11; Nephi did read, 43-23.
Moses, law of, engraven on plates of brass, 8-16; commandments according to, 35-22, 60-10, 136-3; 128-5; why given, 73-4; observed until fulfilled in Christ, 92-24.
Mosiah, king of Zarahemla, 130-12, 131-19.

Mosiah, last king of the Nephites, son of king Benjamin, 134-2; made king, 135-10, 138-30, 147-ch. 6:4; reads record of Zeniff, 182-5; reads account of Alma, 182-6; dissensions during reign of, 184-5; discourses upon king-craft, 191-5; urges representative government instead of monarchy, 193-25; causes election of judges, 194-39; translates and keeps Jaredite records, 190-13, 485-1; death of, 194-46; last of the Nephite kings, 194-47; laws established by, 195-1, 196-14, 368-22.

Mosiah, sons of, 189-34; numbered among unbelievers, 187-8; seek to destroy church, 187-10; are rebuked by an angel, 187-11; converted, they labor in the ministry, 189-32; go on mission, 189-1, 190-7; a record of their ministry among the Lamanites, 237; meet Alma, 237-1; commissioned by the Lord, 238-10; establish churches, 255-4; accompany Alma to Zoramites, 274-6; were men of God, 317-18.

Mountains, tumbling to pieces, seen in Nephi's vision, 20-4; to be carried up, 42-11, 416-10; shall cover persecutors, 93-5; holy, of the Lord, 103-15; of the Lord's house, 74-2; obey command in the name of Jesus, 113-6.

Mount Zion, nations fight against, 95-3.
Mourning, among people of Nephi, 266-4, 416-23.
Mouth, draw near with, while hearts are far from the Lord, 97-25; words from the Lord's, 100-2.
Mulek, son of Zedekiah, brought to the land of promise, 373-10; all Zedekiah's sons slain except, 380-21.
Mulek, city of, captured, 326-26; retaken, 329-26.
Mulek, land northward called, 373-10.
Muloki, in prison, 247-2; preaches, 250-11.
Multitude, fell to earth at Christ's appearing, 421-12; overcome with joy when Christ prays, 433-18.
Murderer, wo unto the, 69-35.
Murders, secret, must be destroyed in land of promise, 72-15; forbidden, 95-32; by degenerate Nephites, 518-10.

Nahom, a place in Arabia, burial-place of Ishmael, 33-34.
Nails, prints of in Savior's hands and feet, 421-14.
Narrow, neck of land, 358-5; pass or passage, 323-34, 328-9, 463-29, 464-5.
Nature, the God of, suffers, 42-12.
Nazareth, city of, seen in Nephi's vision, 18-13.
Neas, planted, 152-9.
Neck of land, narrow, joining land northward to land southward, 254-32; ships

INDEX 559

launched by, 358-5; fortified, 367-7; Jaredites built large city by, 497-20.
Nehor, proclaims against the church, 195-3; withstood by Gideon, 195-7; slays Gideon, 195-9; condemned by Alma, 196-14; executed, 196-15; followers of, after the profession of, 232-16, 18, 234-15, 236-11, 249-4, 259-28, 29.
Nehor, city of, a Jaredite city, 490-9.
Nehor, land of, Jaredite territory, Corihor and followers dwell in, 489-4.
Nehors, Desolation of, 236-11.
Nehors, order of the, 259-28, 29; synagogues after, 249-4.
Neighbor, unjust treatment of, condemned, 98-8, 146-14; false witness against forbidden, 161-23; coveting property of, forbidden, 161-24; man should love his, 179-15, 426-43.
Nephi, Book of, First, 1.
Nephi, Book of, Second, 49.
Nephi, Book of, Third, 399.
Nephi, Book of, Fourth, 456.
Nephi, son of Lehi, birth and education of, 1-1; makes a record, 1-2, 2-17; character of, 4-16; to be led to land of promise, 4-20; chosen to be a ruler, 4-22; faith of, 5-15; asks Laban for the plates of brass, 6-24; with his brothers hides in cavity of rock, 6-27; smitten by his elder brethren, 6-28; protected by an angel, 6-29; slays Laban, 8-18; secures the plates, 8-24; induces Zoram to join the company, 9-34; returns to Jerusalem for Ishmael and family, 11-ch. 7:2; bound by cords, 12-16, 39-11; vision of, 17-1; explains olive-tree as symbol for house of Israel, 28-12; marries, 31-7; breaks his bow, 32-18; commanded to build a ship, 34-8, 38-4; filled with power of God, 38-52; brothers of, receive shock, 38-53; crosses ocean with his father's company, 39-9; arrives at promised land, 40-23; makes plates, 40-1; preaches Christ, 48-21, 50-10, 92-23, 92-1; with a large company flees from Laman and Lemuel, 60-7; made ruler and called king, 61-18; comments on Isaiah's prophecies, 89-1; prophesies concerning last days, 95-1; dies, 108-12.
Nephi, son of Helaman, 365-21; made chief judge, 366-37; resigns, 368-1; preaches with his brother, Lehi, 369-14; preaches to Lamanites, 370-18; goes to land of Nephi, 370-20; imprisoned with Lehi, 370-21; prison in which confined, shaken, 370-27, 371-31; encircled as if by fire, 370-23; and Lehi, converse with angels, 371-36, 39; persecutors of, overshadowed by cloud of darkness, 371-28, 34, 40; persecutors of, told to repent, by Aminadab, 371-38; persecutors of Lehi and, rebuked by voice from heaven, 371-29; faces of Lehi and, did shine as angels' faces, 371-36; converts many, 372-50; goes to land northward, 373-6; returns to Zarahemla, 376-1; deplores ascendency of Gadianton band, 376-4; laments he had not lived in Lehi's day, 376-7; prophecies of, 376-2; prays on his garden tower, 377-10; teaches multitude from tower, 377-12; predicts calamity except people repent, 377-19; arouses opposition, 378-5; reveals secret murder of the judge, 380-27; names murderer of the judge, 382-26; hears voice from heaven, 383-3; is given great power, 384-7; conveyed away from persecutors by the Spirit, 384-16; invokes famine in the land, 385-4; prays for rain, 385-10, 386-17; disappears, 399-3, 402-9.
Nephi, grandson of Helaman, 399-2; receives plates, 399-2; sign of the Lord's birth promised to, 400-13; visited by angels daily, 414-18; casts out devils, 414-19; raised his brother from the dead, 414-19; did many miracles, 414-20; called from the multitude by Jesus, 422-18; with eleven others given authority to baptize, 422-22; is baptized, 437-11; baptizes his associates of the twelve, 437-12; first among the twelve, 437-4.
Nephi, son of Nephi the disciple, 456; historian of his times, 456; dies, 457-19.
Nephi, city of, 60-8; Nephites flee to, 153-15; Limhi and his people return to, 174-1; Lamanites in, 256-11; chief city of land of Nephi, 314-20; Amalickiah takes possession of, 315-31.
Nephi, land of, named after Nephi, 60-8; Mosiah the first, flees from, as directed by the Lord, 130-12; Lamanite armies come from, 133-13; Ammon and brethren go to, 147-6; Limhi king of, 147-9; Zeniff had knowledge of, 152-1; people of Noah carried back to, by Lamanites, 171-15; Amulon and Lamanites search for, 180-35; sons of Mosiah go to, to preach to Lamanites, 189-1; Aaron goes to, 191-3; Amlicites join Lamanites in, 199-24; king Lamoni desires Ammon to accompany him to, 247-1; Aaron led by the Spirit to, 251-1; nearly surrounded by water, 254-32; sons of Mosiah tell of mission in, 265-20; people of Ammon brought from, 337-3; Lamanites flee to, 347-38.
Nephi, plates of, see **Plates**.
Nephihah, made chief judge, successor to Alma, 204-17; dies, 323-37.
Nephihah, city of, 322-14; Nephites flee to, 326-24; captured by Amalickiah, 326-26; attacked by Lamanites, 348-5; retaken by Moroni, 355-26.
Nephihah, land of, Moroni goes to, 354-14; Moroni leaves, 356-30.
Nephihah, plains of, Nephites pitch tents in, 355-18.
Nephites, all who were not Lamanites, 108-13; declared by Jacob to be more wicked than Lamanites, 111-35; Enos prays that record of, be preserved,

INDEX

126-13; believers called, 201-11; armies of, assemble in Jershon, 301-4; fight for their liberties, 301-9; fight, not for power but for homes and rites of worship, 304-45; taught to defend themselves, even to bloodshed, 317-14, 304-46; fortify Ammonihah, 318-4; fortify Noah, 319-13; attacked at Noah, 320-21; many sail forth in ships of Hagoth, 358-6; repent, 367-15; in fear of Lamanites, 368-20; had corrupted the laws, 368-22; impenitent, 372-2, 375-31; converted by Lamanites, 373-5; and Lamanites in mutual friendliness, 373-6; may be destroyed except they repent, said the Lord, 397-17; again disbelieve and become hardened, 401-1; all converted, 408-1; and Lamanites converted, 456-2; return to homes, 410-1; have peace after subduing the Gadianton band, 411-3; fall into dissension and form tribes, 413-2; prosper during period of righteousness, 456-7; fair and delightsome people, 456-10; factions arise among, 458-36; become proud and vain, 459-43; exterminated as a nation by Lamanites, 470-10, 472-2; killed who will not deny Christ, 510-ch. 1:2; become depraved, lustful and barbarous, 518-9; declared to be without civilization, 518-11.

Neum, a prophet, predicted Christ's crucifixion, 41-10.

New Jerusalem, to be established, 440-22, 444-23; a, to come down from heaven, 503-3.

Nimrah, son of Akish, 494-8; flees from his father's kingdom and joins Omer, 494-9.

Nimrod, son of Cohor, 490-22.

Nimrod, valley of, 480-1.

Noah, son of Zeniff, 147-9; becomes king, 155-1; buildings erected by, 156-8; becomes a wine bibber, 156-15; hardens his heart against word of God, 157-29; imprisons Abinadi, 159-17; orders that Abinadi be slain, 160-1, 166-1; accuses Alma of sedition, 170-33; life of, spared by Gideon, 170-8; flees with his people before Lamanites, 170-9; commands men to desert wives and children, 171-11; burned to death, 171-20; priests of, abduct daughters of Lamanites, 172-3.

Noah, a Jaredite, son of Corihor, 490-14, 15; captures Shule, 490-17; slain, 490-18.

Noah, the patriarch, flood in days of, 220-22, 445-9; Jaredite barges tight like ark of, 488-7.

Noah, land, and city of, 235-3, 319-12; fortified, 319-13; Lehi in charge of, 319-17.

Nobility, claim to, asserted by king-men, 325-8, 17, 18, 326-21.

Nothingness of men, the, 388-7, 142-5, 143-11.

Nurture, and admonition of the Lord, 125-1.

Oath, and sacred ordinance, 324-39; evil and secret, 290-27, 29, 374-21, 25, 375-30, 459-42, 492-15, 20, 498-33; between Nephi and Zoram, 9-33, 35, 37; of the people of Ammon, 332-11, 14, 337-8; Mormon repents of his, 467-1.

Offering, sacrificial, 3-7, 10-9, 136-3; burnt, done away by Christ, 418-19.

Ogath, site of a Jaredite camp, 508-10.

Olive-tree, Israel compared unto, by Lehi, 16-12, 17-14, 28-7, 12, 29-16; allegory of the wild and tame, 115-3.

Omega, Alpha and, the Lord so called, 418-18.

Omer, a Jaredite king, 479-30, 491-1, 492-11, 493-1.

Omner, son of Mosiah, 189-34; see **Mosiah,** sons of.

Omni, son of Jarom, 129-15; makes record on the plates, 129-1.

Omni, Book of, 129.

Onidah, hill, 277-4; place, 313-5.

Onihah, city, destroyed at time of the crucifixion, 417-7.

Only Begotten of the Father, the, 90-12, 228-5, 9. See also **Christ.**

Opposition, must needs be, 53-11, 54-15.

Ordained, of God, the twelve apostles, 20-7; by Alma, one priest to fifty members, 169-18; priests and elders, by Alma, 210-1; ministers, by Nephi, 415-25; manner in which the disciples ordained priests and teachers, 510-ch. 3.

Order, all things to be done in, 144-27.

Ordinances, associated with law of Moses, 92-30; a type of the order of the Son of God, 229-16; strict observance of, chronicled, 269-3.

Ore, for tools, 34-9; on promised land, 40-25; Nephi made plates of, 40-1; precious, 61-15, 110-12; records on plates of, 176-27; work in all kinds of, 373-11; dug and used by the Jaredites, 498-23.

Orihah, son of Jared who came from the great tower, 479-32, 488-14; anointed king, 489-27; righteousness of, 489-30; his many children, 489-2.

Outer darkness, to be suffered by spirits of the wicked, 295-13.

Ox, found in the land of promise, 40-25; lion to eat straw like the, 103-13.

Paanchi, son of Pahoran, contends for the judgment-seat, 359-3; condemned to death, 360-8.

Pachus, wicked king of Nephite dissenters, 354-6; slain, 354-8.

Pacumeni, son of Pahoran, contends for the judgment-seat, 359-3; submits to the voice of the people, 360-6; appointed chief judge and governor, 360-; slain by Coriantumr, 361-21.

Pagag, firstborn son of the brother of Jared, 489-25.

INDEX 561

Pahoran, son of Nephihah, 324-39; contention among the people concerning, 324-2; refuses to permit alteration of the laws, 324-3; opponents of, called king-men, 324-5; supporters of, called freemen, 324-6; writes letter to Moroni, 352-1; his faithfulness and patriotism, 352-9; joined by Moroni, 354-6; returns to the judgment-seat, 357-44; dies, 359-2.

Pahoran, son of Pahoran, contends for the judgment-seat, 359-3; made chief judge, 359-5; murdered by Kishkumen, 360-9.

Paradise, 67-13, 295-12, 457-14.

Path, straight, and straight and narrow, 14-20, 104-9, 105-19.

Pearls, for ornament and display, 458-24.

Penitent, the, to be blessed, 262-21, 265-18, 300-23, 24.

Perdition, the son of, 451-32, 455-7.

Perverse. generation, and wicked, see Generation.

Persecution, inflicted by unbelievers, 186-1; forbidden by Nephite law, 196-21.

Pestilence, unbelievers to be destroyed by, 63-15, 71-6, 158-7; withheld because of prayers of righteous, 220-22.

Plain, and precious scriptures taken away, 23-26, 28, 25-40.

Plainness, Nephi delights in, 89-4, 103-3, 106-6; of the word of God, 23-24, 29, 106-5, 110-11.

Planets, witnesses for God, 272-44.

Plates, of brass, history, genealogy, and scripture engraven upon, 5-3, 6-24, 8-24, 23-23, 130-14, 420-17; contain five books of Moses, 10-11; prophecies of Joseph written upon, 57-2, 58-15; Nephi had brought after separating from Laman and his people, 60-12; the sons of Benjamin taught concerning, 134-3; delivered to Alma, 191-20; contained scriptures and genealogies, 288-3; Nephi, the grandson of Helaman, given charge of, 399-2.

Plates of Nephi, two sets of, 15-2, 4, 62-30; made from ore, 40-1; Mormon made an abridgment from, 132-3; king Benjamin attests that records are true, 134-6; Mosiah given charge of, 135-16; contain the teachings of Jesus, 448-7; Mormon instructed by Ammaron to take possession of, 460-4; hid up in hill Cumorah, 469-6.

Plates, the larger, also called the **other plates,** and the **other plates of Nephi;** contain more of the secular history, 15-4, 41-4, 58-14, 62-29, 33, 108-3, 113-13, 125-26; delivered, with the smaller plates, to Chemish, 130-8; Mormon finishes his record from, 132-4, 133-9; Helaman commanded to keep record on, 288-2; Nephi, grandson of Helaman, makes record from, 409-10.

Plates, smaller, also called **these plates;** contain more of the sacred or ecclesiastical history, 11-ch. 6:3, 15-4, 16-1, 40-1, 3, 60-4, 62-30, 107-1, 113-13, 125-27, 127-2, 129-14, 129-1, 131-25, 132-3; part called the plates of Jacob, 113-14; full, 132-30; Mormon adds, to his record, 132-6.

Plates, gold, twenty-four, Jaredite record, brought by Limhi's explorers, 150-9, 176-27; received by Mosiah, 177-14; Alma speaks to Helaman concerning, 289-21; Moroni takes account of Ether from, 478-2; record of Brother of Jared upon, 484-21; not to be revealed until after Christ, 485-1; to whom to be shown, 487-ch. 5:2.

Prayer, and fasting, for Alma, 188-22; teaching of Aaron on, 252-16.

Prayers, of the righteous delay destruction, 220-22; of Alma, 268-17; Zenos concerning, 280-3; people admonished to pray for mercy, 283-18; when vain, 283-28, 512-ch. 7:6; the Lord's, 426-9; in families, 435-21; in the name of Jesus, 437-6, 514-26; an evidence of faith, 438-22; disciples united in, and fasting, 449-1; the church met often for, 511-ch. 6:5.

Pride, Gentiles lifted up in, 94-20; churches corrupted because of, 99-12; and love of gold, 109-16; Nehor lifted up in, 195-6; and other sins, 197-32; enters the church, 366-33; ends the condition of people having possessions in common, 458-24.

Priestcraft, and iniquities, 71-5; forbidden, 95-29; introduced among the people, 196-12.

Priesthood, the holy order of God, 229-18, 300-2, 379-18.

Priests, Jacob and Joseph consecrated, 62-26, 109-18; of churches of men contend one with another, 98-4; king Benjamin appoints, 146-3; wicked, of Noah, 171-23; labor for their own support, 186-5, 197-26; ordained of God, 227-1; Alma consecrates, 234-13; and false prophets, 458-34; manner of ordination of, 510-ch. 3.

Prison, Alma and Amulek cast into, 232-17; destroyed at miraculous deliverance of Alma and Amulek, 233-27; in Middoni, 247-3; Nephi and Lehi cast into, 370-21; shaken at miraculous deliverance of Nephi and Lehi, 370-27.

Prisoners, held by Moroni for exchange, 328-8; Lamanite, compelled to bury their dead, 331-1; put to work, 331-3, 336-25; exchange of, proposed by Ammoron, 333-1; conditions for exchange of, proposed by Moroni, acceded to by Ammoron 333-11, 334-20; upwards of 2,000 slain in their rebellion, 342-14; sent to Zarahemla, 342-16; converted, set at liberty, 409-4; taken by Lamanites from the tower of Sherrizah, 518-7.

INDEX

Probation, this life a state of, 54-21, 69-27, 226-24, 298-4; continue until end of, 107-9; days of, past, sorrow over, 392-38.

Proclamation, gladsome, by Limhi to his people, 148-17; by Lachoneus, to assemble people for defence against Gadianton robbers, 405-22.

Procrastination, of day of repentance, 283-33, 35.

Promised land, see **Land of Promise.**

Promises, according to the flesh, 71-2, 72-17; of God, extended to Lamanites, 217-16, 218-24; to people of Nephi verified, 322-21; people led away by Akish through fair, 492-17.

Prophecies, concerning signs of Christ's birth fulfilled, 399-4; of Abinadi and Samuel the Lamanite, fulfilled, 461-19, 462-10.

Prophecy, of Nephi concerning the Jews, 89-4.

Prophets, Jews understand the, 89-5; rejection of, 96-5, 122-8; persecutors of, perish, 92-3; words of, searched, 113-6; Jews killed the, 114-14; many, in days of Enos, 127-22; labor diligently, in days of Jarom, 128-11; Jaredite, in the reign of Shule, 490-23; Jaredite, given liberty to travel, by king Shule, 491-25; Jaredite, brought about repentance, 491-26; Jaredite, cry repentance to people of Heth, 495-28; persecuted, even to death by people of Heth, 495-29.

Prosperity, of the church, in days of Helaman, 365-25.

Punishment, no, where there is no law, 69-25; Sherem speaks of eternal, 124-18; everlasting, the wages of the wicked, 138-33.

Pure, in heart, 112-2; blessed, 424-8.

Quaking, of the earth, 20-4, 388-9, 416-12.

Queen, wife of king Lamoni, counsels with Ammon, 244-3; widow of king Lehonti, marries Amalickiah, 315-35.

Queens, nursing mothers to people of Israel, 72-9.

Rabbanah, a Lamanite title of honor, 241-13.

Raiment, disciples admonished to take no thought for, 427-25, 28.

Raising, of the dead, by Christ, 140-5, 449-15; by Nephi, grandson of Helaman, 414-19; by the Nephite disciples, 456-5. See also **Resurrection.**

Ramah, hill, same as hill Cumorah, 508-11.

Rameumptom, the holy stand of the Zoramites, 275-21.

Ranks, based on wealth, 411-12.

Rebellion, of Laman and others, upon the waters, 39-9, 49-2; of Corihor, the Jaredite, 489-4; of Cohor, and Noah, 490-15; of Jared, 491-2; of Akish, 492-13; of Heth, 495-26; caused by secret combinations, 499-15.

Reckoning of time, changed by Nephites after sign of Christ's birth, 402-8.

Record, of Lehi, Nephi's abridgment of, 2-17, 40-1; genealogy in, 10-1; of the Jews, angel's prophecy concerning, 23-23; of Mormon, delivered to Moroni, 132-1, 472-1; Nephite, coming forth of, a sign, 442-5, 486-17; omissions from Nephite, supplied by command of Christ, 445-7.

Records, God able to preserve, 126-15; of Jaredites, brought by king Limhi's explorers, 150-9, 478-2; Nephite, many kept, 364-13, 409-9; hid up in the hill Cumorah, 469-6, 508-11.

Redemption, through the Messiah, 53-6, 55-26, 133-8, 218-27, 476-12; plan of, 226-25; from sin, 369-10; brought to pass, 471-7.

Red Sea, Lehi arrives at, 3-5; Moses smote, 379-11.

Remission, of sins, look forward for, 211-6; for repentant, 227-34, 229 16; baptism unto, 516-11.

Remnant, of House of Israel, 98-2; to hear gospel, 102-3; of seed of Jacob, 311-23, 410-24, 440-16, 443-12, 22, 469-24, 472-ch. 7:10; of seed of Joseph, 311-23, 410-23, 420-17, 429-12, 503-6.

Repentance, way to, prepared, 17-18; of Gentiles, 26-5, 63-12, 102-2; temporary, of Laman and Lemuel, 40-20; men called to, 54-21, 68-23, 94-27, 143-10, 216-12, 423-32, 514-31, 516-8; and baptism, 104-11, 208-49; punishment without, 139-38, 395-1, 498-1; reward of, 140-12, 185-29, 389-22; voice from heaven calls to, 371-29.

Restoration, of Israel, 102-5, 103-8; of Israel, sign of beginning of, 454-1; of all things to their proper order requisite with justice, 297-2.

Resurrection, necessary by reason of the fall, 67-6; of all men, 68-22, 223-41, 448-4; power of the, 73-25, 114-11, 122-9, 515-41; of Christ of universal application, 281-22, 394-15, 471-6; of the dead, 162-35, 164-20; the first, 164-21, 168-9, 296-17; meaning of, 225-8, 296-18; Aaron speaks on, 250-9; a space between death and the, 296-21; of Christ redeems mankind, 165-7, 394-17; of many saints, 395-25, 446-9.

Revelation, from God in a sealed book, 96-7; not to be despised, 114-8.

Rich, unrighteous, condemned, 69-30, 70-42, 99-15, 144-23; people of church become, through righteousness, 197-29; Lamanites and Nephites became, 373-9.

Riches, seek kingdom of God before, 110-18; king Benjamin had not sought, 137-12; become slippery, under the curse, 392-31, 461-18.

INDEX

Righteous, do not murmur, 31-3; are favored of God, 36-35; need not fear, 48-22; shall not perish, 93-8.
Righteousness, God will visit Israel because of, 42-11; God's ways are, 51-19; perfect knowledge of, 68-14.
Riplah, hill, 303-31.
Riplakish, ancestor of Morianton, a Jaredite, 479-23; his wicked reign, 496-4; his death, 496-8.
Ripliancum, waters of, 508-8.
River, seen in vision of Lehi, 13-13; source of, 13-14, 21-16; explanation of vision of, 30-26.
Roads, many built in days of Lachoneus, 411-8.
Robbers, see **Gadianton Robbers.**
Robe of righteousness, prayed for by Nephi, 59-33.
Rock, figurative of strength in righteous, Christ called the, 29-15, 59-30, 60-35, 70-45, 100-28, 423-39.
Rocks, rent at death of Christ as foreseen in Nephi's vision, 20-4; rending of, predicted by Samuel the Lamanite, 394-21; rent to pieces as predicted, 416-18.
Rod of iron, in vision of Lehi, 14-19; in vision of Nephi, 19-25; meaning of, 29-23.
Root, of Jesse, 85-10.
Ruler, Nephi wrongly accused of desiring to make himself a, 33-38, 39-10, 60-3; God makes Nephi a, 4-22, 6-29, 61-19; Mosiah proclaimed a, by king Benjamin, 135-10, 138-30.
Rulers, covered because of iniquity, 96-5.
Rumors, of wars, 20-2, 21-21, 27-15, 90-12, 474-30.

Sabbath, observed by people of Nephi, 128-5, 169-23; remember the, 161-16.
Sack-cloth, garb of humility and penitence, 157-25, 385-9.
Sacrament, of bread and wine, Christ administers, 434-3; emblems miraculously provided, 439-3; none to partake unworthily, 435-28; Christ administered to Nephites often, 449-13; blessing on bread, 511-ch. 4; on the wine, 511-ch. 5.
Sacred things, the records, interpreters, etc., so called, 41-5, 108-4, 288-2, 289-14, 292-47, 324-38, 358-1, 399-2, 459-48, 469-6.
Sacrifice, Christ a, for sin, 53-7; burnt, offered by people of king Benjamin, 136-3; an infinite and eternal, 282-10; of broken heart and contrite spirit instead of burnt offerings, 418-20; of women and children to Lamanite idols, 466-14, 467-21.
Saint, man becomes, through atonement, 141-19.
Saints, of God, church called, 26-12; a gulf between the wicked and, 30-28; of the Holy One, 68-18; cry of blood of, shall ascend, 92-3, 99-10; all, shall dwell with God, 517-26.
Salem, Melchizedek, king of, 229-17.
Salt, of the earth, useless if its savor be lost, 424-13, 432-15.
Salvation, all the earth shall see, 42-17, 441-35; is free, 52-4; none barred, 94-24; Lamanites might have, 126-13; through faith, 140-9, 145-7, 223-40; by the atonement, 142-6, 206-21; not by the law of Moses alone, 161-28; to be declared to every nation, 165-28; the reward of the righteous, 218-28; the day of, near, 229-21; ye have procrastinated the day of, 392-38.
Sam, one of Lehi's sons, 3-5, 4-17, rebellion against, and brethren, 11-6, 201-6; Lehi rejoices because of, 13-3, 14; blessed by Lehi, 58-11; accompanies Nephi into the wilderness at separation from the Lamanites, 60-6.
Samuel, prophet of Israel, mentioned by Christ, 440-24.
Samuel, the Lamanite, 389-2; prophesies destruction to unrepentant, 390-5, 392-38; prophesies of Christ, 390-6; specifies signs of Christ's birth and death, 393-3, 394-20; calls for repentance, 395-1; converts many, 397-1; escapes persecutors, 397-6; prophecy of, fulfilled, 446-10, 461-19, 462-10.
Sanctification, result of penitence and obedience, 366-35, 209-54, 229-12, 522-33.
Sanctuaries, 99-13, 234-17, 250-6.
Sariah, the wife of Lehi, 3-5, 9-1, 13-14; complains against Lehi, 9-2.
Satan, see **Devil.**
Savior, the, see **Christ.**
Scarlets, desired by the abominable church, 22-8.
Scattering, of Israel, predicted, 16-3, 17-14, 29-17, 46-3, 63-11, 71-6, 90-15.
Scent, of corpses, 236-11, 506-23.
Scorner, to be consumed, 98-31.
Scourge, Lamanites a, to Nephites, 5-24, 61-25.
Scriptures, all, for profit and learning, 43-23; engraven upon the plates of brass, 58-15; wresting of, forbidden, 229-20; searching of, taught by Christ, 445-1.
Sealed, book shall be, 96-7.
Sealing, power given to Nephi, son of Helaman, 384-7.
Seantum, murderer of the judge, accused, 382-26; confesses, 383-37.
Sebus, the water of, 239-26.
Secret combinations, of Akish, 492-13. See also **Gadianton Robbers.**
Seed, the word compared to, 278-28.
Seeds, of every kind, carried by Lehi's colony, 13-1, 31-11, 39-6; planted by Lehi's people, 40-24; sown by Nephi's people, 60-11; carried by Jaredites, 480-41, 3.

Seer, 56-6, 151-13, 190-16; covered because of iniquity, 96-5.
Seezoram, chief judge, murdered by his brother, 382-23.
Senine, gold coin, a day's wage for a judge, 221-3, 222-5, 7.
Senum, silver coin, value of, 221-3, 222-6.
Sepulchre, Christ laid in a, for three days, 90-13.
Sermon, the, on the mount, repeated, 423 to 429.
Serpent, raised by Moses, 91-20, 379-14. See also **Devil.**
Serpents, fiery flying, a scourge, 37-41, 89-29; poisonous, a scourge to the Jaredites, 495-31; destroyed, 497-19.
Servant, of Laban, Zoram, 8-20; Ammon, a, to king Lamoni, 239-25; of Teancum, 327-33; of the devil, 512-11.
Servants, unprofitable, 137-21; of Lamoni scattered by Lamanites, 239-27.
Seth, a Jaredite, son of Shiblon, 479-11; brought into captivity, 499-9.
Shame, of sinners on day of judgment, 225-15; to be forgotten, 444-4.
Shared, a Jaredite, battles with Coriantumr, 505-23; slain, 505-30.
Shazer, a camping place for Lehi's people, 31-13.
Sheaves, symbolical of reward of labor, 261-5; the Lord's people to be gathered as, 440-18.
Sheep, people of God likened to, 49-25, 396-13; disobedient not Christ's, 207-38; of other folds, of Christ, 430-17, 1.
Shelem, a mount, place of the Lord's manifestation to the brother of Jared, 482-1.
Shem, land of, 463-20.
Shem, a Nephite chieftain, slain at Cumorah, 470-14.
Shemlon, land of, 154-7, 172-1.
Shemnon, one of the twelve disciples, 437-4.
Shepherd, one God and one, 25-41; one fold and one, 49-25, 430-17; as sheep having no, 207-37; Christ, the good, 207-38, 39, 208-41, 209-57, 60, 377-18; the devil a, 207-39.
Sherem, denies Christ, 123-1; demands a sign, 124-13; is stricken and dies, 124-15, 20.
Sheum, a variety of food-plant, 152-9.
Shez, a Jaredite king, son of Heth, 479-25; attempts to restore the broken nation, 496-1; death of, 496-4.
Shiblom, a Nephite chieftain, slain at Cumorah, 470-14.
Shiblon or **Shiblom,** a Jaredite king, son of Com, 479-12; brother of, puts prophets to death, 499-5; death of, 499-9.
Shiblon, a son of Alma the younger, 274-7, 292-1; goes on mission to Zoramites, 274-7; commandments of Alma to, 292-1; with his brothers is successful in the ministry, 320-30; takes charge of the sacred things, 358-1; dies, 358-10.
Shiblon, a coin, 222-15.
Shiblum, a coin, 222-16.
Shilom, city of, 149-21, 152-8.
Shilom, land of, 147-ch. 7:5, 154-8; many buildings erected in by king Noah, 156-13.
Shim, hill, wherein Ammaron deposited the sacred engravings, 460-3; sacred records taken from by Mormon, 467-23; mentioned in record of Jaredites, 493-3.
Ship, Nephi commanded to build a, 34-8; Lehi and his colony put forth to sea in, 39-8.
Ships, built by Hagoth, 358-5; thought to have been lost, 358-8.
Shiz, a Jaredite, the brother of Lib, 506-17; his vengeful oath, 507-24; slain by Coriantumr, 509-30.
Shule, Jaredite king, son of Kib, 479-31, 489-7; restores kingdom to his father, 490-9; reigns as king, 490-10; righteousness of, 490-11; captured by Noah, 490-17; regains kingdom, 490-18; protects the prophets, 490-24.
Shum, a coin, 222-5.
Shurr, valley of, camp of Coriantumr, 507-28.
Sidom, land of, 233-1.
Sidon, river, or waters of, 460-10; baptisms in, 203-4; wilderness at head of, 254-29, 302-22.
Siege, of robbers against people of Nephi, 407-16; of Coriantumr against army in wilderness, 505-5.
Signs, of Christ's birth, 92-3, 393-3, 400-13; of Christ's death, 41-10, 394-20, 415-3, 416-20; a, demanded by Sherem, 124-13; of the gathering of Israel, 442-1; secret, received by Kishkumen, 362-7.
Signs, secret, used to promote wickedness, 374-22.
Silks, 22-7, 203-6, 494-17, 498-24.
Silver, 22-7; found on land of promise, 40-25; workmanship in, 61-15; Nephites rich in, 128-8, 197-29.
Similitude, Abraham and Isaac a, 113-5.
Sin, Lord cannot look upon with the least allowance, 308-16; unpardonable, the, 124-19, 293-6.
Sins, warning against, 69-38, 70-45; remission of, 92-26, 125-2; see **Remission of sins;** of the world, Lamb of God taketh away, 212-14; Jesus Christ slain for, 421-14.
Siron, land of, 293-3.
Skins, of the Lamanites, dark, 61-21, 201-6; garments made of, 318-6; of righteous Lamanites become white, 403-15.
Slaughter, of Amlicites, 199-18; of Gadianton robbers, 407-11; of Nephites, 467-21, 470-10; of Jaredites, 508-15.

INDEX 565

Slavery, king Limhi offers to submit to, 148-15; people of Ammon offer to submit to, 264-8; forbidden by law, 264-9.
Slings, Nephites armed with, 198-12. See also **Weapons.**
Slothfulness, decried, 350-14.
Snare, of the adversary, 178-9, 224-6.
Society, of the robbers, secret, 404-9, 494-6, 500-22.
Solomon, temple of, Nephite temple patterned after, 61-16; sins of, 111-23.
Son of righteousness, 93-9, 447-2, 495-22. See also **Christ.**
Soothsayers, condemned, 443-16.
Sorceries, 197-32, 461-19.
Souls, final state of, 30-35; between death and resurrection, 295-7.
Spies, of Alma, 199-21; of Helaman, 338-22.
Spirit, the Great, Ammon thought to be, 240-2; explained by Aaron, 252-9.
Spirit, of God, came down from heaven, 372-45; kings to be wrought upon by the, 42-12; truth made known by the, 208-46.
Spirit, of the Lord, Nephi caught away in, 17-1; in form of a man, 18-11; will not always strive with man, 93-11; one with Christ and the Father, 224-44; does not dwell in unholy temples, 368-24. See also **Holy Ghost.**
Spirits, of all men at death taken to God, 295-11; will be restored to body, 67-12; unclean, see **Devil.**
Stain, figurative of wickedness, 206-21, 257-12.
Standard, of liberty raised by Moroni, 326-20.
Star, new, predicted as sign of Christ's birth, 393-5; appears, 400-21.
Statutes, see **Law of Moses.**
Steel, swords of, 7-9, 490-9; Nephi's bow of fine, 32-18; workmanship in, 61-15.
Sting, of death, 252-14, 471-5.
Stone, the, Jews will reject, 114-15; with engravings brought to Mosiah, 131-20; to be prepared by the Lord for Gazelem, 290-23.
Stones, Lehi builds altar of, 3-7; Nephi makes fire with, 34-11; Mosiah translates by means of the two, 190-13; sixteen, prepared by brother of Jared, 482-1; two, given to brother of Jared by the Lord, 484-23.
Stratagem, of Moroni, 328-10, 333-3; of Antipus, 339-30; Manti taken by, 346-28.
Stripling, soldiers, Helaman's army of, 333-22, 341-57.
Stubble, wicked shall be as, 48-15, 93-6, 447-1; wicked churches to be consumed as, 48-23.
Sun, appeareth to stand still, 388-15.
Sword, of Laban, 7-9, 61-14, 108-10, 133-13, 135-16.

Swords, of the Jaredites, found by Limhi's explorers, 151-11; of the Anti-Nephi-Lehies buried, 257-12, 258-17.
Synagogues, none to be barred from, 94-26; Alma and Amulek preach in, 236-13; after the order of the Nehors, 249-4; the poor cast out of, among the Zoramites, 276-2; hypocrites in, 426-5.
Task-masters, 181-9, 19.
Taxes, light under king Benjamin, 137-14; of people of Limhi, 148-15; heavy, levied by Riplakish, 496-5.
Teacher, Jacob a, 70-48; king Benjamin ceases to be, 138-29.
Teachers, Jacob and Joseph consecrated, 62-26, 109-18; corruption because of false, 99-12; ordination of, 510-ch. 3.
Teachings, of Jesus to Nephites, not a hundredth part written, 448-6. See also **Christ, teachings of.**
Teancum, a Nephite commander slays Morianton, 323-35; meets army of Amalickiah, 326-29; camps in borders of Bountiful, 327-32; slays Amalickiah, 327-34; decoy march by, 329-22; sets prisoners to work, 331-3; slays Ammoron, 356-36; is slain, 356-36.
Teancum, city of, 466-3.
Tempest, during voyage of Lehi, 39-13; God to visit Israel with, 42-11; unbelievers to be destroyed by, 63-15; nations to be visited by, 95-2; at death of Christ, 394-23, 415-5.
Temple, Nephi builds, 61-16; Jacob teaches in, 109-17, 2, 110-11; Mosiah summons people to, 135-18; people assembled near, in Bountiful, at time of Christ's appearing, 421-1.
Temptation, of Christ, 140-7, 163-5, 212-11; by the devil, 21-17, 19, 284-39; admonition to avoid, 291-33, 426-12, 435-18.
Tents, departure of Lehi with, 31-12; in land of promise, 40-23; of Nephi's colony, 60-7; Lamanites' custom of dwelling in, 126-20; pitched around temple, by king Benjamin's assembly, 136-5.
Teomner, a Nephite officer under Helaman's command, in ambush, 345-16.
Testimony, words of Nephi a, 92-28; a few to bear, of the Nephite record, 96-13; of two nations, to be a witness of God, 101-8; of Alma, concerning Christ, 212-13; of three, concerning the Nephite record, 96-12, 487-ch. 5:3; of three and of eight, see forepart of this Book.
Thanks, to be given to God, 213-23, 291-37, 419-10.
Things, all, see **All things.**
Three Nephite Disciples, the, never to taste of death, 452-7, 457-14; minister among Nephites, 453-16, 456-5; taken from people, because of wickedness, 472-10; minister to Mormon and Moroni, 472-11.
Throne, of God, all to stand before, 100-23, 112-8.

Thunder, predicted, as a visitation at time of Christ's death, 20-4, 42-11; to be visited upon the wicked, 93-6; at death of Christ, 415-6.
Tidings, glad, of great joy, to king Benjamin, 140-3.
Timber, of curious workmanship, in building the ship for Lehi's company, 38-1; for defense of cities, 321-2, 331-4; land without, 363-5; attempt to restore growth of, 364-9.
Time, Nephite reckoning of, changed after Christ's birth, 402-8.
Timothy, grandson of Helaman; raised from the dead by his brother, Nephi; one of the twelve disciples, 437-4.
Tithes, paid by Abraham to Melchizedek, 229-15; the Lord robbed of, 447-8.
Title of liberty, raised by Moroni, 310-12; dissenters compelled to hoist, 326-20.
Tongues, gift of, 217-21; of children loosed, 449-14.
Tools, Nephi finds ore to make, 34-9; among Nephites, 128-8; among Jaredites, 498-25.
Torment, endless, nature of, 68-19, 100-23, 122-10, 141-25, 225-17.
Tower, colony of Jared came from, 131-22, 479-33; of the great, 190-17; sufficiently high to reach to heaven, 375-28; the great, 478-3; erected by king Benjamin, 136-7; Limhi discovers Lamanites from, 172-8; Nephi's, in garden, 377-10.
Towers, erected by Moroni as part of fortification, 321-4.
Traditions, Nephite, Lamanites swore to destroy, 126-14; Lamanite, incorrect, 134-5; baseness of Lamanite, 237-9; prophecies called foolish by Korihor, the anti-Christ, 269-14; Lamanite, wicked and abominable, 396-7.
Transfiguration, seeming, of the three disciples, 453-15.
Translation, gift of, 151-13; gift of, among the Nephites, 217-21.
Traveler, none can return from grave, 51-14.
Treasures, hearts upon their, 69-30; cursed because of wickedness, 391-19.
Tree, in vision of Lehi, 13-10; river near, 13-13; iron rod leads to, 14-19; desirable fruit of, 13-10, 14-15; of life, 19-25; 29-22, 30-28, 226-21, 298-3; remnant to be grafted in the true olive, 29-16.
Trees, obey, through faith, 113-6.
Tribes, of Israel, word of God to, 101-12, 429-15, 465-18; Nephites separate into, 413-2; united against king Jacob, 413-11; agree not to fight each other, 414-14.
Tribes, the lost, 429-15, 430-20, 1, 444-26.
Tubaloth, Lamanite king, 360-16.

Unalterable, are the decrees of God, 297-8.

Unbelief, inability to understand because of, 184-3; miracles cease because of, 514-37.
Unchangeable, Being, an, 476-19, 517-18.
Unclean, nothing, in presence of God, 17-21, 30-34, 213-21, 223-37, 380-25.
Unpardonable sin, 124-19, 293-6.

Vainness, and frailties and foolishness of men, 69-28.
Valley, of Gideon, etc., see **Gideon,** valley of, etc.
Vapor, of darkness, Israel to be visited with, 42-11, 48-18.
Variableness, in God, no, 476-9.
Vengeance, of God, 443-21, 465-15, 473-20; blood of saints to cry for, 196-13, 492-22; 493-24; sword of, 475-41.
Vessel, inward, to be cleansed, 350-23, 351-24; the virgin, a precious and chosen, 211-10; the Lord's ministers called chosen, 514-31.
Vessels, of the Lord, be ye clean that bear the, 441-41; of Jared, see **Barges.**
Victory, thanks to God for, 347-33; over death and the grave, 163-8, 165-8, 252-14, 266-28, 471-5; over the devil, 236-21.
Vineyard, servants of the Lord to prune his, 122-2; planted by king Noah, 156-15.
Virgin, the, 211-10; seen in vision of Nephi, 18-13, 15, 18.
Virtue, dear above all things, 518-9.
Visage, of the Lord's servants to be marred, 442-44.
Vision, of Lehi, 2-8, 9-4, 13-2, 49-4; of Nephi, 17-1; of Amulek, 215-20, 219-7; of the father of Abish, 245-16; knowledge given through, 59-23.
Visionary, man, Lehi a, 4-11, 9-2, 4.
Voice, raised to God, 60-35; of the people, judges chosen by, see **Judges;** of the people, against Amlici, 198-7; of an angel like thunder, 292-7; from heaven, in protection of Lehi, and Nephi, 371-29; of the Lord to the people, following the crucifixion, 417-1, 419-3; of the Father, proclaiming the Christ at the time of his visitation to the Nephites, 421-3; hills and mountains tremble at the Lord's, 388-9.
Vultures, many bodies of Lamanites and Amlicites devoured by, 200-38.

Wade, wading, through affliction, 34-1, 211-5, 214-14, 332-15, 366-34.
Wages, according to works, 202-27; of wicked, 208-42; of the Nephite judges, 221-1.
Wanderers, in a strange land, 229-23, 263-36.
War, among descendants of Lehi, foreseen in Nephi's vision, 20-2, 21-21; in the great and abominable church, predicted, 47-13; among nations subject to the mother of abominations, 27-16; and contentions among Lehi's descendants, records of, on the larger or other

INDEX 567

plates, 41-4, 62-33; after return of the Jews from captivity, 90-12; among people of Nephi, predicted, 92-2; between Nephites and Lamanites witnessed by Enos, 127-24; attested by Omni, 129-3; attested by Abinadom, 130-10; attested by Amaleki, 131-24; as recorded by Mormon, 460-8, 470-8; caused by strife and crime, 322-21.
Warfare, Helaman writes Moroni about, 337-2.
Wars, final, among Jaredites, 508-8; final, between Nephites and Lamanites, 470-8.
Watch, and pray continually, admonitions to, 230-28, 435-15.
Watchman, shall sing, 159-22, 441-32.
Water, fountain of filthy, seen in Nephi's vision, 21-16; meaning of Lehi's vision of, 30-26; from the rock, by the power of God in Moses, 36-29, 91-20; Christ to be baptized by, 104-5; Alma and Helam buried or baptized in, 168-14; Zarahemla nearly surrounded by, 254-32; large bodies of, in the land northward, 363-4; Jaredites driven forth, 344 days upon the, 488-11; bitter fountains cannot give good, 512-11.
Waters, many, seen by Nephi in vision, 22-10; Irreantum means, 34-5; Cumorah in land of many, 469-4; of the Red Sea divided, 36-26; of Sidon, corpses cast into, 201-3, 307-22; of Sebus, Ammon at the, 240-34, 239-26; of Mormon, see **Mormon,** waters of.
Wealth, church members gain, through faithfulness, 197-31.
Weapons, made by Nephites, 128-8; by Jaredites, 498-27; Nephites armed with, 198-12; laid down by people of Ammon, 258-17; by Lamanites, in remorse, 258-25, 260-14; buried, 258-17, 260-14, 396-9.
Well Beloved, a title of the Christ, 372-47.
Whirlwinds, persecutors to be carried away by, 93-5; wicked carried away by, at death of Christ, 416-16.
Whisper, out of the dust, the Nephites to, 94-16.
Whore, of all the earth, the abominable church, 26-10, 11, 12, 47-13, 14, 72-16, 99-18.
Whoredoms, wo unto them who commit, 69-36; divine commands against, 95-32; many go astray because of, 99-14; excuse themselves in committing, 111-23; call to repent of, 455-ch. 30:2; Morianton unjust to himself because of, 497-11.
Wicked, Nephi spake hard things against the, 31-2; shall not destroy the righteous when the fulness of God's wrath is poured out, 48-16; nations to be destroyed, 36-37; the, shall be cast out, 165-2; call to come out from the, 209-57; judgments of God will overtake the, 460-5.
Wickedness, many go astray because of, 99-14; afflictions because of, 203-3, 417-7.
Wilderness, Lehi departs from Jerusalem into, 3-4; Ishmael's daughters mourn because of affliction in, 33-35; children born in, 35-20, 39-7, 52-1, 55-1; Nephi and a company flee into, at time of the division into Nephites and Lamanites, 60-5; of Hermounts, Lamanites driven into, 200-37.
Will, of God, operative upon Mormon, 132-7.
Wine, oppressors of the covenant people to be drunken with blood as with, 64-18; the iniquitous to be drunken but not with, 96-4; buy, without money, figurative of salvation, 70-50; made in abundance by the wicked king Noah, 156-15; Limhi sends, to Lamanites, 177-10; Laman, one of Moroni's soldiers, takes, to Lamanites, who become drunken, 335-8, 14.
Wine, sacramental, Jesus commanded his disciples to bring, 434-1; miraculously provided at the administration by Jesus Christ, 439-5; manner of administering, 511-ch. 5:1.
Wisdom, of God, 67-8, 97-22; of wise shall perish, 97-26; of men, foolishness, 69-28; God has all, 263-35; admonition to learn, in youth, 291-35.
Wise, learned think they are, 69-28; must consider themselves fools, to be acceptable to God, 70-42; the, who are puffed up and sin shall be thrust down to hell, 99-15; the, may be confounded by children, 278-23; angels appeared unto, as the time of Christ's birth drew near, 398-14; man builds on rock, 428-24.
Witchcrafts, to be cut off, 443-16.
Witness, blood of the innocent a, 231-11; false, forbidden, 161-23.
Witnesses to the Book of Mormon, three, to attest truth of the book, 96-12, 73-3, 487-3, 4; others than the three, 96-14, 97-22. See The Testimony of the Three and also of the Eight Witnesses in forepart of this Book.
Wives, unrighteous desire for many, 108-15; David and Solomon had many, 111-24; hearts of, broken because of wickedness of their husbands, 111-35; husbands who love their, commended, 112-7.
Woe, eternal or endless misery and, 50-13, 216-11, 369-12, 377-16.
Wolf, to dwell with lamb, 103-12.
Wolves, true shepherd sees that they enter not, 209-59; false prophets as in sheep's clothing but are ravening, 428-15.
Women, of Lehi's company bore children in the wilderness, 34-1, 35-20; God delights in the chasity of, 111-28; taught

to spin, 154-5; toil and spin, 373-13; fed upon flesh of husbands by barbarous Lamanites, 518-8.

Wonders, signs and, to be manifested by Christ, 93-13; many shown, as time of Christ's birth drew near, 398-13.

Wood, people taught to work in, 61-15; fine workmanship of, 128-8.

Word, of God, according to the, 36-31; of Christ, the obedient feast upon, 105-20; of God, the iron rod, 19-25; wo unto those who reject the word of God, 96-14; of God, shall hiss forth, 101-3; of God, nourished by the, 122-7.

Words, of Mormon, the, 132.

Words, of the book are of those who have slumbered in the dust, 96-9; of the book, God to bring forth, 96-14.

Work, great and marvelous, the Lord's, 26-7, 91-17, 100-1, 443-9; a marvelous, among the Gentiles, 47-8; a marvelous, and a wonder, 97-26; the Lord's, not yet finished, 101-9; of the Father, commencement of, 444-26.

Workers, of iniquity, denunciation of, 207-37.

Workmen, curious, 373-11.

Works, men to be judged by their, 30-32.

Worship, princes shall, 45-7; of the Father by the Jews in Christ's name, 91-16; of the Father by the Nephites in Christ's name, 113-5; of God before the altar by people at Sidom, 234-17; strange, of the Zoramites, 274-12; not confined to sanctuaries, 280-2; sacred privileges of, 324-39.

Writing, given to Moses, 56-17; by the finger of God on the wall of the temple, 219-2.

Writings, of the kings, 129-14.

Yesterday, today and forever, God the same throughout, 17-18, 52-4, 97-23, 101-9, 275-17, 476-9, 521-19.

Yield, not, to sin, or temptation, 59-27, 93-10, 413-5, 477-28.

Yoke, of the abominable church, 22-5.

Zarahemla, people of, 130-14; had come from Jerusalem, 130-15; people of, unite with people of Mosiah, 131-19; Limhi sends men to search for, 150-7; people of, numbered with Nephites, 183-13; landing place of people of, 254-30.

Zarahemla, land of, 130-13, 199-24; Lachoneus gathers his forces in, 405-22, 23; land southward called, 495-31.

Zarahemla, city of, burned at time of the crucifixion, 415-8; rebuilt, 456-8.

Zedekiah, king of Judah, 1-4, 10-13, 130-15; Mulek, son of, 373-10; sons of, except Mulek, slain, 380-21.

Zedekiah, one of the twelve disciples, 437-4.

Zeezrom, a lawyer, accuses Amulek and Alma, 221-31; questions Amulek, 222-21; questions Alma, 225-8; encircled about by pains of hell, 231-6; sick at Sidom, 233-3; converted and healed, 234-6; preaches the gospel, 234-12, 274-6.

Zemnarihah, a chieftain of the robbers, 407-17; fails in his designs against Nephites, 408-22; starts with his people for land northward, 408-23; is intercepted and hanged, 408-28.

Zenephi, lawless army of, 519-16.

Zeniff, grandfather of Limhi, 147-9; sent as a spy, 152-1; became leader of his company, 152-3; repulses invading Lamanites, 153-14, 155-19; confers kingdom upon his son Noah, 155-1.

Zeniff, record of, 152; received by king Mosiah, 177-14; read to the people by direction of king Mosiah, 182-5.

Zenock, predicted that Christ would be lifted up, 41-10; his testimony of the Son of God, 280-15; predicted destruction at time of the crucifixion, 420-16.

Zenos, spoke of burial of Christ, 41-10; spoke of the three days of darkness, 41-10; gave parable of the tame olive-tree, 115-1, 122-1; words of, must come to pass, 122-1; spoke concerning prayer and worship, 280-3; testifies of destruction to occur at the crucifixion, 420-16.

Zerahemnah, a leader of the Lamanites, 301-5; surrenders to Moroni, 306-8; attempts to kill Moroni and is scalped, 306-12; begs for mercy, 307-19.

Zeram, sent out as a spy, 199-22.

Zerin, mountain, removed, by faith of the brother of Jared, 502-30.

Ziff, 156-8.

Zion, supporters of, to be blessed, 24-37; opposers of, to be destroyed, 47-14, 63-13, 72-13, 95-13; law to go forth from, 74-3; laborer in, 95-31; devil's doctrine that all is well in, 99-21.

Zoram, the servant of Laban, 9-35; marries, 31-7; a true friend to Nephi, 52-30; blessed by Lehi, 52-31; accompanies Nephi in the separation of Nephites and Lamanites, 60-6.

Zoram, a chief captain among Nephites, 235-5.

Zoram, head of the dissenters, 273-59.

Zoramites, 108-13; separated from the Nephites, 273-59; build synagogues, 274-12; their Rameumptom, 275-21; strange prayers of, 275-15; converts cast out by, 284-6, 8; prepare for war against people of Ammon, 285-10; converts from among, given land, 285-14; become Lamanites, 301-4; made captains of Lamanites, 316-5; lead Lamanites away, 401-29.

www.ingramcontent.com/pod-product-compliance
Lightning Source LLC
Chambersburg PA
CBHW030257080526
44584CB00012B/353